P9-DEA-389

THROWN UNDER THE OMNIBUS

ALSO BY P. J. O'ROURKE

Modern Manners
An Etiquette Book for Rude People

The Bachelor Home Companion
A Practical Guide to Keeping House Like a Pig

Republican Party Reptile
Confessions, Adventures, Essays, and (Other) Outrages

Holidays in Hell
In Which Our Intrepid Reporter Travels to the World's Worst Places and Asks, "What's Funny About This?"

Parliament of Whores
A Lone Humorist Attempts to Explain the Entire U.S. Government

Give War a Chance
Eyewitness Accounts of Mankind's Struggle Against Tyranny, Injustice, and Alcohol-Free Beer

All the Trouble in the World
The Lighter Side of Overpopulation, Famine, Ecological Disaster, Ethnic Hatred, Plague, and Poverty

Age and Guile Beat Youth, Innocence, and a Bad Haircut
"I Was Tragically Hip and I Recovered! You Can Too!"

Eat the Rich
A Treatise on Economics

The CEO of the Sofa
One Year in the Life of a Man Who Said, "Mind If I Put My Feet Up? I Think I Will Take This Lying Down."

Peace Kills
America's Fun New Imperialism

On The Wealth of Nations
A Minor Mister Opines upon a Master's Magnum Opus

Driving Like Crazy
Thirty Years of Vehicular Hell-Bending Celebrating America the Way It's Supposed to Be—with an Oil Well in Every Backyard, a Cadillac Escalade in Every Carport, and the Chairman of the Federal Reserve Mowing Our Lawn

Don't Vote—It Just Encourages the Bastards
A Treatise on Politics

Holidays in Heck
A Former War Correspondent Experiences Frightening Vacation Fun

The Baby Boom
How It Got That Way . . . And It Wasn't My Fault . . . And I'll Never Do It Again

THROWN UNDER THE OMNIBUS

A Reader

P. J. O'Rourke

Atlantic Monthly Press
New York

Published simultaneously in Canada
Printed in the United States of America

FIRST EDITION

ISBN 978-0-8021-2366-4
eISBN 978-0-8021-9140-3

Atlantic Monthly Press
an imprint of Grove Atlantic
154 West 14th Street
New York, NY 10011

Distributed by Publishers Group West

groveatlantic.com

15 16 17 18 19 10 9 8 7 6 5 4 3 2 1

To Tina

For the daughters, the son, the moon, and the stars

And malt does more than Milton can
To justify God's way to man.

—A. E. Housman

CONTENTS

The Baby Boom (*2014*)

INTRODUCTION

There's a long-term problem with being a writer, and the problem is all the things that, over the long term, I've written. How would you like to have the twaddle and blather you talked forty years ago preserved in detail, set down in black and white, and still extant someplace?

I once had hope that the fashion for recycling would rid me of my printed past. But what artisan—however modest his art—can bear to think that his life's work amounts to no more than the one-one hundredth part of the local Boy Scout paper drive? So there's still a heap of it in an attic closet.

Then came digitization, when everything one has ever written or said or, for all I know, thought is embalmed and heaped in the infinite attic closet of the Internet.

Sooner or later somebody will discover those closets and these skeletons. I might as well publish them myself. Also, I'm being paid for it. The business of trading embarrassment for something of value is an ancient custom, dating back to the murky beginnings of *The Oprah Winfrey Show*.

Examining my musty work I see evidence that I was once younger than anyone ever has been. And on drugs. At least I hope I was on drugs. I'd hate to think that these were my sober and well-considered thoughts. It is, I guess, interesting to watch the leftist grub weaving itself into the pupa of satire and then emerging a resplendent conservative blowfly. Also interesting is the career arc. I start out making cruel fun of a second-rate American president and wind up making cruel fun of a second-rate American president.

And that is all the interest I can summon. I wonder how many people in the so-called creative fields stand before their accumulated professional efforts and think that the thing they've been doing for the past four decades is a thing for which they have no particular talent. Not enough, to judge by the too copious output of various mature painters, poets, and architects. Hardly ever do we hear these people exclaim, "My pictures don't look like anything," "My poems don't rhyme," or "This isn't a building, it's the box a building comes in."

Fortunately, I discovered journalism. Talent hasn't been a question since. But I didn't mean to be a journalist. I meant to be a genius. I was going to produce an oeuvre so brilliant, important, and deep that no one would ever understand it. Pooh on *Finnegans Wake*. ". . . riverrun, past Eve and Adam's, from swerve of shore to bend of bay, brings us by a commodius vicus of recirculation back to Howth Castle and Environs . . ." Anybody can read that. Here's a line from a play I wrote in 1968: "vIvAvIvAvIvA vIvAvIvAvIvA vIvAvIvAvIvA."

Unfortunately I didn't have the knack for literature. It seemed that a certain number of English professors had to have written brilliant, important, and deep PhD dissertations on how no one would ever understand you. Also, it helped to be dead.

To tell the truth, I didn't even mean to be a writer. I meant to be a race-car driver, except I didn't have a race car. Or I meant to be a rock star, except I couldn't sing or play an instrument. (I know, I know, there are so many who never let that stop them, but I was naive.) Or I meant to be a soldier of fortune except the entry-level job in that field was a stint in Vietnam and, jeez, they were actually shooting at you over there. What I meant *not* to be was just a college student. How bourgeois. I did spend the summer of 1966 working as a railroad brakeman, and that seemed to me to be the coolest job that a fellow who knew all the verses to "If I Had a Hammer" could possibly have. I wanted to quit college and stay a brakeman forever, but (this never seemed to happen to Neal Cassady) my mother wouldn't let me.

So I had to find something I could be while also being a college student and something that didn't require expensive equipment, difficult skills, or courage under fire. Writing was the obvious choice.

I decided that I would, over the summer of 1967, write a novel. I wasn't sure how long something had to be before it was considered a novel so I looked around for the briefest acceptable example of the type. I settled on Oscar Wilde's *The Picture of Dorian Gray.* In point of learning the craft, I would have been better off reading the book. Instead, I counted the words in it, multiplying the average per page by the total of pages to arrive at the figure 50,000. There were 130 days in my summer vacation. If I wrote 384 words a day I would be within 80 words of a complete novel by fall. And, so, every night after work and every noontime when I got up on Saturdays and Sundays, I would sit down and write 384 words. Oh, sometimes it was 380 and sometimes 390, but usually I was pretty close to my mark. And in September I indeed had something that was . . . just awful.

I have not been able to reread it, partly because of severe wincing but partly because I couldn't type and all 49,920 words are scrawled in longhand (also execrably spelled and punctuated with mad abandon). The text concerns, as much as I can determine or remember, being young in Ohio. Fair enough, since I'd never been anything other than young in Ohio (though I had visited Chicago and been to Florida twice). I believe the protagonist visits Chicago and goes to Florida twice. The problem with the book is that I saw being young in Ohio as a horror beyond telling and my prose proved the case.

When I got back to school in the fall, I gave my opus to Jerry Bovim, the only real writer I knew. Jerry hadn't actually published anything, but I could tell Jerry was a real writer because, although he was not yet thirty, he was already drinking himself to death. (I still have some of Jerry's fragmentary manuscripts, and the sad truth is that he *was* a real writer. Indeed, he might have been another John Kennedy Toole if only he'd killed himself after he'd completed something instead of before.) Jerry wrote a long critique, a largely charitable assessment in which he expounded upon the difficulties of the picaresque novel, the challenges of first-person narration, and the need for consistency in fictional point of view. He allowed that some of my characters were effective, was indulgent with my attempts at plot development, and even went so far as to say "the thing as a whole is rather likable." But at the end of his commentary he appended this postscript: "It has just occurred to me that there is, however, the dreadful possibility that your book is supposed to be serious."

MODERN MANNERS

(1983, revised edition 1989)

"A gentleman is one who never inflicts pain."
—Cardinal Newman

"Unintentionally."
—Oscar Wilde

What Are Manners?

Manners are a way to express altruism in daily life. Either that or manners are a way to screw people over without their knowing it. Anyway, manners are what your mother always wanted you to have. Whether your mother is a noble idealist or a scheming bitch is something that must be decided by you.

How Can Good Manners Be Identified?

Good manners are a combination of intelligence, education, taste, and style mixed together so that you don't need any of those things. Good manners have a number of distinctive qualities. First, they can be learned by rote. This is a good thing; otherwise most rich men's daughters could not be displayed in public. Secondly, manners do not vary from culture to culture or place to place. The same polite behavior that makes you a welcome guest in the drawing rooms of Kensington is equally appropriate among the Mud People of the fierce Orokaiva tribe of Papua New Guinea—if you have a gun. This is the advantage of Western-style manners. Citizens of Westernized countries still have most of the guns.

Another distinctive quality of manners is that they have nothing to do with what you do, only how you do it. For example, Karl Marx was always polite in the British Museum. He was courteous to the staff, never read with his hat on, and didn't make lip farts when he came across passages in Hegel with which he disagreed. Despite the fact that his political exhortations have caused the deaths of millions, he is today more revered than not. On the other hand, John W. Hinckley Jr. was only rude once, to a retired Hollywood movie actor, and Hinckley will be in a mental institution for the rest of his life.

How Do Good Manners Work?

Manners exist because they are useful. In fact, good manners are so useful that with them you can replace most of the things lacking in modern life.

Good manners can replace religious beliefs. In the Episcopal Church they already have. Etiquette (and quiet, well-cut clothing) is devoutly worshipped by Episcopalians.

Good manners can replace morals. It may be years before anyone knows if what you are doing is right. But if what you are doing is nice, it will be immediately evident. Senator Edward Kennedy, for instance, may or may not be a moral person, but he is certainly a polite one. When Miss Kopechne seemed to be in trouble, Senator Kennedy swam all the way to Edgartown rather than run up a stranger's phone bill calling for help. You should be the same way yourself. If you happen to be on a sinking ship with too few lifeboats, take one and slip quietly away. There's going to be a terrific fuss among the drowning passengers, and it's rude to deliberately overhear an argument which is none of your concern.

Good manners can also replace love. Most people would rather be treated courteously than loved, if they really thought about it. Consider how few knifings and shootings are the result of etiquette as compared to passion.

And good manners can replace intellect by providing a set of memorized responses to almost every situation in life. Memorized responses eliminate the need for thought. Thought is not a very worthwhile pastime anyway. Thinking allows the brain, an inert and mushy organ, to exert unfair domination over more sturdy and active body parts such as the muscles, the digestive system, and other parts of the body you can have a lot of thoughtless fun with. Thinking also leads to theories, and theoretical correctness is always the antithesis of social correctness. How much better history would have turned out if the Nazis had been socially correct instead of true to their hideous theories. They never would have shipped all those people to concentration camps in boxcars. They would have sent limousines to pick them up.

Thinking is actually rude in and of itself. Manners involve interaction with others. You cannot, for instance, think and listen to what other people are saying at the same time. And what most people have to say doesn't merit much thought; so if you *are* caught thinking, you really have no excuse.

As a result of thinking's innate rudeness, thinking people are not often popular. Although the Curies were extremely famous, they were rarely invited out socially. They were too thoughtful. Also, they glowed.

The fact that good manners require interaction is finally their most useful trait. Manners force us to pay attention to the needs, desires, and hopes of other people. If you have good manners you will never become narcissistic and self-obsessed. A self-obsessed person is to be pitied; there are so many interesting people in the world, and while he's not paying attention to them, they will probably rob and cheat him.

The Fundamentals of Contemporary Courtesy

The purpose of old-fashioned manners was to avoid attracting attention. The reason for this was that old-fashioned manners were possessed by only a few hundred rich people. These few hundred rich people didn't want all the hundreds of millions of poor people to notice who had the money. If the rich, polite few started attracting attention, the poor, rude many might get together and commit mayhem the way they did in Russia. The heck with that, said rich people.

But nowadays there are hundreds of millions of rich people, and poor people have been pretty much rendered harmless by drugs and sleeping on sidewalks. Plus it's getting so you can't tell rich from poor anyway, what with Nigerian illegal immigrants selling Rolexes on street corners and Gloria Vanderbilt putting her name on blue jean behinds. The problem modern people have is trying to be special. Therefore, the purpose of modern manners is to attract as much attention as possible.

Greetings

The importance of conspicuousness in modern life has led to the phenomenon of "greeting inflation." Once, even the closest friends greeted each other with a polite bow. Today such reticence is almost extinct. A loud "Sweetheart," a slap on the back, chuck on the arm, tousling of hair, and a cheerful "Have a nice day!" will do if you don't know a person at all. But if you have even the slightest acquaintance with someone, it is usual to embrace him physically no matter what the circumstances. If you're carrying a briefcase or package, just throw it into the gutter. This makes a dramatic gesture of good fellowship.

If you actually know someone's name, twin kisses on both cheeks are expected and should be accompanied by some highly original term of endearment. "I love you" or "You're my best friend" isn't nearly strong enough. In California, where manners are more modern than anywhere else, people say, "I'd murder my parents to have lunch with you" or even "I'm so glad to see you that I'm going to give you gross points in my new movie." (The latter statement is a lie, by the way.)

Rebuffs

At one time there was not only an etiquette of greeting people but also an etiquette of not greeting them. This ranged in degree from the coldly formal bow to the "cut direct." The cut direct was delivered by looking right at a person and not acknowledging his acquaintance or even his existence. This is no longer done. It has been replaced by the lawsuit. Opposing parties in a lawsuit (and other enemies) are expected to greet each other like lovers—especially now when it's so fashionable for hostesses to invite people who hate each other to the same dinners. If the enmity is minor or philosophical in nature, argument—or, better, tableware throwing—may resume after a drink or two. But if the hatred is deep and well occasioned, the mutual detestors are expected to chat amicably throughout the evening.

Hat, Cane, and Gloves

What to do with your hat and cane is a perennial awkwardness when greeting people. If the cane is necessary, it should be replaced with a crutch, which will gain you much more sympathy.

A hat should be taken off when you greet a lady and left off for the rest of your life. Nothing looks more stupid than a hat. When you put on a hat you are surrendering to the same urge that makes children wear mouse ears at Disney World or drunks wear lampshades at parties. Wearing a hat implies that you are bald if you are a man and that your hair is dirty if you are a woman. Every style of hat is identified with some form of undesirable (derby = corrupt ward heeler; fedora = male model; top hat = rich bum; pillbox = Kennedy wife, et cetera). Furthermore, the head is symbolically identified with the sexual organs, so that when you walk down the street wearing a hat, anyone who has the least knowledge of psychology will see you as having . . . a problem. A hat should only be worn if you are employed as a baseball player or are hunting ducks in the rain.

Gloves present another problem, especially when shaking hands. Men must always remove their gloves before a handshake. There is a good reason for this. A man can be very accurately judged by his hand. A soft hand indicates a lazy, unemployed person. A hard, calloused hand shows that a person is an ignorant and dull manual laborer. A cold, clammy hand means that a person is guilty and nervous. And a warm, dry hand means a person is incapable of feeling guilt and has the nerve to pull anything on you. A woman never removes her gloves. There's a good reason for this, too. A woman can also be very accurately judged by her hand, and why would she want to be?

The Handshake

Despite the popularity of more effusive forms of greeting, the handshake is omnipresent. It is now extended to everyone—men, women, old people, young children, and, especially, pet dogs.

It's important to develop a limp and affected handshake. A firm, hearty handshake gives a good first impression, and you'll never be forgiven if you don't live up to it. Also, a firm, hearty handshake inspires confidence in others. People who go around inspiring confidence in others are probably looking to sell them something. You don't want to appear to be that sort.

Farewells

Much more important than greeting people is saying good-bye to them or getting them to say good-bye to you or getting rid of them somehow anyway. The one thing that can be safely said about the great majority of people is that we don't want them around. Be sincere and forthright about the problem. Take the person you want to get rid of aside and tell him he has to leave because the people you're with hate him. Say, "I'm sorry, Fred, but you can't sit down with us. Molly and Bill Dinnersworth hate you because you're so much smarter and more successful than they are."

This is nasty and flattering at the same time. And it makes life more interesting, which, if you're too sophisticated to just want attention, is the point of existence.

In Public

If you don't manage to get rid of everyone and end up having to go somewhere with a group of people, make sure the couples are separated and that each partner is escorted by somebody new. This will give everyone something different to fight about later.

Generally speaking, a man is supposed to walk to the left of a woman and also keep himself between her and the curb. Of course, it is frequently impossible to do both. But the great thinkers of all ages have been unanimous in their admiration of paradox.

Unless he is helping her into an ambulance or a paddy wagon, a man is never supposed to touch a woman in public. That is, he shouldn't if he's married to the woman. Nothing is more deleterious to the spirit of romance than watching a married couple hold hands.

If a man is walking down the street with two women, he should keep them both on his right and not appear between them like an acrobat taking a bow. Every authority on etiquette mentions this precept. But what no authority on etiquette mentions is how a man can manage to get two women in the first place. The best idea is for him to convince his wife or girlfriend to talk a friend of hers into a threesome. Most likely the result will be physically and emotionally disastrous. But everyone will get something juicy to tell the psychiatrist and something to romanticize in a diary or memoirs. Again, life is made more interesting.

It's no longer de rigueur for a man to burden himself with anything heavy that a woman is carrying, especially not a mortgage or someone else's baby. Nor should a man necessarily hold a door for a woman, unless it is a revolving door. It's not good manners to hold a revolving door, but it is lots of fun when other people are trapped inside.

Restaurants, Taxicabs, and the Theater

When entering a restaurant, a man should allow the woman to precede him to their seats. This lets her find a friend whose table she can stand at and chat for half an hour while the man gets a chance to glimpse the prices on the menu and has a clear shot to bolt for the door when he sees those prices.

A wise woman allows a man to enter a taxicab ahead of her so she can slam his hand in the door if he's been acting like an ass.

At the theater, concert, or ballet, a man allows a woman to take her seat first. He then holds her coat on his lap, along with his own coat, her purse, her umbrella, both programs, and any other personal effects. Safely hidden behind this mound of belongings, he can go to sleep.

The Importance of Being on Time

Whatever type of event you're attending, it's important to be on time. Being on time should not be confused with being prompt. Being prompt means arriving at the beginning. Being on time means arriving at the most interesting moment. Excepting love affairs, that moment is rarely the beginning.

"On time" is between midnight and four a.m. in New York, even for an eight o'clock play. Between midnight and four a.m. the actors will be getting drunk in a bar, and they'll be much more fun to talk to than when they're up on the stage.

In most other urban areas, "on time" is between twenty minutes and an hour late. This gives everyone else time to be late, too, and they'll appreciate it.

In the country being on time more nearly approximates being prompt. But don't overdo it. Being early is an unpardonable sin. If you are early, you'll witness the last-minute confusion and panic that always attend making anything seem effortlessly gracious.

In California, "on time" doesn't mean anything at all. An appointment for a meeting at three o'clock on Tuesday indicates there won't be a meeting and there might not be a Tuesday. Few words and no numbers have any meaning west of the Nevada border.

At Home

One popular way to avoid the problem of being on time is to stay at home and conduct your life over the telephone. This is very chic in New York. Even New Yorkers who occasionally go outdoors have taken to telephoning every person they know once a day and twice if any of them has anything awful to say about the others.

Living over the telephone has a number of advantages. It saves on cab fare and clothing budgets, and love affairs can be conducted without the bother of contraception or hairdressers. In fact, with judicious use of answering machines, a love affair can be conducted without the bother of ever talking to the loved one.

Making Up in Public

It's bad manners to apply cosmetics in public. It reminds people that you need them.

Smoking in Public

Smoking was once subject to all sorts of polite restrictions, but now it's just illegal. Therefore, there's only one remaining rule of etiquette about smoking in public: make sure you don't smoke anywhere else. Smoking is an inexpensive and convenient means of showing fashionable contempt for middle-class rules and regulations. Smoking also looks good. People who don't smoke have a terrible time finding something polite to do with their lips. But, when no one's around to see you, it doesn't matter what you do so there's no point in smoking then.

If someone asks you not to smoke, tell him you have no intention of living to be an embittered old person. But thank him for his concern.

Nonchalance

Nonchalance about health and well-being is what gives smoking its charm. That same nonchalance is at the heart of all really good manners. The most fundamental lesson of etiquette is "be unconcerned." Proper behavior means always giving the appearance of unperturbed grace. This appearance is much easier to achieve if you really *don't* care about anything. And this is why people always seem to be on their best behavior right before they commit suicide.

Code of A Modern Gentleman

1. Never strike anyone so old, small, or weak that verbal abuse would have sufficed.
2. Never steal anything so small that you'll have to go to an unpleasant city jail for it instead of a minimum security federal tennis prison.
3. Remember, the truth is rude. Consider the truth about where babies come from, especially some people's.
4. Never be unfaithful to a lover, except with your wife.
5. Never transmit a sexual disease in public.
6. Women and children should be protected in every tax-deductible way.
7. Don't pull on a crewneck sweater with a lit cigarette in your mouth.

Important People: When to Stand Up, When to Sit Down, and When to Roll Over and Play Dead

An important person should be treated exactly like anyone else holding a gun at your head.

Fortunately there aren't many important people. To be important a person must be able to have an effect on your life. But the anarchy, entropy, and confusion in what's left of Western civilization make it difficult for anyone to have any effect on anything. Therefore this section is about people who are *called* important rather than people who *are* important. The headwaiter at Ma Maison, IRS auditors, and your immediate superior at work are important enough to be treated under separate headings.

People Who Are Important "To Me"

Some people who are called important are the "to me" kind of important, as in, "My parents are important to me." If it is necessary to explain that someone is important to you, that explanation is all you are socially obligated to do for him. He isn't that important.

Famous People

Other people who are called important are actually famous. Of course, they aren't important, either. And it would be hard to think of anything less important than some of them. A lamprey is more important than Bianca Jagger. But it is not a lie to call famous people important, because it isn't they to whom we are referring. It's their fame. Fame is very important. Modern society is without any concept of dignity, worth, or regard. Today the only thing which sets one person apart from another is his or her degree of fame.

Social obligations to the modern or famous type of important people are enormous and complex. We must be as obsequious as possible to famous people and do everything in our power to make them like us. Fame is a communicable disease. And if you kiss the ass of someone who's got it, you may catch it yourself.

Introductions

In order to meet famous people and give them the opportunity to take advantage of you, an introduction is necessary. Asking for their autograph or running up to their restaurant table and gushing over their latest cause for notoriety ("I *loved* your divorce!") won't do.

The perfectly correct and most formal introduction is: "Mr. Awfulpics, may I present Mr. Climby" or "Mr. Grosspoints, may I present you to Miss Bedable." Or use the word "introduce" instead of "present." It's almost as correct and not as stupid sounding. The less famous person is presented to the more famous person. But men are always presented to women no matter how many times the man has appeared on the cover of *Time* and no matter how obvious it is that the woman wants to sleep with him just because he has. The only circumstance in which a woman is presented to a man is if that man is president of the United States—and who'd want to sleep with *him*?

Children

Children are never introduced at all unless the famous person has a thing for them and you have one paid for and ready at the time.

Subfamous People

Of course, the very formal method of introduction is never used by sophisticated people because sophisticated people have never had occasion to read a book of etiquette. Besides, most of them know each other already. But it is wise to use the most ceremonious forms with people such as game-show hosts, rock-star wives, daytime television personalities, Cher's boyfriends, and others who might be insecure about their social status because they have none.

Otherwise, introductions are tailored to the circumstances and to the amount of fame involved. If there is no fame involved and you're just introducing one worthless friend of yours to another, you can say simply, "Don't you guys know each other?" and walk away.

Insignificant Friends

When you want to introduce an insignificant friend to a famous person, you probably don't really *want* to at all. It's hard to do what you really want all the time but, like every difficult task, it results in a feeling of great accomplishment and satisfaction. Just leave your friend standing there like furniture while you chat happily with the MTV veejay, mafia hit man, or elected official.

If you owe money to the friend or are married to him or her and taking this tack will get you in trouble, you can say, "Oh, by the way, Mr. Panflash, this is Alice. We went to the same child psychiatrist back in Lake Forest." If you have an ancient acquaintance with someone not worth knowing, most people will at least pretend to forgive you—the way they would pretend to forgive you for a birth defect or the wrong racial background. Of course, your spouse—whom you met two weeks ago in a health club—may be perplexed by this explanation, but that's what your spouse gets for trying to marry up.

Ambitious Friends

Introducing an ambitious friend to a famous person is more tricky. It's not done unless the friend is so ambitious that he might be of use to you someday. Ambitious people are a lot more annoying than worthless people. Strategically, you don't want to alienate the friend but, tactically, you don't want to be remembered for foisting that friend on your famous acquaintance. Say, "Mrs. Greedagent, this is my friend Mark. He's involved in a lot of really interesting cable TV projects." You've used the phrase "cable TV projects"—international code words for "unemployed and on the make"—so the celebrity cannot claim she wasn't warned. Change "cable TV projects" to "video art" if you think it will be a really long, long time before your friend is famous himself.

When Two People Are Both Important

Introducing important people to each other is much more satisfying than introducing them to video artists. One approach is to do everything you can to make them attractive to each other and hope that you will receive a sort of social "finder's fee" if they hit it off. They won't. The social habits of famous people are like the sexual practices of porcupines, which urinate on each other to soften the quills. A more interesting thing to do is to make sure the two important people loathe each other right from the start: "Ana Plotless, this is Bret Leadpart. Bret thinks your novels are very good—of their kind . . . Bret, Ana has told me that she's heard you're very famous—in Japan." This way you'll become the conduit for all sorts of wonderful maliciousness between these two august souls.

When One Person Is Important and the Other Person Is "Interesting"

The most delightful introduction you can make is to introduce an important person to someone he or she is going to find sexually interesting. This introduction is made in two parts. First you prep the sex object: "Kiki, save the drugs for later. I'm going to introduce you to Antonio. Antonio is a famous photographer . . . Yes, he does lots of fashion—Paris *Vogue*." Then you march Kiki over to your well-known friend. "Antonio, you're going to love this girl. She once made Warren Beatty bleed out the ears." Kiki's name is not a necessary part of the transaction.

Introducing Yourself

There is only one person you can never introduce to the famous and that is yourself. Therefore it's good to cultivate the affections of professional sycophants such as publicists, movie agents, and freelance writers for *Vanity Fair* magazine. These people are understandably short of friends, and, if you are kind to them, they'll let you get the benefit of celebrity acquaintance while they do the fawning and toadying necessary for such acquaintance to be achieved.

Making Famous People Comfortable

Once you've met a famous person, say something that will make you remembered: "Cornelia Guest! Oh, my gosh, Miss Guest, I know it's polite for a gentleman to remove his hat when he meets a lady, but for you, I feel I should do something more, like take off my pants!!!"

Then shut up. Famous people think they want to be treated like regular people. This is not true. Famous people also think they are special and wonderful. This is even less true. The best course of action is to go ahead and treat them as if they are ordinary (because, boy, are they ever) but now and then throw something into the conversation to show that you share their completely wrongheaded opinion of their own wonderfulness: "Gosh, Cornelia, you make liposuction *come alive*!"

When the famous person you've met is not in your immediate company, ignore him or her completely. This is the modern use of the "cut direct" mentioned above. Whereas, in former times, the cut direct was used on enemies, it has now evolved into a polite way to show respect for famous friends. It is an article of faith among celebrities that they are constantly pestered by the public. Of course there are so many celebrities, and so few of them are celebrated for anything, that most of the time the public can't be bothered. But it's only common courtesy to act as though the famous people you know are so famous that the public is very bothered indeed. You don't want to be seen as part of that public. Wait for the celebrities to pester you. They will soon enough. If they weren't infantile self-obsessed hogs for attention, then our kind of society never would have thought they were important in the first place.

THE BACHELOR HOME COMPANION

(1987, revised edition 1993)

"If dirt was trumps, what hands you would hold!

—Charles Lamb

We Are All Bachelors Now

This book is addressed to the true bachelor, an adult male and a gentleman, who has never married and never intends to.

We are a select group, without personal obligation, social encumbrance, or any socks that match. We breathe the cold, pure air of solitude—of Olympus, of Parnassus, and of the basement where all the pipes are frozen because nobody turned up the thermostat. We have no need, unless puzzled by a meat loaf recipe, for dull, cloying familial ties. We are free to drop everything and mount our Rocinante on a moment's notice. (Although sometimes it takes a little longer than a moment because we can't remember which laundry the shirts are at.)

Sherlock Holmes was portrayed as a bachelor. So was Raffles the Gentleman Cracksmith. Sir Isaac Newton and Giacomo Casanova were bachelors, also Saint Paul, President Buchanan, Nietzsche, Oliver Goldsmith, George "Chinese" Gordon, Voltaire, and almost all the popes. King Henry VIII kept trying to be one. The Lone Ranger, Sam Spade, and Jesus Christ will always be bachelors, not to mention Clarabell, Mayor Koch, and Daffy Duck.

We are our own men, aloof and independent, unchocked wheels in a world of cogs and gears. We do as we damn well please. And we don't belong to any immune-deficiency high-risk groups either.

We also don't exist.

What's become of the bachelors of yore? The old salts? The Oxford dons? The misanthropic billionaires wedded solely to greed? Well, some of us turned out to belong to that immune-deficiency high-risk group after all (Daffy Duck for one, I'll bet). Some of us broke down and got married and are paying a fortune in child support. And the rest of us turned into "singles."

We've given up cigarettes and are attempting to cut down on saturated fats. We live in condominium apartment complexes with heather-tone wall-to-wall carpeting. We try to meet girls at aerobics classes. And we're in transactional analysis, dealing with our conflicted feelings about making a commitment.

Therefore this book is really addressed to assistant district sales managers, Dekes and Phi Delts in off-campus housing, divorced guys, young men who've been told to get the hell out of the house by their parents, and any fellow whose girlfriend won't marry him because her first husband was such a bummer. That is, to every male in a house without pot holders.

This book is also addressed to husbands whose wives have discovered careers, self-fulfillment, or Visa cards with astronomical credit ceilings. Like the rest of us, these "grass bachelors" must face that Augean stable whose name is kitchen.

In fact, this book is even addressed to the traditional housewife and mother who, in her heart, would like to put the kids in the dog run and go play golf. Go ahead. Throw a wad of baloney in there and grab your Pings. It doesn't matter. Home life in our society has already disintegrated. Small children come home to find their parents (which, stepfolks included, can number as many as ten) gone to jobs, love affairs, racket ball courts, or detox centers. Old people are forced by uncaring progeny (and their own incessant complaints about what's on TV) to live in the confines of golden-age communities. Even newlyweds don't spend much time together, now that few marriages outlast the appliance warranties.

Motherly landladies and devoted kitchen help have disappeared, too—off playing seniors tennis and cheating the welfare agencies. We are all discovering anew what any ancient bond servant (or Mom, if we'd been listening) could have told us: keeping house is as unpleasant and filthy as coal mining, and the pay's a lot worse.

So when it comes right down to it, this book is addressed to everybody. We are all bachelors now, "strangers in a home we never made."

How I Became a Bachelor Housewife

I always wanted to be a bachelor when I grew up. My friends may have had fantasies about raking the yard, seeing their loved ones in pin curlers, and cleaning the garage on Sundays, but not me. I saw myself at thirty-eight lounging around a penthouse in a brocade smoking jacket. Vivaldi would be playing on the stereo. I'd sip brandy from a snifter the size of a fish tank and leaf through an address book full of R-rated phone numbers.

It never occurred to me that the penthouse would be littered with dirty socks, damp bath towels, old sports sections, and empty pizza boxes. I'd have to dig through all that stuff to find the brocade smoking jacket, and then it would need treatment with complicated spot removers. Lounging around the penthouse in an undershirt is not the same. Besides, it isn't a penthouse. Who can afford a penthouse in a job market filled with wildly competitive married guys supporting three ex-families?

I think I'll skip the brandy. You shouldn't drink on an empty stomach. I looked in the refrigerator—nothing in there except half a bottle of flat tonic water, two withered limes, and one more empty pizza box. (The brandy snifter got broken in the dishwasher anyway.)

Of course, bachelors can just go hang out in fancy restaurants all night. And I would if I weren't broke from buying new clothes. You know how it is with us fashion-conscious bachelors, always trying to keep up with the latest sartorial trends. Well, sort of. Actually, I have to buy new clothes because I destroy all my chinos and boxer shorts every time I go to the laundromat.

I used to do this with bleach and fabric softener. These made enormous piebald blotches and great big holes in my clothes. Being a suave bachelor and all, I felt it beneath my dignity to stand in a laundromat reading the instructions on the bottles. Not to mention the instructions on the machines. I might as well try to land a DC-10. What on earth is a "prewash cycle"? Prewash means "before washing." Before washing is when the clothes are scattered all over the floor. Why would I want to put money and bleach in a washing machine then? If anyone ever designs washing machines for bachelors, there will be one big dial with two settings: DIRTY and DON'T BREATHE.

Now, I just use lots of detergent. If some is good, more must be better, and a whole box should be great. (Another thing about washing machine instructions, they're printed on the inside of the washing machine lid. This is not where you want the instructions when the machine is spewing foam all over the laundromat and you can't even get near it, let alone open the top.) The clothes *do* get clean. True, they're stiff, have chunks of solidified laundry soap in the pockets, and smell like *eau de Fab*. But that doesn't matter because I'm going to ruin them in the dryer.

The way dryers work is you put wet clothes in, run the dryer for an hour, and take wet clothes out. Leave these mildewing in a laundry bag for a couple of days, and they'll smell every bit as bad as they did before you washed them. What I recommend is insert a hundred quarters in the coin slot and go watch football games. When you come back the clothes will be dry and just the right size—if you own a doll collection. Like most bachelors, I don't.

So I go out and buy new chinos and new boxer shorts and try to save money by cooking at home. However, it's hard to make even a simple omelet with flat tonic water, withered limes, and empty pizza boxes.

The problem with grocery shopping is it lacks an element of surprise. Wait until you're very hungry before going to the store. This way you'll make lots of surprising impulse purchases. It's like Christmas when I get the grocery bags home. I don't know what might be in there—a ten-pound bag of pistachio nuts, jars of pickled squid, tinned guava jelly, goat pâté. However, it's hard to make a simple omelet with pistachio nuts, pickled squid, guava jelly, and goat pâté, too. This means another trip to the store.

Why does everything come in Giant Size, King Size, and Holy Roman Empire Size boxes? A package of macaroni as big as a Japanese car is not what I need. And I don't understand unit pricing. There's the price, the unit price, the sale price, but what does the damn thing *cost*? And I can't find stuff. Whatever I want is always thirty brands of sugar-frosted cereal away from where I am. Supermarkets should arrange it so important purchases like peanut butter, roach spray, and cigarettes are in one place, while everything else is off in a married-couple annex with the fabric softeners and breakfast foods. (Do people really feed their children purple cornflakes shaped like movie monsters? Are they mad at the kids, or what?)

I go to delicatessens because they'll bring me what I ask for. "Give me a six-pack of eggs," I say.

Bachelor cooking is a matter of attitude. If you think of it as setting fire to things and making a mess, it's fun. It's not so much fun if you think of it as dinner. Fortunately, baloney, cheeseburgers, beer, and potato-chip dip provide all the daily nutrients bachelors are known to require. I mean, I hope they do.

I have several specialties. Instant coffee is one. Simple omelets are another. My recipe: add contents of refrigerator to two eggs and cook until everything stops wiggling. A bachelor friend of mine has an interesting variation. Mix last night's Chinese takeout food with your scrambled eggs. (Remove fortunes from fortune cookies first.) He calls it Egg Foo Breakfast.

I also make a stew. I put meat, beef bouillon, potatoes, celery, carrots, onions, and a splash of red wine into a large pot. When it begins to simmer I go watch football games until all the ingredients boil down to a tarry mass. Then I phone out for pizza or Chinese.

Nomenclature is an important part of bachelor cooking. If you call it "Italian cheese toast," it's not disgusting to have warmed-over pizza for breakfast.

Pizza for breakfast is one of the great examples of bachelor freedom. And, as a bachelor, I'm free to eat pizza anywhere I want—in front of the TV or on the bed or in the bathtub. I also eat, at least to judge by where I find leftovers, in the hall closet and under the couch.

I find a lot of things under the couch whenever I clean up, giant dust bunnies mostly, but mysterious things, too—rubber beach toys, copies of *Livestock Breeding Quarterly*, "Souvenir of the Seattle World's Fair" pen and pencil sets.

Maybe there are other people who live in my house and I don't know about it. I certainly don't remember putting a cigar out in the soap dish or using that new Vivaldi CD as a drink coaster or hiding my cuff links behind the thesaurus. What are my dress shoes doing in the toilet tank? Why has somebody been scaling fish on the bedroom rug?

A lot of bachelor time that married people believe is spent paging through address books is really spent using T-shirts as dust cloths and getting vacuum-cleaner cords tangled in footstools. Or thinking up reasons not to. I think, "Dirt is superficial, a matter of appearances." I think, "If you can't see dirt, it doesn't really exist." No fair looking behind the stereo speakers.

I keep the light low. Not hard when your windows need washing as badly as mine do. Also I'd be risking my neck to wash windows in my fifth-floor apartment. What if I dropped something? A paper towel soaked in Windex might kill from that height. No use washing the dishes either. The automatic dishwasher breaks everything. I tried using paper plates, but the dishwasher made a mess of those, too.

Being a bachelor has turned me into a housewife, a lousy housewife. And now I have a different perspective on the traditional woman's role in society. A housewife has to be a chemist, engineer, mechanic, economist, philosopher, and workaholic. That's just to pick up after herself. I shudder at what it must be like when there are kids, pets, and somebody like me in the home. Therefore it is with profound respect that I ask for advice from my women friends.

"What should I do about that green fungus in the bread box?" I ask.

"I don't know," they tell me. "You'll have to talk to my husband. He does the cooking at our house. I'm pretty busy with my career."

Bachelor Entertaining

One of the best things about bachelorhood is that no one expects hospitality from us. We're obviously selfish people or we'd be married and holding up our end of the car pool. Furthermore, society is a free market and we are a scarce commodity. Every hostess in America is wracking her Rolodex for unattached dinner guests.

As long as our looks don't actually gag a cat, we're invited everywhere. In return, all we have to do is keep our fingers out of wedding rings. Ours is the life of the happy drone. The whole hive of civilization is busy feeding us and keeping us amused.

Nevertheless, there are moments when bachelors are expected to act the host. Sometimes lovers or parents corner us, sometimes we give in to misplaced whims of congeniality, and sometimes twenty old SDS buddies show up on the porch, drugged and armed.

There are three types of entertainment a bachelor is traditionally called on to provide:

1. Love trysts
2. Dinner parties
3. Enormous drunken blowouts

Money is your best weapon. Take all your guests to a restaurant and let the restaurant people clean up the mess. If you get someone stupid on the MasterCard 800 number, maybe you can convince him that your telephone number is your credit limit. If this fails, try postponing the event in hope of atomic war. Atomic war is much overrated as tragedy, compared to what an enormous drunken blowout can do to your house. If atomic war fails, follow the directions below.

The Love Tryst

The proper love tryst has three elements:

1. Drinks
2. Cozy meal
3. Interesting excuse

The interesting excuse is not actually interesting. It just gives your date an excuse for not saying good-bye when she ought to. Usually it's a videotape of something highbrow like a Truffaut remake of *Francis Joins the Navy*. With any luck you won't see the end of it.

The important thing in a love tryst it to make your home tug at your date's heartstrings. Women like to think every bachelor is one of the Lost Boys who wandered away from Neverland while Peter and Wendy weren't looking.

Turn your place into a female's idea of a mess, which is to say clean it. Women know we can't take care of ourselves, and they think this is adorable. But that doesn't keep them from blanching at the sight of soap scum. Now muss your home with boyish clutter. Hang neckties from cute places like the refrigerator-door handle. Stick your ski hat on top of a lampshade. Leave a half-empty wineglass on a table next to a burned-down candle and sheets of stationery covered with crossed-out lines of poetry. (Steal them from Rupert Brooke.) Toss your tuxedo on the floor. And use a wastepaper basket for an ice bucket. This is what women mean when they say, "His place was a fright." If your place is *really* a fright, they won't stay long enough to talk about it.

Be sure all towels and sheets are clean. And make your bed, no matter how strange this seems. Women make their beds each morning and they assume everyone—criminals on the lam, animals in their burrows—does the same. It isn't hard, once you have the knack. Just keep tucking in the end parts of things until their middle parts get smoothed out and flat. But be sure to move around the bed as you do this. If you stand in one place and tuck, you'll wind up with all the blankets completely under the mattress.

Now wreck dinner. There are two forms of the intentional dinner muff. Using the first method, have all the ingredients for a good dinner ready but don't start cooking until your date arrives. Throw meat that's still wrapped in butcher paper into the oven without a pan. Cram the brown-and-serve rolls into the toaster. As with housecleaning, if you're really incompetent, your date will feel obliged to take over. This, however, is a mean thing to do to a woman and, believe me, she'll know it.

The second method is better. Have the dinner under way before your date arrives, and make sure it's terrifying. Fix baloney soup and pickled beet salad with ouzo and sheep cheese dressing. And make sure all of it, including the salad, catches fire during drinks. Then just when the gruesome slop is supposed to be served, a prearranged pizza delivery boy shows up at the front door.

The Perfect Little Dinner Party

Why spoil it by showing up? Let people ring your doorbell for a while and go away puzzled but probably relieved. Or be a bully. When you invite your guests, they'll say, "Is there anything I can bring?" Tell them, "Yes, a salad, a vegetable dish, dessert, and an eight-pound standing rib roast—medium rare." Voilà, dinner is served.

If this doesn't work, serve what you can muster and distract like mad. Serve unshucked oysters as hors d'oeuvres. Put the table someplace unusual, like out in the yard in the snow. Dress your dog as a butler. Make guests cook their own live lobsters on weenie forks in the fireplace. If you keep people busy and confused, they're liable to think they're having fun.

The Enormous Drunken Blowout

Here's an event where bachelor expertise pays off. Bachelors know all about parties. In fact, a good bachelor is a living, breathing party all by himself. At least that is what my girlfriend said when she found the gin bottles under the couch. I believe her exact words were, "You're a disgusting, drunken mess." And that's a good description of a party, if it's done right.

Every society needs to blow off steam. Classical Greece had its Dionysia. Ancient Rome had its bacchanals. But modern America seems to have gotten off the track. We are the only culture to ever develop a type of festivity where you get cornered by a pipe-smoking psych prof who's a bug on nuclear winter.

To turn a dumb soiree into a dangerous bash, the first consideration is time. Don't choose an ordinary time like Saturday night. Have your party at eleven on a weekday morning. The purpose of parties is fun. And *anything* is fun when you're supposed to be working. Other good times for a party are during college exams, jury deliberations, hospital stays, and any time during a marriage.

A good excuse for a party is usually not what you think. Birthdays, weddings, family reunions, and other occasions with an atmosphere of obligatory joy are a bore. Some of the best parties are after funerals. Fun and happiness are not synonymous. Happy people don't need fun. Fun takes your mind off things. If you have a wonderful marriage, beautiful children, a great job, and you're sure you'll go to heaven when you die—why would you want to take your mind off *that*? But the rest of us need lots of fun.

Whatever the occasion, do not neglect alcohol. No other refreshment will do. Yes, alcohol kills brain cells, but it's very selective. It kills only the brain cells that contain good sense, shame, embarrassment, and restraint. Wield a heavy hand at the bar. Spike the white wine. Forget all the soft drinks and most of the mixers; these contain dangerous amounts of water. Water is no fun unless you're throwing people into a swimming pool. You don't want your guests to get *half* drunk. They might suddenly remember the babysitter, try to drive home, and kill themselves. If a guest is able to make it to the end of your driveway, you've unleashed a dangerous maniac on America's highways.

You also need to have your party in the right kind of place, a place that's too small. You have to pack people together to make them act silly. Try this experiment with house cats. Observe what five house cats do in a living room. Now observe what they do in a laundry sack. This is why parties on boats and in bathtubs are always successful. But any unusual place, regardless of size, is good. High dangerous places like roofs and bridges are excellent. Caves, abandoned warehouses, and beachfront motels during hurricanes are also great. The party spirit responds to any bizarre locale. A bachelor apartment qualifies.

Lots of noise and lots of people are a must for a good party. Make sure some of these people hate each other. Otherwise there will be no chemistry. What would the universe be like if there were only positively charged protons and no negatively charged electrons? Nothing would happen. The most basic molecules couldn't exist. The world wouldn't have hydrogen, let alone cute blond girls in short skirts. Chaos takes organization.

Not every kind of noise will do either. You can't play RUN-D.M.C. if you're feting the Capitol Hill set. To pick the right music, determine your party crowd's median age. Then play hit songs from the most mentally retarded period of their lives—when they were in their teens.

One Final Point

In order to make sure the party gets completely out of hand, you'll need "party catalysts." Drugs are okay, but things for the guests to throw at each other are better, also legal. Have plenty of things available to throw, and if no one takes the hint, throw them yourself—Jell-O cubes, snowballs, wet paper towels. Things that squirt are good, too—seltzer bottles, warm champagne. If that doesn't get things going, bust up the furniture.

REPUBLICAN PARTY REPTILE

(*1987*)

A POPULAR JOKE FROM THE 1930S:

A boy is hitchhiking on a country road. A car stops for him and the driver asks, "Are you a Republican or a Democrat?"

"Democrat," says the boy, and the car speeds off.

Another car stops and the driver asks, "Are you a Republican or a Democrat?"

"Democrat," says the boy, and the car speeds off.

This happens three more times, and the boy decides he's giving the wrong answer. The next car that stops is a convertible driven by a beautiful blonde. "Are you a Republican or a Democrat?" she asks.

"Republican," says the boy, and she lets him in.

But as they're driving along, the wind from the open top begins to push the blonde's skirt higher and higher up her legs. And the boy finds himself becoming aroused. Finally he can't control himself any longer. "Stop!" he hollers. "Let me out! I've only been a Republican for ten minutes and already I feel like screwing somebody!"

Myths Made Modern

Twelve Romances from the Hellenic Golden Age Turned into a Dozen Stories about Greek Love

Apollo and Daphne

Apollo is the son of Jupiter, who is president of the gods, and Latona, an old girlfriend of Jupiter's whom he never married. Apollo is the god of handguns, Blue Cross coverage, and elaborate home stereo systems. Also, he is the god of getting a dark and even tan.

Apollo's first love was a girl named Daphne, and this came about because of the anger of Cupid, the god of interpersonal relationships. Apollo, as befits a god, possesses perfect marksmanship. In fact, it was his celestial hand that steadied the .44 caliber pistol when the Son of Sam murdered all the pale girls who weren't carrying adequate medical insurance. And it was also Apollo who guided the shots that hit John Lennon because of the awful mixing quality on the Plastic Ono Band album. Apollo was chaffing Cupid about that deity's recent change to automatic weapons, which Cupid insisted was necessary to keep up with the fast-paced shifts in modern emotional involvement. Apollo was saying that Cupid could not hit the long side of a supertanker with an Uzi, so Cupid let him have it with one of his deep-felt emotional-commitment rounds. Then Cupid fired a couple of the bullets that make women want careers. And these struck Daphne, who was a beautiful tennis-court nymph. Apollo was immediately smitten with Daphne, but she wanted to go to law school. Apollo followed Daphne around and pestered her and phoned her in the middle of the night all the time until Daphne became annoyed and called upon Diana, the goddess of women who are searching for self-fulfillment, and asked that august deity to turn her into a female Family Court judge. Apollo wept when he saw the transformation. But he still loved Daphne, and to this day, whenever Apollo spies a case of child abuse where the youngster's injuries aren't covered by a private or corporate medical plan, he has the parents arrested and their case placed on Daphne's court docket.

Io

Juno is the first lady of Olympus and the goddess of acting like a married woman. She keeps a close eye on her husband, Jupiter. One day while Juno was straightening up around heaven she saw a large smog cloud descend over the usually sunny climes of Southern California. Juno suspected Jupiter of causing this smog to conceal some activity of his. So she called upon Zephyr, an arctic air mass high-pressure zone causing local high winds and cold temperatures, to blow the smog away. Then Jupiter was revealed in a motel room with a Datsun. Juno guessed that the Datsun's form concealed some fair beauty, transformed for concealment's sake. And she was right, for it was Io, daughter of the Imperial Valley irrigation sprinkler system god Inachus. Jupiter had been dallying with her all afternoon in the motel.

Juno quickly joined her husband and praised the beauty of the compact car in his room. Jupiter claimed that he had just created it from a bedspring and a room-sized refrigerator unit on commission for a Japanese car company. Juno asked to have it as a gift. What could Jupiter do? He was loath to give his girlfriend to his wife, but how could he refuse Juno such a trifling request as a new Japanese car, especially one that got such good mileage? So he consented. Juno was still suspicious, however, and took the car to Argus to be closely watched.

Now, Argus was a beast with a hundred eyes and at least that many concealed microphones and wiretaps. He worked for the Central Intelligence Agency, even though he wasn't supposed to because its charter forbids domestic operations. Anyway, Argus never slept or at least didn't sleep very well unless he took two Nembutals, which his doctor had forbidden him for fear that he was developing a barbiturate dependency. So Argus kept Io under round-the-clock surveillance.

Jupiter was very upset by these developments, and so he called for Mercury. Mercury presides over big business, professional wrestling, running political campaigns, and illegal dumping of toxic waste—over all things, in other words, which require cleverness, dexterity, and two sets of account ledgers. Mercury is also the United Parcel Service delivery truck driver of the gods and wears a winged cap and wingtip shoes. Jupiter instructed Mercury to go to Argus and "lean on him a little." So Mercury pretended to be from the staff of a Senate subcommittee investigation and read to Argus from a book of government rules and regulations about clandestine intelligence operations for hours until every one of Argus's eyes closed and he was asleep. Then Mercury had him blown up by a right-wing Cuban expatriate group.

So Io escaped and drove down the highway to Palm Springs, but Juno sent a gas shortage to afflict her and she had to wait for hours and hours in a gas line in Compton, and her hubcaps were stolen. At last Jupiter interceded and, by promising to pay no further attentions to Io, convinced Juno to relent. Which she did, and furthermore Juno even went so far as to get Io a good part in a new thriller movie from Paramount, where we will be seeing her soon in a car chase all over Asia Minor.

Hero and Leander

Leander was a youth from Santa Monica, and Hero lived many miles away in Laurel Canyon, where she was a priestess of Venus, the goddess of mixed doubles, eye makeup, and random rape slayings. Every weekend Leander used to marathon-run all the way from Santa Monica to Laurel Canyon. But one weekend the weather wasn't very good and Leander decided to lift weights instead. And he never saw Hero or called her again. Some weeks later Hero saw Leander marathon-running with another girl, and she was so despondent that she began marathon-running also and now she feels a lot better about herself.

Diana and Actaeon

Diana is the virgin (with men, anyway) goddess of female self-actualization. She is also the protectoress of wives who have shot their husbands in the back of the head with a .38 after fifteen or twenty years of marriage and then get off with a plea of self-defense by saying their spouse used to whip them with a belt.

One day Actaeon, a noted job hunter, was out looking for work and accidentally saw Diana naked, or, some say, even worse, in a pretty, frilly dress. Diana turned Actaeon into an employer, and he was set upon by OSHA investigators who made him post danger signs in six languages over all his drill presses and give every member of his bookkeeping staff a hard hat and build a new $40,000 restroom for women workers with couches where they could lie down if they were having their periods. Eventually he was hounded into bankruptcy.

Pygmalion

Pygmalion was a fashion photographer who was homosexual and hated women. However, he had one model whom he had discovered while she was waiting tables in Redondo Beach, and he fixed her hair and did her makeup and showed her how to dress, and when he was done she was so beautiful that he fell in love with her even though he was queer. So Pygmalion prayed to Venus, the style and leisure section goddess, to transform the fashion model into a human woman, and—miracle of miracles—it was done. They both lived happily ever after until the fashion model met a movie actor and ran off to Kauai with him.

Orpheus and Eurydice

Orpheus was the son of Apollo and the muse Car Stereo. When Orpheus was a boy his father presented him with a Sony Walkman and a collection of Bix Beiderbecke tape cassettes. Nothing could withstand the charm of this music. Not only were Orpheus's friends and relatives entranced by the tunes but even the stock market could be lulled into a day of light trading by the fine melodic improvisations of Beiderbecke's cornet and the prime rate could be induced to drop a point or more.

Orpheus fell in love with the beautiful Eurydice, but unfortunately she stepped on a cancer cell during their honeymoon and was killed by a bad movie plot. Orpheus went to the underworld in search of his bride. There he found his way barred by the great three-headed dog Cerberus, who has one head representing inadequate gun control, another head representing unemployment, and a third head representing judicial leniency and backlogged court calendars. Cerberus relented, however, when Orpheus let him wear the Walkman on his unemployment head and listen to "In a Mist." After that Orpheus talked to a number of underworld figures and many of them turned out to be real Beiderbecke fans too. They agreed to let Eurydice out of the movie contract where she had to die from the special kind of cancer that only actresses get (and which lets them keep their looks even after they're supposed to have been on chemotherapy for six months). The only condition was that Orpheus was never to look at the videotapes of what Eurydice had been doing while she was associating with reputed members of organized-crime families. But Orpheus couldn't resist taking a peek, and it ruined their marriage.

Penelope's Suitors

Penelope was the wife of the war hero Ulysses, who had been an officer in Vietnam. He was overseas for a long time and Penelope felt like he was *never* coming back. So she had a lot of suitors. But Ulysses did come back, and when he did he killed all of Penelope's men friends. And he would have gone to jail if the jury hadn't decided that he was suffering from post-Vietnam stress syndrome and therefore had been temporarily insane.

Echo and Narcissus

Echo was a sauna, Jacuzzi, and hot-tub nymph who never had anything original to say, and Narcissus suffered from a narcissistic personality disorder and was somewhat neurotic. They dated for a while but it didn't really work out. She's got a job now as a production assistant at Lorimar and he's trying to make it as a male model.

Pyramus and Thisbe

Pyramus was the best-looking boy and Thisbe was the cutest girl in all of Tarzana Junior High School. But even though they lived right next door to each other their parents wouldn't let them date because each family thought the other family wasn't Jewish. So the only way Pyramus and Thisbe could get together was at the tennis club or at parties or in school or at the beach or in the shopping mall or at dances or on the weekends.

One night Pyramus and Thisbe agreed to meet secretly on the boardwalk in Venice. Thisbe got there first, but before Pyramus came to meet her she was chased by a Mexican street gang, and as she ran away she dropped her purse. Pyramus arrived shortly, and when he came to the place where he was supposed to meet Thisbe he saw her purse where it had fallen with all of its contents spilled out on the sidewalk. "Alas," spoke Pyramus, "Thisbe has been chased by a Mexican street gang and doubtless raped and will now have all sorts of hang-ups about sex and will have to go to group therapy sessions and also her birth-control pills are lying here on the ground and have been crushed by roller skaters and she's probably not going to want to fuck anyway until she gets the prescription refilled. I guess I'll turn queer." But Thisbe had escaped from the gang of Mexicans and was returning to the place where she had vowed to meet Pyramus just as Pyramus tried to pick up a member of another Mexican street gang. So they both got raped.

On the very spot the three Fates, Clotho, Lachesis, and Atropos—who stitch the cloth of human destiny into slacks and have the cuffs altered to determine man's life span—have caused a mulberry tree to be planted with berries red as blood. But this has nothing to do with our story and was the result of an earlier car wreck.

Pluto and Proserpine

Proserpine was the beautiful daughter of Ceres, goddess of farm price supports and of balancing economic development with ecological concerns. Proserpine used to hang around with Pluto, an underworld big shot. They eloped and were married in Reno and then Pluto carried her off either to Hell or to the 1948 Democratic National Convention—it being difficult to tell the difference in the matter of smoke and noise. Ceres was wroth. She searched everywhere for her daughter and in her anger she caused wheat rust and weevils and leaf blight and soil erosion and a really incompetent

Department of Agriculture bureaucracy under the Truman administration, thus bringing much distress to mankind. At long last the whereabouts of Proserpine came to light during the Senate's Kefauver Committee hearings on organized crime. Ceres sent her lawyer to make a deal with Pluto, and in return for immunity from federal prosecution Pluto allowed Proserpine to visit her mother during the spring and summer at the Ceres family truck farm near El Centro. And that is how the different seasons of the year came into being. Thus, to this day, for half the year we have floods and droughts and depressed prices on the commodities market and the rest of the time we have drug smuggling, extortion, murder, and theft.

Cupid and Psyche

The myth of Cupid and Psyche is a difficult myth to understand. Psyche was a beautiful young girl whom the god of liking people a lot fell in love with by accident when he shot himself in the foot. They got married, but it was an open marriage and Psyche wasn't supposed to see Cupid hardly at all. However, as it turned out, she saw quite a lot of him and caught more than a little grief from his possessive mother, Venus. Everything turned out all right in the long run, though, and Psyche was made an immortal by having her picture on the cover of *People* magazine.

The true meaning of this myth can only be understood by spending years in analysis with a Freudian psychiatrist who needs words like "psyche" to explain vague things he probably shouldn't be poking his nose into anyway.

Venus and Adonis

Part of Cupid's problems probably have to do with the fact that his mother, Venus, once fell in love with Adonis, a professional skier, and Cupid witnessed that young man's death in a chairlift accident. Venus was greatly grieved and transformed the fallen slalom racer into an eternal personal vibrator. As a result, Cupid still has ambivalent feelings about the active expression of female sexual needs.

Ship of Fools

(July, 1982)

I never did get it, what this trip was all about. I stood at the rail of the cruise ship *Alexander Pushkin* staring out at the vast rolling shore of the Volga. Here or there was a patch of grain, not high enough even in late July to conceal the line of furrows plowed straight downhill in the most erosion-producing way possible. And here or there was a skinny cow in an untidy hectare of pasture. But most of the land looked empty, unsown, ungrazed, uncultivated. And all around me were minds just as fallow.

I was on something called the Volga Peace Cruise, a sixteen-day trip to the USSR featuring a nine-day boat ride from Rostov north up the Don, through the Don-Volga canal, and on up the Volga River to Kazan. The 160 passengers were all Americans. Most were antinuke activists and peace-group organizers with sixties leftover looks. Others were products of the Old Left. The peaceniks talked about peace, mostly in terms of atomic holocaust. The leftists talked about peace, mostly in terms of Soviet-American relations. The entire program of the "peace cruise" consisted in the bunch of us talking about peace. And the Soviet government had provided five Russian "peace experts" to talk about peace too.

I asked some of my fellow passengers what the point was.

"Atomic holocaust is the most important issue facing mankind," said the peaceniks.

"Atomic holocaust and Soviet-American relations," said the leftists.

What about dissident Russian peace activists? Was anyone interested in talking to them?

"There is no need for dissident peace organizations in the Soviet Union," said the leftists. "The Soviet Union already has the largest peace organizations in the world. In America dissident peace organizations are important because American foreign policy is prowar. But the Soviet Union is propeace because twenty million Soviets died in World War II."

"Well, if we *see* any . . ." said the peaceniks.

Did anyone expect the Soviet "experts" to say anything everyone hadn't heard Soviet experts say already?

"Soviet-American relations are very important," said the leftists.

Were we going to convince those experts that their government ought to pull its troops out of Afghanistan?

"Huh?" said everyone.

Or maybe the leftists would convince the peace activists to take a more political view of things?

"What leftists?" said the leftists.

Friday, July 16, 1982

I was attracted to the Volga Peace Cruise by a half-page advertisement in the February 27, 1982, issue of *The Nation* magazine. It read, in part, "Find out for yourself what's going on in the Soviet Union capital and heartland as you join *The Nation* this summer on an exciting, affordable Soviet excursion."

I have a sneaking love for the old-time left and that compendium of their snits and quarrels *The Nation*. Mind you, I'm a registered Republican and consider socialism a violation of the American principle that you shouldn't stick your nose in other people's business except to make a buck. Still, Wobblies, Spanish Civil War veterans, the Hollywood Ten touch the heart somehow.

But, to tell the truth, I'd never met any Old Leftists. I expected them to be admirable and nasty, like Lillian Hellman, or brilliant, mysterious, denying everything, like Alger Hiss, or—best of all—hard-bitten and cynical but still willing to battle oppression, like Rick in *Casablanca*. I did not expect them to be the pack of thirty fussing geriatrics I met at Kennedy Airport, misplacing their hand luggage, losing their way to the ladies' room, barking at the airline personnel, and asking two hundred times which gate we'd have to be at in three and a half hours.

They were leftists all right. In between palsies of fretting, they'd tell you how wonderful the Soviet Union was: pensions were huge, housing was cheap, and they practically paid you to get medical care. Believe me, you haven't been bored until you've been buttonholed by a seventy-year-old woman who holds forth all afternoon on the perfidies of American foreign policy *and* shows you pictures of her grandchildren. These were people who believed everything about the Soviet Union was perfect, but they were bringing their own toilet paper.

Saturday, July 17

The ad had promised excitement, and surely entering the Soviet Union would be exciting. The Russians are famous for making border crossing an exciting event. But we just stood in line for four hours. "You can understand the delay," said a lady who had complained all night about everything on the flight to Moscow. "So many reactionary forces are trying to destroy the Soviet Union." If reactionary forces are vulnerable to understaffing and inept baggage handling, they don't stand a chance at the Moscow airport.

There was only one faint thrill when we handed in our passports to the officer in the little glass passport-control booth. He was maybe seventeen with a tunic too large around the neck and a hat too big by half. He made an awful face and shouted, "Num? Fuss num? Plas oaf burf? Dat oaf burf?"

One of my tour group members had been born in Kiev. She said her "plas oaf burf" was Russia.

"Dat oaf burf?"

"1915," she said.

"When leaf?" hollered the passport officer.

"1920."

"Reason leaf?" he yelled.

I swear she sounded embarrassed. "I don't know. My parents did it."

Then we got on a smoky, gear-stripped bus and rode past blocks of huge, clumsy apartment buildings and blocks of huge, clumsy apartment buildings and blocks of huge, clumsy apartment buildings, through the smoggy Moscow twilight, through half-deserted streets. No neon lights, no billboards, no commotion, not much traffic, everything dusty-looking and slightly askew, and everything the same for an hour and a half.

"Some people," said a leftist lady with orange hair and earrings the size of soup tureens, "say the Soviet Union's depressing. I don't know *how* they can say that."

We pulled up in front of an immense glass-curtain-walled modern hotel, a perfect Grand Hyatt knockoff, and I headed for the bar. It was pretty much like any bar in a Grand Hyatt. There was a big drunk man there, red-faced and bloated. He seemed to speak English. At least he was yelling at the bartender in it. "A glass of schnapps," he said. He got vodka.

"How long you been here?" I said.

"Hahahahahahaha," he said. "I'm from Frankfurt!"

"Scotch," I said to the bartender. "Where've you been?" I asked the drunk. The bartender gave me vodka.

"Fucking Afghanistan!" said the drunk. Afghanistan? Here was some excitement.

"Afghanistan?" I said, but he fell off his stool.

Sunday, July 18

My tour group of leftists met with another three or four groups in the Moscow hotel. The others were mostly peaceniks. I don't know how my group got involved in the peace cruise or how I got put in with them. They certainly weren't from *The Nation.* "*The Nation* prints too much anti-Soviet propaganda," said a potbellied man smoking a pipe with a stupid bend in the stem.

In fact, there was no one from *The Nation* on the cruise except one assistant editor in the book-review department. The excursion ad had run, I found out later, in large part because *The Nation* received a commission for each passenger it signed up. The ad had listed a number of other sponsors: Fellowship of Reconciliation, National Council of American-Soviet Friendship, Promoting Enduring Peace, Women's International League for Peace and Freedom, and World Fellowship League. A few passengers in the other tour groups were from those organizations, but most seemed to be representing tiny peace organizations of their own. And if you didn't stick socks in their mouths right away, they'd tell you all about it.

First, however, a visit to Lenin's tomb. It's real dark and chilly in there, and you march around three sides of the glass case, and it's like a visit to the nocturnal-predators section at the Reptile House with your grade-school class—no talking!

"He has the face of a poet," said our beautiful Intourist guide, Marya. He certainly does, a nasty, crazed, bigoted face just like Ezra Pound's.

None of the leftists so much as sniffled. This offended me. I can get quite misty at the Lincoln Memorial. And I had to explain who John Reed was when we walked along the Kremlin wall. "Oh, that's right," said the orange-haired lady, "Warren Beatty in *Reds.*" Today she wore earrings that looked like table lamps. "Isn't it wonderful?" she said, presenting Red Square as if she'd just knitted it. "No crowds!" The square was cordoned off by soldiers.

Back to the hotel for another big drink.

We spent the rest of the day on a Soviet version of a Gray Line tour, visiting at least thirty places of no interest. For the uninitiated, all Russian buildings look either like Grand Army of the Republic memorials or like low-income federal housing projects without graffiti. There are a few exceptions left over from the czars, but they need to have their lawns mowed. Every fifteen feet there's a monument—monuments to this, monuments to that, monuments to the Standing Committee of the Second National Congress of Gypsum and Chalk Workers, monuments to the Mothers of the Mothers of War Martyrs, monuments to the Inventor of Flexible Belt Drive. "In the foreground is a monument to the monument in the background," Marya narrated.

During a brief monument lacuna, Marya said, "Do any of you have questions that you would like to ask about the Soviet Union?"

"Where can I get a—" But the leftists beat me to it.

"What is the cost of housing in the Soviet Union as a percentage of worker wages?" asked one.

"What is the retirement age in the Soviet Union?" asked another.

"What pension do retired Soviet workers receive as a percentage of their highest annual work-life salary?"

"Is higher education free in the Soviet Union?"

"What about unemployment?"

Marya answered, pointed out a few more monuments, and asked, "Do any of you have other questions you would like to ask about the Soviet Union?"

Exactly the same person who'd asked the first question asked exactly the same question again. I thought I was hearing things. "What is the cost of housing in the Soviet Union as a percentage of worker wages?"

And that flipped the switch.

"What is the retirement age in the Soviet Union?"

"What pension do retired Soviet workers receive as a percentage of their highest annual work-life salary?"

"Is higher education free in the Soviet Union?"

Marya answered the questions again. The third time it happened she began to lose her composure. I could hear her filling up empty places in the sightseeing landscape. "Look, there's a building! And there's another! And over there are several buildings together! And here [sigh of relief] are *many monuments*."

All the time we were in Russia, at every opportunity, the questions began again, identical questions with identical wording. I'm proud to say I don't remember a single one of the answers. Except the one about unemployment: "There is no unemployment in the Soviet Union. The Soviet constitution guarantees everyone a job." A pretty scary idea, I'd say.

Later in the trip, when I'd fled the bus tours and was wandering on my own, the lumpier kind of Russian would come up and ask me questions—not the "You are foreign?" sort of questions but rapid, involved questions in Russian. Perhaps because my hair was combed and I wore a necktie (two Soviet rarities) they thought I had special access to the comb-and-necktie store and must therefore be a privileged party official who knew what was what. I've wondered since if they were asking me, "What is the cost of housing in the Soviet Union as a percentage of worker wages?"

Monday, July 19

One of the bus questioners stood next to me as we waited to board our flight to Rostov. She looked out at the various Aeroflot planes standing on the tarmac and managed a statement that was at once naive, gratuitous, patronizing, and filled with progressive ardor. "Airplanes!" she said. "The Soviet Union has thousands and thousands of airplanes!"

I never did find out what this lady looked like. She was only about four foot eleven, and all I ever saw was a skull top of hennaed hair with a blur of fast-moving jaw beneath it. She had that wonderful ability some older people have of letting her mind run right out her mouth.

"Well," she'd say, "here I am with my seat belt buckled up just sitting right here in the airplane seat and folding my hands in my lap and I'll move my feet over a little so they're on top of my flight bag and pull my coat up over my shoulders, whoops, I'm sitting right on it but I'll just wiggle around a little like this and pull it over my shoulders . . ." For *hours*, all the way to Rostov.

The peaceniks, especially the older peaceniks, were more visually interesting than the leftists. Somebody ought to tell a sixty-year-old man what he looks like in plastic sandals, running shorts, and a mint-green T-shirt with a Kenneth Patchen plagiarism silkscreened on the front.

The peaceniks were sillier acting than the leftists too. There was a pair of Quaker ministers with us, man and wife. But they were not Quakers as one usually pictures them. They had "gone Hollywood." Imagine a Quaker who came up to you in the LA airport and tried to get a donation for a William Penn button. Not that they did that, but it always looked to me as though they were about to. Anyway, this couple bore different last names. When we got aboard the ship in Rostov, a passenger went to return a book to the husband.

"I'm sorry," said the wife at their cabin door. "He's not here."

"But can't I give the book to you?" asked the passenger. "It belongs to your husband."

"We're *not* the same persons," said the wife.

My cabin mate was no leftist. "I'm not pro-Soviet," he said as he watched me unpack a necktie with little duck hunters all over it. "I'm a retired peace activist. I mean I'm not retired from peace activism—you know what I mean." He had spilled a bottle of Campho-Phenique in his luggage and had gastrointestinal trouble from the food and wouldn't use the air-conditioning because it might give him a cold, so all the way to Kazan our cabin smelled like the bathroom at a Vicks factory. Three bus tours after we met he told me, "This country is just like a big club. Did you know there's no unemployment? The Soviet constitution guarantees everyone a job!"

Tuesday, July 20

Fortunately there were other people to talk to. Actually, you couldn't talk to most of them because they were Russians and didn't speak English—what you might call a silent majority. On the plane to Rostov I'd sat next to a fellow named Ivor. He spoke only a bit of English but was a good mime. He got it across that he was an engineer. I got it across that I was an American. He seemed very pleased at that. I should come and stay with his family. I explained about the cruise boat, showing him a picture of it on the brochure. I did a charade to the effect that I'd better stick close to the boat. He gave me an engineering trade magazine (in Russian, no illustrations), and I gave him some picture postcards of New York. We parted in a profusion of handshakes at the Rostov airport.

The boat stayed at the dock in Rostov until midnight Tuesday. They have plenty of monuments in Rostov, too, and tour buses were lined up on the quay. I could hear someone asking inside one of them, "What is the cost of housing in the Soviet Union as a percentage of worker wages?"

I was just being herded into that bus when someone grabbed my arm. It was Ivor. "Come on," he gestured. I escaped down the embankment. We got on a boat packed to the scuppers with Russians and went for a two-hour excursion on the Don. Ivor bought a bottle of champagne and began a labored explanation punctuated with hand wavings and flurries of picture drawing in my reporter's notebook.

His father had been on the front lines when the armies of the East and West had met in Germany in 1945. Apparently the Americans had liberated every bottle of alcoholic beverage between Omaha Beach and the Oder-Neisse Line and really made the welkin ring for their Red comrades in arms. "Anglish—*poo,*" said Ivor. "Francis—*poo,*" but the Americans, they were fine fellows, plenty of schnapps, plenty of cognac, plenty of vino for all. And they could *drink*, those American fine fellows. So Ivor's "vada" had made him promise (point to self, hand on heart) if (finger in air) Ivor ever met American (handshake, point to me) he must buy him much to drink. *Da?* (Toast, handshake, toast again, another handshake.)

Standing behind Ivor was a giant man well into his sixties, a sort of combination Khrushchev and old Arnold Schwarzenegger. He was staring hard at me, cocking an ear to my foreign language. He wore an undershirt and a suit coat with a line of medals out across the breast pocket, "*Deutsch?*" he asked me sternly.

"*Nyet deutsch,*" I said. "American."

He beamed, I mean just *beamed*. "Ally!" he said. It was his only English word. He pulled out a wallet with what I guess were commendations and an honorable discharge. "*Amerikanskii* ally!" he said and slapped my shoulder. Eight-ounce glasses of brandy must be bought for Ivor and me.

I toasted him with *my* only Russian word—"*Tovarishch!*" He brought forth a tiny grandson and had him shake hands with me.

"Now the little one can say he met an American," Ivor more or less explained. I toasted the big guy again. He pledged a long toast in return, and, as I understood Ivor's translation, we'd drunk to the hope that America and Russia would be allies again in a war against China.

I bought more cognac. Ivor bought beer. The big fellow bought even more cognac.

When the boat docked Ivor and I went to a beer hall, a basement where they lined up half-liter mugs and squirted them full with a rubber hose from four feet away. Everyone grabbed half a dozen mugs at a time and drank one after the other while standing at long wooden tables. There was no communication problem now. We discussed women ("Ah, beautiful. Oh, much trouble"), international politics ("Iraq—*poo*. Iran—*poo*"), the relative merits of socialism versus a free-market system ("Socialism—enough responsible, *nyet* fun. Captialism—*nyet* enough responsible, plenty fun"), and, I think, literature ("*And Quiet Flows the Don—poo,* too long"). Then we went to another bar on top of a Russian tourist hotel and had even more to drink. I didn't want to let my side down. And there were Ivor's father's feelings to be considered.

Ivor and I embraced, and I staggered back to my stinking cabin to pass out. The woman with her brains between her teeth was standing at the top of the gangplank. "I hope you're not one of those people who's going to see the Soviet Union through the bottom of a vodka glass," she said.

The Enemy Among Us

Of course, we had plenty of Russians aboard the boat too. There were five of the advertised experts. I'll change their names in case some reconstructed quote or poetic exaggeration of mine is misconstrued to mean that one of these Soviets might be "turned" by the CIA. No one deserves to be pestered by surreptitious Yalies who couldn't get into law school.

Two of the experts were really journalists. Natalia was a pleasant blond woman of about forty. She didn't have much to say. Nikolai was a sturdy guy in his midthirties, completely Western in dress and manner. He had lived as a foreign correspondent in Switzerland and Austria for seven years, wore a bush jacket like any other foreign correspondent, and was as bluff and hard-drinking as any newspaperman. I gathered this wasn't much of an assignment. Nikolai took no notes at the peace confabs, and Natalia took only a few.

A third expert, Orlonsky, was a sinister-looking type with a half-Russian, half-Tartar face and slitlike eyes. He turned out to be a bored economist from the Soviet Institute of U.S. and Canadian Studies who was along to brush up on his English in preparation for some academic conference he was going to in San Francisco. The Institute of U.S. and Canadian Studies is supposed to have subscribed to the *Village Voice* for six years in an attempt to find out about life in America's rural areas. But Orlonsky seemed to be a look-alive fellow. He wanted to talk about America's marvelous demand-side goods-distribution system and did our Reagan administration economic institutes have screws loose or what? Also, where did our automobile industry go? But the Americans wanted to talk about peace and Soviet-American relations.

Two more official-expert types were Dr. Bullshovich from the USSR Academy of Sciences Institute of World Economy and International Relations and Professor Guvov from the department of philosophy and sociology at Moscow U. Dr. Bullshovich was a lean, dry character with a Jesuitical wit that was lost on his audience. Between formal peace activities he hid somewhere. Guvov was a doctrinaire buffoon who looked like a Hereford cow and was a big favorite with the leftists. "He is not a professor," one of the crew members told me later. "He is, you would call it, instructor. He should be teaching military schools."

Besides the experts there were thirty or more officers, sailors, waitresses, stewards, and cruise personnel. Some of the higher-ranking crew members spoke English but usually didn't let on. They preferred to stare blankly when the Americans began to complain. And the Americans did complain, the leftists worst of all. Between praise of the Soviet Union it was "It's too noisy, too rough, too breezy. The chair cushions are too hard. And what's that smell? This food is awful. Too greasy. Can't I order something else? I *did* order something else. Didn't someone say I could order something else? I'm sure I can order something else if I want to, and, young lady, the laundry lost one of my husband's socks. They're expensive socks and one of them is lost."

Translating the complaints, or pretending to, were a half dozen Intourist guides. They began to have a haunted look before we were two days out of port.

Very Early Wednesday Morning, July 21

When I came to, after the Ivor expedition, I stumbled into the ship's bar. We'd cast off while I was asleep, and motion of the boat combined with motion of my gullet. I couldn't have looked well. Nikolai was sitting on a stool next to one of the Intourist guides, a dark, serious type named Sonya. I gripped the bar with both hands and tried to decide which of the impossible Russian soft drinks would be easiest to vomit. "You need vodka," said Nikolai, motioning to the barmaid. I drank the awful thing. "Now," said Nikolai, "how did you get that President Reagan?"

"I voted for him," I said. "How did *you* get Brezhnev?"

Nikolai began to laugh. "I do not have this great responsibility."

"How are you liking the Soviet Union?" asked Sonya.

"I'm not," I said.

She was worried. "No? What is the matter?"

"Too many Americans."

Sonya kept a look of strict neutrality.

"I have not met many Americans," said Nikolai. "They are all like this, no?" He made a gesture that encompassed the boat, winked, and ordered me another vodka.

"Not exactly," I said.

"Perhaps they are just old, a bit," said Sonya with the air of someone making an obviously fallacious argument. "But," she brightened, "they are for peace."

"Yes," I agreed. "They are progressive. They are highly progressive. They are such great progressives I think I have almost all of them talked into defecting."

"No, no, no, no, no," said Nikolai.

Much Later Wednesday Morning, July 21

We docked on a scruffy island somewhere up near Volgodonsk. One of the U.S. peace experts, a pacifist from the American Friends Service Committee, got up a volleyball game against the crew. "Now let's play and let's play hard," he told the American team. "But don't forget we're playing for *fun*." The Russians trounced them.

That night the Russians took me out onto the darkened fantail, where they had dozens of bottles of beer, cheese, bread, and a huge salted fish.

Sonya was concerned about my Republicanism. "You are not for peace?" she asked.

"I during Vietnam War struggle for peace very much [talk with the Russians for a while and you fall into it too], rioting for peace, fighting police for peace, tear gassed for peace," I said. "I am tired of peace. Too dangerous."

Orlonsky began to laugh and then shook his head. "Vietnam—too bad."

"Land war in Asia," I said, "very bad. And some countries do not learn from an example." All of them laughed.

"And in Middle East," said Sonya, mirthfully pointing a finger at me, "some people's allies do not learn also."

"War is very bad," said Nikolai. "Maybe U.S. and Soviet Union go to war over Lebanon—ha, ha!" This seemed to be a hilarious idea. The Russians all but fell out of their chairs.

"With all of Middle East how do you pick only ally without oil?" said Orlonsky.

I said, "With all of Europe how do you pick Poland?"

"You wish to make trade?" said Nikolai.

"Also, in deal, you can have South Africa," I said.

"We will tell Reagan you are a progressive," said Orlonsky.

"P. Cheh. [P.J.] was making faces at the *Pravda* news today. I do not think he is a progressive," said Sonya.

"Oh, he is a progressive," said Nikolai. "You remember, Sonya, he has almost all Americans on ship ready to defect."

Marya made a strangled noise in the back of her throat. Sonya turned very sober. "Progressives," she sighed. "Everything must be made perfect for them."

Thursday, July 22

Our first scheduled conference took place while we sailed through the remarkably scum-filled Tsimlyansk Reservoir. The conference coordinator was a short, broad, overvigorous American woman in her sixties. Let's call her Mrs. Pigeon, so she won't sue, and also because too much truth doesn't go with travel writing. Mrs. Pigeon was an authority on the education of children, and, in fact, had the personality of a teacher—the sort of teacher who inspires any feeling child to sneak back in school at night and spray-paint the halls with descriptions of the human love act.

Mrs. Pigeon introduced the Soviet experts and their two American counterparts, Reverend Bumphead (not his real name) and the volleyball coach, Nick Smarm (not his real name). Nick was a politician, but the sort who would run for city council in Youngstown on an antidevelopment, pro-ecology ticket. He smiled too much. The Reverend Bumphead was a young man of Ichabod Crane lank. I never caught his denomination. My guess is Zen Methodist. He was either growing a beard or didn't know how to shave.

Mrs. Pigeon opened the proceedings in a patronizing tone that propelled me back through twenty-five years to the vile confines of the fourth grade. It was a beautiful afternoon, hot sun, clear sky, and just the right crisp breeze. The conference was being held on top of the cruise boat, but the 120 or so participants had jammed themselves in under the shade deck, where they were surrounded by superstructure on three sides and the air was stifling.

The peaceniks took notes. I had a vision of newsletters, reams and reams of mis-stapled copier paper Xeroxed when the boss wasn't looking, vomiting forth from the tepid organizations these people represented. "My Interesting Peace Voyage Through the Soviet Union"; "An Interesting and Enjoyable Visit to the USSR with Peace in Mind"; "Not *War and Peace* but *Peace and Peace*" (one of the clever ones); "Peace in the Soviet Union and an Interesting Trip There Too." Maybe America could be bored into nuclear disarmament.

Nick Smarm began to speak. It was the standard fare. He laid the greater part of the blame for a potential international nuke dukeout on the

American doorstep. What he was saying wasn't wrong, at least not in the factual citations he made. But suddenly and quite against my will I was angry. To stand in front of strangers and run your country, *my* country, down—I didn't care if what Nick said was generally true, I didn't care if what he said was wholly, specifically, and exactly true in every detail. I haven't been that mad in years. I had to leave, go below. I was ashamed of the man. And it occurred to me that I would have been ashamed if he were Russian and we were on the Mississippi. That big fellow with the medals down his suit coat, my ally, he wouldn't have done such a thing on the *Delta Queen*.

I had a drink and went back. Reverend Bumphead from the Princeton Coalition for Disarmament was speaking now. He said exactly the same thing.

"Now it's time for all of us to ask Nick Smarm and Reverend Bumphead some interesting questions," said Mrs. Pigeon.

"Mr. Smarm," said a fat man, "now this is just a hypothetical question, but the way you were describing how the arms race is mostly the fault of the United States, couldn't I, if I were a red-baiter type, say that—just hypothetically now—you were a paid Soviet agent?" And he hastily added, "Please don't anybody take my question literally!" They took his question literally. The fat man was smothered in literalism. Squeals of indignation wafted toward the banks of the Don.

"What a terrible thing to say!" shrieked one of the leftist ladies. I'll bet she was pissed—all those friends of hers acting as Soviet agents for years, and no one ever offered to pay *them*.

I was about to put in a word for Pudgy, but it was too late. He was already overapologizing to Nick.

"What is the cost of housing in the Soviet Union as a percentage of worker wages?" asked a leftist. Reverend Bumphead didn't know the answer to that, so Mrs. Pigeon answered the rest of the questions.

Very Early Friday Morning, July 23

I tried to explain my patriotic seizure to Nikolai. "Wouldn't you feel the same?" But I didn't seem to be getting through.

I gave up. We had more drinks. About twenty minutes later Nikolai said to me, "I did not think Nick's speech was so interesting." He pulled a deadpan face. "I can read *Pravda*."

Friday, July 23

Ashore in Volgograd we were taken to Mamayev Hill, where umpteen million people died defending the place when it was still named after Stalin.

One of the leftists chaffed me for wearing a suit and tie again. I mean, we were going to visit a mass grave.

The leftists had their wreath, but watching them present it in their bowling shirts was more than I could bear. Besides, there was a fifty-two-meter-high statue of "Mother Russia" on top of the hill, and it's pretty interesting if you've never seen a reinforced-concrete nipple four feet across.

It wasn't until that afternoon, after four days on the boat, that I discovered there were real Americans aboard. Some ordinary tourists had stumbled into this morass of the painfully caring and hopelessly committed. By price or by accident they had picked this tour, and they were about as happy as if they'd signed up for a lemming migration.

When I came back from Mamayev Hill, I saw a normal-looking, unagitated person stretched out on the sundeck in a T-shirt from Air America, the old CIA-run Southeast Asia airline. "What got you on this tour?" he asked, when I stared at the logo.

"I guess masochism," I said and looked again at the T-shirt.

He puffed out his chest. "*This* ought to shake the bastards up."

He was one of a dozen New Mexicans, all friends, traveling together on a private tour. Until now they'd had a wonderful time in the USSR. They said it was a fine place as long as you could drink like a Russian and leave like an American. But they'd taken this cruise without any idea of the peace that lay in store for them, and since they'd come on board they'd barricaded themselves in the promenade deck lounge and had kept the leftists out with loud Western accents and the peaceniks away by smoking cigarettes. Smoking cigarettes seems to alarm peace activists much more than voting for Reagan does.

The New Mexicans had become special pets of the barmaid. They were allowed to take glasses, ice, bottles, and china forward to the lounge. She wouldn't take tips from them, but Billy, a Santa Fe architect, had gone to the market in Rostov and brought the girl an armload of flowers. She blushed to the clavicle.

The New Mexicans were amazed at their fellow passengers, not in the matter of politics, but because the passengers were so rude to the crew. "And to each other," said Sue Ann, a real estate developer. "I've never heard husbands and wives carp at each other like that in my life."

When it came to politics, Tom, a former AID officer with the State Department in Vietnam, said, "After all, there hasn't been a *great big war* since the A-bomb was invented."

"I live in Alamogordo," said Sue Ann. "I'll bet that shakes the bastards up." Indeed, that did bother some of the peaceniks, though the Air America T-shirt didn't—not one knew what it was.

Soviet-American Relations in Action

That evening at dinnertime, seven or eight young Russians from the local Soviet-American friendship club were ushered on board by Mrs. Pigeon. I noticed they gobbled the meat. Their president was a stiff young fellow, a future first secretary of the Committee for Lies About Grain Production if ever there was one. He had a guitar about two times bigger than normal and a watchful mien. But the others were okay. I sat between Alexei, a construction foreman who looked to be twelve, and Boris, an engineer (practically everyone in Russia is an engineer, just like our sanitation engineers are).

Alexei wanted to talk about rock and roll. His English was no worse than the average *Rolling Stone* reviewer's. "Abba—too nothing. Hard rock! Yay! Led Zeppelin! Yay! And Kiss!! I most like—hard, hard rock! You know of Time Machine?" He was very excited that an American recognized the name of the top Russian rock group. "Good like Beatles. But is best hard rock America, yay! Is only too bad always rock stars so many dying of too much liquor and . . ."—he shot a glance at the president—"and of other things."

Boris wanted to talk about cars. In his opinion Russia needed much, much faster cars. "I want fast car," he said.

The Americans wanted to talk about peace and Soviet-American relations.

We went to the boat-deck music room after dinner with about ten Americans, mostly leftists, and Marya to help translate. There was one lady among the leftists I had not noticed before, though she was markedly ugly. It was not the kind of ugliness that's an accident of birth but the kind that is the result of years of ill temper, pique, and petty malice. These had given a rattish, shrewish, leaf-nosed-bat quality to her face.

The president said, "We are thankfully welcomed of being here. English ours is not so well. But is practicing now you with more." Then each of the Russian kids introduced himself and said his profession as best he could.

The ugly woman took aim at Alexei and said with great acerbity, "How many women construction workers are there in the Soviet Union?"

Alexei tried to answer. "Is construction worker training in mostly male, men I am meaning, but is also some girls if . . ." He got no further.

"Girls?!" shrieked the old bitch. "*Girls*?! We don't call *women* girls! That's an insult!" The Russian kids stared at her, mystified. The hag turned on Marya. "You explain to them that calling women girls is a demeaning thing to do."

Marya said something placating in Russian. The president tried a halting apology, but the ugly woman interrupted. "One thing I'd like to know." She glared at Alexei's denim trousers. "Why do young people all over Europe, even in the socialist countries, pick up that awful American popular music and those sloppy blue jeans?"

Marya made what sounded like a pained verbatim translation. All the Russian faces in the room froze into the great Russian public face—serious but expressionless, part poker face and part the face the troops made on *You'll Never Get Rich* when Phil Silvers asked for volunteers.

It isn't easy to get a sober Russian to do anything on impulse, but I took Marya by the cuff and convinced her we'd better get some beer from the bar. The room was still silent when we returned. The president wouldn't take a drink, but the rest of the Russians seemed glad enough to bury their faces in beer. The ugly woman sat smugly, still waiting for a reply. The other Americans were getting embarrassed. Finally, the woman's husband spoke up. He was wearing his running shorts and Kenneth Patchen T-shirt again. "What is the cost of housing in the Soviet Union as a . . ."

Something had to be done. I stood up. "I think it's very unfair for us to monopolize the comradeship and international goodwill of these Soviet young people," I said. "There is another group of Americans in the lounge who are eager to discuss Soviet-American relations with our guests, and—"

"Oh, yes!" said Marya, and she began to point to the hallway and chatter in Russian. The New Mexicans were a little surprised to see us, but their hospitality didn't falter.

"We are thankfully welcomed of being here," said the president. "English ours is not so—"

"The hell with that," said Tom. "Play us a song on that thing." And it was a pretty good song, and Sue Ann even got him to have a drink when he finished.

Saturday, July 24

There was another peace conference under the shade deck, and this time it was the Russians' turn to speak. I was slightly late, due to sheer reluctance. Mrs. Pigeon was opening the session. "It is better to get these answers from Soviet experts than from our press," she was saying as I walked in. I walked back out again and had a beer. Actually, I had three.

When I returned, Guvov, the buffoon, had wound up his speech and was answering a question about whether Solzhenitsyn was just a bad writer or a spy too. He was wearing a hilarious pair of ersatz Levi's with TEXAS JEAN printed on a salad-plate-sized plastic patch on the ass. "Solzhenitsyn painted the Soviet Union only in dark colors," he said. The leftists clapped vigorously. "Criticism," said Guvov, "leads to the problems of democracy."

Time for more beer.

It seemed to be dawning on a few of the peaceniks that something was askew. When I returned from the bar the second time, one of them was addressing Guvov. "A lot of the Americans on this trip have admitted the errors of American foreign policy. How come none of the Soviets have admitted any Soviet errors?"

"We don't criticize the foreign policy of our government," said Guvov, "because we hundred-percent agree with it and approve of it." The questioner gasped. But the leftists all clapped, and so did quite a few of the peaceniks.

That was it for me and peace. I apologize, but this reporter did not attend any more peace functions of any kind.

Loath Boat

The leftists and peaceniks spent most of every day talking. They were not arguing. They were not analyzing. They were not making observations. What they were doing was agreeing with each other—in feverish spasms of accordance, mad confabs of apposition, blathers of consonance. On Reagan, on the weapons freeze, on the badness of Israel, on the dangers of war, on the need for peace, they agreed.

I decided these people were crazy.

I watched my cabin mate write a letter to his wife. It was a political exhortation. "We Americans must repudiate the Reagan administration . . ." This to his wife of thirty years.

Crazy. And stupid too.

One, who was from the deep Midwest and looked like Millicent Fenwick, told me, "You know, if the people who put Reagan in office prevail, they're going to take the vote from women."

As we were going through the locks of the Don-Volga canal the woman with the direct connection between her cerebral cortex and her mouth came nattering up beside me at the rail. "Isn't it marvelous?" she said, staring at a gigantic blank wall of concrete. "They're such wonderful engineers in the Soviet Union." I agreed it was an impressive piece of work. "Marvelous, marvelous, marvelous, marvelous," she said. She peeked over the side. "And where *do* they get all the water?"

The Intourist guides were at wits' end, the Soviet experts were becoming testy, and the crew was clearly disgusted and getting into the grog ration earlier each day.

The ship's doctor, a blowsy, mottle-eyed, disbarred-looking fellow, had taken to experimenting on the diarrhea symptoms half the Americans were suffering. Marya gave an elaborate burlesque of accompanying him as the translator on his rounds. The Russians would not explain the joke, but I know one peacenik had gone to him with the malady and received a laxative and a glass of 200-proof neutral grain spirits. I did not see that person again for thirty-six hours.

Sunday, July 25

Sunday I was drunk.

What Was Going On in the Soviet Capital and Heartland as We Joined *The Nation* This Summer on an Exciting and Affordable Soviet Excursion?

I know I'll never understand what the Americans thought they were doing in Russia, but I'm almost as confused about what the Russians thought they were letting them do.

Obviously the Volga Peace Cruise was approved. Unapproved things unhappen in the USSR. But though the Soviets had approved it, they didn't seem very interested. In one of the cities where we docked, a local reporter came aboard and talked to Nick Smarm. When Nick finished excoriating the U.S. and began pointing out that the Soviet Union was also engaged in the arms race, the reporter simply stopped writing. This was the total media attention given us.

I suppose we were under surveillance. I noticed that Sonya took complete notes during the conferences, but it seemed to me she was paying most attention to what her countrymen said. Some peaceniks suspected their rooms had been searched. One woman had found her bags a little too neatly closed and zipped. Another woman's copy of *Peter the Great* disappeared.

"Do not bother to look for it," said one of the Intourist guides, when the woman made a stink. "It has doubtless slipped behind the folding bunk when the steward lady has been making the bed. It is most difficult to look under there so steward lady will do it for you during dinner." This sounded suspicious. But the book did not mysteriously reappear after dinner, not even with certain pages torn out, so maybe it was just lost.

Neither I nor the outspokenly pro-American New Mexicans were bothered. One day Nikolai and Sonya took me on a nice but pointless speedboat ride up the Volga, and I assumed this was when my cabin was to be searched. But I'd used the old Ian Fleming trick of fastening a human hair with spit across my locker door and it was still there when I got back.

If anything was happening to the leftists, they weren't talking. But one of them, the woman who was embarrassed to have left the Soviet Union as a child, had relatives in Moscow, whom I know she visited. When we went through customs at the end of the tour, she was searched completely and questioned so long that the plane had to be held for her. Our tour leader claimed it was because she'd lost one of her currency exchange receipts.

Whatever the official Soviet attitude toward us may have been, the private Russian attitude was manifestly clear. The Russians, when they'd had a few drinks, would repeatedly make declarations starting, "I am not an anti-Semite, but . . ." And, at least to judge by last names, many of our tour members were Jewish.

One of the crew, in the most confidence-imparting stage of drunkenness, told me, "You know Brezhnev is married to a Jew. Many members of the Presidium are married to Jews. This is why we cannot be so firm with the Israelis."

But the peaceniks and the leftists were blind to this, or passed it off as anti-Zionism only. Their only serious concern was with the CIA. They were convinced there must be a CIA agent aboard. I suggested the fat man, surely an agent provocateur. But they'd decided he was okay, since he'd apologized to Nick. Someone said the leftists suspected me—that coat and tie. I asked Nikolai who he thought it was. "All of them," he laughed.

Monday, July 26

I think the Russians had decided, both privately and officially, that these Volga peace cruisers were inconsequential people, unable to influence American policy in any important way.

When we docked in Togliatti, the leftists were very eager to see the Lada automobile plant there, one of the most modern factories in the Soviet Union. They were swooning to meet genuine "workers." But it wasn't on the schedule. Our Intourist guides made a halfhearted attempt to convince the local Intourist office to allow a tour, but it was too big a group, too many officials would have to be contacted, it would take too long to arrange, and so on. The leftists were pretty sore, and went so far as to make no excuses for the Soviet system this time.

But meanwhile Nikolai had somehow got in touch with the Lada plant management and informed them that I worked for *Car and Driver* magazine. I'm only a contributing editor there, and even if I were editor in chief I wouldn't have much sway over the FTC, DOT, and Reagan administration executive orders that keep the Russians from exporting cars to us. But I was a representative of the real world nonetheless. And that afternoon there was a big chauffeured car waiting at dockside to take me, the only admitted Republican on board, for a personal tour of the Lada plant.

All the Rest of the Days on the Trip

By Tuesday the twenty-seventh I'd come to the end of the tour, at least as a sentient being. There were still two days left to the cruise and six days left in Russia, but I was gone.

The place just wears you out after a while. There is not a square angle or a plumb line in all the country. Every bit of concrete is crumbling from too much aggregate in the mix, and *everything* is made of concrete. I saw buildings with the facades falling off that were still under construction. And everything that's well built turns out to be built by somebody else. Moscow Airport was built by West Germans, the Grand Hyatt knockoff by the French, the Lada plant by Italians, and the very boat was made in Austria.

The air pollution in the cities is grotesque. No machine seems to run well. And the whole of commerce visible on the Volga consisted of carting sand and phone poles from one port to the next.

The New Mexicans had a contest: a bottle of champagne to be won by the first person who saw a crane with an operator in it. No one won. Every building site we saw was three-fourths deserted. I asked Orlonsky where the workers were, but he turned sly on me. "Perhaps they are at lunch." It was 10:30 in the morning.

What little of the old and charming architecture is left is rotting, sitting neglected, waiting to be torn down for its lack of modernism. Russia stinks of dirty bodies and evil Balkan tobacco and a disinfectant they must distribute by the tank car daily, some chemical with a moldy turned-earth stench as though vandals had been at it in the graveyard or mice had gotten into the mushroom cellar.

In the end, every little detail starts to get to you—the overwhelming oppressiveness of the place, the plain godawfulness of it.

We put in at Ulyanovsk, birthplace of Lenin. Not an easy city to find your way around in. Take Lenin Avenue to Lenin Street; go straight to Lenin Square, then left along Lenin Boulevard to Lenin Place and Lenin Lane. Don't miss the monument to Lenin's sister's dog.

And there's no reason to find your way around. There's nothing there. We were shitfaced drunk in the bar by noon. The New Mexicans and I were crazed now with the desire for a cheeseburger, mad for the sound of a pedal steel guitar, would have killed for a six-pack of Budweiser and a ride down the interstate at 100 miles an hour in a Cadillac Coupe de Ville. But there was nothing to be done, nothing to do but drink. So we drank and told jokes: old jokes, bad jokes, dirty jokes.

We were interrupting the progressives' dinner now. The leftists and the peaceniks were mad. But only Mrs. Pigeon had the courage to approach. What were we laughing about?

"Sex," said Sue Ann.

"Now, what's so funny about sex?" said Mrs. Pigeon.

"Well, if you don't remember, honey . . ." And Mrs. Pigeon retreated. We began to sing. We sang "Silver Threads and Golden Needles" and "Danny Boy" and

My mother sells rubbers to sailors,
My dad pokes the heads with a pin,
My sister performs the abortions,
My God how the money rolls in.

The progressives could not get the Russians to stop us. Instead, the Russians came back from the fantail and began to sing too, loud Russian songs with stamping and pounding of glasses. Then some of the peaceniks came up and then a few more, and they began to sing along. They sang "America the Beautiful" and "God Bless America" and every verse to "The Star-Spangled Banner," a most cacophonous sound. We danced, and the ship's band tried to play jitterbug. And the Russians gave toasts, and we gave toasts.

To the American Eagle,
The higher she goes, the louder she screams,
And who fucks with the eagle best learn how to fly!

And the Russians said:

To Mother Russia,
Who comes here with the sword
Dies by the sword!

And someone said, "From one bunch of sons of a bitches to another." And we drank everything that came to hand, the doctor's neutral grain spirits included, and sang and danced and drank some more until we passed out on top of the tables in a triumph of peace and Soviet-American relations.

There's nothing at all to the rest of the trip except a huge gray-and-green hangover with a glimpse of the White Kremlin making my head ache in Kazan and the band piping us ashore in the morning with, most appropriately to my mind, "The Battle Hymn of the Republic." Then a flight to Moscow, rough weather all the way, and back to that Grand Hyatt hotel.

There was a Russian disco band in the lounge, balalaika music played on electric guitars and set to a Donna Summer beat. The New Mexicans went on to Leningrad, and I was left sitting alone in the bar waiting for my plane home a day and a half hence. An English tourist sat down next to me. "Been here long, have you?" he said. "Been all around the country?"

"I've been to the fucking back of the moon!" I said. "Scotch," I said to the bartender. He gave me vodka.

How to Drive Fast on Drugs While Getting Your Wing-Wang Squeezed and Not Spill Your Drink

When it comes to taking chances, some people like to play poker or shoot dice; other people prefer to parachute jump, go rhino hunting, or climb ice floes, while still others engage in crime or marriage. But I like to get drunk and drive like a fool. Name me, if you can, a better feeling than the one you get when you're half a bottle of Chivas in the bag with a gram of coke up your nose and a teenage lovely pulling off her tube top in the next seat over while you're going a hundred miles an hour down a suburban side street. You'd have to watch the entire Iranian air force crash-land in a liquid-petroleum gas storage facility to match this kind of thrill. If you ever have much more fun than that, you'll die of pure sensory overload, I'm here to tell you.

But wait. Let's pause and analyze *why* this particular matrix of activities is perceived as so highly enjoyable. I mean, aside from the teenage lovely pulling off her tube top in the next seat over. Ignoring that for a moment, let's look at the psychological factors conducive to placing positive emotional values on the sensory end product of experientially produced excitation of the central nervous system and smacking into a lamppost. Is that any way to have fun? How would your mother feel if she knew you were doing this? She'd cry. She really would. And that's how you know it's fun. Anything that makes your mother cry is fun. Sigmund Freud wrote all about this. It's a well-known fact.

Of course, it's a shame to waste young lives behaving this way—speeding around all tanked up with your feet hooked in the steering wheel while your date crawls around on the floor mat opening zippers with her teeth and pounding on the accelerator with an empty liquor bottle. But it wouldn't be taking a chance if you weren't risking *something*. And even if it is a shame to waste young lives behaving this way, it is definitely cooler than risking *old* lives behaving this way. I mean, so what if some fifty-eight-year-old butt head gets a load on and starts playing Death Race 2000 in the rush-hour traffic jam? What kind of chance is he taking? He's just waiting around to see what kind of cancer he gets anyway. But if young, talented you, with all of life's possibilities at your fingertips, you and the future Cheryl Tiegs there, so fresh, so beautiful—if the two of *you* stake your handsome heads on a single roll of the dice in life's game of stop-the-semi—now *that's* taking chances! Which is why old people rarely risk their lives. It's not because they're chicken, they just have too much dignity to play for small stakes.

Now a lot of people say to me, "Hey, P.J., you like to drive fast. Why not join a responsible organization, such as the Sports Car Club of America, and enjoy participation in sports car racing? That way you could drive as fast as you wish while still engaging in a well-regulated spectator sport that is becoming more popular each year." No thanks. In the first place, if you ask me, those guys are a bunch of tweedy old barf mats who like to talk about things like what necktie they wore to Alberto Ascari's funeral. And in the second place, they won't let me drive drunk. They expect me to go out there and smash into things and roll over on the roof and catch fire and burn to death when I'm sober. They must think I'm crazy. That stuff scares me. I have to get completely shitfaced to even think about driving fast. How can you have a lot of exciting thrills when you're so terrified that you wet yourself all the time? That's not fun. It's just not *fun* to have exciting thrills when you're scared. Take the heroes of the *Iliad*, for instance. They really had some exciting thrills, and were they scared? No. They were drunk. Every chance they could get. And so am I, and I'm not going out there and having a horrible car wreck until somebody brings me a cocktail.

Also, it's important to be drunk because being drunk keeps your body all loose, and that way, if you have an accident or anything, you'll sort of roll with the punches and not get banged up so bad. For example, there was this guy I heard about who was really drunk and was driving through the Adirondacks. He got sideswiped by a bus and went head-on into another car, which knocked him off a bridge, and he plummeted 150 feet into a ravine. I mean, it killed him and everything, but if he hadn't been so drunk and loose, his body probably would have been banged up a lot worse—and you can imagine how much more upset his wife would have been when she went down to the morgue to identify him.

Even more important than being drunk, however, is having the right car. You have to get a car that handles really well. This is extremely important, and there's a lot of debate on this subject—about what kind of car handles best. Some say a front-engined car; some say a rear-engined car. I say a *rented* car. Nothing handles better than a rented car. You can go faster, turn corners sharper, and put the transmission into reverse while going forward at a higher rate of speed in a rented car than in any other kind. You can also park without looking, and you can use the trunk as an ice chest. Another thing about a rented car is that it's an all-terrain vehicle. Mud, snow, water, woods—you can take a rented car anywhere. True, you can't always get it back, but that's not your problem, is it?

Yet there's more to a good-handling car than just making sure it doesn't belong to you. It has to be big. It's really hard for a girl to get her clothes off inside a small car, and this is one of the most important features of car handling. Also, what kind of drugs does it have in it? Most people like to drive on speed or cocaine with plenty of whiskey mixed in. This gives you the confidence you want and need for plowing through red lights and passing trucks on the right. But don't neglect downs and 'ludes and codeine cough syrup either. It's hard to beat the heavy depressants for high-speed spinouts, backing into trees, and a general feeling of not giving two fucks about man and his universe.

Overall, though, it's the bigness of the car that counts the most. Because when something bad happens in a big car—accidentally speeding through the middle of a gang of unruly young people who have been taunting you in a drive-in restaurant, for instance—it happens very far away, way out at the end of your fenders. It's like a civil war in Africa; it doesn't really concern you too much. On the other hand, when something happens in a little bitty car it happens right in your face. You get all involved in it and have to give everything a lot of thought. Driving around in a little bitty car is like being one of those sensitive girls who writes poetry. Life is just too much to bear. You end up staying at home in your bedroom and thinking up sonnets that don't get published till you die, which will be real soon if you keep driving around in little bitty cars like that.

Let's inspect some of the basic maneuvers of drunken driving while you've got crazy girls who are on drugs with you. Look for these signs when picking up crazy girls: pierced ears with five or six earrings in them, unusual shoes, white lipstick, extreme thinness, hair that's less than an inch long, or clothing made of chrome and leather. Stay away from girls who cry a lot or who look like they get pregnant easily or have careers. They may want to do weird stuff in cars, but only in the backseat, and it's really hard to steer from back there. Besides, they'll want to get engaged right away afterward. But the other kinds of girls—there's no telling what they'll do. I used to know this girl who weighed about ninety pounds and dressed in skirts that didn't even cover her underwear, when she wore any. I had this beat-up old Mercedes and we were off someplace about fifty miles from nowhere on Christmas Eve in a horrible sleet storm. The road was a mess, all curves and big ditches, and I was blotto, and the car kept slipping off the pavement and sliding sideways. And just when I'd hit a big patch of glare ice and was frantically spinning the wheel trying to stay out of the oncoming traffic, she said, "I shaved my crotch today, wanna feel?"

That's really true. And then about half an hour later the head gasket blew and we had to spend I don't know how long in this dirtball motel, although the girl walked all the way to the liquor store through about a mile of slush and got all kinds of wine and did weird stuff with the bottlenecks later. So it was sort of okay, except that the garage where I left the Mercedes burned down and I used the insurance money to buy a motorcycle.

Now, girls who like motorcycles will do *anything*. I mean, really, *anything you can think of*. But it's just not the same. For one thing, it's hard to drink while you're riding a motorcycle—there's no place to set your glass. And cocaine's out of the question. And personally, I find that pot makes me too sensitive. You smoke some pot and the first thing you know you're pulling over to the side of the road and taking a break to dig the gentle beauty of the sky's vast panorama, the slow, luxurious interplay of sun and clouds, the lulling trill of breezes midst leafy tree branches—and what kind of fun is that? Besides, it's tough to "get it on" with a chick (I mean in the biblical sense) and still make all the fast curves unless you let her take the handlebars with her pants off and come on doggy style or something, which is harder than it sounds; also, pants-less girls on motorcycles attract the highway patrol, so usually you don't end up doing anything until you're both off the bike, and by then you may be in the hospital. Like I was after this old lady pulled out in front of me in an Oldsmobile, and the girl I was with still wanted to do anything you can think of, but there was a doctor there and he was squirting antiseptic all over me and combing little bits of gravel out of my face with a wire brush, and I just couldn't get into it. So take it from me and don't get a motorcycle. Get a big car.

Usually, most fast-driving maneuvers that don't require crazy girls call for use of the steering wheel, so be sure your car is equipped with power steering. Without power steering, turning the wheel is a lot like work, and if you wanted work you'd get a job. All steering should be done with the index finger. Then, when you're done doing all the steering you want to do, just pull your finger out of there and the wheel will come right back to wherever it wants to. It's that simple. Be sure to do an extra lot of steering when going into a driveway or turning sharp corners. And here's another important tip: always roll the window down before throwing bottles out, and don't try to throw them through the windshield unless the car is parked and you're outside it.

Okay, now say you've been on a six-day drunk and you've just made a bet that you can back up all the way to Cleveland, plus you've got a buddy who's getting a blow job on the trunk lid. Well, let's face it, if that's the way you're going to act, sooner or later you'll have an accident. This much is true. But that doesn't mean you should sit back and just let accidents happen to you. No, you have to go out and cause them yourself. That way you're in control of the situation.

You know, it's a shame, but a lot of people have the wrong idea about accidents. For one thing, they don't hurt nearly as much as you'd think. That's because you're in shock and can't feel pain or, if you aren't in shock, you're dead, and that doesn't hurt at all so far as we know. Another thing is that they make great stories. I've got this friend—a prominent man in the automotive industry—who flipped his MG TF back in the fifties and slid on his head for a couple hundred yards, then had to spend a year with no eyelids and a steel pin through his cheekbones while his face was being rebuilt. Sure, it wasn't much fun at the time, but you should hear him tell about it now. What a fabulous tale, especially during dinner. Besides, it's not all smashing glass and spurting blood, you understand. Why, a good sideswipe can be an almost religious experience. The sheet metal doesn't break or crunch or anything—it flexes and gives way as the two vehicles come together with a rushing liquid pulse as if two giant sharks of steel were mating in the perpetual night of the sea primordial. I mean, if you're on enough drugs. Also, sometimes you see a lot of really pretty lights in your head.

One sure way to cause an accident is with your basic "moonshiner's" or "bootlegger's" turn. Whiz down the road at about sixty or seventy, throw the gearshift into neutral, cut the wheel to the left, and hit the emergency brake with one good wallop while holding out the brake release with your left hand. This'll send you spinning around in a perfect 180-degree turn right into a culvert or a fast-moving tractor-trailer rig. (The bootlegger's turn can be done on dry pavement, but it works best on top of loose gravel or schoolchildren.) Or, when you've moved around backward, you can then spin the wheel to the right and keep on going until you've come around a full 360 degrees and are headed back the same way you were going; still, it probably would have been easier to have just kept going that way in the first place and not have done anything at all, unless you were with somebody you wanted to impress—your probation officer, for instance.

An old friend of mine named Joe Schenkman happens to have just written me a letter about another thing you can do to wreck a car. Joe's on a little vacation up in Vermont (and will be until he finds out what the statute of limitations on attempted vehicular homicide is). He wrote to tell me about a fellow he met up there, saying,

> *This guy has rolled (deliberately) over thirty cars (and not just by his own account—the townfolks back him up on this story), inheriting only a broken nose (three times) and a slightly black-and-blue shoulder for*

> *all this. What you do, see, is you go into a moonshiner's turn, but you get on the brakes and stay on them. Depending on how fast you're going, you roll proportionately. Four or five rolls is decent. Going into the spin, you have one hand on the seat and the other firmly on the roof so you're sprung in tight. As you feel the roof give on the first roll, you slip your seat hand under the dash (of the passenger side, as you're thrown hard over in that direction to begin with) and pull yourself under it. And here you simply sit it out, springing yourself tight with your whole body, waiting for the thunder to die. Naturally, it helps to be drunk, and if you have a split second's doubt or hesitation through any of this you die.*

This Schenkman himself is no slouch of a driver, I may say. Unfortunately, his strong suit is driving in New York City, a place that has a great number of unusual special conditions, which we just don't have the time or the space to get into right here (except to note that the good part is how it's real easy to scare old ladies in new Cadillacs and the bad part is that Negroes actually *do* carry knives, not to mention Puerto Ricans, and everybody else you hit turns out to be a lawyer or married to somebody in the mob). However, Joe is originally from the South, and it was down there that he discovered huffing glue and sniffing industrial solvents and such. These give you a really spectacular hallucinatory type of a high where you think, for instance, that you're driving through an overpass guardrail and landing on a freight-train flatcar and being hauled to Shreveport and loaded into a container ship headed for Liberia with a crew of homosexual Lebanese, only to come to find that it's true. Joe is a commercial artist who enjoys jazz music and horse racing. His favorite color is blue.

There's been a lot of discussion about what kind of music to listen to while staring doom square in the eye and not blinking unless you get some grit under your contacts. Watch out for the fellow who tunes his FM to the classical station. He thinks a little Rimsky-Korsakov makes things more dramatic—like in a foreign movie. That's pussy-style. This kind of guy's idea of a fast drive is a seventy-five-mile-an-hour cruise up to the summer cottage after one brandy and soda. The true skid-mark artist prefers something cheery and upbeat—"Night on Disco Mountain" or "Boogie Oogie Oogie" or whatever it is that the teenage lovely wants to shake her buns to. Remember her? So what do you care what's on the fucking tape deck? The high, hot whine of the engine, the throaty pitch of the exhaust, the wind in your beer can, the gentle slurping noises from her little bud-red lips—that's all the music your ears need, although side two of the first Velvet Underground album is nice if you absolutely insist. And no short jaunts either. For the maniacal high-speed driver endurance is everything. Especially if you've used that ever popular pickup line "Wanna go to Mexico?" Especially if you've used it somewhere like Boston. Besides, teenage girls can go a long, long time without sleep, and believe me so can their parents and the police. So just keep your foot on it. There's no reason not to. There's no reason not to keep going forever, really. I had this friend who drove a whole shitload of people up from Oaxaca to Cincinnati one time, nonstop. I mean, he stopped for gas but he wouldn't even let anybody get out. He made them all piss out the windows, and he says that it was worth the entire drive just to see a girl try to piss out the window of a moving car.

Get a fat girlfriend so you'll have plenty of diet pill amphetamines and you'll never have to stop at all. The only problem you'll run into is that after you've been driving for two or three days you start to see things in the road, great big scaly things twenty-feet high with nine legs. But there are very few great big scaly things with nine legs in America anymore, so you can just drive right through them because they probably aren't really there, and if they are really there you'll be doing the country a favor by running them over.

Yes, but where does it all end? Where does a crazy life like this lead? To death, you say. Look at all the people who've died in car wrecks: Albert Camus, Jayne Mansfield, Jackson Pollock, Tom Paine. Well, Tom Paine didn't actually die in a car wreck, but he probably would have if he'd lived a little later. He was that kind of guy. Anyway, death is always the first thing that leaps into everybody's mind—sudden violent death at an early age. If only it were that simple. God, we could all go out in a blaze of flaming aluminum alloys formulated specially for the Porsche factory race effort like James Dean did! No ulcers, no hemorrhoids, no bulging waistlines, soft dicks, or false teeth . . . *Bash! Kaboom! Watch this space for paperback reprint rights auction and movie option sale!* But that's not the way it goes. No. What actually happens is you fall for that teenage lovely in the next seat, fall for her like a ton of Trojans, and before you know it you're married and have teenage lovelies of your own—getting felt up in a Pontiac Trans Am this very minute, no doubt—plus a six-figure mortgage, a liver the size of the Bronx, and a Country Squire that's never seen the sweet side of sixty.

It's hard to face the truth but I suppose you yourself realize that if you'd had just a little more courage, just a little more strength of character, you could have been dead by now. No such luck.

A Cool and Logical Analysis of the Bicycle Menace

And an Examination of the Actions Necessary to License, Regulate, or Abolish Entirely This Dreadful Peril on Our Roads

Our nation is afflicted with a plague of bicycles. Everywhere the public right-of-way is glutted with whirring, unbalanced contraptions of rubber, wire, and cheap steel pipe. Riders of these flimsy appliances pay no heed to stop signs or red lights. They dart from between parked cars, dash along double yellow lines, and whiz through crosswalks right over the toes of law-abiding citizens like me.

In the cities, every lamppost, tree, and street sign is disfigured by a bicycle slathered in chains and locks. And elevators must be shared with the cycling faddist so attached to his "moron's bathchair" that he has to take it with him everywhere he goes.

In the country, one cannot drive around a curve or over the crest of a hill without encountering a gaggle of huffing bicyclers spread across the road in suicidal phalanx.

Even the wilderness is not safe from infestation, as there is now such a thing as an off-road bicycle and a horrible sport called "bicycle-cross."

The ungainly geometry and primitive mechanicals of the bicycle are an offense to the eye. The grimy and perspiring riders of the bicycle are an offense to the nose. And the very existence of the bicycle is an offense to reason and wisdom.

Principal Arguments That May be Marshaled against Bicycles

1. *Bicycles Are Childish*

Bicycles have their proper place, and that place is under small boys delivering evening papers. Insofar as children are too short to see over the dashboards of cars and too small to keep motorcycles upright at intersections, bicycles are suitable vehicles for them. But what are we to make of an adult in a suit and tie pedaling his way to work? Are we to assume he still delivers newspapers for a living? If not, do we want a doctor, lawyer, or business executive who plays with toys? Saint Paul, in his First Epistle to the Corinthians, 13:11, said, "When I became a man, I put away childish things." He did *not* say, "When I became a man, I put away childish things and got more elaborate and expensive childish things from France and Japan."

Considering the image projected, bicycling commuters might as well propel themselves to the office with one knee in a red Radio Flyer wagon.

2. *Bicycles Are Undignified*

A certain childishness is, no doubt, excusable. But going about in public with one's head between one's knees and one's rump protruding in the air is nobody's idea of acceptable behavior.

It is impossible for an adult to sit on a bicycle without looking the fool. There is a type of woman, in particular, who should never assume the bicycling posture. This is the woman of ample proportions. Standing on her own feet she is a figure to admire—classical in her beauty and a symbol, throughout history, of sensuality, maternal virtue, and plenty. Mounted on a bicycle, she is a laughingstock.

In a world where loss of human dignity is such a grave and all-pervading issue, what can we say about people who voluntarily relinquish all of theirs and go around looking at best like Quixote on Rosinante and more often like something in the Macy's Thanksgiving Day parade? Can such people be trusted? Is a person with so little self-respect likely to have any respect for you?

3. *Bicycles Are Unsafe*

Bicycles are top-heavy, have poor brakes, and provide no protection to their riders. Bicycles are also made up of many hard and sharp components which, in collision, can do grave damage to people and the paint finish on automobiles. Bicycles are dangerous things.

Of course, there's nothing wrong, *per se,* with dangerous things. Speedboats, race cars, fine shotguns, whiskey, and love are all very dangerous. Bicycles, however, are dangerous without being any fun. You can't shoot pheasants with a bicycle or water-ski behind it or go 150 miles an hour or even mix it with soda and ice. And the idea of getting romantic on top of a bicycle is alarming. All you can do with one of these ten-speed sink traps is grow tired and sore and fall off it.

Being dangerous without being fun puts bicycles in a category with open-heart surgery, the war in Vietnam, the South Bronx, and divorce. Sensible people do all that they can to avoid such things as these.

4. Bicycles Are Un-American

We are a nation that worships speed and power. And for good reason. Without power we would still be part of England and everybody would be out of work. And if it weren't for speed, it would take us all months to fly to LA, get involved in the movie business, and become rich and famous.

Bicycles are too slow and impuissant for a country like ours. They belong in Czechoslovakia.

5. I Don't Like the Kind of People Who Ride Bicycles

At least I think I don't. I don't actually know anyone who rides a bicycle. But the people I see on bicycles look like organic gardening zealots who advocate federal regulation of bedtime and want American foreign policy to be dictated by UNICEF. These people should be confined.

I apologize if I have the wrong impression. It may be that bicycle riders are all members of the New York Stock Exchange, Methodist bishops, retired Marine Corps drill instructors, and other solid citizens. However, the fact that they cycle around in broad daylight making themselves look like idiots indicates that they're crazy anyway and should be confined just the same.

6. Bicycles Are Unfair

Bicycles use the same roads as cars and trucks yet they pay no gasoline tax, carry no license plates, are not required to have insurance, and are not subject to DOT, CAFE, or NHTSA regulations. Furthermore, bicyclists do not have to take driver's examinations, have eye tests when they're over sixty-five, carry registration papers with them, or submit to Breathalyzer tests under the threat of law. And they never get caught in radar traps.

The fact (see no. 5, above) that bicycles are ridden by the very people who most favor government interference in life makes the bicycle's special status not only unfair but an outright incitement to riot.

Equality before the law is the cornerstone of democracy. Bicycles should be made to carry twenty-gallon tanks of gasoline. They should be equipped with twelve-volt batteries and a full complement of taillights, headlamps, and turn signals. They should have seat belts, air bags, and safety-glass windows too. And every bicycle rider should be inspected once a year for hazardous defects and be made to wear a number plate hanging around his neck and another on the seat of his pants.

7. *Bicycles Are Good Exercise*

And so is swinging through trees on your tail. Mankind has invested more than four million years of evolution in the attempt to avoid physical exertion. Now a group of backward-thinking atavists mounted on foot-powered pairs of Hula-Hoops would have us pumping our legs, gritting our teeth, and searing our lungs as though we were being chased across the Pleistocene savanna by saber-toothed tigers. Think of the hopes, the dreams, the effort, the brilliance, the pure force of will that, over the eons, have gone into the creation of the Cadillac Coupe de Ville. Bicycle riders would have us throw all this on the ash heap of history.

What Must Be Done about the Bicycle Threat?

Fortunately, nothing. Frustrated truck drivers and irate cabbies make a point of running bicycles off the road. Terrified old ladies jam umbrella ferrules into wheel spokes as bicycles rush by them on sidewalks. And all of us have occasion to back over bicycles that are haplessly parked.

Bicycles are quiet and slight, difficult for normal motorized humans to see and hear. People pull out in front of bicycles, open car doors in their path, and drive through intersections filled with the things. The insubstantial bicycle and its unshielded rider are defenseless against these actions. It's a simple matter of natural selection. The bicycle will be extinct within the decade. And what a relief that will be.

The King of Sandusky, Ohio

My grandfather was King of Sandusky, Ohio. His father, King Mike the First, had ruled a small farm ten miles from town. There was a period of great disorder in Sandusky then, due to the City Ordinance of Succession. The throne of Sandusky cannot pass through a female heir. King Jim, who ruled in the year of my grandfather's birth, 1887, had no sons and no brothers, nor had he had any paternal uncles. So the question of inheritance fell among an array of quarreling cousins, one of whom (though, I believe, only by marriage) was my great-grandfather Mike. But Mike was good with a broadsword and had friends at the county courthouse. Eventually he was appointed Chancellor of the Exchequer at one of the local banks and conquered a lumberyard and a livery stable. King Jim was old and growing senile and my great-grandfather had himself declared Royal Protector by taking care of the old king's house and yard and making sure he always had a carriage if he wanted to go for a ride in the country. When King Jim died in 1901 my great-grandfather knew where all the legal papers were, and, with the help of my young grandfather, the future Crown Prince Barney, he fought a pitched battle with the other claimants and cousins in an office downtown. He was greatly outnumbered by his rivals, but they were leaderless and quarreled among themselves, and while they were consulting a lawyer they had hired, King Mike set upon them with archers and most of them were slain. A few retired on pensions, however, and one moved to California.

King Mike died in 1920, and his oldest son, my great-uncle Will, became King of the Farm, but it was my grandfather who was placed upon the throne of Sandusky. This was not in strict adherence to the Succession Ordinance, but few men ever defied my grandfather and lived or did not have a business failure.

Under the reign of my grandfather, Sandusky grew in power and prosperity. A grain elevator was built and a factory and then another. My grandfather was always at war. He conquered Norwalk, Fremont, Tiffin, and Oak Openings State Park, where there was a battle that lasted nearly two days in the dark and tangled woods of the bird sanctuary. In 1942 he defeated

Port Clinton, using archers—as his father had—and massed infantry armed with pikes and swords at the bridge on Route 4. The mounted knights he fought, whose number made up nearly all the nobility and royal family of Port Clinton, were shot down with arrows or forced over the guardrail and drowned in their heavy armor before anyone could get to them with a powerboat. It's a lesson I've never forgotten. Cavalry is important for mobility's sake and for swift forays, but the true strength of an army lies in its well-trained foot soldiers. Also horses have to be fed and groomed every day and usually boarded at a stable on the outskirts of town.

King Barney commissioned a navy for Sandusky, with three-masted galleons. And he fought sea battles at Put-In Bay, at North Bass Island, and even at the mouth of the Maumee River, in Toledo harbor. Thus my grandfather wrested much of the freighter traffic in western Lake Erie from the Businessmen Princes of Toledo and Detroit, Michigan. He also fended off attacks from the barbarians who came down out of Canada in their war ferries. They wore no armor, only hats, and fought with axes, but they were fearsome warriors nonetheless and were driven from our shores only after they had sacked many fishing camps and a boat dock. There was an uprising, too, among the peasants who were in a labor union at the Willis Overland plant, and my grandfather put down that rebellion with great force. And he quarreled with the deacon of the largest Presbyterian church in town, a man who commanded powerful forces and wanted to enforce the Eighteenth Amendment, which commanded Prohibition and caused a great schism in Ohio. My grandfather, at last, seized all the deacon's property and foreclosed on some empty lots and small businesses that he owned, distributing them with his customary largess to the earls and counts who owned restaurants and bars and had fought loyally by the king's side. He took for himself a Buick dealership. And built a palace for the royal household on Elm Street. By the time I was born, in 1957, King Barney ruled nearly all of north-central Ohio from Lorraine to Bucyrus and as far west as Perrysburg. What he hadn't conquered by sword and fire had been annexed by the city government, and dukes and barons from surrounding towns swore fealty to my grandfather, even, in some cases, sending their own children as hostages on vacation visits to the royal court. Where, of course, they were treated with the greatest courtesy.

King Barney, though fierce in war, was at heart a kindly man, loved by his subjects. Very few were the times when he threw anyone into the dungeon at the Buick dealership, and only then when they had committed some heinous crime. And he hated to order an execution. Even when Leonard of Fostoria married my second cousin Duchess Connie and treated her cruelly, and was cast into the dungeon and broke $300 worth of distributor caps and taillight lenses which were stored there, Grandfather did not have him killed but just talked him into joining the Marine Corps.

My grandfather King Barney had five children. Crown Prince Bob was the oldest; then my father, who bore the title Prince of New Car Sales and was also the Captain of the Royal Guard; then Princess Annie; then Prince Larry, who ran the used-car lot; and my youngest uncle, Prince Fred. My father married Princess Doris, whose father had been the Emperor of Michigan City, Indiana, but who had been deposed in the stock-market crash of 1929. Her family had fled Indiana, and her brother Sam took refuge in a monastery owned by the New York Central Railroad, where he became Chief Abbot and a freight-train engineer. Her sister Dorothy married a real estate salesman from Chicago who was very successful because he was the duke of a suburb.

I led an idyllic childhood, partly at the court of my grandfather the king and partly at his summer cottage. I was trained in the arts of warfare and at falconry and baseball and playing the trumpet. My father was a great favorite with the people. It was assumed that someday he would be king, since Uncle Bob had no male heirs. Oddly, I must have been nearly ten before I realized that I myself was therefore in line for the crown. And it was not long after I had made that realization that my father was tragically struck down. There had been trouble at the car dealership. A White Castle restaurant across the street had rebelled, and my father and my Uncle Larry, who was his chief lieutenant, gathered their troops and some of the mechanics from the garage and laid siege to the Amazon waitresses. It was only a glancing blow of a halberd that struck my father's helmet, and Prince Larry told me that in the victorious glow of the burning lunchroom my father complained of nothing but a slight headache. But that night he suffered a cerebral hemorrhage and went into the hospital and died. A hundred lancers on horseback and many people in a long line of cars accompanied him to his grave in Woodlawn Cemetery, where our family owned a plot.

Less than a year later my mother married again, to Count Ralph, a minor nobleman from a shopping center on the south side of town. And thus began the intrigue that was to mark the next dozen years of my life.

At first I didn't care much one way or the other about my new stepfather. He seemed nice enough, in a way, but he drank too much beer and his armor was the cheap foreign kind. And he did not have a charger of his own. Anytime there was an argument with a neighbor over feudal obligations like keeping their lawns nice, he would have to rent a horse in order to settle the quarrel with a jousting match. But I didn't really mind him. Anyway, I was much too busy with the Grade School Wars. They caused great destruction and suffering, especially to substitute teachers. My grandfather should have put a stop to these fights, but he was growing old and he never recovered from the death of my father, who was his favorite. He began to grow feeble after that and wound up in a royal nursing home. And my uncle Bob, the crown prince, cared about nothing but business and golf.

There were three grade schools in the local school district, and we were at war with each other constantly. And the four public high schools in Wood County were fighting each other also. Not to mention the two parochial high schools, each of which had elected its own pope. And this caused rioting among the Polish and Italian people who worked in the factories. At school we fought with wooden pikes and swords. Most of our parents wouldn't let us have real swords until we were sixteen. Although some kids who had paper routes saved up and bought them anyway. We had real arrows, though. And I was grazed on the arm once and had to have stitches.

The school wars were exciting. They were fought from classroom to classroom. I was one of the leaders, of course, because I was of royal blood. But I was in the sixth grade, so I was only a lieutenant. Still, I led my men in many sword fights, especially on the staircases. We would fight up and down the staircases. They were the best places for sword fights. Our school, McKinley School, was a big building, like a fortress, and we fought from barricades across the corridors, and even the principal couldn't get us to behave. Once we were besieged by the kids from Nathan Hale Grade School, and they drove us to the second floor and conquered our gym. We might have starved if the girls hadn't had to go home when the streetlights came on. And they were able to get back into the school auditorium that night because there was a PTA meeting and they came with their parents. We hoisted picnic baskets full of provisions up from the auditorium floor to the balcony, and so we survived until morning. We had new sword fights on all the staircases that next day and drove the Nathan Hale kids back to their own neighborhood. We captured one of their sixth-graders, who used to be in my class but his parents moved. He was a spy, and we proved it with a trial by fire, and he died in the hospital. After that our grade school couldn't fly the yellow safety pennant on our flagpole under my family's royal banner. The yellow safety pennant meant no student had been hurt that year and had a picture of Amber the Safety Elephant on it.

I was so busy that I didn't notice that Count Ralph, my stepfather, was conspiring against me until my grandfather died and Uncle Bob was crowned King of Sandusky. This made me crown prince, and I always led my class when we marched to school assemblies or to drop our contributions into the March of Dimes collection. Count Ralph's first plot was to poison my uncle so that I would be king and he could be appointed regent until I was twenty-one. He tried this at a weenie roast but King Bob only vomited and the poison hot dog did not have time to do its work.

But then my stepfather decided upon a different and more treacherous scheme. I believe he realized that I knew about the poisoning attempt, for I had spied on him when I worked after school at his hardware store in the shopping center. And he knew I had come to hate him because he would not buy me an English racer bicycle and because he continually ranted and raved at me for not cleaning up after my brace of coursing hounds. He and my uncle came to a rapprochement. And despite my warnings to the king, Count Ralph was made my protector and Head of the Royal Guards. It became clear to me that the two of them were in league when my cousins Prince Buster and Prince Kevin were waylaid on the street and killed by a hit-and-run driver. This left no other male heir but me, and if I could be gotten out of the way, King Bob's grandson, my second cousin Prince Dickie, could be made crown prince. I knew, also, that Count Ralph was aiding my uncle in urging City Council to change the laws of royal succession. Either way I would never become king. They couldn't kill me outright, not yet. It would look bad in the papers. But they were going to get rid of me somehow. My mother was weak. She feared for my safety, but she also wanted to save her marriage and was afraid of what the neighbors would say if she got divorced. I went to my uncles Prince Larry and Prince Fred, whose sons had been murdered. I asked them for help raising a troop of armed men. I could muster a hundred boys from McKinley School and at least my own patrol from my Boy Scout troop, but we were poorly armed and had no siege engines or cavalry. But my uncles were scared they'd lose their jobs. Only Princess Annie was any help. She gave me a packet of poison to spread on the fabric of my stepfather's sport coat. But I lost it on the way home.

There was nothing to do but flee, so I sought sanctuary at the home of my mother's brother, the Duke of Evanston, Illinois.

This was not a happy time of my life. I was among strangers whose customs and manner of dress were unfamiliar to me. And it was a cliquish high school. I didn't fit in. Then the duke, my uncle, had a massive coronary. I had hoped that he and his son, my cousin Eddie, would help me raise an army. Perhaps, also, Reverend Stevens at Evanston United Methodist would declare a crusade, and I could return to Sandusky and topple Uncle Bob from the throne. Cousin Ed was a bully and I had never liked him, but he had powerful friends on the football team. But my hopes were dashed, and instead of raising an army I was caught in a quarrel between my cousin, the new duke, and his mother, who still held the purse strings of the ducal treasury at the local branch bank and would not let Duke Eddie have even his own checking account. And Lady Sue, Eddie's sister, was contemplating a totally unsuitable marriage to a commoner, a bread-truck driver. And, worse, this man was a heretic, a Seventh Day Adventist whose family had been slaughtered in the general massacre of Adventists the year before. He had escaped only because he had been out in the garage trying to fix a lawn mower when it happened. But he lived in fear for his life and planned to emigrate to the colonies in Wisconsin, where he hoped religious toleration would be found. And he planned to take Lady Sue with him. No one had time for me, and I never did make many friends in school.

Before my senior year, I decided to return alone to Sandusky. I knew I faced likely death or imprisonment in my bedroom on some slight pretext. Nor did I have any plan. Uncle Sam tried to convince me to become a railroad monk. But I must have a life of action, and if I could not find some way to succeed in Sandusky, then perhaps I would become a brigand and live in the forest and rob picnickers.

Once I was home, however, a streak of good fortune came my way. My high school was in the wealthiest part of town, but our athletic teams were not very good and in the various skirmishes and battles with the other schools in the parking lots after football games we had lost many dead and wounded. We had no archers, our single troop of lancers was decimated, and our infantry was a rabble of kids whose parents were not very well off. Because I was still, in name at least, crown prince, it was easy to get elected to Student Council. And since no one else wanted the job, I became chairman of the Battle and Pillage Committee. I knew there was no way that I could form our high school's dispirited and disorganized army into an effective fighting force, not even against other high schools, let alone against my uncle the king and my stepfather and his Royal Guards—especially since my stepfather had grounded me for a month for getting a speeding ticket. Still, with even a few troops I had some options open. You see, of the six high schools in the Sandusky area there was one, Scott High, which was nearly all colored. We were at peace with them, just then. And, in fact, since they were in an isolated part of town, they were at war with no one but some eastside rednecks who were high school dropouts anyway. But what I did was bully our Student Council president—a little bespeckled fellow and a great coward—into making belligerent noises toward Scott High on the pretext of a Negro family or two moving into our school district. We could not beat them in a set-piece battle. I knew that. But their school was far enough away from ours that it would not come to outright war for a while, I felt sure. Then, one night, I took a dozen of my best and most trusted swordsmen and we dressed ourselves as colored people, wearing gauntlets and keeping our visors down so that no one could see the true color of our skin. Then I led a small raid on some houses in a nice neighborhood near our school. We burned the places to the ground and killed the families, being sure to perform the worst mutilations on the bodies. It got a lot of coverage on television, and the first result was a much larger military budget for my army. We took, in fact, all the money from the prom decorations fund—everything that had been made from car washes and bake sales for a whole year. I purchased arms and horses and even a siege engine or two, which did much to raise morale.

The kids at Scott High denied they'd done the killings, of course, and, of course, we called them liars and threatened war. But threats were as far as I let it go just then. Instead of attacking Scott High, my little band of raiders and I made another attack pretending to be colored. This time we attacked houses near Libby High School. My school and Libby had been at war for years, and I thought, rightly, that a "colored" outrage would give us cause to unite with them against the Negros. I won't go on with all the details, but in such a way I eventually brought all five of the white high schools, even the Catholic ones, into a unified force. We made terrible war on the Negros and they, vastly outnumbered, were beaten in battle after battle and driven back into the center of the slum where they lived.

That spring the four other military commanders and I sat in parlay to plan a final attack, a complex action along converging lines, which is the hardest type of battle plan to make. The strategy, drafted by myself, was, if I may say so, excellent. It would take too much time to detail it here, but, briefly, the plan was to use our cavaliers not as the primary fighting force (such as was then the custom among high schools) but for the purpose of continual short feints to turn the Negro flanks between poised companies of our five-school infantry, which I had drilled. And while our archers held the colored center pinned down, we would cut their troops to ribbons from each end. By means of this battle we intended to wipe out all the remaining colored people in Sandusky, for we planned to slaughter the prisoners and children.

I held precedence at this council, by virtue of my inheritance and tactical ability, but I knew that with the end of the colored war we would all fall back to quarreling with each other. And I also knew that some of the other high school commanders had no love for me. At least two, in fact, wanted to command a united army of high school students and use it to take control of the city just as I planned to. Therefore I made a diplomatic move unbeknownst to my comrades in arms. I arranged a secret meeting with the leader of the colored forces. I told him of our intention to massacre his people, and he was very upset about it. But I offered to make an arrangement with him. If he would ensure that his troops killed each of my four co-commanders, then I would allow him to surrender on liberal terms with no massacre or rape or looting by the white armies. He agreed, and I showed to him the exact position that each commander would be occupying during the battle. He swore that he would do his best to see that each was killed.

It was a terrific fight. Every Negro person in Sandusky had armed himself as best he could with knives and shovels and rocks and bottles, and the police had cordoned off that whole part of town so that we could fight without tying up traffic. Of course, the colored troops were no match for our mounted knights, and our archers and crossbowmen cut them down in waves. But they fought well, giving no quarter and asking none. And, while they fought, the captain of their high school's guard fulfilled his promise to me and sent his best knights in at just the place I had told him so that by midafternoon three of my rivals were dead and the other so badly wounded that he had to go home. I alone was left in charge of the field, and when the Negroes at last began to wave white bedsheets attached to broom handles and garden rakes, I called a halt to the killing. I gave the colored people a place to live, between the freight yard and the river, on the edge of downtown as far south as the Delco battery plant, and they remain loyal subjects to this day.

Now I was in uncontested command of a battle-seasoned army of three thousand men, and I could have turned them at any time against my stepfather's Royal Guards and won the issue, I had no doubt. But the time was not yet ripe. For one thing it would have been against the law and I might have been sent to reform school if the police caught me doing it. And for another thing, my uncle, though not so popular as his father had been, still had public opinion on his side. The thing to do instead, I thought, was to force King Bob to make *me* head of the Royal Guard, as was my birthright. But that was impossible so long as my protector and stepfather, Count Ralph, lived. Nor did I trust my younger uncles, either of whom might be made protector in his stead. So I had Prince Fred and Prince Larry murdered and would have done the same for Count Ralph. But my stepfather was too well protected for that, and there would have been no doubt in anyone's mind as to who had ordered it done. So I decided to pick a quarrel with him and kill him in a public duel.

It happened at the dinner table. Mom had just brought in the roast when Count Ralph, unhinged by my taunts while we'd been eating salad, drew his rapier and, made clumsy by his anger, thrust into a bowl of potato salad. I leapt on my chair and, grabbing the pull-down light fixture in my left hand, slashed at him with the heavy saber I had carried to the table for just this purpose. I missed and cut one of the dining-room drapes in half. Ralph parried my backstroke and cut me beneath the arm. I kicked a gravy boat at his chest and, as he flinched, caught him with a glancing blow that cut off his ear and killed my sister Jill. He had his dagger out by now, but dagger and rapier were no match for my heavier weapon, and I backed him into the family room, slashing furiously at his bleeding head. He did me some damage, I must say. I was wounded again in the thigh and lost a finger of my left hand to his knife. But I laid open his chest right through the sport shirt so that a strip of flesh fell open like a flap. Ralph ran out the back door onto the patio. I could have skewered him then, from behind, but I wanted a death that was face-to-face. He poked through the screen as I came out after him, and I stumbled off the steps. He would have had me if he'd been quicker, but he was too fat from beer and too soft from sitting watching TV every night. I regained my footing and we went at it for a moment more until I had him backing away into the yard. It was then that he tripped on the lawn chair and fell backward into it like he was sitting down. His head went back, and I gave a mighty slash and severed it from his body.

King Bob had no choice after that but to make me Captain of the Royal Guards. I accused most all of them of corruption, cheating on their income tax, or violating parking regulations, and had them executed. I replaced them with my own soldiers. Now I'm waiting for my uncle to die. I believe Princess Annie is going to poison him. And then I'll be king and move out and get a place of my own and buy a four-wheel-drive Jeep.

HOLIDAYS IN HELL

(1988)

"Wherever you go, there you are."
—Buckaroo Banzai

A Ramble through Lebanon

October 1984

I visited Lebanon in the fall of '84, which turned out to be pretty much the last time, for the next five or six years, that an American could travel freely in Lebanon with only a risk (rather than a certainty) of being kidnapped. Somehow I had convinced Vanity Fair *to let me do a "travel" piece on the holiday pleasures of Beirut and its environs. What follows is, with a few parenthetical addenda, the article I wrote, an article that* Vanity Fair, *understandably, decided was too odd to publish.*

"Bassboat." "Bizport." "Passboot." "Pisspot." It's the one English word every Lebanese understands and no Lebanese can say. The first, deepest, and most enduring impression from a visit to Lebanon is an endless series of faces, with gun barrels, poking through the car window and mispronouncing your travel documents.

Some of these faces belong to the Lebanese Army, some to the Christian Phalange, some to angry Shiites or blustering Druse or grumpy Syrian draftees or Scarsdale-looking Israeli reservists. And who knows what the rest of them belong to. Everybody with a gun has a checkpoint in Lebanon. And in Lebanon you'd be crazy not to have a gun. Though, I assure you, all the crazy people have guns, too.

You fumble for passes and credentials thinking, "Is this Progressive Socialist or Syrian Socialist National Party territory? Will the Amal militia kill me if I give them a Lebanese Army press card? And what's Arabic, anyway, for '*Me? American*? Don't make me laugh'?"

The gun barrels all have the bluing worn off the ends as though from being rubbed against people's noses. The interesting thing about staring down a gun barrel is how small the hole is where the bullet comes out, yet what a big difference it would make in your social schedule. Not that people shoot you very often, but the way they flip those weapons around and bang them on the pavement and poke them in the dirt and scratch their ears with the muzzle sights . . . Gun safety merit badges must go begging in the Lebanese Boy Scouts.

On the other hand, Lebanon is notably free of tour groups and Nikon-toting Japanese. The beaches, though shell-pocked and occasionally mined, are not crowded. Ruins of historical interest abound, in fact, block most streets. Hotel rooms are plentiful. No reservation is necessary at even the most popular restaurant (though it is advisable to ask around and find out if the place is likely to be bombed later). And what could be more unvarnished and authentic than a native culture armed to the teeth and bent on murder, pillage, and rape?

One minor difficulty with travel to Lebanon is you can't. There's no such thing as a tourist visa. Unless you're a journalist, diplomat, or arms salesman they won't let you in. And if you believe that, you'll never understand the Orient. Type a letter saying you're an American economist studying stabilization of the Lebanese pound or something. (Sound currency is one thing all factions agree on. The Central Bank is the best guarded and least shelled building in Beirut.) I had a letter saying I was studying the tourism industry in Lebanon.

"The *tourism* industry?" said the pretty young woman at the Lebanese Consulate.

"Yes," I said.

"*Tourism*?"

I nodded.

She shrugged. "Well, be sure to go see my village of Beit Mery. It's very beautiful. If you make it."

Middle East Airlines is the principal carrier to Beirut. It flies from London, Paris, Frankfurt, and Rome—sometimes. When the airport's being shelled, you can take a boat from Larnaca, Cyprus.

There are a number of Beirut hotels still operating. The best is the Commodore in West Beirut's El Hamra district. This is the headquarters for the international press corps. There are plenty of rooms available during lulls in the fighting. If combat is intense, telex Beirut 20595 for reservations. The Commodore's basement is an excellent bomb shelter. The staff is cheerful, efficient, and will try to get you back if you're kidnapped.

There's a parrot in the bar at the Commodore that does an imitation of an incoming howitzer shell and also whistles the "Marseillaise." Only once in ten years of civil war has this bar been shot up by any of the pro-temperance Shiite militias. Even then the management was forewarned so only some Pepsi bottles and maybe a stray BBC stringer were damaged. Get a room away from the pool. It's harder to hit that side of the building with artillery. Rates are about fifty dollars per night. They'll convert your bar bill to laundry charges if you're on an expense account.

Beirut, at a glance, lacks charm. The garbage has not been picked up since 1975. The ocean is thick with raw sewage, and trash dots the surf. Do not drink the water. Leeches have been known to pop out the tap. Electricity is intermittent.

It is a noisy town. Most shops have portable gasoline generators set out on the sidewalk. The racket from these combines with incessant horn honking, scattered gunfire, loud Arab music from pushcart cassette vendors, much yelling among the natives, and occasional car bombs. Israeli jets also come in from the sea most afternoons, breaking the sound barrier on their way to targets in the Bekáa Valley. A dense brown haze from dump fires and car exhaust covers the city. Air pollution probably approaches a million parts per million. This, however, dulls the sense of smell.

There are taxis always available outside the Commodore. I asked one of the drivers, Najib, to show me the sights. I wanted to see the National Museum, the Great Mosque, the Place des Martyrs, the Bois de Pins, the Corniche, and Hotel Row. Perhaps Najib misunderstood or maybe he had his own ideas about sightseeing. He took me to the Green Line. The Green Line's four crossings were occupied by the Lebanese Army—the Moslem Sixth Brigade on one side, the Christian Fifth Brigade on the other. Though under unified command, their guns were pointed at each other. This probably augurs ill for political stability in the region.

The wise traveler will pack shirts or blouses with ample breast pockets. Reaching inside a jacket for your passport looks too much like going for the draw and puts armed men out of continence.

At the Port Crossing, on the street where all the best whorehouses were, the destruction is perfectly theatrical. Just enough remains of the old buildings to give an impression of erstwhile grandeur. Mortars, howitzers, and rocket-propelled grenades have not left a superfluous brushstroke on the scrim. Turn the corner into the old marketplace, the Souk, however, and the set is a Hollywood back lot. Small arms and sniper fire have left perfectly detailed havoc. Every square inch is painstakingly bullet nibbled. Rubble spills artfully out of doorways. Roofs and cornices have been deftly crenulated by explosion. Everything is ready for Ernest Borgnine, John Cassavetes, and Lee Marvin in a remake of *The Dirty Dozen,* except the Lebanese can't figure out how to remove the land mines.

We went back and forth across the Green Line six times, then drove into Beirut's south suburbs. This area was once filled with apartment buildings housing the Moslem middle class. The buildings were destroyed by Israeli air strikes during the invasion of 1982. Modern construction techniques and modern warplanes create a different kind of ruin. Balconies, windows, and curtain walls disintegrate completely. Reinforced concrete floors fold like Venetian-blind slats and hang by their steel rebars from the buildings' utility cores. Or they land in a giant card-house tumble. Shiite squatter families are living in the triangles and trapezoids formed by the fallen slabs. There's a terrible lack of unreality to this part of the city.

Outside the areas controlled by the Lebanese Army the checkpoints are more numerous, less organized, and manned by teenagers in jeans, T-shirts, and Adidas running shoes. They carry Russian instead of U.S. weapons. Some belong to the Shiite Amal militia, others to the even more radical Hezbollah. All have strong feelings about America. Fortunately, they can't read. One even held my Arabic press credentials upside down, picture and all, and tipped his head like a parakeet to see if I matched my inverted photo. At the most dangerous-looking checkpoints, Najib said something that made the guards laugh and wave us through.

"Najib," I said, "what are you telling them?"

He said, "I tell them you travel for pleasure."

Finally, we got to a place where we could go no further. Down the street the Sunni Moslem Mourabitoun militia was having it out with the Shiite Amal militia—part of the long-standing Sunni/Shiite dispute about whether Muhammad's uncle Abbas or Muhammad's son-in-law Ali should have succeeded the Prophet and, also, about who gets the take from the southside gambling joints.

West Beirut can also be toured on foot. You'll find the city is full of surprises—a sacking of the Saudi embassy because of long lines for visas to Mecca, for instance, or shelling of the lower town by an unidentified gunboat or car bombs several times a day. Renaults are the favored vehicles. Avoid double-parked Le Cars. Do not, however, expect the population to be moping around glassy-eyed. There's lots of jewelry and makeup and the silliest Italian designer jeans on earth. The streets are jammed. Everyone's very busy, though not exactly working. They're rushing from one place to another in order to sit around drinking hundreds of tiny cups of Turkish coffee and chat at the top of their lungs. The entire economy is fueled, as far as I could see, by everyone selling cartons of smuggled Marlboros to each other.

It turns out I didn't miss much on Najib's style of guided tour. The Bois de Pins, planted in the 1600s by Emir Fakhr al-Din to protect Beirut from encroaching sand dunes, had all its foliage blown off by Israeli jets and looks like a phone-pole farm. The Place des Martyrs, so-called because eleven nationalists were hanged there by the Turks in 1915, is right on the Green Line and now all that much more aptly named. Most of the buildings on the Corniche have literally been face-lifted. The old American embassy is here, in the same state as U.S. Middle East policy. The British embassy down the street is completely draped in anti-bomb nets imported from Belfast. Hotel Row was ravaged at the beginning of the civil war in 1975. The high-rise Holiday Inn is a delight to the eye. Who, when traveling around the earth faced with endless Holiday Inns, has not fantasized about blowing one to flinders? The National Museum is bricked up and surrounded with tanks—no nagging sense of cultural obligation to tour this historical treasure trove. I couldn't find the Great Mosque at all.

A surprising lot of Beirut stands, however. A building with a missing story here, a lot with a missing building there, shattered this next to untouched that—all the usual ironies of war except with great restaurants.

The Summerland Hotel, on the beach in the ruined south suburbs, has good hamburgers. The wealthy Moslems, including Shiites, go here. All Shiites are not stern zealots. Some have string bikinis. And, like an American ethnic group with origins nearby, they wear their jewelry in the pool. (It was at the Summerland where the Amal militia feted its American captives during the 1985 TWA hostage crisis.)

Downtown on the Corniche you can lunch at the St. Georges Hotel, once Beirut's best. The hotel building is now a burned shell, but the pool club is still open. You can go waterskiing here, even during the worst fighting.

I asked the bartender at the pool club, "Don't the waterskiiers worry about sniper fire?"

"Oh, no, no, no," he said, "the snipers are mostly armed with automatic weapons—these are not very accurate."

Down the quay, pristine among the ruins, Chez Temporal serves excellent food. A short but careful walk through a heavily armed Druse neighborhood brings you to Le Grenier, once a jet-set mob scene, now a quiet hideaway with splendid native dishes. Next door there's first-rate Italian fare at Quo Vadis. Be sure to tip the man who insists, at gunpoint, on guarding your car.

Spaghetteria is a favorite with the foreign press. The Italian specials are good, and there's a spectacular view of military patrols and nighttime skirmishing along the beachfront. Sit near the window if you feel lucky.

Addresses are unnecessary. Taxi drivers know the way and when it's safe to go there. Service at all these establishments is good, more than good. You may find ten or a dozen waiters hovering at your side. If trouble breaks out, the management will have one or two employees escort you home. When ordering, avoid most native wines, particularly the whites. Mousar '75, however, is an excellent red. Do not let the waiters serve you Cypriot brandy after the meal. It's vile.

The Commodore also has restaurants. These are recommended during fighting. The Commodore always manages to get food delivered no matter what the situation outdoors.

Nightlife begins late in Beirut. Cocktail hour at the Commodore is eight p.m., when U.S. editors and network executives are safely at lunch (there's a seven-hour time difference). The Commodore is strictly neutral territory with only one rule. No guns at the bar. All sorts of raffish characters hang about, expatriates from Palestine, Libya, and Iran, officers in mufti from both sides of the Lebanese Army, and combatants of other stripes. I overheard one black Vietnam veteran loudly describe to two British girls how he teaches orthodox Moslem women to fight with knives. And there are diplomats, spooks, and dealers in gold, arms, and other things. At least that's what they seem to be. No one exactly announces his occupation—except the journalists, of course.

I met one young lady from Atlanta who worked on a CNN camera crew. She was twenty-six, cute, slightly plump, and looked like she should have been head of the Georgia State pep squad. I sat next to her at the Commodore bar and watched her drink twenty-five gin and tonics in a row. She never got drunk, never slurred a word, but along about G&T number twenty-two out came the stories about dismembered babies and dead bodies flying all over the place and the Red Cross picking up hands and feet and heads from bomb blasts and putting them all in a trash dumpster. "So I asked the Red Cross people," she said, in the same sweet Dixie accent, "like, what's this? Save 'em, collect 'em, trade 'em with your friends?"

Everyone in Beirut can hold his or her liquor. If you get queasy, Muhammad, the Commodore bartender, has a remedy rivaling Jeeves's in P. G. Wodehouse's novels. It will steady your stomach so you can drink more. You'll want to. No one in this part of the world is without a horror story, and, at the Commodore bar, you'll hear most of them.

Dinner, if anyone remembers to have it, is at ten or so. People go out in groups. It's not a good idea to be alone and blonde after dark. Kidnapping is the one great innovation of the Lebanese civil war. And Reuters correspondent Johnathan Wright had disappeared thus on his way to the Bekáa Valley a few days before I arrived.

If nabbed, make as much noise as possible. Do not get in anyone's car. If forced in, attack the driver. At least this is what I'm told.

Be circumspect when driving at night. Other cars should be given a wide berth. Flick headlights off and on to indicate friendly approach. Turn on the dome light when arriving at checkpoints. Militiamen will fire a couple of bursts in your direction if they want you to slow down.

Clubs, such as the Backstreet near the Australian embassy, keep going as late as you can stand it. There's some dancing, much drinking, and, if you yell at the management, they'll keep the Arab music off the tape deck. Cocaine is available at about fifty dollars a gram and is no worse than what you get in New York.

Beirut nightlife is not elaborate, but it is amusing. When danger waits the tables and death is the busboy, it adds zest to the simple pleasures of life. There's poignant satisfaction in every puff of a cigarette or sip of a martini.

The jokes are funnier, the drinks are stronger, the bonds of affection more powerfully felt than they'll ever be at Club Med.

East Beirut is said to also have good restaurants and nightclubs. But the visitor staying on the West Side probably won't see them. No one likes to cross the Green Line at night. And, frankly, the East isn't popular with the West Side crowd. All the window glass is taped, and the storefronts are sandbagged over there. It gives the place a gloomy look. No one would think of doing this in the West. It would be an insult to the tradition of Oriental fatalism, and nobody would be able to see all the cartons of smuggled Marlboros stacked in the window. Anyway, the East Side Christians are too smug, too pseudo-French, and haven't been shelled enough to turn them into party reptiles.

To travel to the rest of Lebanon you just hail a taxi. The country is only one hundred and twenty miles long and forty miles wide, and no Lebanese cabdriver has to call home to ask his wife if he can take off for a couple days. Settle the price first. This won't be easy. It's not the way of the Levant to come to the point. I asked Akbar, one of the Commodore's taximen, how much he'd charge to take me through the Israeli lines and into South Lebanon.

"I have been in this business twenty-seven years," he said.

"Yes," I said, "but how much is it going to cost me?"

"I will tell you later."

"Give me a rough idea."

"Would you like a coffee?"

"What's your hourly rate?"

"Across the street—fine rugs at the best price. I will get you a discount."

"What do you charge by the mile?"

"I have a cousin in Detroit."

"Akbar," I shouted, "what's it going to cost?!"

"If you do not like my price, I tell you what," Akbar gestured grandly, "you do not hire me anymore again."

Make sure your driver knows English well enough to translate. Lebanese English is often a triumph of memorization over understanding. "I come from the village of Baabdat," the driver will say in quite an acceptable accent, "it is very beautiful there in the mountains."

"Right," you'll say, "but you'd better pull over, that guy behind the sandbags is leveling an antitank gun at us."

"You do?" the driver will say. "Is that in Texas? I have a nephew in Houston."

Wherever you go, it's important to leave early in the morning. Those who think the war is dangerous have not seen the traffic in Beirut. It's a city of a million people with three stoplights and these aren't working. There are some traffic cops, but they are on no account to be minded as they tend to wave you into the path of dump trucks going sixty miles an hour. All driving is at top speed, much of it on the sidewalks since most parking is done in the middle of the streets. The only firm rule is: armored personnel carriers have the right of way.

Once outside Beirut there are, of course, other difficulties. The only land route into the Israeli-occupied south goes through the Chouf Mountains to a crossing point in the town of Bater, which is separated from Beirut by forty miles of armed Druse. You can also take a boat to Sidon from the Phalange-controlled docks in East Beirut if you're a Christian. I am, but there seemed to be some difficulty anyway. First they said they would have to ask Israeli permission because I was a journalist. Next they told me they didn't speak English. Then they quit speaking French.

On the way to Bater my driver took me past "Green Beach," the former U.S. Marine emplacement where a truck bomb had killed 241 Americans the year before. It's as defensible a position as the bottom of the airshaft in the Plaza Hotel. There's hardly a spot in Lebanon from which you can't fire a gun and hit it. Don't get out of the car. The beach is now an Amal military base under heavy guard because it's next to the orthodox Shiite women's bathing area. They wear ankle-length chadors in the water, which may explain the lack of a world-class Shiite women's swim team.

In the Chouf Mountains, the land is green and exquisite, cut through with precipitous gorges. Even the steepest slopes have been terraced and planted with fruit trees, vineyards, olive groves, and gun emplacements. The road is narrow with no railings or shoulders, and traffic is slow because the Druse are usually moving artillery around preparing to blast the Phalangists on the coast. Be sure to keep a mental note of such things. It's considered good manners to convey information about military movements to the next faction down the road. This takes the place of celebrity gossip in Lebanese small talk.

The Druse militiamen were good-natured. "Do you speak Arabic?" asked one. I shook my head, and he said something to another soldier who poked face and gun into the car and shouted, "He just said he wants to fuck your mother!"

I said, "He should see my mother."

Laughter all round.

The Druse villages are built in the Ottoman style, graceful, foursquare sandstone buildings with balconies, arched windows, and fifteen-foot ceilings. The low-pitched hip roofs are covered in red tile. Tidy gardens surround each house. Peasants in white skullcaps and baggy-crotched jodhpurs ride donkeys along the road. Herds of goats meander in the streets. It's all quite timeless except for the videocassette rental stores, unisex hair salons, and Mercedes-Benz sedans all over the place.

The Bater crossing was another matter. A couple hundred Lebanese, mostly old people, women, and children, were jammed into line behind barbed wire, waiting for the crossing to open. Several hundred more squatted in the dirt or milled about disconsolate. These, apparently, did not have their papers in order. Some had been there for days. A few tents had been provided but no toilets. There was no running water and no food other than what people had brought with them. Soldiers from the Israeli-hired South Lebanon Army were yelling, pointing guns, and threatening everyone. The sun was hot. A few of the women and all of the babies were crying. The smell was horrendous.

There seemed to be no way to tell when the crossing would open. My driver, Akbar, didn't have any ideas. I was not about to get in line behind the barbed wire. It looked too much like Bergen-Belsen. No one in sight, as far as I could tell, was in charge of anything but pistol waving.

On top of an embankment about a hundred yards on the other side of the crossing was a machine-gun nest with the Star of David flying over it. I took my passport out and, holding it shoulder high, walked through the barbed wire and tank traps. I fixed the South Lebanon Army guards with a stare I hoped would remind them of the recent Grenada invasion. "*American,*" I said. They backed away, and I headed as coolly as I could for the muzzle of the Israeli .50-caliber machine gun now being pointed at my chest.

Israelis are not well liked in West Beirut. During 1982 the Israelis besieged the Moslem part of town. There was no electricity and little food or water. The shelling and air strikes sometimes went on for twelve hours at a stretch. Beirut's foreign journalists call the Israelis "Schlomos" and consider them war criminals and also real squares.

Personally, I was glad to confront the only armed maniacs in the Middle East who aren't allowed to shoot U.S. citizens. I hoped they remembered.

"That's *my* helmet you're wearing," I was thinking. "Those are *my* boots, and *I* paid for that gun so you can just go point it at someone else." Not that I said this aloud. The hole a .50-caliber bullet comes out of is *not* small. It looks as if you could put your whole foot in there.

The Israelis motioned for me to come up, and I climbed the embankment. They held the machine gun on me until it became clear I was not a peroxided Iranian. "You must speak to the captain," they said.

He proved to be a boy of twenty-five. "Do you speak English?" I said.

"Gee, sure," said the captain. The Lebanese kept a respectful distance until they saw him talking to me. Then they descended in a horde waving unlikely-looking slips of paper and shouting the interminable explanations of the East. The captain's escort chased them away with shoves and curses.

The women, children, and old folks pressed back with no apparent fear. Finally, they pushed the officer and me under a guard tower. "Welcome to Lebanon" is the phrase everyone uses whenever anything untoward or chaotic breaks loose.

"Welcome to Lebanon," said the Israeli captain. He read my credentials and smiled. "*Tourism*?"

"Yes," I said, "I'm the only tourist in Lebanon."

The captain laughed. "Oh no, you're not. I'm a reservist, you know, and this is my vacation, too."

The Israelis wouldn't, however, allow my car through. I told Akbar to meet me there in two days and then hiked across no-man's-land to a line of taxis on the other side.

There were three stages in crossing the Israeli lines. Once through the checkpoint at Bater, I had to go by taxi to an interrogation center a few miles up the road. From the interrogation center I took a bus eight or ten miles to another checkpoint in Jezzine.

At the interrogation stop I was searched and questioned by Shin Bet, the Israeli FBI. An enlisted man apologized for the inconvenience. Less auspicious-looking travelers were being led off to be grilled in windowless huts.

In Jezzine I was questioned again by the South Lebanon Army, an interesting process since we had no language in common.

I hired another taxi to take me the fifteen miles from Jezzine to Sidon. It took five hours to get through the Bater-Jezzine crossing and a total of eight hours to make it from Beirut to Sidon. Before the war it was an hour drive on the coast road.

Sidon and Tyre, the two coastal cities of southern Lebanon, were once the principal towns of ancient Phoenicia and spawned a mercantile empire from Turkey to Spain. Important archaeological work has been done in both places, exposing six millennia of human misbehavior. Lebanon has been overrun in turn by Canaanites, Egyptians, Assyrians, Babylonians, Persians, Greeks, Romans, Arabs, Crusaders, Arabs again, Turks, French, more Arabs, Israelis, and occasionally U.S. Marines. Perhaps by means of the past one can begin to comprehend the present. Or learn which way to run from the future.

I hired a Palestinian Christian driver named Simon and had him take me twenty-five miles down the lush coast littoral to Tyre. We passed through ten or a dozen Israeli guard posts. These are heaps of sandbags with anxious eyes and many gun barrels sticking over the top. They look down upon a series of "Khomeini gates," cement barriers that jut into the road like meshing-gear teeth and force vehicles to zigzag slowly between them in single file. If you stall in the middle of these, you die.

The roadsides all over Lebanon are piled with trash, the coast road especially so. Beaches and parks are even worse. There's something about a civil war that brings out the litterbug in people.

Tyre is an awful mess of dirty modern architecture, offal, and the detritus of battle. The Elissa Beach Club hotel, on the south shore of the Tyre peninsula, may be one of the few oceanside hotels anyplace where none of the rooms face the sea. But it's clean, the hot water is not actually cold, and the food's passable. Also, there's nowhere else to stay.

Simon went home for the night, and I was left on the hotel's roof terrace about a thousand miles from the nearest example of the Four Freedoms. "I have a cousin in Cincinnati" was the only English anyone could speak. I watched the sun go down behind the ruins of some previous attempt to bring the rule of law to these climes.

I'd hoped at least for a good night's sleep. There'd been quite a few bombs going off in Beirut. I'd heard five the night before, starting with one at midnight in a bar a few blocks from the Commodore and winding up with a spectacular attempt on the life of the minister of education at six a.m. This took windows out for three blocks around and shook the furniture in my room. The minister survived but my repose did not. But this night, it turned out, was the beginning of the Hajj, the Moslem holiday marking the return of the Mecca pilgrims, and the urchins next door celebrated with a six-hour firecracker fight in the street. Then at two a.m. there was a truly horrendous explosion.

No use looking around the next day to see what's been blasted. Everything has been already.

Later I read in the Beirut newspapers that while I was in the south there were four sniping attacks on Israeli patrols, the South Lebanon Army had stormed a section of Sidon, there was a riot at a Palestinian refugee camp near Jezzine, and the coast road was heavily shelled. I noticed none of this. On the other hand, no explosion in Tyre was reported. This illustrates the difficulty, in Lebanon, of knowing what's happening, even to yourself.

In the morning I visited the principal archaeological digs. These are all decorated with small blue and white signs saying the ruins are national treasures protected by the convention of The Hague of 12 May 1954, and in case of armed conflict notify UNESCO. I suppose I should have phoned.

The oldest and most extensive excavation, near the ancient port, has revealed Phoenician house foundations, a Hellenistic theater, a long, colonnaded walk from Roman times, and parts of a Crusader wall. Some pretense is made of keeping these in order. They are guarded by one desultory fellow in a fez. After I'd wandered beyond the palings for an hour, he whistled at me to get out. Nearby a newer dig has uncovered a Roman temple now being used as a garbage dump.

Half a mile or so inland is a much larger site, which I couldn't find mentioned in any guidebooks. Not that there are many Lebanon guidebooks. I couldn't find any in U.S. bookstores. And the Hachette guide I purchased in Beirut was twenty years old. Other than this I was relying on an 1876 Baedeker I found in a New England thrift shop. It was not without useful advice.

> *The transaction of business in the East always involves an immense waste of time, and as Orientals attach no value whatsoever to their time, the European will often find his patience sorely tried.*
>
> *Many travelers rejoice in displaying a stock of revolvers and other arms, which add greatly to their importance in the eyes of the natives, but are not often brought into actual use.*

The larger excavation contains what looks to be an aqueduct, another theater, and a vast Roman necropolis. Simon had come back to get me at the hotel, and I had him drive me into the middle of these ruins. Garbage was being dumped here, too, and burned automobile seats, Pepsi cans, and lots of spent ordnance was mingled on the ground with ancient pot shards and mosaic tile chips. Simon picked up an amphora handle. "How old you think?" I told him about two thousand years. He nodded, "Two-thousand-years-old garbage."

Antiquity hunters have been at work in Tyre. All the Roman tombs are broken open, and many of the fracture marks in the marble are fresh. I peeked inside one grave, and there was a muddle of antique bones. It was, by sheer chance, the only dead body I saw in Lebanon.

I'd been given the name of a Lebanese-American, Billy Hadad, who has a farm on the coast near Sidon. We drove around looking for him. It's hard to know what your driver is doing when he talks to the natives. He'll pull up somewhere and make a preliminary oration, which draws five or six people to the car window. Then each of them speaks in turn. There will be a period of gesturing, some laughter, much arm clasping and handshaking, and a long speech by the eldest or most prominent bystander. Then your driver will deliver an impassioned soliloquy. This will be answered at length by each member of the audience and anybody else who happens by. Another flurry of arm grabbing, shoulder slapping, and handshakes follows, then a series of protracted and emotional good-byes.

"What did you ask them?" you'll say to your driver.

"Do they know of your friend?"

"What did they tell you?"

"No."

Eventually, we were directed to an old fortress-like farmhouse near the shore. There on the terrace was a big American preppie kid in chino pants and a button-down shirt. He looked at me and said, "Awesome. Man, I haven't heard English in months!"

The farm near Sidon has been owned by the Hadads since the time of the Ottoman Turks. Its two hundred and thirty acres are irrigated by springs and planted in avocados, bananas, and other fruit. The house dates from AD 600, with Arab and Turkish additions. It stands on a rock outcrop above a pool in use since Phoenician days. Centuries-old ficus trees grow over the walls, and flowers bloom all around it.

Billy's father was Druse, his mother from Oregon. They met at college in California. In the middle of the civil war Mr. Hadad was killed in, of all things, a skiing accident on Mount Lebanon. Mrs. Hadad took the younger children back to America, and Billy, just graduated from a Connecticut boarding school, came out to Lebanon to manage the property. He has five families, some thirty-five people, working for him.

We had lunch with one of his tenants and sat around a low table under a loggia indulging in Arab table manners. These are the best in the world or, anyway, the most fun. For the midday meal there are a dozen large bowls of things—salad; hot peppers; yogurt; a chickpea paste called hummus; kubbeh, which is a kind of meatball; and things I have no idea the names for. You get a flat loaf of pita bread and make flaps to grab the food. The bread is your napkin, also your plate. We had too much Arak, the regional version of absinthe, and drank endless tiny cups of drug-strength coffee. It's perfectly polite to smoke in the middle of the meal.

The tenant brought out his guns. It's like an Englishwoman showing you her roses. There was a Soviet AK-47, a Spanish Astra 9mm automatic pistol, a Smith and Wesson .38 revolver, an old British military rifle, and a very nice Beretta over-and-under shotgun. This is a modest collection. More militant people have mortars and the like. Serious gunmen favor the rocket-propelled grenade, or RPG, which is something like a bazooka. It's inaccurate and tremendously noisy, a perfect Lebanese weapon.

After lunch we went for a swim. This far south of Beirut the ocean is clean. From out in the water distant rumblings could be heard. I thought it was artillery in the Chouf. "Dynamite fishing," said Billy. (Dynamite is one bait fish always rise to.)

There was a wedding party in a nearby village that night. Lebanese wedding parties are held on the eve of the marriage. Thus the groom is given an excuse for looking green at the altar. A hundred or more chairs had been placed in a circle behind the bride's house. A few lightbulbs were strung in the grapevines and a huge table had been laid with food, Scotch, and Arak.

Parties in Lebanon start slow. Everyone sits primly in the chairs, neither eating nor drinking, and talking only in low voices. Or they would usually. In this case the men and boys must all discuss politics with the American. Every one of them has cousins in Texas.

"Just tell them what you think," said Billy. I couldn't very well do that. After a week in Lebanon what I thought would hardly make fit conversation at a wedding feast.

This was a Christian village. "If the Moslems take over," said a young man (Billy translating), "they'll close the bars during Ramadan. But we won't make them drink at Christmas if they really don't want to." A lather of self-justification followed. Justifying the self is the principal form of exercise in Lebanon. The principal form of exercise for a visitor in Lebanon is justifying American foreign policy. Last year's brief incursion by U.S. Marines, ending in the Green Beach truck bombing, was the first thing everyone asked me about. Moslems wanted to know why the marines had been sent here. Christians wanted to know why they had left. And Druse wanted to know why, during the marines' short stay, they felt compelled to shell the crap out of the Chouf.

My answer to everyone was that President Reagan wasn't sure why he sent the marines to Lebanon. However, he was determined to keep them here until he figured it out, but then he forgot.

Nobody held it against me personally. The Lebanese never hold anything against anyone personally. And it's not considered rude to root for the home team. There were a number of Moslem guests at the party. The villagers had nothing but affection for the Druse Billy Hadad, who towered over most of them. One teenager, summoning all the English at his command, told me, "Billy, il es . . . le homme vert, tu connais, Credible Hulk!" Billy said the only real trouble he's had with his neighbors and tenants was when he tried to convince them that professional wrestling is fake. It's the most popular program on Lebanese TV.

About ten o'clock there was a change in the festivities. Acting on some signal I couldn't perceive everyone suddenly began to drink and shout. A little later the bridegroom was carried in on the shoulders of his friends accompanied by drums, flutes, and the eerie ululation Arab women use to mark every emotional occasion. Awful tapes were put on a large boom box. There was bad Arab music, worse French rock and roll, and Israeli disco music, which is the most abominable-sounding thing I've ever heard in my life. A sister of the bride got in the middle of the circled chairs and did quite a shocking traditional dance.

There was something of the freshman mixer to the party. The young men and women held to opposite sides of the crowd, eyeing each other furtively and being shoved out to dance only after prolonged giggling and conspiracy among their fellows.

"I haven't been laid since I was in Beirut last June," said Billy. "Out in the country it's marriage or death."

Good-fellowship in the Middle East can be a bit unnerving. You'd better get used to being gripped, hugged, and even nuzzled by adult members of your own gender. I was taken aback the first time I saw two fully armed militiamen walking down the street holding hands. Large amounts of Arak aid in acclimation. The sense of affection and solidarity is comforting, actually, when you realize how many of the men throwing their arms around you have pistols in the waistbands of their pants. A Mercedes full of gunmen kept watch on the road.

Eventually I was thrust onto the dance floor and matched with a hefty girl who had me do Arab dances. This was, justly, thought hilarious. But my ancient sockhop dancing made an impression. I gather the locals are not familiar with the Watusi, the Jerk, and the Mashed Potato.

The whole celebration was being videotaped, and every now and then one of the revelers would use the Sony's quartz-halogen light to dry the skin on a snareless Arab drum.

Sometime in the early morning Billy and I returned to his farm. There was protracted questioning from his housekeeper on the floor above. She wanted to make sure we were us before she threw down the door keys. We locked ourselves in with five deadbolts.

The trip back to Beirut was a horror. The Israelis run Betar and the midpoint interrogation center, and conditions there are ugly but organized. However, the clumsy and violent South Lebanon Army has control of the Jezzine checkpoint.

There were about a thousand angry and panicked people in the small town square when I arrived. Most of them were poor Shiites, and all of them seemed to have screaming children and every earthly possession with them. One group of two or three hundred were fighting with fists to get on a bus. Soldiers ran through the crowd screaming and firing Uzis in the air. It was only ten in the morning but already 90 degrees. I looked for Israeli officers. There were none. I sent Simon into the crowd. He returned in a few minutes.

"No ways but bus across," he said.

"How do I get on it?"

"You can not."

I paid him off and sent him home. I was sick with the dysentery every foreigner in Lebanon suffers. My head ached from the wedding party Arak. There was, it appeared, a man with a gun selling bus tickets. But every time he tried to sell one a crowd of three hundred would rush him like a rugby scrum. The man fired his pistol directly over the people's heads. Bullets smacked into nearby masonry. The crowd quailed and ran backward, trampling each other. Then they gathered themselves and rushed the ticket seller again. He grew purple with shouting, reloaded, fired again. The crowd moved away and back like surf. Then with one great surge they chased him on top of a truck.

Most of these people had been camping at Jezzine, if that's the word for sleeping in the streets for days with your children and no food. They were desperate and fully insane. The crowd began running against itself, into walls, up the sides of buildings.

I was at a loss. I might be at Jezzine still if my arm hadn't been grabbed by someone who said, "I ken you're new here." It was a magnificent Scotswoman, tall, thin, and ramrod straight. With her was a gentle-looking Lebanese girl. The woman was Leslie Phillips, head of the nursing school at a medical center near Sidon. She was on her way to get textbooks in Beirut. The girl was named Amal, the same as the militia. It means "hope." She was headed to America for college.

Miss Phillips placed us in a protected corner and said, "I'm going to speak to the man with the gun. I always go straight for the man with the gun. It's the only way you get anywhere in this country." She vanished into the melee. The crowd went into a frenzy again and made right for Amal and me. I suppose I would have been filled with pity if I'd been in a second-story window. As it was I was filled with desire to kick people and I gave in to it.

Miss Phillips was gone for two hours. She emerged from the donnybrook perfectly composed and holding three bus tickets. I asked her what all the shooting was about. "Oh," she said, "that's just Lebanese for 'please queue up.'" An ancient horrible Mexican-looking bus pulled into the crowd smacking people and punting them aside. Amal was carrying a coed's full complement of baggage in two immense suitcases. I handed my kit bag to Miss Phillips, grabbed these, and made for the bus. Or tried to. Three steps put me at the bottom of a clawing, screeching, pileup, a pyramid of human convulsion. I heard Miss Phillips's voice behind me. "Don't be shy," she said, "it's not rude to give a wee shove to the Lebanese." I took a breath, tightened my grip on the suitcases, and began lashing with Samsonite bludgeons at the crowd of women, old men, and children. If you ask me, it *was* pretty rude, but it was that or winter in South Lebanon. I fought my way to the side of the bus. There was a man on top loading luggage and kicking would-be roof rack stowaways in the head, knocking them back on top of the crowd. I hoisted one of Amal's fifty-pound suitcases onto my head, waved a fistful of Lebanese money at the loader, kept hold of Amal with my other hand, and fended off the mob with both feet. This doesn't sound physiologically possible, but it was an extreme situation.

I got both suitcases on top at last. Then we had to scrimmage our way to the bus door in a flying wedge, Miss Phillips leading the way. Just as we were getting aboard, a worse brawl yet broke loose in the throng. One of the

South Lebanon Army guards leapt into the middle of it and began beating people in the face with the butt of his pistol. The crowd exploded. Miss Phillips was heaved inside. I was squashed against the bus door and lost hold of Amal, who was sucked into the maw of the Lebanese. Miss Phillips reached out the bus window and tapped the pistol-whipping soldier on the arm. "Pardon me, lad," she said, "but those two are with me."

The soldier left off his beating for a moment, pushed me into the bus, and fished Amal out of the crowd. I pulled her inside, and the soldier went back to hitting people. Everyone in the crowd was yelling. I asked Amal what they said. "They're all claiming to be someone's cousin," she sighed.

About two hundred people were packed inside the bus, which was built to carry fifty. More kept wiggling in through the windows. It was well over 100 degrees in there. Every now and then a soldier would get in and climb across the top of people to beat one of the illegal passengers. There was more shooting outside. I found myself in a full body press with a Shiite girl. She was rather nicely built but over the top from claustrophobia and shrieking like a ruptured cow. "What's Arabic for 'calm down'?" I yelled.

"As far as I can tell," said Miss Phillips, "there's no such phrase."

We did eventually get under way, the bus backing over people then swaying horribly in blinding dust on the half-lane-wide mountain road. We were only stopped, unloaded, searched, interrogated, and held at gunpoint several times.

Fortunately, the Lebanese are a clean people, even the very poor ones. It wasn't like being packed into a bus on a sweltering day with a bunch of French or anything.

Akbar was waiting at Bater. I found out later he'd also come up from the city the day before and waited all afternoon in case I got thrown out or evacuated or tried to get back to Beirut on foot.

Travel to the North is less arduous. George Moll, the video editor at ABC-TV's Beirut bureau, and I went on a trip to the Bsherri Cedars. Traffic on the coast road north of the city is stalled by checkpoints. Amazing what a few guys standing around with guns can do to create gridlock. "I ♡ Lebanon" bumper stickers are popular with the motorists. "Kill them all—Let God sort them out" T-shirts are popular with the militias.

It's important to remember, when dealing with these militias, that the gunmen are mostly just kids and they're getting a big kick out of the whole thing. I suppose this is only natural when young people lack proper recreational facilities and well-supervised activities to keep them out of mischief. They need sympathy and understanding. Or a sixteen-inch shell from the battleship *New Jersey*.

I wanted to visit the gorge of the Nahr al-Kalb, the River of the Dog, a strategic point on the Lebanese coast just north of Beirut where for more than three thousand years invading armies have carved stelae commemorating their passage. A tunnel for the coast highway now cuts through the gorge wall, and the carvings are reached via a ramp above the traffic. The cuneiform characters of Nebuchadnezzar II, the stela of the Pharaoh Ramses, the Assyrian bas reliefs, a Latin inscription from the emperor Marcus Aurelius, Greek carvings from the Seleucid empire—they've all been completely effaced by air pollution.

Don't go to the famous Jeita Grotto at the source of the Dog River, either. These have been turned into a military training base. Although what kind of military training goes on among a bunch of stalactites lit by colored spot lamps, I can't tell you.

A few miles north of Nahr al-Kalb is the Casino de Liban on Juniye Bay. This was prewar Lebanon's attempt at Monte Carlo and used to have elaborate floor shows featuring plump blondes who were out of work in Europe. You can still gamble there, though just being in this part of the world is a gamble enough for most people. The blondes are gone.

On up the coast road, twenty-four miles from Beirut, is Byblos. Since the Christians were run out of the Beirut airport, the Phalange has taken to landing planes on the highway here. Expect another traffic jam. Byblos was considered by the ancients to be the oldest city in the world. In fact, it has been an established metropolis for at least six thousand years. But Main Street looks like the oldest part of Fort Lauderdale.

By the seaport, however, is an Arab fortification atop a Frankish castle constructed with chunks of Roman temples that had been built over a Phoenician town that was established on the foundations of a Neolithic village—quite a pile of historic vandalism.

The war has not touched Byblos except to keep anyone from coming here. We found one consumptive tour guide playing solitaire in a shack by the entrance to the ruins. He took us through the deserted remains spieling, with pauses only to cough, a litany of emperors, catastrophes, and dimensions.

The Lebanese are chock-full of knowledge about their past. Those who *do* learn history apparently get to repeat it of their own free will. The whole business filled me with inchoate emotions and a desire for lunch.

The Byblos Fishing Club at the base of the Crusader seawall has wonderful food and no other customers. They don't speak English anymore so I went back to the kitchen and picked out what I wanted. Seafood got with dynamite fishing is very tender, it seems. On the wall of the Fishing Club are dusty photos of better days—Ray Milland, Ann-Margret, David Niven, Jean-Paul Belmondo. "Now *this*," said George, "is archaeology."

There's a very good hotel in Byblos, the Byblos-Sur-Mer, whose owner hadn't seen anyone in so long he bought us drinks when we stopped to use the pay phone.

You can proceed to Tripoli on the coast road, but shouldn't. The Arab Democratic Party, which supports Islamic unification, is having a big fight there with the Islamic Unification Party, which is in favor of Arab democracy. And the Syrians are shooting at both of them.

We turned east, toward the mountains, at the Syrian lines near Batrun. There's a medieval Arab castle here that's worth seeing. It sits in the middle of a cement plant.

Once into Syrian-controlled territory the checkpoint scrutiny becomes severe. Ahmed, our driver, began making long explanations to the glowering soldiers. He wouldn't quite confess what he was saying, but I have an idea it went something like: "I have the brother of an important American strongman here and the president of England's cousin. They are traveling in secret as journalists so they may see the justice and resolve of the great Syrian army in its struggle against Zionist oppressors everywhere. Soon they will return to their homeland and tell rich men there to drop a bomb on Tel Aviv."

The Syrian army has dozens of silly hats, mostly berets in yellow, orange, and shocking pink, but also tiny pillbox chapeaux, peaked officer's caps with half a foot of gold braid up the front, and lumpy Russian helmets three sizes too large. The paratroopers wear shiny gold jumpsuits, and crack commando units have skintight fatigues in a camouflage pattern of violet, peach, flesh tone, and vermilion on a background of vivid purple. This must give excellent protective coloration in, say, a room full of Palm Beach divorcees in Lily Pulitzer dresses.

The rest of the scenery is also spectacular—Californian, but as though the Sierras had been moved down to Santa Barbara. The mountains of Lebanon rise ten thousand feet only twenty miles from the sea. You can ski in the morning and swim in the afternoon. Actually, of course, it's raining on the beach that time of year, and the skiing is mediocre at best. But it's the kind of thing that made for great Lebanese travel-brochure writing in the old days.

We drove to Bsherri on the lip of the melodramatic Qadisha Valley, 650 feet deep and only a half mile wide. This is the heartland of the Maronites, seventh century AD Christian schismatics who sought refuge among these dangerous hairpin turns lacking guardrails and speed limits.

Bsherri was the home of Kahlil Gibran and also where Danny Thomas's family comes from. Thus, the two great cultural figures of modern Lebanon, though in many ways opposites (Danny Thomas does not write poetry. Kahlil Gibran never did "spit-takes."), are linked.

We visited Gibran's house above the town. It's probably the world's only example of the California bungalow style carved out of living rock. Interesting but damp. The place is decorated with a hundred or so of Gibran's artworks. He was a dreadful painter—the gentle insouciance of Rodin and the technical abilities of Blake, all done in muddy earth tones. Gibran's coffin is bricked into the wall of his bedroom if that says anything about the guy.

While we were asking directions in Bsherri, a young man named Antoine attached himself to us. He got us into the Gibran house, which was supposedly closed for repairs, then took us home for a Lebanese sit-around with his mother, aunts, sisters, cousins, etc. Hospitality is a must in the Middle East whether anyone wants to have it or not. Pomegranate juice is served, lots of cigarettes are smoked, and tiny cups of coffee are drunk while everyone smiles and stares because you can't speak Arabic and they can't speak English, and Lebanese are the only people in the world who pronounce French worse than Americans.

Antoine's house was extraordinary. Like Gibran's it was carved into the side of a hill. The main room was windowless, floored with layers of Persian carpets and hung wall and ceiling with ornate cloths. There were stuffed falcons, brass things, photographs, and religious statuettes all over the place and a dozen Mafia-Mediterranean-style dining room chairs. Antoine let us know he thought Kahlil Gibran's house was underdecorated. Antoine's mother told us that she'd lost five sons in the war so far, though that may have been the usual polite exaggeration.

Ahmed, though Moslem, was a great hit with Antoine's family. He brought them up-to-date on Beirut politics and then told Syrian checkpoint stories. Syrian checkpoint stories are the Polish jokes of Lebanon.

A Syrian soldier stops a Volkswagen Beetle and demands that the driver open the trunk. The driver begins to open the luggage compartment at the front of the car. "No!" says the Syrian, "I said the *trunk*."

"This *is* the trunk," says the driver.

"I am not a donkey," says the Syrian, pointing to the back of the car. "Open the trunk!" So the driver does as he's told, exposing the VW's engine. "Aha!" says the Syrian, "You have stolen a motor. Furthermore, you have just done it because it's still running."

Another of Ahmed's stories—and he swears this one is true—is about a checkpoint on a hill where the Syrian soldier wanted to inspect a car trunk. "I can't get out," said the driver. "I have no emergency brake, and I must keep my foot on the brake pedal or the car will roll away."

"Don't worry," said the Syrian, "I will sit in the car and hold the brake pedal." So they changed places. "Now open the trunk," said the Syrian. The driver opened it. "All right," yelled the Syrian from inside the car, "is there any contraband in there?"

What the Syrians are looking for in your trunk, by the way, is *Playboy* magazines. Be sure to carry some.

We sat and smoked more cigarettes. Lebanon is not the place to go if you're trying to give that up. Everyone over the age of twelve chain-smokes.

Long-term health effects are not, these days, a major concern, and it's the worst sort of rudeness not to offer cigarettes at every turn. George fell in love with Carmen, Antoine's sister, a beauty of about fifteen. George could talk of nothing else for the rest of the trip but getting married and becoming Maronite. Maybe the feeling was mutual. Antoine took me aside later and asked me if George was a Christian. I assured him that most blond, blue-eyed Americans over six feet tall are not Moslem. He then nicked me, instead of George, for the two hundred Lebanese pounds it allegedly cost to get in the Gibran house.

We went on up into the mountains to the Cedars, one of only three small groves of these trees left. Once the country was forested with them, a hundred feet high at full growth and forty feet in circumference. It was from these the tall masts of the Phoenician galleys were made and the roof beams of Solomon's temple and so forth. The trees in the Bsherri grove look like they need flea collars, and the grounds are a mess.

We found a good hotel, the La Mairie, about ten miles west of Bsherri in Ehden. Ehden is notable for the country's best-looking martyr pictures. There are martyr pictures everywhere in Lebanon. The Phalangists put up photographs of the ox-faced Bachir Gemayel, who got elected president in '82 and blown to bits within the month. The Shiites plaster walls with the face of some dumpy Ayatollah who went MIA in Libya. The Druse have Kamal Jumblatt, who looked dead even before the hit men ventilated his limo. Ehden, however, is the headquarters of the Giants militia, led by the very photogenic Franjieh family. In 1978 the Phalangists attacked the Franjieh home and killed a handsome son, his pretty wife, and their cute little daughter too. If you have to look at pictures of dead people all day, they might as well be attractive.

From Ehden, with light traffic and no mood swings at the checkpoints, it's only two hours back to Beirut.

The remaining great thing to see in Lebanon is Baalbek, site of three immense Roman temples, among the largest in the ancient world. Baalbek, however, is in the Bekáa Valley, where Israeli and Syrian forces are faced off and where Israel has been making periodic air strikes on Syrian missile emplacements. Take sturdy and practical clothing.

Baalbek itself is controlled by an extremely radical pro-Khomeini Shiite group called Islamic Amal. The leader of Islamic Amal is Hussein Musawi. He has close ties to Iran, and many people believe he personally ordered the suicide attacks on the American embassy and the U.S. Marine base at Green Beach.

The Islamic Amal people are so far out there that they think *Syria* is a puppet of international Zionism. When I first arrived in Beirut, the Syrian army had Baalbek surrounded with tanks and was shelling downtown.

I went to Baalbek with ABC's chief Beirut correspondent, Charles Glass, and two drivers, one Syrian and one Lebanese Shiite. (Glass was later kidnapped by radical Shiites, possibly this same Islamic Amal. After two months in captivity, he made a harrowing escape.) The ride over the crest of the Lebanese range is breathtaking. The arid reaches of the Anti-Lebanon mountains rise in the distance. Below is the flat, green trough of the Bekáa, where Syrian and Israeli lines are lost in verdant splendor. The thin neck of the fertile crescent is spread out before you, cradle of the civilization that has made air strikes possible.

At the foot of the descent is the large Christian town of Zahle, a Phalange outpost surrounded by Moslems. The Syrians shell this sometimes, too. Zahle has a good hotel, the Kadri, and an arcade of outdoor restaurants built along a stream in the Wadi Arayesh, or "Valley of Vines."

The road north to Baalbek runs up the middle of the Bekáa. Marijuana fields stretch for miles on either side. This is the source of Lebanon's renowned hashish. Don't try to export any yourself, however. The airport customs officials won't search you when you arrive, but they're very thorough when you leave. Taking hashish out of the country without payoffs is one of the few crimes they still prosecute in Lebanon.

Bedouins from the Syrian desert camp beside the hemp fields. They're not very romantic up close. Their tents are made from old grain sacks, and everything around them stinks of goat.

The ruins of the Roman temples at Baalbek are, words fail me, big. The amount of mashed thumbs and noses full of stone dust that went into chiseling these is too vast to contemplate. The largest, the Temple of Jupiter, is 310 feet long, 175 feet wide, and was originally enclosed by fifty-four Corinthian pillars, each sixty-six feet high and seven and a half feet thick. Only six are left standing now. The temple complex was three centuries in building and never finished. The Christian emperor Theodosius ordered the work stopped in hope of suppressing paganism and bringing a halt to a very lively-sounding cult of temple prostitution.

Once again we found a lonely tour guide who took us around, spouting names and numbers and pointing out things that are extra odd or large.

The ruins are policed by the Syrians, who are doing a better job than the Israelis at Tyre. The captain in charge came up and introduced himself. His English consisted of "Hello." "Hello," he said and shook hands. "Hello," he said and waved good-bye.

Outside the ruins, Baalbek is a tense and spooky place. All the Christians, Sunnis, and Druse have fled. Giant posters of Khomeini are hanging everywhere. There are few women on the streets, and they are carefully scarved and dressed down to the feet. The men gave us hard looks and fingered their weapons. The streets were dirty and grim. Syrian soldiers stayed bunched together. The tanks are still dug in around the city. You cannot get a drink or listen to Western music or dance or gamble, and you'd better not whistle the "Star-Spangled Banner."

The tour guide led us directly from the temples to a souvenir store. There was something appealing about risking one's life to visit a pesthole full of armed lunatics and then going shopping. The store looked like it hadn't been visited since the Crusades, except all the ancient artifacts were new, made this month and buried in the yard for a week.

The nonsense you hear about bargaining in the Orient is, like most nonsense about the Orient, perfectly true. I had not been in the shop three seconds before the owner was quoting prices that would do justice to a Pentagon parts supplier and flopping greasy, ill-made rugs in every direction—like somebody house-training a puppy with the Sunday *New York Times*. There's a charming banter that goes with all this. I mean, I suppose there is. Some of the verbal flourishes of the Levant are lost in a minimal English vocabulary. "Good, huh? Real good, huh? Good rug! Very good!"

"He has a cousin in St. Louis," added the tour guide, helpfully.

It seemed I had to hold up both ends in this legendary duel of wit in the Bazaar. "Tell him," I said to the guide, "his goods are of the greatest magnificence and pleasure flows into my eyes at their splendor. Yes, and I am astonished at the justice of his prices. And yet I must abase myself into the dust at the humbleness of my means. I, a poor traveler, come many miles over great distances . . ." And so forth. Out came bogus Egyptian dog-head statues, phony Roman coins, counterfeit Phoenician doodads, and more and worse and bigger rugs. After an hour and a half I felt I had to pay for my fun. I settled on a small bronze "Babylonian" cow with some decidedly un-Babylonian rasp marks on the casting. I bargained the shopkeeper down from $200 to $30. Good work if the cow hadn't been worth $0.

Charles Glass has spent years in the Middle East and was completely bored by this, however. He said we should go meet Hussein Musawi.

Our Shiite driver was sent to negotiate. After the customary amount of temporizing and dawdle, Hussein consented to see us. We were taken to a shabby and partly destroyed section of town, where we were surrounded by nervous young gunmen. Though whether they were nervous about us or nervous that they might get a sudden invite to make like a human Fourth of July, I don't know. We were marched into a tiny and dirty office and told to sit down. We waited. Then we were marched to a larger office furnished Arab-style with couches around the sides of the room. Khomeini pictures abounded. We were served tea, and Charles and I, though not our Moslem drivers, were very thoroughly searched. Charles's tape recorder was taken apart with special care. Our guards were pleasant, but small talk did not seem the order of the day. We waited some more. Finally, another group of armed young men came and took us through a warren of narrow filthy alleys to a modest and well-protected house. We were put into a small study lined with Arabic books and decorated with more pictures of Khomeini. There were two young men who spoke English waiting for us. They asked in an affable way what was going on with U.S. foreign policy. "After all," said one, "this part of the world has a Moslem majority. Is your government crazy or what?"

Half an hour later Hussein came in and shook hands with everyone. He's a thin man of middle size, about forty-five. He was dressed in a sort of semi-military leisure suit and was very calm and dignified in his bearing but had, I swear it, a twinkle in his eye.

Hussein ordered a gunman to bring us coffee and cigarettes. The young man who spoke English less well acted as translator. "Were you responsible for the bombing of the marine base?" asked Charles. I nearly lit my nose instead of the Marlboro. Hussein answered with equanimity, pointing out that any number of people, including the American Democratic Party, stood to benefit from the attack on the marines.

"How long will this peace last in Lebanon?" asked Charles.

"This is not peace."

"When will there be peace?"

"When there is Islamic justice everywhere," came the answer.

"Everywhere?" asked Charles. "Will there be a place for Christians and Jews under Islamic justice?"

"Islam allows a place for everyone," said Hussein. The translator paused and added on his own, "Except, you know, Zionists and imperialists and other types."

"The Zionists will have to be driven out?"

"Yes."

"That may take a long time," said Charles.

Hussein fixed him with a smile. "Long for you. Short for us."

Hussein expounded upon the destiny of Islam and a believing man's place therein. The translator got himself tangled up with "Allah's great wishes . . . I mean, large would-bes . . . That is . . ."

"The will of God," I suggested.

Hussein turned to me and spoke in English. "Do you understand Arabic?"

"No," I said, "I just recognized the concept."

He said something to the translator, who said to me, "He wants to know if you believe in God."

I didn't think I should quibble. "Of course," I said. Hussein nodded. There was intensity in his look and no little human concern. He continued on subjects theological.

"To get back down to earth for a moment . . ." said Charles.

Hussein laughed. "Oh," said the translator, "all this is very much down to earth."

Charles continued to ask questions. I continued to ponder Hussein. He was practically the first Lebanese I'd met who didn't tell me he had a cousin in Oklahoma City. Although, as it turns out, his brother is a petroleum engineer who used to work in Dallas.

Charles asked Hussein about Jonathan Wright, the missing Reuters correspondent. "I hadn't heard about this," was the reply. "Also he wasn't headed this way."

Hussein told Charles he should study the Koran.

At length we took our leave. As we were being escorted back to our car I noticed a woman on a nearby roof wearing a chador and hanging out lacy black lingerie on the clothesline.

Less than a week after our visit, the U.S. embassy annex in East Beirut got blown up. I hope it wasn't anything we said.

The hotel at Baalbek is the Palmyra, built in the 1870s. It's a massive Ottoman structure furnished with antique carpets and heavy mahogany Victorian furniture. The leather-bound guest register bears the signatures of Louis-Napoléon, the Duc d'Orléans, the empress of Abyssinia, and Kaiser Wilhelm II. There's an air of twilight and deliquescence to the place. Only the owner and a couple old servants are left. No room had been occupied for months, and only an occasional Syrian military officer comes to dinner.

Charles and I sat alone that night in the vast dining room. Pilgrims were still returning from Mecca, and celebratory gunshots sounded outside. "Happy fire" it's called. The electricity guttered in the bulbs and cast the long tables and tall ceiling into gloom. The forces of darkness and barbarism seemed to gather around. It was as though we were the last two Westerners in Asia. We sat up past midnight drinking the bottle of Arak a grizzled waiter had smuggled to us, talking politics and literature and citing apt quotations:

Turning and turning in the widening gyre
The falcon cannot hear the falconer;
Things fall apart; the center cannot hold;
Mere anarchy is loosed upon the world,
The blood-dimmed tide is loosed, and . . .

. . . and you just can't find travel like this anymore.

Among the Euro-Weenies

April–May 1986

The Europeans are going to have to feather their nests with somebody else's travelers checks this year. The usual flock of American pigeons is crapping on statues elsewhere. Sylvester Stallone canned the Cannes Film Festival. Prince won't tour this side of the sink. The U.S. Junior Wimbledon team is keeping its balls on the home court. And transatlantic rubberneck bookings have taken a dive. Some say it's fear of terrorism. Some say it's Chernobyl fallout. Some say it's the weak dollar. But all of that ignores one basic fact. This place sucks.

I've been over here for one gray, dank spring month now, and I think I can tell you why everyone with an IQ bigger than his hat size hit the beach at Ellis Island. Say what you want about "land of opportunity" and "purple mountain majesties above the fruited plain," our forebears moved to the United States because they were sick to death of lukewarm beer—and lukewarm coffee and lukewarm bath water and lukewarm mystery cutlets with mucky-colored mushroom cheese junk on them. Everything in Europe is lukewarm except the radiators. You could use the radiators to make party ice. But nobody does. I'll bet you could walk from the Ural Mountains to the beach at Biarritz and not find one rock-hard, crystal-clear, fist-sized American ice cube. Ask for whiskey on the rocks, and you get a single, gray, crumbling leftover from some Lilliputian puddle freeze plopped in a thimble of Scotch (for which you're charged like sin). And the phones don't work. They go "blat-blat" and "neek-neek" and "ugu-ugu-ugu." No two dial tones are alike. The busy signal sounds as if the phone is ringing. And when the phone rings you think the dog farted.

All the light switches in Europe are upside down. The electrical plugs are terrifying with nine or a dozen huge, nasty prongs, and you'd better wear rubber boots if you come within a yard of them because house current here is about one hundred thousand volts. Not that that makes the appliances work. This electric typewriter I'm pounding, for instance—I'd throw it out the window but it's one of those silly European windows that, when you push it open from the right, comes around from the left and smacks you in the back of the head.

The Europeans can't figure out which side of the road to drive on, and I can't figure out how to flush their toilets. Do I push the knob or pull it or twist it or pump it? And I keep cracking my shins on that stupid bidet thing. (Memo to Europeans: try washing your *whole* body; believe me, you'd smell better.) Plus there are ruins everywhere. The Italians have had two thousand years to fix up the Forum and just look at the place.

I've had it with these dopey little countries and all their poky borders. You can't swing a cat without sending it through customs. Everything's too small. The cars are too small. The beds are too small. The elevators are the size of broom closets. Even the languages are itty-bitty. Sometimes you need two or three just to get you through till lunch.

It's not like the Europeans have been very nice hosts either. The whole month here has been one long shower of shit about America, just because we took a punch at the Libyans. There were huge demonstrations in Germany, Italy, and Spain. In West Berlin twenty thousand young bucketheads turned out. In Barcelona a group of protesters vented their fury on that symbol of American imperialism, a McDonald's. In London thousands of peacemongers blocked the main shopping thoroughfare of Oxford Street, staging sit-down strikes and throwing bottles at the police. Thousands more Brits came out to holler in Manchester, Cardiff, and Glasgow and at the military bases on the Clyde and in Oxfordshire. According to various opinion polls, 66 percent of the British deplored our behavior as did 75 percent of the West Germans, 32 percent of the French, and 60 percent of the Italians. In Belgium a friend of mine was stopped on the street by a policeman and told he should be ashamed to be an American.

The cover story of *Time Out,* London's equivalent to *New York* magazine, was OVER ARMED, OVER EAGER, OVER HERE. A British TV comedy program showed a puppet skit with President Reagan as the Jordanian who tried to blow up an El Al airliner and Mrs. Thatcher as the dim-bulb pregnant Irish girl duped into carrying the explosives. The *New Statesman* ran an editorial explaining how U.S. defense policy can be understood only in light of American football. "Defense, to the average redneck," it said, "means hitting your opponent hard before he sees the ball." An article in the magazine *New Socialist* said that in the U.S. worldview "non-Americans are simply not people," claimed that, "To be President, you have to be mad or an actor," and asked itself, "Does not the United States need a hostile relationship with the Soviet Union to contain discontent at home . . . ?" Another article in the same magazine began, "It is the United States which is clearly the greatest evil to peoples seeking just rights of self-determination." (*New Socialist* is not, by the way, some nut-fudge fringe publication like it would be in the States. It's the official organ of the Labour Party.) As *Paris Match* put it, "*Le point de vue européen était different et tous nos responsables plaidaient pour une action plus discrète.*" Whatever that means.

Actually, the only *discrète* people I've met here were Libyans, the employees of Libyan Arab Airlines in Paris, who never referred to our rocketing and bombing each other as anything but "this difficult situation."

I was talking to the Libyans because I never wanted to go to Europe in the first place. I was headed for Tripoli. It was a dream byline: "From our correspondent on the Line of Death." But daily life kept getting in the way. Taxes were due. I owed a four-thousand-word story to *Gerbil and Pet Mouse Monthly*. My girlfriend was restive. She pointed out I'd forgotten Christmas and that when I'd taken her out for New Year's, I'd taken her out in the backyard to blow off M-80s under the garbage cans.

I set to work with a will, emptying checkbooks, wrestling accountants, interviewing small rodents, scouring the bargain bin at Cartier's. By Monday, April 14, I had everything paid, written, kissed, made up, and in the mail. My safari jacket was packed, my tape recorder loaded. I zipped shut my official foreign correspondent duffel bag, fixed myself a drink, and flipped on the eleven o'clock news. "BOOM!" My foreign correspondent friend Charles Glass was holding a telephone receiver out a window of the Grand Hotel in Tripoli. "We're not sure exactly what's going on," shouted Glass at the phone. I was. Those weren't the Nicaraguan *contras* out there pounding Mad Mo, the terror-bombing Sheikh of Shriek. "It would appear that the United States has launched a military action against Libya," shouted Glass, trying to sound grave. But you could hear the boyish enthusiasm creeping into his voice the way it always does when a reporter manages to get himself right smack dab in the middle of something god-awful.

I could have cried. I did cry. I threw things. I took the first plane to Paris.

Paris had the nearest Libyan embassy or People's Bureau or whatever they're calling them. It looked like military school the way I'd pictured it when my parents used to threaten to send me there. I made four trips to this forbidding crib before somebody there told me the only way I could get a visa to go to Tripoli was to go to Tripoli.

I went back to my hotel and got on the worthless, static-filled French telephone. Air France wasn't flying to Libya just then. British Airways definitely wasn't. Swissair was coy. Maybe it was, and maybe it wasn't. I finally got a reservation on Lufthansa, rushed to the airline's office, and handed over a thousand dollars' worth of funny-colored French bumwad. The ticket agent said, "You have a visa?"

"My visa is waiting for me in Tripoli."

"We cannot take you to Tripoli without a visa."

"I can't get a visa without going to Tripoli."

"You can get a visa in Tripoli?"

"Right."

"But we cannot take you there."

"Why not?"

"You don't have a visa."

You can always reason with a German. You can always reason with a barnyard animal, too, for all the good it does.

I didn't figure an American would be very welcome on the Libyan flag carrier at the moment, unless he wanted to travel naked and in a muzzle. But it was worth a try. I went to the Libyan Arab Airlines office on the Champs-Elysées. There were half a dozen Libyans inside. I picked out a young one behind the counter and began explaining with many worried hand gestures how I had been told by my editor, of a very important magazine, to go directly to Libya no matter what and now I was stranded in this faraway country among foreigners and could not seem to get to Libya by any means, etc. "Oh, my goodness," said the young man, "and right now there is this . . ." He paused and considered the delicacy of my feelings. ". . . this difficult situation."

I'd hate to have to explain this to anyone who was on the *Achille Lauro,* but Arabs are the sweetest-natured people on earth. To meet an Arab is to gain a devoted friend. If you even make eye contact with an Arab, you've got a pal for life. "Would you like some coffee?" said the young man. The other Libyans pulled up their chairs and offered cigarettes. But there was one, with sharp clothes and an equally sharp face, who eyed me narrowly. He said, "What kind of journalistic story is it that you wish to do?"

Well, he had me there. I'd never given it a thought. I just figured, what with guns going off and things blowing up, there'd be plenty of deep truths and penetrating insights. Tragedy and strife produce these things in boxcar lots, as any good reporter knows. Also, I wanted a chance to wear my new safari jacket. You really look like a twink if it isn't adequately dirty and sweat-stained. "Uh," I said, "I'd like to do a *cultural* piece. ("Cultural piece" is a key phrase for foreign correspondents. It means you aren't going to poke into any political leader's Luxembourg bank account or try to find out if his wife has ten thousand pairs of Maud Frizon pumps in the palace basement.)

"There is a great lack of understanding between the Arab world and the United States just now," said the young man behind the counter.

"There sure is," I said.

"Why do *you* think this is?" said the sharp dresser.

The truthful answer would have been, "Because one by one and man to man Arabs are the salt of the earth—generous, hospitable, brave, wise, and so forth. But get you in a pack and shove a Koran down your pants and you act like a footlocker full of glue-sniffing civet cats." We're a frank people, we Americans. But not quite *that* frank. I decided to blame it on Paul Newman.

"It's because of *Exodus*," I said. "*Exodus* was a very popular movie in the United States. Ever since this movie all Americans think everyone in Israel is kind and good and looks like Paul Newman."

"Hmmmmm," said the Libyans. It made sense to them.

"I will call my uncle," said the sharp dresser. "He is an important man at the embassy in Rome."

"I will call the embassy here," said someone else.

"I will book a flight," said the young man behind the counter, and he got me more coffee (the only decent coffee I'd had since I left New York, by the way).

The Libyan Arab Air people squared everything with the Ministry of Information in Tripoli, got me a ticket for that Friday, and told their airport manager at Orly to take me under his wing. All to no avail, however. Come Friday, the French government decided to expel four Libyan diplomats, and I was bumped off the plane.

In the meantime, I was stuck in Paris. A lot of people get all moist and runny at the mention of this place. I don't get it. It's just a big city, no dirtier than most. It does have nice architecture because the French chickened out of World War II. But it's surrounded by the most depressing ring of working-class suburbs this side of Smolensk. In fact, one of these suburbs is actually named Stalingrad, which goes to show that the French have learned nothing about politics since they guillotined all the smart people in 1793.

Frenchwomen, whether pretty or not, all walk around with their noses in the air (and pretty big noses they usually are). I guess this is what's meant by their "sense of style." Where did this sense of style thing get started? The French are a smallish, monkey-looking bunch and not dressed any better, on average, than the citizens of Baltimore. True, you can sit outside in Paris and drink little cups of coffee, but why this is more stylish than sitting inside and drinking large glasses of whiskey I don't know.

I was exhausted the night I arrived and couldn't think of any place to go except Harry's New York Bar. Harry's is a 1930s hangout left over from the days when Hemingway used to stop in while taking a break from pestering large animals, such as his drunk friend F. Scott Fitzgerald. At least the drinks at Harry's aren't microscopic. I had three and called for the "carte de menu." I'd forgotten that Harry's doesn't serve food.

"We do *not* serve food," said the waiter, cocking a snook. There was a ferocious pause, "except hot dogs." Thus, on my first night in this capital of international gastronomy, I dined on two hot dogs and five Scotches.

The next night I called my girlfriend who was back in the States and, no doubt, happily contemplating the sterling silver Elsa Peretti refrigerator magnet I'd bought her to make up for Christmas. She's spent a lot of time in Paris. "Where's a good place for dinner?" I asked.

"There's the Brasserie Lipp on the Boulevard Saint-Germain," she said, "or La Coupole in Montmartre."

"Not La Coupole," I said. "I've been there before. That's the place that's crowded and noisy and smells bad and everybody's rude as hell, isn't it?"

"I think you just described France," she said.

Actually, it was Brasserie Lipp I'd been to before. I remembered the minute they stuffed me behind a hankie-size table between the pissoir and a trolley full of sheep cheese. I ordered steak, and they brought me sauerkraut.

Nobody's French is *that* bad, not even mine. But Parisians never deign to understand a word you say in their own language, no matter how loud or often you pronounce it. They insist on speaking English until you wonder if the whole thing is a put-up job. Maybe they just take a couple of years of Frog Talk in high school like the rest of us and can no more speak French themselves than they can make ice cubes.

I also went to the Louvre. Big deal. The *Winged Victory of Samothrace* looks like somebody dropped it. And the *Mona Lisa* has a sheet of bullet-proof glass in front of it, covered with smudgy nose prints. Besides, I think if something is going to be as famous as the *Mona Lisa,* it ought to be bigger. Do not, however, miss the Peter Paul Rubens Unabashed Sell-Out and Philistine Sycophant Room on floor two. In 1622 Queen Marie de' Medici commissioned Rubens to paint about two dozen Greyhound bus–size canvases celebrating every moment of her worthless life. The series runs from Queen Marie's birth, attended by all the hosts of heaven, to her marriage to the king of France when they invited every figure in ancient mythology including Io the cow. These paintings take win, place, and show in the international hilarious fat girl derby.

At least the French weren't rioting about American imperialism. In fact, it was hard to tell *what* the French thought about our little experiment in Libyan bomb tag. (You're "it," Muammar, and no taps back.) The French official position was all over the map. It was "a question of national sovereignty" one day and "we weren't consulted in advance" the next. Then it was "we don't approve of such methods" followed by a hint that they would have approved of such methods after all if we'd only used bigger bombs. The French are masters of "the dog ate my homework" school of diplomatic relations.

French unofficial position, that is, the opinion of taxi drivers, bartenders, the concierge at the hotel, and those old women they keep in the bathrooms, was no easier to figure out. I'd ask and get a nudge, a smirk, pursed lips, shrugged shoulders, knowing rolls of the eyes, waved hands, knit brows—the whole panoply of Froggy visual tics.

Maybe it *is* fun to sit outside in Paris and drink little cups of coffee. You can watch the French grimace and posture. And then you can guess what they're saying to each other.

"I think, Antoinette, for me the croissant has the aspect existential. It is bread, the staff of life, but no? And yet, there is the paradox marvelous. Because the bread itself, it is a lifeless thing. Is it not true? We must order croissants."

"No, no, no, no, Jacques. To think as this is to make the miscomprehension of the universe, its nature. To order the croissants would be an act inconceivable. An action of the most bourgeois type . . ."

Who gives a shit what the French think.

After I was kicked off the plane to Libya, I went to visit my friend in Bruges, the one who was under instructions from the police to be ashamed. We spent the weekend looking for fun in Belgium, which is an isometric exercise. That is, it's a strain and you get nowhere.

A hotel desk clerk gave us the name of the one local hot spot. It was called "The Korral" or "Sixes Gun" or some such bogus American moniker like they put on everything over here when they want you to think you're going to get something un-European, like a good time. It was a crowded place where they played French rock and roll (which sounds like somebody's chasing Edith Piaf around the old Peppermint Lounge with an electric hedge trimmer).

My friend was trying to explain that you don't put sweet vermouth in a martini when a little scene caught my eye. Standing by the door was a Belgian greaser, a young hard guy with a modified skinhead haircut, dressed all in black and carrying a motorcycle helmet. He was running through all the usual teenage tough-kid postures and checking out the room to make sure all the other kids understood how unconcerned he was with their opinion. Perched on a railing in front of him, with her legs wrapped around his butt, was an adorable blonde girl about sixteen years old. She was kissing and nuzzling her cool beau, who would peck her briefly then swig his beer and check the room again.

In the breast pocket of her blouse the girl had a little toy stuffed rabbit. After another offhand kiss from her boyfriend, she took the rabbit out, held it in her hand, and whispered in the boy's ear. I couldn't hear what she said and they were speaking Flemish anyway, but I could tell what was going on.

"I want a real kiss."

"Yeah, okay."

"Now the bunny wants a kiss."

"Knock it off."

"The bunny wants a kiss soooooooo bad."

"Come on, knock it off."

"If the bunny doesn't get a kiss, *somebody's* going to be very cross."

The greaser kid scoped the room with mean but panicked eyes. Then he kissed the bunny.

On Monday I went to the UK to make one more attempt to get to Libya before I started kissing toy bunnies myself. I got a reservation on Lufthansa again. I figured I'd just lie, show them my old Lebanese visa with a lot of Arabic squiggles on it. Germans respond well to lies. At least, they always have historically.

Then I went to the ABC News bureau in London where a phone line was open to the Grand Hotel in Tripoli. I talked to my old Lebanon buddy the ABC video editor George Moll.

"Get your ass down here!" said George. "This is great! And bring some salami, okay? And cheese. And potato chips and pretzels."

"And cigarettes!" said a voice in the background. "A carton of Marlboros."

"Two cartons!" said another voice. "And a carton of Salems and chocolate bars and Cokes!"

"And bring pita bread!" said George.

"Pita bread? What the hell do you want with pita bread? You're surrounded by Arabs," I said. "You can't get pita bread?"

"You can't get *anything*," said George. "And for chrissake bring booze!"

"How can I do that? They'll kill me."

"Naw," said George, "they'll just rough you up. Anyway, they won't catch you. It's easy. Just get a six-pack of soda water, the little bottles, the kind with the screw tops. And fill them up with vodka and screw the tops back on and put them back in that plastic collar thing."

"Are you sure you should be telling me this over the phone?"

"If they can't make pita bread, what the fuck do you think their phone taps are like?" said George. "So, anyway, what's happening?"

"Nothing much," I said. "It's raining. And everybody's yelling at Margaret Thatcher about the F-111s and . . ."

"Not up there," said George. "I mean, what's happening down *here*? They won't let us out of the hotel."

Loaded with three times the European Economic Community's import limit on tobacco and foodstuffs and stinking like a delicatessen, I got as far as Frankfurt. Then a telex came through from Libya that all foreign journalists who could count higher than ten were expelled.

Back in London—tired, discouraged, and a little drunk—I called an old girlfriend from college. She and I had been through a lot together back when the U.S. was taking a punch at the Vietnamese and I was the one blocking the streets and screaming about American imperialism. (Morality was so much simpler when I thought the government was trying to kill *me*.) This girl is married now, with a family. So it wasn't anything, you know . . . I mean we'd hardly seen each other since she moved to England fifteen years ago. I just longed for a friendly face. (Where do they keep the motels in Europe, anyway?)

"You're bloody *mad*!" she shouted. "All you Americans are *mad*! All you want to do is put McDonald's all over the earth and start World War III!"

And this from someone who was born and raised in Great Neck, Long Island. Well, if I was going to get barked at, it might as well be by a person who does it for a living. I went to see Meg Beresford, general secretary of the Campaign for Nuclear Disarmament.

In England, even the peace movement has a bureaucracy, and the CND is the central organizing body for all those demonstrations the Brits are always having against cruise missiles, Polaris submarines, atomic power plants, and other things that can or do blow up. In England, everything has a musty old tradition too. It was the CND who, nearly thirty years ago, devised that semaphore of Nuclear Disarmament initials, the ☮. Thus, the "footprint of the American chicken" is really a European invention.

Meg told me that the phones at CND had been ringing off the hook on the day of the air strike and that the demonstrations against the raid had been highly spontaneous. She said the air strike was "a foolish way to try to deal with terrorism" and that people in England had "a feeling that Libya is rather a small actor" in the terror pageant and that the effect of the raid "will be to bring terror to our streets."

What I didn't understand, I said, was the emotional intensity of the demonstrations. Big civilized countries had been launching punitive raids on misbehaving weedy little native powers since . . . well, at least since the redcoats shot up Lexington and Concord.

Meg said that when the F-111s were launched from English soil, the British realized for the first time "what those bases were for."

This made the British sound a little thick.

Meg claimed the apparent attempt to kill Qaddafi himself had upset people, "like watching one of those John Wayne movies."

When a European mentions John Wayne, you know you're going to get an earful.

Meg admitted there was "resentment at American culture." She said, "Western democracies feel there is nothing immoral about spreading that kind of system, spreading Western-style democracy." She paused. "McDonald's everywhere."

Will somebody please tell me what's the matter with McDonald's? It's not like the Europeans don't line up by the millions to eat there. Maybe McDonald's food isn't the best thing for you, but roasted goose liver smooshed up with truffles isn't either. And has anyone ever smoked a joint and had a "*pâté de foie gras* attack"?

"There is," said Meg, "at the back of the American psyche the feeling that the American way is the best."

As opposed to what? As opposed to living in seedy, old, down-at-the-heels England with an eighteenth-century class system and seventeenth-century plumbing? Or as opposed to lining up for pita-bread ration cards in a half-assed African sandlot run by a fanatical big mouth with a dishtowel on his head?

"What do you think we *should* be doing?" I asked Meg.

"Sitting down in a really serious way to solve the Middle East problem is what Reagan should be doing."

"What if it won't solve?" I said. "I know the source of this terrorism is the Israeli-Palestinian problem. And that's a place where two wrongs don't make a right. But it's also a place where two *rights* don't make a right."

"The Palestinian problem has to be treated in a much more serious way," said Meg.

The Europeans are great ones for solving problems by taking them more seriously.

She said there was a need for a "definite Middle East policy that's not involved with violence." (Which would be a first in three or four thousand years.) "Something," said Meg, "that other European countries with more experience and understanding could get involved with . . . The UN has to be the place where these things ultimately get solved."

I mean, the UN has done such a bang-up job on the Iraq-Iran War, for instance, and the Pol Pot holocaust. They've really got things straightened out in Namibia and Afghanistan too—with the help, of course, of those European countries with more experience and understanding.

I don't mean to pick on Meg Beresford, really. She is obviously a decent person and committed as all get-out to international niceness. But she herself said, musing on the booze-addled States-side Micks who give the IRA guns and money, "If the U.S. feels morally justified in bombing Libya, Britain should feel justified in bombing the U.S."

"Damn right," I said. "Any dumb potato head who's dragged those rotten ancestral quarrels to his new home in America deserves no better than to get a British laser bomb targeted on his South Boston bar." (That is, assuming the British *have* laser bombs, and assuming the British have the capability to launch a transatlantic air strike without U.S. aid. Which they don't.)

I left CND even more depressed than when I'd arrived. Not over anything Meg said, it's just that why are all high-minded causes so dowdy? The CND offices were an earnest muddle of desks and cubicles and unpainted bookshelves with piles and stacks and quires and reams of those mimeographed handouts that swarm around all do-good organizations like flies on cattle. The better the cause, the worse the atmosphere. And what cause could be better than saving the whole of mankind from nuke vaporizing? You could bottle the dumpy glumness at CND and sell it to . . . well, to the English. London is a quaint and beautiful city—if you stick to the double-decker tourist buses. But the CND offices were out in the East End, in the aptly named district of Shoreditch. Dr. Johnson said, "When a man is tired of London, he is tired of life." But these days he might just be tired of shabby, sad crowds, low-income housing that looks worse than the weather, and tattoo-faced, spike-haired pea brains on the dole.

Meanwhile, the Soviet Union was trying to poison half the world with its Chernobyl atomic power plant. But was anybody blocking Oxford Street or calling Gorbachev's energy policy "a game of Cossacks and Rabbis"? It just didn't seem fair.

I decided to go to West Berlin. Berlin was close to the scum cloud of cesium, iodine, and other isotopes that will light up your thyroid and give your kids three heads. Maybe I could make some sense of the Europeans in this isolated, beleaguered, and slightly radioactive outpost of freedom. And maybe I could peek over the Iron Curtain and get a look at what we've been protecting these Euro-weenies from since 1945.

That wasn't hard. The boundary between East and West is shockingly apparent from the air. The plane descended to 9,500 feet, the permitted altitude through the air corridor to Berlin, and there it was—a thick streak of raked-dirt minefield following, with painful accuracy, the medieval zigzag border between the kingdoms of Hanover and Prussia.

There was a slide-show change in the landscape. Crisp paved highways turned to muzzy gravel roads. The little towns were suddenly littler. Surburban sprawl evaporated. The distinctive fishbone patterns of parking lots disappeared. The lush, ditzy quiltwork of private farmland gave way to big, rational, geometric collective fields, where the crops looked thin. The constraints, the loss of liberties were visible from nearly two miles up.

Upon landing the scenery changed back. Suddenly you were in the world again, at least the slightly fussy, slightly tiresome European version of it.

It was May Day, and when I checked into my hotel, I asked the desk clerk if there were any big Red doings scheduled.

"Yes," she said, "in the Platz der Republik there is always a large program."

"Where's that?" I asked.

"Oh, just down the street."

"In *West* Berlin?"

"Oh, yes."

"Don't they have a big May Day thing in *East* Berlin? I mean, this is the main communist holiday."

"No, I don't think so," said the desk clerk, "not so much over there. The demonstrations are usually on this side."

The Platz der Republik is a wide, grassy square near the Brandenburg Gate. The "large program" was a sort of political fair put on by one of West Berlin's left-wing trade-union organizations. There were no pony rides or Ferris wheels, but there was food, beer, a bad rock band singing memorized American lyrics, and a hundred booths and tents filled with haymows of those high-minded mimeographed leaflets. The booths seemed like the world's worst carnival games. "Hurry! Hurry! Hurry! Hit the clown on the nose, and win three hundred pounds of literature denouncing U.S. intervention in Nicaragua and a 'Ban NATO' button!"

It was fascinating to wander among the posters and banners and displays of elaborately captioned photographs and be absolutely ignorant of the language. German, to me, looks like what worms do under rocks. There were lots of photos of dirty and tired-looking workers, but I couldn't tell if they were exploited victims of capitalist oppression or heroic comrades struggling to build the joyful new world of socialism. The dead babies in blast wreckage were definitely victims of capitalist oppression. They just didn't have a Kiev-ish look about them. In fact, I saw no reference to Chernobyl. It had been almost a week since the accident started, and the plume of loathsomeness sprouting from the Ukrainian steppe had, that very day, reached its greatest extent. But there were plenty of poster-paint cartoons of Uncle Sam with dog fangs. Usually he was gnawing on someone foreign-looking.

And fifty feet away was the Berlin Wall.

West Berlin is the city that Iggy Pop once moved to because New York wasn't decadent enough for him. I was expecting at least *Cabaret* or maybe *Götterdämmerung* performed by the cast of *La Cage aux Folles*. Forget it. We bombed the place flat in WWII, and they rebuilt it as a pretty good imitation of Minneapolis. The downtown hub of West Berlin, the Europa Center, is a perfectly modern business/shopping/entertainment complex. As a result, the hot tip for an evening of merriment is to cruise the mall. Furthermore, they serve you bologna for breakfast.

On Saturday there was finally a demonstration in West Berlin protesting the Chernobyl mess. Eight or ten thousand people participated, but this was only half the crowd that rallied against the Libya strike. None of the placards or banners even mentioned Russia by name. And the whole thing was a thoroughly spiritless affair.

Everyone gathered in the Europa Center in front of the Aeroflot airline office. A couple of chants were begun, but nobody took them up. Then the crowd marched. It marched a mile out toward the Technical College, a mile down toward Adenauer Platz, and a mile or so back toward downtown, where it petered out in some obligatory speech making. Apparently this was a standard route. On the way, the crowd passed the American cultural center, which was blocked off by tall wire-mesh barricades and a tripe cordon of riot police. There was nothing in the least anti-American about this demonstration, but the authorities seemed to be worried that the protesters would turn and storm the cultural center from pure force of habit.

As I slogged along, bored and footsore, I talked to the English-speakers in the bunch. They said it was a shame I'd missed the Libya demo. That one was much more interesting.

"How come?" I asked.

They got all excited and told me West Germany was "a colony of the United States." They told me the La Belle discotheque terrorist bomb that killed an American soldier in Berlin was probably a setup. "Perhaps this bombing was necessary to bomb Tripoli." And they told me . . . Shit, they told me all sorts of things. Basically, they told me off.

I'm sorry. I quit. I just don't have the stomach to go through my sheaves of scribbled notes and piles of garbled tape cassettes again just to shake out three more quotes about what a sack of bastards Americans are.

The day before I left Berlin, I ran into a dozen young Arab men on the street. They were trotting along, taking up the whole sidewalk, accosting busty girls and generally making a nuisance of themselves. One was beating on a snareless drum, and the others were letting loose with intermittent snatches of song and aggressive shouts. They descended on me and loudly demanded cigarettes in German.

"I don't speak German," I said.

"Are you American?" said one, suddenly polite.

"Yes."

"Please, my friend, if you don't mind, do you have a cigarette you could spare?"

I gave them a pack. "Where are you from?" I asked.

"West Beirut," said the drum beater.

"I've been there," I said.

"It is wonderful, no?"

Compared to Berlin, it is. "Sure," I said. They began reminiscing volubly. "What are you doing here?" I asked.

"Our families sent us because of the war. We want to go back to Beirut but we cannot."

I told them I guessed I couldn't go back either, what with the kidnapping and all. They laughed. One of them stuck out his middle finger and said, "This place sucks."

"You should go to America," I said.

"There is only one bad thing about America," said the drum beater. "They won't let us in."

Back in London, I was having dinner in the Groucho Club—the in spot for what's left of Britain's lit glitz and *nouveau* rock *riche*—when one more person started in on the Stars and Stripes. Eventually he got, as the Europeans always do, to the part about "Your country's never been invaded." (This fellow had been two during the Blitz, you see.) "You don't know the horror, the suffering. You think war is . . ."

I snapped.

"A John Wayne movie," I said. "That's what you were going to say, wasn't it? We think war is a John Wayne movie. We think *life* is a John Wayne movie—with good guys and bad guys, as simple as that. Well, you know something, Mister Limey Poofter? You're right. And let me tell you who those bad guys are. They're *us*. WE BE BAD.

"We're the baddest-assed sons of bitches that ever jogged in Reeboks. We're three-quarters grizzly bear and two-thirds car wreck and descended from a stock market crash on our mother's side. You take your Germany, France, and Spain, roll them all together, and it wouldn't give us room to park our cars. We're the big boys, Jack, the original, giant, economy-sized, new and improved butt kickers of all time. When we snort coke in LA, people lose their hats in Portland, Maine. And we've got an American Express card credit limit higher than your pissant metric numbers go.

"You say our country's never been invaded? You're right, little buddy. Because I'd like to see the needle-dicked foreigners who'd have the guts to try. We drink napalm to get our hearts started in the morning. A rape and a mugging is our way of saying 'Cheerio.' Hell can't hold our sock hops. We walk taller, talk louder, spit farther, fuck longer, and buy more things than you know the names of. I'd rather be a junkie in a New York City jail than king, queen, and jack of all you Europeans. We eat little countries like this for breakfast and shit them out before lunch."

Of course, the guy should have punched me. But this was Europe. He just smiled his shabby, superior European smile. (God, don't these people have *dentists*?)

At Sea with the America's Cup

February 1987

I hear the America's Cup race was the most spectacular sporting event of the decade. You could have fooled me. I was right there in the middle of it on the official press boat, the *Sea Chunder,* getting bounced around and shook silly. I had a psychopathic strangler's grip on the railing and was staring out at the horizon like some idiot Ahab who'd run out of whale bait. All I could see was a whole bunch of ocean and wet, messy waves. Though, as it turned out, I was facing the wrong way, and had to clamber and stumble and crawl on all fours over to the *Sea Chunder*'s other railing. There was a whole bunch of ocean on that side, too, if you ask me.

Way off in the distance, or so I was told, were *Stars & Stripes* and *Kookaburra III.* They looked like two dirty custard-pie slices stood on end. First one tipped one way, then the other tipped the same way, then the first tipped the other way and so did the second.

"Awesome!" "A brilliant tacking duel!" "Superb seamanship!" said the professional boat reporters from *Dinghy & Dock, Flaps Afloat,* and other important journals of the sport. I don't think I'll ever be a real boat reporter. My Rolex isn't big enough. Also, I don't have the color sense. You have to wear orange Top-Siders and a pair of electric-blue OP shorts and a vermilion-and-yellow-striped Patagonia shirt and a hot-pink baseball cap with the name of somebody's boat on it in glitter, plus Day-Glo-green zinc oxide smeared down your nose and around your lips like a radioactive street mime. I do have one loud necktie with little Santas that I wear at Christmas, but this isn't enough to qualify. And professional boat reporters love to hang bushels of stuff around their necks—press passes, dock passes, ballpoint pens that float, cameras, binoculars, and Vuarnet sunglasses on those dangle cords that are supposed to look so cool nowadays but which remind anyone over thirty-five of the high school librarian. Good luck to these men and women if they happen to fall over the side.

Falling over the side, however, was something the boat reporters were disappointingly bad at. While the *Sea Chunder* bucked like a fake Times Square sex act, the boat reporters assumed poses of studied nonchalance, talking boat talk in loud and knowing voices.

It's no use my trying to describe this America's Cup business if you don't understand boat talk. Everything on a boat has a different name than it would have if it weren't on a boat. Either this is ancient seafaring tradition or it's how people who mess around with boats try to impress the rest of us who actually finished college. During the brief intervals on the *Sea Chunder* when I wasn't blowing lunch, I compiled a glossary.

Fore—Front.

Aft—Back.

Midships—You don't know "fore" from "aft" and had better stay where you are.

Bow and Stern—These also mean front and back. Yet although you can go back to the front of a boat, you cannot go aft to the bow (which shows that even boat people get confused by boat talk).

Port—Left. Easy to remember because port wine is red and so's your face if you say "left" instead of "port" on a boat.

Starboard—Right. Not so easy to remember.

Leeward—The direction to throw up in.

Windward—The direction not to.

Avast—A warning that you're talking boat talk or are about to start.

Ahoy—Ditto.

Deck—The floor, except it's also the ceiling and this can be perplexing during bad weather when you're not sure which one you're standing on.

Bulkhead—A wall.

Hatch—A door.

Companionway—A staircase.

Gangway—When you're moving along a wall, trying to stay on the floor, and you go through a door and fall down a staircase, you yell "Gangway!"

Sheets—Ropes and not the things that look like great big bedsheets, which are sails, even though the sheets tend to sail all over the place and the sails are really just big sheets.

Jibs, Mains, Mizzens, Jenoas, and Spinnakers—What you're supposed to call the sails if you're hep.

Cleats, Battens, Booms, Stays, Yards, Gaffs, Clews, and Cheek Blocks—Things on a boat and you don't know what the hell to call them.

But none of this will help you with the most difficult part of boat talk which is how to spell yacht. I've tried "yacth," "yatch," "ychat," and "yot." None of them looks quite right.

Meanwhile, out in the shark-semi-infested Indian Ocean (most of the sharks were back on the Fremantle docks selling *Kookaburra III* sweatshirts for $65), the most spectacular sporting event of the decade dragged on.

If the wind is blowing like stink and everything is working right, a twelve-meter sailboat can go eleven and a half or twelve miles an hour, the same speed at which a bond lawyer runs around the Central Park Reservoir. The *Sea Chunder*—a lumbering diesel the size and shape of a Presbyterian church—can run rings around any twelve-meter ever built. So can a row-boat with a twenty-horsepower Evinrude on the back. The America's Cup is like driving your Lamborghini to the Gran Prix track to watch the charter buses race.

Stars & Stripes and *Kookaburra III* dawdled out to this thing, a buoy, that was floating in the water and from there sailed 3.64 miles to another thing, then turned around and did that seven more times. This took five hours at the end of which everybody was drenched and sick and sunburned, especially me.

Of course they couldn't do it in just any old boat or it might have been over in twenty minutes and cost only a hundred bucks, and what kind of fun would that be? They had to have special twelve-meter boats, which cost $1,000,000 apiece and don't even have a toilet. They also don't have a fridge full of tall cool ones or any tanned wahines in string-knit bathing-suit bottoms.

A twelve-meter is not twelve meters long or twelve meters wide or even wrecked and sunk and twelve meters under the water, no matter how good an idea that would be. A twelve-meter is a boat that conforms to a complex design formula:

$$\frac{L + (2 \times d)\sqrt{s} - F}{.75\pi} = 12$$

In layman's terms this means length (L) of the boat owner's insider-trading securities-fraud-trial transcript plus all the dollars (d) in the world times 2 plus the square root of the Ralph Lauren designer sheets ($\sqrt{s}$) ruined by the crew members sleeping with the spoiled rich girls who follow boat races around minus the number of ugly and embarrassing free (F) boat visors given away by the boat's principal sponsor divided by all sorts (.75π) of snits and quarrels over the rules.

The race ended at last and somebody won, but the *Sea Chunder* was still going UP and *down* and UP and *down* and UP and *down* and oh, God, I had to get to a bathroom, I mean "head." I worked my way along the "deck," holding on to the "bulkhead," and I had just made it to the "companionway hatch" when we hit an extra-messy wave. Blaauuuuughhh. "Gangway," indeed.

There are a lot of mysterious things about boats, such as why anyone would get on one voluntarily. But the most mysterious thing is why rich people like them. Rich people are nuts for boats. The first thing that a yo-yo like Simon Le Bon or Ted Turner does when he gets rich is buy a boat. And, if he's a high-hat kind of rich—that is, if he made his money screwing thousands of people in arbitrage instead of screwing hundreds selling used cars—he buys a sailboat. I don't know about you, but if I got rich I'd buy something warm and weatherproof that held still, like a bar. But not your true cake-eater; he has to have a breeze bucket, a puff-powered moola scow, a wet-ended WASP Winnebago.

Although I don't know why rich people like boats, I do know that many of them deserve no better. And it's all right with me if they spend the privileged hours of their golden days cramped and soggy and bobbing at a clam's pace from Cold Hole Harbor, Maine, to Muck Cay in the Bahamas to Cap de Tripe on the Riviera to Phooey-Phooey in the Solomon Islands. And then there's Fremantle, Western Australia.

Fremantle doesn't seem to fit the mold. I mean, the place is okay, and I was glad to be there as opposed to being on the *Sea Chunder.* But Fremantle is Dayton-on-the-Sea. In fact, Western Australia is Ohio with one side of its hat brim turned up. As soon as I got on solid ground, I went over to the famed Royal Perth Yacht Club. It looked like a cinder-block drive-through bottle store. (Cinder-block drive-through bottle stores are the main architectural features of the greater Perth–Fremantle metropolitan area.) Then I visited the Fremantle docks where the twelve-meters are parked. Welcome to Hoboken, circa 1950. I expected Marlon Brando to saunter out at any moment and have the climactic fistfight in *On the Waterfront.* God knows how the America's Cup race wound up out here. Somebody told me it had to do with the Australians cheating in 1983 and putting tail fins on their boat bottom, but that sounds unlikely. I think the International Sailboat Racing Politburo, or whatever it's called, got Fremantle mixed up with Fort-de-France and thought they were going to Martinique. In Western Australia they don't even know how to make that vital piece of sailboating equipment, the gin and tonic. If you don't watch them, they squirt Rose's lime juice in it.

Australia is not very exclusive. On the visa application they still ask if you've been convicted of a felony—although they are willing to give you a visa even if you haven't been. Australia *is* exotic, however. There are kangaroos and wallabies and wombats all over the place, and even the Australian horses and sheep and house cats hop around on their back legs and have little pouches in front. Well, maybe they don't. Actually I never saw a kangaroo. I saw kangaroo posters and kangaroo postcards and thousands of kangaroo T-shirts. Kangaroos appear on practically every advertising logo and trademark. You can buy kangaroo-brand oleo and kangaroo bath soap, and get welcome mats, shower curtains, and beach towels with kangaroos on them and have kangaroos all over your underpants. But, as for real live kangaroos, I think they're all in the Bronx Zoo.

While I was visiting every bar in Fremantle, trying to recover from my *Sea Chunder* ordeal, I heard the Australians talking about how much they drink and punch each other. True, Australians do drink mug upon mug of beer. But these are dainty little mugs that hardly contain enough beer for one serving of fish-fry batter back where I come from. I could tell the Americans by the way they ordered four or six of these baby brewskis at a time. And the only fight I saw was between two U.S. boat groupies because one threw the other into a swimming pool and ruined his favorite pair of purple boat socks with little pom-poms on the heels.

Australia was like "Australia Nite" at the Michigan State Phi Delt house. The big excitement was driving on the wrong side of the road. Not that I drove on the wrong side. I was over on the right where I was supposed to be. But the Australians were on the left and coming straight at me. After ten or twelve of those lime juice G&Ts, this got very exciting.

I also went to the exciting Royal Perth Yacht Club Ball. The ticket prices were exciting anyway—$300 a pop. The invitation said black tie so I called South Perth Formal Hire and Live Bait and got a polyester quadruple-knit dinner suit with foot-wide lapels and bell-bottoms in the Early Sonny Bono cut. When I arrived at the dance, I was too embarrassed to get out of the car, especially since it was 100 degrees and I was sweating like a hog and the polyester had made my whole body break out in prickly heat. But nobody else in Western Australia owns a tuxedo either. Every guy there was wearing a rented one exactly like mine. We all spent the evening itching and squirming and scratching ourselves like apes.

The R.P.Y.C. buffet, booze-up, and fox trot exhibition had 2,500 guests. This was more than the Royal P's dinky clubhouse or even its parking lot could hold. So the ball was given in an old wool barn that had been decorated to look like, well, an old wool barn. And there was no air-conditioning. Lanolin, ahoy.

At least the Australians weren't dressed the way they usually are, which is in kangaroo T-shirts, khaki short shorts, work boots, and black mid-calf socks. You could tell this was genuine Perth and Fremantle high society because hardly anybody yelled, "G'day, Mate!" They yelled, "Ciao, Mate!" instead.

Australians are friendly, very friendly. I couldn't spend three seconds eating my dinner without one of them butting in at the top of his lungs, "G'day, Mate! Eatin' are ya? Whatzit? Food? Good on ya!" Followed by an enormous backslap right in the middle of my mouthful of boiled lamb brisket (which is either the national dish or just what everything in Australia tastes like). The Australian language is easier to learn than boat talk. It has a vocabulary of about six words. There's *g'day,* which means "hello." There's *mate,* which is a folksy combination of "excuse me, sir" and "hey you." There's *good on ya,* which means "that's nice," and *fair dinkum,* which doesn't mean much of anything. Australian does have, however, more synonyms for vomit than any other non-Slavic language. For example: "liquid laughter," "technicolor yawn," "growling in the grass," and "planting beets." These come in handy for the would-be boat reporter or the would-be Yacht Club Ball society columnist, for that matter.

Stars & Stripes captain and future White House guest Dennis Conner was there, also in a bad tux. He looked like a poster child for the Penguin Obesity Fund. Dennis is supposed to be something of a personality, but with 2,499 other drunks with skin rashes all around it was hard to tell.

In the middle of the wool-barn dance floor, flanked by armed guards, was the America's Cup itself. The America's Saucer, the America's Dinner Plate, the America's Soup Tureen, and the America's Gravy Boat that go with it are presumably held by other yacht clubs. It must be quite a place setting when it's all put together.

I was milling through the crowd of Cup admirers when I bumped into Jimmy Buffett, on tour in Australia and looking, as usual, like a one-man Spring Break. I've known Buffett since he was playing for Coppertone handouts on the beach at Key West. He's a sterling character and so forth, except he's under the misapprehension that sailboats are fun. He nearly drowned me in a sailboat one time when we almost collided with a supertanker off Miami Beach. It was a Gulf supertanker, but it came so close all we could see was the *U.* Anyway, Buffett had written the *Stars & Stripes* fight song "Take It Back" and was in a tizzy of spectator enthusiasm.

"Oh, come on," I said. "This is about as interesting as watching George Bush get ready for bed."

"Goddamn it, P.J.," said Buffett, "you dumb-ass Yankee landlubbing typewriter skipper with your phony-baloney job making fun of everything—this is the most spectacular sporting event of the decade." And he promised to explain twelve-meter racing to me so that I'd feel about the America's Cup like John Hinckley felt about Jodie Foster.

Buffett and I went off to show the Australian bartender what he could do with his Rose's lime juice. And before you could say, "G'day, Mate! Got a fair dinkum hangover? Good on ya!" We were back on the *Sea Chunder,* flopping around like tropical fish on the carpet.

This time I had a better view of the action, not that there was any. "Look!" yelled Buffett. "They're jibing! They're heeling! They're running!

They're reaching! Oh, my God, they're jibing again!" All of which seemed to mean that they weren't doing much.

A twelve-meter is a big boat, some sixty-five feet long, with eleven people sailing it all at the same time. But no matter how much fooling around they do with the ropes and the steering wheel and stuff, the boat just keeps piddling along in the water. Now and then they put up a spinnaker—a great big sail that looks like what happens when a fat girl in a sun dress stands over the air vent at a Coney Island fun house. The purpose of the spinnaker is, I believe, to give the sponsor some place where he can put the name of his company in really gigantic letters.

"Jimmy," I said, "I could probably get into this if they'd *arm* these twelve-meters. You know, maybe twin-mount .50-calibers right up in the pointy part at the front—with tracer bullets."

"P.J.," said Buffett, "shut up."

Fortunately, there was a wild-ass drug scene on the *Sea Chunder.* I was popping fistsful of hyoscine hydrobromide (marketed under the Barf-No-Mor label). Enough of this in your system and you get seriously bent. Your vision goes zoom lens and begins doing *Top Gun* special effects, aborigine didjeridoos start playing in your brain, your temples inflate, and your mouth tastes like Lionel O-gauge track. You don't feel like throwing up. But you do feel like wetting yourself and raping the first mate and eating all the colorful boat clothes. Sailboat racing can be interesting. So was Altamont.

I went downstairs to the *Sea Chunder*'s first floor and had twelve beers to cool out and make myself regular sick instead of hyoscine hydrobromide sick. Also, I figured it was important not to see any more of this America's Cup stuff sober, or I might start thinking about how many starving Ethiopian kids you could feed with just one of these twelve-meters. Of course, that's ridiculous. You can boil *Kookaburra III* for as long as you want, and starving Ethiopian kids still won't eat it.

I spent the rest of the race in the *Sea Chunder* bar watching *Dialing for Dingos* on local TV. Eventually I heard Buffett outside hollering, "We won! We won!" And I guess we did. That's nice. We now have a new national hero, size extra-large. I like it that Dennis Conner, 1987 Athlete of the Year, can't touch his toes or even see them. And twelve-meter racing is the perfect sport for the eighties—snobbish, expensive, and high-tech in a pointless way. You have to be rich even to afford to go see it. I'm sure there are two dozen Hollywood mudsuckers slithering around LA this moment pitching twelve-meter movie ideas. "Like *Karate Kid,*" they're saying, "but with boats."

Already a great national debate has started about where the next America's Cup race should be held. Let me be the first to suggest Aspen. I'll bet these twelve-meters go like a bitch downhill.

Seoul Brothers

December 1987

When the kid in the front row at the rally bit off the tip of his little finger and wrote KIM DAE JUNG in blood on his fancy white ski jacket, I think that was the first time I ever really felt like a foreign correspondent. I mean, here was something really fucking *foreign.*

It wasn't even an act of desperate protest. Opposition candidate Kim Dae Jung hadn't lost the Korean presidential election yet. KDJ was just giving a small pep talk to a group of well-wishers—half a million of them. They spread in every direction out over the horizon, packed flank to flank and butt to loin, all standing at attention in a freezing Seoul drizzle with serious, purposeful expressions on their mugs.

When a Korean political candidate does a little stumping, a little flesh pressing, a little baby kissing, he puts on a sour face, mounts a platform, and stares at the crowd. He's surrounded by Samoan-size bodyguards, his *chap-sae,* or goons, (literally, "trapped birds"). A couple of the goons hold an inch-thick Plexiglas shield in front of the candidate's face. The shield has handles bolted on both ends like a see-through tea tray. The crowd shouts the candidate's name for half an hour, then the candidate yells at the crowd. Korean sounds like ack-ack fire, every syllable has a primary accent: *YO-YO CAMP STOVE HAM HOCK DIP STICK DUCK SOUP HAT RACK PING-PONG!!!!* If the candidate pauses, the crowd responds in unison with a rhymed slogan or with a precise fifteen seconds of waving little paper Korean flags. There's no frenzy in this, no mob hysteria, and it's not a drill or an exercise.

I'd never seen spontaneous regimentation before. And I don't hope to see it again. I was standing on the platform, a couple of goons away from "the DJ," as the foreign reporters call Kim Dae Jung. And I was looking at this multitude, and I was thinking, "Oh, no, they really *do* all look alike"—the same Blackglama hair, the same high-boned pie-plate face, the same tea-stain complexion, the same sharp-focused look in one million identical anthracite eyes. They are a strange northern people who came to this mountain peninsula an ice age ago and have kept their bloodlines intact through a thousand invasions. Their language is unrelated to Chinese or Japanese, closer, in fact, to Finnish and Hungarian. They don't like anyone who isn't Korean, and they don't like each other all that much, either. They're hardheaded, hard-drinking, tough little bastards, "the Irish of Asia."

There was a very un-Irish order to that crowd, however, an order beyond my comprehension—like nuclear fission. There is order to everything in Korea. They call it *kibun,* which means, to the extent it can be translated, "harmonious understanding." Everything in Korea is orderly, except when it isn't—like nuclear fission.

The speech ended, and every single person in that audience pushed forward to be with Kim Dae Jung. I looked down from the platform and saw the kid in the front row wiggle out of his white parka. He was a normal-looking kid (but in Korea everybody is normal looking). He had a sign reading, in garbled English, MR. KIM DJ ONLY BECOME THE 1ST PRESIDENT OF THE WORLD on one side and the same, I guess, in Korean on the other. Then, with a can-do smile, he nipped the digit and began his calligraphy.

The DJ, in a goon envelope, descended to meet his chanting admirers. I tried, without goons, to follow him. I was cross-body-blocked and stiff-armed and went down in a second. I was a one-man zone defense against a football team of 500,000. Squat, rock-hard Korean bodies surrounded me in three dimensions. I was squeezed and heaved and, most of all, overwhelmed by the amazing stink of *kimchi,* the garlic and hot-pepper sauerkraut that's breakfast, lunch, and dinner in Korea. Its odor rises from this nation of 40 million in a miasma of eyeglass-fogging *kimchi* breath, throat-searing *kimchi* burps, and terrible, pants-splitting *kimchi* farts.

I came to the surface of the crowd and went under again like a toddler in surf. I was squashed and tumbled. My foot came out of my shoe. My pocket was picked. Finally, I was expelled from the mass with one collective shove and kick.

This is what Koreans are like when they're happy.

And the Koreans were very happy with their first presidential election in sixteen years. They voted like the dickens—an 89.2 percent turnout. But I couldn't get any of them to tell me why. What was this election supposed to be about?

Practically everybody running for president was named Kim. There was Kim Dae Jung, the opposition front-runner; Kim Young Sam ("Kim: The Sequel"), also the opposition front-runner; and Kim Jong Pil ("Kim: The Early Years"), the opposition straggler. Plus there was the non-Kim candidate, Roh Tae Woo (pronounced "No Tay Ooh" and called "Just Say No" by the foreign press corps). Roh was handpicked by the military dictatorship that's been running South Korea since 1971.

Everybody knew Roh was going to win because Kim the DJ and Kim the Sequel had promised to unite antigovernment opposition behind one candidate, but then they forgot and spent most of the campaign bickering with each other. And Roh was going to win anyway because he had the constituency that votes with M-16s. (When *these* boys make their voices heard in the marketplace of ideas, you'd better listen up.) So the election wasn't about winning.

And the election wasn't about political party allegiance, either. The parties were apparently named at random by pulling two slips of paper out of a hat containing a selection of six words. The Peace and Democracy Party, Democratic Justice Party, Reunification Democratic Party, and New Democratic Republican Party all fielded candidates. If I were a hardworking journalist with a keen eye for detail, I'd sift through my notes now and tell you what Kim belonged to which. But that would be a waste of everybody's time. A Korean political party exists solely to boost the fortunes of its founding candidate and has the average life span of a trout-stream mayfly hatch.

Campaign promises? Kims 1-2-3 promised to promote freedom of expression, work for reunification of North and South, fight corruption, improve the country's god-awful human rights record, raise living standards, and lower taxes. But then that fascist pig Roh Tae Woo went out and promised to do the same and lots more of it. Nobody, Kim or un-Kim, said too much about Korea's near absence of social-security programs, the $140-a-month minimum wage, the seventy-two-hour workweek, or the fact that it's illegal to have an independent labor union. Kim Dae Jung is supposed to be the big liberal in the bunch. When interviewed by a Canadian business magazine, the DJ, that feisty champion of the common man, was quoted as saying, "Of course we want to advocate some social welfare, but we do not want to be excessive . . . If trade unions advocate extreme or radical demands, the law must prohibit this." So the election wasn't about campaign promises.

Why was everybody voting so hard? The only answer I could get from Koreans was "democracy."

"What's this election all about?" I asked.

"Democracy," they answered.

"But what *is* democracy?" I said.

"Good."

"Yes, of course, but why exactly?"

"Is more democratic that way!"

Well, this is heartening to those of us who prefer a democratic system. But I still don't know what they're talking about. "Korea must have democracy," my Korean friends told me. "Democracy is very good for Korea." "Korean people want very much democracy."

I guess democracy is something that if you're going to be really up-to-date, you just can't do without—like a compact disc player. (Actual South Korean experience with democracy, by the way, consists of one thirteen-month period between the April 1960 overthrow of strongman Syngman Rhee and the May 1961 military coup by General Park Chung-hee.)

On election day I cruised Seoul with an old friend from the Marcos-overthrow democracy fad in the Philippines, photographer John Giannini. It was supposed to be a national holiday, but the Koreans went to work just the same, the way they do six days a week, starting before dawn and stopping who knows when. Rush hour doesn't even begin until seven p.m.

Traffic in Seoul is a 50 mph gridlock with nobody getting anywhere and everybody driving like hell. The sidewalks are endless rugby scrums. Elbowing your way through a crowd is Korean for "excuse me." The city is as gray as a parking garage and cleaner than a living room. People stoop and pick up any piece of litter they see. You can spend twenty minutes in an agony of embarrassment trying to figure out what to do with a cigarette butt. And they yell at you if you cross against the light. Everything is made of concrete and glass and seems unrelentingly modern, at first glance. But many buildings have no central heating, and the smell of kerosene stoves pours out of every shop door, mixing with *kimchi* fumes, car smoke, sewer funk, and the stink of industry. It's a tough, homely stench, the way America's ethnic factory towns must have smelled seventy-five years ago (though with regular cabbage instead of *kimchi*).

Giannini and I tried to find the slums of Seoul, but the best we could do was a cramped, rough-hewn neighborhood with spotless, bicycle-wide streets. Every resident was working—hauling, stacking, hawking, welding, making things in sheds no larger than doghouses. Come back in a few years, and each shed will be another Hyundai Corporation. We felt like big, pale drones in the hive of the worker bees.

The voting was just what every journalist dreads, quiet and well organized. There were no Philippine riots, Salvadoran shoot-'em-ups, Haitian baton-twirler machete attacks, or puddles of Chicagoan sleaze running out from under the voting booths. People were standing patiently in line, holding their signature seals, their *chops,* at the ready. Poll watchers from each candidate's party sat to one side, rigid on a row of straight-backed chairs. A reporter who could make an interesting paragraph out of this would get that special Pulitzer they give out for keeping readers awake during discussions of civic virtue. Kim Dae Jung and Kim Young Sam said there was massive vote fraud. But if there was, it was serious, orderly, *Korean* massive vote fraud.

Giannini and I did see one fellow getting roughed up by a crowd outside a polling place. We shoved people, in the Korean manner, until we found someone who spoke English. He told us the fellow being kicked and punched was a suspected government agent. The police came, punched and kicked the fellow some more, and hauled him off. It was certainly the first time I'd ever seen police arrest somebody on suspicion of being a government agent. But that's Korea.

We went out in the country to find people voting in authentic traditional funny clothes. But this, too, was a bore. So we gave up and went to a restaurant—a few floor mats and a kerosene heater in a tent beside the Han River.

The Han is as wide as the Hudson, and its valley is as beautiful as a Hudson River School painting—but more serious, with a gray wash over it. The Koreans are serious about fun, too, thank God. They're perfectly capable of a three-hour lunch, and so are Giannini and I. We ordered dozens of bowls of pickles, garlics, red peppers, and hot sauces and dozens of plates of spiced fish and vegetables and great big bottles of OB beer and mixed it all with *kimchi* so strong it would have sent a Mexican screaming from the room with tongue in flames. By the time we drove, weaving, back to Seoul, you could have used our breath to clean your oven.

After the votes were counted, the Koreans were *not* very happy with their first presidential election in sixteen years. Most citizens responded in the Korean way, by going to work in the morning. But some student radical types decided they'd found a big vote fraud in a ward, or *gu*, office in the Kuro industrial district in southern Seoul.

As usual, I couldn't figure out what was going on. Korea has an infinite capacity to make me feel dumb. This is a whole nation of people who did their homework on Friday night. Even when they don't know what they're doing, they're doing so much of it that they're still going to get an A.

Anyway, the student radicals discovered a locked ballot box under a stack of bread and milk in a truck leaving the Kuro *gu* compound. Local officials gave some lame excuse about how the ballot box had to go to a special vote-counting place, and how the bread and milk truck just happened to be headed that way, and how they'd covered the ballot box to keep the votes from getting cold . . . The students were having none of it. They invaded the five-story Kuro *gu* building, took the local officials hostage, and called for one of those massive violent student demonstrations for which Korea is justly famous.

The way famous, massive, violent Korean student demonstrations work is that the students get a sound truck, turn the volume up to Mötley Crüe, and take turns screaming at themselves. Violent student demonstrators sit around cross-legged in an appreciative half circle and, between screams, holler "*Dok chae tado! Dok chae tado! Dok chae tado!*" which means "Smash the dictatorship." The chant is punctuated with unnerving, blackshirtish synchronized karate chops.

This can go on for days, and at Kuro it did.

Meanwhile, extraviolent student demonstrators were breaking paving stones into handy projectiles, filling *soju* rice-wine-bottle kerosene bombs, building desk-and-filing-cabinet barricades in the Kuro *gu* doorways, and pulling apart some nearby scaffolding to make quarter staves out of iron pipe. A line of command had been created, and all defense preparations were taking place behind a row of stick-wielding young malcontents.

Lack of press freedom in Korea is one of the big student gripes. But the students don't like actual reporters any better than the government does, at least not American reporters. The radicals—in counterfeit New Balance shoes, Levi's knockoffs, and unlicensed Madonna T-shirts—are much given to denouncing American dominance of Korean culture. It took a lot of arguing to get past these ding-dongs. One pair, a dog-faced, grousing fat girl in glasses and a weedy, mouthy, fever-eyed boy, were almost as obnoxious as my girlfriend and I were twenty years ago at the march on the Pentagon. However, they had some oddly Korean priorities. "Don't you step on bushes!" shouted the fat girl as I made my way into the building that they were tearing to shreds.

Inside, firebombs were parked neatly in crates, stones were gathered in tidy piles, more lengths of pipe were laid in evenly spaced rows to booby-trap the stairs, and additional barricades were being carefully constructed on the landings.

Looking down from the roof, I saw little groups of students break away from the chanting and form themselves into squads, squatting in formation. They *dok chae tado*ed for a while then quick-marched to the front lines around the Kuro *gu* compound, where each was given an assigned position and his own firebomb to sit patiently beside. Demonstrators continued to arrive, bringing boxes of food, fruit juice, and cigarettes.

You had to admire the students' industry and organization, if not their common sense. The Kuro *gu* building faced a spike-fenced courtyard with only one narrow gate to the street. There was no way out the back of the place except through the upper-story windows or off the roof. And right next door, completely overshadowing the scene, was a huge police station. Four thousand policemen gathered there that evening, in their distinctive Darth Vader outfits—black gas masks, Nazi helmets, and stiff olive-drab pants and jackets stuffed with protective padding.

The government assault came on Friday morning, two days after the election. It was well under way by the time I arrived at eight a.m. You go to cover a Korean riot story looking more like a Martian than a Woodward or a Bernstein. You wear heavy clothes for protection from the cold and rocks, good running shoes, a hardhat or motorcycle helmet marked PRESS in English and Korean, and the best gas mask you can find on the black market. (It's illegal for civilians to buy them in Korea.)

Korean riot police use the pepper gas developed during the Vietnam War, which is fast becoming a favorite with busy dictators everywhere. I'd been hit with the stuff before, in Panama, but the Koreans lay it on in lavish doses, until the air is a milkshake of minuscule caustic particles. Pepper gas can raise blisters on exposed skin. Any contact with a mucous membrane produces the same sensation as probing a canker sore with a hot sewing needle. The tiniest amount in your eyes and your eyelids lock shut in blind agony. Breathing it is like inhaling fish bones, and the curl-up-and-die cough quickly turns to vomiting. Pepper gas is probably the only thing on earth more powerful than *kimchi*.

There was street fighting going on all around Kuro *gu*, in an orderly way, of course. First the Darth Vader cops form a line with shields interlocked. Then the students run up and throw firebombs at them. The police respond with a volley of pepper-gas rifle grenades. The students throw stones. The police fire pepper gas again and then charge.

The police hardly ever catch a student. That would disturb the *kibun* of the set-piece battle. Instead, there's a squad of volunteers from the police ranks called "grabbers." The grabbers dress in down-filled L.L. Bean–type parkas, jeans, Nikes, and white motorcycle helmets. They carry hippie-tourist-style canvas shoulder bags filled with tear-gas grenades, and swing long batons that look like hiking staffs. Their jackets are all in pleasant shades of beige and baby blue, color coordinated by squadrons. With gas masks in place, the grabbers look like a bunch of mentally unbalanced freelance writers for *Outside* magazine.

The grabbers huddle behind the riot police. As soon as the students break ranks, the grabbers spring out and do their grabbing, beating the shit out of anyone they lay hands on. The beaten students are then led away. Student demonstrators are not often formally arrested in Korea. They are just "led away." What happens to them next is, I hear, even less fun than getting caught in a Kim Dae Jung rally.

Being out in no-man's-land between the students and the police isn't much fun either. Pepper gas grenades were flying through the air, and stones were racketing on the top of my hard hat; plus there was this creepy xxx video rubber-fetish thing all over my face. No gas mask is fully effective against the pepper-gas clouds, and mine looked as if it dated back to the Crimean War. Inside it, I was coughing and weeping and thoroughly panicked, and outside it, barely visible through the scratched and fogged-over eyepieces, was the world's only mayhem with choreography. I had stumbled onstage in mid-performance of some overenthusiastic Asian production of *West Side Story*.

Back at Kuro *gu* itself, the police had retaken the courtyard and the first four stories of the building, but the students were still holding the top floor and roof.

The students don't wear gas masks. They put on those little Dr. Dan and Nurse Nancy cotton face things, and they smear toothpaste on their skin, but otherwise they riot unprotected. The police in the courtyard were firing salvos of gas grenades, twenty at a time, into the fifth-floor windows and onto the roof. The gas bursts looked like albino fireworks. The police also have armored cars with gun turrets that shoot small pepper-gas canisters at hundreds of rounds a minute. Two of these had been set in flanking positions and were raking the rooftop. That the students could even stand in this maelstrom was a testament to Koreanness. But they were not only standing; they were fighting like sons of bitches.

The barricades in the stairwells had been set on fire, and columns of ash were rising above the building. I could see blurred hand-to-hand action inside as windows shattered and pipes and batons flashed. The students were raining everything they could lift on the police. The "Irish confetti" was dancing off upraised shields and bouncing and ricocheting all around in the courtyard. Two fire trucks had been brought through the gate, and their extension ladders were thrust as near to the roof as even a Korean would dare.

A couple of overbrave firemen went scurrying topside in a smoke of stones. The adrenaline-zany kids fended off water blasts with their protest placards and with ordinary umbrellas, the fabric tearing from the spokes in seconds. A stray gas grenade slammed into one of the extension ladders, inspiring vivid gestures from the fireman to his colleagues below.

The otherwise modern cement Kuro *gu* office was topped, Burger King fashion, with a mansard roof of traditional tiles. When the students ran out of stones and bottles, they began pulling loose these fat parentheses of baked clay and sailing them out over the courtyard. Weighing ten pounds apiece and coming from fifty feet in the air, they had the impact of small mortar shells. If you kept your eye on the trajectories, you could move out of the way in time. But to stop watching the sky for even ten seconds was curtains. I saw six or seven cops carried away, heads lolling and blood running out from under their helmets. I turned a shoulder to the building to write that in my notebook, and half a tile flew past me so close I felt the wind through the fly of my Levi's 501s. If I'd been standing one inch to the south, I'd be writing this in soprano.

About 8:45 the police cleared the top floor and the grabbers—or "white-skull police," as the students call them—appeared at the windows waving victoriously. But the cops below were slow on the uptake, and the grabbers got hit with another round of gas.

The students on the roof kept at it. One wild young fool spent the entire battle balanced on the roof tiles, dancing back and forth, chased by streams of water from fire hoses and ducking the gas grenades fired at his head. Every time a grenade missed he'd bow grandly to the police. It's not enough that these guys are better than we are at making cars, ships, TVs, stereos, cameras, computers, steel, and binoculars; now they're building a better Berkeley and Kent State.

The final assault came about nine a.m. There was one double door to the roof, and only four grabbers could get through it at a time. Photographer Tony Suau, with whom I'd covered the Aquino-Marcos election, was standing right behind the first wave. He said the grabbers were obviously scared. And the first four who charged out were flung back inside, bruised and bleeding. But the grabbers persisted, four by four, until they secured the doorway. Then a hundred of them pushed outside.

From the ground it was a Punch and Judy show. The down-bulked grabbers in their helmets and masks were visible only from the chest up behind the mansard parapets. They were thrashing maniacally with their long batons. You could tell when they got a student down—suddenly a stick would be moving in a single arc with burlesque speed: *wack-a-wack-a-wack-a-wack-a-wack*. I saw the bowing kid pulled from his perch and given the Mrs. Punch treatment.

One section of the roof was raised half a story above the other. A dozen determined students held out here, throwing folding chairs, bricks, and roof tiles. For a few last seconds their silhouettes were etched in heroic silliness against the sky.

The paved Kuro *gu* courtyard had been turned into a gravel pit by the battle. Inside the building the air was a mud of smoke and gas. Fires were still burning in some corners, and water from the fire hoses ran in rivulets down the stairs. The police were making the students carry out their wounded. Several were unconscious, and one girl, wrapped in a blanket, had a hand's breadth of skull laid open and a bad, bloodless look to her face.

The students were swollen and red from the gas. They stumbled around, dazed and stupid. The cops were gathering them in Kuro *gu*'s larger rooms, making them prostrate themselves, obeisant like Moslems in prayer but more tightly hunched—children trying to make themselves disappear. These balled-up figures were packed into perfect squares of one hundred. The grabbers strolled over every now and then and gave the kids a few kicks for good measure.

The building had been fought over inch by inch. Every stick of furniture was destroyed, every breakable thing was broken. This was Korea, however—the bathrooms were still spotless.

About one hundred hostages, including several children, were released. They looked thoroughly sick. Nobody seemed interested in them. (According to the next day's official report, twenty-four policemen and forty students were seriously injured. One thousand and five students and student-allied radicals were "led away.")

The captured students were made to "elephant walk" down the stairs and into the courtyard, bodies bowed double, one hand on the waistband of the student ahead. Kicks and swats hurried them along. I noticed the dog-faced girl stumbling by, with glasses missing and a big shiner.

Then the mommy riot began. A dozen middle-aged women arrived at the police lines. They shoved their plump bodies against the riot shields and screeched, "You murderers!" and "Where is my son?!" and "I hate this country!" Then they fell into brief faints, tore their hair, wept, screeched some more, and went into other histrionics—enough for a French actress on a farewell tour. This is not how my mother would have behaved. She would have been there yelling, "Keep the bum!"

That night, the journalists who'd covered the Kuro *gu* riot—having showered and dumped our gas-soaked clothing in hotel hallways—had a long, well-lubricated dinner. Between the blowing of gas-scalded noses and the wiping of gas-curried eyes, we discussed Korean democracy. As I recall, the discussion went something like this:

"What the fuck?"

"Beats the shit out of me."

"Yo, waitress, more whiskey."

When the dinner was over, I went with two photographers, Greg Davis and Tom Haley, for a little constitutional up the hill to Myongdong Cathedral, a few blocks from the restaurant. About a hundred students with the usual rock piles and firebombs were sitting-in up there for no reason anyone was very clear about.

The students had blocked the street on the hilltop in front of the church and weren't going to let us through. "Democracy! Free press!" said Davis, as we flashed our credentials.

"No free press!" shouted student number 30. They'd all given themselves numbers, which they wore pinned to their chests.

"No democracy?" said Davis.

"No democracy!" shouted 30.

Then, out of the gloom, appeared a pair of American preppies, he in tweeds and a necktie, she in a plaid skirt and stadium coat. "Hi!" the boy said brightly. "We're from the International Human Rights Law Group. We're here to observe Korean democracy."

"Ask number 30 about that," said Davis.

Down at the bottom of the hill, riot police were forming up, shield-to-shield, grenade launchers loaded.

"Yeah, you little fuck," I said to number 30. "What do you think about getting democratically hammered, about half a minute from now?"

The members of the International Human Rights Law Group gasped to hear someone speaking to a genuine Korean like that, right in the middle of Korea's first presidential elections in sixteen years. But then they caught a look at the advancing police. The Law Group took off like surprised mice.

Haley, Davis, and I were too slow. We could hear the grenades being fired, half a dozen of them, *KA-CHUNK/CHUNK/CHUNK/CHUNK/CHUNK/CHUNK*. "Incoming!!!" yelled Haley, the last thing he'd be able to say for half an hour. The grenades burst just above our heads.

We ran screaming down an alley, slamming into walls and garbage cans, coughing and gagging, a scum of tears running down our sightless faces. After two hundred yards we collapsed, bent over in pained hacking and gasps. A group of Korean men, earnestly merry with drink, were coming up the other way. They stopped in front of our little spectacle. The lead fellow bowed and said, "You Americans yes what do you think about Korean democracy?"

"Awwwwk ugch ugch ugch," said Haley.

But the Koreans were not making a joke. "What do you think about Korean democracy?" said their leader, gravely.

"Tastes terrible!" said Davis.

They hustled us into a storefront café and bought us a great many large bottles of OB beer. We sat there sneezing and weeping and coughing. They sat there asking, "What do you think about Korean democracy?"

That turned out to be all the English they knew.

The Holyland—God's Monkey House

January 1988

You haven't really seen the Old City of Jerusalem until you've seen it at dawn on a Moslem Sabbath while you're disguised as an Arab and accompanied by a guy who's probably with the PLO, plus two hulking press photographers in unlikely-looking Bedouin headdresses, and all four of you are following the footsteps of Christ down the Via Dolorosa at a jog trot, running in and out of doorways dodging Israeli army patrols.

Old Jerusalem is a medieval city, not an adorably restored medieval city like Heidelberg, but a real one where you can smell the medieval sanitation and smack your head on the dirty, low medieval ceilings. The fortress-fronted, time-soiled limestone houses are built all over each other. The boulevards are steep, twisting, littered, and as wide as a donkey. Some streets are roofed in stone; most have steps cut in the pavement, and they seem more like staircases in a crypt than city avenues. Lamps are few. Signposts date from the Ottoman Empire. Each shadow holds some sinister passage or dwarfish portcullis. The place is the original for every game of Dungeons and Dragons. At dawn in Jerusalem, you could be in any century of human civilization.

The guy who was probably with the PLO, whom I'll call Ahmed, was smuggling me and my photographer friends Tony Suau and John Reardon into the forbidden precincts of the Haram esh-Sharif, the "Noble Sanctuary" enclosing the Dome of the Rock and the al-Aqsa Mosque. Except for Mecca and Medina, these are Muhammadanism's most sacred shrines. Infidels are banned from the Haram's thirty-five acres on Friday, the Moslem day of worship, and this Friday the sanctuary was also being sealed by Israeli soldiers and Jerusalem police. There had been an ugly incident the week before. After midday prayers, some kids displayed the illegal Palestinian flag, burned the flag of Israel (and, of course, the U.S. flag, too), and threw stones. The Israelis responded with clubs and tear gas and, at one point, tossed a gas grenade inside the al-Aqsa Mosque. The result was some coughing and sneezing and lots of international indignation. Today the Israelis would be checking identity cards at the sanctuary's eight gates and letting in only respectable believers.

Tony, John, and I had tried to slip into the Haram before the soldiers arrived. There was only one sleepy Moslem guard on duty at 6:00 a.m. at the Gate of the Tribes. We'd wrapped black and white checked *kaffiyehs* over our heads. But since I was wearing a Burberry trench coat and my friends were carrying thirty pounds of camera equipment, this wasn't much of a ruse. The elderly guard was having none of us. While we were arguing with him, Ahmed stepped out of a crowd of morning prayergoers and took our part. (This happens all the time in the Middle East. No matter whom you're arguing with or what you're arguing about, some stranger will always come to your defense. They're generous with their contention; you never have to argue alone in the Arab world.)

When Ahmed couldn't prevail on the guard, he took us home to a warren of ancient stone rooms (though the furniture was Danish Modern) and served us sticky tea and rolls and bread and coffee thick as syrup.

Several of Ahmed's knuckles were enormously knobbed and one of his fingers was bent at a sickening angle. There were scars around his wrists. He had been imprisoned by the Israelis for four years during the seventies, he said, for "Palestinian activities" and again during the early eighties for helping a friend repair a gun. He said he had been tied in a chair once for five days with a black hood over his head. "It was beautiful when they would take me away to beat me"—he gave us that big grin everyone wears in these parts when they talk about something grisly—"because then I could breathe and see."

Ahmed claimed there would be a demonstration at al-Aqsa and that the journalists, the *sahaffi*, must be inside the mosque to see how Jews treat Moslems in this holy place. He led us through the Arab Quarter to the Via Dolorosa which runs parallel to the Haram's north wall. Then he opened an iron door near the *Ecce homo* Arch—the place where Pontius Pilate, saying "Behold the man," presented a flogged Jesus to the Jerusalem mob. We went through somebody's house, across roofs and down concealed spiral stairs with stone treads worn hollow by a thousand years of escapes and forays. It was a scene from an Indiana Jones movie except the stairs opened into someone's modern bathroom. We went out through the kitchen, down one more flight of steps that were cut into the Haram's wall, and there, framed in a Byzantine Empire back door, was the Dome of the Rock—a big gold cupola rising from an octagon of royal blue tiles and set upon a vast stone platform like a bonbon on a deck of playing cards.

Burnooses were produced to conceal Tony and John's photo gear. I ditched my trench coat. And Ahmed showed us how to fasten the *kaffiyehs* properly with the *ukals,* the tasseled headbands. Then we went, stiff with adrenaline, down the length of the Haram esh-Sharif compound, past guards and policemen and "fellow" Moslems. "*Walk comfortable!*" whispered Ahmed with some irritation. Tony's cameras were clanging under his lumpy robe. Israeli soldiers lined the sanctuary walls and helicopters swayed back and forth overhead.

The dim interior of the al-Aqsa Mosque was the size of a large suburban house lot. There were no furnishings at all except luminous antique carpets spread two and three deep across the floor. Scores of columns, thick as automobiles, supported a roof so high it was nearly invisible. A few of the slippered worshippers knelt alone on prayer rugs; others gathered in small groups along the walls. For the next four hours Tony, John, and I hid in these majestic shadows.

It was unlikely that the Israelis would let anything important erupt again in the Haram or overreact if it did. They'd taken too much flak about the mosque gassing. To put it in Protestant American terms: throwing a tear gas grenade into the al-Aqsa Mosque on a Sabbath was like attacking the Pebble Beach golf course with Agent Orange during the U.S. Open Championship. So we weren't going to see much action. And we weren't really doing our jobs either. Outside the sanctuary, all through the Israeli-occupied territories of Palestine's West Bank and Gaza Strip, there were riots, retaliations, strikes, curfews, stonings, shootings, beatings, shoutings, whinings, and wild excuse makings—the complete folderol of a Mideastern political crisis. Eager, ambitious reporters would have been out there interviewing the pants off everybody and filing serious, indignant, yet balanced and thoughtful pieces. Instead, here we were dressed like ninnies and sneaking around in mosques.

However, dressing like ninnies and sneaking around in mosques is an important tradition among old Arab hands, dating back at least to 1853 when the explorer Sir Richard Burton dressed like a ninny for nine whole months and managed to sneak all the way into the holy Kaaba at Mecca. Like Sir Richard, T. E. Lawrence, and others before us, we were trying to penetrate the soul of the Arab, trying to become one with him and fathom the Mystery of the East. It's just something you have to go through if you're going to be an old Arab hand, like eating a live guppy to get into Sigma Nu.

Shortly before noon, as the mosque was beginning to fill, Ahmed suggested that I go outside and mingle. I thought this was a little *too* P.J. of Arabia, especially since I look about as much like an average American jerk as it's possible to look and speak exactly two words of Arabic. But Ahmed thought I'd pass, thanks perhaps to a high school fistfight which left me with a Levantine nose. "If they start throwing stones," he said, "feel free to join in."

Pulling the *kaffiyeh* down over my forehead to hood my blue eyes, I walked outside into a milling crowd of two thousand Muhammadans. The crowd was all men and boys. Women pray separately in the Dome of the Rock. A few of the men were in churchgoing clothes but most wore jeans and sweaters like my own. My deck shoes—not a popular fashion item with desert peoples—were the only anomaly.

I didn't know quite what to do with myself, so I milled too. Fortunately the Arabs are also fond of lounging. And I lounged for a while—leaning against pillars, sitting on the edge of fountains, that sort of thing. Nobody bothered me; only a couple of small boys looked twice at my yokel face.

The men were chatting or walking alone lost in contemplation. Some strolled in pairs, holding hands. Then the *muezzin* called the faithful and suddenly I was the only person not facing Mecca. Not many O'Rourkes have ever bowed to Mecca, but I did and followed all the gestures and prostrations as best I could, half a beat behind the others, like singing along when you don't know the words.

There was a peculiar casualness to the worship. People ambled in and out of the mosque all through the service. It was God as an informal thing, but a serious informal thing, the way lunch is when you're hungry. A large part of the crowd stayed outside, listening to loudspeakers mounted on al-Aqsa's portico, listening as though they were hearing something they were actually interested in, not a sermon or a scripture reading. I grew up in the prim and glacial ceremonies of the Methodist church—half grammar lesson, half drill inspection. It had never occurred to me that anyone might want to just come and *hang out* at a religious service.

This was no stick-on, decal God here, but a woven-in-the-cloth, blown-in-the-glass deity. In the Holyland, God comes with the territory. And though I don't suppose the Moslems would like to hear it, Israel, too, has God as standard equipment. After all, here it is, the State of Israel, with no other rationale for existence except a promise from God. I wonder what a Methodist homeland would be like—mandatory stay-pressed shirts, federal regulations about keeping feet off furniture, and a prison sentence for anybody with crabgrass in his lawn.

There was, in fact, a demonstration after prayers, though not a very exciting one. Men came out of al-Aqsa and yelled; women came out of the Dome of the Rock and shrieked. An imam, a portly visiting president of the mosque in some West Bank town, was hoisted upon shoulders and carried around the Dome. Dozens of pocket-sized Korans were waved in the air. I demonstrated a bit myself by milling around at a slightly faster pace than I'd milled before.

True to Arab form, the demonstration immediately broke into two quarreling factions. The group hoisting the imam wanted to keep a strictly religious tone of outrage to the proceedings; the other group wanted to wave a small, homemade Palestinian flag and scream at the Israelis. The soldiers along the walls looked tense, and one platoon moved into the enclosure and stood along the edge of the Dome's platform with weapons in array. But they didn't interfere. A few young Moslems made feints at collecting stones to throw but didn't follow through. With nothing to oppose it, the demonstration died down in half an hour.

By the time Tony, John, and I got smuggled out of the sanctuary, it was after three o'clock. Old Jerusalem was a very different place in the afternoon. Israeli soldiers pried at locks with crowbars, trying to force Moslem shopkeepers to end the general strike that started in December while young Palestinian activists darted through the marketplaces warning merchants not to open. Arab boys of ten and twelve were picking up rocks and chunks of cement and yelling encouragement to each other from the roofs. Armored personnel carriers, filled with irritable-looking draftees, squeezed along the few large streets. Islamic fundamentalists barked over PA systems from storefront mosques. Greek monks, Armenian priests, Catholic nuns, and Coptic whatsits lumbered around in full fig like parade floats. Ultra-Orthodox Jews plodded by, wearing ridiculous beaver hats and making sour faces. Jesus-addled German tourists strode overenergetically from one holy hot spot to the next.

At dawn in Jerusalem, you could be in any century. But at midafternoon, you know exactly what century you're in—the twelfth, when everybody was bashing everybody over the head about God.

The rock over which the Dome of the Rock is built is supposed to be the altar where Abraham was going to sacrifice Isaac (until Yahweh explained He was just kidding). David parked the Ark of the Covenant here. And Muhammad is believed to have leapt into heaven with this rock as his trampoline. The hill the rock sits on—indistinguishable from the thousand other dumpy hills of Judea—is called Temple Mount by the Jews, Haram esh-Sharif by the Moslems, and Mount Moriah by the Christians. Solomon's Temple was here and the great Temple complex of Herod, destroyed by the Romans in AD 70. Thus the western wall of the Haram is the Wailing Wall of the Jews, who bemoan their fate on one side of it while the Moslems bemoan theirs on the other. The early Christians considered the place cursed because Jesus predicted the destruction of the temple (a safe enough prediction; the whole of Jerusalem has been destroyed more than thirty times). Score that round of theological debate to the early Christians.

In fact, I think it can be fairly said that *everything* in the Holyland is cursed. The Gaza Strip certainly is. I drove down there to take a look at the place where Israel's current batch of troubles began. The Strip is desolate and, at the same time, one of the most thickly populated places on earth. (Desolately overpopulated, cursed Holyland, blood-soaked home of the Prince of Peace—this region never seems to run out of oxymorons.) Gaza City has the same crowded poverty as Arab Jerusalem, but it's all new and made of cement. The land around it, the mere 140 square miles that make up this gigantic international sore spot, should be a place of gilt-sand beaches and graceful dunes dotted with palms and oasis wells. Instead it's Hell's Riviera with eight refugee camps housing a quarter of a million people.

The Palestinians in these camps were displaced by the 1948 war—the one Paul Newman and Eva Marie Saint won in *Exodus*. Since then they've been "temporarily" sheltered by the jackoff UN; ruled first by useless Egyptian bureaucracy, then by cold-hearted Israeli military fiat; ignored by the Western bloc; exploited by the Eastern bloc; and just left there, like live bait in a geopolitical leg trap, by their fellow Arabs.

In between the refugee camps are some ratty Arab farms. (Palestinians, unlike Israeli citizens, do not get subsidized irrigation water.) Also in between the camps are Jewish settlements. I have no idea why. The Jews have no biblical claim to Gaza except for some exploits of Samson's. ("Then went Samson to Gaza, and saw there a harlot, and went in unto her." Judges 16:1) The settlements are cheerless places surrounded by armed guards and barbed wire and featuring the usual dreadful Israeli architecture—a style that crosses the worker housing of Gdansk with the branch banks of West Palm Beach.

All the refugee camps had been put under curfew, which meant no one could stir outside the shack houses at any time for any reason. The curfew was lifted for only an hour or so a day, the time never announced beforehand. Even then only the women could go outside and get food.

I made my way into the largest of the camps, Jabalia, which houses fifty-two thousand people in what looks like, from a distance, a valley full of packing crates with electrical lines. Entering the camp was a less romantic business than getting into the al-Aqsa Mosque and more dangerous, too. In the occupied territories, unlike Jerusalem, the Israelis were shooting people.

I crawled into Jabalia through a scraggly vineyard and spent an unhappy five minutes with my gut pressed to the sand, trying to look like a grape plant while an armored personnel carrier rolled along a nearby road. I visited an architect there, named Ali, who did not miss the irony of being an architect in a two-room cinder-block house with a corrugated asbestos roof.

I could see daylight all around the eaves in the eight-by-ten-foot living room. There was no heat, and a cold wind was blowing off the Mediterranean. Ali said the camp had been under curfew for seven days. The Israeli-controlled electricity had been cut off twice and at one point the water mains were shut for three days; people had to drink from rain barrels. The food in the camp stores had all run out, and the break in the curfew was not long enough for the women to walk into town and back. Money, too, had about run out, because of the Palestinian general strike and the fact that no one could get to work anyway. However, the United Nations was usually allowed to distribute food to children and nursing mothers once a day. And an informal smuggling network had grown up around the camp perimeters. Nobody was going hungry yet.

Ali counted himself lucky. There were only five in his family. Some people in the camp had households of ten or fifteen. I asked Ali's wife what she was feeding her kids. "Bread and tea for breakfast," she said, "and tomatoes and vegetables that are smuggled." There was no meat or milk. She had no more said that than Ali invited me to stay for dinner. You can't fault Arab manners. It took ten minutes of diplomatic maneuvering to escape imposing on their larder.

"Where are you from?" I asked Ali. Though, of course, since he was only thirty-two years old, he was from nowhere. He was born in the camp. But without hesitation Ali named a little village in what's now Israel proper.

"My father goes to cry there. Nothing is left."

The press stands accused of holding the Israelis to higher moral standards than it holds the other peoples of the Middle East. That's not our fault. Moses started that. Are the Israelis treating the Palestinians any worse than the Palestinians would treat the Israelis if the sandal were on the other foot? Of course not. The Munich massacre and hundreds of killings, bombings, hijackings, rocket attacks, and other vile actions prove it. Unfortunately, morality is not a matter of double-entry bookkeeping.

The Israeli-administered hospital in Gaza City, where Arabs wounded in the rioting are treated, was a pile of shit. The floors were dirty, the bathrooms were dirty, and the little kitchens on each floor were pathetic in their filth. The walls had been painted, a very long time ago, in awful landlord colors. Damp marks spread across the ceilings. Screens were missing from the windows and lightbulbs from the light fixtures. The hospital looked like the "colored" waiting rooms used to look in bus stations down South. The doctors were all Palestinian, but none of them would talk to me for fear of Israeli ire. The patients, however, were pitifully eager to talk, as if exposing their plight would make any difference in the dead-end hatreds of this land. Maybe the Western powers will intervene, said the Palestinians with forlorn hope. But we've done that before. When Godfrey of Bouillon conquered Jerusalem in 1099 he slaughtered all the Moslems and burned the Jews in their synagogue.

I went from bed to bed hearing dreadful stories. A fifteen-year-old who looked twelve, and didn't have an eyelash's worth of down on his upper lip, had been shot through the thighbone an inch below his balls. He said he had been bringing food home when a soldier told him "come here." He did and got shot. He probably wasn't as innocent as that, but any grown man could have knocked this kid cold with a pancake spatula. The slightly larger boy in the next bed had an eye the size of a teacup and bruises like zebra stripes. He said he'd been detained by soldiers and beaten for thirty minutes. In a small room next door were four young men; all had been shot—in the chest, in the side, or in the belly. Only one had been shot in the leg, the traditional shoot-to-wound target. In the ward across the hall was a ten-year-old with a bullet in his rib cage and a man and his teenage son who'd both been beaten senseless, they claimed, in a police station, and an old man who'd been beaten all over and had both his shins broken. And so on.

This is barbarism. I've covered a lot of rioting and civil disorder, and there is no excuse for this kind of civilian hammering by soldiers and police. Panamanian university students can throw a rock in a way that Palestinian boys, who are innocent of baseball, only dream about. The Panamanians have been rioting steadily since last July and only one rioter has been killed. Korean college students are the most organized and determined rioters on earth, and Korean riot cops are no bowl of Sugar Pops. But the Koreans have been at it since June 1987 and the death toll is two.

A few days later Tony Suau and I got into the middle of a little riot, a riotette, in the Kalandia refugee camp on the West Bank, several miles north of Jerusalem. This camp wasn't under curfew, but the Israeli army was running patrols through it and holding down intersections and generally acting like this was downtown Hue in the middle of the Tet offensive.

The enemy was horsing around in the side streets, giving each other noogies and trying to figure out how to tie the *kaffiyehs* over their faces in a genuine fierce-desert-warrior way. They were twelve, thirteen, fourteen years old. I recognized their every move and didn't have to speak a word of Arabic to know what they were saying because this was Tommy, Larry, Gary, Wayne, and me playing war in our backyards in 1959, except for keeps.

Of course the kids were excited to find adult foreigners taking everything they were doing seriously. They delivered long speeches on patriotism as only pubescents can. I believe the 1950s American equivalent would begin, "My old man was on Iwo . . ." And they showed us where to park our car so it wouldn't get hit with stones or rubber bullets.

We followed the kids through a maze of houses and passageways—a modern version of the architecture around the Haram—to an alley on a hilltop that commanded an Israeli control point. There was, among the boys, no future Roger Clemens, but the rocks of Judea are excellent rocks, all pointy and jagged limestone. And the kids get good distance with a run-up underhand throw like a cricket-fast bowler's. Some of them also have, ironically I suppose, the shepherd's sling David the Israeli used on Goliath the Philistine. (*Philistine* and *Palestinian* have the same root in the ancient Egyptian word for natives of the region.) These slings are as potent as a Wham-O slingshot—and almost as accurate.

The kids rushed down the alley. The steel shutters of the closed shops, the bodywork of parked cars, and the tin roofs around the Israeli-held intersection resounded with the merry bang and clatter of a Holyland stoning.

At least the soldiers weren't firing much live ammo that week. Defense Minister Yitzhak Rabin had told them, "The first priority is to use force, might, beatings." And according to the *Jerusalem Post*: "Large numbers of troops are to be concentrated at each trouble spot, where they will fire rubber bullets, charge at the demonstrators, and try to get the leaders, whom they are to beat and detain." Or *try* to beat and detain, since there was fat chance of laying hands on any of these speedy urchins.

The rubber bullets come at you with an untuned guitar string twang and a whistle and hit the pavement and buildings in profound whacks. A couple of these projectiles bounced up by my feet. They're black cylinders about as big as the last knuckle on your thumb, heavy in the hand, and hard as a shoe heel. I cut one open later. It had a steel pellet the size of a .45 slug inside.

The kids darted forward and back, jacked up and grinning with the "drunk delight of battle" that combatants used to get before it was discovered that war is horrible and wrong. The Israelis attempted a charge up the alley, but the kids held the high ground and the soldiers had no cover. Eventually the soldiers made an old man, who'd been driving by, get out of his VW van. They used the van as a rolling shield, pushing it uphill and zinging rubber bullets from behind. The kids (and me and Tony) made a tactical retreat.

I could understand why the Israeli soldiers were showing such anger and fear. It wasn't just the taunting, pesky boys armed with Neanderthal weapons. The whole Kalandia camp was alive with hatred. Moms and doddering granddads were shouting instructions from the housetops. "Jeeps are coming! A platoon is coming up this street! Over here!" Old ladies and little girls rushed out of houses and began throwing up barricades of trash barrels and paving stones they could barely lift. A pretty girl of twelve with an infant on her hip, whom we'd seen by the camp gate, was no idling babysitter. She was a lookout. She came running up the slope, baby a-flap, saying something about troops with tear gas. Doors flew open and the half-pint Geronimos disappeared into labyrinthine Arab domiciles.

The hatred was as universal, as simple, as much a foregone conclusion as God had been at the al-Aqsa Mosque.

Tony and I drove on north and, near Ramallah, caught up with another Israeli patrol just as it was entering the small Al Ama're refugee camp. There was a roadblock on the main street, a single burning truck tire. The Israelis get exercised about roadblocks. They grabbed the handyman at the camp's UN office and made him pour water on the tire and pull it out of the road. None of the Israeli troops looked mature enough to trust with the car keys after dark.

The patrol's commanding officer was a captain, about thirty, and carrying, of all things, a pair of nunchucks. A crowd of catcalling Arab boys had gathered down the street and stones began to fall in among us. The captain moved his patrol toward the boys. Tony and I tagged along. The soldiers had their gas grenades and Galil rifles ready. The boys vaporized.

The captain picked up the pace, trying to catch the kids and shake Tony and me. But, being in full combat gear, he could do neither. The soldiers were rude to us, as armed men often are rude. (And in the Middle East whoever's top dog at the moment is terrifically rude, just as he's terrifically courteous when he's shit-out-of-luck.) The Arab kids stayed always just beyond the next corner, while the soldiers ran faster and faster, around and back and up and down through the twisting streets, sweating like horses.

As the patrol approached an area, the pavement emptied and all the house doors and window shutters closed. As soon as the patrol passed, the doors and windows opened and women and children poked their heads outside, laughing in happy malice. I saw a three-year-old boy step into the road and send mocking kisses at the Israeli soldiers' backs.

After forty-five minutes the soldiers gave up, winded. They returned to the entrance of the camp. By now there were some grudging smiles for Tony and me. The only soldier who seemed to speak English pointed at my notebook and said, "This they see and go wild."

"No, no," I said. "They see this"—I held up the notebook—"and they only go wild two times. They see this"—I pointed to Tony's Nikons—"they go wild ten times. They see TV"—I pantomimed a TV cameraman—"they go wild a *hundred* times!" The soldier laughed and translated for his buddies. They laughed, and gave us some dates and apricots from their packs. We gave them some cigarettes. Then we stood around shrugging amiably with these young men who would have to live their whole lives in this mess. "So much trouble . . . What can be done? . . . Who knows? . . ."

When I'd been in front of the al-Aqsa Mosque, and everyone was bowing toward Mecca and praying, I prayed too. And I repeated that prayer when we left Al Ama're. Actually, it wasn't exactly a prayer. It was more a sort of chat with God. I said, "God, the next time you're looking for people, you know, to receive Revealed Truth and everything and be the Anointed of the Lord like the Christians and the Jews and the Moslems are, *please,* God, don't choose lapsed Methodists from Ohio. *Choose somebody else.*"

Third World Driving Hints and Tips

During the past couple years I've had to do my share of driving in the Third World—Mexico, Lebanon, the Philippines, Cyprus, El Salvador, Africa, and Italy. (Italy is not technically part of the Third World, but no one has told the Italians.) I don't pretend to be an expert, but I have been making notes. Maybe these notes will be useful to readers who are planning to do something stupid with their Hertz #1 Club cards.

Road Hazards

What would be a road hazard anyplace else is, in the Third World, the road. There are two techniques for coping with this. One is to drive very fast so your wheels "get on top" of the ruts and your car sails over the ditches and gullies. Predictably, this will result in disaster. The other technique is to drive very slow. This will also result in disaster. No matter how slowly you drive into a ten-foot hole, you're still going to get hurt. You'll find the locals themselves can't make up their minds. Either they drive at 2 mph—which they do every time there's absolutely no way to get around them. Or else they drive at 100 mph—which they do coming right at you when you finally get a chance to pass the guy going 2 mph.

Basic Information

It's important to have your facts straight before you begin piloting a car around an underdeveloped country. For instance, which side of the road do they drive on? This is easy. They drive on your side. That is, you can depend on it, any oncoming traffic will be coming straight at you on your side of the road. Also, how do you translate kilometers into miles? Most people don't know this, but one kilometer = ten miles, exactly. True, a kilometer is only 62 percent of a mile, but, if something is one hundred kilometers away, read that as one thousand miles because the roads are 620 percent worse than anything you've ever seen. And when you see a 50 kph speed limit, you might as well figure that means 500 *mph* because nobody cares. The Third World does not have Broderick Crawford and the Highway Patrol. Outside the cities, it doesn't have many police at all. Law enforcement is in the hands of the army. And soldiers, if they feel like it, will shoot you no matter what speed you're going.

Traffic Signs and Signals

Most developing nations use international traffic symbols. Americans may find themselves perplexed by road signs that look like Boy Scout merit badges and by such things as an iguana silhouette with a red diagonal bar across it. Don't worry, the natives don't know what they mean, either. The natives do, however, have an elaborate set of signals used to convey information to the traffic around them. For example, if you're trying to pass someone and he blinks his left turn signal, it means go ahead. Either that or it means a large truck is coming around the bend, and you'll get killed if you try. You'll find out in a moment.

Signaling is further complicated by festive decorations found on many vehicles. It can be hard to tell a hazard flasher from a string of Christmas-tree lights wrapped around the bumper, and brake lights can easily be confused with the dozen red Jesus statuettes and the ten stuffed animals with blinking eyes on the package shelf.

Dangerous Curves

Dangerous curves are marked, at least in Christian lands, by white wooden crosses positioned to make the curves even more dangerous. These crosses are memorials to people who've died in traffic accidents, and they give a rough statistical indication of how much trouble you're likely to have at that spot in the road. Thus, when you come through a curve in a full-power slide and are suddenly confronted with a veritable forest of crucifixes, you know you're dead.

Learning to Drive Like a Native

It's important to understand that in the Third World most driving is done with the horn, or "Egyptian Brake Pedal," as it is known. There is a precise and complicated etiquette of horn use. Honk your horn only under the following circumstances:

1. When anything blocks the road.
2. When anything doesn't.
3. When anything might.

4. At red lights.
5. At green lights.
6. At all other times.

Roadblocks

One thing you can count on in Third World countries is trouble. There's always some uprising, coup, or Marxist insurrection going on, and this means military roadblocks. There are two kinds of military roadblocks, the kind where you slow down so they can look you over, and the kind where you come to a full stop so they can steal your luggage. The important thing is that you must *never* stop at the slow-down kind of roadblock. If you stop, they'll think you're a terrorist about to attack them, and they'll shoot you. And you must *always* stop at the full-stop kind of roadblock. If you just slow down, they'll think you're a terrorist about to attack them, and they'll shoot you. How do you tell the difference between the two kinds of roadblocks? You can't.

(The terrorists, of course, have roadblocks of their own. They always make you stop. Sometimes with land mines.)

Animals in the Right-of-Way

As a rule of thumb, you should slow down for donkeys, speed up for goats, and stop for cows. Donkeys will get out of your way eventually, and so will pedestrians. But never actually stop for either of them or they'll take advantage, especially the pedestrians. If you stop in the middle of a crowd of Third World pedestrians, you'll be there buying Chiclets and bogus antiquities for days.

Drive like hell through the goats. It's almost impossible to hit a goat. On the other hand, it's almost impossible *not* to hit a cow. Cows are immune to horn honking, shouting, swats with sticks, and taps on the hind quarters with the bumper. The only thing you can do to make a cow move is swerve to avoid it, which will make the cow move in front of you with lightning speed.

Actually, the most dangerous animals are the chickens. In the United States, when you see a ball roll into the street, you hit your brakes because you know the next thing you'll see is a kid chasing it. In the Third World, it's not balls the kids are chasing, but chickens. Are they practicing punt returns with a leghorn? Dribbling it? Playing stick-hen? I don't know. But Third Worlders are remarkably fond of their chickens and, also, their children (population problems notwithstanding). If you hit one or both, they may survive. But you will not.

Accidents

Never look where you're going—you'll only scare yourself. Nonetheless, try to avoid collisions. There are bound to be more people in that bus, truck, or even on that moped than there are in your car. At best you'll be screamed deaf. And if the police do happen to be around, standard procedure is to throw everyone in jail regardless of fault. This is done to forestall blood feuds, which are popular in many of these places. Remember the American consul is very busy fretting about that Marxist insurrection, and it may be months before he comes to visit.

If you do have an accident, the only thing to do is go on the offensive. Throw big wads of American money at everyone and hope for the best.

Safety Tips

One nice thing about the Third World, you don't have to fasten your safety belt. (Or stop smoking. Or cut down on saturated fats.)

It cures a lot of worries about long-term consequences, being in a place where average life expectancy is forty-five minutes.

PARLIAMENT OF WHORES

(1991)

Abracadabra, thus we learn
The more you create, the less you earn.
The less you earn, the more you're given,
The less you lead, the more you're driven,
The more destroyed, the more they feed,
The more you pay, the more they need,
The more you earn, the less you keep,
And now I lay me down to sleep.
I pray the Lord my soul to take
If the tax-collector hasn't got it before I wake.

—Ogden Nash

Preface: Why God Is a Republican and Santa Claus Is a Democrat

The subject of this book is government because I don't have to do anything about it.

I am a journalist and, under the modern journalist's code of Olympian objectivity (and total purity of motive), I am absolved of responsibility. We journalists don't have to step on roaches. All we have to do is turn on the kitchen light and watch the critters scurry. If I were a decent citizen instead of a journalist, I would have a patriotic duty to become involved in the American Political System and try to reform or improve it. In that case I would probably do my patriotic duty about the way I did in the 1960s, before I was a journalist, when my involvement with the American Political System consisted of dodging the draft. All this is by way of saying that if you are a nonjournalistic American and don't want to read this book because it's about government, just buy it and let it lie around your house like *A Brief History of Time*.

I decided to write about the United States government after I had spent some years writing about awful things that happen to foreigners overseas. It occurred to me that some pretty awful things happen to us right here. Furthermore, they happen in English, so that I could ask people why they were doing the awful things or getting the awful things done to them. Then, when the people told me and I didn't understand, at least I'd know that I didn't understand and wouldn't get confused by the language barrier and maybe think I did.

I also found the sheer, boring, gray dullness of government a challenge to my pride as a reporter. "I," I thought, "I alone—master that I am of the piquant adverbial phrase and the subordinate clause *juste*—can make this interesting. Why, combine my keen eye for detail with my sharp nose for the telling particular, and the reader will get . . . a faceful of minute observations. Yes, I can paint the drab corridors of power in the party hues of lively prose, dress the dull politicos in motley, and cause the Mrs. O'Leary's cow of governmental insipidity to kick over the lantern of public indignation and set the town ablaze." I am not the first journalist to make this mistake.

Anyway, I thought I'd observe the 1988 presidential race and then go to Washington for the first six months of the new administration, learn everything there is to know about government, and write a book. But the six months turned into two years. I'm not sure I learned anything except that giving money and power to government is like giving whiskey and car keys to teenage boys. And what resulted was not so much a book as a great digest of ignorance.

Grant me at least that it is an ambitious failure. In the following volume I have tried to do a number of things. I have tried to write a kind of Devil's Civics Text in which, like a voodoo doctor teaching poli-sci, I give unnatural life to a description of American government. I have also tried to present a factual—data-filled, at any rate—account of how this government works. Which is complicated by the fact that it doesn't. So I've tried to present a factual account of how the government fails, too. Finally, I've attempted to compose a dissertation on what we Americans expect from our government and how—like parents or fans of certain sports teams—we intend to maintain those expectations even if it kills us. And, several times in the past, it has.

I have tried to keep the book reasonably free of personalities. Not that this was possible in a political system (a socioeconomic system, for that matter) as fame-driven as ours. I had to mention the president by name, though I was tempted not to. I've always admired the way the movies of the 1930s and 1940s would only show the president character from the back. It was more respectful. Either that or movies were made by Republicans in those days.

I preferred to concentrate on systems and institutions, not because people aren't important, but because people are important, in Washington, so briefly. There was a time not long ago when day could hardly break without asking permission from Don Regan, and now, for all I know, he's hosting a talk radio show in Anaheim. I concentrated on institutions because in order to concentrate on persons I'd have had to keep revising and revising until the moment these pages went to press, and I'd still wind up with a book as dated as a Jody Powell joke.

Having said that, I was reading my manuscript (book buyers may not realize it, but we writers often do read what we write, although some of us just wait for the movie version), and I noticed that Senator Daniel Patrick Moynihan is singled out for criticism in three different chapters. I have nothing in particular against the senator from New York. There are plenty worse in the nation's upper house—John Kerry, Edward Kennedy, Christopher Dodd, Claiborne Pell, Alan Cranston, and the appalling Howard

Metzenbaum, to name just six. Senator Moynihan's triplicate appearance is mostly coincidental. So—Paddy to Paddy—I apologize, Senator. On the other hand, Daniel Patrick Moynihan is the archetypal extremely smart person who went into politics anyway instead of doing something worthwhile for his country. So maybe he owes all of us an apology, too.

This book is written, of course, from a conservative point of view. Conservatism favors the restraint of government. A little government and a little luck are necessary in life, but only a fool trusts either of them. Also, conservatism is, at least in its American form, a philosophy that relies upon personal responsibility and promotes private liberty. It is an ideology of individuals. Everyone with any sense and experience in life would rather take his fellows one by one than in a crowd. Crowds are noisy, unreasonable, and impatient. They can trample you easier than a single person can. And a crowd will never buy you lunch.

But although this is a conservative book, it is not informed by any very elaborate political theory. I have only one firm belief about the American political system, and that is this: **God is a Republican and Santa Claus is a Democrat.**

God is an elderly or, at any rate, middle-aged male, a stern fellow, patriarchal rather than paternal, and a great believer in rules and regulations. He holds men strictly accountable for their actions. He has little apparent concern for the material well-being of the disadvantaged. He is politically connected, socially powerful, and holds the mortgage on literally everything in the world. God is difficult. God is unsentimental. It is very hard to get into God's heavenly country club.

Santa Claus is another matter. He's cute. He's nonthreatening. He's always cheerful. And he loves animals. He may know who's been naughty and who's been nice, but he never does anything about it. He gives everyone everything they want without thought of a quid pro quo. He works hard for charities, and he's famously generous to the poor. Santa Claus is preferable to God in every way but one: there is no such thing as Santa Claus.

The Mystery of Government

What *is* this oozing behemoth, this fibrous tumor, this monster of power and expense hatched from the simple human desire for civic order? How did an allegedly free people spawn a vast, rampant cuttlefish of dominion with its tentacles in every orifice of the body politic?

The federal government of the United States of America takes away between a fifth and a quarter of all our money every year. That is eight times the Islamic zakat, the almsgiving required of believers by the Koran; it is double the tithe of the medieval church, and twice the royal tribute that the prophet Samuel warned the Israelites against when they wanted him to anoint a ruler.

> *This will be the manner of the king that shall reign over you . . . He will take the tenth of your seed, and of your vineyards . . . He will take the tenth of your sheep . . . And ye shall cry out in that day because of your king.*

Our government gets more than thugs in a protection racket demand, more even than discarded first wives of famous rich men receive in divorce court. Then this government, swollen and arrogant with pelf, goes butting into our business. It checks the amount of tropical oils in our snack foods, tells us what kind of gasoline we can buy for our cars and how fast we can drive them, bosses us around about retirement, education, and what's on TV; counts our noses and asks fresh questions about who's still living at home and how many bathrooms we have; decides whether the door to our office or shop should have steps or a wheelchair ramp; decrees the gender and complexion of the people to be hired there; lectures us on safe sex; dictates what we can sniff, smoke, and swallow; and waylays young men, ships them to distant places, and tells them to shoot people they don't even know.

The government is huge, stupid, greedy, and makes nosy, officious, and dangerous intrusions into the smallest corners of life—this much we can stand. But the real problem is that government is boring. We could cure or mitigate the other ills Washington visits upon us if we could only bring ourselves to pay attention to Washington itself. But we cannot.

During the 1988 presidential campaign deep-thinking do-gooders at some tax dodge called the John and Mary R. Markle Foundation set up a commission to study the electorate and discovered that 49 percent of the public didn't know Lloyd Bentsen was the Democratic vice presidential nominee. That is good news for Lloyd Bentsen—he now only has to make 51 percent of the public forget he was ever on the Dukakis ticket. But the Markle commission members were not so pleased. They called the information "astonishing" and claimed it "suggests a wide-spread, glacial indifference" to elections.

This is an insult to glaciers. An Ice Age would be fascinating compared with government. We'd be wondering whether to update our snowblowers and trying to figure out if using rock salt to keep ice floes off our driveways would kill the herbaceous borders. We'd be *interested* if glaciers were the problem. "American voters today do not seem to understand their rightful places in the operation of a democracy," said the Markle commission. Wrong again. It's democracy that doesn't understand its rightful place in the operation of us—to shut up and get out of our faces.

Government is boring because political careers are based on the most tepid kind of lie: "I'll balance the budget, sort of." "I won't raise taxes, if I can help it." Of course politicians don't tell the truth: "No, I *can't* fix public education. The problem isn't underfunding, teachers' unions, overcrowding, or lack of computer equipment in the classroom. The problem is your damn kids." But neither do politicians tell huge, entertaining whoppers: "Why, send yours truly to Capitol Hill, and I'll ship the swag home in boxcar lots. You'll be paving the roads with bacon around here when I get done shoveling out the pork barrel. There'll be government jobs for your dog. Leave your garden hose running for fifteen minutes, and I'll have the Department of Transportation build an eight-lane suspension bridge across the puddle. Show me a wet basement, and I'll get you a naval base and make your Roto-Rooter man an admiral of the fleet. There'll be farm subsidies for every geranium you've got in a pot, defense contracts for Junior's spitballs, and free day care for Sister's dolls. You'll get unemployment benefits for the sixteen hours every day when you're not at your job, full disability benefits if you have to get up in the night to take a leak, and Social Security checks will come in the mail not just when you retire at sixty-five but when you retire each night to bed. Taxes? Hell, I'll have the government go around every week putting money *back* in your paycheck, and I'll make the IRS hire chimpanzees from the zoo to audit your tax returns. Vote for me, folks, and you'll be farting through silk."

Government is also boring because in a democracy government is a matter of majority rule. Now, majority rule is a precious, sacred thing worth dying for. But—like other precious, sacred things, such as the home and family—it's not only worth dying for; it can make you wish you were dead. Imagine if all of life were determined by majority rule. Every meal would be a pizza. Every pair of pants, even those in a Brooks Brothers suit, would be stone-washed denim. Celebrity diet and exercise books would be the only thing on the shelves at the library. And—since women are a majority of the population—we'd all be married to Harrison Ford.

Furthermore, government is boring because what's in it for us? Sure, if we own an aerospace contracting company, a five-thousand-acre sugar-beet farm, or a savings and loan with the president's son on the board of directors, we can soak Uncle Sucker for millions. But most of us failed to plan ahead and buy McDonnell Douglas, and now the only thing we can get out of government is government benefits—measly VA checks and Medicare. We won't get far on the French Riviera on this kind of chump change. Besides, the French look at us funny when we try to buy *pâté de foie gras* and Château Margaux '61 with American food stamps.

Government is so tedious that sometimes you wonder if the government isn't being boring on purpose. Maybe they're *trying* to put us to sleep so we won't notice what they're doing. Every aspect of our existence is affected by government, so naturally we want to keep an eye on the thing. Yet whenever we regular citizens try to read a book on government or watch one of those TV public affairs programs about government or listen to anything anybody who's in the government is saying, we feel like high school students who've fallen two weeks behind in their algebra class. Then we grow drowsy and torpid, and the next thing you know we are snoring like a gas-powered weed whacker. This could be intentional. Our government could be attempting to establish a Dictatorship of Boredom in this country. The last person left awake gets to spend all the tax money.

Boredom isn't the only problem, of course. American lack of interest in government is well developed, but American ignorance of government is perfect. Almost everything we know about the workings of Congress, the presidency, the Supreme Court, and so forth comes from one high school civics course and one spring vacation when Dad took the family to Washington, D.C. On the trip to Washington we learned that the three branches of government are the White House, the top of the Washington Monument, and the tour of the FBI building. In the high school civics class we learned just how long an afternoon can be made to seem with the help of modern educational methods.

I can remember everything about my civics course—what classroom it was in, who taught it, which of my friends were in the class with me, where I sat, and what the brassiere of the girl who sat next to me looked like when I peeked down the armhole of her sleeveless blouse. About the civics I remember nothing. There must have been tiny subliminal messages printed between the lines of my textbook saying, "Go ahead, take another look, she must be a 42D."

That was twenty-six years ago, but things have not changed much. I got a copy of a current high school civics book, *American Civics*, published by Harcourt Brace Jovanovich. I'm told it is one of the nation's most widely used texts. The heft of the thing, its awkward shape and inept cover art, the glossy, teen-resistant paper—all of this gave me what I can only describe as a backup of the memory's septic system. I was all of a sudden swamped with powerful, involuntary recollections of dreary class discussions, irksome pop quizzes, and desiccated spring afternoons.

American Civics is, of course, completely up-to-date. Its blurry, stilted photographs of people in unfashionable clothes are printed in color instead of black and white. Its page layouts have been tarted up with cartoons, pastel type, and *USA Today*–style lists of "fun facts" to suit the attention span of the *Sesame Street* generation. And, dispersed throughout the book are little boxed items such as this:

> *CAN YOU GUESS?*
>
> One of our Presidents had a serious physical handicap.
> Who was he?
> *Answer is on page 578.*

(The answer is not, by the way, "Ronald Reagan and his handicap was Nancy.")

American Civics has also trimmed its sails to the prevailing ideological winds. It has a section with the infelicitous title "Upsetting America's Ecology" and another section that says, "The Reverend Jesse Jackson ran a strong campaign for the 1984 and 1988 Democratic Presidential nominations." There's a photo of a man in a wheelchair above the caption, "Disabled doesn't mean unable," and in the "Living Documents" appendix at the end—tossed in with the Mayflower Compact, the Gettysburg Address, and the Emancipation Proclamation—is some screed from a women's rights conference in 1848 called the Seneca Falls Declaration.

What's more, the authors of *American Civics* assume their students are as ignorant of everything as they are of government. Thus, among such traditional chapter headings as "How a Bill Becomes a Law" and "Our Federal Court System," we find "Your Family and You" and—I'm not kidding—"Using Television as a Resource" and—I'm still not kidding—"Civics Skills: Reading a Help Wanted Ad." (Though I suppose ignorance is relative. Few seventeen-year-olds today need to peek into the armhole of a sleeveless blouse to find out what a brassiere looks like.)

Underneath the moral and typographical frills and lessons in how to use a phone, however, *American Civics* is the same font of monotony, the same bible of ennui that civics books have always been. I defy anyone to read two paragraphs of it without incurring a strong desire to join Posse Comitatus or the Symbionese Liberation Army or some other group that promises to kill high school civics teachers. I also defy anyone to read two paragraphs of it and tell me what he or she just read.

There are, of course, other sources of information on government available to literate adults. I have in my hand—or, rather, in both my hands, because it is 793 pages long and weighs more than a cinder block—*The Power Game: How Washington Works* by Hedrick Smith. This comes with a gold-foil sticker on its cover saying, AS SEEN ON PBS. Just four little words, yet oh how they catch the heart.

The Power Game seems to contain everything that Hedrick Smith, in his long career as a *New York Times* reporter, has ever heard or seen in Washington, including—I'm not sure about this, but the literary styles are similar—the entire District of Columbia phone book. *The Power Game* is—and I'm quoting the dust-flap copy so you know I'm telling the truth—"an eye-opening inside portrait of how Washington, D.C., really works today." It's a very different kind of book from *American Civics*. Where *American Civics* is amazingly boring, *The Power Game* is . . . words fail me . . . an eye-opening inside portrait of how Washington, D.C., really works today.

Our Founding Fathers lacked the special literary skills with which modern writers on the subject of government are so richly endowed. When they wrote the Declaration of Independence, the Constitution, and the Bill of Rights, they found themselves more or less forced to come to the point. So clumsy of thought and pen were the Founders that even today, seven generations later, we can tell what they were talking about.

They were talking about having a good time: "We hold these Truths to be self-evident, that all Men are created equal, that they are endowed by their Creator with certain unalienable Rights, that among these are Life, Liberty and the Pursuit of Happiness."

"This is living!" "I gotta be me!" "Ain't we got fun!" It's all there in the Declaration of Independence. We are the only nation in the world based on happiness. Search as you will the sacred creeds of other nations and peoples, read the Magna Carta, the *Communist Manifesto,* the Ten Commandments, the *Analects* of Confucius, Plato's *Republic,* the New Testament, or the UN Charter and find me any happiness at all. America is the Happy Kingdom. And that is one good reason why we who live here can't bring ourselves to read *American Civics* or *The Power Game* or even the daily paper.

As it is with us, so it was with the Original Dads. Their beef with Triple George? He was *no fun.*

"He is, at this Time, transporting large Armies of foreign Mercenaries to complete the works of Death, Desolation, and Tyranny, already begun with circumstances of Cruelty and Perfidity, scarcely paralleled in the most barbarous Ages, and totally unworthy the Head of a civilized Nation."

Totally.

There are twenty-seven specific complaints against the British Crown set forth in the Declaration of Independence. To modern ears they still sound reasonable. They still sound reasonable, in large part, because so many of them can be leveled against the present federal government of the United States. Maybe not the "Death, Desolation, and Tyranny" complaint (unless you're deeply opposed, on fight-for-your-right-to-party grounds, to coca-plant eradication in Bolivia and Peru), but how about:

". . . has erected a Multitude of new Offices, and sent hither Swarms of Officers to harass our People, and eat out their Substance."

George III was a piker compared with FDR or LBJ.

Or: ". . . has called together Legislative Bodies at Places unusual, uncomfortable, and distant . . . for the sole Purpose of fatiguing them into Compliance with his Measures."

Every American president does that to the House and the Senate.

". . . has refused his Assent to Laws, the most wholesome and necessary for the public Good."

Our Congress won't pass a balanced-budget constitutional amendment or any legislation banning people over thirty from wearing spandex bicycle shorts.

". . . has endeavored to prevent the Population of these States; for that Purpose obstructing the Laws for Naturalization of Foreigners; refusing . . . to encourage their Migrations hither."

Tell a Vietnamese boat person, a Hong Kong shopkeeper, or a migrant worker from Mexico that this doesn't describe U.S. immigration policy.

". . . has kept among us, in Times of Peace, Standing Armies."

Certainly.

". . . has combined with others to subject us to a Jurisdiction foreign to our Constitution, and unacknowledged by our Laws."

Federal regulatory agencies, for instance.

". . . Depriving us, in many Cases, of the Benefits of Trial by Jury."

If we cross one of those regulatory agencies.

". . . Cutting off our Trade with all Parts of the World . . ."

. . . is what our trade quotas and tariffs do.

". . . Imposing Taxes on us without our Consent."

Nobody asked me if I wanted a 1040 Form.

". . . Taking away our Charters, abolishing our most valuable Laws, and altering fundamentally the Forms of our Governments."

So say states' rights conservatives.

". . . has plundered our Seas, ravaged our Coasts . . . and destroyed the Lives of our People."

All the tree huggers believe this.

And lastly:

". . . has excited domestic Insurrections amongst us."

In Watts, Bensonhurst, that Mohawk reservation in upstate New York, and my house since I married into a family full of Democrats.

American Civics calls the Declaration of Independence a "living document." All too true.

The Constitution is an equally forthright piece of work and quite succinct—twenty-one pages (in the *American Civics* E-Z-reader large-type version) giving the complete operating instructions for a nation of 250 million people. The manual for a Toyota Camry, which only seats five, is four times as long. And, thanks to the pro-growth economic policies of the vigorously libertarian—not to say completely impotent—Continental Congress, the Constitution is not translated from Japanese.

An hour's perusal of our national charter makes it hard to understand what the argle-bargle is about. The First Amendment forbids any law "abridging the freedom of speech." It doesn't say, "except for commercials on children's television" or "unless somebody says 'cunt' in a rap song or 'chick' on a college campus."

The Second Amendment states that "the right of the people to keep and bear arms, shall not be infringed," period. There is no mention of magazine size, rate of fire, or to what extent these arms may resemble assault rifles. All rifles were assault rifles in those days. Furthermore, if the gun laws that Massachusetts has now had been in force in 1776, we'd all be Canadians, and you know what the weather in Canada is like.

There is no reference to abortion whatsoever in the Constitution, not so much as an "I'll pull out in time, Honey, honest." The Tenth Amendment tells us, "the powers not delegated to the United States by the Constitution, nor prohibited by it to the States, are reserved to the States respectively, or to the people." This means the power to drive the nation crazy over a gob of meiotic cells that wouldn't fill a coke spoon and, on the other hand, the power to murder innocent babies that haven't even been born yet are—just as the amendment says—"reserved to the States respectively, or to the people."

The Constitution is not hard to understand. Although the quality of reasoning degenerates in the later amendments. The Sixteenth Amendment is particularly awful: "The Congress shall have the power to lay and collect taxes on incomes, from whatever source derived."

And Section 4 of the Fourteenth is very silly: "The validity of the public debt of the United States, authorized by law . . . shall not be questioned."

The Twenty-sixth Amendment, giving the vote to eighteen-year-olds, must have been drafted by people who'd never met any eighteen-year-olds or, worse, by people who were eighteen.

And then there is the—from a male point of view—tactically foolish Nineteenth Amendment: "The right of citizens of the United States to vote shall not be denied or abridged by the United States or any State on account of sex."

This made women stop protesting a trivial wrong to their gender—exclusion from the electoral process—and allowed them to focus their indignation on more serious forms of injustice, such as the fact that women suffer discrimination and harassment in the workplace, are paid less than men, are rarely promoted to the highest levels of corporate or professional responsibility, and this year's hemlines make their legs look fat.

There are also a few gimmicks and dodges in the Constitution, such as Section 4 of the presidential disability and succession amendment, which says that the vice president "and a majority of either the principal officers of the executive departments *or of such other body as Congress may by law provide*" (italics my own) can declare the president incompetent. If I'm reading this right, it means that with the help of pals in the House and Senate, Dan Quayle and the principal officers of the Fort Wayne, Indiana, Elks Club can send George Bush to the bughouse and declare a national golf emergency.

But, on the whole, the text is easily glossed. The single exception being Article Two, Section 1: "The electors shall . . . vote by ballot for two persons . . . The person having the greatest number of votes shall be the President . . . and if there be more than one who have such majority, and have an equal number of votes, then the House of Representatives shall immediately choose by ballot one of them."

This was later modified by the rather more confusing Twelfth Amendment: "The person having the greatest number of votes for President, shall be the President, if such number be a majority of the whole number of Electors appointed; and if no person have such majority, then from the persons having the highest numbers not exceeding three on the list of those voted for as President, the House of Representatives shall choose immediately, by ballot, the President."

The idea seems to be to make the election of a president so complicated and annoying that no one with an important job or a serious avocation—that is, no one presently making any substantial contribution to society—would be tempted to run for the office. So far, it's worked.

Otherwise, only one important question is raised by the Constitution, a question implicit in its preamble.

"We the people of the United States, in order to form a more perfect Union, establish justice, insure domestic tranquility, provide for the common defense, promote the general welfare, and secure the blessings of liberty to ourselves and our posterity . . ."

The question being, "Are we done yet?"

The first objective was achieved in 1865 when we squashed the rednecks. The result was a definitely more perfect union. Compare it, for example, with the Union of Soviet Socialist Republics or the AFL-CIO. We've established about as much justice as the country can stand—maybe more. (Perfect justice being a thing none of us would care to confront.) Domestic tranquility we don't have, but how we'd get any without violating every clause of this document that is supposed to ensure it I can't imagine. The common defense is so well provided for that even such uncommon things as Saudi Arabians are defended by it. In the matter of promoting the general welfare, we have—to judge by the welfare rolls—done it too well. The blessings of liberty are so manifestly secured to ourselves that we seem weighed down by the things, and lately are attending AA meetings, joining strict religious cults, and formulating personal diet and exercise regimens to ease the burden. And, as for posterity, that's why birth control was invented.

So when can we quit passing laws and raising taxes? When can we say of our political system, "Stick a fork in it, it's done"? When will our officers, officials, and magistrates realize their jobs are finished and return, like Cincinnatus, to the plow or, as it were, to the law practice or the car dealership? The mystery of government is not how Washington works but how to make it stop.

The Winners Go to Washington, D.C.

I, embarking on my attempt to make government comprehensible, and the Bush administration, embarking on its attempt to make government, arrived in Washington at about the same time in early 1989.

Many reporters, when they go to work in the nation's capital, begin thinking of themselves as participants in the political process instead of as glorified stenographers. Washington journalists are seduced by their proximity to power, and that was me. Power had my lipstick smeared and was toying with my corset hooks before I even got off the Trump Shuttle.

Newsmen believe that news is a tacitly acknowledged fourth branch of the federal system. This is why most news about government sounds as if it were federally mandated—serious, bulky, and blandly worthwhile like a high-fiber diet set in type.

All of Washington conspires to make reporters feel important—a savvy thing to do to people who majored in journalism because the TV repair schools advertised on matchbook covers were too hard to get into. The U.S. government, more than any other organization on earth, takes pains to provide journalists with "access" to make the laptop Saint-Simons feel that they are "present at the making of history." Of course, the same high honor can be had by going around to the back of any animal and "being present at the making of earth."

If you can get accreditation to the Congressional Press Galleries—which, when you're employed by a "major news outlet," is about as difficult as falling asleep in a congressional hearing—you receive a photo ID tag to wear on a chain around your neck. Everybody who's anybody in Washington wears some kind of ID tag on a chain around his neck, so that the place looks like the City of Lost Dogs. I wore mine everywhere until one day in the shower, when I had shampoo in my eyes, the chain caught on the soap dish and I was nearly strangled by my own identity. This happens a lot to members of the Washington press corps.

Within days of getting to Washington I began to write pieces featuring all the access I had and frequently mentioning that real political figures, some of them so important you'd actually heard their names, spoke directly to me in person. Thus, readers were left with an indelible sense of "A politician talked to him? What the hell else does a politician ever do to you except take your money?" I even got a part-time slot on one of those public affairs TV shows that air at 6:00 a.m. on Sunday mornings. It was a sort of farm-team *McLaughlin Group,* but it gave me a chance to say things like "Washington journalists are seduced by their proximity to power."

Washington is a fine place for journalists to live as well as to brownnose. It has plenty of the only kind of people who can stand journalists—other journalists—and plenty of the only kind of people journalists get any real information from—other journalists. It is, like most journalists themselves, not very big (Washington is smaller than Memphis, Tennessee) and not as sophisticated as it thinks. And it's pretty. Washington has lots of those Greek- and Roman-style buildings that practically make you feel like a senator just walking up the steps of them. Senators, in particular, are fond of this feeling, and this is one reason official Washington escaped the worst effects of modern architecture. That plus the fact that steel and glass skyscrapers are relatively cheap to build, and cost effectiveness is not a concept here. As Article One, Section 9, paragraph 7, of the U.S. Constitution says, "No money shall be drawn from the Treasury, but in consequence of appropriations made by law." So it's obvious what the whole point of lawmaking is.

But Washington, though it costs taxpayers a fortune, is itself inexpensive —at least compared to New York or Los Angeles. In Washington journalists can afford to live almost as well as people who work for a living. Those stories about crack wars and the "murder capital of America" are nonsense, of course—as long as you stay in the part of Washington that concerns itself with real wars and being the regular capital. This is the part that extends northwest along Connecticut, Massachusetts, and Wisconsin avenues from the tourist attractions on the Mall to the Maryland suburbs—the "white pipeline." People do occasionally venture outside this zone, people who come in to do your cleaning or mow the lawn.

Numerous demonstrations, marches, PR stunts, and other staged events are held in Washington to give journalists an excuse for not covering real events, which are much harder to explain. Barely a weekend passes without some group of people parading in the capital to protest the piteous condition of those inevitable victims of injustice, themselves.

One Saturday it's opponents of abortion dragging little children along to show they hadn't been killed. The next Saturday it's advocates of abortion dragging little children along to show they'd been born on purpose. The homeless come and make themselves at home around the Washington Monument. The Vietnam veterans are veteran gatherers at the Vietnam Veterans Memorial. Earth Day organizers litter the streets with posters and pamphlets calling for trash to be recycled. The AIDS Memorial Quilt is unfolded, and the Cancer Sampler and Car-Wreck Duvet are probably coming soon.

For the people in government—rather than the journalists who pester it—Washington is an early-rising, hardworking city. It is a popular delusion that the government wastes vast amounts of money through inefficiency and sloth. Enormous effort and elaborate planning are required to waste this much money. At 10:30 on weekday nights Washington bars and restaurants are as empty as synagogues in Iraq. I have never gotten up so early in Washington—or stayed up so late—that somebody wasn't already awake and jogging by beneath my apartment window. On my first full day in Washington I saw an astonishingly beautiful young woman, slim, doe-eyed, and still dewy from a hinterland childhood, the kind of girl who would be streaking like a Tomahawk cruise missile through the New York fashion-model and dance-club world. She was reading *Defense News* on the Metro at 7:45 a.m.

People in government jobs, especially political appointees and high-level bureaucrats, are customarily at their desks by eight in the morning and are still there at six at night. They return calls, are courteous over the phone, prompt in their appointments, and helpful to the point of obsequiousness.

Government people work so hard for the curious reason that their output can't be measured. There are plenty of ways to determine bad government, but good government is hard to quantify. How can streets be too clean or crime rates too low? A poverty threshold is easy to establish, but nobody's ever too rich. The casualties of war are simpler to count than the augmentations of peace. And that's why government employees work so hard—since output can't be measured, input has to be.

People in government are also a cheerful and indefatigably optimistic bunch. At first I was mystified. Government work would seem to be a run in a hamster wheel. Government can do nothing, at least nothing right. For instance, the deficit is terrible, but lower spending will hurt the poor, and higher taxes will lead to a recession causing more people to become poor and get hurt by the lower spending needed to bring taxes down to end the recession, and so on. But since government rarely succeeds, it hardly ever fails. And government programs aren't necessarily designed to go anywhere. Like the joggers beneath my window, who are the people who run those programs, they just go. The results—sweat, ruined knees, America as a second-rate world power—don't matter. It's the effort that makes the action worthy. Frank Lavin, who was the director of the Office of Political Affairs in the Reagan White House (notice my access), told me, "People who believe in government regulation and intervention in life—for them government is a church." And people who are truly committed to government exhibit the same dull self-satisfaction and slightly vapid peace of mind as do devout churchgoers. They also know their business is never going to be bought by Sony.

Washington's optimistic enthusiasm, dreadfully wholesome energy, and overabundance of media types are never more evident than when a fresh batch of optimistic enthusiasts and wholesomely energetic dreadfuls is sucked into town by a new presidential administration and all the media types rush there to meet them.

This was particularly true in the case of George Bush. Usually journalists suffer a brief, syrupy infatuation with an incoming chief executive. But everybody had such a crush on George that you began to wonder if the *New York Times* editorial board wasn't maybe driving by George's house in the middle of the night and pining out the car window or sneaking into the Kennebunkport Yacht Club to leave anonymous poems in his locker.

First the jerk disappeared—the tall schmo with the nasal lockjaw, the one who was running for president but nobody could figure out why because he kept getting his tongue in a clove hitch and calling every whatchamajigger a "thing." He vanished without a trace. You'll remember that until the beginning of January 1989 George Bush was a skinny, inconsequential doofus, an intellectual smurf and moral no-show who'd wound up in the White House by default. Then one day I saw in the newspapers that the president-elect was a seasoned Washington professional, a man who knew where all the levers and pedals and remote-control channel changers of government were located, plus he was a symbol of unity and strength reaching out to Americans of every hue, stripe, and polka-dot pattern and gathering us together in an immense bipartisan hug, cuddle, and smooch.

Next George was applauded like an Academy Award–winning actor with cancer for his proposed cabinet appointments. (This being before the U.S. Senate decided that former senator John Tower was too drunk and silly to be secretary of defense but not quite drunk and silly enough to be a senator again.) In fact, only two of Bush's nominees were other than mundane. There was William Bennett, who had been so much fun as Reagan's secretary of education. You had to love a man who'd made that many schoolteachers mad. Bennett always seemed about to say, "Anybody who doesn't know what's wrong with America's schools never screwed an el-ed major." However, now Bennett was to be "drug czar." Would his scholastic background help? Would he make dead crack addicts stay after life and write, "I will not be killed by rival gangs of drug dealers" one hundred times on the blackboard? Then there was Jack Kemp, the proposed secretary of Housing and Urban Development. But was it a bold stroke or a mean prank to make the only real conservative in the crowd go down to the ghetto and explain the Laffer curve?

Anyway, for the moment, the media were treating Bush's cabinet picks as if they were the nine worthies, the three wise men, and two surefire ways to lose weight without dieting. And this was nothing compared with what had happened to Barbara Bush: apotheosis. Now, Barbara Bush was reputed, on good authority, to be a nice woman, warmhearted, funny, sensible, and all the things we usually say about our mothers when they're listening. But it wasn't as though she'd actually done anything or even said much. Barbara Bush, it seemed, was elevated to secular sainthood strictly on the basis of gray hair and a plump figure. And such is the remarkable speed of fashion in Washington that, within hours of the swearing in, snowy bouffants and comfortable tummies appeared everywhere among the politically chic. A few extra pounds were spilling over the waistband of my own boxer shorts.

Even the Dan Quayle market was—very temporarily—up. This is the fellow who was supposed to answer the question once and for all "Can a person be too dumb for government?" But in February 1989 columnists and commentators were mumbling about what a hardworking senator Dan had always been. The *Wall Street Journal* went so far as to call him "an avid reader . . . not just of newspaper clips or an occasional magazine piece, but of real live books." Quick to note a vogue in toadying, the *New Republic* offered a Quayle Revisionism Award, only to have readers write in suggesting the prize be given to the *New Republic*'s own senior editor, Morton Kondracke, for saying Dan Quayle was "well-informed, intelligent, candid and engaging."

There was a giddiness in the District of Columbia during inauguration week, and not just among Republicans dizzy from victory and cheap, warm domestic Inaugural Ball champagne. Liberals were sidling up to each other and confessing profound relief that Puckermug Micky Dukakis was back in Boston with a huge, poorly balanced Massachusetts state budget about to fall on his head. Garry Trudeau had run out of punch lines for his *Doonesbury* comic strip and was stuck with an "invisible George" joke, about a president so hopelessly visible that he seemed to show up everyplace except *The Oprah Winfrey Show*. Jesse Jackson and George Bush looked to be on the verge of starting their own two-man Operation PUSH chapter. Jackson said Bush's inaugural speech "set exactly the right tone." And the *Tehran Times*—this is true—welcomed George Bush to the White House and opined that he'd "acted wisely" at the onset of his administration.

On inauguration day anti-Bush demonstrators were thin on the ground. A smattering of ERA signs were held aloft along the parade route. A few devoted peace buffs were camped across from the White House in an anti-nuke vigil that they'd vowed to continue until the world didn't blow up. The homeless were nowhere to be seen. I suppose the police had told them to go home. The *Washington Post* devoted only fifteen column inches to "alternative" celebrations in its special Saturday inauguration section. And I saw just one protester outside an Inaugural Ball, a lonely flake in pigtail and knapsack with a message about the Super Bowl hand-lettered on notebook paper: "If Joe Montana Passes Like Dan Quayle Speaks, the Bengals Will Win." (They didn't.) The *liberal* liberals, the serious hemorrhaging valentines, the real giveaway-and-guilt bunch, had disappeared into the same black hole as the jokes about Barbara looking like George's mother. Alas, the pinkos—they'd lost to the guy who lost to George. They weren't even ranked anymore.

Of course, in those bastions of GOPery, where you'd expect the welkin to ring, there were rung welkins all over the place. At a Republican National Committee staff party at the Grand Hyatt, the crowd was young, integrated, drunk, loud, and seemed to have lost its copy of "The How to Act Like a Republican Manual." A large can of men's hair-styling gel had been discovered in the hotel suite's bathroom, and people were being tackled at random. "Mousse him! Mousse him!" went the cry. Someone would go down in a pile-on and emerge with improbable hair spikes projecting above pin-striped suit jacket.

A clean-cut person in his middle fifties with very good posture walked in. "It's the general!" yelled the RNC staff. "Hey, General! Hi ya doin', General?! MOUSSE HIM!!!" He came out looking pretty good, too. Later I remember somebody, possibly me, weaving down the hotel hall with a large cigar in one hand and a larger drink in the other, shouting, "We had all the money! Then we won all the votes! Now we've got all the fun!" while his wife kicked him and threatened to call security.

It had been a long while since there was this much good cheer and auld lang syne at a presidential inauguration. You'd have to go back to 1961, when Jackie was a tomato and Jack was giving the world a nudge and a wink, and the New Frontier stretched before us full of challenge, potential, and shoving people into swimming pools. (Although it's instructive to remember what happened in the late sixties and early seventies when we reached the unexplored regions of that New Frontier—war, drugs, STDs, disco music, and about a billion ruined marriages.)

George Bush looked like he'd be a cozy president, old shoe, *gemütlichkeit*. This wasn't the same as having a smug little wiseacre or a big Hollywood movie star in the White House. The first word of George Bush's inaugural address was *hey*. (That is, of course, after he'd said "Thank you, ladies and gentlemen," because this is a president who minds his manners.) "Hey, Jack, Danny," said George, looking around at Congressmen Jack Brooks and Dan Rostenkowski as though he'd just stepped up to the podium at a Monday Rotary lunch. "Mr. Chief Justice, Mr. President, Vice President Quayle, Senator Mitchell," George continued, "Speaker Wright, Senator Dole, Congressman Michel, fellow citizens, neighbors, friends . . ." For a moment it seemed as though the president might just keep on greeting people for hours, like a little kid trying to include everybody in the God-bless section of his bedtime prayers: ". . . colleagues, compatriots, associates, acquaintances, distant cousins, people who graduated from high school about the same time I did . . ." But he stopped himself, gave the world a goofy smile, and delivered a speech we'd all heard a hundred times before but never from a president of the United States. It was a speech we'd all heard a hundred times from our dads.

> *This country has a meaning beyond what we can see . . . our strength is a force for good . . . We are not the sum of our possessions. They are not the measure of our lives... We have more will than wallet; but will is what we need . . . The final lesson of Vietnam is that no great nation can long afford to be sundered by a memory . . . A president is neither prince nor pope, and I do not seek "a window on men's souls." In fact I yearn for a greater tolerance, an easygoingness about each other's attitudes and way of life.*

Most dads don't have Peggy Noonan speech writing for them, so their phrases aren't so orotund and rhetorically balanced, but it's the same lecture in the den.

> *You should thank your lucky stars you were born in the United States of America. Money isn't everything. Hard work never killed anybody. Family is family so quit picking on your little brother. And I can't follow you around for the rest of your life keeping you out of trouble, so use your common sense and don't do anything stupid—it would break your mother's heart.*

Then the Reagans blew out of town. The herds of anchorfolk covering this on TV did their best to make the departure damp-eyed, but you could practically hear the nationwide sigh of relief. They are really lovely, lovely people, the Reagans, and we enjoyed their stay, we really did, but, well, you know . . . They *have* been here quite a while, and they're frankly not getting any younger. And they're a bit—let's be truthful—la-di-da, especially her. When you come right down to it, it's great to have them out of the way so we can spend Sundays padding around in our bathrobes with the funny papers all over the place and can leave the TV on during dinner if we want.

Which is apparently what the Bushes were doing. Twenty-eight members of the Bush family spent the first night of the Bush presidency at the White House. "You kids cut that out! Go to sleep this minute! No pillow fighting in the Green Room, you'll break the gosh-darned antiques!"

During the inaugural parade Bush kept darting in and out of his limousine, and the crowd reacted as if he were the early Beatles. These pop-outs were much better received than the Jimmy Carter business of walking the whole parade route. We Americans like our populism in small doses and preferably from an elitist. A Democrat populist might mean what he says and take our new Toro away because a family down the street can't afford the self-starting kind with the de-thatching attachment. A Republican populist is only going to indulge in the popular types of populism and will then get back in his Cadillac and behave.

Dan Quayle stayed in his Cadillac entirely and broadcast cheery greetings to the parade viewers over the car's built-in PA system: "Section A . . . stand 21, how are you? Hello, Section B." (These are actual quotes.)

It was worth going to the Inaugural Balls on Friday night just to see hundreds of newspaper reporters in bad tuxedos and mortal pain from rented dress shoes. I went to two of the things, which is about all a non-elected human being can bear. Ball procedure consists of standing around chatting amicably in itchy clothes if you're a man or, if you're a woman, standing around chatting amicably in clothes that parts of you are about to squeeze out of. You can't drink because the bar is two hundred fifty thousand Republicans away from where you are. And you can't dance because the music is being played by marines on sousaphones. This must be what entertainment was like in the nineteenth century, before fun was invented.

The Young Americans Ball at the J. W. Marriott Hotel was particularly crowded, and the Young Americans were horribly well behaved. I'd bet most of them weren't even on drugs. This may be just as well. What kind of hallucinations would these clean-cut juveniles have? "Oh, man, I was staring at these clouds, and they looked just like falling bond yields." Though I'm a conservative myself, I worry about the larval Republicans. They should act up now and get it over with, otherwise misbehavior may come upon them suddenly in middle age, the way it came upon the protagonist of Thomas Mann's *Death in Venice* and, also, Gary Hart.

The Maine and Indiana Ball at Union Station was better, full of the most reassuring kind of grown-ups, who looked like grown-ups used to look thirty years ago—happy, prosperous, solid, sensible, a little boring, and not about to turn up in a Bret Easton Ellis novel. It was worth hundreds of hours of psychoanalysis and a prescription for Valium just to walk around among their merry, placid faces and ample cummerbunds.

Dan Quayle arrived at Union Station about 10:30 wearing a smile that said—as only an open, honest, corn-fed Midwestern smile can say—"Fuck you." Who can blame him? There was terrific press bias against Quayle during the election because most journalists worked harder at college than Dan did and all it got them was jobs as journalists. Marilyn Quayle was there, too, looking—it was indeed a strange week in Washington—great. She had her hair done up in something my wife said was a chignon, and whatever it was, it made Marilyn look considerably less like a Cape buffalo than usual. Though actually I admired the Cape buffalo look. I have an idea that—like the Cape buffalo—if Marilyn Quayle gets furious and charges, you've got only one shot at the skull. You wouldn't want to just wound her.

The next night the president's campaign manager, the supposedly cold-blooded Lee Atwater, staged an immense rhythm-and-blues concert at the Washington Convention Center auditorium. This was more or less Atwater's first official act as the new Republican National Committee chairman—inviting Sam Moore, Percy Sledge, Bo Diddley, Albert Collins, Joe Cocker, Ron Wood, Willie Dixon, Etta James, Dr. John, Stevie Ray Vaughan, Delbert McClinton, Billy Preston, and about a dozen other blues musicians to entertain, of all things, the GOP faithful.

I'd like to travel back in time to January 1969, when Richard Nixon was being inaugurated, and Pigasus, the four-footed Yippie candidate, was being inaugurated, too, and the country was a mess, and so was my off-campus apartment. And I'd like to tell the self that I was then: "Twenty years from today you will watch the chairman of the Republican National Committee boogie down on electric guitar. And he's going to duck walk and do the splits and flip over backward and sing "High Heel Sneakers" at the top of his lungs. And when he gets finished, the president of the United States—a Republican president—is going to be pulled up on stage by Sam Moore of Sam and Dave and presented with an electric guitar with THE PREZ painted on the front. And the president of the United States and the chairman of the RNC are going to trade blues licks in front of a crowd of eighty-five hundred big squares in a deep groove."

I'd like to know what I would have thought, that is, after I got over the shock of seeing myself come back from the future so jowly and with an ROTC haircut.

Anyway, the concert sounded like Jesse Jackson had been elected, except the music was better. Jackson would have felt compelled to have boring Sting there and some Suzanne Vega and Tracy Chapman depressive types and dreary Rainbow Coalition stuff, too, probably featuring "Hava Nagilah" played by a marimba band. The Republicans were under no such constraints.

When President Bush entered the auditorium, no one played "Hail to the Chief." Instead, the 1967 Bar-Keys instrumental "Soul Finger" had been chosen as the presidential theme. Bush walked, as he'd have to for at least the next four years, inside a hollow square of stiff-necked fellows with long-distance looks and pistols in their armpits. But within the Secret Service phalanx you could see one bright, white head swaying and nodding to the beat. Barbara Bush didn't sit down all night.

Atwater, whose health problems were still a year away, proved to be an excellent guitar player and a, well, very enthusiastic vocalist. The evening's master of ceremonies, the president's son Marvin, bellowed into a microphone: "They call Frank Sinatra the chairman of the board, but they call Lee Atwater THE CHAIRMAN OF THE REPUBLICAN NATIONAL COMMITTEE!!!"

"I taught Lee everything he knows about that kind of dancing," said George Bush. "I know when to shut up and when to say something," continued Bush, "And this is a time to shut up." Though he didn't quite. He wanted to talk about how he'd thrown the White House—the "People's House" he insisted on calling it—open to the public that morning and how, even after these people had been waiting outside in the cold for what must have seemed like forever, they didn't complain. They looked around in awe "just like me and Barbara."

"We've got a little present for you," said Sam Moore.

"Dancing lessons, I hope," said the president half under his breath. And there was a smile of real pleasure when he saw the guitar. It almost looked as though "THE PREZ" knew how to play it.

And then the music began again. All across the auditorium thousands of Republicans were coming out of their tuxedo jackets. The convention center was wall-to-wall in a pattern of jiggling suspenders over soaking-wet dress shirts, like a huge attack of extra Y chromosomes. Did they have rhythm? No. But this is America. You can achieve anything in America. Republicans might even achieve a little soul.

We'd had eight years of talk about patriotism and family values from a man who saw less combat in the service than I saw as a hippie and whose children spent his whole administration exiled to the *Good Morning, America* gulag. Now there was an actual household in the White House, one where Dad really was a war hero.

Our country was all smiles and handshakes with the USSR. The first faint blush of political freedom was visible in Eastern Europe. Wars were petering out in Afghanistan and Angola. Central America was idling in neutral. The economy was OK. It seemed to be a genuinely promising moment in the history of the nation, a moment for—as Dr. Johnson said about second marriages—"the triumph of hope over experience."

Agricultural Policy: How to Tell Your Ass from This Particular Hole in the Ground

The federal government began formulating agricultural policy in 1794, when the residents of western Pennsylvania started the Whiskey Rebellion in response to an excise tax on corn liquor. The agricultural policy formulated in 1794 was to shoot farmers. In this case, the federal government may have had it right the first time.

Like most Americans nowadays, my experience with agriculture is pretty much limited to marijuana plants under a grow light in the closet of my off-campus apartment. I did, however, once help artificially inseminate a cow.

I had this half-baked friend, a complete city slicker, who—out of the blue—decides he's going to raise cattle. So he buys a farm and he buys some cows. And I'm up visiting him when it's time for the cows to get in a family way.

Now this is not done like I might have thought, with a cow and a bull in a heart-shaped stall and some Barry White tape cassettes. It turns out breeding cattle is like teenage pregnancy but more so. Not only isn't the bull around to help raise the calf, he's not even there to get the cow knocked up.

What happens instead is there's this liquid nitrogen thermos bottle full of frozen bull semen. (Let's not even *think* about how they get that.) And there's this device that looks like a giant hypodermic needle . . .

Anyway, my friend got this real farmer, Pete, to come in and actually do the honors.

So, while I'm holding the cow's head and my friend is holding the cow's middle, Pete takes this freezing cold syringe thing and inserts it into a very personal and private place of the cow's.

Then what Pete does is he sticks his arm into an even more personal and private place of the cow's—all the way up to the elbow.

Now, Pete does this not to make a pornographic beastiality video, but so that he can feel the tip of the inseminator tube through the cow's intestine wall and guide that tip into the cow's uterus.

It was a pretty gruesome thing to watch and, since I was up at the cow's other end, I'm glad to say I *didn't* watch it.

But I'll tell you one thing—I will *never* forget the look on that cow's face.

It was the same look that I got on *my* face—for the same reason—when I read the 1990 omnibus farm bill.

Every five years or so the U.S. Congress votes on a package of agricultural legislation that does to the taxpayer what Pete did to the cow.

The last farm bill cost American taxpayers over $100 billion in direct out-of-our-paycheck-into-the-feed-bag costs and another $50 billion in higher prices we paid at the supermarket. This was the Food Security Act of 1985. "Yes, officer, the stereo, the TV, and the coin collection are gone but, thank God, the refrigerator wasn't raided."

The new farm bill will only cost about $50 billion, although there's no telling what any farm bill is really going to cost. The 1981 farm bill was budgeted at $12 billion and ended up costing $60 billion, and the 1985 bill was supposed to represent a substantial cut in 1981 allocations.

You see, if the weather's bad and we have lots of droughts and freezes, we'll have to give disaster aid and crop-insurance payments to farmers, and the farm bill will end up costing us more. On the other hand, if the weather's good and we have plentiful harvests, we'll have to buy up surplus commodities and pay farmers to cut down on planting, and the farm bill will end up costing us more. And if—God forbid—the weather is good some of the time and bad some of the time—if, in other words, the weather is *normal*—then we can all just start backing toward the barn door and mooing for frozen bull sperm.

But all this money goes to poor farmers laboring from sunup to sundown on millions and millions of farms across the nation, doesn't it?

No.

In the first place, there aren't millions and millions of farms in America. There are about two million if you use the very inclusive Bureau of Census definition of a farm as any place with $1,000 or more annual gross sales of farm products. My off-campus apartment closet would have qualified if the grow lights hadn't blown the fuse box. There are, in fact, only about 314,000 full-time commercial farms in the U.S. These are farms that have gross annual sales of over $100,000. These are also the only farms where farm income exceeds income from nonfarm sources, such as factory jobs, retirement benefits, or sticking up 7-Eleven stores.

Nor are farmers, in general, poor. Farm-family income has exceeded average family income in America for more than twenty-five years. And federal farm spending doesn't go to poor farmers, anyway. The largest farms in America, those with gross receipts of more than $500,000, receive 60 percent of all price-support money.

So what are our Department of Agriculture tax dollars buying for us? A Department of Agriculture. The USDA has 106,000 employees, one for every three full-time farms in the country.

These 106,000 people would be more useful to the farm economy if we sent them out to hoe weeds. But they can't go; they're too busy doing things like administering the Federal Wool and Mohair Program. According to the U.S. General Accounting Office report to Congress on the 1990 farm bill, "The government established a wool and mohair price-support program in 1954 . . . to encourage domestic wool production in the interest of national security." Really, it says that. I guess back in the fifties there was this military school of thought that held that in the event of a Soviet attack we could confuse and disorient the enemy by throwing blankets over their heads. Then, while they were punching each other in the dark and trying to figure out who turned the lights off, we'd have time to run into our missile silos and destroy Russia with ICBMs. From 1955 to 1980, $1.1 billion was spent on wool and mohair price supports, with 80 percent of that money going to a mere six thousand shepherds and (I guess) moherds. This is $146,400 per Bo Peep. And, let me tell you, she didn't lose those sheep. They're off at boarding school in Switzerland.

Then there's the U.S. Honey Program, instituted in 1952 to stabilize honey prices (you remember how the American economy was almost brought to its knees by wild swings in the price of honey) and to "maintain sufficient bee populations for pollinating food and fiber crops." The honey program spends $100 million a year on about twenty-one hundred beekeepers—more than $47,000 each. For that kind of money, hell, *I'll* go sit in the flowers and wiggle around and get pollen all over my butt.

James Bovard, policy analyst at the libertarian Cato Institute and author of the book *The Farm Fiasco,* notes that between 1985 and 1989 government spending on rice farms was equal to $1 million for every full-time rice farmer in America and that the annual subsidy for each American dairy cow is between $600 and $700—greater than the per capita income of half the world's population.

Walter Williams, an economics professor at George Mason University, points out that since 1985 federally mandated attempts to boost citrus prices have resulted in the destruction (or use as cattle feed) of three billion oranges and two billion lemons (which explains why we so rarely hear about a cow with scurvy).

And Congressman Dick Armey, in an article for *Policy Review* entitled "Moscow on the Mississippi: America's Soviet-Style Farm Policy," says the 1985 farm bill paid farmers *not* to farm sixty-one million acres—an area equal to Ohio, Indiana, and half of Illinois—and that the amount we've spent on farm subsidies in the past ten years is enough to have bought all the farms in thirty-three states.

"Moscow on the Mississippi" is an apt phrase. U.S. farm policy is coercive, collectivist, and centrally planned and has been since 1929, when that wild radical Herbert Hoover created the Federal Farm Board in an attempt to corner the commodities market and control farm prices.

The New Deal successor to the Federal Farm Board was the Commodity Credit Corporation, or CCC, one of the Roosevelt era's Goldilocks programs, so-called because it barged in on the taxpayer fifty years ago, and *it's still there.* The CCC is empowered by its 1933 charter to "undertake activities for the purpose of increasing production, stabilizing prices, and insuring adequate supplies; and to facilitate the efficient distribution of agricultural commodities." A more Brezhnevian set of instructions to a government agency is hard to imagine.

U.S. farm policy is, along with North Korea and the Stanford liberal arts faculty, one of the world's last outposts of anti–free market dogmatism. Congressman Kika de la Garza, who is the exasperatingly powerful chairman of the House Agriculture Committee, wrote in the Capitol Hill newsletter, *Roll Call,* that "most Americans believe the unique nature of agriculture—the lengthy production cycle, dependency on the weather, susceptibility to price swings, etc.—justifies a certain level of government involvement." But you can say the same thing about the unique nature of selling Mazda Miatas. Why isn't the government giving $50 billion to car dealerships?

A GAO report on federal dairy policies contains this sentence: "The federal government first developed dairy policies when low milk prices appeared to threaten the adequacy of the nation's milk supply." Which is insane. Everybody from wife-bartering savages to Michael Milken knows that low prices mean surplus, not shortage. Yet this statement appeared in a GAO report criticizing the federal dairy programs for *not* being "market oriented." Meanwhile, the dairy farmers themselves, through their lobbying organization, Dairymen, Inc., issue position papers that sound like extracts from Albanian newspaper editorials: "Dairymen enthusiastically supports a strong and flexible federal milk marketing order program. Such a program is essential for the maintenance of orderly marketing of milk in fluid and manufactured dairy product markets."

Thus, while America was fighting Commies all over the world, communism grew apace in our own back forty. American farm policy is exactly what, during the McCarthy era, people were jailed, fired, and blacklisted for advocating in this country—unless, of course, they were American farmers.

This being America, we haven't pursued Marxist goals with tanks, secret police, and gulag camps; we've used money. And the result has been a uniquely American totalitarian screw-up. Instead of terrible shortages, we've created gross overproduction. Instead of making people dirt poor, we've made them filthy rich.

As with anything that's had too much attention from the government, farm policy is a mess and a tangle, an immense dog's breakfast of programs, laws, and regulations. The farm policy briefing package prepared by the Library of Congress for U.S. senators and representatives begins with a "Glossary of Agricultural Terms" forty pages long.

But farm policy, although it's complex, can be explained. What it can't be is believed. No cheating spouse, no teen with a wrecked family car, no mayor of Washington, D.C., videotaped in flagrante delicto has ever come up with anything as far-fetched as U.S. farm policy.

To begin with, there is the concept of parity—the deep thought behind all of the USDA's price- and income-support measures. Parity is the idea that the price farm goods bring ought to be the same, now and forever, in inflation-adjusted dollars, as the price farm goods brought in the years 1910 through 1914. Parity was conceived in the twenties, when increased mechanization and better seeds and fertilizers were causing agricultural prices to fall. Farmers liked the fact that they could grow more stuff. But they didn't like the fact that other farmers could grow more stuff, too, and that all the stuff being grown was therefore less rare and valuable. The farmers wanted the calendar turned back to those golden pre–world war days, when—as they remembered it—a peck of wheat sold for a bushel of money, and every load of manure was pitched by a hayseed Vanderbilt.

The U.S. government is a sort of permanent frat pledge to every special interest in the nation—willing to undertake any task no matter how absurd or useless. So our government obliged the farmers, or tried to, and parity was born.

If we applied the logic of parity to automobiles instead of feed and grain, a typical economy car would cost forty grand; $43,987.50 is what a 1910 Nash Rambler cost in 1990 dollars. And for that you got a car with thirty-four horsepower, no heat, no A/C, no tape deck or radio, and no windows. If farm parity were a guiding principle of human existence, we'd not only have lousy, high-priced economy cars, we'd have a total lack of civilization. Cheap, plentiful food is the precondition for human advancement. When there isn't enough food, everybody has to spend all his time getting fed and nobody has a minute to invent law, architecture, or big clubs to hit cave bears on the head. Agriculture prices have been falling, relative to the prices of other goods and services, not since the 1920s, but since the Paleolithic age. And it's a good thing. Otherwise we wouldn't grow food, we'd *be* food.

The government has any number of ways of inflicting parity on taxpayers and food shoppers. For example, there's the "nonrecourse loan." This is a loan farmers can get from the government using their crop as collateral. But the government sets the value of that collateral not by the crop's price but by what the crop's price *ought to be* in a dream world full of parity and happy farmers. Say wheat is selling for $3.50 a bushel, but the USDA thinks farm life would be a more fulfilling experience if the price were $4. So the USDA sets the "nonrecourse loan rate" at four bucks, and farmers can get a loan of $4 for every bushel of wheat they've got lying around. Then if America happens to suffer a terrible outbreak of toast weevils and the price of wheat goes up to $10 a bushel, farmers can pay back their $4 loans, sell the wheat for $10, and bank the profits.

But if everybody in the United States suddenly goes on an all-meat diet and the price of wheat drops to fifteen cents, the farmers can blow off the loans, make the government eat the wheat, and not even get an ink smudge in their credit histories. It's an absolutely no-risk business transaction, like doing real estate deals with your dog. "Beach front? You don't want beach front, Fido. I've got some prime dumpside acreage, chicken bones and dead rats all over the place. I'll trade you straight up."

Or if a nonrecourse loan is too complicated for the farmer, the government has another program, called "loan-deficiency payments." In this program the government pays the farmer *not* to take a nonrecourse loan.

The "conservation reserve program" is almost as simple. The government gives annual payments to the farmer in return for the farmer removing highly erodible land from production—as if erosion weren't doing that already. A farmer on the conservation reserve program will doubtless want to be on the "acreage conservation program," too. That way the government will pay him up to $3,500 a year to practice soil conservation in general. This is like going into a Dairy Queen and giving the owner money to keep his ice cream freezers plugged in.

"Marketing orders" are used to keep farm prices high at the retail level. The growers of various commodities are encouraged to get together and fix the price for which their commodities will sell. In other industries there's a name for people who do this: felons. Some marketing orders are enforced by "marketing quotas." Growers decide how much growing each grower can do. If shoeshine boys tried this, you'd only get one loafer polished during shine-business slumps.

During the mid-1980s the dairy industry had its own plan to limit production, the "whole herd buyout." Dairy farmers decided there was too much cheap milk at the supermarket. Hell, even homeless welfare babies were drinking moo juice. So the government bought and slaughtered 1.6 million dairy cows. How come the government never does anything like this with lawyers?

Farm-product bargains are also eliminated by means of the "commodity import program." Our government gives foreign governments grants and loans to buy stuff grown in the U.S., stuff that would otherwise be a glut on the domestic market. I guess we should be thankful that similar programs have not been undertaken by the governments of Colombia, Bolivia, and Peru.

While some government programs are making farm products more expensive to buy, other programs are making farm products cheaper to produce. For example, farmers get cut-rate credit to the extent that the federal government now controls half of all farm debt. Farmers also get subsidized crop insurance. And, for those farmers who didn't feel like buying subsidized crop insurance but had a crop failure anyway, there are free disaster benefits.

This conflict between policies that send prices up and policies that drive prices down results in the need for a third category of policies that do nothing at all. These are the famous programs that give farmers money for not farming. In the "payment-in-kind program" the farmer is given the excess farm products that other farmers grew in return for not growing any of his own. In the "paid acreage diversion program" the more farming the farmer doesn't do, the more the government pays him. And in the best program of all, "0/92," the farmer does absolutely nothing and gets 92 percent of all the payments and benefits he could have possibly gotten from the largest crop he could have possibly grown. A USDA scheme like this gives every government agency something to shoot for. With 0/92 as an inspiration, Health and Human Services will probably dream up a way for us taxpayers to catch clap from whores without getting laid.

Just when you think the farm issue can't get sillier, here comes Willie Nelson pounding on the gut fiddle and adenoidaling away at Farm Aid. Yes, Willie and such thoroughly improbable acts as L. L. Cool J, Guns N' Roses, Iggy Pop, and Lou Reed (hey, there's a bunch of sheep in fishnet stockings out here, they've got drugs, and they say they're with the band) have raised a few more bucks for the farmers who just euchred Congress out of $50 billion.

There are farm families in need of charity, of course. But singling out farmers and getting all soggy-nosed and soak-eyed over their plight has less to do with facts than with romantic nostalgia for a pastoral ideal that never existed. Throughout history farm life has been brutish, dirty, and mostly stupid. Not that any of us would know. This country is so urbanized we think low-fat milk comes from cows on Nutri/System weight-loss plans.

According to the *Statistical Abstract of the United States,* about 1.3 million people in America define themselves as farmers. But there are 4.1 million secretaries. These secretaries are poorly paid, hold jobs that provide little satisfaction or chance for advancement, are frequently working mothers, and often the sole support of their families. Where's the "Lend a

Short Hand" concert for them? Where are the famous ode-yodelers singing "Momma Was a Hard-Typing Gal"? Why'd farmers get cinematic encomiums like *The River*, *Country*, and *Places in the Heart* while secretaries got nothing but *Nine to Five*?

Farming has always carried emotional freight. Thomas Jefferson, caught in a moment of rare idiocy arguing against the industrialization of the United States, said, "Those who labor in the earth are the chosen people of God . . . whose breasts He has made a peculiar deposit for substantial and genuine virtue." This, by the way, from a gentleman farmer who owned two hundred slaves and kept at least one of them as his mistress.

The farm lobby makes good use of such lofty forms of nonsense and, also, of less lofty forms of nonsense, such as congressmen. For instance, sugar growers donate about half a million dollars a year to congressional election campaigns, and the dairy industry donates $2 million. Even though only 46 out of 435 congressional districts are controlled by farm votes, farmers have gained heavy leverage on Capitol Hill by combining rhetoric, ready money, and a talent for political logrolling that dates back to the Constitutional Convention, when Southern farmers managed to get slaves counted as three-fifths of a voter without letting any slaves do three-fifths of the voting. As a result of this disproportionate influence, 25 percent of the net income U.S. farmers receive is in the form of direct cash payments from the government. The only other businessmen who put this kind of lip clamp on the public teat are defense contractors. And at least when we give billions to defense contractors, we get something back for it, Star Wars or something. Maybe we don't need Star Wars, maybe it doesn't work, but at least the defense contractors were thinking of us. They made, you know, a gesture. But we give billions to farmers and don't even get a basket of zucchini on the front porch.

Our that-ain't-hay farm policy is useless. Even Willie Nelson acknowledges that four hundred thousand small farms have gone out of business since he began giving his Farm Aid concerts, and I don't think we can blame all four hundred thousand on Willie's awful music. A 1988 Government Accounting Office report concluded that one quarter of the bankruptcies among Farmers Home Administration borrowers were the result not of any credit crunch, but of an excess of cheap, subsidized loans.

Agricultural economist Clifton B. Luttrel estimates than an old-fashioned money-vomiting Great Society–style welfare system to keep needy farmers in business would cost only $4 billion a year, less than half what current programs cost.

I went to see Pete, the dairy farmer who'd helped my friend get his cow pregnant. Pete's family has been dairy farming in New England all this century, and dairy farmers, as a group, have been on the receiving end of great federal largess—on the order of $6 billion to $7 billion a year. Pete, however, had just sold his cows and was subdividing his land to build vacation homes. I had a very short interview with Pete.

Me: As the result of price supports, product purchases, marketing orders, and other federal dairy programs, how much better off are local dairy farmers?
Pete: There are only two local dairy farmers left.
Me : Are they better off?
Pete: Nope.

U.S. farm policy, besides not doing what it's supposed to, does do what it isn't supposed to, and lots of it—the law of unintended consequences being one piece of legislation Congress always passes.

Many farm-program payments are doled out according to an "acreage base." This is the amount of land on a farm that's planted in a particular crop. In order to protect their acreage base and continue getting government payoffs, farmers are forced to practice "monocropping"—planting the same thing every year instead of rotating crops to replenish soil nutrients. Monocropping requires more chemical fertilizers, which pollute groundwater, and more pesticides and weed killers, which cause severe side effects, such as Meryl Streep appearing in front of congressional committees to complain about what's in her food.

The acreage-base system also discourages experimentation with new crops, such as canola (vegetable oil) and kenaf (paper pulp), both of which show enormous potential as dinnertime child disciplinary threats. ("No TV until you finish your kenaf.")

Other farm-program benefits, such as "deficiency payments," are paid on the basis of yield rather than acreage. The more you grow, the more you get paid. Yield-based deficiency payments for feed corn, combined with disaster payments based on yield projections, encourage farmers in drought areas to plant the highest yielding varieties of corn rather than the varieties that are most drought resistant. Meanwhile, wind erosion blows the top three inches of North Dakota into downtown Duluth.

Farm programs even make American foreign policy more screwed up than it is already—not an easy thing to do. The USDA sugar program spends a quarter of a million dollars per year per American sugar grower. This to keep the sugar industry healthy in a climate unsuited to producing sugar. These subsidies and the sugar-import quota that goes with them cost sugarcane-growing U.S. allies such as the Philippines more than $800 million a year in lost revenues. That's $319 million more than we pay the Philippines to rent our military bases there.

And while the USDA is spending $10 billion a year to increase farm income, the same government agency is spending $20 billion to make food affordable to poor people through the Food Stamp program. A moron, an imbecile, an American high school student can see there's something wrong with this equation. Just give the $10 billion to the poor people, and let them buy their own damn food from the farmers.

I spent two and a half years examining the American political process. All that time I was looking for a straightforward issue. But everything I investigated—election campaigns, the budget, lawmaking, the court system, bureaucracy, social policy—turned out to be more complicated than I had thought. There were always angles I hadn't considered, aspects I hadn't weighed, complexities I'd never dreamed of. Until I got to agriculture. Here at last is a simple problem with a simple solution. Drag the omnibus farm bill behind the barn and kill it with an axe.

At Home in the Parliament of Whores

Hundreds of miles from the ambitions and deceits of Washington there is a little town in New Hampshire where I live. This town is tucked under the arm of an impressive mountain and is surrounded by resplendent gauds of foliage in the autumn and wreathed in downy coverlets of snow all winter long. Delicate spires of colonial church steeples nick the cloud-chased New England sky, and a pellucid trout stream rolls and chuckles in the shadow of the old woolen mill, now a historical landmark. A mere fifty-one hundred souls make their home here. There's not a stoplight or a parking meter to be seen. The whole town could be a Norman Rockwell painting come to life if Norman Rockwell had been better at depicting towns that have convenience stores on half the street corners and are filled with pseudo–Cape Cod tract houses, each with a snowmobile for sale in its front yard.

Still, my little town—let's call it Blatherboro—is as decent a place as you will find in America. In 1989 the Blatherboro Police Department received twenty-nine reports of lost property. In the meantime, town residents turned fifty-nine items of lost property in to the police. The citizens of Blatherboro are decent to the point of defying arithmetic.

The citizens of Blatherboro are also employed. Virtually no one in the town is out of work or stays that way long. The town welfare officer, a very practical lady, has been known to come by people's houses early in the morning and *take* them job hunting. Only sixty-three Blatherboro households required any charity in 1989, and that charity was, as the word indicates, charity. The $21,000 that the town spent on public assistance was all supplied by private donations.

Blatherboro's residents are educated and sensible—literate enough to support three local weekly newspapers and sensitive enough to their neighbors' feelings to make sure that no very juicy news appears in any of the three. They are a calm, law-abiding lot. Shootings, stabbings, rapes, and so forth are unheard of in Blatherboro (though there is a certain amount of discreet wife beating and child abuse, especially during the midwinter doldrums). The last murder of any note took place in 1919 and is still discussed with indignation.

Blatherboro is a nice town, but not so nice as to be eerie. The people of Blatherboro are good people but not dreadfully good. Blatherboro is an uncommonly comfortable place for comfortably common people, like me, to live. It is an economy class Shangri-la.

The government of Blatherboro is as homey and reasonable as Blatherboro itself. There is a traditional New England town meeting held once a year. Here the business of democracy is disposed of in one sitting. And here I go to do my civic duty and help dispose of it.

There is nothing at all of a Rockwell painting to a real New England town meeting, and nothing of a Robert Frost poem either. "Whose woods these are I think I know . . ." Hah. Whose woods are whose everybody knows exactly, and everybody knows who got them rezoned for a shopping mall and who couldn't get the financing to begin construction and why it was he couldn't get it. And you'd hardly use our town meeting as a calendar photograph. It's held in the high school gym, a windowless space barely large enough for full-court basketball, redolent of damp socks and painted two-tone yellow in the two worst tones of yellow ever seen.

This political arena is filled with folding metal chairs of an ingeniously uncomfortable design. The front rows of the folding chairs are occupied by elderly know-it-alls in lime-green blazers—business executives who retired (much to the relief of their respective businesses, no doubt) and moved to Blatherboro to reside in their summer homes year-round. These former items of corporate deadwood spend most of their day basking in the warm glow of New Hampshire tax policy. (New Hampshire tax policy is to not have any taxes—there is no state or local income tax and no sales tax either.) And the rest of the time they devote to thinking up great ideas and swell notions for improving everything in Blatherboro, especially the efficiency of its government.

Sitting in the back rows of the folding chairs and standing around the gymnasium walls are the Blatherboro natives, ranging in type from deer-poaching swamp Yankees to frayed Emersonian Brahmins and including a large number of working-stiff French Canadians. The natives live in fear that the improvements in efficiency proposed by the blowhard retirees will send the one tax New Hampshire does have, the town property tax, soaring. This property tax keeps soaring anyway, despite the fact that every single person at the town meeting has a plan to reduce taxes.

The Blatherboro selectmen (who are the equivalent of city councilmen, except this isn't a city and there's no council) and the Blatherboro town manager sit at a folding table facing the earnest crowd, and the town moderator stands behind a podium and calls on people. Members of the local Boy Scout troop carry microphones to the orators in the audience, and a combination of bad PA system and typical gym acoustics produces a voice of the *populi* that is more *pox* than *vox*.

Despite the minimal nature of Blatherboro town government and, indeed, the minimal nature of Blatherboro, and despite the goodwill, good sense, and good New England parsimony of Blatherboro's residents, the result of the annual town meeting is always a stupid and expensive mess.

Much of the stupidity is common to all government. There are certain subjects about which people are incurable boneheads. Humans apparently cannot rationally consider what constitutes a danger to humanity or how likely any given danger is to occur. Thus, Blatherboro has fifteen police officers—the same ratio of police to population as New York City. The annual Blatherboro police budget is $425,000. This in a town that, in 1989, had 520 crimes, of which 155 were minor incidents of teenage vandalism. The cost of police protection against the remaining 365 more or less serious malefactions was $1,164 each—more than the damage caused by any of them.

On the other hand, almost everything in Blatherboro is built out of wood. Half the town is too rural to have fire hydrants, and a lot of the town is too cheap to have smoke detectors. Every home has a fireplace, most have woodstoves, and quite a few have wood-burning furnaces so that in March 1989, for example, there were three chimney fires in four days. But the Blatherboro Fire Department is a completely volunteer organization with an annual budget of less than $50,000.

People are also very stupid about what makes people smart. The local school system, which serves Blatherboro and the nearby town of Quaintford, isn't very bad. But it isn't any good either. The Blatherboro-Quaintford School District Annual Report expounds at length on "competency-based programs," "whole-language instruction," and "curriculum coordination" and devotes a dozen pages to discussing "budget objectives" and listing the various administrators, speech pathologists, special-education consultants, and so forth that are thought necessary to modern education. But nowhere does the annual report remark on the fact that the high school's ninth grade has 124 students, while the high school's tenth grade—whose denizens are of legal age to leave school—has 79. This is a 36 percent dropout rate, about the same as the dropout rate in most inner-city slums.

The Blatherboro-Quaintford schools have a total of only 1,488 students, kindergarten through twelfth grade, yet there is a complete school-district office with a staff of fifteen people, including a superintendent of schools, an assistant superintendent, and a business administrator. And there are an additional twenty-eight principals, assistant principals, counselors, aides, and other people who don't actually teach anything on the school-system payroll.

Blatherboro's annual per-student spending is over $5,000—almost three times the national average for state college tuitions. If Blatherboro's parents and taxpayers were as serious about education as they—and every other parent and taxpayer in America—always say they are, they could gather the youngsters into miniature academies of perhaps fifteen students each and hire $75,000-per-year private tutors to teach them. In the academic-infested groves of New England, $75,000 would hire a fine tutor. Alternatively, Blatherboro students could be packed off to the local Catholic schools, where they'd get a better education—and a good, sharp rap on the knuckles if they showed any need for counseling—for less than half the price.

City planning is also beyond Blatherboro's ken. The town has a Planning Board, a Board of Adjustment, a building inspector, a Conservation Commission, and a Historic District Commission, and the place still looks like hell. Of course, there are patches of twee and precious prerevolutionary beauty, as there are in all old New England towns. Sections of Blatherboro are so overrun with white clapboard and green shutters that if a man were to unzip his fly the Historic District Commission would probably make him put green shutters on either side of that too. But the rest of the place looks like every other piece of overpaved, cheap-jack, fake-front highway sprawl in the nation. I don't happen to mind this sprawl myself, at least not in theory, because in theory I'm a private-property strict constructionist. But I do mind all the boards and commissions and employees of the town wasting my money failing to prevent it.

Besides the ordinary and general kinds of idiocy, the Blatherboro Town Meeting also deals in some witlessness specific (but no doubt not unique) to Blatherboro.

The retired blowhards had gotten together with the Blatherboro elected officials, the members of the Chamber of Commerce, and all the other people in town whose method of torturing their neighbors is good citizenship and decided that the town offices were too small. Too small for what was not explained, though the selectmen gave an elaborate presentation, complete with slide show, detailing just how much too small. The proposed solution was to sell the snug and handsome little Town Hall that sits on the Blatherboro common and sell the Mayberry RFD storefront police department down the street and buy an empty factory building out on the east side of town and put everybody in there. This would cost $1.3 million but would, it was said, save the town money in the long term.

The Town Flake stood up to speak. He is an old and addled gentleman with hair in long, white tangles—WASP dreadlocks. He's been making a complete and utter pest of himself at town meetings for over thirty years. He owns his own mimeograph machine and runs off reams of smudgy philippics accusing town government of incompetence and waste. He knows all the regulations in *Robert's Rules of Order* and uses them until he has to be shushed by the moderator or shouted down by the townspeople. And he is always and invariably right on every issue. "Save money in the long term! Save money in the long term!" said the Town Flake with high scorn. "Government's always full of ideas to *save money in the long term*. Just why is it that government never has a single, solitary idea about saving money *now*?" The Town Flake was shushed by the moderator.

A very old lady wanted to know, if we were going to sell the town office, were we also going to sell the World War I monument on the common? It was patiently explained to her that monuments (or commons either) don't get sold. Whereupon another even older lady asked, if the town office got sold, did the World War I monument go with it? The question would come up twice again in the debate.

Someone else wanted to know why a factory couldn't go in the factory building—and provide jobs and pay taxes. To which the selectmen replied that the economy's a bit slow in New England these days, and no business is likely to buy the factory.

"Well, if no business is likely to buy the factory, who the heck is going to buy the Town Hall and the police station?" hollered the Town Flake.

The arguments continued for two hours. And these arguments were, in their effect, much more persuasive against democracy than for buying the factory or keeping the Town Hall. It is remarkable, on close inspection, what a lousy way to get things done democracy is. Not that democracy necessarily makes the wrong decisions. Private enterprise can do this with equal or greater ease. But in a democracy the decision-making process must be listened to. The great thing about the invisible hand of the market is not that it's invisible but that it's silent.

Buying a factory to put the town government in was at last voted down, 241 to 207.

Debate now moved to whether the town should spend $1.7 million to build a new water tank.

The Town Flake pointed out that one reason the tank would be so expensive is that the town intended to build it in a valley with pumps instead of on a hill with gravity. He was shushed by the moderator.

New Hampshire is—with the exception of tropical rain forests (which I hear won't be around much longer)—the wettest place on earth. When the snow melts in spring there's not a basement in the state that you can't launch a boat in. A summer day without rain is considered something to tell your grandchildren about. You cannot walk half a mile in a straight line anywhere in New Hampshire without drowning in a stream, lake, beaver pond, or somebody's flooded cellar. Yet the town of Blatherboro was running out of water. This was a stupidity beyond the range of local talents. Anything as astonishingly dumb as this must have the federal government involved in it somehow. And, indeed, it did. Congress had passed the Safe Drinking Water Act of 1982, which assumed that people in small towns were too far removed from Senate subcommittee hearings and presidential fact-finding commissions to know whether their drinking water was safe. Federal law now mandates that all water taken from surface sources in small towns everywhere must be filtered and chlorinated whether it needs to be or not.

So Blatherboro is obliged to build an entire new water system. The $1.7 million water tank is the first step in a three-phase construction program that will eventually cost the town $6.2 million. Never mind that that's enough money to drill a nice, new, clean, private artesian well for every household in town.

The only thing more depressing than democracy at work is democracy not allowed to. The debate on the water tank had just begun when the town's attorney pointed out that if Blatherboro didn't comply with federal water regulations, the town would be fined $25,000 per day. The water tank was approved by a grudging 251 to 108.

Next was an article "To authorize the Board of Selectmen . . . to apply for, accept and expend any and all Federal or State grants, gifts or funds that may become available during the ensuing year." This was passed overwhelmingly, as well it might have been, with loud shouts of "Aye!"

There followed an hour-long argument about whether to close a small section of the old Town Road. The blowhard retirees claimed that the road should be closed because the town natives liked to run their four-wheel-drive vehicles through there at all hours of the night, and the town natives argued that the road should be kept open because they liked to run their four-wheel-drive vehicles through there at all hours of the night. The natives won on a voice vote by being able to yell "Nay" louder with no teeth than the retirees could yell "Aye" with false ones. After that the $4 million town government operating budget was passed with no debate whatsoever, the reasoning being that the thing had already been debated at public Budget Committee hearings, although no one had attended them. There was one "Nay" from the Town Flake.

With these mundane matters out of the way, it was time for the gist of the town meeting, the big fight everybody was waiting for, the keen excitement and high drama of quarreling about sewers.

It really is impossible to overstate the tedium of government. As boring as civics classes were back in high school, they were a bacchanal compared with civics itself. The next six hours of the Blatherboro Town Meeting were devoted to bickering about whether the Department of Public Works should have exclusive authority to approve sewer-line hookups. Of course, I have used the words *quarrel, fight,* and even *bicker* in a strictly poetic sense. I doubt that in the course of the evening's long and brutal fray so much as a voice was raised except by the Town Flake, and then only to calling-the-dog level. A town meeting is tedious with that amazing and inexplicable tedium of a large number of people behaving themselves in public. It is the opposite of a mob or a riot, the flip side of human collective behavior. Taking part in a New England town meeting is like being a cell in a plant.

Nevertheless, there were very strong feelings about effluvia in Blatherboro. An article was proposed that, if passed, would require that a Special Town Meeting be convened to approve any expansion of the town sewer system costing more than $50,000. The idea was not to save money on sewers. User fees and hookup charges already reimburse the town for all sewer costs. The purpose of the proposal was, instead, to control growth. Every commercial, industrial, or housing development of any size would need to be approved by the town as a whole or wind up swimming in its own waste. Specifically, this article was aimed at stopping a golf course and condominium complex already under construction on the west side of town. The golf course developer had been punctilious in meeting the town's Planning Board, Board of Adjustment, Conservation Commission, and Historic District Commission requirements and in obeying all applicable state and federal laws. The golf course and condo complex owner had needed to obtain forty-seven permits from eleven different government agencies in order to start construction. But he had done so. An all-sewage Special Town Meeting was the last possible way to stop the plaid pants and spiked kiltie shoes.

As I mentioned before, I hold private property rights to be sacred—in theory. Which is like saying I'm rich—in Bulgaria. In theory we're all lots of things: good, kind, and, above all, consistent. I hold private property rights to be sacred in theory, but in practice I had thrown in with the anti–golf course faction.

To be fair, we weren't opposed to the golf course for any Pals-of-the-Animals, Eco-Stalinist reasons. Most of us play golf. We didn't have any cutesy-artsy objections to seeing trees cut down. It's a lot easier to shoot a deer on a 350-yard par-four fairway than it is in the deep woods. And we weren't opposed to growth itself—in theory. But the sad truth of local government, like the sad truth of national government, is that people are no longer an asset. Humans do not benefit the modern state. Total 1989 Blatherboro town expenditure—including the town's share of county government and school system costs—was $9.5 million, or about $1,860 per person. Almost all this money was raised through property taxes and automobile registration fees. A typical new family moving to Blatherboro, with a mom, dad, and two kids (for families still come in that configuration in New Hampshire), would be buying a town-house condominium with a tax-assessed value of $100,000. The current property tax rate on that condominium is $2,860 a year. If the new family owns two late-model cars, registration fees (which are based on the blue-book value of the automobile) would be about $340. Add in a few miscellaneous levies and charges, and the new family ends up contributing approximately $3,500 per annum to the Blatherboro town coffers. But that is almost $4,000 less than what the town will spend on these people. A family of four must own at least a quarter of a million dollars' worth of property to carry its own weight in the Blatherboro town budget.

Theory is important, sure, but it shouldn't get between a man and his wallet. You can't serve theory for dinner. People have a *theoretical* right to do what they want with their property, and people have a *theoretical* right to move into my town. *But* . . .

It was at this moment, in the middle of the Blatherboro sewer debate, that I achieved enlightenment about government. I had a dominion epiphany. I reached regime satori. The whole town meeting was suddenly illuminated by the pure, strong radiance of truth (a considerable improvement over the fluorescent tubes).

It wasn't mere disillusionment that I experienced. Government isn't a good way to solve problems; I already knew that. And I'd been to Washington and seen for myself that government is concerned mostly with self-perpetuation and is subject to fantastic ideas about its own capabilities. I understood that government is wasteful of the nation's resources, immune to common sense, and subject to pressure from every half-organized bouquet of assholes. I had observed, in person, government solemnity in debate of ridiculous issues and frivolity in execution of serious duties. I was fully aware that government is distrustful of and disrespectful toward average Americans while being easily gulled by Americans with money, influence, or fame. What I hadn't realized was *government is morally wrong*.

The whole idea of our government is this: if enough people get together and act in concert, they can take something and not pay for it. And here, in small-town New Hampshire, in this veritable world's capital of probity, we were about to commit just such a theft. If we could collect sufficient votes in favor of Special Town Meetings about sewers, we could make a golf course and condominium complex disappear for free. We were going to use our suffrage to steal a fellow citizen's property rights. We weren't even going to take the manly risk of holding him up at gunpoint.

Not that there's anything wrong with our limiting growth. If we Blatherboro residents don't want a golf course and condominium complex, we can go buy that land and not build them. Of course, to buy the land, we'd have to borrow money from the bank, and to pay the bank loan, we'd have to do something profitable with the land, something like . . . build a golf course and condominium complex. Well, at least that would be constructive. We would be adding something—if only golf—to the sum of civilization's accomplishments. Better to build a golf course right through the middle of Redwood National Park and condominiums on top of the Lincoln Memorial than to sit in council gorging on the liberties of others, gobbling their material substance, eating freedom.

What we were trying to do with our legislation in the Blatherboro Town Meeting was wanton, cheap, and greedy—a sluttish thing. This should come as no surprise. Authority has always attracted the lowest elements in the human race. All through history mankind has been bullied by scum. Those who lord it over their fellows and toss commands in every direction and would boss the grass in the meadow about which way to bend in the wind are the most depraved kind of prostitutes. They will submit to any indignity, perform any vile act, do anything to achieve power. The worst off-sloughings of the planet are the ingredients of sovereignty. Every government is a parliament of whores.

The trouble is, in a democracy, the whores are us.

GIVE WAR A CHANCE

(1992)

Like many men of my generation, I had an opportunity to give war a chance, and I promptly chickened out. I went to my draft physical in 1970 with a doctor's letter about my history of drug abuse. The letter was four and a half pages long with three and a half pages devoted to listing the drugs I'd abused. I was shunted into the office of an army psychiatrist who, at the end of a forty-five-minute interview with me, was pounding his desk and shouting, "You're fucked up! You don't belong in the army!" He was certainly right on the first count and possibly right on the second. Anyway, I didn't have to go. But that, of course, meant someone else had to go in my place. I would like to dedicate this book to him.

I hope you got back in one piece, fellow. I hope you were more use to your platoon mates than I would have been. I hope you're rich and happy now. And in 1971, when somebody punched me in the face for being a long-haired peace creep, I hope that was you.

The Death of Communism

Berlin, November 1989

Four days after the surprise-party opening of East Germany's borders people were still gathering at the Berlin Wall, smiling at each other, drinking champagne, and singing bits of old songs. There was no sign of the letdown with which every sublime experience is supposed to conclude. People kept coming back just to walk along the freshly useless ramparts. They came at all sorts of hours, at lunch, dawn, three in the morning. Every possible kind of person was on promenade in the narrow gutter beside the concrete eyesore: wide hausfraus, kids with lavender hair, New Age goofs, drunk war vets in wheelchairs, video-burdened tourists, Deadheads, extravagant gays, toughs become all well behaved, art students forgetting to look cool and bored, business tycoons gone loose and weepy, people so ordinary they defied description, and, of course, members of the East German proletariat staring in surprise—as they stared in surprise at everything—at this previously central fact of their existence.

Even West Berlin's radicals joined the swarms. West Berlin had the most dogmatic agitators this side of Peru's Shining Path, but that was before November 9. Near the restored Reichstag building I overheard a group of lefties amicably discussing nuclear strategy with a half dozen off-duty U.S. GIs.

"Ja, you see, tactical capability mit der cruise missiles after all vas not der Soviet primary concern . . ."

"Sure, man, but what about second-strike capability? Wow, if we hadn't had that . . ."

All in the past tense. A British yob, who certainly should have been off throttling Belgians at a football match, came up to me apropos of nothing and said, "I fucking 'ad to see this, right? I 'itched 'ere from London and got these chunks off the wall. You think I can't pay for the fucking ferry ride back with these? Right!"

At the Brandenburg Gate the East German border guards had shooed the weekend's noisy celebrators off the Wall. But the guards weren't carrying guns anymore and were beginning to acknowledge their audience and even ham it up a bit. Somebody offered a champagne bottle to a guard and he took a lively swig. Somebody else offered another bottle with a candle in it, and the guard set the candle on the Wall and used a plastic cup to make a shield around the flame.

The people in the crowd weren't yelling or demanding anything. They weren't waiting for anything to happen. They were present from sheer glee at being alive in this place at this time. They were there to experience the opposite of the existential anguish which has been the twentieth century's default mood. And they were happy with the big, important happiness that—the Declaration of Independence reminds us—is everybody's, even a Communist's, unalienable right to pursue.

The world's most infamous symbol of oppression had been rendered a tourist attraction overnight. Poland's political prisoners were now running its government. Bulgaria's leadership had been given the Order of the Boot. The Hungarian Communist Party wouldn't answer to its name. Three hundred thousand Czechs were tying a tin can to the Prague Politburo's tail. And the Union of Soviet Socialist Republics was looking disunified, unsoviet, and not as socialist as it used to. What did it mean? The Commies didn't seem to know. The Bush administration didn't either. And you can be certain that members of the news media did not have a clue. Ideology, politics, and journalism, which luxuriate in failure, are impotent in the face of hope and joy.

I had booked a hotel room in East Berlin. When I arrived at the West Berlin airport a taxi dispatcher said the border crossings were so busy that I'd better take the subway to the other side. The train was filled with both kinds of Berliners, and stepping through the car doors was like walking into a natural history museum diorama of Dawn Man and his modern descendants. The Easterners look like Pleistocene proto-Germans, as yet untouched by the edifying effects of Darwinian selection. West Germans are tall, pink, pert, and orthodontically corrected, with hands, teeth, and hair as clean as their clothes and clothes as sharp as their looks. Except for the fact that they all speak English pretty well, they're indistinguishable from Americans. East Germans seem to have been hunching over cave fires. They're short and thick with sallow, lardy fat, and they have Khrushchev warts. There's something about Marxism that brings out warts—the only kind of growth this economic system encourages.

As the train ran eastward, West Berliners kept getting off and East Berliners kept getting on until, passing under the Wall itself, I was completely surrounded by the poor buggers and all the strange purchases they'd made in the West. It was mostly common, trivial stuff, things the poorest people would have already in any free country—notebook paper, pliers and screwdrivers, cornflakes, and, especially, bananas. For all the meddling the

Communist bloc countries have done in banana republics, they never seem to be able to get their hands on any actual bananas.

The East Berliners had that glad but dazed look you see on Special Olympics participants when they're congratulated by congressmen. The man sitting next to me held a West German tabloid open to a photo of a healthy fraulein without her clothes. He had that picture fixed with a gaze to make stout Cortez on a peak in Darien into a blinking, purblind myope.

At the Friedrichstrasse station in East Berlin, passport examination was perfunctory and the customs inspection a wave of the hand. I walked outside into a scene of shocking, festive bustle. Though, to the uninitiated, I don't suppose it would look like much—just squat, gray crowds on featureless streets. But there are never crowds in East Berlin. And the crowds had shopping bags. There's nothing to shop for in East Berlin and no bags in which to put the stuff you can't buy. Taxi drivers saw my luggage and began shouting, "You want taxi?!" "Taxi, ja?!" Imagine shouting that your services are for hire in East Berlin. Imagine shouting. Imagine services. I heard laughter, chatting, even giggles. I saw a cop directing traffic with bold and dramatic flourishes. I saw border guards smile. It was a regular Carnival in Rio by East Berlin standards. And, the most amazing thing of all, there was jaywalking.

I had been in East Berlin three years before. And I had been standing on a corner of a perfectly empty Karl-Marx-Allee waiting for the light to change. All Germans are good about obeying traffic signals, but pre-1989 East Germans were religious. If a bulb burned out they'd wait there until the state withered away and true communism arrived. So I was standing among about a dozen East Germans, meaning to follow the custom of the country, but my mind wandered and without thinking I stepped out into the street against the light. They all followed me. Then I realized I'd walked into the path of traffic, the only traffic that there'd been on Karl-Marx-Allee for the past ten minutes—a speeding army truck. I froze in confusion. The East Germans froze in confusion. Finally I jumped back on the curb. And they did too, but not until I'd jumped first.

In 1986 I'd come through the border at Checkpoint Charlie, and getting in was a dreary and humiliating experience similar to visiting a brother-in-law in prison. There was much going through pairs of electrically locked doors and standing before counters fronted with bulletproof glass while young dolts in uniforms gave you the fish-eye. There were an inordinate number of NO EXIT! signs, and I remember thinking the exclamation points were a nice touch.

You had to exchange twenty-five perfectly good West German marks, worth about fifty cents apiece, for twenty-five perfectly no good East German marks, worth nothing. I thought I'd see how fast I could blow my stack of

East marks on the theory that the test of any society's strength and vigor is how quickly it Handi-Vacs your wallet.

I walked to Unter den Linden, old Berlin's Champs-Elysées. The city was empty feeling, no construction noise, no music, no billboards or flashing lights. There were plenty of people around but they all seemed to be avoiding one another like patrons at a pornographic movie theater, and, although it was a beautiful spring day, the East Berliners were moving with their shoulders hunched and heads turned down as though they were walking in the rain. The women were frumps but the men bore an odd resemblance to trendy New Yorkers. They had the same pallor and mixing-bowl haircuts. They wore the same funny, tight, high-water pants with black clown shoes as big as rowboats and the same ugly 1950s geometric-patterned shirts buttoned to the neck. Except the East Berlin guys weren't kidding. This wasn't a style. These were their clothes.

Unter den Linden's six lanes served only a few deformed East German Wartburg sedans and some midget Trabant cars. The Trabants had two-cycle engines and made a sound like a coffee can full of steel washers and bees. They looked like they were made of plastic because they were. Other than that the traffic was mostly blimp-sized double-length articulated buses progressing down the vacant avenue at the speed of Dutch elm disease.

The store windows were full of goods, however: a fifty-bottle pyramid of Romanian berry liqueur, a hundred Russian nesting dolls, a whole enormous display devoted entirely to blue plastic toothbrushes with the bristles already falling out. The huge Centrum department store smelled as though the clothes were made from wet dogs. The knit dresses were already unraveling on their hangers. The sweaters were pilling on the shelves. The raincoats were made out of what looked like vinyl wallpaper. And there were thirty or forty people in line to buy anything, anything at all, that was for sale.

I went to a bar in the showplace Palace of the Republic. It took me thirty minutes to be waited on although there were two bartenders and only five other patrons. The two bartenders were pretty busy washing out the bar's highball glass. I was amazed to see "Manhattan" listed on the drink menu and ordered it and should have known better. There was some kind of alcohol, but definitely not whiskey, in the thing, and the sweet vermouth had been replaced with ersatz sloe gin.

Next, I stood in line for half an hour to see what Marxism could do to street-vendor pizza. It did not disappoint. The word *cottony* is sometimes used to describe bad pizza dough, but there was every reason to believe this pizza was really made of the stuff, or maybe a polyester blend. The slice—more accurately, lump—had no tomato whatsoever and was covered in a semiviscous imitation mozzarella, remarkably un-cheese-like even for a coal-tar by-product. Then there was the sausage topping. One bite brought a flood of nostalgia. Nobody who's been through a fraternity initiation will ever forget this taste, this smell. It was dog food.

I went back to Checkpoint Charlie. You weren't allowed to take East German money out of the country. I don't know why. It's not like there was anything you could do with it in the West. The bills are too small for house-training puppies. But East Germany was total in its totalitarianism. Everything was banned that wasn't compulsory. Anyway, when I went through customs a dour official in his early twenties said, "Have you any currency of the German Democratic Republic?"

"Nope," I said. "I spent it all."

He looked skeptical, as well he might have. "Empty pockets, bitte," he ordered. I had twenty-one marks left over.

"Well, I'm coming back tomorrow," I said.

His expression changed for a moment to boyish amazement. "You *are*?" He resumed his governmental frown. "This once I will allow you to retain these currencies because you are coming back tomorrow," he said and rolled his eyes.

I did come back and this time couldn't find anything at all to spend money on. The only excitement available in East Berlin seemed to be opening the subway car doors and getting off the train before it came to a complete halt. But I couldn't figure out how to pay the subway fare so I couldn't even spend my money on this. I walked back toward Checkpoint Charlie with forty-six marks in my pocket. Then I did something my capitalist soul had never allowed me to do before in my life. I crumpled up money and threw it in a garbage can.

There was no question of throwing money away on my 1989 visit to East Berlin. The glimmering new Grand Hotel, standing on that very corner where the garbage can had been, accepted only hard currency. In return you got food you could swallow and Johnnie Walker Scotch at the bar (although something described as "cod liver in oil" still lurked on the restaurant menu).

There had been changes for the regular citizens of East Berlin as well. There were three or four times as many shops on the streets, some with pseudo-boutique names like "Medallion," "Panda," and "Joker." The stuff for sale was awful enough, but there was more of it. Thus at least half the law of supply and demand was being obeyed—if something's lousy, it's always available. The first lineup of shoppers I saw turned out to be waiting for an antiques shop to open. The new Wartburg 353 models even had styling—not much styling and that borrowed from 1960s Saabs, but styling nonetheless.

However, the real change was the lack of fear, a palpable physical absence like letting go of your end of a piano. My note taking—which in 1986 would have sent passersby scuttling like roaches surprised in a kitchen—now went unremarked. American reporters were all over the place, of course. And in every hotel lobby and café you could hear East Germans griping loudly to the reporters while the reporters loudly explained to the East Germans how all this was feeling to the people of East Germany.

There were pictures everywhere of the new East German leader Egon Krenz, just as there'd been pictures everywhere of the old East German leader Erich Honecker. But these weren't the lifted chin, stalwart forward looker vanguarding the masses photos. Egon—who resembles a demented nephew of Danny Thomas's—was shown spreading hugs around, tousling toddler moptops, and doing the grip-and-grin at various humble functions. He was politicking, plain and simple. The Commies didn't quite have it right yet: they take office and *then* they run for it. But they're trying.

Personally I missed the old East Berlin. The only thing East Germany ever had going for it was a dramatic and sinister film noir atmosphere. When you passed through Checkpoint Charlie the movie footage seemed to switch to black and white. Steam rose from manhole covers. Newspapers blew down wet, empty streets. You'd turn your trench coat collar up, hum a few bars of "Lili Marleen," and say to yourself, "This is me in East Berlin."

That's gone now and the place is revealed for what it's really been all along, just a screwed-up poor country with a dictatorship. The dictatorship part is understandable, but how the Commies managed to make a poor country out of a nation full of Germans is a mystery. The huge demonstrations that had shaken East Germany for the past several months had one characteristic that distinguished them from all other huge demonstrations in history—they never began until after work. I went to one of these at Humboldt University. The students were demanding economics courses. It was hard to reconcile this with my own memories of student protest. We were demanding free dope for life.

The students were also protesting the opening of the Wall. Not that they were against it. But they were furious that the East German government might think this was all it had to do. One picket sign showed a caricature of East Berlin's party boss Günter Schabowski naked with a banana stuck in every orifice and a balloon reading, "Free at last!" No one made any attempt to break up the rally. Soldiers and police were there, but they were applauding the speakers.

Even though the guard dogs and the machine-gun nests were gone, the east side of the Berlin Wall was still pristine, smooth whitewashed precast reinforced-concrete slabs a foot thick and ten feet high and separated from the rest of the city by thirty yards of police. On the west side, the Wall was in your face and covered with graffiti paint as thick as ravioli.

I went out Checkpoint Charlie—with nobody worrying over what I might do with my East German marks—and turned right on Zimmer Strasse, what Berliners call "Wall Street" because the Wall runs along the old curbstone, leaving only a sidewalk in front of the West Berlin buildings.

There was a steely, rhythmic noise that, for a moment, I thought might be some new Kraftwerk-style Euro synthesizer music (Berliners are horribly up-to-date with that sort of thing). But it was the sound of hundreds of people going at the Wall with hammers, chisels, picks, sledges, screwdrivers, and even pocket knives. The chipping and flaking had progressed in a week until long, mouse-gnawed-looking ellipses were appearing between the slabs with daylight and occasional glimpses of East German border guards visible on the other side. I saw thirty schoolchildren on a class excursion with their teacher, all beating the Wall in unison with rocks, sticks, and anything that came to hand.

I talked to a man in his sixties who was going along the Wall with a rucksack and a geologist's hammer. He'd escaped from the East in 1980. He'd been in prison over there for his political opinions. He gestured at the layers of spray-painting, the hundreds of symbols, slogans, and messages ranging from John Lennon quotes to "Fuck the IRA." "I want one piece of every color," he said.

A twenty-year-old West German named Heiko Lemke was attacking the Wall with a set of professional stonemason's tools. In two days he'd made a hole big enough to pass a house cat through, even though the police had twice confiscated his cold chisels—the West German police. During a one-minute breather Lemke said he was an engineering student, a supporter of the Christian Democratic Party, didn't want history to repeat itself, and was going to come back to the Wall on the weekend with some serious equipment.

Two American teenagers, Neville Finnis and Daniel Sheire, from Berlin's English-language JFK High School were attempting to rip the top off one section of the Wall with their bare hands. The Wall is capped with six-foot-long two-hundred-pound half-pipes cast in ferro concrete. These need to be lifted nearly a foot in the air before their edges clear the cement slab and they can be heaved to the ground. Neville and Daniel straddled the wall, in postures that would bring dollar signs to the eyes of any hernia surgeon, and lifted. When that didn't work, two more JFK students got up on the Wall and lifted Neville and Daniel while Neville and Daniel lifted the half-pipe. "Go for it! Go for it!" they yelled at each other. It was an American, rather than a scientific or methodical, approach. The half-pipe landed with a great thump. The political message was clear to all the JFK students. "Yeah!" shouted one. "Let's sell it!"

The East German border guards didn't interfere. Instead they came up to openings in the Wall and made V-signs and posed for photographs. One of them even stuck his hand through and asked would somebody please give him a piece of the concrete to keep as a souvenir.

The hand of that border guard—that disembodied, palm-up, begging hand . . . I looked at that and I began to cry.

I really didn't understand before that moment, I didn't realize until just then—we won. The Free World won the Cold War. The fight against life-hating, soul-denying, slavish communism—which has shaped the world's politics this whole wretched century—was over.

The tears of victory ran down my face—and the snot of victory did too because it was a pretty cold day. I was blubbering like a lottery winner.

All the people who had been sent to gulags, who'd been crushed in the streets of Budapest, Prague, and Warsaw; the soldiers who'd died in Korea, and my friends and classmates who had been killed in Vietnam—it meant something now. All the treasure that we in America had poured into guns, planes, Star Wars, and all the terrifying A-bombs we'd had to build and keep—it wasn't for nothing.

And I didn't get it until just then, when I saw that border guard's hand. And I think there are a lot of people who haven't gotten it yet. Our own President Bush seems to regard the events in Eastern Europe as some kind of odd dance craze or something. When I got back to the United States, I was looking through the magazines and newspapers and it seemed that all I saw were editorial writers pulling long faces about "Whither a United Germany" and "Whence America's Adjustments to the New Realities in Europe." Is that the kind of noise people were making in Times Square on V-E Day?

I say, shut up you egghead flapgums. We've got the whole rest of history to sweat the small stuff. And those discredited peace creeps, they can zip their soup coolers, too. They think Mikhail Gorbachev is a visionary? Yeah, he's a visionary. Like Hirohito was after Nagasaki. We won. And let's not let anybody forget it. We the people, the free and equal citizens of democracies, we living exemplars of the Rights of Man tore a new asshole in International Communism. Their wall is breached. Their gut string is busted. The rot of their dead body politic fills the nostrils of the earth with a glorious stink. We cleaned the clock of Marxism. We mopped the floor with them. We ran the Reds through the wringer and hung them out to dry. The privileges of liberty and the sanctity of the individual went out and whipped butt.

And the best thing about our victory is the way we did it—not just with ICBMs and Green Berets and aid to the Contras. Those things were important, but in the end we beat them with Levi's 501 jeans. Seventy-two years of communist indoctrination and propaganda was drowned out by a three-ounce Sony Walkman. A huge totalitarian system with all its tanks and guns, gulag camps, and secret police has been brought to its knees because nobody wants to wear Bulgarian sneakers. They may have had the soldiers and the warheads and the fine-sounding ideology that suckered the college students and nitwit Third Worlders, but we had all the fun. Now they're lunch, and we're number one on the planet.

It made me want to do a little sack dance right there in the Cold War's end zone. We're the best! We're the greatest! The only undefeated socioeconomic system in the league! I wanted to get up on the Wall and really rub it in: "Taste the ash heap of history, you Bolshie nosewipes!" But there was nobody left to jeer at. Everybody from East Berlin was in West Berlin watching Madonna music videos.

Return of the Death of Communism

Nicaragua, February 1990

On the morning of the twenty-sixth, the day after Violeta Chamorro's victory over Danny Ortega, I walked into the Inter-Continental hotel in Managua and Bianca Jagger was sitting alone in the lobby. Bianca had been ubiquitous during the election campaign. There was Bianca looking smart in an unconstructed linen jacket and yellow socks to match, Bianca looking serious with press pass and camera, Bianca looking thoughtful listening to Jimmy Carter, Bianca looking concerned conferring with Senator Christopher Dodd, Bianca looking committed in simple tennis shoes and neatly mussed hair, Bianca looking important wearing sunglasses after dark. But this morning Bianca looked . . . her age. Here we had a not very bright, fortyish, discarded rock-star wife, trapped in the lonely hell of the formerly cute—one bummed-out showbiz lefty.

I was feeling great myself, ready to turn somersaults over the Ortega defeat, full of good cheer and pleased with all the world. But then the forlorn, sagging little shape of Bianca caught my eye and, all of a sudden, I FELT EVEN BETTER.

I hadn't come to Nicaragua prepared for such bliss. Like most readers of papers and watchers of newscasts, I thought the Sandinistas were supposed to win this one. I'm a member of the working press; you'd think I'd know better than to listen to journalists. But there's a little bit of the pigeon in every good confidence man. I even believed the February 21 ABC–*Washington Post* poll that had Ortega leading Chamorro by sixteen percentage points. That is—I blush to admit this—I accepted the results of an opinion poll taken in a country where it was illegal to hold certain opinions. You can imagine the poll-taking process: "Hello, Mr. Peasant, I'm an inquisitive and frightening stranger. God knows who I work for. Would you care to ostensibly support the dictatorship which controls every facet of your existence, or shall we put you down as in favor of the UNO opposition and just tear up your ration card right here and now?"

Furthermore, when I arrived in Nicaragua I found an Ortega political machine that was positively Bushian in its relentless drumming on the issue-free upbeat. Danny's smiling (I presume they used a photo retoucher) face and Danny's heartthrob-of-the-poli-sci-department mustache were everywhere to be seen. As was Danny—pestering babies, attempting dance steps, wearing Ed Begley Jr. the-dog-was-sick-on-the-carpet shirts, and tossing free baseballs into crowds of squealing totalitarianism fans. The Sandinistas' black and red, Doberman-mouth party colors were painted anyplace paint could stick. Sandinista songs played from every radio. The Danny for president slogan *todo sera mejor* (meaning "everything will be better" and not, as I momentarily thought, "major dried toads") was as perfect an all-purpose campaign promise as I have ever heard. There were Sandinista music videos with singing and dancing that could send Paula Abdul back to wagging pom-poms for the LA Lakers. And there were Sandinista ad campaigns tailored to every segment of the electorate. A billboard for city youth (the voting age is sixteen in Nicaragua) showed a moonstruck couple in Ortega T-shirts walking hand in hand toward a voting booth beneath the headline "When you do it for the first time, do it for love." Banners for the countryside showed a fierce portrait of Ortega with the motto *Daniel Es Mi Gallo,* "Daniel Is My Fighting Cock." (These can now be profitably recycled by the Kentucky Fried Chicken franchise outlets soon to open in Nicaragua.)

I confess I believed the Sandys had all the corners nailed down, and I spent the last couple of days before the election committing that original sin of journalism, "writing the lead on the way to the ballpark." What was I going to say about a loathsome Sandinista victory? I supposed I'd have to natter on about the unfair advantages of using state resources for party ends, about how Sandinista control of the transit system prevented UNO supporters from attending rallies, how Sandinista domination of the army forced soldiers to vote for Ortega, and how Sandinista bureaucracy kept $3.3 million of U.S. campaign aid from getting to UNO while Danny spent three million donated by overseas pinks and millions and millions more from the Nicaraguan treasury, etc.

But this seemed like weak-tea, crybaby stuff. No, I thought, I'll have to go shoveling in the manure pile of political science, trying to uncover the appeal that Marxism and other infantile worldviews still hold for people. One nice thing about being a conservative, at least I wouldn't feel betrayed by the masses. Democracy is only one of human liberty's safeguards and not always the most effective one. Back in the U.S. we've got a House of Representatives full of bed-wetting liberals to prove it.

The Dog Is Dead but the Tail Still Wags

That was what I planned to call this article. (It's still a good title—I'll save it for a description of GOP performance in this year's midterm congressional elections.)

Thus I was in a grim frame of mind when I went to the press conference held by that most ex- of America's ex-presidents, Jimmy Carter. The press conference was at the Sandinistas' imposing media complex, one of the few buildings in Managua that won't fall down if you piss against the side of it. This propaganda palace was built with money donated by patsy Swedes, named after their bumped-off prime minister, Olof Palme, and hence called, by the small contingent of conservatives present, the "Good Socialist Press Center."

Carter was the head of one of the three principal international election-monitoring groups that were fluttering around Nicaragua pronouncing everything they saw fair and equitable. There was the UN ("the turkeys"), the OAS ("the chickens"), and Carter's group, the Council of Freely Elected Heads of Government ("the geese").

What Carter thought he was doing, besides proving there are worse things than marines that the U.S. can send to Nicaragua, I don't know. But there he was, the man who gave the store away in the first place, still grinning like a raccoon eating fish guts out of a wire brush and still talking in that prissy, nose-first, goober-grabber accent, except this time in Spanish: ". . . new-WAY-vuh KnickerRAH-wuh deh-muh-crat-TICK-uh . . ."

Carter oozed moral equivalence. "There have been serious problems in the campaign process on both sides," said Carter. "We have to give credit to the Nicaraguan people for establishing an excellent electoral process," said Carter. "If the election is certified as honest and fair, the United States should lift sanctions," said Carter. It's a shame Jimmy was too young to be an international observer at Germany's elections in 1932. "We have to give credit to the German people for establishing an excellent electoral process." Maybe he could have given Hitler some help rearming.

The "press" at the press conference was a dirty and confused bunch, even by press corps standards. Inspection of credentials showed most of them to be correspondents for the Xeroxed newsletter of the Berkeley High-Colonic Liberation Front or television reporters from the Ann Arbor Reincarnation for Peace Coalition's public-access cable program. When a genuine newsman asked Carter about a report of UNO poll watchers being arrested, the backpack journalists hissed.

A number of celebrity fellow travelers were in Nicaragua for the vote-off—Jackson Browne, Jimmy Cliff, the Sandinistas' Washington lawyer Paul Reichler, and Ed Asner, who didn't look like he'd missed any meals due to the injustice of the capitalist economic system. But the real show was the *sandalistas,* prosperous, educated lefties from the United States who've flocked to Nicaragua for a decade to . . . well, to *help.* Although it's something of a puzzle why rebellious middle-class Americans went to Nicaragua to help Sandinistas wreck Central America, instead of, say, going to South Africa to help Boers chase schoolchildren with whips, or to Uganda to help Idi Amin eat people.

Some say the *sandalistas* are just young and dumb. But those folks are only half right. At first glance the Birkenstock Bolshies seem young. They wear "youth" clothes and have adolescent body language—constantly distributing hugs and touches and squirming with emotion rather than sitting still in thought. But, looking closely at the uniform ponytails and earrings (many of the women wear them too), I noticed the tresses that were still long in back were ofttimes gone on top, and the lady *sandalistas,* their underarm hair was streaked with gray.

A number of college-age kids were present, too—earnest and homely and not at all the type who would have been lefties in my day of high-fashion revolt. In 1968 these kids would have been in the ham radio club or Future Stenographers of America.

The Ortega-snugglers were dressed as though they were going to a Weather Underground Days of Rage costume party. They were all in jean skirts and drawstring pants, clogs, folk-art jewelry, and tie-dyed tank tops—fashions fully twenty years out of style. I wonder what my hip friends and I in the Summer of Love would have thought about people wearing zoot suit jackets and reet pleat pants with key chains dangling to the ground.

The Carter press conference was on Saturday morning, the day before the election. That afternoon I attended a less complacent press conference given by the Center for Democracy at the Inter-Continental Hotel. The same bunch of backpack journalists were here, too, hissing even before anybody asked a question. Some of these lifestyle leftovers had gone so far as to don the red and black Sandinista neckerchief, an item of apparel identical to that worn by the Boy Scouts of America. In Nicaragua the effect was of a scout troop gone deeply, seriously wrong, growing older and older but never graduating to Explorer and earning merit badges in "Lenin," "marijuana," and "poor hygiene."

I hadn't been keeping up to speed on Nicaraguan nonsense and had no idea why the lefties were heckling the Center for Democracy. The center is one of those painstakingly bipartisan, painfully fair organizations that I usually heckle myself. CFD was the first election-monitoring group invited to Nicaragua. It was invited by both sides and had been observing the election campaign since the spring of last year. But now the CFD's credentials were downgraded so that its observers couldn't enter polling places, and more than fifty CFD observers had been denied Nicaraguan visas at the last minute.

The trouble was, the Center for Democracy had gotten caught telling the truth. CFD observers were at a UNO rally in the town of Masatepe on December 10, 1989, and they saw a Sandinista mob set upon Chamorro supporters with machetes. The mob killed one person and chopped the arms off a couple of others while the Sandinista police stood around like potted palms. Now, it's all right for observer groups to observe such things, that's what they're there for. But if the Sandinistas had wanted truth-telling groups, that's what they would have asked for. The OAS observers at the Masatepe rally obligingly waffled and claimed "both sides" were to blame. But the CFD delegation—which included such dyed-in-the-hair-shirt liberals as Bob Beckel—was outraged by the Sandinista attack and said so.

Thus the press conference questions directed to Center for Democracy president Allen Weinstein weren't questions at all but diatribes capped with little rhetorical inquisitions such as, "How are you going to overcome your bias?" and, "Don't you think it's idiosyncratic that yours is the only observer group complaining about credential problems?" after which half the press conference attendees would clap. One particularly impassioned and bearded fellow named Carlos, a professor at Glendale College in California, where he teaches "Chicano Studies," explained how the fact that the CFD was an observer group in the first place and came to Nicaragua at all proved its members had no respect for Nicaraguan sovereignty.

I'd gone to Nicaragua with the head of the National Forum Foundation, Jim Denton. Forum has been sponsoring interns from newly de-communized Eastern Europe, bringing them to the United States so that they can see how democratic institutions work and can learn to avoid making terrible mistakes like electing Jimmy Carter. Denton took two of these interns, Slawek Gorecki from Poland and Martin Weiss from Czechoslovakia, to Managua. Jim and I thought the *sandalistas* were funny. Martin and Slawek did not. They were sickened and enraged that citizens of a free nation would go somewhere to promote dictatorship. Even more than disgusted, they were mystified. Trying to explain American lefties to Martin and Slawek was like—simile fails me—trying to explain American lefties to two reasonable and intelligent people who'd never seen any.

Martin and Slawek—and Jim and I, too, for that matter—preferred meeting with Commandante Raphael Solis, president of the Sandinista National Assembly. Here was a comprehensible scumbag, somebody who was making a buck off the evil he espoused.

Solis was master of the world-weary idealist act—lots of rueful smiles and care-laden brow rubs. His manners were gracious and welcoming, his grin warm and genuine. Solis said he was confident of an Ortega victory and of a large majority in the new National Assembly. But was he? With the improved sensitivity and increased intelligence that hindsight brings, I detect some loyal-opposition bullpen warm-up from Solis. He claimed he was looking forward to national reconciliation and hoped the UNO parties would play a part in it. He dismissed the statement by Interior Minister (and head of the secret police) Tomás Borge that the Sandinistas were "prepared to lose the election but not to lose power."

"That is," said Solis with the aplomb of a born politician, "campaign rhetoric." He touted a "*perestroika* atmosphere" in Nicaragua, predicted "foreign-policy compromises," and, in response to needling from Slawek, he said, "As to the changes in Eastern Europe, I haven't heard any criticism from the Sandinista leadership. We think these changes are positive, democratic." And he went on to claim that Nicaragua would be making the same changes soon and, also, had made them already.

At sunrise on election morning we headed around Lake Managua and north into the mountains, visiting polling places in Sebaco and Matagalpa and little villages in between. Then we drove farther north to Jinotega in what had been Contra territory. Everywhere we went it was the same: awful roads through beautiful scenery to lousy towns. The whole country is cracked, shattered, dirty, worn-out. Everything dates from the Somoza era or before. Ten years of revolution have produced nothing but the Olof Palme Press Center. Even the lamest People's Republic cosmetic touches were missing. Sandinista graffiti is the only fresh paint in Nicaragua. The nation looks—and smells—like that paradigm of socialism, a public restroom.

The voting was done in dingy schoolrooms with all the window glass broken or missing and bare wires running across the ceiling to fifteen-watt lightbulbs. Every voter had the ballot-marking process explained to him personally so that the election went forward at the speed of mammal evolution. People were waiting in line by the hundreds to vote.

Each polling place was run by a brisk, snippy, managing Sandinista woman of middle age, the kind of woman who, in a free society, is known as "my first wife." Denton, Martin, Slawek, and I didn't have the proper credentials to enter polling places, but we did anyway and, for the most part, got away with it—though at the price of being treated like ex-husbands.

The UN, the OAS, and the Carter group were all going around doing about the same thing we were in the way of checking for vote fraud. That is, they popped their heads in and made sure there was no Sandinista with a pistol in a toddler's ear saying, "Vote for Danny or the rug monkey gets it." We didn't see any cheating like that, and the UN, the OAS, and the Carter group said they didn't either.

We did see a truckload of soldiers being hauled around to vote. "Who are you for?" we yelled. "*Cinco! Cinco!*" they shouted, holding up five fingers to indicate they were voting for the fifth line on the ballot, the Sandinistas. "Uno," said one little fellow in the back, and they all giggled and made as if to pummel him.

In the village of San Ramon we saw some horseplay. The men and women had decided to get in separate lines. Then the line of men shoved the line of women off the school porch and into the rain. The women confided to us that the men were going to vote for Ortega.

And we saw former Democratic presidential hopeful Bruce Babbitt standing around at one polling place, looking clueless. Jim Denton said, "That's Bruce Babbitt," but for the life of me I couldn't remember who Bruce Babbitt was. I guess this tells us all we need to know about Bruce's political future.

The only Nicaraguan we heard complain was a guy who wasn't allowed to vote because he was drunk. "He admits that he's drunk," the Sandinista policeman told us. "Everybody makes mistakes," the drunk told us. And we told the policeman, "They let Teddy Kennedy vote in the Senate."

When we came back through Sebaco late in the afternoon, some of the same people who'd been standing in line to vote at seven that morning were still waiting. "We've been in line since four in the morning, since three in the morning, since two in the morning," one person told us with cheerful rural vagueness about time. "And if it is necessary we will stay here until . . . *ten*!" said another man, naming the latest hour of the evening he could think of offhand.

Of course people don't stand in line for twelve hours in drizzly weather at the ass end of nowhere to vote for the status quo. So there were three hints I'd been given that Ortega might lose. But there's no getting through to the highly perceptive. It wasn't until another journalist told me the Sandinistas were in trouble that I believed it.

We'd gone back to the Olof Palme center to wait for returns. Around 11:00 p.m. a network television newsman with (don't be shocked) left-wing connections came by looking agitated. "P.J., I was just over at Sandy headquarters and something's gone seriously wrong," he said, meaning the opposite. "All of Ortega's people are really upset. The early returns show them getting . . ." Getting what the billboard said when you do it for the first time, you should do it for love.

The UNO people had heard the same buzz and were in a mood of contained but swollen hope. Chamorro's coalition was holding its election-night party at a restaurant in one of Managua's few remaining middle-class enclaves. The crowd was a model of bourgeois propriety. Occasionally someone would stand on a chair and say, "*Viva UNO*" in a loud voice, but that was about it. The place was all clean shirts, hearty handshakes, polite honorifics, and, "How's your brother in Miami?" It was difficult to picture these decent, hardworking, prosperous, commonsensical people overthrowing a government. Sometimes it's hard to remember that bourgeois propriety is the real revolutionary force these days. All over the world we're bringing down dictatorships—or at least forcing them to go condo.

The Sandinista "victory party" was, on the other hand, a massive street disco populated by kids who in the U.S. would have been selling crack, getting the name of their favorite heavy metal band tattooed on their butts, or planning a drive-by shooting. These are the last people on earth that *sandalista* types would consort with back home. But all sorts of big, homely, dirty-haired American girls in stained T-shirts and dweeby little chicken-necked American boys in ripped jeans were fraternizing like hell with the lumpen Nicaraguans. (Who were dressed in their Sunday best, by the way.)

There was no evidence that Danny was in difficulty at the street dance, really no trace of politics, except the general air of thuggishness that hangs over all "mass" political movements. Lots of beer and cane liquor was being consumed and much smooching in the shadows was being done and fistfights and lunch blowings were beginning to dot the crowd. After half an hour of walking around with our hands over our wallet pockets, we decided our little group of *wingtipistas* belonged back at the Chamorro party or—even better by the standards of the bourgeois propriety revolution now afoot—asleep in our beds.

I awoke to the sound of lugubrious Spanish on the television. It was Danny Boy giving his concession speech, old Landslide Daniel. I understand Jimmy Carter had tracked Danny down in the middle of the night and told him—loser to loser—the jig was up. The Sandinistas had done everything they could to ensure the validity of this election in the eyes of the world. Now they had to eat what they had cooked.

Danny's speech was a long one. There are no brief excuses for communism. And it was punctuated with more pauses for dramatic effect than a high school production of *Macbeth.* Lined up behind Daniel was most of the Sandinista *nomenklatura,* pouting and sniffling and generally looking like dear Uncle Bill had died and left his fortune to the cat. At the end of Danny's speech, he and his pals raised their fists in the air and warbled the Sandinista battle anthem, the one with the last line about Yankees being "the enemies of all humankind," singing us farewell in the manner of the Mickey Mouse Club, except this crowd couldn't carry a tune on a shovel. The TV cameras pulled back to show the Olof Palme press corps singing along through their tears.

Me, I was singing myself, making up little tunes and dancing and capering around.

Benjamin Linder was blown to a flinder,
Dennis Wilson run o'er by a train,
Now it's hasta luego to Danny Ortega,
And United Fruit's come back again!

I rushed out to gloat. I especially wanted to gloat over the Americans—the ripe-suck liberals and MasterCard Marxists—see them backing and filling and blowing smoke out their pants cuffs. At the Inter-Continental, across the lobby from Bianca, Paul Reichler was excusing the Nicaraguan people to the news media, saying they had "voted with their stomach." The poor misguided fools. I suppose they should have voted with their asshole, Paul Reichler. A few yards away that human rum-blossom Senator Chris Dodd was telling reporters the election "wasn't a victory for UNO. The Nicaraguan people just wanted change." Yes, yes. And the 1988 presidential race wasn't a victory for Republicans either. The American people just wanted Michael Dukakis ground into a heap and sold as fiber supplement.

Driving through the streets of Managua, seeing American hippie-dips all fiddle-faced and dejected, it was hard to resist the temptation to yell things out the car window. "Get a job!" Or, "What's the matter with your legs, toots, don't you know 'Fur is dead'?" In fact I couldn't resist it. My favorite thing to do was just make a little pistol motion with my hand and shout, "Nicolae Ceauşescu!!!"

I headed for the Olof Palme center to rank on the backpack journalists. Oh, it was almost too sweet for telling, how they bellyached and sourpussed and went around in sulks. Carlos, the professor of "Chicano Studies," tried to look on the sunny side. "We can't abandon the people of Nicaragua," he said with a straight face, and, "The struggle will continue. People will be even more committed." But in the end, Carlos was reduced to racism in his attempt to explain why the polls said Danny would win but the voters said otherwise. "It's the Latino culture," said Carlos. "People love to say one thing and do another."

The younger *sandalistas* looked like they'd just seen Lee Atwater open for the Grateful Dead. They weren't angry, really, just deeply, deeply disappointed. Here they'd blown their semester break and Mom was going to have a cow when she got the VISA bill for the plane ticket, and then the Nicaraguan people went and let them down like this. But the old *sandalistas,* the New Left geezers, they looked like they'd gone to hell in a bong. It's into the trash can with this sixties litter, and you could see they knew it. They looked like Abbie Hoffman was looking the last couple years of his life, as though every night when they go to sleep a BMW chases them through their dreams.

And in that BMW, or hoping to be there soon, were all the regular Nicaraguans down at the Eastern Market.

Were they surprised that UNO won? They laughed. "We expected victory, especially the mothers," said a mother.

"All the mothers are happy," said another mom.

"We hope Violeta fulfills her promises," said the proprietress of a shoe store. "Or we'll get rid of her too," she added in the tone of an experienced democrat.

"If Ortega doesn't give in, the people will rise up," said a cobbler. "We have *other countries* that will help us." And he nodded toward the Congressional Press Gallery ID I was wearing around my neck.

"What about the polls?" I asked. "Why were they so wrong?"

"People were afraid," said a man in a barbershop.

"The same old experts who always come here came here and gave us the same old results they always give," said the barber.

Another customer began yelling, "All we had to eat was old lard and the kind of sugar they feed to cattle!"

And that set off a passing drunk who may have been confused about geopolitics—or maybe not—but, anyway, had the right attitude. "Tomorrow, Japan!" he shouted.

Postscript

Today, of course, Danny Ortega and his Sandinistas are back. Let this go to show that all political joy is fleeting. Danny has been president of Nicaragua since 2006. He's not quite as bad as he used to be. In fact, he's to the right of New York City mayor Bill de Blasio on issues such as abortion and allowing carriage horses to pull buggies. Ortega hasn't interrupted Nicaragua's steady, if slow, recovery from Marxist impoverishment. (Per capita GDP was $244 when he was thrown out. It's currently $1,851.) But Danny is back. I suppose the only Christian thing to do is hope that Bianca is happy now.

Dispatches from the Gulf War

Jordan, August 1990

War! War! Bloodred savage war! Cry havoc and loose the dogs of ditto. Saddam Hussein—he's worse than Hitler, worse than Stalin, worse than waking up wearing a wedding ring next to Roseanne Barr. He invaded Iran. He invaded Kuwait. He even invaded some parts of the country he already lives in, that's how crazy Saddam Hussein is. He's got chemical weapons filled with . . . with . . . *chemicals.* Maybe he's got the Bomb. And missiles that can reach Riyadh, Tel Aviv, Spokane. Stock up on nonperishable foodstuffs. Grab those Diet Coke cans you were supposed to take to the recycling center and fill them with home heating oil. Bury the Hummel figurines in the yard. We're all going to die. Details at eleven.

It's lots of fun being in the panic industry. If you can't convince the world to love you, then scaring everyone out of their Bart Simpson Underachiever-and-Proud-of-It T-shirts is the next best way to get attention and feel needed. My fellow members of the news media and I have been pursuing this strategy with zest since August 2. "Horror Show," "Talk of War," "Must This Mean War?," "Should War Come: A Scenario," read the headlines. *Time* ran a cover bannered "Is the World Ready for This?," showing a photo of what looks like a cellular phone wrapped in a table napkin wearing Ray-Bans and a shower cap but which was labeled "U.S. soldier testing chemical warfare gear in Saudi Arabia." The daily papers and the nightly news are festooned with maps—arrows going every which way, little silhouettes of tanks and planes, and proposed casualty figures that look like long-distance phone numbers.

The U.S. government has also been pretty good at spreading alarm—not to mention money and guns—all over the place. We are sending 250,000 troops, six hundred fighter planes, three naval carrier groups, and twenty-six B-52 bombers to the Persian Gulf, a little late to save Kuwait, maybe, but just in time to rescue the U.S. defense budget. One well-placed ICBM and Saddam Hussein would get the message, but that wouldn't prevent Congress from taking all our Stealth Bomber money and giving it to naked National Endowment for the Arts performance artists to rub on their bodies while denouncing male taxpayers.

Everybody's been cashing in on Hussein Hysteria. The Soviet Union is accumulating points in the civilized-nation lookalike contest. The UN thinks it might finally have found something to do for a living. My girlfriend plans to make a fortune selling "FUQ IRAQ" bumper stickers. Literary agents are lining up hostage tell-alls and sending faxes to Baghdad instructing trapped Americans to have poignant thoughts and spiritual insights and to get tortured a little, if possible. So many TV camera crews have descended on the Middle East that Arab authorities are rushing to tourist hotels to check the Gideon Bibles—Exodus, chapters 7 through 12—on the subject of plagues: blood, frogs, lice, flies, dead cattle, boils, hail, locusts, darkness, firstborn sons, and, yep, network anchormen. Of course, Jesse Jackson is on hand, warning the world in light verse couplets about a situation "Where the price of oil would go up/And the price of blood would go down." The occasion being too solemn for rhyme.

So I figured I'd better get over there. I've been to the Middle East three whole times before and know several words in Arabic, including *la* ("no") and *Ayna akrab mal'ab golf?* ("Where's the nearest golf course?"), therefore I'm an expert, too, and can put things into perspective, give you a clearer picture of unfolding events, and maybe relieve some of the unnecessary fears and needless anxieties stirred up by cynical, sensationalistic journalists like me.

I know what you readers are saying to yourselves. You're saying, "P.J., P.J., how can you possibly tell us what these people are going to do? Here they are gadding about in their mothers' nightgowns, playing with pop beads and going, 'Muhammad this' and 'Muhammad that,' when they've got to know Ali is pushing fifty and has Parkinson's disease and couldn't go half a round with Razor Ruddock."

Well, that just shows how ignorant of Arabic culture you readers are. Ali could go the distance with Ruddock any day of the week standing on one foot, I don't care whose disease he's got. Besides, the Arab peoples possess an ancient and highly developed civilization that is in many ways more sophisticated than our own. For instance, they invented algebra. And this is why we have to go to war with Saddam Hussein this minute and bomb the shish kebab out of him before he invents trig and chemistry and the whole of America flunks high school.

Sending everything we've got short of Dan Quayle in a National Guard uniform to the Middle East to keep Saddam Hussein from doing whatever it is that he hasn't managed to do already is called "being the world's policeman." There's a lot of argument about this, mostly from American newspaper editorial writers who like to begin paragraphs with "America isn't the world's policeman." But you'll notice that when Kuwait got invaded, nobody called Sweden.

So here we are, running around armed to the eyeballs in the same kind of weather you can get at the laundromat by putting two quarters in the dryer, while our domestic economy deflates like a cheap beach toy. And do we hear any thank-yous?

I hadn't even gotten out of the Kennedy Airport Royal Jordanian Airline first-class lounge (a windowless room with two bottles of Johnnie Walker, no ice, a bowl of pistachios, and a television permanently tuned to *Wheel of Fortune*) before a Jordanian started in on me: "When Israel invades Sinai, did America send troops? When Israel invades the West Bank, did America send troops? When Israel invades Lebanon, did America send troops?" Of course he was being very unfair. We didn't send troops but we *did* send arms, matériel, and a great deal of financial assistance. Albeit we sent them to Israel.

At the baggage carousel in Amman, a Jordanian-American businessman, when asked where the *bureau de change* was, answered with an impassioned defense of Saddam Hussein. "Again and again and again Iraq asked Kuwait to quit violating OPEC guidelines. Again and again and . . ."

I bought a copy of the *Jordan Times*. They wanted the Cold War restarted:

> *. . . it is most unfortunate that the Soviet glasnost and perestroika policy has meant giving the Americans more leeway to do what they want with the smaller countries in the world . . .*

Like, you know, save their butts.

At my hotel an organization called the Child Welfare Committee of the General Union of Voluntary Services was handing out press releases about a "Women's and Children's March" to protest the trade embargo on Iraq: "Such a blockade constitutes no less than an act of savagery, unprecedented in recent history . . ."

The march was organized by the same kind of earnest, whole-grain busybodies we have in the States, wearing Birkenstock sandals and primitive jewelry and arriving at the demo in their husbands' Volvos. They were trying to get seven or eight hundred kids under twelve to quit dropping, losing, and smacking each other over the head with printed signs reading, "ARAB WORLD IS MY WORLD," "IRAQI CHILDREN = ARAB CHILDREN," "HOW MANY KIDS' LIVES FOR A BARREL OF OIL?" and "DO NOT KILL MOM."

Do-gooders are always hard to figure, but watching the Women's and Children's March was—considering the porky guy with the poison gas who stands to benefit—like being a spectator at an Earth First! spotted owl shoot.

And one more thing I discovered on my first day in Jordan: the Jordanian-American Friendship Society has been dissolved. (Though its president, Mohammad Kamal, admitted, "The organization . . . has really been dormant since its establishment.")

America is the world's policeman, all right—a big, dumb Mick flatfoot in the middle of the one thing cops dread most, a "domestic disturbance."

To the uninitiated, what Iraq did to Kuwait seems like regular war. Country A whacks Country B, which screams bloody murder, dragging Countries C, D, and E into the fray. But within the large, noisy, and exceedingly fractious family of Arabs, it's not that simple. Iraq, Kuwait, Jordan, Syria, Saudi Arabia, and so forth are hardly nations as we understand the term. They are quarrels with borders.

Until 1918 the Arabian peninsula was ruled by the Ottoman Empire, so called because it had the same amount of intelligence and energy as a footstool. When the Turks backed the wrong horse in World War I, the French and English divvied up the region in a manner both completely self-serving and unbelievably haphazard, like monkeys at a salad bar. The huge, senseless notch in Jordan's border with Saudi Arabia, for instance, is known as "Winston's Hiccup" because the then head of the British Colonial Office, Winston Churchill, is supposed to have drawn this line on a map after a very long lunch.

The British were fans of one Hussein ibn Ali, the Grand Sharif of Mecca, who led the Arab revolt against the Turks that Lawrence of Arabia claimed to be such an important part of. The British wanted to make members of Hussein's Hashemite family kings of whatall and whichever. They crowned Hussein himself King of the Hejaz, the Red Sea coast of the Arabian peninsula. They put his son Faisal on the throne of Syria. But the French threw a fit, so the Brits moved Faisal to Iraq. And Faisal's brother Abdullah—grandfather of the King Hussein we've got these days—was given the booby prize of Transjordan, an area previously known as "to-hell-and-gone-out-in-the-desert" when it was called anything at all.

In the 1920s, Ibn Saud—the man who put the "Saudi" in Saudi Arabia—chased Hussein ibn Ali out of the Hejaz. This is why the Jordanians hate the Saudis.

The Jordanians should hate the Iraqis, too, because the military government that Saddam Hussein now runs killed every available member of the Iraqi branch of the Hashemite family in 1958. But Jordan and Iraq are both too busy hating Syria for Syria's attempt to achieve Arab hegemony by allying with Iran, invading Lebanon, and trying to gain control of the Palestine Liberation Organization.

The PLO, meanwhile, nearly toppled King Hussein in 1970, whereupon the king, with Iraqi support, exterminated thousands of Palestinians. Thus the Palestinians should hate the Jordanians and vice versa, but since 65 percent of Jordanians *are* Palestinians, it's easier for everybody to hate Israel.

Which still doesn't explain why the people in Jordan are furious at the United States for coming to the aid of Kuwait. Unless it does.

Amman is a pretty dangerous place for an American to go—you wouldn't believe the traffic. Everybody in Jordan drives everywhere at top speed. They parallel park at sixty miles an hour. And Jordanians never touch the brakes, turn signals, dimmer switch, or even the steering wheel. All driving is done by horn.

Amman's street layout was designed using the splatter technique popular with action painters of the post–abstract expressionist school. The idea of numbering buildings and naming streets has been taken up, but in a grudging, desultory manner, the way baby boomers practice dental flossing.

There are no major intersections in Amman. Instead there are roundabouts, from which radiate four, six, eight, twelve, or thirty avenues. There's really no telling because, although it's possible to enter a roundabout from virtually any street in the city, it's not possible ever to exit again.

This is why I missed a special Rotary Club of Jordan meeting called to protest America's unfairness to Iraq. I had been eager to see the results of backslapping Rotarian boosterism applied to Islamic *jihad*: "Okay, fellows, any member who hasn't drunk the blood of an infidel dog since the last meeting has to stand on his chair and sing 'I'm a Little Teapot.'"

Rotary International is just the thing for Amman, a bland, clean, busy, humdrum, commercial city, a kind of Arab Brussels, although perched on spectacular hills.

The buildings are all cement block made to look like limestone, except for some made of the limestone the cement's supposed to look like. By day the whole town is the color of those afternoons at the beach when you can't tell where the sea ends and the sky begins, and by night it's alive with the headlights of drivers lost in roundabouts. All the modest one- and two-floor cement homes have metal rebars left sticking up from their roofs like whiskers—a Third World symbol of hope, meaning the residents are planning to make enough money to add another story to the house. Even the poorest parts of the city are tidy and unodoriferous, thanks, in part, to huge subsidies Jordan receives from the oil-rich Gulf states such as Kuwait.

But subsidies or no, pictures of Saddam Hussein were beginning to appear on the smaller and shabbier storefronts and in the rear windows of taxicabs. Copies of that old anti-Semitic forgery *The Protocols of the Elders of Zion* were stacked next to the cash register in an expensive bookstore. And, according to the *Amman Star,* University of Jordan students "from all political trends" were condemning "Arab traitors, Saudi Arabia, and Kuwait for inviting foreign troops into Arab and Islamic lands," and calling for "a battle of honor against the United States, the Zionists and all other treacherous forces."

The students had formed something called the Preparatory Committee for the General Union of Jordanian Students. One of their spokesmen said the Gulf crisis "pushed us to political extremism that hopes for an Arab-American confrontation that will lead to redrawing the map of the Arab world." In which case I hope they get New Jersey.

I did manage to find—by just leaving my car in a roundabout and walking—the University of Jordan, a handsome, shady campus filled with polite kids. The members of the infelicitously acronymed PCGUJS said, however, that only the head of their Information Sub-Committee was authorized to make statements to the international press. To my relief, they couldn't find him.

Most of the students at UJ were dressed like students anywhere, or better than that, Jordan being more or less a Mediterranean country and quite stylish. But about a third of the women students were wearing no makeup, scarves covering all their hair, and drab ankle-length dresses. This in adherence to fundamentalist Muslim rules of decorum which mean, basically, dressing the way middle-aged dads with teenage daughters think girls should. To judge by the amount of fiddling, tugging, and adjusting of the scarves, it was a fashion that had just come in. It's been a long time since I was in college, so maybe I've forgotten how these things work, but a campus fad for looking like a Russian cleaning lady and acting like a nun seems odd.

When I got back to my hotel Saddam Hussein was on the English-language TV news, pestering a group of British expats he had stuck somewhere in Baghdad.

"Your presence here and in other places is best to avoid the scourge of war," said Saddam through a not very competent translator. "Are you having recreational facilities?" Not waiting for an answer, he suggested they take a group photograph "about preserving the memory of this time," then said, "Let's put this on TV!" as though struck with a remarkable inspiration having nothing to do with the video cameras, soundmen, and lighting crews in the room. Saddam reached out with a beefy mitt and petted the head of a freckled little English kid later identified as Stewart Lockwood. "Are you playing volleyball with Iraqis?" asked Saddam, pawing the youngster's face, kneading his cheeks, and playing with his nose. Young Stewart—sturdy chap—bore it all with more disgust than fear. A week later I was in Abu Dhabi, watching English-language news again, this time about Jesse Jackson's return from putzing around in Iraq. And there was poor Stewart, now gripped by Jesse like a pet being taken to the veterinarian and giving Jackson exactly the same look he'd given Saddam. If we're serious about achieving world peace, we could start by getting international political leaders to leave Stewart Lockwood alone.

I drove out to Ruwayshid, the Jordanian checkpoint where the refugees from Iraq and Kuwait were beginning to arrive in large numbers. It's 250 kilometers through desert waste. Those of us brought up on Disney *The Living Desert* films expect time-lapse blooming century plants and lizards with funny tongues pursuing bugs all over the place. But in fact this desert looks like house plants do after six months in a bachelor's apartment. It's flat and featureless with nothing sentient visible. At noon the temperature is in the hundreds. Dust devils slop back and forth in dirty spirals across the plain. And the whole is bathed in a nasty shimmy of mirage. Mirage being not an optical illusion of a palm-fringed oasis, but the constant glare of hot sunlight reflected by an even hotter layer of air along ground that's too hot to talk about.

There is one real oasis 100 kilometers from Amman, Al Azraq, a nasty littered collection of concrete-block buildings with a salt marsh and about fifteen half-dead date palms. This was Lawrence of Arabia's headquarters and, for five dinars, an ancient worthy will tell you, "This was Lawrence of Arabia's headquarters."

Beyond Al Azraq the desert gets worse, all covered with small chunks of basalt that absorb and compound the nauseating heat. This is the Black Desert, where even Bedouin caravans wouldn't go, because the sharp, heated stones destroyed the feet of their camels. After another 75 kilometers the desert gets worse yet. Solid lava flows with the texture of piles of razor blades are interspersed with lumps of basalt now big as chairs and sofas. And if you roll down your car window swarms of tiny flies cover every part of your exposed flesh.

Lawrence called Al Azraq a "luminous silky Eden," and by the time you get back from Ruwayshid it actually looks that way.

This two-lane asphalt highway across the desert is the only ground link to Iraq, and there was plenty of blockade violating traffic on it. The Iraqis seemed to be running every old tanker truck they could get started, trying to get cash for their oil in Jordan. But the return traffic was not exactly a good-buddy, that's-a-big-10-4 version of the Berlin airlift. Many of the trucks headed toward Baghdad were empty, very few seemed to be carrying food, and a number of them were loaded with two-by-fours or immense rolls of pulp paper, playing what part in the war effort I'm not sure.

The road is straight and paved in a sort of folk-craft blacktop. The truck drivers go right down the center crown to avoid as many potholes as they can, and nobody dawdles out here. It is a memorable experience to roll head-on with a closing speed of 240 kilometers per hour at a fully loaded eighteen-wheel gasoline truck being driven by somebody dressed like Yasir Arafat.

The rest of the traffic coming toward me was made up of refugees. I guess I'd expected them to be pushing all their belongings in baby carriages or something, the way movie newsreel refugees always were when I was a kid. That type of refugee would sizzle and pop open like a weenie on a grill in this climate. Besides, these were affluent refugees—at least they had been until recently—in Chevrolet Caprice Classics, 200-series Mercedes, Peugeots, and BMWs. And they were very modern refugees, people making a run for it not because Stukas were strafing their villages but because their bank cards wouldn't work in Kuwaiti cash machines anymore.

Every refugee car carried suitcases tied on the roof, the immense vinyl suitcases of the underdeveloped world, big as folded-up rollaway beds. Each car was more splendidly loaded than the last, bearing huge swollen stacks of luggage, and every moment that these stacks stayed in place was a tribute to Middle Eastern knotwork. But now and then some vast baby-blue portmanteau would pitch loose and go vaulting down the highway berm like a rectangular Olympic gymnast, until it exploded—an underwear bomb.

Less affluent refugees were packed into buses. And refugees less affluent than that were standing in the back of open trucks. You'd see one of these trucks pulled to the side of the road for a piss break, its occupants scattered across acres of featureless landscape, squatting in their *dishdasha* robes to preserve some modesty during the call of nature.

At the Ruwayshid checkpoint thousands more refugees were arguing with officials and one another, standing in petrified lines, wandering around bedraggled, or patiently hunkering in whatever shade they could find. They were contained in a five-acre barbed-wire space with a dozen smelly cement buildings between two border-guard posts that looked like turnpike tollbooths. The compound was covered with shit and litter and aflutter with the Oriental mania for making copies of documents in triplicate and stamping everything with rubber stamps six or seven times. There seemed to be some food and water available, and a mosque where, when the *muezzin* made the midday call to prayer, nobody went.

These were the lucky refugees. Out in the desert toward Iraq, beyond the Jordanian border guards who refused to let me pass, were thousands and thousands more people with no shelter at all—thirsty, hungry, and desperate to get into Ruwayshid, the first-class section of hell.

I talked to a Jordanian named Abnan abu Sherke who'd waited two and a half days out there. He owned a store in Kuwait that he had abandoned and had five thousand dinars in a Kuwaiti bank, which were gone forever, and he'd driven 1,750 kilometers so far trying to get back to his family in Jordan.

"We are Arabs," said Mr. Sherke in a pleasant and conversational tone of voice. "We are very happy because Iraq is face-to-face with the U.S. I have the admiration for Saddam Hussein. I lose everything but I am happy."

The next day I drove the new four-lane desert highway out to Aqaba, Jordan's only port and a would-be Red Sea tourist resort that looks like a Bulgarian's idea of Fort Lauderdale.

This is another crucial chink in the international cordon that's supposed to convince Saddam Hussein to act like Václav Havel. At the quays I counted two ships loading Jordanian phosphate, one rusty tramp steamer from Bombay, and a grossly overloaded car ferry full of Egyptian refugees headed for Suez. If Saddam is going to feed a nation of eighteen million people by way of Aqaba, they'd better start eating Egyptians and their automobiles.

In an absolutely empty souvenir shop downtown the doddering owner told me, "Jordan is a friend to all nations." His thirty-year-old son said, "You know almost all the taxes you pay in America go to Israel, eighty percent." He said he wasn't anti-Semitic, either, because he'd gone to college in Romania and had a Jewish girlfriend there for six months.

I drove back to Amman by the old mountain route, 360 kilometers of goats in the right-of-way and spectacular cliff-top views of the Dead Sea that will kill you in a second if you take your eyes off the road. I passed through Wadi Musa, a mile of flat sand between cliffs as tall as the Empire State Building. Here are the Springs of Moses, where he struck the rock with his staff and brought forth water. And here are picturesque Bedouins with their flocks and tents and dreams of running a grocery store in Detroit.

I traversed the ancient lands of Ammon and Moab and Edom and viewed the sites of King Solomon's Mines and the Palace of Herod where Salome danced for the head of John the Baptist. The mountain highway follows the same path that the Roman road took two thousand years ago, beside the ruined line of Crusader castles with remains of Byzantine, Ottoman, and British forts in between. It's a kind of Grayline Tour of failed foreign policy initiatives.

These heights above the Jordan valley, along the great rift that runs from Africa almost to Europe, are the home and hearth of the entire world's culture. The oldest remains of fixed human habitations—houses from eleven thousand years ago—have been found here in Beida and Jericho. These people buried dead children in jars under their living room floors. No kidding. I checked up on it at the Archaeological Museum in Amman—evidence that not only the Arab world but our entire civilization was founded by crazy people.

Near Wadi Musa, about 95 kilometers north of Aqaba, I stopped for a few hours to look at the ruins of Petra. This was the great stronghold of the Nabataean Arabs who flourished from the fourth century BC until the first century of the Christian era by straddling the caravan route from Arabia Felix to the Tigris-Euphrates valley. They made their money by helping themselves to some of everything that went by—a previous example of vast, unearned wealth in the Middle East.

The Nabataeans used their swag to build Petra, which can be reached only by traveling down the floor of an unnerving canyon called the *Siq*—three hundred feet deep and barely wide enough for three people to walk abreast. At the end of this passage is a two-square-mile city of tombs, temples, houses, and public buildings all carved into the face of living rock in the most elaborate Greek and Roman styles. It is a monumental hidey-hole, a thing done by mad children with unlimited resources.

Trade routes shifted. Petra lost its livelihood. The very location of the place was forgotten, and it wasn't rediscovered until the early nineteenth century. Bedouins were still building their cooking fires in the palaces of Petra until a few years ago, when the Jordanian government's Department of Antiquities shooed them out. They come back to water their flocks and lead tourists around. A kid of about fourteen was showing me a spectacular Doric cavern with a strong smell inside. "Is here was the great temple," I said in profound and solemn pigdin, "and now is used to pen goats." The Bedouin kid looked at me like I was a big dope. I had some better idea what to use it for?

United Arab Emirates, September 1990

The situation down in the Gulf States is, of course, very different from that in Jordan. For one thing, the guy who stamped my passport at the Abu Dhabi airport was wearing a wristwatch worth more than my car. Also, we've got a quarter of a million troops around here keeping the locals from being pounded like cheap veal, so they're very pro-American. Well, sort of pro-American. "The foreign forces will leave the area as soon as the reasons for which they came are ended," said the United Arab Emirates defense minister Sheikh Mohammed bin Tashid in an interview with the UAE *Khaleej Times*, which also ran an editorial blaming the whole Gulf crisis on "big powers."

> *The big powers have only themselves to blame for what is happening now. Greedy for money they and unscrupulous arms dealers in Western countries have supplied Iraq with all the weapons now being pointed at themselves.*

So maybe they're not very pro-American, but they're very pro–not getting pounded like cheap veal. The exiled defense minister of Kuwait told the *Gulf*

Times that he'd order an immediate attack on Iraq if he were commanding the U.S. troops in Saudi Arabia, and as I got into the elevator to go to my room at the Abu Dhabi Sheraton, a Kuwaiti in a perfectly pressed *dishdasha* and carefully draped *ghutra* headdress began to speak to me in high-speed Arabic: "America something-something-something-something." I shrugged and he held up an admonishing index finger. "Quickly! Quickly!" he said.

The Gulf is a place that does not surrender itself easily to mere description. The weather, to begin with, is so bad in September that people *long* for the interior of Saudi Arabia. When I was there the temperature was over 110 degrees every day, but with a dampness that can't be possible under skies as blue as a vinyl swimming-pool liner. The windows of my hotel room were frosted like an iced-tea pitcher. One afternoon the humidity was actually 100 percent, at which point air isn't even vapor. I was breathing soup. A poison gas attack would be wholly redundant here.

Everything is air-conditioned, but not for comfort. An air-conditioned car is like a space suit. Step outside it for more than a few seconds at midday and you get dizzy, sick, and as wet as if you'd been flushed down a toilet.

And there's the architecture. Abu Dhabi is new, really new, with a half million people packed into an unrelenting pre-post-modernism worse than Epcot Center. I've seen a photograph of old Abu Dhabi. There was a mud fort, of exactly the kind used as the set of *Beau Geste*. There was a mud mosque. There was the home of the British colonial officer and a few Bedouin tents. That was it. That was the whole town. The picture was taken in 1966.

Now buildings tower, ooze, and mushroom in every shape that concrete can be poured. Some are trimmed in chrome and smoked glass like the coffee tables in time-share condos, and others make a daffy nod to Islamic tradition with pointless pointed arches opening to nowhere or senseless spreads of mosaics on ceilings instead of floors. My hotel was supposed to evoke, with rounded crenelations and brown tints, the mud fort in the center of town. But it only succeeded in looking like a grain elevator.

The city is laid out in an uncompromised grid which should make it easy to get around in even during the twilight 500SEL Benz-lock. But, instead of a few numbered addresses like Amman, there are none, and no concept that a street, once named, should keep that name for any length of its existence. Thus in a downtown as simple as a tic-tac-toe board, I lost the whole Saudi embassy, and two street maps, the concierges at three hotels, the Avis rent-a-car girl, the marines on duty at the U.S. embassy, several shopkeepers, an imam at a mosque, and the guards at the ambassador of Saudi Arabia's own residence were unable to direct me there.

When I did find the Saudi embassy, two days later, it was a big and obviously expensive building with not only no style but no discernible front. The reception room was bare except for chrome and Naugahyde conference-room chairs, one dusty Formica-topped table, and a standing ashtray. The floor was cheap terrazzo, the walls shabby stucco, but the ceiling was covered with rococo plasterwork painted in pink and aqua and highlighted with gold leaf. On the wall was an official Saudi government map of the Arabian peninsula, which—in case you think the Kuwait fracas is the last we're going to hear from this neck of the woods—indicated disputed borders with the UAE, Oman, Qatar, and Yemen.

There is no charm in Abu Dhabi. As the *Economist Business Traveler's Guide to the Arabian Peninsula* puts it, "There are virtually no 'sights' as such." And the only place I've ever seen with worse aesthetics or a greater taste for flash and fake was Jim and Tammy Bakker's Heritage Village USA. To which place the UAE bears other similarities as well. "Oil wealth has also reinforced the religious basis of society in the Emirates," says a locally printed tourist booklet. "Today, in the cities, no one need walk further than half a kilometer to the mosque."

There are beautiful gardens, however, along all the streets and in every open space, all brought to blooming, verdant life by that thing which, in the desert, is more precious than gold—money. Even the superhighways have gardens. The road that runs 130 kilometers to the oasis of Al Ain in the mountains on the Oman border is irrigated and landscaped the entire way, sleeved in date palms and tamarisk trees and flowering shrubs, the plants tended by brown, sweating people from Pakistan, Bangladesh, India, and Egypt. Only here and there can you see what's behind the mask of greenery, which is nothing, the true, complete nothing of the sand desert. There are not only no plants or animals but not even any objects, just creeping, blowing, red-blond sand in dunes that rise as high as three hundred feet.

I went, in the early mornings when I could almost stand the heat, to the *suqs,* the open-air markets in Abu Dhabi and Dubai. Though almost nothing is manufactured in the Emirates, or, really, anywhere in the Arabian Peninsula, shops were stuffed with goods, a barbaric splendor of merchandise —truly barbaric. That is, synthetic fabrics of astonishing ugliness, shoddy housewares, bad appliances, every kind of electronic gimcrack known to East Asia, a million overpriced Rolexes, garish nylon carpets in lampoons of Persian designs, gold necklaces with medallions bigger than salad plates, gems cut and set like carnival prizes, furniture to make a Mafia wife wince, and table lamps Liberace wouldn't have owned.

We think of a barbarian as somebody with a bone in his nose. But, in fact, a barbarian is more likely to have his nose full of a Hong Kong Shalimar knockoff. I wonder if all the polyester and highway beautification will weather as well as the ruins of Petra.

But, never mind. World peace and international order must prevail, so we're going to sacrifice ourselves and our treasure . . . Well, not actually our own personal selves. More like eighteen- to twenty-year-old selves who couldn't find worthwhile civilian jobs. And the treasure is borrowed, like the rest of the national debt. But you know what we mean. We're going to make the same brave, selfless sacrifices to save the Arabs from Saddam Hussein's crazed aggression that we made to save the Jews from Hitler's death camps, the Cambodians from Pol Pot's massacres, and the Poles, Hungarians, and Czechoslovaks from Stalin's terror . . . That is, the same brave, selfless sacrifice that we were going to make as soon as the Jews, Cambodians, Poles, Hungarians, and Czechoslovaks struck oil.

"Somewhere in Eastern Saudi Arabia," January 1991

This is the first globally broadcast, real-time, live, on-camera, televised war. It's so televised, in fact, that increasing CNN's Nielsen share seems to be an allied war aim only slightly less important than degrading Saddam Hussein's command-and-control capability. However, what you're reading is, as you may have noticed, print. My report is not electronic, maybe not even electric. To judge by the sound of this rented typewriter, I've got one of the early IBM diesel models. These words are thus as out-of-date as the U.S. State Department's tilt toward Iraq in the last Gulf war. By the time you read this we may be up to our Kevlar underpants in the kind of bloody trench warfare not seen since the French got their crepes folded at the Somme. Or we may be drinking Saudi near-beer out of the open-toed slippers of Saddam Hussein's harem concubines in liberated Baghdad. Who knows? Truth is the first casualty of war, but, in this particular conflict, print journalism took the second hit.

What you're reading is not only out-of-date, it's hastily written and disorganized, too. This is war, for chrissake. At least that's my excuse. Actually, the best thing about this war has been all the new excuses generated by the Pentagon briefing officers. These will doubtless prove handy to Americans in all walks of life, especially schoolkids who haven't done their homework.

"My book report impacted harmlessly in an unpopulated area."

"I can't tell you what happened in 1812, we're waiting on the bomb-damage-assessment reports."

"I'm sorry but units of elite Republican Guards were dispersed and dug in around my algebra problem."

I arrived in Saudi Arabia thirty-two hours after the war began having taken a sixteen-hour flight in the cargo hold of an Air Force C-141 Starlifter. There were 126 other journalists on the trip. Now that Twisted Sister has disbanded, the C-141 Starlifter is the single noisiest thing on earth. The journalists couldn't hear themselves think. Of course there's nothing unusual about 127 journalists not thinking, but the Starlifter was so loud that the journalists couldn't talk. And 127 journalists silent for sixteen hours is another first for this war.

We had a brief stop in Frankfurt, where we received what the air force called "a hot Italian food meal" followed by everybody's last Scotch until the war is over. We landed "somewhere in eastern Saudi Arabia," which means the port area of Dhahran on the Persian Gulf about 180 miles south of the Kuwaiti border—as Saddam Hussein has surely figured out by now. Then we were herded into a U.S. military briefing where it was explained to us that we could do absolutely nothing as journalists without U.S. military permission to do it, and whatever it was that we got permission to do, we might not be able to do that either.

In fact—as of this writing—the military has been reasonably helpful in dragging journalists out to places of moderate discomfort and/or mild danger and letting those journalists ask Oprah Winfrey–quality interview questions. But the military press office—the Joint Information Bureau, or JIB—has a strictly grade-school field-trip mentality with much posting of rules, schedules, and little lists of things reporters are expected to bring along. The JIB will be requiring notes from our parents next.

Reporters used to covering "low-intensity conflicts"—where we took taxis to the fighting and it was the U.S. military advisers who weren't supposed to be there—are, in a word, bored. But, in an un-low-intensity conflict, bored is the way to be. It means you're still alive. Besides, what's really hurting journalism around here isn't military censorship, it's military jargon. Spend more than an hour at the JIB and you begin calling the staircase "a foot-impelled bi-directional vertical transport asset."

I haven't been to the front yet. There are more than seven hundred journalists here—far more newsmen than there is news—and there's only room for about one hundred of them on the military "pools" covering the troops. Also, I'm here as a radio journalist but am not even sure which part of a tape recorder takes the pictures.

I'd been trying to get a Saudi Arabia visa since Iraq invaded Kuwait last August, but when the name of your magazine means "a large rock that moves around" and its pages are filled with pictures of Madonna wearing cookie tins on her chest, you don't get taken as seriously as the guys from *Time*. John Lyons, an old friend of mine at ABC radio, got me a slot as an emergency incompetent broadcast correspondent, and I'm left in the rear manning the phones and explaining the Gulf crisis to Blitzo Bob and Rocket Jaw Jim on the WONK Morning Drive-Time Zoo.

That's all right. The rear is where the action's been. We call it "Club Scud." We've had missile attacks almost every night. When the first attack came, ABC-TV producer Derwin Johnson and I got in a car and began driving around Dhahran looking for missile damage. We heard sirens and saw flashing lights on one of the main roads. We rushed to the scene and discovered a car wreck. Then we heard more sirens and saw other flashing lights. We rushed to that scene and discovered another car wreck. We saw four or five smashups that night, including one involving a police car. When the air-raid sirens go off everybody starts looking at the sky instead of the road, and Saddam Hussein's most fearsome weapon of the war's first week was the unguided Chevrolet Caprice Classic sedan.

The first sign of a Scud attack is a deep, vibrant *whoosh* from the Patriot antimissile missile being fired. Then there's a *crack* when the Patriot breaks the sound barrier, followed by a light in the sky and a huge *boom* from the Scud being destroyed. After that there's a brief pause followed by an incredibly loud air-raid siren, which our hotel sets off to let us know that the Scud attack that has just happened is expected soon. This sends the Filipino waiters and Indian busboys into a panic. They go running down the stairs to the air-raid shelter, colliding, on the way, with journalists running up the stairs to see the Scud fireworks from the hotel roof. Getting out on the roof is the third most dangerous thing about the Scuds—after car wrecks and falls on the staircase. You have to go through the blacked-out kitchen of the Chinese restaurant on the top floor, and there's considerable danger of falling into a big pot of stewed cat.

A Scud only carries about 250 pounds of explosives which—assuming the Patriots don't get it first—would create a blast a hundred yards wide at the most. These missiles are being lobbed into an area of eastern Saudi Arabia that's roughly fifty miles long and thirty miles wide. That's 4,626,400,000 square yards. The actual chance of taking a direct Scud hit is two in a million. Don't tell CNN this, however. Its nightly Scud watch—called the "Range-Finder Show" for its comments on where the missiles seem to be headed—is about all we have in the way of entertainment here.

Not only is this the first live televised war, it's also the first war ever covered by sober journalists. There is nothing available in Saudi Arabia with more "command-and-control capability" than O'Doul's. Which explains why a lot of the coverage from here seems a bit, well, sober. (Some of us journalists have discovered, by the way, that what we'd thought for years was the pain of genius was, in fact, a hangover.)

Coverage from here has been sober and—as sobriety often is—uninformative. After five months of the United States being about as involved with another country as it's possible to get, most folks back home still don't know what Saudi Arabia looks like. Sand and camels, they think. Sand and Marlboros and Pepsi would be more like it. Eastern Saudi Arabia looks like Arizona would if Arizona had beautiful beaches. There's the same big sky, the same sparse vegetation, and the same modern architecture—most of it ugly, just like in Phoenix.

Local mores do not, however, allow for much in the way of beach blanket bingo or *Sports Illustrated* swimsuit-edition photo ops. And there are no movie theaters, nightclubs, discos, or rock concerts either. And no Victoria's Secret catalogs or even lingerie ads from the *New York Times Magazine*. But there are superhighways, supermarkets, and malls. Most of the power shoppers are men. What few women you see are all in black, veiled up past the forehead and draped down to the ground. When the women want a better look at things in the market, they pull the hems of their veils out and over the merchandise like nineteenth-century photographers taking tintypes.

Saudi Arabia is perhaps the richest country on earth, and there are some big houses here and some Mercedes-Benzes that aren't much smaller. But it's not an ostentatious nation. Saudi men all dress the same no matter their wealth or importance. They wear sandals and a long nightshirt of a *dishdasha* or *thobe,* in white cotton or brown wool according to the season. They wear white or red-checked *gutra* headdresses held in place by the *igal* headband, a cord that was once used by Bedouins to hobble their camels. Status is told by the details—a Rolex watch, a Mont Blanc pen, a gold Dunhill lighter.

Saudi mansions are built close to each other. The two- or three-story houses are always plastered white and usually roofed in red tile. The architecture is grand in scale but austere in form—a sort of large, dull cousin of the Spanish colonial style. Each home is enclosed in a small garden. You don't see the slew of leisure toys with which rich Americans clutter their yards. There are no ski boats, ATVs, dirt bikes, camper vehicles, ultra-light airplanes, hang gliders, or whatnot. The desert comes right up to the garden walls.

Not that Saudi Arabia is all desert. There are large oases along the Persian Gulf coast. These contain thousands of date palms in a landscape so ripe, wet, and buggy that it could come out of central Florida. Except that these groves of palm trees have been occupied by the same clans of strict and pious Arabs for fourteen centuries. Imagine Disney World without the Disney and without the world.

Most native Saudi Arabians are adherents of the orthodox Sunni Muslim Wahabi sect. Wahabis are strict like old-fashioned American Baptists—no drinking, dating, mixed dancing, or movie going. But the Wahabis are not looney televangelist-with-a-gun fanatics of the Ayatollah Khomeini stripe. The religious practices and attitudes of Saudi Arabia are no more peculiar than those of Billy Graham. A churchgoing, small-town American from forty years ago would be perfectly familiar with the public morality here. Only the absolute segregation of the sexes would seem strange. And I'm not so sure about that. At O'Rourke family Thanksgiving dinners in the fifties all the men were in the living room watching bowl games and the women were in the kitchen washing dishes.

During the nine days that I've been here I have, of course, spent most of my time watching CNN to see what's happening to me. But I've also managed to visit the markets, or *suqs*, in the various towns along the Gulf coast—Dammam, Al Khubar, Qatif, Tarout. It's nice for an American to be someplace where people love the country they come from—a big change from being in America.

I've tried to get some "man in the *suq*" radio interviews but without much success. People are shy of the tape recorder. But they're eager to shake hands, say *Marhaba* ("Hello"), buy me a cup of coffee, and ask about the war. "You are the journalist but now we will interview *you*," said a wholesaler in the Dammam fruit and vegetable market. I asked why he wanted to do that. "Because you have talked to too many people"—an accurate solecism if ever I've heard one. The people in the market wanted to know how dangerous the Scuds were, how the air war was going, when the ground war would start. They said they didn't trust the information they were getting. They wanted to talk to a newsman and hear the real story. I asked where they were getting this information that they didn't trust. "From the news," they said.

People in eastern Saudi Arabia are still worried about poison-gas attacks. Nobody here goes anyplace without a gas mask. The masks come in imitation leather shoulder bags. Every man on the street has one. Dhahran looks like it's hosting an international convention of purse snatchers. Nothing could be further from the truth. There is virtually no crime in Saudi Arabia. You can leave the key in your car ignition here and leave your wallet and watch on the car roof. This is one of the most honest places on earth and for good reason. Under Shari'ah religious law murder is considered a mere civil matter, involving monetary compensation of some kind, but theft can be punished by amputation of a hand. There's also no begging or importuning or wheedling of any kind. I don't know what they amputate for this offense, but whatever it is, I suggest we start cutting it off in New York City.

The Dhahran area seems a bit empty and, at the same time, overpopulated with foreigners—sort of like Paris in August. Many local residents have decided that Scud month is a good time to visit relatives down around Yemen somewhere. But other than light traffic and ever-present gas masks, life is normal. Food prices have actually gone down and the only notable shortage is of AA batteries. This tells us that the U.S. troops are moving up to the front. As the troops leave, they empty the battery racks, stocking up to keep their Walkmans running. This is—one more first—the first war where everybody gets to pick his or her own theme music.

In case you're wondering, a gallon of premium gasoline costs 58 cents, and, no, you don't get your windshield washed. The gas stations are just like ours, including the bathrooms. Most bathrooms in this part of the world are Turkish style—you put a foot on either side of a hole in the floor and hunker down. But Saudi Arabian gas stations are equipped with American facilities. Some of the local people are unaccustomed to using these, however, which leads to footprints on the toilet seats.

U.S. troop morale seems to be ridiculously good. I ran into some members of the 101st Airborne Division buying art supplies in downtown Al Khubar. I'd say that indicates confidence (not to mention a previously little-suspected creative bent among our nation's paratroopers). The soldiers, sailors, marines, airmen, coast guarders, and whatever in Dhahran are cheerful. Maybe they're cheerful because they're not off in hell's outhouse somewhere sleeping in sand holes and eating MREs (Meals Ready to Eat or, as they're called, "Meals Refused by Ethiopians"). But from what we've been seeing in the "pool" reports and hearing from the reporters who've been to forward positions, the troops up there are in a pretty good mood, too.

It's important to remember that the 1991 U.S. military is not made up of Oliver Stone and his hootch-torching platoon of hopheads. These young men and women were barely born then. They're the Reagan Kids. They took one look at the sixties leftovers which littered their childhoods and said, "Give me a haircut and a job." They've got skills, training, education, and if they'd just quit calling me "sir" and telling me, "You're the same age as my mom," they'd be the salt of the earth.

One more thing about this generation of soldiers—they grew up in video arcades. It's no coincidence that watching the Gulf War's high-tech weapons on our TV screens is so much like watching computer games. This war is the daddy of all Mario Brothers, the Gog and Magog of hacker networks, the devil's own personal core dump. And our soldiers have an absolutely intuitive, Donkey Kong–honed, gut-level understanding of the technology behind it. Thank God they do. It's why we're winning. So here's what you folks back home can do to help with the war effort. If you happen to have any kids and they're outdoors exercising in the fresh air and sunshine, give them hell: "YOU GET IN HERE RIGHT NOW AND PLAY NINTENDO!" The future of our nation may depend on it.

Gulf Diary

January 28 through February 8, 1991

Monday, January 28, Dammam Suq

It's supposed to be a male-dominated society in Saudi Arabia, but I'm not so sure. There are amazing dresses for sale in the stores here—loud-colored silks and violently patterned satins with gold embroidery and gem-stone trimmings. Under those black *abayas* Saudi women are wearing important fashion statements. There are also a lot of jewelry stores with big gold necklaces and big ruby bracelets and diamond rings so large that you'd practically have to wear them on both hands at once just to lift them. I'm a married man. If this were *really* a male-dominated society, the jewelry stores would be stocked with plastic pop beads and the only thing the dress shops would sell is aprons. Plus the prices would be easier to read.

Since the time of the Crusades we in the West have been using "Arabic numerals." But the numerals actually used in Arabia are different. The 1 is the same, but an Arabic 2 looks like a backward 7. A 4 is a backward 3. A 7 is a 6. A zero is a 5. And a little dot is a zero. I don't know why the numbers are different, but I can guess. I'll bet if we went back and examined the Crusaders' expense-accounts, we'd find out that Richard the Lionheart got skinned.

Tuesday, January 29, Half Moon Bay

Oil is so important in Saudi Arabia that thoughts of "Liquid MasterCard" seem to pervade everything. The U.S. Consulate in Dhahran hands out a pamphlet to visiting Americans. The pamphlet gives tips on tourism and recreational activities. A suggested picnic outing: "The beaches nearby are open to the general public and afford a good view of the oil terminal."

Wednesday, January 30, Al Khubar

One of the pleasures of going someplace where people don't speak English is making fun of the English the people don't speak. Many of the commercial signs in Saudi Arabia are printed in English—more or less. I've seen the "Decent Barber Shop" and the "Meat Cow Fresh Butcher Shop," also "Wow" brand toilet paper, a fast-food restaurant advertising "humburgers" (ham being illegal), and a fancy model of running shoe called, in all innocence, "Crack."

Of course, when it comes to truly not speaking English, it's impossible to top the U.S. Department of Defense. The DOD calls a metal nut—the metal nut that goes on a bolt—I'm not kidding about this—a "hexaform rotatable surface compression unit."

A more peculiar feature of Saudi Arabia is intersection art. There are lots of traffic circles, and in the middle of each traffic circle is . . . something. Devout Muslims don't approve of statues of people, so there aren't any of those. But, just in the Al Khubar area alone, there is a giant cement Arab coffeepot (a symbol of hospitality), a scale model of the Space Shuttle (because a Saudi prince was a crew member on one mission), a real twenty-foot-long fishing boat mounted on a concrete plinth, a large jet airplane engine in a glass case, and an entire mosque, utterly isolated and unreachable on its island in the highway. There's also a lot of abstract stuff, such as a huge metal spiral (representing oil prices?) and two immense stucco triangles flanking what appears to be the robot vacuum cleaner from *The Jetsons*. What I have not seen in a traffic circle—and don't think I will see—is a monument to the first Saudi Arabian who learns how to signal a turn.

Thursday, January 31, International Press Headquarters, Dhahran

There don't seem to be a lot of celebrities protesting against this war. New Kid on the Block Donnie Wahlberg did wear a "War Sucks" T-shirt at the Grammy awards, but that's about it. In fact, I've heard that Jane Fonda has decided to maintain public silence on the subject of Desert Storm. Getting Jane Fonda to be quiet—this alone makes fighting Iraq worthwhile.

The Saudi Arabian beach resort of Khafji has been retaken. Which leaves us with the question: What do Saudi Arabians do at a beach resort? The women are dressed in tents, you can't get a beer to save your life, and it's hard to play beach volleyball when you trip over your *dishdasha* every time you serve. As much as I can figure, the only amusement that's available in Khafji is the one we've just witnessed—shooting Iraqis.

You may wonder what the job of being a Gulf War journalist is like. Well, we spend all day broadcasting on the radio and TV telling people back home what's happening over here. And we learn what's happening over here by spending all day monitoring the radio and TV broadcasts from back home. You may also wonder how any actual information ever gets into this loop. If you find out, please call.

Friday, February 1, International Press Headquarters, Dhahran

Dogs are considered "unclean" in Saudi Arabia. Which, if you think about it, is true so far as it goes. Sport does like to get mud on the bedspread and roll in stuff on the lawn. But camels are *not* considered unclean in Saudi Arabia. This leads me to believe that the Saudi Arabians know something about house training animals that we do not.

Members of the press corps have been trying to figure out what the U.S. military means when it talks about "air supremacy." We think it means that American air force pilots bombing Iraq are the only people in the world who can take a long trip by air and not have to change planes in Atlanta.

The so-called pool system of reporting the war is causing a lot of frustration. The U.S. military puts together groups, or pools, of reporters—one reporter from each kind of media. Then the military takes these pools on little trips to see things. This is like not being able to go to a football game unless Joe Montana invites you personally. If the pool system were used in dating, two hundred people would . . . well, it would be the 1960s all over again. If we got our news at home the way we're getting it here, the only time you'd know about a fire would be when kids playing with matches phoned the local newspaper before they lit the living room drapes.

Sunday, February 3, Dhahran Air Base

I was interviewing some British Tornado pilots who've been flying missions deep into Iraq—missions that sometimes take four or five hours. And I asked them the question that was foremost in *my* mind: "Isn't that a long time to go without taking a leak?"

It turns out the pilots do have "relief sacs." But they're wearing so much clothing—flight suits, G-suits, chemical-weapon-protection suits—that it takes them ten minutes just to get ready to use these aerial bedpans. So they avoid liquids for a couple of hours before they fly, and, so far, only one Tornado pilot has actually relieved himself over Iraq. And, no, he did not target civilian areas.

Monday, February 4, the Road to Abqaiq

Out in the Saudi desert I came across one of the strangest road-hazard signs I've ever seen. I was driving through a region of huge sand dunes, and every mile or so there would be a triangular sign—the kind that says SLOW, CHILDREN or DEER CROSSING in the States. But these signs said SAND DUNES. Sand dunes drift at a rate of about thirty feet a year. Saudi Arabians are fabulously bad drivers, but even they should be able to avoid something that's moving at less than one millionth of a mile per hour.

Wednesday, February 6, King Fahd Air Base

I was with a couple of U.S. Air Force officers, and they were complaining how everything has to be shipped in here—food, water, even the most primitive construction materials. While they were grousing I was looking around at all the bunkers, gun emplacements, and air-raid shelters built out of sand bags—thousands and thousands of sand bags. "Well," I said, "I bet there's one thing you guys can get locally . . ."

"You're *wrong,*" said the air force officers. "We know what you're going to say, but the sand here isn't the right kind of sand to make sand bags—too powdery." So the U.S. military is *shipping sand to Saudi Arabia*.

Because of the time difference, we get the late-night TV talk shows here early in the morning. Arsenio Hall by himself is alarming enough at 8:00 a.m. but this morning he had Sandra Bernhard on and, whoa, talk about something that doesn't go with breakfast. At least she makes the troops feel a little better about there being no USO shows here.

We've been having an informal competition to come up with the worst movie idea based on this war so far. Here's a strong contender: A group of American war correspondents somehow gets trapped behind enemy lines, and they have to complain and exaggerate their way out of Iraq.

Thursday, February 7, Hofuf

This is an ancient oasis town a hundred miles off into the Saudi desert, and it's one of the few places in this country that retains any character or visual charm. It has narrow-roofed streets in the *suq*. There's a bit of Ottoman Empire architecture left mid the concrete-block modernism. And Hofuf has one of the world's largest mud forts, a place that looks like . . . one of the world's largest mud forts.

It must have been interesting to live here. I guess when you grow up in a mud fort, Mom yells, "You kids take your shoes off before you leave—I don't want you tracking our house all over the outdoors."

Friday, February 8, International Press Headquarters, Dhahran

I watched Secretary of State Baker's speech to the House Foreign Relations Subcommittee the night before last, and I actually heard the secretary say that America will help rebuild the economy of Iraq after this war. Mr. Secretary, I just can't tell you what enthusiasm your plan has inspired here in Saudi Arabia. First, let's give the Iraqis Michael Milken so he can set up a Baghdad junk-bond market. Then we'll send in Michael Dukakis for a repeat performance of his Massachusetts Miracle.

As everyone knows, the U.S. military censors our "news pool reports." We're not supposed to tell specific locations—cities, military bases, etc. We're only allowed to name the country or, at most, the general region of that country.

One of my radio pool-report tapes came back from the censors with a so-called red flag and a note saying, "You cannot mention 'Thumerate' in Oman." I'd never heard of Thumerate. In vain I searched the map of Oman for Thumerate. Finally I played the tape back. What the military censors were sure was a city or vital base—Thumerate—was an air force colonel from North Carolina saying, "*The emirate* of Oman."

We keep hearing about Iraq's "elite Republican Guard." Well, if they're so elite why don't they have better jobs than sitting around getting the stuffing bombed out of them in Kuwait? And what are they guarding anyway—big charred wrecks of buildings and blown-up bridges? And one more thing—how many of these elite Republican guards are really Republicans?

At the Front, Early February 1991

Halfway through a ninety-minute flight to the front lines aboard a C-130 Hercules cargo plane, Colonel Clay Bailey, commander of the U.S. Air Force's 317th Tactical Airlift Wing, said, "The crew calls this plane the 'Franken-Herc.'"

I asked why.

"Because it was patched together from two other C-130s that crashed," said the colonel with the large smile that military men get when they're scaring civilians.

The inside of a Hercules is like an airborne basement, with wires, pipes, and ductwork covering whatever you call an airplane's walls and ceiling. There's room for 42,000 pounds of cargo. Colonel Bailey wouldn't tell me what this cargo was, a secret which made me sincerely hope his crew would avoid air turbulence, let alone enemy antiaircraft fire.

The cargo was in wooden boxes held in place by what looked like oversized women's hairnets. Each net-full rested on a metal plate as wide as the plane, and the plates sat on a wheel-covered deck—a kind of reverse skateboard or roller floor that allows the cargo to be rapidly shoved out the back when the plane lands or even when it doesn't land, if parachutes are used.

We were flying at 6,000 feet with fighter planes somewhere above and below us so that we were the tuna fish in a giant airlift sandwich. There was nothing to see from the cockpit except winter desert haze—endless murky gray-brown ground and murky gray-blue sky with a smudge of horizon in between. We seemed to be inside a bad Mark Rothko painting. But if I looked straight below us and concentrated, I could pick things out, things that looked like random scatterings of runes or Arabic letters—wiggles and dots in the sand. The wiggles were berms—bulldozed ridges of sand pushed up around the tents, tanks, guns, and trucks, which were the dots. Berms are this war's trenches. You get dug in, but first you get bermed up. There was nothing actually random about the wiggles. This was a modern front with soldiers and weapons carefully spread around thousands of square miles. It is to the front lines of past wars as today's pro football defense is to the way football was played in the 1950s. The troops don't just line up and crouch anymore.

At first a modern front didn't seem impressive, and then I realized how long I'd been looking at wiggles and dots while flying by at 300 miles an hour. This is a big, but uncrowded, war. The sky isn't black with airplanes. The ground isn't honeycombed with bunkers. Everything in this war is so powerful, so fast, and has so much range and reach that a roomy bloodbath is required.

The C-130 landed on a mile-long blocked-off section of a two-lane highway about fifteen miles from the Iraqi border. The plane came in at the same angle that's used for bobsled runs. The pavement was only twenty feet wider than the landing-gear track. This is not a large margin of error when crosswinds are blowing, and they always are. Outside the scenery was similar to that photographed on Mars by the *Viking* spacecraft—so similar as to be identical and I think a NASA audit is called for.

The land was hard-packed grit the color of blood and diarrhea. It was strewn with mud-pie-looking rocks and was so awful in its perfect flatness that I thought I could see the curvature of the earth. Anywhere I stood I seemed to be standing on high ground. The horizon fell away in every direction. I got dizzy when I stared into the distance.

A cold and arid wind seemed to come from every direction at once. A few tents had been pitched. They had grit all over them and drifts of grit coming in under the tent flaps. A few soldiers were there, grit all over them too. One of the air force officers had just come back from a yearlong tour of duty in Greenland. "When I got off the airplane in Greenland," he said, "I thought, 'I've found the end of the earth.'" I asked him what he thought now. "I've found the other end."

Army Specialists Forest Chester of Aberdeen, Washington, Michael Lindstrom of Reno, Nevada, and Sherrie Murry of Lyons, Georgia, were using a tent pole to scratch a map of the United States into the dirt, making the outline as nearly life-size as they could. They'd been five months in Saudi Arabia without leave, and they'd been a month in this particular Satan's parking lot. The fact that I was writing for *Rolling Stone* magazine was the most interesting thing they'd heard in days, although that wasn't saying much. They wanted me to please tell country/folk singer John Prine to do another album, quick.

Listening to Walkmans is about the only fun American troops are having in a place where there's no booze and most of the women either are covered with the front-hall rug or they outrank you. By now every American soldier has listened to every cassette and CD in Saudi Arabia at least twice. I was talking to a sergeant in a Dhahran record store, a black woman from Chicago. She said, "Who's that girl who's got the song that goes 'da-da-da-da-da' forever?"

I said, "Suzanne Vega?"

"Yeah," she said. "I'm even going to listen to her."

Peacenik types say there would be no war if people truly understood how horrible war is. They're wrong. People don't mind a little horror. They can even be enthusiastic about it if the horror is happening to somebody else. But everybody hates to be bored and uncomfortable. If people truly understood how much sleeping on rocks, how much eating things rejected by high school cafeterias, how much washing one body part at a time in cold water, and how much sheer sitting around in the dirt war entails, we'd have world peace.

The, speaking of dirt, dirty little secret of this war is that we all privately hoped the Israelis would get fed up with being Scud-whipped and break down, drop the big one, and fuse the sands of Iraq into one vast sheet of glass so we could go in there and finish this thing with Windex. That isn't going to happen. And so the war drags on—a whole three weeks now. Jeez, this thing is turning out to be longer than the Ken Burns Civil War miniseries on PBS.

Boredom aside, U.S. troop morale seems to be fine, whatever that means. You'll notice that the term "morale" is never used except in reference to soldiers or people in analogous positions, such as employees of large corporations or prison inmates. Even educational institutions have "school spirit" or "the mood on campus" rather than "morale." Nobody ever talks about the morale of participants in a passionate love affair, nor does the word come up in discussions of wild drinking sprees, marathon poker games, or visits to whorehouses in Bangkok.

"Morale" apparently means "how well people are doing when they're not doing well at all." In that sense, U.S. troop morale is, as I said, fine. Nobody has painted a peace symbol on his helmet. And nobody—except journalists dealing with the military's Joint Information Bureau—has threatened to frag an officer. Everybody has a pretty good idea why he's here. And just about any pfc can articulate it better than President Bush: A whole bunch of U.S. citizens are facing a tinpot dictator with the fourth-largest army in the world so that the tinpot dictators with the fifth-, sixth-, seventh-, and eighth-largest armies in the world won't dis Uncle. Or anybody else. One of the war's favorite T-shirts bears a *Ghostbusters* logo with Saddam Hussein in place of the ghost. "Who Ya Gonna Call?" it says, and below that are the numbers 001, the international telephone access code for the United States.

Morale is particularly fine in the air. Air forces own the franchise for this war so far. Even the crews from the British Tornado fighter-bomber wing which has had four of its planes shot down were full of smiles and sangfroid. A half dozen Tornado fliers were trotted out to endure the press. When asked the inevitable age-of-sensitivity "How does it feel?" question, the crew members gave answers better suited to a gardening column than the Phil Donahue show.

"One of the things that obviously you can't train for and get used to is the amount of flak and missiles coming up," said pilot Richard Goodwin. "It does look very, very spectacular."

"I'm still amazed at the sort of sparkling lights of the antiaircraft fire and the missiles and so forth," said Goodwin's navigator Dave Chatterson, "and I stupidly enough still find them quite pretty."

A lieutenant colonel in the Kuwaiti Air Force—who'd managed to escape to Saudi Arabia in his A-4 Skyhawk last August—was even more cheerful. "It's, kind of, happy feelings to get into Kuwait," he said. "After six months we didn't see Kuwait. And then we fly inside Kuwait. You see the country. At the same time, you know, we bomb our country." Though this didn't seem to upset him. "But we try to avoid to bomb which is populated areas," he added.

Morale is fine and boredom is preferable to getting shot, but Saudi Arabia is off the hit parade. Very few people who came here for Desert Storm will be coming back on vacation. It's not that the Saudis aren't fighting. Saudi troops—uncouth-looking fellows who seem to be from the boonies of Asir and the Yemen border—fought well if not wisely at the battle of Khafji. (The Saudi brass have explained to everyone who will listen that they didn't allow the Iraqis to slip into Khafji and they won't do it again, also it wasn't their fault and furthermore it was part of a plan.) But the drab sanctimoniousness of Saudi Arabia is getting on everybody's nerves. There's no noise, no fun, no movies, no Christmas, and our military chaplains have to be called—that word again—"morale officers."

Our Father, who art in . . . um . . . the gym at the base . . . Give us this day our daily hobby and leisure-time activities . . . And forgive us if we get in a bad mood.

And civilian Saudis themselves aren't acting much like American civilians would if the fourth-largest army in the world were massed on the Canadian border. Nobody is up in the master-bedroom window with his duck-hunting shotgun or out fixing punji sticks in the lawn shrubbery. The Saudis aren't doing much of anything, which is par. They pray five times a day and everything shuts down for about five hours at every prayertime—you figure it out. All real work in Saudi Arabia is done by dark-skinned poor people—from India, Egypt, Thailand, and the Philippines. (Of course, you could make a somewhat similar argument about the U.S. military, but don't make it in front of General Powell.) There's a standing wager in the press corps, a free bottle of postwar champagne to the first person who sees a Saudi lift anything heavier than money.

The entire Saudi civilian war effort in Dhahran has consisted of half the Saudis leaving town, even though Dhahran is separated from the front by 180 miles of desert and the U.S. Army, Air Force, and Marines. I talked to an Indian who was managing a Dhahran sportswear store. About two-thirds of the shops on the block were closed. I asked when they'd shut. "From the beginning of the war," he said.

"Was it the Scud missiles that scared the shopkeepers away?"

"Oh, no," said the Indian. "Just the war. They never know what is going to happen."

"Where'd they go?" I said.

"Maybe some went to Jiddah. Maybe some are sleeping at home. All the stores open here, they are open by Indians and Filipinos."

I said, "I guess it's too far for you to go back home?"

He frowned and shook his head and said it wasn't too far at all. "My sponsor has my passport." He couldn't leave.

So far no pejorative term has been coined for Iraqis. There's no "Gook" or "Kraut" or "Nip" for this war. And the only Iraqi jokes I've heard, I've heard on the telephone from back home. As a matter of fact there's only one war joke going around in Saudi Arabia.

What's the name of the Saudi national anthem?

"Onward, Christian Soldiers."

Gulf Diary

February 11 through February 25, 1991

Monday, February 11, Dhahran

One thing all of us here sincerely regret is that John Tower was not confirmed by the Senate as U.S. secretary of defense. You can bet we'd be able to get a drink in Saudi if Good-Time Johnny Tower were in charge of Desert Storm. Either that or we'd be fighting this war someplace where we could—New Orleans during Mardi Gras, for instance.

Tuesday, February 12, Dhahran Air Base

Ever since bombs were invented it's been customary to personalize them with messages written on the shells: "Stick this in your mustache, Saddam," that sort of thing. We've been trying, however, to improve the quality of bomb graffiti, make it a little more clever. Not that we've had much success so far.

STEALTH PILOTS DO IT IN THE PLACE WHERE YOU LEAST EXPECT THEM TO DO IT
IF YOU CAN READ THIS, YOU'RE DEAD
MY OTHER BOMB IS ATOMIC

Anyway, we're open to suggestions.

Wednesday, February 13, Dhahran

An Iraqi air-raid shelter was hit by American bombers. Initial estimates from Baghdad of the casualty figures ranged from 40 to 1,500. This illustrates a persistent problem in the Middle East. The zero was invented by the Arabs, but so were the next six or eight zeros after that. Americans should be warned that you will hear a lot of numbers coming out of this part of the world, but don't count on them.

Thursday, February 14, Dhahran

It's Valentine's Day, time for romance. And what could be more romantic than sex toys? We've been trying to figure out what Saudi Arabian sex toys would be . . . edible veils? Inflatable plastic airline tickets to Europe? But in a country where a man may have as many as four wives, the most popular marital aid is probably ear plugs.

Have you noticed Saddam Hussein's furniture? You can see it in the background in his CNN interview or when he's having a photo opportunity with international peace-pest diplomats—Cosa Nostra Rococo. Now we know why the Iraqi Air Force disappeared—they didn't want to get the white velvet upholstery in their MiG cockpits messed up flying combat missions.

If we want to demoralize the population of Iraq and sap their will to fight, we ought to show them videotapes of the South Bronx, Detroit City, and the West Side of Chicago. Take a look, Iraqis—this is what we do to our own cities in peacetime. Just think what we're going to do to yours in a war.

Friday, February 15, Dhahran

Maybe Kuwait really *was* a threat to Iraq. I talked to a Kuwaiti Air Force colonel who thought it had been. He explained that Kuwait was using all its oil money to buy things for its citizens while Iraq was using all its oil money for military hardware. "Iraq," the colonel said, "either had to bring its citizens up to the Kuwaiti level or bring Kuwaiti citizens down to the Iraqi level." In other words, Kuwait caused the war by shopping too much. This leaves us with little hope for world peace as long as wives are allowed to hold credit cards in their own names.

I passed a Saudi bus on the highway last night. U.S. soldiers had written in the dust on the back and sides. "Iraq sucks," said one message, but most of the graffiti was hometowns—Mobile, El Paso, Detroit, Des Moines. And way up in the corner of the bus's back window one soldier had written the name of that quintessential hometown of almost all us Americans—"Suburbia."

Sunday, February 17, Riyadh

I drove to the Saudi capital to attend a couple of the military briefings in person. The only road map I had was in Arabic. I had a little trouble finding my hotel, just off Squiggle Street at the corner of Long Squiggle and Tall Squiggle.

The journalists in Riyadh are more earnest, whiney, and weenie-like than the journalists with the troops in Dhahran. One long-haired worrywart who was with either the *Village Voice* or National Public Radio was concerned that we were bombing every one of the government buildings in Baghdad. "Are we going to leave Iraq without *any* government departments?" he asked the briefing officer indignantly.

Not all the reporters in Riyadh are like that, of course; the British newspaperman sitting next to me said, "We'll leave them the Department of Tourism—'See the Ruins.'"

We're used to not getting much information during the question-and-answer periods at the military briefings. But today a reporter asked a Saudi general, "What's the weather like in Saudi Arabia in March?"

"I will try to find this out for you," the Saudi general said.

Monday, February 18, Wadi as Sahba

I got stuck out in the desert. I pulled off the road to take a leak and my car went down in the sand like the *Lusitania.* I didn't have a shovel. I tried to dig the car out with a hubcap—the car went in deeper. I tried to put brush and rocks under the wheels—the car went in deeper. I had the car in the sand up past the doorsills by the time the Saudi police happened by. They almost got their car stuck in the sand, too. They didn't have any rope so they flagged down a trucker. He didn't have any rope either so we used one of the canvas straps from his freight load. We got my car out, but the canvas strap became completely snarled in my front bumper and tangled in the police car's back axle and none of us had a knife. We spent the next half hour sawing at the cargo strap with the edge of a flattened soft-drink can.

America has all the guns and Saudi Arabia has all the money, but it's no wonder the Japanese are ruling the world.

Wednesday, February 20, Dhahran

I read today on the AP wire that our loyal NATO ally Turkey is sending two generals and three colonels to Saudi Arabia. No soldiers or anything, just generals and colonels. "Forward, me!" "About my face!" "I am hereby recommending that a medal for heroism be awarded to me for saving the life of everyone under my command by sitting in a Riyadh hotel room."

Between 350 and 400 Iraqi soldiers just surrendered to U.S. helicopters flying hundreds of feet in the air. Not long before, another group of Iraqi soldiers had surrendered to three *Life* photographers. The Iraqis seem willing to surrender to anything. The Saudis have promised that all prisoners of war will be given adequate food and shelter, kept away from the fighting, and released when the war is over. Adequate food and shelter? Kept away from the fighting? Released when the war is over? The press corps must have surrendered months ago.

Thursday, February 21, Dhahran

Personally, I'm coming back to the United States as a big supporter of nuclear power plants. It's worth the risk just to make sure that this part of the world *never* has any political, strategic, or economic significance again. That done, we can use the Middle East for the purpose to which it is so ideally suited—dumping nuclear waste. Watch out for the nine-legged camels.

Every time I look at American TV I see these "defense experts"— former generals now being paid large fees to go on *Nightline* and talk about the Gulf War. Well, I'm a former hippie. Maybe I can get a job as a "protest expert."

Ted Koppel will say: "P.J., does your expertise as a retired long-haired butt-head lead you to think that the protesters will continue to beat drums outside the White House or will they begin chanting 'No Blood for Oil'?"

And I'll say, "Well, Ted, I believe that we will see continuation of a primarily drum-focused activity here although we cannot rule out the possibility that the protesters may eventually utilize 'Draft Neil Bush' signs. We know they have the capability."

Friday, February 22, Dammam

I've mentioned before that Saudi Arabia is an incredibly honest country—as well it might be, since they cut your hand off if you're caught stealing. But although there seems to be no theft here, there are enormous padlocks on all the shops and offices—sometimes four or five of them on a single door. Maybe there's a side to Saudi Arabia I don't know about. Whatever, I've decided to stay out of neighborhoods full of one-handed men.

Monday, February 25, Dhahran

One terrible problem confronting Iraqi troops is finding something white to wave when surrendering. They've run out of pocket hankies. The Iraqi army doesn't issue bedsheets. And, since the Iraqi soldiers have been at the front lines for a long time without adequate supplies, their underwear is, frankly, not white anymore. If antiwar organizations want to stop the fighting in the Gulf, they should send Clorox to Iraq.

We hear the Iraqi army is systematically blowing up buildings in downtown Kuwait City. If the architecture in Kuwait resembles the architecture in Saudi Arabia, the Iraqi army will have done one good deed, anyway. As soon as the Iraqis have all surrendered, let's send them to New York and let them take a whack at Trump Tower.

Riyadh and the Desert, Late February 1991

Certain of the ancient moral philosophers—Norman Mailer comes to mind—hold that every man should experience war because war, like love, is one of the central mysteries of life.

Central? Let's hope not. Mysterious? And how. Even the most modern and baffling romances, with their diseases, divorces, custody battles over the dog, and years spent afterward in therapy and Woody Allen movies are not more mysterious than combat. For example, during the past week and a half we've been facing the worst threat of this war so far—peace. Giving the Iraqi armed forces a chance to go home, simonize their tanks, and think up new ways to amaze the world is the most terrifying imaginable outcome to the Gulf conflict.

But we were reasonably confident that bloody, murderous peace wouldn't break out. We'd managed to survive Saddam Hussein's first call for a cease-fire, "The Dog Ate Kuwait" peace initiative, which he presented last week. Then there was the Soviet-brokered "I'll Pull Out in Time, Honey, Honest" peace plan. We endured that. So we figured we could get through George Bush's noon on February 23 deadline. And, indeed, as I write this, on Sunday, the twenty-fourth, word comes that the ground war has started. Word also comes that we're going to learn nothing about that ground war. The secretary of defense tells us we are entering a period of "media blackout." Thus war grows more mysterious still. And so does war reporting. Here I sit scribbling trivia while the most serious events of a generation take place so close that I can see the haze from the oil-well fires in Kuwait.

War is mysterious but never more so than when it involves two of life's other big mysteries, Saudi Arabia and the U.S. military mind.

Nothing about the U.S. military—except killing bad guys—makes sense. The military mind is unfathomable even in the most minute and specific details of its operation. Inside each MRE field-ration kit there's a pouch containing salt and pepper, gum, napkins, other odds and ends, and a pack of matches. The matchbook cover is plain olive drab and bears the message: "These matches are designed especially for damp climates but they will not light when wet."

As for Saudi Arabia, the English-language newspaper here, *Arab News,* has an Islamic agony column where readers can write in with the kind of questions Ann Landers would get if she were a Muslim scholar.

Q. What lesson do we draw from knowing that a certain person died in the toilet?

The answer being no particular lesson. But some of the replies in the *Arab News* leave a Westerner feeling that he has encountered a mentality almost as foreign as the one which produced the MRE matchbook:

A. The rule is that when you put your socks on in the morning you should have a full ablution, washing your feet. Then before that ablution is invalidated, you put on your socks . . . If you need to do ablution again that day, you need not take off your socks. You simply wet your hand and, using your fingers, you pass them over the top of your feet.

Simply as a physical locale Saudi Arabia is incomprehensible. It's not a matter of "What are we doing in this place?" It's a matter of "What is this place doing in existence?" The two-hundred-mile stretch of desert between the Persian Gulf and the Saudi capital Riyadh is so scruffy, flattened-looking, and devoid of physical features that it hardly seems to be part of nature. The land appears to have been cleared by a bulldozer the size of the Hoover Dam. It's God's Vacant Lot. There's a whole section of Saudi Arabia called the Rub al Khali, the "Empty Quarter," and the frightening thing is, this isn't it. The Rub al Khali is somehow emptier yet.

An ugly four-lane highway runs through the ugly desert from Dhahran to Riyadh. Junk is strewn all along it—rusted mufflers, empty water bottles, waste paper, lengths of cable, old truck tires, construction detritus, and a thousand bright pink and yellow plastic shopping bags floating like jellyfish on the breeze.

We Americans are long trained in highway citizenship. It's been thirty-five years since I threw something out a car window without guilt. I'd forgotten the pure exhilaration of littering and found myself heaving Coke cans and half-eaten sandwiches into the ether at every opportunity.

The other signs of human life along the Riyadh road are oil wells and oil storage tanks, a few plumber's nightmare petrochemical factories, and an occasional gas station.

The view in Saudi Arabia, when there's anything *to* view, is utilitarian, industrial, and dumpy—grimly practical stuff. But what is the practical result of all this practicality? There's no clue in Riyadh. It is a city with two million people and uncountable wealth, and there is no reason on earth to go there. A large, glossy picture book, *The Kingdom of Saudi Arabia*, commissioned by the Saudi government itself, says of Riyadh: "With its flyovers and tree-lined boulevards, its first-class hotels and . . ."

Here is a glowing official description of a nation's capital, and the first thing that the first sentence mentions is highway overpasses.

Rightly so. Riyadh is almost all new, with the worst kind of urban newness—a grid of lifeless streets in a cage of freeways, and every little rectangle is filled with modern architecture. There are miles of the usual high-rise concrete and steel self-storage-in-the-sky buildings. But the Saudis can afford the creative kind of modern architecture, too. You can always tell when modern architecture is being creative—the rest of the thing looks like the same old curtain-wall rabbit hutch but the roof is nutty. Lumpy roofs, wavy roofs, roofs in curlicues, and roofs puckered in the middle like assholes—Riyadh has them. Also, like Abu Dhabi and Dubai, it has modernism that gives a nudge and a wink to Arab traditions—giant cement Bedouin tent shapes serving no purpose and enormous onion-shaped arches in the middle of nowhere. And there are all the other varieties of contemporary design Habitrail Modern, Brobdingnagian Lego Block, Behemoth Tinker Toy, Cheese Grater of the Titans, plus some of those buildings that are—who knows why—wider at the top than they are at the bottom.

The Saudis are guaranteeing the safety of surrendering Iraqi troops, and they're also providing asylum to everybody who ever got kicked out of architecture school.

Only a few of the traditional mud houses of the Najd, or central Arabian highlands, are left in Riyadh, and the Saudis are tearing these down as fast as they can. The flat-roofed buildings are reddish-beige, the color of a frostbitten nose. More vertical and austere than American adobe homes, each is a sort of private tower keep with only a few small, deep-set, and shuttered windows. The floors are made of palm-trunk beams covered in layers of thatch. Simple pie-crust and pinking-shear patterns are traced around the edges of the roofs. By watching the demolition work I acquired a sort of X-ray vision. Where walls were toppled, I could look inside the houses and see the steep switchback staircases with their mud steps leading to snug whitewashed rooms with borders around the windows and doors painted in brilliant blues and greens.

Near the demolition site I found several dozen Filipino construction workers shoveling wet dirt and straw into a cement mixer. They were building a brand-new mud structure. This, I was given to understand, would be ready for tours in a month—the traditional architecture of Old Riyadh painstakingly reconstructed within two hundred yards of Old Riyadh being torn down.

I drove southeast out of the capital, following a line of oasis towns in the riverless riverbed of the Wadi as Sahba. Each town was a miniature of Riyadh in its up-to-date ugliness and sat in a nasty little tangle of date palms that looked like the cat had gotten into the potted plants.

The road was two-lane here and the driving was, as it is everywhere in Saudi Arabia, horrific—conducted at absolute top speed with no thought for consequences. Though there were plenty of consequences to be observed. Amazing car wrecks lay beside the road, sometimes a dozen of them in a mile, things you would never know had been cars if a couple of car wheels weren't sticking up out of them. Whole Chevrolets were crumpled like gum wrappers. And these wrecks had taken place without collision on a perfectly straight and level road that is absolutely free of obstructions. Cars just somehow go blooey and wind up in a wad beside the highway.

Running parallel to the road was a railroad track that was also perfectly straight and level and absolutely free of obstructions. And—sure enough—amazing train wrecks lay beside the rails, things that you would never know had been trains if a couple of train wheels weren't sticking up out of them.

I stopped in one of the oasis towns to get gas and some more Coke cans to throw out the window. There was a Bedouin kid, about fifteen, at the little store. Most Saudis are—whether they take their socks off during ablution or not—fastidiously clean, and they are polite to the point of cold formality. But this kid was pesky and dirty and determined to practice his nonexistent English. "Riyadh? Riyadh? Riyadh?" he said. Yes, I'd come from Riyadh. "Is seeing George Bush?! George Bush?! George Bush?!" George Bush is a president. Riyadh is a capital. So naturally I'd seen him there. Then the kid tried to sell me something. It was a photograph of a girl—with her veil off. I've been here so long I blushed.

Turning back toward the Persian Gulf, I drove northwest through the 150-mile-long Ghawar oil field. The whole way I could see an immense natural gas burnoff flaring on the horizon like the pillar of fire that guided the Hebrew tribes by night when they were fleeing from Egypt. Above the flame was a huge vertical cloud like the pillar of smoke that guided the Hebrew tribes by day. But the Hebrew tribes wound up in Israel and the oil wound up here. God let the Hebrews take a serious wrong turn.

Is this empty, dusty, cheerless, oily, fun-free place making the American military crazy? Here's another mystery of war—no. Even being in the American military isn't making the American military crazy. I visited an army motor pool where the soldiers had—with the exception of a few forays into the shockingly dull local town—been confined for five months to one vast expanse of asphalt surrounded by razor wire. Specialist Hefner of St. Mary's County, Maryland, and Specialist Jonas of Bay City, Texas, both streaked with grease like zebras, were happily wrenching on a large truck. "She's our best mechanic," said Specialist Hefner of Specialist Jonas, who had left a baby behind in the States to come do this. Specialist Jonas gave a shy smile of nondenial. "We don't like it here too much—nothing to do," said Specialist Hefner. But that was all I could get out of them in the way of complaints, although Specialist Hefner did allow that the Saudis "drive like fools."

At Saudi Arabia's main Persian Gulf port facilities in Dammam, I talked to Captain Johnny L. Sawyer from Detroit, Michigan, commander of the 551st Transportation Company. His job is to unload boats. Captain Sawyer said, "When we initially arrived here, we worked the soldiers eighteen hours a day, gave them four to six hours rest, at most, and put them back to work.

There weren't any complaints whatsoever. That's seven days a week, and we've been doing that for the past six months. They're down to a twelve-hour schedule now but we still have soldiers that are willing to work extra hours without being told. They stay behind just to finish a job." Captain Sawyer had been in the army for thirteen years and had come up through the ranks. "The quality of the soldiers, from then to now," he said, "has improved drastically. I don't think that a soldier that we would have called standard then would be allowed to join the army today."

I talked to a medical officer at one of the British field hospitals. He'd been in Vietnam and this was his first contact with the American military since. "I was astonished when I got here," he said. "Every American soldier I met was tidy, cheerful, eager to help, glad to be here—well, not precisely *glad*, but you know what I mean. This had not been my experience in Vietnam. It is as if the American soldiers here come from a different nation."

And that is one last mystery of war—where did the addled, sniveling, pointless America of the past quarter century go? There's no trace of it in these parts. The catchphrases of this war are "I'll make it happen," "not a problem," "good to go," and "hoo-ah!," a sort of all-purpose noise of enthusiasm. When the chairman of the Joint Chiefs of Staff visited here, the soldiers asked him for his autograph. A sense of doing something worthwhile and important has even infected a few members of the press corps. Some reporters were ready to check into the local clinic after experiencing a strange and frightening choked-up feeling when looking at the American flag.

At the King Fahd Air Base, west of Dhahran, there's a small sign posted in one of the buildings taken over by the U.S. Air Force:

GIVE WAR A CHANCE

Missile Attack on Dhahran, February 25, 1991

We couldn't go to war, but war came to us. Two days into the ground assault on Iraq the majority of the press corps was stuck, as usual, in the press headquarters at the Dhahran International Hotel. There was a Scud missile attack on Monday night, one of dozens since the war began. We didn't think much about it. Some of the technicians on the outdoor TV platforms—where you see correspondents stand with the silly blue-domed roof of the hotel's pool cabana in the background—watched the Scud go down. They thought it hit near the local shopping center and we joked that Saddam Hussein was targeting Dhahran's only decent record store. Then we went back to the work of pretending we knew more about this war than people watching television in Cleveland.

The missile had, indeed, struck right behind the record store, going through the roof of a warehouse that had been converted to a billet for U.S. troops. We heard nothing about this at the press headquarters. Almost two hours later I was driving to Dammam and I saw hundreds of blue police lights blinking in clusters around the shopping center. A half dozen helicopters hung in the sky with their searchlights moving back and forth like blackboard pointers. And ambulances were rolling away in long and frighteningly silent convoys.

Saudi police blocked the road. I parked and followed a crowd of robed Saudi onlookers, some of them holding hands, most of them speaking in whispers. They moved across a half mile of open fields toward the shopping center. It didn't seem like a disaster scene. What had been the warehouse with more than one hundred Americans inside didn't look like a building that had been blown up. I thought I was staring at a construction site. The framework of steel girders was mostly still standing. Some of the I-beams were twisted or collapsed, but the ventilation ducts and the electrical conduits remained in place. What I didn't understand was that there had been a roof and walls. And these were utterly blown away.

There was really nothing else to see except slightly panicky Saudi police and very serious American troops. Twenty-eight soldiers were killed and ninety-nine were wounded—more American casualties caused by one unlucky Scud strike two hundred miles behind the lines than had been suffered in the whole rest of the war to date.

Kuwait City, March 1991

As befits a short war, it didn't take me long to readjust to peace—three minutes and forty seconds to be exact, the length of one Billy Idol music video. I was drunk and lying on a hotel bed in Rome. In the previous forty-eight hours I had managed to get myself out of the reeking, scrambled mess of Kuwait, back to the ugly, sterile, unwelcoming Saudi capital of Riyadh. From there I'd driven across hundreds of miles of stupid desert in a disposable diaper of a Korean rental car and finagled a ride out of Dhahran on an airliner chartered by an English TV company to take its people and gear to the next place foreigners decide to get killed.

It didn't seem like it had been a short war at that particular moment, not after two months with the arrogant, lazy Saudi Arabians and nothing to drink. We charter passengers were into the Johnnie Walker miniatures before the plane cleared the runway, and grown men, adult broadcasting executives with serious jobs in a large corporation, were kneeling in their seats, trying to swill from three or four little Scotch bottles at once and screaming out the windows at the diminishing landscape, "FUCK YOU, YOU MOVING TEA TOWELS!"

Anyway, as I was saying, I was lying on a hotel bed in Rome, and I flicked on the television, and there was MTV showing a Billy Idol video.

Billy was really going at it, running around the stage in a most histrionic way, thrusting his fist into the air, stamping his feet, and making violent and emphatic faces at the camera. It was a dramatic performance but confusing to my woozy intellect. What, I wondered, was Billy Idol being dramatic *about*? I'd just spent the past week in a burned-up, blown-up, looted city where there was no food or water, seeing mangled bodies and hearing stories of murder, rape, abduction, etc. It made me get drunk and lie on the bed without taking my shoes off. But Billy Idol seemed to have experienced something much more dramatic, so much more dramatic that it made him strip half-naked, dye his hair platinum, wear a bunch of jewelry, and jump around like an ape.

"Billy Idol concerts are," I thought, "obviously worse than war."

Kuwait did have a better light show. There is nothing else in the world (I'm glad to say) quite like four or five hundred burning oil wells casting a lambent glow upon a nighttime desert landscape. The flames come up out of the wellheads in soft, thick, billowing shapes like clouds or turds or cake batter. The fires are scary when you glance at them but terrifying if you keep looking. That is, the fires seem to be big and close. Then you stare into the perspectiveless desert and realize they are fifteen or twenty miles away and are therefore enormous beyond comprehension. You can hear them across all that distance. There's no reassuring, ordinary crackle and roar in the noise the fires make, and no blast of heat. Instead the sound is a steady, sucking rumble of the whole atmosphere being dragged toward the conflagrations. And beyond the fires that you see are the fires you can't see, brightening the horizon on all sides like a dozen simultaneous dawns breaking on one very bad day.

I had a lot of time to look at the oil-well fires because on the third night of the ground war I spent six hours with forty-five other journalists and a half dozen British army officers being held at gunpoint in the middle of the Kuwaiti desert.

Not by Iraqis, of course. The Iraqi army was in high-speed rewind. We were under arrest by a Saudi colonel who was furious that the British didn't have the correct paperwork for escorting a convoy.

Our mission to bring pool journalists from Dhahran to Kuwait City was not moving with the same efficiency and precision as the rest of the allied Gulf War operations. The British military escort was made up of retired officers who had volunteered to aid the Gulf War effort and had come to do so at their own expense. They were an affable lot but, well, retired. They were armed with Lee-Enfield bolt-action rifles of a vintage suitable for port wine, and they didn't have two-way radios or even maps. They put the eighteen-vehicle convoy together with the slowest things at the back so that the trucks all lost sight of the cars within minutes. The main purpose of the convoy was to get the British Independent Television Network's satellite dish into Kuwait. The first thing the British officers did was leave that dish behind. The second thing they did was take a wrong turn leaving Dhahran and head south toward Qatar instead of north toward Kuwait City. It took us eight hours to reach the Kuwaiti border, a three-hour drive.

It was dark by the time we passed through the well-shelled town of Khafji and its abandoned Saudi customs post. We could hear artillery fire in the distance now, and every few hundred feet we'd pass a burned Iraqi tank or personnel carrier.

Shrapnel was scattered everywhere on the road, causing a half dozen blowouts. And more time was wasted when young journalists—members of that generation so handy with keyboards, modems, and electronic what all—had their first encounters with screw jacks and lug wrenches. Then we got arrested.

The Saudi colonel, who looked like a cross between Omar Sharif and Mr. Potato Head, had a platoon of soldiers line up across the road and level their rifles at us. "YOU DO NOT HAVE THE PERMISSIONS! HOW CAN YOU BE COMING HERE WITHOUT THE PERMISSIONS WHEN I AM THE PERSON WHO IS MAKING THE PERMISSIONS FOR YOU TO COME HERE?! YOU MUST GO BACK TO DHAHRAN AND GET THE PERMISSIONS FROM ME THERE TO COME HERE AND GIVE ME PERMISSIONS!!!" shouted the Saudi colonel.

In vain it was explained to the colonel that this was an official British military convoy, that the British were Saudi Arabia's allies, that this was Kuwait and not Saudi Arabia anyway, and that we could hardly go back and get permission from him in Dhahran when he was here.

The electronic-minded young journalists fetched a satellite phone and its bulky antenna dish out of their car, set it up in the middle of the road, and phoned the Kuwaiti minister of information at his exile home in Tarif. The minister told the colonel the convoy could proceed, whereupon the colonel hung up on the minister of information and threatened to shoot the satellite phone with his submachine gun.

In the midst of this argument a metallic-blue Ferrari 328 came humming through our convoy, its thousand dollars' worth of tires and its three inches of ground clearance apparently immune to jagged metal fragments. This was just a couple of Kuwaiti refugees determined to get home before the liberation rush. They didn't even slow down for the gun-pointing soldiers, who jumped to get out of the Ferrari's way.

In the end it turned out what the Saudi colonel wanted was a sufficiently abject and humble apology from the British officers for, I guess, failing to fill out, in triplicate, the Request for Permission to Help Keep the King of Saudi Arabia from Getting the Holy Kaaba Stuffed up His Butt.

Apology delivered, the Brits led our convoy directly into downtown Kuwait before realizing that the city had not actually been reconquered.

Iraqi jeeps, trucks, armor, and artillery pieces were lying on their tops and sides all along the Kuwait City expressways as though somebody had spilled Saddam's toy box. The Iraqis who'd been inside all seemed to be gone, in one sense of the word or the other. In place of the Fourth-Largest Army in the World we saw cruising teens. This was the Kuwaiti Resistance. One group of five pulled up in a Buick Park Avenue, happily brandishing AK-47s out the windows of Dad's car. They were dressed just like teenagers would dress if the cool kids at the high school got to form their own partisan army—one guy favored the Rambo look, another was dressed like Little Steven, two others were got up in Mutant Ninja Turtle garb, and one fellow, who wasn't quite with the program, seemed to have stepped out of a J. Crew catalog. They were hunting for Iraqis or people who looked like they might be Iraqis or people who had collaborated with Iraqis or had thought about collaborating. And I wouldn't be surprised if they were also keeping an eye out for the algebra teacher who gave too many pop quizzes. Small arms fire could be heard coming from various places in the lightless city. It was a teenage dream come true: bad guys invade your neighborhood and you and your best friends get to stay out late, kill them, skip school, and impress girls. The Kuwaiti Resistance fighters welcomed us effusively.

The Brits decided we should go to the International Airport even though we'd been hearing on the shortwave radio about a tank battle there. Fortunately, this was over but lots of jumpy U.S. Marines were patrolling the airport perimeter, and it was a shock to their systems when they came across us, totally lost, in eighteen civilian vehicles packed with camping gear, foodstuffs, bottled water, and people in Banana Republic clothes. It must have looked like the Adventure Tour travel business had gotten completely out of hand.

Going back into the city at 6:00 a.m., we could see that the Iraqis had left in brainless panic. All their wrecked military equipment was pointed in the same, Baghdad-ward, direction. Allied air strikes had caused some of the destruction but traffic accidents had caused more. Jeeps had smashed into tanks. Tanks had rammed bridge abutments. Armored personnel carriers had rear-ended ambulances. A truck towing a howitzer had jackknifed and collided with itself. And a T-55 Soviet tank came a cropper on a highway divider and wound up high-centered, three and a half feet in the air.

Iraqi defenses had been abandoned with the same comic haste. Guns, ammunition, canteens, helmets, even shoes were left behind. Tea kettles were still sitting on paraffin burners. I found somebody's uneaten dinner—a pot full of chicken and rice, or rice and cat maybe, white meat anyway. The defenses themselves were pathetic. The Iraqis had built miles of low dirt berms across the main road from Saudi Arabia. These were little more than speed bumps, and were supposed to . . . to what? . . . signal allied armor, "Slow, War Zone"?

Every highway overpass had a little pillbox built on it—four feet square and three feet high with no roof or back wall. These tiny redoubts were made of crumbly local bricks pasted together with a few dabs of mortar. Hundreds of them pimpled the city in places the Iraqis had, by some mysterious thought process, decided were strategically important. Thus the roofs of all the hotels had pillboxes but the roofs of other tall buildings didn't, and while expressways were defended, roads with two-way traffic were not.

Iraqi soldiers had made sad little nests in these emplacements—lined them with stolen blankets, chunks of foam rubber, old clothes, canned goods taken from local homes, pictures of pretty women torn from magazines, and other bits of unmilitary junk. The local soccer stadiums and Kuwait's only ice-skating rink had also been fortified, the fortifications consisting of one row of sandbags placed in front of each principal entrance.

Members of the Kuwait Resistance showed me a twenty- by thirty-foot model of Kuwait City in the basement rec room of a mansion that had been occupied by Iraqi staff officers. The model was made of sand with blue-dyed sawdust from the Persian Gulf. Roads were indicated with gift-wrap ribbon, and the principal buildings and military installations were represented by Lego blocks. Handsome navy-blue construction-paper arrows showed U.S. forces coming ashore into conveniently located minefields, while much larger and more festively lettered red arrows showed Iraq's reinforcements arriving from somewhere in the direction of the rec room's projection TV. It seemed Saddam Hussein had let the defense of Kuwait be planned by the prom decorations committee.

The Iraqis were better at destroying Kuwait City than they were at keeping hold of it. But they weren't really good at this either. Again their first concern was with the hotels, as if allied forces would never be able to effect a real conquest without room service. The Iraqis tried to set all the hotels on fire, but in many cases they used diesel oil, which is not the best arson accelerant. The hotel where I found a room had survived pretty much intact except that a thick layer of greasy and insoluble oil soot had settled on every chair, table, towel, bedsheet, and toilet seat. After a couple of days, all the reporters staying there looked like they had passed out in a tanning booth.

Downtown had experienced plentiful random artillery fire, as if children had had tantrums with tanks and mortars. But the big triple cocktail onion–looking pointy water-tower things that are the symbol of Kuwait City proved too sturdy for Iraqi gunfire, or maybe just too hard to hit when whole sides of city blocks offered themselves as targets. The *suqs* with their flammable jumbles of shops had been successfully torched. And anything complex and vulnerable, such as the power stations, the desalinization plants, and the main telephone switchboard, was thoroughly ruined.

But what the Iraqis were really good at was looting. Every store and office and an enormous number of homes had been sucked clean of all possessions. Nothing was left behind except the trash of deliberate vandalism and, in some cases, piles of human shit. The Hilton Hotel had been taken to pieces room by room. It looked like all the rock bands in the world had stayed there at the same time.

The city was not, however, extensively booby-trapped. The Iraqi soldiers were evidently so stupid and eager to leave that it was hard to imagine them having the forethought to wire up surprises. "All boobies, no traps," was the consensus. And most of us quit worrying about dirty tricks. Besides, there was so much untricky dangerous stuff lying around the city—live bullets and artillery shells, loose mortar rounds, unexploded American cluster bombs, and so forth. An NBC camera-crew member lost some fingers fondling a land-mine detonating cap he'd picked up as a souvenir. And mines were going off on the city beaches with fair regularity, turning some unwary Kuwaitis into what the GIs call "pink mist." I was helping dismantle one of the small pillboxes on the Hilton's roof, getting bricks to level a satellite dish. There was a wooden carton sitting in the pillbox. I lifted the lid and found enough RPG—rocket-propelled grenade—rounds to put me, bricks, and satellite dish in permanent earth orbit. I closed the lid carefully and extinguished my cigar.

The Hilton is next door to the American embassy, and a couple days later U.S. Special Forces came and "swept" the hotel to make sure a small thermonuclear device wasn't hidden in the basement or anything. I saw one of the Special Forces guys later in the hotel lobby. "Hey, we found a booby trap!" he said in the perky, enthusiastic, pumped-up way nineteen-year-old Special Forces guys have of saying these things.

"Good for you," I said. "Where was it?"

"In a big box of RPGs, in that first gun emplacement on the edge of the roof. You know, the one with some bricks missing off it. There was a hand grenade with the pin out in there. Man, if anybody had jiggled that box . . ."

I briefly got religion. "God spared me for a special reason," I thought and felt very good about myself. "I must be going to accomplish something very important in life, something that will benefit all mankind."

My ABC producer friend Derwin Johnson said, "There were two fucking dozen other people on that roof! It's probably one of *us* who's going to invent a vaccine to prevent Jim Morrison revivals."

On Thursday afternoon, February 28, about six hours after the U.S. declared a cease-fire, the victorious armies began to roll into Kuwait City. The Arab contingents were firing their guns in the air and the Kuwaiti

Resistance fighters responded by firing *their* guns in the air and then the other Kuwaitis picked up all the leftover Iraqi guns and started firing these in the air, too. People were singing, dancing, clapping their hands, and beating on car horns. The women began ululation, that fluttering liquid animal sound made somewhere in the back of the throat, and the women's kids joined in with a more familiar plain screaming of heads off.

An impromptu parade was begun past the American embassy, but there wasn't anyplace that the crowd wanted to parade *to*, so the parade turned in ever tightening circles in front of the embassy and finally just stopped and became a crowd. The crowd yelled, "George Push! George Push! George Push!" Someone had already spray-painted "Thank you for George Push" across the American embassy wall, and the "P" had been carefully crossed out and the spelling corrected. A donkey was led down the street with an Iraqi helmet tied on its head and "Saddam Hussein" painted on its flanks. The first American soldiers showed up and everyone had to kiss them and shove babies into their arms and get the soldiers to autograph Kuwaiti flags. Kuwaiti flags were everywhere and at least a dozen little girls wore Kuwaiti-flag dresses—one red sleeve, one green sleeve, white down the middle, and a black triangular yoke at the neck. Their mothers must have been stitching these all through the war. There were plenty of American flags, too, one with a picture of Marilyn Monroe sewn over the stripes. And across an intersection downtown a thirty-foot banner had been strung, reading—in answer to the U.S. and European antiwar protesters' "No blood for oil" slogan—BLOOD FOR FREEDOM.

Then there was a great noise and wind, and descending from the sky into this melee came a huge American army helicopter down onto the roof of the U.S. embassy. The helicopter disgorged a squad of Army Rangers to roaring, stentorious cheers. It was the fall of Saigon with the film run backward.

A lot of people were crying, and I was one of them. A young Kuwaiti came out of the crowd, and he was crying, and he grabbed me by my notebook and, with that immense earnestness that you only have an excuse for a few times in your life, he said, "You write we would like to thank every man in the allied force. Until one hundred years we cannot thank them. What they do is . . . is . . ."—words failed him—". . . is *America*."

Not everything was quite so saccharine as that in Kuwait City, of course. Earlier in the day, on the other side of the Hilton Hotel, some scores had been settled. Kuwaiti Resistance kids shot up an apartment building that was supposed to be full of Iraqi collaborators. The Kuwaitis dragged out three ordinary-looking middle-aged men, one howling for mercy and two looking grim. "They are Sudanese Intelligence," said one Resistance kid. Though any review of Sudan's recent history would render that phrase oxymoronic. The suspects were shoved into a Toyota Supra and taken off to

I'd-rather-not-think-where. Later I saw another alleged collaborator arrested at bazooka-point. That was a quick giveup.

Palestinian guest workers, many of whom had had the bad taste to chortle over the Iraqi conquest of their Kuwaiti employers, were a particular target of the Resistance. Roadblocks were set up all over town to ferret out the Pals. The roadblocks were manned—boyed, to be exact—by nervous kids with automatic weapons. It was like being back in Beirut except these militants wanted to hug you for being American instead of shoot you for it. Considering that the Kuwaitis were as bad as the Lebanese about gun safety, getting hugged was probably as dangerous.

Some of the Palestinians weren't playing things smart. I found one of them standing in line with a jerrycan at a gas station. He was being insulted by the Kuwaitis on either side of him. Instead of making excuses or becoming suddenly Syrian, he jumped out of line and started shouting at me: "Why you Americans come here and do this, why you don't come to the West Bank as we have been waiting for since 1962?!" I presume he meant '67 but, whatever, it didn't seem like the most politic tack to be taking at the moment. The Kuwaitis apologized to me and pulled the Palestinian back into the gas line so they could insult him some more.

As joyful as the Kuwaitis were, they were just that furious. It was a difficult frame of mind to understand at first, though happy anger is probably more common and less contradictory than it sounds. Every Kuwaiti I spoke to had had members of his or her family beaten, killed, or simply taken away. The hospital morgues were filled with the remains of tortured Kuwaitis, many unidentifiable. Every cemetery had a swath of new graves, mostly filled with men, the birth dates on the tombstones painfully contemporary, and the death dates beginning August 2, 1990.

I visited a mass grave where two hundred some Kuwaitis were interred and these were only the bodies that family members had been able to retrieve and bury by stealth. In another cemetery I found a man tending the graves of his uncle and his uncle's son-in-law. Each tomb had an improvised wooden marker and a bottle stuck neckdown into the dirt with a verse of the Koran rolled inside. The man stood between the bare-earth mounds with his hands at his sides and spoke very quietly. His expression was of enormous, almost hysterical resignation, a kind of smile of grief. He said his uncle's body had burns from a clothes iron and from cigarettes. There were marks of electrical wires. His fingers had been chopped off. His eyes gouged out. Finally he had been shot in the head. The son-in-law had been tortured with an electric drill, then scalped, then shot in each eye.

"They were taken away on January 17," said the man in the cemetery. That was the day the air war began. "The bodies were left at hospitals on January 19," he said. "These people were not Resistance." He paused and then said in the same quiet voice, "Iraqi occupying soldiers should be given back to the Kuwaiti people."

When the Iraqis tried to leave Kuwait City, early on the second day of the ground war, they headed en masse up the road to Basra using both sides of the six-lane highway. About thirty-five miles north of the city, near a low rise called the Mutlaa Ridge, this bugout was spotted by U.S. Navy A-6 attack planes. These navy pilots must fly New York City traffic helicopters in civilian life, because they knew exactly what to do. They went right to the spot on the crest of the ridge where the road narrows from six lanes to four and plugged that bottleneck with cluster bombs.

The panicked Iraqis tried to drive around the burning wreckage and became bogged down in the sand. The traffic jam spread out and backed up until it was nearly a half mile wide, more than a mile long and contained at least fifteen hundred vehicles. Then all the airplanes that the U.S. Navy, Marines, and Air Force could muster came in and let loose with everything they had. One navy pilot called it "shooting fish in a barrel," but it was more like sticking a 12-gauge shotgun into a goldfish bowl.

The wreckage was still smoldering four days later. It didn't look like a battlefield. There were some Iraqi army vehicles in the mess—tanks opened up like bean cans and armored personnel carriers turned into giant hibachis. But most of the transport had been stolen, stolen in a perfectly indiscriminate frenzy of theft that left the ground covered with an improbable mixture of school buses, delivery vans, sports coupes, station wagons, tank trucks, luxury sedans, fire engines, civilian ambulances, and semi-tractor trailers. I saw a motor scooter, a Geo Tracker, and—the vehicle that would be my personal last pick for something to escape in—a cherry-picker crane. It looked like a bad holiday traffic jam in the States except charred and blown up, as though everybody in hell had tried to go to the Hamptons on the same weekend.

Allied burial details were moving through the wreckage, but some bodies were still lying crispy and twisted in agony. I felt sorry for the poor dead bastards, but it was a reasonable, detached kind of sympathy that came from the went-to-college part of the brain. I was intellectually obligated to feel sorry for them, but after seeing what they'd done in Kuwait City, I had more of an Old Testament feeling in my heart.

> *Then did I beat them as small as the dust of the earth, I did stamp them as the mire of the street, and did spread them abroad.*—II Samuel 22:43

Of course I didn't do this personally, but my tax dollars helped. I caught myself giggling in the carnage. This supposedly formidable and certainly ruthless army had not only run from a fight like a flock of hens, it had also tried to carry with it every item of portable swag in the emirate. The killing field was littered not so much with corpses as with TVs, VCRs, Seiko watches, cartons of cigarettes, box lots of shampoo and hair conditioner, cameras, videotapes, and household appliances. School desks, tea sets, stuffed animals, silverware, an accordion, and a Kuwaiti family's photo album were all being dragged back to Iraq. I saw a pickup-truck bed full of women's ball gowns and another truck stacked with Pampers. A hot-wired camper van sat with two cans of club soda resting in the dash-mounted drink gimbals. The camper bunks were filled with men's boxer shorts, the price tags still on them, and the whole—camper van, club sodas, underpants, and all—was punched full of tiny holes like a cheese grater from cluster-bomb shrapnel.

Six days after the liberation of Kuwait the Kuwaitis were still celebrating outside the U.S. embassy, firing every available weapon in the air, including the .50-caliber dual-mount machine guns on the Saudi and Qatari personnel carriers. It's one thing to get plinked on the head by a falling pistol bullet, but a .50-caliber slug plummeting from the sky at terminal velocity could go right through you to the soles of your feet. One American marine told me that sixteen people had been killed by "happy fire" so far, but a U.S. Army officer said it was more like 150. All the press corps' telephone and television satellite uplinks were on the roof of the Hilton and rounds were beginning to land up there. One bullet came down between the feet of ABC executive Neil Patterson, who started handing out helmets and battle gear to everybody on the ABC payroll. The most dangerous thing I did during the entire war was cook spaghetti sauce on a camp stove on the Hilton roof without wearing my flak jacket.

Finally, one of the ABC satellite technicians—a Brit and a veteran of the Special Air Services—could stand it no more and leaned over the roof parapet and bellowed at the trigger-crazed Kuwaiti merrymakers, "STOP IT! STOP IT! STOP IT! PUT THOSE FUCKING GUNS AWAY AND GO GET A MOP AND A BROOM AND *CLEAN THIS COUNTRY UP*!"

I went out to the Kuwait International Airport, or what was left of it, to try to get home. While I was sitting out there next to the burned ruins of the International Terminal, a Saudi business jet arrived guarded on all sides by U.S. Cobra and Apache helicopters. The crown prince of Kuwait was returning home after a comfy exile in Tarif.

The next thing I knew the tarmac was covered with sleek Kuwaitis in perfectly draped *dishdashas*. They were shaved and scrubbed and their gold wristwatches sparkled in the sun. A U.S. Air Force enlisted man, sitting next to me on a broken couch that had been dragged out of the rubble of the first-class lounge, said, "When the fat guys in the bathrobes come back, you know the war is over."

I hitched a ride to Saudi Arabia on a New Zealand Air Force C-130. The members of the flight crew were all in their twenties and filled with leftover joy of combat. They let me stand on the flight deck as they brought their 132-foot wingspan, 100,000-pound airplane down to a hundred feet and began chasing camels and goats across the desert at 300 miles an hour. The scattered tamarisk bushes were coming at us like uncountable fastballs in a batting cage. The camels gave out pretty quick but the billies and nannies and kids were inspired to remarkable sprints of goat turbo-terror. The vast destitution of the Dahna Sands spread out in an infinity around us. "Wall-to-wall fuck-all, eh?" shouted the Kiwi pilot. He and his crewmates had smiles as wide as their skulls. This was the stuff that made it all worth while, to be in absolute charge of 17,200 horsepower, to have, gripped in your fists, the whole might of science, of industry, of civilization's mastery of the world—*our* civilization's mastery of *this* world. "HOOOOO-AH!!!" as the Gulf troops say.

We popped over the top of a little ridge, and there was a Bedouin camp on the other side. I watched a boy about nine or ten years old come running out from one of the goat-hair tents. We were so close I could see his expression—thrill and fear and awe and wonder combined. His whole life he'll remember the moment that sky-blackening, air-mauling, thunder-engined steel firmament of war crossed his face. And I hope all his bellicose, fanatical, senseless, quarrel-mongering neighbors—from Tel Aviv to Khartoum, from Tripoli to Tehran—remember it too.

ALL THE TROUBLE IN THE WORLD

(*1994*)

"I read somewhere that the sun's getting hotter every year," said Tom genially. "It seems that pretty soon the earth's going to fall into the sun—or wait a minute—it's just the opposite—the sun's getting colder every year."

—F. Scott Fitzgerald,
The Great Gatsby

Multiculturalism

Former Yugoslavia, Fall 1992

In former Yugoslavia all manner of ethnic, religious, and cultural minorities were fully empowered—with guns.

I watched as Serbian Chetnik nationalists tried to take the village of Golubic from Bosnian-Herzegovinian Muslims. The unspellables were shooting the unpronounceables.

I was in a slit trench on a hill behind Bosnian lines. Golubic is—or was—a trim group of tile-roofed stucco houses set in little gardens along the Una River. A rail line ran beside the riverbank, with engine and freight cars blown up on the tracks. The Una was the shade of blue that children color rivers, and its waters were speckled with rapids like dabs of white enamel. The afternoon was without wind or cloud. No leaf turned or branch swayed along Golubic's tidy lanes. The place seemed to be a miniature of itself, and the war, a war on a model-train layout.

I had a perfect view of the fighting, except there was nothing to see. High-power weapons and high-speed fire scatter modern soldiers, and camouflage and smokeless explosives render those soldiers invisible. If artists still painted pictures of battles, a battle would look like an ordinary landscape with small pockmarks and some large, charred holes. Nor is there "din of battle" anymore. No trumpet calls or rallying cries or even shouts and screams could be heard in Golubic, just desultory gunfire. The putter of a machine gun would echo between the house walls. Then a pause. Then some answering thumps and pops. The Serbian artillery was a couple miles away. I could hear it go off. Later I'd hear an explosion, but usually I couldn't see where. Sometimes a shell would whistle overhead. Now and then a puff of dust would rise in the valley but with the sound of impact so delayed that cause and effect seemed disconnected. A few rifle shots were coming in my direction, I guess. Flying bullets don't, in reality, make noise. Though once in a great while I'd hear the adventure-movie sound of a ricochet in the rocks nearby.

Golubic is in a corner of northwest Bosnia known as the "Bihac Pocket," a Muslim enclave some forty-five miles in circumference containing 320,000 people who were being shelled by Serbs. To the east and south of Bihac were the rebellious Bosnian Serbs who controlled two-thirds of Bosnia. To the west and north were the rebellious Croatian Serbs who controlled one-third of Croatia. The Muslims were surrounded. But, then, so were the Serbs. Beyond the Croatian Serbs were Croatian Croatians, and beyond the Bosnian Serbs were more Bosnian Muslims. Thus it was across the map of ex-Yugoslavia: concentric circles of combat, murder, and rapine.

I drove to Bihac with London *Times* reporter Ed Gorman, a television reporter I'll call Tom Lamson, and a Croatian translator, Kadi, who pretended to be Serbian when we were stopped by Serbian soldiers. It was easy for Kadi to pretend to be Serbian because Serbs and Croats are so much alike that they can only tell each other apart by religion. And most of them aren't religious. So the difference between Serbs and Croats is that the Serbs don't go to Eastern Orthodox services and the Croats don't attend Mass. And the difference between Serbs and Muslims is that five times a day the Muslims don't pray to Mecca.

On the fifty-mile drive from Croatian-held territory into Bihac five kinds of armies had set up seven checkpoints. In the very middle of these was the United Nations Protection Force, UNPROFOR. Most UNPROFOR troops come from nations that don't normally teach lessons in civic order to Europe—Jordan and Nigeria, for example. In this particular sector the UN soldiers were from Czechoslovakia, which at that time was itself disintegrating. The Czechoslovaks doubtless wished to be home shooting each other instead of here unable to shoot anyone. UN peacekeepers aren't allowed to fire their weapons unless they come under an attack so severe that they're probably already dead. What UNPROFOR is protecting isn't clear. Certainly not itself. The UN checkpoint was on a hill with no cover, exposed in every direction and within a Daisy air-rifle shot of both Muslims and Serbs. The Czechs had AK-47s and a formidable-looking armored car. But their helmets were baby blue and the armored car was painted toilet-bowl white.

Inside Bihac was another UN group, a six-man military observer team. The officer in charge was testy. He'd been under fire for seven weeks. "It's been quiet today," he said. There was an explosion several blocks away. "Right on cue," said the officer. We tried to ask him about the strategy of the civil war. Were the Serbs trying to occupy Bihac or neutralize it? Was the siege a bargaining ploy, something to be given up so Europe would turn a Neville Chamberlain eye on a partitioning of Bosnia? Would the Bosnians . . . "I've given up trying to figure out why. I just report," said the officer. The UN observer team's mission in Bihac was to talk to the Serbs by radio phone and arrange a cease-fire, the officer said. But the Serbs weren't returning his calls. "Sitting here, getting shelled, waiting for the phone to ring," he said, "that about sums up our situation." The observers had a logbook recording the assaults, bombings, and artillery attacks on the area. Each page was ruled in vertical columns: DATE, TIME, LOCATION, DAMAGE, CASUALTIES. The column headed ACTION TAKEN BY THE UN was empty.

Bihac proper has a population of forty-five thousand, plus refugees. Farms butt against the business district, and beyond the farms is a spread of outlying villages such as Golubic, three miles away. The villages and the town have yet to grow together in modern suburban sprawl. Bihac looks cute to American eyes, as if built in the three-quarters scale of Disneyland's Main Street. The architecture is worth a picture postcard—vaguely antique and Palladian, though not much of it predates New York's Museum of Natural History. The atmosphere is generalized European. Bihac could be in Austria or Bavaria or Tuscany or, for that matter, in the new Euro Disney theme park in France. The mosque seemed out of place. So did the artillery damage.

The civilian response to the shelling in Bihac was appealingly civilian. All the windows in the center of town were sandbagged, but the sandbags were made from pillowcases in paisleys and plaids and bold geometric prints. A protective barrier around the Bihac Hotel had been built out of old refrigerators filled with sand.

Bihac had been under siege since April. Casualties among civilians had been fairly light to date: 315 dead and 1,500 wounded. The farmers in the Una valley were still getting in crops. Factories still operated. Red Cross and UN relief convoys were making it through. Everybody in Bihac said Bihac couldn't survive the winter, but nobody talked about surrendering. All the shade trees had been girdled and would be dead and ready to cut for firewood by the first snowfall. A little bit of ammunition was arriving on night flights from Croatia. Mortar shells were being manufactured in local machine shops using shotgun shells for detonators and explosives scavenged from bombs left behind by the Yugoslavian air force. The land mines also looked homemade—rusty metal objects the shape of Mallomars and the size of hubcaps with precarious spring-mounted trigger mechanisms on top. The Bosnian soldiers set rows of these across the highways. To let our car pass they would boot the mines aside with a nonchalance combining kick-the-can with kick-the-bucket.

Gorman, Lamson, and I drove to the outskirts of Golubic. A few shells were falling, but it was hard to say how close. The locals weren't diving under things. We had flak vests. But wearing a flak vest only makes you realize how much more there is to vestments than a vest. The areas of my body that I like best weren't covered at all. I wanted flak briefs and flak mittens and flak socks and a flak bag to stick my head into.

A Bosnian soldier led us up a farm road to the trench above the fighting. He was wearing a Yugoslav National Army uniform with a little blue ribbon tied to his left epaulette to show he was in the Bosnian forces. The road ran along a ridgeline behind a hedgerow. The Serbs held the other side of the valley. Years ago TITO had been spelled out in painted rocks on the hill over there. The enormous letters were still faintly visible. The four of us trotted in a crouch—the soldier nimbly, the three reporters less so and making the trumpeting breath noises of chain smokers. Running in a flak vest is like going for a jog with your mattress box spring. The vest weighs thirty pounds and is made of solid Kevlar plates which ring like dinner dishes when rapped with your knuckles. The vest front is formed in one smooth carapace and is not meant to be worn over a whiskey gut. I know why there are no fat turtles.

Every couple hundred yards there was a gap in the hedge, and here we'd have to run across one at a time. We'd pull up in a crowd before the opening, politely trying not to be the third or fourth to go. The theory is that snipers don't see the first two runners in time to shoot.

It's not a good idea for a journalist to wear khaki pseudo-military journalist clothes in a war zone. You look too much like something that's supposed to be shot, such as a journalist. On the other hand, white ducks and a madras shirt catch the eye and I wish I'd packed my duck-hunting camo duds.

Gorman, Lamson, and I spent all afternoon in the slit trench, peering through the shrubbery at the indiscernible mayhem in Golubic. At one point a haystack caught fire. Later a couple of stray pigs wandered down a street. And an hour or two after that, in the middle of a fusillade, a farmer left his house and ambled over to his barn. Except for various explosions, this is all we saw. But we weren't bored. Violence is interesting. This is a great obstacle to more worthwhile journalism.

We spent the night at the fridge-fortified hotel. It was a splendid fall evening with amber light on the horizon blending off into cobalt blue around a waning moon and air as cool as clean sheets (something the hotel didn't have). We stood outside drinking the local beer, leaning against the refrigerators, and listening to the shells hit around town. The cars on the street drove by fast, keeping their lights off so as not to attract snipers. When it was dark we went into the hotel bar and ate goulash by candlelight. "When there's electricity, there's no water," said the waitress, "and when there's water, there's no electricity." We commiserated. Life must be very difficult. "It's hard to make espresso," she said.

Zagreb, the capital of Croatia, is even more of an ordinary European place than Bihac. The driving is just as frantic but the cars aren't being shot at. The service is mediocre but due to socialism, not siege. There is an old town of regulation charm, a hilltop cathedral inspiring the standard awe, and the usual handsome public square with a statue of a brave dead guy where you'd expect it to be.

You don't see many soldiers in Zagreb, not as many as you saw in peacetime Eastern Europe under communism. Some of the snapshots displayed in the instant-photo store windows are from the front—groups of men arm in arm next to something blown up. A few buildings have their windows X-ed with masking tape as though giants had been playing tic-tac-toe. At the newsstands the gun magazines are on the front racks. Those are all the signs of war in Zagreb, and the fighting is only thirty miles away. Maybe Europeans have greater sangfroid than Americans. But there's a lot of fighting in Detroit and things are quiet in Bloomfield Hills.

In the evening everyone goes to the cafés that line the steep streets near the cathedral. The cafés are chic. Numerous young men of military age were sitting around in fancy jeans and sneakers. I asked Kadi the translator whether these guys felt any duty to join the Croatian army. "No," she said.

It is a peculiar feature of the contemporary era that a large portion of our horrors are optional. A couple of days later I was on the Bosnian border in Slavonski Brod, a Croatian city being shelled by the Serbs. I was in the Arcade Bar drinking in the middle of the day with the twenty-six-year-old owner, Vinko. A lean-to made of timbers as thick as railroad ties shielded the front window. Vinko wore a diamond stud in his left ear and pants with enough pleats to make a concertina. Some music more current than I am was on the stereo. "War makes no sense," said Vinko.

"There's no pressure on young men to go fight," said a girl at the bar.

"I'd go fight if everyone else would go," Vinko said.

I'd talked to a soldier in Bihac, a captain in the Bosnian army who was from Serbia and not Muslim. He had been in the Yugoslav Federal Army. He said he sat out the war in Slovenia and sat out the war in Croatia and sat out the first part of the war in Bosnia "until Bosnians decided if Bosnia was just for Muslims. When they said it was for everybody who would fight, I joined." Then he told a virulently anti-Gypsy joke.

As the war repels a certain number of Yugoslavs, so it attracts a certain number of foreigners. The government press office in Zagreb was full of chirpy volunteers from places like Cleveland, Ohio. College-age children of Croat emigrants, they were skinny, Gap-clad citizens of a 90210 planet in some other solar system than gory Balkan peasant feuds. Nonetheless they were willing to come back and help Yugoslavia destroy itself.

A blond Bosnian guerrilla fighter from Las Vegas seemed to live in the bar of my hotel. He wore steam-ironed battle dress with an ascot and a beret. His hair was combed into a ducktail. He told a lot of war stories, carried maps to illustrate them, and claimed he was about to lead a supply convoy into central Bosnia. He'd be leaving very soon, as quickly as possible, any day now. In the evenings I'd hear his voice above the tavern din, "Did you see me on *Good Morning America*?"

A freelance journalist cornered Gorman, Lamson, and myself one night. He'd been shot in the leg. In Sarajevo. Just a few days ago. "In these very jeans." His Levi's were, indeed, torn at the knee. He'd had quite a lot of other adventures in Sarajevo. And before that he'd been in Lebanon. He'd had his throat cut and been thrown down a well there. Or was it shot and pitched off a building?

Many of the other soi-disant journalists had had no previous experience at all. I met one photographer who was just out of college and on assignment for an avant-garde Swiss art magazine named *NKKKK* or *XOX* or some such. He'd driven his daddy's car, alone, into Serbia, across Croatia, down into the middle of Bosnia, and back out again. He looked twelve, which is all I can think of to account for his not being entirely dead.

Mixed with the liars and greenhorns was the usual war-side crowd of UN bumf shufflers, international aid agency deadwood, and other people who tangle up humanitarian assistance and get in the way of charitable help, plus the shills for peace—Greens, Buddhist monks, members of U.S. congressional fact-finding missions, and, of all things, an Iranian human rights group.

There's another kind of person who comes to a war, though not often enough. Ed Gorman and I met him at a UN checkpoint, standing beside a tractor-trailer with vast red crosses painted on the side. His name was Mick Rhodes and he was waiting for some fighting on the highway to end so he could deliver a load of food and medical supplies to beleaguered Muslims. Rhodes was a Yorkshireman, a long-haul truck driver by trade, as wide as he was high and with a serious belly. He had any number of tattoos, hair as short as Sinéad O'Connor's, and, across the bridge of his nose, a scar shaped like the business end a broken pint mug. Mick Rhodes looked like a football hooligan. He'd been listening to BBC radio back in Yorkshire and heard an interview with a Yugoslav Red Cross official who said drivers were needed.

"They were asking for drivers to cross the lines," said Mick, "because they can't use their own guys. That's why we're all expats." He motioned to some fellow drivers, every one of whom looked like he could clear the foreign fans from a European Cup match with a sidelong glance. Mick's company had given him six months off, and here he was. "I'm away from home ten weeks at a time normally," he said. "The only difference here is that this time I'm getting shot at as well." I asked him which was worse, that or the road traffic in Turkey. "Turkish traffic," he said. He had a wife and six kids at home. His wife was a bit nervous but "knew this was what I wanted to do."

"Have you ever done anything, any volunteer things, like this before?" asked Gorman.

Mick laughed. "No, not me. That is, not counting a few loads of donated food for Romanian orphans during the civil war there."

Gorman and I went for a Sunday drive in the pokey Croatian countryside. The land north of Zagreb is hilly but well populated, as clean as Switzerland and as dull as Idaho. Prosperous, compact, and photogenic farms cover the slopes. Heidi and her dotty granddad could have sauntered out of any one of them, although nothing that interesting happened. Ed tried to make a case that the countryside was "eerily quiet." But Ed has never been in Boise on a Sunday. Besides, the graffiti on the battlements of Ptuj castle belied him: LED ZEPPELIN, DOORS, JANIS JOPLIN.

We came to the border of Slovenia on a two-lane road in the middle of nothing. Here were a pair of prefabricated metal buildings of the cheaper kind, looking like they'd come from Ikea Home Border Posts. The border guard had to lock up his kiosk and crossing gate and unlock his office and sit down and do ten minutes of paperwork and three minutes of passport stamping to give me my Slovenian visa. Meanwhile, tractors and farm wagons took an unpaved detour around the checkpoint.

Inside Slovenia everything is identical to Croatia, except that the money and flags have the Slovenian coat of arms on them, as do posters, bumper stickers, baseball caps, and T-shirts. These appear to be manufactured by the same company that makes the sweatshirts, ashtrays, dish towels, scarves, and decorative ceramic wall plaques that have the Croatian coat of arms on them in Croatia. Ditto for Bosnia. And ditto, no doubt, for Serbia, Montenegro, Macedonia, Kosovo, and whatever other pieces this country is falling apart into. There may be a dark capitalist conspiracy behind the war in Yugoslavia but it's led by the world's tchotchke industry, not the international arms cartel.

We were back in Croatia twenty miles later and had to go through another complete set of border formalities and currency exchanges. Ed asked for imported beer at a roadside café. "Well," said the proprietor, "*Slovenian* beer is imported now." Next we stopped at Kumrovec, Tito's birthplace. Kumrovec is a supposedly authentic restoration of a nineteenth-century Balkan farm village—a Marxist peasant hero's version of Colonial Williamsburg. Nobody was there. A tour guide rushed out and showed us around in several languages we didn't speak. The souvenir shop was closed. The guest book in the Tito homestead was nearly devoid of recent signatures. One man had printed, in large, slashed pen strokes, "VUKOVAR!"—a Croatian city where 264 people had been massacred by the Serbs. But was this inscription a message of Titoist resolve, a plea to Tito's spirit, or a curse on Tito? At any rate, ex-Yugoslavians weren't flocking to Kumrovec in gratitude for the thirty-five years that Tito spent keeping them from killing each other.

Tito kept Yugoslavs from killing each other by doing it for them. This is the same technique used by the Romans, Byzantines, Ottomans, Austro-Hungarians, Nazi Germans, and everyone else who's had the misfortune to rule the Balkans. The locals have to be provided with an ample supply of new grievances, otherwise old grievances come to the fore. In Tito's case, one of the new grievances was Tito.

Although Tito himself was of mixed Croat/Slovene/son-of-a-bitch background, his World War II partisan troops were mostly Serbs. In 1946, 100,000 anti-Tito Croat refugees were handed over to Tito by the British. Tito's partisans then killed something between 40,000 and all of them, with the usual number of women, children, and old people included. Of course, the partisans had their reasons. The Croats, under raving nationalist Ante Pavelić, had established a Nazi puppet state in 1941 and killed as many as 350,000 Serbs.

Tito tried to eliminate Balkanization in the Balkans by proscribing the nationalism of Serbia, Slovenia, Croatia, Bosnia, Macedonia, and Montenegro while, at the same time, carefully apportioning the number of government and Communist Party jobs given to each nationality. Everyone was supposed to be a Yugoslavian ("South Slav") and get together and sing one national anthem, "Hej, Sloveni" ("Hey, Slavs"). This worked about as well as you'd expect a country with a national anthem called "Hey, Slavs" to work.

Now, in the bookstores of ex-Yugoslavia, you can buy maps showing—with pie graphs, color lithography, and percentages worked out to the third decimal place—precisely how many people of each ethnic group live exactly where in this place that used to be a country. And in a Zagreb souvenir shop I saw an Ante Pavelić poster for sale, his portrait embellished with cartography showing the extensive boundaries of "Greater Croatia 1941–1945."

If you look at a topographical map of the Balkans, you'll see nothing that would serve as a natural boundary and no area—no plain, valley, coastline, or mountain fastness—coherent or extensive enough to put a boundary around. It was a confused region before nations or even people existed—not big enough to be a subcontinent, too big to be a peninsula, wrinkled, creased, puckered, the cellulite thigh of Europe.

To this bad hash of terrain came a worse omelet of population. The Balkans separate Asia from the West, divide the steppes from the Mediterranean, lie athwart the road from Baltic ice and snow to Adriatic topless beaches. Most of the roving bands, nomadic tribes, pillaging hordes, and migrating populations of Western history have passed through the Balkans. Every time they did, they'd tell their most objectionable members to go camp around the corner. Then the band, tribe, horde, or population would sneak off.

The Christians hate the Muslims because Christians were peons under the Ottomans. The Muslims hate the Christians because Muslims were pissants under the Communists. The Croats hate the Serbs for collaborating with the Communists the same way the Serbs hate the Croats for collaborating with the Nazis, and now the Bosnians hate the Montenegrins for collaborating with the Serbs. The Serbs hate the Albanians for coming to Yugoslavia. Everybody hates the Serbs because there are more of them than anyone else to hate and because, when Yugoslavia was created in 1918 (with the help of know-it-all American president Woodrow Wilson), the Serbs grabbed control of the government and army and haven't let go yet. And everybody hates the Slovenes, too, for getting out of this civil war after only ten days.

Yugoslavia's ethnic wounds are also, unfortunately, infected with idealism. There's a surplus of intellectuals in the region. Yugoslavia, like the rest of Eastern Europe, has more artists, writers, and teachers than it has art, literature, or schools. In the resultant mental unemployment, idealism's bad ideas flourish.

First, there is the bad idea of nationalism, that every little group of human twerps with its own slang, haircut, and pet name for God should have a country. Then there's the bad idea of what the government of that country is supposed to do: kill everybody whose hair looks different. And finally there is the worst idea of all, a belief common to the benighted people in underdeveloped areas everywhere from the Bosnian hills to America's universities: that nationhood is a zero-sum business. The thing that makes Croatia rich makes Serbia poor. But Japan is powerful without natural resources. Singapore is important without physical territory. And Luxembourg wields enormous influence and barely has people. Modern nations do not triumph by conquering territory or dominating strangers. War doesn't work anymore. To become major players upon the international stage, Yugoslavians would be better off selling Yugos.

Between Zagreb and Belgrade the Serbs and Croats fought their war on the turnpike. It's an ordinary-looking toll road with guardrails, median strips, service plazas, and long, straight lanes of pavement. The guardrails have been crushed by tanks, the median strips dug up for trenches, the service plazas reduced to ruins, and the pavement gashed with shell holes. The Croatians still give out toll tickets at one end of the road, but the tollbooths at the other have been blown to pieces. Ed Gorman and I drove ninety miles east on this thoroughfare to Slavonski Brod. There was no other traffic, just an occasional UN blue hat or Serbian Chetnik waving us over to check our papers. The highway runs down toward the Danube through the flat, open country of the Sava River valley. The scenery, except for tile roofs and Lombardy poplars, is exactly Midwestern.

Someday, maybe, the various constituent parts of America will become "empowered" the way Serbia and Croatia are. Someday Aryan Nation, NOW, the VFW, Act Up, AARP, Native Americans, Right to Life fetuses, people with Hispanic surnames, the blind, the deaf, the rest of the differently abled will have their dreams come true. Having made the drive to Slavonski Brod I now know what America will look like when it happens.

Slavonski Brod is a city of seventy-five thousand on the Croatian side of the Sava River. The Croatian-allied Bosnian Muslims were still holding a couple dozen square miles on the opposite riverbank. The Bosnian Serbs had been shelling Slavonski Brod since March. The downtown was even more boarded-up, empty, and burned-out than the downtown of an American city that size. But quieter—until shells landed. Those were loud as hell. Since the city was escapable, an unsurprisingly large number of its residents had escaped, and the rest stayed off the streets during intervals of artillery fire. The shells arrived mostly in the daytime and mostly on the hour. The day before we arrived there had been eleven separate barrages—a total of 130 shells, 60 of which landed in the city and 70 in the surrounding villages. Sometimes the artillery fire was supplemented with Soviet-made Frog missiles or MiGs dropping cluster bombs.

The attacks seemed to have no particular target and no specific purpose. The rail line and the river bridges were being ignored by the gunners or missed by remarkable margins. I suppose the Serbs were trying to frighten and demoralize the people of Slavonski Brod. And, of course, kill them. The locals were good at keeping their heads down. So far only seventy-two civilians had died, although twenty-five of those were children.

The people of Slavonski Brod couldn't seem to make up their minds about whether they were frightened and demoralized. "You want to ask us if we see the end," said a woman in the Croatian government press office, one of the few businesses still operating downtown. "We don't," she said. "There is very little hope." Then she told us morale was high.

The people of Slavonski Brod were certainly irritated that Sarajevo was getting so much media play. "All attention is paid to Sarajevo. All the supplies and all the aid goes to Sarajevo," the president of Slavonski Brod's executive council said peevishly. Gorman and I did our best to explain that there is a big difference, in terms of journalistic melodrama, between being surrounded on three sides and being surrounded on four.

Outside the gates of Slavonski Brod's hospital the tree trunks were covered with black-bordered pieces of paper announcing deaths—Post-it notes from the grave. Casualties from the fighting across the river are brought here—Croats, Bosnian Muslims, captured Serbs—some 6,500 of them in the past year, 752 of whom have died. Heavily built wooden barriers covered the hospital doors, and sandbags blocked the lower windows. All the patients and medical equipment had been moved into the basement. A few ordinary sick people were there, but most of the cases were the gory infirmities of war—young men who'd had large chunks of something blown off or blasted into them. Their beds were lined up end to end down the smelly, narrow basement corridors, making a kind of Lincoln Tunnel rush hour of mutilation and pain. The operating tables were in the furnace rooms with barely enough space below the pipes and ducts for the surgeons to stand upright. X-ray machines, autoclaves, and oxygen bottles were jammed hodgepodge between plumbing and electrical fixtures. Every spare corner was filled with the cots, hot plates, and hanging clothes of doctors and nurses who stay for three-day shifts. Coming and going was too dangerous to do it more often than necessary. The hospital had taken eight direct hits, and two staff members had been killed on the grounds. Most of the work—not only medical procedures but cooking and laundry—was done at night when the danger was less. And every night the hospital tried to evacuate twenty to thirty patients, driving them out of town at top speed in blacked-out ambulances. No one said so, but I'm sure a certain number of those patients must have wound up back at the hospital, that much the worse for a traffic accident.

The chief janitor's office had been taken over by the hospital administrator Dr. Ivan Balen. He was in his forties and looked like an American doctor, but more tired, and he smoked.

"Everything is very sad and terrible," said Dr. Balen—the answer to every question I had meant to ask him.

Tom Lamson and I thought we'd better visit Serbian territory. What with besieging Sarajevo, shelling Slavonski Brod, setting up concentration camps, shooting civilians, and engaging in ethnic cleansing the Serbs were not winning the war of publicity.

The Serbs controlled the old Yugoslav National Army, the JNA, and, when Yugoslavia deconstructed, Serbia and the Serb militias that Serbia supports in Croatia and Bosnia wound up in control of the tanks, airplanes, and heavy artillery. The reason Serbia has acted so viciously in this war is "why the dog licks his balls." Because it can.

We drove on the Belgrade turnpike again about halfway to Slavonski Brod, then turned south on a two-lane road to Banja Luka, thirty miles inside Bosnia.

Banja Luka, with two hundred thousand people, is the largest Serb-controlled city in Bosnia. Back in Zagreb we'd heard dramatic tales about the drunken, thieving, trigger-happy, rape-inclined behavior of Serb irregulars at the checkpoints. But they were pleasant enough to us. One gave me a lapful of walnuts he'd stolen off some vanished Muslim's tree.

On close inspection the Serbs *are* a little different from the Croats. The Serbs look more like John Belushi and the Croats look more like the rest of the cast of *Animal House*. Not that either are a lot of laughs. Although we did pick up one hitchhiking Serb soldier who did a comic turn trying to get both himself and his AK-47 into our tiny backseat. Or it would have been comic if I'd been sure the thing was unloaded.

Serbian territory is also distinguishable from the rest of Yugoslavia. There's less bomb and artillery damage since the Serbs have all the bombs and artillery. And the international embargo seemed to be working. Well, not exactly *working*, because the fighting was worse than ever, but the Serbs have been reduced to using horse carts and bicycles to save fuel. There were more cars on the road in besieged Bihac than there were here among the besiegers.

Banja Luka seemed to be about the same kind of place as Slavonski Brod except we weren't allowed to look at it. We were ushered to military headquarters and there put under escort. We told Kadi to ask if we could get a peek at some starving concentration-camp prisoners, ethnic cleansing, and murder of innocent Muslims. I trust she put the request in more diplomatic terms. The answer was no. But the Serbs would take us to see a mosque, just to show us that it was perfectly unmolested, which—not counting four bullet holes in a ground-floor window—it was. It was also closed. And the Serbs let us talk in private to the local representative of the UN High Commissioner for Refugees.

The UNHCR man was a very young Greek, cleanly dressed and neatly barbered but speaking with such exhausted resignation that, if you closed your eyes, you could imagine he was a refugee himself. There were twenty-five or thirty thousand Muslims left in the city, he said. The Bosnian Serbs refused to recognize these people as refugees because they weren't, technically, in a war zone and weren't, technically, away from home. Under UN bylaws, of which there are many, the young Greek couldn't do much about this. The local authorities were giving him some cooperation in protecting the Muslims. "Yeah—back and forth," he said. The Serbs needed UN help because winter was coming. "They are also sick and tired of being the bad guys in the war." One hundred and twenty Muslims had been killed in Banja Luka since April, most of them in April and May. There were still incidents of beatings and so forth. The Muslims were afraid to come out of their houses. "My house has been robbed twice in the past three days," said the Greek. "There was nothing there to steal. Maybe it's intimidation." He told us the situation was "not so bad" in Banja Luka, leaving to our imaginations what the bad places were like.

Back at the military headquarters we endured an hour-long peroration from a Serb major. He was determined that the Bosnian Serbs should achieve that status of victimhood so coveted in modern politics. The Serb major claimed that three hundred to seven hundred rockets and artillery shells a day were being fired at Bosnian Serbs from the Croatian side of the Sava. (I had driven practically the length of this river twice. No such thing was happening.) The serb major said, "These attacks haven't been provoked, as we have no aspirations in Croatia." (They occupy a third of it.) "Five hundred mujahideen from Iran are in Bihac." (Keeping a very low profile.) "We are against ethnic cleansing." The major explained that what had been reported in the international press as ethnic cleansing was just "movement of migration in some settlements."

All this was conveyed to us through a Serbian translator, a teenage girl who seemed on the point of tears at hearing this litany of Serbian travails. Or maybe she had allergies. The major presented us with a thirteen-page document, written in English and titled "Jihad Must Be Stopped." A sample of the text:

> *By and order of the Islamitic fundamentalists from Sarajevo, the healthy Serbian women from 17 to 40 years old are getting set apart and subjected to an especial treatment. According to their sick plans of many years, these women have to be fecundated by orthodox Islamitic seeds in order to make the raising generation of janizaries on the spaces which from now on surely consider as theirs/Islamitic Republic/more numerous.*

The major assured us that forty thousand Serbs were being held in Muslim concentration camps in Bosnia. "Where?" said Lamson, because outside Sarajevo and Bihac the Muslims seemed barely to have enough of Bosnia left to hide forty thousand of themselves. "Many small private camps," said the major.

The major produced a former prisoner. His name was Risto Dukis, a dirty kid of fifteen with bristly hair and large, light brown eyes. Risto seemed a bit startled, like someone brought up on stage from a quiz-show audience. He was from a little village called Jezero, which had been overrun by the Bosnian Muslim military. The Muslims had held him for two months. He didn't know where his mother and father were and had no idea what had happened to them. He was a high school student. When he grew up he wanted to be, he said, "a worker."

Risto said he'd been out in a field on a weekend morning when he'd been taken prisoner by some thirty Muslim soldiers. They questioned him, beat him, and made him dig a hole that they said would be his grave. They stood him on a table under a tree, as if to hang him, and shook the table.

When he was properly terrified they took him away and beat him until they got him to say he was a Serbian scout. He was kept alone for three days in the basement of a school, then taken to an army barracks, where he was beaten again and forced to make another confession. He slept on a pile of old uniforms for a month. They gave him rice or beans or soup twice a day. Then he was sent to a camp where there was no solid food, only soup and tea. He was beaten by Muslim refugees and forced to do hard labor. Finally there had been a prisoner exchange, and he was released.

Risto said that he knew one of the Muslims who captured him. And this was the man who threatened his life. He was a forest worker from a neighboring village. "He knew my parents," said Risto. "He drank coffee in my house." Risto said that the man had told him, "We used to be good friends, and now you are collaborating with the Chetniks."

"Did the man believe that?" asked Tom Lamson.

Risto said he thought so.

"Had you had any unpleasant experiences with Muslims before?"

"No. I wouldn't have expected them to treat me like that."

"Do you hate them?" asked Tom.

"So I hate them," said Risto.

"What will you do now?"

"Well, if I catch them, I will do exactly the same." Tom asked him if he had any idea why all this was going on. "Muslims blame Serbs," said Risto. "I think the Serbs aren't guilty. I blame the Bosnian president." (Though I don't think Risto, any more than I, could remember that august personage's name.)

Risto seemed believable. And his story was the Yugoslavian civil war in a nutshell: past and present wrongs inspiring wrongs of the future, bigotry feeding on bigotry, violence begetting violence, and in the middle of it all the Risto Dukises—innocence defiled.

"The morning you were captured," said Lamson, "what were you doing out in that field?"

"Oh, I was scouting for the Chetniks," said Risto.

Famine: All Guns, No Butter

Somalia, December-January 1991–92

I flew to Somalia in a small chartered plane shortly after U.S. troops had landed in Mogadishu.

Good intentions were being combined with—how rare this mixture is—good deeds. Food was being shipped to the country and international peacekeepers were being sent to deliver the food.

"Feed the hungry" is one of the first principles of morality. Here it was in operation. So where *were* the starving children of Mogadishu? Where were the pitiable little fellows with the gone-away expressions, faces already turned to some less painful world, limbs as thin as the lines of type in a newspaper obit column, and bellies gravid with death? A glance at these tykes racks the soul. They are the emblem of Third World misery, the inevitable cover of news magazines, the constant subject of videotape on *Eyewitness News*. I half expected to be met by a delegation of them at the Mogadishu airport.

What I met with instead were guns. Arrayed around the landing strip were U.S. guns, UN guns, guns from around the world. Trucks full of Somalis with guns came to get the luggage. These were my guns, hired to protect me from the other Somalis with guns. And I thought I might get a gun of my own besides, since none of these gunmen—local, foreign, or supranational—looked like they'd mind shooting me.

Everything that guns can accomplish had been achieved in Mogadishu. For two years the residents had been joining, dividing, subdividing, and rejoining in a pixilation of clan feuds and alliances. Previously Somalia had been held together by the loathsome but stable twenty-two-year reign of dictator Siad Barre. But Barre gained loathsomeness and lost stability, and when he took a walkout powder in January 1991, all and sundry began fighting each other with rifles, machine guns, mortars, cannons, and—to judge by the look of the town—wads of filth.

No building was untouched, and plenty were demolished. It was a rare wall that wasn't stippled with bullet holes and a peculiar acre that lacked shell damage. Hardly a pane of glass was left in the city. There was no potable water and no electricity. At night the only illumination was from tracer bullets. Mogadishu's modern downtown was gone, the steel and concrete architecture bombarded into collapse. The old city was deserted rubble, a no-man's-land between two envenomed clan factions. Rubbish was dumped atop wreckage everywhere and goats grazed on the offal. Mounds of sand had blown through the streets. Sewage welled up through what pavement was left.

The destruction had squeezed people into the roads, where they built market stalls from pieces of scrap wood and flattened olive-oil cans—market stalls which seemed to sell mostly pieces of scrap wood and flattened olive-oil cans. Young men waving AK-47 assault rifles pushed among the crowds. Rusted, dent-covered, windshieldless pickup trucks with gun mounts welded into their beds sputtered down what remained of the right-of-way, outnumbered by donkey carts and overtopped by pack camels.

It was a scene of Paleolithic ruin except for the modern weapons. The Somalis used to paint the outside walls of their shops with crude pictures of canned goods, television sets, photocopiers, and the like. Cartoon murals on abandoned storefronts were the only evidence that the twentieth century had produced anything pleasant.

Compared to Mogadishu, starving children would be cute. In fact, somewhere in the psychic basement of the sob-sister sorority house, in the darkest recesses of the bleeding heart, starving children *are* cute. Note the big Keane-painting eyes, the etiolated features as unthreatening as Michael Jackson's were before the molestation charges, the elfin incorporeity of the bodies. Steven Spielberg's E.T. owes a lot to the Biafran-Bangladeshi-Ethiopian model of attractive suffering.

It's easier to advertise our compassion for innocents in misery than it is to face up to what happened in a place like Somalia. What happened was not just famine but the complete breakdown of everything decent and worthwhile. I spent two weeks in Somalia and never saw a starving child, not because they didn't exist but because they were off somewhere dying, pushed into marginal spaces and territories by people with guns. Going to Somalia was like visiting the scene of a crime and finding that the murderer was still there but the body had fled.

The world has enough food. In 1990 the World Hunger Program at Brown University published a book, *Hunger in History*, edited by Lucile F. Newman. World Hunger is the kind of program (and Brown the kind of university) that would, I think, be eager to tell us if the world didn't have enough food. But they don't tell us this. In the book's final article, "On Ending Hunger: The Lessons of History," Robert W. Kates and Sara Millman say that "global food sufficiency" was reached in the 1960s and that, as of the mid-1980s, the world was "nearing diet sufficiency," by which they mean the earth has enough protein, carbohydrates, vitamins, minerals, and whatever else is currently supposed to be good for us to go around.

The modern era has witnessed an enormous increase in food, an enormous increase in people being fed—and an enormous increase in famine. This would seem to defy physical law.

When a thing defies physical law, there's usually politics involved. Drought, floods, crop failures, and insect pests have played a part in some modern famines, but none of these famines was *caused* by nature. The Chinese famine of 1958–61, the worst famine in history, had nothing to do with weather or "acts of God." In fact, it could be said to have resulted, literally, from an act of godlessness—the imposition of Marxist theory on traditional peasant agriculture. The same thing caused the Ukrainian famine of 1932–34 and the Cambodian famine of 1975–79.

Some famines were deliberately created. The Nigerian government used starvation as a weapon of war against the Biafrans. The Ethiopians did the same thing to the Eritreans, and the Muslim Sudanese are doing it now to their Christian and animist countrymen.

Some famines came not from political organization but from lack thereof. A government can't very well provide famine relief when there is no government, as there was none in China in the late 1920s.

And some famines have political causes of maddening complexity. The British in Bengal in 1943 had no weird ideas or evil designs. But they wanted to keep rice supplies out of the hands of possible Japanese invaders, and they wanted to feed the masses in Calcutta and keep the vital industries there running. So the British confiscated rice that was stored in rural Bengal. This set off a price panic, and mass starvation followed, even though there was no great scarcity of food.

Indeed, famine can occur when and where there's a food surplus. Sylvia Nasar, in an article on the political causes of famine in the January 17, 1993, *New York Times*, says, "one of the worst recent famines—Bangladesh's in 1974—took place in a year of unusually high rice production." Unfounded rumors of a rice shortage caused prices to double. Then the government of the "People's Republic of Bangladesh," led by self-styled socialist Mujibur Rahman, set about making things worse. The army was sent to arrest hoarders, "convincing people," says Ms. Nasar, "that [Mujibur] had lost control and fueling the price surge." The price surge led to a huge black market. Black marketeering exacerbated the already wonderful corruption of the Mujibur regime. And people starved for no reason. Ms. Nasar adds, "The United States contributed by announcing that it would withhold food aid to punish Bangladesh for, of all things, selling jute to Cuba."

Plenty is no guarantee against famine, but neither does scarcity guarantee that famine will happen. Indian economist Amartya Sen was one of the first scholars to argue against regarding famine as a natural disaster. His 1981 book *Poverty and Famines* was, in academic circles, whatever the academic-circle equivalent is of a new animated Disney feature. Using the 1943 Bengal famine as his principal example, Sen proved (as well as anything can be said to be proved in the social sciences) the political nature of food distribution in modern society.

Later Professor Sen studied the 1983–84 drought in sub-Saharan Africa. He found that Sudan and Ethiopia had experienced, respectively, 11 percent and 12½ percent declines in food production. Those countries suffered severe famines. But Botswana had a 17 percent decline in food production, and Zimbabwe had a 37½ percent decline, and there wasn't any famine in either place. The reason was that Sudan and Ethiopia didn't mind if certain troublesome portions of their populations starved to death while Botswana and Zimbabwe did mind.

Apparently most portions of Somalia's population were troublesome to somebody.

In order to go to Somalia, I took a job as a radio reporter for ABC news. It wasn't a country I could cover by myself. News organizations had to create fortresses for themselves in Mogadishu and man those forts with armies.

ABC sent in its most experienced fixers, men known in the news business (and not without respect) as "combat accountants." The accountants hired forty gunmen and found a large walled house that used to belong to an Arab ambassador. The house was almost intact and close to the ruins of the American embassy, which—the accountants hoped—would soon be occupied by U.S. Marines.

Satellite dishes, telephone uplinks, editing equipment, half a dozen generators, fuel, food, water, beer, toilet paper, soap, sheets, towels, and mattresses all had to be flown in on charter planes from Nairobi. For some reason we wound up with five hundred boxes of Kenyan chocolate chip cookies that tasted like bunion pads. Cooks, cleaning people, and laundry men were employed, as well as translators—dazed-looking academic types from the long-destroyed Somali National University.

Some thirty of us—journalists, camera crews, editors, producers, money men, and technicians—were housed in this compound, bedded down in shifts on the floor of the old audience hall while our mercenaries camped in the courtyard.

It was impossible to go outside our walls without "security" ("security" being what the Somali gunmen—gunboys, really—liked to be called). Even with the gunmen along, there were always people mobbing up to importune or gape. Hands tugging at wallet pockets. Fingers nipping at wristwatch bands. No foreigner could make a move without setting off a bee's nest of attention—demanding, grasping, pushing crowds of cursing, whining, sneering people with more and worse Somalis skulking on the fringes of the pack.

One of the first things I saw, besides guns, when I arrived in Mogadishu was a pack of thieves creeping through the wreckage of the airport, sizing up our charter cargo. And the last thing I saw as I left was the self-appointed Somali "ground crew" running beside our taxiing plane, jamming their hands through the window hatch, trying to grab money from the pilot.

A trip from our compound to Mogadishu's main market required two kids with AK-47s plus a driver and a translator who were usually armed as well. The market was walking distance but you wanted a car or truck to show your status. That there was a market at all in Mogadishu was testimony to something in the human spirit, though not necessarily something nice, since what was for sale was mostly food that had been donated to Somalia's famine victims. CONTRIBUÉ PAR LES ENFANTS DE FRANCE said the stenciled letters on all the rice sacks. (Every French schoolchild had been urged to bring to class a kilo of rice for Somalia.)

Meat was also available, though not immediately recognizable as such. A side of beef looked like seventy pounds of flies on a hook. And milk, being carried around in wooden jugs in the hundred-degree heat, had a smell that was worse than the look of the meat. But all of life's staples, in some more or less awful form, were there in the market. If you had the money to get them. That is, if you had a gun to get the money. And a whole section of the market was devoted to retailing guns.

I wanted to buy a basket or something, just to see how the ordinary aspects of life worked in Somalia in the midst of total anarchy and also, frankly, to see if having my own gunmen was any help in price haggling. I was thinking I could get used to a pair of guys with AKs, one clearing a path for me and one covering my back. I'd be less worried about crime in the States, not to mention asking for a raise. And, if I happened to decide to go to a shrink, I'll bet it would be remarkable how fast my emotions would mature, how quickly my insights about myself would grow, how soon I'd be declared perfectly well-adjusted with two glowering Somali teens and their automatic weapons beside me on the couch.

They were, however, useless at bargaining for baskets. Nobody gets the best of a Somali market woman. Not only did the basket weaver soak me, but fifteen minutes after the deal had been concluded she chased me halfway across the marketplace screaming that she'd changed her mind. My bodyguards cringed and I gave up another three dollars—a sort of Third World adjustable basket mortgage.

She was a frightening lady. Ugly, too, though this was an exception. Somali women are mainly beautiful: tall, fine-featured, and thin even in fatter times than these. They are not overbothered with Muslim prudery. Their bright-colored scarves are used only for shade and not to cover elaborate cornrows and amazing smiles. Loud cotton print sarongs are worn with one shoulder bare and wrapped with purposeful imperfection of concealment. There is an Iman fashion plate doppelgänger carrying every milk jug. You could do terrific business with modeling agencies hiring these girls by the pound in Somalia and renting them by the yard in New York.

The men, perhaps because I am one, are another matter. They're cleaver-faced and jumpy and given to mirthless grins decorated with the dribble from endless chewing of qat leaves. Some wear the traditional *tobe* kilt. Others dress in Mork and Mindy–era American leisure wear. The old clothes that you give to charity are sold in bulk to dealers and wind up mostly in Africa. If you want to do something for the dignity of the people in sub–Saharan countries, you can quit donating bell-bottom pants to Goodwill.

When we emerged from the market our driver was standing next to the car with a look on his face like you or I might have if we'd gotten a parking ticket just seconds before we made it to the meter with the dime. Shards of glass were all over the front seat. The driver had been sitting behind the wheel when a spent bullet had come out of somewhere and shattered the window beside his head.

Mogadishu is almost on the equator. The sun sets at six, prompt. After that, unless we wanted to mount a reconnaissance in force, we were stuck inside our walls. We ate well. We had our canned goods from Kenya, and the Somalis baked us fresh bread (made from famine-relief flour, no doubt) and served us a hot meal every night—fresh vegetables, stuffed peppers, pasta, lobsters caught in the Mogadishu harbor, and local beef. I tried not to think about the beef. Only a few of us got sick. We had a little bit of whiskey, lots of cigarettes, and the pain pills from the medical kits. We sat out on the flat tile roof of the big stucco house and listened to the intermittent artillery and small-arms fire.

Down in the courtyard our gunmen and drivers were chewing qat. The plant looks like watercress and tastes like a handful of something pulled at random from the flower garden. You have to chew a lot of it, a bundle the size of a whisk broom, and you have to chew it for a long time. It made my mouth numb and gave me a little bit of a stomachache, that's all. Maybe qat is very subtle. I remember thinking cocaine was subtle, too, until I noticed I'd been awake for three weeks and didn't know any of the naked people passed out around me. The Somalis seemed to get off. They start chewing before lunch but the high doesn't kick in until about three in the afternoon. Suddenly our drivers would start to drive straight into potholes at full speed.

Straight into pedestrians and livestock, too. We called it "the qat hour." The gunmen would all begin talking at once, and the chatter would increase in speed, volume, and intensity until, by dusk, frantic arguments and violent gesticulations had broken out all over the compound. That was when one of the combat accountants would have to go outside and give everybody his daily pay in big stacks of dirty Somali shilling notes worth four thousand to the dollar. Then the yelling really started.

Qat is grown in Kenya. "The Somalis can chew twenty planes a day!" said a woman who worked in the Nairobi airport. According to the Kenyan charter pilots some twenty loads of qat are indeed flown into Mogadishu each morning. Payloads are normally about a ton per flight. Qat is sold by the bunch, called a *maduf*, which retails for $3.75 and weighs about half a pound. Thus $300,000 worth of qat arrives in Somalia every day. But it takes U.S. Marines to deliver a sack of wheat.

I went to the Marine Corps encampment at Mogadishu Port on the day before Christmas. The docks and quays and warehouses had been so heaped with wreckage and muck that the first pieces of military equipment the marines landed were bulldozers. The marines plowed away the debris and sprayed the wharves with firefighting equipment from the U.S. Navy ships. It took three scrappings and hosings before Mogadishu was only as dirty as an ordinary seaport. Then the marines built a twenty-foot high wall of cargo containers around the space they'd cleared, not so much for military reasons but to make a sort of citadel of hygiene.

Only one of the port's warehouses had enough corrugated tin left on top to provide shelter. This was pinked with galaxies of bullet holes. Somalis must have stood inside and fired through the roof for the sheer noise of it. Seven or eight hundred marines were sleeping here, their mosquito net–draped cots in rows as close as auditorium chairs. It was 100, 110, 115 degrees every day in Mogadishu, with air so humid that the wind felt like shaving lather. Even in our thick-walled, shaded house the only way I could sleep was to lie naked on the mattress with an electric fan pointed at me. There were no fans in the warehouse and not even much of that hot, sopping breeze.

A branch of some reasonably fir-like plant had been set up by the warehouse doors, its needles decorated with miniature Tabasco bottles, Chiclets, and other of the less-esteemed items from the MRE ration packs. In place of a star was a plastic envelope of beef stew. The navy claimed it would try, the next day, to get some turkey in from the ships' galleys. And satiric carols had been composed.

On the first day of Christmas,
The Marine Corps gave to me
Forty injections for tropical disease . . .

The troops were crabbier than they'd been in the Gulf War. They were sticky and dirty and bored. They had no showers, no hot meals, and, even with female military personnel all over, no private place to take a crap. But all these conditions had existed in Saudi Arabia and for months on end. The problem in Somalia was more abstract. This was the first large-scale military operation in history to be launched for purely altruistic reasons. Nobody knew how to go about such a thing. In a war against hunger, what do you do? Shoot lunch?

I went out on patrol with a squad of marines. I borrowed one of the flak vests that make jogging around in the Mogadishu weather truly miserable. I skipped the Kevlar helmet, which feels like a hollowed-out bowling ball. Neither the jacket nor the helmet will stop an AK-47 round, just slow it down, and I didn't want any slow bullets in my head.

The patrols were being made because the marines, when they weren't unloading boats or guarding aid convoys, couldn't think what else to do. We went in open Humvee trucks to the most battle-frayed parts of town. The idea was, I guess, to look for snipers and goons and people too blatantly displaying arms and to see if anyone wanted to shoot marines, then shoot them first. Hard to say what the average Somali—the man-in-the-gutter, if you will—thought about this. There was a large group hanging out at the entrance to the port, begging. Sometimes they tired of begging and threw stones until a few marines rushed out and beat them with truncheons, then they'd beg again. But when we stopped our trucks in the ravaged downtown a solitary old man said, in a carefully enunciated shout, "Shoot everybody who makes trouble! We like peace! Long life to America!" This was in front of the city's only Christian church. Someone had tried to brick up the doors and windows. Someone else had pillaged the place.

Schools had long ago disappeared in Mogadishu, and the streets were filled with kids, not starving but good and dirty. The kids would put things out in the road when they saw us coming—bricks, stones, pieces of pipe. Then, when we drove closer, they'd run out and snatch this stuff back. They were playing "roadblock." They liked to try out their English. Earlier that day, when I was driving to the port, a little boy had leaned in my window, flashed an enormous winning smile, and said, "I will kill you." The kids seemed to like the marines, however. Sometimes a marine would open an MRE packet and scatter its contents. In return the kids would point to certain buildings and yell to the effect that snipers were inside.

The marines said the kids were sometimes right. We gave a Humvee ride reward to one ten-year-old who, a couple days before, had shown the marines where a machine-gun-equipped Toyota pickup—a "technical," as it's called—was hidden. The marines had shot its occupants.

The kids would run in packs behind the speeding Humvees, their sandals flapping like applause. If there's ever a ten-kilometer-in-shower-flip-flops Olympic event, it will be won by a prepubescent Somali.

The kids also act as mine canaries. Suddenly they *aren't* running behind the Humvees, suddenly they all disappear, then the marines know they're in a conclusively dangerous place. For instance, the "Green Line," so called after the famous boundary in Beirut, though Mogadishu's Green Line isn't a line but a whole area so fought over that there's nothing left to fight over. Then there's the "Bridge of Death" (actually a culvert) and "Bermuda," for the triangle of the same name, because if you go in there you'll never come out.

Like many people with a mean streak the Somalis have a way with nicknames. A thoroughgoing bad hat may be called *Mattukaday*—"man who's never been seen in a mosque." There is a warlord yclept "Fuji" for inscrutability and a doctor who goes by "Cholera." A particularly hasty defeat of one subclan is remembered as "Kuwait." The most congested intersection in the city is named "Kamakazi Corner" not from the driving but because of suicidal quarrels that break out among the gunmen there. Siad Barre was known as "Big Mouth" due to his speeches, and his cronies were called "Four Pockets" in honor of their ability to line same.

We got out of the Humvees and began to patrol on foot. Mogadishu has a sort of Capitol Hill from when there used to be a government. The way the marines had said the kids sometimes vanished, the kids vanished that way here. The marines went down the street in a hollow rectangle, the men on the right side checking the walls and windows above the men on the left and vice versa. One man was walking backward in the rear. One man was darting ahead, his M-16 preceding him around corners.

A minibus full of young Somali men nosed into an intersection in front of us. There was a big grinding of gears and the Somalis sped backward at cartoon speed.

We went into a ruined government office. Two marines flopped in the doorway behind us and sealed the entrance. Two men went up the steps, scanned the hallways, and pressed back against the walls. Two more men shouted, "Coming up!" and went on to the next floor, the patrol leapfrogging thus until we were on the roof.

The whole mess of Mogadishu spread below us. The place probably never did amount to much, though it's more than a thousand years old. In the distance the blue and yellow stripes of desert meeting surf were pretty enough, albeit the land was covered with thornbushes and the ocean infested with sharks. Wide strips of dirt with tree stumps were visible where handsome avenues might once have been. Maybe the narrow Omani stone houses near the port used to evoke the charm of *Arabian Nights*, if you didn't mind that they were built by slave-trading elephant murderers. They were slums now. And the rest of Mogadishu, what was left of it, was a joke. The taller buildings, nearly all of them abandoned, were built in that ever present Third World *wog moderne* style, cement puns on Le Corbusier. Siad Barre had constructed an immense reviewing stand for himself, but its grandeur was foiled by its perfect resemblance to a parking garage. The Italians, who were the colonial power in southern Somalia from the 1880s until 1960, had put up a fake Middle Eastern castle on a bluff above the harbor, giving the old part of town a "Seven Package Tours of Sinbad" look. Here and there were bogus classical monuments from when Mussolini was in charge, notably a vaulted gateway to nowhere with dumpy proportions and lots of fasces on it. The post-imperialist Somalis had done as well as they could to go one better than this item, and in the center of a roundabout near the airport stood a huge, ill-crafted, out-of-plumb, Taco Bell–facade concrete thing with peeling white paint and big blue letters reading ARCH OF POPULAR TRIUMPH.

The marines came down from the roof of the government building, retracting their pickets like a coiling snake. You don't realize how much paper there is in a government until you see it all busted out of its filing cabinets and spread in drifts down floors and through courtyards. Then it seems as though government must be nothing but paper, and I suspect the Somali government wasn't much more than that. Paper and, of course, guns—the guns are still in working order.

Our patrol went on up the hill to the parliament building. This had been subjected to something more like evisceration than looting. The very marble of the floors had been pulled up, and the electrical fixtures had been yanked with such vehemence that the wires were pulled right out through the plaster, leaving vertical trenches in the walls. The National Assembly chamber had been stripped of carpet and decor. Its floor was covered with human excrement. All the chairs and desks had been torn from their mountings. Somalia's seat of government had been soundly trashed. How many people in how many countries have wanted to do this? Somalis gave in to the temptation.

Where did this strange nation come from? The Somalis have a joke: God was bored. So He created the universe. But that was boring, too. So God created Adam and Eve. But He was still bored. So God created the rest of the human race. And even then He was bored. So God created the Somalis. He hasn't stopped laughing since.

As with all nomads, Somalis come basically from nowhere. Roving, quarreling, pillaging bands of Somalis show up in the Horn of Africa—the biblical land of Punt—about the same time that roving, quarreling, pillaging bands of Normans show up for the Battle of Hastings. The Somalis are, and seemingly always have been, divided into clan families. There are six of these: Dir, Isaaq, Hawiye, Darod, Digil, and Rahanweyn. They hate each other. Not that those are their only hatreds. The two worst Somali warlords extant at the time of my visit, Mohamed Farah Aidid and Ali Mahdi Muhammad, were both Hawiye. Each clan family is divided into numerous subclans. They hate each other, too. And each subclan is likewise split and irked. The first Europeans, visiting Mogadishu in the sixteenth century, found the then tiny city already riven into warring clan sectors.

Back when one culture could say what it thought of another without risking a massive Donna Shalala explosion, the 1911 edition of the *Encyclopaedia Britannica* (the only reference work I really trust) opined, "The Somali are a fighting race and all go armed . . . They are great talkers, keenly sensitive to ridicule, and quick tempered . . . love display . . . are inordinately vain and avaricious . . ." And, said *Britannica*, "The Somali have very little political or social cohesion." In fact, the basic unit of Somali society is something called the "diya-paying group," *diya* being the Arabic word for blood money.

Besides the members of the six clan families, there are other nonclan Somalis known as *sab*, or "low." These are hunters, barbers, leather workers, metalsmiths, and other productive citizens much looked down upon by nomads. Noble camel thieves think *sab* vocations are degrading. The six clans themselves are divided in prestige according to degree of idleness. The Dir, Isaaq, Hawiye, and Darod call themselves "Samale," from whence comes the name of the country. The Samale clans consider themselves to be strictly nomads—fighters and herdsmen. They call the Digil and the Rahanweyn "Sab clans," and *Rahanweyn*, in Somali, means merely "large crowd." The Sab are farmers, and nomads regard farms with the same violent distaste I have for law offices.

The gunmen who are currently destroying Somalia, who are wrecking the livelihoods of innocent Somalis and robbing them of their sustenance, are largely Samale. And many of the people who are starving are Sab. It is one of Somalia's plentiful supply of grim ironies that the victims of its famine are the people who grow its food.

Of course the nomad clansmen doing the wrecking and robbing aren't traditional nomads any more than a Toyota pickup truck with a machine gun mounted in its bed is a traditional element of a caravan. But the Samale don't need any "men's movement" wildman weekends to get in touch with their inner warrior. Somali became a written language only in 1972. Just a few miles from the main towns you see itinerant families of Darod and Dir who could pass for Mary and Joseph on their flight into Egypt. Here all the men are dressed in *tobe* kilts, with sword-length daggers in the waistbands, and the women are wrapped in homespun instead of Kenyan chintz. The camel bridles, donkey blankets, pannier baskets, and milk jugs have been made by hand. The nomad life is possessed of almost as much honest, natural, rough-hewn folksiness as a New England crafts fair. Only the occasional flash of a bright yellow plastic wash bucket tells you what millennium you're in.

I have a friend, Carlos Mavroleon, who works as a freelance TV reporter for ABC and who has spent a lot of time among nomads in the Muslim world. Carlos found a very good translator and went off with a minimum of security and baggage to the far parts of the Somali desert to talk to the real Samale. They were shy of strangers—given current events in Somalia, they'd be crazy if they weren't—and it took Carlos several days of lolling around making gifts of tea and tobacco before the nomads would chat. Finally they invited him into their camp, and, when a suitable length of pleasantries had been exchanged, Carlos asked the nomads, "How has this war affected you?"

"Oh, the war is terrible!" they replied. And they told Carlos that just last week some goats had been stolen and a month before a valuable camel was lost. It was a very horrible war indeed. More goats might be lost at any time and only a couple of years ago a wife had been carried away.

Carlos said he didn't realize for a while that the war the nomads were talking about was the war they had been conducting, time out of mind, with the next subclan down the wadi. "No, no, no," said Carlos, "I mean the big war in Mogadishu."

"Oh, *that* war," said the nomads, and there were shrugs all around.

Carlos liked the Somalis. "Men in skirts killing each other over matters of clan," he said. "People call it barbaric savagery. Add bagpipes and a golf course, and they call it Scotland."

And, like good Scots Presbyterians, the Somalis can be religious fanatics when they feel like it. Sayyid Muhammad 'Abdille Hassan, known as the "Mad Mullah," fought the British Empire to a standstill in northern Somalia in the Dervish Wars of 1900 to 1920. The British were forced to withdraw to coastal garrisons, causing famine among the Somali clans who were not allied with the Mullah. An estimated one-third of the population of British Somaliland died during the Dervish Wars, a period that Somalis call "the Time of Eating Filth."

The British never intended to rule Somalia but found themselves continually forced to intervene in Somali affairs to ensure the supply line to their strategic outpost at Aden. In the words of I. M. Lewis in his *A Modern History of Somalia*, "The problem of the future status of these areas was complicated; no one friendly or fully acceptable . . . seemed to want them." And they still don't. Various internationalist schemes were attempted, which is where Italian Somaliland came from. The Mad Mullah was unimpressed. During World War I he wrote a letter to the British commissioner at Berbera:

> *You . . . have joined with all the peoples of the world, with wastrels, and with slaves, because you are so weak. But if you were strong you would have stood by yourself as we do, independent and free. It is a sign of your weakness, this alliance of yours with Somali, menials, and Arabs, and Sudanese, and Kaffirs, and Perverts, and Yemenis, and Nubians, and Indians, and Russians, and Americans, and Italians, and Serbians, and Portuguese, and Japanese, and Greeks, and cannibals, and Sikhs, and Banyans, and Moors, and Afgans, and Egyptians . . . it is because of your weakness that you have to solicit as does a prostitute.*

Seventy-five years before the fact, Sayyid Muhammad was able to accurately predict the composition, effectiveness, and moral stature of today's UN.

The Mullah is still revered in Somalia. And the day I arrived in Mogadishu a flyer was being distributed in the local mosques showing a servile Somali rolling out a carpet for a pair of armed men mounted tandem on a horse. One man was marked with a cross and the other with a Star of David. Two fighting men on one horse was the seal of the Knights Templar, a Christian military order formed in the twelfth century to fight Muslims in the Crusades. Sense may be short in these parts, but memory is long.

So here we were on another crusade, this time one of compassion (though Richard the Lionheart thought his cause was compassionate too). Enormous stores of food aid were arriving in Mogadishu, food donated by international governments and by private charities. Armed convoys were being formed to deliver that food. It takes a lot of weapons to do good works (as Richard the Lionheart could have told us). And this is not just a Somali problem. We have poverty and deprivation in our own country. Try standing unarmed on a street corner in Compton handing out twenty-dollar bills and see how long you last.

I went with an ABC camera crew on the first convoy to Jalalaqsi, 120 miles north of Mogadishu up the Shebelle River. For the sake of making America's allies look less worthless, the Italian army was given the escort job. A company of Italians in Fiat jeeps and troop carriers led a dozen aid-agency food trucks. Two U.S. Army platoons in Humvees brought up the rear.

The convoy was not a work of logistical genius. It left town a day late because (my American military sources swear this is true) the Italians lingered too long over lunch. Then the Italians, who in their own country are homicidally fast drivers, insisted on a twenty-mile-per-hour convoy speed. They also took three meal breaks. Then one of the Italian drivers fell asleep at the wheel and ran into practically the only tree in the Somali desert. After the sun went down, the convoy got off course somehow. I'm not exactly sure what happened, but I believe the lead driver saw what he thought were the lights at the Jalalaqsi airstrip and headed toward them, but those were actually the lights of the last vehicles in the convoy. Anyway, we wound up with an enormous merry-go-round of trucks, jeeps, and Humvees circling in the desert.

The trip took fourteen hours. Then, with thousands of square miles of parched sand in every direction, the Italians found a mudflat for us to camp in.

The Somalis had been busy, too. Before we even left Mogadishu, the Italian colonel in charge of the convoy had caught one of the Somali drivers draining the radiator of his own truck. That way he'd have a "breakdown" en route and his cargo would be "stolen." A number of other such sabotages were detected. The Somalis were also quarreling with each other, and their qat-addled driving was bad even by Italian standards. Then, during meal break three, the Somalis decided they couldn't eat Italian rations and they couldn't eat American MREs. They would have to leave the convoy, go to a local village, and get Somali food.

"This is a famine, goddamn it," said an American sergeant. "There *isn't* any Somali food. If there *was* any Somali food, we wouldn't have to fucking *be* here."

The Italian colonel said he wanted to shoot all the Somali drivers.

An American lieutenant commented, "I'm quitting the army. I'm going on welfare. I'll sell the cars to my folks, sell the house to my sister, and get benefits. This thing sucks—helping people who don't give a shit."

ABC's Somali employees had also claimed they needed special food. The Kenyan canned goods we were going to pack for them might have pork inside. They wanted a million shillings. Which they got. But they didn't buy any food with it. And, when we weren't looking, they ate all of ours. We had to get the ABC satellite phone out, set it up in the mudflat, and trade soldiers long-distance calls to Mom for MREs.

We didn't have any camping gear either, and when we got ready to go sleep in our trucks, we found our gunmen already stretched out on all the seats, roofs, and hoods. I took three Halcion tablets and lay down in the mud, and I understand the entire Italian and U.S. military presence in Jalalaqsi was kept awake all night by my snoring.

When the sun came up, we could see a refugee squatter camp stretching for a mile along the Shebelle. These people were not starving; that is, they weren't starving *to death*. Their misery had not quite reached the photogenic stage. But they were living in huts no bigger than the houses children make by putting a blanket over a card table. These homes weren't even hovels, just little humps in the landscape formed with sticks bent in half-circle hoops and covered with grain sacks and pieces of scrap cloth.

The refugees had none of the proud shyness that Carlos had found among the nomads. You could approach these people at random, and they were only too glad to talk. They had nothing to do but talk.

I talked to a woman named Habiba Osman. She had fled from the fighting in someplace called "Burrui," which I cannot find on a map. She was a Hawiye, a member of the Hawadli subclan, and had been chased away from her home by other Hawiye, members of the Abgaal subclan. She had nine children, she said, holding up four fingers, and she was forty-five. Her husband, Muhammad, stood in the background. They were getting one portion of coarse cornmeal a day. It was hard to eat. They made it into porridge.

I counted her possessions: a wooden bowl, a long pestle for cracking grain, an empty two-gallon olive-oil can, an aluminum pot, a few aluminum dishes. The goats and camels had been stolen.

I went to watch one of our convoy trucks unload food for the Save the Children charity in Jalalaqsi. The town itself hardly existed anymore, though it hadn't been ruined by the war or abandoned by its population. It was just—like the rest of the Somali nation, citizenship, and culture—a neglected, entropic, crumbling mess. The Save the Children headquarters was a tumbledown school sitting in a small yard inside the high walls with which everything needs to be surrounded in Somalia. The food we'd brought to them was something called Unimix, a sort of Purina Famine Chow made of 50 percent corn, 30 percent beans, 10 percent sugar, and 10 percent oil, all ground together. It makes a nourishing gruel when stirred into water, if you can find clean water. A great number of Somalis had to be hired to unload the food: some to carry the fifty-pound sacks, more to stand around yelling commands, and even more, armed with long switches, to argue with the others and take swipes at townspeople who gathered in a nosy cluster around the truck.

Save the Children had managed to keep some food coming into Jalalaqsi. In the midst of the worst chaos they had eight kitchens operating to feed kids. They were able to do this, they said, because they worked closely with clan elders. More importantly, there isn't much of a thieves' market for Unimix. Save the Children was losing only 10 percent of its food shipments. But, even so, as many as ten children a day were dying in the refugee camp where I talked to Habiba Osman.

Several reporters were interviewing a Save the Children aid worker. One of the reporters must have flunked journalism school because he asked a question that went straight to the point. "Who cares?" he said, looking around at the wretchedness, squalor, muddle, and despair. "Back in the United States, in the rest of the world, who really cares about these people?" The man from Save the Children started to laugh. He was possessed of Christian charity—or Muslim or Jewish or whatever. The idea that someone could look at this suffering and *not* care was absurd to the aid worker, utterly ridiculous. So he laughed.

Much uglier jokes were available. About food, for instance. It was all over the place. In fourteen hours of travel the previous day, we'd never been out of sight of the stuff. The American sergeant yelling at the Somalis for trying to grocery-shop in a famine was wrong. Just as I'd been wrong about parched sands when I'd seen our bivouac area. The Shebelle River valley is wet and fecund and contains the richest farmland in Somalia. The road from Mogadishu traversed miles of corn and sorghum, the fields marked out with animal skulls set on stakes. (Scarecrows, maybe, or scarepeople. I saw a human skeleton beside the pavement.) Even in the drier areas, away from the river, there were herds of cows and goats. We'd been carrying thousands of pounds of food relief through thousands of acres of food.

It was not a supply-side problem they had in Somalia, as our drivers and gunmen pointed out to us that afternoon when they refused to take us back to Mogadishu. They said they'd be robbed and shot. "But," we said, "you knew we were coming to Jalalaqsi, and you knew we'd have to go home. We talked about this before we left. We asked for volunteers. You weren't afraid then," we said. They said they'd changed their minds.

So we left the little army that our corporation had hired with the larger army that our tax dollars pay for and hitched a ride to Mogadishu on a relief agency plane.

Somalia is amazingly roofless. Almost every building we flew over had its ceiling off. How much of this was from neglect and artillery and how much from looting of corrugated tin sheets I don't know, but you could look right down into the rooms and hallways, and it made the entire country seem like a gigantic game board of Clue. Probable correct answer: Everybody. In the dung heap. With an AK-47.

Beautiful beaches, however. As we came into Mogadishu we could see miles of tawny sand with not a hotel or time-share condominium in sight. At this very minute some real estate developer is probably saying, "We got your two baby-boom major obsessions here: oceanfront property and weight loss. Bingo, it's the new Hilton Head."

On New Year's Eve I went with another convoy west a hundred miles to Baidoa, this time with U.S. Marines in the lead. We made the trip in three hours despite long sections of road that weren't there anymore. Marines drive like qat-influenced Somalis except they don't litter. American troops in Somalia were scrupulous about not tossing empty water bottles out Humvee windows or scattering MRE trash on patrol. They policed their areas and always left the campground cleaner than they found it. We tried to explain to the marines that the locals *wanted* those water bottles and MRE scraps. Somalia is so bad that making a mess improves the place.

The land was less fertile here than in Jalalaqsi. Western Somalia is one great thorn scrub savannah gradually rising toward the mountains of Ethiopia and utterly featureless except for two gigantic limestone rocks, Bur Acaba and Bur Eibi, which jut out of the surrounding plain as big and steep and out of place as ski resorts. But, although this was desert, it had wells and irrigated fields, and between the fields was grazing land dotted with cows, goats, and camels. Again, we were never out of the sight of food. And never out of the sight of hunger either.

Children were begging frantically by the roadside, pointing to their bellies and making terrible faces. Older boys twirled rags to attract attention. That they had enough energy for theatrics meant they were among the better off. We weren't going to stop for them anyway. The road was famous for bandits.

On New Year's Day we would come back down this highway without marines. The beggars were gone, and in their place were a dozen freelance roadblocks. These were lengths of iron pipe, each balanced on an oil drum and counterweighted with a chunk of concrete. Half a dozen armed creeps lurked in the thornbush shade while one harmless-looking fellow squatted by the drum, ready to raise the pipe and obsequiously wave you through—unless you looked as harmless as he did, in which case you'd be robbed and shot. We'd found some doughtier gunmen than the Jalalaqsi bunch, and we had a dozen of them with us in three trucks. We drove fast right at the blockades with much scowling and bristling of gun barrels and we were unmolested.

We went on the trip to Baidoa to see George Bush, who was making the kind of high-speed kiss-and-promise tour of Somalia that seemed, I thought, indistinguishable from presidential campaigning—as though the man had suffered complete memory loss, forgot he was beaten the previous November, and forgot he was in the wrong country besides.

Baidoa had been completely destroyed: "Somollified," as we'd taken to calling it. And it stank with the same smell poverty has around the world—stale smoke and fresh shit. The only buildings left intact were the fortified charity offices. The charities also had the only vehicles left running, all filled with gunmen and sporting the flags and logos of various relief agencies. A total innocent, set down in these environs, would say by the look of things that Baidoa had been conquered and pillaged by the Red Cross, OxFam, and CARE.

We found lodgings of a sort in Baidoa at the Bikiin Hotel, named not after the bathing suit but, very approximately and very unaccountably, after the capital of China. The Bikiin was a disintegrating thatch-and-cement establishment that served dirty plates of spaghetti and warm Kenyan beer. But it had the one thing you want most in Somalia—a high wall. It also had an antiaircraft gun and a howitzer outside the front gate.

No rooms were to be had, not that we wanted one of the dank little cubicles. And there were no bathrooms that we would go into more than once voluntarily. We commandeered an empty hut at the back of the compound, made pallets on the floor, and draped mosquito nets around as best we could. We got our gunmen squared away, fed on the spaghetti and staked out around our trucks. Then we found a table and some chairs and set these out under a palm tree.

There were four of us ABC employees: a reporter from New York, a South African soundman, a cameraman from Cairo, and me. We'd requisitioned two bottles of Scotch from the ABC emergency larder. Huge red clouds rolled through at sunset like blood pouring into water. The sky turned ruby then maroon then mahogany then black. A breeze came up. The temperature went down to only ninety degrees. The clouds blew away again and there was a moonless equatorial sky undimmed by the lights of civilization or anything resembling it. The sky was so clear that the starlight cast shadows, and so many sparkles and glitters and glints appeared above us that it looked like something really expensive had been dropped and shattered in heaven—God's Steuben ashtray, maybe.

We began to drink and think big thoughts. What the hell were we doing here? We thought that, for instance. And we thought, well, at least some little bit of good is being done in Somalia. The director of the Baidoa orphanage had told us only one child died in December. Before the marines came, the children were dying like . . . "Dying like flies" is not a simile you'd use in Somalia. The flies wax prosperous and lead full lives. Before the marines came, the children were dying like children. Would this last? No, we thought. Everything will slip back into chaos as soon as the marines are gone. But to do some good briefly is better than doing no good ever. Or is it always? Somalia was being flooded with food aid. The only way to overcome the problem of theft was to make food too cheap to be worth stealing. Rice was selling for ten cents a pound in Somalia, the cheapest rice in the world. But what, we thought, did that mean to the people with the fields of corn and sorghum and the herds of goats and cattle? Are those now worth nothing, too? Had we come to a Somalia where some people sometimes starved only to leave a Somalia where everybody always would?

We had some more to drink and smoked as many cigars and cigarettes as we could to keep the mosquitoes away—mosquitoes which carry yellow fever, dengue, lymphatic filariasis, and four kinds of malaria, one of which is almost instantly fatal. Was this the worst place we'd ever covered? We thought it was. We had, among the four of us, nearly forty years' experience of journalism in wretched spots. But Somalia . . . tiresome discomfort, irritating danger, amazing dirt, prolific disease, humdrum scenery (not counting this night sky), ugly food (especially the MREs we were chewing), rum weather, bum natives, and, everywhere you looked, suffering innocents and thriving swine. True, the women were beautiful, but all their fathers, brothers, uncles, husbands, and, for that matter, male children over twelve were armed.

Still, we thought, this wasn't the worst New Year's Eve we'd ever spent. We had a couple more drinks. We certainly weren't worried about ecological ruin, shrinking white-collar job market, or fear of intimacy. All that "modern era anomie" disappears with a dose of Somalia. Fear cures anxiety. The genuinely alien banishes alienation. It's hard for existential despair to flourish where actual existence is being snuffed out at every turn. Real *Schmerz* trumps *Weltschmerz*. If you have enough to drink.

But what do you do about Somalia? We had even more to drink and reasoned as hard as we could.

Professor Amartya Sen says, "There has never been a famine in any country that's been a democracy with a relatively free press. I know of no exception. It applies to very poor countries with democratic systems as well as to rich ones."

And in the *New York Times* article featuring that quote from Professor Sen, Sylvia Nasar says, "Modern transportation has made it easy to move relief supplies. But far more important are the incentives governments have to save their own people. It's no accident that the familiar horror stories . . . occurred in one-party states, dictatorships or colonies: China, British India, Stalin's Russia." She notes that India has had no famine since independence even though the country suffered severe food shortages in 1967, 1973, 1979, and 1987.

Says Professor Sen, "My point really is that if famine is about to develop, democracy can guarantee that it won't." And he goes on to say that when there is no free press "it's amazing how ignorant and immune from pressure the government can be."

Well, for the moment at least, Somalia certainly had a free press. The four of us were so free nobody even knew where we were. But how do you get Somalia one of those democratic systems Amartya Sen is so fond of? How, indeed, do you get it any system at all? Provisional government by clan elders? Permanent international occupation? UN trusteeship? Neocolonialism? Sell the place to Microsoft? Or . . . Or . . . Or . . .

We were deep into the second bottle of Scotch now, and boozy frustration was rising in our gorges along with the MRE entrées. It's all well and good to talk about what can be done to end famine in general. But what can be done about famine specifically? About this famine in particular? About a place as screwed-up as Somalia? What the fucking goddamn hell do you do?

There's one ugly thought that has occurred to almost everyone who's been to Somalia. I heard a marine private in the Baidoa convoy put it succinctly. He said, "Somalis—give them better arms and training and seal the borders."

Environment

The Outdoors and How It Got There
Peruvian Amazon, Summer 1993

Why are we worried about nature's welfare? How did we get to be enamored of the outdoors? Just go into it for a minute, and no fair taking the indoors with you. Doff the little Donna Karan frock, that rumpus room for your torso. Shed those lacy Christian Dior knickers, gazebo for your butt. Eschew your Joan and David pumps, small personal floors for feet. Enter nature as you, indeed, entered nature. Then get arrested. Police, we mustn't forget, are part of nature, too.

But let's say you're on your own land and properly secluded, and the kids are at camp, and the cleaning lady has gone home, and today isn't the day the boy comes to mow the lawn, and your husband's too busy watching ESPN to notice. Go outdoors and cavort. Scamper through the foundation plantings. Roll in the gladiolus. Vault the lawn furniture. Romp 'neath clothesline and bird feeder. You'll learn about yourself. And what you'll learn is that *you itch*.

Ticks, lice, fleas, mites, poison ivy, poison oak, mosquitoes, blackflies, deerflies, horseflies, sunburn, prickly heat, allergies, rashes, and fungal infections . . . One thing that's certain about going outdoors: when you come back inside, you'll be scratching.

With me it was chiggers.

I was in an Orejón Indian village on the Sucusari River in the Peruvian Amazon. A few slapdash thatch-topped shacks were set around a weedy common. The jungle stood behind with its excess of greens: celadons, olive drabs, chartreuses, envies, gullibilities, golf courses, and Saint Patrick's Day parades. The locals lolled in their hammocks. Midday hush obtained. The sky was a fine, light, equatorial blue with just a few tubby cumulus clouds as pretty as foam on a beer.

It was Eden, a scruffy Eden, Eden after the apple had been eaten but before anybody realized they'd have to go to work. Anyway, there was a one-room schoolhouse in the village and a beautiful schoolteacher barely out of her teens and very shy. I was thinking, if I were a younger man, maybe I'd get into this ecology stuff. With altruistic enthusiasm born of undying love, the two of us could save a rain forest and a half. And rescue mountain ranges. And give the Heimlich maneuver to an occasional small continent. While I was thus woolgathering, one of the beautiful schoolteacher's tiny charges booted a soccer ball into my knee.

It was 95 degrees. I'm as old as the president of the United States. I have a body like a sack of gummy bears. And it's been thirty years since I was a third-string forward on my high school's JV soccer team. But such is male vanity that for the next half hour I was America's one-man World Cup team battling a half dozen midget Pelés. Running through the verdure, I got chiggers. Who got the schoolteacher, I can't say. She wandered away unimpressed.

I'd flown to Peru from Florida. There's a corner of Miami International Airport devoted to off-brand Latin American airlines: Cha-Cha Air, Trans Mato Grosso, Malvinas National, Aero Tierra del Fuego, and so forth. American "eco-tourists," seeking solitude in untrammeled wilderness and lonely communion with the natural world, jammed the ticket counters. There's a look about these sightseers. They haven't been out in the weather enough to get skin-cancerous, and they haven't been in an office or shop for fourteen hours a day either. Theirs is the healthy glow of people without enough to do. They are in their thirties or forties but sit on the airport floor cross-legged as though they were fifteen. They touch each other a lot and make prolonged eye contact, and their conversations are filled with little noises of affirmation. The men are not actually unshaven but look as though they are nerving themselves not to shave. The women wear their hair plain and their faces scrubbed and go undecorated except for large pieces of "native" jewelry—that is, jewelry from cultures where women spend as much time dolling themselves up as they can spare from baby having and yam-field tilling.

Why do the eco-tourists have neon-blue hiking shorts? And fluorescent-purple windbreakers? Caution-signal-yellow sweat socks? Crap table–toned fanny packs? Hojo roof–tinted luggage? T-shirts the hue of sex dolls? What is the connection between love of nature and colors not found in ditto?

Ahead of me in line was an all-female tour group, bound for the Amazon, as it were. They talked about being an all-female tour group. This, they told each other, was meaningful. Also meaningful were herbal medicines, spiritual healings, astral projections, auras, and other things not subject to empirical observation or experimental proof. Natural creatures showing appreciation of nature by holding natural science in contempt—nature *is* mysterious.

"Party of ten women?" said the Peruvian airline ticket agent.

"Party of ten *loud* women!" said one of the women, loudly.

I'd signed up for my own Amazon trip more or less at random. I had a pile of tour-company brochures, each saying the rain forest was a marvel and all promising "experiences you'll never forget." I guess the people who write the brochures—or the people who read them—haven't had many such experiences or the tour companies would tout "experiences you'll wish you could remember more of," those being the fun kind. The brochures also pointed out that I wouldn't be exploring for oil or cutting down tropical hardwoods. In fact, I'd be doing the rain forest a kind of favor by going there and thanking it for sharing. And every brochure had a large picture of a poison frog. I don't know why this was a selling point.

I hoped, of course, to be thrown in with, well, ten loud women, for instance. But no luck. News of coup attempts and Shining Path excesses had given Peruvian adventure travel too adventurous a name just then. I wound up with just four other people on a tour designed for thirty.

We landed in Iquitos, an old rubber boom city far back behind the Andes and reachable only by river or air. It was late at night and violently hot. The air was wet and immobile. We stood around in a cement-floored hall decorated with murals of Machu Picchu, which we were nowhere near, and ads for "Inca Cola." The baggage handlers threw our luggage in all directions. A clutter of begging musicians played the Simon and Garfunkel Andes theme, leaving me with that "I'd-rather-be-a-hankie-than-a-snot" tune stuck in my head for a week.

The ten loud women were assembled by their tour guide and led loudly away. The guide for my tour, Julio, came to get us in a bus made of wood, like one of those arts-and-crafts-store toys that people without children give to kids. "The lush rain forest of the Amazon wilderness supports the most prolific and diverse array of flora and fauna found anywhere in the world," began Julio.

"Where can we get a beer?" said Tom, an ex–rodeo rider. Tom turned out to be a Republican. His wife, Susan, may have been one, too. (Ever since the Republican party got overexcited about fetus empowerment at the 1992 convention, it's been hard to get women to admit this.) If so, we were the first eco-tourist group with a Republican majority since Teddy Roosevelt explored the Amazon in 1913.

The fourth member of our party, Michael, was the executive editor of a publishing house in New York and had just commissioned a book from an old college friend of mine. "I know what *you're* doing," Michael said to me. "You're writing an article viciously satirizing large plants. Don't anybody do anything plantlike. He's taking notes." Michael was traveling with the marketing director of his company, Shelley, who'd come to the Amazon because of a lifelong fascination with three-toed sloths.

"Their top speed is 1.6 miles per hour," said Shelley. "They sometimes spend their entire existence in one tree. They only come down to shit. And they only have to do that once a week. They lead a wonderful life."

Julio looked confused. "The Amazon rain forest occupies over two and a half million square miles and includes major portions of nine South American countries," he said. "There are eleven hundred tributaries to the Amazon river system, which contains sixty-six percent of all the earth's river water. It has been calculated that the Amazon contributes twenty percent of the oxygen . . ."

It took us two days to make Julio stop this. We knew that we'd gotten through to him when he quit saying "Amazon rain forest" and started saying "jungle."

"We *really* need some beer," said Susan.

"Or some of that Peruvian coca-leaf tea," I said.

"And we need to know how to get the little bags up our nose," said Michael.

We had a few hours' sleep in an Iquitos hotel that was trying hard to be clean and air-conditioned. Then we went to find coffee on Iquitos's modest esplanade. We watched the sun advance in a giant sky over an immensity of water and herbage. It was a noble vista, grand and calm and reaching off past the two-mile-wide river into a vast distance. A blush of haze obscured the horizon, giving an impression of true endlessness, as though the earth really were flat and you could see all of it from Iquitos. It was like a vision of, to be honest, Illinois. It was especially like a vision of Illinois in the flooded summer of 1993.

Iquitos is not as majestic or as dull as its surroundings. It's a mildly pleasant city of 250,000, fairly tidy and not completely impoverished. The architecture is low and pastel, arranged in an orderly grid with the houses blank and flush against the sidewalk, Latin style. Monument-filled plazas appear at regular intervals, although I don't think anything monumental has ever happened in Iquitos. There's one novel feature, a floating slum named Belén full of tenement rafts and pushcart boats and beer cellars on stilts. Belén is sometimes called the Venice of the Amazon, but not very often.

Iquitos has a feel, a very Estados Unidos feel, of being a place with no reason to be in that place, like most towns in . . . Illinois. Iquitos was founded in the mid-1700s by Jesuits in order to pester local Indians with religion. The Indians, of course, have long ago all been pestered, many to death. Modern Iquitos dates from the rubber boom of the late nineteenth century. The famous rubber baron Fitzcarraldo made a fortune here, or lived here, or passed through. Local history is obscure on the point. Anyway, *Fitzcarraldo*, the movie, was shot in Iquitos. "Signs of the great opulence of those rubber boom days may still be seen in mansions and edifices," said my guidebook. By which was meant, I think, that there's an old hotel with balconies and that some of the narrow, squat, fin de siècle stucco town houses have doorways decorated with Portuguese tiles.

Iquitos is the nethermost deepwater port on the Amazon, twenty-three hundred miles upstream. But not many oceangoing freighters call anymore. It's a seventeen-day trip from the Atlantic, and there's no pressing reason to make it. Rubber comes from factories now. Iquitos exports some Brazil nuts, some plywood, some tobacco, some mahogany, and photos of poison frogs. Most of the locals seem to make their living in the open-air market, selling each other the same enormous catfish—a shovel-nosed thing the size of a bunk-bed mattress and marked with the dun-colored camouflage that was used in the quite-different environment of Desert Storm. There is oil being looked for in the region, however. And some has been found already. Another boom approaches, perhaps. More decorative tiles and hotels with balconies are on their way. In fact a skyscraper was even started in Iquitos. But the contractors were building it between two of the eleven hundred tributaries that contain 66 percent of the earth's river water, which means 66 percent of the earth's river mud, and the thing began to sink. The empty shell stands eight or ten stories high, moldy and just slightly out of plumb.

Julio collected us in the clapboard bus and took us to the tour-company dock. Here we got on board a very long and narrow boat with an absurd palm-frond roof. The boat had a large outboard motor dropped in a well near the stern and a little steering wheel at the bow connected to the engine by thirty-foot strands of scraping, twanging coat-hanger wire.

We went fifty miles down the Amazon in three and a half hours, traveling not quite fast enough to water-ski but fast enough to dangle a hand over the side and not get it eaten by piranhas. The big sun and big clouds made dapples of Impressionist light on the water, and the breeze was as good as that moment in a noontime parking lot when the car AC finally kicks in. The fashionably earth-toned river complemented the green jungle verge. It was a scene of inordinate charm that stretched along the Amazon's banks . . . and stretched and stretched and stretched—uniform, unvarying, same, and identical for fifty miles. Fortunately, the boat driver sold beer from a cooler.

And the boat had an interesting bathroom. It was a little outhouse past the stern of the ship, hanging over the water aft of the outboard motor. To get there you had to climb across the top of that outboard, its propeller churning horribly below. Then, when you pulled up the toilet-seat lid, you realized you were right over the engine's rooster-tail wake—death douche.

Our tour company's lodge was tucked up a creek in the jungle. Tree-trunk pilings supported a ramble of thatch and board buildings all roofed in the same manner as the boat. One tennis court–size screened area enclosed a dining room and a bar. Guitars leaning in a corner threatened folk music. The rooms themselves were just partitioned nooks, open beneath the roof. Mosquito nets covered the beds. There was no electricity or plumbing, and the showers were fed from gravity tanks full of river water more or less warmed by the sun.

Michael called the style of the lodge "primitive *primitif*." Although this tour company is owned by an urban corporation, the people who run it and who built its facilities are either Indians or *ribereños*, the poor people who live along the riverbanks and are a mixture of Indian, Spaniard, rubber planter, river boatman, and whatever. It would be interesting to know what people who live in humble circumstances think of creating humble circumstances for people who live in luxury to visit. But they were too polite to say.

Whatever the employees' opinion of their tasks, they accomplished them with grace. The lodge had ice for drinks, plenty of hammocks, fresh fruit, fried plantains, wonderful little Peruvian potatoes, and excellent (very large) catfish fillets. And, except for a biology professor from Lima and his assistant, we were the only guests. There was twice as much staff as us. A perfect wilderness adventure, or it would have been except Julio inveigled us into a nature hike.

Some people would think it odd to go all the way to the Amazon and never get out and take a close-up look at . . . Yow! Did you see the size of that bug?! Personally, I believe a rocking hammock, a good cigar, and a tall gin and tonic is the way to save the planet. From a recumbent, and slightly buzzed, perspective, Mother Earth is a fine specimen of womanhood. And the environment is something for which everyone should give his all, if somebody will go get my wallet.

I have accumulated a three-foot stack of books and articles about the rain forest. (Just think of the dead trees. And, by the way, do you send a decorative arrangement of cement to a plant funeral?) From this reading material, I gather that, if the rain forest disappears, we'll have to get our air in little bottles from the Evian company and biodiversity will vanish and pretty soon we'll only have about one kind of animal and with my luck that will be the Lhasa apso. The indigenous peoples will all become exdigenous and move to LA, and this will be tough on them because it's hard to use a car phone when you've got a big wooden disk in your lower lip. Furthermore, we'll never discover all the marvelous properties of the various herbal treasures that are found in the rain forest, such as Ben & Jerry's Rainforest Crunch. Also, rain forests are disappearing so fast that by the time you read this they're probably gone.

In my reading about the rain forest, however, I have found very little description of what it is like to *be* in a rain forest. You'd think something so wet, hot, and biological would stink like boiled Times Square, but it doesn't.

Jungle has a nice fresh scent, the reason being that there's so much life in the jungle that anything which dies or is excreted or even gets drowsy is immediately a picnic for something else.

A tree keels over and it's termite Thanksgiving. A termite slows up and it's lizard hors d'oeuvres. The lizard takes a nap—kinkajou lunch. And so on up the food chain—and back down it. There's a spider in the jungle so big it eats birds. The ravenousness of rain forest appetites is such that the floor of the jungle is nearly bare. If you don't count ants. And you can't. There are ants in numbers large enough to confuse the people who calculate national debt. There are ants all over every leaf and stem (not to mention every shoe and sock), ants all over the ground and around all the tree trunks, and ants climbing in droves up the jungle vines. Which is something they don't tell you in the Tarzan books: he went *ahhEEEahhEEEahhEEEahh* as he swung through the jungle because he had ants in his loincloth.

There are ants as big as AA batteries and ants as small as, well, ants. Leafcutter ants regularly go forth in columns of ten thousand to pick up dime-sized bits of foliage and carry these back to their nests for the purpose, I believe, of making public-television nature movies. My guidebook asked me to imagine that the half-inch leafcutter ants were six feet long. I have my own fantasy life, thank you. Anyway, my guidebook insisted, each of these six-foot creatures would be capable of carrying 750 pounds and move at fifteen miles an hour. Which makes the leafcutter ant nature's lawn tractor.

The intense, even NBA-like competition among living things in the rain forest means that almost every plant and animal has some kind of stinger, barb, thorn, prickle, spur, spine, poison, or angry advocacy group back in the United States boycotting your place of business. There's a fierce competition for the nutrients in the ground, which is why rain forest soil is notoriously poor and easily damaged by horticulture. The tremendous hardwood trees of the jungle, rising 120 feet with prodigious rocket-ship tail-fin buttresses and trunks as big around as tract houses, are rooted in earth where you couldn't grow petunias.

But what it is like to actually *be* in the rain forest is hot and sticky. When you get out of your hammock and go nature hiking, you're immediately covered in sweat. Your underwear clings, your shirt clings, your pants cling, and things that *EEK!* aren't part of your clothing cling to you. You're also immediately covered in bugs. And the rain forest is, as its name would imply, rainy. Hence, *WHOOPS!* slippery. You're immediately covered in mud too.

While we were trying to remove the sweat, bugs, and mud with handkerchiefs, moist towelettes, and Deep Woods Off (in the environmentally friendly pump containers), Julio was showing us insects that look like sticks and frogs that look like leaves and moths that look like birds and lizards that look like anything they sit on. There seem to be problems with personal identity in the jungle.

The rain forest is not, however, scary, not even in the dark. Though the rain forest is dense, tangled, and filled with remarkably icky things, the conifer woods of Maine are spookier. Not to mention the bushes of Central Park. Maybe this is because anacondas aren't really inclined to attack people (probably because we taste like towelettes and Deep Woods Off) and the *ribereños* have eaten most of the crocodiles. Or maybe it's because the largest land mammal anywhere nearby is the capybara, a sort of giant guinea pig. But I think it's the sound. The jungle sounds exactly like the jungle sounds in every jungle movie. There are even distant drums, though these turn out to be from popular songs being played on the lodge staff's boom box. Even in the middle of the night, when you have no idea where you are, it's impossible to believe there isn't someone selling popcorn and Milk Duds right around the corner.

Actually, right around the corner was someone collecting bats. The biology professor was stringing fine mesh nets across the jungle paths. These are invisible to bat radar. The bats get as tangled up as jungle hikers who have come around a corner and walked into a fine mesh net full of angry bats.

The professor extracted the bats—and us—and held the bats with wings outspread so we could examine them in the light of Tom and Susan's video camera.

Why do people spend so little time contemplating the ugliness of nature? How many ordinary humans can get all the way through even the most fabulous sunset without getting up for a beer or going inside to check the evening news? But you can watch an enraged Jamaican fruit bat trying to bite a professor from Lima for hours. A Jamaican fruit bat looks like a colonel in the rat air force. And it's got a set of teeth on it that you could use to perform an appendectomy. If I were Jamaican, I'd keep the fruit out in the garage or maybe rent a mini-storage space. There was another bat, I didn't catch the name, which ate pollen or pollinated plants or did something in the pollen line. Anyway, it had a tongue that was a surprise. If bats wore blue jeans, this fellow would be able to get change out of his hip pocket with his tongue. It must make bat date night interesting.

All these bats were furious, swiveling their necks and snapping their heads from side to side, trying to get at the professor's fingers, taking thumb-sized chunks out of the air with their jaws. And all these bats were male; and, in the throes of their fury, they had erections—tiny, pink bat penises sticking out of their fur. Some feminist theory of something-or-other was being validated here, maybe. Susan and Shelley declined to comment.

For those of us who were not enraged male bats, however, the jungle wasn't very sexy. That cannot, of course, be literally true, given the reproductive riot and galloping fecundity around us. But, for average *norteamericanos,* the prospect of romance was something like moving our beds into a sauna, dumping bug spray on the hot rocks, and making love under down quilts.

The gummy swelter of the rain forest only gets worse after dark. When the sun goes down, the air is becalmed, and a humid, gagging smother settles upon the body. Sundown makes the heat get worse, and so, for that matter, does everything else. When the rain comes, the air gets so dense you could serve it as flan. When the wind blows, the atmosphere is as horrid as ever; there's just more of it. And, when the sun comes up again, it brings the heat of the day.

We got up early the next morning (or would have gotten up if any of us had been able to sleep) and went bird-watching, an activity I don't understand. Watch birds *what*? The birds of the Amazon have wonderful names, however.

Undulated tinamou
Horned screamer
Laughing falcon
American finfoot
Wattled jacana
Plumbeous pigeon
Mealy parrot
Common potoo
Ladder-tailed nightjar
Pale-tailed barbthroat
Gould's jewelfront
Black-eared fairy
Spotted puffbird
Lanceolated monklet
Yellow-billed nunbird
Red-necked woodpecker
Ocellated woodcreeper
Pale-legged hornero
Common piping guan

And these are very useful if, for instance, you're writing an epic poem about the Bush administration secretary of the interior and need a rhyme for "Manuel Lujan." But don't ask me which birds are which. And don't ask anybody else either. There's always the horrible chance that they'll tell you. And seventeen hundred species of birds are found in Peru alone.

Cinnamon-rumped foliage-gleaner
Black-spotted bare-eye
Ash-throated gnateater
Screaming piha
Amazonian umbrellabird
Lesser wagtail-tyrant
Black and white tody-flycatcher
Golden-crowned spadebill
Bright-rumped attila
Social flycatcher
Violaceous jay
Orange-fronted plushcrown
Cocoa thrush
Giant cowbird
Short-billed honeycreeper
Variable seedeater
Purple-throated fruitcrow

I did like the flocks of parrots. They'd all sit together in a tree saying, in unison, "I'm a pretty boy!" No. But I don't see why, with patience, they couldn't be trained to do so.

It was strange to see parrots, toucans, macaws, and cockatoos flying around without perches, cages, or a jungle covered in newspapers. Actually, the toucans and macaws weren't *that* wild. They were hanging around the lodge, squawking and begging. A macaw ate the shutter release off Shelley's camera, and one of the toucans stuck its huge beak into Michael's coffee cup, slurped the contents, and got jittery and irritable.

When we came back from bird-watching (a bit irritable ourselves), Julio found a sloth for Shelley. It was in the top of a cecropia tree reading a letter from Bill Clinton asking it to come to Washington and help reinvent government. Really, it was doing even less than that, although it was doing it upside down, which I think should count against the sloth's slothfulness. I find even *getting* upside down fairly laborious.

Shelley had never seen a live sloth. They can't be kept in captivity because, although sloths eat the leaves from some thirty kinds of trees, any given sloth will eat leaves from only a couple of those kinds, so you'd have to take thirty giant rain forest trees around everywhere with your captive sloths. Tom had a telescope, we set this on a tripod, and Shelley looked through the lens. "Oh, he's beautiful!" she said. She was wrong. The sloth had a long, awkward, gawky body of the kind basketball players had before steroids were discovered. Julio gave a sharp whistle, and the sloth turned its chalky face—very slowly—in our direction. A green smear of leaf slobber was spread around its mouth.

Sloths move at the speed of congressional debate but with greater deliberation and less noise. Shelley's sloth stared at us for half an hour and, having decided we were a surprise, headed for cover. One triumvirate of sloth claws came unhooked from a tree branch and a sloth leg swung down like fudge batter dripping from a spatula until another tree branch was languidly encountered and methodically grasped. Then a second sloth limb repeated these motions, then a third, until at last the sloth had all its appendages located elsewhere and thereto the sloth head and body proceeded at a stately pace.

Our notions of grace have been so influenced by slow-motion videotape that sloths seem to be graceful. In fact, they're just slow. But Shelley disagreed. She wants to start a Sloth Circus. "This is a circus strictly for adults," said Shelley, "very soothing—Windham Hill calliope music. The clowns are all dressed in business suits. They don't fall down, they get tripped up by little clauses in contracts. And all the stunts are leisurely. On a high wire in the center ring, the circus sloths sleep late on Sunday morning, then read the *New York Times*."

We, too, had a leisurely morning, although Julio had a long list of experiences we'd never forget and were supposed to be having. We finally consented to go in a small speedboat to look for dolphins. There are two kinds of dolphins in the Amazon. Estuarine dolphins look like slimmed-down versions of the Sea World type, as if Flipper'd been doing extra laps and had given up leaping for fish between meals. Amazon River dolphins, however, are pink, a too-vivid parody of flesh, like the Crayolas of that name. You don't get a good look at pink dolphins because they don't jump. They just roll to the surface, presenting an indistinct mass of plump tissue—drowned and bloated corpses given unnatural animation, scuba zombies. The *ribereños* say that the pink dolphins sometimes take human form and appear as beautiful maidens who entice young men ("Want to go out for sushi?"). The dolphin maiden lures her prey to the riverbank. Then the fellow disappears forever. The *ribereños* consider it bad luck to kill Amazon River dolphins. And even worse luck to date them.

The estuarine dolphins travel in pods and are more inclined to Greenpeace fund-raising antics. Unfortunately, we couldn't find any estuarine dolphins, and after a couple of hours on the river we resorted to desperate measures. And here is some news about our friends the aquatic mammals—they actually *do* like Judy Collins. Michael started it. He sang "Who Knows Where the Time Goes," and three dolphin fins appeared. Tom and Susan and I tried "Someday Soon," and there was a blowing and bubbling astern. Michael and Shelley sang "Suzanne," and a minute later, thirty yards off our bow, two dolphins launched themselves into the air with excellent hang time.

We tried "Smoke Gets in Your Eyes" by the Platters. Nothing. "Can't Help Falling in Love" by Elvis. Nothing. "Alley Oop" by the Hollywood Argyles. Nothing. But then all six of us (Julio knew the words in Spanish) warbled "Both Sides Now." If dolphins had Bic lighters or a way to hold them or anything to stand up on, the dolphins would have been standing up holding Bic lighters and singing, "Fromupanddownandstillsomehowits-cloudsillusionsIrecall," in squeaky, fast-forward voices.

"Time for a civilization hike!" said Michael. "Enough of bugs! Birds! Great big fish! We've got to get away from this hustle and bustle of nature and spend time in restful human society—get in touch with our *outer* selves." Julio took us to meet a friend of his, José, a man in his seventies who lived on a farm along the banks of the Amazon. José had a few acres of sugarcane and a few acres of pasture for cows and water buffalo. He grew mangoes and bananas. And he had chickens and relatives everywhere underfoot.

Ribereño dwellings are built on posts about grandchild-high. Sometimes there is an enclosed room, but usually the home is open on at least three sides—all porch and no house. One interior wall separates kitchen from parlor. The construction materials are rough boards and tin sheets. There's only a little furniture: a table, a bench, a couple of stools, and maybe an heirloom mantel clock. There is always, however, a framed marriage photograph hand-tinted in Amazon River dolphin color.

The kitchen stove is just cement or stones with palm wood burning on top and a grill propped over the coals. A catfish the size of a golf bag is normally roasting on this grill. The smoke goes any which way. There is no chimney. Tethered out front will be two or three dugout canoes of a pattern begging to be made into coffee tables and sold at Crate and Barrel. And, if the family is well-off, there will be a square-sterned, factory-made canoe or johnboat with an outboard motor.

Julio's friend had a yet more prized possession, a fifty-year-old sugarcane press set up in a shed next to his house. The press was operated by a water buffalo pushing a tree-limb crank in a circle around the floor, the water buffalo being lured in this orbit with offerings of pressed sugarcane. The cane juice was collected in a bucket and the bucket was emptied into an enormous copper pan, the shape of a backyard television satellite dish and fully as large—probably the largest piece of metal this side of Iquitos that wasn't a roof. The pan nestled atop a circular stone forge burning at a temperature I estimated to be almost as great as that inside my mosquito netting at night at the lodge. As the cane juice boiled down, José skimmed the impurities with an old spaghetti colander. What was left was molasses, a huge amount of it.

Molasses has only so many uses. I didn't figure the locals were *that* fond of pancake syrup. I asked Julio a discreet question. And, yes, José did make bootleg rum, a huge amount of it. We could get some for a dollar a liter. We did.

After a long nap we went on an Indian Embarrassment Tour. We hiked ten minutes through the jungle to a muddy clearing. Here the tour company had paid members of the once fierce Yagua tribe to build a traditional communal house. It was a fifty-foot-long, twenty-foot-high, loaf-shaped construction thatched all the way to the ground. It looked like a big pile of leaves. There were no windows. The inside looked like the inside of a big pile of leaves. The Yagua were wearing skirts that looked like piles of leaves, too, sort of vegetable dirndls. They had streaked their faces with Max Factor, donned fish-bone and parrot-feather necklaces, and stuck Indian-type things in their hair. The women covered their breasts with something that resembled a large baby's bib, made of cotton and not, I think, part of the original Yagua dress code.

We were supposed to "trade" with the Yagua. The tour-company brochure had been firm on this point. We were encouraged to bring "trade items" such as clothing, fish hooks, pocketknives, and the like. But we weren't supposed to try to give the Yagua money. "Money is not of much use on the river," said the brochure in a palpable untruth. We consulted among ourselves and discovered we'd all brought stupid T-shirts. I'd gone to my local gun-nut store and gotten some with big Stars and Stripes across the fronts and mottoes such as TRY TO BURN *THIS* FLAG, ASSHOLE! The Yagua brought balsa wood carvings and decorated gourds and various items of jewelry made from parts of animals that hadn't been, our brochure was careful to assure us, killed or anything like that. "They do not kill animals for this purpose," said the brochure, "but use the leftovers from their kitchen."

The Yagua were bored. So, for that matter, were we. Michael grew up on the Texas border and speaks Spanish, or used to. He said his vocabulary had evaporated with years of living in New York and using his Spanish for nothing but reading the cigarette and hemorrhoid medication ads on the subway. Michael told a half dozen small Yagua children that Tom and Susan and Shelley and I were "*bestias—no humanos*." He said they could tell because we were so big and old and still could not speak one word that they could understand. We came from a frightening place with little bitty rivers ("*poquitos mini-ríos*"). It was very far away and filled with T-shirts. And we ate—nouns failed him—cigarettes and hemorrhoid medication.

One old man had pulled out all the stops in the authentic-dress business. He had a grass skirt so elaborate he was lucky he hadn't been declared an endangered ecosystem from the waist down. The old man produced an eight-foot blowgun and some darts made from thin wooden splinters as long as a hand, with a little cotton wool wrapped around one end and the other end dipped in a poison frog—devil's Q-Tips. The blowgun itself was crafted from a thin, ruler-straight sapling that had been split and hollowed and bound back together with rattan. The old man took the blowgun, aimed it at a tree, and missed six times. Tom said he'd like to try and hit the tree on first puff. Then we were truly embarrassed. I only hope the Yaguas cheated us hugely on the T-shirt deals. As we left, the children lined up and waved happily. "*¡Adios, no humanos!*"

We walked around the corner to where the Indians really lived—in wood and tin houses like everyone else. A radio playing mariachi music was hooked up to a car battery. They were all wearing stupid T-shirts.

The next morning we took our big thatched boat, our water-borne Trader Vic's, and went downstream to the town of Orellana at the mouth of the Napo River. Orellana was named for Francisco de Orellana, one of Pizarro's captains and the first European to travel the length of the Amazon. He left the Andean foothills of Ecuador in 1541, made his way down the Napo to the main river, and reached the Atlantic over a year later, having a terrible time the whole trip. The members of Orellana's expedition nearly starved to death, which means they must have been bad wing shots, inept nut gatherers, and remarkably poor fishermen. Or maybe, being good Catholics, they thought they were supposed to eat fish only on Fridays. Anyway, they raided Indian villages for food. Orellana's tales of village women who fought back (he made them out to be very large women, inasmuch as they managed to kill some of his soldiers) are the reason for the river's "Amazon" name. The Spaniards were eventually reduced to eating the soles of their boots "boiled with herbs," and they should have been glad Nikes weren't invented.

The town of Orellana has a population of four hundred, electricity for a couple of hours a day, a muddy plaza with a concrete monument to shoe-nibbling conquistadors, an ugly modern clay brick church, and a few stucco buildings painted with swimming pool paint. In the plaza a dozen men were cutting boards from jungle hardwood, or, rather, one man was cutting while eleven or so watched. A log fifteen feet long and a yard in diameter had been laid on the grass and a chain saw had been turned into a handheld lumber mill. One horizontal lengthwise cut was taken off the log. Then a series of parallel lines about two inches apart were drawn on the level surface. The chain-saw operator began to take fifteen-foot-long slices off the log, freehand. The other men stood around holding their noses. The log was from a moena tree, a relative of the rosewood, and it smells like a fart when it's cut.

The moena is not, for olfactory reasons, one of the trees causing the rain forest to be cleared by greedy lumber companies. Interesting that a tropical plant should equip itself, probably hundreds of thousands of years ahead of time, with a defense mechanism against Danish modern furniture makers.

The real industry in Orellana is gathering tropical fish. The rain forest is the principal source of kissing gouramis, neon tetras, marbled hatchetfish, and suchlike. It is a little-known fact that the bottom of the Amazon is covered with small plaster castles, toy treasure chests, and miniature deep-sea divers who make bubbles.

Michael and Tom and I discovered more bootleg rum. There's a great variety of rum in the Amazon—there's *trago* and *agua ardenté* and *cachasa* and *mezchal del caña de azucar*. Sometimes the rums are flavored with fruit juices and vine saps. The specialty of Orellana was a rum mixed with fermented wild honey. This makes an alleged aphrodisiac called *rompe calzon*, or "bust underwear." Maybe it was my age or maybe the damp, prickly, rash-inducing nature of the underwear that was supposed to be busted, but *rompe calzon* had no effect on me, though I tried it in ample dosage.

After another long nap (the boat having meanwhile traveled up the Napo and into the Sucusari River), we arrived at the tour company's second camp. Here a really sophisticated effort at simplicity had been made. The camp was nothing but one large, wobbly bamboo platform with a roof of palm leaves. Narrow mattresses lay on the platform with a little tent of netting over each. And there was a poison frog in the washbasin.

It was a male frog, said Julio. He could tell because of the eggs. The eggs of the poison frog are carried on the male's back. It's a nineties, caring kind of poison frog.

The Sucusari camp was decorated with twee balsa plaques carved by previous tourist groups. (Balsa *isn't* a tropical hardwood. It's very soft.) The plaques bore the names of the travelers and memorialized principal incidents of their travels—"Remember the time the canoe tipped over!"—and often contained brief poems on the order of

Though the bugs made noise,
Our trip was full of joys,
Because the monkey howls,
And the wise owl hoots,
Taught us that it's,
Bad to pollute.

A pet capybara named Margarite was kept at the camp. The capybara is the world's largest rodent, a four-foot-long, hundred-pound member of the guinea pig family. (Note that no one ever claims he or she is being "used as a capybara.") Margarite had about as much personality as a guinea pig. Although the camp cook said that sometimes when visitors were swimming in the river Margarite would jump in the water and nip female tourists on the rump.

"Last one in gets to live to maturity!" said Michael. Margarite didn't molest Susan or Shelley, and Julio assured us that the piranha of the upper Amazon aren't really dangerous. They hardly ever eat anybody, he claimed. Indeed, at Orellana we'd seen half a dozen kids swimming in the river. Of course, we don't know how many kids there were to begin with. Another rare thing, said Julio, was an attack by the candiru catfish. This is the famous tiny, spined catfish which swims right up a part of the male anatomy that just thinking about makes me wince too hard to type, and it can only be removed by surgery. "That almost never happens," said Julio. He didn't get in the water himself.

Tom and I tried a dugout canoe, a small one—a difficult craft to maneuver, especially since, with two well-nourished North American males aboard, the whole thing was underwater. A dugout is much superior to a conventional manufactured canoe because you can get soaking wet without bothering to capsize it.

But we were coming perilously close to having fun, and that is not the point of eco-tourism. So we went to the Orejón Indian village and I got chiggers.

Chiggers are a kind of mite or, rather, the larvae of a mite, and they are only a hundredth of an inch long. It's hard to keep an eye out for them. They crawl on your body and find some hot, damp spot (which, in the Amazon, is everyplace) where your clothes are tight (I have apparently grown too fat for my socks) and there they release an enzyme, the evolutionary purpose of which is to make you tear your Friends of the Earth membership card into small pieces, these being what the chigger larvae actually feed upon.

The only thing you can do about chiggers is not scratch them. And you can drink three six-packs of beer and not take a whiz while you're at it. No Sirens calling to Ulysses, no Lorelei enticing Rhine boatmen to destruction, no pink dolphin maiden breathing heavy through her blowhole at the local swains ever produced a desire as overpowering as the yen to scratch a chigger bite. By comparison, a sailor in port after six months at sea has a mere partiality to feminine companionship. Madonna has half a mind to get some publicity. And politicians are this way/that way about getting reelected. And never has there been such delight in surrendering to a temptation or achieving a goal. The next thing you know, you've been scratching for two and a half hours and your legs are blood salad.

Chiggers are supposed to drop off after about four days. But mine seemed to migrate north instead and establish themselves in a less socially acceptable area for scratching. And my chigger itches persisted for weeks so that, when I was back in the real world, engaged in the ordinary activities of adulthood—giving a speech, visiting a museum, serving as an usher at a friend's wedding—I would be suddenly overwhelmed by an uncontrollable desire to thrust both hands down the front of my trousers and make like I had a bad case of Arkansas pants rabbits.

I blame my chiggers on Theocritus, who invented the pastoral poem in the third century BC. Theocritus was from Syracuse, the large, urbane Greek colony in Sicily, and he spent his career in Alexandria, the most cosmopolitan metropolis of the ancient world, the capital of arts, ideas, and sophistication, the Seattle of its day.

Theocritus was a city boy, but as a youth he lived for a while on the Aegean island of Cos. A school of medicine had been founded there by Hippocrates in the fifth century BC, and various cultural institutions had grown up around the school. Cos was, in effect, a college town. Like many of us who went to college in a cute place, Theocritus had fond memories of amusing locals, of young love in wholesale quantities, of long, gabbing walks in the woods with friends, and of how idyllic everything looks when you're supposed to be in chem lab. Hence:

Ah, sweetly lows the calf,
And sweetly the heifer,
Sweetly sounds the goatherd with his pipe,
And sweetly also I!

—*"Idyll IX"*

This type of lyric, with its remarkable lack of percipience about barnyard noises, folk music, and self, was brought to full development in the first century BC by Virgil.

Oh, if you'd only fancy life with me in country poverty . . .
And shepherding a flock of kids with green hibiscus!
Piping beside me in the woods you'll mimic Pan

—*"Eclogue II"*

From Virgil a line of direct descent runs for two thousand years to John Denver.

Virgil had, at least, grown up on a farm, though not an unprosperous one, and actual labor was done by the slaves. He spent most of his adult life as a court favorite of the emperor Augustus.

Successful men of affairs (or, in the case of the modern ecology movement, their children) customarily spout nostalgia for simple times and places—catching bullhead with dough balls on bent pins, sprawling in the hayloft atop the milkmaid, running through meadows barefoot, stepping in things. To this piffling wistfulness, Virgil added the element of utopian idealism. He envisioned a pastoral Eden.

The carrier too will quit the sea, no naval tree masts
Barter their goods, but every land bear everything,
The soil will suffer hoes no more, nor vines the hook.
The sturdy plowman too will now unyoke his team,
And wool unlearn the lies of variable dye.

—*"Eclogue IV"*

Christians have traditionally interpreted "Eclogue IV" as predicting the birth of Christ and the new age that will follow (hence Virgil's role in Dante's *Inferno* as the only good pagan in hell). But advocates of a very different kind of New Age like Virgil's idea even better. Edward Abbey wrote a novel, *The Monkey Wrench Gang,* about pro-bucolic activists who wreck construction machinery to stop progress. Abbey would be a saint to environmentalists if saints got recycled instead of going to heaven. In 1986 Abbey said that he had "hope for the coming restoration of a higher civilization: scattered human populations, modest in number, that live by fishing, hunting, food gathering . . . that assemble once a year in the ruins of abandoned cities for great festivals of moral, spiritual, artistic and intellectual renewal."

Of course, Theocritus, Virgil, and people who put sugar in bulldozer fuel tanks don't hold Western civilization's majority brief on nature. At least they didn't used to. There are 305 mentions of wilderness in the Revised Standard Version of the Bible, none of them laudatory. In the Old Testament, six Hebrew words are translated as *wilderness*. The literal meanings of the words are "a desolation," "a worthless thing," "a sterile valley," "an arid region," "a haunt of wild beasts and nomads," and "an open field." In the New Testament the two Greek words for *wilderness* both mean "lonely place."

The terms we have inherited for paradise don't indicate that our ancestors had any inclination toward eco-tourism after death or even in their daydreams. *Paradise* has its root in the Old Persian word for "enclosure." *Eden* comes from the Hebrew "delight." *Valhalla* is "Hall of the Slain." *Olympus* is a ninety-eight-hundred-foot mountain in Thessaly that nobody had bothered to climb or they would have known the gods weren't up there. *Heaven* doesn't have anything to do with earth at all; it's the firmament. And, to borrow a term from one of those non-Western cultures that's supposed to be so in tune with the ecosystem, *nirvana* means "extinction."

While paradises tend to be alfresco, they are not at all wild, except for Valhalla, which is wild but indoors. The traditional Muslim seven heavens sound like a visit to Van Cleef and Arpels followed by an encounter with paparazzi flash cameras: (1) Silver, (2) Gold, (3) Pearl, (4) White Gold, (5) Silver and Fire, (6) Ruby and Garnet, and (7) Divine Light Impossible for Mortal Man to Describe.

Until very recently ordinary people spent most of their time outdoors—farming, hunting, gathering nuts and berries, pillaging the countryside in armed bands. The more contact people actually have with nature, the less likely they are to "appreciate" it in a big mushy, ecumenical way. And the more likely they are to get chiggers.

James Fenimore Cooper was the son of a wealthy land agent. He went to Yale. He lived most of his life in Scarsdale except for seven years spent as the American consul at Lyons. Cooper wrote the *Leatherstocking Tales* idealizing pioneer life and particularly the life of that pioneer ideal Natty Bumppo. In Cooper's 1827 book, *The Prairie,* Bumppo says, "They scourge the very 'arth with their axes. Such hills and hunting grounds as I have seen stripped of the gifts of the Lord, without remorse or shame! . . . how much has the beauty of the wilderness been deformed in two short lives!"

Cooper's contemporary President Andrew Jackson was an actual backwoodsman. Jackson, in his 1829 inaugural address, says, "What good man would prefer a country covered with forests and ranged by a few thousand savages to our extensive Republic, studded with cities, towns, and prosperous farms, embellished with all the improvements which art can devise or industry execute."

The concept of "nature" is itself, so to speak, artificial. Are RingDings elf food? Is Wal-Mart part of the spirit world? For people who live in what we would call "the state of nature"—for Yaguas, Orejóns, *ribereños*, me when I'm fishing in Michigan—nature is nothing in particular. It's meat locker, wastepaper basket, patio, and toilet.

Perhaps I should say nature is nothing *in general*. Man alone in the wilderness—with nothing but a camper-back pickup, a cooler full of Bud Light, and a cellular phone between him and the raw power of the elements—is not thinking of nature as an abstraction. His interest in the natural world is highly specific: "Shit, I'm out of ice."

When those who have a purpose for being outdoors encounter those who are outdoors because of how earthy the earth is, some conflict of interest ensues. Witness the strained relations between loggers and owl enthusiasts or between k. d. lang and pot roast. At the very least the lover of shrubbery will get kidded. Roderick Frazier Nash (author of *Wilderness and the American Mind,* eminent environmentalist scholar, prominent spokesman for ecological ethics, and a man so devoted to nature that he read enough James Fenimore Cooper and presidential inaugural speeches to find the quotes I used above) was fed a line and swallowed the hook, the worm, and the bobber.

> *I had the opportunity to talk, through an interpreter, with a man who hunted and gathered in the jungles of Malaysia. I tried without success to discuss wilderness. When I asked for an equivalent word I heard things*

like "green places," "outdoors," or "nature." Finally, in desperation, I asked the interpreter to ask the hunter how he said "I am lost in the jungle." . . . The interpreter turned to me and said with a smile that the man had indicated he did not get lost in the jungle. The question made as little sense to him as would asking an American city dweller how he said "I am lost in my apartment."

Personally, I have been lost in my apartment any number of times. I have a friend, Gilbert, who is a hunting guide in New Brunswick and a member of the Micmac tribe. One day he and I were lost in a vast alder bog on one of those overcast days without shadow to give bearing. Gilbert said, "Indians never get lost—although sometimes the *path* wanders."

For most of history, mankind has managed to keep a reasonable balance between thinking nature is adorable and thinking it wants to kill us.

Virgil's soppy lyric to his true love aside, the original Greek Pan was born completely covered in hair, with a goat's beard, hooves, and horns. His mother, the nymph Callisto, was so frightened that she ran off and left him to the care of whatever welfare agencies Olympus had. A sudden spasm of fear in the wilderness is supposed to be caused by a glimpse of Pan, hence the word *panic*. Many of the traditional attributes of Satan are traceable to Pan. Our image of Pan as a frolicsome, pipe-tooting gadabout in need of a leg wax is a late classical invention. And the notion of Pan, as a nature deity, being more or less the God of Everything—"pantheism"—is the result either of a misidentification with the Egyptian god who created the world, ram-headed Chum, or of etymological confusion between the name Pan, which means "pasturer," and *pan*, the neuter form of the Greek adjective *pas*, meaning "all" or "everything." Pan's actual position in mythology was something akin to baby-brother-of-the-president-during-the-Carter-administration.

The wild Anglo-Saxons were, if anything, less fond of wildness than the Greeks. In *Beowulf* the monster Grendel and his rather more monstrous mother are said to "dwell in a land unknown, wolf-haunted slopes, windswept headlands, perilous marsh-paths, where the mountain stream goes down under the mists of the cliffs." We'd declare it a national treasure and lobby to have it protected under the Wilderness Preservation Act. Loss of habitat is threatening endangered monster species everywhere.

Our own pilgrim forefathers didn't enjoy camping, were not exhilarated by fresh air, and found little fascination in contact with indigenous cultures. Pilgrim leader William Bradford, in his *History of Plimoth Plantation*, writes of arrival in the New World.

They had now no friends to welcome them nor inns to entertain or refresh their weatherbeaten bodies; no houses or much less towns to repair to,

> *to seek for succour . . . what could they see but a hideous and desolate wilderness, full of wild beasts and wild men . . .*

Gardens provide a clue to a society's attitude toward nature. The first mention of a garden in Western literature is in the *Odyssey,* where Homer describes the palace grounds of King Alcinoiis of Phaeacia. These seem to have been covered entirely in fruit trees, grapevines, and vegetable plots—more a greengrocer's than an arboretum. The early Greeks didn't garden. They farmed, but not for fun. Cimon planted the first pleasure garden in Athens in the fifth century BC. The early Romans didn't think much of herbaceous borders either. In the third century BC Cato the Elder recommended growing cabbages. Nothing like a "naturalistic" garden would be seen in Europe for another two millennia.

Art, also, gives us some idea of what people consider worth noticing in the world. Pure landscape painting was known to the Romans, but apparently as a novelty. Pliny, in his *Natural History,* goes out of the way to mention a painter in the time of Augustus who introduced a style that included "sacred groves, woods, hills, fishponds, straits, streams and shores, any scene in short that took his fancy." But pictures without people, gods, or important animals in them didn't recur in Europe until Dürer made some watercolor sketches in the fourteenth century, and it was another three hundred years before anybody sold a lumpy mountain prospect, an overdressed sunset, a big wave getting a rock wet, or a quaint stretch of cart-track mire with gnarly tree nearby.

From the very beginning of the Renaissance, however, there were dangerous stirrings in that wild, untamed segment of nature, the intelligentsia. In 1336 Petrarch hiked up Mount Ventoux, near Avignon. Supposedly, no one before him had made such a trip just to see the view. Once on top, Petrarch opened a copy of St. Augustine's *Confessions* (obviously, a different kind of climbing gear was carried in the Trecento) and happened upon the passage where Augustine rails against those who "go about wondering at mountain heights . . . and to themselves they give no heed."

Suitably abashed, Petrarch scuttled back downhill. But during his brief sojourn upon the Ventoux peak, the poet stood astride the medieval and modern ages—the first European to climb a mountain for the heck of it and the last to feel like a jerk for doing so.

A mush-pot sentimentality about things natural was growing. Loon-June-Moon infected the best minds. By the 1500s Montaigne was raving about the natives of lately discovered America, calling them "men fresh sprung from the gods."

Montaigne had a servant who had gone as a soldier or a seaman to Brazil and probably to the Amazon basin. The Indians' dwellings are described as "very long, with a capacity of two or three hundred souls, covered with the bark of great trees, the strips fastened to the ground at one end and supporting and leaning on one another at the top . . . whose covering hangs down to the ground and acts as the side." This is the communal house that the Yagua don't want to live in anymore. And the servant says he never saw Indians who were "palsied, bleary-eyed, toothless or bent with age." Probably true enough. In Stone Age societies such venerable folks are what we call dead.

The rest of the information from Montaigne's source sounds like wishful thinking or a crib from "Eclogue IV."

> *This is a nation . . . in which there is no sort of traffic . . . no name for a magistrate or for political superiority, no custom of servitude, no riches or poverty . . . no occupations but leisure ones. The very words that signify lying, treachery, dissimulation, avarice, envy, belittling [are] unheard of.*
>
> *The whole day is spent in dancing.*
>
> *They live in a country with a very pleasant and temperate climate.*

And Montaigne believed every word. He says:

> *What we actually see in these nations surpasses not only all the pictures in which poets have embellished the Golden Age and all their ingenuity in imagining a happy state of man but also the conceptions and the very desire of philosophy.*

From this bosh it is but the jot of a pen nib to the twaddle of Jean-Jacques Rousseau. In his *Discourse upon the Origin and Foundation of the Inequality among Men* (1754), Rousseau converts Primitivism from a telling of tall tales into a theory of political science. "Let us begin therefore, by laying aside facts, for they do not affect the question," says Rousseau with a frankness rare among modern political ideologists. Rousseau then gives us a picture of *au naturel* man "satisfying the calls of hunger under the first oak, and those of thirst at the first rivulet . . . laying himself down to sleep at the foot of the same tree that afforded him his meal; and behold, this done, all his wants are completely satisfied."

Not only are all his wants satisfied, he's taking great care of his body. "Man . . . in a state of nature where there are so few sources of sickness, can have no great occasion for physic." Since the complete requirements of human health and happiness can be provided by a tree and a creek, Rousseau concludes that the whole rest of history has been a waste of time: "It is evident . . . that the man, who first made himself clothes and built himself a cabin, supplied himself with things which he did not much want."

Shack and shift are bad, says Rousseau, because we become convinced we can't live without them even though he, Rousseau, has just proven to us that we can and that we don't like getting dressed or going indoors anyway. Therefore all progress and even thought is wrong. "As there is scarce any inequality among men in a state of nature, all that which we now behold owes its force and its growth to the development of our faculties and the improvement of our understanding."

Nobody likes to take responsibility for himself. Our troubles are always someone else's fault. Rousseau perfects this idea. It wasn't just another person who did us dirt, it was *every* other person since the foundation of Ur. Civilization is to blame.

Any person who has spent time outdoors actually doing something, such as hunting and fishing as opposed to standing there with a doobie in his mouth, knows nature is not intrinsically healthy. Kill an animal and inspect its hide and innards. You'll find it has been prey to ticks, lice, fleas, and all the other things that, at the beginning of this chapter, I predicted would assail a naked suburbanite. You'll see that it has been the victim of injuries and diseases as well. Nor are people who live in places without electricity, sewage treatment plants, penicillin, and dental checkups as Rousseau's imagination or Montaigne's household help would have them. European male oppressors may have brought smallpox and VD to the Third World, but they did not bring malaria, yellow fever, sleeping sickness, river blindness, plague, or chiggers. And what kind of person sleeps under an oak tree filled with ripe acorns, spending the whole night being pelted with rock-hard nuggets falling from fifty feet in the air? As for eating those missiles, my encyclopedia says, "The Acorns of the oak possess a considerable economic importance as food for swine."

William Rose Benét, scholar, essayist, and founder of the *Saturday Review,* defined *primitivism* as:

> *. . . a persistent tendency in European literature, art, and thought since the 18th century . . . to attribute superior virtue to primitive, non-European civilizations . . . Later primitivism expanded to include among the objects of its enthusiasm the violent, the crude, undeveloped, ignorant, naïve, non-intellectual or sub-intelligent of any kind, such as peasants, children, and idiots.*

It's interesting how many of these words—other than "violent"—apply to Henry David Thoreau. Montaigne was a naff and Rousseau a screwball. But it's Thoreau who's actually taught in our schools. And it is into the wet, dense muck of *Walden* that Roderick Nash, Edward Abbey, and the party of ten loud women have dipped their wicks.

Thoreau took the bad ideas and worse ideals of the primitivists, added the pitiful self-obsession of the romantics, and mixed all of this into transcendentalism, that stew of bossy Brahmin spiritual hubris.

The transcendentalists were much devoted to taking the most ordinary thoughts and ideas and investing them with preposterous spiritual gravity. They saw the divine in everything, even in long, boring lectures about how everything is divine. Any random peek into the essays of Ralph Waldo Emerson will show you the method by which "Don't Litter" has been turned into an entire secular religion.

In 1845 the twenty-eight-year-old Thoreau (having failed to read Rousseau closely enough) built himself a little cabin near Walden Pond in Concord, Massachusetts. The land was owned by Emerson and was about as far out of town as the average modern driving range. Thoreau frequently went to dinners and parties in Concord, and, according to his list of household expenses in *Walden*, he sent his laundry out to be done. Thoreau lived in his shack for two years devoting his time to being full of baloney.

> *I had three pieces of limestone on my desk, but I was terrified to find that they required to be dusted daily, when the furniture of my mind was all undusted still, and I threw them out the window in disgust.*

> *I have always been regretting that I was not as wise as the day I was born.*

Or maybe he was on drugs.

> *My head is hands and feet.*

We have here the worst sort of person, the sanctimonious beatnik. Thoreau is the progenitor of the American hipster arrogance we've been enduring for the past century and a half. And he is the source of the loathsome self-righteousness that turns every kid who's ever thought "a tree is better looking than a parking lot" into Saint Paul of the Recycling Bin.

> *But I have since learned that trade curses everything it handles; and though you trade in messages from Heaven, the whole curse of trade attaches to the business.*

> *Our inventions are wot to be pretty toys, which distract our attention from serious things . . . We are in great haste to construct a magnetic telegraph from Maine to Texas; but Maine and Texas, it may be, have nothing important to communicate.*

> *The New Hollander goes naked with impunity, while the European shivers in his clothes. Is it impossible to combine the hardiness of these savages with the intellectualness of the civilized man? [Thoreau died of TB.]*

All of the above is from the first hundred-odd pages of *Walden* and I defy any thinking adult without an airsickness bag to go further.

Being pathologically high-minded can have unfortunate side effects. The painter George Catlin, who traveled in the American West in the 1830s, was one of the first advocates of creating large national parks. But Catlin was so fond of things just the way nature made them that he thought Indians should be put in the parks, too.

One hundred and sixty years later, in a Sierra Club book called *Lessons of the Rainforest,* Kenneth Iain Taylor is arguing that the Indians of the Amazon should be subjected to the same zoo-animal treatment. "For the wisdom necessary to save the rainforests is contained only in the complete traditional systems that these people practice," claims Taylor. "Nor can we expect these ancient ways of forest preservation to be continued by acculturated, integrated, or assimilated people stripped of their traditions and crashing around the forest with firearms and chainsaws and outboard motors." Waterskiing tournament at three. Natives not eligible.

Among the unfortunate side effects of high-mindedness is the Amazon ecology tour, which Michael, Shelley, Susan, Tom, and I were still on. And we were thinking deeply about the whole business of suffering extreme discomfort in the interests of personal pleasure. Psychology has a name for this.

Julio was meanwhile pointing out that the rain forest is upside down. That is, jungle vegetation is so dense that sunlight, growing space, nutrients in the form of decomposing plant matter, and even rain itself are most available at the top of the rain forest, in the canopy. Usually, if you want to see a profusion of disgusting life-forms, you look under a rock. In the jungle you climb a tree. Plants called hemiepiphytes germinate in the treetops, then send roots down to the earth instead of branches up to the sky. True epiphytes never touch ground at all. Their roots just dangle in the air creating a messy snarl and collecting detritus—making their own potting soil. This humus may get thick and rich enough to host a colony of earthworms, and the tree upon whose limb this natural window box is sitting will sprout roots from its branch (grow a foot on its arm like Thoreau had heads on his feet) to take advantage of the soil. Orchids are epiphytes. If we lose the rain forest, we'll lose the earth's principal source of prom corsages. Think of all the poor girls getting bouquets of genetically engineered celery pinned to their spaghetti straps.

With such profuse herbage occupying the sky, snakes, lizards, bugs, and the more agile mammals have moved there too. And Julio was determined that we should see them. Some well-meaning foundation (not the American Acrophobia Association) has built a system of platforms and rope bridges in the jungle canopy. We hiked for an hour from the Sucusari camp and arrived at a great big tree with a staircase around it, the kind of thing Scarlett O'Hara might have descended in *Gone with the Planet of the Apes*. At the top of these stairs was the first platform. It was about high enough above the ground to test the thesis that a cat always lands on its feet, if you didn't care about the cat. From here we were supposed to walk a rope bridge sixty or eighty feet long to another big tree with stairs, climb these, cross a second rope bridge, climb more stairs, traverse another bridge, and so forth until we were 120 feet in the air and consumed with nausea, vertigo, terror, and the nagging worry "Is it sweat or have I wet myself?" I say "we" but just Susan and I were doing the worrying. Altitude didn't bother Michael, Tom, Shelley, or Julio. And they had that kind sympathy and solicitous attitude that people who aren't afraid of heights always show to those who are.

"See how the ropes wiggle when I do the Boogaloo!"

"Ever read *The Bridge of San Luis Rey*?"

"If you look straight down, you can see the puke from the last group that was up here."

Mankind is supposed to have evolved in the treetops. But I have examined my sense of balance, the prehensibility of my various appendages, and my attitude toward standing on anything higher than, say, political principles, and I have concluded that, personally, I evolved in the backseat of a car.

"Ninety percent of the rain forest's photosynthesis is taking place here in the canopy," said Julio. Susan and I were certainly green. "More than half of the rain forest's species live in the canopy." But I didn't see any. All I saw were two carefully placed feet—my own—and ten white knuckles gripping things. "Twice as many insect species are found here compared to ground level." Which is great news when you haven't got a hand free to swat them.

Our tour company had a third jungle camp near the canopy walkway, and as soon as we got there, Michael, Tom, and especially I began looking for more bootleg rum. This time we turned up something called *haya huasca* instead. It came in an old Coke bottle with a wooden plug in the top and was made from herbs and bark and such. Michael said that, as best he could translate, it was supposed to "make us throw up and see the future."

We didn't get sick and we certainly didn't see the future, or I would have kept my eye on yen fluctuations and would be rich. It was a mild drug, producing just a few sparks of light and some glowing auras at the edges of the field of vision and delivering a minor inner bliss, a little psychic wet kiss. That is, I thought it was a mild drug until Susan and I began urging everyone to climb back to the top of the canopy walkway and "dig the sunset."

And it's amazing up there when you're looking at something besides your fingers and shoes—like swimming through the tops of trees, like riding green surf. Sure the rope bridges sway, but so do Mother's arms. I even looked down, though there was nothing to see. The jungle is so thick, I don't think you could fall through it. (I was talked out of trying.) If you did fall, you'd probably become an epiphyte human with all your roots—wife, kids, the mortgage—dangling in the air.

I went so far as to examine how the canopy walk was constructed, that's how filled with courage I was. Each rope bridge was made, not with ropes, really, but with four steel cables—two to form the footpath and two to be used as handrails. Rope crossties ran between the cables at intervals, like ribs in a ship hull. Nylon mesh netting was strung between the crossties, then ordinary cheap Home Depot aluminum ladders were laid flat between the footpath cables with wooden planks over the ladder rungs, and that was it. The cables were attached to the trees by half hitches and clove hitches, oregano hitches, sheet and pillowcase bends, and knots you couldn't get ZZ Top beards into. It looked like hippie engineering to me. I'm a veteran of the *Whole Earth Catalog* era, and I've watched a lot of geodesic domes and yurts and such flop over on their sides and go *fttttt*. But with *haya huasca,* who cared?

Besides, there was a sunset the color of eco-tourist hiking shorts. And, with dusk, all those species Julio had been talking about arrived: fat, black lizards with butts shaped like canoe paddles, big yet nearly invisible Esmerelda butterflies with perfectly clear wings, iguanas the size and shape of scaly green dachshunds, a thousand tree frogs saying "Wyatt Earp," dragonflies as lacy and complicated and rather larger than Victoria's Secret lingerie, and hummingbirds that could actually carry a tune. Well, maybe that last was the *haya huasca*. I'll bet Thoreau really *was* on drugs. It certainly is the easy way to make the ecosystem better, at least to look at. And drugs would excuse sentences like "I have always been regretting that I was not as wise as the day I was born."

I was beginning to get a few insights of that type myself. I started looking at the multitude of insects, the astounding number of them, the great smacking gobs and oodles, the scads and lashings of bugs galore. They wandered all across each other and every surface and right through the air across no surface at all and all over me. I decided that God had created the world for bugs. Whatever we have in the way of Old and New Testament was plagiarized from some original buggy text. It was bugs who lived in the Garden of Eden (full of *rotten* fruit and *dead* animals). And the bugs had probably eaten . . . everything, the whole damn tree of knowledge included.

By sheer weight of numbers they are obviously God's chosen creatures. There had, no doubt, been a little bug Moses. What would the Ten Bug Commandments be? "Go forth and multiply," certainly. Maybe, "Thou shalt find a porch light and bump into it for hours."

About then the *haya huasca* began to wear off. This was probably a good thing. Unfortunately, it wore off before Susan and I managed to get down from the canopy walk. And there we were in the pitch dark, frozen in terror like a pair of reverse suicides with the whole police and fire departments (Shelley and Michael and Tom) urging us to step out on a ledge.

Haya huasca made me believe strange things but no stranger than the things more sensible Americans believe cold sober. Susan and Shelley were excited to discover that one of the Orejón Indians who had helped build the canopy walkway was a *brujo*, a male witch or shaman. Shelley's family had been Jewish for five thousand years, and Susan's, Christian for two thousand. About these creeds they were reasonably skeptical, but the *brujo* they'd met ten minutes ago . . . I'm being unkind. The *brujo* seemed to be a nice man, very dignified with sad and commonsensical eyes. I'm sure he was, in his way, as devout as ever was Reverend Lackland, the incredibly boring pastor of Monroe Street Methodist Church, which I attended as a child in Toledo, Ohio.

In fact, the *brujo*'s spiritual cleansing ceremony was at least as tedious and lengthy as Methodist Sunday school. Most religious services seem to be so. Is ennui the sacrifice God wants us to make to Him? Is He pleased by an offering of fidgets, guilty dozings, and daydreams of releasing white mice in the choir loft? Wouldn't we better glorify God by enjoying the blessings of His creation, by, say, getting on the green in three and two-putting? Of course, there aren't many golf courses in the Amazon.

The *brujo* sat each of us on a stool. Then he took a little bouquet or broom made of dried leaves of the *shacapa* plant and flicked us all over while softly whistling something that reminded me only a little of Simon and Garfunkel. He finished by blowing cigarette smoke all over our persons. Susan and Shelley looked blissful, though they are ardent nonsmokers.

What we had experienced was "like a dry shower," said the *brujo* later, Julio translating. The fellow had been a *brujo* for thirty-five years. You become a *brujo* by altering your diet, by "leaving out all pleasure foods," and by fasting. "Your visions become your lunch" was Julio's literal translation. Also, you drink *haya huasca*.

Julio said he'd fallen into the Amazon once while wearing knee-high rubber boots. The boots had filled with water and pulled him under, and he'd nearly drowned. He went to a *brujo* who cured him of being frightened of the river, a cure that apparently lasted longer than my cure of being scared of heights. Of course, I was using *haya huasca* without professional supervision. Also, said Julio, his mother had once begun to lose weight, and a *brujo* informed her that Julio's father had secretly married another woman and that the second wife was putting a curse on Julio's mom. I'd think a secret second wife would pretty much be a curse in her own right. Anyway, the *brujo* removed the curse, and I bet he was cheaper than my divorce lawyer. A team of *brujos* could do no harm in matters like the Woody Allen–Mia Farrow custody case.

The next morning, spiritually dry-cleaned and tuned in to that great National Public Radio station which is nature, we went for a last peek at the ecology. We took one of the square-sterned canoes equipped with a small outboard and half-paddled, half-motored up a narrow inlet to a lake with water the color of espresso.

The jungle loomed over us in the most looming sort of way. We saw some disgusting insects and some awful lizards and a snake, albeit a small and phlegmatic snake. Snakes are my least favorite thing, not counting rope bridges 120 feet in the air. Tom was contemplating a spider the size of a Bass Weejun. "Nothing dies of old age around here, does it?" said Tom.

"These black water areas are the habitat of electric eels," said Julio. "They grow to be six feet long and can generate six hundred volts of direct current at about one-half to three-fourths ampere, enough to stun a horse." We are all hoping for the development of wind- and solar-powered eels soon.

"Julio," I said, "does the Amazon have any legendary monsters—Yeti, Bigfoot, Nessie, the Jersey Devil, anything like that?"

"No," said Julio. So maybe the Amazon natives recognize the essential benevolence of nature even in this most violently competitive and sanguinary biological niche. Or, maybe when you've got six-foot electric eels and tiny catfish that swim up your pecker, you don't need legendary monsters.

And yet I was surprised again by the unscary, nonmysterious, subthreatening nature of the rain forest. The fake-seeming safari noises, the floral arrangements growing on tree branches, the Disney World–like lack of odors, the angelfish in the minnow nets, and now, looking around, I realized the jungle was filled with houseplants. Most of the greenery on our windowsills was bred from tropical stock. Terror is difficult to experience surrounded by ficus trees, dumb cane, Christmas cactus, spider plants, philodendrons, and Boston ferns as though you were visiting the overheated apartment of a maiden aunt.

On the lake we motored between lily pads two yards across. According to my guidebook, these can "support the weight of a small child," although there are certainly laws about trying that. Then we crossed a dozen acres of white water hyacinths, our outboard prop getting thoroughly tangled in beauty and fragrance. Several trees along the shore were filled with the hanging nests of oropendolas, a tropical oriole that makes its own birdhouses from woven vines and twigs. And they are no better at it than kids taking a crafts program at summer camp. Oropendola nests look like oversize sheep scrotums. Another tree was full of saddle-backed tamarind monkeys bouncing around like flying puppies. It seems the more evolved an animal is, the more time it spends playing. Which does not explain why I'm at the typewriter, unless it does. Or maybe we don't know what worm fun and snail recreation look like. They may be having a riot. And in one more tree we saw a pair of speckled owls, perched on a branch, asleep with their heads leaned together, cuter than thrift-shop salt-and-pepper shakers. Then came the best sight of all, a blue morpho butterfly, a big hand span of a butterfly in an indescribable tint—a Day-Glo pink of a blue, an international signal orange of a blue. Eco-tourists in the Miami airport wouldn't wear this blue. A color not found in nature was finding itself in nature right in front of us, floating in that scatterbrained way butterflies do, just beyond our bow.

We came back from the lake and down to the mouth of the Sucusari River and out into the mile-wide Napo. Here black drapes of rain approached in the sunshine. Wide fields of clear sky appeared between vast storm clouds. There were lightning strikes and a rainbow at the same time. It was an encyclopedia of weather.

The rain swept toward our canoe, and we made for the nearest house. It was a one-room shack but a big one, and this was a good thing because it was a big family that owned it, and all of them had run inside, too. Thirty of us must have been in the shack, and "rain" does not describe what was happening outside. The difference between a downpour in the temperate zone and a downpour in the tropics is the difference between stepping into the shower and being thrown into the pool. Or, rather, having the pool thrown on you.

The shack was humble even by *ribereño* standards. The only furniture was a table. A few newspaper ads decorated a wall. But they had rum, and Michael and I had cigarettes. And they also had a liquor called *clabo huasca*. It was not quite as potent as *haya huasca*, but it did cast a happy glow upon the scene. The kids brought out their pets to show us: a bat (cute as bats go, certainly cuter than those we'd seen in the bat professor's hands), some puppies, a baby peccary that looked like a cross between a hamster and a wart hog, and a flock of chachalacas, noisy little jungle turkeys. The parents beamed. The young men turned on a boom box. The young women flirted a bit. We drank more rum and *clabo huasca* and smoked more cigarettes and had a little fiesta until the sun came out.

Our hosts were migrants from the impoverished and rebel-bothered mountains of Peru. They'd come as squatters and cut a little homestead from the jungle. Julio's parents had come to the Amazon for the same reason and so had many *ribereños*, and many more are on the way. It is these decent, hardworking, hospitable, pleasant people who are destroying the rain forest. They are not doing it in quite so rapid or spectacular a manner as the timber companies or the big Brazilian ranchers. But there are a lot more poor people in South America than there are well-capitalized corporations. Knotty pine will make a comeback and mahogany will go out of fashion. Everybody will die of high cholesterol from eating too many hamburgers and beef prices will go down. The timber companies and the ranches will disappear, but the poor will still be there.

I have a photograph taken in 1887 showing my grandfather, his parents, and his nine siblings lined up in front of a one-room unpainted shanty on a forty-acre dirt farm in Lime City, Ohio. The roof was made of wooden shingles instead of corrugated tin, and due to climatic differences, the shack my great-grandad built had more in the way of walls, but other than that, the old O'Rourke plantation was indistinguishable from the mansion of our hosts on the Napo.

I'm sure great-grandfather Barney O'Rourke would have liked to move to a passive solar bungalow in the Berkeley Hills, carefully recycle his trash, use only appropriate technology in his certified organic garden, and bicycle to his job at the university teaching a course in Sustainable Development. But it wasn't an option. Among other things, I don't think Barney could read.

When we were back in the Iquitos airport, waiting for our plane to Miami, the ten loud women reappeared. I gathered from their loud chat that they'd been on a tour boat docking at various places along the river, probably the same places we'd seen. They seemed to have had a meaningful time, full of auras and so forth, and heck, we'd seen some auras ourselves. But one of the women was carrying a polished wooden box with a glass front, and inside the box was a dead and mounted blue morpho butterfly. I looked again, to make sure my imagination wasn't creating a too-perfect irony. But Michael, Shelley, Tom, and Susan saw it too.

"Oh, yes," said Julio, "the ecology groups are always bringing back snake skins, animal pelts, caiman skulls, all those sorts of things."

Theocritus, Virgil, James Fenimore Cooper, Montaigne, Rousseau, Edward Abbey, Henry David Thoreau, John Denver, and ten loud women—quit pestering your mother.

PLAGUE

Sick of It All
Haiti, December 1993

Does even plague have politics? *Everything* has politics. Political means could be used to prevent almost all deaths from childhood diarrhea. Diarrhea is spread by contaminated water. Public sanitation is, like personal security, national defense, and rule of law, one of the few valid reasons for politics to exist. Lowly, semicomic diarrhea kills 2,866,000 people a year worldwide, 2,474,000 of them children under the age of five. But celebrities aren't wearing brown ribbons on their tuxedo lapels at the Academy Awards or marching down the Mall in Washington carrying signs reading DIARRHEA—IT CAN BE CONTAINED.

I went to the Washington headquarters of the Pan American Health Organization (PAHO), this hemisphere's branch of WHO. I talked to Christopher J. Drasbek, PAHO's "Regional Technical Officer, Expanded Program for the Control of Diarrheal Diseases." Mr. Drasbek is one of those people who—with clumsy title, on modest salary, in an office shared by two other colleagues—accomplishes the actual good in the world.

Mr. Drasbek took time from the mounds of paperwork that accrue in any kind of good done in a bureaucracy (and also time, it occurred to me later, from his lunch hour) to tell me just how easily politics could rid the globe of 2,500,000 deaths.

"What would it cost," I asked, "to clean up the world's drinking-water supplies?"

"We don't even have to do that," said Mr. Drasbek. "All we need are Oral Rehydration Salts." He pulled some foil packets out of a desk drawer. "These cost eight to ten cents apiece." He explained that diarrhea kills by dehydration. The salts in the foil packet restore the body's electrolyte balance, the degree of salinity in the body's cells. Thus, the cells are able to retain fluid.

You mix one packet of the rehydration salts into a liter of clean water and get the patient to drink as much of the liquid as possible. This Oral

Rehydration Therapy, or ORT, is given for as long as the diarrhea lasts. ORT alone, with no other treatment, is enough to prevent death from diarrhea, even from cholera. "Usually, to rehydrate a child, it takes two packets," said Mr. Drasbek. In other words, between sixteen and twenty cents. So, for five hundred thousand dollars, 2,474,000 lives could be saved each year. This is about half the cost of a thirty-second Super Bowl advertising spot—an apt comparison, since Gatorade is more or less a commercial version of Oral Rehydration Therapy.

A packet of Oral Rehydration Salts contains glucose (corn sugar) to help the small intestine absorb the salts, sodium bicarbonate otherwise known as baking soda, a small amount of potassium chloride, and ordinary table salt. A homemade oral rehydration solution can be prepared by mixing eight level teaspoons of sugar or honey and half a teaspoon of salt in a liter of clean water. ORT is one of the unheeded medical miracles of the twentieth century. A dozen years ago there were over 5,000,000 annual childhood deaths from diarrhea.

But that still leaves enough dead kids every year to populate Kansas. What government is so politically screwed-up that it can't get a little boiled sugar water and a pinch of salt to sick babies? Well, there's Haiti. According to PAHO the average Haitian child has seven episodes of diarrhea a year and only a one-in-six chance of receiving Oral Rehydration Therapy.

I flew to Port-au-Prince on December 22, 1993. You'd expect the Christmas decorations in Haiti to be little Santas with pins in them. It's been a long time since Saint Nick brought the Haitians much. And, in a deforested country undergoing an international oil embargo, even sticks and coal would look good in the stockings—if Haitians had socks. However, Haiti's yuletide is greeted with the usual red and green gewgaws and tinsel festoons. Christmas trees are fashioned from the branches of Norfolk pines. JOYEUX NOËL is spelled out in Mylar letters. The radio plays reggae, calypso, and merengue covers of all the noted carols. And I didn't see a doll with needle marks anywhere in the country.

Making figurines of one's enemies and torturing these playthings has nothing to do with Haiti or voodoo. It is a piece of European superstition brought to the New World by those mysterious savages the French. Haiti has no need for such elaborate fancy goods of evil. Sturdy, utilitarian forms of wrong are readily available—the city water system, for instance.

For most Haitians the only source of water is a public well or tap. Downtown Port-au-Prince is served by one slimy concrete outdoor sink, a sort of horse trough with faucets. Here water is available only between eight p.m. and five in the morning. The women and girls carry it home in five-gallon plastic buckets. That's forty-some pounds of water balanced on the heads of people who don't weigh much more than that themselves. And they're carrying it through unlit streets.

These streets are heaped with trash as high as the women's bucket tops. A long mound of putrefying dreck will stretch for a block to an intersection, then turn the corner and continue for half a block more—a giant disposable traffic island. Not that it gets disposed of. According to the Pan American Health Organization, as of June 1993, Port-au-Prince had twelve garbage trucks in running condition. This to collect an estimated sixteen thousand tons of solid waste produced daily in the capital. Every now and then the locals try to burn the refuse, but the result is a parody of the North American landfill debate—biodegradability versus incineration. In Haiti's climate everything is biodegradable. And the ooze of tropical rot defeats the fires. The trash piles stay just as large, with guttering flames adding a new stench to the miasma.

I saw two of the twelve garbage trucks. One was parked downtown, and garbage men were behind it with shovels. The first garbage man would scoop a load of filth and dump it at the feet of the next garbage man who would pass it to another. There was no garbage in the truck. The Metropolitan Solid Waste Collection Service occupied a modernistic gray and white building with expanses of tinted glass. A long row of truck garages was attached. Here another, very clean, garbage truck was parked on a wide, smooth asphalt driveway. The Collection Service's building was spotless, the grounds were tidy, and, at two-fifteen on a Tuesday afternoon, nobody was there.

I'd been in Haiti for about six hours when I gave up the idea of investigating infant diarrhea or Third World sanitation or medical care in underdeveloped nations. Haiti was too far gone in entropy. Investigating public health, when the public obviously didn't have any, left me nothing but that public to investigate. If the politics of disease are to be understood, particularly in the dreadful countries where this understanding is most needed, then the politics of total collapse have to be understood first. You can boil the water, but how do you boil history, social structure, economics, and religion?

And, as it is with disease, so it is with hunger, crowding, pollution, hatred, poverty, and so on. All these problems are knotted and tangled together. Haiti is as good a name as any for the snarl.

I took the long list that I'd made of health experts and government officials and NGO directors I'd meant to interview and put it in the glove compartment of my rented Jeep. My driver and translator, Dumarsais, asked, "Who do you want to go talk to?"

"Let's just drive around," I said.

The mystery of Port-au-Prince's trash heaps is that there are so many really immense holes in Port-au-Prince's streets. Putting one into another would create a certain leveling, at least, if not sanitation.

The streets and roads of Haiti are so bad that they almost seem to have been made so on purpose. The mere dragging and scraping of axles and undercarriages should lower some of the great humps, and chunks of disintegrating vehicles should fill a few of the ruts. "Haitian roads are a free massage," said Dumarsais.

Maybe there are deconstructionist road crews who go out at night and wreck the macadam, gangs in the pay of the Port-au-Prince spare parts and car repair industry. But I don't think so. Several long and exceptionally dirty blocks of the capital are given over to shade tree mechanics (minus the shade and the trees). It's difficult to tell their wares from plain scrap metal and harder to decide whether the autos they're hammering on are being put back together or beaten apart. We needed a new gas cap for the Jeep. Numerous experts came forward offering fittings ranging in size from a hubcap to a thimble, and one proffered the top of a juice bottle.

Or perhaps Haiti has guerrilla organizations so impoverished that they cannot lay hands on guns, bombs, or even knives and are reduced to terrorizing the establishment with shovels. The pavement in front of the very house of Lieutenant General Raoul Cédras, head of Haiti's military junta, had been torn up, leaving a dusty and rock-strewn gap in his suburban street. (The house was an unprepossessing stucco villa in the hills above Port-au-Prince, identifiable only by a large number of soldiers standing, decidedly not at attention, outside its gate.)

During the time I was in Haiti, Haitians were blaming such things as lousy water and roads on the international embargo. The embargo had been instituted the year before in an attempt to return elected president Jean-Bertrand Aristide to power. But, looking around Port-au-Prince, it's evident that lousiness is nothing new. The oldest buildings are wooden frame structures out of a New Orleans French Quarter attacked by termites instead of decorators. These houses are so rotted and gaping they seem to be wayward theatrical sets, held up by concealed props and guy wires. The newer buildings are random jumbles of concrete covered in battered signs: AVE MARIA DRY CLEANERS, SKYLAB ICE CREAM, SACRED HEART ART & SNACK, SUPER MARRIAGE NUMBERS BANK. The storefronts were brightly colored once, maybe, but now are wholly grimy, like Kandinskys painted in the dirt.

The waterfront is an idle mess. Most of the docks are too rickety to hold a middle-size reporter. The harbor is a slough of wet rubbish. The ocean itself is stained the color of tea-bag seepage. Everything is worn-out. The tap-taps, the little buses made from pickup trucks, are exuberantly so—covered with chipped decorations, dented ornaments, and scratched-up paintings and slogans. The open-air markets are woefully so—filled with more crud and dust than goods. The people are in between—always hail-fellow-well-met and as carefully dressed and laundered as circumstances allow but tired, frayed, and thin.

Little cheerless cement houses of the lesser bourgeoisie are scattered haphazardly up the hillsides. They all have high walls with broken glass embedded in the tops or, sometimes, upended conch shells. The streets, empty lots, and open spaces of even the better neighborhoods are spread with trash.

The downtown parks are weed-grown and deeply littered, the railings knocked over, the statues of the heroes oxidized to the indistinctness of lead soldiers and dripping with pigeon muck. The only clean thing in the city center was the empty presidential palace, a mediocre beaux arts design in the middle of ample, well-tended grounds. A single chrome kitchen chair sat unaccountably on the lawn.

Dumarsais and I went to buy fuel at the gasoline black market, which was hardly clandestine. Sales were conducted by the side of Boulevard Harry Truman down the street from the Haitian Chamber of Commerce. Gas from open 55-gallon oil barrels was sloshed into cans, buckets, and plastic washbasins. All purchases guaranteed filtered through a dirty cloth. It was the only place in the country where I didn't see people smoking. One of the customers was a police officer in a squad car, and he seemed to be paying full price. In Haiti even corruption is inefficacious.

I spoke to an outbound American missionary couple at the Port-au-Prince airport, nice people from my native corner of Ohio. The wife talked about Haitian boat people. "I'd float out of here on a matchstick if that's the only chance I thought I had." She and her husband were cheerfully headed to Uganda.

As for plague, the whole of Haiti is a disease vector—of physical, mental, and moral illnesses.

On the night after Christmas in an alley of Cité Soleil, Port-au-Prince's largest slum, one Issa Paul was murdered, presumably by supporters of Haiti's exiled president. The next night the same alley was set afire, presumably by supporters of the junta that exiled Aristide. Paul was a member of the Front for the Advancement and Progress of Haiti, or FRAPH, pronounced like the French word for hitting somebody. FRAPH does the bidding of the Haitian military. Cité Soleil is a center of enthusiasm for Aristide. A good-size chunk of Cité Soleil burned down.

Cité Soleil has become a squalor chestnut in the U.S. media. It is more crowded, needy, and pathetic than other places most American journalists have been, not counting singles bars in the 1970s. Whenever something awful is happening in Haiti (and something awful always is), we are given a description of this vast shantytown built on the mud flats of Port-au-Prince Bay where 150,000 people, give or take a zillion, live in a kind of poverty the news always describes as "abject." Considering America's treatment of Haitian boat people, the cliché is too appropriate: abject, from *abjectus*, Latin for "thrown out." The reporters tell us how the residents of Cité Soleil swim in mire when it rains and choke in dust when it doesn't and go hungry in either case. Then we are treated to a reflection on the irony of the place-name "Sun City."

"Cité Soleil" is not ironic. After the ouster of dictator Jean-Claude "Baby Doc" Duvalier, the name of the slum was changed to honor Radio Soleil, the Catholic station instrumental in Baby Doc's fall. Baby Doc's father, François "Papa Doc" Duvalier, built Cité Soleil in the 1960s and named it after his own wife: Cité Simone. That was ironic.

Cité Soleil is not the worst slum in the world. A lot of people around the globe live this way. Cité Soleil is about as bad as parts of Dhaka or Rio, better than all of Mogadishu, and, although South Central Los Angeles is more attractive looking, I have walked through Cité Soleil at three in the morning and been bothered by nothing worse than my conscience. But, in another way, all Third World slums are more terrible than the CNN videotapes can make them out to be. You can't smell television.

Cité Soleil is low, muddled, close-set, overpeopled, and made from such an oddment stew of cast-off materials that, at first, the eye registers nothing but confusion. The smells are what's clear: sweat, shit, piss, puke, rotting offal, burning rubbish, spoiled cooking oil, rancid fry-fire smoke, kerosene vapors, cheap cigarette fumes, the bad breath of diseased teeth, and the body odor of lesions and sores all underlain with something more subtle, something with a scent reminiscent of Watergate.

Even for a government project, Cité Soleil is a horror. There are no water pipes to speak of, no sewers at all, only a few electrical wires, and the oil embargo has given the military an excuse for not running electricity through them. There isn't so much as a latrine or an outhouse in Cité Soleil. When I went there a few days before the fire, the first thing I smelled was an open area in the midst of the hovels, about half an acre heaped in ordure and slime and dotted with squatting kids. "This is where people go to crap," said Dumarsais. "The children go in the daytime, the grown people at night." Goats and pigs were nibbling in the excrement as they nibble in all such piles of waste in Haiti, and it certainly moves one in a vegetarian direction when goat or pig is on the menu.

Cité Soleil was laid out with a few main roads running perpendicular to the bay. The roads are on causeways of rubble and fill. Between and below them, housing was constructed in the mud. The building material was cement block and the design inspiration was horse sheds of the less spacious kind. The old historic homes of Cité Soleil are long rows of three-walled cubicles perhaps ten feet square with no windows, doors, or chimneys, unless you count the missing fourth wall as one of each. Around these hovels, worse hovels grew up, tiny shacks made of anything that will stand or lay flat—packing-crate staves, lengths of pipe, plywood scraps, cardboard, the tin from gallon cans. The siding of one residence is the wallpaper of the next. The space between the dwellings, when there's any at all, is so narrow that walking must be done in a tango slide.

It is as though thousands and thousands of kids have all built forts on the same vacant lot—the raggediest kids ever on the worst vacant lot you can picture. And they've gotten their parents to come play, too. By which I mean, Cité Soleil, though remarkably bad, is also remarkably cheerful, noisy, and welcoming.

Haitians are not, of course, simple, happy folk who don't notice misery the way we would. But pulling a long face and railing at fate (or Americans—and the two can be hard to distinguish in these parts) isn't the fashion in Haiti.

However, at 7:30 on the morning after the fire, Cité Soleil was no longer cheerful, though still noisy. An area about the size of three football fields had burned, leaving perhaps a thousand people hovel-less and an indeterminate number dead. The only thing left of the nothing these people had owned was the corrugated metal of the hut roofs. Young men were collecting the tin sheets and piling them together with a racket like a high school theater group's attempt to make thunder sound effects offstage. Two hysterical women and one crippled old lady sat in the smoldering ash. A little girl held a burned baby doll (with absolutely no pins in it). Dumarsais found me someone who could speak English.

"What happened?" I asked.

"I don't know," he, probably wisely, said.

People were picking through the debris. Some had found charred pop bottles. They might be able to get the deposits back. One woman had the very sensible idea of gathering armloads of the ruins and selling them as charcoal.

Cité Soleil is grossly flammable. The more so because the drivers of Port-au-Prince's tap-taps live there. Since the embargo, the tap-tap drivers have been squirreling supplies of gasoline in their homes. The whole slum should have burned to the ground. But, in Haiti, nothing works right.

A Port-au-Prince radio station gave a Christmas concert. The music was admirable. The staging was clever. But the cash bar didn't even have a horizontal surface. Refreshments were served circle tag–style from the middle of a crowd of thirsty audience members by a woman with a cigar box full of change, a man with a bottle, another man with several plastic cups, and a third man with a table knife and a block of ice. Whenever the woman was cornered, the man with the bottle had been tackled elsewhere. When the bottle was seized, the cups had escaped. By the time a cup had been nabbed I found myself on the extreme outskirts of the crowd and had to reenter the scrum to get back to the woman with the cigar box. I finally achieved a nearly complete drink only to be caught out by the man with the ice, a hockey puck–size chunk of which splashed all my liquor on the ground.

Getting on my plane to Haiti in New York, the sound of "We will begin pre-boarding . . ." was drowned by the trampling of Haitians, all of them aware of the probable fate of checked luggage in the Port-au-Prince airport and therefore toting their complete movable possessions and some major appliances as hand baggage. More than an hour later a stewardess was still standing at the aircraft's forward bulkhead, with her hairpins come loose and her face the shade of raspberry yogurt, holding the intercom phone in a World Wrestling Federation grip and shouting repeatedly, "The-captain-cannot-take-off-until-all-carry-on-items-have-been . . ."

The grandiose Louis-Napoleon-style building of Haiti's Department of Agriculture is half burned down. Haitians—who, like most people having a hard time, are fond of the fantastic—say the army burned it to destroy records of illegal atomic-waste dumping done by foreign governments in Haiti. But a foreigner has more humdrum suspicions concerning, perhaps, fire hydrants which only work after eight p.m.

At a New Year's Eve party in the Oloffson Hotel, midnight slipped by without the band noticing or anyone exclaiming, "Happy New Year!"

The military junta's effort to win the hearts and minds of Haiti's citizens consisted of suddenly, on January 1, changing the name of Cité Soleil back to Cité Simone. Replacing the street names was more than the army could handle. But the Cité Soleil tap-taps were supposed to put Cité Simone signs on their roofs. I saw one tap-tap with a brick-shaped hole in its windshield and a "Cité Simone" placard so hastily done the paint was still wet. I asked the driver what had happened, and he said, as the man at the fire had, that he didn't know. But another tap-tap driver claimed one of the army's plainclothes goons, or "attachés," had said—referring to President Aristide or the Cité Soleil fire or maybe to everything in general—"What you like is gone, so the name is changed."

"Nothing sounds stupid here," said a left-wing French priest in a Chicago Bulls T-shirt who had just finished telling me a very stupid story about how multinational corporations choose the president of the United States and the Pentagon employs twenty million people.

The only orderly thing I saw on the Port-au-Prince streets was a neat and level line of bullet holes down the side of an automobile, and these had been also to no avail. The car was in running order and waiting in line to get gas.

In the wealthy suburb of Pétion-Ville, anti-American graffito appeared, aptly mispunctuated: FUCK US.

Even rudeness doesn't work in Haiti. I went to the Iron Market, a city block–size shed of steel beams and sheet metal, a tinker's and tinsmith's Carnegie Hall. It was from here that Haiti's tourists used to bring home mahogany carvings of surpassing insipidity and garish canvases showing improbable congregations of addled-looking jungle animals. The tourists were gone but plenty of people were still on hand to pester them. An insistent young man named Jesse laid hold of me. He claimed great powers as an interpreter, purchasing agent, porter, and general factotum, and he could probably cook and take Pitman shorthand. I told him to buzz off. "Be nice to me," said Jesse, with perfect frankness. "Someone else will just come along and bother you." Dozens were waiting to do so.

Jesse led me through a Minotaur's palace of handicrafts. The awful tourist stuff was there but with no one but the tourists to blame for it winding up in American dens and rec rooms. A hundred kinds of wonderful things were also for sale—coarse Mardi Gras masks, fine embroidery, cheerful little painted wooden boxes, large solemn polished wooden trays, beautiful tortoiseshell bracelets that U.S. Customs will confiscate, and silhouettes of strange voodoo spirits cut from the flattened sides of oil drums which will show up clearly on your baggage X-rays and scare the hell out of airport security personnel. Haiti's abstract soapstone sculptures could give a refresher course to Henry Moore, if he weren't dead. Among the dross of mahogany figurines were individual pieces as well whittled as netsuke. The excellence of the palm-frond weaving made Baby Doc's old nickname "Baskethead" seem almost a compliment. Handsome goatskin rugs were spread across the Iron Market's floor (although these were best appreciated with the ocular rather than olfactory sense). Furniture was available, too, clunky enough to be called fashionable country pine in *Elle Decor*, but better made and cheaper. For eight chairs and a dining room table long enough to bowl duckpins on, the kickoff bargaining price was $750.

I tipped Jesse, and Dumarsais took me to a gallery owned by Issa El Saiëh, whose family, in an example of frying pan/fire emigration, had come to Haiti from Palestine. A thousand paintings were for sale in what had once been a living room, dining room, and sun porch. Issa had portraits with the wide-eyed, startled, straight-ahead impact captured usually only on driver's licenses. He had historical scenes executed with masterful-but-crude technique as though the French academic school had used house-painting brushes. There were Edenic landscapes of a Haiti so unlike the real thing that it hurt worse to see them than to look at Cité Soleil. The pictures of voodoo spirits or saints, the *loas*, made surrealism so much Hallmark sympathy-card art. And the animal paintings appeared to be illustrations for fables Aesop thought it best not to tell.

Issa told me about the various painters, how one hung in New York's Metropolitan Museum, another was collected by a Rockefeller, a third had just sold out an exhibit in Switzerland. One painter seemed to have been strongly influenced by Henri Rousseau. "You know, I have to laugh when people say things like 'strongly influenced by Henri Rousseau,'" said Issa.

"This is Haiti. That guy's never seen a Henri Rousseau or had a chance to. You know what influenced him? Tarzan. Go to his studio and you'll see stacks and stacks of Tarzan comics."

There was another painter I particularly liked, an impressionist who used such large blocks of pigment that the effect was almost of cubism, who had Gauguin's colors and a deft use of heavy black line like Rouault. "Oh, that's the janitor," said Issa. "Give him five bucks."

I couldn't see Issa's gallery or the Iron Market, and then think Haitians were lazy or in any way slow thinking. Even the tap-tap buses bespoke acuity and gumption in their tags and slogans.

I WANT TO BE
I WANT TO BE FREE
BACK TO REALITY
WELCOME TO AIR
AMI DE TRAVAIL
THAT'S WONDERFUL
CRY FREEDOM
OZONE
EXODE 14:14 (referring to the Bible verse "The Lord will fight for you, and you need only to be still.")

All over the city I saw signs: COLLEGE DESCARTES, COLLEGE PYTHAGORAS, COLLEGE ALBERT EINSTEIN, COLLEGE ISAAC NEWTON, TWO-WAY ENGLISH SCHOOL, and COLLEGE MIXTE ALPHA—VERITABLE CENTRE DE FORMATION INTELLECTUELLE—ORDRE DISCIPLINE SUCCES.

Haiti is not screwed-up because Haitians are screwed-up. Haitians are courteous. "Accident do for everything," said the waiter when I let loose an oafish gesture and knocked the sugar bowl halfway across my hotel's dining room.

Haitians are funny. When journalists rushed to Haiti in the fall of 1993 to cover reaction to the Governors Island Accord that was supposed to put Aristide back in power, the staff of the Port-au-Prince Holiday Inn took a look at the reporters and posted a sign in the lobby: OUR EVENING DRESS CODE HAS BEEN TEMPORARILY SUSPENDED IN HONOR OF OUR FRIENDS IN THE MEDIA.

And Haitians are law abiding, when there is law to abide. Along the unmarvelous sidewalks of the Rue des Miracles, dozens of moneychangers stood with large wads of U.S. dollars in hand. "I'd like to see someone try that in New York City," said Dumarsais, who once lived in Brooklyn.

"Is there much crime in Haiti?" I asked.

"Why would we have crime in Haiti?" said Dumarsais. "We have the police and the army to do that for us."

The headquarters of that army is a modest two-storied, balconied affair sitting cater-cornered from the Presidential Palace. It looks colonial, which makes sense since the Haitian army is a sort of colonial occupying force, though with nothing to occupy but its own country. The parade ground consists of a parking lot, and security is provided by a few very slack sentries, or maybe these are just soldiers standing around the front door.

A public waiting room, which seemed to have a lot of wives or girlfriends in it, is separated from the offices of the high command by a glass half-wall partition less elaborate than that which protects an American liquor-store clerk. I was ushered inside by, of all things, a Canadian, Lynn Garrison, honorary consul of the Republic of Haiti.

Garrison is convinced that the military is misunderstood and that Aristide is a commie nut. Both of which may be true. Whether that means the military is any better than we think or Aristide any worse than what usually governs Haiti, I can't say. Personally, I've always thought the Haitians made a mistake not going communist. Look how well escapees from Cuba are treated by the U.S. The Haitians also made a mistake being black. Look how well escapees from British journalism are treated by the *New Yorker* and *Vanity Fair*. Anyway, it's too late now for Haiti to become part of the Red Menace.

Garrison led me upstairs to a sitting room with French windows opening to the second-floor balcony. On that balcony was a crèche. Mary, Joseph, and Jesus looked American. Garrison pointed at the parking lot. "Schoolchildren," he said, "come here after dark to read their textbooks under the streetlamps."

Garrison made his case against Aristide, calling the little priest a symptom of the absurd expectations Haitians have about changes in government. After the fall of the Duvaliers in 1986, he claimed, there were crowds in the streets shouting, "We've had democracy for seven days—where's the food, where's the jobs?" (Which didn't sound so absurd to a reporter who's covered U.S. presidential elections.) And Garrison accused Aristide of complicity in the horrible reprisals against Duvalier supporters. This may be fair. In 1993 the *New York Review of Books*, not noted for its right-wing politics, ran three articles of Homeric length about Aristide. The author, Mark Danner, was largely praiseful but also described Aristide's constituents killing Duvalierists by "necklacing" them—shoving old car tires down over their shoulders to pin their arms to their sides and then setting them on fire.

Their remains were left lying in the sun to be further abused, or in some cases their charred corpses were paraded through the streets like war trophies.

Then Danner recounted an interview with Aristide.

> *"I stood and marveled at the justice of the people," Father Aristide told me as he sat in his church that March . . . He smiled patiently at my surprise, and at the inevitable question: How could he, a priest, call such acts "justice"? . . . "One must know when to look at the acts of the people and judge them as a psychologist, not as a priest," he replied, and then, a bit more heatedly, "Our consciences should be clear."*

Garrison made his case for the army, calling them the "only structural element that can do anything in the country," though the single example he gave of a thing they had done was the approval of some tree planting by an international organization. Anyway, "only element that can do anything" is the excuse always given for uniformed bully boys in the Third World. Never mind that since independence Haiti hasn't been in a real war with anyone except the Dominican Republic and hasn't fought at all since 1855, if you don't count battling the 1915–1934 American occupation, which was done by Haitian peasants, not the army. But then Garrison told me something that really was illuminating, something that explained the whole relationship between armed might and corruption in Haiti. Full colonels in the Haitian army are paid 5,000 gourdes a month, U.S. $417. Enlisted men make 83 bucks.

The public moralists at Americas Watch issued a report in February 1993 detailing rights violations by Haiti's military. In a long list of harassments, injustices, beatings, and occasional murders, one item caught the eye as painfully typical. It seems that most of Haiti's pigs had to be slaughtered in the early 1980s because of an outbreak of African swine fever. Various international aid agencies have been trying to rebuild the ham population ever since—teaching pork-chop husbandry, providing adopt-a-piglet services for rural cooperatives, and so forth. Said Americas Watch: "Soldiers . . . took advantage of their new power after the coup to steal pigs from peasant groups . . . In [the town of "X"], a soldier [named "Y"] was the worst offender . . . he came home from the capital a few days after the coup firing his gun into the air. He got some friends together and they stole a pig to feast upon. In the following days [Y] and his group stole more than 60 pigs in [X]. This encouraged other military supporters to steal pigs."

I was in X myself and the area did seem pigless, also politicized. The head of an aid agency in Port-au-Prince had told me pig distribution was being broken up by the military, lest it somehow lead to rural insurrection. "Every time they see a pig," said the agency head, "they think there is a group of peasant organizers near." An aid worker in X confirmed this, saying, "Whenever anyone is working directly with peasants he or she is suspected by the authorities." Not that those suspects weren't pretty far gone in political paranoia themselves. Someone else in X told me the whole swine-fever episode had been a plot by American pig monopolies.

Haitians aren't screwed-up, but everything political, intellectual, and material around them is. Even so, some Haitians have molded comfort and success from this poor clay. I was surprised to see a Jaguar sedan in Port-au-Prince, surprised because most of Haiti's rich drive Range Rovers, the roads being what they are. Enough of these rich exist to people the fancy suburb of Pétion-Ville, five miles into the mountains from downtown. Reasonably fancy suburb, anyway. While some of the houses are very large, none could be said to be distinguished. And none could be said to be attached to a sewage system either.

The bars on the windows of the houses in Pétion-Ville are very attractive —elaborate scrollwork lattices. Similar filigrees, called *vèvè*, are used in voodoo ceremonies to represent the *loas*. The designs are drawn on the floor of the voodoo temple with flour, coffee, ashes, or even gunpowder to invoke a *loa*'s power. Some scholars of voodoo trace the *vèvès* back to the Dahomey, or to the Arawak tribes who occupied pre-Columbian Haiti. Others claim the *vèvès* derive from eighteenth-century French embroidery motifs, china patterns, and wrought iron.

Many of the residents of Pétion-Ville are mulattoes. Haiti has a history of race warfare, not between blacks and whites—because the whites all fled or were killed at independence—but between blacks and mulattoes. Under French rule many mulattoes were freedmen, often rich and educated. The mulattoes owned slaves themselves, and blacks haven't forgotten it. Since Haiti became a free country mulattoes have dominated the nation's economy and often pulled its political wires, and blacks haven't forgotten this either. Meanwhile Haiti's only sustained contact with whites was an invasion by U.S. Marines and an even more devastating—through the introduction of AIDS alone—invasion by tourists and charity givers. Yet Haiti is integrated in a way not seen in the United States except in soft-drink television commercials.

At the radio station Christmas party, every skin shade possible was represented from sable to much lighter than my purple Irish sunburn. And the music was multicultural enough to baffle David Byrne. Wispy little French cabaret songs were sung in a big American way by someone who looked like Nat King Cole. "White Christmas" and "Silent Night" were crooned in the Gaulic manner by Maurice Chevalier's double. Then came RAM, a Haitian voodoo rock band led by an American, Richard Morse, who owns the Oloffson Hotel. RAM is so diverse, it has a song on the *Philadelphia* movie soundtrack.

The New Year's Eve party at the Oloffson was more eclectic yet. Mulatto businessmen and industrialists came with their pale-skinned wives; so did members of the black elite, whose families rose to wealth through the government and armed forces. There were embassy personnel in the crowd, aid workers, journalists, wandering hipsters, artists, musicians, regular and irregular Haitians of all kinds, even an absurdly dressed group of French holidaymakers, the seeming victims of a very shady travel agency.

Since Graham Greene set his novel of Papa Doc terror, *The Comedians*, there in 1966, the Oloffson has been an emblem of everything that is strange, gothic, incomprehensible, and outré about Haiti, although nothing else in the country resembles it. The Oloffson is a meandering white folly of Victorian gimcrack covered in hundreds of layers of paint, all the paint missing from everything else in Port-au-Prince. It's built into the side of a hill, so that the back of its ballroom is the face of a cliff. The names of various famous people who have stayed there are inscribed on the hotel room doors: IRVING STONE, LILLIAN HELLMAN, ANNE BANCROFT, and, too rightly, CHARLES ADDAMS.

RAM, of course, performed again. Richard Morse was dressed in khaki with a military officer's cap and a big cigar. Except for his ponytail and normally shaped face, Morse looked a good deal like Haiti's de facto dictator General Raoul Cédras. RAM played a song that has caused the band political trouble. One radio station was shut down for broadcasting it. "You're just playing this same song over and over," the soldiers told the station manager (a kind of armed playlist criticism with which Top 40 listeners can, in a way, sympathize). Translated from the Creole, the offending lyrics are: "I only have one son/And he's been forced to leave the country." At the back of the crowd a natty gentleman in a very good suit was standing on a chair, digging the tune. Dumarsais told me this was the richest man in Haiti.

Are Haiti's wealthy the cause of its disease and anguish? Are they just bloodsuckers, sweat jobbers, and bums on the plush? Doubtless some are. And maybe some are only making a living. Are they in cahoots with the military? As if they have a choice. Armed partnership negotiation is at least as effective as armed music reviewing. Anyway, sharing the wealth is not going to solve Haiti's problems. With a $370 annual per capita GNP, every Haitian would wind up with . . . $370.

Maybe Haiti is really not screwed-up at all. If we take the longest possible view of human existence—which allows us to ignore such unpleasant details as life and death—Haiti is normal. Haitians live the way the great majority of people have lived throughout history, like the cattle of stronger men. Haiti has an unwritten Bill of Rights (no matter, since only 35 percent of Haitians can read) to the effect of "Who can, may." The government exists solely to benefit the governors. The enforcement of law consists of force only. The elite is divorced from its fellow countrymen and feels the same responsibility toward the other party that, after a divorce, most of us feel. In a society where commonweal does not exist, there are no duties, only exactations to be avoided, and no freedoms, only privileges to be grabbed. There can be no such thing as "public services" because nothing in the country is truly public. Everything is somebody's fief. And every fief must be exploited if the exploiter cares to survive. Haiti is so dangerous and unstable that loyalties to clan and alliances for power have to take precedence over civic virtue. Anyway, how can civic virtue exist without *civis*? The votes of Haitians count for nothing. Their labors go for naught. And the entire business of their nation, from colonial times to the present, has been conducted in French, a language 90 percent of Haitians don't understand. Haitians are no more citizens in their own country than Anglo-Saxons in Norman England, helots in Sparta, or Republicans in Chicago.

So how did Haiti get to be so normal? The French settled on the western end of Hispaniola in 1641 in an attempt to quell—or get in on—Caribbean pirate activity. The French soon discovered that Saint-Domingue, as they called their colony, was better suited to sugarcane growing than plank walking. By the late eighteenth century Saint-Domingue was exporting 177 million pounds of sugar a year. Its commerce with the mother country made up a third of all French foreign trade and provided the single greatest source of French government revenue. Saint-Domingue was counted the richest colonial possession in the world.

The trouble was that sugar plantations required large numbers of unhappy people. Growing sugarcane is miserable labor done in a wretched climate. Tending, carting, and pressing the cane, boiling down the molasses, and refining the sugar are all hard work. And harvesting the cane is a nightmare business of stooping through a tropical marsh swinging a machete and making snakes and rats mad.

To harvest enough sugarcane to make a few bottles of rum, the way the *ribereños* do in the Amazon, is one thing. But to harvest enough to make 177 million pounds of sugar, and for someone else's profit, is another matter entirely. No one in his right mind wants to work on a sugar plantation. The SDS types who joined the Venceremos Brigades to help Castro with his cane harvests in the 1960s are living testimony. Thus slaves were imported to Haiti, and a lot of them. By the time of the French Revolution, Saint-Domingue was estimated to have a population of 32,000 white people; 24,000 freedmen, mostly mulattoes; and 480,000 slaves. This was as many slaves as there were in the entire thirteen colonies during our own Revolution, and in a country the size of Maryland.

For Saint-Domingue, the first steps on the road to liberty were not exactly a freedom march. In 1789, after the Declaration of the Rights of Man, the white planters grew frightened that the new National Assembly in France might grant the vote to mulattoes or even abolish slavery. They convened a Colonial Assembly in order to declare themselves to have no political rights whatsoever. They claimed to be under direct rule of the king. This set off a slave rebellion, which set off another rebellion by mulattoes, who claimed loyalty to the National Assembly. The mulattoes fought both the Colonial Assembly and the slaves.

In 1792 the government of France sent a civil commission to Saint-Domingue to straighten out this mess. One of the commission members was a Jacobin named Sonthonax who dismissed the Colonial Assembly, quarreled with the National Assembly loyalists, infuriated the governor general, got on the wrong side of the army garrison, and ended up siding with the rebel slaves.

Sonthonax, in a good move, considering who his allies were, announced the end of slavery. The blacks left the plantations. The whites left the country. And such chaos ensued that even some of the slave rebellion's leaders, among them Toussaint L'Ouverture, deserted to the Spanish troops who had invaded from the other side of the island. Then the British invaded, too. And at this point—though I have been back and forth through Haitian histories a number of times—I lose count of how many people were fighting each other.

In 1794 Toussaint L'Ouverture redeserted to the French governor general's side. Toussaint was a freed slave of minor education and unimposing looks, but he possessed that military genius which seems to come to men sometimes out of nowhere, as it did to Spartacus and Sam Nunn. Toussaint chased away the Spanish immediately, expelled the last of the British in 1798, and used political maneuver to rid himself of Sonthonax and the remaining powerful whites. He then defeated the mulattoes, killing some of their leaders and exiling the rest. By 1801 Toussaint was in complete control of Haiti.

And he didn't know what to do.

Given Haiti's economy and the lack of skills and sophistications among its inhabitants, the only recourse seemed to be to put people back to work on the plantations. This Toussaint did by means of forced labor, although now the workers were supposed to be entitled to a share of estate proceeds, and they were, of course, theoretically free.

Perhaps this policy would have created stability and prosperity sufficient to allow Haiti to evolve into a veritable Arkansas of the Antilles. But the world's other resident military genius from out of nowhere, Napoleon, decided on reconquest in 1802.

The commander of the French invasion, General Leclerc, brought along his wife, Napoleon's extremely annoying sister Pauline. Leclerc was thus eager to spend as much time as possible out campaigning. He overran Haiti in a few months and nabbed Toussaint. Then Napoleon made the mistake of reinstituting slavery in Guadeloupe and Martinique. Haitians could take a hint. All hell broke loose.

By December 1803 the French had been driven from the country. Of the forty-three thousand troops Napoleon sent to Haiti, thirty-five thousand had died, most, including Leclerc, from—speaking of the political aspects of disease—yellow fever or malaria. Toussaint was also killed, in a tropics-to-temperate-zone exchange of ills, by pneumonia in a French prison cell. Independence was declared on New Year's Day, 1804, by Toussaint's lieutenant Jean-Jacques Dessalines. He stood on the beach at Gonaïves and tore the white stripe out of the French tricolor and had the remaining sections sewn together to create the Haitian flag. Then he massacred the French whites who had been stupid enough to remain in Haiti during all of the foregoing.

Dessalines, like Toussaint before him, could think of nothing to do with Haiti but return it to the plantation system. Haitians were not pleased with Dessalines's decision. An enlisted man shot him.

In 1807 Haiti was divided between an illiterate ex-slave military commander, Henri Christophe—who crowned himself Emperor Henri I in the North—and a French-educated mulatto, Alexandre Pétion—who made himself the president of a republic in the South. Christophe continued the tradition of absolute rule and plantation service. Pétion had liberal ideas about franchise rights, land reform, and teaching agricultural methods by example. Here was an experiment to see which system of government would best benefit the Haitian people.

Neither.

Christophe invented a nobility for his fellow army officers—Comte de Limonade and Duc de la Marmelade among the titles. Everybody else got to live under the feudal peonage that Europe had just spent a thousand years getting rid of. Christophe grew nasty, paranoid, and self-indulgent, as those who possess an excess of power invariably seem to do. Haitians who could, fled to the more lenient regime of Pétion. Meanwhile Christophe spent the wealth from the plantations of his little empire on knee breeches, gilt furniture, and royal carriages from Europe; on the huge, carelessly named Sans Souci palace; and on a string of cyclopean fortifications. The largest still stands, the Citadel of Laferrière. It's on the top of one of Haiti's tallest mountains. The walls are 140 feet high and 30 feet thick. This stronghold once mounted 365 cannon and cost, the Haitians say, twenty thousand peasant lives in the building. It was meant to repel foreign enemies. They never came.

By 1820 the North was in rebellion. Then Christophe had a stroke that left him paralyzed from the waist down. The gleeful army mutinied. In Haiti, being a defeated political figure does not result in fat lecture fees and large publishing advances, at least it didn't before Aristide. Christophe shot himself.

Things didn't go much better for Pétion. He and his fellow mulattoes had what contemporary meddlers in poverty would call "high self-esteem" and "good workplace communication skills," et cetera. But the mulattoes had favored slavery and therefore possessed no moral standing with the majority of their countrymen. That majority had been through half a generation of war mingled with repression almost as onerous as what they'd suffered during bondage. The mood of most Haitians under Pétion was akin to the mood of boys just out of school in June. Going back to cutting cane, even their own cane, must have seemed as bad an idea as mowing the lawn once seemed—really, still seems—to me. Also, Christophe, angered by the desertions of his populace and hopping with megalomania, kept threatening to invade the South. The wherewithal of the Pétion government had to be spent on defense. The republic went broke. Pétion worried himself to the point of illness. He wasted away in 1818 saying he was sick of life.

Jean-Pierre Boyer was elected to replace Pétion and took over the whole country when Christophe died. He signed a foolish treaty with France agreeing, in return for international recognition, to pay Haiti's ex-landowners huge reparations. When the bill for this came due, Haitians, yet again, were sent to the plantations by force. They rebelled. Boyer resigned and sailed for Jamaica in 1843.

Major Charles Hérard replaced Boyer. According to *Black Democracy: The Story of Haiti* by H. P. Davis, Hérard "entered the capital on March 21st amid an extraordinary demonstration of popular approval." He promptly invaded the Dominican Republic, lost the war, blew his popularity, and in April 1844 "sailed for Jamaica."

Three presidents followed in the next three years until General Faustin Soulouque was elected in 1847, supposedly because he was too idiotic to bother anybody. Soulouque crowned himself "Emperor Faustin I," named 624 princes, dukes, and other nobles, and initiated a court etiquette so elaborate that after a joke the chamberlain would announce, "His majesty is laughing. Gentlemen, you are invited to laugh also." Soulouque sailed for Jamaica in 1859.

Then came General Fabre Geffrard, who sailed for Jamaica in 1867. And Major Sylvain Salnave, who was tried and shot in 1869. And Jean-Nicolas Nissage Saget, who actually served out his constitutionally mandated term and left office peacefully. This so confused the nation that there was a coup d'état anyway. General Michel Domingue sailed for Jamaica in 1876.

The next president, Pierre Boisrond-Canal, sailed for parts unknown. (Jamaica being, apparently, full to the brim with ex-leaders of Haiti.) J. N. Leger, in *Haiti, Her History and Her Detractors,* says the people showed great sympathy for Boisrond-Canal and "cheered him as he left the wharf."

So it went for Haiti through another eleven chief executives, only one of whom gave up power on purpose, until we arrive at the case of Vilbrun Guillaume Sam. "General" Sam was "elected" "president" in 1915, that date being the only thing in his career which doesn't require quotation marks. Once Sam was installed, the usual rebellion got under way outside Port-au-Prince, and the usual political opponents were locked in the national prison. Revolutions in Haiti don't normally involve much fighting. The standard procedure is for the leader of the rebellion, when he feels strong enough, to send a small force of men into the capital. The rebels attack various government buildings, and the government troops either fight back or don't according to whether they think the revolution is likely to succeed. Sam, however, committed a rules-book violation and had all his political prisoners slaughtered. The public was wroth. Sam had to hide in the French legation. A mob gathered there. In the words of H. P. Davis:

> *The mob remained without the gates, but a small body of well-known citizens, after courteously explaining to the French minister that the people were no longer to be baulked of their revenge, entered the house and, finding Sam under a bed in a spare room on an upper floor, pulled him down the stairs, dragged him along a driveway, and threw him over an iron gate to the mob.*

Sam was torn to pieces.

It was then that the United States bowed to the kinds of pressure that the United States is forever being pressured to bow to—in Kuwait, Somalia, Bosnia, and Haiti right now—and intervened. The U.S. Marines were sent to straighten things out in short order. They stayed nineteen years. And everything in Haiti has been fine ever since.

Washington Irving called Haiti "one of the most beautiful islands in the world" (although he went on to say "and doomed to be one of the most unfortunate"). As recently as 1936 Alec Waugh said that the country was "of extraordinary natural beauty, which might almost have inspired Rousseau's dreams of the ideal state of nature." (Waugh was talking about Jean-Jacques Rousseau, rather than Henri, but "Tarzan" was still what he meant.) Haiti doesn't look like that anymore. In the hills the deforestation is complete, as though the geography had been sanded. What green is left is down in the cracks and crevices of the landscape awaiting some cook-fire-building or charcoal-making equivalent of Zip-Strip. On the plains a few big trees are left, looking like amputee veterans of a botanical war. The Haitians cut off one limb at a time to keep their fuel supply growing as long as possible.

There are no zombies working the fields in Haiti. No one's working the fields at all. It is impossible to tell a Haitian farm from a brush patch, although there is a shortage of cultivatable land in Haiti and all those brush patches are, in fact, farms. A few banana trees will appear in a chicken-infested thicket of weeds with, here and there, a patch of cassava, sorghum, sweet potatoes, chickpeas, or corn, and, in the mountains, maybe a half-wild coffee bush or two. Why aspire to agricultural surplus when soldiers will just steal your pigs? And most of the farmers don't own their land or don't have clear title to it. A title would, anyway, be under the power of those august local officials—mayors, army officers, and government-appointed *chefs de section*—who can read and write. And the document would be in French besides.

Dumarsais and I traveled to the Haitian countryside, driving north from Port-au-Prince on a road known as "the goat path." This climbs the quite-dry Montagnes Trou d'Eau and the once green Montagnes Noires to Haiti's central plateau. The initial ascent is steeper than college tuition and made via zigzags like a Washington polygraph. At no point is the road wide enough for two vehicles to pass safely, and at some points nothing at all can pass without mortal risk. There are two brief sections of guardrail, thought-provokingly dented. What has gone on at the curves that don't have guardrails?

Beggars appeared along the roads of the central plateau, also soldiers. I saw many more soldiers in the middle of the country than I saw at the border. Going into the mountains we were stopped at three military checkpoints and questioned at each, the information on our passports and press cards laboriously copied by officers who held the pencil stubs as though they were large power tools.

The soldiers were nice enough. I was headed for the outhouse at the army garrison in Mirebalais when a private motioned for me to stop. He ran back into the barracks. I could see him through the unglazed, unscreened window as he opened a large vinyl suitcase. He returned with a precious commodity he'd brought from home, toilet paper.

It was hours after dark when we arrived in the town of "X." I'll call it Pignon, which is a real town elsewhere in Haiti, as are Bombardopolis, Ditty, Mme Joie, Marché Canard, and Moron. We'd been delayed when a truck ahead of us went into a rut so deep that it fell over on its side.

The army barracks in Pignon were completely unlit. A soldier came out of the moon shadows and motioned us into a large, dusty room empty except for three straight chairs and a table. Eventually another soldier arrived with a candle. He was followed by a wide man in a loud sport shirt. This was the lieutenant. He wore a huge gold watch of elaborate design. And what a great rogue of a pig thief he must have been, if the watch was real, which it wasn't.

The lieutenant, with the aid of the candle, my flashlight, and a Bic, solemnly read every entry and exit stamp in my passport. I wish I knew what he thought. As the result of a busy reportorial weekend in the aftermath of the opening of the Berlin Wall, I have something like fifteen East German visas in there. "I'm in Haiti to cover the terrible health effects of the U.S. embargo," I ventured.

"Thousands of children are dying," said the lieutenant, his tone indicating even an East German spy could understand that.

I wouldn't, I hoped, see any dying children. But I did want to see the Pignon town clinic that treated them. We went there to wash up by Eveready light. The clinic had all the normal plumbing fixtures, but running water came from only one tap sticking out of a wall in a rear supply room. I stood over a drain and sluiced myself with a bucket.

We slept in a small house that the clinic owned. A broken exercise bicycle stood in the corner of my mud-walled room. What CARE flub, Peace Corps mix-up, or kink in charitable intentions had put it here?

In the morning the porch of the clinic was full of patients, mostly women and children, all dressed in their best clothes because not much happens in Pignon. Getting sick is an occasion. Thirty-five to forty people a day are usually treated. The clinic is run by one of the international aid agencies. The agency works in cooperation with Haiti's Ministry of Health. The Ministry of Health is one of this unhealthy nation's largest employers. About one-fifth of the country's civil servants, some eighty-nine hundred people, are on its payroll. And 62 percent are in administrative positions.

The Pignon clinic, however, couldn't be called a patronage plum. It was a humble structure, superior to its surroundings only by virtue of a poured-concrete floor. The dispensary was untidy, with medical supplies stacked wherever space could be found. The examining rooms were not very clean. A refrigerator was used only to keep things from getting lost or rat eaten. There'd been no electricity since the international embargo began.

The clinic had a little laboratory, not much more complicated than my boyhood chemistry set. But twenty-five tests could be performed, including cancer biopsies and Pap smears. There was a gas oven to sterilize the equipment for simple operations such as cleaning and suturing tropical country life's endemic machete wounds. There was a delivery room, its walls decorated with sexy posters promoting breast feeding. Only very difficult births took place here, maybe three a month. Midwives attended the rest. The clinic staff had made friends with the midwives, convincing them to wash their hands and so forth. The midwives had even been enlisted to sell safe water for infant formula to the mothers for a penny or two a jug.

One of the midwives came up and gave me a kiss. She was a very old woman with no teeth but real gold earrings and a face that was a nest of smile lines. Her fame seemed to rest on having had triplets.

The clinic even had a dental chair. Treatment was all by extraction as far as I could tell by observing the locals. A dentist, a volunteer from France, came by every so often to yank the really difficult teeth.

The Pignon clinic had no doctor and only moderate hopes of getting a nurse. Until then, the clinic was run by a nurse's aide. The aide did not know how many people lived in the area his clinic served. Haiti does not yet suffer from information overload. But the Pan American Health Organization estimates that the population of the central plateau is over 473,000 and says there are just forty-four health centers, mostly the doctorless kind. The hospital nearest Pignon (and hospital is stretching the term) is several hours away over worse roads than we had come in on.

But Haitians don't die of the fancy hospitalized maladies which afflict the sanitized and healthy. They don't live long enough. Life expectancy is fifty-five years. And the mortality rate among children under five is 13.5 percent. These kids expire from the most prosaic causes—a cough, the runs. And here the nurse's aide was able to perform the kind of wonders practitioners at Mayo can only pray for. He could clear lungs with decongestants and cure most respiratory infections with cheap antibiotics. And he had reduced diarrhea cases to fewer than three a week.

"How?" I asked.

"Safe water."

"But how do you get safe water?"

"Chlorine."

"Where can you get chlorine?"

"Five drops of Clorox in a gallon," said the nurse's aide. "That's all."

The nurse's aide said foreign donations were down. Dumarsais blamed it on the embargo. He said people were mixed up about what they should or shouldn't do for Haiti. But I think people are mixed up about Haiti, period. We like to give to hopeful or heroic causes. Note how few charitable campaigns are targeted at "Muddling Through." The clinic used to provide medicine for free but now sometimes had to sell it. "What if people can't pay?" I asked.

"We open a line of credit," said the nurse's aide.

"And what if people can't pay off the credit line?"

The aide seemed puzzled by my question. "Those who can," he said, "pay back. Others just can't." A nurse's aide in Haiti has come up with an eight-word national health-care program. The plan the Clinton administration presented to Congress was fourteen hundred pages long.

The Pignon clinic has been operating since 1978. Before that the only medical treatment in the area was from—as the nurse's aide put it—"a not-trained woman who gave injections." The success of the little clinic, all the things it accomplished with facilities and skills that wouldn't do to treat an American for a hangover, was wonderful. But this is a sad kind of wonder. It should be this easy to save the millions of other dying kids, kids so unfortunate they don't even have the luck to live in Pignon.

Pignon had no stores or shops. The only thing that marked it as a town was a town square. An aberrant bit of government attention had been paid to this plot of land. The bare earth was overlain with a maze of cement curbs and walkways to make a formal garden without the garden. And cement benches had been placed around it as though Haiti lacked spots to sit and do nothing.

There was nothing with any charm in Pignon, except every one of its residents. They waved each time they saw us, inquired after our well-being and comfort, and insisted that I wear an absurd straw hat while I wandered around in the sun—lest, I suppose, my weird red skin pop like a weenie's on a grill. Not that they had any weenies. Or grills either.

When we had a flat on our Jeep, two chairs were brought out so Dumarsais and I could sit in the road while half of the town's men went to work repairing the tire with scraps of rubber and a vulcanizing oven improvised from an old piston head.

No one begged or stared. Only one kid could have been labeled pesky, and he was cute about it. The very pariah dogs were friendly. Or maybe they'd given up even the hope of having anything to bite.

Of course, the humans in Haiti have hope. They hope to leave. Back in Port-au-Prince, I asked Dumarsais to take me to the wharf in Cité Soleil where boat people embark. I stood on one of the dock's few planks and looked at a wooden sloop that seemed to have been built with a hammer and a penknife. The vessel was maybe thirty feet long with a shallow draft and an awkwardly wide beam. The hull looked soggy with age. The sails appeared to have been sewn from grain sacks. There was no cabin or shelter of any kind. "Put a couple of hundred people on board," I said, "and it's going to be an unpleasant cruise to Florida."

"Ha!" said Dumarsais. "It's for fishing. The refugees don't use those." He turned me around and faced me toward the shore. A couple of twelve- or fifteen-foot lorries were sitting swaybacked on a mud bank. Their hulls had been eaten by rot. I could see daylight through their sides. "*That*," said Dumarsais, "is what people go to Florida in."

And for those who cannot get to Florida, there is heaven or, anyway, voodoo.

Someone at the bar at the Oloffson Hotel had said to me, "You'll never understand Haiti if you don't understand voodoo."

"Can you explain it to me?" I asked.

"You wouldn't understand."

Dumarsais took me to a voodoo temple, or *hounfò,* a few blocks from the pier. This was a room about thirty feet by thirty feet, a grand space for Cité Soleil, and decorated in a manner that owed something to the sacramental and something to party time. The ceiling was covered with small paper flags, crêpe bunting, and inflated beach balls. The walls were painted putt-putt golf green and arrayed with *vèvè* symbols and with pictures of the *loas* the *vèvès* represent.

Loas, though descended from African pantheons, are identified with Catholic saints. Saint John the Baptist is Jan Batis Trasetonm, the Virgin Mary is Metrès Ezili, Saint George is Ogou Chango, and the Three Kings are Simbi Boua, Simbi Nandezo, and the rap-group-sounding Simbi 3 Kafou. The saintly *loas* were depicted here in a carnival-booth art style, and combined with the cagelike *vèvès*, they gave the *hounfò* the look of a canonized sideshow menagerie.

In the center of the room was a pillar of stepped-back, ziggurat design like a Sunday school illustration of the Tower of Babel. This was the *potomitan,* the ladder by which *loas*' spirits descend into the *hounfò*. Most of a voodoo ceremony's rituals and dances center upon it. It was decorated with ribbons and with drawings of eyes and other symbols. There's a hint of the maypole in the *potomitan*, though May is not the season when nature awakes from a long sleep in Haiti. Nature may not ever do that in Haiti again.

The members of this *hounfò* were adherents of Bizango, one of a number of voodoo organizations in Haiti. They are called "secret societies," but the secret is only that they have some private ceremonies and passwords, as do the Free and Accepted Masons, which, if you think about it, are no more strangely named.

The *houngan*, or priest, wore a shirt and tie and looked as if he might *be* a Mason, a thoughtful small businessman, the kind who does a lot of volunteer work. Indeed, his title in this Bizango chapter was the unexotic one of president. He asked me if I would like to see the altar. It was actually a room, no bigger than a kitchen pantry, lit only by a few small oil lamps. A confusion of sacrifices were in here, pieces of velvet and satin, items of clothing, vases, pottery cups, flags, artificial flowers, foodstuffs, bottles of rum, and, in the center of these, a cross swathed in dark-colored draperies. It was as though, in collecting these sacred objects, the worshippers had tried to touch upon every aspect of existence, including reality—a number of long and nasty-looking knives were thrust into the dirt floor in front of the cross.

I'm not of mystical inclination. Aside from the occasional prayer-in-time-of-medical-tests, I am rooted in the profane. Nevertheless, I was affected by the reliquary. Voodoo is a syncretic religion. All its myriad labors of inclusion and reconciliation were enshrined here. If it was just a closet in a slum, it was a closet with a story. People from dozens of Africans societies, with their hundreds of deities, had been abducted by aliens and taken to a place that might as well have been another planet. Here they were subjected to the worst indignities by people the color of grubs and slugs. These pasty tyrants claimed that the son of their own god said everybody was equal. This god and his kid and the kid's mother were all filled with infinite mercy and love, but, if you didn't convert, they baked you in an oven when you died.

Whatever the various African words for "bullshit" are, slaves in Haiti must have spoken them frequently. And yet those slaves studied Christianity, and they studied all their own multifarious creeds. From this metaphysical slumgullion they created something upon which they could agree, just as they created a language, Creole, in which they could agree they agreed. Thus a measure of comfort, hope, and social structure arose in conditions that would have driven less decent and intelligent people—me, for instance—into atheistic rage. What voodoo's nameless apostles accomplished makes the labors of the early church fathers at the First Council of Nicaea seem a mere keeping of minutes at a PTA meeting.

I said something to this effect to the *hounfò*'s president. He opened a narrow door next to the altar room. "I don't think any outsider has ever seen this," said Dumarsais. There was a small space inside, little more than a cupboard. This was the sanctum sanctorum of the chapter. I confess that to me it looked like more of the same spiritual jumble sale. But an electric charge of reverence ran through Dumarsais. And the president himself seemed awed. I had to be satisfied with feeling honored.

Dumarsais said there was a meeting of the chapter that night, a ceremony only for the initiates, but the president said we could come. And so at nine o'clock we returned. The street was empty except for our Jeep. No one and nothing stirred aboard in Cité Soleil.

The *hounfò* was lit by a single lantern. About forty-five people were inside. They ranged in age from early twenties to the indeterminate venerability that comes so early to Haitians. The men wore identical gray smocks trimmed in crimson, the peasant smocks of eighteenth-century France but in dress-parade version. The women wore archaic peasant dresses in the same colors. Everyone had a red kerchief tied at the neck, and one was loaned to me.

People sat around the margins of the room, smoking cigarettes and talking. An old woman swept the packed-earth floor. Branches from some aromatic plant had been piled around the *potomitan,* like a combination room freshener and preparation for an auto-da-fé. I couldn't tell exactly when the ceremony began. The president, now wearing the sequined shirt of a salsa bandleader, came in. And three men began to play on a graduated set of congas. But the president didn't burst into song. He spoke in conversational tones. A young man moved through the crowd anointing the congregation with something like Aqua Velva, pouring so much of it on our hands and heads that the room smelled like one giant fourteen-year-old boy learning to shave. Someone else had a censer on a chain, incense fumes pouring out, and he used it very differently than in a Catholic Mass, swinging the vessel between the legs of the men and under the skirts of the women.

Candles were distributed and lit. The president, punctuating his remarks with a gourd rattle, made one general prayer to the *Gran Mèt,* the Big God. Voodoo is, at its heart, monotheistic. But God is conceived—quite reasonably, given Haitian experience—as remote. He is too la-de-da for daily affairs. Once obeisance had been made to the *Gran Mèt*, all further invocation was aimed at the more workaday *loas*. We prayed to the *loas* represented on the walls, the *loas* to which this particular chapter of Bizango was consecrated. Dumarsais prompted me as to when to kneel, turn, stand, or shut up. Some dancing started. First the men, then the women, then everyone but me circled the *potomitan* in a desultory fashion.

It was an hour and a half before the ceremony took on form. Several people seemed to have been appointed as ritual police. They nudged the others to do the correct thing at the correct time the way Dumarsais nudged me. Late in the evening, the enforcers would also wake those who dozed. A choir was nudged into song. And two angry-acting men entered the dance, one carrying a noose and the other swinging a hide whip.

Voodoo societies had been founded, Dumarsais told me later, for mutual protection in the anarchistic slave communities. The rope and the lash had nothing to do, as I would have thought, with the slave masters. Rather, the whip was a token of self-discipline and the noose stood for catching thieves. The slave masters did not need to be dealt with symbolically, they'd been dealt with in an actual manner in 1804.

The dances grew more practiced and complex—bows and side-slip steps, thigh slaps and arm-waving salutes, turns and bobs and genuflections. If country line dancing were done for some serious purpose to better music by people more coordinated than Houston suburbanites, it would look like this.

And, then again, no it wouldn't. The women rushed into the altar room and came out waving knives. They picked up the branches from the base of the *potomitan* and put them on their heads like laurel wreathes. The drumming quickened. The singing rose in pitch. And a weaving, flailing, cantering dash around the center post began. The speed increased until centrifugal force should have sent the dancers slamming into the *hounfò*'s walls. The man with the whip, a huge person with a shaved head like an artillery shell, stood snapping the plait at the dancers' feet and taking mouthfuls of cane liquor and spraying these over the celebrants. An awful keening chant arose. The frenzy in the darkened room seemed more primordial than Haiti's African heritage. The kingdoms of West Africa date only from the fourth century AD. Maybe this is what the Greek mystery cults did on their lodge nights. Dionysus, that city-state yuppie, invented only wine, not rum, but just such Dionysian furors were described in 408 BC in *The Bacchae* by Euripides. I had no more than thought so when a woman dancer spun out of the crowd straight at me, sweeping her knife through the air and looking perfectly like one of the maenads about to tear her sacrificial victim to pieces. There was the fate of Guillaume Sam to be considered.

But the woman meant me no harm. She didn't even see me. She was possessed, being "ridden by her *loa*," as it is sometimes described. Then another woman was possessed. Then half a dozen women were describing dervish circles and groaning to heaven. One fell on the ground and made pig noises. Some shook and convulsed. Others lost control of arms and legs, and these limbs would then propel them about the room in spastic flips and tosses. They began to speak in tongues. But this was not so impressive. I have a born-again sister who does that. And my own French probably sounds like glossolalia.

Whoever was closest to a possessed woman would (myself excepted) brave the knife blade, run in and catch hold of the ecstatic, and clutch her until the *loa* jumped off or lost interest or whatever. I remember this sort of thing from LSD in the 1960s. And, as with LSD, it was hard to tell whether possession was terrifying or bliss. A bit of both, if memory serves.

For the next couple of hours, dancing waxed and waned and raptures came and went. Then, on some cue I did not see, the crowd faded back to the walls. A delegation of officers and officials went to the small door next to the altar room, the entrance to the holy of holies, and there performed a number of Masonic rituals. My father and all my uncles were Shriners. I know the drill. My instincts about the Bizango president had been right. Later, reading the Haitian voodoo scholar Gérard Alphonse Férère, I discovered that one more thing voodoo had drawn upon was the abandoned Freemasonry of the dead and exiled French slave owners.

When the salutes and incantations were finished, the door of the tabernacle was opened and a cross and three coffins brought out. I'd just looked in there that afternoon. There wasn't space inside for these. The coffins were for an infant, a child, and an adult. The man with the shaved skull raised his rum bottle and took hold of a machete. A woman picked up the cross, and the two of them performed a dance of menace and confrontation—the eternal verities versus Saturday-night fun. The fun seemed to triumph. Another woman put the baby's coffin on her head, and the dance was repeated. She too was vanquished, as was a third woman who danced with the larger, child-sized casket precariously balanced aloft. Finally, four male pallbearers took hold of the biggest coffin, drew daggers from their waistbands, and chased the machete-wielding rum-spitter around the *potomitan*. Death holds trumps. The cross and all the caskets were waltzed through a macabre cotillion, a Busby Berkeley eschatology.

In the end the coffins were stacked crisscross fashion with daggers and candles arrayed in front of them and a crucifix drawn on the earth in flaming rum. Each member of the congregation came forward to make elaborate gestures of respect, to knock several times on the lids of the coffins and place a cash offering on the polished wood. "The grave is just one more thing we have to go through," said Dumarsais. And, considering what Haitians have been through already, I could see his point.

The last act of the ceremony was for the coffins to be run up and down the streets of Cité Soleil. Whether this was to exhibit Bizango's victory over death or just to scare the neighborhood, I couldn't tell. But Dumarsais said to me, "There is no real protection in Haiti without voodoo."

When the coffins had been brought home—carried backward into the *hounfò* and backward through the sanctuary door—the members all embraced each other. Each of them hugged me and clasped my hand. Then, though it was two in the morning, it was time to talk. A voodoo society is also a social club and a mutual aid organization and even a community bank. Everyone had his say. They asked me to speak, too.

All I could manage was "Thank you." But what I really wanted to tell the voodoo celebrants was "I wish all of you could come to the United States and live there. You're an immense improvement on the other people who go to Florida. And, if Americans are worried that immigration will cause overpopulation, ecological problems, and such, then we could arrange a trade. You sail north. And we'll get a bunch of crabby families in Winnebagos, drug smugglers, Disney executives, Palm Beach divorce lawyers, 2 Live Crew, time-share condo salesmen, Don Johnson, Miami Beach aerobics instructors, William Kennedy Smith, kvetching retirees, and teenage gang members and send them back to Haiti on the same boat."

AGE AND GUILE BEAT YOUTH, INNOCENCE, AND A BAD HAIRCUT

(*1995*)

A FORGOTTEN HERO OF THE TROJAN WAR

Thersites only clamour'd in the throng,
Loquacious, loud, and turbulent of tongue:
Awed by no shame, by no respect controll'd,
In scandal busy, in reproaches bold;
With witty malice studious to defame;
Scorn all his joy, and laughter all his aim.
But chief he gloried with licentious style
To lash the great, and monarchs to revile . . .
Spleen to mankind his envious heart possess'd,
And much he hated all, but most the best.

—Alexander Pope's
translation of *The Iliad*

A Few Thoughts on Humor and Humorists

(*Foreword to a 1980* National Lampoon *anthology*)

The most important thing in life is to have a sense of humor. A sense of humor is more important than food, because if you have a sense of humor, you can laugh even though you're starving, while if you laugh too hard on a full stomach, you'll throw up.

It's often said that "laughter is the best medicine." This actually isn't true. Penicillin is the best medicine, followed by tetracycline and the sulfa drugs. But, judging by what a joke the Carter administration's State Department turned out to be, laughter *is* the best foreign policy. In fact, laughter serves many purposes. Laughter is the way we cope with conflicting emotions. For example, your mother is dying of cancer. You're sorry she's dying, but she's been in pain, so you're also relieved by the prospect of her imminent demise. Why not kid her about it? Put on a little skit—wear her bedpan on your head and use the oxygen tent noises to pretend you're Darth Vader. Laughter alleviates fear, too. Your mother really won't mind dying now, especially if the bedpan was full and she saw you stick your head in it.

Humor can be an effective substitute for aggression, the way it was for Roberto Duran in the second—"*No Mas*"—Sugar Ray Leonard match. Sugar Ray may have won the fight, but it was Duran everybody laughed at. And humor can also be used as a defense. Humor was used as a defense in the trial of mass murderer Richard Speck. Speck's attorneys claimed their client should be freed because one of the investigating officers, upon entering the building where all the dead nurses were found, was heard to say, "There's something funny going on here."

Still, what is amusing to one person may seem simply squashed flat and run over in the road to another. And what is considered unattractive and sad by some may be peeled up and sailed through the window of the girl's gym by others. What do we really mean by the word *humor*? Consider the following list of common colloquial phrases involving mirth.

When people say:	They actually mean:
"That's funny."	*"That's not funny."*
"Don't make me laugh."	*"That's not funny."*
"That's not funny."	*"That's funny."*
"She has a wonderful sense of humor."	*"Don't make me laugh."*

Yet there are many things that *do* make people laugh, and sometimes people laugh for no apparent reason. For instance, let's examine a room full of teenage girls at a slumber party. They are all giggling. Let's examine them very carefully. (We'll say we're doctors, or something.) What are these girls giggling about? They're probably discussing sex. Perhaps their humor is a means of coping with fear, like the time you spilled a bedpan all over your dying mother. But there's no reason for young girls to be afraid of sex. We'll be gentle. Of course, we're old and gross, so maybe they're using humor as a defense mechanism like Richard Speck did. But Richard Speck was convicted. And we will be too if that was Mom and Dad who just pulled in the driveway.

Even if the causes of laughter cannot be exactly defined, there are still several recognizable types of humorous activity. There is *parody,* when you make fun of people who are smarter than you; *satire,* when you make fun of people who are richer than you; and *burlesque,* when you make fun of both while taking off your clothes. But the key to all types of humor probably lies in the folk saying "I didn't know whether to laugh or cry," or possibly in the folk saying "I didn't know whether to shit or go blind." The latter would seem to be an easy choice, but the truly funny person may have trouble making up his mind. For a real humorist is a special sort of person, a man apart, different from the rest of us. He brings to everyone around him the wonderful and unexpected gift of laughter. Think of him this way: If all the world were a church and all the people in the world were silent prayers going up to heaven, the humorist would be a fart from the pulpit.

The Welsh National Combined Mud Wrestling and Spelling Bee Championship

Mucking about in the Fforest Fawr, Llanddewi Brefi, Pontrhydfendigaid, and Other Orthographically Challenged Places

(*Car and Driver, 1984*)

Author's note: *In late 1983 a party of sixteen* Car and Driver *staff members, friends, and dependents drove nine off-road vehicles across the pavement-free middle of Wales. Ostensibly, our mission was to test a cross section of American four-wheel-drive products against their British, German, and Japanese counterparts. In fact, what we were doing was illustrating the central idea of all automotive journalism: getting money to do what one would spend money to do if one hadn't found a way to be paid for doing it.*

A Ford Bronco II, a Chevrolet S-10 Blazer, a GMC S-15 Jimmy, a Jeep Cherokee, a Land Rover, two Range Rovers, a Mercedes-Benz Geländewagen, and a Mitsubishi Montero were used on the trip. Since these are now long outdated, I have excised the technical chatter about them. Wales, on the other hand, has not had a major redesign since Owen Glendower got whupped at Harlech Castle in 1409.

You might think off-road driving in the British Isles would be a matter of: "Very good, sir. We'll have Mrs. Twickham take down her front trellis, and you can motor about in her rose garden, then turn sharp at the rookery, and go right through the privet hedge and into the vicar's kitchen yard." But it's not like that at all. Even though Britain has a population density about double that of Macy's toy floor at Christmastime, there are still vast tracts of empty moor, fen, bog, wold, and other kinds of wilderness that the Brits have funny names for.

The really tough part, however, is getting out of London. The Limeys just can't shake their national dyslexia about which side of the road is for tailgating and which is for head-on collisions. And I can't remember to list to port. But I have, I think, finally come up with the proper mnemonic device; what you have to do is think of yourself as a well-dressed Socialist: "Keep left, look right. Keep left, look right." See? This makes driving in England a snap as long as you don't have to pass, change lanes, go through roundabouts, or shift gears.

The English also have a road-numbering system based on the Duke of Wellington's cribbage scores. Thus it was in a dither of confusion, occasional naked fear, and also rain and jet lag that we made our way fifty miles west up the Thames to the village of Streatley. There, with hoots of relief from the Yanks, we got off the paved road and into some nice safe precipices, cliffs, and escarpments.

A remarkable geological feature called the Ridgeway begins at Streatley. The Ridgeway is a narrow fold of chalk highlands that stretches west for forty miles along the crest of the Berkshire Downs and into northern Wiltshire. The country falls away in perfect symmetry on either side, and the view of England is too wonderful to be fact. If you were the kind of child who created imaginary worlds on your bedspread, this is what you saw from your knees.

The Ridgeway has been in use as a thoroughfare since 3000 BC, and it is still in better shape than most streets in New York. Even so, wet grass, slippery chalk soil, and gale-force winds blowing up off the Salisbury Plain made the going tricky. I had no more than sighed with relief to be out of traffic when I became what's known as "cross-rutted," meaning I got the front wheels into a set of ruts that were headed toward Lisbon and the back wheels into a set pointed at Reykjavik. As a result, I spun. I barely dropped anchor in time to avoid committing an act of civil disobedience protesting the General Inclosure Act of 1801. That is, I nearly hit a fence.

At midday we stopped in Wantage, birthplace of Alfred the Great (AD 849), which like most English villages is possessed of a millennium's accumulated cuteness. We needed lunch, and we also needed enough petrol for our Afrika Korps–sized expedition. If you're planning an off-road jaunt in England, or anywhere else, you might try it with fewer people and vehicles. We went through the Midlands and Wales at about the same rate of speed as Geoff Chaucer's Canterbury package tour. It was fun, though, carrying our own house party with us, and the Wantage pubs appreciated the 2,000 percent increase in custom.

Back on the Ridgeway, we did some serious rooting about in the truffle pit of history. Here, between Wantage and Swindon, is the immense White Horse, a 365-foot-long, 130-foot-wide equine figure carved into the chalk hillside. Alfred the Great supposedly dug the thing himself, as a memorial to the drubbing he gave the pagan Danes at nearby Ashdown. More likely it's twice as old as that and was the totemic emblem of some gang of Celtic biker types. Anyway, it gives its name to the fine valley below, the Vale of White Horse, and also to the White Horse Tavern on Hudson Street in New York, where Dylan Thomas drank himself to death in 1953. A fine description of the area (the vale area, not Hudson Street) was left by Thomas Hughes in *Tom Brown's Schooldays.* (And the Scotch was left by us in the Land Rover. Oops. It gets awfully cold and windy out in the middle of history.) Actually, the White Horse is not best viewed from the Ridgeway heights. From up there it looks like something you might get yourself into on a golf course and need a chalk wedge to get out of again. There is a nice hill alongside, however, where Saint George slew the dragon. (Unanswered questions: Was it dragon season? Is it sporting to slay them when they aren't on the wing? Was Saint George careful to extinguish all dragon-breath fires and pick up the spent lance tips and empty mead cans in his dragon blind?) No grass will grow on the place where the dragon's blood was spilled. This is because people walk around on it all the time, looking for the place where grass won't grow.

Back closer to where the whiskey and the cars were is an ancient hill fort called Uffington Castle. Nothing is left of it now except the turf mounds where the ramparts stood. Eerie to think of my blue-painted ancestors squatting here among the watch fires and plotting the same kinds of things my cousins are plotting tonight in some Belfast pub.

A bit farther along the Ridgeway is Wayland's Smithy, a New Stone Age "long barrow" of prodigious size. Presumably it was a burial chamber, but it may have been used for prehistoric games of nude stoop tag. There is, after all, much we don't know about the peoples of ancient Britain.

A Saxon legend of later date makes the barrow home to Wayland Smith, a blacksmith. If your horse threw a shoe while you were riding along the Ridgeway, you were supposed to leave a silver coin on a stone, whistle three times, and turn your back; Wayland would then shoe your horse and take the money. However, this does not work with a pound note and a Land Rover. But who wants a horseshoe pounded into his Land Rover's tire anyway?

By now we were full to the gills with history, and practically empty of Scotch, so it was time to push on to the night's lodgings. These were in Cowbridge, seventy miles away across the Severn and down the Welsh coast past Cardiff.

We'd planned to get on the M4 at Swindon and speed across the Severn Bridge in time to get really stupid and loud before dinner, but the high winds we'd been fighting all day caused the bridge to be closed. We had to make a massive detour up the Severn estuary, forty miles to Gloucester, then seventy miles back down to Cowbridge.

It was nearly eleven by the time we got there, so we had to settle for getting loud and stupid during dinner instead of before. The people at the Bear Hotel were lovely, though. That is, they didn't evict us at gunpoint. *Caveat gobbler,* however, about UK food, especially if you're tired and have had a few and are in the giggling sort of mood where you order what sounds funny on the menu. I ordered "whitebait," which turned out to be a plateful of deep-fat-fried guppies. The nearest McDonald's was 153 miles away, in London.

The sun (and the whitebait) came up the next day, and we pushed west to Port Talbot, where Richard Burton went to high school. Port Talbot bears a striking resemblance to Muncie, Indiana. We then avoided Swansea, where Dylan Thomas failed to drink himself to death because he didn't get home from New York in time, and motored inland along the river Neath to Aberdulais, where, according to local history, nothing much has ever happened.

In Aberdulais we left the pavement and turned onto the Sarn Helen, the principal Roman road linking north and south Wales. The name comes from Helen, wife of Magnus Maximus, who was Roman emperor for about five minutes in AD 383. Either that, or the name comes from *Y Lleng,* Welsh for "the legion," or from *elin,* which means "angle," or from anything else you can think of. Although the Sarn Helen is much newer than the Ridgeway, it's in much worse shape. The Ridgeway has good natural drainage, and it remained in active use until the early 1800s; but maintenance on the Sarn Helen stopped in AD 410, when the emperor Flavius Honorius took time out from being chased around Italy by Alaric the Visigoth to write a letter to the Britons telling them to take care of their own damn roads.

The Romans made a better road than anyone ever has since. For a primary road like the Sarn Helen they dug parallel ditches more than eighty feet apart and excavated the soil between them. Then they laid in a sand-and-quarry-stone foundation bound on either side by tightly fitted curbs of dressed and wedged stone blocks. On top of this foundation they built an embankment four or five feet high and fifty feet wide, constructed of layers of rammed chalk and flint and finished with a screened-gravel crown two feet thick.

Even so, 1,573 years of neglect have taken their toll. The road has worn down and topsoil has accumulated along it, and the Sarn Helen has turned from an embankment into a ditch. There are washouts and mud holes and boulders in the ditch, too. But the Sarn Helen *is* still there. I doubt we'll be able to say the same about 1-95 in the year 3556.

Our first problem, however, was the work of man and not nature. Some farmer had dropped a big oak across the right-of-way—one of those very tangly and many-branched oaks. Apparently, it was felled on purpose to keep such trendies as ourselves from lurking about and luring sheep and daughters to chic London nightspots. Fortunately, among our horde of traveling companions was Roger Crathorne, demonstrations manager for Land Rover, Ltd. Roger is one of the most accomplished off-road drivers ever. Also fortunately, Rovers have winches. Roger used the winch on his Range Rover and the winch on the Land Rover to create something that looked like what I flunked in high school trig. Then he deftly set the oak back among its roadside mates, while the rest of us stood around and gaped and drank Bloody Scotches. (A Bloody Scotch is what you drink when you want a Bloody Mary but don't have any vodka. It's just like a regular Bloody Mary, but with Scotch instead of vodka, and without tomato juice, Worcestershire sauce, Tobasco, or celery sticks. You drink it right out of the bottle.)

Once past the tree blockade, we drove uphill through gullies so narrow that the bigger vehicles were digging mud with their door handles until we achieved a crest from which rustic beauty positively vomited forth—mist upon the heather, scudding clouds above, tree trunks artfully gnarling, all the usual stuff. A ruined stone house commanded the hill. There were arrow slits built into its walls. This farmstead stood fortified against . . . Saxons? Normans? Roundheads? Pesky neighbors with unruly kids? Probably lots of things. For centuries these hills ran wild with—well, with wild hill runners.

We traveled along heights fenced four hundred years ago by practitioners of the lost art of building dry stone walls, then entered the great pine woods known as the Fforest Fawr, and took a wrong ffork somewhere and got lost in an open-pit coal mine. This was neither interesting nor scenic. But we picked up the Sarn Helen again in a little town called Onllwyn.

Now the going turned dirty. There was nothing in the scenery to warn us, but the Sarn Helen became as bad a road as I've ever been down in anything except a metaphor. We were in rolling, pleasant upland. Parts of Beverly Hills look more ferocious. But the track across this peaceful greenery was vicious slop, broken only by chapel-width boulders and ruts where you could lose Kareem Abdul-Jabbar. The roadbed bucked and dipped like an amateur prostitute, and the bank angle tipped to the limits of a protractor's descriptive abilities. All this was spiced with greasy, knife-sharp ledges of shale, oleaginous grass clumps, Olympic-sized mud puddles, and just plain great big holes.

Half an hour in, soldiers began appearing. They sloughed toward us along the road, muddy and exhausted-looking. One of the Brits among us claimed they were candidates for some special commando force. He said they're put out at the end of the Sarn Helen with one extra pair of dry underpants and a piece of zwieback or suchlike, and, if they find their way back alive, they're in.

At the end of the Sarn Helen we forded the quick headwaters of a river and found ourselves looking down into what may be the most beautiful valley on earth. It is a wide and gentle-sided dell done up in all the most exquisite shades of green—emerald, hunter, loden, apple, jade, and olive—with tiny farms curling up each slope as though some wonderland were cupped in vast angelic hands.

But enough aesthetic palaver. If we had wanted beauty, we'd have been riding women, not cars and trucks . . . *Ouch! Stop! Ouch! Ouch!!* (It's important, when writing macho-type automotive journalism, to do it where your girlfriend can't see over your shoulder.)

From the beautiful valley we followed secondary roads northwest to Llandovery, getting caught in a herd of sheep along the way. The sheep were being drovered in the time-honored dog-nipped fashion, except that modern Welsh sheep have big iridescent-orange patches spray-painted on their sides for identification. This would certainly spoil the looks of any Staffordshire pastoral china figurines depicting Daphnis and Chloe his shepherdess love. The sheep looked as if they had been hanging out in the New York subway system.

Llandovery, an old center for Welsh drovers (sheep cowboys), had great charm in a sober Methodist way. All the more sober since we missed pub hours.

From Llandovery we went north up the river Tywi into the Cambrian Mountains. From their peaks we could see Cardigan Bay, twenty-five miles in the distance. The Cambrian Mountains were the hideout of Twm Sion Catti, the Welsh Robin Hood. The difference between the Welsh Robin Hood and the English Robin Hood is that Twm stole from everybody. Also, he had a sense of humor instead of a Maid Marian. According to my guidebook to South Wales, Twm once went into an ironmonger's shop and asked to buy a cooking pot. The storekeeper showed him one.

"No," said Twm. "That has a hole in it."

"I don't see a hole," said the storekeeper.

Twm took the pot and jammed it down over the storekeeper's ears. "If there's no hole," said he, "how'd I get your head in it?" Then Twm cleaned out the store.

A teeny but perfectly maintained byway led through the mountains past the Llyn Brianne Reservoir to a small chapel called the Soar y Mynydd. We paused while *Car and Driver*'s editor David E. Davis had his picture taken in the pulpit and I pondered why some Celts got John Wesley and dirty old coal mines while other Celts got whiskey recipes and popes with swell hats. If you ask me, the Welsh couldn't spell well enough to find the boat to Dublin.

Outside the chapel was a steep hill, its bottom third a smooth, wet, and naked rock face. The proper driving technique here was to take a fast run at it and stand on the gas and pray. We side-slipped and slithered. It was like trying to stuff a snake up a drainpipe. But we all made it to the top, I with my eyes closed.

Then it was national debt-size ruts and bogs as soft as a politician's conscience as we descended to Llanddewi Brefi, site of the sixth-century synod where Saint David refuted the Pelagian heresy. By this act he saved all of Western Europe from a religion that sounds like a skin disease.

In Tregaron that night, at the Talbot Inn, a wedding breakfast was being held in the bar. It had been going on for ten hours. Welshmen like Mr. Davis put great stock in Welsh singing, but to my Irish ears it sounds like men jumping off chairs into a bathtub full of frogs. As soon as dinner was over, Philip Llewellin, who was serving as our chief of reconnaissance and native gillie on this trip, decided to prove to the wedding party that, although he is only half Welsh, that half is from the throat to the liver. Of course the rest of us had to help. Our tab outran the wedding's within an hour, and by midnight we were as drunk as any leek-wearing Taffy you could find in a day's ride by sheepback. Pubs in the UK, it's true, close their doors at 11:30, but what does it matter as long as you're on the inside of them when they do? The landlord waxed fond with our spending abilities and slapped down two bottles of whiskey, gratis, on our table. (The landlord's wife slipped in and prudently took one bottle back.) This whiskey was, I swear to you, named "Old Sheep Dip" right on the label, which proves once again that Protestants will drink anything. (Methodists serve grape juice at communion, you know.)

We finally put a stop to Philip's singing, so he began to tell stories. Llewellin is a marvel at this. "The rise and fall of empires, the passing of ages and eons, 'tis but the wink of the eye, a cloud across the sun, a breeze playing in the summer wheat . . ." He was quoting Shelley's "Ozymandias" when I left him at 3:00 a.m.

As I tucked myself into bed, the wedding party was beginning a giant brawl in the street below. I dozed off to the merry sounds of police whistles and breaking crockery. (How do you tell the bride at a Welsh wedding ceremony? It's important, because she's the one you're not supposed to punch in the face.) In the morning Llewellin looked as though he'd been on the losing side, but he couldn't remember whether he'd gotten into the fight or just finished the bottle of Old Sheep Dip.

We refueled in Pontrhydfendigaid (pronounced "huh?") and took a gravel road back east into the huge stretch of grazing lands known as the Great Welsh Desert. Not many people live here, and I'm not so sure about those who do. Every time I got out of a car to relieve myself, the sheep would start backing toward me, looking over their shoulders expectantly.

About noon we left a rough gravel drovers' road and attempted to strike out across the great moor on the divide of the Cambrian Mountains. Llewellin, in the Cherokee, was in the lead at the top of a hill when, *squish,*

Cherokee and Philip all but disappeared. Now, how can the top of the hill, where we were, be wetter than the bottom of the hill, whence we came? It is the miracle of the peat bog. (Peat, by the way, is found only in Celtic countries because God realized the Celts were the only people on earth who drank so much that they would try to burn mud.) Our hill had once been a basin where constant flooding encouraged the growth of ferns and their ilk. Dead fern bodies accumulated in a waterlogged mass that finally even other ferns couldn't grow in. Sphagnum moss took over. This can grow in the vilest muck. Layer after layer of sphagnum was laid down until the bog began to rise above the level of the surrounding land. By all rights this mound should have begun to drain and turn itself into a nice dry hummock or knoll, but instead the collected sphagnum acted as a giant sponge and swelled prodigiously with rainwater so that after seven thousand or eight thousand years we had a convex swamp thirty feet high at its peak. We also had a stuck Llewellin. Crathorne charged to the rescue with his Range Rover and went down too. Then I put the Blazer in, because three is a lucky number. We spent an hour and a half winching one another out.

The only way across such mire is to use an actual boat anchor on the end of your winch line and pull yourself across, but it would have been irresponsible and dangerous for us to have tried something like that, plus we might have missed lunch. So we gave up four-wheeling. We took a drive around the Elan Valley reservoirs instead and paused to view the great Edwardian edifice of the Claerwen Dam. It looks like Hadrian's Wall never did but should have. The reservoirs are a sore point with the Welsh, however. Their water goes to Birmingham, England, where water rates are much lower than they are in Wales. Also, the reservoirs cover a cottage where Shelley lived in 1812, and the Welsh don't hold with throwing cold water into the windows of poets' houses.

And that was it for us. Sunday afternoon was waning, and we were all due back in London that night. From the Elan Valley we continued east via normal roads. On our way to the English frontier we stopped at Rhayader for a delicious lunch. There we were set upon by punk rockers and thrashed nearly to death.

Actually, that last sentence is a lie. I just put it in to keep readers from being jealous. I mean, we're out wallowing in fun all the time, while you have to stay home and buy magazines. So I thought if I told you we all got beat up, you wouldn't get mad at us and go buy *Motor Trend* or anything.

Besides, I'm an honorary Welshman now. And as Gerald the twelfth-century archdeacon of Brecon said in *Descriptio Cambriae* ("The Description of Wales"): "A formal oath never binds them. They have no respect for their plighted word, and the truth means nothing to them . . . To a people so cunning and crafty this seems no great burden, for they take it all very lightly."

BAD SPORTS

Fly-Fishing

(*Rod and Reel*, *1987*)

I'd never fly-fished. I'd done other kinds of fishing. I'd fished for bass. That's where I'd get far enough away from the dock so that people couldn't see there was no line on the pole, then drink myself blind in the rowboat. And I'd deep-sea fished. That's where the captain would get me blind before we'd even left the dock and I'd be the one who couldn't see the line. But I'd never fly-fished.

I'd always been of two minds about the sport. On the one hand, here's a guy standing in cold water up to his liver throwing the world's most expensive clothesline at trees. A full two-thirds of his time is spent untangling stuff, which he could be doing in the comfort of his own home with old shoelaces. The whole business costs like sin and requires heavier clothing. Furthermore it's conducted in the middle of blackfly season. Cast and swat. Cast and swat. Fly-fishing may be a sport invented by insects with fly fishermen as bait. And what does the truly sophisticated dry fly artist do when he finally bags a fish? He lets the fool thing go and eats baloney sandwiches instead.

On the other hand, fly-fishing did have its attractions. I love to waste time and money. I had ways to do this most of the year—hunting, skiing, renting summer houses in To-Hell-and-Gone Harbor for a Lebanon hostage's ransom. But, come spring, I was limited to cleaning up the yard. Even with a new Toro every two years and a lot of naps by the compost heap, it's hard to waste much time and money doing this. And then there's the gear needed for fly-fishing. I'm a sucker for anything that requires more equipment than I have sense. My workshop is furnished with the full panoply of Black & Decker power tools, all from one closet shelf I installed in 1979.

When I began to think about fly-fishing, I realized I'd never be content again until my den was cluttered with computerized robot fly-tying vises, space-age Teflon and ceramic knotless tapered leaders, sterling silver English fish scissors, and thirty-five volumes on the home life of the midge. And there was one other thing. I'm a normal male who takes an occasional nip; therefore, I love to put funny things on my head. Sometimes it's the nut dish, sometimes the spaghetti colander, but the hats I'd seen fly fishermen wear were funnier than either and I had to have one.

I went to Hackles & Tackles, an upscale dry fly specialty shop that also sells fish print wallpaper and cashmere V-neck sweaters with little trout on them. I got a graphite rod for about the price of a used car and a reel made out of the kind of exotic alloys that you can go to jail for selling to the Soviet Union. I also got one of those fishing vests that only comes down to the top of your beer gut and looks like you dressed in the dark and tried to put on your ten-year-old son's three-piece suit. And I purchased lots of monofilament and teensy hooks covered in auk down and moose lint and an entire L.L. Bean boat bag full of fly-fishing do-whats, hinky-doovers, and whatchamajigs.

I also brought home a set of fly-fishing how-to videotapes. This is the eighties, I reasoned, the age of video. What better way to take up a sport than from a comfortable armchair? That's where I'm at my best with most sports anyway.

There were three tapes. The first one claimed it would teach me to cast. The second would teach me to "advanced cast." And the third would tell me where trout live, how they spend their weekends, and what they'd order for lunch if there were underwater delicatessens for fish. I started the VCR and a squeaky little guy with an earnest manner and a double-funny hat came on, began heaving fly line around, telling me the secret to making beautiful casting loops is . . .

Whoever made these tapes apparently assumed I knew how to tie backing to reel and line to backing and leader to line and so on all the way out to the little feather and fuzz fish snack at the end. I didn't know how to put my rod together. I had to go to the children's section at the public library and check out *My Big Book of Fishing* and begin with how to open the package it all came in.

A triple granny got things started on the spool. After twelve hours and help from pop rivets and a tube of Krazy Glue, I managed an Albright knot between backing and line. But my version of a nail knot in the leader put Mr. Gordian of ancient Greek knot fame strictly on the shelf. It was the size of a hamster and resembled one of the Woolly Bugger flies I'd bought except in the size you use for killer whales. I don't want to talk about blood knots and tippets. There I was with two pieces of invisible plastic, trying to use fingers the size of a man's thumb while holding a magnifying glass and a Tensor lamp between my teeth and gripping nasty tangles of monofilament with each big toe. My girlfriend had to come over and cut me out of this with pinking shears. Personally, I'm going to get one of those nine-year-old Persian kids that they use to make incredibly tiny knots in fine Bukhara rugs and just take him with me on all my fishing trips.

What I really needed was a fly-fishing how-to video narrated by Mister Rogers. This would give me advice about which direction to wind the reel and why I should never try to drive a small imported car while wearing boot-foot waders. (Because when I stepped on the accelerator I also stepped on the brake and the clutch.)

I rewound Mr. Squeaky and started over. I was supposed to keep my rod tip level and keep my rod swinging in a ninety-degree arc. When I snapped my wrist forward I was giving one quick flick of a blackjack to the skull of a mugging victim. When I snapped my wrist back I was sticking my thumb over my shoulder and telling my brother-in-law to get the hell out of here and I mean right now, Buster. Though it wasn't explained with quite so much poetry.

Then I was told to try these things with a "yarn rod." This was something else I'd bought at the tackle shop. It looked like a regular rod tip from a two-piece rod but with a cork handle. You run a bunch of bright orange yarn through the guides and flip it around. It's supposed to imitate the action of a fly rod in slow motion. I don't know about that, but I do know you can catch and play a nine-pound house cat on a yarn rod, and it's great sport. They're hard to land, however. And I understand cat fishing is strictly catch and release if they're under twenty inches or belong to your girlfriend.

Then I went back to the television and heard about stance, loop control, straight line casts, slack line casts, stripping, mending, and giving myself enough room when practicing in the yard so I wouldn't get tangled in my neighbor's bird feeder.

After sixty minutes of videotape, seven minutes of yarn rod practice, twenty-five minutes of cat fishing, and several beers, I felt I was ready. I picked up the fin tickler and laid out a couple of loops that weren't half bad if I do say so myself. I'll bet I cast almost three times before making macramé out of my weight forward Cortland 444. This wasn't so hard.

I also watched the advanced tape. But Squeaky had gone grad school on me. He's throwing reach casts, curve casts, roll casts, steeple casts, and casts he calls squiggles and stutters. He's writing his name with the line in the air. He's making his dry fly look like the Blue Angels. He's pitching things forehand, backhand, and between his wader legs. And, through the magic of video editing, every time his hook-tipped dust kitty hits the water he lands a trout the size of a canoe.

The videotape about trout themselves wasn't much use either. It's hard to get excited about where trout feed when you know that the only way you're going to be able to get a fly to that place is by throwing your fly box at it.

I must say, however, all the tapes were informative. "Nymphs and streamers" are not, as it turns out, naked mythological girls decorating the high school gym with crepe paper. And I learned that the part of fly-fishing I'm going to be best at is naming the flies:

Woolly Hatcatcher
Blue-Wing Earsnag
Overhanging Brush Muddler
Royal Toyota Hatchback
O'Rourke's Ouchtail
P.J.'s Live Worm-'n-Bobber

By now I'd reached what I think they call a "learning plateau." That is, if I was going to catch a fish with a fly rod, I had to either go get in the water or open the fridge and toss hooks at Mrs. Paul's frozen haddock fillets.

I made reservations at a famous fishing lodge on the Au Sable River in Michigan. When I got there and found a place to park among the Saabs and Volvos the proprietor said I was just a few days early for the Hendrikson hatch. There is, I see, one constant in all types of fishing, which is when the fish are biting, which is almost-but-not-quite-now.

I looked pretty good making false casts in the lodge parking lot. I mean no one doubled over with mirth. But most of the other two thousand young professionals fishing this no-kill stretch of the Au Sable were pretty busy checking to make sure that their trout shirts were color coordinated with their Reebok wading sneakers.

When I stepped in the river, however, my act came to pieces. My line hit the water like an Olympic belly flop medalist. I hooked four "tree trout" in three minutes. My back casts had people ducking for cover in Traverse City and Grosse Pointe Farms. Somebody ought to tie a dry fly that looks like a Big Mac. Then there'd be an excuse for the hook winding up in my mouth instead of the fish's. The only thing I could manage to get a drag-free float on was me after I stepped in a hole. And the trout? The trout laughed.

The next day was worse. I could throw tight loops. I could sort of aim. I could even make a gentle presentation and get the line to lay right every so often. But when I tried to do all of these things at once, I went mental. I looked like Leonard Bernstein conducting "Flight of the Bumblebee" in fast forward. I was driving tent pegs with my rod tip. My slack casts wrapped around my thighs. My straight line casts went straight into the back of my neck. My improved surgeon's loops looked like full Windsors. I had wind knots in everything including my Red Ball suspenders. And two hundred dollars' worth of fly floatant, split shot, Royal Coachmen, and polarized sunglasses fell off my body and were swept downstream.

Then, mirabile dictu, I hooked a fish. I was casting some I-forget-the-name nymph and clumsily yanking it in when my rod tip bent and my pulse shot into trade deficit numbers. I lifted the rod, the first thing I'd done right in two days, and the trout actually leaped out of the water as if it were trying for a *Field & Stream* playmate centerfold. I heard my voice go up three octaves until I sounded like my little sister in the middle of a puppy litter, "Ooooo that's-a-boy, that's-a-baby, yesssssss, come to daddy, wooogie-woogie-woo." It was a rainbow and I'll bet it was seven inches long. All right, five. Anyway, when I grabbed the thing some of it stuck out both ends of my hand. I haven't been so happy since I passed my driver's license exam.

So I'm a fly fisherman now. Of course I'm not an expert yet. But I'm working on the most important part of fly-fishing technique—boring the hell out of anybody who'll listen.

BIRD HUNTING

(*Men's Journal, 1994*)

Some of the best bird covers in New Brunswick are old garbage dumps. The word *cover,* used in the sense of hunting ground, is a variant of *covert* although there is nothing MI-6ish or Mossad-like about game birds as far as I can tell.

Birds do not go to the dump because they're thinking that's the last place I'd look for creatures of natural beauty and untamed grace. Nor do they need to. Given my faculties as a sportsman and the skills of my dog, birds could hide in the foyers of New Brunswick bed-and-breakfasts, in bowls of wax fruit.

Birds go to the dump because—I hate to break this to Friends of the Earth—animals have no aesthetics. Eels congregate in the sludge on the bottom of New York harbor. Trout bite on feather, fur, and tinsel dry flies as ugly as Barbie clothes. To a raccoon a trash can is Paris in May. Rabbits desert the most elaborate nature refuges to visit your messy and unweeded vegetable garden. Wild geese adore golf courses, even the unfashionable public kind. And there is nothing, it seems, more gorgeous and fascinating to a deer than the headlights of an oncoming car.

Considering animal taste, I'm not sure I want to know why birds are attracted to dumps. And considering my own taste—gin slings, madras pants, Ed McBain novels, Petula Clark recordings—I'm not sure I want to know why I'm attracted to bird hunting. But I will try to make sense of the matter.

I've been shooting in New Brunswick for a decade. Usually eight or ten of us make an outing in the fall. We are an ordinary lot, halfway through life's actuarial leach field and moderately well fixed. We're not likely to be tapped for a Benetton ad.

Some of us are avid hunters and deadly shots, and some of us had a gun last year that didn't fit and needed a different choke and the safety kept sticking. I was using the wrong size shot and too light a load. I'm beginning to get arthritis in my shoulder. I had a new bifocal prescription. My boots hurt. The sun got in my eyes.

This is not one of those men-go-off-in-the-woods hunting trips full of drink, flatulence, and lewd Hillary Clinton jokes. For one thing, some of us aren't men. A couple of us aren't even Republicans. We pack neckties, sports coats, skirts, and makeup (although I don't think anyone wears all four). There is little of the Cro-Magnon in this crowd. Though there *is* something about three bottles of wine apiece with dinner and six-egg breakfasts . . . Did somebody step on a carp? And you've heard about Hillary whispering to Bill, "Give me ten inches and hurt me!" So he made love to her twice and appointed David Gergen White House communications director.

Our New Brunswick sojourn is not a wilderness adventure either. We're no Patagonia-clad apostles of the Rio Summit out getting our faces rubbed in Mother Nature's leg hairs. And we're too old to need a thirty-mile hike, a wet bedroll, and a dinner of trail mix and puddle water to make us think life is authentic. If we'd wanted to push human endurance to its limits and face the awesome challenges of the natural elements in their uncivilized state, we could have stayed home with the kids.

No. We spend the first half of the shoot in the deep woods but at a good lodge with an excellent chef. The chef not only cooks six-egg breakfasts and Bordeaux-absorbent dinners but packs delightful lunches for us, for example moose sandwiches, which are much better—also smaller—than they sound.

For the second half of the shoot we drive to the Bay of Fundy and stay at a handsome inn where the sensible innkeepers bring out the old bedspreads and second-string towels so there will be no need to apologize for the mess left by gun cleaning, dog brushing, and male pattern baldness. The innkeepers also let us into their kitchen to cook what we've killed. Some of us may not be brilliant shotgunners, but we are all serious game cooks even though I'm not really used to cooking on a commercial gas range and those copper-bottom pans the inn has heat up, I think, too fast and shouldn't there be some kind of government standards or warning labels or something concerning butter flammability?

The Regal Woodcock

What we are hunting in New Brunswick is mainly woodcock, *Scolopax minor,* sometimes called "bog sucker" or "mud bat"—a chunky, neckless, blunt-winged, mulch-colored bird with a very long beak and a body the size, shape, and heft of a beefsteak tomato. Rereading that sentence I see I have failed to capture in prose the full measure of the woodcock's physical attractiveness. Probably because it looks like a knee-walking shorebird in urgent need of Jenny Craig. It does have lovely eyes. And a wonderful personality, too, for all I know. Anyway, the woodcock is, in fact, a cousin of the sandpiper and the snipe but makes its home on less expensive real estate.

Woodcock live in the alder patches that occupy, in horizon-knocking profusion, the numberless streambeds and vast marsh bottoms of New Brunswick's flat, damp topography. Alders are a pulpwood shrub whose branches grow in muddled sprays like bad flower arrangements. Hunting in young alder thickets is like walking through something with a consistency between Jell-O and high hurdles. Old alder thickets, which grow as high as twelve feet, present grim, decaying vaults of face-grabbing, hat-snatching limb tangles. But the alder thickets where the woodcock nest and feed are those, like us, in their middle years. And these have all the bad features of alders young and old plus a greasy mud footing and foliage which, even in late fall, is as dense as salad.

Once such a mess of alders has been entered it becomes impossible to tell the time of day or where you are supposed to be going or from whence you came, and the only thing you know about your direction is it's not the one your dog is headed in.

Every now and then, deep within an alder patch, you come upon a dump. The overturned cars and abandoned refrigerators are, at least, landmarks. And if you've been in the alders long enough, they're a positive delight to the eye. The old woodsman's adage about getting lost is "always go uphill." This is a problem in New Brunswick, which doesn't have much in the way of uphills; indeed the entire province seems to be on a downhill slope. Anyway, from my own experience, the only thing going uphill when you're lost does is give you a better view of no place you've ever seen before.

The woodcock are in the alders because the soil there is full of earthworms, which is what woodcock eat. The flavor of all birds is influenced by diet. A Canada goose shot in a field of corn is a treat. A Canada goose shot on the fourth green and filled with fertilizer and lawn chemicals is disgusting. Fish-eating ducks taste like fish that have been eaten by ducks. And I'm told "eating crow" is not an empty phrase. Woodcock are delicious. This raises the worrying thought that we should really be hunting and frying night crawlers. They are certainly easier to find and kill. But worm-digging gear is not going to look stylish in an Orvis catalog.

You need a dog to hunt woodcock. Most pointing dogs can be trained to do it, but the breed of choice is the Brittany, a knee-high orange and white canine about as long as he is tall with no tail worth the mention and looking like an English springer spaniel with a better barber and a marathon running hobby.

Brittanys were bred in the eponymous province of France about 150 years ago specifically for woodcock hunting. They have a character that is both remote and excitable—yappy and grave at the same time. Brittanys are very intelligent, whatever that means in a dog. Does a very intelligent dog have a unified theory of table scraps or a good and logical explanation for humping your leg?

What a Brittany has, in fact, is an intense, irrational, foolish, almost human desire to hunt woodcock. He possesses several techniques. He can run into the alder cover and flush a bird that is much too far away. Flushing is what a hunter calls it when a dog scares a bird silly and makes it fly. The bird will then fly in any direction that your gun isn't pointed. This as opposed to pointing, which is when a dog scares a bird even sillier and makes it sit down. The Brittany can also run into the alder cover and *point* a bird that is much too far away. When a Brittany points he goes absolutely rigid and still (and does so in a way that makes him look like he's about to hike a dog football or moon a dog sorority house rather than in that paw up, tail out, King Tut tomb painting posture dogs have in *Sports Afield* photographs or on place mats from the Ralph Lauren Home Store). The Brittany is wearing a bell around his neck. The idea is to keep track of the dog in the woods by following the noise of the bell. Then, when the dog goes on point, the bell will stop ringing, and you're supposed to head directly toward the complete silence. You see the problem. Brittanys may be intelligent, but the people who thought up the bell were, to put it bluntly, French.

The Brittany can also do what it's supposed to do and hunt right in front of you—"working close" as it's known—in which case he'll walk over the top of the woodcock leaving you to flush it yourself by almost stepping on the thing, whereupon it will fly straight up in your face with an effect as nightmarish as a remake of Hitchcock's *The Birds* starring Ted Danson and Whoopi Goldberg.

When everything goes exactly right, which is none of the time, the Brittany will go on point someplace where I can see him do it. I'll "walk up" the woodcock, which will take flight at an obliging distance. The woodcock has powerful breast muscles and is capable of almost vertical ascent. It will rise above the alders beating its wings so fast that its feathers make a loud whistling sound. Then, in a motion called towering, the bird will pause for a moment before flying away. This is when I take my shot. And, assuming that the alders haven't jammed my hat down over my eyes or knocked the gun out of my hand and assuming that I remembered to load the gun in the first place and that I haven't stepped on the dog while walking up the bird and gotten myself bitten on the ankle, then—if my hand is steady and my aim is true and nothing blocks the way—I'll miss.

I regard it as armed shopping, a gentle pastime, if you think about it. Going to the grocery store is what's bloodthirsty. Consider all the Perdue oven stuffers you've bought for dinner over the years. How many of them had any chance of getting away? You mighty nimrod, you—every chicken you stalked, you killed. Whereas for me, there's hardly a bird that comes before the barrels of my gun that doesn't get off scot free. Nay, better than free. The bird receives an education about what those orange and white and hairy—and pink and winded and pudgy—things are doing in the woods. I am a university for birds.

Birds, of course, do get shot on these trips, even if not by my gun. And the dog is actually as important to finding dead birds as he is to missing live ones. Woodcock possess almost perfect camouflage, and, while difficult to see when living, they—for some reason—disappear completely into the leaf mold once they've been killed. It is hard to imagine what Darwinian benefit there is to an invisible corpse. Though there may be one. If the thing that eats you can't find you when you're ready to be eaten, maybe that gourmand will give up on the whole enterprise. It's a modification of the oyster defense mechanism, which is to look incredibly snotlike at mealtime. Anyway, there are a number of interesting evolutionary questions about woodcock. How'd they lose the beachfront condo? Why would anyone migrate to New Brunswick? And how come they eat worms? Is it a bet or something? According to Guy de la Valdène's authoritative text on *Scolopax minor, Making Game* (Clark City Press), the woodcock has lived in North America since the middle Pleistocene, for a million and a half years. But there were no earthworms on this continent until the seventeenth century. They were introduced in potted plants from Europe and Asia. Before 1600 were the woodcock sending out for Chinese? Also, birds are supposed to be direct descendants of dinosaurs. So why aren't woodcock extinct? My guess is it's because whatever killed the dinosaurs was wearing new bifocals. I don't suppose we'll ever know for sure. Any more than we'll ever know for sure whether the tyrannosaurus went: *PEEP*

That dogs are able to find birds, alive or dead, is not surprising. Dogs more or less "see" the world through their olfactory sense. (Therefore what I look like to a dog after a long day in the alders is something I won't dwell on.) Woodcock—to judge by my dog's behavior—must smell to a Brittany like coffee in the morning or Arpège at night.

The surprising thing is that hunting dogs don't leap on the live birds or gobble the dead ones. The whole point of breeding bird dogs is to come up with a pooch who—contrary to every imaginable predator instinct—*doesn't* catch his prey. He lets you, with your shotgun, do it for him. (Or not, as the case may be. It is a fact known only to bad shots that dogs smirk).

Suppose you sat a seven-year-old boy on the end of a dock with a fishing pole, and every time the bobber went under you grabbed the rod and landed the fish. Suppose you got the child to put up with this all day and not only put up with it but like it.

V. S. Naipaul, in his history of Trinidad, said (apropos of what I don't remember and God knows why V. S. Naipaul, of all people, would bring up the subject) that Sir Robert Dudley, circa 1600, illegitimate son of the Earl of Leicester, was noted "for being the first of all that taught a dog to sit in order to catch partridges." A remarkable man was Bob.

And pointing is only half of what dog breeders have accomplished. The dog also retrieves. Imagine—to put this in terms comprehensible to the lowest common denominator of male readers—you found a Victoria's Secret model in your front yard, wearing her professional attire, and intensely interested in affection. And suppose you carefully picked her up, being sure not to hug her too tightly or return any intimate caresses, and delivered her to your next-door neighbor, the guy who's had your Skill Saw since last February and always lets his crabgrass go to seed.

I have no idea what dogs get out of hunting. And, come to think of it, I don't have much idea what people get out of hunting either.

Partly it's a social thing. All of us on the trip are good friends, and it's nice to be off together in a place for which our bosses and offices can never quite figure out the area code. ("Where was that you said you were going? New Zealand? New Orleans? New Guinea? New Jersey?") But we could go to each other's houses and turn off the phones and run through the shrubbery in our old clothes, if we wanted.

There's nature appreciation. But, though New Brunswick has some appealing coastal vistas and some handsome salmon rivers, the province is not a scenic wonder, and the land we hunt is hardly pretty. Still, we do appreciate it. There's something about being out in nature with a purpose—even if that purpose is only to pester dogs and scare feathered creatures—that makes you pay more attention to the outside world. A hike is such a pointless thing, no matter how wonderful the view. You might love the way your house looks but you wouldn't just walk around and around in it. When you hunt you have to keep a careful eye on weather, terrain, foliage, and dangerous animals such as me if I happen to be in the cover with you swinging my gun around in every direction trying to get the safety to release. There's even a religious aspect to detailed examination of the outdoors. The universe, on close inspection, seems hardly to have been an accident. Or, if it is an accident, it's certainly a complexly ordered one—as if you dropped mushrooms, ham, truffles, raw eggs, melted butter, and a hot skillet on the kitchen floor and wound up with a perfect omelet. That said, alder patches are something God created on a Monday, after a big weekend.

Hunting also produces a good, solid sense of false accomplishment. After a long day of bird getaways and gun bungles, of yelling at dogs and yourself, you really think you've done something. You don't get this feeling from any other recreation. Probably it's a throwback to the million years or so that man spent thumbing through the large stone pages of the Paleolithic L. L. Bean catalog. The cave paintings of Lascaux, after all, depict bison hunts, not tennis matches.

The fact that my friends and I don't have to hunt to get food may actually be our reason for hunting. Fun can be defined as "anything you don't have to do." Or is that right? You have to eat. And eating is the one sensible (if you're not counting calories or the fire extinguisher mess from the little problem I had with sautéing) thing that we do on this trip.

Woodcock, like most game meat, is almost fatless and can be cooked as rare as steak without a chicken tartare effect. Woodcock has a slightly liverish flavor, but it is liver to make a Neoplatonist of you. This is the cosmic ideal of liver, liver in the mind of God or, anyway, in the mind of Mom—liver that tastes like your mom thought you should think it tasted.

The only real meat on a woodcock is the breast. When cleaning a woodcock you can split the breast skin with your thumbs and pull the muscle off the carcass. Take this, cut it in half, and roll the halves around in a hot frying pan in good olive oil with a little salt and pepper and maybe a dash of Worcestershire sauce and a sprinkle of rosemary, and you've got . . . something nobody else in the house will touch. It's ugly as a sea slug and smells like tripe, but it tastes superb. We use the drumsticks as hors d' oeuvres, a kind of snob's answer to buffalo wings. Really serious woodcock cooks sauté the "trail," the intestines, and serve them on toast. We're not that serious.

We have meals of high-savored woodcock. And we have meals of delicate-tasting ruffed grouse, whose meat is to Kentucky Fried as the fresh-baked baguettes of Provence are to ballpark hot dog rolls. And we have meals of wild duck, the piquant flesh of which bears not the slightest resemblance to the Donald-flavored item that's bought in stores. Served with all these are steaming heaps of fiddlehead ferns picked from the nearby woods and bowls of piping New Brunswick potatoes, small as golf balls and sweet as pies, and rolls and buns and scones and jiggling plates of wild foxberry jelly and pots, tubs, and buckets of strong drink and desserts aplenty besides.

Here at last is something I really *am* good at. I can tuck in with the best of them. And I get better every year. I have the new holes punched in my belt tongues and the let-out pants seats to prove it.

When dinner is over we yaw and waddle away from the table and back to our rooms for one more drink or five and to make some truly inventive excuses for our shooting—"I was thinking about my ex-wife and I pulled the trigger too soon"—and to tell each other various bits of highly improbable avian lore. Then we are up again at dawn to hunt.

The Noble Grouse and the Lordly Duck

Ruffed grouse, or partridge as it's called in New England, *Bonasa umbellus,* is an airborne special forces commando chicken. It's about the size of a chicken. It looks like a chicken. It acts like a chicken—scratches, pecks, and does a chicken walk. But it's decked out in camouflage khakis and browns. And it can fly, which is something a chicken can't do. (I know because a fighter pilot friend of mine was once in a argument at the officers' club as to whether chickens couldn't fly or just didn't want to. Someone drove to a local chicken farm, bought a chicken, got in an open cockpit biplane, took the biplane to three thousand feet, and tossed the chicken out. To this day there is a large dent in one of the Quonset huts on that air base. But that story's better after dinner.)

Grouse prefer a more gentlemanly sort of country than woodcock. Grouse like old apple trees on overgrown farmland, brushy edges of conifer forests, and patches of hawthorn shrubs. These last are filled with sinister barbs, but you don't have to go into them. You can send the dog. Nicer hunting ground does not mean nicer hunting, however. I have been consistently outwitted by ruffed grouse. Not that this is any compliment to the bird's intelligence. I have been consistently outwitted by my VCR and my tuxedo bow tie. Nonetheless, for an animal with a . . . well, with a bird brain, the grouse is sagacious. Three of us were hunting a field one afternoon, and the man on the right put up a grouse. Instead of flying away and inviting a shot, the grouse hopped over the man's head and flew straight for the middle hunter at eye level, thereby keeping either from being able to shoot without hitting the other. Repeating the tactic, the bird darted around the middle hunter and flew at me. And, when the bird got past me, it broke into every-which-way flight maneuvers and reached the woods untouched. A grouse can walk almost as fast as it can fly and will trot away from most encounters, silent and invisible. The bird rarely holds. And grouse droppings, or "chalk," smell more like grouse than grouse do so you'll often find your dog has spent ten minutes pointing bird shit.

When the grouse does get up, it flies with a tremendous bass note flutter of wings, a tremolo played on a tuba, a noise so startling that you're likely to shoot your hat.

As do many game animals, grouse seem to check the calendar. They can be flapping around in scads and passels the day before hunting season opens, and the next morning they're as rare as intelligent television. The locals in New Brunswick hunt grouse on the ground, waiting until the birds come out on the country roads at dusk to gravel, that is, to swallow the small stones that birds need for their gizzards, to break up food in lieu of chewing. Then the locals blow the heads off the grouse with full-choke twelve-gauge shotguns. It's very unsporting to shoot a game bird on the ground, and we disdain this manner of hunting utterly. Unless we need the grouse for dinner. Or we've had a bad day. Or it's after 3:00 p.m.

The peculiar thing about grouse is their learning curve. Savvy as they are where they're hunted, in locales where they're rarely or never shot, they are sap-green patsies. Some of our usual party went to northern Maine a dozen years ago to hunt grouse at a lodge where most of the customers were after deer, moose, or bear. We found the grouse sitting in rows on tree limbs. Spruce grouse, which are darker and differently marked, are famous for this kind of behavior. Spruce grouse not only look like chickens but are dumb enough to fly to a Sunday dinner and surrender. But these were ruffed grouse and no amount of shouts and dog barks would budge them. We had to throw sticks to make them fly, and, when even this didn't work and we broke down and shot one off its perch, the next bird in line just shuffled over and took the deceased's place.

One of our New Brunswick guides, Tom, who is Indian, says that when he was a kid his family was too poor to afford shotgun shells and he used to hunt grouse by sneaking up behind them with a noose on the end of a stick. I wouldn't believe this from anybody but Tom, who is a chief of one of the local bands of Micmac and a practitioner of traditional medicine and spent a year traveling around the United States on a Ford Foundation grant, comparing tribal religious ceremonies. Tom has a shocking ability to see things in the woods and get up close to them. And he can walk through an alder patch without getting poked in the eye by a stick. Tom is a very convincing man.

Unfortunately, Tom is also a very convincing man when you're out with him in the far middle of those god-awful gloomy alder thickets and the sun has gone down and you've got no idea how to get back to the car and he starts telling you about the *Tjno,* a giant Indian who turned wild and if you stumble into his territory he'll catch you and make you work for him. That is, if you're a woman or a child. "Husbands," said Tom, "the Tjno eats." Tjnos are now, I suppose, mostly employed as divorce lawyers.

There are also *Pugalatmooj* in the woods—little people who taught the Micmac how to make canoes and arrowheads. They sound a bit like leprechauns but more useful and less likely to make fools of themselves appearing on St. Patrick's Day cards.

Another of our guides, Robert, is a retired RCMP officer and an expert on ducks. He can call ducks, shoot ducks, make duck decoys, name from memory every kind of duck found in North America, and give each kind its Latin moniker. Robert can tell you everything you want to know about ducks except why anyone would ever go hunt them.

The idea of duck hunting is to get up about the time that people who are having fun go to bed and get dressed in dirty flannels, itchy thermal underwear, muddy hip boots, clammy rain ponchos, and various other layers of insulation and waterproofing, then clamber, trudge, wade, paddle, stumble, flounder, and drag yourself miles into a swamp while carrying coolers, shell boxes, lunch buckets, flashlights, hand warmers, Buck knives, camp stoves, toilet paper, a couple of dogs, and forty or fifty imitation ducks, then sit in a wet hole concealed by brush cuttings and pine boughs until it's dark again and you can go home.

Meanwhile the weather will either be incredibly good, in which case the ducks will be flying in the clear sky thousands of feet above you, or incredibly bad, in which case the ducks will be landing right in front of you but you won't be able to see them. Not that any actual ducks are required for this activity, and often none are sighted. Sometimes it's worse when they are. The terrible thing about duck hunting is that everyone you're with can see you shoot and see what you're shooting at, and it is almost impossible to come up with a likely excuse for blasting a decoy in half.

Last year I was in Bosnia covering the war there for *Rolling Stone*. And I was hunkered down in a muddy trench behind a pile of shrubbery and tree branches watching tiny Serbs attack in the distance. "This seems familiar," I thought. It was, indeed, the very image of duck hunting (although for some reason, this time, the ducks had the guns).

And sure enough, one month later to the day I was hunkered down in a muddy trench behind a pile of shrubbery and tree branches with Robert and my pals. It was pissing down rain. I'd forgotten my pocket flask. Somebody had left the sandwiches in the bottom of the canoe and they'd turned into bread and mayonnaise soup. The glass liner had broken inside the coffee thermos. Everybody was out of cigarettes. And the dog had rolled in something awful. Of ducks, there were none. Not even any bottom-feeding coot, the recipe for which is

PLANKED COOT

> *Arrange bird on a 1-inch-thick kiln-dried oak plank. Roast in oven for two hours at 350°, basting every 20 minutes with a red wine, olive oil, vinegar, and garlic clove marinade. Throw the coot away and eat the plank.*

It is only natural that war and hunting are of a kidney. Hunting has been intimately connected with warfare since the beginning of civilization. And before the beginning of civilization there probably wasn't a difference. The traditional leisure activity of archers and lancers and knights and such, when not killing people, was to kill other things.

We don't need hunting in the modern world. It makes the wilderness so primitive. It upsets actresses and sensitive undergraduate types. And, anyway, we can easily bag a cheeseburger out the window of our car. But we do need war. At least I assume we do—to judge by the amount of it that's going on in the world at any given moment. And it's my theory that the entire purpose of the annual hunting trip is to make war look, comparatively speaking, like fun.

Deep-Sea Fishing

(*Men's Journal, 1992*)

Imagine a serious, highly competitive, physically demanding outdoor sport that you can play while sitting in a chair drinking beer. Deep-sea fishing is as close as a middle-aged man gets to heaven—unless he's not watching his cholesterol.

I was on the boat *Lucky Too* with Captain Jay Weed and mate Scott Genereux. We were sixteen or eighteen miles out of Key West, just past the big coral reef that runs from left to right below the Florida Keys like the line under an arithmetic problem. The seas were tall and disorderly. The water was such a deep Brooks Brothers suit color that it looked false—blue-tinted contact lenses on a brown-eyed woman. The wind was up and the sky was filled with tumbling dryer loads of clouds. The *Lucky Too* is a thirty-four-foot fiberglass cabin cruiser with a 212-horsepower diesel engine. It's purpose-built for sport fishing. But even with this much size and power the boat was topping and bobbling and slobbering around.

Captain Jay was looking for fish. I have no idea how. Maybe he knows their ways from years on the open sea, or maybe they leave their phone numbers on channel buoys. Mate Scott was walking on the heaving deck as though it were so much Kansas sidewalk. He was baiting hooks and tending lines and generally exhibiting the kind of nautical competence that makes such landlubbing forty-four-year-olds as myself feel like shoes for an eel.

Everybody on the boat had a job. My job was to not throw up. This is the one, entire skill to being a deep-sea fisherman—not punting your bran muffins. Though you have to have a thick spot in your wallet, too. Deep-sea fishing isn't cheap. A good boat charter costs between $400 and $550 a day plus six-packs and a lunch to blow and a minimum 15 percent tip to the mate if you expect to go out on that boat again and not wind up trolling schools of pizza anchovies. I must admit I was good at deep-sea fishing. What with a prescription anti-seasickness patch behind my ear and *Men's Journal* footing the bill, I was, in fact, a regular damn athlete.

We were fishing with four rods, seven-foot-long fiberglass poles as thick as rake handles at the butt. Until something bites, these rods sit in holders built into the side rails of the boat. Captain Jay trolled at four or five knots (a knot being pretty much like a mile-per-hour, but more expensive). The lines from the rods are baited with fish bigger than what I used to catch and cook in my Midwestern boyhood. Two lines drag directly behind the boat, one on the surface and another weighted on a "deep troll" rig to fish sixty or eighty feet under water. The remaining two lines are held away from the boat by a pair of steel outriggers, which lean over the ocean like high-tension wire towers built by drunks.

The *Lucky Too* has, on its aft deck, a pair of fighting chairs—barber chairs without the barbers. At the front of a fighting chair's seat cushion, in line with your crotch, is a socket to hold the base of the fishing rod. Now and then there'd be a sizzle, and line would start hurling off one of the reels. Scott would grab the rod, make sure it was a fish on the hook and not a lobster pot or an overboard beer cooler, then hand it to me. I'd fit the rod into the socket and get busy.

There's a lot of excitement when a fish strikes, most of it for the fish, of course. Some game fish leap out of the water when hooked. Some even leap as high as fish do in the photographs on charter boat brochures. And a big fish will run the monofilament out like a teenage daughter on a Visa card credit line. You reel a few times first, to set the hook. After that you "work" the fish with a pumping motion—pulling back on the rod with all your weight then reeling like the world's champion egg white stiffener as you bring the rod back down. It's important not to give the fish any slack, though we're talking strictly in physical terms. You can have any kind of emotional relationship you want with the fish.

As soon as you've reeled as much line as you can, the fish will run it out again and you'll pull back on the rod and start over. You do that between a dozen and a hundred times while trying not to think to yourself, "If it weren't such a big fish and I weren't paying so much to catch it, this would be as much fun as pushing a stalled car to the nearest turnpike exit."

We were fishing for sailfish, which, had we caught any, we would have thrown back. There aren't enough sailfish anymore, and they are so prized as a catch that most sportsmen let them go. This probably sounds insane if you're not a fisherman, but that's the "catch and release" philosophy: don't kill these animals, just annoy the hell out of them. We were also fishing for mackerel, especially the big king mackerel or kingfish. These would be sold cheap on the dock because mackerel are, frankly, very mackerel-flavored. Smaller fish such as cero mackerel, little sharks, et cetera, would also be thrown back. There is, all told, a certain futility to deep-sea fishing. But it's a satisfying futility, like having sex with birth control.

Hooking a big barracuda was very satisfying indeed. Very futile, too. I mean, I wasn't going to eat the thing. Barracuda taste like a cat-food salad, and they give you ciguatera, an awful disease. And I wasn't going to get it mounted as a trophy. Why would I have something that's as ugly as a divorce hanging on my wall? I just wanted to haul this scaly SOB up to the stern and give him a fish version of an IRS audit.

I'd been losing kingfish to barracuda all afternoon. A thirty-pound king mackerel would take the bait, jump in the air in a manner spectacular enough to be worth exaggerating later, and put up an admirable (if you admire fish) fight. Then I'd begin reeling it in and here'd come the barracuda. They'd snap and flash and trouble the water. By the time I got my mackerel into the boat, I'd have only half a fish and not the cheerful half either. If I got a barracuda itself on the line, its own brothers, its pals, its school-of-fish mates would do the same thing, gobbling cannibal chunks of flesh. Barracuda are the lawyers of the sea.

But the big barracuda I caught must have come off the William Kennedy Smith defense team. There wasn't a bite mark on him. He was about three and a half feet long. And he weighed twenty-some pounds, most of which was jaw muscle and the rest of which was teeth. Of course we let him go. Anything as nasty as that must serve some purpose in maintaining the balance of the earth's ecosystem. Probably it eats ecologists.

You see, deep-sea fishing has nothing to do with the enchantments of nature. Our friend and fellow intellectual the dolphin, for instance. With the help of various activist groups he has achieved everything except the vote and abortion rights. But out in blue water the dolphin is a fish thief and welfare cheat. A hooked game fish is an easy mugging, a finned food stamp to a dolphin. Barracuda take a percentage, *vigorish.* But a dolphin makes one swipe at a kingfish the size of a golf bag—a kingfish you've been fighting for half an hour—and leaves nothing but the head. Anybody who's seen this will think again before getting into the Sea World swim tank with smiling, playful Flipper.

Nor does deep-sea fishing have anything to do with nature's brilliant design. I watched for an hour while the same tern flew down and snatched our bait and then flew away until the monofilament line yanked the fish from its beak. Then the tern would come back and do it again. Like a modern American with a government benefit, the tern couldn't figure out there was a string attached.

Deep-sea fishing is about nature that is mean and stupid. And let us not forget futile. I suppose this is what Hemingway was getting at in *The Old Man and the Sea.* (Though Ernie could have sent in a dolphin as soon as the codger hooked the marlin and saved us all some reading time in high school.)

Mean, stupid, futile—nature and middle-aged men have a lot in common. This is one clue to the pleasures of deep-sea fishing. And another clue is that, in order to deep-sea fish, you have to travel to someplace far away from wives, children, jobs, bills, and stationary exercise bicycles—Costa Rica, Cabo San Lucas, Bimini, Cozumel, or the like. I picked Key West because I'd had fun there in the 1970s. At least I think I did. It's all blurry now. But I remember catching record-size hangovers in bars with three bathrooms: "Men," "Women," and "Drugs." It was a dirty little island back then, populated with the flotsam of the seven seas and the jetsam of trailer parks uncounted.

But I hadn't seen Key West in almost ten years. The place has changed. Time-share resorts have been built where historic liquor stores once stood. Tennis courts blot the swamps. And there's a Santa Fe–style restaurant where a perfectly good parking lot used to be. Key West has become a "travel destination," filled with—of all things—families. There are families everywhere, ambulating in sunburned clumps: fussing mom, bored kids, dad with his eyeball fused to the camcorder. And they're wearing clothes in colors from the spectrum of visible light's dreaded "vacation band." These are resort clothes, clothes with too many zippers, too many drawstrings, too many pleats, buttons, pouches, snaps, pockets, buckles, straps, epaulets, and elasticized hems; clothes so divorced from normal sartorial function that the Bermuda shorts might as well have three leg holes. And every item of apparel is covered with designer logos like smallpox scars.

Scattered among the families are double-scrubbed, peach-faced college students, fun-having as hard as they can, getting mirth-filled and perky on three light beers. It's amazing how decent, middle-class Americans, enjoying themselves in a harmless way, create a more repulsive atmosphere than dope smugglers, drunks, sex deviants, and cokeheads ever did. Key West's main street, Duval, used to have five or six terrible bars, two flophouses, and a Cuban lunch counter. It is now flanked with unbroken lines of souvenir T-shirt stores. Sample slogan: "My Buns Got Toasted in Key West."

In the midst of these emporiums is local sing-along king Jimmy Buffett's Margaritaville,™ a sanitary and wholesome nightspot with menu items named after Jimmy's songs. It is so different from the places in Key West where Buffett actually used to drink that the device of simile is strained. Suppose the present-day Elizabeth Taylor were given her original part in a remake of *National Velvet.* It is that different.

Margaritaville™ has a souvenir T-shirt store of its own, naturally, where all manner of Buffett memorabilia may be purchased. What a shame this never occurred to the great musicians of the past. Think what Wagner could have done with a Götterdämmerung Outlet—adjustable Valkyrie hats with foam rubber horns, life-size inflatable Rhine Maidens, and personalized, gold-plated Nibelungen rings.

Better to be out with nature however mean and stupid. And she was particularly so the next day, with a sky like the bottom of an old frying pan and waves as big as hospital bills. The first thing we caught, though it was large and full of fight, wasn't even a fish. A poor pelican snatched our bait and had to be pulled to the boat and unhooked. It was a wet and difficult business for Scott to get ahold of so much angry bird without bird or Scott being too badly hurt. When the pelican was freed it turned as perverse as a human and hung around the *Lucky Too,* looking expectant.

We caught nothing else that morning except a couple small yellowtail snappers, which displayed the same color combinations as Key West tourists. The boat was being shaken like a bad dog. And the real excitement was trying to take a leak in the *Lucky Too*'s tiny head. I attempted to wedge myself into position, pushing a hand against the ceiling and a foot against the deck, another foot against one bulkhead, and the other hand against the wall behind me, but this left no appendage free to undo my zipper. The only comfortable way to piss would have been to sit down on the toilet and have the head filled with Styrofoam packing peanuts to hold me in place.

I tried to eat lunch but the cooler was chucking ice cubes into my lap, my sandwich got blown out of my hand, and my beer leapt out of its gimbal holder and spilled into my Top Siders. I didn't have a chance to vomit; my food was doing it for me.

There are times, deep-sea fishing, when even the meanest and stupidest middle-aged man wonders if he wouldn't be happier back at the office losing a fortune in leveraged buyouts. Then we got into the blackfin tuna. We found them just on the edge of the reef, where the ocean turns from abysmal blue to a perfect grass green as though you'd been watering the lawn and just couldn't stop and now the front yard is thirty feet deep. Blackfins aren't very big fish, never more than forty pounds. They weigh less than the paperwork from a real estate deal, but they've got as much fight in them as any condo salesman. Blackfins don't do any graceful leaps or acrobatics, either. No one ever made a 1950s table lamp with a ceramic base in the shape of a battling tuna. They strike in a quiet, solid way as though you'd hooked the dock. And working the fish, pulling it back to the boat, is a matter of enough sit-ups to make Jane Fonda ditch the exercise business and marry a rich guy. Tuna are deadweight when you're reeling them and torpedoes when you aren't. One moment of inattention and your line is headed for Cuba. And, when you finally do get the tuna to where it can be gaffed, it shakes its head back and forth like a girl meeting William Kennedy Smith in a bar and dives, going for the bottom faster than T-bill yields.

We caught a bunch of them—beautiful fat parabolas of fish, dark-spined with brass highlights along the flanks. The sun came out and the wind went down a little. Flying fish sped down the valleys between the waves. A loggerhead turtle swam by, brown as a Havana cigar and big as a breakfast nook. The boat quit rocking so badly or I quit minding so much. I had another two or three beers. Scott took a fillet knife, grabbed one tuna by the tail, and cut out long, thin, garnet-colored strips of meat—the freshest sushi in the world. Captain Jay turned the *Lucky Too* toward Key West, and I settled into a haze of exhausted and slightly alcoholic bliss. One of the quiet joys of middle age is knowing exactly where you are in the food chain—above tuna, below souvenir T-shirt stores.

GOLF

(Men's Journal, 1992)

The smooth, long, liquid sweep of a three wood smacking into the equator of a dimpled Titleist . . . It makes a potent but slightly foolish noise like the fart of a small, powerful nature god. The ball sails away in a beautiful hip or breast of a curve. And I am filled with joy.

At least that's what I'm filled with when I manage to connect. Most of my strokes whiz by the tee the way a drunk passes a truck on a curve or dig into the turf in a manner that is more gardening than golf. But now and then I nail one, and each time I do it's an epiphany. *This* is how the Australopithecus felt, one or two million years ago, when he first hit something with a stick. Puny hominoid muscles were amplified by the principles of mechanics so that a little monkey swat suddenly became a great manly engine of destruction able to bring enormous force to bear upon enemy predators, hunting prey, and the long fairway shots necessary to get on the green over the early Pleistocene's tar pit hazards.

Hitting things with a stick is the cornerstone of civilization. Consider all the things that can be improved by hitting them with a stick: veal, the TV, Woody Allen. Having a dozen good sticks at hand, all of them well balanced and expertly made, is one reason I took up golf. I also wanted to show my support for the vice president. I now know for certain that Quayle is smarter than his critics. He's smart enough to prefer golf to spelling. How many times has a friend called you on a Sunday morning and said, "It's a beautiful day. Let's go spell potato"?

I waited until I was almost forty-five to hit my first golf ball. When I was younger I thought golf was a pointless sport. Of course all sports are pointless unless you're a professional athlete or a professional athlete's agent, but complex rules and noisy competition mask the essential inanity of most athletics. Golf is so casual. You just go to the course, miss things, tramp around in the briars, use pungent language, and throw two thousand dollars' worth of equipment in a pond. Unlike skydiving or rugby, golf gives you leisure to realize it's pointless. There comes a time in life, however, when all the things that do have a point—career, marriage, exercising to stay fit—start turning, frankly, golflike. And that's when you're ready for golf.

The great thing about starting golf in your forties is that you *can* start golf in your forties. You can start other things in your forties but generally your wife makes you stop them, as Bill Clinton found out. Golf does not require tremendous strength or endurance. You can drive a little car around on the playing surface—something you can't do on a tennis court. Although, the way I play tennis, it wouldn't hurt.

Golf has gravitas. You play it with your pants on. There's nothing sadder than seeing a short, winded, aging ofay—me—on a basketball court. Although watching our presidential candidates out for a morning jog is close. Picture George Washington and Abraham Lincoln puffing around in their underwear. We'd be a slave-owning southernmost province of Canada except that King George and Jeff Davis would have laughed themselves to death.

I'm already a fool, I don't need to look the fool besides. I want my secretary to walk into my office and find me putting into an overturned highball glass. That's stylish. I don't happen to have an office. But I might get one and what would my secretary think if she walked in and found me batting grounders into the kneehole of my desk?

You can play golf first thing in the morning. I've noticed, for men my age, more and more of the important things happen at that hour of the day: golf, heart attacks, delivery of the *Wall Street Journal,* and—intermittently—erections.

You can smoke or drink on a golf course without interrupting the game, and you can take a leak—something you can't do on a squash court and shouldn't do in a swimming pool.

I wanted a sport with a lot of metaphors. I'm a journalist. We journalists like to draw upon the common fund of human experience when we express our many important ideas. And what's more common or better funded than sports? Sports metaphors are the bricks of journalistic prose. Sports similes are the mortar. Sports analogies are the trowel, or maybe the hod carrier . . . You get the idea. "Tinker to Evers to Chance." "Hang time." "He shoots! He scores!" "'Roid Rage." Without sports metaphors American journalism would experience, as it were, sudden death.

But I was running out of valuable athletic clichés. Would beach volleyball say much about proposals for federal health care reform? Could I use mumblety-peg comparisons to explain the North American Free Trade Agreement negotiations? Golf, however, is ideal for these purposes. "Christian fundamentalists put a wicked slice in the Republican party platform." "Somebody should replace the divot on the back of Al Gore's head." "Let's go hit Congress with a stick."

I also wanted a sport with a lot of equipment. All truly American sports are equipment intensive. Basketball was strictly for hoop-over-the-barn-door

Hoosiers and Jersey City Y's until two-hundred-dollar gym shoes were invented. And synchronized swimming will never make it to network prime time because how often do you need new nose plugs? I'm an altruistic guy, in my own Reaganomics way. Sports gear purchases are about all that's keeping the fragile U.S. economy alive, and you'd have to get into America's Cup yachting or cross-country airplane racing to find a sport that needs more gear than golf. I've bought the shoes, hats, socks, pants, shirts, umbrellas, windbreakers, and plus fours—all in colors that Nirvana fans wouldn't dye their hair. Then there are the drivers, irons, putters, and the special clubs: parking-lot wedge, back-of-the-tree mashie, nearby highway niblick. MasterCard has installed a plaque on the wall of its headquarters to commemorate my taking up golf.

Actually, I was forced to become a golfer. As a middle-aged affluent Republican, it was beginning to look strange that I didn't play. People were casting aspersions on my sex life. What with not being out on the golf course at the crack of dawn and not being soused at the nineteenth hole until all hours of the night—I might have one. Where I live in New Hampshire, if that kind of thing gets around, you can be drummed out of the local GOP and lose your Magic George Bush Decoder Ring.

Thus I prevailed upon a friend of mine to take me to his country club. There—once it was established that I'm only half Irish and that, although my name technically ends in a vowel, it's silent—I was graciously allowed to play as a guest. This is another thing I like about golf, the exclusiveness. Of course most country clubs exclude the wrong kinds of people, such as me. But I hold out the hope that somewhere there's a club that bans first wives, people in twelve-step programs, Sting, the editorial board of the *Washington Post,* and Ross Perot.

I played nine holes, and I must admit, for a complete tyro, I wasn't bad. I'll now proceed to tell you about every stroke on every hole. And that's one more swell thing about golf, it provides ammunition for the social bore. Who doesn't love cornering others with tales of action and adventure starring the self? But racquetball, for instance, has limits in this regard: "I hit it. She hit it. I hit it. She hit it really hard." And so on. Golf, on the other hand, is picaresque. A good golf bore can produce a regular *Odyssey* of tedium. And golf allows banal sports chitchat to be elevated to the plane of theoretical physics. An absolute lunkhead—the guy from work who files "The First National Bank" under *T* for "The" and thinks John Donne is a toilet cleaner—turns into Stephen Hawking on the subject of golf. Note this passage from Jack Nicklaus's *Golf My Way*:

> *When the club's face looks to the right of the direction in which the head is traveling, the ball spins around an equator tilted from left to right and thus curves to the right during flight.*

I'll do you a favor and *not* tell you about every stroke. Or any stroke at all. Though I got off some very nice drives. True, they didn't land on the correct fairway, but that was due to wind. And I will stand mute on the subject of technique except to say I learned that many chip shots are best played with a sharp kick from the toe of a golf shoe. And if you cut a hole in your pants pocket you can drop a ball down your trouser leg and "discover" that your shot landed remarkably close to the green. And putting, for a person of my socioeconomic background, is best done by envisioning the cup as being behind a little windmill or inside the mouth of a cement whale. I also found out that all the important lessons of life are contained in the three rules for achieving a perfect golf swing:

1. Keep your head down.
2. Follow through.
3. Be born with money.

There's a fine camaraderie on a golf course—lumbering around with your fellow Republicans, encompassed by a massive waste of space and cash, bearing witness to prolific use of lawn chemicals, and countenancing an exploitative wage scale for the maintenance employees. Golf is the only sport known to have inspired an indignant left-wing poem. It was written by one Sarah Norcliffe Cleghorn in 1915.

The golf links lie so near the mill
That almost every day
The laboring children can look out
And see the men at play.

Just show me an indignant left-wing poem about softball or bungee jumping. And our local mill has been converted to a shopping mall, so the kids are still there.

Golf is also the only sport God is known to play. God and Saint Peter are out on Sunday morning. On the first hole God drives into a water hazard. The waters part and God chips onto the green. On the second hole God takes a tremendous whack and the ball lands ten feet from the pin. There's an earthquake, one side of the green rises up, and the ball rolls into the cup. On the third hole God lands in a sand trap. He creates life. Single-cell organisms develop into fish and then amphibians. Amphibians crawl out of the ocean and evolve into reptiles, birds, and furry little mammals. One of those furry little mammals runs into the sand trap, grabs God's ball in its mouth, scurries over, and drops it in the hole.

Saint Peter looks at God and says, "You wanna play golf or you wanna fuck around?"

And golf courses are beautiful. Many people think mature men have no appreciation for beauty except in immature women. This isn't true, and, anyway, we'd rather be playing golf. A golf course is a perfect example of Republican male aesthetics—no fussy little flowers, no stupid ornamental shrubs, no exorbitant demands for alimony, just acre upon acre of lush green grass *that somebody else has to mow.*

Truth, beauty, and even poetry are to be found in golf. Every man, when he steps up to the tee, feels, as Keats has it . . .

Like stout Cortez when with eagle eyes
He star'd at the Pacific—and all his men
Look'd at each other with a wild surmise—
Silent, upon a peak in Darien.

That is, the men were silent. Cortez was saying, "I can get on in two, easy. A three-wood drive, a five-iron from the fairway, then a two-putt max. But if I hook it, shit, I'm in the drink."

EAT THE RICH

(1998)

"In this state of imbecility, I had, for amusement, turned my attention to political economy."

—Thomas De Quincey,
Confessions of an English Opium Eater

Love, Death, and Money

I had one fundamental question about economics: Why do some places prosper while others suck? It's not a matter of brains. No part of the earth (with the possible exception of Brentwood) is dumber than Beverly Hills, and the residents are wading in gravy. In Russia, meanwhile, where chess is a spectator sport, they're boiling stones for soup. Nor can education be the reason. Fourth graders in the American school system know what a condom is but aren't sure about 9 × 7. Natural resources aren't the answer. Africa has diamonds, gold, uranium, you name it. Scandinavia has little and it's frozen besides. Maybe culture is the key, but wealthy regions such as the local mall are famous for lacking it.

Perhaps the good life's secret lies in civilization. The Chinese had an ancient and sophisticated civilization when my relatives were hunkering naked in trees. (Admittedly that was last week, but they'd been drinking.) In 1000 BC, when Europeans were barely using metal to hit each other over the head, the Zhou dynasty Chinese were casting ornate wine vessels big enough to take a bath in—something else no contemporary European had ever done. Yet, today, China stinks.

Government does not cause affluence. Citizens of totalitarian countries have plenty of government and nothing of anything else. And absence of government doesn't work either. For a million years mankind had no government at all, and *everyone's* relatives were naked in trees. Plain hard work is not the source of plenty. The poorer people are, the plainer and harder is the work that they do. The better-off play golf. And technology provides no guarantee of creature comforts. The most wretched locales in the world are well supplied with complex and up-to-date technology—in the form of weapons.

Why are some places wealthy and other places poor? It occurred to me, at last, that this might have something to do with money.

But I didn't know anything about money. I didn't know anything about money as a practical matter—did I have enough to pay the mortgage? And I didn't know anything about money in a broad or abstract sense. I certainly didn't know anything about economic theory. And I wasn't alone in this.

I couldn't answer the central question of this book because I was an economic idiot. I got to be an economic idiot by the simple and natural method of being human. Humans have trouble with economics and not just because economic circumstances sometimes cause them to starve. Humans seem to have an innate inability to pay attention to economic principles.

Love, death, and money—these are the three main human concerns. We're all keen students of love. We are fascinated by every aspect of the matter, in theory and in practice, from precise biological observations of thrusting this and gaping that to ethereal sentimentalities marketed in miles of aisles at Hallmark stores. No variety of love is too trivial for exegesis. No aspect of love is so ridiculous that it hasn't been exhaustively reviewed by the great thinkers, the great artists, and the great hosts of daytime talk shows.

As for death, such is the public appetite for investigation of the subject that the highest-rated television program in America is about an emergency room. The most hardheaded and unspeculative person has his notions of eschatology. The dullest mind can reason extensively about what causes kicking the bucket. Dying sparks our intellectual curiosity.

But money does not. All we care about is the thing itself, preferably in large amounts. We care a very great deal about that. But here our brain work stops. We don't seem to mind where our money comes from. And, in an affluent society, we don't even seem to mind where our money goes. As for larger questions about money, we shrug our shoulders and say, "I wish I had more."

Why is it that we are earnest scholars of amorousness and necrosis but turn as vague and fidgety as a study hall in June when the topic is economics? I have several hypotheses, none of them very good.

Love and death are limited and personal. Even when free love was in vogue, only a certain number of people would allow us to practice that freedom upon them. A pious man in the throes of Christian agape may love every creature in the world, but he's unlikely to meet them all. And death is as finite as it gets. It has closure. Plus the death ratio is high, 1:1 in occurrences per person.

Economics happens a lot more often and involves multitudes of people and uncountable goods and services. Economics is just too complicated. It makes our heads ache. So when anything economic goes awry, we respond in a limited and personal way by searching our suit-coat pockets to see if there are any wadded up fives inside. Then we either pray or vote for Democrats, depending on our personal convictions of faith.

Or maybe economics is so ever present, so pervasive in every aspect of our lives that we don't really perceive it. We fail to identify economics as a distinct entity. We can watch a man slip and fall and almost never hear him say, "Goddamned gravity!" And we can watch a man fall ten times and not see him become interested in how gravity works. Almost never does he arise from the eleventh tumble saying, "I went down at a rate of 32 feet/second^2—the force being directly proportional to the product of the earth's mass times my weight and inversely proportional to the square of the distance between that patch of ice on the front steps and my butt." And so it is with economics. No amount of losing our jobs or our nest eggs sends us to the library for a copy of John Maynard Keynes's *The General Theory of Employment, Interest, and Money*.

The very pervasiveness of economics keeps us from getting intellectual distance on the subject. We can view death from afar for an average of 72.7 years if we're a male American, and 79.5 years if we're a female. Although love is notorious for fuddling the brain, there is matrimony to cool the passions or, failing that, sexual climax will work in the short term. But there is no such thing as a dollargasm. Money is always with us. What am I going to do to take my mind off money? Go shopping? Drink and drugs will cost me. I suppose I can play with the kids. They need new shoes.

Constant money worries have a bad effect on human psychology. I'd argue that there is more unbalanced thinking about finance than about anything else. Death and sex may be the mainstays of psychoanalysis, but note that few shrinks ask to be paid in murders or marriages. People will do some odd things for political or religious reasons, but that's nothing compared to what people will do for a buck. And if you consider how people spend their dough, *insane* hardly covers it.

Our reactions to cash are nutty even when the cash is half a world away and belongs to perfect strangers. We don't ridicule people for dying. Or, in our hearts, despise them for fooling around. But let a man get rich—especially if it happens quickly and we don't understand how he did it—and we can work ourselves into a fit of rage. We aren't rational and intelligent about economics because thinking about money has driven us crazy.

I'm as much of a mooncalf as anyone. I certainly had no interest in economics as a kid, as kids don't. Children—lucky children at least—live in that ideal state postulated by Marx, where the rule is, "From each according to his abilities, to each according to his needs." Getting grounded equals being sent to a gulag. Dad in high dudgeon is confused with Joseph Stalin. Then we wonder why so many young people are leftists.

I had no interest in economics at college, either. I belonged to that great tradition of academic bohemia which stretches from the fifteenth-century riots of François Villon to the Phish tours of the present day. For university hipsters, there is (no doubt Villon mentions this in his *Petit Testament*) nothing more pathetic than taking business courses.

My friends and I were above that. In our classes we studied literature, anthropology, and how to make ceramics. We were seeking, questing, growing. Specifically, we were growing sideburns and leg hair, according to gender. It did not occur to us that the frat-pack dolts and Tri-Delt tweeties, hurrying to get to Econ 101 on time (in their square fashion), were the real intellectuals. We never realized that grappling with the concept of aggregate supply and demand was more challenging than writing a paper about "The Effects of Cool Jazz on the Poetry of Edgar Allan Poe." What the L-7s were being quizzed on was not only harder to understand than Margaret Mead's theories about necking in Samoa, it was also more important. The engine of existence is fueled by just a few things. Unglazed pottery is not among them.

If the Rah-Rah Bobs and Pin-Me Sallys had been taking Love or Death courses, we would have been right there with them. But money was a different matter. We weren't interested in money. Actually—what we weren't interested in was work. Maybe we guessed that it would be a lot of work to b.s. our way out of memorizing such formulae as:

$$\text{Price Elasticity} = \frac{\%\ \text{Change in Supply}}{\%\ \text{Change in Price}}$$

Not that we weren't up to the task: "Like, price—that equals wasting natural resources and the pollution thing, if you're into the whole capitalist, monopoly rip-off, man."

And, of course, we *were* interested in money. I remember we'd get excited whenever we had any. It's just that we were determined not to earn it. We would never go in search of money. Money was something that would come looking for us after we'd choreographed our world-shattering modern-dance recital or mounted our famous empty-gallery show of preconceptual post-objectivist paintings or when our folk-rock group, Exiles of Dayton, learned to play "Kumbaya." And we weren't going to "sell out" no matter how much money was lavished upon us.

Business majors intended to (it was a loaded phrase in those days) "make money," and they were going to do this even if it involved some activity that wasn't a bit artistic, such as running IBM. We artsy types would have been shocked if anyone had told us (and no one had the nerve) that making money was creative. And we would have been truly shocked to learn that a fundamental principle of economics—"Wealth is created when assets are moved from lower-valued to higher-valued uses"—is the root of all creativity, be it artsy, IBMsy, or whatever.

"Putting money first" was crass. It was as if you'd gone to a party with dozens of wild, swinging chicks and, instead of drinking Mateus and making small talk about Jean-Paul Sartre, you just whipped out your unit. Except we would have thought that was a blast. But go into business? Never.

If you don't count selling drugs. Which we were all doing. We knew everything about price elasticity when it came to pot, not to mention aggregate supply and demand. In point of fact, we hirsute weirdos probably had more real business experience than any business major on campus. And one more thing—we all fancied ourselves to be Marxists. As a philosophic recipe, Marxism is a cannelloni of the economical, stuffed with economics, and cooked in economic sauce.

Still, we were not interested in economic ideas. And, to be fair, the business majors weren't, either. Econ was not something they took because they were fascinated by the elegant complexities of economic relationships or because mankind cannot survive without economic activity. They took econ and forgot everything in the text so they could get a job from somebody else who took econ and forgot everything in the text.

I turned into a square myself, of course, as everyone who lives long enough does. I got a job as a journalist—but without ever considering that journalism was a business. (Although I would have been unpleasantly surprised to get a hug instead of a paycheck at the end of the week.) And I continued to ignore economic issues even though I had a press pass to the most spectacular extravaganza of economics in this century.

It was the 1970s, and the economy was changing almost as often as bed partners. The Great Depression may have been more dramatic, but it was a one-trick pony. In the '70s, globalization suddenly included the other three-quarters of the globe. The places that used to make our windup toys were making our automobiles. Everything was being imported—except oil, which had hitherto been given away free with a windshield wash and a set of highball glasses at most brand-name gas stations. Then, one day, you couldn't buy oil for money. Not that there wasn't plenty of money around in the '70s. It just didn't happen to be worth anything. We had a previously unimaginable combination of fever inflation and hypothermia business slump. You could make more money buying Treasury bills than you could make breaking into the Treasury. The gold standard disappeared from the scene. Maybe it joined a cult. International currency-exchange rates were determined with mood rings. The most powerful nations in the world had, at their helms, an amazing collection of economic nincompoops—Nixon, Carter, Mao, Harold Wilson, Georges Pompidou, Leonid Brezhnev. And the electronic-media revolution was under way so that bad ideas about economics were spreading around the world at neural speed.

I dozed through it. And I was covering politics, too. Even I realized that money was to politicians what the eucalyptus tree is to koala bears: food, water, shelter, and something to crap on. I made a few of the normal journalistic squeaks about greed and self-interest, and let the thing slide.

It wasn't until the 1990s, when I'd been a foreign correspondent for ten years, that I finally noticed economics. I noticed that in a lot of places I went, there wasn't anything you'd call an economy. And I didn't know why.

Many of these countries seemed to have everything—except food, water, shelter, and something to crap on.

I decided to go back to the econ texts I'd finessed in college and figure things out. And my beatnik loathing returned full-blown. Except this time it wasn't the business majors I despised; it was the authors of the books they'd had to study. It turns out that the econ professors were economic idiots, too.

Looking into a college textbook as an adult is a shock (and a vivid reminder of why we were so glad to get out of school). The prose style is at once puerile and impenetrable, *Goodnight Moon* rewritten by Henry James. The tone varies from condescension worthy of a presidential press conference to sly chumminess worthy of the current president. The professorial wit is duller than the professorial dicta, and these are dulled to blunt numbness by the need to exhibit professorial self-importance. No idea, however simple—"When there's more of something, it costs less"—can be expressed without rendering it onto a madras sport coat of a graph and translating it into a rebus puzzle full of peculiar signs and notations. Otherwise the science of economics wouldn't seem as profound to outsiders as organic chemistry does. And then, speaking of matters economical, there's the price of these things—$49.95 for a copy of *Economics*, fifteenth edition, by Paul A. Samuelson and William D. Nordhaus.

Economics has been, as its edition number indicates, in use as an econ text forever—that is, since 1948, which counts as forever to the baby boom generation. The book is considered a fossil by many economists, but it has been translated into forty-six languages, and more than four million copies have been sold. *Economics* was what the current leaders of international business and industry were afflicted with in school. And here was another shock. Professor Samuelson, who wrote the early editions by himself, turns out to be almost as much of a goof as my friends and I were in the 1960s. "Marx was the most influential and perceptive critic of the market economy ever," he says on page seven. Influential, yes. Marx nearly caused World War III. But perceptive? Samuelson continues: "Marx was wrong about many things . . . but that does not diminish his stature as an important economist." Well, what would? If Marx was wrong about many things *and* screwed the babysitter?

Samuelson's foreword to the fifteenth edition says, "In the reactionary days of Senator Joseph McCarthy . . . my book got its share of condemnation." I should think so. *Economics* is full of passages indicating that Samuelson (if not William-come-lately Nordhaus) disagrees with that reactionary idea the free market. The chapter titled "Applications of Supply and Demand" states that "crop restrictions not only raise the price of corn and other crops but also tend to raise farmers' total revenues and earnings." Increase your corn profit by not growing corn? Here's a wonderful kind of business where everybody can get rich if they'll just do nothing.

In the chapter "Supply and Allocation in Competitive Markets," the book seems to be confused about the very nature of buying and selling. "Is society satisfied with outcomes where the maximal amount of bread is produced," it asks, "or will modern democracies take loaves from the wealthy and pass them out to the poor?" Are the rich people just going to keep those loaves to grow mold? Why would they produce "the maximal amount of bread" to do that? Or are we talking about charity here? If so, let us note that Jesus did not perform the miracle of the loaves and taxes. We all know how "modern democracies take loaves from the wealthy." It's the slip-ups in the "pass them out to the poor" department that inspire a study of econ.

It was not reassuring to learn that the men who run the companies where our 401(k)s are invested have minds filled with junk from the attic of Paul A. Samuelson's *Economics*.

There were newer texts than *Economics* for me to look at, and what they said wasn't so obviously wrong. But then again, what they said wasn't so obvious, period. Here are the first three sentences of *Macroeconomics* by David C. Colander (donated by Eric Owens, who lives next door to me and is taking econ at the University of New Hampshire): "When an artist looks at the world, he sees color. When a musician looks at the world, she hears music. When an economist looks at the world, she sees a symphony of costs and benefits." Somebody change the CD, please.

The textbooks weren't good. This sent me to the original source material, the classics of economic thought. But here I had to admit, as I was tacitly admitting thirty years ago, that I don't have the brains to be a Tri-Delt. *The Wealth of Nations, Das Kapital, The General Theory of Whatchmacallit* were impressive works and looked swell on my bookshelf, but they put me to sleep faster than the economic news of the '70s had.

There were, of course, popular books on economics, but the really popular books were about extraordinary people doing extraordinary things and getting fabulously wealthy or going to jail—preferably both. I was interested in ordinary people doing ordinary things and getting by. And the less popular but more worthwhile books on economics all seemed to presume that I'd made it through something like *Economics* without blowing a fuse.

So I gave up trying to be smart about economics. I decided that if I wanted to know why some places were rich and other places were poor, I should go to those places. I would visit different economic systems: free market, socialist, and systems nobody could figure out. I'd look at economically successful societies: the U.S., Sweden, Hong Kong. I'd look at economically unsuccessful societies: Albania, Cuba, Tanzania. And I'd look at societies that hadn't decided whether to be successful or not: Russia and mainland China. I'd wander around, gape at things, and simply ask people, "Why are you so broke?" Or "How come you're shitting in high cotton?"

BAD CAPITALISM

Albania 1997

Albania shows what happens to a free market when there is no legal, political, or traditional framework to define freedoms or protect marketplaces. Of course there's lots of violence—as you'd expect in a situation where the shopkeepers and the shoplifters have the same status under law. And, of course, there's lots of poverty. Theft is the opposite of creating wealth. Instead of moving assets from lower-valued to higher-valued uses, theft moves assets from higher-valued uses to a fence who pays ten cents on the dollar for them. But capitalism conducted in a condition of anarchy also produces some less-predictable phenomena. Albania has the distinction of being the only country ever destroyed by a chain letter—a nation devastated by a Ponzi racket, a land ruined by the pyramid scheme.

A pyramid is any financial deal in which investors make their money not from investing but from money put into the deal by other investors, and those investors make money from the investors after that, and so on. It's the old "send five dollars to the name at the top of the list, put your own name at the bottom of the list, and mail copies to future ex-friends." If I want to make fifty dollars from my five dollars, ten new dupes must be recruited. If each of them hopes to make fifty dollars, a hundred suckers will be needed, then a thousand, and hence the "pyramid" name. If a pyramid scheme grows in a simple exponential manner—10^1, 10^2, 10^3, etc.—it takes only ten layers of that pyramid to include nearly twice the population of the earth. And 9,999,999,999 of these people are going to get screwed because the guy who started the pyramid has run away with all the five-dollar bills.

When communist rule ended in Albania, in 1992, the nation was broke and was kept from starving only by foreign aid and remittances from Albanians in Italy, the U.S., and elsewhere. But the people of Albania still managed to scratch together some cash. Like American baby boomers, they were worried about the future. So, like baby boomers, they invested. The Albanians invested in pyramid schemes. The pyramids grew. People were getting rich, at least on paper. And then, in 1997, the pyramids collapsed.

Albanian reaction to the financial disaster was philosophical—if your philosophy is nihilism. Violent protests occurred all over the country. The Albanian government banned public meetings. The protests became more violent. The government reacted to this by authorizing the military to shoot at crowds. The military responded to that by deserting in droves. Soldiers had money in the pyramid schemes too, and were just as mad as anyone else. The violent protests turned into armed rebellions. The government lost control of every military base in the country. By spring the Albanian army was reduced to perhaps one intact unit, numbering a hundred soldiers. The entire defense arsenal was looted.

There'd been plenty to loot. Albania's Communists had required every man, woman, boy, and girl to undergo military training. Estimates of the number of weapons loose in the country ranged as high as 1.5 million. And the Albanian defense ministry admitted that a whopping 10.5 billion rounds of ammunition had been stolen—more than three thousand bullets for every person in the nation. Heavy weapons were also pilfered—artillery, missile launchers, and high explosives. Some of these were taken by local Committees for Public Salvation, but most wound up in less responsible hands. The National Commercial Bank in the city of Gjirokaster was robbed with a tank.

Korce, near the border with Greece, was terrorized by gangs of masked men. Outside Fier, on the seacoast plain, twenty people died in a shoot-out between criminals and armed villagers. The southern port of Vlore was taken over by a gangster chief named Ramazan Causchi, who preferred to be called "the Sultan."

At least fourteen thousand Albanians tried to escape to Italy by commandeering boats. One thousand two hundred people squashed into a single purloined freighter. The president of the country himself, Sali Berisha, stole a ferry to send his son and daughter to Brindisi, Italy. Prison guards deserted and six hundred inmates broke out of Tirana's central prison. Among the escapees was the head of Albania's Communist Party, the wonderfully named Fatos Nano. (Nano exhibited the pattern of recidivism common to ex-convicts by campaigning hard during Albania's elections in June 1997. He is now prime minister.)

U.S. Marines and Italian commandos evacuated foreign nationals by helicopter. Humanitarian aid ceased. The International Committee of the Red Cross threw up its hands. "This is almost like Somalia," said an ICRC official. In four months more than fifteen hundred people died and tens of thousands were injured. Theft slipped into pillage. The railroad to Montenegro was stolen—the track torn up and sold for scrap. Pillage degenerated into vandalism. Schools, museums, and hospitals were wrecked. And vandalism reached heroic scale. Bridges were demolished, water-supply pumping stations were blown apart, power lines and telephone wires were pulled down. Albania came to bits.

I went to Albania in July 1997. Flying over the Albanian Alps on the trip from Rome to Tirana, I could see that something was historically wrong with Albania. The villages are not tucked into the fertile, sheltered valleys the way the villages of Austria, Switzerland, or even Bosnia are. The villages of Albania are right up on the treeless, soilless, inconvenient mountaintops. Before ski lifts were invented, there was only one reason to build homes in such places. A mountaintop is easy to defend.

The Tirana airport had one runway and a small, shabby, whitewashed concrete terminal building with a random planting of flowers outside. There were no visa or immigration formalities. Presumably, few people were trying to sneak into Albania to get social benefits. Customs agents did run my bag through an X-ray, however. Searching for something to steal, I guess. With all the ordnance available in Albania, they couldn't be looking for weapons.

I'd found a translator and driver by calling the Hotel Tirana and hiring the front-desk clerk's boyfriend. I'll call him Elmaz. He met me in the airport parking lot in his uncle's worn-out Mercedes. Elmaz said Tirana was thirty minutes away. We drove toward town on a four-lane turnpike that—"Five kilometers long," said Elmaz—promptly ended. "Is only highway in country," said Elmaz. The buckled, pitted two-lane road that followed was full of cars, trucks, and horse carts—an amazing number of them for such a supposedly obliterated economy. Scores of wrecked trucks and cars lined the road. Albania has so many wrecks that all the horse carts are fitted with automobile seats, some with center consoles and luxurious upholstery.

The landscape was the Mediterranean usual, a little too sun-baked and sublimely mountained for its own good. The fields, however, were only half-sown in midsummer, and out in those fields and up along the hillsides were hundreds of cement hemispheres. Each dome was about eight feet across and had a slit along the base. All the slits faced the road. It seemed to be a collection of unimaginative giant penny banks.

These are self-defense bunkers. Elmaz said there are 150,000 of them in the country. They're everywhere you look. They are Albania's salient feature. The shop at the Hotel Tirana sells alabaster miniatures as souvenirs—model igloos, though the gun slots seem to indicate flounder-shaped Eskimos. In the cities, some of the bunkers have cement flower planters molded onto their tops, a rare combination of civil defense and gardening. Larger bunkers appear along the beaches and at other strategic spots. The mountains are riddled with fortified tunnels, and even the stakes in Albania's vineyards are topped with metal spikes so that paratroopers will be impaled if they try to land among the grapevines.

Albania's longtime Communist leader Enver Hoxha (pronounced Howard Johnsonish: "Hoja") ordered all this after the Soviet Union's 1968 invasion of Czechoslovakia. He was sure Albania was going to be invaded next. Hoxha called for "war against imperialism, against the bourgeoisie, social democrats, national chauvinists, and modern revisionists . . . They hurl all sorts of foul invectives on us. This gladdens us and we say: Let them go to it! Our mountains soar up higher and higher!"

But who'd want to invade Albania? Or so I was thinking as Elmaz and I drove past Albania's Coca-Cola bottling plant. There, peeking out from behind a ten-foot fiberglass Coke bottle on the roof, was a sandbagged machine-gun nest. Maybe Hoxha wasn't crazy.

In the event, the pillboxes were no use against the force that actually invaded Albania, which was the force of ideas—though not exactly the same ideas that sparked the Declaration of Independence, to judge by what Elmaz showed me over the next week. Elmaz was studying to be a veterinarian. Everything had been stolen from his school: books, drugs, lab equipment, even parts of the buildings themselves. "We are without windows, without doors," said Elmaz. "We study with only desks and walls." The desks had been stolen, too, but the faculty had found them in local flea markets and bought them back. "All the horses we have were shot," said Elmaz.

Across the road from the veterinary school was a collective farm that once had five thousand cattle. "They stole five thousand cows!" I said, amazed at the sheer get-along-little-doggy virtuosity needed to rustle a herd that size in Albanian traffic.

"No, no, no," said Elmaz. "They could never steal so many cows in 1997."

"How come?"

"Because they were all stolen in 1992 when communism ended."

How could mere confidence games lead to total havoc? And why did pyramid schemes run completely out of control in Albania? It took about an hour to find out. Elmaz drove me to see Ilir Nishku, editor of the country's only English-language newspaper, the *Albanian Daily News*.

"Why were the pyramids so popular in Albania?" I asked Nishku. "Were people just unsophisticated about money after all those years of communist isolation?"

"No," said Nishku, "there had been pyramid schemes already elsewhere in Eastern Europe, and they had collapsed before the Albanian ones were started. People in Albania knew about such things as the failure of the MMM scheme in Russia."

"Then how did so many Albanians get suckered in?" I asked.

And the answer was simple. "People did not believe these were real pyramid schemes," Nishku said. "They knew so much money could not be made honestly. They thought there was smuggling and money laundering involved to make these great profits."

The Albanians didn't believe they were the victims of a scam. They believed they were the perpetrators—this being so different from the beliefs of certain Wall Street bull-market investors in the United States.

"My family had two thousand dollars in the pyramid schemes," said Elmaz. It was their entire savings.

Nishku told me the first Albanian pyramid scheme was started in 1991 by Hadjim Sijdia. Sijdia Holdings offered 5 percent or 6 percent interest per month, 60 percent to 72 percent a year—way too much, especially considering that Albania was then in a period of low inflation. But Sijdia Holdings had some real investments, and although Hadjim Sijdia was jailed in Switzerland for fraud, he managed to get out and somehow repay his debts.

Following Sijdia Holdings, however, came schemes with a primary business of scheming. There were about nine large pyramids in Albania. Three of them—Sude, Xhaferri, and Populli—had no real assets at all. By 1993 small-business owners had gotten the idea and began creating mini-pyramids all over the country. Free enterprise can be free of all sorts of things, including ethics, and competition drove the promised rates of return high and higher. At one point the Sude pyramid was offering interest of 50 percent a month.

"The pyramid schemes," said Ilir Nishku, "created the idea that this is the free market and just four years after communism, we could get rich. They created the wrong idea that *this* is capitalism."

"Everyone was sitting in cafés," said Elmaz.

Albania's economic statistics looked great: 9.6 percent growth in 1993, 8.3 percent in '94, 13.3 percent in '95, 9.1 percent in '96.

"Albania's economy chalks up the fastest growth rate on the continent," chirped the slightly clueless *Bradt* travel guide.

The very clueless *United Nations 1996 Human Development Report* for Albania declared, "The progress in widespread economic well-being reported in the *1995 Human Development Report for Albania* has continued, forming a social basis for human development."

Something called the *Eurobarometer Survey* said the Albanians were the most optimistic people of eastern and central Europe.

Even Enver Hoxha's ancient widow, Nexhmije (pronounced . . . oh, who cares), waxed positive on capitalism. Released from prison in December 1996, she had a new bathroom installed in her apartment. Jane Perlez of the *New York Times* interviewed the communist crone: "'This is the good thing about the consumer society,' [Nexhmije] said, showing off some pink Italian tiles. 'Though it's very expensive, you can find everything.'"

The glory days lasted until February 1997. Then five of the big pyramids collapsed, and all the little ones did. Four other major pyramid schemes quit paying interest and froze accounts. An estimated $1.2 billion disappeared, more than half the Albanian gross domestic product. "Where did all that money go?" I asked Nishku.

He began ticking off possibilities: Swiss banks? The Albanian government? Money-laundering operations in Cyprus? Turkish Mafia? Russian Mafia? Italian Mafia? "We don't know," he said.

I asked Nishku if there was any possibility that people would get their money back.

He said, "No."

The best place in Albania from which to admire capitalist freedoms gone wrong is the Hotel Tirana's balcony bar overlooking Skenderbeg Square in the center of Albania's capital city.

"Sheshi Skenderbej" is an all-concrete piazza the size of a nine-hole golf course. A dozen streets empty into it. From each street come multitudes of drivers going as fast as they can in any direction they want. Cars head everywhere. Cars box the compass. They pull U-ies, hang Louies, make Roscoes, do doughnuts. Tires peel and skid. Bicycles scatter. Pushcarts jump the curbs. Pedestrians run for their lives. No horn goes unhonked. Brakes scream. Bumpers wallop. Fenders munch. Headlight glass plays jingle bells on the pavement. There's lots of yelling.

Until 1990, Albanians were forbidden to own motor vehicles. They didn't know how to drive. They still don't. Every fourth or fifth car seems to have an AUTOSHKOLLE sign on the roof, and not a moment too soon. Now there are 150,000 automobiles in Albania. If you've ever wondered why you don't see beaters and jalopies on Western European streets, why there are no EU junkyards, it's because the junk is in Albania. Elmaz said, "When we were first open to Europe, we bought used cars. Very used cars. After one year . . ." He pursed his lips and made the *kaput* noise.

The bad cars of Europe are in Albania. And the hot cars. An unwashed Porsche 928 lurching inexpertly through the square seemed a probable example. Its huge V-8 was being gunned to piston-tossing, valve-shattering rpms. Even a mid-1980s model 928 would cost an average Albanian sixteen years' salary.

An American wire-service reporter was teasing Elmaz about used-car shopping: "I'd like to get a Renault Twingo, maybe. A '95 or '96. For about a thousand dollars? One that hasn't been rolled."

"Ha, ha, ha," said Elmaz in the kind of laugh that indicates nobody's kidding. "I know someplace."

The wire-service reporter, who seemed to be rather too well informed on various matters, said that pot cost thirty dollars a kilo in Albania. And the *Economist* magazine's business report on Albania said that in March 1997, a fully automatic Kalashnikov assault rifle could be bought on the streets of Tirana for as little as three dollars.

"*Everyone* is surreptitiously armed," said the wire-service reporter. Or not so surreptitiously. I saw a middle-aged man in civilian clothes walking along what used to be Boulevard Stalin, holding his five-year-old son by one hand and an AK-47 in the other.

Such are Second Amendment freedoms in Albania. And First Amendment freedoms lag not far behind in their extravagance. Each evening during the first weeks of July 1997, a couple hundred royalists would march into the chaos of Skenderbeg Square, bringing traffic to a new pitch of swerve and collision.

I watched the royalists set up podium and loudspeakers on the steps of a Soviet-designed cement blunder that used to be the Palace of Culture. They unfurled the heart-surgery-colored Albanian flag, bearing the image of what's either a two-headed eagle or a very angry freak-show chicken. The royalists shouted into the microphone such things as, "We will get our votes, even by blood!" The volume was enough to drown out the loudest car crashes. Then, at greater volume yet, they played a recording of the Albanian national anthem, which is as long as a Wagner opera and sounded like it was being played by a drunken brass band.

The royalists were demonstrating on behalf of one Leka Zogu, who thinks he's the king of Albania. He'd just been defeated (80 percent of the voters said "*jo*") in a national referendum on restoring the monarchy. Not that Albania ever had a monarchy. The country wasn't even a country until the twentieth century. It was a backwater of the Ottoman Empire from the 1400s on and a back-farther-water of the Byzantine Empire before that.

Leka Zogu's father, Ahmed Zogu, overthrew what passed for the government in 1924, crowned himself King Zog I in 1928, pimped the country to Mussolini, and skipped into exile one step ahead of Axis occupation in 1939. Leka was two days old at the time. Since then the younger Zogu has sojourned in Rhodesia and South Africa, been thrown out of Spain over an arms-dealing scandal, and spent a brief jail stint in Thailand for gunrunning.

After an hour or so of royalist racket, Leka Zogu's motorcade arrived, flashing the kind of suction-cup roof lights that people buy when they want you to think they belong to the volunteer fire department. This sloppy parade of Mercedes sedans shoved into the rumpus of Skenderbeg Square, and the royal himself popped out in one royal beauty of a leisure suit. Leka (in the Albanian language the definite article is a suffixed *u* or *i* so "Leka Zogu" translates as "Leka the Zog") stood at the microphone like a big geek—six feet eight inches tall, chinless, and bubble-bellied. He mumbled a few words. (His majesty's command of Albanian is reported to be sketchy.) Then he booked. Wide guys patted lumpy items under their clothes. All the Benzes tried to turn around at once, which would have created still worse traffic mayhem if that had been possible.

A few days before I got to Albania some of Leka's supporters got so enthusiastic that they started a gun battle with the police. The shooting went on for fifteen minutes, although only one person was killed, because the two sides weren't near each other. The police were in a soccer stadium several blocks from the demonstration.

Capitalism is pursued in Albania with the same zest—not to mention the same order and self-restraint—as driving, gun control, and politics.

Hundreds of cafés and bars have opened, whacked together from raw timber with the carpentry skills of 1960s hippie commune dwellers. The rude structures are built on any handy piece of open ground and "have occupied even school yards in the capital," says the *Albanian Daily News,* old copies of which, along with every other form of litter, carpet the city streets. Private garbage collection is not yet up and running in Tirana, but private garbage disposal is fully operational. Every public space is covered with bags, wrappers, bottles, cans—and the booze shacks and pizza sheds that sold them.

Gardens have been obliterated by jerry-building, monuments surrounded, paths straddled, soccer pitches filled from goal to goal. The Lana River is walled from view, not that you'd want to look. The bar and café squatters have used pickaxes to make haphazard connections with waste pipes and water mains. The Lana has crossed the lexicological line between *river* and *open sewer*. And what used to be Youth Park, a huge area of downtown greenery, has become the world's first dining and leisure shantytown.

But it's gambling that's the real meat and drink. It's done on the same confounding electronic video-card-playing devices that the Pequot Indians are using to reconquer Connecticut. Albania is a country that, from 1986 to 1990, imported sewing machines, electric stoves, and hot-water heaters numbering a total of zero. And Tirana is a city with electricity as reliable as congressional-committee testimony. But there they are: the very latest examples of wallet-Hoovering technology from America, available everywhere and, through some miracle of Mafia-to-Mafia efficiency, functioning smoothly all day.

Albania is also a country where the poverty line is $143 a month for a family of four. Eighty percent of Albanians are living below that line. And what looks like 80 percent of Albanians are standing in front of bleeping, blinking games of chance feeding 100-lek coins—fifty-cent pieces—into the maw. The most common commercial sign in Tirana is AMERICAN POKER.

The second most common sign is SHITET. Appropriately. Although it actually means "for sale." Appropriately. Or perhaps it should be "up for grabs," whatever that is in Albanian. Maybe it's "Amex." I went to an American Express office to get some money, and they were completely taken aback. They would never have anything so snatchable as money right there in an office. For money you go to the Bank in the Middle of the Street. Here—everyone being surreptitiously armed—great wads of money are being waved around, some of it peculiar. I got a few greenbacks with the green on the backs more of a pants-at-a-Westport-cocktail-party shade than usual and a twenty with something dark and odd about the presidential portrait. Was Andrew Jackson in the Jackson 5?

The thousands of tape cassettes being sold in the middle of the street are counterfeit, too. At least I hope so. I'd hate to think anyone was paying royalties on Bulgarian disco and Turkish rap. The Marlboros are real, however, and cost less than they do when they fall off the back of a truck in Brooklyn. The clothes fell off a truck, too, I think, though not, unfortunately, a Brooks Brothers semi. Albanians have the Jersey Dirt Mall mode of dress figured out. Like everything else, these duds are sold mid-street, from racks mingled with car accidents, royalists, money, guns, and automated five-card draw.

Reading over what I have written, I fear I've made Albanians sound busy. They aren't. Even their gambling is comparatively idle—exhibiting none of the industry shown by the old bats in Atlantic City with their neatly ordered Big Gulp cups of quarters and special slot-machine yanking gloves.

There are lots of skulking young men in groups on Tirana's corners and plenty more driving around in cars with no apparent errand or evident destination. It's not a mellow indolence. I saw one guy cruising in his Mercedes, an elbow out the window, a wrist cocked over the steering wheel, riding cool and low. But his trunk lid was open, and chained in the boot was a barking, gnashing, furious 150-pound German shepherd.

Men in Albania hold each other's hands too long in greeting, a gesture that seems to have less to do with affection than disarmament. They kiss each other on the cheeks, Italian-style, but more Gotti than Gucci. Everybody stares. Nobody steps out of your way.

The Albanians have a Jolly Roger air. You could give an eye patch and a head hankie to most of the people on the street and cast them in *Captain Blood.* Not to demean a whole ethnic group or anything, but like most Americans, the only Albanians I'd ever heard of were Mother Teresa and John Belushi. An entire country full of Mother Teresas would be weird enough—everybody looking for lepers to wash. But imagine a John Belushi Nation—except they're not fat, and they're not funny.

"They'll rob you," said the wire-service reporter as we—pretty idle and indolent ourselves—ordered another round at the Balcony Bar. "Don't carry your wallet." Then a neophyte television producer walked up and announced that he'd gone out to tape some local color and hadn't made it to the city limits before he lost a car, a TV camera, and $5,000 in cash.

A whole family lived in front of the Hotel Tirana, doing nothing. Between the hotel entrance and Skenderbeg Square was a quarter-acre patch of what used to be grass. Therein camped, from dawn to dark, a very big and fat woman; a very small and bedraggled woman; several skinny, greasy men; and approximately a dozen seriously unkempt children. The big woman spent all day spraddle-legged on a tablecloth, playing cards with the skinny men. The small woman spent all day wandering back and forth across the packed-dirt lot. Every time a hotel guest stepped outside, the children descended upon him or her, begging in a horde or, if begging was to no avail, thrusting little hands into pockets and purses, and grasping at whatever the hotel guest was carrying. Otherwise the children swatted and kicked each other. Sometimes the children would go over to the big woman, who'd also give them a swat. And if the tykes obtained money, they'd return to the big woman, and she'd snatch it.

The family had a puffy, sallow baby with the scorched blond hair that is a sign of malnutrition. The infant seemed to be eight or ten months old but didn't appear to be able to hold its head up. It never cried. A ten- or eleven-year-old boy was the principal caretaker. He squeezed the baby to his chest with one arm while he chased the other children around, giving them karate chops and kung fu kicks. Meanwhile, the baby's appendages wagged and jiggled in all directions.

Between martial arts exhibitions, the baby was left alone on a sheet of cardboard on Skenderbeg Square's tumultuous sidewalks. Passersby were supposed to leave coins. Occasionally they did.

"They are Gypsies," said Elmaz. But *Gypsy* is the preferred local bigotry epithet, the N-word of the Balkans, with the added advantage that it can be used on anybody darker than Kate Moss.

The translator who worked for the wire-service reporter said he'd questioned the child-care boy about the baby. The boy had said, "His mother was going to throw him away. But she gave him to us. Now we're taking care of him."

There is not, so far as I was able to discover, an Albanian Child Abuse Hotline. "That's because it would be jammed with how-to calls," said the wire-service reporter.

"What the fuck is with this place?" said someone else at the bar. And I do not have an answer for that.

All of Albania's rich and varied social life comes to a halt promptly at 10 p.m., when the shoot-to-kill curfew began.

The Organization for Security and Cooperation in Europe had sent an Italian-led contingent of some seven thousand troops to enforce it.

The OSCE troops arrived in April 1997 in their scout cars and personnel carriers. The situation in Albania was so bad that having Italians tooling around in armor-plated vehicles actually made the streets safer. Now, after 10 p.m. in Tirana, everything was quiet. No, not quiet. There was continual gunfire coming from the maze of Tirana's back streets. And the gunfire set off Tirana's dogs. As a result I spent the night thinking, first, about stray Kalashnikov slugs and the Hotel Tirana'a floor-to-ceiling windows: "Gosh, I wish I had a room on a lower floor." Then thinking about what a really large number of loud dogs Tirana has: "Gosh, I wish I had a room on a higher floor." I ended up back at the balcony bar, fully exposed to both the bullets and the barking, but at least I had gin.

Tirana was not quiet at night, but it was invisible. Nothing moved on the main streets. And most of the town's electricity was out so I couldn't see it moving, anyway. I gazed into a stygian void with just an occasional tracer shell arcing across the night sky. Make a wish?

Albania is a little place the size of Maryland, with a population of 3.25 million. Albania is little, and Albania is out of the way, blocked from the rest of the Balkan Peninsula by high, disorderly mountain ranges, and, until this century, cordoned from the sea by broad, malarial swamps. Seventy-five percent of the land is steeps and ravines. In the north, the Albanian Alps rise in such a forbidding confusion of precipices that they are known as the *Prokletije,* or Accursed Mountains. In the eighteenth century, Edward Gibbon called Albania "a country within sight of Italy which is less known than the interior of America." As late as 1910, geographical authorities were saying that certain districts of Albania "have never been thoroughly explored." And considering the neophyte TV producer's experience, they won't be explored soon.

This isolated, outlandish place emerged from World War II run by the isolated and outlandish Communist guerrilla chieftain Enver Hoxha. In 1948, Hoxha broke his alliance with Tito because Yugoslavia wasn't being pro-Soviet enough. In 1961, Hoxha broke his alliance with Khrushchev because the Soviet Union wasn't being pro-Soviet enough. In 1978, Hoxha threw out the Red Chinese for having played Ping-Pong with the U.S. And by the time Hoxha died in 1985, Albania wasn't on speaking terms with anyplace but North Korea and maybe the English Department at Yale. Hoxha's successor, Ramiz Alia, stayed the loony course for a while, but in 1990, with communism going into a career slump all over the globe, Alia tried some reforms.

The Albanians' response to a sudden introduction of personal autonomy and individual responsibility casts an interesting light on the human psyche. They ran like hell. According to Balkans expert James Pettifer, "Over 25,000 people seized ships moored in Durres Harbor and forced them to sail to Italy." Thousands of others fled to Greece or occupied the grounds of Western embassies in Tirana. University students pulled down the gigantic gilded statue of Enver Hoxha in Skenderbeg Square, and the Alia government had to dismantle and hide the nearby statues of Stalin and Lenin. There was repeated food rioting, widespread destruction of public property, and extensive looting of everything owned by the government—and everything was.

Then things got better. Dr. Sali Berisha, whom Pettifer calls a "leading cardiologist" (Albania *has* a leading cardiologist?), was elected president. The Communists were jailed. In Pettifer's words, "The new government . . . embarked on a program of privatization and the construction of a free-market economy."

But this privatization being programmed and this free-market economy being constructed were based on only one industry: pyramid schemes.

Although Albania seems inaccessible, it has been, over the past three millennia, repeatedly accessed. Albanians have had the misfortune to live too close to the kind of folks who can't seem to resist invading things—even things like Albania.

Albania has been invaded by various Greek city states, Macedonia, Rome, Byzantium, Slavic hordes, Byzantium again, Bulgarian hordes, Byzantium one more time, Normans, Christian Crusaders, Charles I of Anjou, Serbs, Venetians, Turks, and Fascists. Durres, historically the principal city of Albania, has changed hands thirty-three times since the year 1000.

Albania has been invaded, yes. Conquered, no. While the rest of the Balkan Peninsula was being Hellenized, Latinized, Slavo-fied, or Turkey-trotted, Albanians stayed Albanian. Their language is the last extant member of the Phrygo-Thracian family of tongues once spoken by peoples from the far side of the Black Sea to the eastern Adriatic.

The highland areas of Albania have been claimed by various nations but governed by none. Authority has always rested with the *Mal,* the Albanian word for tribe and also—to give some idea of the cozy relationship among Albanian clans—the Albanian word for the mountain that each village is on top of.

The tribalism that has disappeared from the rest of Europe (or been reduced to what tartan you wear on your golf slacks) is still a prime fact of existence in Albania. Tribal identification transcends the theological hatreds so avidly pursued in the rest of the Balkans. There are tribes with both Christian and Muslim members. "The true religion of the Albanian is being an Albanian," said nineteenth-century nationalist Pashko Vasa.

Tribal identification transcended atheism, too. In the 1960s, twenty-eight of the fifty-two members of the Albanian Communist Party's central committee were related by blood.

Blood being the key word. Albania is remarkable for the number and persistence of its blood feuds. As soon as a boy is of age, he is liable to become a Lord of Blood, a *Zot i Gjakut,* with responsibility for killing members of the clan who killed members of his clan, who killed members of their clan, and so forth—a sort of pyramid scheme of death.

Men who are "in blood" can spend years shut up inside their fortified houses. Girls, however, are let off the hook unless they swear to be virgins and wear men's clothes. Lest anyone accuse the Albanians of utterly eschewing all rule of law, this takes place under the auspices of the *Kanun Lek Dukagjini,* the Law of Lek, a voluminous compendium of tribal custom and practice dating back at least to the 1400s, copies of which may be purchased at book stalls in Tirana.

According to James Pettifer, who wrote an essay on the subject for the *Blue Guide* to Albania, anthropologists estimate that there are some two thousand blood feuds going on in Albania and that as many as sixty thousand people are involved. (The *Blue Guide* is one of the few tourist manuals with a good section on the ins and outs of vendetta killing.) In 1992, a man was beheaded with an ax in a Tirana hotel lobby—revenge for a murder his father had committed in a northern village more than forty years before.

The Albanians certainly have preserved their culture. Whether this is a good idea is a question that can be decided only, of course, by Albanians. But in these times of multicultural zeal, it may be worth noting that the Albanian language did not have a proper alphabet until 1908. The country didn't get a railroad until 1947. The first Albanian university was founded in 1957. And there is an Albanian proverb to the effect that a woman must work harder than a donkey because a donkey feeds on grass, while a woman feeds on bread.

Culture is an important factor in determining the economic success of a nation. But, that said, what else is there to say? Germany got rich with a culture as barbaric—a couple of world wars and a Holocaust prove it—as anything ever seen. Tibet stayed poor with a culture so wonderful that half of the movie stars in America want to move there. And how do you change a culture anyway? We could wire Albania for cable and let its citizens see how the rest of the world lives. Jerry Springer should give them some good ideas.

Albania did not improve upon inspection. Even the animals in the Tirana zoo had been stolen. The monkeys were gone from Monkey Island. The aviary was empty of birds. All the large ruminants had been "eaten," said Elmaz. Only two lions, a tiger, and a wolf remained in captivity. No one had had the guts to steal them—although several young men seemed to be gearing themselves to the task. The bars on the wolf's cage had been pried back. One young man stuck his hand inside, shouted, and snatched the hand back. The wolf ignored him, and the men went down the hall to tease the tiger and lions.

In the middle of downtown Tirana, two hundred yards from Skenderbeg Square, is a block-long hole in the ground. Garbage fires smolder at the bottom. This is where Sijdia Holdings was going to build Albania's first Sheraton hotel with pyramid-scheme investments. Only the hole for the cellar was completed. An enclosed staircase rises from the bottom of the hole to street level where there's a door with a neon sign above it, CLUB ALBANIA.

The nearby apartment buildings that housed the country's Communist elite were built in the clean, austere International style of twentieth-century cities everywhere, but they're crumbling. Where big chunks of stucco have fallen away, primitive rubble-wall construction is visible, ready to explode with the structures' weight in the next little earthquake.

Apartments for the common folk were built much worse. Elmaz's mother had had the unenviable job of teaching geography to students who, as far as they knew, would never be allowed to leave the country. She lived in a block of flats with four stories of haphazardly laid masonry courses. Flaking mortar oozed from every joint. The bricks looked like they'd been dug from beds of clay with canoe paddles.

The Hotel Tirana, which went up in 1979, was so badly designed that the Italian entrepreneurs who later took it over had to add a separate tower as a fire escape. Short gangways lead from the tower to an emergency exit on each floor. This outside stairway created security problems, however, so the tower was encased in steel mesh. Now if there's a fire at the Hotel Tirana, the result will be hundreds of guests in an enormous fry basket.

Near the Lana River is a neighborhood called the Block, once reserved for Enver Hoxha's inner circle. Their idea of luxury was semisuburban, the kind of semisuburb you're trying to convince your parents to move out of before their car gets stolen. But the Hoxha residence looks like the house of a really successful Chicago dentist. There's something of the Chicago prairie style to its broad but ill-proportioned windows, clumsy, deep-eaved roof, and dumpy fieldstone terracing—call it Frank Lloyd Left.

Hoxha's daughter Pranvera is, in fact, an architect. I don't know if the Hoxha homestead was her work, but other evidence indicates she's at least as addled as her dad was. She designed what used to be the Enver Hoxha Memorial a couple of streets away. It is immense, concrete, and circular with steep conical exterior walls used these days for daring cardboard-under-the-butt slides by local preteens. It once contained, says the *Blue Guide*, "more or less everything that Hoxha ever touched or used." It now contains the USAID office, which is more useful. I think.

Elmaz and I drove forty kilometers west of Tirana to Durres, passing a complex of greenhouses from which both houses and green had been removed. We saw two summer palaces King Zog had built for himself, completely ransacked. The very paint seemed to have been stolen off the walls.

Durres was, at the time, Albania's only working port. And in that port were exactly two ships. One was a Chinese-built destroyer that had been "bought" from the Albanian navy. At any rate, $6,000 had changed hands. Now the *Khajdi* was a discotheque, paneled inside with the same rough wood used in the beer halls and gambling hells of Tirana's Youth Park. Something had gone wrong in the bilge, however, and the *Khajdi* was listing so far to starboard that you felt you'd had more than enough to drink the moment you stepped inside. Business was bad, the proprietor reported.

The other ship was a beached freighter missing hawsers, hatches, portholes, and anything else that could be filched, including anchors. A couple of men had shinnied up the foremast and were trying to pry a brass knob off the top. A gang of boys ran around the deck playing pirates or, if you think about it, not actually playing. Technically speaking, they *were* pirates.

Elmaz said the looting had pretty much stopped, at least in the thirty or forty kilometers around Tirana. I asked him whether the OSCE force had imposed law and order. He didn't think so. "They are just driving around and sitting in cafés like everyone else," he said. I asked him if the government had managed to quiet things down. It didn't have an army anymore, but it still had the secret police, actually the too-well-known police, the Sigurmi, left over from the Hoxha regime and now renamed, with euphemistic masterstroke, the National Information Service. But Elmaz didn't think the police had done much except pester Sali Berisha's political opponents.

"Then what stopped the looting?" I said.

"They were finished," said Elmaz.

A little before curfew on my last night in Albania, I was sitting in a café with the wire-service reporter and a couple other fellow hacks. "Albanians are just like anybody else," I was saying.

"They're crazy," said the wire-service reporter.

"No, they're not," I said. "They just have a different history, different traditions, a different set of political and economic circumstances. They're acting exactly the way we would if we . . ."

There was an Albanian family at the next table: handsome young husband, pretty wife, baby in a stroller, cute four-year-old girl bouncing on her dad's knee. The girl grabbed the cigarette from between her father's lips and tried a puff. Mom and Dad laughed. Dad took the cigarette back. Then he pulled a pack of Marlboros from his shirt pocket, offered a fresh cigarette to the little girl, and gave her a light.

BAD SOCIALISM

Cuba 1996

I got my first look at Havana at dawn, from the window of my room in the Hotel Nacional. The city was gray with the grizzled markings particular to tropical desolation. Bright colors were bleached to dirty pearl. There were ashen streaks from leaking roofs and dark whorls left over from stagnant puddles. Mildew spread across walls like a living soot.

Even from ten stories up, I could see holes in everything: holes in roofs, holes in streets, holes where windows ought to be. There were holes in everything, and chunks missing from everything else. Chunks had fallen from balconies, cornices, porticoes, marble and granite facades. The city blocks were missing chunks of buildings. Some of the remaining buildings were missing so many chunks I thought they were abandoned until I saw the hanging laundry. And the laundry was full of holes.

Cuba looked like it had lost a war. And it had—the Cold War. But Albania had lost the Cold War, too, and Tirana, as I'd see a year later, was a colorful, noisy place this time of day: cafés were full, cars collided, street vendors shouted their wares. Havana was silent.

I watched enormous breakers tumbling against the seawall of the Malecón, Havana's oceanfront boulevard. Thousands of gallons of gray brine sloshed over the holes and chunks in its concrete pavement. Torrents of dingy sea foam flushed against the Malecón's paintless old town houses. Very few *tuberos*, those brave souls who try to escape from Cuba aboard tied-together inner tubes, would be out today. They'd be washed right back into somebody's living room. And a very crummy living room, to judge by what I could see.

I was feeling pretty crummy myself. I'd arrived the previous midnight and gone straight to the Nacional's bar and started drinking *mojitos*. This was Cuba-fan Ernest Hemingway's second favorite drink, after the wake-up slug out of a hidden gin bottle. A *mojito* is made by mixing too much sugar with too much rum in not enough soda water and adding crushed mint leaves and lime juice. It sounds disgusting and, believe me, the next morning it is.

The walls of the bar were decorated with black-and-white photographs of celebrities visiting the Nacional, all of them, except a couple second-string European intellectuals, before the Castro era. Bad rumba music boomed from the girlie show in the hotel nightclub.

After five or eight *mojitos* I went to the john. If you were designing a socialist system—a nation in which everyone had the same social status—wouldn't eliminating restroom attendants be the first thing you'd do? And if I were designing a socialist system (what a hobby), I'd at least let the masses visit the hotel that they all supposedly own in common. But ordinary Cubans can't enter the Nacional or its several acres of seaside gardens unless they are, for instance, restroom attendants.

A few Cubans manage to sneak in. When I went upstairs at 3 a.m., there was a North American–type fellow in the elevator with a young woman, a girl, really, maybe sixteen years old. She was clean and clean-cut, soberly dressed, without jewelry or makeup, wholesome of manner and apparently a prostitute. At least the elevator operator thought so. He ordered her out. She was not a hard-looking girl, but a hard look crossed her face as she left.

I rented a car for an exorbitant amount of money. The car-rental company's manager spoke at length about Cuban-American friendship and how the citizens of both countries desired peace and mutual cooperation, "except for a few fascists such as Barry Goldwater and that Oklahoma bomber." The manager seemed to have done pretty well in the revolution. "According to my Rolex . . . ," he said, noting the time on my rental contract. And I got to hear about how he liked women with large bottoms.

He gave me the keys to a dirty and dented Japanese sedan. It had a Toyota nameplate, but, looking at the fit and finish, I'd say I doubt it.

I drove through Habana Centro. In 1991, Fidel Castro told Mexican journalist Beatriz Pages, "The other Latin-American countries have tens of millions of beggars; Cuba has none. In other Latin-American countries, you see children cleaning car windshields, running among the cars to do that." I stopped at a red light. Children ran among the cars, cleaning windshields.

Not that there were many windshields to clean. Traffic in Havana was mostly a matter of bicycles and pedestrians who had grown so used to empty streets that someone who looked both ways before crossing was probably a paranoid schizophrenic. People dawdled along, peddling at four miles an hour in the passing lanes and pushing baby strollers down highway exit ramps. Old ladies stood in the middle of the avenue puzzled that there should be someone who wanted to get by.

There were, however, still traffic police, hundreds of them, one on almost every corner. And traffic rules were completely in force, though stoplights were burned out and street signs were illegible with corrosion. It was, for instance, almost impossible to make a legal left turn in Havana, and all the streets in the city seemed to go one way to the left. These streets are numbered odd east-west and even north-south. I was inclined to give up *mojitos* when I found myself at the corner of Tenth and Eleventh streets.

Habana Centro looked like 1960 Cleveland after a thirty-seven-year strike by painters and cleaning ladies. But the old city, La Habana Vieja, was beautiful. Cuba's Spanish-colonial architecture is classical and restrained, less Taco Bell influenced than Mexico's. And unlike the rest of the Caribbean, Cuba's old buildings are made of stone. The island has, during its history, suffered various periods of neglect, such as the present one. Maybe the Cubans were trying to design things that would look good as moldering ruins.

The tourist areas of the old town had been cleaned up, and somewhat more cleanup was in progress. A number of museums and government-owned restaurants were open and were, as *Fodor's* Cuba guidebook says of one such, "decorated with antique furniture recovered from the great mansions of the local bourgeoisie." Tactfully put. Outside of the tourist areas, however, there was a fair danger of experiencing some freelance socialism; you might find that *you* were the local bourgeoisie from which something got recovered.

Later in the morning, Havana's streets grew crowded, but not with a madding crowd. Nobody was doing much of anything or going anywhere in particular. Thousands of people were just hanging around in the middle of a weekday in a country where, by law, there's no unemployment. Some people were walking dogs. All the dogs were old and small, the kind kept by rich women for purposes of baby talk. Maybe the dogs had been left behind when the rich women fled the revolution—thirty-seven-year-old miniature schnauzers forced to pawn their costume-jewelry collars and have their fur clipped at barber colleges.

The dogs didn't look happy. The kind of meat that goes into dog food would be eaten by people in Cuba, if there were any of it to be had. The people didn't look happy, either. There was an edge and an attitude among the idling mobs in Havana. They gave out lots of hard looks, and, when foreign women were around, grabbed their testicles, and made hisses and sucky lip noises.

But when I actually met the Cubans—and I met a lot of them at a gas station after I drove the Toyota into a big hole, causing a front wheel to fold like a paper plate with too much potato salad on it—they were swell. They were pleasant, helpful, cheery, polite. They all had relatives in America. And an American woman told me that when she went out alone, the noises ceased. Or nearly ceased. The men grabbed their testicles in a formal and courtly manner.

The gas station was one of the few visible instances of anybody doing anything for a living. The Cuban government has not only eliminated the concept of unemployment, it's eliminated the concept of jobs, if you don't count begging or pestering strangers to buy "genuine Cohiba cigars" that "a good friend of mine sneaks out of the factory." Either the fellow who sneaks Cohibas out of the factory has an unusual number of good friends, or Cohiba sneaking is Cuba's largest industry.

There was little honest economic activity on the streets of Havana, only occasional kiosks selling cigarettes and newspapers, which they were mostly out of.

At a few prescribed spots in the city, there were arts-and-crafts markets. The arts and the crafts looked like they were made by accountants, lawyers, university professors, and other famously unhandy types who'd been out on the patio with dull tools trying to turn pieces of scrap wood into Che Guevara wall plaques and cigarette boxes with CUBA IS BEAUTIFUL carved on the lids in a desperate attempt to get U.S. dollars.

The dollars were provided by a few tourists watched over by more than a few tourist police. Membership in this branch of the constabulary being proclaimed, in English, on the breast pockets of their uniforms. The tourist police did not, however, enforce fashion law. The tourists wore NBA balloon shoes on noodle legs, pie-wagon-sized jogging shorts, and idiot logo T-shirts.

The Cubans, poor as they were, looked much better. Not that their clothing was good. It seemed to be from American relatives who had gone to Price Club and put together large boxes of practical duds. But the Cubans wore that clothing well—tight where tight flattered, artfully draped where artful draping was to the purpose, and when all else failed, the clothes were simply absent. There were bare midriffs, wide skirt slits, buttons undone to the navel.

Cubans are stylish. Cubans are even glamorous, especially the women. And some of the women were entirely too glamorous for the middle of the day. Because there was a certain economic activity on the streets of Havana, and lots of it. Flocks of women stood along major roads plying the trade. "Why is that girl hitchhiking in her prom dress?" I heard a tourist ask.

The whores were budding in Cuba, and everything else was old, withered, blown, used up. Even the Young Pioneers, solemn kids in red kerchiefs doing calisthenics in the park, seemed to be obsolete children, products of some musty, disproven ideas about social hygiene. Tired, stupid slogans—SOCIALISM OR DEATH—were painted everyplace. The paint on the signs was peeling. All the paint in Cuba was peeling.

Of course, there was a good neighborhood in Havana. There always is in these places. Miramar is on the beach to the west of downtown. The streets were lined with royal palms and also with new BMWs. The cheerful mansions had been built in the style that's called Spanish if you live in Pasadena. These were perfectly maintained and lavishly gardened, and every one of them was owned by a Cuban government institution, a foreign corporation, or an embassy, and so were the cars. In between the cheerful mansions were mansions of little cheer. The Castro government "recovered" these and turned them into housing for "the people." It was part of the liberty, equality, and fraternity espoused by the Cuban revolution. The fraternity in question must have been the one portrayed in *National Lampoon's Animal House*. Much of Miramar looked like the Deltas had been living in it for the past seventy-four semesters. They'd all gotten crabby and gray. And they'd run out of beer.

Nighttime was better in Havana. The city had so few lights that after dark I hardly noticed the electrical blackouts.

There were some privately owned restaurants. The food was good, and I could get a meal for five dollars. However, it did have to be dollars. No one in Cuba was interested in pesos. Even beggars checked to see if the coin being offered was American. The private restaurants were allowed no more than twelve seats, and only family members could be employed. This was as far as the Cuban government had been willing to go with capitalism among its own citizens. It will be interesting to see how this model works if it's applied to other free enterprise undertakings, such as airlines. Mom will begin beverage service as soon as Junior gets the landing gear up.

The big restaurants were nationalized, and in a nation that's suffering severe food shortages, this meant that only rice and beans were available to foreigners who had dollars. Ha, ha, ha. Hard-currency joke. I could get anything I wanted—lobster, steak, Cohiba cigars actually made by Cohiba, and rum older than the prostitutes sitting at all the other tables with German businessmen. The catch was, not only couldn't Cubans afford these things, neither could I. In the Floridita, where the daiquiri was invented and where the New York City price of drinks was apparently also invented, cocktails cost five dollars—more, at the black-market exchange rate for dollars, than most Cubans make in a week. I was also in constant danger of being serenaded. Guitar players roam Cuba's restaurants in packs. They know one song, "Guantanamera." The complete lyrics are:

"Guantanamera, Guantanamera,
Guan-tan-a-meeeeera, Guantanamera."

This unofficial national anthem was popularized by noted Cuban patriot Pete Seeger.

Was I missing something? Cuba is famous for its charm. I decided to hire a guide. Maybe he could find me some. Roberto, as I'll call him, took me to Hemingway's house in the village of San Francisco de Paula. It's a white stucco plantation-style manor on a hilltop with twenty-two acres of land, a guest cottage, and a swimming pool. I must remember to write harder.

There's a three-story tower with a den at the top where Hemingway could go and think big thoughts. ("Where is that gin bottle?") And in the toilet off the main bedroom, there's a pickled lizard on a shelf. The lizard got into a fight with one of Hemingway's cats. The cat won, but the reptile fought so bravely that Papa felt the need to immortalize it. The liquid in the container was low. It looked like somebody had taken a few nips out of the lizard jar. On second thought, I'm not sure I have what it takes to be a major author.

Hemingway's widow donated the house to the Castro government. And Britain donated Hong Kong to China.

Roberto was chatty, full of official, government-approved information. On the way to San Francisco de Paula, we passed the dirty, bedraggled worker housing that everywhere mars the Cuban landscape. The buildings are nothing but concrete dovecotes: six-story-high, hundred-yard-long stacks of tiny apartment boxes open on one end. They must have staircases, but I couldn't see any. Maybe the government comes along at night and plucks up people and puts them in their pigeonholes. "The workers made these!" said Roberto. Though, if you think about it, workers make everything. "The government gives them the construction material," he said. "Then they rent for twelve years. And then they own them!" In other words, you get a free home in Cuba as long as you build it and pay for it.

When we drove into La Habana Vieja, Roberto pointed at a gutted hotel: "These are special worker brigades, doing this construction. They can work sixteen hours a day." This must have been one of the other eight. Everyone was sitting around smoking cigarettes. "They get extra rations," said Roberto, "a big bag with soap, cooking oil, rice, beans . . ." Roberto sounded as if he was describing the contents of a big bag from, say, Tiffany's.

"In 1959 there were six thousand doctors in Cuba," said Roberto, apropos of nothing. "Three thousand of them left after the revolution. Yet we are training new doctors. By the year 2000 there will be sixty thousand doctors in Cuba!" But Roberto could only talk government talk so long. He couldn't stay off the real subject, what was on every Cuban's mind all the time: the economic mess. "You see these cabdrivers?" he said, pointing to a line of tourist-only taxis. "People need to earn dollars. These drivers may be doctors."

"In Cuba," said Roberto, "anything you want is available—for dollars." But people are paid in pesos, even if they work for foreign companies, which Roberto, in fact, does. The national tourist service isn't owned by the nation anymore. It's been sold to overseas investors. These people pay $300 a month for Roberto's services. But they don't pay Roberto. They pay the Cuban government. The Cuban government then pays Roberto 150 a month, in pesos.

Figuring out what the Cuban peso is worth is a complex economic calculation. To put it in layman's terms, a pretty close approximation is nothing. Pesos are of use almost exclusively for buying rationed goods. The Cuban rationing system is simple: they're out of everything. Although you can get a really vile pack of cigarettes for ten pesos. Think of Roberto's salary as a carton and a half of smokes.

Roberto was able, however, to earn dollars through tips. Cadging these being, of course, the subtext to his economic discourse. He used to be a teacher but couldn't live on the pay. His wife is a chemical engineer, but her chemical plant shut down three years ago. While we were walking around the old town, Roberto met another engineer, now working as a carpenter for dollars—building the table under which he'd get paid.

"Just to feed ourselves," said Roberto, "we have to go to four markets. The ration store for, maybe, rice. Then the government dollar store—this is very expensive. Then the dollar market where farmers can sell what they grow if they grow more than the government quota. And then the black market."

We drove down Avenida Bolívar, through what had been Havana's shopping district. Hundreds of stores stood closed and empty, the way they've been since 1968, when the last small businesses were nationalized. "That is where the Sears store was," said Roberto, pointing to the largest empty building. "But now we have nothing to sell."

Every so often Roberto would snap out of it and resume the official patter: "Over there is a memorial to Julius and Ethel Rosenberg. Perhaps you have a monument to them in North America?" I said I didn't think so. But mostly, Roberto wanted to talk about free enterprise. He and his wife were sleeping on the mattress his mother bought when she got married: "It has been repaired over and over. We get the TV sometimes from Miami—oh, the 'Beatty Rest' mattresses! And what good prices!"

Roberto was optimistic. He kept showing me new family-owned restaurants. "Look, there's one!" He pointed to a pizza parlor. "There's more!" He pointed to several pizza parlors. In Cuba, capitalism's thin edge of the wedge comes plain or with pepperoni.

Roberto thought small private retail shops would be opening soon. He thought the government's new "convertible peso," which is pegged 1:1 to the dollar, would become the national currency. He was even enthusiastic about the fees the Cuban authorities were beginning to charge, such as highway tolls. "Maybe we will get better service," he said. Roberto told me that the economy had "come back since the low point of '94, a little," and that this was due to the private businesses. "The only thing the government controls now is the taxes," said Roberto.

He was wrong. Fidel Castro, in his 1996 year-end speech to the Cuban National Assembly, described the economic reforms thus: "We legalized robbery." Castro then did, indeed, announce an income tax on the self-employed.

That night, after Roberto had been sufficiently tipped, I went to a bar on the east side of Havana harbor with a European reporter who's lived for years in Cuba. He thought economic reform was over. He said the authorities were "still emphasizing that outside investment is 'not vital,'" and that they "still think the state sector can be made 'more efficient.'" He quoted a Canadian diplomat: "The pace of economic reform in Cuba is determined by the learning curve in economics of Fidel Castro. And he's a slow learner."

As we talked, a young Cuban woman came out on the terrace. She ignored us in a very unprostitutional way, chose a chair just within earshot, and began avidly appreciating the city skyline. "I'd buy it if she were a tourist," whispered the reporter, "but Cubans do not go to dollar bars for the view."

There is one vibrant, exciting, and highly efficient sector of the official Cuban economy: the police. I was driving through the Vedado neighborhood in western Havana absolutely desperate to turn left. Finally, I just went and did so. Almost a mile away, in an entirely different section of town, a policeman walked out into the street, flagged me down, and wrote me a ticket for the transgression. There's a space provided for this on the rental-car papers, and the fine comes out of the deposit.

The traffic-cop omniscience was creepy enough, but I happened to be on my way to visit a dissident couple. Well, "dissident couple" is a little dramatic. They hadn't actually dissented about anything. They just wanted to leave Cuba. They went to Sweden and applied for asylum. But the generous Swedish refugee policy does not extend to refugees from progressive, socialist countries to which Sweden gives millions of dollars in foreign aid. They were sent back. And now they were in permanent hot water.

They lived in a shabby tower block with a ravaged elevator, piss stink in the stairwells, bulbs filched from the lobby light fixtures, and even the glass stolen from the hallway windows. And in Havana, this was a good place to live. The apartment had been inherited from a parent, a parent who had been an official in the revolutionary government. "Come on Friday," the couple had said. "We don't have power outages then."

There were five rooms—small rooms (you couldn't flip a pancake in the kitchen without standing in the hall), but five rooms nonetheless—and a bathroom (when the water was running). And not too many of the louvers in the jalousie windows were broken. Carlos and Donna—not their real names of course—come from families that had been prosperous (families that now, incidentally, won't speak to them). The low, narrow-walled living room was filled with too much big, dark furniture from a more expansive age, like a Thanksgiving dinner for twelve put in the microwave. I felt claustrophobic although I was five stories in the air and could see the ocean shining in the distance.

Carlos and Donna are not allowed to hold jobs, but they each speak four languages and so are able to get work as guides and translators with the various groups of academics, philanthropists, conference delegates, and film-festival attendees who are forever traipsing through Cuba looking for international understanding and a tan.

"You have to earn dollars anyway here," said Carlos. "'Dollars or Death' is what everyone says." He showed me their ration books, which have categories for everything from tobacco to clothing. So far in 1996, only one liter of cooking oil per family had been available. Eggs were plentiful at the moment—fourteen a month for the two of them. Carlos and Donna also got two bars of soap a month, some months. There was virtually no meat, and it was inedible. "All red meat has been nationalized," said Carlos by way of explanation. Cuban nationalization does to goods and services what divorce does to male parents—suddenly they're absent most of the time and useless the rest. Cubans can't even get real coffee from the ration stores. They get coffee beans mixed with the kind of beans you get in tortillas. This tastes the way it sounds like it would and gives everyone stomach cramps.

The few legitimate delights of Cuba—coffee, rum, cigars—require not just dollars but lots of dollars. And even this doesn't always work. The Montecristo coronas I bought in a government shop had the flavor and draw of smoldering felt-tip pens.

Carlos and Donna had had one other brush with the law. Besides committing the heinous crime of trying to move, they were also caught with dollars. Until mid-1993 it was illegal for Cubans to own dollars. Given what the peso was worth, that meant it was illegal for Cubans to have money. Carlos and Donna found sixty dollars tucked in a book they'd inherited. They dressed in their best clothes and, being fluent in French, tried to pass themselves off as foreigners at a beachfront hotel. "To get a decent cup of coffee," said Donna. But the hotel waiter wasn't fooled. Perhaps the two bars of soap a month was the giveaway, this being more than most French tourists use. As Carlos and Donna walked home, they were arrested.

They escaped any serious jail time, maybe because of their foreign-diplomat connections. But they were threatened with six or seven years' imprisonment. And a year later the block captain—the government snitch who resides on every Cuban street—called them in and threatened them with imprisonment again. "When dollars became legal," said Carlos, "everyone was happy." I wasn't so happy thinking about all those people who were locked up for years sometimes, just for having one or two dollars.

"Still, I don't have any hatred against the system," he said. "But this is just for myself, for my own sake—I don't want hatred to destroy me."

"When we couldn't leave," said Donna, "we were in despair for a while. Then we became involved in the charity work of the church, in their hospitals. This created new meaning."

"We're happy now," said Carlos.

But they don't have children. They felt too cut off from Cuban society for that. Carlos doesn't even know if his parents are still alive.

"The revolution brought some benefits," said Carlos, "at least at first. There was better housing, but it was gotten by giving away what had been stolen from others. The health care is free—and worth it. I can go to the doctor, but he can do nothing for me. This is why the Catholic Church must have its own hospitals. The education is free, too. But it's indoctrination. This is not a real education. Then they make the students work on the sugar harvest. Of course, the students wreck the agriculture. They don't care. They don't know what they're doing."

Carlos and Donna thought it was important that people know what a disastrous and terrifying place Cuba is. "Not for the sake of future revenge," said Donna, "but because of the frailty of memory. People will forget how bad it was, the way they're already forgetting in Russia. But more important, they'll forget why it became that way."

It will take a lot of forgetting. Socialism has had a nasty reign in Cuba. Hundreds of low-level supporters of the ousted Batista regime were executed, and thousands were jailed. Homosexuals, Jehovah's Witnesses, and people with AIDS antibodies have been sent to concentration camps. Critics of the government are forced into internal exile or confined in mental hospitals. The Americas Watch human rights group has said that Cuba holds "more political prisoners as a percentage of population than any other country in the world." Freedom House, a pro-democracy organization whose board of trustees runs an ideological gamut from Jeane Kirkpatrick to Andrew Young, says, "There is continued evidence of torture and killings in prison and in psychiatric institutions . . . Local human-rights activists say that more than 100 prisons and prison camps hold between 60,000 and 100,000 prisoners of all categories." (This is about twice America's generous rate of per capita incarceration.) How many of those categories are political? Well, from a socialist point of view, all of them. And any normal Cuban is probably going to wind up in jail sooner or later anyway, because, according to Amnesty International, serious offenses in Cuba include "illegal association," "disrespect," "dangerousness," "illegal printing," and "resistance." Castro himself was in jail for a while under the previous administration and in a 1954 letter from his cell he wrote: "We need many Robespierres in Cuba."

Maybe the potential for disaster lurks in all socialism, but what had caused this potential to be realized in Cuba and not, for instance, in Sweden? I asked Carlos and Donna if there was something fundamentally different about Cuba's socialist ideology? Or had evil people simply taken control of socialism in Cuba?

"Neither," said Carlos. "It's because of power. They have total power. Think what you yourself would do if you had total power over everyone."

Not a pretty picture, I admit. And I'm not even a socialist. Socialists think of society as a giant, sticky wad. And no part of that gum ball—no intimate detail of your private life—can be pulled free from the purview of socialism. Socialism is inherently totalitarian in philosophy.

In Cuba, the authorities have a Ken Starr grand jury–like right to poke into every aspect of existence, no matter how trivial. Imagine applying Marxist theory to rock and roll, this being what the *Union de Escritores y Artistas de Cuba*, or UNEAC, the official labor organization for creative types, is supposed to do. Karl Marx said in *Das Kapital*, "Nothing can have value without being an object of utility. If it be useless, the labor contained in it is useless, cannot be reckoned as labor, and cannot therefore create value." Roll over Beethoven, indeed.

Professor Dr. Jose Loyola, who was, according to his business card, "*Compository Musicologo*" and "*Vice Presidente Primero*" of UNEAC, talked to me about utility. Specifically, he talked about trying to get Cuban elements into rock and roll to offset imperialist U.S. influences. Sex, drugs, and cha-cha-cha? Professor Dr. Loyola's office was in a splendid nineteenth-century town house, the kind of house that should belong to a rock star. Although I had visited an actual Cuban rock star, Santiago Feliu. Feliu lived in what looked like a graduate student's off-campus apartment.

The UNEAC town house had been spoiled by the cheap partitions and wobbly chrome-leg chairs loved by bureaucracies everywhere, and by photographs of Fidel where art used to hang. While we sat in the part of the former dining room that was now the professor-doctor's stuffy office, the power went out repeatedly.

I asked how musicians got into this union. They submit an application with curriculum vitae listing their important concerts, the rewards and prizes they've won, and the recordings they've made. Then a commission made up of three or four "prestigious musicians" meets and decides upon acceptance or rejection. Which is just the way most people get into the business everywhere.

LEAD RAPPER WITH CREW Da Thug Murderz
PERFORMED Public park in South Bronx, Cell Block D Riker's Island
CITATIONS Many, mostly from NYPD narcotics squad
ATTACHED DEMO CUT, "Kill Yo MoFo"

Mick? Elton? Do we let him in?

I asked what UNEAC did for its members. "The prestige of the organization opens many doors," said Professor Dr. Loyola. "It promotes the work of the artists and takes care of some of their, ah, material problems." In other words, you starve if you aren't in UNEAC.

"What if you aren't a member?" I asked.

"Oh, most artists aren't members," said Professor Dr. Loyola. "There are fourteen thousand professional artists in Cuba. Only four thousand are members. The other ten thousand have the government's Ministry of Culture to promote their work." The way our government's National Public Radio plays "Kill Yo MoFo" by Da Thug Murderz on *All Things Considered*.

"What kind of problems do musicians face in Cuba?" I asked.

"Material problems."

"Material problems?"

"Maybe," said the professor doctor, "if we had stores where they could buy their instruments, it would be better."

"Could be," I said.

"Some people get musical instruments from the Ministry of Culture," he ventured and changed the subject. "Before, there were many empirical musicians in Cuba. Now they have formal training. Now there is a kind of upgrading school for empirical musicians." And what a shame this wasn't the practice in America's rural South during the time of Huddie Ledbetter and Lightnin' Sam Hopkins. They wouldn't have been so "downbeat" if they'd been able to get work in the New York Philharmonic orchestra.

"What does UNEAC do," I asked, "if an artist gets in trouble with the government?"

"If he is right, we will help him out. And if he is not right, we will help orient him in the correct direction," said Professor Dr. Loyola with a perfectly straight face.

Since 1959 the Cuban government has been "orienting" everybody in "the correct direction," thereby making a total mess of the Cuban economy. And one of the things that's so messy about it is that there's no way to measure how messy it is.

There are simply no reliable Cuban economic statistics. Everybody, Cuban officialdom included, agrees that Cuba's economy has shrunk by at least a third since the 1980s. But a third of what? Cuba's per capita gross domestic product for the year 1995, for example, has been calculated at \$2,058 by dissident Cuban economists, \$2,902 by the Cuban government, \$3,245 by wishful-thinking leftist American academics and—the highest estimate of all—\$3,652 by the U.S. Department of Commerce. Now the per capita GDP in Cuba is about \$1,200, according to the National Bank of Cuba, or \$1,480, if you believe the CIA's *The World Factbook,* while the *Columbia Journal of World Business* thinks the figure may be as low as \$900. Nobody knows. Just as nobody knows what the peso is worth.

The black-market rate in March 1996 was 21 pesos per dollar. But there was something wrong with that rate. Just two years before, the rate was 150 pesos per dollar. And dollars hadn't gotten any less necessary or much more available. Latin American scholar Douglas W. Payne thinks the

Cuban secret police took over the black market. Or maybe the Cuban government was using the new convertible peso—which, though printed in bright tropical hues, is essentially counterfeit U.S. money—to flood the currency exchanges. "There will arrive the day when money will have no value," Fidel Castro once said in a fit of Marxist utopianism. But apparently he meant it.

I went into the Ministry of Trade's product showroom, and there, offered for wholesale export to the world, were coconut shells painted to look like turtles, baskets that seemed to have been woven by people wearing catcher's mitts, posters for obscure brands of rum, pictures of Che Guevara, and Aunt Jemima rag dolls in half a dozen sizes.

The Cubans may not be good with their hands, but they're very skillful with blame. They blame the Soviet Union. And not without reason. When the Soviet bloc collapsed, the Cubans lost somewhere between $4 billion and $6 billion a year in grants, subsidies, and trade concessions. Taking the low figure, that's a dollar per person per day for everyone in the country. You can live for less than that in Cuba, and almost everyone has to.

Of course, the Soviets used to get something in return for this aid. They got sugar and cobalt and nickel. Which is why it was always easy to get a plate of sugared cobalt and nickel at Moscow restaurants in the 1980s. Plus, the Soviets got to be a huge pain in the ass to the United States. But what the Cuban government got was the luxury of perfect shiftlessness. The Castro government took boatloads of money from the Soviet Union and took all the businesses, industries, and land in Cuba, too.

So the Soviet Union is to blame for Cuban poverty because the Soviet Union fell apart, which means that everything is really America's fault. Everything usually is. Cubans have been blaming their troubles on the United States at least since independence in 1902 and probably since Columbus set course too far south and missed becoming an American citizen. Even as José Martí was leading the struggle for freedom from Spain, he was denouncing the United States as a "monster." And he was living in the United States at the time.

My tour guide Roberto told me that the explosion of the battleship *Maine* was just an "American pretext to get into the Cuba-Spain war." No matter that's how Cuba won.

On the other hand, the United States has been less than an ideal next-door neighbor. "Just at the moment I'm so angry with that infernal little Cuban Republic that I would like to wipe its people off the face of the earth," said Teddy Roosevelt in 1906. American armed forces occupied Cuba from 1899 to 1902, and from 1906 to 1909. There was further military intervention in 1912 and threats of more, plus an invasion by proxy at the Bay of Pigs in 1961. And a U.S. trade embargo, in force since that year, certainly looks to the Cubans like a "wipe its people off the face of the earth" gesture.

The Cubans estimated that as of 1996, this embargo had cost them between $38 billion and $40 billion. That happens to be much less than they'd received from the Soviets for doing the things that got them embargoed. But we're talking politics here, not sense. Then in 1996 came the Cuban Liberty and Democratic Solidarity Act, or Helms-Burton Act, as it's called, after its respective sponsors in the U.S. Senate and House. This passed by whopping majorities because Cuba had just shot down two private planes carrying anti-Castro exiles who had a habit of dropping leaflets on Havana. Probably the leaflets contained dangerous information about the price of mattresses in Miami. Helms-Burton tightened the embargo by imposing sanctions not only on those who trade with Cuba but on those who trade with those who trade with Cuba and those who date them and their friends and pets. Or something.

And the Cubans were steamed. All over Havana, walls had been painted with six-foot cartoons depicting Senator Jesse Helms as Hitler and Uncle Sam as Hitler, and Jesse Helms as Hitler again. The Cubans didn't seem to know what Rep. Dan Burton looked like. Come to think of it, I don't either.

Of course the embargo is stupid. It gives Castro an excuse for everything that's wrong with his rat-bag society. And free enterprise is supposed to be the antidote to socialism. We shouldn't forbid American companies from doing business in Cuba, we should require them to do so. Bring them ashore with marines if necessary. Although I guess we've tried that.

And the Cubans are stupid for rising to the bait. There's another little island next to a gigantic, powerful country that threatens to invade and enforced an embargo for decades. And Taiwan has done okay.

I went with two American newspaper reporters to interview a Cuban economist, Hiram Marquetti, a professor at the University of Havana and an industrial-planning consultant to various state companies and government agencies. I wanted to see what it was like talking to an "expert" who wasn't allowed to tell me the facts and maybe wasn't allowed to know them.

Marquetti, looking grave, said the U.S. embargo had cost Cuba $42 billion, upping the amount a couple of billion dollars from what Cuban Foreign Ministry adviser Pedro Prada said in his book *Island Under Siege* (available in English in hotel gift shops and complete with an appendix: "Opponents of the Blockade," listing Danny Glover, Cyndi Lauper, and Cheech Marin).

Marquetti, looking graver, admitted things were lousy. Malnutrition was evident in some sectors of the population. During the last few years, he said, the average Cuban's intake of vitamin A was down 35 percent, iron down 40 percent, and vitamin C down 15 percent. The last item is interesting in a country where citrus trees are basically weeds.

Marquetti, looking graver yet, said, "The highest percentage of disposable income goes to food, usually more than 50 percent. We need the free market to complete the supply." But he also said that this free market and the dollars that make it work "do not necessarily have to do with the opening of the economy." He claimed that "dollarization" was about Cuba acquiring "new technology, expertise in company management, and access to new markets." It was not about any actual Cubans acquiring any actual money.

"Total foreign investment, including contracts, has been $2 billion since 1992," said Marquetti, now looking proud. Though my European journalist friend thought only about $750 million had ever really been spent, and a *New York Law Journal* article cited estimates as low as $500 million. "Nickel mining provides $50 million a year in salaries alone, though such figures are not usually released, for security reasons," said Marquetti, looking sly and confidential.

The newspaper reporters were getting bored. "What effect is dollarization having on families and society?" asked one of them. Said Marquetti, looking bureaucratically oblivious, "Number one: foreign investment. Two: intensive development of tourism. Three: opening to foreign trade."

Sis has been out hitchhiking and someone made a foreign investment in her. It's all part of Cuba's intensive development of tourism. And, gosh, is she open to foreign trade.

"What about the prostitutes?" said the other reporter. "There are rumors that the government turns a blind eye because of the dollars they bring in."

All at once, Marquetti looked human and, indeed, rather enthusiastic. "They are very inexpensive," he said. "They are very educated. They are very young and very pretty. Cuba is a country that attracts tourism for cheap sex," he said, stopping just short of a wink. Marquetti tried to look grave again. "Since the crisis there has been a negative social impact, but you can't eliminate it through repressive means." It's not like these girls are scattering mattress-price leaflets. "We have to look for other solutions, such as education." But he'd just said they *were* educated. "Some sectors of Cuban youth, they view prostitution as a solution to their economic problems."

As for Hiram Marquetti himself, he was selling his report on the Cuban economy—five dollars per copy.

Before the revolution, annual per capita income in Cuba was $374; that's about $1,978 in current dollars. So Cuba is poorer than it used to be, although the poverty is spread around a little more. Castro's government is as dishonest as the prerevolutionary government was. The modern corruption involves more greed for power than passion for lucre, but that's actually worse. And the depraved sex is still available if you can sneak the whores past the elevator operators.

Getting more people to sneak whores past elevator operators was, so far, the best the Cuban government had been able to do in terms of a plan to improve the economy. Tourism was supposed to be the salvation now that Soviet aid had vaporized and sugar was selling for less per pound than garden loam. About 700,000 tourists a year were visiting Cuba, an increase of more than 100 percent since 1990. The Cuban government expected foreign companies to invest an additional $2.4 billion in tourist facilities by the year 2000. This would double the number of hotel rooms on the island. And every one of those rooms will be occupied, I predict, by somebody as ticked off as I was.

Because Cuba does not quite have the tourism thing figured. When I checked into the Hotel Nacional, I was given the manager's room, in which he was living. I was given another room. The key card didn't work. The bellhop went to get another key card. Then the safe didn't work—no small matter since Americans can't use credit cards in Cuba and have to conduct all business in cash, an awkward lump of which I was carrying.

When I returned from the hotel bar bloated with *mojitos*, the key card didn't work again. I went down to get another. The elevator took ten minutes to arrive. The new key card didn't work. I went back. The elevator took another ten minutes. That key card didn't work, either. The maid let me in.

I was awakened at dawn the next morning by a series of chirpy phone calls from the government tourism service in the downstairs lobby. CubaTrot or Havan-a-Vacation or whatever it was called had a driver and a translator and a guide and something else, maybe a circus elephant, waiting for me, bright and early, ready and willing, all set to take me anywhere I wanted to go, except back to bed. None of which stuff I had ordered.

At dawn on the second morning the operator called saying I "must go to reception immediately." When I went downstairs the desk clerk said, "It was nothing." When I went upstairs the key card didn't work. At dawn on the third morning it was a wrong number. On the fourth morning it was someone jabbering expressively in French.

At least I was always awake in time for breakfast. Every day I ordered coffee, toast, and orange juice, and I never got the same thing twice. I traveled to a beach resort in Trinidad on the Caribbean coast, and at dawn the phone rang—a hang-up. I ordered coffee, toast, and orange juice, and got coffee, orange juice, and a cheese sandwich with ketchup on it. The next morning at about seven, a room-service waiter arrived at my door, unbidden, with a plate of dinner buns. As I was checking out, there was an irked Canadian couple at the front desk saying, "We got a message. You told us, 'Call from Toronto,' nothing else, eh? We're thinking there's maybe something wrong at home. So we try and we try, and we get through, eh? And it costs us fifty dollars. And nobody's called us at all."

I had driven to Trinidad on the *autopista,* which is a six-lane . . . a four-lane . . . sometimes a two-lane . . . The Russians never got around to finishing it. And it's not like there are any lane divider lines painted on it anyway. The *autopista* runs from Havana southeast through the middle of the island. There was so little traffic that cows grazed on weeds coming up in the pavement cracks. I had stumbled into a radical ecologist's daydream. Or so it appeared until I'd pass some East German tractor-trailer spewing a mile-long cloud of tar-colored exhaust.

You have to watch out when you drive in Cuba, but you never know what you're watching out for. It could be anything. Potholes, of course, some of them big enough for a couple of chairs and a coffee table. Then there are the people who leap out from the side of the road frantically, desperately, even violently trying to sell you one onion. Or a string of garlic. Or a pale, greasy-looking hunk of something. Lard? Flan? Pound of flesh? (It turned out to be homemade cheese.)

At every major road junction there were scores of hitchhikers, not the prostitute kind but regular folks, whole families among them. Cuba's national transportation system barely exists. Says *Fodor's* guide, "Be prepared to wait three days for the next available bus." Standing among the people with their thumbs out were the traffic police. They stopped cars and trucks (though not those with *tourista* license plates) and made them take passengers.

Cops helping you bum a ride—now here was the revolution the way I had it planned thirty years ago when I was smoking a lot of dope. Except, not exactly. The reason so many people were hitchhiking in the middle of nowhere was that they'd been sent there to work on the sugar harvest. I don't recall that the workers' paradise of my callow fantasies contained any actual work.

That sugar harvest was going on all around me. Or, rather, not going on. I'm no agricultural expert, but I'm almost certain that leaning against fences, walking about with hands in the pockets, and sitting on stalled tractors smoking cigarettes are not the most efficient methods of cutting sugarcane.

Much work had been done, however, painting propaganda slogans. SOCIALISM OR DEATH appeared on almost every overpass. What if the U.S. government had slogans all over the place? I tried to come up with a viable campaign. My suggestion, AMERICA—IT DOESN'T SUCK.

As for "Socialism or Death," after a couple of weeks in Cuba, I was leaning toward the latter option. To which the Castro government's response is: Death? Yes. No problem. That can be arranged. But, *first,* socialism!

I turned off the *autopista* onto a raggedy strip of pavement through the Escambray Mountains. The sun went down, and suddenly traffic materialized —gigantic Russian trucks driven without sense, headlights, or any idea of keeping to the right on the road. I emerged from the mountains at Cienfuegos. Says *Fodor's*: "The people of Cienfuegos . . . constantly tout it as '*la Linda Ciudad del Mar*' (the lovely city by the sea)." They're lying. From here it was a thirty-mile drive through coastal mangrove swamps on a road covered with land crabs. Every time I went over one, it made a noise like when you were ten, and you spent two weeks making a plastic model of the battleship *Missouri*, and your dad stepped on it in the dark. I tried avoiding the crabs. They scuttled under the wheels. I tried driving at them. They stayed put. The road smelled like thirty miles of crab salad going bad.

It was almost 10 p.m. before I got to my hotel on the beach, the Ancon. But the buffet was still open. They were serving crab salad. I went to the bar.

In the morning the ocean sparkled, the sand gleamed, the cheese sandwich with ketchup arrived. Bright-pink vacationers frolicked in the surf or, rather, stood on the beach discussing whether to frolic in the surf, having seen large numbers of stingrays the last time they frolicked.

The Ancon was filled with middle-aged Canadians having the middle-aged Canadian idea of fun, which consisted mostly of going back to the buffet for seconds on the crab salad. The architecture was modernistic. The rooms were comfortablistic. The food was foodlike.

There are worse tourist facilities in Cuba, namely all of them. The Ancon is top of the line. I inspected the other beach hotels near Trinidad, and I had driven out to see those along the *playas del este* outside Havana. Most were stark. Some were dank and unclean. And one spread of tiny prefabricated cottages with outdoor sinks and group bathrooms looked like nothing so much as a portable toilet farm.

Cuba serves the very lowest end of the international holiday market. When some waiter in Paris recites the *plats du jour* like he's pissing on you from a great height, you can extract your mental revenge by picturing him, come August, on Cuba's *Costa del Fleabag*, eating swill in a concrete dining hall.

I wandered around the Trinidad region. I went to see the Iznaga Tower, an early-nineteenth-century neoclassical structure with seven arched and columned setbacks tapering to 140 feet at the pinnacle—monumental but so delicately proportioned that the whole thing seemed about to take flight. It looked like a spaceship designed by Palladio. The purpose of this beautiful and subtle artistry, which took ten years to construct, was to keep the slaves from goofing off. The plantation owner would get up on top and give everybody the hairy eyeball. The tower was no longer in use. With the block-captain system, the chattel labor now spied on itself.

I drove through the Valle de los Ingenios (Valley of the Sugar Mills, as it's romantically called) and over the Escambray Mountains again. As late as 1967, anti-Castro guerrillas were extant here. The Cuban government prefers to call them "bandits." Back in Trinidad, in what used to be a church, there's the marvelously named Museum of the Struggle Against Bandits, which should certainly open a branch in the U.S., maybe on Wall Street.

Not much was actually in the museum. The centerpiece was a beat-up pleasure boat supposedly captured from the CIA. Two suspiciously new and definitely Soviet machine guns had been mounted on its deck with unlikely looking half-inch wood screws. The rest of the displays were mostly devoted to photographs of Cuban soldiers "martyred by bandits." One of these poor soldiers was named O'Really.

Not much was actually in Trinidad, either. It's very old, if you like that sort of thing. Trinidad was founded in 1514 by Diego Velázquez de Cuéllar, the conquistador of Cuba. Although Cuba didn't really take much conquering. Confiscador would be more like it. The local heyday was in the eighteenth century, when Trinidad was a major slave port. Then better slave off-loading facilities were built in Cienfuegos. Not much has changed in Trinidad since, and this gets the guidebooks excited. *Fodor's* goes on at some length about how this "marvelous colonial enclave" has not been "polluted with advertising, automobiles, souvenir shops, dozens of restaurants and hotels, and hordes of tourists milling through the streets." Which, translated, means nobody's made a centavo here in two hundred years.

The buildings around the main square were patched and painted. The buildings not around the main square weren't. Practically everything was one-story high and built flush against tiny, crooked streets paved in stones as large as carry-on luggage.

I got lost driving back to the hotel. The streets were becoming even tinier, and the people standing around in those streets were not looking full of glee that UNESCO had declared Trinidad a World Heritage Site. In fact, they looked depressed and mean. I was getting more than the usual number of cold stares and catcalls, and just when I'd thought to myself, "I wouldn't care to stop here," I stopped there.

The starter motor whined uselessly. The car was inert. A crowd of impoverished Cubans gathered around me. I was frantically looking up "Placating Phrases" in the *Berlitz* when I realized the rude noises and gestures had stopped. The people in the crowd were smiling. And not the way I would have smiled if I'd found a moneyed dimwit trapped in my barrio. "*El auto es busto,*" I explained, opening the hood in that purposeful way men have when we don't know what we're doing.

"*Mi amigo es mecanico,*" said a fellow in the crowd. He and two of his friends grabbed the fenders and pushed the car down the block and around a corner. A big guy about my age came out of a house, shook my hand, and removed the car's air filter. While the big guy probed the carburetor, the crowd went to work. One kid brought tools. Another kid sat in the driver's seat and worked the ignition on the big guy's instructions. Two young men rolled a barrel of gasoline up the street and tipped some into the tank. An old man came out of another house with a pitcher of water. He checked the level in the battery cells and filled the windshield-washer reservoir while he was at it. A second man removed the distributor cap and inspected the points. He pulled the spark-plug wires and looked into their sockets. A third man detached the fuel line and began sucking on it, spitting the gasoline into the street. The big guy took the fuel pump apart. The distributor cap man disappeared for a while and returned with some scavenged spark-plug sockets, which he spliced onto the old spark-plug wires. Other people checked the radiator and the oil. "I have an aunt in Union City, New Jersey," said someone. That was the extent of anybody's English.

After an hour the big guy shook his head. It couldn't be fixed. Which was fine with me. The car smelled like dead crabs, and I'd get another one from FlubaTour at the hotel. But now I had a problem in diplomacy. My crowd of mechanics didn't want to take any money. I could, I gathered with some translating help from a cabdriver, pay for the gasoline. Gasoline was hard to get. But as for working on the car, well, they hadn't fixed it. But they should get some money for their time, I said. They shrugged. They looked at the ground. They were embarrassed, time being the only thing everyone's got lots of in Cuba. It was with negotiating effort worthy of Jimmy Carter fishing for a Nobel Peace Prize that I managed to get their price up to fifty dollars.

Che Guevara believed that socialism would create a "New Man," someone who worked not for personal gain but for the good of humanity in general. All the murders, imprisonings, harassments, and deprivations of Cuba have supposedly been aimed at creating this New Man—somebody who would act like the big guy. Except the big guy wasn't one of them. He had a handmade sign hanging over his door: PARKING 24 HOURS I CARE FOR YOUR CAR I DO SOME REPAIRS ON BICYCLES MOTORCYCLES AND CARS, written, with obvious hope of future capitalist imperialism, in English.

From Beatnik to Business Major:

Taking Econ 101 for Kicks

After two years of wandering around in different economic locales, trying to look at various societies from an economic point of view, and generally poking my nose into other people's business, I thought I should make another attempt to answer the question, "What am I talking about?" I went back to the books about economic theory and the college econ texts, and even Samuelson's dreadful *Economics*. And this time I was . . . still bored, I'm afraid. And I was still overwhelmed. But the tedium had become more interesting, if that makes sense. And my incomprehension was better informed.

Reading about economics after watching a lot of economic activity is like reading the assembly instructions after the Christmas toy has been put together. Certain significant patterns begin to take shape in the mind—even though the instructions are still gobbledygook and the toy doesn't work.

I make no claim to understand economics. But I have begun to understand how economics is understood. This is how economics is understood after two semesters at most colleges:

- I. There are a lot of graphs.
- II. I'd better memorize them.
- III. Or get last year's test.

And this is how economics is understood after three drinks at most bars:

- I. There are only so many things in the world, and somebody is taking my share.
- II. All payment for work is underpayment.
- III. All business is crime.
    - A. Retailers are thieves.
    - B. Wholesalers are pimps.
    - C. Manufacturers are slave drivers.

IV. All wealth is the result of criminal conspiracy among:
  A. Jews.
  B. The Chinese.
  C. Pirates in neckties on Wall Street.

And here is how economics is understood by followers of John Maynard Keynes:

THE KEYNESIAN EQUATION—SHOWING THE RELATIONSHIP BETWEEN AUTONOMOUS EXPENDITURES AND THE EQUILIBRIUM LEVEL OF INCOME

Where equilibrium level of income (Y) equals aggregate autonomous expenditures [Consumption (C) plus Investment (I) plus Government Expenditure (G) plus the total of Exports (X) minus Imports (M)] times 1 divided by the marginal propensity to save (mps) where mps equals 1 minus the marginal propensity to consume (mpc). Thus:

$$Y = \frac{[1]\ [C+I+G+(X-M)]}{1-mpc}$$

It's hard to imagine applying the above formula to any ordinary economic question, e.g., should I put my bonus in a certificate of deposit or buy new stereo speakers?

When we look at economics in general terms, all of us feel as though we're confronting an enormous piece of machinery that we can't comprehend and don't know how to operate. In fact, we feel like we're being run through that machinery. We are wheat, rice, and corn being delivered to the Nabisco factory, and we're going to come out the other end definitely toasted, possibly shredded, and, maybe, we hope, coated with sugar.

Yet, although this is how we feel, this is not how we behave. When we engage in any specific economic activity—when we buy, sell, mooch, or work—each of us acts as if he knows what he's doing. Even Fidel Castro does. In July 1997, *Forbes* magazine estimated Castro's net worth to be $1.4 billion.

So we do understand economics. We just think we don't. And sometimes, unfortunately, we're right.

Economists claim to study production, distribution, and consumption. But production requires actual skills and so can't be taught by economics professors, because they'd have to know how to do something. And consumption is a very private matter. Consider the consumption of toilet paper, condoms, frozen pizza-for-one eaten straight out of the microwave in the middle of the night, and cigarettes in the carport when your spouse thinks you've stopped smoking. Therefore, economics tends to concentrate on distribution.

When economists say "distribution," however, they mean the distribution of everything, not just the distribution of such finished products as the pizzas and the microwave ovens to thaw them. There is also the distribution of raw materials—the seeds and fertilizer needed to grow the pizza toppings and the petrochemicals necessary to make the wood-grain plastic laminates decorating the ovens. Then there's the distribution of labor—the effort required to freeze the pizza and round up all the microwaves. And the distribution of capital—the money required to buy plastic laminates and market pizzas that taste like them. There's distribution of ideas, too. (Whose idea was it to put pineapple chunks on a pizza?) And there's even distribution of space and time, which is what grocery and appliance stores really sell us. They gather the things we want in a place we can get to on a day we can get there and, voilà, a fattening midnight snack.

All these things that get distributed are called "economic goods." To an economist, anything is an economic good if it can be defined by the concept of "scarcity." And the economist's definition of scarcity is so broad that practically everything can be called scarce. Air is an economic good. If air gets polluted, we have to pay for catalytic converters and unleaded gasoline to make it breathable again. Even if the air is free, we have limited lung capacity. The more so if we've been out in the carport huffing Camels. Air is an economic good for each of our bodies, and we hope that body is using the air economically—getting lots of O_2 into the bloodstream, or whatever, and not just making farts with it.

From an economist's point of view, everything is scarce except desires. Random sexual fantasies are not economic goods. But if we try to act on them, they rapidly become economic (or highly uneconomic, as the case may be). Goods are limited; wants are unlimited. This observation leads economists to say that the fundamental purpose of economics is finding the best way to make finite goods meet infinite wants (though it never seems to work with random sexual fantasies).

While trying to make finite goods meet infinite wants, economists spend a lot of time mulling over something they call "efficiency." Economists explain efficiency as being the situation where an economy cannot produce more of one good without producing less of another good. If you have two jobs, you've probably reached labor efficiency. You can't put in more overtime on job A without putting in less overtime on job B or the child-welfare authorities will come to your house. You're efficient, although neither of your bosses may think so.

The example of efficiency that economists usually give is guns and butter. A society can produce both guns and butter, they say, but if the society wants to produce more guns, it will have to—because of allocation of resources, capital, and labor—produce less butter. Using this example you'll notice that at the far reaches of gun-producing efficiency, howitzers are being manufactured by cows. And this is just one of the reasons we can't take economists too seriously.

In fact, efficiency is a condition that's never been achieved, as you've seen from watching your job A and job B coworkers. Economists don't really know much about efficiency, and neither does anyone else. Doubtless the citizens of eighteenth-century England thought they were producing as many lumps of coal and wads of knitting as they possibly could. One more coal miner would mean one less stocking knitter. Then, James Watt invents the steam engine. Pretty soon, coal carts are hauling themselves, and knitting mills are clicking away automatically, and everybody has more socks and more fires to put wet, smelly stocking feet up in front of. Efficiency is constantly changing, and economists can't keep up with this because they have to grade papers and figure out what Y equals.

One thing that economists do know is that the study of economics is divided into two fields, "microeconomics" and "macroeconomics." Micro is the study of individual economic behavior, and macro is the study of how economies behave as a whole. That is, microeconomics concerns things that economists are specifically wrong about, while macroeconomics concerns things economists are wrong about generally. Or to be more technical, microeconomics is about money you don't have, and macroeconomics is about money the government is out of. These two concerns seem hopelessly meshed in real life, and therefore I've tangled them together in this book.

Economists also make a distinction—for no good reason I can figure—between "inputs" and "outputs." Inputs are the jobs, resources, and money we use in order to make the outputs we want, such as money, resources, and jobs. All outputs, even shit, heartbreak, and enormous illegal profits, turn out to be inputs: manure, movie plots, and capital investment in video-poker machines in Tirana.

Two additional unimportant economic terms are "supply" and "demand." Scarcity has already explained these. There's lots of demand and not much supply.

Economists measure supply and demand with curves on graphs. When the supply curve goes up, the demand curve goes down. But how true is this? Do I get less hungry because I know I have a freezer full of pizza? My experience with the microwave at 2 a.m. argues otherwise. And can we really know how much people want something? The kid "really, really, really" wants a snowboard. Does he really want it? Or after three times falling on his butt at Mount Barntop, is he going to leave the thing propped in the carport for the next twenty years? As for the supply curve, the concept of efficiency shows us that we don't know how many snowboards can be produced, or how cheaply, and if we wait until next winter, they may be giving them out free with Burrito Supremes.

So far, from an examination of the basic principles of economics, we've learned that things are scarce. We knew that. Fortunately the less-basic principles of economics are more interesting.

HOW TO READ A GRAPH

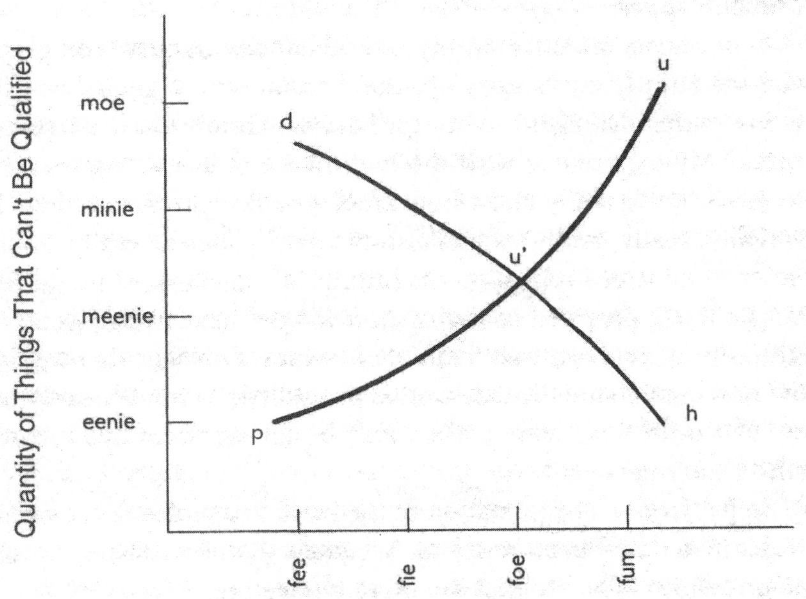

Where: *pu* = number of pages of econ text devoted to graphic analysis and *du'h* = number of econ students asleep in lecture hall

Ten Less-Basic Principles of Economics

1. The Market Is Never Wrong.

A thing is worth what people will give for it, and it isn't worth anything else. If you have some shares of Apple Computer and you go into the NASDAQ market offering those shares for $1,000 apiece, you may be brilliant. Apple stock may be worth $1,000, easy. And all the NASDAQ customers may be idiots for buying Apple at a mere thirty dollars. A Macintosh is a much better computer than an IBM PC. But, smart as you are and dumb as everybody else is, the market says your shares didn't sell. And the market is right.

Also, a thing may be "priceless." You'd rather die than trade your Macintosh for an IBM. But that's still a price, albeit a very high one.

2. So You Die. Things Still Cost What They Cost.

It's no use trying to fix prices. To do so, you must have a product that can't be replaced, and you must have complete agreement among all the people who control that product. They're greedy or they wouldn't have gotten into the agreement, and they're greedy so they sneak out of it. This is what was wrong with Paul Samuelson's idea about crop restrictions, and this is why the members of OPEC are still wandering around in their bathrobes, pestering camels.

Any good drug dealer can tell you that to ensure a monopoly, you need force. To ensure a large monopoly, you need the kind of force only a government usually has. And it still doesn't work.

The government of Cuba, with force aplenty at its disposal, decided that beef cost too much. The price of beef was fixed at a very low level, and all the beef disappeared from the government ration stores. The people of Cuba had to hassle tourists to get dollars to buy beef on the black market, where the price of beef turned out to be what beef costs.

When the price of something is fixed below market level, that something disappears from the legal market. And when the price of something is fixed above market level, the opposite occurs. Say the customers at suburban Wheat Depot won't pay enough for wheat. The U.S. government may decide to buy that wheat at higher prices. Suddenly there's wheat everywhere. It turns out that people have bushels of it in the attic. The government is up to its dull, gaping mouth in wheat. The wheat has to be given away. The recipients of free wheat in the Inner City Wheatfare Program hawk the wheat at traffic lights, and what they get for it is exactly what people are willing to give.

3. You Can't Get Something for Nothing.

Everybody remembers this except politicians. Lately, it has been the fashion for American politicians to promise that government revenue—taxes—can be cut while government benefits—expenditures—remain intact. Benefits might even get larger. This will be done through efficiency, as if politicians are all going to invent the steam engine. Though, to the extent that steam is hot air, predictable jokes are invited.

Politicians have trouble giving up the idea of something for nothing; it's such a vote catcher. A government can give most people something for nothing by taxing the few people with money. There are never enough of those people. And the people with money are the people with accountants, tax lawyers, and bank accounts in Luxembourg, so they end up not paying their taxes. Or, even if they do pay their taxes, the people with money are also the people who know how to manipulate the system. Therefore, instead of the situation that Samuelson posited in *Economics* where "modern democracies take loaves from the wealthy and pass them out to the poor," we get a situation where loaves are taken from the wealthy and tickets to subsidized opera performances at the Kennedy Center are passed out to the rich.

A government can give all people something for nothing by simply printing more money. This doesn't work, because it makes all the money worth less, as it did in Weimar Germany, Carter America, and Yeltsin Russia. Inflation is a tax on the prudent, who watch the value of their conservative bank account and savings bond investments disappear. It's a subsidy for the Wall Street scam artists who can borrow money for harebrained speculatory schemes and pay it back later with money that no longer has any value. And it's a punishment to the old and the poor, who live on fixed incomes and who can't expect to get a big cost-of-living adjustment retrieving soda cans from trash baskets.

Finally, a government can give us something for nothing by running a deficit, by borrowing money from everybody and then giving everybody his money back, plus interest. This is obviously stupid and exactly what we've been doing for decades in the United States. Deficits are less immediately painful than high inflation or huge taxes, although eventually they lead to one or the other, or both. In the meantime, we're not getting anywhere. If all our investment money is tied up in loans to the government, that money is going to be spent on government things, such as financing the Inner City Wheatfare Program. Our investment money can't be spent on research and development to create a genetically engineered wheat-eating squid to turn that worthless wheat into valuable calamari.

4. You Can't Have Everything.

If you use your resources to obtain a thing, you can't use those same resources to obtain something else. That's called fraud (or having a credit card). In economics it's called "opportunity cost." When you employ your money, brains, and time in one way, it costs you the opportunity to employ them in another. Opportunity costs fool people because they're unseen. When we observe money being spent, we're impressed. We gasp with awe at the huge new Federal Wheat Council headquarters in Washington, D.C. We don't admire the vast schools of squid feeding in our nation's wheat fields—because they aren't there. The main cost of government expenditure is not taxes, inflation, or interest on the national debt. The main cost is opportunity.

5. Break It and You Bought It.

Being fooled by hidden costs is the source of a lot of economic confusion. War is often spoken of as an economic stimulant. World War II "pulled America out of the Depression." Germany and Japan experienced "economic miracles" after the war. Somebody is not counting the cost of getting killed and wounded. Besides, if destruction were the key to greater economic productivity, every investor on Wall Street would be learning Albanian.

6. Good Is Not as Good as Better.

Almost as bad as costs that go unnoticed are benefits that get too much attention. It's great if everybody has a job. Computers are taking jobs away. We could guarantee full employment if we removed computers—and electricity, too—from the communication industry and hired people to run all over town and fly around the world, telling our friends and business associates what we want to say.

When James Watt invented that steam engine, thousands of ten-year-old boys who had been hauling coal carts were put out of work. However, this left them free to do other things, such as live to be eleven.

7. The Past Is Past.

Another thing that gets too much attention is money that's already been spent. In economics this is called "sunk costs." It doesn't matter that you blew everything you made selling Apple at $1,000 a share on a scheme to genetically engineer squid. What matters is whether you can make any money off those squid now or convince people that the squid will make money in the future, so that those people will buy the fool company. This is called "marginal thinking," and on Wall Street it means almost the exact opposite of what we usually mean when we call someone a marginal thinker.

8. Build It and They Will Come.

Ralph Waldo Emerson was referring to better mousetraps, and the idea that the world would beat a path to your door for one tells us something about housing conditions in the nineteenth century. The underlying notion is stated formally in economics as Say's Law (after French economist Jean Baptiste Say, 1767–1832): "Supply creates its own demand." More is better. Any increase in productivity in a society causes that society to get enough richer to buy the things that are produced.

This works even in an economy as screwed up as Cuba's. The Cuban authorities allowed limited free-market sales of food, and this increased food production. Despite the extreme poverty of Cubans, that food did not sit around unsold.

9. Everybody Gets Paid.

People want to get something for what they do, although what they want to get may not be money—it may be sex or salvation or an opportunity to apply Marxist theory to rock and roll. Everything is a business.

This is the "public choice" theory of economics. One of its founders, James M. Buchanan, won the 1986 Nobel Prize in economics for his work on understanding politics as an economic activity. Politicians don't measure profits in cash. The gain that they want is an increase in power. Thus the socialists of Cuba are just as greedy as the pirates of Albania.

In order to increase their "power income," politicians have to pass more legislation, expand bureaucracies, and broaden the scope of government power. A politician who claims he's going to cut the size of government is saying he's going to creep up on himself and steal his own wallet.

10. Everybody's an Expert.

Of all the principles of economics, the one that's most important to making us richer (or more powerful or whatever) is specialization, or as Adam Smith, who discovered the principle, called it, "division of labor."

Milton Friedman uses a pencil as an example. A pencil is a simple object, but there's not a single person in the world who can make one. That person would need to be a miner to get the graphite, a chemical engineer to turn graphite into pencil lead, a lumberjack to cut the cedar trees, and a carpenter to shape the pencil casing. He'd need to know how to make yellow paint, how to spray it on, and how to make a paint sprayer. He'd have to go back to the mines to get the ore to make the metal for the thingy that holds the eraser, then build a smelter, a rolling plant, and a machine-tool factory to produce equipment to crimp the thingy in place. And, for the eraser itself, he'd have to grow a rubber tree in his backyard. All this would take a lot of money. Yet a pencil sells for nine cents.

The implications of division of labor are surprising, but only if we don't think about them. If we do think about them, they are, like most economic principles, a matter of common sense. There are, however, a few things about economics that don't seem to make sense at all. Todd G. Buchholz, in his book *New Ideas from Dead Economists*, says, "An insolent natural scientist once asked a famous economist to name one economic rule that isn't either obvious or unimportant." The reply was "Ricardo's Law of Comparative Advantage."

The English economist David Ricardo (1772–1823) postulated this: If you can do X better than you can do Z, and there's a second person who can do Z better than he can do X, but can also do both X and Z better than you can, then an economy should *not* encourage that second person to do both things. You and he (and society as a whole) will profit more if you each do what you do best.

Let us decide, for the sake of an example, that one legal thriller is equal to one pop song as a Benefit to Society. (One thriller or one song = 1 unit of BS.) John Grisham is a better writer than Courtney Love. John Grisham is also (assuming he plays the comb and wax paper or something) a better musician than Courtney Love. Say John Grisham is 100 times the writer Courtney Love is, and say he's 10 times the musician. Then say that John Grisham can either write 100 legal thrillers in a year (I'll bet he can) or compose 50 songs. This would mean that Courtney Love could write either 1 thriller or compose 5 songs in the same period.

If John Grisham spends 50 percent of his time scribbling predictable plots and 50 percent of his time blowing into a kazoo, the result will be 50 thrillers and 25 songs for a total of 75 BS units. If Courtney Love spends 50 percent of her time annoying a word processor and 50 percent of her time making noise in a recording studio, the result will be 1 half-completed thriller and 2.5 songs for a total of 3 BS. The grand total Benefit to Society will be 78 units.

If John Grisham spends 100 percent of his time inventing dumb adventures for two-dimensional characters and Courtney Love spends 100 percent of her time calling cats, the result will be 100 thrillers and 5 songs for a total Benefit to Society of 105 BS.

JOHN GRISHAM AND COURTNEY LOVE EACH SPEND EQUAL TIME WRITING AND COMPOSING						
	THRILLERS		SONGS		BS PRODUCTION	
John Grisham	50.0	+	25.0	=	75	
Courtney Love	.5	+	2.5	=	3	
					78	Total BS

JOHN GRISHAM SPENDS ALL HIS TIME BASHING THE LAPTOP KEYBOARD AND COURTNEY SPENDS ALL HER TIME CATERWAULING AND PLINKING GUITAR STRINGS						
	THRILLERS		SONGS		BS PRODUCTION	
John Grisham	100	+	0	=	100	
Courtney Love	0	+	5	=	5	
					105	Total BS

(Just to make things more confusing, note that Courtney Love loses 40 percent of her productivity by splitting her time between art and music, while John Grisham loses only 25 percent of his productivity. She has the "comparative advantage" in making music because her opportunity costs will be higher if she doesn't stick to what she does best.)

David Ricardo applied the Law of Comparative Advantage to questions of foreign trade. The Japanese make better CD players than we do, and they may be *able* to make better pop music, but we both profit by buying our CDs from Sony and letting Courtney Love tour Japan. And if she stays there, America has a definite advantage.

Comparative advantage is a rare example of the counterintuitive in economics. It's also unusual because it requires a little arithmetic to understand. We think of economics as strangled in math because of the formulas and graphs filling most economics textbooks. But you can (and I did) search the entire founding volume on economics, Adam Smith's *An Inquiry into the Nature and Causes of the Wealth of Nations,* without encountering a mathematical formula. In *New Ideas*, Buchholz quotes Alfred Marshall, the preeminent economist of the late nineteenth century (and a mathematician).

1. Use mathematics as a shorthand language, rather than as an engine of inquiry.
2. Keep to them until you have done.
3. Translate into English.
4. Then illustrate by examples that are important in real life.
5. Burn the mathematics.

We don't need to know math to understand economics, because economics isn't about abstract principles, it's about microwave ovens, cow howitzers, steam engines, wet knitting, snowboards, mousetraps, and Courtney Love on permanent tour in Japan. And this brings us to one more economic exception to common sense and a thing that requires all sorts of mathematics from us every day: money.

Why is this soiled, crumpled, overdecorated piece of paper bearing a picture of a rather second-rate president worth fifty dollars, while this clean, soft, white, and cleverly folded piece of paper is worth so little that I just wiped my nose on it? And what exactly is a "dollar"? If it's a thing that I want, why do I prefer to have fifty grimy old dollars instead of one nice new one? This isn't true of other things—puppies, for instance.

But money is not a puppy; it's not a specific thing. Money is a symbol of things in general, a symbol of how much you want things, and a symbol of how many things you're going to get. Money is a mathematical shorthand for value (and per Alfred Marshall, we seem to burn the stuff).

But what is value? The brief answer is "complicated." Value varies according to time, place, circumstance, and whether the puppy ruined the rug. Plus, there are some things upon which it is difficult to place a value. This is why we don't use money to measure all of our exchanges. Kids get food, clothing, and shelter from parents, and in return, parents get . . . kids. Important emotional, philosophical, and legal distinctions are made between sex and paying for sex, even if the socially approved sex costs dinner and a movie.

We need economic goods all the time, but we don't always need money for them, and it's a good thing, since for most of human existence, there wasn't any. Money didn't exist, or, rather, everything that existed was money. If I sold you a cow for six goats, you were charging it on your Goat Card.

Anything that's used to measure value, if it has value itself, is "commodity money." Societies that didn't have fifty-dollar bills picked one or two commodities as proto-simoleons. The Aztecs used cocoa beans for money, North Africans used salt (hence "salary"), medieval Norwegians used butter and dried cod, and their ATM machines were a mess.

Some commodities are better as money than others. Movie stars would make bad money. Carrying a couple around would be a bother, and you'd have to hack a leg off to make change. Precious metals, however, make good money and have been used that way for more than five thousand years.

Metal commodity money is portioned out by weight. A coin is just a hunk of metal stamped to indicate its heft. From weighing money to making coins is a simple step, but a couple thousand years passed before the step was taken. Nobody trusted anybody else to do the stamping.

When coins *were* invented, the distrust proved to be well founded. The first Western coins were minted by the kingdom of Lydia, in what is now Turkey, and were made of a gold-silver alloy called electrum. It's hard for anyone but a chemist (and there weren't any) to tell how much gold is in a piece of electrum versus how much silver. The king of Lydia, Croesus, became proverbial for his wealth.

In China, the weight of bronze "cash" was supposed to be guaranteed by death penalties. A lot of people must have gone to the electric (if they'd had electricity) chair. A horse cost 4,500 "1-cash" coins during the Han dynasty (206 BC to AD 220) and 25,000 cash during the Tang dynasty (AD 618–907).

Kings, emperors, and even lowly congressional representatives have expenses. It is to a government's advantage to pay for those expenses with funny money. One reason that money violates common sense is that governments commonly do crazy things with it.

Another reason that money violates common sense is that we don't have to use real commodities as money. We can use pieces of paper promising to deliver those real commodities. This is "fiduciary money," from the Latin word *fiducia,* trust.

In Europe, paper money was developed privately, in the thirteenth century, from bills of exchange traded among Italian merchants and from receipts given by goldsmiths to whom hard money had been entrusted for safekeeping. We still use such private money when we cash a traveler's check.

Public fiduciary money was first printed in Sweden. Swedish commodity money came in the form of copper plates. Thus, in Sweden, a large fortune was a *large* fortune. In 1656 the Stockholm Banco began issuing more convenient paper notes. The bank issued too many notes, and the Swedish government went broke.

In 1716, Scotsman John Law helped the French government establish the Banque Royale, issuing notes backed by the value of France's land holdings west of the Mississippi. Banque Royale issued too many notes, and the French government went broke. But the most extensive Western experiment with paper money took place right here. In 1775 the Second Continental Congress not only created paper money but passed a law against refusing to accept it. The Continental Congress issued too many notes and . . . A subtle pattern begins to emerge.

All fiduciary money is backed by a commodity, even if the backers are lying about the amount of that commodity. Historically the commodity most often chosen has been gold. By the nineteenth century, the major currencies of the world were based on gold, led by the most major currency, the British pound. This was a period of monetary stability and, not coincidentally, economic growth. There are people who think we should go back on the gold standard, and not all of them have skinny sideburns, large belt buckles, and live on armed compounds in Idaho. Money ought to be worth *something,* and gold seems as good as whatever.

But there's that endlessly perplexing relationship between money and value. The high value of gold is a social convention, a habit left over from the days when all bright, unblemished things (people included) were rare. Gold may go out of fashion. A generation may come along that, to the surprise of its parents, regards gold as gross or immoral, the way current twenty-year-olds regard milk-fed veal. And gold is a product. Different ways to get huge new amounts of it may be discovered. This happened to the Spanish. When they conquered the New World, they obtained tons of gold, melted it down, and sent it to the mint. It never occurred to them that they were just creating more money, not more things to spend it on. Between 1500 and 1600, prices in Spain went up 400 percent.

Presented with the enormous wealth of America's oceans, fields, and forests, Spain took the gold. It was as if someone robbed a bank and stole nothing but deposit slips.

Gold is an irrational basis for currency, but the real problem with fiduciary money—from a government standpoint—is that it's inconvenient. A currency that can be converted into a commodity limits the amount of currency that can be printed. A government has to have at least some of the commodity or the world makes a laughingstock out of its banknotes—"Not worth a Continental."

So if a government can lie about the amount of a commodity that is backing its currency—as the Stockholm Banco, Banque Royale, and Continental Congress did—why can't a government lie about everything? Instead of passing a law saying one dollar equals X amount of gold, why not pass a law saying one dollar equals one dollar? This is "fiat money" (from the Latin for being forced to drive a cheap, unreliable car), and it's almost the only kind of national currency left in the world.

Fiat money is backed by nothing but faith that a government won't keep printing money until we're using it in place of something more important, such as Kleenex. Concerning this faith, the experiences of Weimar Germany, Carter America, and Yeltsin Russia make agnostics of us all. The only thing that protects us from completely worthless money is our ability to buy and sell. We can move our stock of wealth from the imaginary value of dollars to the fictitious value of yen to the mythical value of stock shares to the illusory value of real estate, and so forth. Our freedom to not use a particular kind of money keeps the issuers of that money— *honest* wouldn't be the word—moderate in their dishonesty.

I subjected myself to a large dose of economic theory because I'd finally realized that money was as important as love or death. I thought I would learn all about money. But money turns out to be strange, insubstantial, and practically impossible to define. Then I began to understand that economic theory was really about value. But value is something that's personal and relative, and changes all the time. Money can't be valued. And value can't be priced. I should never have worried that I didn't know what I was talking about. Economics is an entire scientific discipline devoted to not knowing what you're talking about.

Trying to observe economic practice showed me that I needed to learn some economic principles, and trying to examine economic principles showed me that I'd better look at the practice again.

How to Make Nothing from Everything

Tanzania 1997

The problem in some places is how to reform an economic system. The problem in more places is how to get one. The World Bank claims that some two billion of the world's citizens live on $1 a day or less. These people have livelihoods governed by the plain rules of subsistence. They don't buy, sell, or trade much because they don't have much to buy, sell, or trade. They're poor.

And nowhere have people been poor longer or more thoroughly than in Africa. According to World Bank statistics, the ten poorest countries on earth are all African. Not one of the fifty-three members of the Organization of African Unity—not even diamond-infested South Africa or oil-soaked Libya—has a decent general standard of living. And this is the continent where man evolved, where the first great civilization arose. This is the human hometown.

I went to Tanzania in February 1997. Probably every child whose parents weren't rich enough has been told, "We're rich in other ways." Tanzania is fabulously rich in other ways.

The Tarangire reserve is a thousand square miles of branching river valleys sheltering some of the last great elephant herds in the world.

To the northwest, the wildlife-covered Serengeti Plain stretches away forever, oceanic in its flatness. The only landmarks are the kopjes, wind- and rain-polished bubbles of granite ranging from back porch to state capitol building in size. At night lightning bolts can be seen eighty miles away on the shores of Lake Victoria.

The nearby Ngorongoro Crater is a collapsed twin of Kilimanjaro, a mountaintop chasm 1,500 feet deep and ten miles across, containing a miniature perfect universe of grassland and rain forest.

One dawn I rode a dizzy-pitched, rut-ulcerated switchback road into the crater. Maasai boys were leading a hundred cattle down to a salt lick. The young herdsmen were dressed in pairs of plaid blankets, with one worn as kilt and the other as toga. Beadwork swung at their necks and dangled from the piercings at the tops and bottoms of their ears. Each carried a long stick with the war-lance aplomb young boys give to long sticks. The air was clean and sharp. The clear sky was just beginning to light up. The cowbells plinked like a half-audible cheery tune. There are probably worse things to be than a Maasai boy taking cattle into the Ngorongoro Crater at dawn. Although the usual Maasai diet of curdled milk and cow's blood wouldn't provide enough roughage for an American my age.

There is an all-day, all-night rush hour of animals in Tanzania: Cape buffalo jam, zebra lock, and wildebeest backup. Thomson's gazelles bound about, each with a black swoop on its side—enough like the Nike trademark to raise questions about sponsorship. Warthogs scuttle with their tails up straight in the air, endlessly acknowledging some foul in the game of hogball. Hyenas are all over the place, nonchalant but shifty, in little groups meandering not quite aimlessly—greasers at the Y dance. Hippos lie in the water holes in piles, snoring, stinking, sleeping all day. The correct translation for the Greek word "hippopotamus" is not "river horse" but "river first husband." And lions doze where they like, waking up every day or two to do that famous ecological favor of culling the weak, old, and sick. (Do lions ever debate the merits of weak versus old versus sick? "Call me an epicure if you like, but I think the sick wildebeest have a certain piquancy, like a ripe cheese.")

The nation of Tanzania might seem to be a Beulah Land—if you stick to the parks and the game preserves, and get back in your hotel by sunset. It can be done. I have a fatuous article from the March 2, 1997, Sunday *New York Times* travel section in which some publishing-industry pooh-bah tells how he and his wife flew in chartered planes to the Ngorongoro and the Serengeti, "and returned dazed by the wealth of wildlife and the vastness of the terrain."

But, putting the tourist daze aside, Tanzania is a truly poor country. I arrived at Kilimanjaro Airport, near that mountain but not much else. It was evening, time for the overseas flights to land, and mine had, and that was it. The airport is one of those grand, reinforced concrete 1970s foreign-aid projects now going grim from mildew and falling to pieces. Surely it is one of the few international airports without a visible clock. There are no hustling taximen or begging children outside the door. It costs fifty cents to enter the airport grounds, and they can't afford it.

A safari guide named John collected me in the minivan in which we'd spend the next two weeks. It was a beaten, slew-wheeled, butt-sprung vehicle. John managed to keep it working (except for flat tires and getting stuck, and a rear hatch that sprang open in a remote corner of the Maasai Steppe with a lion on one side of the road and an irritated mother elephant on the other).

We drove for an hour and a half through the smoky African night. *Smoky* is not an adjective chosen for artistic, evocative reasons. According to Tanzanian government figures, 90 percent of the country's energy generation is from wood fires. Virtually all the cooking, heating, lighting, and manufacturing in Tanzania is accomplished by the same method Boy Scouts use on hot dogs at campouts.

We arrived on the outskirts of Arusha, the principal city in northern Tanzania. Here was another stained and flaking assistance-to-developing-nations structure—the best hotel. No air-conditioning, no screens, and not much happening in the bar.

In the morning we drove to Arusha proper, a low sprawl of neglected stucco buildings, with here and there a large government office made of the inevitable aid-donor concrete. Half the businesses downtown had something to do with doing something with tourists, and the rest sold used refrigerators. The thin and sluggardly traffic was made up of colonial-era Land Rovers and large, woebegone trucks with obscure South Asian brand names. A few trucks were full of farm produce. A few were full of people. All the others were broken down by the side of the road, with men lying under them, occasionally working on the truck mechanicals, but usually sleeping. In the center of town, in a traffic circle where one bus seemed to be permanently circling, was a monument to the fact that Arusha is halfway between Cairo and Cape Town.

Outside the small business district, the roads were lined with scrap-wood and palm-thatch stalls, some with signs that overreached the mark—HOLLYWOOD BAR—others selling modest goods, such as scrap wood and palm thatch. Vendors who couldn't afford sheds sold goods more modest yet: pieces of bicycle tire and strips of rubber cut from old inner tubes. There were a few industrial buildings at the city's edge, but nothing industrious seemed to be happening in them. An open-air market was busy but looked more full of people than goods. John laughed and pointed out a Christian revival tent next to a brewery.

The Tanzanian men wore shirts and slacks that had a clothing-drive look but, if so, they were picked from the Goodwill bin with more taste than most Seattle bands show and more use of detergent, too. The Tanzanian women had on T-shirts or Western blouses, but also *kangas*—yard-wide, twelve-foot lengths of brightly printed cotton cut in two to make a skirt and shawl. The *kangas* were spotless, even when the women were working in the fields (something Tanzanian women have an equal opportunity to do; in fact, there seems to be an affirmative-action program in force). It's not a dirty country—if you don't count dust.

It's not a squalid country. There are no droves of the crippled and diseased, no beseeching for alms, no pestering of strangers, no evident public violence. Tanzania is not a nation suffering social collapse, but I'm not absolutely sure I mean that as a compliment. There's the sad possibility that they just don't have the cash for booze, drugs, and handguns.

Seeing the people in Arusha going about their business—or lack thereof—should have been more depressing than it was. Describing the English poor of 150 years ago, George Eliot noted "the leaden, blank-eyed gaze of unexpectant want." But with Tanzanians, there is a twinkle in that gaze. The women walk down the roads bearing all the burden of Tanzanian material possessions. These are few enough, but still a lot to carry on your head. And more often than not, the women are smiling. Their *kangas* sway and billow. The printed cloths are embellished with slogans or catch phrases, such as PENYE KUKU WENGI HAKUMWAGWIMTAMA: "Don't dry the millet where the chickens are." Children rush home from school as gleefully as if they were headed for rec rooms full of Sega games and *Anastasia* videos. (Tanzanian kids all wear school uniforms, in case you think that regulation is the answer to all ills.) Just the names of things in the country are cheerful: the No Competition Grocery, the New Toyota Shoe Shine, the Buy-n-Bye Minimart, and a long-distance motor coach christened So What. Merchants are nice to the point of chagrin over any commercial aspect of a visit to their stores. One shop had an apologetic sign posted in the window:

YOU ARE MY FRIEND
YES
YOU ARE MY RELATIVE
YES THANK YOU
BUT MY BUSINESS DOES NOT KNOW YOU

A few weeks after I left the country, Hillary and Chelsea Clinton came to Arusha on a fly-through tour of Africa. The silly young daughter of the president of the United States told an audience at Kilimanjaro Airport that in America "we have a big problem with people not thinking they have a future. Young women and young men . . . there's a lot of hopelessness." The Tanzanians were too nice to pelt her with dirt clods.

Beyond the town, people were even poorer. Arusha is green, irrigated by the waters of Kilimanjaro's smaller companion Mount Meru, which hulks 15,000 feet over the city. The farmland is lush, but the farms are hodgepodges: a banana tree here, a cassava plant there, here a maize stalk, there a bean sprout, everywhere a chicken (and several children chasing it). Hollow logs hang lengthwise in the branches of the taller trees. Fetishes of some kind, I assumed, but I had the sense to ask John.

They're beehives. One whole chapter in the *Tanzanian National Budget* is devoted to beekeeping. People can't afford sugar. Sugar sells for twenty-eight cents a pound.

The average Tanzanian smallholding is less than one and a quarter acres. The homesteads are just shacks topped with sheets of tin or one-room bunkers built from very irregular concrete blocks made, one by one, in wooden molds.

Farther west, the land gets worse, rocky and dry and barren as a stairwell. Goats seem to be the only crop. Here, people don't have the luxury of shacks. The tiny houses are thatch roofed, with walls made from stick-work lattices, the spaces between the sticks filled with little rocks, and the whole plastered over with mud if—water being scarce—the family can afford mud.

Women sat by the side of the road, hitting rocks with stumpy hammers, making gravel by hand—to give some idea of the value of labor in Tanzania. Little boys stood resolutely in the middle of nowhere next to gunnysacks of charcoal that the passing trucks can't burn and the walkers and bicyclers can't carry. If you wonder where all the old, fat-tired, one-speed, backpedal-to-brake American bicycles went, the Huffys and the Schwinns, they're in Tanzania, complete with reflectors, mud flaps, rocket-shaped battery lamps, and handlebar baskets with little brothers stuffed in them.

The road to the Rift Valley is paved and reasonably smooth from lack of traffic, but it's only as wide as an alleyway. At Makuyuni ("Place of the Fig Tree"—and there's not one) is the turnoff to Tanzania's most important tourist attractions: the Ngorongoro Crater, the Olduvai Gorge, the Serengeti. And at Makuyuni, the pavement illogically ends. We headed west across the Rift Valley on a road that was just a pile of rocks—like driving lengthwise on a New England stonewall. We were slammed so badly inside the van that John steered out into the arid, rutty bush, where we were engulfed in dust, dropped into holes, and launched aloft by boulders. John went back to the road until we could take it no more, then back to the bush. And so we traveled to Ngorongoro, veering from the Scylla of African topography to the Charybdis of the Tanzania Highway Department, a journey of thirty-odd miles that took three hours.

In the Rift, the Maasai still live with their livestock inside corrals of piled thornbush, in flat-topped, windowless hovels made from straw smeared with cow dung and entered through a crawl hole.

The Greek Cynic philosopher Diogenes is said to have slept in a barrel. And supposedly it was a happy revelation to him that he could drink out of his cupped palms and thus throw away one more possession, his cup. But Diogenes had a barrel, a fairly complex piece of technology. Compared with the way some Tanzanians exist, Diogenes was a Sharper Image customer.

Statistically, there are poorer countries than Tanzania; that is, countries so chaotic that all their statisticians have been chased up trees—Liberia, Somalia, Congo—and countries which are so reclusive—North Korea—that it's impossible to tell what's going on. But Tanzania is right at the bottom of the aforementioned barrel, which would probably have to be imported from an industrially advanced nation. According to the *World Bank's 1996 World Development Report*, Tanzania is poorer than Uganda, poorer than Burundi, poorer than godforsaken Chad. Haiti is 80 percent wealthier than Tanzania. Papua New Guinea is almost ten times more prosperous, never mind that some of its citizens have not discovered the wheel.

Tanzania is so poor that its poverty is hard to calculate. Eighty-five percent of the workforce is employed in agriculture, if *employed* is the word. They grow things. They eat them. This does not generate W-2 forms or register on the stock exchange that Tanzania doesn't have. ("Money and capital markets" are to come "in the near future," says the Ministry of Finance.)

As with Cuba, there's a sad econometric debate about Tanzania's per capita gross domestic product. Tanzanian government figures (with their foggy population counts and a Tanzanian shilling with an exchange rate varying between worth-little and worthless) work out to approximately $128 a person a year. The World Bank believes it's about $117. The CIA, in its *1997 World Factbook,* estimates Tanzanian per capita GDP at $650. But this is from the organization that—as late as 1989—thought the Soviet Union's per capita GDP was nearly as high as Britain's. The CIA uses something called the purchasing-power-parity (PPP) method to measure gross domestic product. PPP is supposed to compensate for the lower living costs found in poorer countries. It's like having your boss tell you, "Instead of a raise, why don't you move to a worse neighborhood—your rent will be lower and so will your car payments, as soon as someone steals your Acura."

Let's take the Tanzanians' own figures—it's their country after all: $128 per capita GDP. And here we see the fallacy on the bottom line of utopian economic ideas. If theoretic social justice were enacted—if all the income in this nation were divided with perfect equality—everybody would get thirty-five cents a day. This (using the PPP method, by the way) is half a pack of Sportsman cigarettes and nine ounces of dried beans.

I mentioned the thirty-five-cents figure to an American friend, who said, "Christ! You can find that much lying in the road." Not in Tanzania you can't. There's nothing on or near the roads. The things we throw away—broken scraps of plastic, bits of tin sheeting, snips of copper wire—are collected by the Maasai and made into the centerpieces of beadwork necklaces and bracelets. These are sold by old women at the tourist spots for about a dollar apiece. Sell one and that's three days of per capita gross domestic product.

There are probably better ways to measure extreme poverty than GDP. Tanzania has a population slightly less than California's and is slightly more than twice California's size, and Tanzania has 1,403 miles of paved roads. The District of Columbia has 1,104 miles (although, to be fair, our capital has worse potholes than their capital does). Telephone lines for Tanzania's approximately 29 million people number 85,756. Cell phone service, I was told, was coming "next month," which is when you usually get a dial tone. Outside the cities, there are no phones, just three shortwave-radio call stations.

I sat in a hotel bar one night, listening to the howling, shrieking distortions of a ham-radio set on which a frantic husband in the Serengeti was explaining that the tour guide's jeep had gone into a hyena den, and he thought his wife's spine was fractured. Garbled plans were being made to fly the wife hundreds of miles to Nairobi, Kenya, for medical treatment. At last count, there was one doctor for every 28,271 people in Tanzania, and, I suppose, 28,270 patients were in line ahead of the poor woman with the fractured spine.

Only 260,171 Tanzanian households or businesses have electricity, and that electricity arrives with the frequency and predictability of Publishers Clearing House sweepstakes wins. Speaking of such, the average Tanzanian receives 2.14 pieces of mail per annum. In 1990, the most recent year in which the Tanzanian government has managed to count these things, 3,314 cars, 2,385 four-wheel-drive vehicles, and 6,445 trucks were imported.

Five percent of Tanzania's teenagers are enrolled in high school (though this is better than the percentage of American high school students actually paying attention). The average Tanzanian family devotes 70 percent of its expenditures to food. In Cuba, where they claimed the American embargo was starving them, that figure was 50 percent. And a U.S. family allots about 14.5 percent of its spending to food—$6,592, which is 1,739 Big Mac meals and a large order of fries, and may explain why Americans are so fat. Tanzanians are not. According to the World Bank, 29 percent of Tanzanian children age five or less are underweight.

Why is Tanzania so poor? The nation is by no means overpopulated. The countryside is mostly dry plains and mild badlands, a sort of tropical South Dakota with seacoast, but it's not infertile. Tanzania is a net exporter of edibles. Agricultural products make up 75 percent of foreign-trade earnings. Forty percent of the country is meadow or pastureland, enough to supply all the burgers missing from local lunch breaks. And Tanzania has resources: tin, phosphates, iron ore, coal, diamonds, gemstones, gold, natural gas, and nickel, says the CIA's *World Factbook*, and salt, gypsum, and cobalt, adds the U.S. State Department's *1997 Country Commercial Guide*. Plus, there's said to be hydroelectric potential. (I did notice a lot of water running downhill—as water tends to do.)

Tanzania has not suffered the wars, civil and otherwise, that have riven sub-Saharan Africa. It did fight one brief conflict against Uganda, in the good cause of ousting Idi Amin. But peace has been the general rule since independence. Domestic peace, as well. Tanzania isn't wracked by tribal conflicts. Julius K. Nyerere, the high-minded and high-handed schoolteacher who ruled the country for its first twenty-four years, opposed tribalism and was helped in his opposition to tribes by the fact that Tanzania has more than 120 of them. None is large enough to predominate. Besides the well-known Maasai, there are the Ha, the Hehe, the Gogo, etc., etc. It's silly enough to murder somebody because he's a Serb or a Croat, but to kill a person for being a Gogo is much too absurd for the sensible and even-tempered Tanzanians.

Tanganyika, as it used to be called, did not have a very bad colonial history, as those things go. The Germans arrived late, in 1885, and left early, in 1918, after muffing World War I. Local people fought the Germans persistently—in the Hehe Rebellion of 1891, the Maji Maji War of 1905, and a variety of other spirited (and oddly named) uprisings. The British took over Tanganyika as a League of Nations protectorate rather than as a colony, so the Tanganyikans were spared the influx of wastrel coffee planters, lunatic white hunters, and Isak Dinesen that plagued Kenya. Resistance to British rule was nonviolent and well organized, and the Brits left in 1961 with a minimum of puling and fuss.

Tanzania does have various of the other evils on which Third World poverty is blamed—corruption, for instance. Tanzania has that. But so do Newt Gingrich and Al Gore. The wild, venal jobbery of politicians doesn't, by itself, make a country poor. Nor does colonial exploitation. Virginia and Massachusetts were colonies, too, and more effectively exploited than Tanzania was.

Then there's socioeconomic lag, the late introduction of the ideas that propel the developed world. Yet Tanzania, or at least its coast and its islands such as Zanzibar, were exposed to science, math, and technology by Muslims beginning in the eighth century. That's eight hundred years before anybody who could read or recite multiplication tables arrived in North America. True, Arab traders came for the purposes of stealing slaves and pillaging ivory. But the harbingers of civilization rarely go anywhere in order to deliver Girl Scout cookies. The poverty of Tanzania is a puzzle.

Lack of education is, of course, a problem. But Tanzania's literacy rate is estimated to be almost 68 percent. Even if that estimate is optimistic, the proportion of Tanzanians who can read and write now is higher than the proportion of Europeans who could do so at the beginning of the Industrial Age. Also, illiterate is not ignorant. The most backwoods of Tanzanians speaks a tribal tongue or two, plus Kiswahili and, often, English. At my tourist hotel on the rim of the Ngorongoro, I asked the bartender why Tanzania was so poor. He said "lack of education" and then held forth with a fifteen-minute dissertation on the mathematics of the exchange rate that left me heavily shortchanged and in some doubt about his theory.

One answer is that Tanzania is *not* poor—by the standards of human experience. Admittedly, these are grim standards, but until creatures from other planets really do invade, we have no others. The World Bank claims that 48 percent of rural Tanzanians and 11 percent of the country's city dwellers are living in "absolute poverty," which the World Bank defines as an "income level below which adequate standards of nutrition, shelter, and personal amenities cannot be assured." But when and where on earth were the poor ever guaranteed three hots and a flop, let alone "personal amenities"? According to the Organization for Economic Cooperation and Development, Tanzania's current per capita gross domestic product is something like Japan's or Brazil's at the beginning of the nineteenth century, and about the same as that of India or China in 1950.

Tanzanians live the way people usually have since we quit being apes. No, they live better. Tanzanian life expectancy is approximately 52 years. Life expectancy in the United States was 52.6 years in 1911. The infant-mortality rate in Tanzania is 84 deaths per 1,000 live births. The American infant-mortality rate was 85.8 as recently as 1920.

After we had crossed the Rift Valley, John and I drove to the Olduvai Gorge, where Louis and Mary Leakey did their archaeological work, showing just how ancient mankind is. More than a million years ago *Homo erectus*—who resembled modern man at least as much as Neil Young does—was wandering around here on open savannas very similar to those of modern Tanzania.

The hominid tools on display in the museum at the Olduvai Visitor Center are not reassuring as to the lifestyle of our early relations. You'd have to be an expert to tell they're tools at all and not just stones that broke funny. Of course, there's always the possibility that the Leakeys were pulling our leg and Ralph Reed is right, and man was created by divine miracle last Wednesday at noon. Anyway, the stuff that Grandfather Erectus was working with in his Paleolithic basement shop gives you a second thought about what poverty really means. I wouldn't care to be turned loose in the African underbrush with nothing but a couple of sharp rocks—not even for an hour and knowing that John was parked back by the road with our box lunches.

Man was born into a state of nature, and nature, I'm sad to report, is woefully underdeveloped in an economic sense. The wildlife herds were sad reminders that there are only two ways to obtain a thing: either agree upon a price for it or take it by butting heads. Wildebeest depend upon the latter method. Due to a lack of pockets, wildebeest cannot carry cash or credit cards. Among animals, only marsupials have pockets, and then just to keep their babies in. And there are various difficulties, practical and theoretical, with an economic system based on inch-long blind and hairless kangaroos.

No medium of trade is one reason that wildebeest aren't very productive. No brains is another. About the only thing wildebeest can do to increase productivity—of crap and other wildebeest—is eat more. This they accomplish to the best of their ability, standing around all day with their choppers in the groceries. Leaves and grass aren't much more nutritious for them than they are for us. Consider how much lettuce and oat bran you would need to gain weight. Consider how much a 500-pound wildebeest would.

Wildebeest also sleep, but not peacefully. A significant minority of creatures on the African veldt aren't grazers or browsers, or members of PETA. They're hungry, too. And buff. Running down a 500-pound herbivore is an excellent exercise program. Plus, John said that cheetahs and leopards will kill—as will many a lesser hunter in a duck blind—for fun. So wildebeest wake up a lot in the night, and when they wake up, they eat. They mate, of course. Once a year. Fun-o. They migrate to find other things to eat. They go to water holes, but these are haunted by crocodiles, lions, jackals, wild dogs, hyenas, and minibuses full of tourists waiting to see the violence and strong-language portions of safari. That's about it for the wildebeest lifestyle. The young ones frisk, but they get over it.

Nature is poor, and the Tanzanians haven't gotten nearly far enough away from nature. Coming back from the Serengeti, John and I drove by a small airport. There were vultures on the landing strip—never a good sign. We descended into the Rift to the marshy village of Mto-wa-Mbu, which means "Mosquito River," a name of stunning obviousness, like calling Kansas "Flat State."

We went to the market, a jolly, if unhygienic, huddle of teetering sheds and precarious vegetable heaps. I was taking notes on food costs. This nosiness might have raised suspicions or hackles elsewhere, but Tanzanians have experienced more than three decades of foreign-aid mavens, development experts, and academic investigators of Third Worldery. They got with the program at once. Three or four helpful loafers showed me into every corner of the bazaar, and merchants gave price quotations with the speed and facility of NYSE specialist brokers.

The market smelled. The whole of Tanzania smells. It's an odor of smoke and spoiled milk with undertones of compost and beef jerky. Amazingly, it's not a bad smell. But it's not the smell of success.

Along the main street, Mto-wa-Mbu resembles a ghost town in the American West—if cowboys had had a marvelous sense of color, and also if they'd stuck around. Mosquito River is fully populated. Its leaning, sagging, dilapidated buildings are made of cinder block. This isn't usually a "rickety" building material but, with lack of mortar and abstention from use of the level or plumb bob, a tumbledown effect can be achieved.

All the small towns in Tanzania look like hell. The crudity of ordinary things is astonishing: fences, gates, window frames, doors, and let's not mention toilets. Every place is makeshift, improvised, jury-rigged, askew (and, in the case of toilets, amok). Americans are so querulous about mass production that we forget the precision afforded by machinery. *Handmade* often means made with ten thumbs. Examine the shelves you put up in your garage. Now take a log and a machete and build them.

Lots of things are started in Tanzania. Not much is finished. Scattered everywhere are roofless masonry walls—literally a few bricks shy of a load. Paint appears on the fronts of buildings but never on the sides or backs. The country seems as if it were built by hippies. And in a sense, it was.

Julius Nyerere was born two years after Timothy Leary. Nyerere, called *Mwalimu,* "the teacher," was elected president of Tanganyika in 1962, just when Professor Leary began advocating LSD use at Harvard. Nobody has ever accused Nyerere of being drug-addled. He's lived an abstemious life (although he does have twenty-four grandchildren). But some of the same generational fluff filled the skulls of both Julius and Tim.

Nyerere embraced the collectivist ideology that ran riot in the twentieth century, and from this embrace was born a particularly spacey and feckless socialism call *ujamaa,* or "familyhood." Excerpts from Nyerere's writing sound like a 1969 three-bong-hit rap from somebody going off to found an organic jojoba bean–growing commune: "Our agricultural organization would be predominately that of cooperative living and working for the good of all . . . Some degree of specialization would be possible, with one member being, for example, a carpenter." Dig it. "If every individual is self-reliant . . . then the whole nation is self-reliant." Heavy.

The 1967 Arusha Declaration, a government manifesto cataloging the right-on goals and groovy ideals of *ujamaa,* states that agriculture and animal husbandry are where the Tanzanian economy is at. Industrialization would mean a bummer money trip. In the words of the tuned-in *Mwalimu,* "We make a mistake in choosing money—something we do not have—to be the big instrument of our development." Development being something else they do not have.

Issa G. Shivji, a law professor at the University of Dar es Salaam, has written an article summing up *ujamaa.* He says, "There were two central premises of this ideology: equality of human beings and developmentalism." Equality is the thirty-five cents a day mentioned earlier. Developmentalism sounds like some even worse offshoot of Scientology. "The problem," Shivji continues, "was that the ideology of *ujamaa* was not supported by any explicit social theory," and that the Tanzanian government "pursued this policy logically and consistently."

In other words, *ujamaa* worked as well as rigidly adhered to nonsense usually does. Slogans were coined, such as the Hitlerish "*Uhuru na Kazi,*" which sounds even more Hitlerish when translated: "Freedom and Work." Price controls were instituted, lasting until 1986. In 1981 farmers were being forced to sell corn to the government for 20 percent of market value, and that market value was nothing to write to Iowa about. In Mto-wa-Mbu, price-uncontrolled corn now sells for twenty-three cents a pound. Local industries were nationalized, foreign companies were expropriated, and compensation for these takings was, in the words of the U.S. State Department, "extremely slow and ponderous." Much of commerce met the same ponderous, if not so slow, fate. East Indian and Arab minorities were the targets. The history textbook used in Tanzanian public high schools blandly states, "The monopolistic position of Indian wholesale traders was abolished."

A program of "villagization" was begun. The idea was to persuade rural Tanzanians to move to eight thousand "familyhood villages," *ujamaa vijijini,* where the government could provide them with water and education, and, by the way, keep an eye on everybody. The planned communities did not fulfill the plan. The water didn't arrive; neither did the education, nor the people who were supposed to move there. When persuasion wouldn't work, force was used. By the end of the '70s, more than 65 percent of the population in the Tanzanian countryside had been deported to the *ujamaa vijijini* gulag. But, this being Tanzania, the population just wandered away again and built houses of their own in the bush.

Other vaporous ideas were being tried. According to *Ideology and Development in Africa,* a terribly fair-minded book published by the Yale University Press in the early '80s, "There was a sharp reorientation of medical outlays away from high-cost, Western-model, curative medicine and toward rural, paramedical, and preventive health care. By 1974 the fraction of the health budget allocated to hospitals had dropped from 80 percent in the late 1960s to 50 percent," with results such as the hyena hole/fractured spine crisis I overheard on the shortwave radio.

Meanwhile, the Tanzanian economy went concave. Tanzanian National Accounts figures indicate that the per capita GDP has yet to return to its 1976 level. And the purchasing power of the legal minimum wage fell 80 percent between 1969 and 1987. So another answer to the question "Why is Tanzania so poor?" is *ujamaa*—they planned it.

They planned it, and we paid for it. Rich countries have been underwriting Tanzanian economic idiocy for thirty-seven years. There's a certain kind of gullible and self-serious person who's put in charge of foreign aid (e.g., ex-head of the World Bank Robert McNamara; I rest my case). This type was entranced by modest, articulate Julius Nyerere and the wonderful things he was going to do. American political-science professor Ali Mazrui dubbed it "Tanzaphilia." In the midst of the villagization ugliness, Tanzania was receiving U.S. Official Direct Assistance (or ODA, as it's called by the succor/sucker professionals) of $300 million a year in big, fat 1975 dollars. That was twenty dollars a person—probably what it cost to build a *vijijini* hovel, catch a Tanzanian, and stick him inside.

Scandinavian countries were particularly smitten, seeing in *ujamaa* a version of their own sanctimonious social order, but with better weather and fewer of those little meatballs on toothpicks. By the early 1990s, Sweden, Norway, and Denmark together were sending Tanzania more than $320 million a year.

Then there is the aforementioned World Bank, financed by the United States, Japan, and other wealthy nations. Its purpose is to loan money to underdeveloped areas, and I can't understand why it won't loan money to me, as I am in many areas quite underdeveloped. The World Bank charges interest rates like your dad does when you borrow a twenty. Thirty-three percent of the projects funded by the World Bank are considered failures by the bank itself. The World Bank thus operates on bad business principles. And moral principles of the same ilk. Villagization was just fine with the World Bank; in fact, it had already proposed something on that order in the reams of busybody economic advice with which international organizations pester the globe. How would we like it if the Organization of African Unity told us to get out of our suburbs and move to Detroit?

The World Bank loaned Tanzania oodles of money. More oodles were loaned by other kindly aid agencies. Tanzanians now have a total foreign debt equal to almost two years' worth of everything produced in the country. Tanzania is $7.4 billion in hock. The money will be repaid . . . when Rush Limbaugh becomes secretary-general of the UN.

But don't worry, the International Monetary Fund is on the case. If a country gets in trouble by borrowing too much from places like the World Bank, then it qualifies for an IMF loan. As long as Tanzania promises to abide, more or less, by free-market guidelines and doesn't print more worthless paper money than it absolutely has too, the IMF will "help."

Tanzania has been smothered in help. It's received loans, grants, programs, projects, an entire railroad from the Chinese government (running 1,200 miles to nowhere in particular), and just plain cash. In 1994, by World Bank tally, foreign aid made up 29.1 percent of the Tanzanian GDP, more than the budget of the Tanzanian government.

Tanzania is said by Africa scholar Sanford Ungar to be "the most-aided country in all of Africa." In the period immediately after independence, Tanzania was getting half a billion dollars a year in aid. Between 1970 and 1989, the CIA estimates, another $10.8 billion arrived. According to the World Bank, $5.4 billion more was given between 1990 and 1994. This is more than $20 billion, without even trying to pump the figure by adjusting for inflation.

John told me that good farmland in Tanzania sells for a million shillings an acre, about $1,650. Since there are 29 million Tanzanians, $20 billion would have bought each family a larger-than-average farm plot, and everybody could have gone back to doing what they were doing before *ujamaa* was thought of. The biggest reason that Tanzania is poor is that we've paid them to be so.

John and I took the hammering ride back across the Rift. When I got green from being jiggled, John said, "*Safari* means 'hard journey.'" Dust devils the size of major league ballparks roamed across the Maasai homesteads. The Maasai didn't bother to glance at these swirling circles of debris, which hit us with high-speed curtains of dirt and filled our van like a window planter. The Rift Valley is the work of continental drift. Africa is being pulled apart. Some day, Tanzania will float away from Rwanda, Burundi, Congo, and Uganda. And Tanzanians deserve the move. Tanzanians deserve a lot of things.

Tanzanians certainly don't deserve what they've had since 1961. The scum tide of *ujamaa* has receded, but it's left behind such things as the awful road to Makuyuni we were on. *Ujamaa* has also left the Tanzanian public mind strewn with intellectual jettison. The national budget, in its "Agriculture" section, asserts that the government is encouraging "private sector participation in production," and, in its "Land" section, claims that the government seeks "to ensure equitable distribution and equal access to land by all citizens." So you're encouraged to farm your private plot, and everyone else is encouraged to farm it, too. The high school history book gives the following analysis of economic history: "General Tyre Corporation built one tyre factory for the whole of East Africa in Arusha. But soon after this decision, another corporation, Firestone, built a similar factory in Nairobi. This meant the competition of imperialist capital." And even John, who was completely sensible, said, "We have lots of bananas, but we don't do anything with them—just use them for food."

John did tell me, however, that nobody even thought about trying to put the Maasai into *ujamaa* villages. Say what you will against the blood sports, people who spear lions for fun are well prepared for political rough and tumble.

And Julius Nyerere apologized, which is more than most '60s icons have bothered to do. When he relinquished the presidency in 1985, he said, in his farewell speech, "I failed. Let's admit it."

We drove on from Makuyuni to the Tarangire River basin on the far edge of the Maasai Steppe. The Maasai are fit and towering, despite what is—by the standards of Tanzania itself—a life of extreme hardship. They customarily knock out a couple of their children's teeth so that the kids can be force-fed when they get lockjaw. Administering a liquid diet is easy enough, because Maasai cuisine is nothing but, basically, gravy. It would be food suicide for any other people and may cause even the Maasai a certain amount of indigestion. They call Europeans *iloredaa enjekat*, "those who confine their farts with clothing." The Maasai try to avoid pants and other items of Western apparel. They stick to their tartan wraps. From toddler to granny, they possess a martial bearing. No Maasai man goes outdoors without a lance or quarterstaff. As a result of this public dignity, seeing a Maasai engaged in any ordinary activity—riding a bicycle, walking down the road with an upside-down dishpan on the head, drinking a soda pop—is like seeing a member of the Joint Chiefs of Staff skateboarding. But the Maasai do know how to wear plaid-on-plaid. Ralph Lauren is history if the Maasai ever get start-up capital and a marketing plan.

This brings us to a sadder question than "Why are the Tanzanians so poor?" which is "Why do we care?" An economist would answer that a Maasai line of "LionKill" sportswear would drive down the price of Ralph Lauren Polo clothing and that we, as consumers, would profit. But the idea that the increased productivity of others benefits ourself is not something most noneconomists understand or believe. It would be nice to think that we worry about Tanzanian poverty out of some *ujamaa*-like altruism—or maybe it's not so nice to think that, considering the results of *ujamaa*. Anyway, altruism toward strangers is mostly a sentimental and fleeting thing—a small check dashed off to Save the Children. Twenty billion dollars' worth of it is rare. In the cold war days, of course, we were giving money to Tanzania on the theory of: "Pay them to be socialist so they won't be communist and figure out what the difference is later." But now, I'm afraid, the sad truth is that we care about Tanzanians because they have cool animals.

And they do. John and I spent most of our days together driving around and looking at them. The minivan had a kind of sunroof on legs that, instead of sliding out of the way, popped up to form a metal awning. Thus, while John drove, I would stand in the back and, holding the awning's supports, be bounced and jiggled around like some idiot of the Raj in a mechanical howdah. Then, John would shout things such as, "Elephant!"

And I would shout, "No kidding!" because the elephant was twenty feet from us, walking across the road without so much as a sideways glance for traffic. It was an enormous solitary bull. His back was powdered with the dust that elephants fling over themselves to ward off bugs, a pink dust in this case, collecting in the deep gray wrinkles and making his hide look like an old actress betrayed by her pancake base. The bull's tusks were as long as playground slides and so thick that bowling rather than billiard balls could have been carved from them, if such a thing were thinkable nowadays. He was the most impressive living creature I've seen—for about a minute. Then he got more impressive, growing an immense erection for no reason. (I hoped it was for no reason. A mad infatuation with our minivan would have been unwelcome.) "Fifth leg," said John.

The elephant walked off into a forest to strip the bark from the legal-pad-colored fever trees and snap the branches off for snacks. Elephants leave a real mess in the woods. They leave a mess wherever they go. You can see how, in a country supported by humble agriculture, the big browsing animals get killed, and not just by poachers. We love elephants in North America, where they never get into our tomato plants or herbaceous borders, much less destroy the equivalent of our fax machines and desktop computers.

On the other side of the forest and keeping their distance from the tourist track were three more big browsers: black rhinos. There used to be thousands of rhinoceros in Tanzania. Now there are not. The poachers did get the rhinos, as they've gotten most of the rhinos in Africa, all because middle-aged men in Asia believe the powdered horn is a natural and organic Viagra.

The Cape buffalo are still around in droves, however. Their horns don't seem to do anything for Asians. And it's harder to kill them. The Cape buffalo is just a cow, but a gigantic and furious one—the bovine as superhero, the thing that fantasizing Herefords wish would burst upon the scene between feedlot and Wendy's.

Most of the animals were not shy. They've discovered that the round-footed noisy things on the roads do not claw or bite, and are not—on their outsides, anyway—tasty. We were able to drive to within tollbooth-change-tossing distance of some young lions lying on a sandbank at a water hole.

"These are stupid young males," said John in a tone that (he being as fiftyish as I) implied the unlikelihood of any other young male type. "They are hunting badly. A female would be behind the sand, not on top of it." The lions didn't seem to care. They didn't seem to care about us, either. And they didn't care about the half dozen other jeeps and vans full of tourists that, seeing us seeing something, eventually gathered around.

A trip to the game lands of Tanzania isn't a lonely, meditative journey. Everything I saw was also being ogled by dozens of other folks from out of town, and they were reeling off enough videotape to start a Blockbuster chain devoted solely to out-of-focus fauna. But the tourists pay money, and money is what it takes to keep the parks and preserves more or less unspoiled and to buy the bullets to shoot poachers. If the animals of Africa aren't worth more alive to rubberneckers than they're worth dead to farmers, pastoralists, and rhino-horn erection peddlers, then that's that for the *Call of the Wild*. (Besides, romantic as it may sound, how solitary do you want to be in the presence of stupid young lions?)

One of the lions got up, walked a couple of steps away, took a leak, and—with no thought for the grace and style that Western-educated people so admire in African wildlife—lay down again in the piss.

At the next water hole, we saw a pair of lions dozing in the midday heat. A herd of wildebeest surrounded them, evidently thirsty yet mindful of trespassing's consequences. "But every now and then," said John, "one of them forgets."

The male lion was crashed out on his back, immobile. The female was lying prone and panting hard. "They have just mated," said John. "Lions mate every six minutes and then gradually decreasing until it's every half hour, every hour, every few hours, and so on for seven days."

John had a variety of information about the sex lives of animals. "Do you know why there are so few giraffes?" he asked at a moment when we had quite a few in sight. "They have no natural enemies," John continued. "Their hooves are too sharp. Their legs are too strong, not like wildebeest or zebras. But there are wildebeest and zebras everywhere." He paused. "The guidebooks will not tell you this, but giraffes are homosexual." John had no more said this than the two giraffes closest to us—one definitely female and the other very emphatically male—began to (and never has this slang term been used with more scrupulous precision) neck.

"You're wrong about *these* giraffes," I said. "They're going to mate."

"Not yet," said John. "She has to kick him first."

On a riverbank meadow in the Tarangire, we came across a huge troop of baboons, more than a hundred of them. They were, well, monkeying around—lollygagging, dillydallying, scratching their heads and other body parts, putzing, noodling, airing their heels, and chattering all the while. About what I don't know. But John told me baboons are a favorite food of the big cats. Baboons aren't much different than we were in *Australopithecus* days. I wondered if this troop was us four million years ago. If so, the baboons are probably plotting revenge upon the predators. "As soon as we evolve, we take the lion habitat and *pave its ass.*"

But not just yet, I hope. Tanzania has creatures of such breath-catching magnificence that they turn the most hardened indoorsman mushy about the mysteries of nature. It happened to me when I saw a mother cheetah stretched under a gum arabic tree with four cubs a couple of weeks old. The mother cheetah bore a startling resemblance to my high school sweetheart from St. Ursula's, Connie Nowakowski—the same tawny coloring, the same high cheekbones, the same little uptilt of the nose, and the exact, the identical eyes. Connie died in her thirties, years ago, and it would be just like her to come back as a cheetah. She'd love the drama, and the coat looks great. But how any male cheetah got four cubs—or even a hand-job—from Connie Nowakowski is one of the mysteries of nature.

A full quarter of Tanzania's geography is some kind of conservation area. For so poor a country, this is a remarkable bit of eco-conscious forbearance. It's not like the big game couldn't be put to use. "Are wildebeest edible?" I asked John.

"Yes."

"How about Cape buffalo?"

"Yes, yes."

"I'll bet a gazelle steak is nice."

"Oh, yes."

"Are warthogs any good to eat?"

"Yes," said John, "delicious."

I wasn't even going to ask about elephants. Lions, anyway, are horrible. I had a lion steak once, at a German restaurant during "Wild Game Week." The flavor was militant liver.

Keeping the conservation areas conserved is not just a matter of Tanzania sucking up to the International Wildlife Fund. Vast sections of Tanzania are infected with sleeping sickness borne by the tsetse fly. Sleeping sickness does not bother wild animals, but it does kill people and—something that's more economically important in Tanzania than people are—domestic cattle. The Sierra Club's travel guide to East Africa says, "A good number of African parks undoubtedly owe their existence not to an animal that humans wanted to preserve, but to one we couldn't get rid of." The tsetse is the size of a housefly but manages a bite like an enraged fox terrier. Dozens of them would get in the minivan and hang out behind the dome light and under the sun visors, waiting for their chance. Tobacco fumes seemed to be the only effective repellent. Cigarette packs should come with a printed message: "Smoking may prolong life in areas of tsetse fly infestation."

If we want to save Tanzania's wildlife, we'd better do something about its poverty. Otherwise the Tanzanians may give up on safari tourism, spray the Ngorongoro, the Serengeti, and the Tarangire with DDT, and start playing the *Bonanza* theme song. Who wouldn't rather be a cowboy than a busboy?

In fact, no matter why we're appalled by Tanzanian poverty, we'd better do something about it. There's suffering humanity to be considered. And that suffering humanity will be us if we're not careful. Only a few million of the world's people are relatively wealthy, but two billion live like the Tanzanians. One of these days those two billion are going to figure out that they can buy guns in Florida without much of a background check.

On my last night on safari, I gathered an armload of Serengeti beer and went to sit on the small terrace of my ground-floor hotel room. There was a stretch of flowering shrubs on the other side of a knee-high wall and, beyond that, miles of pitch-dark Africa. I heard a *crunch-crunch* in the decorative landscaping. Then a *crunch-crunch, crunch-crunch*. I turned off my room lights. It was a moonless night, but I thought I could see something moving. I got out my travel flashlight, its beam about as wide as a finger. I shone it this way and that, and then down along the ground, and there was a pair of eyes. They were big, round, red eyes, and they seemed to be very far apart. I shone the flashlight around some more, and there was another pair of eyes. And a third. *Crunch-crunch, crunch-crunch*. The eyes were coming in my direction. I ran into the room and pulled the screen door shut.

As if that was going to help. The glass slider wouldn't budge. I chugged a Serengeti and thought . . . I don't know what I thought. I went back out on the terrace and said, "Ahem," and, "See here, you animals . . ." I aimed the flashlight directly into the scarlet orbs and wiggled it vigorously. The eyes kept coming. The crunching got louder.

The eyes came up to within three feet of my wall. Then they seemed to turn away, and in my flashlight beam I saw the enormous head of a Cape buffalo, scarfing the bougainvillea. I switched the room lights back on. Here was the animal "considered by hunters to be the most dangerous of the big game" (said my *Brant Guide to Tanzania*). In fact, here were three of them. And they were acting like well-mannered parochial-school football players in the lunchroom cafeteria line—at the expense of the hotel's gardening staff. The Cape buffalo were unperturbed, not interested in me, and eating everything in sight. They munched their way next door. I had another beer. It goes to show how even the most wrathful of earth's residents can be rendered dull and domestic—if the chow is good.

How is Tanzania supposed to get rich? Well, there are "improvements in agricultural yield," always a favorite with development-aid types. The British Labour government tried this after World War II in what was known as "the groundnut scheme." The Brits decided that Tanganyika was going to become the world's foremost producer of groundnuts—that is to say, peanuts. They selected three huge sites and cleared the land by running a chain between two tractors, pulling the chain through the bush, and destroying thousands of acres of wilderness. Thirty-six and a half million British pounds were invested, an amount nearly equal to the whole Tanganyikan government budget from 1946 to 1950. It was then discovered that peanuts wouldn't grow in Tanganyika.

The current Tanzanian government budget contains more pages on agriculture than would ever be read by anyone, except a journalist in a hotel room with dysentery and nothing but a copy of the current Tanzanian government budget. But the only mentions of land *ownership* in the budget are an admission that buying land entails "lengthy and bureaucratic procedures" and this weasel sentence: "A new land law being formulated proposes to introduce different structural arrangements." Julius Nyerere (apologizing again) has said it was a mistake to collectivize the individual small farms, the *shambas*. But it's a mistake that hasn't been corrected. John said that farms must be bought "informally." (Another note from the budget: "FISHERIES—the sector still faces problems from dynamite fishing.")

I did see one swell coffee plantation, Gibb's Farm, at the foot of the Ngorongoro Crater. This is run by English people and has thousands of neatly clipped coffee bushes lined in parade file. A smoothly raked dirt road winds up through the property with woven-stick barriers stuck in the drain gullies to hinder erosion. A profusion of blossoms surrounds the main house. The very picture of a Cotswold cottage yard has been somehow created from weird, thorny African plants, which need to be irrigated every minute. The English will garden the ash heaps of Hades if hell lets them.

I suppose the farms of Tanzania could all look like Gibb's Farm, but it turns out that Gibb's Farm doesn't make any money as a farm but prospers because upscale tourist lodgings have been installed. So there's tourism.

According to the U.S. State Department's *Country Commercial Guide*, "Tourism is currently the second-largest foreign-currency earner for Tanzania, after coffee." (Actually, as mentioned, the largest foreign-currency earner for Tanzania is foreign aid. But never mind, with Republicans in Congress foreign aid is not a growth industry.) All the tourists I talked to were voluble in their praise of Tanzania—as soon as they'd recovered enough from their road trips to form words. And Tanzania's tourist hotels produced $205 million in revenue in 1995. But that's only 6.7 percent of the country's GDP. This compared to the 6 percent of GDP produced by Tanzania's "transport and communication sector." Tanzania doesn't have any communication. As for transport, according to the same State Department guide that talks up tourism, "It takes approximately three days to travel by road from the capital, Dar es Salaam, to the second-largest city, Mwanza," a distance of about 500 miles.

I talked to the manager of a luxury hotel near Mto-wa-Mbu, a Kenyan whom I'll call Shabbir, and his friend, a Tanzanian named, let's say, Mwambande, who ran the plush tented camp down the road. Shabbir said it was difficult to get these resorts to work. What was going on in his kitchen right now "was hell." And at another hotel in Tanzania, I did watch a waiter just arrived from the sticks being utterly confounded by a soda-can pop top. I asked Shabbir and Mwambande if tourism could make a country like Tanzania rich. Shabbir didn't think so. He was leaving for better opportunities in Vietnam. Mwambande didn't think so, either, but more optimistically. "Tourism acts as a showcase," he said. "It helps people come see a place for them to invest."

They explained that tourism itself isn't very profitable for Tanzania because so much of what's spent is "yo-yo money." The foreigners arrive via foreign-owned airlines in planes built by foreigners. They stay at hotels constructed with foreign building materials, ride around in foreign-made cars, and eat food imported from foreign places. The money rolls in, pauses for a moment, and rolls back out.

Some of the foreigners are, indeed, rich people. "Is the Tanzanian government giving them any incentive to invest?" I asked.

"Oh, yes," said Mwambande, "if you build a plant here you get a five-year tax holiday."

"But," I said, "it normally takes a new enterprise five years to make a profit." Mwambande and Shabbir laughed. "And what about after the tax holiday?" I said. "What are taxes like then?" Mwambande and Shabbir laughed and laughed.

In a February 10, 1997, story about a Tanzanian crackdown on illegal tour operators, Kenya's *East-African* newspaper mentioned these taxes just in passing: "a hotel levy (20%), sales tax on food (15%), sales tax on fresh juices and cakes (30%), stamp duty (1% of turnover), withholding tax on goods and services (2%), training levy (10% on expatriate employees' taxable income), payroll levy (4% on gross taxable income of all employees), vocational education training agency tax (2% on gross taxable income of all employees)."

Forget about tourism. How about trade? Trade benefits everyone. Anytime I've got something you want more than I want it, or vice versa, and we swap instead of steal, the economy is improved. But trade in Tanzania has—surprise—its problems, too. Starting right at the dock. Says the State Department's *Commercial Guide*: "The Customs Department is the greatest hindrance to importers throughout Tanzania. Clearance delays and extralegal levies [note diplomatic wording] are commonplace." And until a couple of years ago, Tanzanians, like Cubans, weren't allowed to have real money. They had to make do with Tanzanian shillings, which no one wanted.

The current Tanzanian government (which is to say, the same old government after some shady elections to stay current looking) claims to have a "trade liberalization policy." But that government shows no understanding of what trade is. It talks about local industries "facing stiff and often unfair competition from imports." That's the point. Back in the States, we'd be driving DeSotos and browsing the Web with room-size Univacs if it weren't for the Japanese. The Tanzanian government also claims that "the domestic market is now more or less saturated with imports." Sure. Until the early 1980s there were only nine computer installations in the country, and a ban on importing computers wasn't completely lifted until 1994.

Nor does "trade liberalization" seem to be aimed at people doing the actual trading. A story in the Dar es Salaam *Guardian* began, "Petty traders along Ali Hassan Mwinyi Road . . . yesterday received a city commission notice to quit the area in five days—and a demolishing grader erased their kiosks a few hours later." Or if bulldozers won't do it, a value-added tax is being instituted this year. An exaction of between 14.2 and 17.5 percent will be charged on the sale of most goods and services. Still, trade does happen. I went to the largest and most prosperous-looking store in Arusha. I'll give it the moniker Safari Barn. It sold souvenirs to tourists. A Maasai warrior in full fig stood sentry by the door, looking as quietly mortified as a Coldstream Guard placed at attention in front of a Victoria's Secret outlet.

The souvenirs were beautiful: black wood carvings of hippos, rhinos, Cape buffalo, giraffes. (Could America's unemployed carve squirrels and mice this well?) And Safari Barn also sold the best *kangas* I'd seen. I picked out one with orange hearts and black wiggle lines like a Keith Haring print. SEMENI MNAYOJUA MSIKAE MKAZUA, said the slogan along the material's edge. I asked the saleswoman to translate. She blushed, the blood rising in her dark complexion and turning her cheeks maroon. John began giggling. "It means," he said, "'Don't sit down and spread your legs and tell everything you know.'" Besides the *kangas* and wood carvings, there were comely Maasai beads, sparkling "Tanzanite" gemstones, and a terrific selection of masks. Literally terrific, most of them, with gobbly teeth and vexed expressions, and fulsome trimmings of what I hoped wasn't human hair. "What are these masks used for?" I asked another saleswoman. You can't come back from Africa without a mask. But I might be shy about having certain ceremonies represented around the house.

"Mostly they're for dancing," said the saleswoman.

"What kind of dancing is done in this one?" I said, pointing to a handsome white striped false face with a box for a mouth and nose.

She hesitated: "Dancing . . . at night."

I got an antelope mask.

I talked to the man who owned Safari Barn, whom I'll call Nisar. By his faintly Middle Eastern speech and pallor (and wow of a wristwatch), I judged him to be a foreigner. But, though Europeans are rare, Tanzanians cover all skin-color bases. There is a sizable population with roots in India, Persia, and Oman, plus people of mixed African-Arab and whatever-whichever ancestry. Nisar's family had been in Tanzania for six generations.

Nisar said Julius Nyerere's "economics were no good." The British tradition of understatement survives in Tanzania. Although only sometimes. "I have queued for a loaf of bread for two weeks," said Nisar. "Under Nyerere, even if I had enough money for a dozen Rolls-Royces, if I drove a Mercedes, I'd go to jail for seven years—languish in jail." So he hated Nyerere's guts. No. "Nyerere destroyed tribalism in Tanzania," Nisar said and claimed he encountered no prejudice for being non-African. He praised Nyerere's insistence that everyone speak Kiswahili: "It unified the nation."

Safari Barn was successful, said Nisar, because "I poured money into Tanzania when others were afraid to spend a shilling." It was hard getting Safari Barn built. Nisar's description of working with Tanzanian contractors was like Shabbir's description of work in the hotel kitchen. Nisar had received no tax holidays, no subsidies. To get them, he would have had to go to Dar es Salaam and hang around. "'The minister is here.' 'The minister is there.' 'The minister is gone for a week.' It could take a month to see the right guy. I'm a one-man show here." Then, Nisar said (without a *but* or a *however* or an *even so*), "Tanzania is the best country in Africa. And I have traveled all over. If there is a food shortage in Tanzania, people won't riot. There has never been that tradition here. They will get through it. They will share, help each other. They will organize to complain. They will have meetings. They are very political. But not violent. This is not a violent country." He paused and thought that over for a second. "These people," said Nisar, "are so damn lazy."

Well, not lazy—not when half the teenage girls in the country are walking around with five-gallon buckets on their heads. Five gallons of water weigh forty pounds. But Tanzanians are *country*. Rural labor is hard and long, not busy-busy. Cassava plants don't crash on deadlines. Chickens don't form quality teams. The sun does not take work home at night. And Tanzanians are political but, again, not in a way an American always understands. During the 1995 elections, John had run for the legislature, the Union Assembly, on the opposition NCCR ticket. But he couldn't remember what the party's initials stand for. (National Convention for Construction and Reform, incidentally.) Tanzania has been ruled by Nyerere's CCM Party (*Chama Cha Mapinduzi*, Party of the Revolution) since independence. Tanzania is a one-party state but has dozens of political parties. According to Louisa Taylor, Africa correspondent for the Canadian *Ottawa Citizen*, "Every party stands for clean government and well-equipped hospitals, good roads, and higher crop yields, and all are equally vague on how they would make it so."

Even when making it so is a simple matter. I was talking to an expat Brit who'd come to East Africa as a colonial administrator after World War II. I said, "That washboard from Mto-wa-Mbu to Makuyuni—all they'd have to do is send a road grader over it." (The one from Ali Hassan Mwinyi Road seems to be available on short notice.)

"Oh, less than that," said the Brit. "They used to just drag a big log behind a tractor—up and back. The fellow'd get to one end and turn around and go back to the other. Took all the corrugation out. You'd watch for the dust cloud having gone your way and then take off. I'd run my little MG right up to the Ngorongoro rim."

The dysfunction of Tanzania is comic, depending on the cruelty of your sense of humor. Here is an exhibit label from a Tanzanian Museum:

The Soda Bottle (ancient)
The soda bottle which in use up to 1959. This bottle contain a marble and rubbering which jointly (wished) as stopper for the gas.

Then you take a swig of the locally produced purified water and notice brown, gelatinous things floating in your own bottle (modern).

John and I visited a high functionary of the Tanzania Chamber of Commerce, Industry and Agriculture, Arusha branch.

"What does the Chamber of Commerce do?" I asked.

"Our main activity is getting new members," said the functionary.

"Is the Chamber doing anything to attract business to Arusha?" I asked.

"We haven't reached that level yet," said the functionary. "I think Arusha has everything to attract business."

"Except telephones," I mentioned.

"Telephones will be privatized next year," he said. "Arusha has two million people in the whole town." He thought about that. "Arusha has three hundred thousand people. It is second to Dar es Salaam in importance. If all goes well, it might become first important."

"Do you have any brochures?"

"We used to have the newsletter, but of recently, we have not done any printing."

"But *what* does the Chamber of Commerce actually *do*?"

"We are a pressure group," said the functionary with emphasis.

"Have you been a successful one?"

"We have! To some good extent. The Chamber of Commerce played a big role in formulating the budget. We were invited to Dar es Salaam to give our opinion. We complained about the postal-service box rent going from three thousand shillings to fifty thousand shillings."

"Did they change the rate back?"

"No."

The Chamber of Commerce office was located in a long, tin-roofed shed adjacent to the former headquarters of the East African Community, or EAC. The latter building is of a truly stupendous international-donor type, featuring not only discolored concrete but also oxidized aluminum, rust-stained stainless steel, and a row of empty flagpoles all bent at different angles. The EAC was an attempt by Tanzania, Kenya, and Uganda to form a common market, and it fell apart when Kenya's president, Daniel arap Moi, started getting huffy and Uganda's dictator, Idi Amin, started eating people. But nothing in Africa that receives foreign assistance ever really goes away, and the EAC continues to exist in the guise of East African Cooperation. In the parking space reserved for the EAC's deputy secretary was a BMW. In the executive secretary's parking space was a new Mercedes sedan. These plenipotentiaries are members of what Kiswahili-speaking Africans call *wa-Benz,* "People of the Fancy German Cars." So the comedy of errors has a happy ending—for some folks.

And not for others. When John isn't guiding, he and his wife live in northwestern Tanzania, on an informally purchased farm near the Burundi border. They have two grown sons and did have two young daughters, but the five-year-old girl had died a couple months before John and I met. She had malaria. John took her to the local dispensary, where she was injected with a massive dose of something, and she went into a coma. When the girl had been unconscious for five days, medics at the dispensary said she needed a tracheotomy. The nearest surgeon was a hundred kilometers away. John told the medics to radio ahead and hired a car. The drive took all day. By the time John and his daughter arrived, the surgeon—the only surgeon, in fact the only doctor—at the hospital had left. "Oh, the doctor goes home around five," said the hospital staff. "Go get him!" said John. And they said, "We don't know where his house is." John hired another car and searched for hours. Meanwhile, his daughter died.

I flew to the capital of Tanzania, wherever that may be. "In 1973 it was decided to move the capital city from Dar es Salaam on the coast to Dodoma in the center . . . a dry and desolate area," says the *East Africa Handbook*. The move to Dodoma is "anticipated around the turn of the century," says the *Globetrotter Travel Guide to Tanzania*. "Dodoma is now the official capital of Tanzania, displacing Dar es Salaam," says the *Brant Guide to Tanzania*. "Some government offices have been transferred to Dodoma," says the CIA's *1997 World Factbook*. And an article in the February 20, 1997, Dar es Salaam *Guardian* begins, "Dodoma branch members of the Tanzania Chamber of Commerce, Industry and Agriculture have asked the government to clarify a minister's statement that Dodoma is not the country's legally recognized capital."

Anyway, I flew to Dar es Salaam. A jolly soldier rummaged through my carry-on baggage, airily dismissing my pocketknife as a possible weapon and telling me that the woman operating the metal detector was his sister. I was ushered into the "boarding lounge" for the requisite two- or three-hour wait before anything airplane-like happens in Tanzania. Warm soft drinks were for sale by a young lady with no change.

As I walked to the tired prop plane, John was on the roof of the airport, shouting good-bye. He'd been waiting the whole time outside in the heat to see me off.

The plane flew over Mount Kilimanjaro. Hemingway begins "The Snows of Ditto" by noting that there's a frozen leopard carcass at the top. "No one has explained what the leopard was seeking at that altitude," writes Hemingway. A clean, well-lighted bathroom is my guess.

In Dar, as knowing travelers call it, I was met by a driver named Nzezele (pronounced "Nzezele"). Dar es Salaam is a seaport without the bustle and sin that implies. Probably due to lack of ships and sailors. A few rusty tubs are moored in the harbor. Much of the commerce with nearby Zanzibar is still conducted in sailing dhows. Goats graze in the main rail yard.

Dar sports some stucco buildings in the art deco style but with Arabian embellishments: horseshoe arches and crenellated roof lines, all in a poor state of repair, as if a sheikh had come to Miami Beach with the District of Columbia's public school system maintenance staff. The dusty moderne, however, is being supplanted by dusty glass boxes. Here and there are signs of history, or history's ugly half sister, politics: a squatty palace built by the sultan of Zanzibar when he ruled the city and a small, tile-roofed, half-timbered Lutheran church, a misplaced molecule of Bavaria, from before Tanzania was Tanganyika, when it was German East Africa. The predominant tint of the city is beige, a color with a bad name for being middle class and bland, but Africa can use some bourgeois dullness. And there is a nine-hole golf course right downtown.

Traffic dribbles around unimpeded by many stoplights, none of those being at the busier intersections. Buses and taxis bear pictures of Bob Marley. Pedestrians wear T-shirts emblazoned with Rastafarian slogans. BACK TO AFRICA is—confoundingly—a popular slogan in Tanzania.

There are some nice houses up on Oyster Bay, but not ridiculously nice. There are some slums out in Kariakoo, but not horribly slummy. The neighborhoods where Nzezele told me to lock the car door wouldn't make a New Yorker button his wallet pocket. A Swedish expat told me that he'd been robbed once. The big wad of Tanzanian shillings that it takes to amount to twenty dollars had been picked from his jeans. A crowd chased the thief, who dropped the money. Bystanders picked it up and brought it back to the Swede, asking him to count it, to make sure it was all there. The crowd chasing the thief caught him and beat him to death.

There's no garbage on the streets in Dar, no rats, no stray dogs. There are some beggars, but they're halfhearted. Dar es Salaam has a clunky charm. The International Cashew and Coconut Conference was being hosted February 19–21. You'd be nuts not to sign up. And you have to love a city with a thoroughfare named Bibi Titi Mohamed Street.

Of course, Dar es Salaam has its troubles. The city is out of water. Hundreds of women stand in line at the few open taps, their plastic buckets making brightly colored dots in the pathos. The problem is not drought or depletion of ground supplies. Dar's water system has a 40 percent leakage rate.

The February 19, 1997, *Guardian* carried a story about corruption—in all senses of the word—at a city-hospital morgue: "Certain persons had raised objections that hospital staff were preventing relatives from picking up bodies of identified persons until they paid either fees or consideration to the staff." The hospital had been forced by "congestion of dead bodies" to put some corpses "outside the cold room . . . Nurses, doctors, patients, and passersby were exposed to a choking smell, which invited swarms of flies from all directions." A photo accompanying the story showed the garbage truck in which the bodies were hauled away.

Does poverty lead to this kind of thing, or does this kind of thing lead to poverty? It is a question that economists have not answered. Maybe there's some inherent cultural failure that is keeping Tanzania poor. But even if that's so, there are legal and political failures helping poverty abide. We don't know if we can change culture. At least we don't know if we can change it for the better. But we do know we can change other things. More freedom and responsibility can be given to individuals. I went to the government of Tanzania to see if it was doing any of that.

And here was an odd glimmer of hope. Poor and shabby countries ought to have poor and shabby governments. They usually don't.

There is some misappropriated opulence in Tanzania. The compound where the president lives has a house and grounds that make Bill Clinton's Pennsylvania Avenue residence look like the place where Bill grew up. But the actual government of Tanzania is run out of the same colonial administration offices constructed by Germany ninety years ago, and they haven't been mopped since Kaiser Bill.

The buildings are on the harbor in a line along the Strand (renamed Wilhelms Ufer by the Germans, renamed Azania Front by the English, renamed Kivukoni Front by the Tanzanians). They are substantial train-shed-like wood and stucco structures with a few architectural flourishes—arabesque lintels and tile-roofed porches—indicating a Germanic attempt to go native.

I went to the Bureau of Statistics, President's Office, Planning Commission at 3:30. Just too late. Everyone had gone home, although there was one man left in a large, dusty room stacked with copies of government publications and pamphlets, many of them yellowing and dating back to the '60s. These were for sale, but for some reason, the man couldn't sell them to me. But he showed me several that he said would be excellent for me to buy, including the *Tanzanian Statistical Abstract* (most recent available: 1994), the *Tanzanian Budget* (most recent available: 1994), and the *National Accounts of Tanzania from 1976 to the Present* (the present, in Tanzania, being 1994). He then gave me a heartfelt speech about current politico-economic conditions in Tanzania, of which I didn't understand much. As the American accent tends to flatten most vowels into an *uh,* the Tanzanian accent tends to flatten most consonants into a sound somewhere between an *l, n, t, d,* and *r.* He did wind up, however, by saying, "Until that, you can pour aid in, and all you'll get is . . ." He pantomimed a fat man.

There was exactly such a fellow at the bar in the Sheraton that night, in the very largest size of Armani clothes, with a great deal of jewelry. It's rare to see a stout Tanzanian, but, now that jail time for driving a Mercedes is no longer the practice, it happens. And when Africans use the phrase "big man," it's not a metaphor. The big man had his cell phone, his Filofax, his double Johnnie Walker Black, and a pile of U.S. dollars on the bar in front of him and coolly left them lying there as he made frequent trips to the pay telephone, because Tanzania didn't have cell phone service yet.

I went back to the Bureau of Statistics at 9:30 the next morning. Just too early. No one had arrived yet. I wandered unchallenged through the offices, a dark bafflement of low warrens and vaulted passageways with broken tile underfoot and crazed and damp-stained plaster on the walls. It gave a sinister impression until I noticed that the place was furnished with beat-up Ikea-modern furniture and bulletin boards covered with photos of kids, cutout newspaper cartoons, and postcards from vacationing pals. The government offices of Tanzania look like what would happen if Franz Kafka designed the national PTA headquarters.

I found the correct person to sell me the *Statistical Abstract* and national accounts summary, but he explained that what I really wanted was the *Rolling Plan and Forward Budget for Tanzania for the Period 1996/97–1998/99 Volume I.* "Stacks and stacks of them have just been printed," he said. He didn't have any, however. He sent me, with Dungeons and Dragons directions, through the building to an office with its number Magic Markered on the door. Here, another bureaucrat did have the budget. His desk was covered with copies. "Stacks and stacks of them," he pointed out, but he wasn't authorized to sell me one. "You should go to the planning commission," he said. Although that's where I thought I was.

I got in the car and told Nzezele that we needed to go to the planning commission. He drove me the thirty feet there. At the planning commission a puzzled security guard, a puzzled secretary, and someone else who was puzzled considered my request, and after a closed-door consultation with a boss, they pointed me down a long hall containing several motorbikes and a lot of automobile tires. I emerged into a courtyard with extraordinarily grimy paint. Something good was cooking nearby. I climbed a couple of flights of creaking, swaying stairs, crossed a shaky breezeway, and found myself in the office of the head of environmental planning. A rattling air conditioner was creating a dank environment. He told me he had "only a very few" budget copies. I told him—just between ourselves—about the fellow in the next building who had stacks and stacks of them on his desk. He made a note. I may have set off an enormous turf war within the Tanzanian bureaucracy.

Anyway, the head of environmental planning said that he couldn't give me a budget. I looked disappointed, and he immediately offered to loan me his personal copy on the condition that I bring it back the next morning. So I spent a festive night at the Sheraton copying Tanzanian budget information into a spiral notebook.

Not that I was missing much. The nightlife in Dar es Salaam consists of a few tourists being robbed of their running shoes on the downtown beach. Besides, contained in the *Rolling Plan and Forward Budget* were further glimmers of hope. Right on page 2 the document states, "The government is being reoriented to play the role of facilitation of development other than continue being seen as 'provider' of development." The English may have gotten out from under them, but this is still a clear explanation of what government should do. Compare it to the Republican "Contract with America." And for brevity and bluntness, it tops anything that's come out of the Oval Office since Nixon yelled "Fuck" on the Watergate tapes.

There are lots of honest admissions in the Tanzanian budget: about civil-service reform "launched in 1992–93 against a background of grossly overstaffed, underpaid and barely performing workforce," and about poverty—"The living conditions of the majority of the people, particularly in rural areas, are quite alarming." And no easy, *It Takes a Vijijini* solutions are proposed. The budget says "poverty-borne problems" must be "tackled," but "this needs to be achieved under conditions of macro-economic stability." Which may be translated as, "Curing poverty equals allowing people to get rich." This very simple equation has eluded some of the deepest thinkers of the world's advanced nations.

Naturally there is also claptrap in the Tanzanian budget—the mealy mouthing about property rights that I mentioned before and scary sentences such as "expenditure management control system will be enhanced by setting up five additional sub-treasuries, bringing the total to 10." But taken as a whole, as an example of a government going on public record, the *Rolling Plan and Forward Budget* might almost be called refreshing.

The Tanzanian government has an idea, a slight inkling of what to do—or, rather, what not to do. Often, the most important government action is to leave people alone. That brings us to what we prosperous Westerners should do for Tanzanians. We should leave them alone, too.

Not the cheap, easy kind of leaving them alone. There are plenty of charities and causes in Tanzania that could be supported—and lavishly, if we're the kind, decent folks we like to think we are. Individuals can be helped. But can you "help a nation"?

Official Development Assistance has funded disasters and fostered attitudes of gross dependence. Yoweri Museveni, the president of Uganda, says his country "needs just two things. We need infrastructure and we need foreign investment. That is what we need. The rest we shall do by ourselves." This is the "if we had ham, we could have ham and eggs, if we had eggs" philosophy. Or as Nzezele put it as I was leaving Dar after having given him a large and not very well-earned tip, "When you get back to America, if you find that you have any extra money, could you send me a wristwatch?"

Delivering our cash to a dictatorial and silly government was bad, but even worse was delivering our big ideas about centralization, economic planning, and social justice to a country that had 120 university graduates at the time of independence. Not that the Tanzanians didn't understand our big ideas; they understood them too well. They just had no experience with how bad most big ideas are. They hadn't been through Freudianism, Keynesianism, liberalism, www.heavensgate.com, and "Back to Africa." They don't have ten thousand unemployable liberal arts majors sitting around Starbucks with nose rings.

There's even some evidence that getting ahead in the world comes from a lack of big ideas. Call this the Bell-Dip Theory. The United States is arguably the most successful nation in history, but not—by any argument—the smartest. Japan, even in a recession, is an economic powerhouse, but we're talking about a people in love with Speed Racer, whose most sophisticated art form is the haiku, an itty-bitty poem on the order of

An old pond.
A frog leaping in.
Sit on a pickle.

Tanzania is one of those places called "developing countries," as if the Family of Nations had teens, as if various whole geographical regions were callow, inarticulate, clumsy, but endearing—you know, going through an awkward phase.

And that's about right. Every twenty-four hours of Tanzania is like a crib sheet on adolescence. There's the dewy-aired, hopeful dawn. All is beautiful. All is fresh. Then, as the day goes on, the dust rises. The noise builds. Everything is seen in a too-vivid light. The glaring inadequacies of life are revealed. Enormous confusion develops. There's a huge stink. And just when you've really had it—when you're ready to call for the International Monetary Fund's equivalent of "grounding," when you're about to take away the keys to the goat or something—the whole place goes to sleep for eighteen hours.

How to Make Everything from Nothing

Hong Kong 1997

How a peaceful, uncrowded place with ample wherewithal stays poor is hard to explain. How a conflict-ridden, grossly overpopulated place with no resources whatsoever gets rich is simple. The British colonial government turned Hong Kong into an economic miracle by doing nothing.

Hong Kong is the best contemporary example of laissez-faire. The economic theory of "allow to do" holds that all sorts of doings ought, indeed, to be allowed, and that government should interfere only to keep the peace, ensure legal rights, and protect property.

The people of Hong Kong have been free to do what they wanted, and what they wanted was, apparently, to create a stewing pandemonium: crowded, striving, ugly, and the most fabulous city on earth. It is a metropolis of amazing mess, an apparent stranger to zoning, a tumbling fuddle of streets too narrow and vendor-choked to walk along, slashed through with avenues too busy and broad to cross. It is a vertical city, rising 1,800 feet from Central District to Victoria Peak in less than a mile; so vertical that escalators run in place of sidewalks, and neighborhoods are named by altitude: Mid-Levels. Hong Kong is vertical in its building, too, and not just with glossy skyscrapers. Every tenement house and stack of commercial lofts sends an erection into the sky. Picture Wall Street on a Kilimanjaro slope, or, when it rains, picture a downhill Venice.

And rain it does for months. Hong Kong in monsoon season has a climate like boiled Ireland. Violent air-conditioning wars with humid heat in every home and place of business, producing a world with two temperatures: sauna and meat locker. The rainwater overwhelms the outgrown sewer system, which fumes and gurgles beneath streets ranged with limitless shopping. All the opulent goods of mankind are on display in an air of shit and Chanel.

It is a filled-in city, turgid with buildings. The Sham Shui Po district of Kowloon claims a population density of more than 425,000 people per square mile—eighteen times as crowded as New York. Landing at Kai Tak Airport, down one thin skid of Kowloon Bay landfill, you fly in below clothesline level, so close to apartment windows that you can watch women at bathroom mirrors putting on their makeup. You can tell them that their lipstick's crooked.

There is no space in Hong Kong for love or money, at least not for ordinary kinds of either. A three-bedroom apartment in Central rents for $1,000 a month, but there isn't room in any of those bedrooms to have sex even with yourself. The whole home will be 700 square feet, less than ten yards long by eight yards wide, with windows papered over because, outside those windows, a hand grab away, are the windows of the apartment next door. And anything you're going to fix in the kitchen had better be something that can be stood on end—like a banana. This is how middle-class people live. Poor people in public housing will have three generations in a fifteen-by-twenty-foot room.

But when they come out of that room, they'll be wearing Versace and Dior—some of it even genuine. Hong Kong is a styling city, up on the trends. Truly up, in the case of platform sneakers. You can spend an entertaining afternoon on Hollywood Road watching teens fall off their shoes. Over the grinding hills, in the blood-clot traffic, men nonetheless drive their Turbo 911s. The S-Class Mercedes is the Honda Civic of Hong Kong, and for the soccer-mom set, a Rolls and a driver is a minivan.

Jesus, it's a rich city. Except where it's Christ-almighty poor. Hong Kong is full of that "poverty midst plenty" stuff beloved of foreign correspondents such as myself who, when doing a Hong Kong piece, rush from interviews with day-laboring "cage men" in barred flophouse partitions to dinners in the blandly exclusive confines of Happy Valley's Jockey Club, where I could sample the one true Hong Kong luxury—distance between tables.

But those poor are going to *get* rich. Just ask them. You can call the old lady selling dried fish on the street on her cell phone.

The *bippity-beep* of cell phones all but drowns the air-conditioner racket. And each time a cell phone rings, everyone within earshot goes into a self-administered frisk, patting himself down to find the wee gadget. You can go weeks without talking to an answering machine, because you're not really dialing a telephone, you're dialing an armpit, purse, shirt pocket, or bikini top.

The cell phone has to be there, or somebody might miss a deal. Everything's a deal. In a store you ask, "What's your best price?" then "What's your Chinese price?" and on from there. I was trying to buy a bottle of cognac in a little restaurant. The owner produced a brand I'd never heard of for $100 and a brand nobody's ever heard of for $80. I got my friend Annie, who let fly in Cantonese, and we had a bottle of Remy for one dead U.S.

Grant. "I didn't know you were going to bring my sister in here," said the owner. "*Hwa-aaah!*"

It's a Cantonese exclamation halfway between *oy vey* and *fuhgedaboutit*. Which is Hong Kong in a nutshell—a completely foreign city that's utterly comprehensible. It's a modern place, deaf to charm, dumb in the language of aesthetics, caught up in a wild, romantic passion for the plain utilitarian. The only traditional touches are the catawampus walls and whichaway entrances dictated by *feng shui*, the art of placing things so as to ensure luck and not disturb spirits. One building in Repulse Bay has an enormous square hole in its middle so that a certain invisible dragon can get from the mountain to the sea. Knowing Hong Kong, it was probably a scam with a paid-off fortune-teller helping architects and construction companies boost their fees. Some of Hong Kong may believe in geomancy, but it was my local bookstore in New Hampshire that had thirteen *feng shui* titles.

Everything else quaint within reach in Hong Kong has been torn down. Just a few poky colonial government buildings are left. Landfill has pushed the waterfront a thousand feet into Victoria Harbor. Ferry terminals block the water views, and tides are cramped into a raging flume between Central and Kowloon.

The statue in Statue Square is of a business manager, the nineteenth-century chief executive of the Hong Kong and Shanghai Bank. Behind the square, the Hong Kong and Shanghai Bank Building itself rises. Here the local taste for functionalism has been carried to an extreme that arrives at rococo: a massy, looming, steel Tinkertoy of a thing with its whole construction hanging, suspension-bridge fashion, from eight enormous towers. Very functional indeed, whatever that function is. Maybe to be expensive. It cost a billion dollars to build.

To the west is Jardine House, an aluminum-skinned monolith covered with circular porthole windows—Thousand Assholes, as it's known. To the east is the I. M. Pei–designed Bank of China Tower—all big diagonals and tricky, skinny angles. Its purpose was to be the tallest building in Asia, which it was for about five minutes before being overtopped by Central Plaza a few miles away, and then by twin towers—the tallest enclosed structures in the world—being built in Kuala Lumpur.

A competitive place, Southeast Asia. And it attracts some types that can compete with anything I've seen. I sat at dinner one night between a tough-as-lug-nuts young woman from the mainland who lives in New York and deals in used motor oil—sparkling table talk—and a large and equally adamantine chick from the wrong side of somewhere's tracks in America. I turned to the suicide blonde.

"I'm uh arht cunsultunt," she said.

"Come again?"

"Uh *arht* cunsultant."

"That's interesting. Who do you art-consult for?"

She named a large Saudi prince.

"What kind of art does the prince like?" I asked.

"Nineteen-cenchury reuhlist—you know, Uhmerican."

"Any particular artist?"

"Andrew Wyeth."

I'd been under the impression that Andrew Wyeth was still alive—rare in a nineteenth-century artist. And you'd think Hong Kong would be a strange place to look for one of his paintings. But who knows? They shop hard in Hong Kong. Buy hard. Sell hard.

They drink hard, too. On Friday nights, police are posted in the Lan Kwai Fong bar district because people have actually been crushed to death there during happy hour. Nobody takes it easy in Hong Kong. The only idleness visible is on Sundays, when thousands of the city's overworked Filipino maids come to Central, spread cloths and plastic sheets up and down the sidewalks, and picnic in the least attractive and most heat-baked part of town.

The Filipino maids are Hong Kongese, too. They're in Central because it's practical to get there on the subways, trams, and buses. Hong Kong is a practical place, down to earth, or, rather, down to concrete. The complimentary city guide in my hotel room gave advice on pricing whores and noted, "Some of the conservative hotels don't allow a man to toddle in with a rent-a-bird in the middle of the night. But as you can imagine there are plenty of 'cheap guest houses.'"

In the window of an antiques shop, I saw an ivory carving of the familiar row of monkeys: SEE NO EVIL, HEAR NO EVIL, SPEAK NO EVIL but this one had a fourth monkey with his hands over his balls: FUCK NO EVIL.

City of hardheads. City of rough tongues. You're a *gweilo* right to your face, meaning a white goblin or foreign ghost or old devil or any number of other things, according to how it's said (none of the meanings being complimentary). You can give back as good as you get, however (or try to, since *gweilos* are famously dim). For instance, the Cantonese really can't distinguish an *l* from an *r*. "Ah, you ordered flied lice," said Annie's *gweilo* husband, Hugh. "That's *fried rice,* you plick," said Annie.

I met two women who seemed barely into their twenties but were the publisher and the sales manager of a prominent Hong Kong business magazine.

Publisher: "You're really well dressed."

Sales manager: "For a journalist. We understand you're a popular writer."

Publisher: "In Japan."

City of straight faces. I was looking at some animal figurines representing Chinese astrological signs. The ancient woman behind the shop counter asked, "What year you born?"

"1947."

"*Hwa-aaah*. Year of pig! Good luck!"

"Oh, 'Good luck! Good luck!'" I said. "That's what Chinese always say to shopping *gweilos*. Stolen Ming dynasty grave offerings: 'Good luck!' Can of tuna fish: 'Good luck!' Lacoste shirt: 'Good luck!'"

"Not so!" she said. "Some years bad luck."

"Such as?"

"Year of buffalo."

"Which year is that?"

"This one."

"This one" being 1997. I had come to Hong Kong to watch the best contemporary example of laissez-faire be surrendered to the biggest remaining example of socialist totalitarianism.

Hong Kong was (and, to be fair to its new commie rulers, remains, for the moment) socialism's perfect opposite. Hong Kong doesn't have import or export duties, or restrictions on investments coming in, or limits on profits going out. There's no capital-gains tax, no interest tax, no sales tax, and no tax breaks for muddle-butt companies that can't make it on their own.

The corporate tax in Hong Kong is 16.5 percent of profits. The individual tax rate is 15 percent of income. Hong Kong's government runs a permanent budget surplus and consumes only 6.9 percent of gross domestic product (compared with the 20.8 percent of GDP spent just by the federal government in the U.S.). The people of Hong Kong have not been paylings of the state. They've owned their own. They've been able to blow it, Dow Jones it, start a sweater factory, hire, fire, sell, retire, or buy the farm. (And there actually are some little-bitty farms in the New Territories.)

Hong Kong has never had democracy, but its wallet-size liberties, its Rights-of-Man-in-a-purse, have been so important to individualism and self-governance that in 1995 an international group of libertarian think tanks was moved to perhaps overstate the case and claim, "Hong Kong is the freest nation in the world."

Free because there's been freedom to screw up, too. Hong Kong has no minimum wage, no unemployment benefits, no union-boosting legislation, no Social Security, no national health program, and hardly enough welfare to keep one U.S. trailer park in satellite dishes and Marlboro Lights. Just 1.2 percent of GDP goes in transfers to the helplessly poor or subsidies to the hopelessly profitless.

Living without a safety net, people in Hong Kong have kept a grip on the trapeze. The unemployment rate is below 3 percent. In America, a shooting war is usually needed to get unemployment that low. The "natural rate" of unemployment is considered to be about 5 percent in the U.S., which rate would cause natural death from starvation in Hong Kong. But they aren't dying. Although smoking is the city's principal indoor athletic activity, life expectancy in Hong Kong is about seventy-nine years, compared with seventy-six in the States. And the infant-mortality rate is comparable to our own. This from people who consider crushed pearls, dried sea horses, and horns from the dead rhinos of Tanzania to be efficacious medicine. Even the babies are too busy to die.

Economic growth in Hong Kong has averaged 7.5 percent per year for the past twenty years, causing gross domestic product to quadruple since 1975. With barely one-tenth of 1 percent of the world's population, Hong Kong is the world's eighth-largest international trader and tenth-largest exporter of services.

I'm not exactly sure what "exporter of services" means, unless it's fly-by dim sum, but, anyway, it's a fine statistic and helped make dinky, terrifying Kai Tak Airport the third-busiest passenger terminal in the world and the second-busiest air-cargo center. And Kai Tak's solitary runway sticks out into a container port that's the world's most busy of all.

Hong Kong's per capita GDP is $26,000. Average individual wealth is greater than in Japan or Germany. It's $5,600 greater than what Hong Kong's ex-colonial masters back in Britain have, and is creeping up on the U.S. per capita GDP of $28,600. Besides Americans, only the people of Luxembourg and Switzerland are richer than those of Hong Kong. And these are two other places where capital is allowed to move and earn freely.

True, there has been an "Asian crisis" since the above statistics were compiled. The Hong Kong stock market has flopped. Indonesia, Thailand, Malaysia, South Korea, and maybe Japan are experiencing depressions. The entire business world of Asia is supposed to be in ruins. But a mere continent-wide financial collapse is unlikely to faze the people of Hong Kong.

Hong Kong's economy was destroyed by the Japanese occupation of World War II, destroyed again by the UN embargo on trade with the Communists in 1951, and almost destroyed a third time by worry about the 1997 handover to China. The territory has been squeegeed by typhoons, squished by mudslides, toasted by enormous squatter-camp fires, and mashed by repeated refugee influxes. Hong Kong has no forests, mines, or oil wells, no large-scale agriculture, and definitely no places to park. Hong Kong even has to import water. So in Hong Kong they drink cognac instead, more per person than anywhere else in the world. They own more Rolls-Royces per person, too. So what if there's no space at the curb? They'll hire somebody fresh from the mainland to drive around the block all night.

Why did the British allow this marvel of free enterprise? Why did Britain do so little to interfere with Hong Kong's economic liberty? This is especially hard to answer because, back in London, an ultra-interfering socialist Parliament had taken charge after World War II. This government would bring the UK's own economy to a halt like a hippo dropped on a handcart.

Actually, the British did piss in the colonial soup when they could. The crown government held title to almost all the land in Hong Kong and the New Territories, and dealt it out slowly to keep sales revenues high. Thus the crowding in a place which, in fact, comprises some 402 square miles of dry ground—enough, in theory, to give everybody a bean-sprout garden. Instead, half the population is stuck in claustrophobic government housing. Then in the '70s, one of Hong Kong's thicker governors, Sir Murray Maclehose, set aside 40 percent of the colony as parkland—cramped comfort to the fellow living in 300 square feet with his wife, mother, kids, and their Tamagotchi pets.

But the British never tried to install a European-style Pampers-to-Depends welfare system in Hong Kong. Maybe the Labour MPs were unwilling to invest vast quantities of groundnut scheme–type pinko planning genius in a place that could be gobbled up at any time by the pinko planning geniuses on the mainland. Maybe the colonial administrators were overwhelmed by the number of refugees from pinko planning coming into town. Maybe the mother country was too broke from ruining its own economy at home. Or maybe the Brits just didn't care about pushing social justice down the throats of people who were, after all, only Chinese.

On the other hand, the British were not irresponsible. The "doing nothing" mentioned at the beginning of this chapter is a relative term. Laissez-faire isn't Tanzanian administrative sloth or Albanian popular anarchy. Quite a bit of government effort is required to create a system in which government leaves people alone. Hong Kong's colonial administration provided courts, contract enforcement, laws that applied to everyone, some measure of national defense (although the Red Chinese People's Liberation Army probably could have moved in anytime it wanted), an effective police force (Hong Kong's crime rate is lower than Tokyo's), and a bureaucracy that was efficient and uncorrupt but not so hideously uncorrupt that it wouldn't turn a blind eye on an occasional palm-greasing illegal refugee or unlicensed street vendor.

The Brits built schools and roads. And the kids went to school because they knew if they didn't, they'd have to hit that road. And the UK gave Hong Kong a stable currency, which it did totally by cheating—first pegging the Hong Kong currency to the British pound and then, when everyone got done laughing at that, pegging it to the U.S. dollar at a rate of 7.8:1. Now when there's any money-supply dirty work to be done, Hong Kong can blame everything on Alan Greenspan.

Hong Kong was also fortunate in having a colonial government which included some real British heroes, men who helped the place stay as good as it was for as long as it did. The most heroic of these was John Cowperthwaite, a young colonial officer sent to Hong Kong in 1945 to oversee the colony's economic recovery. "Upon arrival, however," said a *Far Eastern Economic Review* article about Cowperthwaite, "he found it recovering quite nicely without him."

Cowperthwaite took the lesson to heart, and while he was in charge, he strictly limited bureaucratic interference in the economy. He wouldn't even let bureaucrats keep figures on the rate of economic growth or the size of GDP. The Cubans won't let anyone get those figures, either. But Cowperthwaite forbade it for an opposite reason. He felt that these numbers were nobody's business and would only be misused by policymaking fools.

Cowperthwaite has said of his role in Hong Kong's astounding growth: "I did very little. All I did was to try to prevent some of the things that might undo it." He served as the colony's financial secretary from 1961 to 1971. In the debate over the 1961 budget, he spoke words that should be engraved over the portals of every legislature worldwide; no, tattooed on the legislators' faces.

> *In the long run the aggregate of decisions of individual businessmen, exercising individual judgment in a free economy, even if often mistaken, is less likely to do harm than the centralized decisions of a government; and certainly the harm is likely to be counteracted faster.*

Even *Newsweek* has been forced into admiration: "While Britain continued to build a welfare state, Cowperthwaite was saying 'no': no export subsidies, no tariffs, no personal taxes higher than 15 percent, red tape so thin a one-page form can launch a company."

During Cowperthwaite's "nothing doing" tenure, Hong Kong's exports grew by an average of 13.8 percent a year, industrial wages doubled, and the number of households in extreme poverty shrank from more than half to 16 percent.

"It would be hard to overestimate the debt Hong Kong owes to Cowperthwaite," said economist Milton Friedman. And it would be hard to overestimate the debt Hong Kong owes to the Chinese people who sanctioned and supported what Cowperthwaite was doing or, rather, doing not. Because Hong Kong didn't get rich simply as a result of freedom and law. Economics is easier than economists claim, but it's not as easy as that. Chinese culture was a factor in Hong Kong's success. And yet, almost by definition, Chinese culture must have been a factor in mainland China's failure. Culture is complex. Complexities are fun to talk about, but, when it comes to action, simplicities are often more effective. John Cowperthwaite was a master of simplicities.

Yeung Wai Hong, publisher of Hong Kong's most popular Chinese-language magazine, *Next,* has suggested erecting a heroic-scale statue of John Cowperthwaite. (To be paid for by *private* subscription, thank you.)

In less than one lifetime, Hong Kong created the environment of comfort and hope that every place on earth has been trying to achieve since the days of *Homo erectus* in the Olduvai Gorge. And Hong Kong's reward? It has been made a "Special Administrative Region" of the People's Republic of China.

At midnight on June 30, 1997, the British sold six million five hundred thousand souls. No, gave them away. Nearly a London-full of individuals, supposed citizens of the realm that invented rights, equity, and the rule of law, got Christmas-goosed in July. Hong Kong was on the cuffo, a gimme, an Annie Oakley for the mainland Communists.

At the stroke of twelve, I was watching TV in my Hong Kong hotel room. The handover ceremony was being broadcast from the hideous new convention center three-quarters of a mile away. A British military band wearing hats made from Yogi and Smokey and Poo played "God Save the Queen." The Union Jack went south. Prince Charles had just given a little speech. "We shall not forget you, and we shall watch with closest interest as you embark on this new era of your remarkable history." In other words, "Good-bye and bolt the door, bugger you."

Outside, on my hotel-room balcony, the floodlit convention center was all too visible on the harbor front, looking like somebody sat on the Sydney Opera House. Directly below the balcony, a couple thousand not very noisy protesters stood in the rain in Statue Square, looking like somebody was about to sit on them. They were listening to democracy advocate Martin Lee. Mr. Lee was a member of the first freely elected legislature in the history of Hong Kong. And the last. It was unelected at midnight. Mr. Lee was speaking without a police permit. And speaking. And speaking. Every now and then a disconsolate chant of agreement rose from the crowd. Mr. Lee kept speaking. No one bothered to stop him.

Back inside, on the TV, president of China Jiang Zemin was speaking too—introducing himself to his instant, involuntary fellow countrymen with a poker-faced hollering of banalities in Mandarin. "We owe all our achievements most fundamentally!!! To the road of building socialism!!! With Chinese characteristics!!! Which we have taken!!!" he said, interrupting his speech with episodes of self-applause, done in the official politburo manner by holding the hands horizontal and moving the fingers and palms as if to make quacky-ducky shadow puppets.

The big men on the convention-center podium—Jiang, Prime Minister Li Peng, and Foreign Minister Qian Qichen—seemed to have made their own suit jackets at home.

Tung Chee-hwa, the Beijing-appointed chief executive of the new Hong Kong Special Administration Region, came to the microphone next, making pronouncements that combined a political-reeducation-camp lecture ("Our thoughts and remembrance go, with great reverence, to the late Deng Xiaoping") with a Dick Gephardt speech ("We respect minority views but also shoulder collective responsibility . . . We value plurality but discourage open confrontation. We strive for liberty but not at the expense of blah, blah, blah.").

This also was said in Mandarin, which is not the native tongue in Hong Kong. In fact, no one uses it here, and having the HK chief executive lipping away in an alien lingo was like hearing an American politician speak meaningless, bizarre . . . it was like hearing an American politician speak.

Outside on the balcony again (covering the Hong Kong handover required a journalist to give his utmost—what with AC-chilled binocs fogging in the tropical heat and a minibar running low on ice) I watched the HMS *Britannia* pull away from the convention-center dock. A nondescript, freighter-shaped vessel painted white, *Britannia* looked to be more an unfortunate cruise-ship choice than a royal yacht. It steamed through Victoria Harbor, hauling butt from now-foreign waters. On board were the last British governor of Hong Kong, the aristocrat currently known as Prince of Wales, any number of other dignitaries, and, I hope, a large cargo of guilt.

Would the Limeys have skipped town if Hong Kong was full of 6.5 million big, pink, freckled, hay-haired, kipper-tucking, pint-sloshing, work-shy, layabout Labour-voting . . .

Or maybe Hong Kong just wasn't one of those vital, strategic places worth fighting for—like the Falklands. Maybe the Poms intervene militarily only where there's enough sheep to keep the troops entertained.

Why didn't the British give some *other* island to China. Britain, for instance. This would get the UK back on a capitalist course—Beijing being more interested in moneymaking than Tony Blair. Plus, the Chinese have extensive experience settling royal family problems.

Or why didn't Britain *sell* England to Hong Kong? Hong Kong can afford it, and that way anyone who was worried about the fate of democracy in the Special Administrative Region could go live in Sloane Square, and the rest of England could be turned into a theme park. There's quaint scenery, lots of amusements for the kiddies ("Changing of the Wives" at Buckingham Palace is good), and plenty of souvenirs, such as, if you donate enough money to the right political party, a knighthood.

But this didn't happen. And the people of Hong Kong (unless they were very rich) were stuck in Hong Kong. Sure, they had British passports. But these were "starter passports"—good for travel to . . . Macao. Of course, they could have gotten passport upgrades. For a million Hong Kong dollars, they could have gone to Toronto. Very fun.

Oh, let's give the Limeys a break. It's not as if we Americans gave a damn, either. We could have threatened to stealth-bomber the Red Chinese or, for that matter, Margaret Thatcher when she started gift-wrapping Hong Kong for Deng Xiaoping. We could have told China to go kiss Boris Yeltsin's ass if it wanted to be a most-favored nation. And we could have handed out 6.5 million green cards.

Imagine 6.5 million savvy, hardworking citizens-to-be with a great cuisine. What a blessing for America. And how we would hate them. Pat Buchanan would hate their race. The AFL-CIO would hate their wage rate. The NAACP would hate their failure to fail as a minority. And Al Gore would hate 6.5 million campaign contributors who didn't have to sneak pro–free trade money to the Democratic National Committee anymore but could go right into polling booths and vote Republican.

The surrender of Hong Kong was a shameful moment. But if you missed Martin Lee's soggy peroration in Statue Square, you might never have known it. The stock market was still on a swell, up 30 percent from a year before, with bulging, steroidal gains in the so-called red chips, the mainland holding companies promoted by the ChiComs. Trade and foreign investment were at unexampled heights. No one was running from the real estate market. Tiny condominiums in unglamorous districts were going for $500,000.

A five-day weekend was declared, though no one closed shop. Retail sales were 30 percent to 40 percent above the usual. Important people had flown in from all over the globe. I saw the back of Margaret Thatcher's head in my hotel lobby.

On July 1 ("Dependence Day," I guess) people who should have known better sent messages of cheer, fulsomely printed in the *South China Morning Post.*

> *China has made important commitments to maintain Hong Kong's freedom and autonomy.*
>
> —Bill Clinton

> *Hong Kong can be an even better place in which to live and work.*
>
> —Madeleine Albright

> *I feel pretty relaxed about it.*
>
> —*George Bush*

Skyrockets splattered in the evening skies. The British Farewell Ceremony for ten thousand invited guests had featured not only bands from the Scots Guards, Black Watch, and various other men without pants, but also the Hong Kong Philharmonic Orchestra and (I saw this) a dance troupe with performers dressed as giant deutsche marks, enormous circuit boards, and huge powdered wigs. At the other end of the lifestyle continuum, there was a One Nation Under a Groove 11 p.m. to 9 a.m. rave.

In between were thousands of parties, from impromptu expat booze-ups in the Wan Chai lap-dancing district to dinners with courses incalculable by abacus at Hong Kong mogul David Tang's China Club. Here the whole food chain was ravaged, from depth of sea slug to bird's-nest height.

The China Club is decorated colonial style in big-wallah mahogany, except the walls are covered with Mao-era socialist-realism art, and the waiters and waitresses are dressed as Red Guards. Meaning? I have no idea.

I also have no idea why my hotel kept giving me handover gifts: a bottle of champagne, a coffee-table book about Hong Kong titled *Return to the Heart of the Dragon* (less ominous-sounding in Chinese, I gather), and a silver mug bearing crossed British and Chinese flags, and inscribed:

Resumption of Sovereignty
To
China
1 July 1997
Hong Kong

To which I intend to have added:

Bowling Tournament
2nd Place

Whimsical handover T-shirts, many making hangover puns, were for sale around the city, as were such humorous novelties as "Canned Colonial Air—Sealed Before June 30th." I suppose the same sort of things were being marketed in Vienna in 1938: "Last Yarmulke Before *Anschluss,*" and so on. Maybe in occupied France, too: "Vichy Water," ha-ha.

There were grumbles in Hong Kong, of course, such as dissident-ish shows by artists objecting to censorship, in case there was going to be any. Martin Lee and his fellow Democratic Party members gave a glum press conference, at which they promised to keep representing their electoral districts, even if they didn't anymore. And a certain amount of fretting in the press was seen, but mostly of the affectless editorial page kind that mixes

AFTER GENOCIDE—WHITHER RWANDA? with AFTER GRETZKY—WHITHER HOCKEY? Hong Kong, on the whole, was awfully cheerful.

Why weren't 6.5 million people more upset about being palmed off to an ideology-impaired dictatorship that has the H-bomb? Even one of Taiwan's top representatives in Hong Kong was quoted saying, "As a Chinese person, I think it is a good thing that Hong Kong is coming back to China." Chiang Kai-shek, please.

There is the colonialism issue. How did the Chinese of Hong Kong really feel about being ruled by England? It's a complex question. Or, as a number of Chinese people said to me, "No, it isn't." Being an American, and an Irish-American to boot, I was, maybe, told certain things that the English didn't hear. "We hate the English," for instance.

When a Chinese friend said that, I said, "Wait a minute, I was in Vietnam not long ago, and nobody seemed to hate Americans. If the Vietnamese can forgive Americans for napalm, carpet bombing, Agent Orange, and what all, surely you can forgive the English for the odd opium war and some 'Land of Hope and Glory' karaoke."

"It's a different thing," said my friend. "You just killed the Vietnamese; you never *snubbed* them."

Hong Kong's people are also realists. Calling in to complain on the *Larry King Show* wasn't going to do much. Thus the tepid response to the handover's endless television and newspaper "streeters," the interviews with random locals: "Excuse me, I understand you're about to get secret police in your neighborhood. Would you care to tell the world how much you hate Jiang Zemin?"

There are real reasons for Hong Kong's realism. In 1945 the population of the territory was only 1.2 million. Today, the whole city is filled with refugees and children of refugees. Until 1980, Hong Kong had a "touch base" asylum policy where, basically, anyone from the mainland who made it to downtown could stay. The Chinese who fled the civil war, the communist takeover on the mainland, and the lunatic deprivations and slaughters that followed know that there's only one real safe haven: money.

And they're serious about making it. The hours posted on the door of the fashion-forward department store Joyce are MONDAY–SATURDAY 10 A.M.–7 P.M., SUNDAY AND PUBLIC HOLIDAYS 11 A.M.–6 P.M. Take two hours off for Christmas. And the in-case-of-typhoon notice in my hotel room read:

> *Signal Number 9 and 10: When these signals are hoisted, extreme weather conditions will prevail, meaning that the typhoon is centered over Hong Kong. May we suggest that while you are confined indoors, you enjoy the facilities of our restaurants and bars.*

Finally, the residents of Hong Kong were putting a good face on things because . . . what the hell else were they going to do? There's a joke they tell in Shanghai about the Hong Kong handover. Mao asks Zhou Enlai and Deng Xiaoping, "How do you get a cat to bite a hot pepper?"

Zhou says, "You hold him down, pry his jaws open, and shove the pepper into his mouth."

Mao says, "No, that's force. We want the cat to bite the pepper of his own free will."

Deng says, "You take the pepper, wrap it in a delicious piece of fish, and, before he knows it, the cat has bitten the pepper."

Mao says, "No, that's trickery. We want the cat to know he's biting the pepper."

Zhou and Deng say, "We give up. How do you make a cat bite a hot pepper?"

"It's easy," Mao says. "Stick the pepper up the cat's ass. He'll be *glad* to bite it."

EAT THE RICH

We're so close to being rich. Everybody in the world could be rich as hell. The benighted masses of India could quit pedaling bicycle rickshaws and start dragging Lear jets through the streets of Calcutta. Native tribes in the Brazilian rain forest could be *singing* in the rain. Eskimos could give up clubbing baby seals and devote their arctic vastness to building an Olympic-quality ice dancing team.

When we're all wealthy, Sally Struthers will be featured in magazine ads headlined, "You Can Send This Child to Summer Weight-Loss Camp or You Can Turn the Page." CARE packages will contain oyster forks and truffles. And altruistic musicians will hold benefit concerts to raise enough money to pay the Rolling Stones to retire.

Money won't solve all our problems. But money will give us options—let us choose the problems we want to have. Leisure conglomerates may open franchises in Bosnia and Herzegovina where Muslims and Serbs can blast each other in paintball wars. Self-destructive individuals will still exist, but instead of dying from drug overdoses in pay-toilet stalls, they will be able to expire in luxury at the Chateau Marmont like John Belushi. The Taliban fundamentalists might continue to keep women in seclusion, but they could do so by opening a Bergdorf Goodman's in Kabul. They'll never see those wives again.

All this is possible because the modern industrial economy works. Obviously it works better in some places than in others. But it works, even in the poorest areas. Côte d'Ivoire now produces almost as much per capita wealth as the United States did when the Monroe Doctrine was declared, and Egypt produces more. America did not consider itself a poor country during the 1820s, and, in fact, at that time it was one of the world's most prosperous nations.

Extensive research has been done on the history of this industrial economy, much of it by the Organization for Economic Cooperation and Development. The OECD was founded by the Marshall Plan countries in the wake of World War II, and its purpose is what its name says. The OECD wants to make everyone rich as hell, although it never quite confesses to this in its literature.

In 1995 the OECD published a book by economist Angus Maddison titled *Monitoring the World Economy 1820–1992*. Maddison has been studying economic growth since the 1950s, and has examined and weighed the subject's statistics and statistical estimates. On the strength of these, Maddison calculates that until the Industrial Revolution, economic growth was paltry. Measured in 1990 U.S. dollars, the world Gross Domestic Product went from $565 per person in 1500 to $651 per person in 1820. That was an increase in wealth of about 27 cents a year.

But after the Industrial Revolution, something wonderful happened. The total world GDP grew from $695 billion in 1820 to almost $28 trillion in 1992. This planet had the same amount of arable land in 1992 as it had in 1820, and, arguably, fewer natural resources. Plus, population had grown from a little more than 1 billion to nearly 5.5 billion. But even so, world GDP per capita swelled from $651 to $5,145. Prosperity increased by $26 a year. Wealth has been growing a hundred times faster than it did before the Industrial Age.

The modern economy works, and we know how to make it work better. Free markets are extremely successful. The evidence is there for anyone who wants to look. Hong Kong, with 6.5 million people in 402 square miles, has an annual GDP of $163.6 billion. Tanzania, with 29.5 million people in 342,100 square miles, has a GDP of $18.9 billion.

Even a free market with lots of tax baggage and regulatory impediments is much better than a market that isn't free. Sweden has about the same amount of arable land as Cuba, a similar range of natural resources, a worse climate, and a couple million fewer people. But Sweden's GDP is more than eleven times the size of Cuba's.

And the free market trumps education and culture. North Korea has a 99 percent literacy rate, a disciplined, hardworking society, and a $900 per capita GDP. Morocco has a 43.7 percent literacy rate, a society that spends all day drinking coffee and pestering tourists to buy rugs, and a $3,260 per capita GDP.

We know what to do, and we know how to do it. So what's wrong with the world? To a certain extent, it's the same thing that's wrong with me. Because the prosaic, depressing, and somewhat shameful fact is that the secret to getting ahead is just what my parents told me it was.

The whole miracle of the modern industrial economy is based upon the things that our folks were trying to drum into our heads before we went off to college to grow hairy and bearded—or, as the modern case is, get pierced eyebrows and neck tattoos. It's the advice we received at the dinner table while the Jell-O dessert puddled and our friends were waiting for us at the mall. It's the clumsy set-piece speech our parents made in the heart-to-hearts they'd spring on us when we were really high. It's what we heard in capital letters when we brought home grades that looked like a collection of *Baywatch* bra cup sizes or wrecked the car.

- Hard work
- Education
- Responsibility
- Property rights
- Rule of law
- Democratic government

Actually, most parents didn't get all those items into the lecture. In fact, I've never heard of a parent saying, "Listen here, if I catch you running around without property rights again, I'll take away your cell phone." But when our parents said, "Be honest," they were assuming that property rights were real. And when our parents said, "Obey the law," they were making a logical inference that the law existed and that it merited obeying. And many of our parents had served in the military, defending democracy, and would remind us of this at length.

Of course, by "hard work" our parents didn't mean that we should be doing the hard things that constitute work for the poor people in the world. Few parents hope that their children will get jobs carrying forty-pound buckets of water on their heads. Our parents wanted us to do hard work that was intelligent, fulfilling, and promised advancement in life. (Although they also wanted us to mow the lawn.) The hard work was linked to education.

However, billions of people don't have a chance to get an education, and some of them, like religious fundamentalists and deconstructionist college professors, don't believe the education when they get one. This is one reason that dinner-table parental advice is difficult to apply to the earth's impoverished masses. There are also billions of people who don't have property rights, not to mention property. Or the property rights are arbitrary, and the property can be taken away by anybody with a gun or a government title. These billions of people have trouble being responsible because being responsible means thinking of the future. They haven't got one.

Rule of law is crucial. And it has to be good law, not Albania's Law of Lek. So if what our parents tell us is going to be globally effective, Mom and Dad will need to bring world leaders into the dining room. All the presidents, prime ministers, dictators, generals, chairman of idiot political parties, lunatic guerrilla chieftains, and fanatical heads of crazed religious sects will need to squeeze around the imitation Queen Anne mahogany veneer (with extra leaves in) and get a real talking-to.

Then there is democracy to be considered. Democracy is a bulwark against tyranny—unless the *demos* get tyrannical. People can vote themselves poor.

So now all the people on the planet are coming over to the house. And when they get there, what they're going to do is . . . exactly what we did. They're not going to listen.

There is a worldwide pigheadedness about money. There is a willful and even belligerent ignorance concerning ways and means. There is a heartfelt and near universal refusal to understand the basic economic principles behind the creation of wealth.

Not all this ignorance is irrational. Some people profit from economic privation. Economists, for instance. John Maynard Keynes couldn't have become a big shot, guiding government intervention in business and finance, if it hadn't been for the Great Depression. And Alan Greenspan is a success because we all lost our wallets when inflation scared our pants off.

We fear the power that others have over us, and wealth is power. We're afraid that Kathie Lee Gifford is going to make us sew jogging suits for thirty cents an hour. But are the rich really scarier than the poor? Take a midnight stroll through a fancy neighborhood, then take a midnight stroll a few blocks from the U.S. Capitol. Sure, we can get in trouble in Monte Carlo. We can lose at roulette. We can get suckered into a shady business deal with Princess Stephanie's ex-husband. But we're more likely to be mugged in the District of Columbia.

Not that we should begrudge the crimes of those poor people. They're just practicing politics on a small scale. If they'd listen to their own political leaders, they'd put down the gun and pick up the ballot box, and steal from everybody instead of just us.

Political systems must love poverty—they produce so much of it. Poor people make easier targets for a demagogue. No Mao or even Jiang Zemin is likely to arise on the New York Stock Exchange floor. And politicians in democracies benefit from destitution, too. The United States has had a broad range of poverty programs for thirty years. Those programs have failed. Millions of people are still poor. And those people vote for politicians who favor keeping the poverty programs in place. There's a Matt Drudge conspiracy theory in that somewhere.

Many religions claim to admire poverty. And some religions even advocate the practice of being poor. (Although all those religions seem willing to accept large cash donations.)

You'd think that businessmen, in the search for new customers, would always be opposed to impecuniousness. But Kathie Lee Gifford is not alone in depending on destitute workers to take pay-nothing jobs.

Then there is a certain kind of environmentalist who thinks that human deprivation means plant and animal wealth. Tanzania's experience of rhino-subsidizing rich tourists versus rhino-killing impoverished poachers argues against this. (And an Asia where every man could afford Viagra would be the best thing that could happen to the rhinoceros.) But many "Greens" still believe that increasing human prosperity is wrong. For example, the famous population-control advocate Paul Ehrlich has said, "Giving society cheap, abundant energy . . . would be the equivalent of giving an idiot child a machine gun."

Finally, general poverty benefits specific wealth. If most people are broke, that's great for the wealthy few. They get cheap household help, low ancestral-manor real estate prices, and no crowds on Martha's Vineyard. This explains the small, nasty plutocracies in impoverished countries. Maybe it also accounts for the rich socialists prominent on the political landscape of wealthy countries for the last two centuries.

I began by asking why some parts of the world are rich and others are poor, and I naturally had prejudices about what the answers would be. I favored the free market, not because I knew anything about markets, but because I live in a free (or nearly free) country, and I'm a free man (as long as I call home frequently), and it works for me. I was skeptical about the ability of politics to deliver economic benefits because I did know something about that. I'd been writing about politics, at home and abroad, for years. I had a low opinion of the political trade and its practitioners. And I considered culture, as an economic factor, to be a joke. How is ballet going to make the Tanzanians wealthy?

I was stupidly surprised to find out how important law is. Law, of course, derives from politics. And a political system is ultimately a product of a society's attitudes, ideas, and beliefs—that damned conundrum, its culture.

Which brings me back to the free market. I started out looking at the free market in terms of its effectiveness, its "efficiency," as an economist would say. I ended up looking at the free market as a moral device. My initial prejudice was right in one respect. The most important part of the free market is the *free* part. Economic liberty cannot be untangled from liberty of other kinds. You may have freedom of religion, if the rabbi can get off night shifts on Fridays. You may have freedom of assembly, but where are you all going to go if it rains?

The U.S. Constitution is (at least I hope it is) a statement of American cultural values. The First Amendment implies a free market. Six of the remaining nine articles in the Bill of Rights defend private property specifically. And two of the others concern rights reserved to the people, some of which are certainly economic rights. We are a free-market nation, though the electors and the elected sometimes forget it.

A belief in the free market means a belief that people have an innate right to the fruits of their endeavors, and the right to dispose of the fruit the way they see fit, as long as other people don't get pasted in the face with a rotten peach.

There are people who don't believe this. Some of these people are just bad. They steal. Some of these people are "nationalistic" and think it's okay to take things from other people if they live more than a peach toss away or speak another language or have a different religion or look funny. And the kings, emperors, and so forth who ruled mankind during most of history were under the impression that everything belongs to kings, emperors, and so forth.

Now that the kings and emperors have been shot or reduced to pathetic ceremonial posts, the most common reason given for not believing in economic liberty is that the free market is unfair. Socialists, Social Democrats, American liberals, and all other kinds of economic levelers think that unconstrained industry, agriculture, and commerce lead to the exploitation of people who aren't very good at these things.

A little bit of immoral wealth and a great deal of unconscionable poverty is supposedly thereby created.

It was Adam Smith in *The Wealth of Nations* (published with happy coincidence in 1776) who originally argued that a free market is good for everybody. Smith seems to have been the first person to realize that all voluntary exchanges increase prosperity. Wealth is created by any swap. It may seem like an even trade, but each trader gives up something he values less in order to receive something he values more. Hence the wealth of both traders grows. When Neolithic spear makers did business with Neolithic basket weavers, the spear makers were able to carry things around in a manner more convenient than skewering them on spear points, and the basket weavers were able to kill mastodons by a method more efficient than swatting them with baskets.

The free-market outcome benefits all. It's moral. And the beautiful thing about this morality is that we don't have to be good to achieve it. In the most, perhaps only, famous passage from an economics book, Adam Smith states, "It is not from the benevolence of the butcher, the brewer, or the baker, that we expect our dinner, but from their regard to their own interest." Smith saw that a man's selfish concern with his own well-being is a desirable, indeed, a splendid thing for society. "[He] intends only his own gain," wrote Smith, "and he is in this . . . led by an invisible hand to promote an end which was no part of his intention." That end is economic progress.

The general morality of the free market, however, does not answer the specific objection of unfairness. Economic liberty leads to differences in wealth. And the differences are enormous. The "wealth gap" is the subject of a critical debate about economics. The perception of unfairness is the reason that enormous numbers of the world's decent and well-meaning people, in fact the majority of them, do not rush to embrace the free market in its totality. Complete economic liberty would mean a system like Hong Kong's under John Cowperthwaite with no barriers to trade or capital flow, and no barriers to labor flow, either; no check on immigration, no minimum wage, no cost controls, and no attempt to create a fair society. This is a daunting prospect, and it's not just Fidel Castro who's daunted by it.

Socialists and capitalists naturally take opposing sides on the question of how economically fair life should be. But so do various political parties which claim to be pro-market. So do theologians and philosophers. And so do ordinary people when they're voting for school-bond issues or deciding how much to cheat on their taxes.

Fairness is a potent emotional issue, but how is fairness to be delivered? It's hard to build a political structure that provides economic fairness. The map is full of failed attempts. When a government controls both the economic power of individuals and the coercive power of the state, we get, at best, Mainland China, a place that violates a fundamental rule of happy living: never let the people with all the money and the people with all the guns be the same people.

There is another difficulty with political control of the economy which keeps even the best-behaved governments from using resources well. This problem was explained by the economists Milton and Rose Friedman in their book *Free to Choose*. The Friedmans argued that there are only four ways to spend money.

Spend your money on yourself.

Spend your money on other people.

Spend other people's money on yourself.

Spend other people's money on other people.

If you spend your money on yourself, you look for the best value at the best price—knockoff Pings on sale at Golf-Fore-Less. If you spend your money on other people, you still worry about price, but you may not know—or care—what the other people want. So your brother-in-law gets a Deepak Chopra book for Christmas. If you spend other people's money on yourself, it's hard to resist coming home with real Pings, a new leather bag, orange pants with little niblicks on them, and a pair of Foot-Joy spikes. And if you spend other people's money on other people, any damn thing will do and the hell with what it costs. Almost all government spending falls into category four. This is how the grateful residents of Ukraine got Chernobyl.

Also, if fairness is important, what is really fair? We may say something like, "People have a right to food, a right to housing, and a right to a good job for decent pay." But from an economist's perspective, all those rights involve making finite goods meet infinite wants. Unless the fair society generates tremendous economic growth—which societies that put fairness first have trouble doing—the goods will come from redistribution. Try rephrasing the rights statement thus: "People have a right to *my* food, a right to *my* housing, and a right to *my* good job for *my* decent pay."

Accepting the free market allows us to avoid the political abuse and financial mismanagement inherent in trying to design an economy that's fair. It also allows us to see that economies can't be designed. Economics is the measurement of how human nature affects the material world. The market is "heartless." So are clocks and yardsticks. Saying that economic problems are the result of the free market's failure is like gaining twenty pounds and calling the bathroom scale a bum.

Adam Smith recognized that markets are self-organizing. Man has a "general disposition to truck, barter, and exchange," wrote Smith. If people are protected from coercion by other people, and from coercion by that agglomeration of other people known as the state, human brains and greed create economic growth. "The strength of the mastiff is not in the least supported either by the swiftness of the greyhound, or by the sagacity of the spaniel," wrote Smith. "Among men, on the contrary, the most dissimilar geniuses are of use to one another."

I had thought that economic problems were the result of ignorance about economics. I was wrong. I asked a friend who's knowledgeable in the field: "Why is the concept of the 'invisible hand' so difficult to comprehend?" He said, "It's invisible." The hardest thing to understand about economics is that it doesn't need to be understood. My beatnik friends and I, when we were in college, were perfectly justified in expending our intellectual energy on love and death instead of money.

But there was one thing that we did need to learn. And still do. And it's a piece of knowledge that seems to contradict psychology, life experience, and the dictates of conscience: economics is not zero sum. There is no fixed amount of wealth. That is, if you have too many slices of pizza, I don't have to eat the box. Your money does not cause my poverty. Refusal to believe this is at the bottom of most bad economic thinking.

True, at any given moment, there is only so much wealth to go around. But wealth is based on productivity. Without productivity, there wouldn't be any economics, or any economic thinking, good or bad, or any pizza, or anything else. We would sit around and stare at rocks, and maybe later have some for dinner.

Wealth is based on productivity, and productivity is expandable. In fact, productivity is fabulously expandable, as Angus Maddison has shown in *Monitoring the World Economy*. Yet a person who is worried about fairness can look at Maddison's figures and say that they are just averages. Per capita

GDP does not show us who actually got the cash. The worrier about fairness can recite the old saw: "The rich get richer and the poor . . ."

"Get entertained by *People* magazine stories about divorces among the rich." That is not how the worrier was going to finish his sentence. "Get lower mortgage rates because banks have more money to lend." That is not it, either. "Get better jobs because there's more capital to be invested in businesses." No, the cliché is, "The rich get richer, and the poor get poorer."

Except there is no evidence of this in recent history. Per capita GDP is a tricky figure and doesn't tell us much about the well-being of individual people. But there are other statistics that don't present the same problems of averaging. Life-expectancy and infant-mortality rates do tell us how things are going for ordinary folks. No matter how rich a nation's elite, its members aren't going to live to be 250 and wildly skew the numbers. And a country can't fake a low infant-mortality rate by getting a few rich babies to live while letting all the poor babies die.

The United Nations study *World Population Prospects: 1996 Revision* contains historical statistics on life expectancy and infant mortality. Figures are given for Most Developed Regions, Less Developed Regions, and Least Developed Regions. The last being places that are truly poor, such as Tanzania. In the early 1950s the richest countries had an average infant-mortality rate of 58 deaths per 1,000 live births. By the early 1990s the average was down to 11. During the same period the infant-mortality rate in the poorest countries dropped from an average of 194 deaths per 1,000 to 109 per 1,000. Infant-mortality rates declined in both rich and poor countries, and so did the gap between those rates. A difference of 136 deaths per 1,000 had diminished to a difference of 94 deaths forty years later. This is still too many dead babies (and it's hard to imagine a number of dead babies that wouldn't be too many, unless the fair-minded worrier is also a zealous pro-choice advocate). But infant-mortality rates give us some hopeful information about world economic growth. Yes, the rich are getting richer, but the poor aren't becoming worse off. They're becoming parents.

Life expectancy tells the same story. In the early 1950s, people in rich countries lived, on average, 66.5 years. By the early 1990s they were living 74.2 years. In the poorest countries, average life spans increased from 35.5 years to 49.7 years (which, somewhat unnervingly, was my exact age when I wrote that sentence, and I was glad I didn't live in Tanzania and had to die that night). Anyway, the difference in life expectancy between the world's rich and poor has decreased by 6.5 years. The rich are getting richer. The poor are getting richer. And we're all getting older.

So if wealth is not a worldwide round-robin of purse snatching, and if the thing that makes you rich doesn't make me poor, why should we care about fairness at all? We shouldn't.

Fairness is a good thing in marriage and at the day-care center. It's a nice little domestic virtue. But a liking for fairness is not a noble sentiment. Fairness doesn't rank with charity, love, duty, or self-sacrifice. And there's always a tinge of self-seeking in making sure that things are fair. Don't you go trying to get one up on me.

As a foundation for a political system, fairness may be no virtue at all. The Old Testament is clear on this point. The Bible might seem an odd place to be doing economic research, especially by someone who goes to church about once a year, and only then to give the Easter Bunny time to deliver Peeps. However, I have been thinking—in socioeconomic terms—about the Tenth Commandment.

The first nine Commandments concern theological principles and social law. Thou shalt not make graven images, steal, kill, etc. Fair enough. But then there's the Tenth Commandment: "Thou shalt not covet thy neighbor's house, thou shalt not covet thy neighbor's wife, nor his manservant, nor his maidservant, nor his ox, nor his ass, nor anything that is thy neighbor's."

Here are God's basic rules about how we should live, a very brief list of sacred obligations and solemn moral precepts, and right at the end of it is, "Don't envy your buddy's cow."

What is that doing in there? Why would God, with just ten things to tell Moses, choose, as one of them, jealousy about the livestock next door? And yet, think about how important to the well-being of a community this Commandment is. If you want a donkey, if you want a pot roast, if you want a cleaning lady, don't bitch about what the people across the street have. *Go get your own.*

The Tenth Commandment sends a message to socialists, to egalitarians, to people obsessed with fairness, to American presidential candidates—to everyone who believes that wealth should be redistributed. And the message is clear and concise: Go to hell.

If we want the whole world to be rich, we need to start loving wealth. In the difference between poverty and plenty, the problem is the poverty, not the difference. Wealth is good.

You know this about your own wealth. If you got rich, it would be a great thing. You'd improve your life. You'd improve your family's life. You'd purchase education, travel, knowledge about the world. You'd invest in worthwhile things. You'd give money to noble causes. You'd help your friends and neighbors. Your life would be better if you got rich. The lives of the people around you would be better. Your wealth is good. So why isn't everybody else's wealth good?

Wealth is good when a lot of people have it. It's good when a few people have it. This is because money is a tool, nothing more. You can't eat or drink money, or wear it very comfortably as underwear. And wealth—an accumulation of money—is a bunch of tools.

Tools can be used to do harm. You can break into a house by driving a forklift through a picture window. You can hit somebody over the head with a hydroelectric turbine. Tools are still good. When a carpenter has a lot of tools, we don't say to him, "You have too many. You should give some of your hammers, saws, screws, and nails to the guy who's cooking omelets."

Making money through hard work and wise investment is a fine thing to do. Other ways of making money aren't so bad, either, as long as everybody who's in on the deal is there voluntarily. Better sleazy productivity than none. As terrible as Albania's pyramid schemes were, Albania's riots were worse.

And the Hong Kong of John Cowperthwaite shows that even the most resolutely free-market system makes use of private means for the public weal. If the United States radically reduced the size of its government, eliminated all subsidies, price controls, and corporate welfare, and abolished its entitlement programs, we'd still pay taxes. And those tax revenues would be spent—ideally—on such reasonable things as schools, roads, and national defense, in case the British invade again and try to hand over Wall Street to the Red Chinese.

Or take the real-world example of two kids who graduate from college with honors. One is an admirable idealist. The other is on the make. The idealist joins Friends of the Earth and chains himself to a sequoia. The sharpie goes to work for an investment bank selling fishy derivatives and makes $500,000 a year. Even assuming that the selfish young banker cheats the IRS—and he will—he'll end up paying $100,000 a year in taxes: income tax, property tax, sales tax, etc.

While the admirable idealist has saved one tree (if the logging company doesn't own bolt cutters), the pirate in a necktie has contributed to society $100,000 worth of schools, roads, and U.S. Marines, not to mention Interior Department funding sufficient to save any number of trees and the young idealists chained thereto.

And if the soulless yuppie cheats the IRS so well that he ends up keeping the whole half million? That cash isn't going to sit in his cuff link box. Whether spent or saved, the money winds up invested somewhere, and maybe that investment leads to the creation of the twenty-first century's equivalent of the moldboard plow, the microchip, or the mocha latte. Society wins. Wealth brings great benefits to the world. Rich people are heroes. They don't usually mean to be, but that's their problem, not ours.

Almost everyone in the world now admits that the free market tells us the economic truth. Economic liberty makes wealth. Economic repression makes poverty.

Poverty is hard, wretched, and humiliating. Poverty is schoolgirl prostitutes trying to feed their parents in Cuba. Poverty is John driving around in the Tanzanian night looking for the doctor while his daughter dies. But what poverty is not is sad. Poverty is infuriating. These things don't have to happen. These conditions don't need to exist. We can't solve all the problems of life, but we can solve the problem of gross, worldwide material deprivation. The solution doesn't work perfectly. The solution doesn't work uniformly. Nonetheless, the solution works. If we can't fix everything, let's fix the easy stuff. We know how to get rid of poverty. We know how to create wealth. But because of laziness, fear, complacency, love of power, or foolish idealism, we refuse to do it.

We think we can dabble in freedom—allow a few of its liberties and leave our favorite constraints in place. We think we can screw around with the free market—skip its costs and get all of its benefits anyway.

There is a joke that President Reagan used to tell to illustrate the attitude that some people have toward the blessings they get from freedom and private property.

A traveling salesman is staying overnight with a farm family. When the family sits down to eat, there's a pig in a chair at the table. The pig has three medals hanging around its neck and a wooden leg. The salesman says, "Um, I see a pig is having dinner with you."

"Yep," says the farmer. "That's because he's a very special pig. You see those medals around his neck? Well, the first medal is from when our baby son fell in the pond and was drowning, and that pig dove in, swam out, and saved his life. The second medal, that's from when our little daughter was trapped in a burning barn, and that pig ran inside, carried her out, and saved her life. And the third medal, that's from when our oldest boy was cornered in the stockyard by a mean bull, and that pig ran under the fence, bit the bull's tail, and saved the boy's life."

"Yes," says the salesman, "I can see why you let that pig sit right at the table and have dinner with you. And I can see why you awarded him the medals. But how did he get the wooden leg?"

"Well," says the farmer, "a pig like that—you don't eat him all at once."

THE CEO OF THE SOFA

(2001)

"All generous minds have a horror of what are commonly called 'facts.' Who does not know fellows that always have an ill-conditioned fact or two which they lead after them into decent company like so many bull-dogs."

—Oliver Wendell Holmes

"It's a Person!"

(*1997*)

"It's a person! I suppose that's the modern thing to say," I said, as I doled out cigars to celebrate the birth of my beautiful—*and* intelligent, capable, and fiercely independent—daughter. But I am a traditionalist at heart. I've bought the requisite box of stogies.

However, as a traditionalist, I'm beginning to wonder about this tradition. None of my relatives, business associates, or barroom pals has given away a corona on the occasion of nativity that I can recall. Everybody's familiar with the custom, but I don't think I've ever seen the customary gesture made. In fact, I believe my entire knowledge of the convention is based on old comic strips, gags from the Pleistocene era of TV comedy, and a couple of dusty boxes of cheroots with pink and blue cigar bands that were in the display case at the drugstore where I had an after-school job in 1964.

I've consulted libraries, etiquette books, and friends who are replete with arcane knowledge. The only thing I've learned for certain is that, at the christening, I should not give a cigar to Father O'Malley. Urban VIII (reigned 1623–1644) wrote a papal bull forbidding priests to smoke cigars.

I called *Cigar Aficionado*—the *Vogue* magazine of the fashion for big smokes—and asked George Brightman, director of business development, why I should be dispensing gaspers. He said he thought it was "rooted in something British—a naval officers' tradition, maybe." Mr. Brightman suggested I call Simon Chase at Hunters & Frankau, Great Britain's most prestigious firm of cigar importers. Mr. Chase said he thought it was "something the English do to imitate Americans. I believe it comes from your side rather than our side." I called Molly E. Waldron at the Tobacco Institute in Washington. No one there knew the answer so Ms. Waldron called Norm Sharp at the Cigar Association of America. The only information Mr. Sharp had was from a seventeen-year-old newspaper clipping saying, "Cigars were so rare and treasured in the late seventeenth and eighteenth centuries that . . . they were used as expression of deep emotional appreciation," and "The birth of a boy was considered a most important event . . . so fathers who could afford to celebrated by giving their friends cigars as a way of expressing happiness." The source named in this clipping was the Tobacco Institute in Washington.

A certain interrogational circularity was setting in. Why do I give a guy a cigar because my wife had a baby? As the most knowledgeable salesman at that best of cigar stores, Georgetown Tobacco, said, "You're not going to give him a lollipop."

I'm probably better off making things up. As I've found out from years of journalism, this is often the case. Perhaps I'm offering cigars to drive away evil. The cigar does seem to be anathema to ideological types whom I don't want bothering my little darling. Although smoke is not an infallible charm against them. V. Lenin bought cigars at Zino Davidoff's father's store in Geneva. A bill still exists—marked *Not paid,* of course.

Anyway, that theory does not explain why I'm bestowing the gifts. The flow of presents should run in the other direction at blessed event time—as per three wise men and a newborn babe no doubt almost as adorable as mine. And my wife and I *have* made quite a haul. In fact, if I see one more bootie, blankie, snugglie, jammie, hatsie, pantsie, or shirtsie covered in twee, cloying, dwarfish bears, I'm going to need a bottle myself. Preferably Dewar's. I understand bunnies and chicks, but why bears? Bears are not cute. Bears are bad-tempered predators. Bears eat garbage. Bears smell.

And so do cigars. Maybe the association of cigars with paternity has to do with masking diaper odor. Not that anyone would smoke a cigar anywhere near Daddy's little precious. But maybe cigars are an excuse for fathers to go stand in the garage when diapers need to be changed. A cigar can buy you a whole hour, as opposed to the ten minutes you get from a Camel. Or maybe cigars are a Planned Parenthood policy, a method of spacing births. As long as Dad has cigar breath, the next child is not likely to be conceived soon.

This still doesn't tell me why I'm doing the giving instead of the receiving. There's the obvious Freudian thing. Freud is supposed to have said, "Sometimes a cigar is just a cigar." But that leaves what a cigar is the rest of the time open to Freudian interpretation. By proffering cigars I'm saying, "I made a baby. Here is an object symbolizing how the deed was done. Let me know if your wife needs a baby, too." Then there's the potlatch aspect. To show what big men they were, Indians of the Pacific Northwest used to give away or burn valuable goods. With cigars you can do both.

A new father is a very big man. He feels like one of those bond moguls of the 1980s. That is, he feels lucky to get out on parole, even if it's only to the garage. But he also feels important and powerful. Cigars are indicators of power and importance. Although I don't know why. Where I grew up they were indicators of old men playing gin rummy. Perhaps it's because a cigar is such a good theatrical device. Light a big one and puff on it, and you're immediately doing an excellent impression of pompous, portly middle age.

And when the puffing is done by one of us who actually *is* pompous, portly, and middle-aged, the impression is particularly good.

The cigar as a stage prop to signify plutocracy has been in use at least since Charlie Chaplin's silent films *City Lights* and *The Gold Rush*. And various propped-up stagy plutocrats—Arnold Schwarzenegger, Michael Douglas, Jack Nicholson—are still making good use of it. As did Bill Clinton, who—I have seen photographs that prove it—*leaves the band on his cigar*. I think this says everything that needs saying about the late Clinton presidency.

But I've gotten off the subject. We may never know why a man presents cigars with a birth announcement. But we will know what kind of cigars he's presenting. And here comes the cigar-bore monologue: "The El Fumigatore Malodoro Grande is a big, noisy, wide-bodied smoke. It has an earthy, dirty flavor of wadded-up plant leaves with an undertone of cedar chips from the bottom of the gerbil cage and a loud, stupid finish when the exploding device inside goes off." Actually, I don't know how to talk that kind of talk. I'm one of those people who can't figure out why wine-tasting columns don't mention getting drunk. That *is* the point. Nobody would pay $300 for a bottle of '89 Château Cheval-Blanc if it didn't pack a wallop. And nobody would inhale the fumes of smoldering vegetable matter from a Cohiba Esplendido if the smoke didn't contain nicotine.

The fact of the matter is, I'm distributing drugs to commemorate the arrival of my daughter. This would make more sense if nicotine were a drug that produced uncontrollable impulses to set up trust funds for infants or immunized guests against the noises caused by colic. Nonetheless, the alkaloid $C_{10}H_{14}N_2$ does provide a nice little buzz, the kind of high that allows you to keep your wits about you, so you know just how long to linger in the garage until the nappies are clean and the burping has been administered.

Cigars are a mere narcotic. And I am a democrat—in the small *d* sense—about getting stoned. Yet I confess to a measure of snobbery concerning distinctions among cigars. I can't buy a box of Phillie Blunts. The kind of people who hollow out their cigars and fill them with marijuana are not a presence in my social set. And I can't buy any of the good Dominican and Honduran imports because they're all gone—purchased by au courant types trying to look like Arnold Schwarzenegger, Michael Douglas, or, more realistically, Ronald Perelman. Besides, I have the most wonderful baby on earth. Only the best will do. And Cuba still makes the best cigars.

Maybe it's the soil or the climate. Maybe it's the comely Cuban maidens rolling the cigars on their . . . actually, they roll them on tables. Maybe it's just more $C_{10}H_{14}N_2$. But importing Cuban cigars is illegal. There's a cautionary tale about cigar smuggling in the December 1997 issue of *Cigar Aficionado,* although a possible dodge is mentioned. A customs agent interviewed at New York's JFK airport gives his opinion that body-cavity concealment is "still too extreme for cigars." The mind, however, boggles and so do other parts of the anatomy. This certainly would be a bad way to smuggle *lit* cigars.

So I didn't get any Cubans. Specifically, I didn't get a box of Montecristo No. 4 coronas. And where I didn't get them—which I can't tell because then I'd not only be committing a crime but engaging in a criminal conspiracy—was from a certain well-known foreign country. An outfit there will ship cigars in a box labeled MADE IN MEXICO, and it's not a lie because the box *is* made in Mexico.

Finally I possessed some cigars worthy of my fabulous kid. At $13 apiece, they'd better be. And then I faced another problem. To whom should I give them? Although tobacco is very stylish now, many of my friends are still stuck in the outmoded nineties health fad and haven't resumed smoking. As for the chic new breed of puffers I know, I sincerely approve of them. A shared vice is a pleasure. It's also a pleasure to watch a thirty-five-year-old financial hotshot turn pea green as he pretends to enjoy a Romeo y Julieta Belicosos. And, concerning halitosis among the increasing number of my female acquaintances who indulge, I'm a husband and father and shouldn't be kissing around anyway. But, all that said, giving really scarce, really good cigars to modish neophytes is like casting pearls before debutantes. They'll enjoy it, but I will not.

I can't help suspecting that the trendsetters don't know an El Rey Del Mundo from a White Owl. And seeing four inches of a Havana H. Upmann stubbed out in the ashtray at a martini bar is enough to make a real addict cry (or steal the butt). This leaves, as recipients of my cigar largesse, men with palates as blackened, clothes as smelly, and suit lapels as full of little singe holes as my own. Most of these fellows are older and richer than myself. They already have cigars, they already have children, too, and grandchildren to boot. I've thought it over and decided to hell with them.

I am parting with my cigars very slowly, parceling out just one per day, right after dinner. And every evening, for the next twenty-five nights, you'll find me with a demitasse of good coffee, a snifter of fine brandy, and a celebratory smoke, in the garage.

Kid Pro Quo:

Management Tips from Mothers with Toddlers

(2000)

In the 1970s there arrived in the American workplace something that would change the business world forever. This thing would prove more important than Arab oil embargoes, dim-bulb Carter-era monetary policies, or even the desktop computer. It wore lipstick. Although only if it wanted to. Until about 1978 the majority of adult female Americans did not have a job, even when they were supposed to during World War II. Why is a matter of debate. Sexual discrimination, social tradition, and lack of economic opportunity doubtless played their parts.

My own opinion (and I have known a number of adult female Americans personally and am married to one) is that women decided to go to work because they felt like it.

Anyway, the results have been spectacular. The Independent Women's Forum, a nonpartisan pro–free market think tank very much devoted to having women do what they feel like doing, has collected statistics on the subject. Between 1960 and 1994 women's wages increased ten times faster than men's. Females are currently starting businesses at twice the male rate, and women-owned enterprises are growing more quickly than the overall economy. In 1973 only 11 percent of corporations had women on their boards of directors; now 72 percent do. In 1970 the legal profession was 95 percent male. Today there's a 29 percent chance that your wife's divorce lawyer will be . . . your wife.

Some professions are, in effect, controlled by women, who make up 51 percent of editors and reporters, 66 percent of PR "men," and 62 percent of the psychologists telling us to get over it about the Mrs. making more than we do. Even the federal government's Glass Ceiling Commission, created by the Civil Rights Act of 1991 to bird-dog the remaining boys-only boardrooms, had to admit that women are getting along all right. The commission conceded that the two economic sectors expected to grow most at the beginning of the new century—service/trade/retail and finance/insurance/real estate—are well on their way to becoming hen parties.

No ethnic subculture or immigrant population has ever swept capitalism off its feet the way women have. The last time any group rose so quickly to the top was when men first got jobs and the only competition was from woolly mammoths.

What accounts for the distaff triumph? Of course, as every son, brother, boyfriend, and husband knows, women are smarter than we are. But it can't be only that. Looking around at my fellow males I realize *everything* is smarter than we are—the copy machine, for instance. And, when I was working, the copier never got promoted ahead of me. Although, as I recall, it did have a nicer cubicle.

The fact is women possess a certain body of arcane knowledge, an eons-old set of complex skills, an ancient esoteric understanding that no one else has. This profound wisdom and well-learned craft is shrugged off by the ignorant (i.e., me) in the single dismissive phrase *good with kids.*

Or I used to shrug it off. But one day I came home from New York and was fuming into my martini about childish articles editors, infantile managing editors, and a publisher who was a spoiled brat when what should my eyes behold but—a spoiled brat. *My* spoiled brat. There was my daughter Muffin, age two and a half, in the middle of the living room shouting *no,* kicking the furniture, and otherwise acting like every corporate executive since the great Ice Age Inc. takeover of Woolly Mammoth Ltd. in 11,000 BC.

Then my wife breezed into the room and did something involving a sippy cup and a Barney tape. Peace reigned. During that reign of peace I had a brilliant insight. Well, brilliant for a man.

Women are successful in the business world because the business world was created by men. Men are babies. And women are . . . *good with kids.*

So if I want to be successful in the business world, I need to be good with kids too. But how to go about this? Well, I could undertake to become principal care provider for Muffin. But there's our daughter's welfare to be considered. I have no idea how many Ring Dings and packages of beer nuts a toddler needs each day. And are diapers supposed to be changed three times a week or only twice?

I could ask my wife how to be good with kids. She's certainly good with the one who is, at the moment, contentedly singing along with a fuzzy *Tyrannosaurus rex*. (I'll bet the Microsoft antitrust division wishes it could get the Justice Department to do this, although, actually, in that case the *Tyrannosaurus rex* is Janet Reno. Which shows there is an exception to the good-with-kids rule; Janet would scare the hell out of Muffin.) My wife also rose higher on the corporate ladder than I ever did, before she resigned to run our wholly owned subsidiary of Toys "Я" Us. But would my wife tell me how to be good with kids? Does Macy's tell Gimbels? (Since Gimbels—like me as a freelance writer—is out of business, apparently not.)

Instead I decided to buy books about raising children. But not just any children. Not babies—anybody with a dairy farm, a chain of rug-cleaning establishments, and 200,000 shares of Procter & Gamble can raise a baby. And not teens—raising teens is the business of the police and the National Association of Television Broadcasters' Code of Standards and Practices. I bought books about the most crucial and difficult periods in child raising: the God-Awful Ones, the Terrible Twos, the Threes That Are So Bad There's No Name for Them. I bought books about raising the variety of kid that I am absolutely clueless about raising: ours.

Of course, I chose books that were written by women. I remember the disaster that ensued when a generation of parents listened to Dr. Benjamin Spock. Trying to gain management acumen from Spock's ultra-permissive *Baby and Child Care* would result in running a brokerage house full of people in bell-bottoms eating peyote and handing out stock certificates for free on the street. I also wanted books that received high marks from women readers, so I consulted the Average Customer Review page at the Amazon.com website, looking for things like: *I am still using the "respectful" techniques I learned from this book.* (Note the sly use of quotation marks.)

Here's what I picked.

- *1,2,3 . . . the Toddler Years: A Practical Guide for Parents and Caregivers* by Irene Van der Zande
- *Parenting Your Toddler: The Experts' Guide to the Tough and Tender Years* by Patricia Henderson Shimm and Kate Ballen
- *Your One-Year-Old: The Fun-Loving, Fussy 12- to 24-Month-Old* by Louise Bates Ames, PhD, Frances L. Ilg, MD, and Carol Chase Haber

Was I imagining it or did the lady at the bookstore cash register look suspicious? "My wife is going to a Theta reunion in Bloomington, Indiana," I said, "for the *whole weekend.*" I placed a concealing copy of *Sports Afield* in my shopping bag and slipped home. I opened *Your One-Year-Old* at random and . . . the shock of recognition was so severe that the gin bottle almost dropped from my hand. Listen to these excerpts from the chapter titled "Characteristics of the Age."

- He seems to want *everything,* to prefer everybody else have nothing.
- A busy little person. Though much of his activity is purely . . . bumbling around from one spot to another.
- Almost anything may attract his attention, and then he almost seems to have to respond, without rhyme or reason.

- Extremely self-involved. He relates to others if and when it pleases him.
- All too likely to put on a full-fledged temper tantrum over what may actually be only a minor frustration.
- Can be seen as enchanting if the viewer appreciates an almost total egocentricity.

Is that not the most brilliant description of a boss ever limned? Especially of, I'd say, the nation's boss, Bill Clinton.

Nor does women's sagacity stop at mere keen observation. The books I bought wade right in and tell you how to deal with the SOB you work for.

"You control him," says *Your One-Year-Old,* "by controlling the surroundings and by just not having too many things around that will get him into difficulty." White House interns, for example.

"If you do use language to motivate him," the book continues, "keep it very simple, and use words of one syllable only." The most famous boss-motivating monosyllable is, naturally, the *Yes*. But its opposite, the *I will get right back to you on that,* works too, because, as *Your One-Year-Old* says, "he has such a very short attention span." And try "Your golf game looks real good," and "You've lost weight." *Your One-Year-Old* points out that "Whatever gives comfort is worth its weight in gold." Naps are also suggested. They worked with President Reagan.

The three books are full of good advice about how to make people who think they're in charge think they actually are. Never ask your boss a yes-or-no question.

"*No* becomes his favorite word even when he wants to say *yes,*" states *Parenting Your Toddler.*

"He quite typically says 'no' instead of 'yes,' 'down' instead of 'up,'" notes *Your One-Year-Old.*

"There's almost always a way to give . . . a choice," vouchsafes *1,2,3 . . . the Toddler Years.* "Notice," the book continues, "that these questions are all offered in the form of closed questions." One of the examples given, since we're using President Clinton as our specimen awful boss, is rather too pertinent.

> *"Do you want to wear your red pants or your blue pants?" It's important before asking the question to decide what choices we're willing to live with. Open questions such as "What do you want to wear?" lead to answers we may not be willing to accept, like, "Nothing!"*

The closed question—it is so easy, so obvious, and yet every one of the Joint Chiefs of Staff forgot to ask Bill Clinton, "Do you want to stay out of the Balkans or not get involved in former Yugoslavia?" The problem is, the Joint Chiefs are guys.

The books are equally savvy about temper tantrums. Says *Your One-Year-Old,* "The less they bother you, chances are the less frequently they will occur. It is not much satisfaction to play to an uninterested audience."

Parenting Your Toddler gives six rules for dealing with tantrums:

1. Don't punish.	("I quit.")
2. Don't reward.	("I quit. Sob. Sob.")
3. Don't bribe.	("I'll quit if you ask me to.")
4. Don't placate.	("You don't really want me to quit, do you?")
5. Don't leave the room.	("I quit. F— you.")
6. Don't have a tantrum yourself.	("I quit. F— you. I'm suing.")

Then the text goes on to posit a strategy worthy of Napoleon, if Napoleon had been a woman. But he wasn't, so he wound up getting fired and moving to Saint Helena. The strategy is: just name the feelings that caused the tantrum. "Once your toddler calms down, explain in short sentences why he gets angry."

Let's try using the example that *Parenting Your Toddler* gives, about putting crayons away, with some minor modifications to aid Napoleon's case.

Napoleon should have said, "General Wellington and General Blücher, you got really mad when I said it was time to put Louis the Eighteenth away. It's okay to be angry; next time you can tell me this. You can say, '*Napoleon, we get mad when you escape from Elba.*' I will listen to you. And you know that no matter how mad you get at me, somebody stinky is always going to run France."

Just naming things seems ridiculous to a male. But think how often females make it work around the house: *Because I'm your mother* or *Oh, no, you don't, you're a married man.*

Equally effective for dealing with tantrums, and with almost all other lousy executive behavior, is a technique that women invented at a very early date—distraction. "Not right now, Adam, I've got to go fig-leaf shopping. Why don't you have an apple instead?" Or, as *Your One-Year-Old* puts it, a "new and interesting object if offered may prove to be a satisfactory substitute for the thing he really wanted. Or a total change of scene . . . may help him forget his frustration." Hence the importance of the business jet, which, you'll recall, came into use in the middle seventies just when large numbers of women were gaining influence over America's executive suites. If the corner-office carpet apes get completely out of control, put them on the G-5.

Besides sage advice, the books contain a variety of real-life anecdotes to help better understand how corporate and professional life looks to women. It looks like a playdate gone horribly wrong. Thanks to the following item from *Parenting Your Toddler,* I now know everything about telecommunications networks and am ready to go toe-to-toe with the sharpest gal in the industry.

> *Lily walked into her friend's house and her eyes immediately lit upon a beautiful new doll. Lily quickly said, "Joan, I'll share your new doll." Joan, who obviously had heard that sharing was a good thing, replied, "Oh, yes, we'll share the doll." Lily then grabbed the doll and ran into a corner with it, saying, "Now, we are sharing."*

I suppose women thought men would never read these books. Or women thought these books would be read only by the kind of man who bikes to his job at the organic food co-op—not a threat to their corporate promotion. Anyway, women are spilling the beans here. Peruse the following passage, allegedly about biting, from *1,2,3 . . . the Toddler Years.* First, however, we will substitute *account supervisor* for "eighteen-month-old," *new executive assistant* for "four-year-old sister," *PalmPilot* for "doll," and *vice president of account services* for "Mama."

> *Account Supervisor Kenny stood quietly watching his new executive assistant. It's possible to guess at the sort of thoughts going through Kenny's head. "I wonder about this girl here. I know what she looks like . . . I know what she smells like . . . but what does she taste like? I'll just find out . . . Wow, she made a big noise! And she dropped that PalmPilot she never lets me play with. Uh-oh! Looks like the vice president of account services is real mad at someone . . . Who, me?"*

You members of the business sisterhood should be more careful about putting your secrets into print. Or at least you should make a pretense of actually using these books to raise kids. I've noticed you never look at them. When anything untoward happens in our house you call your mother. "Mom," you say, "I'm having a terrible problem with bedtime. It's just, *No, no, no! More bottle! More bottle!* Nothing seems to work. What did you used to do?"

And your mother says, "I used to hide your father's gin."

What You Learn from Having Kids

(2001)

You learn you're a total idiot. You experience an epiphany of true and perfect ignorance the moment the scary nurses in the delivery room—masked like Yemeni harem wives—hand you your wet, red, screaming bundle of joy. You learn you don't know a thing about life. Why, here is the most important of all things about life. Here is life itself. And—EEEEE, IT'S ALIVE!!!—you don't even know how to hold it. One hand for the baby's bottom, one hand under its back, and then, with your third hand, you . . .

The nurses quickly snatch the baby back. You don't know a thing. Maybe you've been to graduate school. Maybe you've been around the world. Maybe you can hack into the company's Human Resources Department files and find out which of the senior VPs is in the federal witness protection program. You're able to pronounce the last names of every placekicker in the NFL. And you don't know an effing thing. An effing thing, literally. You don't know where babies come from. Oh, intellectually you know. But you don't really know until someone near and dear to you has a baby and you are forced by the callous laws of modern male sensitivity to be there when it happens. Babies come from *there*?! Whole babies?! Head and everything?! Ouch.

You learn you're a total idiot, and then you learn you've married a genius. You thought you and your wife had an equal amount of information about babies. After all, you attended the same birthing classes. (Although she, maybe, wasn't hiding a beer under her sport coat.) As far as you could tell, your wife believed a baby was, mainly, a possible impediment to making partner at the law firm. Suddenly she understands exactly what to do when the baby cries, poops, screams, spits up—actions that babies are capable of performing all at the same time and continuously, if there's an important baseball game on TV.

You've married a genius. In fact, you've married into an entire race of geniuses—women. Aunts, mothers-in-law, female cousins, your wife's sorority sisters, random old ladies from the neighborhood descend upon your house to tell you you're a total idiot. "That's no way to hold a baby!" they say and quickly snatch the baby back. Should you be insulted by this? Or should you watch the Yankees get their bucket kicked by the Red Sox? Don't be an idiot.

You probably thought you loved women before. Hah! That was mere admiration from afar—sort of paging through the Victoria's Secret catalog of love, thinking swell thoughts without actually *knowing* women. As a father you learn what these adorable cupcakes are capable of. They're capable of forgiving you for getting them pregnant. What would you do to a person who forced you to spend nine months shaped like a bowling pin? That's a bowling pin that can't have a cigarette or a martini and at the end of nine months has to, basically, pass a kidney stone the size of a cantaloupe. You'd murder him. And consider breast-feeding. Not the earth-mother Madonna-and-child scene of maternal bliss you thought, huh? Here's a wonderful, beloved, helpless little creature depending for its very existence on biting my wife in a sensitive place. And for twenty hours a day.

Then there are diapers and burp cloths and belly button scabs and all the rest of the icky goo of life that women plunge right into, armed with nothing but a Handi-Wipe and a smile. Women can cope with dreadful messes and misbehaviors and turn around and excuse and exculpate the person who made them. This is a wonderful thing. Although, considering the recurrent dreadful messes and misbehaviors in American politics, it also explains why women weren't allowed to vote until fairly recently.

Becoming a father also teaches you that you are, personally, a religious fundamentalist and antiabortion fanatic. This information comes as something of a surprise to those of us who hadn't been to church since, um, my mother got married, kind of late, and who had always regarded abortion clinics as a sort of emergency date-night resource—where you take a *really* bad girlfriend on the *very* last date. But the first time your little inchoate blob pops up on the sonogram screen and you shout, "He looks like me!" it's all over between you and NOW. Never mind that the baby comes out wet, red, screaming, crying, pooping, spitting up—he (actually, as it turned out, she) looks like me (which, mercifully, she doesn't—except for, as my wife points out, the wet, red, screaming, crying, pooping, spitting-up part). What can abortion advocates be thinking? Babies are so soft, so tender, so sweet . . . Wait, I know, they want to *eat* my baby. Be gone, you imps of Satan! Which brings us to the religious stuff.

A lot of praying goes into becoming a dad, and it's not just praying for the Viagra to kick in. "Please, God, let my wife be all right. Please, God, let the baby be all right. Please, God, don't forget—ten fingers, ten toes. And, oh, yeah, just one head. And, God, don't let me blow chunks and pass out in the delivery room." By the time it's over, you owe the Big Guy. Not to mention what you owe the hospital and the doctor, plus college tuition is coming up fast—further reasons for prayer.

However, don't be frightened that fatherhood will make you vote the Christian fundamentalist ticket. Fatherhood also turns you into a big mush of a liberal. I am a Cro-Magnon Republican of long standing. Yet I can now be reduced to a puddle of compassionate tears by *It Takes a Village*. Perhaps I exaggerate. But I did used to think welfare mothers were irresponsible jerks for trying to raise kids without a job, without an income, without a good home, without a husband to blow chunks and pass out in the delivery room. Now I think welfare mothers are irresponsible jerks who should be given the Congressional Medal of Honor. And I am enraged by any government policy that might . . . What do you mean the Reagan administration declared that ketchup counts as a vegetable in school lunches? Don't tell me the guy has Alzheimer's, I'll go out to California and *knock* some sense into his head. These days, I believe the Department of Transportation should require bicycle helmets for children going to bed.

And that is what you learn just in the first two days of being a father. This is nothing compared to what you learn later. For instance, when Muffin got old enough to watch children's television, I learned what my hobby is going to be when the kids are grown up and out of the house. I'm spending my retirement years tracking down all the people involved in children's television programming and shoving the Teletubbie with the sexual-diversity issues in their ear. Except Maria on *Sesame Street*. She's still a babe. I've had a crush on her since the show started thirty years ago and my artsy-fartsy MFA friends and I would get together every afternoon and smoke dope and goof hysterically on the Cookie Monster. Which tells you everything about the intellectual level of children's television, not to mention the intellectual level of children.

A child has the same amount of brains as a pot-fumed graduate student. In fact, a child has the same amount of brains as every other member of the nitwit human race. This is why I get *There was a farmer had a dog/And Bingo was his name-o* stuck in my head for a week just the way Muffin does. Except I don't feel obliged to sing B-I-N-G-O out loud all day, although the clapping part is rather compelling: B-I-N-*clap-clap,* B-I-N-*clap-clap*—.

Anyway, all mankind's ideas and interests, all human aims and motives, are exhibited, fully formed, in a three-year-old child. The kid is just operating on a smaller scale and lacks the advantage of having made enormous soft-money campaign contributions to political candidates.

Speaking of whom, no one who is a parent was able to bear watching the Bush/Gore debates.

"You did!"

"Did not!"

"Did too!"

"Did not either, you big booger!"

There are plenty of politicians—and business executives and other VIPs—who wouldn't surprise me a bit if they proudly announced to the media, *I made BM!* and then expected to get a Tootsie-Pop for their efforts.

Think of the actors, musicians, athletes, models, gossip-column nuisances, people with body piercings, and moron climbers of Mount Everest whose whole lives consist of being a brat on a swing set: "Look at me! Look at me! Look at me! No hands!" Or, in case of the Everest climbers, no fingers.

And then there are all the adults who won't go to sleep at night and then wind up in other people's beds, where they don't belong.

When Saint Augustine was formulating his doctrine of Original Sin, all he had to do was look at people as they are originally. Originally, they're children. Saint Augustine may have had a previous job—unmentioned in his *Confessions*—as a preschool day-care provider. But it's wrong to use *infantile* as a pejorative. It's the other way around. What children display is *adultishness*. Children are, for example, perfectly adultish in their self-absorption. Tiny tots look so wise, staring at their stuffed animals. You wonder what they're thinking. Then they learn to talk. What they're thinking is, *My* Beanie Baby!

I was trying to point out the glories of a sunset to Muffin the other day. "Look at all the colors," I said.

"Why?" she asked.

Because they're so beautiful, I said.

"Why?" she asked.

Because the sun is going down, I said.

"For *me*?"

But children are cute when they do these things, an indication of the enormous amount of detailed thought that God put into the creation of the universe. He made children cute so we wouldn't kill them.

Fatherhood teaches you to hate humanity—except your kids, because they're so darn cute, and except everybody else who has kids. You bond with these people immediately no matter who they are and no matter how much you would detest them under other circumstances. This parent-to-parent pact is a powerful force. It caused World War II. Roosevelt had kids. Stalin had kids. Hitler didn't have kids. Hey, what's Adolf doing sneaking into the Safeway express line with eleven items while Uncle Joe has Svetlana wrapped around his neck screaming for M&Ms? "Screw that," said Franklin, "I'm invading Normandy."

It's parent solidarity that keeps my wife from leaving me when I spend all day watching the Red Sox instead of spooning strained peas, wrangling diapers, fumbling with jammie buttons, and reading *The House at Pooh Corner* over and over and over . . .

"Again!" says Muffin.

. . . until I snap. "And then it was hunting season and Christopher Robin shot the stupid bear and skinned him and cooked him and ate him."

"Waaaaaaah!!! Poooooh!!!"

And I am heartbroken. I've just learned one more thing. I'm in love. One pout puts my emotions into a theater full of junior high school girls watching 'N Sync. One smile and I feel like Elvis in a Percodan factory. I knew nothing about being in love before. I thought it had to do with Elizabeth Hurley in a garter belt, maybe. No. True love is feeling absolute, genuine bliss at hearing the words, "I made BM! Can I have a Tootsie-Pop?"

Kids love, too. And here is another example of God's attention to detail. He makes children just stupid enough that what they love is you. They love you with an unalloyed, complete, and trusting love. Even if you did kill Pooh.

Of course the kind of love I knew about when I knew nothing about love is still around. This led to me becoming a father for a second time. And then you really start to learn things.

Anybody can have one kid. Having one kid is like owning a dog—albeit a dog that stays a puppy for twenty-two years and never learns to fetch anything but credit card bills and nose colds. But going from one kid to two kids is like going from owning a dog to running a zoo.

It takes about two hours per meal to feed Muffin and Poppet, three hours to get them dressed, with an additional hour for finding lost shoes. It takes two hours to get them undressed, two more hours for bathtub, bath tantrums, and bathroom mop-up, an hour to get them into their Dr. Dentons, and three hours of reading *The House at Pooh Corner* to put them to sleep. By this point it's one in the morning. And yet, in most American families, both parents work. When? And why does America's economy do all right in spite of this?

Don't ask me. I already get enough questions at home from Muffin. Most notably, upon the arrival of Poppet, "Why did you bring home a baby?"

Because I'm opposed to materialism. And having a family cures it. When a one-year-old careens across the living room, knocks over a Waterford crystal vase, smashes an antique Chinese ginger jar lamp, and pukes on the embroidered silk upholstery of the Chippendale settee, what is the reaction of a family man? "Get the video camera! She's *walking*!"

Having kids defines fun down—just in time for middle age when having fun isn't much fun anymore anyway. I used to think booze and sex would bring me joy. Now it's a nap. Or a business trip to a Motel 6 in Dayton. Where I can go to the john in peace. Wow, a dry towel. And twenty-six channels to myself.

It's important to have somebody around the house who's in trouble besides me. I rarely miss the toilet bowl. Actually—I'm informed by a reliable source that I'm married to—that's a fib. But I rarely miss with No. 2. There's the absolute and unconditional affection I receive—from the makers of Pampers, Play-Doh, Legos, Froot Loops, et cetera. I get an excuse to indulge in a longtime private fantasy and build a major Barbie collection. No, scratch that.

The noblest calling in life is to shape and form a worthy human character. Mrs. O says that's why she wanted to get married, but so far it hasn't worked on me. And there's the matter of ensuring a kind of immortality. Everyone wants to live forever, and a couple of bored kids can make one rainy Saturday afternoon seem like eternity. Plus I felt I owed it to the world to become a total idiot. Smart people cause so much trouble. I'll bet the folks who invented the atomic bomb weren't taking care of the kids that day. If they had been, the residents of Hiroshima would have been pelted with Pampers, Play-Doh, Legos, and Froot Loops, instead of radiation and a shock wave.

Actually, by becoming a father I've learned that I'm too much of a total idiot to explain anything, let alone why people have kids. In fact, I'm such a total idiot that I'm trying to talk Mrs. O into starting on a third.

Summer

(*2001*)

For nine long months the memory of summer lays its hold upon me. Lolling days of sun. Cares brushed away by gentle zephyrs. Pellucid twilights. Sultry evenings—especially when the window AC unit goes out. Madras and poplin and white after Memorial Day. Specifically, white thighs and calves. There's cruising the islands: Mykonos, Ibiza, Staten. That night in Monte Carlo? A Chevy Monte Carlo. I didn't break the bank, but I did back into an ATM machine. What about those merry golf outings? Always bogeyed the eighth hole, the one with the spiral ramp and the windmill. Long walks on the beach. Soft sands, soft promises, and a soft roll of flab spilling over my swim-trunk waistband. Mornings on horseback, or on Lawnboy anyway. The scent of fresh grass clippings. And the smell the electric weed whacker makes when its nylon cord gets snarled. Summer, the fragrant time: flowers, new-mown hay, musk, and whatever else was in that aftershave my high school girlfriend gave me. More long walks on the beach—we never did find the car keys. And, best of all, the famous summer moon. That old lady walking her dog was sure surprised when I stuck my butt out the passenger-side window.

But throw nostalgia aside. Another summer is here. How did a twenty-five-pound dead raccoon get under the cover of the aboveground pool? The living is easy. The charcoal is damp. We're out of lighter fluid. And we're going to get this summer off to a great start as soon as we get home from the emergency room and the gasoline blaze in the Weber dies down. Summer is for adventure. Summer is the season of sights and sounds. Did Aerosmith always sound this bad? And what a sight they're getting to be.

This summer I'm going to do the things I've always meant to do. Plant a topiary garden. Learn Italian. Read *Middlemarch*. Use the nine mandated days of paid vacation before August or lose 60 percent of accumulated holiday time in the subsequent calendar year. And visit my wife's parents in Des Moines.

I'm going to spend more time with the kids this summer. Like I've got a choice. Muffin has to be taken to tennis lessons at 9, swim lessons at 10, tai kwan do lessons at 11, soccer practice at 1, gymnastics at 2, playdate at 3, and a birthday party at a Chuck E. Cheese restaurant in a suburb on the other side of the moon at 4. Don't let me forget to stop and buy a gift. Also, I'll have plenty of time with the kids on the way to Des Moines while they spill grape juice, break the Gameboy, and throw up in the SUV. And, by the time we get back . . . Gosh, where did the summer go?

More to the point, why are we sad when it's gone? Everybody claims to love this time of the year and yet consider:

Summer school
Summer camp
Summer job
Summer love
Summer rental
Summer reruns
Summer soldiers and sunshine patriots
Summer stock performances of *Annie Get Your Gun*

As an adjective, "summer" is no compliment. The second-rate, the unimportant, the flimsy, and the stupid predominate from June to September.

Summer is the season of big dumb movies and big dumb books and big dumb me turning crab-boil red at the shore. Nature tricks us with its benign looks, and we wander around outdoors unwary as we'd never be in December. Nobody gets chandelier stroke, coat-and-hat-burn, or cool rash. Summer is when we're not paying attention. We get confused about things. Daylight savings versus the 401k. You think you'll retire on a bank account full of extra sunshine after dinner. Temperatures go up, IQs go down. Ghettos do not burn in January and neither do large overfertilized patches of grass in my front yard.

The very bliss adults feel at the advent of summer is half-witted. We're forgetting that we're not ten. There comes no lovely day in spring when the doors of America's businesses fly open and employees rush away singing:

Office is out! Office is out!
Management let the monkeys out!
No more faxes! No more phones!
No more taking laptops home!

And, come autumn, adults do not move to a different and perhaps more interesting cubicle where a new and maybe more lackadaisical quality team supervisor will be in charge. Adult life doesn't even have a proper summer. It just has a period of hot weather with more houseguests, more houseflies, and no fewer house payments. Summer is a sham. Summer is a hoax. Summer, if we think about it, is . . .

But let's stop thinking. It's summer. There may be nobler times of year, but no one's made a movie called *Endless February*. There never was a "Mud Season of Love." And no pop songs have been written about slush and driveway salt.

Summer isn't worthwhile. Bless it. The worthwhile things get on our nerves enough the other three-quarters of the annum. Let's see what Duty looks like in a thong bikini. Let's find out if Honor can water-ski. Summer is inconsequential. But we know what "take the consequences" means. We don't get much done in the summer. But what are we, do-gooders? And, if what we do isn't good, is the world worse off without it? Summer promises us nothing. Couldn't we all use a little more of that in our lives? Summer makes us act foolish. So? How much fun have you had acting serious?

The major religions of the world do not have their high holy days in summer, for good reason. The Goddess of Winter is stern and self-disciplined. The Goddess of Fall is fruitful and wise. The Goddess of Spring is full of hope. But the Goddess of Summer is . . . naked, if we can get her to drink two more Mai Tais.

Summer is pointless. That's the point. Summer is useless. Who wants to feel used? Summer is dumb. And so am I. Looks like one more perfect summer.

35th Anniversary of Elaine's Restaurant

(1998)

Elaine's is a haven for writers. You know how insecure and timid we writers are. The great thing about Elaine's is the safety. For instance, I'm safe from the food. Every other place in New York seems to be specializing in some horrible gustatory fad: Tibetan dirt salads or Provençal escargot sorbets. God help us if Manhattan restaurateurs ever discover the anthropophagite entrées of the New Guinea highlands. But Elaine never serves me a fish that isn't dead yet or a Bolivian guinea pig terrine. In fact, at Elaine's I'm safe from physical excitement of any kind. Elaine realizes that we writers live our whole lives on paper in the sincere hope of never having to live them anywhere else. There are no fistfights. And anyone who's seen Elaine slam-dunk a paparazzo is unlikely to start one. There is no "pickup" nonsense. If you go home from Elaine's with someone, you're probably married to her—or anyway someone you know is.

I'm safe from romance and adventure at Elaine's. And, more important, I'm safe from literature. Writers attract bores the way booze attracts writers.

I spend ten hours slicing at a Gordian knot of a book chapter, and then I get cornered by the counterman at Starbucks who went to the Iowa Writers' Workshop and wants to discuss mimetic distance and objective correlatives. At Elaine's people know better. They're writers themselves. They know what to say. They say, "How much was the advance?"

I should have gone into the time-share vacation condominium business with Uncle Ned. But Elaine doesn't think so. She takes writers seriously; she respects me for being one. I suppose she's been wrong about other things in her life, too, but it's great that there's one place where I'm safe from being thought of as, mainly, a failed time-share vacation condominium salesman. And no matter how much money Uncle Ned makes, he won't be able to get a good table at Elaine's—unless he buys the movie rights to my book.

Venice vs. Vegas

(2000)

Las Vegas is one of the most peculiar cities in the world but apparently that's not enough. Las Vegas has decided to become all the world's other peculiar cities, too.

The gambling capital already has Paris Las Vegas and New York New York. In the Nevada version of the City of Lights, waiters never mock you for ordering in the local lingo. If something smells like a smoldering Doberman, you can safely call the fire department; it's not an existentialist smoking a Gauloise. And at New York New York you experience a wonderful, heartwarming phenomenon that the native Gothamite will never know: parking.

So far so good with the urban impersonators on the Strip. Although one might prefer that the cities chosen were cities that really needed replacing, not to mention roulette and girlie shows. I suggest Dayton Ohio Las Vegas and Tehran Tehran.

But now there's something much more ambitious in the middle of the desert—Venice. A fellow named Sheldon Adelson has built The Venetian resort and casino. And according to its brochure, when Adelson announced his plans for The Venetian, he said, "We're not going to build a 'faux' Venice. We're going to build what is essentially the *real* Venice."

Anyone who can make a bagel and a lot of noise can create a convincing New York. And Paris as we know it today is mostly a recent fabrication. It's the product of urban renewal in the 1870s when the French government undertook an innovative program of slum clearance by killing all the members of the Paris Commune. But Venice is another matter—heir to Byzantium, progenitor of Marco Polo, patron of Titian, and inspiration to Lord Byron, who

> *Look'd to the wingèd Lion's marble piles,*
> *Where Venice sate in state, throned on her hundred isles!*
>
> —Childe Harold's Pilgrimage *Canto IV, stanza I*

And they should get that wingèd lion treated, because marble piles sound very painful.

Anyway, there is a mystery to Venice, a soul, an essence—quite a strong essence on a hot August day when the tide is low in the Adriatic. Phew!

When I met Sheldon Adelson at The Venetian I told him, "You didn't get the smell right."

"Can't do everything," he said. Although he certainly has tried. Pulling into the Ducal Palace's driveway, you can see St. Mark's Square, the clock tower with its clockwork Moors, the twin columns topped by St. Theodore and the wingèd lion of St. Mark that needs Preparation H, the Campanile, the Sansoviniana Library, the Ca' d'Oro palace, the Bridge of Sighs, and the Rialto. This is a lot more than you can see from the original Ducal Palace's driveway, especially since it doesn't have one.

Considering the desiccated landscape around Las Vegas, a city with an average rainfall of 4.2 inches a year, I would have thought Sheldon Adelson faced a major obstacle to building "the *real* Venice." After all, what was the main physical feature causing Venice to be Venice? Barbarians, as it turns out. Venice is built on a mud bank in the middle of a lagoon and is up to its Venetian blinds in water—because of barbarians. Attila the Hun chased the Italians out there in AD 453. So Sheldon Adelson was in luck. Las Vegas is filled with barbarians, particularly the kind who wear black socks and sandals and T-shirts and shorts to restaurants at night and leave their baseball caps on during dinner.

What is it with Americans? America's malls are full of clothing stores. America does almost nothing but shop. Then why are Americans dressed like my three-year-old daughter when she's allowed to choose her own clothes? Except Americans are much fatter. Italians don't look like this. You don't catch Italians going into the Basilica di San Marco in flip-flops and a halter top with extra butt hanging out of their Speedos. But I digress. Venice *vs.* The Venetian. Is Venice as romantic as I remember it being, after nine Bellinis at Harry's Bar? Will video poker ever inspire a novella by Thomas Mann? Would it be easier to read than other Thomas Mann stuff?

Now some people might think that Venice *vs.* The Venetian would be no contest. After all, Venice is the most romantic city on earth. I remember when I was first married—an evening in one of those beautiful mahogany *motoscafo* water taxis, coming back from Harry's with my bride to the Excelsior Hotel on Lido Beach . . .

It might have been a heck of a night if I hadn't had nine Bellinis and wound up hanging over the gunwale.

Then there's the matter of taking one's wife to Venice at all. Wives *will* want one of those Murano glass chandeliers that's the size of a sailing dinghy even though our dining room ceiling is less than eight feet high, and this would leave all the handblown dangling glass chandelier stuff dragging in the butter dish.

Plus there's the matter of getting a chandelier into the overhead bin on the return flight. Furthermore, Murano chandeliers cost as much as . . . as much as the water-taxi fare from where the autostrade runs out of dry land to the dock at the Gritti Palace Hotel.

That's where my wife and I stayed three years later when we *drove* to Venice (we weren't thinking that out) with our toddler daughter. And let's not talk about what the Gritti Palace costs. A phone number. That's in dollars. The trail of zeros from the Italian lire hotel bill spilled off one receipt page and filled two others.

However, we did have a good time, even though there is practically nowhere in Venice that you can push a stroller without going into the drink or carrying it up and down the stairs on those cute little bridges, Venice being woefully behindhand in Americans with Disabilities Act compliance.

And you can't take the toddler out of the stroller because Italians are too nonchalant—or too short on tort lawyers—to put guardrails along the canals. Also, the balusters on the cute little bridges are spaced so far apart that toddlers are tempted to run a quarterback draw even on fourth down and ten. The one time we did let go of Muffin's hand, in the middle of St. Mark's Square, a Japanese tourist handed the child an open bag of bird feed, and ten thousand filthy pigeons reenacted the climactic ten minutes of Alfred Hitchcock's *The Birds* on our baby daughter's head. Don't order squab in Venice—or, come to think of it, for God's sake, *do*.

Las Vegas was a very different experience. For one thing, I was alone. And I had a good-sized wad of cash—a financial windfall resulting from my wife's failure to buy a Murano chandelier. (Hint to husbands wishing to avoid chandelier purchases: When you go to the Murano glass shops take a two-year-old. And turn her loose. This is expensive, but not as expensive as the chandelier. Your wife won't have time to buy anything anyway because all three of you are going to get the bum's rush from every glass shop on the island.)

But is The Venetian "essentially the *real* Venice"? For a Venice that's on the wrong continent, in the middle of a dust bowl, and was built last year, The Venetian is surprisingly authentic. The Campanile, for instance, is fake, but so's the one in really real Venice. The original Campanile, completed in 1173, collapsed in a heap in 1902, and a replica was constructed in its place.

The Venetian's architectural unity is marred by a large, ugly, modern parking garage. Ditto Venice's. The Autorimessa Comunale is on the Piazza Roma, and getting a space in it is more of a crap shoot than anything in Las Vegas. Then there's Giorgio Armani, Dolce & Gabbana, Donna Karan, and Calvin Klein. Are these brands for sale along the Grand Canal in Venice or along the Grand Canal in The Venetian? Both. Plus The Venetian's Grand Canal is not only indoors, it's on the second floor. I'd like to see Venice's famed Renaissance architect Jacopo Sansovino pull that off. Not that I'd let him try. When Sansovino was building his namesake Libreria Sansoviniana in 1545, the roof fell in and Sansovino went to prison for a while. Nevada has too many tort lawyers for Sheldon Adelson to let something like that happen. And Adelson's Libreria Sansoviniana is not, like Sansovino's, filled with musty old books that you aren't allowed to touch. It contains Madame Tussauds Celebrity Encounter. You aren't allowed to touch things there either, but who'd want to touch a wax Wayne Newton?

However, back to the Grand Canal. The gondolas don't actually go anyplace in the indoor version, just back and forth. But they don't actually go anyplace in the outdoor version—just around in circles until your wallet is empty and your head is ringing with a pidgin English rendition of "That's Amore." And the American tourists in the Las Vegas gondolas look less uncomfortable than the American tourists in the Venice gondolas because, in Las Vegas, the gondolier isn't some sneering foreigner in suspiciously tight pants; he's a nice out-of-work actor or musician who feels just as dumb in the gondola as you do. Furthermore, the water in the Las Vegas Grand Canal is clean, chlorinated, and shallow. And if you do fall in, so what? There are enough coins on the bottom to play the slots for hours.

Most of the things that aren't authentic about The Venetian's Venice are, like the smell, an improvement. The ten thousand filthy pigeons of St. Mark's Square have been replaced with fifty trained white doves that are released for a brief flyby, on the hour, from 1 to 4 p.m. In the Grand Canal food court you can get—as opposed to authentic octopus in its own ink—pastrami with mustard on rye.

The suite we had at the Gritti Palace was half the size of the single I stayed in at The Venetian. The Venetian's room decor was not equal to the gilded ceiling mirror and ormolu bidet rococo of the Gritti, but I didn't mind. And I would have minded even less if I'd had, as we did in Italy, a two-year-old girl along. The walls of our rooms at the Gritti were covered with paintings of the very naked mythological type. "Where their clothes go, Daddy? What's that? What's that? What's *that*?" And the Las Vegas Rialto Bridge has—bless those tort lawyers again—metal bars between the balusters to keep toddlers from getting a first down in the clean, chlorinated lagoon.

Las Vegas gambling is a terribly vulgar affair, of course. I certainly thought so after losing all my Murano savings at blackjack. But maybe some better-bred, more white-shoe sort of games of chance could be developed to suit the refined taste of those who appreciate nine Bellinis at Harry's Bar.

Sending the children to Brown and betting that they don't become communists is a possibility, as is marrying chorus girls without getting prenuptial agreements.

And the entertainment at The Venetian C2K nightclub wasn't very good. A "tribute show" featured some guy who did pop music impressions, including all the stages of the Elvis career. But it could have been worse. An Italian doing impressions might have run through all the popes.

So our next European vacation is going to be spent in the Mojave. And yet . . . and yet . . . there's something about the damp, smelly, expensive Venice of old. Maybe it's the gleam in my wife's eye (although I suspect that's the Murano chandelier), or maybe it's the thought of what Shakespeare's *The Merchant of Las Vegas* would be like.

Act I, Scene III

SHYLOCK TO ANTONIO: If you repay me not on such a day,
In such a place, such sum or sums as are
Express'd in the condition, let the forfeit
Be nominated for an equal pound
Of your fair flesh. . . .

Enter "Porsche," scantily dressed.

A *pound* of flesh? Here's *a hundred and sixteen pounds!*
With a pair of D-cups! And get a load of these gams!

Talking Points for a Discussion Between My Wife and Me About Whether to Spend Our Next Vacation in Venice or Las Vegas

VEGAS	vs. VENICE
GONDOLIERS	
Wear authentic straw hats	Wear leather jackets and talk on cell phones
SEAT BELTS IN GONDOLAS?	
Yes	*Scusi?*
TORT LAWYERS	
Too many	Not enough
ELVIS IMPRESSIONS	
Too many	Not enough
WAX WAYNE NEWTONS	
Too many	Not enough
BRIDGE OF SIGHS	
Connects shopping mall with parking garage	Provides Byron's view of wingèd lion with painful itch
RODEO IN TOWN?	
Yippie-ki-yay!	No, but a big roundup was under way with police corralling Nigerian hawkers of knockoff Prada bags
"KOOKED CLUMS IN FRIED PAN" ON MENU?	
No	*Si, buono!*
KEY LITERARY WORK	
Script for *Viva Las Vegas* — asks existential question, "Who was Elvis impersonating?"	*Across the River and Into the Trees*—portrait of the artist when he's over the hill and into the Bellinis
KEY LITERARY WORK YET TO BE WRITTEN	
Death in Las Vegas — late-in-life Thomas Mann attempts a second career as a stand-up comic at the Dunes	*Fear and Loathing in Venice*—machine-gun-toting carabinieri make short work of Raoul Duke and his Samoan attorney
DRAW ON 16 IF DEALER HAS FACE CARD SHOWING?	
Don't know	*Non capisco*

Blind (Drunk) Wine Tasting, with Christopher Buckley

(2001)

A wide variety of wines were sampled, ranging from the reputedly splendid to the allegedly pitiful. Selection of the better stuff was done by V, proprietor of a quietly chic potables emporium in Washington, D.C. Lesser plonk was chosen on the basis of weird names and ugly labels. Additional expertise came from the pages of Hugh Johnson's *Pocket Encyclopedia of Wine,* 1999 edition. This book was chosen because it is wide-ranging, authoritative, concise, and the only wine guide for sale at the local card and gift shop.

The blind tasting was conducted in two rounds. The first commenced at 3:45 p.m., with both participants well lunched and purely uninebriated. The second round began at . . . well, no one remembered to consult the time, but it was much later, after all of the No. 5 and most of the No. 7, described below, had been consumed.

There was no spitting into little cups. A hefty gulp of every wine was taken and then some in many cases. Palates were cleansed with bites of liver pâté and puffs on Montecristos.

Christopher (or perhaps it was I) claims to recall—from some comparative lit class taken a generation ago—that when the Babylonian gods sat in assembly they thought it incumbent upon themselves to debate each judgment twice—once sober and once blitzed. A good idea, and never better than when judging wine.

We were taking notes. The tasting comments are presented verbatim—more or less, since the notes begin to become illegible even before the No. 7 Lynch-Moussas is reached in the first round. Here's what I have been able to decipher.

1. Los Vascos

   Les Domaines Barons de Rothschild (*Lafite*)
   Cabernet Sauvignon, 1997
   Chile, $8.99

V's comments: "A more Californian than Bordeaux taste."

POCKET ENCYCLOPEDIA OF WINE: Two stars (*out of four*); no vintage info. Wines of Los Vascos are "fair but neglect Chile's lovely fruit flavours in favour of firm structures." Of Chilean wine generally: "Its problems . . . above all [are] old wooden vats."

Sober Tasting

C.B. (*whose wife once took a wine-tasting course, sloshes wine around, holds it up to light, and explains that if the wine sticks to the side of the glass it has "legs"*)

P.J. (*looks skeptical*)

C.B. Good legs, jejune nose, almost flippant. Acidic in a bad way.

P.J. What the man said.

C.B. Nicotine bitterness; deep, almost asphalty finish.

P.J. Bark mulch undertones.

Drunk Tasting

P.J. Bland, sweet-smelling, not evil.

C.B. But pretty evil.

P.J. Blandly evil.

C.B. Box wine or Livingston Cellars.

P.J. Box.

Conclusion (after labels had been revealed): Old wooden vats.

2. Livingston Cellars

"Burgundy" (no vintage)
Modesto, California, $3.99

V: "It's made by Gallo. They took their name off."

PEW: E&J Gallo, one to two stars. Livingston not rated separately. "Having mastered the world of commodity wines (*with eponymously labeled 'Hearty Burgundy,' 'Pink Chablis,' etc.*) . . . is now unleashing a blizzard of regional varietals."

Sober Tasting

C.B. No legs, no nose.

P.J. No tits.

C.B. Tutti-frutti (*he spits it out*).

P.J. (*who does not spit it out*) Yuck.

Drunk Tasting

C.B. Really bad.

P.J. A new flavor of candy that Lifesaver decided not to market.

C.B. Flunks the "stuck with boring relatives" test. Flunks the "altar boy communion wine" test. That is, flunks the "time when you'll drink anything" test. I'm not sure it would be transubstantiated if consecrated.

P.J. My guess is Skouras.

C.B. Really *Greek,* or Livingston, or box wine. It's exotically bad.

Conclusion: When the varietal blizzard strikes, don't duck into a wine bar.

3. Codice

Rioja, 1997
Spain, $7.49

V: "Bordeaux method with Tempranillo grape. A bit lighter, tarter than California wines. Wood flavor, rusticity."

PEW: "Spain and Portugal joined the EU (*and, as far as most of their wine is concerned, the twentieth century*) only thirteen years ago."

Sober Tasting

C.B. Okay legs, chlorine nose.

P.J. YMCA pool.

C.B. Better than it tastes.

P.J. Huh?

C.B. Daring to be really bad, but not quite managing.

Drunk Tasting

P.J. Fruity smell.

C.B. If fruit were a medicine.

P.J. Drinkable.

C.B. Acceptable, complex. Ariel or Livingston Cellar.

P.J. (*who, not long ago, had been to Spain, where he swilled Rioja and was thus cheating*) Codice.

Conclusion: CB's mistaking Codice for Ariel dealcoholized wine—a subconscious plea for the Twelve-Step Program?

4. Carruades de Lafite

Pauillac, 1996
Bordeaux, $61.99

V: "Youthful Bordeaux. Flavors of vanilla from oak. To drink or to age." Suggests serving with steak.

PEW: The second wine of the four-star Lafite-Rothschild. Not rated separately. The '96 is a recommended vintage. Of Pauillac generally: "Very varied in style."

Sober Tasting

C.B. No legs.

P.J. (*who has a slight cold*) Nose is subtly bad.

C.B. Ugly nose. Chalky complexion . . . You know this trick about wine tasting? If you're at a loss, describe someone who's in the room.

P.J. I'll have you know that this nose has been broken three times. Twice in fistfights.

C.B. Manly nose.

P.J. And once in a riding accident.

C.B. Okay, okay, I'm sorry.

P.J. Well, actually, it was the pony at the church carnival.

C.B. Let's have a drink. (*They do.*) Subtly good.

P.J. Tastes okay. Kind of stinks.

Drunk Tasting

P.J. Smells too sweet, tastes too bitter.

C.B. Cloying nose, mildly annoying taste. It's getting worse.

P.J. Awful.

C.B. Skouras?

P.J. Skouras.

Conclusion: As for serving it with steak—Philly cheese steak comes to mind.

5. Château Cheval Blanc

Saint-Emilion Grand Cru, 1989
Bordeaux, $299.99 (*magnum*)

V: "Made with the Cabernet Franc grape, as were the great nineteenth-century Bordeaux. An exceptional vintage year. Violets with cassis. Well-ripened, lots of structure. Leathery, woody, rich, length in palate."

PEW: Four stars (*indicating "grand, prestigious, expensive"*). "Intensely vigorous and perfumed . . . For many the first choice in Bordeaux."

Sober Tasting

C.B. Has legs. Nose is (*smiles*) whew! Licorice, tar.
P.J. Tar?
C.B. Wow, is that complex! Don't quote me. Is it the Big Boy?
P.J. We'll have to drink several glasses to be sure.
C.B. P.F.G.
P.J. Is that a technical term?
C.B. Pretty f—ing good.
P.J. It's the Big Boy.
C.B. Definitely the Big Boy.

Drunk Tasting

None was left.

Conclusion: The English Huswife, published in 1648, says, "The wines that are made in Burdeaux are . . . the most full gadge and sound Wines." Mr. Buckley and Mr. O'Rourke think like the English Huswife and, by this stage, spell like her too.

6. Skouras

"Mediterranean Red" (no vintage)
Peloponnese, Greece, $5.99

V: "The American importer designed his own label. He drew a sketch of sailboats and sent it to Greece. The printed labels came back with pictures of kites on them."
PEW: Two to three stars, Mediterranean Red not rated separately. Of the Peloponnese generally: "Vines mostly used for currants."

Sober Tasting

C.B. Sudsy legs.
P.J. Smells too pleasant.
C.B. Tastes very fruity. Way fruity. Juicy Fruit.
P.J. Château Wrigley.
C.B. Inviting you home. Almost playful.
P.J. You're cut off.

Drunk Tasting

C.B. Sweet. Terrible.
P.J. Creepy.
C.B. Livingston Cellars.
P.J. Don't know, don't care.

Conclusion: Be especially wary of Greeks bearing gifts of wine.

7. Château Lynch-Moussas

Pauillac, 1996
Bordeaux, $29.99

V: "Good vintage, full-ripened. Deep, rich, passionate flavor."
PEW: Two stars; '96 recommended vintage. A fifth growth but "making serious wine."

Sober Tasting

P.J. (*drinking deeply*) Either real good . . . or not.
C.B. Thick, almost Bulgarian legs. Pug nose. (*He, too, drinks deeply.*) And yet, and yet . . . not the Big Boy, but a Lady-in-Waiting.
P.J. A little sharp, a little bitter.
C.B. A little pipsqueaky.

Drunk Tasting

C.B. Fine, dignified nose. I like it a lot. It's grown, blossomed, since last time.
P.J. (*at that stage when he suddenly thinks he can talk wine talk—and probably Chinese*) Perfumy. Big. Tannin. A game wine, but too young.
BOTH (*more or less in unison*) Definitely Carruades. Unless it's Lynch-Moussas.

Conclusion: Buy some.

8. Frog's Leap

Cabernet Sauvignon, 1996
Napa Valley, $29.99

V: "Rich, with structure and complexity, but not at top of California level. Not overly weighty."
PEW: Two to three stars; '96 a recommended vintage. "Small winery, charming as its name (and T-shirts)."

Sober Tasting

C.B. Extremely leggy. Ghastly nose. (*He drinks.*) Upchucky.

P.J. No flavor at all and yet it tastes bad.

C.B. Wine I'd serve to houseguests I was trying to get rid of.

Drunk Tasting

P.J. Actually, I think it has a better nose than number 7. (*He stubs out his Montecristo in the pâté plate.*) But shrieks of raw youth.

C.B. Probably Lynch-Moussas.

Conclusion: The only bad wine that got markedly better as C.B. and P.J. got markedly stewed. Consider this when serving those houseguests—who are probably wearing Frog's Leap T-shirts.

9. Meerlust Merlot

Stellenbosch, 1995
South Africa, $19.99

V: "Acidic in a good way."

PEW: Three stars. "South Africa is the seventh-largest wine producer in the world—but as a consumer remains a mainly beer-drinking nation."

Sober Tasting

C.B. Slimy legs.

P.J. A lot like number 8.

C.B. Forceful nose. Bad in a new way. Slatternly.

P.J. I disagree. Bad without dirty thrills or novelty.

Drunk Tasting

C.B. Awful. Dignified nose. Taste a nasty surprise.

P.J. Eeeeeuw. God! Harsh. South African?

C.B. Let's hope it's the Ariel.

Conclusion: Mainly a beer-drinking nation.

10. Manischewitz

Concord Grape (*no vintage*)
Naples, New York, $3.49

V: "No comment."

PEW: Not rated. Concord grape generally used for "mostly grape juice and jelly . . . strong 'foxy' flavour, off-putting to non-initiates."

Sober Tasting

C.B. (*recoils*)
P.J. Really, really awful. Explains why Jewish people don't drink much.
C.B. Hypoglycemic finish.

Drunk Tasting

C.B. Manischewitz.
P.J. Manischewitz. (*Bottle is poured down sink.*)

Conclusion: Possibly all right with peanut butter.

11. Ariel

Dealcoholized Cabernet Sauvignon, 1997
Napa Valley, 1997

V: (*Didn't know what to say.*)
PEW: Doesn't say anything.

Sober Tasting

C.B. Chocolate nose.
P.J. Chocolate-covered oak, with gym shoes.
C.B. A soupçon of gym shoe.
P.J. Odd flavor, completely different from, and even worse than, the "bouquet."
C.B. Sweet and sour doggy bed. Paint.
BOTH Livingston Cellars.

Drunk Tasting

P.J. Time to hose out the kennels.
C.B. Awful. Awful.
BOTH Ariel!

Conclusion: The theory that alcohol is what makes booze taste bad is hereby exploded.

12. Franzia "Mountain Burgundy"

(*no vintage*)
Ripon, California, $9.99 for 5-liter box. (Price per 750 cl is $1.50—cheaper than some water.)

V: (*winced*)
PEW: One star, "Mountain Burgundy" not rated separately. "Penny-saver wines."

Sober Tasting

C.B. I'm having trouble with this nose.
P.J. Mine's been broken three—
C.B. You said that.
P.J. Sorry.
C.B. Aggressively unpleasant.
P.J. I *said* I was sorry.
C.B. The wine.
P.J. Oh, come on. Tastes okay. Pretty good cheap-drunk material.
C.B. Sangria material.

Drunk Tasting

C.B. Smells bad.
P.J. Tastes worse.
BOTH Box wine.
P.J. (*peeking*) It's the most popular wine in America.
C.B. No.
P.J. Says so right on the box.

Conclusion: Avoid the sangria.

13. Rosemount Estate

Cabernet Sauvignon, 1997
Perth, Australia, $9.99

V: "User-friendly. Good price. A riper, sweeter style of Cab, more Californian or New World."

PEW: Two to three stars; no vintage information; Cab S not rated separately. "Australian ideas and names are on all wine-lovers' lips . . . Even growers in the south of France listen carefully to Australian winemakers."

Sober Tasting

C.B. Good legs.
P.J. Oh, cut that out.
C.B. Ambiguous nose.
P.J. The kind of nose shared by both good and bad wines.
C.B. Uh, yes.
P.J. Kind of winey-smelling.
C.B. Lots of tannin.
P.J. Bitter.
C.B. Shanghai Tang.

P.J. Not very good, but let's drink some more of it.
C.B. Headachey finish.

Drunk Tasting

C.B. Promises more than it can deliver.
P.J. Sort of loud and upside down.
BOTH Australian.

Conclusion: Loud, upside down.

It was Mr. Buckley and Mr. O'Rourke's fondest hope that, if they got drunk enough, wine would cease to be a qualitative matter and become a quantitative issue. They aspired to stifle wine snobbery and reduce all tiresome oenophilic queries to the basic question: "Is there more?" They failed. In fact, drinking seemed to sharpen their critical skills. The bad wines got mostly worse as the bacchanal wore on. And, more's the pity, so did the good ones. Messieurs Buckley and O'Rourke both felt just terrible the next day and were forced to admit to the wisdom of their friend V, who had disparaged the entire idea of the Blind (Drunk) Wine Tasting. "Wine," said V, "is to enhance food, enliven the mind, lubricate conversation, and enrich life. If you do all that, drunkenness will come naturally. And anyway, for getting drunk, vodka is better."

The Memoir

(2001)

After years of effort in the author trade, I discover an ideal topic, an inexhaustible subject of discourse, a literary inspiration—me. I'll write a memoir. I don't know why I didn't think of this ages ago. It will be liberating to sit down at the typewriter and just be myself, as opposed to being, say, Anne Rice, which I don't have the clothes for.

Even though my memoir is still in the idea stage, I'm full of enthusiasm. I'll give the secret of my success—the success I plan to have as a memoir writer. As far as I can tell, the secret is thinking about myself all the time. No doubt my memoir will be inspirational, inspiring others to think about themselves all the time. They'll see the meaning in their lives—they've been meaning to write a memoir, too.

So what if it's a crowded field? My memoir will stand out. It will show readers a side of life they little guessed at, the side with the writer sitting in his boxer shorts surrounded by six empty coffee cups and three full ashtrays playing Go Fish with the dog.

Maybe readers *had* guessed at that. But I'm going to recount my personal struggles, such as having to come up with things to write about all the time. I've spent decades looking for stories that would interest other people. I've surmounted enormous obstacles—thinking about other people, just for instance.

But enough about them. This isn't going to be a mere self-help book. This is the story of how one young man grew up to be . . . a lot older. That is probably the most serious issue I need to work through in my memoir. The issue being that I haven't really done much. But I don't feel this should stand in my way. O. J. Simpson wrote a memoir, and the jury said he didn't do anything at all.

There's also a lot of anger I need to deal with. I'm angry at my parents. For memoir purposes, they weren't nearly poor enough. They weren't rich either. And they failed miserably at leading colorful lives. My mother did belong to Kappa Kappa Gamma, which is a secret society, I guess. And my father was a veteran of the Pacific war, but the only casualty in his battalion was one fellow crushed by a palm tree. Furthermore, we lived in Toledo, Ohio. I suppose I could write a comic memoir. But in today's society there are some things you just don't make fun of, and chief among these is yourself.

My parents also neglected to abuse me. They're gone now, alas. (Downside: no publicity-building estrangement when memoir is published, to be followed by tearful reconciliation on *Oprah*. Upside: I'm an Adult Child of the Deceased.) I've thought about asking my wife's parents to abuse me, but it seems too little, too late. I did have a stepfather who drank.

Perhaps I'll keep the section on my childhood brief, just emphasize that I'm a survivor. That's what's unique about me, and there are six billion people in the world who know how unique I feel. This should guarantee excellent sales. And—here comes that literary inspiration again—memoirs do sell. Readers want to know what real people really did and really felt. What a shame that the writing geniuses of the nineteenth century wasted their time making things up. We could have had Jane Austen Reality Prose: *Got up. Wrote. Went out. Came back. Wrote some more. Vicarage still drafty.*

Modern book buyers have become too sophisticated for imaginary romance and drama. They want facts: Roswell, New Mexico; the missile that shot down TWA flight 800; the Republican majority in the Florida popular vote. Unfortunately, I don't have many facts like that, but I do have some terrific celebrity gossip. I've read all their memoirs.

I also know about some awful things my friends have done. I've noticed, while memoir reading, that one of the main points of the genre is ratting on your pals. I was going to gather that material together and commit it to paper. Then I realized that other memoir writers, as a class, seem to have very few friends who weigh 200 pounds and own shotguns.

Probably confession is a safer route. I've done all kinds of loathsome deeds myself and am perfectly willing to admit them, if it sells books. But thumbing through my memoir collection, I noticed another thing. Good memoir writers only confess to certain of the more glamorous sins—drastic sexual escapades, head-to-toe drug abuse, bold felonies after the statutes of limitation have run out. Nobody confesses to things that just make him look like a jerk-o. Nobody admits he got up at 4 a.m. with a throbbing head after five hours of listening to the kid's pet squeaking in the exercise wheel and drowned the gerbil in the toilet. Most of my transgressions fall into this category and will need to be excised. I don't want to get caught writing one of those "unauthorized autobiographies."

This brings me to the other little problem I'm having with the story of my life, which is remembering it. There were the 1960s. I recall they started out well. Then there were the 1970s. I recall they ended badly. In between, frankly, I am missing a few candles on the cake. Also there were the 1950s, when nothing memorable happened, and the 1980s, when everything memorable was happening to somebody else. And the 1990s went by in a blur. But, no worries, I've been keeping a diary: *Got up. Wrote. Went out. Came back. Wrote some more. Drowned the gerbil.*

Maybe I can make up for my lack of reminiscences by inserting various vivid fantasies I've had. But this is cheating on the memoir form, since I'm admitting that those things—the *New York Review of Books* swimsuit issue, for example—never happened.

Or perhaps I should go back to all those challenges I've faced. I've had to endure enormous prejudice. True, since I'm a middle-aged white male Republican, the enormous prejudice came from me. But I still had to endure it. This is one reason that learning to love myself was another huge challenge. But I've overcome that too. Although, now that I'm completely self-infatuated, I keep waiting for me to give myself a raise. It's been a bitter disappointment.

Thank goodness. Bitter disappointments are crucial to memoirs. Thinking of something to write in this memoir has been a bitter disappointment so far. That means I can write about not being able to write. Should be good for a chapter, if I can make it sound bitter enough.

Wait. I'm forgetting spiritual transformation. I've been touched by an angel—and a big one, too, all covered in glitter. It got me right in the forehead three months ago, when the dog knocked over the Christmas tree.

And I have a good title: *My Excuse for Living*. That should count for something.

Anyway, I'm not daunted. The memoir is the great literature of the current era. All that we ask of art, the memoir provides. Beauty is truth, truth beauty, and if we can get a beauty to tell the truth, then Kathryn Harrison's *The Kiss* is all ye need to know. Art justifies God's ways to man like *The Art of the Comeback* does. God is going to fry Donald Trump in hell, and He is perfectly justified. As with all art, the memoir holds a mirror up to life, and if there are some lines of cocaine on that mirror, so much the better. Out of chaos the memoir brings order—a huge order from a major bookstore chain, it is to be hoped. The memoir is nature's handmaiden and also nature's butt boy, bagman, and patsy if *Behind the Oval Office* by Dick Morris is anything to go by. The memoir exists on its own terms, art for art's sake, if you happen to be named Arthur—vide *Risk and Redemption: Surviving the Network News Wars* by Arthur Kent. The memoir speaks to us; indeed, it won't shut up. *Vita brevis est, memoir longa.*

And mine is going to be really long. I've got a major book happening here. After a whole ten minutes spent wrestling with my muse, I've made a vital creative breakthrough. I now know how to give my memoir the moral, intellectual, and aesthetic impact that the works of Shakespeare, Goethe, Dostoyevsky had on previous generations. As with all insights of true originality, it's very simple. It's called lying.

Excuses for Republicans

(2000)

Republicans are always short on excuses for who they are and what they do. So I've drawn up a list of excuses for Republicans. It can be printed on a handy three-by-five card and carried in a suit pocket or slipped into a golf bag.

I. Five Excuses for Republican Cigar Smoking

1. I can identify my clothes by smell. That way, when I'm getting dressed in the dark, I don't accidentally wind up in a Norma Kamali skirt and a pair of Joan and David lizard pumps.
2. Cigars produce more secondary smoke. Thus antismoking types are killed off faster.
3. I'd feel like a jerk serving brandy and Freedent.
4. Tell the following anecdote: Years ago I was on the porch of a little inn on the coast of Maine. An old lady was sitting in a rocker. I asked would she mind if I smoked a cigar. "Young man," she said, "when I was a little girl my mother told me never to object when a man lights a cigar. 'Where there are cigars,' said my mother, 'there is money.'"
5. Cigars are the way I relax and unwind. They're better for my health than drinking.

II. Five Excuses for Republican Drinking

1. If I stopped drinking and smoking, it would add ten years to my life. But it would add them to the wrong end.
2. "I was drunk" is a better excuse than "I was stupid."
3. Weddings, funerals, divorces, hostile takeovers, bankruptcies, tax audits, drops in the NASDAQ, weekends with the family—I'm an occasional drinker.

4. When you've been through as many weddings, funerals, divorces, hostile takeovers, bankruptcies, tax audits, drops in the NASDAQ, and weekends with the family as I have, you've got some memories you'd like to lose. Drinking causes memory loss.
5. There's another excuse, but I forget it.

III. Five Eccuses for Republicans Driving Sports Cars That Cost More than Their Fathers Ever Made in a Year

1. A high-powered executive in a high-pressure job may not have time to sail his yacht or fly his plane, but driving a fine performance vehicle is a way for him to relax and unwind twice a day just going back and forth to work. (The president of Porsche once actually said this in an interview. Claim he said it to you.)
2. When I was in high school I promised myself that someday I would get one of these babies. Lots of people abandon their youthful ideals.
3. When a thing gives you honest unalloyed pleasure, you can't think of it in terms of monetary expense.
4. It's really an investment.
5. Anyway, it's cheaper than marrying a woman half my age.

IV. Five Excuses for Republicans Marrying Women Half Their Age

1. Because I can.
2. She loves me for my money—and that's true love.
3. She believes my stories about the sixties.
4. If she tries to screw me in the divorce, I'll fire her dad.
5. She's mellow. She's laid-back. She doesn't care if I smoke, drink, drive like hell, and stay out all night.

V. FIVE EXCUSES FOR EVERYTHING ELSE REPUBLICAN

1. My wife won't let me.
2. I'm in the middle of a terrible divorce.
3. After I gave up smoking and drinking and sold the Porsche and quit running around with women half my age, I had to do *something*.
4. One thing I've learned in all my years of experience—never make excuses.
5. I used to be a Democrat.

Unpublished Introduction to the 25th Anniversary Edition of Hunter S. Thompson's *Fear and Loathing in Las Vagas*

(Unpublished at the Request of My Friend, HST)
(1997)

Not much happens in *Fear and Loathing*. That's the amazing thing about the book. Here is a famously colorful era's finest specimen of the picaresque—a genre that, according to William Rose Benét, "deals sympathetically with the adventures of clever and amusing rogues"—and what gives? The rogues aren't clever. Amusing is not the word for them. They accomplish little roguery. The author shows them no sympathy. And of adventures they really have none. Two men in early middle age visit Las Vegas while intoxicated. They frighten a few people (mostly each other), are rude to bystanders, and astonish a cleaning lady. Two rental cars and several bedrooms and bathrooms are left the worse for wear. A couple of large corporations are cheated of modest sums. As for serious malefaction, there is possession of controlled substances, a (poorly) concealed weapon, possible sexual contact with a woman who may be underage, and a skipped hotel bill. In a century marked by countless unspeakable crimes, we may speak of these, and they don't count.

Fear and Loathing in Las Vegas is a bloodcurdling adventure where no one is murdered, robbed, imprisoned, or hanged. The only hairsbreadth escape is from a speeding ticket and DWI citation. And at the end of the story comes not triumph or tragedy or revenge or contrition but status quo ante like a TV sitcom. But Hunter Thompson is such a genius that it's a thrilling saga. A thrilling saga in which nothing much happens—a fitting example of the picaresque for the Now Generation. One of the things Hunter did in this book was write a coda to, an obituary for, the nonsense of the 1960s.

It's important to recall that in the part of the 1960s known as "The Sixties" nothing much happened.

The war in Vietnam was widely and vigorously protested. And nothing happened, the war went on. Blacks rioted in the slums. Nothing happened, the slums are still there. Mysticism was practiced, psychedelics were ingested, consciousness was everywhere raised. Nothing happened. Hundreds of thousands of people gathered at Woodstock. Nothing whatsoever happened. And we were all freed from sexual prudery and repression. And nothing happened—at least nothing very splendid, though there were plenty of illegitimate children, venereal diseases, and hurt feelings.

We see the protagonists of *Fear and Loathing* in 1971, in the wake of this great generational blow-off, wallowing in the inanity of the times. It would be a masterly period piece if Hunter had decided to go no further. But Hunter is nothing if not a gone cat. Instead, the book is an entire description of all life as complete senseless idiocy.

Good and evil are a ridiculous mess. We hear much about the "vicious," "twisted" "swine" who control American society and who threaten Raoul Duke and his three-hundred-pound Samoan attorney. But the only people we see being vicious or twisted or swinish are that attorney and Duke. Authority is described as nasty and corrupt. And nearly all the ancillary characters in the book, even the hotel clerks, are portrayed as authority figures. Yet these people are largely honest, forbearing, even hospitable. "Let's have lunch!" says one hotel clerk as Raoul Duke absconds.

Threats are, indeed, made to Duke and the attorney, but only by innocents such as the carload of Oklahoma tourists who've had "Shoot! Scag! Blood! Heroin! Rape! Cheap! Communists!" screamed at them. And when we encounter actual "pigs"—as Duke calls law officers—they turn out to be, at worst, bemused. "What the hell's *goin' on* in this country?" a small-town Georgia DA quite reasonably asks when Duke and the attorney tell him narcotics addicts are everywhere, working in pairs and slitting people's throats. And when Duke is apprehended drunk, stoned, and driving at 120 mph, the California highway patrolman is downright kind. And has a sense of humor: "I get the feeling you could use a nap."

There is a terrific loneliness throughout the book. The protagonists are not friends. Duke shows occasional protective impulses toward the attorney. He forgoes an opportunity to electrocute him. The attorney threatens to carve a Z in Duke's forehead. Duke locks the attorney in a bathroom. No explanation is given for these two being together. But neither mentions any other emotional bond. The only romance is when the attorney seduces a runaway who obsessively draws Barbra Streisand and has come to Las Vegas to present her portraits to the star. This, it hardly needs saying, comes to a sad end.

Duke and the attorney profess no moral, religious, or philosophical principles. The attorney makes no statement of conscience except to call Duke a "filthy bastard" for proposing to prostitute the Barbra Streisand artist. And Duke seems actively opposed to belief. He goes so far as to blame the failure of 1960s utopianism on "the desperate assumption that somebody—or at least some *force*—is tending that Light at the end of the tunnel." The only credo in *Fear and Loathing* is freedom in its most reductive and alienated sense, "a gross, physical salute to the fantastic *possibilities* of life in this country."

Hunter gives us a harrowing portrayal of the human condition as absurd. This is anomie writ wide and deep. Compared to *Fear and Loathing in Las Vegas,* Albert Camus's *L'Étranger* is a lame jailhouse whine, and Samuel Beckett's *Waiting for Godot* is a puppet-theater skit about idleness and boredom. Thompson alone captures the—how else to put it?—fear and loathing that are at the root of the contemporary essence.

And he makes us laugh at it. This is something we're unlikely to do during *Waiting for Godot* performances, even if we're as high as Raoul Duke. Hunter takes the darkest questions of ontology, the grimmest epistemological queries, and just by posing them sends us doubled over in fits of risibility, our sides aching from armpit to pelvic girdle, the tops of our legs raw from knee-slapping, and beer spitting out of our noses.

Hunter performs this philosophical legerdemain by creating a pair of empty clowns who seem to have the brains of marmosets but who speak with the mouths of poets. They are utterly insensitive, lawless creatures who are nonetheless agonized by the dilemmas of being and nothingness. It's as if two of the Three Stooges had discovered Søren Kierkegaard and William Butler Yeats.

Then Thompson fills his clowns with drugs. Drugs let us see things differently. Drugs give us new viewpoints. Drugs provide us with alternative perceptions, thousands of alternative perceptions, all of them wrong. Thus we see the futility of relying on the mind when facing the abyss. Contort the mind however we will, it cannot do the job. What's more, drugs are all about the self. Thus we see the futility of ego. Drugs are potent agents of change, but they only change me. They have no effect on the outside world. So there everything is, just the way it's always been, and I'm all changed—like somebody who shows up at a funeral dressed for an orgy. And Thompson fills his clowns with drugs so they can be clowns while also, presumably, being normal (well, more or less normal) men. If you want a truly frightening idea, consider Raoul Duke and the three-hundred-pound Samoan attorney doing all the things they do in *Fear and Loathing* sober.

Hunter Thompson takes two fools, incapacitates them, sends them on a farcical quest after a material manifestation of something—the American

Dream—that has an immaterial existence, and sends them to look in the wrong place besides. After two-hundred-odd pages of perfect and lyrical writing about that "nothing much," which twentieth-century hipsters insisted on thinking was the central fact of reality, the fools are back where they started.

Like all true comedy, *Fear and Loathing in Las Vegas* is a cautionary tale. Live in a universe that stops at the end of your nose, and this is the life you will lead. Lead a life where you believe in nothing, and this is the universe you will live in.

PEACE KILLS

(2004)

Next year we are to bring the soldiers home
For lack of money, and it is all right.
Places they guarded, or kept orderly,
Must guard themselves, and keep themselves orderly.
We want the money for ourselves at home
Instead of working. And this is all right.

It's hard to say who wanted it to happen,
But now it's been decided nobody minds.
The places are a long way off, not here,
Which is all right, and from what we hear
The soldiers there only made trouble happen.
Next year we shall be easier in our minds.

Next year we shall be living in a country
That brought its soldiers home for lack of money.
The statues will be standing in the same
Tree-muffled squares, and look nearly the same.
Our children will not know it's a different country.
All we can hope to leave them now is money.

—Philip Larkin,
"Homage to a Government"
(England, 1969)

Why Americans Hate Foreign Policy

I was in Berlin in November 1989, the weekend the wall opened. The Cold War was over. The ICBMs weren't going to fly. The world wouldn't melt in a fusion fireball or freeze in a nuclear winter. Everybody was happy and relieved. And me, too, although I'm not one of those children of the 1950s who was traumatized by the A-bomb. Getting under a school desk during duck-and-cover was more interesting and less scary than the part of the multiplication table that came after "times seven." Still, the notion that, at any time, the USSR and the USA might blow up the whole world—my neighborhood included—was in the back of my mind. A little mushroom-shaped cloud marred the sunny horizon of my future as an internationally renowned junior high school football player. If *On the Beach* was for real, I'd never get tall enough to date Ava Gardner. What's more, whenever I was apprehended in youthful hijinks, Mutually Assured Destruction failed to happen before Dad got home from work. Then, in the fall of 1962, when I was fifteen, Armageddon really did seem to arrive. I made an earnest plea to my blond, freckled biology-class lab partner (for whom, worshipfully, I had undertaken all frog dissection duties). "The Cuban missile crisis," I said, "means we probably won't live long. Let's *do it* before we die." She demurred. All in all the Cold War was a bad thing.

Twenty-seven years later, wandering through previously sinister Checkpoint Charlie with beer in hand, I felt like a weight had been lifted from my shoulders. I remember thinking just those words: "I feel like a weight has been lifted . . ." A wiser person would have been thinking, "I feel like I took a big dump."

Nastiness was already reaccumulating. I reported on some of it in ex-Soviet Georgia, ex-Yugoslav Yugoslavia, the West Bank, Somalia, and Iraq-ravaged Kuwait. The relatively simple, if costive, process of digesting the Communist bloc was complete. America needed to reconstitute its foreign policy with—so to speak—a proper balance of fruit and fiber. The serious people who ponder these things seriously said the new American foreign policy must include:

- Nation building
- A different approach to national security
- Universal tenets of democracy

This didn't occur to me. Frankly, nothing concerning foreign policy had ever occurred to me. I'd been writing about foreign countries and foreign affairs and foreigners for years. But you can own dogs all your life and not have "dog policy." You have rules, yes—Get off the couch!—and training, sure. We want the dumb creatures to be well behaved and friendly. So we feed foreigners, take care of them, give them treats, and, when absolutely necessary, whack them with a rolled-up newspaper. That was as far as my foreign policy thinking went until the middle 1990s, when I realized America's foreign policy thinking hadn't gone that far.

In the fall of 1996, I traveled to Bosnia to visit a friend whom I'll call Major Tom. Major Tom was in Banja Luka serving with the NATO-led international peacekeeping force IFOR. From 1992 to 1995 Bosnian Serbs had fought Bosnian Croats and Bosnian Muslims in an attempt to split Bosnia into two hostile territories. In 1995 the U.S.-brokered Dayton Agreement ended the war by splitting Bosnia into two hostile territories. The Federation of Bosnia and Herzegovina was run by Croats and Muslims. The Republika Srpska was run by Serbs. IFOR's job was to "implement and monitor the Dayton Agreement." Major Tom's job was to sit in an office where Croat and Muslim residents of Republika Srpska went to report Dayton Agreement violations.

"They come to me," said Major Tom, "and they say, 'The Serbs stole my car.' And I say, 'I'm writing that in my report.' They say, 'The Serbs burned my house.' And I say, 'I'm writing that in my report.' They say, 'The Serbs raped my daughter.' And I say, 'I'm writing that in my report.'"

"Then what happens?" I said.

"I put my report in a file cabinet."

Major Tom had fought in the Gulf War. He'd been deployed to Haiti during the American reinstatement of President Aristide (which preceded the American un-reinstatement). He was on his second tour of duty in Bosnia and would go on to fight in the Iraq war. That night we got drunk.

"Please, no nation building," said Major Tom. "We're the army. We kill people and break things. They didn't teach nation building in infantry school."

Or in journalism school, either. The night before I left to cover the Iraq war I got drunk with another friend, who works in TV news. We were talking about how—as an approach to national security—invading Iraq was . . . different. I'd moved my family from Washington to New Hampshire. My friend was considering getting his family out of New York. "Don't you hope," my friend said, "that all this has been thought through by someone who is smarter than we are?" It is, however, a universal tenet of democracy that no one is.

Americans hate foreign policy. Americans hate foreign policy because Americans hate foreigners. Americans hate foreigners because Americans *are* foreigners. We all come from foreign parts, even if we came ten thousand years ago on a land bridge across the Bering Strait. We didn't want anything to do with those Ice Age Siberians, them with the itchy cave bear–pelt underwear and mammoth meat on their breath. We were off to the Pacific Northwest—great salmon fishing, blowout potluck dinners, a whole new life.

America is not "globally conscious" or "multicultural." Americans didn't come to America to be Limey Poofters, Frog Eaters, Bucket Heads, Micks, Spicks, Sheenies, or Wogs. If we'd wanted foreign entanglements, we would have stayed home. Or—in the case of those of us who were shipped to America against our will, as slaves, exiles, or transported prisoners—we would have gone back. Events in Liberia and the type of American who lives in Paris tell us what to think of that.

Being foreigners ourselves, we Americans know what foreigners are up to with their foreign policy—their venomous convents, lying alliances, greedy agreements, and trick-or-treaties. America is not a wily, sneaky nation. We don't think that way. We don't think much at all, thank God. Start thinking and pretty soon you get ideas, and then you get idealism, and the next thing you know you've got ideology, with millions dead in concentration camps and gulags. A fundamental American question is "What's the big idea?"

Americans would like to ignore foreign policy. Our previous attempts at isolationism were successful. Unfortunately, they were successful for Hitler's Germany and Tojo's Japan. Evil is an outreach program. A solitary bad person sitting alone, harboring genocidal thoughts, and wishing he ruled the world is not a problem unless he lives next to us in the trailer park. In the big geopolitical trailer park that is the world today, he does.

America has to act. But, when America acts, other nations accuse us of being "hegemonistic," of engaging in "unilateralism," of behaving as if we're the only nation on earth that counts.

We are. Russia used to be a superpower but resigned "to spend more time with the family." China is supposed to be mighty, but the Chinese leadership quakes when a couple of hundred Falun Gong members do tai chi for Jesus. The European Union looks impressive on paper, with a greater population and a larger economy than America's. But the military spending of Britain, France, Germany, and Italy combined does not equal one third of the U.S. defense budget. The United States spends more on defense than the aforementioned countries—plus Russia plus China plus the next six top defense-spending nations. Any multilateral military or diplomatic effort that includes the United States is a crew team with Arnold Schwarzenegger as coxswain and Nadia Comaneci on the oars. When other countries demand a role in the exercise of global power, America can ask another fundamental American question: "You and what army?"

Americans find foreign policy confusing. We are perplexed by the subtle tactics and complex strategies of the Great Game. America's great game is pulling the levers on the slot machines in Las Vegas. We can't figure out what the goal of American foreign policy is supposed to be.

The goal of American tax policy is avoiding taxes. The goal of American health policy is HMO profits. The goal of American environmental policy is to clean up the environment, clearing away scruffy caribou and seals so that America's drillers for Arctic oil don't get trampled or slapped with a flipper. But the goal of American foreign policy is to foster international cooperation, protect Americans at home and abroad, promote world peace, eliminate human rights abuses, improve U.S. business and trade opportunities, and stop global warming.

We were going to stop global warming by signing the Kyoto protocol on greenhouse gas emissions. Then we realized the Kyoto protocol was ridiculous and unenforceable and that no one who signed it was even trying to meet the emissions requirements except for some countries from the former Soviet Union. They accidentally quit emitting greenhouse gases because their economies collapsed. However, if we withdraw from diplomatic agreements because they're ridiculous, we'll have to withdraw from every diplomatic agreement, because they're all ridiculous. This will not foster international cooperation. But if we *do* foster international cooperation, we won't be able to protect Americans at home and abroad, because there has been a lot of international cooperation in killing Americans. Attacking internationals won't promote world peace, which we can't have anyway if we're going to eliminate human rights abuses, because there's no peaceful way to get rid of the governments that abuse the rights of people—people who are chained to American gym-shoe-making machinery, dying of gym shoe lung, and getting paid in shoelaces, thereby improving U.S. business and trade opportunities, which result in economic expansion that causes global warming to get worse.

As the nineteenth-century American naval hero Stephen Decatur said in his famous toast: "Our Country! In her intercourse with foreign nations may she always be in the right; but our country, right or wrong, should carry condoms in her purse."

One problem with changing America's foreign policy is that we keep doing it. After the Cold War, President George H. W. Bush managed to engage America—in spite of itself—in the multilateralism of the Gulf War. This left Saddam Hussein exactly where we found him twelve years later. Like other American achievements in multilateralism, it wasn't something we'd care to achieve again. The East Side of midtown Manhattan, where a decent slum once stood, is blighted by the United Nations headquarters. And, in the mountains of the Balkan peninsula, the ghost of Woodrow Wilson wanders Marley-like, dragging his chains and regretting the deeds of his life.

President Bill Clinton dreamed of letting the lion lie down with the lamb chop. Clinton kept International Monetary Fund cash flowing into the ever-criminalizing Russian economy. He ignored Kremlin misbehavior from Boris Yeltsin's shelling of elected representatives in the Duma to Vladimir Putin's airlifting uninvited Russian troops into Kosovo. Clinton compared the Chechnya fighting to the American Civil War (murdered Chechens being on the South Carolina statehouse Confederate-flag-flying side). Clinton called China America's "strategic partner" and paid a nine-day visit to that country, not bothering himself with courtesy calls on America's actual strategic partners, Japan and South Korea. Clinton announced, "We don't support independence for Taiwan," and said of Jiang Zemin, instigator of the assault on democracy protesters in Tiananmen Square, "He has vision."

Anything for peace, that was Clinton's policy. Clinton had special peacemongering envoys in Cyprus, Congo, the Middle East, the Balkans, and flying off to attend secret talks with Marxist guerrillas in Colombia. Clinton made frantic attempts to close an Israeli-Palestinian peace deal. What if the Jews control the Temple Mount and the Arabs control the movie industry? On his last day in office, Clinton was still phoning Sinn Fein leader Gerry Adams. "Love your work, Gerry. Do you ever actually kill people? Or do you just do the spin?"

Clinton was everybody's best friend. Except when he wasn't. He conducted undeclared air wars against Serbia and Iraq and launched missiles at Sudan and Afghanistan. Clinton used the military more often than any previous peacetime American president. He sent armed forces into areas of conflict on an average of once every nine weeks.

Then we elected an administration with adults in it—Colin Powell, Dick Cheney, and Donald Rumsfeld. Gone was the harum-scarum Clinton policymaking apparatus with its frenzied bakeheads piling up midnight pizza boxes in the Old Executive Office Building. They disappeared, along with the clinically insane confidants—vein-popping James Carville, toe-sucking Dick Morris—and the loose haircuts in the West Wing and the furious harridan on the White House third floor.

President George W. Bush's foreign policy was characterized, in early 2001, as "disciplined and consistent" (Condoleezza Rice): "blunt" (the

Washington Post), and "in-your-face" (the Carnegie Endowment for International Peace). Bush began his term with the expulsion of one fourth of the Russian diplomatic corps on grounds of espionage. He snubbed Vladimir Putin by delaying a first summit meeting until June 2001, and then holding it in fashionable Slovenia.

On April 1, 2001, a Chinese fighter jet, harassing a U.S. reconnaissance plane in international airspace, collided with the American aircraft, which was forced to land in Chinese territory. Bush did not regard this as an April Fools' prank. By the end of the month he had gone on *Good Morning America* and said that if China attacked Taiwan, the United States had an obligation to defend it.

"With the full force of American military?" asked Charlie Gibson.

"Whatever it took," said Bush.

The president also brandished American missile defenses at Russia and China. The Russians and Chinese were wroth. The missile shield might or might not stop missiles, but, even unbuilt, it was an effective tool for gathering intelligence on Russian and Chinese foreign policy intentions. We knew how things stood when the town drunk and the town bully strongly suggested that we shouldn't get a new home security system.

In the Middle East, Bush made an attempt to let the Israelis and the Palestinians go at it until David ran out of pebbles and Goliath had been hit on the head so many times that he was voting for Likud. In Northern Ireland, Bush also tried minding his own business. And Bush quit negotiating with North Korea about its atomic weapons for the same reason that you'd quit jawing with a crazy person about the gun he was waving and call 911.

We saw the results of Clinton's emotional, ad hoc, higgledy-piggledy foreign policy. It led to strained relations with Russia and China, increased violence in the Middle East, continued fighting in Africa and Asia, and Serbs killing Albanians. Then we saw the results of Bush's tough, calculated, focused foreign policy—strained relations with Russia and China, increased violence in the Middle East, continued fighting in Africa and Asia, and Albanians killing Serbs. Between the first year of the Clinton administration and the first year of the Bush administration, we went from attack on the World Trade Center to World Trade Center attack.

Further changes could be made to U.S. foreign policy. For a sample of alternative ideas, we can turn to a group of randomly (even haphazardly) chosen, average (not to say dull-normal) Americans: the 2004 Democratic presidential hopefuls. By the time this is read, most of them will be forgotten. With luck, all of them will be. Nonetheless, it's instructive to recall what ten people who offered themselves as potential leaders of the world deemed to be America's foreign policy options.

Incessant activist Al Sharpton pleaded for "a policy of befriending and creating allies around the world." The way Sharpton intended to make friends was by fixing the world's toilets and sinks. "There are 1.7 billion people that need clean water," he said, "almost three billion that need sanitation systems . . . I would train engineers . . . would export people that would help with these things."

Ex–child mayor of Cleveland Dennis Kucinich promised to establish "a cabinet-level Department of Peace." The secretary of peace would do for international understanding what the postmaster general does for mail.

Former one-term senator and erstwhile ambassador to New Zealand Carol Moseley Braun said, "I believe women have a contribution to make . . . we are clever enough to defeat terror without destroying our own liberty . . . we can provide for long-term security by making peace everybody's business." Elect me because women are clever busybodies. This is the "Lucy and Ethel Get an Idea" foreign policy.

Massachusetts's thinner, more sober senator, John Kerry, said that he voted for threatening to use force on Saddam Hussein, but that actually using force was wrong. This is what's known, in the language of diplomacy, as bullshit.

Previous almost–vice president Joe Lieberman indignantly demanded that Bush do somewhat more of what Bush already was doing: "Commit more U.S. troops," create "an Iraqi interim authority," and "work with the Iraqi people and the United Nations." Perhaps Lieberman hadn't gotten over coming *this* close to the office next to the oval one. Perhaps Lieberman was suffering from a delusion that he was part of the current presidential administration. But after 9/11 Americans wanted to kiss the Supreme Court for its 2000 Florida electoral vote decision. Imagine having a Democrat as commander in chief during the War Against Terrorism, with Oprah Winfrey as secretary of defense. Big hug for Mr. Taliban. Republicans are squares, but it's the squares who know how to fly the bombers, launch the missiles, and fire the M-16s. Democrats would still be fumbling with the federally mandated trigger locks.

Onetime governor of insignificant Vermont, Howard Dean, wanted a cold war on terrorism. Dean said that we'd won the Cold War without firing a shot (a statement that doubtless surprised veterans of Korea and Vietnam). Dean said that the reason we'd won the Cold War without firing a shot was because we were able to show the communists "a better ideal." But what is the "better ideal" that we can show the Islamic fundamentalists? Maybe we can tell them, "*Our* president is a born-again. You're religious lunatics—*we're* religious lunatics. America was *founded* by religious lunatics! How about those Salem witch trials? Come to America and you could be Osama bin Ashcroft.

You could get your own state, like Utah, *run* by religious lunatics. You could have an Islamic Fundamentalist Winter Olympics—the Chador Schuss."

Since the gist of Howard Dean's campaign platform was "It Worked in Vermont," he really may have thought that the terrorists should take up snowboarding. On the other hand, the gist of General (very retired) Wesley Clark's campaign platform was "It Worked in Kosovo." Kosovo certainly taught the world a lesson. Wherever there's suffering, injustice, and oppression, America will show up six months late and bomb the country next to where it's happening.

The winner of South Carolina's JFK look-alike contest, John Edwards, and the winner of Florida's Bob Gramm look-alike contest, Bob Gramm, said that America had won the war in Iraq but was losing the peace because Iraq was so unstable. When Iraq was stable it attacked Israel in 1967 and 1973. It attacked Iran. It attacked Kuwait. It gassed the Kurds. It butchered the Shiites. It fostered terrorism in the Middle East. Who wanted a stable Iraq?

And perennial representative of the House of Representatives Dick Gephardt wouldn't talk much about foreign policy. He was concentrating on economic issues, claiming that he'd make the American Dream come true for everyone. Gephardt may have been on to something there. Once people get rich they don't go in much for war making. The shoes are ugly and the uniforms itch. Someday Osama bin Laden will call a member of one of his "sleeper cells"—a person who was planted in the United States years before and told to live like a normal American—and . . .

"Dad, some guy named Ozzy's on the phone."

"Oh, uh, good to hear from you. Of course, of course . . . Rockefeller Center? . . . Next Wednesday? . . . I'd love to, but the kid's got her ballet recital. You miss something like that, they never forget it . . . Thursday's no good. I have to see my mom off on her cruise to Bermuda in the morning. It's Fatima's yoga day. And I've got courtside seats for the Nets . . . Friday we're going to the Hamptons for the weekend . . ."

But how, exactly, did Gephardt plan to make everyone on earth as materialistic, self-indulgent, and overscheduled as Americans? Would Gephardt give foreigners options on hot dot-com stocks? That might have worked during the Clinton years.

As of early 2004 there was one foremost, pressing question in U.S. foreign policy, and America didn't seem to have the answers for postwar Iraq. Then again, what were the questions?

Was there a bad man? And his bad kids? Were they running a bad country? That did bad things? Did they have a lot of oil money to do bad things with? Were they going to do more bad things?

If those were the questions, was the answer "UN-supervised national reconciliation" or "Rapid return to self-rule"?

No. The answer was blow the place to bits.

Critics say we didn't do enough thinking about the problem of postwar Iraq. I say we blew the place to bits—what's the problem?

If there is something we didn't do enough thinking about—something we haven't done enough thinking about for sixty years—it's fascism. The genius of fascism is to turn people into a mob. Baath Party fascism did a good job. Fascism doesn't use only the stick; it uses the carrot as well, albeit in a brutal fashion. There's a lot of being hit over the head with root vegetables involved in fascism. But Hitler would have ended up painting carnival sideshow posters in Bavaria if a mob of Germans hadn't thought they were getting something out of fascism. And how do you plan for a mob? Do you buy *The Martha Stewart Book of Gracious Rioting*?

Americans have been surprised by Iraqi fascism, although we are familiar enough with other evil ideologies. Communism still persists in Cuba, North Korea, and the minds of a million university-type intellectuals. Religious extremism waxes worldwide. But communists do bad things for a purpose. They have a vision of a utopia where everyone shares everything and you give your Lawn Boy to a family in Chad. And religious extremists do bad things for a purpose. They have a vision of a utopia where everyone goes to heaven together. So what if you have to die to get there? You have to die to get to heaven anyway. Fascism, however, is a pointless ideology—the grasp of power for power's sake. The fight against fascism seems like Dad's war, Granddad's war. Fascism should be out-of-date in the purposeful, task-oriented world of today. Never mind Slobodan Milošević, Vladimir Putin, the Palestinian Authority, Somali warlords, China's politburo, the Saudi royal family, murderous Hutu rabble, and Newt Gingrich's career arc.

Fascists do bad things just to be bad. "I'm the baddest dude in Baghdad," Saddam Hussein was saying, "the baddest cat in the Middle East. I'm way bad." This was way stupid. But fascists *are* stupid. Consider Saddam Hussein's weapons of mass destruction. He didn't have any. How stupid does *that* make Saddam? All he had to do was say to UN chief weapons inspector Hans Blix, "Look where you want. Look beneath the couch cushions. Look under my bed. Look in the special spider hole I'm keeping for emergencies." And Saddam Hussein could have gone on dictatoring away until Donald Rumsfeld is elected head of the World Council of Churches.

Instead, we blew the place to bits. And a mess was left behind. But it's a mess without a military to fight aggressive wars; a mess without the facilities to develop dangerous weapons; a mess that cannot systematically kill, torture, and oppress millions of its citizens. It's a mess with a message—don't mess with us.

Saddam Hussein was reduced to the Unabomber, Ted Kaczynski, a nutcase hiding in the sticks. The terrorism his cohorts practice is terrifying, hence its name. Killing innocent people by surprise is not called "A Thousand Points of Light." But as frightening as terrorism is, it's the weapon of losers. When someone detonates a suicide bomb, that person does not have career prospects. And no matter how horrific the terrorist attack, it's conducted by losers. Winners don't need to hijack airplanes. Winners have an air force.

Kosovo

November 1999

America is the winner in the new era of highly moral conflicts—just wars, good wars, wars to end . . . other wars. I covered a couple of these, in Kuwait in 1991 and Somalia in 1993. But I didn't stick around for the aftermaths, and, it will be remembered (especially by Iraqi Shiites of the Basra region), neither did America. It wasn't until the NATO occupation of Kosovo that I got a chance to see what happens when the ancient tradition of invasion is stood on its ear. Contrary to a million years of human instincts, conquest now entails giving rather than taking territory while exploiting the victor's labor and resources to heap booty on the conquered.

The air war against Yugoslavia had been declared a victory. Kosovo was being run by the UN, NATO, and other forces for good. Forces for good and plenty of them—here are some of the more than three hundred well-meaning organizations that were active in Kosovo at the end of 1999: Humanity First, Emergency Corps of the Order of Malta, Center for Mind Body Medicine, Associazione Amici Dei Bambini, Mother Teresa Society, Saudi Joint Relief Committee, American Jewish Joint Distribution Committee, Iranian Relief Committee, Vietnam Veterans of America Foundation, and the World Society for Protection of Animals. So, could Serbs and Albanians now live together peacefully?

A young Albanian and former Kosovo Liberation Army fighter said yes. Well, what he actually said was, "When you hate this much maybe you would kill them all, but we will try to live with them, which shows what kind of people we are."

Something else that showed what kind of people they are was the "NATO" brand bubble gum for sale locally, with bubble gum cards depicting victims of Serb atrocities, KLA martyrs, Albanian refugees, and a cruise missile direct hit on Serbian police headquarters in Pristina.

But the KLA veteran did not look like someone who had been chewing over blood vengeance since his first Halloween. He looked like a slightly bored, faintly irritated member of a tenant committee. Which he was, except that the committee was petitioning the Norwegian army instead of a landlord.

"A sewer line is blocked," said the tenant committee chairwoman. "Heating oil supply is low. We need more garbage containers."

"We will not have everything for everyone," said a beleaguered Norwegian infantry captain.

The captain was in Kosovo Polje, site of the Battle of Kosovo, where the Ottoman Turks threw the Serbs out of Kosovo in the first place, in 1389. Now Albanian Kosovars had done it again—this time by squatting rather than fighting, in a housing complex that used to be 80 percent Serb and had become 80 percent Albanian. The Norwegians were on hand to prevent murder, and also to provide more garbage containers.

"The level of hatred will always exist," said the KLA veteran. "But we are a peaceful nation and we will try to live with them—if the people who did bad things are punished."

"Thank you for controlling the youths who were throwing stones," said the Norwegian captain.

"We try," said the chairwoman.

Battle-hardened combatants beating their swords into complaints about water pressure and their spears into requests to fix the electrical wiring—it was a dream conflict for liberals, a peace-on-earth, goodwill-to-men, Kris Kringle of a military action. Kosovo was the war the war haters loved. Bianca Jagger, Susan Sontag, Barney Frank, House Democratic Whip David Bonior, the late Minnesota senator Paul Wellstone, and various other usually reliable advocates of peace seemed to have been drinking at the VFW Hall and getting "Semper Fi" tattooed on their biceps. "I harbor no second thoughts on the morality of our course," Senator Wellstone said. "My only regret is that our action has been less effective than I would have hoped."

Such a regret, of course, depends upon what was hoped *for*. If we hoped to increase wartime destruction, we were very effective. Normally the victor in a war does most of the damage, but in Kosovo everybody got to destroy things—losers, winners, and neutral nations alike.

The locals explained how to tell the difference between the piles of rubble. When the destruction was general, it was Serbian. Serbs surrounded Albanian villages and shelled them. When the destruction was specific, it was Albanian. Albanians set fire to Serb homes and businesses. And when the destruction was pointless—involving a bridge to nowhere, an empty oil storage tank, an evacuated Serb police headquarters, and the like—it was NATO trying to fight a war without hurting anybody.

However, if we hoped to protect ethnic Albanians, we were, as Senator Wellstone mentioned, less effective. In fact, we were less effective at protecting ethnic Albanians than Slobodan Milošević had been. According to the U.S. State Department, an estimated ten thousand Albanians were killed and 1.5 million were expelled from their homes, most of them *after* the NATO air war began.

On the road from Pec to Istok, in the hills of northwest Kosovo, every single building had been destroyed. Beside the highway, in a gravel patch leveled by a bulldozer, were the graves of nineteen members of the Imeraj family: men, women, and children. The tombs were covered by a type of floral arrangement particular to Kosovo. This is a thin, yardwide disk of foliage with brightly colored blossoms sprinkled on the green background and the whole wrapped tightly in cellophane. Muslim Albanians naturally have no Yuletide decorating tradition and wouldn't understand the horrible free association caused in an American mind—"And to all a good night!"—by these mementos of the Santa War, these giant Christmas cookies of death.

We failed to protect Albanians from Serbs, but we were making up for it by protecting Serbs from Albanians, even though it was Serb persecution of Albanians that caused us to come to Kosovo, thereby giving Albanians an opportunity to persecute Serbs.

In a background briefing a British colonel said, "Out of a prewar Serbian population of thirty thousand, there are eight hundred and seventy-five Serbs left in Pristina."

"Exactly eight hundred and seventy-five?" I asked.

"Exactly." And (more visions of Saint Nick as NATO Supreme Allied Commander, Europe) the colonel knew when the Serbs were sleeping. He knew when they were awake. He had 250 of his men living with the Serbs.

"Living with them and doing what?" I asked.

"Keeping them alive."

Sometimes. On November 29, 1999, three elderly Serbs were pulled from their car in central Pristina. The man was killed, the two women were severely beaten. On October 11, 1999, an Albanian passerby asked a Bulgarian UN worker, in Serbian, "What time is it?" The Bulgarian replied in Bulgarian, a language too similar to Serbian. He was shot to death.

But the forces for good were agreed that Serbs should stay in Kosovo. And so were the forces for bad. Milošević wanted Serbs in Kosovo so he could claim that Kosovo was still part of Serbia. NATO wanted Serbs in Kosovo because, when you're fighting a war to save lives, you've got to save *somebody's*. The UN definitely wanted Serbs in Kosovo. If you don't like multiculturalism, why have a UN? And Senator Paul Wellstone wanted Serbs in Kosovo to show how wonderful multiculturalism can be—if you've got forty-two thousand troops to enforce it.

Six of those troops were bivouacked in an apartment in downtown Pristina to safeguard twenty-four-year-old Maria, two floors up, the last remaining Serb in the building. This was not bad duty. Maria was beautiful. And her mother, visiting from exile in Serbia, was cute, too. It would be a hard test in bigotry for a normal man to hate this pair. Some of the local fellows managed to pass. "What time is it?" they asked Maria on the street.

I asked Maria, "How do you see your future in Kosovo?"

"I don't see it at all," she said. "I just sold my flat. I'm moving to Belgrade."

"Is there any future for Serbs in Kosovo?"

"No."

In perfect agreement with Maria was the KLA commander of the Lap region of northeast Kosovo, Major General Mustafa Remi. That is, Remi would have been a major general except that the KLA was demilitarized and had been disarmed.

"There hasn't been a disarmament," said General (or whatever) Remi, who was wearing a pistol and being saluted by Albanians. "We have only stored our weapons."

I brought up the subject of UN Resolution 1244. This is the piece of paper that set NATO upon the Serbs. The resolution states, with an interesting choice of verb, that "Kosovo can enjoy substantial autonomy within the Federal Republic of Yugoslavia."

"Does the KLA," I asked the general, "still aspire to an independent Kosovo?"

"We don't *aspire,*" said Remi, doing his best—which was very good—to look scary. "We see an independent Kosovo as a reality."

"What if the Western nations don't support this?"

Remi's logic was sound: "I think we are having their support, considering the support that they are offering us."

At Camp Bondsteel, the U.S. headquarters in Kosovo, I interviewed a more affable officer. Camp Bondsteel was an eight-hundred-acre fortified compound in southern Kosovo housing thirty-five hundred U.S. soldiers atop a ridge that dominated a hundred square miles of rolling farmland. At night Bondsteel was lit the way the city on the hill of the Gospels would have been lit if they'd had diesel generators in Saint Matthew's time. By day the earthen tracks and paths were being turned into gravel roads. The tents were being replaced with wooden barracks. The only sewage treatment plant in Kosovo had been built.

"I think the conflict is not over yet," General Remi had told me.

The American officer said, "We learned a lesson in Bosnia. Tents only last three winters."

I asked the officer, "Can you *really* turn this place into a multicultural society?"

"We'll try our best. After all," said the officer with an optimistic, very American smile, "if anybody can do it, *we* can."

Which, back in America we, rather famously, can't.

A bored black private stood guard at another American fortress, Camp Monteith, in southeastern Kosovo. On the subject of local hatreds, he said, "At least if they put you and me in a police lineup, they can tell us apart."

But they can tell Maria, too. "Serbs are identifiable," said Maria. "I can't explain why. It's subtle—facial structure." She told me about a ten-year-old boy, walking down the street, who pulled a knife on her and said, "You are Serb. I kill you." Maria's mother said a little kid ran up to her and pantomimed a throat slitting.

Maybe it's the bubble gum. Or maybe it's history. Peoples who hate each other often seem to be fond of history. The Serbs, the Serbs say, have always been in Kosovo. Except that the Serbs didn't arrive in the Balkans until the sixth century AD. So Albanians, the Albanians say, have always been in Kosovo. Although British historian Miranda Vickers says, "Serbian archaeologists have been hard at work seeking to refute . . . the long-standing Albanian claim for a continuity of descent from the ancient Ilyrians." Anyway, somebody's always been in Kosovo. And somebody else is always showing up, the way the Ottoman Turks did in 1389. The Battle of Kosovo caused a large portion of Kosovo's Serbs to leave for, among other places, Transylvania (making one wonder why the Serbs don't hate vampires rather than ethnic Albanians).

The Serbs reconquered Kosovo in 1912 and committed atrocities against the Albanians, who sided with Germany in 1914 and oppressed the Serbs, who regained control of Kosovo in 1918 and tyrannized the Albanians, who sided with the Germans again in 1939 and crushed the Serbs, who recaptured Kosovo in 1945 and persecuted the Albanians, who rioted in 1981 and beat and robbed the Serbs, who . . .

"Oh," said Maria's mother to Maria with an I-forgot-to-feed-the-cat look, "you got another threatening phone call. A man's voice said, 'What are you waiting for?'"

Food aid was the answer to that question in Gorazdevac, a Serb village in western Kosovo that once had a population of two thousand. The number of residents shrank to about thirty during the air war but had now returned to . . . "Eight hundred," said the village drunk, although 770 seem to be making themselves scarce.

The village headman—or, anyway, the oldest male around—explained that it took five soldiers from the Italian armored brigade in Pec to escort a single villager into the fields. As a result, no winter wheat had been planted, there wasn't enough livestock fodder to last until spring, and—he grew grave—"Yesterday a haystack was set on fire."

"How are people living?" I asked.

"Food aid," he said, serving the Italian soldiers, a son-in-law, me, and the village drunk morning glasses of Sljivovica Manastirka that, if you missed your mouth, could provide a skin peel and an eyelid tuck.

"Can Serbs and Albanians live together peacefully?" I asked.

"We would like to live as before the war," said the headman. "Even though in the past we didn't want to live together, we lived together."

"There is only one God above us!" said the village drunk.

I asked if the Milošević government had been unfair to the Albanians.

The headman's son-in-law answered. "Milošević called for Albanians and Serbs to live together." Two little boys peeked shyly at the yakking men. The son-in-law said he'd named them "Wolf" and "Fearless."

"The Albanians would start a war anyway," said the son-in-law.

The village was a Peter Brueghel painting, if you ignored the villagers in Nikes and the corrugated metal and concrete block that augmented the thatch and the wattle-and-daub. A listing half-timbered gristmill sat athwart a stream. The stream wandered through the main road, and so did pigs.

"The cultural level of Albanians is low. Serbian culture is more high," said the son-in-law.

Luan Mulliqi, the new Albanian director of Kosovo's national Galeria e Arteve—which was up and running in Pristina, although things like water and electricity often weren't—said, "What is a difficult place to live is, for culture, heaven."

Mulliqi was giving me a tour, partly by flashlight, of an exhibit of Kosovar Albanian modern art. Intimations of dread and portraits of corpses pervaded the pictures, although most were painted a quarter of a century before, when Yugoslavia was supposedly a multicultural model to the world. Even the abstracts look worried. One of these was gloomy and terrifying without anything on the canvas except a white billowing shape. "A shroud," said Mulliqi.

The recent artworks, created during the previous year's chaos, were more cheerful. Mulliqi, himself a sculptor, was finishing a piece that incorporated a swatch of the green Astroturf of hope, an array of the tools of reconstruction, and some new wood rafters fastened to an old charred roof beam. A corpse was hanging from those rafters, but it was a cheerful sculpture, comparatively speaking.

Serbs argued that Kosovo's Albanians were cheerful because they were enjoying their martyrdom. "An Albanian with seven sons will sacrifice six for Albanian independence," said the village drunk in Gorazdevac (perhaps making poor young Wolf and Fearless think, "Don't give Dad ideas.")

More likely what Kosovo's Albanians were enjoying was a chance to provide martyrdom to Serbs, especially their immediate neighbors. "Crimes in Kosovo were done by Serbs *here,*" said the KLA vet in Kosovo Polje. "No Serb in Belgrade would know which house Albanians lived in."

In Pasjane, another of Kosovo's Serb villages, the school principal begged to differ, at least about the behavior of the Serbs in his hometown. "There was no killing," he said. "There was no looting." He paused. A large photograph of Slobodan Milošević hung on his office wall. "Well, maybe there was some. But all the dirty people ran away to Serbia. The people remaining in Pasjane are all honest, decent people."

Honest, decent, and furious. Pasjane, in the far southeast of Kosovo, was under intermittent mortar attack from Albanians in the surrounding hills who hadn't gotten the news about storing their weapons. A man had been killed two days before. The other men in Pasjane left the funeral and gathered in the churchyard. They pointed to gravestones damaged by mortar attacks. They pointed to the shrapnel scars on the church.

"This church is from the 1200s."

"This village is from 1340."

"First to fight the Turks."

"Before 1389 all these villages were Serb."

Old hatreds aside, new hatreds were growing apace—hatred for the Americans guarding Pasjane, for example.

A U.S. Army forensics team had come to gather the shell fragments from the lethal mortar attack. The Pasjane Serbs said that they believed the U.S. Army did this to hide something. When the man was killed, they said, an American armored personnel carrier was down the road. The APC turned off its engine just before the mortar shell struck. The Pasjane Serbs thought the U.S. Army was giving a signal to hidden Albanians.

Why couldn't everyone cooperate in Kosovo the way Russian troops and NATO troops were cooperating, which, according to official military sources with whom I spoke, was "fully," even if the Russians had arrived as peace-keeping gate-crashers and even if the Russians were supposed to be perpetrating in Chechnya what the Russians were supposed to be preventing in Kosovo and even if, as one Norwegian enlisted man said unofficially, "the Russians drink on duty"?

"Time is the best medicine," said a colonel in the Russian medical corps who was running a civilian clinic in Kosovo Polje.

"If time is the best medicine," I said, "why don't we all feel better than we did twenty years ago?"

"That," the colonel said, "is a good question."

Another good question was: What really should be done with the Serbs and Albanians? One British soldier, on night patrol through a former Serbian—now sooty ruin—section of Pristina, said, "It's what barbed wire was invented for."

But advocating barbed wire would have embarrassed the forces for good, the participants in the peace blitzkrieg, the elves in the Santa War. So the tenant committee meetings went on.

"We'd like you to take down the Albanian flag on the balcony," said the beleaguered Norwegian captain in Kosovo Polje. "It could be seen as a provocation."

"It's a wedding tradition," said the chairwoman.

"The wedding was last week."

"Flying the flag from Thursday to Monday—that is the tradition," said the KLA veteran.

"Well, tomorrow is Tuesday," said the captain. "And one more thing. There are too many stray dogs. They are creating a health problem . . ."

Said an Italian colonel in Pec, "This is the future of war."

Israel

April 2001

Passover is my idea of a perfect holiday. Dear God, when you're handing out plagues of darkness, locusts, hail, boils, flies, lice, frogs, and cattle murrain, and turning the Nile to blood, and smiting firstborn, give me a *pass*, and tell me when it's *over*.

And the Lord did well by me at Passover—brilliant sunshine on the beaches of Tel Aviv, pellucid waters, no flies in my room at the Hilton, and certainly no lice. I am a firstborn myself but was not the least smitten, not even by the cute waitress at the Hilton's kosher sushi restaurant. I am a happily married man. And by the way, Leviticus 11:10 says, "Of any living thing which is in the waters, they shall be an abomination unto you," an apt description of sushi as far as I'm concerned. But gentiles aren't expected to understand the intricacies of dietary law, although extra complications thereof lead to Passover's main drawback: food and—more important to gentiles—drink.

"I'll have a Scotch," I said to the Hilton's bartender.

"Scotch isn't kosher for Passover," he said. "It's made with leaven."

"Gin and tonic," I said.

"Gin isn't kosher."

"What can I have?"

"You can have a screwdriver—Israeli vodka and orange juice."

"What's Israeli vodka like?" I asked.

"The orange juice is very good."

There was no plague of tourists in Israel. It should have been a period of hectic visitation, with Passover beginning April 7 and the Eastern Orthodox and Western Easters coinciding a week later. But Israel's income from tourism dropped 58 percent in the last quarter of 2000, and to judge by the lineless queues at Ben-Gurion Airport and the empty-seated aisles of El Al, the drop had continued. The marble lobby of the Hilton echoed, when at all, with the chatter of idle desk clerks and bellhops. The din of strife had rendered Israel quiet.

Quiet without portentous hush—traffic hum, AC buzz, and cell phone beepings indicated ordinary life in an ordinary place. Tourism wasn't the only thing there was no sign of in Israel. Demonstrations didn't block intersections, public address systems failed to crackle with imperatives, exigent posters weren't stuck to walls, except to advertise raves. There was no sign of crisis—international or bilateral or domestic political—although all news reports agreed that a crisis raged here, and an economic crisis as well. A 12 percent quarterly decline in gross domestic product was unevident in boarded-up shops and empty cafés, which didn't exist, or in beggars and homeless, who weren't on the streets.

There was no sign of terrorism, not that there hadn't been some. But what doesn't inspire terror, by definition, isn't terrorism. The Carmel Market was crowded, either with people wholly unafraid or with people indifferent to whether they were blown up singly or in bunches. If security was pervasive, it was invisible. Israel, I've heard, is hated fanatically by millions of Muslims around the world, whereas the U.S. Congress is loathed by only a small number of well-informed people who follow politics closely. But a walk around anything in Israel is less impeded by barriers and armed guards than a walk around the Capitol Building in Washington.

There was no sign of war. Plenty of soldiers were to be seen, carrying their weapons, but this is no shock to the frequent traveler. For all that the world looks askance at America's lack of gun control, foreigners love to wave guns around. Nothing about the Israeli Defense Forces is as odd as Italian carabinieri brandishing their machine pistols while grimly patrolling that flashpoint, Venice.

There was, in fact, no sign of anything in Tel Aviv. In particular there was no sign of Israel's vital importance to world peace—except, of course, those signs of vital importance to world peace that one sees everywhere, the lettering here in Hebrew but the trademark logos recognizable enough.

Tel Aviv is new, built on the sand dunes north of Jaffa in the 1890s, about the same time Miami was founded. The cities bear a resemblance in size, site, climate, and architecture ranging from the bland to the fancifully bland. In Miami the striving, somewhat troublesome immigrant population is the result of Russia's meddling with Cuba. In Tel Aviv the striving, somewhat troublesome immigrant population is the result of Russia's meddling with itself. I found a Russian restaurant where they couldn't have cared less what was made with leaven, where they had Scotch, and where, over one Scotch too many, I contemplated the absurdity of Israel being an ordinary place.

What if people who had been away for ages, out and on their own, suddenly showed up at their old home and demanded to move back in?

My friends with grown-up children tell me this happens all the time. What if the countless ancient tribal groups that are now defeated, dispersed, and stateless contrived to reestablish themselves in their ancestral lands in such a way as to dominate everyone around them? The Mashantucket Pequots are doing so this minute at their Foxwoods casino in southeastern Connecticut. What if a religious group sought a homeland, never minding how multifarious its religion had become or how divergent its adherents were in principles and practices? A homeland for Protestants would have to satisfy the aspirations of born-again literalists holding forth about creationism in their concrete-block tabernacles and also fulfill the hopes and dreams of vaguely churched latitudinarians giving praise to God's creation by playing golf on Sundays. A Protestant Zion would need to be perfect both for sniping at abortion doctors in North Carolina and for marrying lesbians in Vermont. As an American, I already live in that country.

Maybe there's nothing absurd about Israel. I wandered out into the ordinary nighttime, down Jabotinsky Street, named after the founder of Revisionist Zionism, Ze'ev Jabotinsky, who wrote in 1923, "A voluntary agreement between us and the Arabs of Palestine is inconceivable now or in the foreseeable future." Thus Jabotinsky broke with the father of Zionism, Theodor Herzl, who, in *Altneuland* (1902), had a fictional future Arab character in a fictional future Israel saying, "The Jews have made us prosperous, why should we be angry with them?" And now the Carmel Market was full of goods from Egypt.

From Jabotinsky Street I meandered into Weizmann Street, named for the first president of Israel, Chaim Weizmann, who in 1919 met with Emir Faisal, future king of Iraq and a son of the sharif of Mecca, and concluded an agreement that "all necessary measures shall be taken to encourage and stimulate immigration of Jews into Palestine on a large scale." Faisal sent a letter to the American Zionist delegates at the Versailles peace conference wishing Jews "a most hearty welcome home."

Turning off Weizmann Street, I got lost for a while among signpost monikers I didn't recognize but that probably commemorated people who became at least as embattled as Jabotinsky, Herzl, Weizmann, and Faisal. I emerged on Ben-Gurion Avenue. The first prime minister of Israel was a ferocious battler. He fought the British mandate, the war of liberation, Palestinian guerrillas, and the Sinai campaign. He even won, most of the time, in the Israeli Knesset. And still he was on the lookout for peace. In the months leading up to the Suez crisis, in 1956, President Dwight Eisenhower had a secret emissary shuttling between Jerusalem and Cairo. Egypt's president, Gamal Abdel Nasser, told the emissary (in words that Yasir Arafat could use and, for all I know, has), "If the initiative [Nasser] was now taking in these talks was known in public he would be faced not only with a political problem, but—possibly—with a bullet."

A bullet was what Yitzhak Rabin got, at the end of Ben-Gurion Avenue, from a Jewish extremist, during a peace rally in the square that now bears Rabin's name. A bullet was also what Emir Faisal's brother, King Abdullah of Jordan, got, from a Muslim extremist, for advocating peace with Israel. Nasser's successor, Anwar Sadat, got a bullet, too.

If bullets were the going price for moderation hereabouts, then I needed another drink. I walked west along Gordon Street—named, I hope, for Judah Leib Gordon, the nineteenth-century Russian novelist who wrote in classical Hebrew, and not for Lord George Gordon, the fanatical anti-Catholic and leader of the 1780 Gordon riots, who converted to Judaism late in life and died in Newgate Prison praising the French Revolution. This brought me to the stretch of nightclubs along the beach promenade. Here, two months later, a suicide bomber would kill twenty-two people outside the Dolphi disco. Most of the victims were teenage Russian girls, no doubt very moderate about everything other than clothes, makeup, and boyfriends.

My tour guide arrived the next morning. His name was a long collection of aspirates, glottal stops, and gutturals with, like printed Hebrew, no evident vowels. "Americans can never pronounce it," he said. "Just call me T'zchv."

I called him Z. I was Z's only customer. He drove a minibus of the kind that in the United States always seems to be filled with a church group. And so was Z's, until recently. "Most of my clients," he said, "are the fundamentalists. They want to go everywhere in the Bible. But now . . ." The people who talk incessantly about the Last Days have quit visiting the place where the world will end, due to violence in the region.

Z was seventy-five, a retired colonel in the Israeli Defense Forces, a veteran of every war from liberation to the invasion of Lebanon. "Our worst enemy is CNN," he said. His parents had come from Russia in 1908 and settled on the first kibbutz in Palestine. Z was full of anger about the fighting in Israel—the fighting with the ultra-Orthodox Jews. "They don't serve in the army. They don't pay taxes. The government gives them money. I call them Pharisees."

As we walked around, Z would greet people of perfectly secular appearance by name, adding, "You Pharisee, you," or would introduce me to someone in a T-shirt and jeans who had, maybe, voted for Ariel Sharon in the most recent election by saying, "I want you to meet Moshe, a real Pharisee, this one."

Z said over and over, "The problem is with the Pharisees." About Arabs I couldn't get him to say much. Z seemed to regard Arabs as he did weather. Weather is important. Weather is good. We enjoy weather. We respect weather. Nobody likes to be out in weather when it gets dramatic. "My wife won't let me go to the Palestinian areas," Z said.

"Let's go to an ultra-Orthodox neighborhood," I said.

"You don't want to go there," he said. "They're dumps. You want to see where Jesus walked by the Sea of Galilee."

"No, I don't."

"'And Jesus, walking by the sea of Galilee, saw two brethren, Simon called Peter, and Andrew his brother, casting a net into the sea' . . . " For a man at loggerheads with religious orthodoxy, Z recited a lot of scripture, albeit mostly New Testament, where Pharisees come off looking pretty bad. When quoting, Z would shift to the trochaic foot —familiar to him, perhaps, from the preaching of his evangelical tourists; familiar to me from Mom yelling through the screen door, "*You* get *in* here *right* this *minute*!"

As a compromise we went to Jaffa and had Saint Peter's fish from the Sea of Galilee for lunch. Jaffa is the old port city for Jerusalem, a quaint jumble of Arab architecture out of which the Arabs ran or were run (depending on who's writing history) during Israel's war of liberation. Like most quaint jumbles adjacent to quaintness-free cities, Jaffa is full of galleries and studios. Israel is an admirably artsy place. And, as in other artsy places of the contemporary world, admiration had to be aimed principally at the effort. The output indicated that Israelis should have listened when God said, "Thou shalt not make unto thee any graven image, or any likeness of any thing." Some of the abstract stuff was good.

I wanted to look at art. Z wanted me to look at the house of Simon the Tanner, on the Jaffa waterfront. This, according to Acts 10:10–15, is where Saint Peter went into a trance and foresaw a universal Christian church and, also, fitted sheets. Peter had a vision of "a great sheet knit at the four corners, and let down to the earth: Wherein were all manner of fourfooted beasts of the earth, and wild beasts, and creeping things." God told Peter to kill them and eat them. Peter thought this didn't look kosher—or probably, in the case of the creeping things, appetizing. And God said that what He had cleansed should not be called unclean.

"Then is when Peter knew Christianity was for everyone, not just the Jews!" said Z with vicarious pride in another religion's generous thought.

A little too generous. To Peter's idea we owe ideology, the notion that the wonderful visions we have involve not only ourselves but the whole world, whether the world wants to be involved or not. Until that moment of Peter's in Jaffa, the killing of heretics and infidels was a local business. Take, for example, the case of John the Baptist: with Herodias, Herod Antipas, and stepdaughter Salome running the store, it was a mom-and-pop operation. But by the middle of the first century theological persecution had gone global in the known world. Eventually the slaughter would outgrow the limited market in religious differences. In the twentieth century millions of people were murdered on purely intellectual grounds.

"Can we go in?" I asked.

"No," Z said, "the Muslims put a mosque in there, which made the Orthodox angry. They rioted, which kept the Christians out. So the police closed the place."

For those who dislike ideology, what's interesting about kibbutzim is that they're such a bad idea. Take an Eastern European intelligentsia and make the desert bloom. One would sooner take Mormons and start a rap label. But Kibbutz Yad Mordechai, three quarters of a mile north of the Gaza Strip, passed the test of ideology. It worked—something no fully elaborated, universally applicable ideology ever does.

I'd never been to a kibbutz. I don't know what I expected—Grossinger's with guns? A bar mitzvah with tractors? Some of my friends went to kibbutzim in the 1960s and came back with tales of sex and socialism. But you could get that at Oberlin, without the circle dancing. I'm sure my poli-sci major pals were very little help with the avocado crop. Anyway, what I wasn't expecting was a cluster of JFK-era summer cottages with haphazard flower beds, sagging badminton nets, and Big Wheel tricycles on the grass—Lake Missaukee, Michigan, without Lake Missaukee.

A miniature Michigan of shrubbery and trees covered the low hills of the settlement, but with a network of drip-irrigation lines weaving among the stems and trunks. Here were the fiber-optic connections of a previous and more substantive generation of high-tech visionaries, who meant to treat a troubled world with water (per Al Sharpton) rather than information. Scattered in the greenery were the blank metal-sided workshops and warehouses of present-day agriculture, suggestive more of light industry than of peasanthood. Yad Mordechai has light industry, too, producing housewares and decorative ceramics. Plus it has the largest apiary in Israel, an educational center devoted to honey and bees, a gift shop, a kosher restaurant, and, of all things, thirteen hundred yards from the Gaza Strip, a petting zoo.

Yad Mordechai was founded in 1943 on an untilled, sand-drifted patch of the Negev. The land was bought from the sheikh of a neighboring village. And there, in the humble little verb of the preceding sentence, is the moral genius of Zionism. Theodor Herzl, when he set down the design of Zionism in *The Jewish State* (1896), wrote, "The land . . . must, of course, be privately acquired." The Zionists intended to buy a nation rather than conquer one. This had never been tried. Albeit various colonists, such as the American ones, had foisted purchase-and-sale agreements on peoples who had no concept of fee-simple tenure or of geography as anything but a free good. But the Zionists wanted an honest title search.

More than a hundred years ago the Zionists realized what nobody has realized yet—nobody but a few cranky Austrian economists and some very rich people skimming the earth in Gulfstream jets. Nothing is zero sum, not even statehood. Man can make more of everything, including the very thing he sets his feet on, as the fellow getting to his feet and heading to the bar on the G-5 can tell you. "If we wish to found a State to-day," Herzl wrote, "we shall not do it in the way which would have been the only possible one a thousand years ago."

Whether the early Zionists realized what they'd realized is another matter. Palestinian Arabs realized, very quickly, that along with the purchased polity came politics. In politics, as opposed to reality, everything is zero sum.

Considering how things are going politically in Zion these days, the following quotation from Herzl should be continued and completed.

> *Supposing, for example, we were obliged to clear a country of wild beasts, we should not set about the task in the fashion of Europeans of the fifth century. We should not take spear and lance and go out singly in pursuit of bears; we should organize a large and lively hunting party, drive the animals together, and throw a melinite bomb into their midst.*

On May 19, 1948, Yad Mordechai was attacked by an Egyptian armored column with air and artillery support. The kibbutz was guarded by 130 men and women, some of them teenagers, most without military training. They had fifty-five light weapons, one machine gun, and a two-inch mortar. Yad Mordechai held out for six days—long enough for the Israeli army to secure the coast road to Tel Aviv. Twenty-six of the defenders were killed, along with about three hundred Egyptians.

A slit trench has been left along the Yad Mordechai hilltop, with the original fifty-five weapons fastened to boards and preserved with tar. Under the viscous coatings a nineteenth-century British rifle was discernible, and the sink-trap plumbing of two primitive Bren guns. The rest of the firearms looked like the birds and cats that were once mummified—by Egyptians, appropriately enough. Below the trench is a negligee lace of barbed wire, all the barbed wire the kibbutz had in 1948, and beyond that are Egyptian tanks, just where they stopped when they could go no farther. Between the tanks dozens of charging Egyptian soldiers are represented by life-size black-painted two-dimensional cutouts—lawn ornaments on attack.

It was the only war memorial I've seen that was both frightening and silly—things all war memorials should be. Most war memorials are sad or awful—things, come to think of it, that war memorials should also be. And this war memorial had a price of admission—which, considering the cost of war, is another good idea.

At the ticket booth was a crabby old guy whom Z greeted with warm complaining, grouch to grouch. Then Z took me to Yad Mordechai's Holocaust museum, which skips pity and goes immediately to Jewish resistance during World War II and Jewish fighting in Palestine and Israel. Yad Mordechai is named for Mordechai Anielewicz, commander of the Warsaw ghetto uprising. The message of the Yad Mordechai Holocaust museum is that the Holocaust memorial is the trench at the other end of the kibbutz.

This is the second wonderful thing about Zionism: it was right. Every other "ism" of the modern world was wrong about the nature of civilized man—Marxism, mesmerism, surrealism, pacifism, existentialism, nudism. But civilized man did want to kill Jews, and was going to do more of it. And Zionism was specific. While other systems of thought blundered around in the universal, looking for general solutions to comprehensive problems, Zionism stuck to its guns, or—in the beginning, anyway—to its hoes, mattocks, and irrigation pipes.

True, Zionism has a utopian socialist aspect that is thoroughly nutty as far as I'm concerned. But it's not my concern. No one knocks on my door during dinner and asks me to join a kibbutz or calls me on the weekend to persuade me to drop my current long-distance carrier and make all my phone calls by way of Israel. And given my last name, they won't.

My last name is, coincidentally, similar to the maiden name of the Holocaust museum docent, who was Baltimore Irish and had married a young man from the kibbutz and moved there in the 1970s. "I converted," she said, "which the Orthodox make it hard to do, but I went through with it. There's a crabby old guy here who sort of took me under his wing. The first Yom Kippur after I converted, he asked me, 'Did you fast?' I said yes. He said, 'Stupid!' You probably saw him on the way in, behind the ticket counter. He's a veteran of the fight for Yad Mordechai. There's a photo of him here, when they liberated the kibbutz, in November 'forty-eight." And there was the photo of the young, heroic, crabby old guy. And now he was behind the ticket counter at the war memorial—not making a political career in Jerusalem or writing a book about the young, heroic days, or flogging his story to the History Channel.

"How cool is that?" said the Baltimore Irish woman running the Holocaust museum.

Z and I had lunch at the kibbutz's self-serve restaurant, where Z took his plate of meat and sat in the middle of the dairy section. In the sky to the south we could see smoke rising from the Gaza Strip—tires burning at an intifada barricade, or just trash being incinerated. Public services weren't what they might be in the Palestinian Authority at the moment. Or maybe it was one of the Jewish settlements in Gaza being attacked, although we hadn't heard gunfire.

These settlements aren't farms but, mostly, apartment clusters. "Are the settlements in the West Bank and Gaza some kind of post-agricultural, post-industrial, high-rise Zionism?" I asked Z. "Or are they a government-funded, mondo-condo, live-dangerously parody of nation building?"

"Pharisees!" said Z and went back to eating.

After lunch we drove to Ben-Gurion's house in Tel Aviv, a modest, foursquare, utterly unadorned structure. But the inside was cozy with twenty thousand books, in Hebrew, English, French, German, Russian, Latin, Spanish, Turkish, and ancient Greek. No fiction, however: a man who devoted his life to making a profound change in society was uninterested in the encyclopedia of society that fiction provides.

Looking at the thick walls and heavy shutters, I wondered if the house had been built to be defended. Then I twigged to the purpose of the design and gained true respect for the courage of the Zionist pioneers. Ben-Gurion came to the Middle East before air-conditioning was invented—and from Plonsk, at that.

We spent the next day, at my insistence and to Z's mystification, driving around the most ordinary parts of Israel, which look so ordinary to an American that I'm rendered useless for describing them to other Americans. American highway strip-mall development hasn't quite reached Israel, however, so there's even less of the nondescript to not describe.

Z and I stood in a garden-apartment complex in Ashdod, in the garden part, a patch of trampled grass. "Here is the ugliest living in Israel," said Z. We went to a hill on the Ashdod shore, a tell actually, a mound of ancient ruins, an ash heap of history from which we had a view of . . . ash heaps, and the power plant that goes with them, which supplies half of Israel's electricity. Ashdod, incidentally, is a Philistine place-name, not a pun. We could also see the container port, Israel's principal deep-water harbor. "This is the place where the whale threw Jonah up," Z said.

We went to the best suburbs of Tel Aviv, which look like the second-best suburbs of San Diego. We spent a lot of time stuck in traffic. Violence in the West Bank had forced traffic into bottlenecks on Routes 2 and 4 along the coast, in a pattern familiar to anyone negotiating Washington, D.C.'s Beltway—living in a place where you're scared to go to half of it and the other half you can't get to.

Israel is slightly smaller than New Jersey. Moses in effect led the tribes of Israel out of the District of Columbia, parted Chesapeake Bay near Annapolis, and wandered for forty years in Delaware. From the top of Mount Nebo, in the equivalent of Pennsylvania, the Lord showed Moses all of Canaan. New Canaan is in Connecticut—but close enough. And there is a Mount Nebo in Pennsylvania, although it overlooks the Susquehanna rather than the promised land of, say, Paramus. Joshua blew the trumpet, and the malls of Paramus came tumbling down. Israel also has beaches that are at least as attractive as New Jersey's.

An old friend of mine, Dave Garcia, flew in from Hong Kong to spend Easter in Jerusalem. "I like to go places when the tourists aren't there," he said. Dave spent two years in Vietnam when the tourists weren't there, as a prisoner of the Viet Cong. "Let's see where the Prince of Peace was born," he said. "It's in the middle of the intifada."

Z drove us from Ben-Gurion Airport to the roadblock between Jerusalem and Bethlehem. The highway was strewn with broken bottles, as if in the aftermath not of war but of a bad party. Israeli soldiers and Palestinian Authority policemen stood around warily. Z handed us over to an Arab tour-guide friend of his who drove a twenty-five-year-old Mercedes and looked glum. Israel had lost half its tourism, but hotels in Palestinian areas were reporting occupancy rates of 4 percent.

The Arab guide parked at random in the middle of empty Manger Square, outside the Church of the Nativity. "There is normally a three-and-a-half-hour wait," he said as we walked straight into the Manger Grotto. The little cave has been rendered a soot hole by millennia of offertory candles. It's hung with damp-stained tapestries and tarnished lamps and festoons of grimy ornamentation elaborate enough for a Byzantine emperor if the Byzantine emperor lived in the basement. I imagine the Virgin Mary had the place done up more cheerfully, with little homey touches, when it was a barn.

The only other visitors were in a tour group from El Salvador, wearing bright yellow T-shirts and acting cheerfully pious. Dave asked them in Spanish if, after all that El Salvador had been through with earthquakes and civil war, the fuss about violence and danger around here puzzled them. They shrugged and looked puzzled, but that may have been because no one in the Garcia family has been able to speak Spanish for three generations, including Dave.

All the dead babies from the Massacre of the Innocents are conveniently buried one grotto over, under the same church. Sites of Christian devotion around Jerusalem tend to be convenient. In the Church of the Holy Sepulcher the piece of ground where Christ's cross was erected, the stone where He was laid out for burial, and the tomb in which He was resurrected—plus where Adam's skull was buried and, according to early Christian cartographers, the center of the world—are within a few arthritic steps of one another. Saint Helena, the mother of the emperor Constantine, was over seventy-five when she traveled to the Holy Land, in AD 326, looking for sacred locations. Arriving with a full imperial retinue and a deep purse, Saint Helena discovered that her tour guides were able to take her to every place she wanted to go;

each turned out to be nearby and, as luck would have it, for sale. The attack of real estate agents in Palestine long predates Zionism.

The Church of the Nativity is a shabby mess, a result of quarreling religious orders. The Greek Orthodox, Armenian Orthodox, and Roman Catholic priests have staked out Nativity turf with the acrimonious precision of teenage brothers sharing a bedroom. A locked steel door prevents direct access from the Roman Catholic chapel to the Manger Grotto, which has to be reached through the Greek Orthodox monastery where there is a particular "Armenian beam" that Greek Orthodox monks stand on to sweep the area above the grotto entrance, making the Armenians so angry that, according to my guidebook, "in 1984 there were violent clashes as Greek and Armenian clergy fought running battles with staves and chains that had been hidden beneath their robes." What would Christ have thought? He might have thought, "Hand me a stave," per Mark 11:15: "Jesus went into the temple, and began to cast out them that sold and bought in the temple, and overthrew the tables of the moneychangers."

It's left to the Muslims to keep the peace at the Church of the Nativity in Bethlehem, just as it's left to the Jews to keep a similar peace at the likewise divided Church of the Holy Sepulcher in Jerusalem. Who will be a Muslim and a Jew to the Muslims and the Jews? Hindus, maybe. That is more or less the idea behind putting UN peacekeeping troops in Israel. This may or may not work. The *Bhagavad Gita* opens with the hero Arjuna trying to be a pacifist. "Woe!" Arjuna says. "We have resolved to commit a great crime as we stand ready to kill family out of greed for kingship and pleasures!" But the Lord Krishna tells Arjuna to quit whining and fight. "Either you are killed and will then attain to heaven," Krishna says, "or you triumph and will enjoy the earth."

Our guide took us to several large gift shops with no other customers, aisles stacked with unsold souvenirs of Jesus' birth. Part of the Israeli strategy in the intifada has been to put economic pressure on the Arabs of the West Bank and Gaza. Fear of death hasn't stopped the Arabs. Maybe fear of Chapter 11 will do the trick. The hopes and fears of all the years reside with badly carved olive-wood crèche sets. Dave and I bought several.

Then our guide took us up a hill to the Christian Arab village of Beit Jala, which the Israelis had been shelling. Large chunks were gone from the tall, previously comfortable-looking limestone villas. Shuttered house fronts were full of what looked like bullet holes, but large enough to put a Popsicle in. "Ooh, fifty-caliber," said Dave with professional appreciation.

"These people," our guide said, "have no part in the violence." Dave and I made noises of condolence and agreement in that shift of sympathy to the nearest immediate victim that is the hallmark of twenty-first-century morality.

"Here a man was sleeping in his bed," said our guide, showing us a three-story pile of rubble. "And they couldn't find him for days later. The Israelis shell here for no reason."

"Um," said Dave, "*why* for no reason?" And our guide, speaking in diplomatic circumlocution, allowed as how, every now and then, all the time, Palestinian gunmen would occasionally, very often, use the Beit Jala hilltop to shoot with rifles at Israeli tanks guarding a highway tunnel in the valley. They did it the next night.

"It's kind of a rule of military tactics," said Dave to me, sotto voce, as we walked back to the car, "not to shoot a rifle at a tank when the tank knows where you are." Unless, of course, scanty olive-wood-crèche-set sales are spoiling your enjoyment of earth and you've decided to attain to heaven.

The owner of an upscale antiquities store back in Bethlehem did not look as if he meant to attain any sooner than necessary, even though his store's air-conditioning unit had been knocked out by Israelis firing on nearby rioters. He arrived in a new Mercedes with three assistants to open his business especially for Dave, his first customer in a month.

The antiquities dealer was another friend of Z's. Z told us that this was the man whose grandfather was the Palestinian cobbler to whom the Dead Sea Scrolls were offered as scrap leather by the Bedouin shepherd who found them—a story too good to subject to the discourtesies of investigative journalism.

The emporium was new, built in the soon-dashed hopes of millennium traffic. The antiquities were displayed with the stark, track-lit modern exhibition drama necessary to make them look like something other than the pots and pans and jars and bottles from people who had, one way or another, given up on this place long ago.

Dave collects antiques, but by profession he's an iron and steel commodities trader. He has also lived in Asia for years. I sat on a pile of rugs and drank little cups of coffee while Levantine bargaining met Oriental dickering and the cold-eyed brokerage of the market floor. The three great world traditions of haggle flowered into confrontation for two and a half hours. Folks from the Oslo talks and the Camp David meetings should have been there for benefit of instruction. Everyone ended up happy. No fatal zero-sum thinking was displayed as banknotes and ceramics changed hands at last. Dave could make more money. And the Arabs could make more antiquities.

Why can't everybody just get along? No reasonably detached person goes to Israel without being reduced in philosophical discourse to the level of Rodney King—or, for that matter, to the level of George Santayana. "Those who cannot remember the past are condemned to repeat it," Santayana said in one of those moments of fatuousness that come to even the most detached of philosophers. In Israel and Palestine, as in Serbia and Kosovo, this goes double for those who can't remember anything else. And everybody *does* get along, after a fashion. Muslims and Christians and Jews have lived together in the Holy Land for centuries—hating one another's guts, cutting one another's throats, and touching off wars of various magnitudes.

The whole melodrama of the Middle East would be improved if amnesia were as common here as it is in the plots of imaginary melodramas. I was thinking this as I was looking at the Dead Sea Scrolls in the solemn underground Shrine of the Book, inside the vast precincts of the Israel Museum. Maybe, I thought, all the world's hoary old tracts ought to wind up as loafer soles or be auctioned at Sotheby's to a greedy high-tech billionaire for display in his otherwise bookless four-thousand-square-foot cyber den. Then I noticed that Z was reading the scrolls, muttering aloud at speed, perusing an ancient text with more ease than I can read Henry James. What's past is past, perhaps, but when it passed, this was where it went.

Z dropped us at the King David Hotel, the headquarters of the Palestinian mandate administration when the British were trying to keep the peace. In 1946 the hotel was blown up by the radical wing of the Jewish Resistance Movement, the Irgun. Some of every group were killed—forty-one Arabs, twenty-eight British, seventeen Jews, and five reasonably detached persons of miscellaneous designation. The Irgun was led by the future prime minister Menachem Begin, who would make peace with Egypt in the 1970s but, then again, war with Lebanon in the 1980s.

On the way to the hotel Z explained why there will always be war in the region. "Israel is strategic," he said in his most New Testamental tone. "It is the strategic land bridge between Africa and Asia. For five thousand years there has been fighting in Israel. It is the strategic land bridge." And the fighting continues, a sort of geopolitical muscle memory, as though airplanes and supertankers hadn't been invented. The English and the French might as well be fighting over the beaver-pelt trade in Quebec today, and from what I understand of Canadian politics, they are.

We were meeting Israeli friends of Dave's at the hotel, a married couple. He voted for Sharon; she voted for Ehud Barak. Dave and I marked our lintels and doorposts with the blood of the lamb, metaphorically speaking, and drank Israeli vodka and orange juice.

"There will always be war," the husband said, "because with war Arafat is a hero and without war he's just an unimportant guy in charge of an unimportant place with a lot of political and economic problems."

"There will always be war," the wife said, "because with war Sharon is a hero and without war he's just an unimportant guy in charge of an unimportant place with . . ."

Also, war is fun—from a distance. Late the next night Dave and I were walking back to our hotel in Arab East Jerusalem. Dave was wearing a Hawaiian shirt and I was in a blazer and chinos. We couldn't have looked less Israeli if we'd been dressed like Lawrence of Arabia (who, incidentally, was a third party to the cordial meeting between Chaim Weizmann and the emir Faisal). Fifty yards down a side street a couple of Palestinian teenagers jumped out of the shadows. Using the girlie overhand throw of nations that mostly play soccer, one kid threw a bottle at us. It landed forty yards away.

On Good Friday, Dave and Z and I walked from the Garden of Gethsemane to the Lions Gate, where Israeli paratroopers fought their way into the Old City during the Six-Day War. We traveled the Via Dolorosa in an uncrowded quiet that Jesus Christ and those paratroopers were not able to enjoy. We owed our peace in Jerusalem to an enormous police presence. This did Jesus no good. Nor did the Jordanian police give Israeli soldiers helpful directions to the Ecce Homo Arch. And our Savior and the heroes of 1967 didn't have a chance to stop along the way and bargain with Arab rug merchants.

Z and the rug merchants exchanged pessimisms, Z grousing about Sharon and the Arabs complaining about Arafat. "The Israeli army tells Arafat where the strikes will come," one shopkeeper said. "They tell him, 'Don't be here. Don't be there.' No one tells me."

I visited the fourteen Stations of the Cross and said my prayers, for peace, of course, although, as a Zionist friend of mine puts it, "Victory would be okay, too." Jesus said, "Love your enemies." He didn't say not to have any. In fact, He said, "I came not to send peace but a sword." Or, anyway, staves and chains.

Then we went to the Wailing Wall, the remnant of the Second Temple, built by the same Herod the Great who killed all the babies buried by the manger in Bethlehem. Atop the Wailing Wall stands the Haram al Sharif, with the Dome of the Rock enclosing Mount Moriah where I had prayed to Mecca a dozen years before, where Abraham was ready to kill Isaac and where, at that moment, Muslims gathered for Friday prayers were surrounded by Israeli soldiers, some of both no doubt also ready to kill. (The Dome of the Rock marks the center of the world for those who don't believe that the center of the world is down the street, in the Church of the Holy Sepulcher.)

In the plaza in front of the Wailing Wall religious volunteers were lending yarmulkes to Jews who had arrived bareheaded. "Well," Dave said, "my mother was Jewish, so I guess that makes me Jewish. I'd better get a rent-a-beanie and go over to the Wailing Wall and . . . wail, or something."

The yarmulkes being handed out were, unaccountably, made of silver reflective fabric. "I look like an outer-space Jew," Dave said.

"I always thought you were Catholic," I said.

"Because of *Garcia*," Dave said, "like *O'Rourke*."

I said, "But I'm not Catholic, either. My mother was Presbyterian, and I'm Methodist. I came home from Methodist confirmation class in a big huff and told my mother there were huge differences between Presbyterians and Methodists. And my mother said, 'We sent you to the Methodist church because all the nice people in the neighborhood go there.'"

"They could use that church here," Dave said.

Dave swayed in front of the wall like the Orthodox surrounding him, although, frankly, in a manner more aging-pop-fan than Hassidic.

What could cause more hatred and bloodshed than religion? This is the Israel question. Except it isn't rhetorical; it has an answer. We went to Yad Vashem, the Jerusalem Holocaust Memorial, and saw what the godless get up to.

There are worse things than war, if the intifada is indeed a war. As of May 2001, 513 Palestinians and 124 Israelis had been killed in what is called the second intifada. About forty thousand perished in the 1992–1996 civil war in Tajikistan that nobody's heard of. From 1.5 to 2 million are dead in Sudan. There are parts of the world where the situation Dave and I were in is too ordinary to have a name.

Late Saturday night the particular place where we were in that situation was the American Colony Hotel, in East Jerusalem, sometimes called the "PLO Hotel" for the supposed connections the staff has. It is the preferred residence of intifada-covering journalists, especially those who are indignant about Israeli behavior. The American Colony Hotel was once the mansion of an Ottoman pasha. Dave and I sat among palms in the peristyle courtyard, surrounded by arabesques carved in Jerusalem's golden limestone. The bedroom-temperature air was scented with Easter lilies and in the distance, now and then, gunfire could be heard.

"This country is hopeless," Dave said, pouring a Palestinian Taybeh beer to complement a number of Israeli Maccabee beers we'd had earlier in West Jerusalem. "And as hopeless places go, it's not bad." We discussed another Israel question. Why are Israeli girls so fetching in their army uniforms? It may have something to do with their carrying guns. But Freud was a lukewarm Zionist and let's not think about it.

After the first Zionist Congress, in 1897, the rabbis of Vienna sent a delegation to Palestine on a fact-finding mission. The delegation cabled Vienna, saying, "The bride is beautiful, but she is married to another man." However, the twentieth century, with all its Freudianism, was about to dawn, and we know what having the beautiful bride married to another man means in today's melodramas. No fair using amnesia as a device for tidy plot resolution.

"Do we have to choose sides?" Dave said. But it's like dating sisters. Better make a decision or head for the Global Village limits. And speaking of sisters, I opened the *Jerusalem Post* on Easter morning and discovered that my sister's neighborhood in Cincinnati was under curfew, overrun with race riots.

9/11 Diary

September 11, 2001

When the Pentagon was hit, Debbie Lehan, the manager of my apartment building in Washington, D.C., and Damon Boone, the building engineer, moved their cars out of the underground garage and parked them to block both ends of the building's horseshoe drive. Of course that was absurd—as if the terrorists had thought, "World Trade Center, Pentagon, and . . . the place on Connecticut Avenue where Naomi Wolf used to live." But by noon all the building's children had been gathered home from school or day care. The children played in the empty half-oval. Career daddies and career mommies hovered. The barricaded driveway was absurd, if you could keep your eyes from misting.

"Better to do *something,*" Debbie said.

Damon unlocked the door to the building's roof. We could see the Pentagon on fire across the Potomac. "It makes me angry, scared, sad all at once," said Damon. According to the theory of terrorism, it was supposed to make him paralyzed with terror.

The traffic on Connecticut Avenue was coming from downtown as if in the evening rush hour. But there was none of the accustomed honking at the District's unsequenced and haphazardly placed stoplights.

Downtown the cars were gone and the stores were closed. Police officers stood in ones and twos. On the corner of F and Fourteenth Streets two businessmen, two messengers, and a panhandler were listening to the panhandler's portable radio. A tape of President Bush's first response to the terrorist attack was being broadcast. One of the messengers said, in the voice people use when they're saying something important, "After today things will never be the same." Then he seemed to have one of those moments that came to everyone on September 11, with jumbled thoughts alike in size but wildly mismatched in weight—pity, rage, and how to get the shirts back from the dry cleaner. "Transportation in the air won't be as fast," he said, in a smaller voice.

At the corner of Fourteenth and Constitution a policeman set out flares to block the street. The policeman took the plastic caps off the flares and tossed the caps aside with the decisive gesture of a man suspending minor public mores in a crisis. A young man on a bicycle stopped at the curb and said to me, "At least the grocery stores are open. But the trucks can't get to the stores. If it's going to be a big international war, I'll just fast."

The young man had a theory that the terrorism had to do with America's pulling out of the UN conference on racism in South Africa, but he was interrupted by a woman indignant that the portable toilets at the Washington Monument were still in use. "They don't know *what* I could be doing in there," she said.

The grass expanse in the middle of the Mall was deserted except for the homeless, suddenly homeless alone. Like everyone else, they seemed subdued, although they didn't stay subdued. The next day, at Eighteenth and L, I would see a ragged man in the middle of the street shouting, "I'll kill all of you people! I don't like any of you!" No one, including the soldiers who were by then everywhere in Washington, paid attention.

Michele Lieber, a lobbyist who lives in my building, had come downtown with me. Alongside the Mall, snack and souvenir trucks were dutifully open. Michele asked a snack-truck proprietor if business was good. "Yes, of course," he dutifully said.

That day, for the first time in my thirteen years in Washington, I saw no protesters. And hardly any were around on Wednesday. A reopened Lafayette Park would feature only an old woman with a sign saying WHITE HOUSE ANTI-NUCLEAR PEACE VIGIL SINCE 1981 and a middle-aged hippie on a similar anti-nuclear sleep-out SINCE 1984. The old woman was talking mostly to herself. "They provoked what happened," she said. The hippie was talking to two adolescent girls with piercings, discussing his pet squirrel.

On Tuesday afternoon even TV crews were mostly absent from the White House vicinity. On Constitution at the Ellipse, ABC White House correspondent Terry Moran was on a lone stand-up, not saying much to the camera. A few people gathered around. "We just got here from Slovakia and everything happened," a tourist said.

Michele and I had walked to the reflecting pool behind the Capitol before we saw any more tourists. A family in sport clothes was standing there looking baffled. I introduced myself to the father, and his first words were (one is grateful for not having a conspiratorial turn of mind), "We're from Slovakia."

"We are a bit concerned," the father said, "but the weather is okay. We had only one day to be here. Tomorrow we are supposed to go to New York."

Michele, on her cell phone, was trying to call friends in New York. She kept getting a recorded message, "Due to the tornado your call cannot go through."

At Bullfeathers, a restaurant on First Street, Representative Don Sherwood, Republican from the Tenth District in Pennsylvania, was having lunch with his daughter. He wanted a session of Congress to be convened at the Capitol that night. "We should be as visible and in-business as possible," he said.

Four or five televisions were on inside the restaurant, their volume turned up. Another congressman and his female aide were in the men's room, the only place quiet enough for the congressman to do a phone interview. The congressman was saying, "We will make the people who did this pay. It is awfully hard to defend yourself from people who have no respect for human life." He seemed to be pulling in two directions—as did the soldiers on the streets the next day, camouflaged for invisibility and wearing blaze-orange traffic control vests.

"We just have to quit being Americans for a little while," said a staffer from the Republican National Committee. "Forget about carrying our Constitution to people who don't give a rat's ass."

Michele and I walked across Capitol Hill. On Massachusetts we met a Senate staffer whom Michele knew. He was jogging. "It was a little hairy when they told us to evacuate," he said. "Then I saw our F-16s fly over, and I felt okay."

We met another Senate staffer who was trying to get his car out of a parking lot that was inside the police cordon around the Capitol. The four of us walked to the Dubliner bar on North Capital Street.

"The congressional leadership," said the second staffer, "has been whisked off to 'an undisclosed location.' As far as I'm concerned they can keep most of them there." This touched on another theory of terrorism: that the organization of society can be attacked by striking at organizations; that we can't organize things ourselves.

"Four Guinness," the first Senate staffer said to the bartender.

"Time to take sides," the second staffer said.

"Time to turn sand into glass," said the first.

Ariel Sharon was on CNN. "It is a war between the good and the bad," said Sharon.

From the Dubliner we took a cab to the Palm restaurant on Nineteenth Street. The bar and the dining room were full. President Bush came on television at 8:30. Everyone has seen, in movies, a restaurant go quiet. I had never before really heard all talk come to a halt and all noise from tableware cease. The customers and staff applauded when the president said, "We will make no distinction between the people who committed these acts and the people who harbor them."

"As I was driving in to open for lunch," the Palm's assistant general manager, Jocelyn Zarr, said, "all the traffic was going the other way. Ten minutes after the Pentagon was hit, I was getting reservations. I'm thinking, 'Aren't these people watching the news?' But they were. They just wanted to be with other people. I told the staff that if anyone wanted to go home, just go. No one did. I opened early. People were streaming in. My only fear was putting a group of people in danger. Once I got past that, I thought, 'The Palm is the center point.' Everyone wanted to come and sit at the bar and talk. Smith and Wollensky called and asked what I was going to do. I said I was staying open. All the evening staff showed up. A friend called and said, 'You shouldn't be working when thousands of people died.' But what else am I going to do?"

On Monday night, September 10, I had finished an article for the *Atlantic* about Israel. Israel is a country that has been under terrorist attack for generations, forever. On Tuesday I didn't want to publish the article. It wasn't serious enough. I was thinking "After today things will never be the same." Lines from W. H. Auden's poem "September 1, 1939" kept coming to mind:

Waves of anger and fear
Circulate over the bright
And darkened lands of the earth

By Wednesday I realized I'd never known what Auden was getting at with that poem, except, perhaps, in "As the clever hopes expire/Of a low dishonest decade." Apt enough, but . . .

Where blind skyscrapers use
Their full height to proclaim
The strength of Collective Man

What's that crap? Or this:

Ironic points of light
Flash out whenever the Just
Exchange their messages

Anyway, Auden repudiated the poem, mostly because of the fatuous line "We must love one another or die." Or just die. And neither agape nor eros is an appropriate response to Osama bin Laden. Also, Auden was the

Englishman who, when World War II loomed, acted as Hitler would have had Englishmen act—he ran to America and stayed there. In Israel, on September 11, things were the same as ever.

September 30, 2001

Traveling to London from Washington twelve days after the terrorist attack, I expected security measures. I'd been told to arrive at Dulles Airport three hours before departure. I was ready for checkpoints where people in flak jackets would use mirrors to look for bombs under cars—although, nowadays, with automotive electronics and the puzzle plumbing of emissions control, everything under cars looks like a bomb. Anyway, the checkpoints weren't there.

At the ticket counter, instead of being asked once, "Hasyourluggagebeenunderyourcontrolatalltimes," I was asked twice. The metal detectors and X-ray machines were operated by the usual dim but friendly minimum-wage security guards, now somewhat less friendly. I was told to hand over my disposable lighter, to prevent, I suppose, any threat of "Do what I say or I'll light this Marlboro and you'll all die—in thirty years due to inhalation of secondhand smoke."

I headed cheerlessly to the designated smoking area, expecting to find a roomful of desperate, fireless people paying black-market prices for Nicorette. Everyone was smoking. I asked for a light, and someone produced a disposable lighter. It seems that if you went through one of the airport's two security portals, you were made to surrender all lighters and matches. But if you went through the other . . .

Concern had been voiced that fear of terrorism could lead to renewed racial profiling. Never mind that the languages of the Taliban—Pashto and Dari—are part of the Indo-European linguistic family and that, if "Caucasian" has any meaning at all, Afghans have a better claim to it than Hungarians or Finns.

The profiling at the boarding gate couldn't be called racial, exactly. The ruddy and the pallid were ushered directly on board, as were the sufficiently black. It was the tanned or swarthy who had to line up for additional questioning. On my flight these included, as far as I could tell, some Hindus, some Filipinos, a Hispanic or two, and a pair of elderly Iranian women wearing chadors in violation of the new American no-unusual-things-on-your-head taboo that has brought grief to Sikhs in the U.S. hinterland. (Not that there hasn't been Sikh terrorism, but it was directed against Indira Gandhi, in retaliation for the Indian army's storming the Golden Temple at Amritsar. This isn't an issue at the moment, but the complexities of building an international coalition against terrorism could lead to India demanding a wholesale revocation of Sikh cab licenses in New York, thereby bringing that city to a halt again.)

An English friend asked me, "Would a bald chap who was sunburned and was gardening and put a tea towel on his head be in trouble in America?"

My plane was two thirds empty. But the unflappable British flight crew was unflapped. I was not subjected to the indignity that an acquaintance suffered on a flight from New York to Chicago. He was made to press the flight attendant call button and identify himself before being allowed to go to the bathroom. This—for a drinking man in the enlarged-prostate years—is a serious violation of civil rights.

The people I know in Great Britain were in the same state of shock and anger as the people I know in America. And, like my American friends, they weren't particularly frightened of a second terrorist strike or of poison gas or germ warfare. But this may be a matter of being old smokers and drinkers, of an age for cardiac arrest and malignancy, with children they'd like to get a damn job, and retirement funds that had gone to hell during the previous year. How much more frightening can life get?

The Brits, however, were more likely to raise the subject of the IRA and say a word about America leading the fight against terrorism while letting the NORAID cans be passed in the bars of Southie and the Bronx. I blamed the Kennedys—always a safe course when questions of bad U.S. political policies are raised. Meanwhile, it's the British themselves who were at the negotiating table with my moron cousins from Ulster. Personally, I'd start the war on terrorism with Gerry Adams. At least we know where he is.

Incidentally, it's ridiculous if you're Irish to claim that you can't fathom the mind-set behind the wild destruction of innocents, the casual self-murder, and the bathos of martyrdom on September 11. Al-Qaeda probably has a Yeats of its own—"A terrible beauty is born."

But there was something going on in Great Britain, among the people I *don't* know, that was more troubling than Northern Ireland home-rule concessions. The September 17 issue of the *New Statesman* ran an amazing editorial leader.

> *Look at the pictures on pages 6–7, showing Americans running in terror from the New York explosions and then ask yourself how often in the past (particularly in Vietnam and more recently in Iraq) you have seen people running in terror from American firepower. American bond traders, you may say, are as innocent and as undeserving of terror as Vietnamese or Iraqi peasants. Well, yes and no.*

To quote more might set off a wave of retribution in America against people wearing derby hats.

I had dinner with the critic and television commentator Clive James and his assistant. The assistant was an able and well-educated young woman who could not be convinced by Clive that, in the matter of moral values, there was such a thing as a superior culture. "They cover their women in the ballroom drapes!" Clive said. "Your dad can have you stoned to death for not marrying some old goat!"

"I wouldn't call it an inferior culture," his assistant said.

"What about Somalia?! What about clitoridectomies?!"

"Of course I'm a feminist," his assistant said. "But I resist the idea of an inferior culture."

It's usually Clive and I who have the arguments. He is, to put it in American terms, a liberal. But he's my age; he remembers when the whole point of being on the left was the effort (alas, misplaced) to forge a superior culture.

I was a guest on a BBC radio phone-in talk show. If the world is mad at America for anything, it should be for invention of the phone-in talk show. The idea of a news broadcast once was to find someone with information and broadcast it. The idea now is to find someone with ignorance and spread it around. (Being ignorant myself, I'm not mad personally.)

A woman named Rhona called and said we didn't have enough empathy for the poor people in the world. We're so rich and they're so poor, no wonder they're angry.

I told her that was a slur on poor people. And anyway, Osama bin Laden is a rich twit.

Rhona said that we are so wealthy and materialistic and they are so deprived. "Here I am," she said, "just an ordinary suburban housewife in a semidetached, and I'm surrounded by all these things I don't need." Privately I was thinking that my moron cousins from Belfast could fix that with breaking and entering. I said, "You're arguing completely beside the point." She was employing a fallacy of relevance, specifically what's called in logic *argumentum ad misericordiam* (although I had to look that up later; what I said on the radio was "So what?").

Rhona accused me of that most grievous of contemporary sins, especially when committed against a woman by a middle-aged man. "Don't patronize me," she said.

Calls and e-mails were nine to one in Rhona's favor, but one stalwart sent this message: "I suspect why ninety percent of callers are not in favor of P.J.'s opinions is because they are out-of-work socialists who have nothing better to do but phone radio stations."

And there are some of their ilk in the United States. Back in Washington, I'd gone to a peace rally on September 29 at Freedom Plaza, near the White House. Several thousand people attended. As I arrived, a man on the speaker's platform was saying, "We cannot permit the president of our country to claim there are only two forces—good and evil. We are not with either."

The Bread and Puppet Theater troupe was carrying a score of what appeared to be eight-foot-high papier-mâché baked potatoes. Asked what this was about, one of the troupe said it represented "naked people being oppressed by clothed people." Asked again, she said the same thing.

Members of another performing arts group were wearing cardboard bird heads and flapping bedsheets. They said they were "the cranes of peace."

A woman asked for signatures on a petition in favor of affirmative action. The National Youth Rights Association had set up a card table with a sign reading LOWER THE DRINKING AGE. Snappy protest rhymes seemed as yet inchoate. Drumming and pogo dancing accompanied the chant "Stop the war/In Afganistan/While we/Still can!"

Another speaker came to the podium and said, "Let us bomb the world with housing." One of those McMansions with the lawyer foyer and the cathedral-ceilinged great room could do real damage.

Vegetarian demonstrators carried large banners illustrated with vegetables. A carrot was captioned "Intelligence." Placards in the crowd read KILLING IS BAD; POVERTY IS TERRIBLE TOO; ABOLISH MONEY FOR A WORLD OF SHARING; and CONGRESS PLEASE KEEP A COOL HEAD. One young man wore a headband scrawled with VICTORY 4 CHECHNYA. Another carried a black-and-red ensign that he said stood for "anarcho-syndicalism," a word I didn't think had been spoken aloud since *Monty Python and the Holy Grail.* "Do you work for the police?" the standard-bearer asked. My work-shirt-and-chinos liberal disguise was ineffective.

A child of nine or ten, wearing a FUCK WAR T-shirt, harangued some police officers. The officers could not keep straight faces. Most of the other demonstrators were of college age with subdermal ink, transdermal hardware, and haircuts from the barber college on Mars. But people my age were present, too, and beginning to resemble Bertrand Russell, especially the women. Then I saw him: a hippie with a walker, wearing a hearing aid. Sic transit generation gap.

Demonstrators tried to burn an American flag. They had trouble lighting it. Maybe their matches had been taken by airport security—or maybe all the antismoking propaganda aimed at the young has come home to roost in a lack of fire-making skills. When the flag at last caught flame, a passerby shoved his way into the crowd. He was a normal-looking man without great height or bulk. He began to throw punches. He was set upon by twenty-five or thirty of the . . . anarcho-syndicalists, I guess. There was a momentary geyser of funny clothes, odd hairstyles, and flopping tattooed limbs. The normal-looking man emerged, slightly winded, carrying the remains of the flag and having received a small scuff on the forehead.

OCTOBER 21, 2001

Six weeks into the War on Terrorism, contemporary war seemed to exhibit the vulgarity that Oscar Wilde said would be needed to make warfare unpopular. That is to say, the opening offensive of this war was directed at the quotidian, the workaday, the commonplace, the vulgar—ordinary people working at their daily jobs in office buildings. And common people, not self-exalted jihad warriors, were showing the bravery and making the sacrifices in Afghanistan as well as the United States. Then, in a more Wildean sense of the world "vulgar," there came the anthrax contamination. A cowflop of a weapon elicited all sorts of bull in response. On October 20 the *Los Angeles Times* devoted 465 column inches to a disease that had sickened fewer people than the corporation that makes the antibiotic by which the disease is cured. Only a few months before, Bayer had withdrawn the anti-cholesterol drug Baycol after it had been linked to fifty-two deaths.

Fortunately, my family doctor, William Hughes, has expertise in the most virulent aspect of anthrax—publicity. Dr. Hughes is married to ABC White House correspondent Ann Compton. He suggested that I get a ciprofloxacin prescription, lest anyone think I was too low in the journalism hierarchy to receive threatening mail. And indeed there were threats in my mail, but only the usual ones from Visa, American Express, and the landlord.

One of the first anthrax attacks was made against the company that owns the *National Enquirer.* The company's name is displayed in large letters on its suburban Florida offices: AMERICAN MEDIA. Supposing that the anthrax contamination is really the work of terrorists, al-Qaeda may be less sophisticated than we feared. "Ah," thought the bin Laden operatives, "*here* is where the American media have their place of headquarters." On the other hand, considering the role of supermarket tabloids in America's life of the mind, al-Qaeda may be more sophisticated than we thought.

Anyway, the media were enormously reassuring, simultaneously telling the public that members of the public won't contract anthrax while giving nonstop coverage to the members of the public who did, will, or might. Then Tom Ridge, the head of the Office of Homeland Security, came on the air, reminding us how much "Homeland Security" sounds like a failed savings-and-loan. Didn't Grandma lose $15,000 in a CD when Homeland Security went under? The media also recounted the complete list of symptoms for all three types of anthrax infection—symptoms that correspond to those of the common cold, the flu, a hangover, acne, and eating the church-picnic potato salad.

According to CNN on October 19, being infected with the intestinal form of anthrax results in "nausea, lack of appetite, and fever." And—if boiling rage counts as fever—so did being on a commercial flight. I had flown on ten during the five weeks after September 11, owing to an author tour for a badly timed collection of light humorous essays. (Not that I'm complaining about being knocked off the medium-well-seller list by people who spent five minutes with Osama bin Laden's brother-in-law in 1976. Especially not after hearing publishing-world scuttlebutt about a certain Manhattan novelist famous for tales of fashion models and drug excess, whose reaction on September 11, it's said, was to exclaim how glad he was that he didn't have a book out. Discriminating readers are *always* glad when he doesn't have a book out.)

Airport security would soon be turned over to the government so that a federal agency could do the same fine job of protecting the nation in the future that the CIA and the FBI did in early September. Meanwhile, "heightened security precautions" were allowing airlines to perfect their technique of treating passengers like convicted felons and providing all the transportation amenities usually accorded to smuggled cockatoos.

At the Los Angeles airport I watched as an elderly, arthritic man was forced to remove his buckle shoes and send them through the carry-on baggage X ray. In Ontario, California, a friend was meeting me at the airport. Of course he couldn't wait at curbside. He had to circle through the arrivals lane while slugs (slugs with valid photo IDs!) delivered my checked bags. On the forth go-round a policeman stepped into the road and told my friend that if he drove by one more time he'd be arrested.

What caused the giant python lines at airport security checkpoints remained a mystery. An acquaintance, a plastic surgeon who specializes in cranial reconstruction, was returning from a conference on head injuries shortly after September 11. His hand luggage contained three human skulls. These passed unnoticed through the X-ray screening.

Doubtless all sorts of civil rights must be sacrificed temporarily in times of crisis. But there is no ACLU for comfort and convenience. A generation hence we'll be living in a world of metal detectors in nudist colonies.

Traveling around the country did, however, allow me to see how different regions of America were coping with current events. On October 9 a local TV anchorman in Washington, D.C., called Islam (using an adjective perhaps left behind by the sudden journalistic shift away from celebrity obsession) "the second most popular religion on earth." It has an amazing Q factor, too, that Islam.

At about the same time, aided by the Internet, there was a cheerful realization nationwide that "Taliban" scans perfectly in "The Banana Boat Song":

Come Mr. Taliban, rid me of Osama.
Air Force come and it flatten me home.
Cruise missile,
Tomahawk,
Half-ton bomb.
Air Force come and it flatten me home.

On October 16, in Austin, Texas, local TV reported that the Austin fire department had responded to a call from a household concerning a "suspicious package." The sole suspicious thing about the package was that it had been mailed from New York City.

On October 19 a chipper announcer for KFWB radio, in southern California, said, "Anthrax news certainly has Orange County people talking . . ." Later that day, at a lunch in Simi Valley, I was sitting next to someone from the Ventura County district attorney's office. He said anthrax alarms were coming in at a rate of one every three minutes, and that the only practical decontamination response would be to have people get naked and be hosed down. That evening, on the set of a public-television book show, T. C. Boyle talked about how he had a certain admiration for acts of "ecotage," but in his fiction he tried to show both sides of the story. He managed never to mention September 11.

I can remember when powdery white substances of sinister origin were doing a lot more damage to America than anthrax had done so far. Circa 1980 America's elite was suffering "nasaltage." It emptied bank accounts, wrecked marriages, ruined thousands of careers, and brought the nation to its knees (with a soda straw over a glass coffee table). But Attorney General John Ashcroft was very firm in stating that anthrax threats are no laughing matter. Pranks and jests concerning anthrax would be treated as serious criminal actions. Thus various larval jokes with "You've got mail" punch lines had to be allowed to die before maturation. And the heavy metal band Anthrax was said to be considering changing its name—presumably to Chicken Pox.

Were we as a nation forgetting what our international critics have been saying about us for years? Aren't we supposed to be a big, terrifying country, a Godzilla of capitalism wrecking the globe? Since when did Godzilla flip out because he might have brushed against something in the mail room while he was devouring Trenton, New Jersey? Since when did Godzilla turn (devastating) tail and scamper to Mexico to buy Cipro over the counter?

I trusted this was a momentary lapse. And I hoped that Osama bin Laden was discovering, amid smart bombs and Delta Forces in Afghanistan, that America isn't scared, America is *scary*. The members of al Qaeda had gotten dressed up in their holy-warrior costumes and gone trick-or-treating at the wrong house.

November 26, 2001

Lo! The intrepid Afghan Taliban fighter of warrior lineage ancient. He who had vanquished countless foes, unassailable in his mountain redoubts, imbued with fanatical resolve, possessed by suicidal courage—and who was now running around Mazar-e-Sharif getting his beard shaved, playing Uzbecki pop music on his boom box, and using Mrs. Afghan Warrior's burka for a bedspread in the guest room, soon to be rented to foreign aid workers.

The fighting in Afghanistan was so brief that CNN Headline News had to delete three bars from its "Target: Terror" score to keep the theme music from outlasting the hostilities. The Soviet Union fought the Afghans for ten years and gave up in ignominious defeat in 1989. What were the Soviets using for weapons—cafeteria buns and rolled-up locker room towels? The United States dropped a lot of cafeteria buns—or emergency food aid that is very like cafeteria buns—on Taliban-controlled areas. Exposure to American school-lunch fare may have been the deciding factor in the radical Muslim demoralization. A country that can make something that dreadful from mere flour, yeast, and water is a country not to be defied.

However it was that we achieved victory, achieve it we did, although to what end remains to be seen. One effect of victory (though very temporary) was to make America's elite even more sanguine about armed conflict than they had been during the 1999 air war on Serbia. SURPRISE: WAR WORKS AFTER ALL, read the headline on the Week in Review section of the *New York Times* for Sunday, November 18, 2001. That same day the *Boston Globe Magazine* ran a cover story titled "The New Patriots: College students support a country at war—and so do their Vietnam-era parents." Of course, there was the possibility that the revived fighting spirit among America's elite had nothing to do with Afghanistan but was a collateral result of Harvard's first undefeated football season since 1913. I believe Harvard played Mount Holyoke, Smith, Li'l Dickens Day Care Center, and several Pop Warner League teams, but I didn't check that.

Meanwhile, what next for our nation? Would we do, after the Afghan war, as we did after the Gulf War and just go home, have a recession, and elect some creepy Democratic governor of an obscure state as the next president? Or would we finish the War on Terrorism? The U.S. Department of State publication *Patterns of Global Terrorism 2000* seemed to offer ample opportunities for pursuing the latter goal.

> *Iran remained the most active state sponsor of terrorism . . . It provided increasing support to numerous terrorist groups, including the Lebanese Hizballah, HAMAS, and the Palestine Islamic Jihad (PIJ) . . . Iraq continued to serve as a safe haven and support to a variety of Palestinian rejectionist groups . . . Syria continued to provide safehaven and support to several terrorist groups . . . Sudan continued to serve as a safehaven for members of al-Qaida, the Lebanese Hizballah . . . Egyptian Islamic Jihad, the PIJ, and HAMAS . . .*

We mustn't forget that this was not a war between Western civilization and the Muslim world. The *Washington Post* certainly hadn't forgotten. The *Post* made absolutely no comment about the real or apparent ethnicity of the person quoted in the following item about anthrax, which ran in the *Post*'s November 1, 2001, issue.

> *"In hindsight, this has been an escalating event," said Mohammad Akhter, executive director of the American Public Health Association. "We will continue to see new cases of anthrax disease."*

I was proud of the *Washington Post* and meant to write a complimentary letter to the editor, but I was too busy phoning in my tip to the FBI.

This was not a war between Western civilization and the Muslim world. There was, nonetheless, interesting reading to be done in *Freedom in the World*, a survey of political rights and civil liberties issued annually since 1955 by the nonpartisan organization Freedom House. Among countries whose populations are predominately (60 percent or more) Muslim, only remote Mali and tiny Benin were rated as "Free." On a scale of 1 (Canada) to 7 (god-awful), no other Muslim country received a score better than 3 in political rights and 4 in civil liberties.

Would we have to fight all those countries? Or could we just give them a hug? A peace vigil was being held each Saturday at noon outside the town offices in Peterborough, New Hampshire, a few miles from the house we own there.

According to the November 15, 2001, edition of the local newspaper, the *Monadnock Ledger*, "One week, when it was rumored that CBS might cover the protestors, 45 people showed up." By Saturday, November 17, the peace protest had, in effect, turned into a victory protest, and eight people were present. There was one sweet-faced, white-haired old lady, and then another who was so much older that she looked as if she might have been doing this sort of thing since the Hitler-Stalin Pact. There was a middle-aged man with hair that was both very long and gone from the top half of his head, a middle-aged woman upon whose features smugness had made an extensive and permanent settlement, a young man whose devil-may-care sideburns clashed with his go-to-hell golf pants, and a tweedy professor type who spent the whole vigil reading *The Nation*. Plus there was a mom in hand-knits trying to keep an eye on a rapidly fidgeting eight-year-old, and an Asian woman of college age who carried a sign reading RETALIATE WITH WORLD PEACE. Considering how world peace has gone for people in many places since the end of the Cold War, that's a harsh sentiment. After a while, the Asian woman wandered off to window-shop.

Most local New Englanders were ignoring the vigil with the perfect obliviousness to all incongruity that has been a New England hallmark since Henry David Thoreau went off to live a hermit's life at Walden Pond but continued to have his mother do his laundry. Only one fellow, flannel-clad, stopped to argue with the pacifists. "What do you do," the fellow asked, "when they strike the homeland? What if they roll right in here with tanks?" I was about to think "Good for you" when the fellow went on to say, "But I'll tell you one thing, I've refused to get the anthrax shots they're trying to give everybody."

So we see at what level debate about a just war and the natural right of self-defense was being conducted. The next morning, in a further sign of the times, Boston's WBZ Radio played a recorded segment by Martha Stewart detailing the intricacies of flag etiquette. The *New York Times* Sunday Styles section could not resist a bow to the New Seriousness—or an Afghanistan hook—even when reviewing the stupidest possible television show.

> *First, network news programs broadcast images of Afghan women removing their burkas . . . A few hours later . . . models had peeled away their clothing and were showing off thong panties as ABC broadcast the Victoria's Secret fashion show . . .*

And the November 20, 2001, issue of the *National Enquirer* had a feature headed "EVEN PETS ARE STRESSED OUT FROM TERRORIST ATTACKS." Here are some of the signs that your dog, cat, or hamster was suffering from the after-effects of 9/11:

- Sadness or glumness.
- Constant fighting with other pets.
- Lapses in toilet training.
- Pet is more needy and constantly seeks attention.

Speaking of constantly seeking attention, Bill Clinton showed up to give a talk at Harvard on November 19, perhaps to share anecdotes about his being a star quarterback on the undefeated Crimson gridiron squad of warrior lineage ancient. The *Boston Globe* didn't mention his football heroics but did give Bill two fulsome stories and a teaser: "Fans flock to Clinton in Hub visit." According to the *Globe,* Bill "blamed himself for not building stronger ties with the Muslim world during the 1990's . . . He said he should have worked harder . . . to support overseas 'nation building.'" In those days of flux and transformation there was comfort in knowing that some things stayed the same. It was still all about Bill. "America can exert influence, he said, by admitting its own faults." Interesting source for that advice. "We cannot engage in this debate," Bill was quoted as saying, "without admitting that there are excesses in our contemporary culture."

During a question-and-answer period Clinton said that he supported the creation of a Palestinian state. It's a good idea. Islamic fundamentalists will need someplace to go. Having them all in the West Bank and the Gaza Strip would allow the War on Terror to be conducted in a compact area with well-mapped terrain and an excellent road system. As long as the Israelis don't get involved. We wouldn't want anybody on our side who was guilty of premature antiterrorism.

Kuwait and Iraq

March and April 2003

Why is Iraq so easy to harm and so hard to help? After eight days of war, U.S. troops had arrived at Karbala, sixty miles from Baghdad. Misery had arrived everywhere. But humanitarian relief had gotten only as far as Safwan and Umm Qasr, just across the border from Kuwait.

I could see one reason that relief had gone no farther. I was on the outskirts of Safwan on March 28, on the roof of a Kuwait Red Crescent tractor-trailer full of food donations. Below, a couple of hundred shoving, shouldering, kneeing, kicking Iraqi men and boys were grabbing at boxes of food.

Red Crescent volunteers provided the boxes, gingerly, to the mob. Each white carton would be grasped by three or four or five belligerents and pulled in three or four or five directions—tug-of-Congolese-civil-war.

Every person in the mob seemed to be arguing with every other person. Giving in to conflicting impulses to push themselves forward and pull others away, shouting Iraqis were propelled in circles. A short, plump, bald man sank in the roil. A small boy, red-faced and crying, was crushed between two bellowing fat men. An old man was trampled trying to join the fray.

The Iraqis were snatching the food as if they were starving, but they couldn't have been starving or they wouldn't have been able to snatch so well. Most looked fully fed. Some were *too* fit and active. Everyone behind the trailer was expending a lot of calories at noon on a ninety-degree day.

Looking out, I saw irrigated patches in the desert, at about the same density as the patches on the uniform of a mildly diligent Boy Scout. The tomatoes were ripe. Nannies, billies, and kids browsed between garden plots. Goat Bolognese was on offer, at least for some locals.

There was no reason for people to clobber one another. Even assuming that each man in the riot—and each boy—was the head of a family, and assuming the family was huge, there was enough food in the truck. Mohammed al-Kandari, a doctor from the Kuwait Red Crescent Society, had explained this to the Iraqis when the trailer arrived. Al-Kandari was a forceful explainer. He resembled a beneficent version of Bluto in the Popeye comics, or Bluto in *Animal House*.

Al-Kandari had persuaded the Iraqis to form ranks. They looked patient and grateful, the way we privately imagine the recipients of food donations looking when we're writing checks to charities. Then the trailer was opened, and everything went to hell.

Al-Kandari marched through the donnybrook and slammed the trailer doors shut. He harangued the Iraqis. They lined up again. The trailer was opened, and everything went to hell.

Al-Kandari waded in and closed the trailer doors again. He swung his large arms in parallel arcs at the Iraqis. "Line up!" he boomed. "Queue!" he thundered—the Arabic-speaking doctor speaking to Arabic speakers in English, as if no Arabic word existed for the action.

Al-Kandari took a pad of Post-it notes and a marker pen from his lab-coat pocket. "Numbers!" he said, still speaking English. "I will give you all numbers!" A couple of hundred shouldering, shoving Iraqi men and boys grabbed at the Post-it notes.

The doctor gave up and opened the trailer doors. I climbed the ladder behind the truck cab to get a better view.

Aid seekers in England would queue automatically by needs, disabled war vets and nursing mothers first. Americans would bring lawn chairs and sleeping bags, camp out the night before, and sell their places to the highest bidders. The Japanese would text-message one another, creating virtual formations, getting in line to get in line. Germans would await commands from a local official, such as the undersupervisor of the town clock. Even Italians know how to line up, albeit in an ebullient wedge. The happier parts of the world have capacities for self-organization so fundamental and obvious that they appear to be the pillars of civilization. But here—on the road to Ur, in the Tigris-Euphrates Valley, where civilization has obtained for five thousand years longer than it has, for example, at a Libertarian Party confab in Phoenix—nothing was supporting the roof.

What I saw, however, wasn't anarchy. British soldiers stood nearby, emirs of everything within rifle shot. The Iraqis did not use weapons or even fists in the aid scramble. Later a British soldier said, "We try to stay out of crowd control, because it looks like we're trying to stop the aid distribution. But we can't let them start fighting." They did start fighting. A few Iraqis hit each other with sticks. They fought, however, at the front end of the truck. British soldiers broke it up.

The Iraqis didn't try to climb into the tractor-trailer or break through its side doors. Red Crescent volunteers, coming and going from the back of the truck, were unmolested. Once an aid box was fully in an Iraqi's control and had been pulled free from the commotion, no one tried to take it. I saw four boxes being guarded by a seven-year-old boy.

I watched a confident gray-haired man push toward the trailer gate. He had wire-rimmed glasses on the end of his nose and a cigarette in the corner of his mouth. He dove for a box, his glasses flying, the cigarette embers burning various *gutra* headdresses and *dishdasha* skirts. He disappeared for the better part of a minute. Then he came out on the other side of the throng, box under one arm and glasses somehow back on his face (but minus the cigarette). The gray-haired man looked around and delivered an open-handed whack to someone who, I guess, had indulged in a late hit.

I stared at the scrum for an hour. Now and then I'd be noticed on the trailer roof. Whenever I caught someone's eye, I was greeted with a big, happy smile. The Iraqis were having fun.

Worse fun was to follow. We were out in the countryside because the first aid convoy to Safwan, two days before, had gone into the center of town and had been looted in a less orderly riot. I left the truck roof and interviewed al-Kandari, or tried to. The doctor was still being importuned for worthless numbers on Post-it notes. "We almost get organized," he overstated, "but then some gangs will come from downtown, by running or by truck." They were arriving already, in anything they could get to move—taxis, pickups, ancient Toyota Land Cruisers, bicycles, Russian Belarus tractors, a forklift, a dump truck.

The men from town promptly climbed into the Red Crescent truck. They threw boxes to their buddies. The volunteers fled. In a few minutes one squad of looters had seventeen aid boxes. The box throwers were dancing and singing in the back of the tractor-trailer. A reporter who'd covered the previous convoy said, "I saw these same guys." He pointed to a wolfish-looking fellow who was pulling the tail of his *gutra* across his face. "You can tell the really bad ones," the reporter said. "They have shoes."

Al-Kandari ordered the driver to start the truck. The British troops cleared the highway. The truck drove back to Safwan with the trailer doors open and looters still inside. The other looters, in their miscellany of rides, gave chase. Men stood on car hoods and in pickup beds, trying to catch boxes being thrown from inside the trailer. Boxes fell, spraying fruit, rice, and powdered milk across the pavement. A flatbed truck passed us, piled with scores of aid boxes. The men standing on the bumpers had shoes. Horn honking, chanting, and other noises of celebration could be heard in the distance.

We drove through Safwan. Boys ran alongside our convoy, managing, with deft coordination of purposes, to jeer and beg at the same time. A reporter tossed a bottle of water to a boy. The boy picked it up and threw it at the reporter.

Safwan's houses, placed higgledy-piggledy, were built of tumbling-down mud brick. The other buildings were squat and lumpish, their walls formed of concrete with too much aggregate in the mix—Baath Party adobe. Signs of economic activity were nil. In the one park, playground equipment was rusty and broken. Trash was everywhere. Hundreds of black plastic shopping sacks blew along the streets, snagging in the rest of the rubbish. The people of Iraq may have nothing, but they have the bag it came in.

Safwan was a dump, but not a ruin. There was little war damage. Coalition forces had destroyed almost nothing but the customs sheds, which hadn't been used since 1991, when the Gulf War cease-fire was signed—as it happened, at Safwan.

In an hour and a half we were back in Kuwait City—in the same geography, on the same oil reserves, with the same people, same language, same religion. But Kuwait City is Houston without beer.

Twelve years ago Kuwait City was a dump *and* a ruin. The Iraqis destroyed what they couldn't steal and left the rubble full of their garbage, including piles of human feces. The hotel where the Gulf War press stayed survived only because it had carpets made from some self-extinguishing synthetic fiber. The Iraqis kept pouring diesel oil on the carpets. The flames kept going out. The hotel stank. There was no electricity. The rooftop cisterns ran dry. The only food was eggs, cooked by the hotel staff over campfires in the parking lot.

Twelve years later in Kuwait City I had tea and smoked salmon sandwiches and tarts and cakes and sticky treats with an American lawyer who has lived in Kuwait for twenty years. He was trapped by the 1990 invasion and forced to hide. He described the convoy of empty trucks that came from Baghdad every day—"all kinds of trucks, dump trucks included"—and returned every night full of swag. He told about the Baghdad buses that were driven to Kuwait carrying members of the "People's Army"—men and women turned loose in the shopping districts to pull down gates, push in doors, and loot. "The Iraqis," he said, "pried up the reflectors between the lanes in the streets and took them back to Baghdad." Then the lawyer spread his hands to take in the magnificence of the restaurant where we were sitting. "Even after all that," he said, "there was a lot left in Kuwait."

The smelly Gulf War hotel and everything else I remembered had been rebuilt or replaced. Freedom accomplishes extraordinary things. And there is an extraordinary list of things that Kuwait is free of. Kuwait is free of the Wahhabi religious idealism that inspires neighboring Saudi Arabia. There is an evangelical church in Kuwait City, a Coptic church, and a Roman Catholic Holy Family Cathedral complex with crosses forty feet high on its gable ends. (I confess to thinking that one way to get a drink in Kuwait was to take communion. But a priest from India drank all the wine.)

Kuwait is free of the lofty goals of pan-Arab socialism that animate the Baath Party. Kuwait is also free of the lofty goals that animate other political parties. Political parties are illegal. To vote in Kuwait one must be basically a son of a family that lived there when oil was something that seeped from the ground and ruined the camel forage. Franchise is denied to women and to most naturalized citizens and to the 62.9 percent of Kuwait's population—mostly guest workers and their dependents—who aren't citizens at all. The national assembly is of dubious political power anyway. Kuwait is more majority-owned than majority-ruled. The relatives of Sheikh Jaber al-Ahmed al-Sabah have held control since the eighteenth century.

As a nation, Kuwait has been, arguably, free of freedom itself. Claimed in turn by Constantinople, Riyadh, and Baghdad, Kuwait has survived by playing Turks off Persians, Arabs off one another, and the English off everyone. Kuwait became a British protectorate in 1899. In 1961 the British were asked to leave and immediately asked to return, to forestall an invasion by a previous Iraqi strongman, Abd al-Karim Qasim.

Now, some would say, Kuwait is an American fief. The Kuwaitis are free of resentment about that. Being an American in Kuwait City was like being a minor celebrity come back home to live. Walking through the souks, I was greeted with shy smiles and hellos from fellow shoppers. Merchants invited me to have coffee *after* I'd bought something. In the luggage souk two shopkeepers left their stores and showed me around until I'd bought what I wanted from a rival. The teller at the bank told me he liked my haircut. As the war neared, hotels and shopping centers put metal detectors inside their doors. As I was going into the Salhiya Mall, a security guard saw me start to empty the many pockets of my safari jacket. He got up, helped me out of the coat, carried it around the detector stanchions unsearched, and helped me put it back on.

The freedom that Kuwaitis do have is the freedom to do what they want. What they want to do is shop, eat, and sit around. The Kuwaitis are among the few peoples on earth—teenagers aside—who don't sneer at these freedoms. Apparently, they never did. Kuwait's Popular Traditional Museum is devoted to recapturing "Old Kuwait"—"old" being before 1951, when bountiful oil revenues arrived. In the museum's corridors are life-size models of bazaars, food markets, coffeehouses, kitchens, and home interiors, all filled with mannequins in period dress, sitting around. Exhibited artifacts include early electric fans, gramophones, Brownie cameras, radios with vacuum tubes, and a set of china commemorating the 1937 coronation of George VI.

In the new Kuwait this freedom of ways and means benefits from means that are prodigious. The McDonald's on Arabian Gulf Street has a doorman and a maître d'. A Mercedes dealership on the west side of town is the size of a county fair. Premium gasoline costs eighty-seven cents a gallon or—to put that in Kuwaiti currency (at US$3.34 to the dinar)—nothing. Lunch lasts from noon to five. The *gutra* on the man in line ahead of me at the McDonald's bore the Dunhill label.

Souk Sharq, on Kuwait Bay near the sheikh's palace, might have been designed by Frank Lloyd Wright, if Wright had been alive in 2000 and in need of a quick bill-payer job. The souk has its own yacht harbor. Inside the marketplace is a wide central aisle, space that in an American shopping center would be given over to booths selling sunglasses and caps with sports-team logos. At Souk Sharq one aisle stall was occupied by the De Beers diamond company.

The souk's grocery store, the Sultan Center, was Balducci's as Costco. Caviar tins were piled to the ceiling. In the food court the Chinese counter had Peking duck to go. At a children's clothing store a toddler play outfit—shirt, jumper, and gym shoes—came to $140 worth of jam mop and chocolate milk sponge. The Kookaï boutique was filled with the latest in the fashionable ethnic look; never mind that Kuwaitis *are* ethnics.

I interviewed a Bedouin the next day. He was tending his camel herd in the desert west of the city. He wore sandals and a sail-sized *dishdasha*. His *gutra* (not from Dunhill) was tucked in manifold gatherings under the *agal* headband. On the back of the Bedouin's riding camel was a carved-wood and tooled-leather footstool of a saddle. The camel's flanks were covered by vividly woven and elaborately tasseled wool provision bags. This was the first time I'd ever seen anyone really use the kind of handicrafts that tourists bring home. The Bedouin milked a mother camel and offered me the bowl. We sat around. He said, "I have three sons in medical school in the United States."

The camel's milk was frothy, light, slightly sweet. It would make an excellent latte. The desert sky was crosshatched with power lines. Oil pumping stations and tank farms could be seen in the distance. There was a six-lane highway behind the desert patriarch. He was Lawrence of New Jersey.

The liberties of Kuwait may be quotidian, but Kuwaitis are serious about them. Even in New Jersey the right to drive isn't exercised with Kuwaiti vigor. I was on that six-lane highway going seventy miles an hour in the left-hand lane, in bumper-to-bumper traffic, when a Mercedes 500SE sedan blinked its lights behind me. I had nowhere to go. The Mercedes driver cut left onto the unpaved shoulder and proceeded at ninety or a hundred down the barely car-width slot between the traffic and the concrete barrier. I could see his taillights wobble. He was terraplaning, gravel surfing, leaving a mile of stone stars in the windshields of the cars ahead.

The small, ordinary freedoms of life are priceless, especially if you remember to have someone else pay the price. Billboards on the backs of Kuwait's city buses show a photograph of a Kuwaiti hugging an American soldier during the 1991 liberation with the caption, in English and Arabic, "We Never Forget."

In early March 2003 most American soldiers were too far from town to be hugged. Also, they were about to liberate in the other direction. I wondered whether the Iraqis would say, "We never forget." If so, in what tone of voice will they say it?

Two days before the war began, the president of the United States gave an inspirational speech.

"I thought the Bush speech was a little bit inspiring," said a PFC at an Army Aviation Chinook helicopter base in western Kuwait.

"Nothing we didn't expect, just a confirmation," a warrant officer said.

"We most definitely have more to look forward to, now, instead of the standstill wait," said a sergeant. She'd obtained, somehow, in a Muslim marketplace, a case of pork sausages, and she was cooking lunch for her platoon in scrounged pans over a jury-rigged propane fire.

"This is just like being home after work," said a platoon member. "We're enjoying ourselves while we can. It's going to be a longer day once combat begins."

Some of the battalion's troops had come from Afghanistan. Kuwait's landscape, they said, was bleaker still. Six sandbags on the floor of each portable toilet said everything about the wind. The soldiers had free weights, laptops (though no Internet access), and once-a-week phone calls home. They said they had CDs with a variety of music: country, heavy metal, rap, bluegrass, gospel, alternative rock. But each soldier listened to one variety, not to the others. There was no "Tenting Tonight" or "Lili Marlene" in the Walkman-headphone army. "Everything is fine, aside from cold showers," said a private.

"One day closer to redeployment," said a lieutenant.

"Your worst day of waiting is better than your best day of combat," said a captain.

Asked about world opinion, peace protests, the UN, and so forth, a helicopter pilot said, "I don't care. We're here to do one thing and one thing only. If they tell me to go hurt someone, I'll go hurt someone."

That was a chilling statement of military professionalism, unless it was a heartwarming testimony to what military professionalism means in a democracy with armed forces under civilian control. Either way, the professionalism was different than it was in Kipling's time. A second pilot, leaving base as a sandstorm blew in, said to the first, "If I don't come back, I'm willing you all my tampons."

"We came here to do a job," said an enlisted man. "It doesn't matter what we think about it, we've got to do it." Then he added, "I'm doing it for my wife and kids."

And each soldier may have been listening to different music, but the soldiers agreed on *not* listening to certain tunes. A member of the popular country-and-western group the Dixie Chicks had stated that President Bush made her ashamed to be from Texas. A gunnery officer collected Dixie Chicks CDs to throw out the window of his Chinook. Also a campaign was discussed to return the Statue of Liberty to the French: "Take the Bitch Back."

The previous week a network anchorman had been scheduled to take a ride on one of the battalion's helicopters. I had happened to be on the base. I asked the private on sentry duty at the landing pad, "Have you seen Peter Jennings?"

"No, sir," said the private. "And I don't much like him, anyway."

At Camp Virginia, in northern Kuwait, amenities were fewer. Hot meals were infrequent. There were long lines for those cold showers. A sergeant took me for a ride in his Bradley fighting vehicle. We went across the desert at terrific speed—"terrific" being about forty-five mph. But in a large armored, tracked vehicle, this is like forty-five mph down the stairs on a cafeteria tray. As we crested a berm, the sergeant said, "Sometimes I don't know why they pay me!" He'd been in Kuwait for six months. Camp Virginia came back into view. "And sometimes," the sergeant said, "they couldn't pay me enough."

His crew wanted to know about *my* pay. "How much do you get paid to come here?" they asked. "Is this fun for you?" An officer from Army Public Affairs shushed them.

I was shown a mobile command-post tent carried by five trucks and big enough for a circus that's given up aerial acts. But inside, it seemed to be a Wall Street bond-trading boiler room. Officers sat at rows of tables, staring at computer terminals. In front of the tables were PowerPoint presentations on three large screens. Map displays showed enemy and coalition military positions in the planned initial combat zone, in Iraq as a whole, and in the entire Middle East.

The tent was windowless, the better to protect against NBC (nuclear, biological, chemical) threats. The other tents were also windowless. Ordinary soldiers, along with headquarters staff, spend a lot of on-duty time staring at computer terminals. And they spend a lot of time inside NBC suits, behind gas-mask lenses, breathing through filters. In the back of the Bradley fighting vehicle, where six combat infantrymen sit, the only peek at the outside is through periscopic slits. The Chinooks themselves, if you stand away from the door gunner's post, don't have a view. Or they don't unless the crew drops the rear-loading ramp. Then you have the disconcerting view you'd get from putting a French window in the floor of your mountaintop house deck. There's something as indoorsy as eBay about the twenty-first-century military. And from all I know about either part of that simile, something as historically transformative.

The military is indoorsy but not homey. The numerous ducts, tubes, and wiring bundles of technology—covered by Sheetrock and acoustic tile in civilian life—are left bare in the army. The hardware seems to expand with exposure. Austere functionality has so overgrown the interior of the Humvee that only four soldiers can fit into that hulking vehicle. Perhaps technology is squeezing humans out of warfare. But will they want to go?

A Chinook helicopter crew took me along on a live-fire exercise, to practice with the door-mounted M-60 machine gun. We flew to a range on the northern Kuwait border where Iraqi military junk from the Gulf War had been hauled. One of every so many rounds in the M-60's ammunition belt magazine was a tracer, which left a Fourth of July rocket trail telling where the bullets were going. I asked if it was like shooting a rifle, aiming precisely, or like shooting a shotgun, leading the target. "It's better than either," said the gunnery officer who'd been collecting Dixie Chicks CDs. "It's like walking the dog!" Bullets ambled along toward a Soviet-era Iraqi tank—trot, trot, trot, and mess in the yard.

Flying back from the firing range, I had a moment of clarity about one of the supposed underlying causes of the conflict in Iraq. The Kuwait desert is as flat as a patio and as big as Connecticut and Rhode Island combined. The entire space appeared to be covered in tanks, artillery pieces, Bradley fighting vehicles, Humvees, transport trucks, and Patriot missile batteries. Streaks of asphalt runway ran in all directions. The tarmac held fighter planes, cargo planes, and hundreds more helicopters: Chinooks, Black Hawks, Apaches, Kiowas. Amid the matériel were Camp Virginia, Camp New York, Camp Pennsylvania, and—the way it looked to me—Camps Other Forty-seven and Camp Puerto Rico and Camp Guam. Military force extended from me to the horizon in every direction, 360 degrees of war. It is much cheaper and easier to buy oil than to steal it.

At dawn on Thursday, March 20, when the first American missiles struck Baghdad, I was asleep in a big, soft bed. My wife, watching late-night news in the United States, called me in Kuwait to tell me the war had started. That was embarrassing for a professional journalist in a combat zone. But I looked around my comfortable hotel room and thought, "We *are* fighting for freedom. In this case, the freedom to go back to sleep in a big, soft bed."

I got out of bed, eventually, and went to interview the random bystanders who have become central to news coverage in the contemporary era. About a third of the stores and businesses in Kuwait City were closed. A bomb-sniffing police dog was digging furiously in a concrete planter outside my hotel, which would have been alarming if the dog hadn't had the unmistakable mien of a pooch who smells something deliciously dead.

The Kuwaitis I talked to were confident and enthusiastic. The proprietor of a fabric shop said, "America is here. I feel no problem in Kuwait."

I went to buy additional pens and notebooks, in case other spokesmen for the "Arab Street" were more loquacious. I asked the stationery-store owner about the onset of hostilities. "This is good," he said. "This is better. I want Saddam finish." He told me about seeing a young Filipina raped by Iraqi troops in 1990, outside his shop door. "I could do nothing," he said. "They loot my store—everything." He put a finger to his temple. "Click," he said. He all but came over the counter with angry enthusiasm. He declared, "I go for a soldier!" Then he sighed. "But my son says, 'You are sixty-seven.'" His Indian shop assistant steered me away from the less expensive pens.

Non-Kuwaiti guest workers were less certain about the war (although the stationery-store assistant did give me a hug after I'd interviewed his boss—and bought two boxes of felt-tips and a dozen steno pads).

"My owner won't let me close," said a Pakistani man at an appliance store. "You ask me, I close. Maybe you will inform him."

The Indian manager of a women's clothing store said, "I think this is not fair. Is for us and everybody, not good. Is bad for Saddam Hussein and very sad because of one person is all this trouble."

"You mean because of Saddam Hussein?" I asked.

"Yes, Saddam."

"But you still don't think this war is good."

"Yes."

I questioned a Filipino clerk at a photo-developing booth about his decision to come to work.

Me: Some businesses are closed.

Clerk: Sometimes they do not open.

Me: But you're open. You're not afraid?

Clerk: Some are a little afraid.

Me: How do you feel about the bombing?

Clerk: (Polite smile.)

Me: The U.S. bombed Baghdad this morning.

Clerk: I did not know about this. (Another polite smile.)

Iraq began firing missiles at Kuwait. Only the first air-raid warning had any effect on the Kuwaitis. When the sirens started, I saw a man in a *dishdasha* come out of an office building and rush nervously toward his car. Fifteen feet from the vehicle he stopped and pressed the door-lock button on his key-chain remote, and then he went back into the office building.

There was a mannequin wearing a gas mask in a store's window display, but it turned out that the store sold equipment to the police and military.

Plastic sheeting and duct tape were displayed in the hardware souk. "Many sales," said a fellow at one of the stalls. "But not because of the war—because of good price."

One of the Kuwaiti soldiers guarding my hotel wanted America to pick up the pace. "Tomorrow, tomorrow, and tomorrow," he exhorted, and made the motion of a baseball umpire calling a runner safe. "Boom!" he urged.

A tiny old lady wrapped in a black *abayah* approached me in the vegetable souk. She had the face of Mother Teresa—or, rather, the face that Mother Teresa deserved but didn't get. "American?" she asked.

"Yes," I said.

She gave me a beatific grin, a smile of hope and blessing, and drew her finger across her throat. "*Saddam!*" she beamed.

There was no sign of fear or patience among the Kuwaitis, any more than there would be among the Iraqis at Safwan. Sermons could be preached about the civilizing benefits and progressive influences of fear and patience.

And I've preached all of them to my three- and six-year-old daughters. I suspect I have one or two elements of the Muslim world in my own home.

But only one or two. An article in *Kuwait This Month* featured the *miswak,* a twig from the saltbrush tree that is employed as a natural toothbrush. "Muslims use it," the article said, "on the recommendations of Prophet Muhammad."

The Prophet is quoted in the text: "Use the *miswak,* for verily, it purifies the mouth, and it is a pleasure for the Lord." Not only is there no separation of Church and State in the Muslim world, there is no separation of Church and dental hygiene.

In *Arab Times,* a Kuwait English-language daily, the law court roundup reported that "S.H.F." was accused of raping "O.S.M." He took her to an apartment for a tryst, then invited some other men to have sex with her. She refused and was raped. S.H.F. was acquitted. The court ruled that "the testimony of the victim cannot be taken into account because during earlier interrogation she had said S.H.F. had sex with her three times and later confessed to having sex five times."

But just when I had decided that the people of the Middle East were as troublesome and confusing as the algebra they invented, there came a glimpse of the brotherhood of mankind, or—apropos of high school algebra—the brotherhood of sophomoric guykind. I was in a phone store when a young Kuwaiti married couple came in. They were in their late teens. She was a beauty, though cloaked to the soles of her feet and veiled to the eyes. A girl who is really pretty—whether she wraps herself in an *abayah,* a nun's habit, or the front hall rug—never wraps herself so that the world can't tell. The boy was tall and gawky and had a foolish grin. A line of hickeys ran up his neck.

The night I returned from Safwan, a missile hit the Souk Sharq. The Kuwaitis claimed it was a "Seersucker" missile. Who names these things—leftover old preppies at the CIA? Next we'll have the Madras Cummerbund missile and the Lime Green Pants with Little Trout Flies missile. I went to Souk Sharq in the morning. Kuwaiti police officers were lifting the crime-scene tape so that all the other guys could have a look at the cool destruction.

The damage wasn't great. But in one perfume shop every bottle had been exploded by the warhead's shock wave. The place reeked of Shalimar. A mature adult American with a perfume store would have been on his cell phone screaming at his insurance agent. The Kuwaiti store owner was sitting in a chair sipping a little cup of coffee. I introduced myself. The owner pointed cheerfully to the wet pile of broken glass. "Special price!" he said.

Being a "unilateral" reporter in Kuwait, rather than a reporter "embedded" with the military, meant that, like everyone else, I watched the war on TV. Except I was too close for comfort—to TV, not war. Cable and broadcast networks had taken over swaths of Kuwait's hotels. I was walking down the hall in the Sheraton and saw a huddle of serious-faced ABC television producers. They were having an animated discussion. Something was up. I moved closer.

"Do you think we should wake Diane?"

"I don't want to wake Diane."

"Maybe we shouldn't wake Diane."

I started to keep a notebook of things said by people who were sitting behind desks on television:

CNN, 3/19, Larry King to John Major: "I don't think the United States has ever started a war."

CNN, 3/20, several hours after the "decapitation strike" against Saddam Hussein: "It is like a brief intermission in some terrible, but real, movie."

CNN, 3/23, concerning a 101st Airborne soldier who threw a grenade into an officer's tent: "We'd like to point out that the soldier is said to have an Arab- or Muslim-sounding last name, but we'd like to point out that at this time this doesn't mean anything at all."

But I gave it up. I'm not prejudiced against CNN. It was just the first station on my hotel-room channel changer.

Every so often, the unilateral reporters were sent on official minibus tours, such as the one to Safwan. Thirty-five or forty journalists would pack into the minibus, pressed against the windows like pickles in a jar. The tours were arranged by the Kuwaiti Ministry of Information. The MOI falls under the purview of Kuwait's Department of Moral Guidance and Public Relations, and *there* is a branch of government that's a boat with two sterns and a big Evinrude outboard engine on each.

The minibuses made a lot of unexplained stops in the desert. At each stop a small, bossy man from the Ministry of Information shouted through a bullhorn: "Everybody get back on the buses."

Nobody got back on the buses.

"We are leaving," shouted the little bossy man.

We didn't leave.

I went to Umm Qasr, Iraq's only deepwater port. I saw Iraq's least successful looter scurrying down a side street clutching a vacuum cleaner hose, a strip of rubber molding, and the kind of small, dirty throw rug you don't mind if the dog chews. I saw Umm Qasr's port facilities. They'd been looted. Umm Qasr was the site of a detention facility for several thousand Iraqi "enemy prisoners of war," or "EPWs" ("POW" having, apparently, acquired too much political cachet for use on Iraqis). We were driven by the detention facility so fast that we couldn't see anything, because, we were told, under the Geneva Convention, prisoners of war are not allowed to be exhibited to the press.

I was also going to keep a notebook of my own thoughts about the war.

- Decapitation strike. Cut head off dinosaur. Dinosaurs have brains the size of walnuts. Leaves a lot of thrashing stegosaurus.
- Was U.S. radio reporter on roof of Nagasaki Hilton in 1945 saying, "Civilian casualties are going to cause problems for the U.S. winning the hearts and minds of the Japanese people"?
- Military bans embed satellite phones. Iraqis listening in. Getting toward April 15. Iraqis asking, "Is this H and R bloc a new coalition?"
- PhD dissertation to be written about the relationship of twenty-four-hour war coverage to reality TV. Glad I'm not in grad school.
- Will Boston Pops give concert featuring TV networks' "War in Iraq" theme music?
- Geraldo expelled for sketching U.S. positions in sand on live TV. Given Geraldo's investigative journalism track record, resulted in Iraqi artillery pounding Damascus.

But I gave that up, too. Geraldo appeared at my hotel, looking dramatically dirty and accompanied by enough equipment and crew to reinvade Iraq. With the Pentagon's blessing, he soon did. "The troops like him," an army public affairs officer explained. And why not? Geraldo is courageous, patriotic, and without him the troops aren't on TV.

Besides, a reporter didn't have to be foolishly brave to feel like a fool during the war. Thousands of Kuwaiti citizens and residents were imprisoned in Iraq in 1990 and 1991. Six hundred and five are still unaccounted for. Kuwait's National Committee for Missing and Prisoner of War Affairs held a reception for POW families and the press. Solemn and formally dressed Kuwaitis presented journalists, who were almost as grubby as Geraldo, with yellow roses, lapel pins, POW/MIA banners, and letters written by family members. One was from "A Daughter of a POW" and was addressed "To the whole world . . . to everyone who live on our good and blessed earth."

Tables of food had been set out. Waiters circulated with glasses of fruit juice. The room was decorated with the yellow ribbons that have gone—in good-thief-on-cavalry fashion—from self-pitying refrain in a country-and-western prison song to international symbol of hope and remembrance. There was no tactful way to escape interviewing the families.

I was with a Lebanese journalist friend who offered to translate. He guided me to two sisters wearing yards of stiff, shiny black cloth, Mona and Naaima. "They're Bedouin women," my friend said, "from a very humble background. You can tell by how dark they are from the sun. This is the only place you'd see them mix with wealthy Kuwaitis." Mona and Naaima's three brothers, ages nineteen to twenty-four, were arrested by the Iraqis in 1990.

"Why were they arrested?" I asked.

"They were in the Kuwait Army," said Mona. Naaima was arrested, too. She was a nurse. The Iraqis asked her to work in a hospital in Iraq. She refused and was sent to prison for four months, first in Basra, then in Najaf, then in Karbala. Her daughter was seven months old. The girl, now a thirteen-year-old in jeans, was at the reception with her mother and aunt. Naaima hadn't known that her brothers were held in the same prison she was. She caught a glimpse of them as she was being moved from Basra to Najaf. Three years ago Mona spoke with a former POW who recalled seeing her eldest brother in prison in 1991. That was all they knew.

"I'm the scum of the earth," I said to my Lebanese friend. "Our business eats these things. We're maggots in people's grief. And we can't even keep a story like this in the news for more than one *Oprah* episode. There's nothing I can do. There's worse than nothing. I'm a beacon of false hope, a Cape Hatteras lighthouse in downtown Raleigh." Or I said something like that, probably not so carefully thought out.

My friend spoke to the two women. They looked at me with concern and said something in Arabic. "They are firm believers in Allah," my friend said. "Whatever their brothers' fate is, they're willing to accept it, knowing that their brothers served Kuwait and served it well."

Baghdad fell. Iraqi rioting commenced. Looting was undertaken in earnest. Twenty-four-hour television coverage turned into the Shopping Channel. The war was over—not the killing, dying part but the part in which I was involved. I could tell by a sign on the bulletin board at the Kuwaiti Ministry of Information press center: FOR SALE—HELMET, U.S. ARMY MEDIUM, LIKE NEW, $100. FLAK VEST, CONCEALABLE, WORN ONCE, $350. And

CNN began covering the murder case against the husband of pregnant Laci Peterson again.

On April 16 I hitched a ride on an air force C-17 cargo plane to the Baghdad airport. Bouncing around in the windowless cargo hold was an Oshkosh fire engine.

"A fire engine?" said the army public affairs officer who took charge of me in Baghdad, and whom I'll call Major Bob. "We've already got a fire engine. What we need is water to put in it."

Thousands of troops occupied the airport. Their water was in one-liter plastic bottles. Sometimes there was a little water left over from drinking. Then a shower could be had by poking holes in the bottom of the water bottle, holding it right side up, and unscrewing the cap.

Hot meals were unavailable. The Meals Ready to Eat are less of a death penalty to the digestive system than they were during the Gulf War, and more of a life sentence to the school lunchroom. The weather was hot and windy in the daytime and hot and windy at night.

Troops and supplies were being flown into the airport's cargo facilities. The passenger terminal, designed by French architects in a "Harrah's Arabia" style, was being used as a bivouac. The combination of no planes at the gates, dull food, nonfunctioning air-conditioning, and snoring people stretched out on uncomfortable boarding lounge furniture made for a shock of the familiar to a frequent flier. Except you could smoke. Except everyone was running out of cigarettes.

There was an ad on the airport wall for the place where Iraq's information minister, Mohammed Saeed al-Sahhaf, used to regale the international press: "Al Rashid—It's More than a Hotel."

"It's a target," an army captain said.

I camped in the airport's administration building, in an office with bookshelves full of Reagan-era Boeing manuals and out-of-date Jeppesen guides to takeoff and landing patterns at international airports. I did not find one for LaGuardia with the World Trade Center towers circled in red. What I found instead was culture, or evidence of it.

Looting by Americans was strictly forbidden. But scrounging was okay, and we didn't have coffee cups. The Iraqi airport administrators had a wall of personal lockers, all carefully locked but with doors subject to persuasion by a Leatherman tool. I found a cup in one locker and—along with a bag of loose tea, a sliver of soap, and a spare pair of socks—the crudely printed cover of an English-language Iraqi edition of *Waiting for Godot.*

Artistic genius, arguably including Samuel Beckett's, has limned the extraordinary experiences of war—terror, desperation, suffering, bravery. Banal discomforts, however, need less brilliant insights to convey them. For example, "sandstorm." The word is too beach, too playground. And Iraq doesn't have sand. It has fine-ground goat droppings and minute particles of gluey clay. When the wind whips up, it's small-craft warnings in the lizard terrarium, a horizontal dirt blizzard. Then the drizzle that comes with spring sandstorms in the Persian Gulf begins, and with every breath the soldiers are fed a slime pie. Months of that and the food and the water, plus those extraordinary experiences of war, such as getting shot at, are wearing.

The lavatory facilities at the airport administration building consisted of one plastic stacking conference room chair with a hole cut out of the seat. It was placed over a bucket behind the TO BAGHDAD sign on the departure ramp.

The soldiers guarding a presidential palace near the airport had been in the Gulf since the previous July. Their lieutenant had been killed in the war. A sergeant told me his wife, unable to get a babysitter, had taken their five-year-old daughter to the lieutenant's funeral in the United States. "One of Daddy's soldiers is on his way to heaven," his wife explained.

"You mean he died," said the little girl. When they got home, the girl took a tablet and pencil and went into her bedroom. The sergeant often receives elaborate scribbles in the mail. Half an hour later his daughter came out and said, "Usually I write Daddy, but you'll have to write this so he can understand it: 'Daddy, be safe. Come home in one piece.'"

Another soldier was carrying a chrome-plated Winged Victory in his pocket. His thirteen-year-old son's soccer team had won the league championship. His son broke the "angel" off the top of the trophy and sent it with a note: "This will protect you."

Sergeant Luis Cubera was a New York City emergency medical technician. Major Bob said, "He was in Tower One when Tower Two got hit."

"It gave me a reason to come back in the army," said Sergeant Cubera.

The palace was called, I think, Abu Abid, but Iraq's presidential palaces are marked with barbed wire and watchtowers, not park service signs or historical plaques. The palace was built on an artificial island in a fishpond big enough for waterskiing. There was a swamped speedboat in the shallows. Some soldiers had removed whip antennas from Humvees and rigged the antennas with communication wire and safety pins. A fish fry was planned.

The palace architecture hinted that Iraq had a heritage. There was a dome and a bunch of pointy arches and some elaborate scribbles in Arabic around the front door, which was three stories high. Scale, proportion, and ornamental detail were those of the Ritz-Carlton Tomb of Hammurabi or the Great Mosque in Disney World's Muslimland.

The palace was badly built. Shoddy rubble-wall construction was skimmed with a thin layer of concrete. Lines were scored in the cement, faking the seams of quarried stone. A missile had blown off the back of the palace, exposing its crawl spaces and utility rooms. The PVC plumbing and low-grade electrical wiring looked like things strewn around by a trailer-park tornado.

Inside, materials were marble, alabaster, mahogany, teak, and mother-of-pearl, elaborately handcrafted by badly skilled workmen. The main reception room was four floors high. A crystal chandelier hung down past two tiers of balconies. I paced off the shadow it cast on the floor. The chandelier was the size of a two-car garage. If a reason to invade Iraq was wanted, felony interior decorating would have done. Imagine Liberace as an inner-city high school basketball star who'd just signed an NBA contract and converted to Islam.

Returning to the airport from the palace, Major Bob and I saw civilians being searched at one of the checkpoints. A village that housed Iraqi airport workers was inside the airport security perimeter. Some of the villagers had fled during the war. Now they were coming back. But they had to be frisked first.

For propriety's sake, the women were asked to frisk themselves. They patted their chadors, or their jeans and T-shirts, with both hands from ankles to shoulders, maintaining a neutrality of expression that was admirable in a forced Macarena.

Najah Raheem, age fifty-one, had been hired by the army to interpret at the checkpoint for three dollars a day.

"What did you do before the war?" Major Bob asked him.

"I was an air traffic controller."

"I'm probably living in your office," Major Bob said.

Najah suggested that we go to the village, called "the French Quarter" because it was built originally for the airport's French construction crews. "They will be eager to talk to you in the French Quarter," Najah said.

"They" was a formidable woman in black who had several of what seemed to be the village elders meekly in tow and any number of small boys and girls peering from behind her cloaks. "Three hundred families!" she said. "Many big families. Smallest families have five children. Ten days—no water, no electricity, no food, no cars."

One of the elders was brought forward to say, "The water main is broken" and "There are no wells."

"Is *this* the new Iraq?" the formidable woman said. "No schools. All night it is dark. We need *one* generator. There is no money. No doctor." She pointed to an old man. He had sores on his feet. He displayed them. "No insulin," the woman said.

Major Bob wanted to know if there had been any looting or threats of violence in the village. "Are you safe?" he asked.

"Safe?" she replied. "Too safe! Ignore safe!"

Major Bob went to the army engineers. "We've got a little hearts-and-minds situation in our own backyard," he said. The officer on duty looked harried. The engineers knew about the problems in the French Quarter, but the French Quarter was hooked into the airport, and they hadn't been able to get the airport's main power and water systems working. Anyway, orders would have to come from above.

"Which means a written report," Major Bob said, eyeing me. Major Bob is an infantry officer by training and inclination. But the army thinks about its field officers what Harvard MBAs think about themselves: they can run anything. "I get to rotate out of public affairs next year," said Major Bob.

The most tendentious journalists don't write to accomplish much except getting read. The most meticulous fact-checking departments don't check actual knowledge. It's remarkable how much about pipelines and electrical grids one reporter can be ignorant of. The report was delivered, and it joined, electronically, a queue of complaints, demands, and emergency appeals.

I went into Baghdad, tagging along on military errands. The city looked more like the target of a trash collectors' strike than the target of shock and awe. There were burned-out military vehicles here and there, but garbage was everywhere. The destruction from the air attacks had been highly specific, though wholesale within its specificity. Uday Hussein's Olympic training facility and supposed personal headquarters was erased, the rubble too flat even for low hurdles. The walls surrounding the complex were untouched. An Interior Ministry building was a ten-story cinder, like the readable ash from a sheet of burned newspaper. Damage caused by the armor attack on the city was noticeable because it was newer, crisper, and more clean-edged than the general deterioration of Baghdad.

The men in the streets were sullen, and they were enthusiastic, and they were both. They stood with their buddies, glaring at American soldiers, and then rushed up to those soldiers to try to sell them something or change money. The women in the streets looked put-upon and harassed. Keeping the kids from playing on the tanks was just one more damn thing. The little boys carried ballpoint pens and wanted to have their arms signed by the soldiers.

Broken glass and twisted window gates from looting were all over the sidewalks. Improvised stalls of tradesmen were all over the sidewalks, too. How much of the trade was in loot I couldn't tell. The citizens of Baghdad were selling a lot of cigarettes and two-liter bottles of Fanta orange soda to one another. They were busy, though not with brooms and mops. I did see one man washing his car, however.

And there was another man, standing by his car in a long line at a gas station, who hid his AK-47 under his *dishdasha* as we drove by. The sound of AK-47s being shot could be heard at a distance from wherever American troops happened to be. Some of the shooting was rhythmic, celebratory "happy fire." Some was not, and came in single shots or short, discordant bursts. The gunfire increased after sundown.

If Kuwait is Houston without beer, Baghdad is Washington, D.C., without Pierre L'Enfant. Wide boulevards have been plopped down anywhere amid an absurdity of monuments and monumental buildings and monumentally bad taste. A photograph of the soccer stadium could convince tabloid readers of an alien invasion. To commemorate victory (of which there was none) in the Iran-Iraq War, Baghdad's parade ground has a pair of boxcar-size hands popping out of the ground, holding crossed swords in a pot metal arch seventy feet high. And there's an identical arch at the parade ground's other end, to commemorate victory some more. The arches were untouched by the recent conflict. They formed a moving testimony to the discipline, training, and self-restraint of the U.S. Army's tank gunners.

An American armored battalion had occupied another Baghdad monument, a hundred-foot-tall split onion dome with both dome halves covered inside and out in bright-blue glazed ceramic tile. "We call it 'the tits,'" said a sentry at the monument's gate.

"Do you know what that is?" asked a reproving captain in whose Humvee I was riding. "It's the tomb of the Iraqi Unknown Soldier."

"Yes, sir," a second sentry said. "You'll find the colonel somewhere over by the, um, 'eggshells.'"

Actually, the Unknown Soldier memorial was back across the river, at the crossed-swords parade ground. The dome sections (which more closely resemble baboon butt cheeks) memorialize *known* Iraqi soldiers—the million or so killed in the war with Iran. Their names and military units are inscribed in profusion around the structure's base, and inside, glass cases are full of the soldiers' belongings. This "Martyrs' Monument" is dedicated to ordinary Iraqis, although, according to the armored battalion's colonel, the only people allowed to visit it under Saddam's rule were members of the Baath Party. One section of the interior was reserved solely for Saddam and his immediate family.

Saddam's family, or their moral ilk, had been using the Martyrs' Monument as a chop shop for stolen automobiles. An Iraqi carpenter hired to repair the car-thief damage was scared to go into the forbidden Saddam zone.

The looting of antiquities from the Iraq National Museum wasn't a good example of America's failure to protect Iraq's heritage. Dug in on the museum's grounds were squadrons of paramilitary *Fedayeen*—not a part of Iraq's heritage that needed preserving. And do you shoot looters? A man running down the street with a two-hundred-pound head of Nebuchadnezzar in his arms can't hurt you. If you shoot someone who's got a Winged Lion of Assyria, he'll turn out to be a museum curator taking it home for safekeeping—or it will be a plastic Winged Lion of Assyria lawn ornament.

American tanks were guarding the National Museum with horse-gone, barn-door-closed acuity. I asked a tank crew, "Do you shoot looters?"

"Our operational orders are supposed to be secret," one crew member said.

"No," said another.

The looting of antiquities wasn't an example of much of anything, considering where the objects in museums come from in the first place. Also, many of the most valuable archaeological treasures were hidden by the museum's staff. Others were trickling back to the museum. The Sumerian Sacred Vase of Warka was restituted by its thieves in June. According to *USA Today,* "The men returned the vase because they realized its importance to Iraq's heritage, officials said."

The official in charge the day I was at the museum, the director of research, Dr. Donny George, said, "Starting from yesterday we've stopped talking to the media." Television camera crews, news photographers, and other journalists had swept through the museum, grabbing images of pillage and snatching quotes from the staff.

One staff member sat atop what archaeologists call—or will call in a thousand years—a midden. The museum's lobby was heaped with crumpled records, letters, bills, and receipts. File cabinets had been pulled into the open space and their locks had been shot open. The locks had been shot open even on some newly delivered file cabinets, empty and still in their shipping wrappers. The staffer, an older man, smoothed pieces of paper. If it was an important piece of paper, he put it in a folder and sighed. If it wasn't, he threw it away and cursed. Every now and then a janitor would shove the discarded papers back into the unsorted pile. The rest of the museum staff sat around.

I'd come to the museum with soldiers from a Civil Affairs battalion. They were reservists with nonmilitary skills—firemen, policemen, engineers. One sergeant was getting his PhD in sociology. With aid agencies yet to arrive, Civil Affairs had the job of fixing everything in Iraq that didn't need to be killed, although Civil Affairs had guns, too. Dr. George gave the soldiers a tour of the museum, and, uninvited, I went with them.

The galleries were a crime scene, but the parts of the museum that weren't open to the public were the scene of something else. Windows were broken. Furniture was smashed. Copiers, coffeemakers, typewriters, and telephones had been thrown around the rooms, and bullets had been fired into ceilings and walls. Bookshelves had been pulled over, and books and publications had been ripped and tossed. Archive photos were torn.

Microfilm was unspooled and festooned like the remains of a ticker-tape parade in negative.

Rows of ancient pots had been staved in. Drawers' worth of carefully cataloged scholarly fragments had been further fragmentized. "Be careful," Dr. George said, "because you might be stepping on antiquities." Thousands-of-years-old crunches sounded under our feet.

The restoration studio was ruined. Tools were bent and broken. This wasn't looting. A gold Lyre of Ur had been stripped of its gold leaf; the lyre itself was on the floor. "Vandalism" was not the word. The Vandals controlled the Mediterranean with their sea power and forced the Roman emperor Valentinian III to make peace. They must have had brains. The people who did this to the National Museum were brainless enough to have gone to college with me. I remember just such a scene visited upon a persnickety landlord of off-campus housing. But I don't think the worst of my keg buddies would have trashed America's heritage. The looted Sumerians themselves, back from the dead and drunk as the lords they were, couldn't get this worked up at a museum.

One of the broken statues looked kind of Greek. "Hellenistic period," I said, in a lucky guess, to Dr. George. He smiled at me and began answering my media queries before I'd had a chance to make any.

"There were three groups of looters," Dr. George said. "First there were the experts." He explained that they had come equipped with glass-cutters and battery-operated saws with stone-cutting blades. They knew what they were after and didn't take replicas or objects that had been overrestored. "Then there were the opportunists." He said that they took whatever they could and did most of the damage. "But then there is a third group—I don't know who they are. I don't understand. They are determined to burn all the libraries and archives in Baghdad, in all the colleges, at Baghdad University. They burned the central library. They burned all the postgraduate studies at the colleges. They burned the library here at the museum—just the library, not the other parts."

While I was interviewing Dr. George, curators from another museum arrived. This was the Museum of Modern Art, formerly known as the Saddam Hussein Museum of Modern Art, now renamed (for the moment, at least), as were the Saddam International Airport, the Saddam City housing project, the Saddam Hospital, and so on. It takes a certain kind of name to name everything after yourself. "P.J." wouldn't do: Pajama International Airport, Pajama City, Museum of Modern Pajamas.

The Museum of Modern Art had been looted, too. "Three or four hours ago we were chasing the looters," one of the curators said. But the staff had managed to get most of the museum's collection locked in the basement. Now, however, Baghdad's sewage system was backing up.

Sewage was flooding into the museum cellar, and Iraq's entire collection of modern art was in peril.

The curators appealed to the Civil Affairs soldiers. "We need trucks," one of the curators said, "to bring the paintings here, where they will be guarded." The men from the Museum of Modern Art said it was America's responsibility. They said it was America's duty. They didn't say it was America's fault. But they were thinking it. And I was thinking that among the things America *didn't* bomb in Baghdad were the sewer outlets into the Tigris.

Major Bob woke me up the next morning. "The Civil Affairs guys scrounged a truck," he said. "We're going to save the modern art of Iraq."

It was a hundred degrees by ten a.m. Iraq's works of modern art tend to the large, also the numerous. We moved them from the mucky basement to the dusty truck as carefully as we could. Seeing a piece from a distance, Major Bob would say, "Now, that's a really bad Chagall"—but it would turn out to be painted in Chagall's extremely late period, when he was dead, and would be signed by someone local. "Well," Major Bob said, "it's their heritage, not ours."

The museum building had been rubbished. A couple of modern sculptures, too big to be hidden, were looking edgy and brutalist and, frankly, improved by the vandalism. Broken glass and shredded exhibit posters covered the entranceway. A young man in a disco haircut, sharply creased pants, and expensive shoes came to the gate. "Can I get into the museum?" he asked.

The sergeant who was getting his PhD in sociology and was cradling an M-16 said, "It's very closed."

We dropped a truckload of art at the National Museum, half a mile away. I stayed behind to talk to Donny George.

Returning on foot, I got lost. Baghdad was, again, like Washington: I didn't have to wander far from the edifices to get into a slum. But rather than leaving the poor to the vagaries of outdated housing stock, the Iraqis had built their slums new. The two-story hovels, with one window apiece, were made of cement blocks left unpainted. There were tiny stores along the street. The shelves were vacant. People were loitering. I heard "Hello, American" several times from kids. I got "Welcome, please" from a couple proprietors of empty stores. There were a few hard stares from young men, who muttered after I'd passed. There were a few fewer wan smiles from old people.

I was in a flak vest that Major Bob insisted I wear for a visit to Baghdad, and my clothes were khaki from dirt. But I was too old to be a soldier, and I didn't have a television camera, so I couldn't be a journalist. I don't know how I appeared to the Iraqis. Mostly I didn't. I was invisible to the majority of people. Seventeen years before, in Belfast, British troops had

had this invisibility. Squadrons in battle gear would patrol the Republican stronghold of Divis Flats, and to the Irish they weren't there. The British have ended up spending nine centuries in Ireland.

I found my way back to the Museum of Modern Art. A television crew from Bahrain had arrived. The soldiers were being interviewed about the importance of Iraq's cultural heritage. An eight-foot canvas depicting an innocent Iraqi being smothered by an American flag and pecked by a bald eagle had just been pulled from the cellar. The TV reporter, Saad al-Hasani, was also an assistant professor of English at the University of Baghdad. I asked him if he knew anything about the "third group" of looters who Dr. George had said were burning libraries.

Professor al-Hasani had gone to stay with relatives in the country during the war. His apartment in Baghdad had been looted. He'd expected that. But someone had carried all his books down to the apartment building's yard and burned them.

"I teach modern theater," he said. "My specialty is Samuel Beckett and the theater of the absurd. I'd always had trouble explaining Beckett to my students. They didn't comprehend the theater of the absurd. Then, after the war in 1991, my students suddenly were starting to understand *Waiting for Godot.* I could tell by the questions they asked in class, by their essays. It was if they were anticipating something. There was a situation in the air. A student came up to me and said, 'This is just like *Waiting for Godot.* Nobody comes. Nobody goes. It's awful. *Nothing to be done.*'"

I told Professor al-Hasani about the book cover in the airport administration-building locker. Would air traffic controllers and aeronautical engineers be reading *Godot,* too?

"Of course," he said.

That evening at the airport a major and a lieutenant colonel from the Civil Affairs battalion drove the truck around scrounging material to build a latrine. The major was a mechanical engineer. The colonel was an electrical engineer. They argued as if they were married.

"We can build a lighter frame if we stress the plywood in monocoque construction."

"Fuck lightness—compression equals strength."

I pounded nails, rather crookedly. It was an innovative outhouse. Cut-down fifty-five-gallon oil drums were set on airport luggage trolleys so that waste cans could be rolled in under the seats.

"You have seen the backside of war," the electrical engineer said.

The next morning Major Bob woke me again. "We're going to the French Quarter with Civil Affairs," he said. I thought proudly about the written report—for a moment. Then the Civil Affairs battalion commander told me our visit had nothing to do with our report informing higher-ups that a visit was needed. "Some Special Forces guys were patrolling through there," he said. "They told command it was a mess. We're only supposed to do an assessment—which is what we did the last time we were there—but we've scrounged some tools, and we were scrounging around in the terminal and found a bunch of antibiotics and medical supplies the Iraqis had hidden."

We were greeted by the village elder who'd said the water main was broken. Without the formidable woman, he was more talkative. He said the American attack on the airport came through the middle of the French Quarter. The area had been defended by Iraqi secret police, but not very well, to judge by the slight shell and bullet damage. The village elder said he'd been a fire chief for thirty years. The French Quarter was not a cap to his career. After a secret-police vehicle was hit by an American rocket, a house caught fire, and the entire block burned down. Ten families were left homeless, but fortunately they were homeless already, having fled from the war.

Tarik al-Wasty, a carpenter and pipe fitter at the airport, had spent the five days of the bombing and assault lying on the floor of his house with his wife and ten children. He showed me a hole where a tank round had come into his garden, and offered me tea. His two-year-old son was still terrified, would sleep only if curled beneath his father, and was coughing continually. A medical corpsman brought some drugs from the Iraqi cache. The corpsmen tried to explain to Tarik, whose English was not good, that steam could be used to help clear the child's chest. Getting a blank stare, the corpsman attempted charades and was prevented from persuading Tarik to boil his toddler in a pot by the family's nine-year-old son, whose English was excellent.

The electrical-engineer lieutenant colonel had discovered fellow electrical engineers among the French Quarter residents. They were probing the innards of a transformer. The mechanical-engineer major had found additional engineers. They were inspecting the water main, which had been crushed by a tank. "I think I know where there's a big piece of pipe I can scrounge," the mechanical engineer said.

Major Bob and I looked at the school. It was the one public building I saw in Iraq that hadn't been looted. There were only a few bullet holes in the walls. The school was decorated with murals of Smurfs and Mickey Mouse drawn, it looked like, by the painter of the Chagalls at the Museum of Modern Art.

The fire chief and some of his friends gave us a tour of the village. The houses were prefab, semidetached, and looked like modest European vacation cottages but with bomb shelters in their yards. Recreation facilities had been provided for the previous construction-worker tenants—a picnic area, a swimming pool, tennis and volleyball courts. The nets were gone. The poles were bent double. The swimming pool was half-filled with chunks of concrete. The picnic area was layered in trash. The fire chief said something about "repairs forbidden" and that the French Quarter had fallen out of favor with Saddam Hussein. If appearances were any indication, so had the rest of Iraq.

"Having looked at the Mideast," Major Bob said, "I realize how the Arabs came up with the concept of zero."

Will a strong Iraq emerge from the chaos? Let's hope not. But will the Iraqi people become part of the modern, free, and prosperous world? That's possible, though I have only one piece of anecdotal evidence to go by. I was riding through Baghdad in the last truck of an army convoy, with a unit that will go unidentified because drinking was a punishable offense for U.S. troops in Iraq. We spotted a man selling beer on the street. "I'd better stop," said the sergeant who was driving, "and check my windshield-wiper fluid level or something."

I jumped out of the truck. "Let me do this," I said. "I've been coming to the Middle East for twenty years. I *know* how to *haggle*."

"How much for the whole case?" I asked the vendor in pidgin and gesture.

"Twenty bucks," he said in English.

Twenty dollars was a fortune in Baghdad at that moment. Also, I didn't have twenty dollars. I had a ten and a bunch of Kuwaiti dinars. The vendor looked askance at the dinars. The soldiers weren't carrying much money, either. They came up with another six dollars among them.

I dickered with the beer merchant. He bargained. I chiseled. We bandied. A crowd gathered to watch. Some teenage Iraqi boys, seeing an Asian-American soldier in the truck, hollered, "*Thigh Cone Do!*" and exhibited awkward kicks.

The seller of beer and I concluded a deal of considerable financial complexity involving U.S. dollars and Kuwaiti dinars, with change in Iraqi dinars at an exchange rate determined by consensus among the purchase's spectators.

Back in the truck, as we tried to catch up with our convoy, I did the math. I had bargained my way from $20 to a final price of $24.50. And the beer turned out to be nonalcoholic.

ON THE WEALTH OF NATIONS

(2007)

"He took only what his superficial mind had the power of taking, and the pith of Smith's thinking must have been left behind. To borrow even a hat to any purpose, the two heads must be something of a size."

—Adam Smith's biographer, John Rae, on a previous author who attempted to appropriate Smith's work

An Inquiry into *An Inquiry into the Nature and Causes of the Wealth of Nations*

The Wealth of Nations is, without doubt, a book that changed the world. But it has been taking its time. Two hundred thirty-one years after publication, Adam Smith's practical truths are only beginning to be absorbed in full. And where practical truths are most important—amid counsels of the European Union, World Trade Organization, International Monetary Fund, British Parliament, and American Congress—the lessons of Adam Smith end up as often sunk as sinking in.

Adam Smith's Simple Principles

Smith illuminated the mystery of economics in one flash: "Consumption is the sole end and purpose of all production." There is no mystery. Smith took the *meta* out of the *physics*. Economics is our livelihood and just that.

The Wealth of Nations argues three basic principles and, by plain thinking and plentiful examples, proves them. Even intellectuals should have no trouble understanding Smith's ideas. Economic progress depends upon a trinity of individual prerogatives: pursuit of self-interest, division of labor, and freedom of trade.

There is nothing inherently wrong with the pursuit of self-interest. That was Smith's best insight. To a twenty-first-century reader this hardly sounds like news. Or, rather, it sounds like everything that's in the news. These days, altruism itself is proclaimed at the top of the altruist's lungs. Certainly it's of interest to the self to be a celebrity. Bob Geldof has found a way to remain one. But, for most of history, wisdom, beliefs, and mores demanded subjugation of ego, bridling of aspiration, and sacrifice of self (and, per Abraham with Isaac, of family members, if you could catch them).

This meekness, like Adam Smith's production, had an end and purpose. Most people enjoyed no control over their material circumstances or even—if they were slaves or serfs—their material persons. In the doghouse of ancient and medieval existence, asceticism made us feel less like dogs.

But Adam Smith lived in a place and time when ordinary individuals were beginning to have some power to pursue their self-interest. In the chapter "Of the Wages of Labour," in book 1 of *The Wealth of Nations*, Smith remarked in a tone approaching modern irony, "Is this improvement in the circumstances of the lower ranks of the people to be regarded as an advantage or as an inconveniency to the society?"

If, in the eighteenth century, prosperity was not yet considered a self-evidently good thing for the lower ranks of people, it was because nobody had bothered to ask them. In many places nobody has bothered to ask them yet. But it is never a question of folly, sacrilege, or vulgarity to better our circumstances. The question is how to do it.

The answer is division of labor. It was an obvious answer—except to most of the scholars who had theorized about economics prior to Adam Smith. Division of labor has existed since mankind has. When the original Adam delved and his Eve span, the division of labor may be said to have been painfully obvious. Women endured the agonies of childbirth while men fiddled around in the garden.

The Adam under present consideration was not the first philosopher to notice specialization or to see that divisions are as innate as labors. But Smith was arguably the first to understand the manifold implications of the division of labor. In fact he seems to have invented the term.

The little fellow with the big ideas chips the spear points. The courageous oaf spears the mammoth. And the artistic type does a lovely cave painting of it all. One person makes a thing, and another person makes another thing, and everyone wants everything.

Hence trade. Trade may be theoretically good, or self-sufficiency may be theoretically better, but to even think about such theories is a waste of that intermittently useful specialization, thought. Trade is a fact.

Adam Smith saw that all trades, when freely conducted, are mutually beneficial by definition. A person with this got that, which he wanted more, from a person who wanted this more than that. It may have been a stupid trade. Viewing a cave painting cannot be worth three hundred pounds of mammoth ham. The mutuality may be lopsided. A starving artist gorges himself for months while a courageous oaf of a new art patron stands bemused in the Grotte de Lascaux. And what about that wily spear point chipper? He doubtless took his mammoth cut. But they didn't ask us. It's none of our business.

Why an Inquiry into Adam Smith's Simple Principles Is Not an Inquiry, First, into Adam Smith

Most things that people spend most of their time doing are none of our business. This is a very modern idea. It makes private life—into which we have no business poking our noses—more fascinating than private life was to premoderns. Adam Smith was a premodern, therefore this book is organized in an old-fashioned way. The man's ideas come first. The man comes afterward. Adam Smith helped produce a world of individuality, autonomy, and personal fulfillment, but that world did not produce him. He belonged to an older, more abstracted tradition of thought.

When a contemporary person's ideas change the world, we want to know about that person. Did Julia Child come from a background of culinary sophistication, or did her mother make those thick, gooey omelets with chunks of Velveeta cheese and Canadian bacon like my mother? I fed them to the dog. What elements of nature and nurture, of psychology and experience developed Julia Child's thinking? But there was a time when thinking mostly developed from other thinking. The thinkers weren't thinking about themselves, and their audience wasn't thinking of the thinkers as selves, either. Everyone was lost in thought. Dugald Stewart, who in 1858 published the first biography of Adam Smith, excused its scantiness of anecdote with the comment, "The history of a philosopher's life can contain little more than the history of his speculations."

Another reason to put the history of Adam Smith's speculations ahead of the history of Adam Smith is that Smith led the opposite of a modern life—uneventful but interesting. He was an academic but an uncontentious one. He held conventional, mildly reformist political views and would have been called a Whig if he'd bothered to be involved in partisan politics. He became a government bureaucrat. Yet the essence of his thinking—"It's none of our business"—will eventually (I hope) upend everything that political and religious authorities have been doing for ten thousand years. In a few nations the thinking already works. There are parts of the earth where life is different than it was when the original physical brute or mystical charlatan wielded his initial club or pronounced his initial mumbo jumbo and asserted his authority in the first place.

The whole business of authority is to interfere in other people's business. Princes and priests can never resist imposing restrictions on the pursuit of self-interest, division of labor, and freedom of trade. Any successful pursuit of these means a challenge to authority. Let people take the jobs they want, and they'll seek other liberties. As for trade, nab it.

A restriction is hardly a restriction unless coercion is involved. To go back to our exemplary Cro-Magnons, a coercive trade is when I get the spear points, the mammoth meat, the cave painting, *and* the cave. What you get is killed.

Coercion destroys the mutually beneficial nature of trade, which destroys the trading, which destroys the division of labor, which destroys our self-interest. Restrain trade, however modestly, and you've made a hop and a skip toward a Maoist Great Leap Forward. Restrain either of the other economic prerogatives and the result is the same. Restrain all three and you're Mao himself.

Adam Smith's Less Simple Principles

It is clear from Adam Smith's earlier (and more celebrated in its time) book, *The Theory of Moral Sentiments,* that Smith was a moral advocate of freedom. But the arguments for freedom in *The Wealth of Nations* are almost uncomfortably pragmatic. Smith opposed most economic constraints: tariffs, bounties, quotas, price controls, workers in league to raise wages, employers conniving to fix pay, monopolies, cartels, royal charters, guilds, apprenticeships, indentures, and of course slavery. Smith even opposed licensing doctors, believing that licenses were more likely to legitimize quacks than the marketplace was. But Smith favored many restraints on persons, lest brute force become the coin of a lawless realm.

In words more sad and honest than we're used to hearing from an economist, Smith declared, "The peace and order of society is more important than even the relief of the miserable." Without economic freedom the number of the miserable increases, requiring further constraints to keep the peace among them, with a consequent greater loss of freedom.

Smith was also aware that economic freedom has its discontents. He was particularly worried about the results of excess in the division of labor: "The man whose whole life is spent in performing a few simple operations . . . generally becomes as stupid and ignorant as it is possible for a human creature to become." We've seen this in countless politicians as they hand-shake and rote-speak their way through campaigns. But it's worth it. Productivity of every kind can be increased by specialization. And the specialization of politics at least keeps politicians from running businesses where their stupidity and ignorance could do even greater harm to economic growth.

Adam Smith's More Complicated Principles

Smith's logical demonstration of how productivity is increased through self-interest, division of labor, and trade disproved the thesis (still dearly held by leftists and everyone's little brother) that bettering the condition of one person necessarily worsens the condition of another. Wealth is not a pizza. If I have too many slices, you don't have to eat the Domino's box.

By proving that there was no fixed amount of wealth in a nation, Smith also proved that a nation cannot be said to have a certain horde of treasure. Wealth must be measured by the volume of trades in goods and services—what goes on in the castle's kitchens and stables, not what's locked in strongboxes in the castle's tower. Smith specifies this measurement in the first sentence of his introduction to *The Wealth of Nations*: "The annual labour of every nation is the fund which originally supplies it with all the necessaries and conveniences of life which it annually consumes." Smith thereby, in a stroke, created the concept of gross domestic product. Without GDP modern economists would be left with nothing much to say, standing around mute in ugly neckties, waiting for MSNBC to ask them to be silent on the air.

If wealth is all ebb and flow, then so is its measure, money. Money has no intrinsic value. Any baby who's eaten a nickel could tell you so. And those of us old enough to have heard about the Weimar Republic and to have lived through the Carter administration are not pained by the information. But eighteenth-century money was still mostly made of precious metals. Smith's observations on money must have been slightly disheartening to his readers, although they had the example of bling-deluged but impoverished Spain to confirm what he said. Gold is, well, worth its weight in gold, certainly, but not so certainly worth anything else. It was almost as though Smith, having proved that we can all have more money, then proved that money doesn't buy happiness. And it doesn't. It rents it.

Adam Smith's Principles: Their Principal Effect

The Wealth of Nations was published, with neat coincidence, in the very year that history's greatest capitalist nation declared its independence. And to the educated people of Great Britain the notion of the United States of America was more unreasonable, counterintuitive, and, as it were, outlandish than any of Adam Smith's ideas. *Wealth* was not light reading, even by the weightier standards of eighteenth-century readers. But it was a succès d'estime and something of an actual success. The first edition sold out in six months, shocking its publisher. Other than this, there is no evidence of Smith's work shocking his contemporaries.

For instance, Smith's suggestion of the economic primacy of self-interest didn't appall anyone. That self-interest makes the world go round has been tacitly acknowledged since the world began going round—a little secret everyone knows. And the worrisome thought that money is imaginary had been worried through by Smith's good friend David Hume a quarter of a century earlier. Indeed the fictitious quality of money had been well understood since classical times. In the two hundred years between the reigns of the emperors Nero and Gallienus, imperial fictions reduced the silver content of Roman coinage from 100 percent to none.

But, though its contents didn't make people gasp, something about *The Wealth of Nations* was grit in the gears of Enlightenment thinking. And that something is still there, grinding on our minds. I could feel it myself when the subject of self-interest came up.

Gosh, *I'm* not selfish. I think about the environment and those less fortunate than me. Especially those unfortunates who don't give a hoot about pollution, global warming, and species extinction. I think about them a lot, and I hope they lose the next election. Then maybe we can get some caring and compassionate people in public office, people who aren't selfish. If we elect an environmentalist mayor, the subdivision full of McMansions that's going to block my view of the ocean won't get built.

And let's face it, the "lower ranks of the people" *do* have too much money. Look at Britney Spears. Or I'll give you a better example, the moneybags buying those châteaux-to-go on the beachfront. You with your four-barge garage and the Martha-bitchin'-Stewart-kitchen that you cook in about as often as Martha does the dishes. You may think you're not the lower ranks because you make a lot of dough, but your lifestyle is an "inconveniency to the society" big time, as you'll find out when I key your Hummer that's taking up three parking spaces.

I know your type. All you do is work all day, eighty or a hundred hours a week, in some specialized something that nobody else understands, on Wall Street or at fancy corporate law firms or in expensive hospital operating rooms. A person has to balance job, life, and family to become a balanced . . . you know, person. This is why my wife and I are planning to grow all our own food (rutabagas can be stored for a year!), use only fair-traded Internet services with open code programming, heat the house by means of clean energy renewable resources such as wind power from drafts under the door, and knit our children's clothes with organic wool from sheep raised under humane farming conditions in our yard. This will keep the kids warm and cozy, if somewhat itchy, and will build their characters because they will get teased on the street.

Okay, yes, I admit that total removal of every market restraint would be "good for the economy." But money isn't everything. Think of the danger and damage to society. Without government regulation the big shots who run companies like Enron, WorldCom, and Tyco could have cheated investors and embezzled millions. Without restrictions on the sale of hazardous substances young people might smoke, drink, and even use drugs. Without the licensing of medical practitioners the way would be clear for chiropractors, osteopaths, and purveyors of aromatherapy. If we didn't have labor unions, thirty thousand people would still be wage slaves at General Motors, their daily lives filled with mindless drudgery. And if there weren't various forms of retail collusion in the petroleum industry, filling stations could charge as little as they liked. I'd have to drive all over town to find the best price. That would waste gas.

Also consider the harm to the developing world. Cheap pop music downloads imported from the United States will put every nose-flute band in Peru out of business. Plus some jobs require protection, to ensure they are performed locally in their own communities. My job is to make quips, jests, and waggish comments. Somewhere in Mumbai there is a younger, funnier person who is willing to work for less. My job could be outsourced to him. But he could make any joke he wanted. Who would my wife scold? Who would my in-laws be offended by? Who would my friends shun?

For the sake of accountability, sensitivity to hurtful language, and all things socially responsible, Adam Smith's flow of goods and services needs to be accompanied by at least the threat of another flow—getting a drink thrown in my face.

Then there is the matter of those goods and services—Adam Smith's gross domestic product. I am as grossly domestic as anyone. Where's the product? How come all the goods and services flow out of my income instead of into it? Of course, I understand that money isn't what's valuable. Love is what's valuable. And my bank account is full of love or something closely related to it, sex. That is, I've got fuck-all in the bank. And if money isn't worth anything, why was Alan Greenspan such a big cheese for all those years? Did he just go to his office and do Sudoku puzzles all day?

None of us, in fact, take the axioms of Adam Smith as givens—not unless what's given to us are vast profits, enormous salaries, and huge year-end bonuses resulting from unfettered markets, low labor costs, increased productivity, and current Federal Reserve policy. Like the AFL-CIO, France, and various angry and addled street protesters, we quarrel with Adam Smith. If this is to be an intelligent squabble we need to examine Smith's side of the argument in full. *The Wealth of Nations* is—as my generation used to say when my generation was relevant—relevant.

The Wealth of Nations, How the High Price of Freedom Makes the Best Things in Life Free

Considering the immense orb of Adam Smith's thinking and his tendency to go off on tangents, *The Wealth of Nations* is surprisingly well organized. Smith divided *Wealth* into five books. He presents his economic ideas in Books 1 and 2. Book 1 addresses production and distribution, and Book 2 concerns capital and profit. Book 3 is an economic history of western Europe showing how various aspects of production, distribution, capital, and profit evolved and how their evolution caused a, so to speak, global warming in the climate of ordinary life. Book 4 is a refutation of economic ideas other than those of Adam Smith. It includes a particularly—too particularly—detailed attack on the mercantilists. And Book 5 is Smith's attempt to apply his ideas to solving problems of government. But since problems are the only excuse for government, solving them is out of the question. For this and other reasons, Book 5 is surprisingly disorganized.

It should be noted that Adam Smith did not create the discipline he founded. What we call economics was invented by François Quesnay and the French physiocrats, whom Smith knew. The physiocrats, however, badly overthought the subject. Quesnay, who was Louis XV's physician, drew an elaborate Tableau Économique, a minutely labeled, densely zigzagging chart—part cat's cradle, part crossword puzzle, part backgammon board. It may have put Smith off the whole idea of graphic representation. The tableau supposedly showed how agriculture is the source of all economic progress, how trade and manufacture do no good for anyone, and how everything—from wagon wheels to Meissen chamber pots—grows, in effect, on trees. Food is the entire basis of living, therefore agriculture must be the entire basis for getting a life. So went the physiocrat reasoning, more or less.

To Quesnay and his fellow courtiers the motive for investigating economics was something between *Pour la France!* and finding a way to kill time while waiting to put leeches on royals. What Adam Smith did was give economics a reason to exist. Smith's inquiry had a sensible aim, to materially benefit mankind, himself by no means excluded.

The Wealth of Nations, Book I

Smith called Book 1 "Of the Causes of Improvement in the productive Powers of Labour, and of the Order according to which its Produce is naturally distributed among the different Ranks of the People," one of those people not being a modern-type book editor, who would have punched up the title.

Smith began by asking two very large questions: How is wealth produced, and how is it distributed? Over the course of the 250-some pages in Book 1 the answers—"division of labor" and "mind your own business"—are explained. But in the meantime Smith answered two even larger questions: Why is everyone equal, and why do we have property rights?

All men are created equal. We hold this truth to be self-evident. Meanwhile it is also self-evident that this truth is wildly untrue. Equality is the foundation of liberal democracy, rule of law, a free society, and everything that the reader, if he or she is sane, cherishes. But are we all equal because we all showed up? It does not work that way at weddings or funerals. Are we all equal because it says so in the American Declaration of Independence, the French Declaration of the Rights of Man, and the UN Universal Declaration of Human Rights? Each of these documents contains plenty of half-truths and untruths as well. The UN proclaims, "Everyone has the right to rest and leisure, including reasonable limitation of working hours." I'll have my wife inform the baby.

High-minded screeds cobbled together by unrepresentative and, in some cases, slightly deranged members of the intelligentsia are not scripture. Anyway, to see what a scripture-based polity gets for a social system we have only to look at the Taliban in Afghanistan or the Puritans in Massachusetts. Everyone has an immortal soul and every soul is of identical value to God, maybe, but that doesn't take us far as a matter of practical political philosophy. And Adam Smith was practical. A footnote of his in *The Theory of Moral Sentiments,* about how his theory was "not concerning a matter of right . . . but concerning a matter of fact," is suitable to all of his philosophy.

When Smith considered how division of labor developed, he briefly directed our attention to an interesting and characteristic quality of man. The most powerful creature to ever stride the earth is the most pitifully helpless. We are born incapable of caring for ourselves and remain so—to judge by today's youth—until we're forty. At the age of two when any other mammal is in its peak earning years, hunting, gathering, and procreating, the human toddler cannot find its ass with both hands, at least not well enough to use the potty. The creativity of a Daniel Defoe couldn't get Robinson Crusoe through the workweek without a supply of manufactured goods from the shipwreck's hold and the services of a cannibal executive assistant.

We must treat other people with the respect due to equals not because we are inspired by principle or filled with fraternal affection but because we're pathetic and useless.

Smith wrote that an individual "stands at all times in need of the co-operation and assistance of great multitudes, while his whole life is scarce sufficient to gain the friendship of a few persons." This nearly left-wing statement was the prologue to Adam Smith's most quoted passage: "It is not from the benevolence of the butcher, the brewer, or the baker, that we expect our dinner, but from their regard to their own interest." Smith wasn't urging us to selfishly pursue wealth in the free enterprise system. He was urging us to give thanks that the butcher, the brewer, and the baker do. It is our good fortune that they are endowed by their Creator with certain unalienable rights, that among these are steak, beer, and hoagie rolls.

Smith's answer to why we have property rights was equally straightforward: "The property which every man has in his own labour, as it is the original foundation of all other property, so it is the most sacred and inviolable." Property rights are not an invention of the rich to keep poor people off their property. Property rights are the deed we have to ownership of ourselves. The property may be modest, but it is inherent. "The patrimony of a poor man," Smith wrote, "lies in the strength and dexterity of his hands." From this humble grasp of hammer and, as it were, sickle comes all free enterprise: "and to hinder him from employing this strength and dexterity in what manner he thinks proper without injury to his neighbour, is a plain violation of this most sacred property."

Any definition of liberty that is not based on a right to property and a right to the same rights as all other people have is meaningless. What we have is ours, and nobody can push us around. This is practically all we mean when we say we are free. Other rights derive from these, when we even bother with those other rights.

Freedom of speech is wonderful, if you have anything to say. A search of the "blogosphere" reveals that hardly anyone does. Freedom of religion is more wonderful, but you can, when you pray, "enter into thy closet, and when thou hast shut thy door, pray to thy Father which is in secret." Jesus Christ himself said so (Matt. 6:6). But most of freedom is a workaday experience, taking place in the material, economic world. Before Adam Smith was even well under way with *The Wealth of Nations* he had proved that we require and deserve an equitable society where we're free from the exercise of arbitrary power and can go to the mall and swipe our Visa cards until the magnetic strips are toasted crisp, if that's what we want.

The Divisibility of Labor

However, the main purpose of Book 1 of *Wealth,* as Smith conceived it, was to show the importance of the division of labor. The purpose of division of labor, wrote Smith, is "to make a smaller quantity of labour produce a greater quantity of work." Smith perceived that the division of labor—specialization—is the original source of economic growth.

Specialization increases economic value. As an example Smith famously used the "trifling manufacture" of a pin. Without specialization and specialists' machinery it would take us all day to make one pin. In an early draft of *Wealth,* Smith noted that if we went so far as to dig in the iron mines, smelt our own ore, and so forth, we could "scarce make a pin in a year." And somewhere a group of hobbyists—contactable via the Internet—is doing just that, to the irritated mystification of their wives.

The Indivisibility of Price

Smith proved his point, and should have left it at that. But here we come to an interesting difficulty in the rational consideration of economics—getting too rational with it. This is economics' original sin, a fault that has existed since economics was conceived. Any student in any econ class knows the problem and has had to memorize various rationalizing formulae that result from—no, are—the problem.

While writing about the increase of economic value, Smith decided to delve into the concept of value itself. He tried to analyze price, and he could not. The price of something is what someone will pay for it, nothing more, nothing less, nothing else. David Hume, in a letter to Smith congratulating him on the publication of *Wealth,* praised the work but noted the error. "If you were here at my fireside," Hume wrote, "I should dispute some of your principles. I cannot think... but that price is determined altogether by the quantity and the demand." Yet to think that went against Smith's inclination to think things through; so he thought things through anyway.

Smith decided that price had "component parts." He settled on three of them: labor, profits of stock (i.e., return on capital), and rent of land. Price theory is a recondite area of economics as people in the stock market, the commodities market, or the market for a house know, and as people in those econ classrooms know to their terror. And Smith's confusions about price were even more confused than modern confusions.

When Smith was trying to put value on price and price on value he didn't have an econ textbook to explain to him the "law of marginal utility." This would be postulated a century later by Carl von Menger, founder of the Austrian school of economics. Translating econ textbook text into English, marginal utility means that we value a good only according to how much we value the specific unit of the good that we most recently consumed, not according to how much we value the good for being so good.

Smith came very close to stumbling on marginal utility when he noted that "Nothing is more useful than water: but it will purchase scarce any thing." With an additional eight ounces of water all we get is a trip to the bathroom in the middle of the night. With an additional eight ounces of gold we get the upfront payment to lease a Lexus. Marginal utility explains why gold, vital to the life of no one except hip-hop performers and fiancés, is so high-priced.

However, the high price we pay for premium bottled water sends the law of marginal utility up the spout. That is where all price theory should go. Witness Adam Smith wrestling with his: "If among a nation of hunters, for example, it usually costs twice the labour to kill a beaver which it does to kill a deer, one beaver should naturally exchange for or be worth two deer." Wait. Can killing a beaver, even in supposition, really be twice as hard as killing a deer? Deer can run like hell. We know where the beaver lives. It built the beaver dam. We've got the beaver's home address. Even if it does take twice as *long* to kill a beaver—wading around in the beaver pond smacking at Bucky's head with the flat side of a canoe paddle—who wants a beaver? It's not like the nation of hunters is wearing a lot of top hats. And after a long day of hunting, take your pick—a juicy tenderloin of venison or beaver soup?

There is an admitted pleasure in watching someone so much more intellectual than oneself going so intellectually wrong. Smith decided that labor was the most important component of price: "Labour alone, therefore, never varying in its own value, is alone the ultimate and real standard." Then, within two pages, he contradicts himself: "the real price of labour . . . is very different upon different occasions." But earlier he'd written, "The real price of everything . . . is the toil and trouble of acquiring it."

Something in the fine philosophical mind of Adam Smith made him resist the mastery of the obvious. There is a statement from the thirteenth century, attributed to Albertus Magnus, that price is what "goods are worth according to the estimate of the market at the time of sale." But before a proposal is made to abandon the complexities of Adam Smith and go back to thinking plain old medieval common sense, it's worth considering some of the other thinking that was common in medieval times. Albertus Magnus preached the eighth Crusade, the last and most pointless. It didn't even try to go to the Holy Land. The eighth Crusade sailed, like an armed Carnival cruise, to Tunis.

Yet there was this about Adam Smith: even when he was wrong he was smarter than other people. Perhaps he was especially smarter than those awful people who always know the "value" of everything and are so eager to tell us its rightful price or its rightful pricelessness.

Labor is not a component of price, which doesn't have components. Things cost what they cost. But by founding the logical structure of *The Wealth of Nations* on the premise of labor—on how we divide it, on how we share its fruits, on the whole toil and trouble of our lives—Smith hit upon the material and moral necessity of our freedom.

Adam Smith, Capitalism's Scourge

Adam Smith cannot be said to have constructed the capitalist system. What he did was provide the logic of a level ground of economic rights upon which free enterprise could be built more easily. And he suggested to the builders that they use the wheelbarrow of free trade, the plumb bob of self-interest, and all the specialized tools of specialization. However, when Smith undertook to consider how free enterprise allocates what it produces—"the Order according to which its Produce is naturally distributed"—he hit capitalism hard enough to make its boiled shirtfront roll up like a window shade.

Some acolytes of Smith might be surprised if they ever read him. He wrote that "the oppression of the poor must establish the monopoly of the rich," and that profit "is always highest in the countries which are going fastest to ruin." About concepts such as "full employment" Smith could make a noise like a John Kenneth Galbraith: "If the society were annually to employ all the labour which it can annually purchase . . . the produce of every succeeding year would be of vastly greater value than that of the foregoing." And Smith could follow that with a worse noise, a Thorstein Veblen of a raspberry: "But there is no country in which the whole annual produce is employed in maintaining the industrious. The idle every where consume a great part of it."

Adam Smith was tough on the landed gentry: "As soon as the land of any country has all become private property, the landlords, like all other men, love to reap where they never sowed." He would have been amused to see the dukes and duchesses of England reduced to keeping circus animals and other attractions on their great estates and letting fat day-trippers waddle through their stately homes, camcording the noble ancestors on the walls.

Smith was tougher yet on the very people who, in his time, were beginning to generate the wealth of nations that he proposed to increase. Despite his personal friendships with merchants and manufacturers in Edinburgh and Glasgow, Smith had a cool loathing for the class.

> *Masters are always and every where in a sort of tacit, but constant and uniform combination, not to raise the wages of labour.*
>
> *Our merchants and master-manufacturers complain much of the bad effects of high wages in raising the price . . . of their goods both at home and abroad. They say nothing concerning the bad effects of high profits. They are silent with regard to the pernicious effects of their own gains. They complain only of those of other people.*
>
> *The interest of the dealers . . . in any particular branch of trade or manufactures, is always in some respects different from, and even opposite to, that of the public.*

Smith was not a fan of what would come to be called lobbying.

> *The proposal of any new law or regulation of commerce which comes from [merchants and manufacturers] ought always to be listened to with great precaution, and ought never to be adopted till after having been long and carefully examined . . . with the most suspicious attention.*

Scandals in the U.S. Congress concerning lobbyist favors and donations would have appalled Adam Smith as much as they appall any good *Washington Post* editorial writer. But Smith, we can assume, would have had enough respect for his readers' intelligence not to feign shock.

And Smith was no enthusiast for the privatization of government functions. Concerning the East India Company and its rule of Bengal, Smith wrote, "The government of an exclusive company of merchants is, perhaps, the worst of all governments for any country whatever."

Adam Smith, Capitalism's Champion

What made Adam Smith different from the later and more foolish critics of capitalism was that he never reasoned backward about the cause of economic disparity. "It is not," Smith wrote, "because one man keeps a coach while his neighbour walks a-foot, that the one is rich and the other poor."

Smith also possessed none of the moral contempt for profit itself that would soon become the laurel wreath crowning every political philosophy pretension. It crowned the pretension of Percy Bysshe Shelley, to give a comic example, and that of Pol Pot, to give a tragic one. The first insurrection in history to style itself "communist" would occur within a few years of Smith's death. It aimed to overthrow the French Revolution's Directory, of all things. The uprising was led by François-Noel Babeuf, who took the name "Gracchus" after Tiberius Gracchus the younger, the second-century BC radical land reformer and would-be dictator of Rome. Tiberius, predictably, was murdered by his opponents. And, predictably, so was Babeuf.

Instead of this sort of thing—sadly familiar to students of modern history—Smith wanted "the establishment of a government which afforded to industry the only encouragement which it requires, some tolerable security that it shall enjoy the fruits of its own labour." Smith did not consider profits to be the same as "pernicious gains." He held that excessive profits were the result of laws that limited or guaranteed trade. A "violent police" was the term he used for such legislative interference in free enterprise.

And even with a brutal constabulary of trade regulations, pernicious gains are to be preferred to pernicious losses. Imagine a world where we went about our daily activities deliberately intending not to profit by them—eating pebbles, wooing the furniture, getting in our car for the sole purpose of driving into a tree.

Smith saw an ordinary rate of profit not as what it ideologically is to the ideological, but as what it actually is to the profit maker, "his revenue, the proper fund of his subsistence." The freedoms of competition force the price the profit maker charges for his goods to be "the lowest at which he is likely to sell them . . . *at least where there is perfect liberty*." The italics are added and the phrase cannot be underscored too heavily. Smith was fostering free enterprise, and he was also nurturing—just in time—resistance to socialism. "Nothing can be more absurd," he wrote, "than to imagine that men in general should work less when they work for themselves, than when they work for other people." And when other people are "The People"—not individuals but an abstraction—the absurdity becomes an insanity.

Adam Smith was not a modern libertarian, but he was a libertarian critic of capitalism. Problems of equality were not to be solved with more laws. In a free market, wages may be too low but, Smith wrote, "law can never regulate them properly, though it has often pretended to do so." Greater capitalist equality was to be achieved with greater equity capital, so that "in consequence of the flourishing circumstances of the society, the real price of labour should rise very considerably."

Likewise the problems of free markets were not to be solved by increased regulation of those markets, but by increased freedom in them: "To widen the market may frequently be agreeable enough to the interest of the public; but to narrow the competition must always be against it." Every law concerning commerce—even the most beneficent, such as the Pure Food and Drug Act—contains an element of narrowing the competition and should be "examined . . . with the most suspicious attention." Congress banned cigarette advertising on radio and TV in 1970, about the same time that the entire nation got stoned on pot. Was Nixon's drug dealer behind the legislation?

Adam Smith, Capitalism's Original Money Maven

Another reason that Adam Smith defended economic freedom, and all the unpleasant questions of money that come with economic freedom, was that he understood money. It was in Book 1 of *Wealth* that Smith, with his seventy-five-page "Digression concerning the Variations in the Value of Silver," may be said to have deflated money, or our notion of it (or any notion that a prolonged discussion of it is interesting). Smith showed that the mercantilist attitude toward the precious metals could be summed up as: "Premium is going for three dollars a gallon! Better fill up the car! Gas won't always be this valuable!" And Smith pointed out that questions of money aren't the questions we should be asking, because "money is the exact measure of the real exchangeable value of all commodities . . . at the same time and place only." The questions we should be asking are about how we can get to a better time and place.

The rich may be piggish, but money is not a Circe that transforms them into creatures with larger gullets than we have. "The rich man consumes no more food than his poor neighbour," Smith wrote, referring to the reasonable prosperity of his time and place. In the unreasonable prosperity of our time and place it's the other way around. The larger the pie wagon the more likely that he or she is living below the government's officially decreed poverty level. Smith stated his meaning better in *The Theory of Moral Sentiments,* in the passage where the invisible hand was originally mentioned.* The rich, he said,

---

*This is not quite true. The most noted two words of Adam Smith's oeuvre were initially used in his essay "The History of Astronomy," probably written when Smith was in his twenties. But there he employed them in a disparaging way. Smith was noting that man has always had some understanding of physics, that "fire burns, and water refreshes; heavy bodies descend, and lighter substances fly upwards, by the necessity of their own nature." Smith averred that not even the ignorant ancients thought "the invisible hand of Jupiter" was "employed in those matters."

Smith did not intend the invisible hand to be understood as it usually is understood, as the agency by which economic liberty automatically produces economic progress. When he meant that, he said it: "government which afforded to industry the only encouragement which it requires." And the one other time that he used the phrase was in Book 4 of *The Wealth of Nations,* in a discourse on the benefits of employing capital "in the support of domestick industry," where Smith—according to his own free trade principles—was wrong.

> *consume little more than the poor, and in spite of their natural selfishness and rapacity . . . [T]hough the sole end which they propose from the labours of all the thousands whom they employ, be the gratification of their own vain and insatiable desires, they divide with the poor the produce of all their improvements. They are led by an invisible hand to make nearly the same distribution of the necessaries of life, which would have been made, had the earth been divided into equal portions among all its inhabitants.*

The economic benefits of wealth in a free market quickly overflow the humble vessel that is Paris Hilton, and they do not trickle down, they pour.

Adam Smith, Capitalism's Therapist

Smith understood the money that people have, and he understood people. Living before the social sciences had split into warring camps (or had claimed the dignity of being sciences), Smith was free to be a psychologist as well as an economist. The word *psychologist* existed in the eighteenth century, but its meaning was "one who treats concerning the soul," or, as Smith most likely would have said, "the imagination." And Smith saw that the human imagination contains darker and more deeply rooted ambitions than greed for cash. In *The Theory of Moral Sentiments* he wrote:

> *To those who have been accustomed to the possession, or even to the hope of public admiration, all other pleasures sicken and decay . . . Place, that great object which divides the wives of aldermen, is the end of half the labours of human life; and is the cause of all the tumult and bustle, all the rapine and injustice.*

And of the Academy Awards and *Us Weekly*.

There is a limit to what people will do for money, but there is no limit to what people will do to go on *The Jerry Springer Show*. Money is not enough. To be called "rich as Croesus" has never been a badge of prestige. The filthy rich king of Lydia wound up a prisoner of Persia's emperor Cyrus. It was Croesus who caused Solon to say that no man should be called happy until he is dead. Or famous.

As for death and glory, there's another ambition that leads to that, plus tumult, bustle, rapine, injustice, and *Us Weekly*. The desire for power pushes a man, Smith wrote, to "the highest degree of arrogance . . . to erect his own judgment into the supreme standard of right and wrong . . . to fancy himself the only wise and worthy man in the commonwealth." Smith managed to describe not only Barbra Streisand but everyone in the world of politics.

There is no toil and trouble as bad as politics. The freedom of the market, though of uncertain fairness, is better than the shackle of government, where unfairness is perfectly certain. And there's an additional factor that makes business superior to politics. Smith saw that a free society tends to disconnect power from pelf. Referring to the Great Britain of his era, Smith wrote, "The person who either acquires, or succeeds to a great fortune, does not necessarily acquire or succeed to any political power, either civil or military. His fortune may, perhaps, afford him the means of acquiring both, but . . . does not necessarily convey to him either." And no amount of current groveling for campaign contributions makes this less true. Politics may be terribly influenced by money, but political power cannot simply be purchased in the marketplace. Ross Perot proved this, happily, as did, less happily, Steve Forbes.

Political powers are different from free market goods. This has to do with the nature of freedom, which is based on equality and self-possession. A citizen of a free country has property rights not only in "the strength and dexterity of his hands" but in the strength and dexterity of his mind. "And to hinder him from employing this strength and dexterity in what manner he thinks proper without injury to his neighbour, is a plain violation of . . ." Voting rights in Florida in 2000, maybe? It's not that we can't be bought, it's that we own certain prerogatives that can't be sold. Our rights are, to use a term from property law that appears in the Declaration of Independence, "unalienable."

Another reason that political powers are different from free market goods has to do with the nature of markets. Unfettered private exchange cannot be limited—as the Chinese government thinks it can—to things. Material items are indivisible from the knowledge of how to make them and the ideas upon which that knowledge is based. All the more so, now, in an "information age." Free markets lead to thinking, that eternal enemy of politicians.

Book 1 of *The Wealth of Nations* is an analysis of the means by which we pursue self-interest and a critique of that pursuit. It is also a warning against pursuing what is worse. Adam Smith did not want us to be like "the common people of England," whom he saw as "so jealous of their liberty, but . . . never rightly understanding wherein it consists."

The Wealth of Nations, Book 2

"Of the Nature, Accumulation, and Employment of Stock" —Let Adam Smith Be Your Market Guru

Investment guides and business motivational books sell in shocking numbers. The *New York Times Book Review* sends them to Coventry in the "Advice, How-To and Miscellaneous" appendix to the best-seller list. But there in Coventry they stay, often for years on end, waxing fat and providing their authors with profits worthy of the fastest among "countries going fastest to ruin." These profits cause the authors of other sorts of books, such as this one, to seethe with envy and declare that the country is going to ruin indeed if investment guides and business motivational books are what sell.

The investing tips are always jejune. The motivating tomes usually are based on one more or less shrewd observation about business that is then plumped and padded, reiterated and restated until a marketable number of pages can be typeset. For instance, "Keep in mind that your competitor is a man of layers. Don't judge him merely by surface appearances. Try to see 'inside the suit,' and understand both the things that make him comfortable and the things that rub him wrong." Hence *What Color Is My Underwear?*, Cooksome Books, 230 pp., hardback, $29.95.

But here is *The Wealth of Nations* with its truly sagacious notice of every aspect of economics and its brainy commentary on all manner of financial concerns. Take an example from Book 2. Hundreds of years before yuppies began installing pseudo-Palladian windows in the profusion of gables that block my view, Adam Smith warned against betting too much "accumulation and employment of stock" on a red-hot housing market.

> *A dwelling house, as such, contributes nothing to the revenue of its inhabitant... If it is to be let to a tenant for rent, as the house itself can produce nothing, the tenant must always pay the rent out of some other revenue . . . Though a house, therefore, may yield a revenue to its*

proprietor . . . it cannot yield any to the public, nor serve in the function of a capital, and the revenue of the whole body of the people can never be in the smallest degree increased by it.

What with Smith's work being in the public domain and all, there's an understandable temptation to wonder if something in the investment guide or business motivational line can't be culled from *The Wealth of Nations*. At the very least there should be material enough for one of those vade mecums for the self-admitted mental deficient, which people seem so unembarrassed to buy—*The Idiot's Guide to the Betterment of Life*, perhaps.

And it just so happens that Book 2 of *Wealth* lends itself perfectly to such projects. Smith's subject is capital, where it is gotten, and how it may be employed to gain whopping returns. This is the stuff of best-sellers on a par with secret sexual techniques of the House of Windsor.

Unfortunately there's a problem. Adam Smith's advice, his how-tos, and, for that matter, his miscellanies are all addressed to the powerful figures who work as secretaries of the treasury, chancellors of the exchequer, chairmen of the Federal Reserve, and governors of the International Monetary Fund and the World Bank. This is not a mass market. On the other hand, the mighty do have sycophants, and maybe they'll all buy my book and give it to Ben Bernanke for Christmas.

Central Banking for Dummies

A central bank is the institution that controls the supply of a country's money. This would be a straightforward matter if it weren't for three facts: Money is imaginary. Banking doesn't involve money. And a central bank isn't a bank.

What the Heck Is Money Anyway?

"Money," Smith wrote, "is neither a material to work upon, nor a tool to work with." Money is make-believe. It's a conjectural idea we have that vaguely approximates value. Using the guesswork of money lets us transfer goods and services in a way that is less cumbersome than barter and less repellent than theft.

Money is the offspring of division of labor and free trade. It is a contentious child. Notions of value cause arguments. This Smith pointed out in a Glasgow University lecture: "The offering of a shilling, which to us appears to have so plain and simple a meaning, is in reality offering an argument to persuade one to do so and so as it is for his interest."

Smith wrote that "money, by means of which the whole revenue of the society is regularly distributed among all its different members, makes itself no part of that revenue." Being imaginary, it can't. "The great wheel of circulation," he continued, "is altogether different from the goods which are circulated by means of it."

We probably shouldn't try to think too hard about the nature of money. In Book 1 of *Wealth,* Smith made an opaque statement that showed the effect of such thinking: "I am always willing to run some hazard of being tedious in order to be sure that I am perspicuous; and after taking the utmost pains that I can to be perspicuous, some obscurity may still appear to remain upon a subject in its own nature extremely abstracted."

And What Is a Bank?

A bank is an institution that doesn't deal in money. If we accept Smith's definition of value as "toil and trouble," banks deal in toil and trouble. Banking is a clever device for storing your toil and trouble. And instead of being charged storage fees, you're compensated for engaging in excess toil and going to extra trouble.

For example, say that, per Book 1 of *Wealth,* you are killing a lot of deer. You're only getting one beaver for every two deer you kill but, nonetheless, you're getting more beavers than you know what to do with. Absent some system of banking, you have to pile the beavers under your bed where they're of no use to anyone. And they stink. Banking allows you to rent the beavers to me with "some tolerable security" of receiving the agreed upon beaver lease revenue and getting your beavers back when I'm finished with my high-profit, beaver-intensive business deal. Money doesn't come into it except insofar as the transaction is more convenient and pleasant if it's conducted in money instead of used beavers.

"It is not by augmenting the capital of the country," Smith declared, "but by rendering a greater part of that capital active and productive . . . that the most judicious operations of banking can increase the industry of the country." What the judicious operations of banking *can't* do is increase the *industriousness* of the country—for instance by lending money to any fool, such as me, who comes along with a lunatic idea for alternative-energy technology based on methane production from rotting beavers. Political advocates of "economic stimulus" often claim that banks ought to do this. And bankers often claim that they've done it. But they shouldn't, and they can't.

There was a banking crisis in Scotland in 1772. Only three of Edinburgh's thirty private banks survived. Every time and place has its equivalent to dot.com–boom Silicon Valley start-ups. Adam Smith described the attitude of investors in 1999 as well as in 1772: "The banks, they seem to have thought, were in honour bound to supply… them with all the capital which they wanted to trade with."

So What Are Banks Really Good For?

They're good for make-believe. Banks are as imaginary as the dollars they lend. Their pillared porticos, their impressive vaults, and their handy time and temperature signs are just symbols. The symbols represent something else we've made up called "contract."

It's fortunate that Adam Smith was free to be a psychologist as well as an economist. Any examination of economics quickly turns into a session on the couch, with dreams to analyze, narcissisms to probe, and family conflicts to be resolved. Money is the child of division of labor and freedom of trade, an active little bastard conceived while we were enjoying some subconscious cooperation. The wedding of property rights to equality before the law also produces an offspring, more widely recognized as legitimate than money, known as valid and binding contract. Bad banking is a bad marriage where contract is being spoiled by the selfishness of private property and the failure of equal rights to assert herself. "When the law," wrote Smith, "does not enforce the performance of contracts, it puts all borrowers nearly upon the same footing with bankrupts or people of doubtful credit." Counseling should be sought. Otherwise poor little contract may start associating with the wrong element, get corrupted by money, and grow up with low self-esteem and self-destructive tendencies. This is what happened to America's Social Security trust fund.

So We Need to, Like, Regulate Banks

Freedom cannot exist without limitation. Adam Smith was not a man to flinch at this conundrum. In his consideration of banking Smith stated his most fundamental free market principle: "If any branch of trade, or any division of labour, be advantageous to the public, the freer and more general the competition, it will always be the more so." However, in his consideration of banking, Smith also stated his most fundamental caveat to that principle: "But those exertions of the natural liberty of a few individuals, which might endanger the security of the whole society, are, and ought to be, restrained by the laws of all governments."

So much is sensible, although you'd never know it to hear the senseless arguments between lawmakers who believe one of these ideas and lawmakers who believe the other. Unlike most politicians Smith was usually able to make his way past the sirens of authoritarianism and the sirens of license without having a head full of wax or needing to be tied to the mast. Smith had a clearer idea of the purpose of law than legislators do. He didn't see writing laws as a contest or a compromise between battling interest groups. He saw writing laws as a way of furthering "that natural liberty which it is the proper business of law, not to infringe, but to support." Sometimes we get that kind of law. And when we do, a lot of bankers go to jail.

What Is a "Central" Bank?

You can't get a debit card that draws on the Federal Reserve Bank, nice as that would be, and never mind that the Bush administration apparently can. A central bank is not really a bank at all but a government agency. Smith called it "a great engine of state." It regulates the amount of money in circulation by, basically, regulating real banks. A nation's currency supply is supposed to be matched to that nation's supply of economic value. If a nation has less circulating money than it has labor and goods, you get a credit collapse and a Great Depression. If a nation has more money than it has labor and goods, you get the 1970s. Which is worse depends upon whether you are more annoyed by double knit, disco, and Henry Kissinger or by claptrap about the Greatest Generation, enormous Medicare expenditures, and your parents.

The purpose of central banking is to prevent the return of disco and to get your parents to shut up. The technical mechanisms by which a central bank does that are beyond the scope of this commentary, not to mention the understanding of this writer. You actually are a dummy if you think you're going to plumb the mysteries of central banking here. The importance of what Adam Smith wrote about central banks was that Smith, as usual, understood the practical principles behind the mystery. He realized that money was not a government asset, but a government liability. He called it "that great but expensive instrument of commerce." And noted that "the stock of money which circulates in any country must require a certain expence, first to collect it, and afterwards to support it."

The Adam Smith Plan for Increased Wealth (of Nations): How Central Banks Can Use Paper Money to Make the Great Instrument of Commerce Work Cheap

The "certain expence" of having a handy medium of exchange made Smith an early advocate of paper money. Not only are precious metals costly to mine, transport, and mint; precious metals also have a real—not just a monetary—value in manufacturing and industry.

Smith went almost literary on the subject. He wrote that "gold and silver money" could be "compared to a highway, which, while it circulates and carries to market all the grass and corn of the country, produces itself not a single pile of either." Paper money would, "by providing, if I may be allowed so violent a metaphor, a sort of waggon-way through the air, enable the country to convert, as it were, a great part of its highways into good pastures and cornfields." (Although now that we really do have a "waggon-way through the air," not many of our interstates have been turned into pastures and cornfields.)

Money is information. In his advocacy of paper money Smith was foreseeing the virtual aspect of the modern economy and all the efficiency that comes from it. Why buy a pricey slab of granite and have information chiseled into it by skilled workmen when information can be encoded almost effortlessly in the ether?

Smith was aware of the danger in what he called "the Dædalian wings of paper money." He was an honest and sane early advocate of paper money, which was not usual. Many eighteenth-century paper money promoters favored paper not because they thought it made money more efficient but because they thought it made money free. The most famous of these was a fellow Scot, John Law. Law proposed a national bank of Scotland which, as Smith put it, "he seems to have imagined might issue paper to the amount of the whole value of all the lands in the country." The Scottish parliament demurred. Law went to Paris and in 1717 concocted the Mississippi Scheme along the same lines. Smith gave a detailed account of Law's operations in a Glasgow University lecture. "The greatest part of the people," he said, "had their whole fortunes in notes and were reduced to a state of beggary." And in *Wealth of Nations*, Smith declared that "the paper currencies of North America" were "a scheme of fraudulent debtors to cheat their creditors."

Many paper currencies issued by many central banks are no better nowadays. Would you like your change in Argentinian pesos? All modern money is paper money but with nothing ensuring its relative value except the promises of a government or, in the case of the euro, the even more nebulous promises of a bunch of governments. We have our paper, or "fiat," money because it's easier for our governments to print more of it in the name of "greater monetary policy flexibility." The quality of money, like the quality of the human body after the age of eighteen, is not often improved by increases in quantity. Smith wrote that "paper money does not *necessarily* increase the quantity of the whole currency." Italics added, alas. In February 2006, Zimbabwe's reserve bank introduced a new fifty-thousand-dollar banknote, and it was not worth enough to buy a beer.

Smith proposed various intelligent limitations on central banking's paper currencies. None of them are of interest to us today because fiat money was beyond even Adam Smith's powers of conception. He thought that money would always be on a gold standard or a silver standard or a standard of some kind. (In Book I Smith wrote about the price of food grains determining "the real value of all other commodities" and was thus in effect suggesting a "market basket" of consumer goods as a currency standard.)

The worth of fiat money is linked to political whims far less substantive than John Law's "value of all the lands in the country." Modern governments have taken the Mississippi Scheme and made it work. Except, of course, when it doesn't.

So There Are Limitations to What Private Banks and Central Banks Can Do to Improve the Economy, but Can't Institutions Like the World Bank Provide the Economic Stimulus We Need to Eliminate Poverty and Aid Developing Nations?

No. Smith put this forcefully in Book 4 of *Wealth*: "I have never known much good done by those who affected to trade for the public good." The explanation for that grouchy outburst is in Book 2 where Smith describes the Ayr Bank, the collapse of which led to the 1772 Edinburgh banking crisis. "It was the avowed principle of this bank to advance . . . capital which was to be employed in those improvements of which the returns are the most slow and distant." This being what the World Bank tries to do. "The operations of this bank," Smith continued, "seem to have produced effects quite opposite to those which were intended." That being how things turn out for the World Bank. Smith wrote that the wonderfully named Ayr Bank, "no doubt, gave some temporary relief . . . But it thereby only enabled [its borrowers] to get so much deeper into debt, so that when ruin came, it fell so much the heavier." And there was no Bono in those days to put everything right.

Owing money to beneficent organizations is not beneficial. It's better to owe money to your scowling uncle or the skinflint down the street. Borrowers are debtors, after all. "The sober and frugal debtors of private persons," Smith observed, "would be more likely to employ the money borrowed in sober undertakings . . . which, though they might have less of the grand and the marvellous, would have more of the solid and the profitable." This maxim applies to everything from programs of foreign aid in the developing world to local city council debates. One new hot dog vendor is better for a town than any number of municipally financed sports stadiums. Smith declared that if the Ayr Bank had succeeded it still would have been a failure, that "this operation, therefore, without increasing in the smallest degree the capital of the country, would only have transferred a great part of it from prudent and profitable, to imprudent and unprofitable undertakings."

A recurring lesson in *The Wealth of Nations* is that we shouldn't get greedy. And no people are as rapacious and grabby as those who work for the public good. They don't want mere millions or billions of dollars to satisfy personal avarice. They seek the trillions of dollars necessary to make life on earth better for everyone. The World Bank should content itself with private good, from which all good things flow.

DRIVING LIKE CRAZY

(2009)

"We drive our cars because they make us free. With cars we need not wait in airline terminals, or travel only where railway tracks go. Governments detest our cars: they give us too much freedom. How do you control people who can climb into a car at any hour of the day or night and drive to who knows where?"

—David E. Davis Jr.

Sgt. Dynaflo's Last Patrol

(1977)

The fervor of automotive brand loyalty in the 1950s must puzzle today's young car enthusiasts no matter how much they love their Honda tuners. It was an era when the wraparound windshield was considered a major technological breakthrough by the American car industry. So what was the Chevy versus Plymouth versus Fix-Or-Repair-Daily argument about? And partisan issues were intra-corporational as well. There were Impala families and Bonneville families, and there may well have been Eldorado Brougham families, but the kids in my neighborhood would have beaten up the kids from those families. Boys of ten or eleven got in heated arguments about the relative merits of cars that were, even then, largely interchangeable and would soon become completely so. I am trying to imagine how I could explain, to someone born in 1999, the fine shade of difference between owning an Oldsmobile and owning a Buick. And what's an Oldsmobile anyway?

I was a Buick brat, born that way, no choice in the matter since my dad sold them for a living. My pulse still races when I see portholes on a fender, though I prefer them on the fender of a Maserati Gran Turismo S rather than on the fender of a Special, Super, Century, or Roadmaster. But I'm getting ahead of myself, passing on a curve, narratively speaking.

In the summer of 1977, I was pleased to hear that Tom Sargent, publisher of *Car and Driver*'s brother magazine *Cycle,* wanted someone to drive his 1956 Buick Special four-door sedan from Florida to Los Angeles.

I'd never written for *Car and Driver,* but on the strength of some drinks I'd had with its new editor, David E. Davis Jr., and the inebriated Oldsmobile/Buick quarrel that had ensued, I volunteered. David E. assigned the photography to the late, and much missed, Humphrey Sutton. Humphrey and I met at a midtown Manhattan restaurant to sketch our route. Just as we were entering the restaurant a taxi came to an abrupt halt, and a motorcyclist behind it came to a halt that was not quite abrupt enough. Rider and bike slid up under the Checker. Considering what publication Tom Sargent was the publisher of, Humphrey and I should have taken this event as an omen rather than an excuse to drink at lunch.

The Buick Special had been stored for the previous few years in a hangar at Sargent's father's home in Crescent City, Florida. Humphrey and I flew to Daytona Beach where Mr. Sargent, senior, picked us up in his Cessna 180. He took us thirty-five or forty miles northwest and landed on a grass strip, coming to a stop right in front of where he'd rolled the Buick onto his lawn. Rolled, not driven. Tom had neglected, until the night before, to inform his dad that we were coming to fetch the car. We almost got the Buick started a number of times before we removed the mouse nest, and the mice, from the carburetor.

Due to Tom's tardy phone call and Humphrey's and my vineous lunch in New York, not much forethought had gone into this expedition. We drove away from Crescent City with an ancient set of filed-down points in the distributor, no tools, no manual, not even a flashlight, and a map of America showing only railroad lines. We did have a Styrofoam cooler full of beer.

"For obvious reasons we called the Buick 'Sergeant Dynaflo,'" I wrote in my original *Car and Driver* piece. But the obvious may need explaining to anyone under forty. Buick was noted for its unique automatic transmission of the Dynaflo name. This was a hydraulic-fluid-filled device with variable pitch blades that delivered power from the 322-cubic-inch V-8 to the rear wheels smoothly, quietly, and, most of all, very slowly.

For other obvious reasons it became clear that the Buick was going to have to be driven from coast to coast on two-lane roads. I no longer remember what became obvious first—the Shake 'n' Bake front-wheel shimmy at fifty miles per hour, the Dynaflo acceleration that meant an inability to reach freeway speed without using a mile of shoulder as part of the merge lane, or the temperature gauge's slow but relentless minute hand movement toward hell.

It's odd to think back and realize that this Buick was only twenty-one years old at the time. A twenty-one-year-old car was an awful lot older then than it is now. Just as, to my mind, a twenty-one-year-old boy is an awful lot younger. At least in the matter of cars, this is not merely old-guy perception. I have a garage full of daily drivers bearing about two decades of vintage. My Porsche 911 will be twenty next year—a few tire and brake pad changes and one valve job and it's as reliable as it was new. (Never mind that the valve job cost more than my first three cars put together.) My wife's 1989 BMW 3-Series convertible is the same way. The top was replaced in the mid-nineties and I had a little suspension work done to take out some clunks. A 1984 Jeep Scrambler, bought new, is still my year-round farm vehicle. All its knobs and switches have fallen off, and it leaves grease patches on the garage floor, but you'd have to drop a thirty-foot oak on it to kill the thing. I've done that too, and it's still running. Next time Al Gore complains about the wasteful and unprogressive nature of the automobile industry, tell him to go find the car from his daddy's days in the Senate and drive it to . . . I can think of several places.

Saturday, June 25, 1977
Crescent City to Nowhere

The Buick Special was, however, beautiful: two-tone turquoise and white with seat covers to match. The weather was splendid. People smiled and waved to us as we rolled through the small northern Florida towns (which, in 1977, snowbirds had not yet left their droppings on). At blue highway speeds the Buick was a big, steady pleasure to drive. We went 150 miles like that, sipping beers and returning salutes. The Buick ran perfectly right up until it didn't.

When the engine went out we were in a godforsaken stretch of piney woods on County Route 98 somewhere around about, but nowhere near, Tallahassee. All of a sudden the car was too quiet, and we weren't going as fast as we should have been. We figured it was the old set of points.

There was a shack about two hundred yards down the road with two broken gas pumps and a sign that said BEER. It was half overgrown with creepers in the front and half sunk into what, these days, would be called wetlands in the back. The scene resembled an EC horror comic *Swamp Thing* title panel, but it was the only building we'd seen for twenty miles, and it did have that sign that said BEER. We pushed the Buick there. I went inside to borrow some tools.

About a dozen hard-visaged, definitely unfriendly, and possibly cannibalistic Southern types were in there, all eyeing me suspiciously. The bartender was a big, nasty-faced old guy with an enormous paunch, a flat-top haircut four inches high, and a cigar turned backward in his mouth. (I assume, but am by no means certain, it was unlit.) I got the idea he didn't like my looks either, but he loaned me a screwdriver and an adjustable wrench.

Humphrey was all business under the hood, tinkering with this and tapping on that. I thought maybe he knew what he was doing until I realized he couldn't find the spark plugs. Buick used to put these lid things over them. After we'd pried one off and given ourselves some spark-plug-wire electrical shocks, we figured maybe it wasn't the old set of points. Maybe it was vapor lock. If you leave vapor lock alone it gets better. This was exactly the kind of mechanical problem that Humphrey and I were good at solving. We decided it was vapor lock and went inside to get a drink.

Humphrey was from England so he thought this bar was quaint, charming in its primitive way, a real piece of Americana. I'm from Ohio and I thought we were going to get killed.

The South was still *The South* in 1977. And the Florida piney woods weren't full of good ole boys in Ralph Lauren Polo shirts who'd made it big developing gated (and de-gatored) golf course communities. The Florida piney woods were full of the kind of rednecks who were beginning to fill that bar—none of them an improvement on the rednecks who had been there already. This was only five years after *Deliverance* hit the theaters and only eight years after the premiere of *Easy Rider,* which I had seen three times when I was trying to be a hippie (and which—from my present perspective of a dad with daughters, surveying the good-for-nothing young men on motorcycles who might want to date them—has a happy ending). I mean, Jimmy Carter had carried the South in '76. They were so primitive down there that they hadn't even evolved into Republicans.

And then there was Humphrey's English accent, a posh accent, one might even go so far as to say a plummy accent. It was a nice accent to have—in England. In the Florida piney woods it was an accent that might not sound, well, you know, *manly*. And Humphrey, after he'd had a few drinks, began to speak—as English speakers the world around do, especially in foreign climes—more loudly. When Humphrey started talking a little louder, people started to look at us a little funny. The louder his talk became, the funnier the looks we got. And just when I was *sure* we were going to get killed somebody asked if that was our old Buick out front with the hood up. We said yes. The room went silent. Then there was, I swear, an audible sound of cracking smiles (revealing a good number of missing teeth). Even the bartender's expression turned faintly cheerful.

"That old Buick quit on ya?" someone else asked. We said yes. There was a rush out the door. Trunk lids popped up, tool cases snapped open, and in minutes our engine compartment was packed with fearsome drunk Florida crackers undoing fuel lines, pulling off plug wires, and wrenching on things that I couldn't see while beer bottles piled up in front of the grille.

Not that any of them were able to get the car started. Humphrey and I went back in the bar and began drinking at a table with the local game warden and José, an immense half-Indian, half-Mexican who'd been the 1959 and '60 Rocky Mountain Professional Wrestling Champion and whose presence in the Florida panhandle was never adequately explained. The game warden said that he himself had had a '56 Buick. "Had one just like it," he said. Several other people said the same thing. In fact, on our entire trip, it was hard to find a man over forty-five who said he *hadn't* had a '56 Buick. And they were fondly remembered, to a car. "You couldn't break 'em with a stick," said the game warden. "That car'll run forever."

Humphrey said he'd settle for tonight.

I asked the warden what the BEER place was called. "Well," he said, "sometimes we call it the 98 Inn and sometimes we call it the 98 Tavern, but mostly we don't call it anything at all. Hell, you're thirty miles from nowhere and forty miles from nowhere else." Then he went off and got into a fistfight.

By midnight Humphrey and I were very drunk. We were talking to a fellow named Jack who was twenty-two and looked like he robbed gas stations to get his heart started in the morning. He had a sharp Appalachian face with various scars and a row of absent dentation. He'd recently shot himself in the stomach over something to do with an estranged wife. He showed us where the bullet had gone in and where it had come out. Now he was living in a trailer with another lady and her five kids, but they were all off at her mother's canning something, so he invited us to stay with him. We were sure he was a homicidal maniac but it was that or sleep in the car.

Jack turned out to be a perfectly amiable guy. It was all we could do to keep him from persuading us to take a little vacation and spend a week down there bait fishing for razorback hogs, or whatever it is they do on vacation in the Florida piney woods. And he did persuade us to share his quart jar of moonshine.

Sunday, June 26
Nowhere to Mobile

Ouch, we woke up. Our friends of the night before had done a fair amount of damage helping us out. There were a lot of loose hoses and wires. Fuel lines were draped over the fenders and the contact arm on the points had been bent double. Humphrey decided that he'd better work on this himself, so he squatted atop the valve covers and sweated and diddled in the distributor for the next two hours. Finally, Jack rounded up yet another local, who took a big screwdriver, jammed it once into the points, slapped on the distributor cap, and started the car first try. "Had one just like it," he said.

Humphrey and I drove south until we found the ocean. We rented a motel room for the day and had showers and a lot of Bloody Marys. And then, God knows why, we went to a water park.

Humphrey thought this was quaint, charming in its primitive way, a real piece of Americana. I thought, between our hangovers and all the Bloody Marys, we were going to drown.

Then we went to Sears and bought some tools that must have seemed at the time as though they would be useful: a large hammer, three unusual sizes of Phillips screwdrivers, a pair of tiny Japanese pliers, and a pry bar.

Just after sundown we got back in the Buick. It was running perfectly now. We drove to Mobile with no problems except that Humphrey turned out to be scared of insects they don't have in England, which is most insects. He nearly put us into a ditch when he got a June bug down his shirt. Also, we couldn't figure out how to work the instrument panel lights so the driver had to open his quarter-ton door every time he wanted to check the speedometer or the gas gauge and this would cause the driver to accidentally yank the steering wheel, sending the car careening across the road into oncoming traffic and making all the water that had leaked out of our busted Styrofoam cooler slosh into our shoes.

Monday, June 27
Mobile to Natchez

We figured that if the points weren't screwed up before, they certainly were now, after being jammed with a big screwdriver. But only one junkyard in Mobile had a '56 Buick, and it had kudzu growing up through its engine compartment, and the distributor was missing anyway. Eventually the junkyard owner found a garage that had a new set of points. We were on our way there when the car quit again. This time we *knew* it was the points. I hitched to the garage and came back with their tow truck. The driver (he'd had one just like it) unhooked the fuel line to the carburetor. There was a vicious reptilian hiss. "Vapor lock," the tow truck driver said. We had a new set of points installed anyway and spent the rest of the day battling vapor lock all across Mississippi.

Back in the 98 Tavern, José the wrestling champion had told us that the one surefire cure for vapor lock was to put wooden clothespins all along the fuel line. We thought that sounded pretty stupid, but by the time we got to Hattiesburg we'd bought two bags of them and had stuck on as many as we could fit. When we stopped for gas in a little town, the station owner opened our hood to check the oil and the half dozen loafers hanging out at his station burst into hysterics. So the clothespins had to go. I thought we should give them another chance. Maybe they'd start to work or something. But Humphrey said he drew the line at getting laughed at if we died in a wreck.

Tuesday, June 28
Natchez to Dallas

We now had the process of unhooking the fuel line and curing our vapor lock down to about one minute, but we'd quit getting vapor lock. And we were just congratulating ourselves when the water temperature hit the bad peg and wouldn't come down. We had to spend an hour and a half cooling off in Louisiana's Kisatchie National Forest. There is absolutely nothing to do in Louisiana's Kisatchie National Forest except sit around and look at the one kind of conifer that grows in the Kisatchie National Forest. Let us call it the Kisatchie cedar. Whether it is rare or endangered I do not know. I do know that after an hour and a half it cries out to be clear-cut.

The engine overheated again as soon as we started the car, and we limped into Clarence, Louisiana, where the proprietor of the sole filling station told us that the Buick's thermostat had "shit the bed." He didn't have any parts or even a garage but he gave us the phone numbers of all the local mechanics and the use of his phone. I called everyone in a thirty-mile radius but no one had a hand free to do the work. Finally, I got one fellow who said, "Hell I had a '56 Buick, and I just tore the damn thermostat out. Threw it away. If you ain't got a gasket, slap some damn cardboard in there. Damn thing'll run forever."

I was embarrassed to admit that I didn't know where thermostats made their home. But the filling station owner did. He made a gasket out of the back of my reporter's notebook and bolted it into the water hose connection where it stuck out on every side, little spiral binding holes and all.

The overheating was fixed, and while we drove toward Dallas that night Humphrey and I debated whether to have the thermostat fixed as well. Buick must have had some reason for putting a thermostat in besides cold mornings in Kansas. Even in Africa or Southeast Asia, where it's always hot, cars have thermostats. At least we thought they did. Maybe thermostats provide back pressure or something in the water pump or somewhere to prevent, you know, surge and gurgling in there. Maybe we'd really need one in the desert where surge and gurgling could be expected to be at their worst. Without a thermostat all the water might swish around too fast in the cooling system, running through over and over again at hundreds of gallons per minute and turning into superheated steam until the whole car blew up like the steamboat *Sultana*. We didn't know.

Wednesday, June 29
Dallas to Nowhere in Particular

The new thermostat—plus labor, fresh antifreeze, a radiator flush, a "water pump inspection," and several other things I couldn't make out on the bill—cost almost (2009 readers, prepare yourselves for a Dr. Evil moment) fifty dollars.

Out beyond Dallas somewhere we came upon something called the *Cadillac Ranch*. A sculptor (soi-disant) had planted ten Cadillacs nosedown in the empty prairie. The Caddys—1951 through 1960—pretty much covered the history of tail fins. About half of each car was sticking out of the ground, on a slant calculated so that the truly enormous fins of the '59 Coupe de Ville formed an equilateral triangle with the earth. Voilà, art. Humphrey and I inspected this cultural treasure and found beer can and condom package indications that the backseats of the sculpture had been used for traditional backseat purposes. You don't see that so much with, for instance, a Rodin.

When we got up toward Wichita Falls we realized we needed a drink and, also, the engine was overheating again. So, as it turned out, was the air-conditioning unit in my motel room. And the desk clerk told us that this was a dry county, and it was fifty miles to the nearest bar or carryout.

Thursday, June 30
Wherever We Were to Tucumcari

The Texas panhandle has to be one of the most featureless landscapes on earth. They have sightseeing buses that take you into Lubbock to see the tree. Or they should. For lack of anything better to do we stopped at a junkyard in Quanah or Goodnight or someplace where the owner had a lot of old Buicks parked in a field. He said our overheating problem had to do with the cylinder head design. "They'd all overheat," he said, "all those '56 Buicks." The next person blamed it all on hot oil in the Dynaflo transmission. Somebody else said the radiators were "too thick and not wide enough." Another said they were "plenty thick but too high." And one man in Barstow claimed that the problem was "this shitty weather we've been having for twenty years." But not one of these people was shaken in his belief that a '56 Buick would "run forever."

Actually, just then, our '56 felt like it would. The temperature gauge was strangely somnolent, and we didn't have a single major problem all day except for the hour or so when our fuel pump was spraying gas all over the hot exhaust manifold.

For thirty miles, approaching Amarillo, Humphrey and I were complaining that the city stank of gasoline. And Amarillo does have a lot of refineries. But the gas smell kept getting worse for thirty miles, leaving Amarillo.

When it eventually occurred to us to stop and look under the hood we found that the tiny rubber gasket under the bolt that holds the fuel pump cap in place had collapsed and gas was squirting out and boiling up in little spitballs on the headers. I have no clue why this didn't turn us into a rolling *Hindenburg*, not even after Humphrey gasped in dismay and let the cigarette drop out of his mouth and fall right in there. I forget what we used to stop the squirting until we'd bought a small rubber washer for two cents at a Tucumcari hardware store. Very possibly it was chewing gum.

Friday, July 1
Tucumcari to Albuquerque

There's a beat-up old road, Route 104, running northwest out of Tucumcari through the desert to Conchas Lake, then up into the Cornudo Hills and across a grassland plateau to the Sangre de Cristo Mountains and Sante Fe. I'd flown to the West but I'd never driven over it. This little 150-mile byway awed me to imbecility. Humphrey said I was dangerous behind the wheel—bouncing up and down in the seat and jabbering about purple mountain majesties above the fruited plain and pointing out all the cows. We had to stop in Sante Fe to have a beer and settle me down.

Other than that it was just another day, with the engine overheating all the time and a new vapor lock problem that happened only on the edge of precipices or in the middle of blind curves. And even when the Buick was running right it was, truth be told, a very ordinary car. Once the museum-piece novelty had worn off, driving it was about as exciting as driving a new Buick. Or it was until we got lost down some lousy dirt roads south of Sante Fe and the car just sort of fell apart. The shocks and springs got Parkinson's disease, and all four wheels broke loose and headed every way but straight. At twenty miles per hour you would have thought we were racing the Baja 1000.

Humphrey had a theory about suspension harmonics or something and claimed that everything would be much better if he just drove faster, which made everything much worse. At least the Buick took to getting vapor lock in front of bars and taverns in all the little towns we went through, and that was good. But by the time we arrived in Albuquerque we were beginning to doubt the wisdom of this enterprise. In fact we were sick to death of the trip and the thing it rode in on.

Saturday, July 2
Drunk All Day in Albuquerque

Saturday we were drunk all day in Albuquerque.

Sunday, July 3
Albuquerque to Somewhere, Utah

Up in the Nacimiento Mountains we had a truly perplexing mechanical problem. We'd stopped for lunch in Cuba, New Mexico. When we came out of the restaurant the car wouldn't start and there was no vapor lock hiss when we opened the fuel line. Humphrey thought maybe the fuel pump had lost prime and was pumping backward. This seemed as likely a story as any. When we took the top off the fuel pump it was blowing bubbles in there.

That, Humphrey told me, was an indication of backward fuel pumping. I took his word for it. Humphrey tried to suck some gas up the fuel line. That didn't work so I tried until I began to giggle from the fumes and get sick.

Speaking of which, the restaurant where we were stalled was halfway along a mile of road between an Apache reservation and a liquor store. The Apaches coming from the reservation paid no attention to us. But the Apaches returning from the liquor store found our huffing and puffing of gasoline fascinating. After an hour we had a John Wayne movie's worth of Apaches surrounding us. Whether they considered us harmless lunatics or thought the opportunity to sniff Mobil premium was a prize worth capturing we could not determine. In fact, we couldn't get much dialogue going with the Apaches at all. Every now and then one would come from the liquor store to our engine bay and announce, "Me, Indian." Then he would act like I had and giggle and get sick. (I realize that "Indian" was, even in 1977, not the sensitive term of ethnic description. But my code of journalistic ethics forbids me from reporting that any Apache said, "Me, Native American.")

Humphrey found a length of radiator hose, which he put over the fuel filler neck and blew into. What this was supposed to do I don't know, but it certainly made him look funny. More Apaches giggled and got sick. After that Humphrey insisted on taking the fuel pump apart. I'd never seen the inside of a fuel pump. (It isn't wildly interesting.) Humphrey claimed that the fuel pump was doing all a fuel pump should. He put it back together. Giggling, sick Apaches were closing in. I tried the starter and the engine caught and ran like nothing had happened, thank God.

We got out of Cuba, over the continental divide, and into the huge Navajo reservation that takes up almost a quarter of Arizona. The landscape opened up, impossibly vast and void, and it dawned on us, for the first time really, that when the next thing broke we might be in serious trouble. We'd go forty or fifty miles without seeing another car and the Buick was overheating worse than ever. We'd bought a five-gallon jerry can in Tucumcari and whenever the gauge went all red we'd stop and one of us would get out and splash down the radiator while the driver gunned the engine. This would hold us for two hours, or one hour in the midday heat, or ten minutes on an uphill grade. We had no business being away from the amenities and attentions of the interstate in this car. We knew that. But we'd started out driving on the back roads because the Buick couldn't make turnpike speed, and these little bypaths had been so quaint and charming in their primitive way, and with such quaint, charming people and so many quaint, charming places to break down in front of and buy beer in that we'd forgotten ourselves and now we were in a real piece of Americana indeed.

Between Kayenta and the Grand Canyon we went a hundred miles without seeing any sign of human life besides each other—and the signs of life in these two humans seemed precarious. Then the sun went down and for the first time since we'd left Florida the temperature fell below seventy degrees. All of a sudden the Buick was a different car. It seemed to exude an aura of strength and dependability, almost as if it might run forever. I was driving, so I put my foot down and—in a Dynaflo way—we took off. If I pushed the old Buick enough past fifty mph all the jitterbug and hootchie-kootchie in the front end went away. Maybe Humphrey was right about "suspension harmonics" (whatever they may be), at least on smooth pavement. And upon smooth pavement we were. We went sixty-five, seventy, eighty miles an hour down these twisting roads, whipping along for all the world like a freshly minted Mercedes-Benz.

We were pulling out onto Route 89 just over the Utah border when some fellow in a late 1960s Datsun Fairlady roadster, of all things, buzzed by doing eighty-five or so, and I lit out, lumbering after him. It was wholly dark by then, and a misty night, and I wonder what the guy thought when he saw that wall of chrome well up in his rearview mirror. He was being overtaken by the past. And the past went by at a hundred miles per hour with door handles higher than his head and two inches of travel left under the accelerator. For me it was a truly exhilarating moment of rapport between man and machine. Then we got vapor lock and the engine conked out.

Monday, July 4
Utah to Las Vegas

We had to go almost a hundred miles up into Utah to find motel rooms. I celebrated America's birthday by awaking in a condition that those who've spent much of their lives on the road in America will recognize. I had no idea where I was. I looked around the anonymous room and there was nothing—no notepad, no matches, no phone book, no area code on the phone—to indicate my location. I turned on the TV. It wasn't working. Usually such disorientation is momentary, or, at worst, you just can't remember the name of the woman snoring next to you. But there was no woman in this case, and my amnesia lasted through shit, shower, and shave. I was beginning to suspect I'd died in my sleep and gone to motel purgatory when I thought to open the door. There was the Buick. Purgatory was not an option.

It was raining. The Buick wouldn't start for a while. Something had gotten wet under the hood and we had to wait for the rain to let up and mop around under there with a motel towel before we got it going. Ten miles down the road it began to rain again and we discovered that we didn't have any windshield wipers. We'd been hearing obscene sucking noises from the brake pedal for a couple of days and we knew there was a problem somewhere in all the tubes and hoses of the Buick's Medusa-head vacuum assist mechanism. But everything seemed to work and we didn't realize that the windshield wipers ran off this system too. I could get the blades to move a little when we were headed uphill and acceleration increased the vacuum pressure. But downhill deceleration did the opposite. The only way to maintain any vacuum pressure at all was to keep my right foot pressed on the accelerator while using my left foot to try to slow down. Since the drum brakes on a '56 Buick are about three times more effective in front than they are in the rear, the back wheels began to slip around. It was not a recipe for safe driving. And, naturally, we were treated to clearing skies up every incline and drenching squalls down every slope until we got back into the desert and began to overheat.

We played it safe through Arizona and Nevada, sticking to Interstate 15 almost to Las Vegas. Then Humphrey insisted that he had to see the Valley of Fire. So we filled the jerry can and headed down a maze of gravel roads into that red sandstone wasteland. I suppose it's very beautiful, if you think you're going to live to tell anybody about it. We were completely alone, and it was 110 degrees in the shade. I was sure that when they found us—our bones picked clean by whatever it is that bothers to live out here—they'd think we were left over from some 1956 Vegas mob slaying. And we did manage to get lost. To add irony to probable death, we'd had a CB radio with us all along. But we'd kept forgetting to have it installed. It was a glum moment out there in the desert when Humphrey and I realized we would not be able to figure out how to connect that radio. Not, literally, for the life of us.

Fortunately we got unlost. Then I decided there was a quicker way to get to Las Vegas than the interstate and we got lost again for a while. Quite a while, actually, so that when we pulled over the top of one more hill and saw the city glistening below us we were almost out of gas, completely out of water, and totally out of patience with each other.

Dirty, half-naked, and our car covered with dust and grit, we weren't sure they'd take us in at the Sands. But the doorman had "had one just like it" and bent our ears for twenty minutes about how nothing ever went wrong with a '56 Buick.

Humphrey and I drank a few drinks in the lobby bar. I went to my room, exhausted. Humphrey ordered a nightcap. This apparently turned into a morning sombrero. (He *was* drinking tequila sunrises.) I came out of my room early in the a.m. and there was Humphrey, more or less where I'd left him, but now accompanied by two scantily sequined young ladies of the type who may be said to have "a rich and varied social life." I must say they were quaint and charming in their primitive way, and each was a real piece of Americana.

Tuesday, July 5
Las Vegas to Los Angeles

There's a 2,400-foot climb up the Barstow incline on the California–Nevada border, and we knew that if we didn't make it before ten in the morning we wouldn't make it at all. So I had to pry Humphrey away from his bosom buddies and pour him into the car. Besides, we were three days overdue in LA and practically broke. (Humphrey had been luckier in love than at craps.)

Somehow we made it to Barstow without seizing up. The temperature gauge was half in the red at exactly fifty miles per hour and if I went even two miles per hour faster the radiator began to boil from engine heat while if I went two miles per hour slower the radiator began to boil from lack of cooling air.

Humphrey was flopping all over in his sleep, flailing at me and falling against the steering wheel. Once, when we were completely boxed in—trucks fore and aft and a car in the left lane—his leg shot out and he stamped on my accelerator foot. We would have crashed if I hadn't given him a swift kick and caused him to curl up on the seat.

It had taken eleven days to cross the country, and we'd had some kind of breakdown every one of those days except this last one. When we got to LA we missed Sargent's home address, went to turn around, and reverse gear gave out. Gave out completely—the Buick couldn't even be pushed backward in neutral. We had to make a circle through the neighborhood and come back to Sargent's house.

I suppose I still love old Buicks. I remember thinking I probably wouldn't try to drive another across the whole grocery store, A&P, Atlantic to Pacific. And I never have. And I never have found out how Tom Sargent got that car out of his driveway.

A Better Land than This

(1984)

Michael Nesmith had been racing in the Baja 1000 for several years and I'd accompanied his team in 1982. Indy 500 legend Parnelli Jones described the Baja off-road race as "like being in an all-day plane crash." In 1983 I was part of a *Car and Driver* magazine road test where we attempted to take five sport sedans the length of the Baja peninsula and destroyed three of them. Baja California was a bad place to race and a worse place to test sport sedans. Therefore, Michael and I reasoned, it would be a swell place for a romantic getaway. Michael invited his then wife Kathryn and I invited my then girlfriend Elena to go on an "off-road road trip." We would take two four-wheel-drive vehicles down the Baja, for fun, attempting to avoid all pavement while camping out along the way. I'm not *blaming* the Baja for Michael's divorce or my breakup. But . . .

I talked the then extant American Motors Corporation (I'm not *blaming* the Baja . . .) into loaning us a pair of their products—a newly introduced SUV model, the Cherokee, and a Jeep CJ with a pickup bed, the Scrambler.

We took these to Michael's race garage in LA. We (by "we" I mean Michael and his mechanics) reinforced the suspensions, bolted in extra spares, fitted the Cherokee with a safari-style roof rack and an electric winch, and wired each Jeep with a set of four auxiliary lights. When the lights were switched on they lit the garage like a Los Alamos A-bomb test.

Mexico has only one brand of gasoline, Pemex, owned by the government. Quality and supply are the same as they would be if the U.S. Post Office was also the gas station. We installed thirty-gallon gas tanks, added backup fuel filters, and packed a case of octane booster.

We also packed oil, coolant, extra radiator hoses and fan belts, a tow strap, jumper cables, fire extinguishers, several sets of wrenches, a shovel, and an air compressor, plus tents, sleeping bags, coolers, twenty gallons of

American water, a camp stove, dried food, a compass, two-way radios, piles of maps and guidebooks, and four snake-bite kits.

In retrospect this strikes me as three snake-bite kits too many. I mean, once I've had to use one snake-bite kit I'm out of there. Hello medevac, good-bye me. On the other hand there was no medevac in the Baja. While you're treating yourself with the first snake-bite kit, I guess the same snake could sneak up and bite you three more times. Even so, for the sake of our love lives, Michael and I would have been better off replacing a couple of the snake-bite kits with a pair of small blue boxes from Tiffany & Co.

Larger gifts from Tiffany wouldn't have fit. The Jeeps were so full that we had to leave a lot of things behind, but only the things we'd be needing. It took us from morning until late afternoon to pack the Jeeps with the other things. On the first day of our journey we made it to Huntington Beach.

On the second day, Tuesday, May 8, we entered Mexico at Tecate and took Route 2 east along the border to the Mesa del Pinal, the pine forests on the western slope of the Juárez Mountains. Here we turned off the road. Forty miles south was Laguna Hanson, the Baja's only lake.

We were lost two hundred yards from the pavement. Lumber is scarce in Baja, and Mesa del Pinal is webbed with woodcutters' roads. Once a way is cleared in the desert it stays clear. The woodcutters' roads overlaid four centuries of cattle trails, mining cuts, Indian paths, and missionary pack routes—all still open to passage, mainly by us. We'd left the compass behind.

Still, it was a beautiful afternoon, sun lighting up the stands of trees, air redolent with incense cedar, piñon pine, sage, and gasoline. I stopped the Scrambler. Gas was pouring out of our custom-fitted tank. A little nest of vent tubes designed to meet some U.S. air pollution regulation had come undone. We would dribble gas the rest of the trip.

Michael got under the car. Elena walked off to photograph the scenery. These uplands look inviting, like Devonshire pastures, but the flapjack-shaped nopal cactus has tiny spines that must be removed by depilatory waxing. Cholla cactus spines are large, barbed, and nearly unextractable. And cholla branches detach so easily they're said to throw themselves at people. Elena was back in a minute.

We kept driving around in the pines. The sun was setting. We got out all our maps. No two agreed on anything. "Laguna Hanson," I read aloud from one of the guidebooks, "is named for an American ranch manager who was murdered there."

We got back in the Jeeps and Elena confessed she'd never spent a night outdoors. I looked over and saw her knuckles gleaming white on the grab handle. I explained that there was nothing to worry about. We had enough food and water to spend weeks lost in the piney woods. Furthermore, Elena had been born in Havana. "You speak the local lingo," I said.

"Are we going to die?" she asked.

We couldn't find any place to pitch camp except the dry washes. These are poor campsites because livestock wander up and down them all night except when they drown during flash floods. A stake bed truck passed by full of drunk and yelling ranch hands. "You see," I told Elena, "we're not that far from civilization. What are they yelling?"

"You don't want to know," she said.

We found the highway again about eleven p.m. We'd penetrated maybe twenty miles into the wilderness.

The Juárez range had climbed gradually from the Pacific, but to the east the descent was immediate. The road peeled down a giant bluff in frenetic switchbacks. There were no shoulders on the highway. Cliffs rose without preamble from one edge of the asphalt and dropped like ruined stockbrokers from the other. Guardrails were few and there were no dents in them, just large holes punched straight through. The only traffic at midnight was enormous diesel trucks doing eighteen-wheel drifts through the turns at seventy miles an hour or, worse, going ten miles an hour in both lanes with their lights out. Clusters of memorial crosses decorated every curve. Sweat greased my palms. My knees shook. I looked at Elena. She lived in New York. Apparently she equated being back on pavement with urban security. Lulled by the familiar noise of honking horns and squealing brakes, she was asleep.

We reached flat land at Mexicali and drove into a fog of chemical spray and fertilizer stink rising from the irrigation canals. We rushed across the border and checked into an American motel.

We were ashamed of ourselves in the morning and returned to Mexico immediately, driving south on the San Felipe road into the delta of the Colorado River. For years Mexico had been arguing with the United States about Colorado water rights. During the Carter administration a treaty had been signed and the United States agreed to divert less of the Colorado's flow. But the Mexican government hadn't completed its channel dredging operations in time. The land Mexico was eager to irrigate was now under four feet of water.

Farther south was El Desierto de los Chinos, the desert of the Chinamen, where nothing grew at all. To the east was a wide salt flat, an eerie mirage of bright sunlight on still water. To the west was sand as bright as the salt, rising to shining hills that merged with brilliant sky, which arched back to the salt's glare until the whole landscape pinwheeled. The temperature was 120 degrees.

About 1900 a group of Chinese immigrants set out across this desert, hoping to find work in the United States. They paid a Mexican guide $100 to lead them. He said he knew where the water holes were. Halfway between San Felipe and the Colorado delta the guide admitted he didn't. They all died, including the Mexican. (Leaving us to wonder how we know the story.)

At El Chinero, where the bodies were buried, we turned west up the San Matias pass, which divided the Sierra Juárez from the Sierra de San Pedro Mártir, the highest range in the Baja. Six thousand feet up in these peaks, a hundred miles from any city, and separated from the road by twenty miles of crag and gorge was a hacienda with a dirt air strip and guest rooms: Mike's Sky Ranch.

Michael and I had been eager to get into bad terrain. We were anxious to try our expensive car modifications. The handcrafted dual front shock-absorber mounts on the Cherokee came loose immediately. Then there was an ugly noise from the Scrambler. I stopped. Water was pouring out of the radiator. One fan blade had bent double and sliced an arc out of the radiator core.

In the Baja 1000 race they attribute such accidents to a special gremlin, the Baja Monster. They say the Baja Monster makes things go wrong no one ever heard of going wrong before. I'd certainly never seen this happen to a fan blade. Actually, like most remote places, the Baja *was* supposed to have a monster. Tibet had the Yeti. The Rockies had Sasquatch. And the monster reported by early travelers in Baja was, rather sadly, Zorillo the rabid skunk.

We towed the Scrambler over the now less attractive rocks and gullies to Mike's.

Mike's Sky Ranch sat in a large valley by a small stream that contained its own species of trout. Wonderful cooking smells came from the sprawl of white adobe buildings. The sun went down between mountains as if into rifle sights and threw a violet cast across the sky. In the last moments of light Kathryn and Elena were delighted by the lambent, darting turns of hundreds of birds suddenly a-flight.

Michael took me aside. He said, "Those are bats."

On Thursday Michael pinched the radiator tubes shut as well as he could. I straightened the fan blade on a rock. There was supposed to be a man with a soldering iron thirty miles away in Valle de Trinidad. He wasn't there. We now had to drive either eighty miles northwest to Ensenada and have the radiator boil from mountain grades or drive eighty miles southeast to San

Felipe and have the radiator boil from desert heat. Kathryn and Elena thought we'd be better off in Ensenada. "They have more jewelry stores there."

The Ensenada radiator shop fixed the Scrambler in ten minutes and charged us eight dollars. You could get anything fixed in the Baja, which was good because everything broke there.

That night we stayed at a new hotel on the Pacific coast at San Quintin. Beach dunes had already destroyed the landscaping.

Below San Quintin Route 1 turned inland and there was a sudden change in scenery. Mesas and granite mountains were replaced by boat-sized sandstone boulders. Wind erosion had ground and drilled these into scary caricatures. The scruffy Sonoran desert foliage gave way to unearthly growths. There were dense spreads of cardón cactus, something like the saguaros in Arizona but more anthropomorphic and much larger. Flocks of vultures perched in the cactus. Sometimes five acres of cardón would have a carrion bird on every arm. There were also forests of boojum—more properly, cirio. The tall, unbranched trees looked like air carrots from Mars. Scattered in the cirio and cardón were copalquins, or elephant trees, whose fat spare-leafed limbs make agonized prehensile shapes. Every child has imagined such a thing outside his bedroom window on a windy night.

Barriers of isolating geography, weather, and seas have turned the Baja into a set of biological atolls. There are hundreds of plants and animals that live nowhere else. More than eighty species of cactus are endemic to the Baja. Cirio trees are found only within a 125-mile radius. The Baja has flowers pollinated not by insects but by bats, and bats that eat fish instead of insects. Isla Santa Catalina in the Sea of Cortés has a rattlesnake species with no rattles. And on Isla Espiritu Santo a race of black jackrabbits has developed. The black fur does not provide protective coloration, much less comfort in the sun. The mutation seems entirely pointless.

Our awe of nature was dulled, however, by garbage all over the place. And the shapely rocks were spray-painted with political party symbols, advertisements, and messages of love. Nature was at its worst here and man wasn't much good either.

There were also, everywhere in the Baja, wrecked cars, hundreds of them, mostly upside down and burned. One guidebook tried to pass these off gaily: "Don't be bugged by those wrecked vehicles here and there along the highway—they're just jalopies abandoned by road construction workers." We stopped for lunch at a little landing strip called Santa Ines. A collection of crashed airplanes was piled behind the cantina.

After 180 miles of living and dead grotesques, Route 1 curved back toward the Pacific and ran along empty beaches through land that looked like the land around Los Angeles would if vanity plates were fatal and bulldozers were free. The beaches end at the town of Guerrero Negro next to

Scammon's Lagoon, the largest of several Baja inlets where all the world's gray whales mate and calve. Whaling ships discovered the lagoon in 1857 and hunted it until grays were thought to be extinct.

Guerrero Negro also had an enormous sea salt harvesting operation. There have been many attempts to get something out of the Baja. The first expedition in 1533 was sent by Cortés to gather pearls at La Paz. The captain was murdered by the pilot, and the pilot was murdered by the Indians. Cortés tried again in 1535. Pearls were found but the pearl divers starved. Agricultural settlements failed in 1603, 1636, 1649, and 1685. Silver mines have been sunk in a hundred places, also mines for gold and lead. In 1868 J. Ross Browne, a reporter for *Harper's Magazine,* wrote that no mine had yet repaid its investment. In 1866 an American land company received a grant of eighteen million acres from the Mexican government and colonization was attempted. The colonists left. There have been onyx quarries at El Marmol, a French copper concession at Santa Rosalia, an attempt to breed pearl oysters on Isla Espiritu Santo, et cetera. They're all gone.

On the outskirts of Guerrero Negro, where the twenty-eighth parallel divides the Mexican states of Baja California and Baja California Sur, was an immense gawky steel constructivist sculpture of a landing eagle. There was a museum at the base with rows of flagpoles and a large amphitheater. All this was built to commemorate the opening of Route 1 in 1973. The museum was abandoned, its windows broken, the sculpture was rusty, and sand filled the arena seats. An osprey and his mate had made a nest in the broken road sign beside the steel eagle.

Inland at mid-peninsula the country changed again, turning to fields of black lava. Tres Virgenes, three perfect volcanic cones, rose in the eastern distance. We traveled eighty miles in this unrelieved scene, then crested a hill and were confronted by the startling tropical luxury of San Ignacia. The oasis occupied a theatrical cleft in the rocks. A lagoon filled the bottom, surrounded by magnificent date palms. Thatch-roofed houses with thick flower gardens were set among the trees. Behind them pale blue and pink adobe buildings faced a broad plaza sheltered by giant Indian laurels. San Ignacio was heaven with bugs.

A colonial baroque mission church filled one side of the plaza. The walls were four feet thick, built from lava rubble, and carefully plastered and painted to imitate dressed stone. The mammoth gilt wood altar and huge murky paintings of Ignatius of Loyola were imported from Spain. Crude local carvings of angel faces decorated the vault above.

The mission was founded in 1728, one of thirty-three missions built by Jesuits, Franciscans, and Dominicans to convert the Baja Indians. The Indians' language had no words for "marriage" or "honesty." They went around naked and did not know how to make pots, weave cloth, or build a hut. They ate insects and lizards and anything else. If a particularly good thing to eat was discovered, they would tie a string around it, swallow the morsel, pull it back up, and pass it to the next person.

In June, when pitahaya cactus fruit were ripe, the Indians gorged themselves, stopping only for naps and to fornicate with everyone, regardless of family ties. During pitahaya season the tribe defecated on large flat rocks so the undigested fruit seeds could be picked out and ground into flour. Father Francisco Maria Piccolo, who in 1716 was the first European to visit San Ignacio, was given some bread baked from this flour. He ate it before discovering its source and was the target of jokes from his fellow missionaries for the rest of his life.

The Indians were not interested in Christianity. It took heroic efforts to gather them into irrigated settlements, introduce them to agriculture and other benefits of civilization, and give them the blessed sacraments. But the missionaries did it. The Indians promptly died. Between the founding of the first Baja mission in 1697 and the expulsion of the Jesuit order from Spanish territories in 1767, the Indian population—with its utter lack of immunity to European, or even New World, diseases—decreased from 50,000 to 7,000. In 1984 only a couple hundred were left near Mexicali.

On the morning of Saturday, May 12, we left San Ignacio by the back way, driving up to the most spectacular view of the oasis, which is from the dump. Then we went across the remaining volcanic highlands to Santa Rosalia, the old French mining concession by the Sea of Cortés. On the town square was a sheet iron church designed by Gustave Eiffel. It was created for the 1889 Universal Exposition in Paris as an example of a "manufactured building." It won second prize and was shipped to Baja by mistake.

Twenty miles south, on the lip of Bahia Concepción, was Rio Mulegé, one of the few Baja rivers that reaches the sea. Mulegé canyon was filled with palms and mangroves backed by naked hills. Man-o'-war birds, whose shape in flight mimicked a pterodactyl's, hung on the thermals. The effect was a museum diorama of the Mesozoic era blown up to horrifying size. The beauty, like so much of Baja's beauty, was hard to bear, a physical assault. It was a relief to look down the highway and see litter and more burned-out, overturned cars.

Under the cliffs along the Bahia Concepción the surf was police-flasher blue. The bay was twenty-five miles long and five miles wide and didn't have a single home on its shores. At the foot of the escarpments, though, if your car would make it, there are campsites on small parabolas of beach.

The water was the temperature of love. The breeze was the temperature of beer. Two kids in a dinghy sold us a kilo of big, perfectly round scallops—the best scallops I've ever tasted. The sun lit the cliff tops purple. Cormorants dove in formation. Pelicans skimmed the tide. It was a moment to justify the whole trip. And a moment was how long it lasted, followed by biting gnats, a soaking dew, and me kicking over the camp stove and setting fire to the beach towels.

Quests and challenges never seem to have a middle until you're in it. Everyone likes to address a challenge. Everyone likes to return from a quest. But the middle is another matter. We were tired, filthy, brilliantly sunburned, and queasy from the constant jolting ride and smell of gasoline. Elena had to be on a plane to New York via Mexico City on Monday, leaving no one to translate. The Baja highway was coming up in chunks from heat and traffic, and, during the previous two years, winter rainstorms had corrugated whole miles of it. All the oil seals on our cars were weeping, every screw and bolt seemed to be working free, and our gear had shaken loose and was rattling maniacally. No amount of octane booster could help the Pemex gasoline, and each hill climb was accompanied by a racking clatter of pre-detonation in the engines.

A little after dawn on Sunday we stopped in Loreto where the Baja's first mission was built. Hanging in the church were excellent, astonishing seventeenth-century paintings of the disciples, the style just shy of El Greco's. They were pulling from their frames and the canvas was rotting beneath the oil. Elena could find out nothing about them. "They are just anonymous," a shopkeeper told her. "There's supposed to be a Michelangelo under one. But we haven't scraped the paint off yet."

We drove two hours to a mountain oasis to see cave paintings, but they had been defaced. No one knows who did the cave paintings either. The Indians told the Spanish they were done by giants.

Back on the highway we climbed the terrible face of the Sierra de la Giganta, the mountains named for those artists, and drove 350 miles to La Paz through an unrelenting span of yuccas and bare grit.

Government and business had been working hard to make La Paz a famous resort though the town has no excuse for existence. Even the oysters John Steinbeck wrote about in *The Pearl* have died off. We checked into the new, big concrete hotel. It seemed to have been jolted too. All the fittings were broken, the carpet was coming untacked, and there were holes in the bedclothes. On the mirror over the bathroom sinks were insincere-looking decals that read "agua potable."

Elena began to get sick at the airport. Kathryn and I were sick an hour later. I looked out my room window and saw the hotel's sewage treatment plant in the same enclosure and nearly indistinguishable from the water purification equipment.

We managed to go out to dinner that night. The special was endangered, Mexican government–protected sea turtle. Sea turtle steaks are the color of those school chalkboards that are supposed to ease eyestrain. "It is like beef," the waiter said, "but with a different smell."

We were sicker yet on Tuesday. La Paz was hosting an International Rotary Club convention. Vendors were out in herds on the *paseo maritimo* along the harbor. Taped mariachi music barked from loudspeakers. La Paz was filling with Americans complaining that the town wasn't authentic enough. We tried to leave.

Three blocks from the hotel Kathryn called me on the radio. "There's something wrong with our car." I asked her if it was engine trouble. "I don't know that much about automobiles," she said. "It's hopping up and down." I looked in the rearview mirror. The Cherokee was hopping up and down.

The front axle assembly where we'd attached our double shock-absorber modification had disintegrated. The nearest Cherokee axle was in San Diego. We bobbed slowly back to the hotel.

We'd set out to travel in places uninhabited and nearly unexplored, to see land unchanged since the first Europeans saw it, to tread where even aboriginal man had barely trod. And we'd wound up with diarrhea at a third-rate luxury hotel in the middle of a Rotary Club convention. It would take a Lear jet, a twin-engine Cessna, two race drivers, six Mexican welders, and the American Motors corporate public relations department to get us home.

An early missionary, Father Juan de Ugarte, once preached to the natives in Loreto on the agonies of hell. His congregation began to laugh. Father Ugarte asked them what was funny, and an old Indian replied, "There must be no lack of firewood in hell. So hell is a better land than this. We would be wise to go there."

It was Baja that was first called "California." The name was a joke. Califia was an Amazon queen in *Las Sergas de Esplandián,* a romance popular in Spain when Mexico was being conquered. California, the island Califia ruled, was "at the right hand of the Indies very close to that part of terrestrial paradise and inhabited by women without a single man among them." Baja too was thought to be an island and Spanish sailors named it "California" after encountering Indian women who washed themselves in urine.

American Motors sent Clay Bintz, fleet manager for its West Coast PR office, to the Orange County airport with two new shock absorbers. The Lear jet owned by Michael's company, Pacific Arts, picked up Clay and Randy Salmont, Michael's race truck codriver, and brought them to La Paz that night.

By nine the next morning Clay had found a man with an arc welder who worked under a tin-roofed ramada in a back alley. Clay held up the shock absorbers and began to mime. Then he stooped and drew pictures in the dirt. The welder and his five assistants clustered around. One peeked under the Cherokee. "Ay, que fucked!" he said. Michael and Kathryn and I went off to find beer and some bathrooms.

The welding crew pushed the Cherokee over a trench. By noon they'd built a new suspension out of scrap metal. An English-speaking neighbor told me, "You found the best welder. There is nothing he cannot repair." The neighbor inspected the discarded custom shocks. "However," he said, "much trouble in life comes from fixing things that are not broken."

Clay and Randy drove us to the airport. The two of them would try to nurse the Jeeps back to the States on Route 1. The Lear was fueled, gleaming, and ready on the crumbly tarmac. Kathryn scampered on board and Michael and I were about to follow. Michael stared wistfully into the desert. "I bet these cars won't make it," he said. He was wavering. He was chickening out on chickening out. "Especially if we went up the Gulf side and into San Felipe on the really bad roads."

Then Barry Connelly, the jet pilot, volunteered to return and fly air support, as he'd done for Michael's '83 Baja 1000 effort. "Just in case you die out there," Barry said. Kathryn stayed on the plane.

If the Cherokee was going to break we wanted it to break as soon as possible. Michael and I drove it hard out of La Paz on Route 1, slamming into ruts and holes and pounding our heads on the roof liner. Clay and Randy followed in the Scrambler. We made it to Loreto in six hours.

The next morning Barry flew back in Michael's Cessna 411 and landed at Bahia de Los Angeles on the Sea of Cortés coast. The rest of us drove another three hundred miles up the highway past Guerrero Negro, then turned east into the wormy rocks and cirio forests on a forty-mile cutoff to the bay.

Bahia de Los Angeles was a perfectly sheltered blonde sand cove about five miles across. Jagged arroyos radiated from it like a circle of dog mouths—bloodred granite pointed with veins of white quartz. This had been the site of a failed silver mine, a dead Indian tribe, and a massive resort development that never happened. There was a small motel there, some houses, and a shack of a gas station. The road built for the resort had come apart so badly that in places we got off and drove through the desert beside it.

The motel was all right. It was too hot to mind the cold showers and we found only one scorpion in the rooms.

Before dawn on Friday we headed back out the cutoff. We planned to take Route 1 north a few miles then get off-road northeast along the Calamajué riverbed. We thought we could reach another cove, Bahia San Luis Gonzaga, by nightfall. Barry would stand by until noon and then fly over our dust trail.

Clay and I took the Scrambler. The ruts and pavement gashes seemed to have grown in the night. The thing to do was to go fast, get "on top" so the Jeep's wheels would hit the far side of the holes before they had time to drop in. At sixty, if you have the nerve, this works on all but the biggest holes. And it was a very big hole we hit. We were tossed out against our shoulder harnesses, dropped back into our seats, and bounced up into the roof. Then there was an ugly noise. Water was pouring out of the radiator again. The same fan blade had bent the same way and cut a second arc through the radiator core.

We pushed and coasted the boiling Scrambler back to Bahia de Los Angeles and woke Barry. He and Clay loaded the radiator into the Cessna and flew three hundred miles to Ensenada, to the same radiator shop. The shop owner had a good laugh, they said. Randy and Michael and I went down to the beach and drank.

It was four in the afternoon when we got the radiator back. Bored and half drunk, we drove a dozen miles out the cutoff and went south on a road into wide broken valleys full of cardón. "Road," in such cases, meant just a place someone else had taken a vehicle. And brought it back, we hoped.

It took us two hours to go twenty-one miles to the ruins of the Mission San Borja. The mission was founded in 1759 to serve the spiritual needs of three thousand Indians. It was named "Saint Borgia" because that appalling family's contributions to the Jesuits financed it. By the time the granite church was complete in 1801 only four hundred Indians were left alive. The settlement was abandoned seventeen years later.

The ruins were not ruins at all. The church stood with huge futility almost perfectly preserved. The nave, at least thirty feet high and maybe seventy feet long, was roofed by an arch built without mortar from oval streambed rocks. Someone had put a color magazine illustration of the Virgin of Guadalupe on the dusty altar.

Here was an enormous monument to blindness and folly, built with the lucre of swine and causing the deaths of thousands of people. Yet there was a feeling of sanctity to the place. Maybe God likes a good joke. I put a couple hundred pesos under a devotional candle.

The sun went down. We raced the cars back to the Bay of LA, sliding sideways into the cactus and getting airborne over piles of rocks. Our ten headlights lit a pantheon dome of roiled silt above the desert floor.

At our motel they'd prepared an enormous meal, sea bass so large that it was cut into porterhouse steaks. All the food in Baja was splendid. The local lobsters were split and grilled slowly over mesquite fires. Delicate flour tortillas and fresh goat cheese were made into quesadillas. There was no refrigeration so everything was exactly fresh (or obviously otherwise). Chickens were, of course, free range and necessarily organic. Steaks were lean, from grass-fed cattle, but well flavored, especially when served ranchero-style with peppers so hot they made your nose run and the top of your head itch. And the Astroturf-colored, odorous sea turtle turned out to be—one might say—endangerously good.

We sat with the motel owner after dinner and had too much to drink. That afternoon out on the long sand spit closing the mouth of the cove there'd been hundreds of shark heads—blue sharks, sand sharks, hammerheads. I asked the proprietor about this. "The local boys cut the sharks up," he said, "and sell them to tourists as scallops. You can always tell the fake scallops. They are so big and perfectly round."

We tried for the Calamajué River again in the morning. This river bottom may be the best road in Mexico—a crown of natural pea stone on a level base of sand. The canyon walls cut through six hundred million years of freshman geology class. There were cliffs of igneous and metamorphic rock, sandstone escarpments, walls of conglomerate, towers of ocean sediment, and upended fields of slate in fracture patterns.

About ten miles from the mouth of the river we turned north to climb over a nameless mountain into Gonzaga Bay. The track here had been graded once and made a fairly good road except it was the wrong one. We were lost for hours, but we didn't mind. We saw two bighorn sheep right beside us by the road, looking indeed like sheep yet in such unsheepish postures, grand as elk and silly as Lambchop the Shari Lewis puppet. The correct road was lousy, but we didn't mind that either. In most places the road was sand with shards of slate embedded like broken bottles on top of a wall. We blew out two of the Scrambler's tires. In other places the road was almost impassable. Alongside one of the most difficult stretches was a 1949 Cadillac coupe, charred and lying on its roof, a Baja version of the frozen leopard in "The Snows of Kilimanjaro."

Gonzaga was a blue eclipse on a beach of moonlight-colored sand ruffed with mangroves. A few American sport fishermen had ramshackle *casas* on the shore. There was no telephone, no mail, and all the water had to be carried in. There was one electric generator hooked to two lightbulbs and the beer cooler. And there was no street in front of the houses, just a landing strip a bit too short for safety.

At the little beach shack restaurant, Alfonsina's, they served us abalone. The restaurant owner unmounted one of the Scrambler's huge, rigid tires with the handle of a lug wrench and the blunt side of a hatchet. Then he patched the tire with an old air mattress repair kit. We slept on the beach just above the high-tide line. The sand was so soft, the air so benign that we needed neither pillows nor blankets.

At sunrise we drove along the coast, up the famously difficult Tres Hermanas road. The going was steep to the limits of adhesion and too narrow for the bodywork, some of which we lost. What seemed to be boulders in the road was, in fact, the road. There were places in these big, loose stones where to lift from the accelerator would be to slide backward, fall over the side, and die.

Randy Salmont took the Scrambler and Michael drove the Cherokee. It took them four and a half hours to go sixteen miles. They picked their way over things neither Jeep had the clearance to pass. This required an exact sense of where each wheel was. The tires had to be carefully put on top of the largest rocks. At some point the Cherokee's undercarriage rolled one stone up atop another and the transmission casing was rammed into the chassis. The driveline's slip shaft was pulled halfway out of the transmission but there was nothing to do except go on, with the gearbox whacking against the floor. The ascents were granite but the downward slopes were slate, cereal box–shaped rocks that made a sound like driving across dinner plates. The temptation was to hit the brakes, but the motor needed to be left in gear to keep any control over the half-accidental slide.

Fear improves the weather. We'd finished the last downhill grade before we realized it was one hundred degrees. Ten feet from us, under a shelf of rock, sat a yellow coyote. He was watching us carefully, but he wasn't going to be spooked away from the only shade in miles. We looked under the cars. It was as if someone had gotten down in the arc welder's trench and gone at them with a sledgehammer from below. Mighty dents appeared in floorboards, oil pans, and gas tanks. Fluids dripped from everything. Edges of fresh-torn metal glittered in the shadows.

But there was nothing tough ahead of us, just fifty miles of good sand road into San Felipe, then 130 miles of pavement to the United States, to working telephones, superhighways, real gasoline, clean drinking water, and successful business enterprises—an orderly, serious, law-abiding society with air-conditioning. The Jeeps would get us back in three hours.

"Let's flip them upside down," Michael said, "and burn them."

Rein*car*nation

(*1998*)

My conscious mind was overwhelmed by a sudden blinding flash of . . . oncoming truck radiator.

Nirvana, from the Sanskrit word meaning *blowout,* is the extinction of desires, passion, illusion, and the empirical self. It happens a lot in India, especially on the highways. Sometimes it's the result of a blowout, literally. More often it's a head-on crash.

I traveled from Islamabad to Calcutta, some 1,700 miles, mostly over the Grand Trunk Road. The Grand Trunk begins at the Khyber Pass and ends at the Bay of Bengal. The road was celebrated in Rudyard Kipling's *Kim* and dates back at least to the fourth century BC (especially in the matter of stoplights and lane markers). Of all the wonders on this ancient route nothing made me wonder more than the traffic accidents.

But first came a phone call from Bill Baker, director of communications programs at Land Rover and responsible for garnering worldwide publicity. When Land Rover introduced the Discovery II in 1998, Bill decided to take the worldwide part of his mandate literally and drive a pair of Discoverys around the world.

"This," Bill said to me on the phone, "will prove they're tough, durable, and can operate under thousands of feet of seawater. Scratch that last part. We'll use a boat. As I was saying, this will prove they're tough, durable, and that automotive journalists can be talked into anything including driving across the most crowded part of the earth during the hottest time of the year at the pace set by Craig Breedlove on the Bonneville Salt Flats."

I told Bill to count me in. I flew to Pakistan and met the Land Rover expedition when it arrived, by way of Baluchistan, fresh from confounding the fundamentalist Shiite clerics of Iran. We stayed in a nice hotel, a place that later became the target of an Islamic extremist terror attack. (But what place in Pakistan hasn't?) There were eight of us: expedition director Iain Chapman, an ex-officer in the British army; Land Rover engineer Mark Dugmore; expedition photographer Nick Dimbly; car journalists Jeremy

Hart, Todd Hallenbeck, and Franco Gionco from Britain, Australia, and Italy, respectively; and Bill and me.

The drive southeast toward the Indian border began pleasantly enough. Traffic was light. It's remarkable how short tollbooth lines are in a country with no money. Groups of squatting men flicking whisk brooms kept the turnpike well maintained. And the pavement surface was excellent—if you don't mind a berm six inches lower than the asphalt so that if you swerve to miss one of the whisk broomers and put a wheel off the road, all the other wheels go into the air.

This did not happen. Although we almost wished it had when we found ourselves trapped in the downtown Lahore train station parking lot. Somehow we'd gotten into the special queue for crippled beggars, bullock wagons, goatherds, and local buses.

"Can you tell us where the border is?" we yelled at a policeman busy directing traffic by hitting it with a long stick. The policeman replied, in perfect English, "No."

"Fortunately," said Bill Baker, "we have the Garmin GPS II Personal Navigator that can show us a route to anywhere on earth and show us our exact position within three meters."

"Well, if it can show us all that," Todd Hallenbeck said, "why didn't it show us we were headed up the arse of that ox on the hood?"

"We were too busy," said Baker, "using the BT Mobile Vehicle satellite phone that delivers full global coverage and allows us to call anywhere in the world."

"Call room service," said Jeremy Hart, "and order ice." It was forty-seven degrees Celsius in Lahore.

"How hot is that in regular temperature?" I asked. No one knew. I picked up the BT Mobile Vehicle satellite phone and called my German mother-in-law in Connecticut. She's used to the metric system. "Hi," I said, "I'm in Lahore. Tell your daughter I'm fine. How hot is forty-seven degrees?"

"*Pffffft,*" said my mother-in-law, "it doesn't get that hot."

Mark Dugmore did the math. It was 116½ degrees in Lahore with 100 percent humidity, which meant that breathing was like drinking coffee through your nose. Our Discovery II had climate control, of course. But once we'd lowered the window to yell at the policeman we couldn't raise it again because there was part of a goatherd and most of a crippled beggar caught in the opening.

Anyway, the Garmin GPS did, indeed, show us our position to within three meters. The problem was that the streets of Lahore weren't three meters wide. In fact one was so narrow that I think we got off the street entirely and into someone's house. But the GPS directed us to the border. Turn right at the armoire. Left at the kitchen sink.

Approaching the Indian frontier from Pakistan, it was clear that the land of the unfathomable was nigh. We went down the single, solitary connecting road between the two countries and there was nothing on it. Not even military fortifications were visible, just one company of crack Pakistani rangers in their jammies because it was nap time.

The only other wayfarers at the Pakistani customs post were two dirty backpackers from Switzerland who were acting like the things that pop out of Swiss clocks every hour. No one was going to or fro. They can't. *Pakistani and Indian nationals are only allowed to cross the border by train,* said my tourist guidebook. This utter lack of customs traffic had not prevented the establishment of fully staffed customs posts on both sides of the boundary.

Getting out of Pakistan was a normal third world procedure. The officials were asleep, lying on the unused concrete baggage-inspection counters like corpses in a morgue—a morgue posted with a surprising number of regulations for its customers. The number-one man roused the number-two man, who explained the entire system of Pakistani tariff regulation and passport control by rubbing his thumb against his forefinger. He then gave a performance in mime of documents being pounded with a rubber stamp.

"Fifty dollars," said the number-one man. I opened my wallet, foolishly revealing two fifty-dollar bills. "One hundred dollars," he said.

Things were very different on the Indian side of the border. Here they had not just an unused baggage-inspection counter but an unused metal detector, an unused X-ray machine, and an unused pit with an unused ramp over it to inspect the chassis and frames of the vehicles that don't use this border crossing.

Our party consisted of people representing four nationalities, in two Land Rovers, with the satellite phone, GPS, several computers, and a trailer filled with food, camping gear, and spare parts. The rules concerning entry of such persons and things into India occupy a book large enough to contain the collected works of Stephen King.

The Indian customs agents were delighted. They'd never had an opportunity to consult their book about so many items. Bandying legal niceties, they fell into happy debate among themselves. Every now and then they'd pause in their arguments with one another to argue with us. An agent would turn a page, point to a paragraph, and say, "You are doing what with these vehicles?"

"We're testing them," we'd reply.

"Oh no, you are not. That would require special licensing."

"We're transporting them," we'd say.

"Definitely no, that is a different permit."

The Land Rovers had already passed the customs inspection of twelve nations, including Bulgaria, without hindrance, delay, or more than moderate palm greasing. The Indian officials heard this explained and clucked and wagged their heads in sympathy for the hundreds of brother customs agents from London to the deserts of Iran who had lost an opportunity to look up thousands of items in a great big book. Everything had to come out of the cars and trailers. Everything had to go through the metal detector, even though the detector didn't seem to be plugged in. And everything had to come back through the X-ray machine, which the customs agents weren't watching because they were too busy looking up items in a great big book.

All this took four hours, during which the seven or eight agents on duty met each hint at bribery with the stare you'd get from an octogenarian Powerball winner if you suggested the twenty-year payout option. The fellow who was recording, in longhand, everything inside our passports did take two cigarettes, but he wouldn't accept a pack.

None of the cases, trunks, bags—unloaded and reloaded in 105-degree heat—was actually opened, except for a wrench set. Perhaps there is one size of wrench that requires a special permit in India. The satellite telephone *did* require a special permit, which we didn't have. The briefcase-sized sat phone went unnoticed. (Engine compartments and undercarriages were inspected, but no one looked under the seat.) Our tire pressures must be checked in case the all-terrain radials were packed with drugs. The Indian government tire gauge wasn't working. We offered our own. We were halfway through checking the tires when we realized nobody was accompanying us. I walked around behind the customs building to take a leak and found drugs to spare. I was pissing on thousands of dollars' worth of wild marijuana plants.

The customs inspection could have gone on forever except that, in India, everything—including the endless cycle of death and rebirth—stops for tea. The customs agents shut their book.

The staggering traffic and whopping crowds of India materialized. We still had 250 miles to go that day to stay on schedule. A brisk pace was required. Think of it as doing sixty through the supermarket parking lot, the school playground, and the Bronx Zoo.

For the greater part of its length the Grand Trunk runs through the broad, flood-flat Ganges plain. The way is straight and level and would be almost two lanes wide if there were such things as lanes in India. The asphalt paving—where it isn't absent—isn't bad. As roads go in developing nations this is a good one. But Indians have their own ideas about what the main thoroughfare spanning the most populous part of a nation is for. It's a place where friends and family can meet, where they can put charpoy string beds and have a nap and let the kids run around unsupervised. It's a roadside café with no side to it—or tables or chairs—where the street food is smack dab on the street. It's a rent-free function room for every local fete. And it's a piece of agricultural machinery. Even along the Grand Trunk's few stretches of toll-booth-cordoned "expressway," farmers are drying grain on the macadam.

Kipling called the Grand Trunk "the backbone of all Hind," claimed that "such a river of life . . . exists nowhere in the world," and said, "It's the Indy 500 with all the infield spectators on the track during the race. And, instead of drivers putting Budweiser on their sponsorship decals, they're drinking it." Or, if Kipling didn't say that, it was only because he'd never been to the Indianapolis 500 so the metaphor eluded him.

Nor was Kipling much on Beatles references. Given visits to the Maharishi Mahesh Yogi, it's easy to see how the Fab Four came up with "Why don't we do it in . . ."

The road is a store, a warehouse, a workshop. We saw a blacksmith who had pitched his tent on a bridge. Under the tent flaps were several small children, the missus working the bellows, and the craftsman himself smoking a hookah and contemplating his anvil, which was placed fully in the right-of-way. The road is also convenient for bullock carts, donkey gigs, horse wagons, pack camels, and the occasional laden elephant—not convenient for taking them anywhere, just convenient. There they stand along with sheep, goats, water buffalo, and the innumerable cows (all sacred, I presume) sent to graze on the Grand Trunk. I watched several cows gobbling cardboard boxes and chewing plastic bags. No wonder the Indians won't eat them.

Dashing through this omnium-gatherum is every kind of motor vehicle you can think of. Or, rather, you can't think of them. Who *would* think of a big automobile factory—India's largest—manufacturing a brand-new 1954 Morris Oxford (the Hindustani Ambassador)? Who'd conceive of a rejected American Bantam design for a World War II scout car rolling off production lines fifty-five years later (the Mahindra Jeep)? Who could envision a Royal Enfield motorcycle with a diesel engine? Let alone the ubiquitous Tata truck, which seems to be a replica of what drove the Burma Road in the war against the Japanese except with a too-tall wood-frame cargo bed and a hideous demon painted on the differential? Tata tailgates bear the message (wholly gratuitous): "Please Blow Horn."

One type of Indian vehicle was a total mystery. It had three wheels, bodywork shaped like a tongue depressor, a grille from a Chrysler Airflow, and a single-cylinder engine with a bore four times its stroke. This power plant was attached to one side of the front wheel steering fork, giving the conveyance the stability of a motorized unicycle. No nameplate was visible. (Who can blame the manufacturer?) We called it an "Ugly." The Uglies were used as taxis, transporting as many as fifteen or eighteen people—for about a hundred yards before the Ugly expired, tipped over, or got squashed by a Tata.

All daytime driving in India is done at full throttle. And Indian drivers respond to nightfall by picking up the pace. Indian pedestrians make a special effort to be present and milling in the road after dark, bringing their household goods and chattel with them. The dimmer switch has not been discovered in India. Night driving proceeds exclusively by high beam, usually only one of them—if there are any lights on the conveyance at all. Chances are there aren't.

Among the many things that suddenly appeared out of the gloom and right in our face was an unilluminated, reflectorless tractor-trailer with a smiley-face death's head and a sign reading HIGH EXPLOSIVES. EXPERT ADVICE GIVEN. NO SMOKING.

The first time you look out the windshield at this melee you think, India really *is* magical. How, except by magic, can they drive like this without killing people?

They can't. Jeeps bust scooters, scooters plow into bicycles, bicycles cover the hoods of Jeeps. Cars run into trees. Buses run into ditches, rolling over on their 1940s-style bread-loaf tops until they're mashed into unleavened chapatis of carnage. And everyone runs into pedestrians. A speed bump is called a *Sleeping Policeman* in Jamaica. I don't know what it's called in India. *Dead People Lying in the Road* is a guess. There's some of both kinds of obstructions in every village, but they don't slow traffic much. The animals get clobbered too, including sacred cows, in accidents notable for the unswerving behavior of all participants. The car in front of us hit a cow—no change in speed or direction from the car, no change in posture or expression from the cow.

It's the lurching, hurtling Tata trucks that put the pepper in the masala and make the curry of Indian driving scare you coming and going the way dinner does. The Tatas are almost as wide as they are long and somewhat higher than either. They blunder down the middle of the road, brakeless, lampless, on treadless tires, moving dog fashion with the rear wheels headed in a direction the front wheels aren't. Tatas fall off bridges, fall into culverts, fall over embankments, and sometimes Tatas just fall—flopping on their sides without warning. But usually Tatas collide, and usually with each other. They crash not just in twos but threes and fours, leaving great smoking piles of vaguely truck-shaped wreckage. What little space is left on the road is occupied by one or two surviving drivers camping out until the next collision comes. Inspecting one of these catastrophes, I found the splintered bodywork decorated with a little metal plaque: LUCKY ENGINEERING.

In one day of travel I tallied twenty-five horrendous Tata wrecks. And I was scrupulous in my scoring. Fender benders didn't count. Neither did old abandoned wrecks or broken-down Tatas. Probable loss of life was needed to make the list. If you saw just one of these pileups on I-95 you'd pull into the next rest stop with clutch foot shivering and hand palsied upon the shift knob, saying, "Next time we fly." But in India you shout triumphantly to Mark Dugmore, Todd Hallenbeck, and Franco Gionco, "That's twenty-five fatals! I had the over! I win today's truck wreck pool!"

Taking the wheel in India was, however, less fun. I had a tendency to beat my forehead against the horn button and weep, "I have a family. I'm fifty. That goat didn't have its turn signal on. My glasses are smudged. I hate the food. We're all going to die."

Fortunately, expedition leader Iain Chapman and Land Rover engineer Mark Dugmore knew what they were doing. Luke 18:25 should be revised to read, "For it is easier for a camel to go through a needle's eye than for a rich man to enter into the kingdom of God, unless the rich man has the good sense to hire Iain Chapman and Mark Dugmore." The younger journalists—Dimbly, Hart, Hallenbeck, and Gionco—were steely nerved as well. And Bill Baker, who is in fact older than I am, was an amazing driver.

Bill, that was particularly amazing when you pulled out from behind two side-by-side Tatas and discovered that the oncoming lane was occupied by two other Tatas with a Premier Padmini microvan wedged between them—closing speed about 120 mph and road shoulder blocked by a dense contingent of women and children.

I have no memory of how Bill got us out of that. But I do remember thinking it was odd what was said in the car at the time. There were no swear words or calls to God or Mommy, just a joint statement on the vagaries of Indian traffic: four people, in unison, going "Whoa."

I also don't remember being crushed to death by a coal truck. We were trapped behind a stupendously overloaded, hilariously top-heavy Tata. Its leaf springs were in the autumn of their suspension life. Every time the truck hit a bump it would tip on two wheels. Bill waited until a bump tipped it away from us, then tried to pass. The truck hit a contrapuntal bump. The last thing I recall was an acre of bituminous-laden Tata bed descending upon us.

The body-on-frame Discovery II was built like the proverbial brick thing of which there were hardly any in India. (And when you do find one, it has a bowl of water instead of a roll of toilet paper. Bring Handi Wipes.) It was doubtless crashworthy, something we—amazingly—did not test. Although we did experience a side mirror fold-in from an express bus, got a Lambretta into the tail gate of the trailer, and had several sacred cow brushbacks (touched by the Pot Roast of God).

We tested the Discovery's off-road qualifications, though not on purpose. We'd go off road abruptly and at high speed because of horrendous events in front of us or because of sudden pavement disappearance. This is not the preferred "tread lightly" method of exploring the wilderness in a sport utility vehicle. Nonetheless the Discovery has excellent rough-terrain capabilities including the all-important capability to not flip over.

The trailer was also great off-road—straight up into the air due to the remarkable things it ran over on Indian pavement. Despite being loaded with spare wheels, tool chests, and jerry cans of diesel fuel, gasoline, and purified H_2O (Indian weight-loss miracle: one tablespoon of tap water with every meal and eat what you want), the trailer planted its landings with gymnastic grace and precision.

Our Discoverys could move ahead quick as stink (not a meaningless cliché in India) and stop faster than the pair of Tatas we saw going in opposite directions who snagged each other's rear wheels and tore each other's axles off. Plus they could maneuver with the agility of a President Clinton policy position. As proof of these assertions, I give you the fact that I lived to write this.

We had to be in Calcutta by the afternoon of June 25, to get the Discoverys into a cargo container for the next leg of the global tour. We left Islamabad on June 20. Our route was 1,710 miles. In five and a half days, we clocked seventy-eight hours of driving time. Thus we crossed the subcontinent at twenty-two miles per hour—on average. This average was achieved by going a million miles an hour for a total of about one of those hours and sitting as still as road kill the other seventy-seven.

Coming east from the border we traveled to the dirty and disorganized town of Chandigarh—pronounced "*Chunder*-gar," Todd Hallenbeck noted, as in the Australian slang for blowing lunch. Brief rest was had at the Budgerigar Hotel (it's motto, no kidding: "Welcome to your nest"). A parakeet in every room? There was something that size in mine but it was a member of the order Insectivora.

Then we made a dash up to Shimla and back through the Himalaya foothills, the Himachals. These foothills are about the size of the Rockies. Highway engineers customarily use switchbacks to decrease grade inclines across mountain slopes. In the Himachals the switchbacks are arranged to maximize vertical ascents and abysmal plunges. Heaps of smoldering Tata wreckage decorated the bottoms of ravines.

Shimla, the famous hill station and summer capital of the British Raj, built at a higher elevation than Kathmandu, was a standard Indian mess of sheet-tin roofing, catawampus concrete block walls, and imperial leftovers. Along the mall there's a row of dusty British-era shops that the British—seeing mountains all around them and not knowing what else to do—built in the alpine style. But the town had a view to die for (or die of, if you leaned against the parade ground's flimsy railings).

Atal Bihari Vajpayee, then prime minister of India, was headed to Shimla. Preparation consisted of someone loudly testing the PA system.

HELLO HELLO HELLO ONE TWO THREE FOUR FIVE
SIX SEVEN EIGHT NINE TEN MICROPHONE TESTING
HELLO HELLO HELLO HELLO HELLO HELLO HELLO

For an hour. This was the crowd warm-up. The speech must have been a dilly. Meanwhile, behind handsome batik curtains, tribal women in full native dress, with nose jewelry the size of baby shoes, were repairing the pavement.

We almost, but not quite, fatally plunged downhill to Dehradun, home of the Indian Military Academy and also the "Windi Ass Shopping Centre." The Hotel Madhuban ("Please do not open window to keep mosquitoes out") was all right, but it didn't have hot water. And all you have to do to make hot water in India this time of year is leave it outside for ten minutes.

Next, we went south to Agra for a peek at the Taj Mahal. It's one of those satisfying tourist destinations that looks just like it's always looked like it would look. An impressive pile built with public funds while a famine scourged the countryside, the Taj was commissioned by Shah Jahan to memorialize his favorite wife, who died in 1629 giving birth to their fourteenth child. If Jahan had really wanted to show his love, he could have cut back on the ginseng and powdered rhino horn.

We had our first glimpse of the famous mausoleum at sunset, from a heap of trash and offal on the bank of the Yamuna River. Mixed into the garbage around our feet were hundreds of miniature clay images of Krishna. These are tossed into the water by devotees upstream in Mathura, the god's supposed birthplace. The holiness of India is impressive. The ground is littered with divinities.

The bridge across the Yamuna into Agra was also interesting—two-way traffic on a one-lane bridge going both ways at once. Three-way traffic was threatened. Splash.

Then it was back on the Grand Trunk to Varanasi, the most holy place in India, where millions of pilgrims come to wash themselves in the purifying Ganges and also to cremate corpses in it. Everybody got up at five in the morning to see this done except me. I figured that, when it came to scary things in the water, the hotel coffee would do.

Varanasi was squalid even by Indian standards. Expedition members had their own reactions. Todd Hallenbeck, an Australian transplanted from California, retained an American can-do sensibility. "Gosh," he said, "you see so many things you'd like to fix."

Franco Gionco, with Latin sophistication, was inclined to excuse the accumulated dreck. "But it is an ancient civilization, very old."

"Certainly smells past its sell-by date," said Jeremy Hart.

Iain Chapman gazed upon all the oddity and impoverishment and made his pronouncement upon India in general: "Surreal pity."

East of Varanasi the driving got harder yet, unhelped by the fact that we were in left-hand-drive cars in a country that drives on the left. A spotter had to be on duty in the death seat saying, at each attempt to pass, "Yes," or "No," or, "Oh, God, no!"

Opportunities to overtake were so few that spotters started modifying their pessimistic assessments. Sometimes the spotter would use the laws of physics and comparisons of relative mass: "Go ahead, nothing but Vespas coming." Sometimes the spotter would try to gauge the legal and social ramifications of possible collision: "Are pigs sacred?" And sometimes the spotter would get distracted by the random nattering in the car.

"Should Prince Andrew marry Sporty Spice?" someone in the backseat would inquire.

"Yes, definitely," the spotter would say, causing the driver to . . .

"Whoa."

This is the India ordinary travelers never see—because they're in their right minds. And we didn't see much of it ourselves. The scenery was too close to view, a blur of cement-block shops and hovels in unbroken ranks inches from the fenders. Yet my map showed open country with only occasional villages meriting the smallest cartographic type size. There are a lot of people in India: 966.8 million as of 1998. I don't know what they want with the atomic bomb. They already have the population bomb, and it's working like a treat.

Nevertheless India, with a population density of 843 people per square mile, is not as crowded as the Netherlands, which packs 1,195 people into the same space. Nobody comes back from Holland aghast at the teeming mass of Dutch or having nightmares about windmills and tulips pressing in on every side.

Poor people who depend on agriculture for a living, as 67 percent of Indians do, take up room. If 67 percent of New Yorkers depended on agriculture for a living, someone would be trying to farm the dirt under the floor mats of your Yellow Cab.

Everything is squeezed together in India to keep it out of the picnic-blanket-sized rice field that's the sole support for a family of ten.

Every nook of land is put to use. At the bottom of a forty-foot-deep abandoned well, which would be good for nothing but teenage suicides in America, somebody was raising frogs. City public restrooms employ the space-saving device of dispensing with walls and roofs and placing the urinal stalls on the sidewalk. No resource goes to waste, which sounds like a fine thing to advocate next Earth Day—except, in the real world of poverty, it means that the principal household fuel of India is the cow flop. This is formed into a circular patty and stuck on the side of the house, where it provides a solution to three problems: storage room, home decor, and cooking dinner.

Therefore, what makes a drive across India insane (and smelly) isn't overpopulation, it's poverty. Except this isn't really true either. The reason for those ranks of shops and houses along the Grand Trunk, and for the cars, trucks, and buses bashing into each other between them, is that people have money to buy and build these things. And the reason for the great smoldering dung funk hanging over India is that there's something to cook on those fires.

When the British left in 1947, India got itself an economy in the socialist closet, an economy in the political bag. The Indians called it the "license-permit-quota raj." The *Economist* magazine once stated, "This has no equal in the world. In many ways it puts Soviet central planning to shame." Indian industries were trapped and isolated by the government. Like an aunt locked in the attic, they got strange. The results can still be seen in the Tata trucks, Ambassador sedans, and motorcycles that Evel Knievel would be afraid to ride. But in 1992 India began to surrender to free-market reforms. Imports were allowed, foreign investment was encouraged, and customs regulations were (amazing as this seems to those who have been through Indian customs) simplified.

By 1998 the Indian economy had been growing for half a decade at about 7 percent a year. As many as two hundred million people had been added to the Indian middle class—a number almost equal to the total middle class of the United States.

India is still very poor. Small boys with hammers make gravel by the side of the road, an activity that must seem worse than school even to small boys and isn't much of a skill-building vocational opportunity either. The people on the Grand Trunk looked in need but not in wretched misery (until they stepped in front of a speeding Tata). There are plenty of flat bellies in India but few of the distended kind that announce malnutrition. And the beggars, whom Western visitors have been taught to expect in legions, arrive only in squads and platoons. A kid selling trinkets in Agra was irked to be mistaken for such. "I'm not a beggar," he said. "You want to buy, you get." Then he named a thievish price.

What is happening in India is what happens every place where an agrarian economy changes into a modern one. The first stage of prosperity is ugly. This is the ugliness that caused William Blake, at the beginning of the industrial revolution, to speak of "dark Satanic mills"—dark satanic mills that were giving people cash, social mobility, and an opportunity to escape a hundred generations of chopping weeds with hoes. Hoeing is not as dark, maybe, as working in a mill, but it's plenty satanic, as anyone with the smallest garden knows.

The quaint and orderly India of old is still there, just beyond the clutter of the Grand Trunk Road. In West Bengal we visited a beautiful farm village full of amusing thatch architecture and cute peasant handcrafts. Here the handsome patina of tradition glowed upon lives that were quiet, calm, and as predictable as famine and the dowry needed to marry off the ten-year-old daughter.

The villagers were friendly enough. But what if a carload of grubby journalists came into my driveway and Nick Dimbly began taking happy snaps while I was scrubbing down the barbecue grill? I preferred the chaos of the Grand Trunk.

The road is a trash basket, as all roads in India are. I saw a dressy middle-aged woman eat a chocolate bar on Nehru Road (the so-called Fifth Avenue of Calcutta). She threw the candy wrapper at her feet with a graceful and decisive motion. And the road is the john. You never have to wonder where the toilet is in India, you're standing on it. The back of a long-distance bus had a sign in Hindi and an elaborate pictogram, the import of which was *Don't crap on the pavement, and wash your hands after you do.*

By day four we were accustomed to the voluminous detritus, but somewhere around the town of Dhanbad (pronounced as it ought to be) we encountered mile upon mile of garbage stretching to both horizons. We were riding through this in awed silence when Jeremy Hart said, "I . . . I don't know what came over me . . . I just put my empty cigarette pack into our litter bag."

Iain Chapman, who was driving, laughed so hard he had to pull over. We pitched all the detritus in the car out the window, litter bag included.

Then the monsoon arrived, eliminating all daylight and firing boiled egg–sized raindrops into the slime on the Grand Trunk Road. "You know you've got pollution when the rain foams," said Bill Baker. The temperature dropped nineteen degrees in five minutes. Which was nice. But if we'd opened the windows to enjoy the frigid eighty-four-degree weather we would have drowned.

Our last night on the road we stayed in an insalubrious government guesthouse. My bathroom was already being used by some of the other guests, each with six legs and a body the length of a hot dog roll. "That's a *good* thing," said Iain. "It means no cobras in your toilet. They would have eaten the bugs."

Just when I thought I wasn't getting it about India, I started to get it less. The next day, we encountered a communist rally. Hundreds of agitated-looking agitators waved red flags and brandished staves. We were a ripe target for the anger of the masses—eight capitalist prats in Land Rovers with a trailer full of goodies protected only by a tarp. We were ignored. It seems the ideological fury of the Communist Party of India (Marxist-Leninist) is directed primarily at the Communist Party of India (Marxist).

The latter runs Calcutta. According to my guidebook, "They have somehow succeeded in balancing rhetoric and old-fashioned socialism with a prudent practicality . . . Capitalism is allowed to survive, but made to support the political infrastructure."

Not that you'd know this by driving into Calcutta, where the infrastructure doesn't look like it could support another flea. Certainly the Howrah Bridge over the Hooghly River can't. It carries sixty thousand motor vehicles a day, and they were all there when we tried to get across at five p.m.

Packed along the filthy opposite bank of the Hooghly were temples to scary gods, a ratty colonial fort, a coal power plant barfing cones of smudge, and the dreariest kind of glass-box office buildings. The city appeared to be an educational diorama: the History of Mess.

I retain nothing but a few disordered and bedlamic images of our entrance into the city: An intersection with a crushed traffic warden's shelter in the middle. A main street with more human beings than I'd ever seen. (One out of five people in the world is an Indian. And, believe me, that person was standing in Nehru Road on June 25, 1998.) A shop that sold what looked like department store mannequins, but they had four arms. A herd of sheep being driven through the traffic. And a very dirty banner advertising "World Environment Day." (Canceled due to overbooking is my guess.)

Jeremy Hart, Todd Hallenbeck, and Franco Gionco flew home. Bill Baker and Nick Dimbly went on to Perth to arrange the next leg of the expedition. I stayed with Iain Chapman and Mark Dugmore to help them load the Discoverys into a cargo container. This took twenty minutes or—adjusting the clock to Indian Daylight Wasting Time—four days.

First the port was closed. Well, it wasn't really closed. I mean, it was sort of closed because the port of Calcutta has silted in and is nearly useless. Only about three ships were there. This didn't keep hundreds of stevedores, shipping clerks, and port officials from coming to work. But there were city council elections that day with attendant rioting. So the police had to suppress voters and weren't available to harass us at the port.

Then the port was closed because it was Sunday.

Then our shipping agents fell into an argument about when to pick us up at the hotel the next day. Not that they disagreed with one another.

"We will go to get them at nine-thirty in the morning," one said.

"Oh, no, no, no, no," said another. "It must be nine-thirty in the morning."

"How can you talk like this?" asked a third, stamping his foot. "The time for us to be there is nine-thirty in the morning!"

We had about ten shipping agents. There's no such thing as hiring an individual in India. In a Bihar village it took the services of two shops, four shopkeepers, and a boy running for change to sell me a pack of cigarettes.

While waiting for the port to open, I wandered the streets of Calcutta. The late-nineteenth-century Writers Building is crumbling and dirty although a row of large, carefully tended potted plants decorates the sidewalk below its windows. Trees, products of less intentional horticulture, grow out of the cracked Edwardian edifice of the nearby Standard Assurance and Life headquarters. Even Calcutta's New Market, built in 1985, seems about to fall down and probably doesn't only because—being nothing but a pile of moldering concrete in the first place—it can't.

Calcutta is a byword for squalor. Most Americans suppose that to tour its precincts is to flush oneself down the toilet of humanity and amble through a human septic system. This isn't true. There aren't that many flush toilets in Calcutta. Anyway, parts of Washington, D.C., are dirtier (Congress, the White House) and Calcutta smells no worse than a college dorm.

The poverty is sad and extensive but at least the families living on the Calcutta streets are intact families—talking to one another instead of themselves. I did see some people who seemed really desperate, addled, and unclean. But these were American hippies at Calcutta's Dum Dum airport. I was standing in the ticket line behind an Indian businessman who stared at the hippies and then gave me a stern look, as if to say, "These are *your* people. Isn't there something you can *do*?"

Calcutta's pollution is more visible than it's fashionable for American pollution to be—smoke and trash instead of microwaves and PCBs. The food sold on Calcutta's streets may be unidentifiable, but it's less likely than New York City hot dogs to contain a cow rectum. The crowding is extreme but you get used to it. You get used to a lot of things: naked ascetics, elephants in downtown traffic, a single file of costumed girls linked by electric wires, with one carrying a car battery and the rest having blue fluorescent tubes sticking out of their headdresses.

I was waiting to cross the busiest street in Calcutta when a four-story temple complex on wheels went by, complete with high priest, idols, acolytes, clouds of incense, blazing torches, and banging gongs. And what I noticed was that I wasn't noticing it. Imagine the pope (and quite a bit of Saint Peter's) coming down Broadway at rush hour and you thinking, *Should I jaywalk or wait for the light?*

There's a certain pest factor in Calcutta, mostly from the touting of roving market bearers. But it's not without its entertainment value. Bearer No. A-49 from the New Market told me not to listen to any of the other bearers because they would get me into their shops and cut my throat. So be sure you get Bearer No. A-49. Accept no other. Lesser merchants, squatting on the street, sell everything from new Lee jeans to brightly colored pebbles and pieces of broken mirrors. The poster wallah's selection included views of the Taj Mahal, photographs of kittens tangled in balls of yarn, and the gore-faced goddess Kali holding a severed human head by the hair.

In the midst of this is the Oberoi Grand Hotel, with guards stationed at the gate holding sticks to use on touts and beggars. At the Oberoi everything is efficient, crisp, clean, and pukka (except when the electricity goes out). The Indians inside seemed as perplexed by the chaos of India outside as I was. I told Alex, the restaurant manager, about the muddle at the port. "Oh, this country," he said, "there are no two ways around it."

We had parked the Land Rovers and trailer in the hotel courtyard. The shipping agents came by to inform us that everything in the vehicles had to be clean and packed exactly as described on the customs documents. Iain, Mark, and I set about amending seventeen hundred miles of dirt and equipment disorder. It was a hundred degrees in the courtyard. A dozen members of the hotel staff gathered to watch us. I don't think they'd seen Westerners do actual work. (And—as far as my own experiences go in the offices and stores of America and Europe—neither have I.) Removing the trailer tarp we discovered an axe had come loose from its lashing and punctured a container of beef stew and a can of motor oil. The trailer bed was awash in petroleum and what Hindus euphemistically call "brown meat."

On Monday we went back to the port, where the customs inspectors ignored everything about our cleanliness and packing except the axe. "What is this?" said the chief inspector.

"An axe," said Iain Chapman.

The officials conferred at length and decided it was so. Then there was a seven-hour delay because of an engine-serial-number discrepancy. The customs inspectors were worried that we'd stolen one of the Discovery IIs from Rover. "*We're* from Rover," said Iain. "These are the only Discovery IIs in Asia, and they can't be stolen because they're both right here." The inspectors returned to their office to ponder this. We sat on the dock.

I asked one of our shipping agents why so many of the Tata truck drivers had decorated their front bumpers with one dangling shoe.

"Oh, for the heck of it," he said.

Finally the Land Rovers were rolled into the cargo container. Things do eventually get done in India. My theory about why they do is that, although making business matters complicated is a great source of fun there, you know how it is with fun. Sooner or later it's time for different fun, such as making family matters complicated. "I am a twenty-one-year-old man involved in a physical relationship with my thirty-six-year-old unmarried cousin for the past six years," read a query to an advice column in a Calcutta newspaper. "It all began when I raped her."

I was sad to see the Discovery IIs go. They weren't broken, an anomaly in this land. And they never burned or exploded, which is more than I can say for Iain when, leaving the docks, the police tried to arrest us because we had padlocks in our possession.

"What the hell kind of thief comes back with the locks instead of the swag?" Iain asked them. Maybe an Indian one, if it would complicate matters.

I remained in Calcutta for a few days after Iain and Mark left, in sort of a paralysis of awe at a dundering muddle of a place that seems in total disorganization but where I couldn't even get lost because everyone with a clean shirt speaks English. And they speak it in a style that is a reminder of India's claim upon the language. There were Indians speaking English when most of America was gibbering in Gaelic, German, or Italian on the wrong side of the Ellis Island fence. Placards ask that Calcutta's subway be treated WITH RESPECT AND AFFECTION. Street signs read, I USE FOOTPATHS, DO YOU?

Indian journalist Gita Mehta says India turns out five million university graduates a year. That's four times the number of bachelor degrees awarded annually in the United States. Yet the ancient guild of scribes still does brisk business outside Calcutta's general post office. Scores of men hunker on the sidewalk writing and reading other people's letters. Forty-eight percent of Indians are illiterate, including almost two-thirds of Indian women.

You walk by a newsstand—a news squat, to be precise—and see the Calcutta *Telegraph*, the Calcutta *Statesman*, the *Asian Age*, the *Times of India*, and stacks of newspapers printed in Hindi and other languages. The *Telegraph* ran a know-how feature on particle physics. A *Statesman* op-ed page had an article on energy efficiency: "The heat rate of the power plant, in layman's terms, refers to how much kilo calorie of heat is required to produce 1 kwp of power." You think you're in a nation of Einsteins until you read the advice columnist's answer to the rapist: "At this stage of life you ought to detach yourself from this cousin to secure a healthy life. Initially your cousin provoked you in the act, and hence it cannot be called rape."

In the midst of Calcutta's street stampede (not a figure of speech, considering cows), there are young hawkers with what look like shoe-shine boxes. What's offered for sale isn't a wingtip buff. The youths crouch in the hubbub, juggle the tiny wheels and springs of wristwatches, and set the timepieces running again. There is a whole street in Calcutta lined with stalls too small and ill-equipped for lemonade sales. Here, artisans with flame-heated soldering irons rearrange the logic on the latest computer circuit boards. Then you look up and see a man walking around wearing a bucket upside down over his head.

Big Love

(2008)

The last time gas prices were going through the roof, or maybe it was the time before last . . . it's hard to keep the cycles of petroleum-cost rafter bashing and basement busting straight. At the moment they're giving away a free fill-up with the purchase of any bank or financial institution. But tomorrow the bill for a gallon of regular may require a restructuring of the international debt market. Don't you dare, however, tell your congressman that you want stable gas prices. If a politician gets to decide what gasoline costs, you know where he's going to stick that price, anatomically speaking.

As I was saying, the last time gas prices were going through the roof, the London *Sunday Times* called me and said they were devoting their automotive section to . . . you got it in one, denouncing cars. Specifically the *Times* was vilifying large SUVs. Would I care to be the piñata at the party and write something in favor of nonsustainable, resource-sucking, planet-boiling, road-hogging murder wagons?

The whole world is angry at America for driving SUVs. Why do we Americans love these monstrous and threatening devices? Barging through traffic in a sport utility vehicle is hardly sporting. The utility of the things is open to question. And they are vehicles mainly in the sense that the Alaska pipeline is a vehicle for oil—most of this pipeline's capacity being needed to keep one Cadillac Escalade topped up.

It has to do with sex. We Americans are not as sexually sophisticated as you foreigners. Therefore a lot of the sex we have results in procreation. We need a place to put the kids. Our families are big. The Bush family, for example, is so big that one presidency wasn't enough for them, let alone one SUV. Dozens of huge, black Chevrolet Suburbans full of Secret Service agents are required to escort the Bush family around.

We have big families, and we're big people. How big I needn't tell you who are annually trampled in Trafalgar Square and butted across Hyde Park by herds of Guernsey-sized American tourists. Michelle Obama, in fact, is considered the Twiggy of America. Even our wispy left-wing intellectual types are . . . you've seen Michael Moore.

We're big people from a big country. We like our elbow room so well that we carry it around with us. We can't stand to be squished together as if we were sitting in the backseat of a Nissan Micra or living in England. And in our big country we're in a big hurry. When we drive an immense Lincoln Navigator we get to where we're going sooner, or at least the front part of our car does, though it may be a long walk to the bumper. Plus, you know what kind of a mess the kids make on long trips. With rear footwells the size of Loch Lomond, we never clean up the soda cans and candy wrappers. We trade in for a new Navigator at ten thousand miles.

An SUV is very safe in a collision—safe for me, because I drive one. You, who don't, are crushed like a garden slug. Although, in fairness, SUVs are equipped with features designed to improve survivability for occupants of the other vehicles involved in SUV crashes. High ground clearance gives you—if you jump out of your Opel Astra and throw yourself flat on the pavement—a better than even chance to survive being run over.

There *is* something of a safety problem with SUVs flipping and landing in ditches on their roofs as a result of encounters with curbs, potholes, or too thickly painted highway center lines. But we Americans don't mind this, given our national propensity to turn the world upside down. Also, we regard these incidents as an answer to the oft-voiced criticism that SUVs aren't really used off-road. This is a baseless attack anyway. America is a country with widespread muck and mire, as you may have noticed in our current presidential election campaign.

Perhaps we SUV owners don't go into the wilderness very often. But such is the weather in America that the wilderness frequently comes to us. Shrubs, trees, surf, sand, and whole chunks of scenery are delivered to our places of residence by hurricane and tornado winds. Our mobile home may blow away but, by gosh, our Dodge Durango is right there in the driveway where we parked it.

America is a practical nation. SUVs provide practical solutions to the problems Americans face. Americans have a lot of baggage—backpacks, fanny packs, laptops, beer coolers, blame for everything that's wrong in the world. Try armor-plating your Mercedes Smart Car.

Americans have cumbersome hobbies. Tie an ultra-light aircraft on your Ford Ka's luggage rack, put a Jet Ski and a dirt bike in the back, and tow a dune buggy. Now you're ready for a typical American afternoon in the park. We don't go in for train spotting or darts.

Animals on the road are another consideration. You have cats, dogs, bunny rabbits. We have moose. (And Sarah Palin.) Hit a moose in your VW Polo and the People for Ethical Treatment of Animals will be picketing to save *you*. (Survive hitting a moose and you run the further risk of Sarah Palin showing up at your house and offering to cook.)

Americans demand convenient parking. Conveniently, SUVs can be parked—*squash, crush*—anywhere.

SUVs provide America with economic stimulus. Replacing parking meters, fire hydrants, street signs, gates, fences, decorative plantings, HANDICAPPED ONLY markers, bumpers, fenders, hoods, and trunk lids that have been backed into by SUVs is a multibillion-dollar business in the United States, and provides tens of thousands of jobs.

Americans are very competitive. America's state and local transport authorities make roads longer and wider. America's automobile companies make cars longer and wider.

And Americans love media attention. Being on television so defines American life that there is now more "reality TV" in America than there is discernible reality. SUVs are easier for television station helicopters to spot during the live televised car chases that all Americans dream of being featured in.

America is also an idealistic nation. Americans drive SUVs for the good of mankind. Think of the vicious wars fought over petroleum resources. SUVs turn oil into dirty air. Nobody fights wars over dirty air. When all the oil is gone the people of the Middle East will be able to go back to being "Sand French." And the sooner America's SUVs use up that oil, the sooner global warming can be halted. Meanwhile, melting of the polar ice caps threatens to put Washington, D.C., under ten feet of water. Is that a bad thing? And whether it is or isn't, you Brit sightseers will be needing an SUV to make your way through the swamped Mall to the submerged Air and Space Museum.

There is, of course, the Freudian aspect of SUVs. Driving an SUV is an affirmation of manhood, an expression of machismo, an undeniably phallic experience. That said, my wife has a much larger SUV than I do. Her GMC Yukon XL was made in America. My Land Rover Discovery was made in Britain. Out of consideration for the amour propre of male writer and male readers alike, perhaps we should drop this subject. (Personally, I think American women like vast SUVs because, standing beside one, they look svelte by comparison. Ouch! No, honey, the Kia doesn't make your butt look big. Honest.)

Speaking of hurt feelings, you'd be better off in England if you had leviathan SUVs like we do. You could have avoided the entire fox hunting ban kerfuffle. Get a Ford Expedition EL. There's room in the back for the horses, the riders, the dogs, *and* the fox. You can slip the whole lot right past the furious people in anoraks.

It's this kind of preservation of freedom that's behind America's passion for SUVs. The real truth is that we need sport utility vehicles to carry our concealed weapons. Sticking them down the waistband of our pants doesn't work with AK-47s, .50-caliber machine guns, bazookas, and so forth. Why do Americans love these monstrous and threatening devices? Because the whole world is angry at America for driving SUVs—and for a few other things we've done lately. We may have to shoot everybody. If anti-Americanism gets any worse, Oprah will be giving away Hummers.

DON'T VOTE: IT JUST ENCOURAGES THE BASTARDS

(*2010*)

"The man of system . . . is apt to be very wise in his own conceit; and is often so enamored with the supposed beauty of his own ideal plan of government, that he cannot suffer the smallest deviation from any part of it.

—Adam Smith

Politics Makes Us Free—and We're Worth It

When I first began to think about politics—when mastodons and Nixon roamed the earth—I was obsessed with freedom. I had a messy idea of freedom at the time, but I had the tidy idea that freedom was the central issue of politics.

I loved politics. Many young people do—kids can spot a means of gain without merit. (This may be the reason professional politicians retain a certain youthful zest; Strom Thurmond was the boyo right down to his last senile moment.) I was wrong about the lovable nature of politics, and even at twenty-three I probably suspected I was wrong. But I was sure I was right about the preeminent place of freedom in a political system.

Freedom is a personal ideal. Because politics is an arrangement among persons, we can plausibly assume that freedom is a political ideal. Our favorite political idealists think so. They've been unanimous on the subject since Jean-Jacques Rousseau convinced polite society that human bondage was in bad taste and John Locke showed the divine right of kings to be a royal pain.

The signers of the Declaration of Independence declared us to be residents of "Free and Independent States." John Adams demanded, "Let me have a country, and that a free country." Tom Paine warned that "Freedom hath been hunted round the globe." And he exhorted us to "receive the fugitive and prepare in time an asylum for mankind." Calling America an asylum may have been a poor choice of words, or not. Thomas Jefferson, in his first inaugural address, preached "Freedom of religion; freedom of the press, and freedom of person." Jefferson was quite free with the person of Sally Hemings. And a dinner toast from Revolutionary War general John Stark bestowed upon New Hampshire a license plate motto that must puzzle advocates of highway safety: "Live Free or Die."

With *Bartlett's Familiar Quotations* as a useful gauge of what we think we think, we find that Emerson poetized, "For what avail the plow or sail, or land or life, if freedom fail?" Hegel weighed in with, "The history of the world is none other than the progress of the consciousness of freedom." As unlikely a character as the crackpot Nietzsche had something to say: "Liberal institutions straightway cease from being liberal the moment they are soundly established: once this is attained no more grievous and more thorough enemies of freedom exist than liberal institutions." The UN Commission on Human Rights comes to mind.

We can survey the arts, where mankind is most blatant in its truths, and find artists taking the broadest liberties. (They are especially free with the use of inevitable fate as a plot device.) We can peruse philosophy, where mankind is less truthful, and not hear freedom denied by anything except free thinking. Theology makes sporadic arguments against free will, with which the devout are freely willing to concur. Science is deterministic and its special needs stepsister social science is more so. But people are free to pick and choose among the determinations of science until they find something they like. I give you Al Gore and you can have him. Perhaps there are scientists who make a sound case for the inevitabilities of biology and such. But we don't know what these geniuses are talking about and very likely neither do they. For example, the important biologist Richard Dawkins has written a book, *The God Delusion,* in which he uses predestinarian atheism to argue that Richard Dawkins is the closest thing to a superior being in the known universe.

The theoretical (as opposed to practical) enemies of freedom are feeble opponents. And we are all but overrun by theoretical allies in freedom's cause. We've got collaborators in the fight for freedom that we don't even want. "The proletarians have nothing to lose but their chains" is the penultimate sentence of the *Communist Manifesto*. And a creepy echo of it can be heard in the refrain of Kris Kristofferson's "Me and Bobby McGee." Mao announced, "Letting a hundred flowers blossom and a hundred schools of thought contend is the policy . . ." Half a million people died in those ellipses.

If we were to give out the proverbial "a word to the wise," the sagacity-testing utterance with which to provide the sages would be "freedom." In the unabridged *Oxford English Dictionary* the noun has fifteen definitions and the adjective "free" has thirty-six. These definitions, along with their usage citations, occupy 189¼ column inches of small and smaller type.

Peter Roget (1779–1869), of *Roget's Thesaurus,* was a physician, a scientist, the secretary of the Royal Society for more than twenty years, and an exhaustingly systematic thinker. He designed his thesaurus (Greek for "treasury") as a reverse dictionary. Instead of listing words and giving their meanings, he listed meanings and gave words for them. Under the heading "freedom" there are more than four hundred entries in twenty-one categories. And "freedom" is only one of the twenty-three headings in *Roget's* "Section I, General Intersocial Volition" of "Division II, Intersocial Volition" of "Class

Five, Volition." It's hard to know whether or not to be thankful that Peter Roget's obsessive-compulsive disorder meds hadn't been invented.

Among the various types and kinds of general intersocial volition, about ten have something to do with political freedom.

freedom in the abstract
autonomy
enfranchisement
toleration
frankness
leisure
laxity
abandon
opportunity
privilege

Several of these may seem beside the point. But "frank," for instance, is from the Old French *franc,* meaning free. We can be frank with the president of the United States. We can honestly and openly say what we think to him. And what we think of him. But in all our name-calling the name we call our president that sticks is "Mr." He's not "Your Excellency" or "Your Highness," nor do we kowtow, genuflect, or curtsy to him. Callisthenes, the great-nephew of Aristotle, plotted to kill Alexander the Great rather than prostrate himself in the Persian manner to the conqueror of the known world.

Then there are the freedoms of leisure, laxity, and wild abandon. Anyone who thinks these have nothing to do with democracy hasn't met the demos. Also, it was not so long ago, during the great political demonstrations of the 1960s, that I was risking my neck—well, risking a conk on the head and a snootful of tear gas—in the battle to create a utopian society where I could lie around all day, utterly heedless and high as a kite.

Freedom, of course, may be considered as an abstraction. I was young enough to be highly abstracted—not to say stoned—when I began to think about freedom. But I wasn't old enough to think. Therefore I can tell you nothing about my abstract thinking on the subject. And so can't a lot of other people, because there are languages in which the word "freedom" doesn't exist. (Not surprising if you think about some of the places languages are spoken.) Richard Pipes, emeritus professor of Russian history at Harvard, who is fluent in a number of tongues himself, makes this point in his book *Property and Freedom* (a perspicacious analysis of what the title says).

Professor Pipes cites the work of M. I. Finley, preeminent historian of classical antiquity (and, incidentally, a Marxist, something Richard Pipes is the opposite of). Finley wrote, "It is impossible to translate the word 'freedom,' *eleutheris* in Greek, *libertas* in Latin, or 'free man,' into any ancient Near Eastern language, including Hebrew, or into any Far Eastern language either, for that matter." Indeed, when the Japanese first encountered Western notions they were hard put to translate "freedom" and ended up using the word *jiyu,* which means something like "getting jiggy with it."

Freedom and liberty themselves don't have quite the same meaning. "Free" is derived from the Indo-European root *pri,* to love. The *p* becomes *f* in Germanic languages, thus *fri* in Old German and *freo* in Old English. The original sense of the adjective was "dear," and it was used to describe those members of a household who had a kinship relation to the master of the house. Since at least the reign of King Alfred the Great, ruled 871–899, the primary definition of "free" has been "not in bondage." You're free because . . . Who loves ya, Baby?

Liberty is probably the better word;* its source is in the Indo-European *leudh,* "to mount up, grow." Hence Latin for children, *liberi,* and German for populace, *Leute*. We the people make *leudh* into *eleutheris* and *libertas*.

Yet the first definition of "liberty" in English is, once again, "exemption or release from bondage." Whatever we mean by our abstract statements about freedom and liberty, the most meaningful thing we're stating is that mankind has a sickening history of slavery.

Enfranchisement is the lively, fortunate, and honorable freedom, for the sake of which our political ancestors pledged their lives, their fortunes, and their sacred honor. Nothing concerning the goal of enfranchisement is ignoble except its excercise. Among those who choose the congressmen, senators, and presidents of the United States we now include people who are not considered mature and responsible enough to have a beer. (If it's any comfort, we should remind ourselves of the purpose of voting. We don't vote to elect great persons to office. They're not that great. We vote to throw the SOBs out.)

Toleration is the best comfort of a free life for most people most of the time, especially if they experience as well as practice it. But tolerance is of minor interest to politics. Politics aspires to a big, positive role in things. And the role of politics in toleration is small except in the usually negative actions of keeping the peace. Yet it was two consummate American politicians who supplied us with a model for the universal formulation of tolerance: "Mind

*But "freedom" is less highfalutin and more of an Americanism. Theodore Parker, a prominent abolitionist, may be partly responsible for the American usage. He is certainly responsible for the American definition of democracy. Parker gave a series of speeches in Boston in the 1850s. Abraham Lincoln's law partner William Herndon attended one of these talks and gave the following transcript to Lincoln, to obvious effect.

A democracy—that is a government of all the people, by all the people, for all the people; of course, a government of the principles of eternal justice, the unchanging law of God; for shortness' sake I will call it the idea of Freedom.

your own business and keep your hands to yourself." These may be rightly called the Bill and Hillary Clinton Rules. Hillary, mind your own business. Bill, keep your hands to yourself.

The ontological freedom known as autonomy isn't part of practical politics, it's all of practical politics—imposing my will and thwarting yours. If the actions of mankind and the events of history turn out to have been foreordained it will be a good joke on politics.

This leaves us with the nub or butt end of politicking: privilege and opportunity. Ignore everything politicians say about opportunity. They're lying. When politicians tout "opportunity" either they are trying to help voters disguise an extortion as a gift or they are the groom of government complimenting the bride of private property while in bed with the socialist maid of honor. And ignore all of politicians' sniffing at and scorn for privilege. Privilege and opportunity are the names for rights—opportunity being rights you'd like to get and privilege being rights you'd like someone else to surrender. A politician doesn't ask if he may have the privilege of a dance; he says he has a right to it.

Our gassing about our rights is almost equal to our gassing about our freedoms when we're puffed full of air concerning our form of government. We're inordinately proud of the Bill of Rights. But it is an odd document.

The First and Sixth Amendments are straightforward enough, reassuring us that we may pray (OMG!), Twitter, kvetch, and be tried in the same court as O. J. Simpson. And the Fifth Amendment says that when we screw up big time we don't have to give our version—like anybody's going to believe us. But the Second Amendment is woefully confusing. (Not that it confuses *me* about gun ownership, in case you were considering a mugging to get my Jitterbug mobile phone.) The principal right that the Second Amendment seems to guarantee is the right to be a soldier. To judge by our various episodes of national conscription—Civil War, World War I, World War II, Korea, Vietnam—this is a right we sometimes have to force people to enjoy.

According to the Third Amendment the Pentagon can't just randomly send the U.S. Marines to sleep on our foldout couch. This is something that, as a home owner, you'd think would be obvious. Although, in fairness, there are people elsewhere in the world who wish they had an amendment keeping the marines out of their house.

The Third Amendment and the Seventh Amendment (concerning jury appeals) are undercut by weasel words: "but in a manner to be prescribed by law" and "otherwise . . . than according to the rules of the common law." The Fourth Amendment (mandating warrants) and the Eighth Amendment (limiting punishments) include strange pairs of modifiers—"unreasonable" and "probable," "cruel," and "unusual"—better suited to a drunken description of my first marriage than to a sober writ of law.

And the message of the Ninth and Tenth Amendments is: you have other rights but you have to guess what they are.

There was opposition to the Bill of Rights. The modern mind expects it to have come from slave owners. But this is too modern. Support for the first ten amendments had little to do with dictionary definitions of freedom and liberty and a great deal to do with qualms that old-line Revolutionary patriots—including Sam Adams—had about the new federal government. Alexander Hamilton, who had other qualms, made a case against the Bill of Rights in that supposed ur-text of American freedoms *The Federalist Papers*.

In *Federalist Paper No. 84* Hamilton put forth various arguments opposing the addition of any bill of rights to the U.S. Constitution. Some of the arguments were weak. Hamilton claimed that the Constitution, as it was, affirmed and maintained the ancient protections of individual liberty embodied in British common law. Maybe. But a more cautious and less expensive way to retain British common law had been available in 1776. Hamilton claimed that previous, precedent-setting bills of rights, starting with the Magna Carta, were merely bargains between a sovereign and his subjects about a ruler's prerogatives. Hamilton felt that no such sharp dealing and unseemly horse trading was necessary in a social contract freely made among equals. But if Nietzsche was right about what liberal institutions do once they're institutionalized—and there's little evidence he wasn't—then Hamilton was wrong. And Hamilton believed the Constitution already included the most important safeguards of freedom: establishment of habeas corpus, prohibition of ex post facto laws, and a ban on titles of nobility. Hamilton was listing the principal instruments in the tyranny tool chest of his era. He didn't foresee the future inventions of oppression such as ethnic cleansing, even though ethnic cleansing of North America was well under way at the time the *Federalist* essays were written.

But Hamilton's other objections to the Bill of Rights were prescient. Don't give the government ideas, he warned.

> *Why, for instance, should it be said that the liberty of the press shall not be restrained, when no power is given by which restrictions may be imposed? I will not contend that such a provision would confer a regulating power; but it is evident that it would furnish, to men disposed to usurp, a plausible pretense for claiming that power. They might urge . . . the provision against restraining the liberty of the press afforded a clear implication that a power to prescribe proper regulations concerning it was intended to be vested in the national government.*

And now we have not only the FCC's naughty involvement in Janet Jackson's wardrobe malfunction but also the gross obscenities of binding and gagging displayed in America's campaign finance legislation.*

Hamilton said that, in the matter of defining a right, "Who can give it any definition which would not leave the utmost latitude for evasion?" Not even God, if you note the various evasions practiced by believers since Genesis. Hamilton said the true security of our freedom "must altogether depend on public opinion, and on the general spirit of the people and of the government." Each of these can be rotten, and occasionally all of them are. Such an occasion arose just seven years after the Bill of Rights was ratified. The Sedition Act made it a federal crime to publish anything about Congress or the president that would bring them into "contempt or disrepute." In other words, the Sedition Act made it a federal crime to publish anything about Congress or the president.

Fortunately the Bill of Rights is flawed in its treatment of only one type of rights—opportunities. It doesn't meddle with the other type—privileges. Perhaps these two categories of rights should be known as "get-outta-here" rights and "gimme" rights or, as they're more usually called in political theory, negative rights and positive rights. The Bill of Rights (and "the idea of Freedom") is concerned mostly with our liberty to say, "I've got God, guns, and a big damn mouth, and if the jury finds me guilty, the judge will pay my bail!" This is a negative right—our right to be left alone, our freedom from interference, usually from government, but also from our fellow citizens when they want us to sober up, quit yelling, put the shotgun down, and go back into the house.

Politicians, in their hearts, are always tepid supporters of get-outta-here rights. For one thing, any and all legislators are being invited to leave. For another thing, strict adherence to negative rights would leave little scope for legislating, something legislators dearly love to do. Gimme rights are more politically alluring. This is how we find ourselves tempted with positive rights to education, housing, health care, a living wage, flood relief, high-speed Internet access, and all the kingdoms of the world, and all the glory of them.

Politicians show no signs of even knowing the difference between negative and positive rights. Blinded by the dazzle of anything that makes them popular, they honestly may not be able to tell. But there's evidence that a confusion of negative and positive rights originally was presented to the public with malice aforethought. President Franklin Roosevelt's "Four

---

*Although, as I write, the Supreme Court has overruled some of this legislation. Corporations, as legal persons, turn out to have the same rights to free speech as we personal persons. Corporations are people? Who knew? This may explain how I got screwed by British Petroleum the other night after a few too many drinks on a Gulf of Mexico beach.

Freedoms" appear to be—at first glance—as natural, well matched, and tidy of composition as the Norman Rockwell illustrations for them.

1. Freedom of speech and expression
2. Freedom of religion
3. Freedom from want
4. Freedom from fear

But notice how the beggar, number 3, has been slipped in among the more respectable members of the Freedom family. "Want *what*?" we ask ourselves.

Saying, as Roosevelt did in his January 6, 1941, State of the Union Address, that "We look forward to a world founded upon four essential human freedoms" and that one of these freedoms is "freedom from want" was not an expression of generosity. Declarations of positive rights never are. There were six million Jews in Europe who wanted nothing but a safe place to go.

Politicians are careless about promising positive rights and cynical about delivering them. Positive rights themselves, in turn, are absurdly expandable. The government gives me a right to get married. This shows I have a right to a good marriage, otherwise why bother giving this right to me? My marriage is made a lot better by my children's right to day care, so the brats aren't in my face all day being deprived of their right to a nurturing developmental environment. Every child has the right to a happy childhood, so I have the right to happy children. Richer children are happier. Give me some of Angelina Jolie's.

The expense of all this makes politicians glad. They get to do the spending. Even negative rights aren't free. They entail a military, a constabulary, a judiciary, and a considerable expenditure of patience by our neighbors. But positive rights require no end of money, and money is the least of their cost. Every positive right means the transfer of goods and services from one group of citizens to another. The first group of citizens loses those goods and services, but all citizens lose the power that must be given to a political authority to enforce the transfer. Perhaps such transfers could be made voluntary. U.S. federal personal income tax receipts in 2008: $1,426,000,000,000. U.S. charitable contributions in 2008: $307,700,000. Perhaps not.

When rights consist of special privileges and material benefits, rights kill freedom. Wrong rights are the source of political power. It's not freedom but power that is the central issue in politics. Only an idiot wouldn't have seen that. And I was one. At least I wasn't alone. In the latter two-thirds of the twentieth century, most of us who involved ourselves in democratic politics claimed that freedom was what we were up to. We claimed it for more than fifty years, from the time of our defeat by Franco in the Spanish

Civil War until the embarrassing moment when those authoritarians Ronald Reagan and Margaret Thatcher led us to victory in the Cold War. Liberals, moderates, and even some conservatives considered the sweeping positive rights created by a half century of social welfare programs to be extensions of freedom, in the opportunity sense. People were being given the opportunity to, you know, not starve to death and stuff.

This wasn't an evil way of looking at things. And not all the programs were bad. But the electorate, the candidates, and we busybody pundits failed to properly scrutinize social welfare programs. It's not that we failed to examine whether the programs were needed or superfluous or well or poorly run. What we failed to look at was the enormous power being taken from persons and given to politics. We insisted on seeing politics through the lens of freedom, as if social legislation were a Polaroid print of quickly developing liberties. We listened only to the freedom track on the electoral stereo. We predicted the future of politics with a horoscope containing just the astrological sign Libra.

We weren't exactly wrong. Living in the midst of the civil rights struggle, during a Cold War with one totalitarian ideology after a real war with another, we understood the value of freedom and the ugly alternative to democracy. But we didn't—or didn't want to—understand power. This was particularly true of my age cohort, the baby boom, and particularly evident in the way we reacted when politicians attempted to use their power to limit our freedom by conscripting us into a war in Vietnam. We challenged the establishment by growing our hair long and dressing like Bozo.

We're a pathetic bunch. And it didn't start with the Beatles, marijuana, and the pill. Recall the coonskin cap. I wore mine to school. Children of previous eras may have worn coonskin caps but they had to eat the raccoons first.

The baby boom's reluctance to attend to the issues of power resulted from the fact that we had some. Freedom *is* power, after all. And, as for freedom, we were full of it. We were the first middle-class-majority generation in history. We had the varieties of freedom that affluence provides, plus we had the other varieties of freedom provided by relaxation of religious convictions, sexual morality, etiquette, and good taste. The social institutions that enforce prudence and restraint had been through a world war, prohibition, depression, a world war part II, and Elvis. They were tired. We were allowed to fall under the power of our own freedoms. And we powered through them. Sixty years on we're still at it, letting not age, satiety, tedium, or erectile dysfunction stand in our way. Yet always at our back we hear the nagging thought that power comes with responsibility.

We don't want that. Has there ever been a generation—a nation, a civilization—more determined to evade responsibility? Probably. The ancient Romans sliced open animals and rummaged in their kidneys and livers in an attempt to avoid owning up to the consequences of empire and toga parties. The Greeks were forever running off to hear the irresponsible babble of the oracle at Delphi, the Larry King of her age. Maybe the Egyptians had an Oprah barge on the Nile where deceased pharaohs could fall to pieces and promise to become better mummies.

Nonetheless we and our contemporaries in the developed countries of the Western world have an impressive record of blame shifting, duty shirking, unaccountability, and refusal to admit guilt or, better, to readily confess to every kind of guilt then announce we've "moved on."

A gigantic global "Not My Fault" project has been undertaken with heroic amounts of time, effort, and money devoted to psychology, psychotherapy, sociology, sociopaths, social work, social sciences, Scientology, science, chemistry, the brain, brain chemistry, serotonin reuptake inhibitors, inhibitions, sex, sex therapy, talk therapy, talk radio, talk radio personalities, personality disorders, drugs, drug-free school zones, Internet addiction, economics, the Fed, PMS, SATs, IQ, DNA, evolution, abortion, divorce, no-fault car insurance, the Democratic Party, diagnosis of attention deficit disorder in small boys . . . The list goes on.

Neither freedom nor power is what I should have been obsessed with for all these years. But it's too late now. I'm a child of my era. And speaking of that era, here are three slogans from 1960s posters that never existed:

BLACK RESPONSIBILITY

SISTERHOOD IS RESPONSIBLE

RESPONSIBILITY TO THE PEOPLE

A Digression on Happiness

American exceptionalism annoys the world. Happiness is the source of the annoyance. Other countries are built upon battle, blood, nationality, culture, language, and territory. America is the exception. Our foundation is pursuit of happiness. It appears in the first sentence of the main body of America's IPO, the Declaration of Independence. Happiness is the one novel feature of the document. And this imaginative mission statement, that we're determined to pursue happiness, comes as something of a surprise after the noble boilerplate of our calls for life and liberty.

We can explore mankind's other covenants, treaties, conventions, protocols, compacts, and concordants, plus all the *corpus juris* of the world, written and unwritten, ancient and modern, and not find happiness.

No talk of happiness appears in England's Magna Carta. The French revolution's Declaration of the Rights of Man fails to address the subject. The European Union's proposed constitution never mentions happiness, although, at 485 pages, it mentions practically everything else including regulatory specifications concerning "edible meat offal" and "lard and other rendered pig fat." The Lisbon treaty that took the place of the rejected EU constitution doesn't supply this want of happiness. The UN's Universal Declaration of Human Rights does state, in Article 24, that "Everyone has the right to rest and leisure, including . . . periodic holidays with pay." Leave it to UN delegates to expect to be paid for their freedom. Anyway, a holiday is not the same as the pursuit of happiness, as anyone knows who's spent a holiday dragging whiney children on a tour of UN headquarters.

The New Testament, arguably the founding text of Western civilization, mentions happiness just seven times and never in a happy context. Peter's First Epistle, to persecuted Christians in Asia Minor, says, "if ye suffer for righteousness' sake, happy are ye." Jesus is quoted as using the word "happy" only once, on the occasion of washing his disciples' feet. We admire the Son of Man but we sons of a gun who populate America do not pursue our happiness in this manner.

The United States is the first—and so far only—among happy nations. "Happy the people whose annals are blank in history books," wrote Thomas

Carlyle. Just ask Americans a question about American history, watch them draw a blank, and you'll see that we are the happy people indeed.

Not that Americans seem very happy at the moment. And maybe Americans never have seemed happy. In his 1741 sermon "Sinners in the Hands of an Angry God," Jonathan Edwards doesn't sound as if he's talking to a cheery crowd.

> *The God that holds you over the pit of Hell, much as one holds a spider, or some loathsome insect, over the fire, abhors you . . . he looks upon you as worthy of nothing else, but to be cast into the fire.*

And now, due to the financial crisis, the mortgage foreclosure crisis, and health care reform, we're not only going to hell, we're broke, homeless, and sick while we're waiting to get in.

Happiness, like the freedom we're so happy to have, is elusive—slippery in physical and conceptual grasp. "I'm happy" doesn't mean "I'm having fun." Remember all the fun you've had. When it was really fun it didn't end up making anybody very happy. "I'm happy" is distinct from those spasms of ecstasy that do not elicit any coherent phrases. "I'm happy" is more or less equivalent to "I'm content," which means "I won't complain because nobody listens to me."

"Happy" is often used as a none too complimentary modifier: "happy-go-lucky," "slaphappy," "happy horseshit," "happy as a pig in same." The catchphrases "one big happy family," "Is everybody happy?," and "I hope you're happy now" are never spoken without a happy smirk of irony. Then there's whatever John Lennon was getting at with "Happiness Is a Warm Gun." Although it's true under certain circumstances. Try defending the perimeter of your outpost in Kandahar by squeezing a puppy.

However, it should be noted that the Declaration of Independence reads, "Life, Liberty, and the Pursuit of Happiness," not, "Life, Liberty, and Whoopee." Jefferson's choosing "the pursuit of" rather than plain "happiness" is a reminder of what happens to the poor suckers who, in their pursuit of happiness, catch the thing. America's legions of minor, temporary tabloid stars can tell the rest of the story, if they survive their stardom.

Happiness is hard to attain, harder to maintain, and hardest of all to recognize. Pick the time of your life when you know you were happiest. You didn't know how happy you were at the time. When the kids were little and you hadn't slept in three years. That first job in Manhattan, being groped by the assistant marketing director and sharing a one-bedroom Avenue X and One Thousanth Street apartment with eleven other people. Those halcyon days at college that you flunked out of.

Old people are forever reminiscing happily about all sorts of things that wouldn't seem conducive to happiness, such as World War II. Will the forsaken recipients of largesse from bilked charities someday wax nostalgic about Bernie Madoff's avuncular ways? The fact that we don't know when we are happy raises the disturbing possibility that you and I are wildly happy right now. I hope my wife doesn't find out.

What's happiness doing in the Declaration of Independence? The original phrase is "Lives, Liberties and Estates," a brief catalog of man's inherent rights that appears several times in John Locke's *Second Treatise of Government*. Locke was one of the Enlightenment's foremost proponents of natural law and the rights it naturally bestows, rights that are so much a part of our nature nothing can take them away, and we can't get rid of them. There were other important natural law theorists, such as Hugo Grotius, Samuel von Pufendorf, Jean-Jacques Burlamaqui. America's patriotic thinkers relied mostly on Locke because he argued the case for people's right to dissolve their government. Also, he was easier to spell. When Thomas Jefferson drafted the Declaration of Independence he was referring directly to chapter IX of the *Second Treatise*, where Locke says that men are "willing to joyn in Society . . . for the mutual *Preservation* of their Lives, Liberties, and Estates, which I call by the general name *Property*." Every educated person understood the reference (moral philosophy not yet having been replaced by civics in the educational curriculum). Many educated persons must have wondered about Jefferson's substitution of laughs for land.

The fact that property wasn't mentioned in the Declaration of Independence still seems odd. The French revolution's Declaration of the Rights of Man lists property second only to liberty, and the French revolutionaries had less respect for other people's property (and less property) than did the signers of the Declaration of Independence.

Jefferson may have been trying to convey the idea that our new nation wasn't going to be a European kind of place. America wouldn't be parceled into aristocratic estates kept intact by primogeniture and entail. Entail is a legal restriction on property, usually land, limiting its inheritance to linear descendants of the owner, and primogeniture is a further restriction that leaves out the girls in the family. Entail was necessary to preserve the power (formerly military, later economic) of the holders of the titles of nobility, which titles the U.S. Constitution would soon ban.

Entail was in bad odor in the late eighteenth and early nineteenth centuries. Rationalist thinkers of the day were ashamed of inherited class distinctions even (sometimes especially) if they were so distinguished. Entailed estates were considered to be the ground from which grew the twisted family tree of peerage occupied by the serpent who urged the rotten fruit of birthright upon Edenic mankind. The metaphor is overfertilized, perhaps, but, said Tom Paine in *Common Sense*, "Original sin and hereditary succession are parallels. Dishonorable rank! inglorious connection!"

Nowadays, when the British royal family is mostly blogfare and titled Frogs and Wops are of no interest to anyone but *Vanity Fair* editors, we wonder at the fuss over entail. Yet in the late 1700s Georgia went so far as to pass a law against such laws, attempting to keep the privileged few from monopolizing the broad cotton fields of Tara. Never mind that for every free household in Georgia the state had approximately thirteen thousand acres of unpopulated land. (And Scarlett O'Hara's father was a bog Irish upstart who won the joint in a poker game.)

More than a decade after America had declared its unentailed independence and made pretensions of nobility illegal, Jefferson was still railing against transgenerational claims on property. In a letter to James Madison, he wrote "*the earth belongs in usufruct to the living*." The italics are Jefferson's and "usufruct" is the legal right to use and enjoy something—pursue happiness with it—during one's lifetime. Tom Paine would make the point again in his 1791 pamphlet *Rights of Man*: "Man has no property in man; neither has any generation a property in the generations that are to follow." Even Jane Austen would comment on the issue. In *Pride and Prejudice* she has the silly Mrs. Bennet say, of the rule that decrees precisely who inherits what, "There is no knowing how estates will go once they come to be entailed." (A remark that advocates of various environmental and conservationalist entails upon land might want to ponder.)

All these proponents of liberty versus heredity were taking their cue from Adam Smith. In *The Wealth of Nations* Smith wrote that the laws of entail "are founded upon the most absurd of all suppositions, the supposition that every successive generation of men have not an equal right to the earth, and to all that it possesses."

America as a place for fresh starts has illustrious intellectual credentials. Not that we'd know it by looking at America's uncouth frontiersmen, woebegone backwoods pioneers, seedy homesteaders, giddy forty-niners, illiterate cowboys, huddled masses of immigrants, and Internet start-up wingnuts.

"Pursuit of Happiness" also may have supplanted "Property" in the Declaration of Independence because of definitional concerns. Locke died in 1704, when "Estates, which I call by the general Name *Property*" was still synonymous with land and land was still synonymous with riches. Until Adam Smith succeeded in improving the world's understanding of economics (if he ever did), land was considered to be the only ultimate source of profit.

The Declaration was written by Thomas Jefferson but it was revised and edited by John Adams and Benjamin Franklin. Jefferson was a devotee of property in the sense of land and chattel (of animal and human kinds). But Adams, although a farmer, had no Jeffersonian vision of America as a pure, agrarian society. Perhaps this was because Adams, unlike Jefferson, made a living from his farm. Adams and Franklin understood that trade, manufacture, and finance would be as significant in America as "real" estate. And Franklin had a personal interest in a type of ownership different from a land title, ownership of what we would come to call intellectual property. (It was not coincidental to Franklin's influence that the power to approve patent rights would be granted in Article I of the forthcoming Constitution, and that the first act passed by the new Congress of the United States would concern patent law.)

Jefferson was often concerned about money, but Franklin and Adams were actually thinking about it. Still, we can understand why, for reasons of popularity and taste, the rights in the Declaration of Independence aren't listed as "Life, Liberty, and Stinking Wealth."

Roger Pilon, chief constitutional scholar at the libertarian Cato Institute, in Washington, D.C., believes there was another reason that property rights were handled with delicacy in the Declaration of Independence. Pilon concludes that Jefferson detected a flaw in the logic of Locke's "unalienable" rights. Property has to be alienable, in a legal sense, or you can't sell it. If we lived in a country where property was unalienable, Steve Jobs and Steve Wozniak would still have the pocket calculator that they sold to raise the money to start Apple. Therefore when we go to work there's nothing on the screen of the computer that doesn't exist at the job we don't have because we're still farming the twenty-acre tobacco patch that our ancestors gypped the Indians out of for beads and trinkets the last time anybody was allowed to buy anything, in the reign of George III.

Property is an important aspect of the pursuit of happiness. Pilon says the founding fathers would have considered this materialistic side of happiness to be, as the founding fathers liked to say, self-evident. Try paying your mortgage with a hug. (Though that's what the U.S. government is helping some people do these days.)

The authors of the Declaration of Independence, the Constitution, the *Federalist Papers,* and the other sources of the American idea of freedom had a materialistic philosophy of independence. And they knew enough philosophy to know that they did.

Jefferson, Franklin, Adams, Hamilton, Madison et al. did not believe that American independence was the same as the independence preached by the so-called cynic philosophers of ancient Greece. The cynics held that independence lay in individual "autarchy" or rigid self-sufficiency. Diogenes was said to have been elated to discover he could drink from his cupped hands and therefore dispense with his mug. But this shows that even the most ascetic pursuit of happiness involves consideration of the material world. (And it shows that Diogenes was a dope who had to found a whole school of philosophy to figure out how to get a puddle to his face.) Diogenes lived in a barrel. "*Whose* barrel?" Jefferson, Franklin, and Adams would have asked. There was nothing cynical about America's founding fathers, in any sense of the word, but nothing naive either.

Pilon maintains that "Pursuit of Happiness" replaced "Property" in the Declaration of Independence not to denigrate material wealth but to expand the idea of materialism. America was established as a way for Americans to make and do things. What sort of things Americans make and do and whether these things lead to great riches, pious satisfactions, or transitory pleasures is nobody's business but our own. America's political institutions are supposed to be the machinery for our making and doing. America is a tool. America is the only place on earth or in history created in order to be both free and teleological. Teleology is the idea that phenomena are guided by a purpose. America is. But—and here's what's new—we Americans get to individually, personally, separately decide on any purpose we want.

What's the point of other nations? It's something of a historical mystery. Conquering the world seems to be a purpose for some nations—fortunately not too many, and fortunately not too often, and most fortunately they always fail. Maybe nations arise to provide their citizens with mutual protection against external and internal threats. If this were the usual case, world history would read like an account of the interrelations of the cantons of Switzerland. Certain nations seem to exist strictly to torment their neighbors or their citizens or both. Other nations are simply . . . there. Notice how in Paris people go to cafés and just sit around all day being French. Or, if they prefer to sit around all night, they can be Spanish and not have dinner until 11 p.m. A friend of mine once said about the rural Turks that they're so lazy they get up at four in the morning to have more time to do nothing. It gives an American the heebie-jeebies. We have to be making and doing. Albeit what we make is often a mess. And what we do is often our undoing. Lately we've added being to making and doing. What Americans are being is famous or infamous (there's no longer a distinction) or fabulous or centered or self-actualized or spiritual or eco-conscious or, frequently, real fat. Anyway, we Americans are very, very busy, and we owe it all to three little words in our Declaration of Independence.

Or maybe that's wrong. Maybe Jefferson, Franklin, and Adams were just happy. Jefferson was famously uxorious. Perhaps his wife, Martha, slipped up to Philadelphia for a dirty weekend. And Franklin landed the Declaration of Independence printing contract. And Adams was working his way through a cask of Madeira. The Declaration's first draft might have read, "Pursuit of Nookie and Graft and I'll drink to That." If it had gone to press this way we'd be a different people, less busy and less happy and more inclined to say such things to each other as "Wealthy Birthday!," "Drunken days are here again!," and "Sexually aroused to meet you."

The Purgatory of Freedom and the Hell of Politics

The best way to have a good political system is to avoid politics. But political disengagement deprives us of opportunities for bitching at politicians and pushing them around. This is occasionally useful and always a pleasure. In our democracy we don't get in trouble by trying to make politicians mad. We get in trouble by trying to make them like us. Our political system goes to hell when we want it to give us things.

There are certain things we may reasonably demand of our political system, of course. But most of these things are negative rights. And often it's the political system itself that's violating those rights. The most sensible request we make of government is not "Do something!" but "Quit it!"

As for our positive rights and the goodies we expect to gain with them, we're confusing politics with Halloween. Politicians don't mind. They love devising programs of incentives and disincentives for the populace. Trick or treat! And a ghouls and goblins political system is fine for those among us who are really scary. But, for the rest of us, don't be surprised if we go house to house—White House to House of Representatives to Senate—and, ringing doorbells as furiously as we may, get nothing but healthy fruit.

If there's something we want, politics shouldn't be our first resort. Politics is all taking, no making. Whatever politics provides for us will be obtained from other people. Those people won't love us.

And we don't love them. When we gain our ends through political takings it's because of a certain bad idea. What we're thinking leads to death, destruction, and taxes. What we're thinking is that we live in a zero-sum world: there is a fixed amount of the things I want, and when anybody has anything I want they've taken it from me.

This is a particularly poisonous idea because for most of history it was true. There may have been a prehistorical moment when all we had to do to get more mastodon meat was walk over the next hill and avail ourselves of some unpopulated spot such as Europe. But civilization is based on land for grazing and crops. There's only so much land. If I'm on it, you're off.

That's the world's shortest history of warfare, and the world's shortest history of class conflict, serfdom, slavery, nationalism, racism, and genocide.

Zero-sum thinking is a name for envy. Ovid, in his *Metamorphoses*, gives an apt description of the "House of Envy" (as a poet in that most zero sum of political systems, the Roman empire, might): "Envy within, busy at the meal of snake's flesh . . . her tongue dripped venom. Only the sight of suffering could bring a smile to her lips. She never knew the comfort of sleep, but . . . looked with dismay on men's good fortune . . . She could hardly refrain from weeping when she saw no cause for tears." I didn't know Hillary Clinton's involvement in politics dated back to the reign of Augustus.

Then one day the idea of zero sum wasn't true. We see its falsehood being revealed by population growth during the late Middle Ages in Europe and India and China (with time-outs for Black Death, massacring invasions, and the Thirty Years' War). The industrial revolution would further this population trend, but the original human anti-Malthusianism doesn't seem to have been the result of science or invention. Adam Smith thought the cause was simple expansion of trade, giving farmers a motive to grow more food than was needed just for eating, reseeding, and the rats.

By now there shouldn't be a zero-sum thought left in our heads. We should be free of all of zero sum's begrudgings. We know we can make more of everything. Energy, to name one. When did our vital supply of lamp-lighting whale oil run out? We didn't notice because we were too busy inventing kerosene and electricity.

Once again India and China (Europe not so much) are showing the way with the vast expansions of their economies. We can bake more pizza (or naan, as the case may be). We can clone more cows. We can raise more plants (under grow lights in the closets of our off-campus apartments). There's even additional beachfront property on its way, thanks to climate change and seaside development in Greenland. Celebrity offers the ultimate disproof of zero sum. The amount of celebrity was always limited by the need for something to celebrate. Click through your cable channels. Not now.

But there is one field of endeavor where zero sum remains the awful truth: politics. Even in the most free and democratic country politics is about power. There's a fixed quantity of power because there's a fixed quantity of me. Power you have over me is power I lose to you. And political power is different from other power because political systems are different from other social systems. A political system has the legal monopoly on deadly force. We're all involved in a variety of social systems, such as that bunch of social snobs with their system of blackballing us at the country club. They're allowed to ban us from the tees but they aren't allowed to pick us off with sniper fire from their clubhouse bar. Governments can. Nothing sums up zero sum like death.

Because government is zero sum there aren't two congressmen wedging their fat butts into the same seat in the House of Representatives. We don't have 300 million Supreme Court justices telling nine old Washington shysters in black bathrobes whether they'll get a lawyer at Gitmo. The chiefs of the Joint Chiefs of Staff aren't all commander in chiefs commanding "Forward March!" to one another until they collide in a group hug.

Political power is awful, and power is awful anyway. Lord Acton, one of nineteenth-century Britain's great defenders of liberty, wrote, "Power tends to corrupt, and absolute power corrupts absolutely." This was in a letter to Anglican Bishop Mandell Creighton, and the subject was papal infallibility (something Acton, a devout Catholic, argued against at the First Vatican Council). If power can do the likes of that to the Holy Father in Rome, just think what it's done to Harry Reid.

We have to be careful about giving power to people—for their own sake, among every other reason. We won't get our power back easily. And when we try to get our power back it isn't pretty: Washington at Valley Forge, Paris during the Reign of Terror, the czar's family in Yekaterinburg.

Nonetheless we are continually tempted to confer power on government—to delegate our power (as some would have it), to alienate our power (as Jefferson would have been more likely to say). And it's not only a desire to escape from our responsibilities that tempts us. The American government is a huge tool, a formidable engine, mighty in its operation and nearly irresistible in its movement (never mind that it doesn't know where it's going). The temptation is to use a tool like this when something needs fixing. Whether the tool suits the task isn't a question we always ask ourselves, as those of us who received Home Depot gift certificates for Father's Day can attest. Maybe we shouldn't change the battery in our wristwatch with the electric drill. But what if it's a cordless DeWalt with a 3/8-inch chuck and fifty different bits?

Or, to put the case differently, the government is a rottweiler ready to be unleashed on your problems. And you've stuffed raw meat down the front of your pants.

One method of being careful with government power is to think about our messy government the way we think about our messy personal lives. There are furious ex-spouses, bitter former lovers, and various outstanding child support judgments. We don't want too much of this in one place, which is why we moved to Phoenix.

America's founding fathers knew enough about messy personal lives to make sure that the chief concerns of the Constitutional Convention were a federalist decentralization of power and a system by which each branch of government would check the other branches of government and balance their power with power of its own. What if all the ex-spouses, former lovers, and kids whose school fees we're supposed to be paying become friends and get the same lawyer? America's founding fathers would have rather moved to Phoenix than let this happen.

It is a good idea for as much government power as possible to be distributed to the smallest possible units of government—the cities, towns, townships, and counties that are scattered all over the United States plus those scattered states themselves. John Sununu, former governor of New Hampshire and chief of staff to President George H. W. Bush, is a cantankerous and truthful man. He's also an engineer. He compares reliance on local government to a goal of mechanical engineering: short control loops. The hot and cold faucets in your shower are a short control loop. If, instead of being located in the shower stall, those hot and cold faucets were in the basement, that would be a long control loop. This is not to say that a short control loop always works. You may be out of hot water. But it's better to stand in the shower fiddling with a useless faucet than to march naked and dripping through the house, amazing the children and shocking the cleaning lady, down two flights of stairs into the grungy basement, and fiddle with a useless faucet there.

If our neighbor on the local sewer commission votes to raise our sewer rates, we can go next door and yell at him or stuff a potato up the tailpipe of his car. Stuffing a potato up the tailpipe of the limousine of the president of the United States is a federal crime, or they'll make it one if I try.

Despite the clear and evident sense of the short control loop argument we are deaf to it. When something's wrong we don't consult the sewer commissioner next door, even if what's wrong is backed-up sewage. We go straight to Washington and, bypassing even the House and the Senate, expect the president himself to take time off from trying to get his limo started and come over to our house with a plunger.

We do this not just because we're morons but because federal government in the United States is more efficient, less corrupt, and harder-working than state and local governments. Illinois. Say no more.

The federal government attracts the best talents in administration, legislation, jurisprudence, and bureaucracy. And those talents are exercised under the greatest scrutiny because the news media pay attention to the federal government. All this makes for a good thing. Of its kind. In the shark tank the juiciest bait attracts the biggest sharks. If that juicy bait happens to be something interesting, such as we the drowning taxpayers, attention will be paid.

The only effective way to keep power decentralized is by making sure our society provides ungovernmental ways of being powerful. The best talents should be offered bait in places other than Washington. Let the good and the great flounce around in the arts, spout pious bilge from pulpits, fill the minds of the young with drivel at great universities, spread patronizing smarm through charitable organizations, and rob all comers in business. Just one ready, necessary thing is needed to set the hook in this lure of decentralization. Thank God for money. And whenever we meet a rich person, however loathsome, we should be sure to say, "Thanks! The disgusting fact of your existence helps spread the manure of life around and keeps it from piling up in one spot, under the Capitol dome."

Political power, however, remains the most powerful of powers, so people will continue to be drawn to it. What kind of people we know too well. The politician's personality has been brilliantly described.

> *A pervasive pattern of grandiosity (in fantasy or behavior), need for admiration . . . beginning by early adulthood . . . as indicated by five (or more) of the following:*
>
> 1. *has grandiose sense of self-importance (e.g., exaggerates achievements and talents, expects to be recognized as superior without commensurate achievements)*
> 2. *is preoccupied with fantasies of unlimited success, power, brilliance*
> 3. *believes that he or she is "special" and unique and can only be understood by, or should associate with, other special or high-status people (or institutions)*
> 4. *requires excessive admiration*
> 5. *has a sense of entitlement, i.e., unreasonable expectations of especially favorable treatment or automatic compliance with his or her expectations*
> 6. *is interpersonally exploitative, i.e., takes advantage of others to achieve his or her ends*
> 7. *lacks empathy: is unwilling to recognize or identify with the feelings and needs of others*
> 8. *is often envious of others or believes that others are envious of him or her*
> 9. *shows arrogant, haughty behaviors or attitudes*

The authors of the above passage had no idea they were writing about politics. They thought they were writing about mental illness. This perceptive analysis of politicians appears on page 717 of the American Psychiatric Association's *Diagnostic and Statistical Manual of Medical Disorders*, fourth edition, under the heading "Diagnostic Criteria for Narcissistic Personality Disorder."

The only thing in the shrinks' notes that might seem odd to a voter is "lack of empathy." Every politician is always telling us how much sympathy, understanding, and fellowship he or she has with us and how deeply he or she is moved by our hopes, our dreams, and our fears. About such too much protestation, Hamlet's mother—no mean politician herself—has an oft-quoted line.

There is an enormously powerful machine that with one wrong turn can kill us all and it's being run by crazy people. What are the chances this will turn out well?

In the meantime it's costing us a fortune. Milton and Rose Friedman, in their seminal work about liberty and market freedoms, *Free to Choose,* showed why government is so expensive. The Friedmans devised what in logic is called a "truth table" to show that there are, logically, only four categories of spending. The table looks like this:

		ON WHOM SPENT	
		You	*Someone Else*
WHOSE MONEY	*Yours*	I	II
	Someone Else's	III	IV

Category I is you spending your money on yourself. Let's take cars as an example of something to spend on and me as an example of someone doing the spending. I have a splendid 1990 Porsche 911—a leftover from my carefree bachelor days—that I got a great deal on, buying it almost new from a dentist who scared himself and bought a Lexus Coupe instead. When you spend your money on yourself you get—as nearly as you can—exactly what you want and you bargain as hard as you can for it.

In *Category II,* when you're spending your money on someone else, you still bargain hard. But you're not quite as concerned about getting exactly what's wanted. Although I'm sure my wife is very fond of the Geo Tracker I bought for her and the kids.

You spend someone else's money on yourself in *Category III,* and I'm on the fence between the Aston Martin DBS coupe that goes for close to $300,000 and letting "someone else" off easy with an Alfa Romeo 8C Competizione spider convertible, a steal at $230,000.

With *Category IV* you're not involved at all. It's not your money and nothing's in it for you. So it might as well be billions spent on jack shit or, as the government called it, "Cash for Clunkers."

All government spending is done in *Category IV*.

There are very few excuses for allowing goods and services to be allocated by political means unless you're trying to get something that isn't yours. And what you get is a Geo Tracker. That's one Geo Tracker for you versus innumerable reasons for the rest of us to prevent you from allocating goods and services by political means. Make that innumerable plus three.

1. Concentrated benefits and diffuse costs.
2. Invisible opportunities.
3. Committee Brain.

One of the things that allows us to be eaten up by our politics is that we are eaten very slowly, one political bug bite at a time. If we were being eaten by a boa constrictor or Kim Jong Il we'd notice. But in a democracy it takes years for us to wake up and say, as Ronald Reagan so memorably said in the 1942 movie *Kings Row,* "Where's the rest of me?" Not until almost forty years later, when Reagan was running for president, did we taxpayers finally come to our senses and ask the same question about our paychecks.

The first secret of our obliviousness to being swallowed is what's called "diffuse costs." A government idiocy may be expensive, but the expense is spread so broadly that none of us feels the nip of that expense very hard. For instance, let's take a government idiocy that's quite expensive and, furthermore, obviously and evidently useless to the nation, and which doesn't even have any political support. Joe Biden. Joe Biden costs us $227,300 a year in salary plus $90,000 for official entertainment expenses. (O'Doul's, because somebody has to keep a clear head during those White House Beer Summits.) Then there are the tens of thousands spent on around-the-clock White House staffers trying to keep Joe Biden's mouth shut and more tens of thousands for shoe shines, black neckties, and Air Force 2 fuel when unimportant foreign leaders die, and at least $20 worth of Secret Service protection. We'll round it off and take a guess and say that Joe Biden costs us $600,000 a year. But there are 300 million of us. Yes, Joe is a complete waste of two-tenths of a cent, but who cares?

Joe does. That is the "concentrated benefits" part of "concentrated benefits and diffuse costs." The two-tenths of a cent means nothing to us, but it's everything in the world to Joe Biden who will bear any burden, meet any hardship, pay any price (well, no, *we'll* pay the price), even go on Bill O'Reilly to remain one and a half heartbeats from the presidency. (The half a heartbeat is the time it will take Nancy Pelosi to wring his neck and become president herself.) And so it goes with other government idiocies even more expensive than Joe such as AIG and Homeland Security.

The expense of politics wouldn't matter so much if it weren't for the opportunities that are destroyed by this spending. Money that's poured down rat holes can't be used to pay the Pied Piper. (Not that the government of Hamelin town *did* pay the Pied Piper.) These destroyed opportunities—or "opportunity costs," as economists call them—are the flip side of zero-sum. It is a source of wickedness to believe that the world contains a fixed amount of resources. Paradoxically, it is a source of wickedness to forget that the world *does* contain a fixed amount of resources, *at any given moment*. The amount of resources is infinitely expandable, but in order to expand it we have to spend the resources we currently have on something other than Joe Biden.

Because our opportunities are lost—so lost they never got anywhere near us—it's easy and maybe comforting to forget about them. These opportunities are certainly invisible to politicians. They don't see the businesses that weren't started, the innovations that weren't pursued, the charitable donations that weren't made, and the beer I didn't drink because a jerk professor and a college-town cop (talk about a fight I don't have a dog in) drank it in the White House backyard.

Meanwhile politicians work themselves into a lather of rationalization about the benefits of government spending. In this they are aided by the more vile kinds of economists such as Paul Krugman and the late John Kenneth Galbraith. Using liberal political-economic reasoning I can prove . . . *anything*. I can prove that shooting convenience store clerks stimulates the economy.

Jobs are created in the high-paying domestic manufacturing sector at gun and ammunition factories. Additional emergency medical technicians, security guards, health care providers, and morticians are hired. The unemployment rate is lowered as job seekers fill new openings on convenience store night shifts. And money stolen from convenience store cash registers stimulates the economy where stimulus is most needed, in low-income neighborhoods where the people who shoot convenience store clerks go to buy their crack.

I am simply flabbergasted that the Democratic majority in the House and Senate isn't smoking crack and shooting convenience store clerks this very minute, considering all the good it does.

The expense of politics is bad, the political destruction of opportunities is very bad, but nothing is as dreadful as the brain of a politician.

Ha. Ha. Ha. What brain? Alas, it's worse than a joke. Taken one by one, politicians are of dull-normal intelligence. But when you put politicians together in governments you get committees. In Congress they even come right out and call the committees committees.

We've all been on committees. We know what happens to intelligence and common sense when a person becomes a committee member—*Committee Brain*.

You live in a neighborhood with a playground. The kids in the neighborhood would like to play tetherball but the playground has no tetherball pole. A committee is formed to raise funds for tetherball: Committee to Raise Funds for Tetherball, CRFT.

CRFT is started by a group of pleasant, enthusiastic, public-spirited neighbors. The minute any of these neighbors becomes a member of CRFT he or she will begin to express his or her pleasant, enthusiastic public spirit by turning into one of the following.

The Martinet

We have to draw up a charter and form a nonprofit corporation with a chairman, a president, vice president, secretary, treasurer, development officer, and human resources executive. And the tetherball pole has to be exactly nine meters high, in accordance with North American Amateur Tetherball Association rules.

The Dog in the Manger

We need to get permission from the County Zoning Board, the City Council, the Parks Department, and adjacent landowners who may complain about tetherball noise. That part of the playground is too damp for tetherball. It might be federally protected wetlands. We can't do any fund-raising without advertising. We can't advertise without raising funds. The kids would rather have a tennis court.

The Person Who Is Stupid Even by Committee Brain Standards

So the rope, like, has a ball on it?

The Worrier

Padded pole, breakaway tether, a lightweight foam ball, and ban on playing after dark or when visibility is poor and when the sun is shining, to avoid UV ray skin cancer damage. The kids should wear helmets and kneepads and safety belts.

The Person with Ideas

If we call ourselves the "Committee to Raise *American* Funds for Tetherball—*Yeah!*" we can use the acronym CRAFTY. Let's set up a challenge grant to erect a second tetherball pole in the inner city. "Midnight Tetherball" could be an alternative to crime for deprived youth. We can also promote tetherball as a way to combat child obesity, which would make us eligible for funding from the Gates Foundation. We'll have a tetherball league—no, three—Adults, Juniors, and Tether Tots. This could be a great Title IX thing. If our daughters are varsity-level tetherball players they'll get into Yale.

The Person with Ideas, None of Which Has Anything to Do with Tetherball

Is the tether biodegradable? Is the pole made from recycled materials? Many playground balls are manufactured in third world countries using exploitative child labor. Let's be sure to utilize organic fertilizer and indigenous plant species when seeding the tetherball play area.

The Bossy Person

Who says the same thing as everyone else on the committee but louder.

The Person Who Won't Shut Up

Who says the same thing as everyone else on the committee but more often.

The Person Who Won't Show Up

Unless his or her vote is crucial, in which case he or she shows up and votes the wrong way.

You

You actually do all the work and call forty people and ask them each to donate $20, and half of them do, and you raise the $400 needed, only to find out you need $400,000 because the House of Representatives' Economic and Educational Opportunities Committee's Select Committee on Opportunities in Physical Education's Subcommittee on Americans with Disabilities Act Compliance requires all tetherballs to be wheelchair-accessible no matter how high the tetherballs fly in the air.

Given the complete dominance of politics by Committee Brain, the wonder is that anything gets done, and the horror is that it does. What government accomplishes is what you'd expect from a committee. "A camel is a horse designed by a committee" is a saying that couldn't be more wrong. A camel is a seeing-eye dog designed by a committee and available free with government grants to people who can see perfectly well but can't walk.

Yet committees are ancient and ubiquitous in our civilization. Moses goes to a business conference with God and the next thing you know, Exodus 32:1, "the people gathered themselves together." And someone says, "All in favor of worshipping a golden calf . . ."

Same thing in the Roman Senate: "All in favor of relinquishing power to Caesar, then stabbing him . . ."

And again in the boardrooms of Lehman Brothers, Merrill Lynch, and Fannie Mae: "All in favor of investing in loans to people who made loans to people who made loans to people with houses that aren't worth pissing on if they catch fire . . ."

Committees persist although their decisions are almost invariably stupid. Therefore committees must provide some value to our civilization with their stupidity. And they do. In fact it could be suggested that our freedoms find their surest protection in stupidity.

We owe the thought to Lord Brougham, another of nineteenth-century Britain's great defenders of liberty. As Lord Chancellor, Brougham led the fights in Parliament that would abolish slavery in 1833 and pass the Reform Bill of 1832 broadening the electorate and making seats in Parliament more nearly representational. Brougham (who, incidentally, had a style of fancy carriage named after him, set the fashion for going to the Riviera, and became himself quite stupid later in life) said, "All we see about us, Kings, Lords, and Commons, the whole machinery of the State, all the apparatus of the system, and its varied workings, end in simply bringing twelve good men into a box."

In other words, what makes and keeps us free is a committee—the jury. Governments have the legal monopoly on deadly force, and, in a free country, the thing that prevents the government from forcing us into prison or onto the lethal injection gurney any time it likes is the need for a jury verdict. Our government cannot inflict any punishment or penalty upon us unless what we have done is so obviously wrong and outrageously bad that even a feebleminded, asinine, obtuse, muddled, stubborn, and silly committee, which never agrees on anything, agrees.

Taxes

Taxes are a good thing. "Every tax," said Adam Smith, "is to the person who pays it a badge, not of slavery, but of liberty. It denotes that he is subject to government, indeed, but that, as he has some property, he cannot himself be the property of a master."

We're tempted to answer Smith with the "We don't need no stinking badges" quote from the movie *Treasure of the Sierra Madre,* but the sage of economic freedom has a point. We cannot be expected to surrender rights in our property—that is, pay taxes—unless we are understood to have property rights, and chief among property rights is our right to the property of ourselves. We're free. Even when taxes are levied by force, first they have to catch us.

Also, taxes caused democracy. When England's Charles I had to go, crown in hand, to beg Parliament for tax revenues, an elected body was able to claim sovereignty and dispatch with the divine right of kings (and King Charles's head).

Our own Revolutionary War was precipitated by taxes. "No taxation without representation" was a slogan among the American patriots, a crowd of whom would protest such taxes at the Boston Tea Party in 1773. (And the original Tea Partiers, like their later-day namesakes, were regarded with contempt by well-placed know-it-alls. Peter Oliver, chief justice of Massachusetts, said of Samuel Adams, "He never failed of employing his Abilities to the vilest Purposes.")

The French Revolution, too, was a result of taxes. Louis XVI needed to raise them and, looking to do so, convened the states-general, a group of delegates from the nobility, the clergy, and the commoners. A cutthroat bunch they proved to be.

We owe a lot to our taxes. But we owe a lot *on* our taxes too. That is why the most surprisingly good thing about taxes is that they are a good deal.

The American government will spend $4 trillion this year. There are an estimated 308.6 million Americans. We each get $12,956. Sure we mostly get it in the form of Sacramento light rail projects that don't go anywhere except Sacramento, sugar beet price supports, contributions to the charity known as GM, Afghanistan troop surges, and interest payments on Chinese-owned T bills. We'd rather have cash. But, still, $12,956 isn't bad.

Let's say you're a family of five: a dad, a mom, and three lovely kids. You're the kind of family we conservatives endorse. You're getting $64,781 from the government. Even Republicans are on the dole. Dad (conservative women are proud to be stay-at-home moms) will have to make a pile of money to pay $65K in taxes.

Although it is unclear just how big a pile dad will have to make to ensure that he's feeding, sheltering, and grooming the America of the future rather than sucking her teat.

Democrats in Congress may lower taxes, for fear that more Republicans will be elected. Or Democrats in Congress may raise taxes for fear more Republicans will be elected before Democrats have a chance to enact a tax hike. The president may make all Wall Street profits greater than the 2009 Madoff-investor average return subject to punitive capitation. Or the president may give another squillion-jillion dollars in bailout funds to all Wall Street firms. The tax code is so confusing that every time a federal appointment is made the appointee has to go before a congressional committee to explain how he got so confused that he didn't pay his taxes. And taxes—and loans to government that will have to be repaid with taxes—come in a variety of types and kinds. Personal income tax receipts fund less than a quarter of federal outlays. Corporate taxes provide a whopping 3.8 percent. Borrowed money accounts for nearly half of what Washington will spend this year. The deficit gap will be closed by revenue from that $9 pack of cigarettes you just bought because thinking about taxes stresses you out.

Natasha Altamirano of the National Taxpayers Union did some complicated mathematics and said, "By my reckoning, somewhere between 85 and 95 million households out of 115 million total have a smaller tax liability than the per capita spending burden." This means that the breadwinners for between one-fifth and one-quarter of American households are shoveling coal in the engine rooms of the ship of state while everybody else is a stowaway, necking with Kate Winslet like Leonardo DiCaprio in *Titanic*.

Ms. Altamirano went on to note that those breadwinners doing all the work are also less likely to be receiving any kind of government monetary assistance and are more likely to have their Social Security benefits taxed.

"If we were to compensate for this," she said, "I imagine that more like 100 million households have a smaller liability than the per capita spending burden." One hundred out of 115 is 87 percent. Our nation is 87 percent mooch, 87 percent leach, 87 percent "Spare (hope and) change, man?"

It may be worse than that or, depending on how greedily liberal you are, better. Let's abandon the complicated mathematics of taxation. We don't understand complicated mathematics. We were liberal arts majors. If we understood complicated mathematics we'd be wealthy hedge fund managers in prison. Let's go to arithmetic. The U.S. gross domestic product for 2009 has been calculated by the Department of Commerce's Bureau of Economic Analysis as $14.2 trillion. The Federal Budget, being $4 trillion, is (divide 4 by 14.2, move the decimal point two places to the right, add the thingy over the numeral 5 on your keyboard) 28.2 percent of the gross domestic product. Let's round down and call it one-fourth. This is our real rate of national taxation. The government makes off with one-fourth of our goods and services. Then the government gives those goods and services back to us. (In a slightly altered form, the way a horse gives the hay we feed it back to us in a slightly altered form.) We each get our $12,956, which is our per-person share of one-fourth of the gross domestic product. But, since the real tax rate on that GDP is 25 percent, each of us has to make $51,824 a year—our per person share of the GDP—to be entitled to call ourselves a tax*payer,* not a tax vampire. And we have to make $259,120 a year if we're supporting a family of five.

Slightly confused by this? Democrats always have been.

How many American households make a quarter of a million bucks? The president's does, and with only two kids. The president is taxing himself. Good. But the rest of the U.S. government's operating expenses are being funded by paycheck withholding on Conan O'Brien's NBC settlement. Plus there's all the money the government has borrowed by taking out a second mortgage on North America, which will soon have the Treasury Department calling the toll-free number for the "debt restructuring services" advertised on late night TV.

The gross unfairness of America's tax system won't lead to class war. Or, if it does, the war will be brief. There are 300 million of us Sponge Bobs and hardly any of the sucker fish we're soaking. On the other hand, young people—with no dependents except their Twitter pals—have to earn only double their age to be ladling gravy to Uncle Sam. They could turn on the government if they started thinking about this (or anything).

The rest of us? We're in the clover. True, we have to "give" 25 percent of our workweek to the IRS. That's ten hours—all of Wednesday and half of Thursday morning. But it's still a good deal and doesn't really leave us overburdened on the job. Nothing gets done on Monday and Friday anyway. Tuesday we had to go pick up our kid from school because a peanut was discovered in the food dish belonging to the fifth grade's gerbil and the whole building had to be hypoallergized. On Thursday, after an early lunch, we left a full cup of coffee in our cubicle and draped our suit jacket over the back of our chair, so it would look like we were around the office someplace, and caught a Nationals game. We don't have to worry that out-of-control federal spending or an insane tax structure will wreck our lives. We've all got government jobs.

More Taxes

I take it back. Taxes aren't a good thing. This is because you're very rich. You're surprised to learn that you're very rich, especially when, like me, you're really broke. But, if you think about it, you know you're rich because only a rich person can afford to pay double for everything.

And you do. The financial bailout, for example. You paid for it once when you discovered that your retirement savings consisted of nothing but a half-eaten chocolate bunny from last Easter, three paper clips, and a dried-up Sharpie. Then you paid for it again with your tax dollars and with the permanent damage done to the American economy when the government pawned everything in the nation because your tax dollars weren't enough to pay for the bailout.

Likewise with the economic stimulus. You write checks to cover your mortgage payment, utilities, insurance premiums, car loan, basic cable, Visa, MasterCard, and American Express bills, and you hand fistfuls of cash to your children and turn them loose in the Abercrombie & Fitch store. Think you're done stimulating the economy? Think again. The president of the United States is also on an economically stimulating spending spree, and he's paying for it with a lien on all the future job and business opportunities that your children will have. This means they won't have them. I hope that your kids, once they've gotten their MBAs, enjoy stocking shelves at the Dollar Store.

What about the new car you paid for with taxpayer funds given to GM and Chrysler? How come it isn't in the driveway? You gave all that money to the car companies and they didn't even send a thank-you note on a scratch-and-sniff card with that new car smell. No, if you want a new car you have to—you guessed it—pay double.

Of course maybe you got something out of the Cash for Clunkers program. And good for you if you did. (Meanwhile, will some liberal brainbox explain to me why it's a good thing to junk a useful machine? How does destroying something that's worth money make us worth more money?)

Paying double for everything didn't start with the financial crisis or even with Democratic control of Congress. Paying double is an integral part of the modern welfare state.

Beginning with welfare. Your tax dollars pay for federal, state, and local welfare programs. Then you pay for your daughter to pursue a career in "holistic dance liberation." You subsidize your son's Internet start-up idea—Buttbook, a Web site featuring all your enemies. Plus there's your perennial bum of a brother-in-law, tweaking on meth in the doublewide and watching Cartoon Network on the high-definition television you paid for.

Same with schools. Your school taxes pay for Alger Hiss Public High School, conveniently right down the street, inconveniently full of heroin and 9mm handguns. So you also pay tuition at Friar Torquemada Parochial High.

At school, home, or work the most important function of government is to protect your person and property. That's what the police department is for. And you get to pay the police *and* pay for burglar alarms, private security patrols, and guard dogs, such as our family's guard dog, Pinky-Wink. (For the information of any prospective burglars, Pinky-Wink isn't really a Boston terrier. He's . . . um . . . a Rhodesian ridgeback, weighing 100 . . . make that 150 pounds. Uh, the kids named him. Stop yapping, Pinky-Wink.)

The second most important function of government, in my opinion, is trash pickup. And people in government can start with themselves as far as I'm concerned. Anyway, municipal garbage collectors pick up the trash from your house. But not until you've sorted it into the proper recycling bins, which you do by picking up the trash from your house. With government, what you don't pay double for in money you pay double for in time and effort.

But usually it's money. When you pay a hospital bill you're really paying two hospital bills—one bill for you because you have a job and/or private insurance and can pay the hospital and another bill, which is tacked onto your bill, to cover the medical expenses of someone who doesn't have a job and/or private insurance and can't pay the hospital. Your tennis elbow underwrites the Alger Hiss Public High School student's 9mm handgun wound.

And never is paying double as doubly troubling as it is in the matter of retirement. You have to pay into Social Security and into your IRA and your Keogh plan and put some money in your savings account too. You have to pay Medicare tax and buy Medicare supplemental insurance and contribute to a medical savings account and make doctor bill copayments besides. And the funding for Social Security and Medicare is so underfinanced and actuarially shaky that you cannot be certain those programs will exist by the time you're eligible for them. And you're sixty-four and a half.

Would you like to know what taxpayers are getting out of this deal? You and me both. How do we benefit from this twinning, this twoing, this duality? Damned if I can figure it out. Barkeep, make that a double.

Why I'm Right

Some people arrive at their political convictions through experience, some through study, some through thought. My political convictions are a result of all three, or, rather, the lack of them.

I was brought up in Republican circumstances, firmly grounded in convention. I was swept out to Marxist sea by a flood of sex. I was trying to impress cute beatnik girls. Then, one day, I found myself beached on the shore of jobs and responsibilities and I was a Republican again. No cognition, cogitation, or will seems to have been involved in my ideological spindrift. As both a radical and a reactionary I was formed by history and institutions. All those beatnik girls had a history. Many of them ended up in institutions.

My maternal great-grandfather owned a farm in downstate Illinois. He was a county sheriff, a stalwart of the GOP, a friend of President McKinley's, and a breeder of harness racing horses. His dying words summarize my family's attitude toward the great sociopolitical issues that would shake the twentieth century: "How did Shorty do at the track today?"

His daughter, my grandmother, was ten when she began accompanying her father to the Republican Party's political conventions in Chicago. She never got over the shock of that blowhard easterner Teddy Roosevelt splitting the party and allowing such a man as Woodrow Wilson—from a Confederate state!—to become chief executive. As far as my grandmother was concerned, Taft was the last real Republican. In a moment of childish innocence I once asked her what the difference was between Republicans and Democrats. She said, "Democrats rent."

My father's family was, if anything, more Republican. My paternal grandfather was a widower, left with a business to run and six small children on his hands. He remarried more in haste than wisdom. The stepmother was insane. She left Uncle Joe out on the back steps until his diapers froze. Grandpa divorced her. But, then as now, there was a political aspect to getting an annulment. (The Kennedys seem to have a vending machine that dispenses them.) According to family story, Grandpa O'Rourke and the local bishop clashed and Grandpa went out and, in one day, joined the Lutheran church, the Freemasons, and the Republican Party. He had a heart attack just before the 1960 elections. At the funeral his sister, my great-aunt Helen, said, "It's a good thing your grandfather died when he did. It would have killed him to see John Kennedy president."

Thus my life would have gone along perfectly well, politically speaking, if it hadn't been for girls. I found them interesting. They found me less so. On my first weekend at college I was walking down an alley with a bar on either side. Each bar had a patio full of students. The girls on one patio were very attractive, their sweaters well filled, their pleated skirts worn daringly above the knee, their blond hair styled in what was called a "sorority flip." They sipped demurely from beer mugs decorated with Greek letters.

But I wasn't athletic or handsome or a Sigma Chi legacy. And I had a feeling that, even if I were, getting such girls into bed would involve attendance at mixers and dances, romantic chat-ups, fumblings under coats in the shrubbery while House Mothers tsked out windows, bestowals of one's fraternity pin or even an engagement ring, and lots of talk about "our future."

The girls on the other patio were fetching as well, in their black leotards and peasant blouses, denim skirts, and sandals. Their long, dark hair was ironed straight. They strummed guitars, smoked unfiltered cigarettes, and drank beer straight from the bottle. I thought, "I'll bet those girls do it."

They did. I went home at Christmas break with my hair grown long, wearing a blue jean jacket with a big red fist emblazoned on the back. My grandmother said, "Pat, I'm worried about you. Are you becoming a Democrat?"

"Grandma!" I said. "Lyndon Johnson and Richard Nixon are both fascist pigs! Of course I'm not a Democrat! I'm a communist!"

"At least you're not a Democrat," said Grandma.

Having donned the clown costume I found it easy to honk the dogma nose, squirt the progressive seltzer, and pile into tiny cars (VW bugs). Soon I really was a communist unless I really was an anarchist or an anarcho-syndicalist or a Trotskyite or a Maoist. I never read any work of political ideology unless by accident, because it was assigned in class. And then I studied it as perfunctorily as any Sigma Chi in the lecture hall. Nothing ensures an obliviousness to theory like the need to get a passing grade on a quiz about it.

I have ex-leftist friends who recall long, intense, fractious political arguments during their university years. But I was at Miami of Ohio, not Berkeley or Columbia. My college friends and I may have begun such discussions, but then the rolling papers were brought out and the debate became over where to get Mallomars.

However, inchoate ideas are often more deeply held than any others. Emerson, for instance, believed intensely in his conception of metaphysics even though, on inspection, he didn't have one. And it's often forgotten what instinctive communal levelers and utopians kids are. After all, they're raised in the only successful Marxist-Leninist economic organization on earth, the family. From each according to his ability. To each according to his need. Outside the home, children spend their formative years under authoritarian, antimaterialistic regimes at school, catechism, summer camp, and Little League. They're taught sharing and caring and "fairness" and a kind of toadying social equality (". . . it's how you play the game"). They're given employment consisting of involuntary volunteer work to fulfill their Boy Scout, or church, or school community service requirements. Maybe they get a job doing some mindless sorting at Dad's friend's FedEx store. They are "part of the solution" and/or they experience proletarian alienation. Then they're sent off to college to learn about freedom and responsibility—freedom to get naked and stoned and responsibility to turn down their stereo after one a.m. It's a wonder that anybody under twenty-five is even a Mikhail Gorbachev.

In my day there was also the war in Vietnam. Proponents of the present war in Afghanistan (myself included) should consider the effect that certain armed conflicts can have on the ideologically impressionable (whether at Berkeley or a Kabul madrassa). Wars need clear arguments of justification, clear strategies of execution, clear objectives. P.S., they need to be won. And the impressionable can't be left wondering just who the winners were. World War I was a dilly in all these respects with ideological consequences less trivial than those of the 1960s.

The Vietnam War's military draft lent extra solipsism to the self-cherishing melodrama of being an adolescent. The government was intent on interrupting my fun to send me to some distant place with a noxious climate to shoot people I didn't know, and, what was worse, they'd shoot back. I had a stepfather at home whom I was perfectly willing to shoot while he snored on the couch. But the government was insensitive to my needs.

I stayed a left-winger for more than a decade. This despite at least three Road to Damascus moments when I should have been converted to better views. During graduate school in Baltimore I worked on an "underground" newspaper. We shrilly denounced war, injustice, and this and that. One evening our office was invaded by a group of young people more radical than ourselves who felt that our denunciations weren't shrill enough. They called themselves, and I am not kidding, the Balto-Cong. They accused us of being capitalist roaders and said they were liberating the oppressor's private property in the name of the people. We explained that they were welcome to it, the private property consisting of about ten thousand dollars of debt, three typewriters, and an old row house from which we were about to be evicted. (Radicals are worse than Democrats; they not only rent but are in arrears on their rent payments.) We were held at knuckle-point and made to undergo a consciousness-raising session that might have gone on who knows how long if a couple of "the people" hadn't stopped by. These were two teenage black kids from the neighborhood. They asked, "What the hell's going on here?" and scared the Balto-Cong away. The neighborhood kids were honors English students who hoped the underground newspaper would provide a venue for their poetry. And I'm glad to say that, thereafter, it did.

A fellow ex-staffer at the newspaper (now also a Republican) tells me that I spent the rest of that night slamming my fist into a beanbag chair and saying, "Spiro Agnew was right!" But I got over it. I had realized there were bad people on the left, but I hadn't realized I was one of them.

Then my student deferment ran out and I was drafted. Standing in my underwear at the draft physical I noticed that I and all the other hirsute children of privilege were clutching thick folders of doctors' letters about asthma, neurosis, back problems, and being allergic to camouflage. The poor kids, with their normal haircuts and the discount store Y-front briefs that came up over their navels, were empty-handed and about to be marched off to war. This told me something about what my radicalism was doing to benefit the masses. But I forget what, because the army doctor told me something more interesting. He told me to get out of there. The army had no use for drug-fuddled hippies.

I remained determined that wealth should be shared with everyone, especially me. But the silent majority tacitly refused to agree and I had to get a job. The pay was $150 a week. I was to be paid every two weeks. I was eagerly looking forward to my check for $300 dollars (as was my landlord). But when payday came I found that, after withholdings for federal, state, and city income tax, Social Security, health insurance payments, union dues, and pension plan contributions, I netted $159.80. I'd been struggling for years to achieve socialism in America only to discover that we had it already.

Usually when I'm asked what made me a Republican I tell that story. But it isn't true. I mean the story is true, but it didn't really change my mind. I went on for years considering myself to be at least a nominal leftist.

I was too busy to be involved in left-wing causes anymore. I had that job. And, truthfully, all causes are boring. They are a way of making yourself part of something bigger and more exciting, which guarantees that small, tedious selves are what a cause will attract. Plus I was finding my work to be about as big and exciting a thing as my own small, tedious self could handle.

And I had begun to notice something else about left-wing causes. Radicals claim to seek what no one claims to want. The collective has been tried in every conceivable form from the primitively tribal to the powerfully Soviet, and "the people" who are thus collectivized immediately choose any available alternative, whether it's getting drunk on Indian Reservations or getting shot climbing the Berlin Wall.

I'd enjoyed all the left-wing rioting. Better yet had been the aftermath back at the crash pad. "We've got to get this tear gas off us. We'd better double up in the shower, Sunshine, to conserve earth's natural resources." But the rioting, along with the Vietnam War, was petering out. Still, I was a man of the left. That was the sort of person I admired. Rick, in *Casablanca,* was a man of the left, and so was, uh, Rick in *Casablanca* . . .

In the end it was silliness, not sense, that turned me back into a Republican. One day in the middle 1970s I was walking along a street and my reflection was caught at an odd angle in a store window so that I saw myself without realizing who I was looking at. I was wearing dirty jeans and a work shirt with mystic chick embroidery on it and a thrift shop peacoat, and my hair was all over the place. I thought, "That guy's looking pretty silly for somebody his age."

Silliness made me a Republican, and boredom helped too. My aging hippie friends were boring. They continued to be convinced that everything was going to be shared soon, so they hadn't gotten jobs. They hadn't gotten married either, although wives were the one thing that did seem to be getting shared. Occasionally they had a kid. They didn't let the diapers freeze. There weren't any. These children, though provided with remarkable freedom from discipline and conformity, didn't seem to give much thanks for it, or ever say thanks, or please, or even "How are you?" My friends were living the lives of unfettered bohemian artists. Except the lack of fetters seemed to tie them to dumps on the Lower East Side. (Rented, not owned.) And where was the art?

These people not only had a great capacity to be boring, they had a great capacity to be bored. Imagine a talent for ennui so well developed that you could be bored by God. It's futile for a political radical to believe in God because politics has all of God's power to shape life and then some. God recused Himself in the matter of free will. Radicals do not. Then there's the egotism of the idealist. If the problems of the world can be intellectually solved by me, what's the intellectual need for Him? Furthermore, the wicked world is so full of wrongs, which radicals are trying to right, thereby making radicals better than that no-good God who created the wicked world. Or would have if He existed. God's like, you know, a square.

My own lack of religious faith persisted even after I'd renewed my faith in other things such as buying instead of renting. If I could summon enough faith to vote for the average Republican, which, by the early 1980s, I was doing, I certainly should have been able to summon enough faith for the Apostles' Creed. But the selfish leftist habit of doubt stayed with me. In 1984 I was in Beirut writing an article about the Lebanese civil war. My friend Charlie Glass, ABC's Middle East correspondent, dragged me out into the Beqaa Valley to interview a terrifying man named Hussein Mussawi, head of a violent fundamentalist Shi'ite militia called Islamic Amal. Mussawi looked at me and asked—in English, which he had theretofore shown no signs of speaking—"Do you believe in God?" I remember wondering if I was fibbing when very quickly I said yes.

Then one day it seemed futile *not* to believe in God. Maybe existence was pointless, though it did have its points for me—writing books, fixing up the house I'd bought in New Hampshire. I'd started hunting again. I'd learned to ski. Maybe I was just too small a part of creation to understand what the larger point was. But if I was so small that my comprehension was meaningless, what did that make my incomprehension? Also, although I could imagine that existence was pointless, I couldn't imagine that it was accidental. Existence seemed too intricately organized. Having led an accidental existence for years I knew what disorganization meant. Never. (Note how often leftists need to admonish themselves with the slogan "Organize!") If the random forces of quantum physics were all that was in play then these forces had dropped butter and eggs and mushrooms and cheese and a Zippo on the kitchen floor and gotten an omelet. Whether I like omelets was neither here nor there.

On the other hand, it was just such an incredulity about things somehow organizing themselves that kept me from embracing all the implications of the free market. "Laissez-faire" was a personal attitude long before I gave it larger significance. Then I remembered a lesson of my leftist days: "The personal is the political." And I began leaving other people alone not only in my life but in my mind.

By the early 1990s my political philosophy was completely elaborated. I didn't have one. I simply thought—and I continue to think—that it is the duty of every politically informed and engaged person to do everything he or she can to prevent politics.

But I was not yet a conservative. I was a Republican and a libertarian. The mutual exclusivity of those two political positions was, I thought, one more proof of the self-negating nature of politics, which should be allowed to take its course until politics is regarded as such a nugatory enterprise that people have to be chased through the streets and tackled and forced to serve as senators, representatives, presidents, and Supreme Court justices. Or maybe, I thought, there should be a game of governance tag where someone has to stay a congressman or senator until he's able to catch someone else and make him "it." If this means legislative halls filled with the helpless and crippled so much the better.

I still think it's a good idea. But that is not conservatism. I became a conservative at 11:59 p.m. on December 4, 1997, the way many people become conservatives. My wife gave birth. Suddenly I was an opponent of change.

Every change was filled with danger. If the temperature in the baby's room changed, I worried. If the temperature in the baby changed, I agonized. Changing my shoes became a matter of great anxiety. Better go to work in my slippers—any noise could wake Muffin. I was tortured by the change from a child who sat up to a child who crawled. Was her speed of development too slow? Was her speed headfirst into the table leg too fast? The change from crawling to toddling was terrible. I wanted to stand with William F. Buckley athwart the tide of history shouting, "Don't swallow the refrigerator magnet!"

Things that once were a matter of indifference became ominous threats, such as refrigerator magnets. And homosexuality. I used to consider erotic preferences a matter of laissez-faire. Then I realized, if my children think homosexuality is acceptable, it could lead them to think something really troubling, that sex is acceptable. Daddy has been down that alley. It took me years to figure out how to be a Republican again. There will be time enough for my kids to learn the facts of life from the priest during Pre-Cana counseling. As for public education's "tolerance" curriculum, the heck with *Heather Has Two Mommies*. How about *Heather Has Two Nannies*. There's a book that could teach children something worthwhile in the way of values.

I have lost all my First Amendment principles about rap songs lyrics. I am infuriated by them. Because I cannot understand a word that hip-hop musicians say. Rappers may, for all I know, be saying, "We need a single-payer national health care system," or, "Home mortgage interest tax deductions subsidize suburban sprawl, increase the burden on transportation infrastructure, and lead to greater production of greenhouse gases."

I am appalled by violence on TV, specifically the absence of it on PBS. "Which perfectly harmless thing is Caillou terrified of today?," I always ask my six-year-old, Buster. "Why isn't Caillou ever terrified of something sensible like a pit bull? Why don't his parents just give him a whack when he whines?"

And what if a purple *Tyrannosaurus rex* shows up in my backyard? The kids will run outside expecting to play games and sing songs and they'll be eaten. What kind of lessons is PBS teaching our children?

Being a parent means suddenly agreeing with Pat Buchanan about everything except immigration. For Pete's sake, Pat, nannies are hard enough to find. Not that I want to do away with Barney, Snoop Dogg, or love (whether it can't speak its name or can't shut up). I am a true conservative. I hate *all* change.

The most recent presidential election was won on a campaign of "hope and change." I was appalled about the change part. We had just, finally, gotten Buster out of diapers. Change is not a good word at our house. Or anywhere else. Change a tire. "You'd better change your ways." Change of life. Any change in a wart or mole.

And hope's no better. You remember your Greek mythology. The box that hope comes in is Pandora's box. After Pandora opens that box and death and disease and all the ills that plague mankind have been loosed upon the world, nothing is left in the box but hope. Is it a good thing when you've got nothing left but hope? How about when you've got nothing left but hope for a government bailout?

Conservatives want things to remain static, to stay just the way they are, not because these things are good but because these things are *there*. When I have to deal with things I know where and what they are. Conservatives are opposed to change not because change is bad but because change is new. It's as modern and confusing as the metric system or the BlackBerry. I don't know how to count the change. And I can't find the OFF button for the hope.

One last thing about change—it's different. No one without children knows how fraught the word "different" is. When used about your child it's never good news. When used by your child it isn't either. If a kid says, "You're different," he means you're crazy. If he says, "I don't want to be different," he means he's going to skip school and shoplift. And when "the spaghetti tastes different" he's about to throw up.

Radicals wish to make a difference. To the born-of-parenting conservative this sounds as sensible as wishing for head lice.

The conservative parent feels the same way about those small, itchy things called ideas. Radicalism is the pursuit of ideas. (A pursuit that, for me, was made all the more tantalizing by the fact that I never came close to grasping one.) Any conservative can tell you that ideas have consequences. Who wants consequences? Conservatism is a flight from ideas. As in, "Don't get any ideas," "What's the big idea?," and "Whose idea was that?"

A flight from ideas might sound like Philistinism but think how valuable the above three phrases are when used on children. Or politicians. And what's so bad about being a Philistine? Putting religious prejudice aside, the Philistines seem to have been respectable people who did well in business. For all we know the reporting on the David and Goliath battle comes to us from some Old Testament version of NPR. And David, what with the poems, the messy love life, the increased centralization of government, was too liberal for my taste.

Furthermore, ideas are not to be confused with facts. One of the great things about being a conservative is that when a decision has to be made—for example, is hiding your spinach under your dinner plate and then trying to feed it to the dog right or wrong?—facts can be consulted. Is it a cardinal sin? A venial sin? Against the law? Or you can just ask mom. A radical can't do this, no matter how many moms are extant. Radicals have to work everything through de novo. Radicals have ideas about sin, law, and motherhood. And the more airy the ideas, the more the answer has to be pulled out of thin air (and the more spinach the dog gets, which doesn't make the dog happy either).

The great moral principles of conservatism, if not self-evident, have at least been entered into evidence by thousands of years of human experience. And the great political principles of conservatism are simple, summarized by the important and perceptive political philosopher Walt Kowalski, portrayed by Clint Eastwood in the movie *Gran Torino*: "Get off my lawn." Then there are the great intellectual principles of conservatism, which are, mmm . . .

Some years ago I was enjoying the conservative pleasures of a driven pheasant shoot in Ireland. Among my hunting companions was a wonderful old fellow named Preston Mann, now pursuing game in paradise. Preston was one of the world's great dog trainers, the proprietor of a splendid hunting club in Michigan, and a crack shotgunner. I'm none of these, in particular the last. I kept missing the pheasants with my first barrel. I generally picked them up with a second shot, but bird after bird escaped my initial blast. Preston was shooting from the next butt and, midst the flap and crackle of pheasants winging toward us, he turned to me and shouted, "P.J. you're thinking about it. It ain't a thinking man's game."

HOLIDAYS IN HECK

(2011)

"I have discovered that all human evil comes from this, man's being unable to sit still in a room."

—Pascal

Introduction: A Former War Correspondent Experiences Frightening Vacation Fun

After the Iraq War I gave up on being what's known in the trade as a "shithole specialist." I was too old to be scared stiff and too stiff to sleep on the ground. I'd been writing about overseas troubles of one kind or another for twenty-one years, in forty-some countries, none of them the nice ones. I had a happy marriage and cute kids. There wasn't much happy or cute about Iraq.

Michael Kelly, my boss at the *Atlantic,* and I had gone to cover the war, he as an "imbed" with the Third Infantry Division, I as a "unilateral." We thought, once ground operations began, I'd have the same freedom to pester the locals that he and I had had during the Gulf War a dozen years before. The last time I saw Mike he said, "I'm going to be stuck with the 111th Latrine Cleaning Battalion while you're driving your rental car through liberated Iraq, drinking Rumsfeld Beer and judging wet *abeyya* contests." Instead I wound up trapped in Kuwait, bored and useless, and Mike went with the front line to Baghdad, where he was killed during the assault on the airport. Mike had a happy marriage, too, and cute kids the same ages as mine. I called my wife, Tina, and told her that Mike was dead and I was going to Baghdad to take his place. Tina cried about Mike and his widow and his children. But Tina is the daughter of an FBI agent. Until she was fourteen she thought all men carried guns to work. She said, "All right, if you think it's important to go."

It wasn't important. And that was that for war correspondence. I decided to write about pleasant places. Fortunately, my previous assignments—Lebanon, the West Bank, the Soviet Union, apartheid-era South Africa, the jungles of the Philippines, Saudi Arabia, Somalia, Pakistan's Northwest Frontier, Bosnia, Kosovo, etc.—set a low bar for pleasant. Unfortunately I had no experience with pleasure travel. I'd always been where people were shooting each other or wanting to shoot each other or—in the case of my side job as a car journalist—trying to die in horrible wrecks. How, I wondered, does one undertake enjoyably going somewhere enjoyable?

Apparently there are rules about traveling for fun. The first rule is to find the most crowded airplane on an airline that regards its customers as self-loading freight. Bonus points if the cabin crew is jocular about this. Nothing but lukewarm diet soda is to be served and that only on flights longer than three hours in duration. Passengers must be very fat, hold babies on their laps, and make certain the infants are suffering from painful ear infections. Passengers should also bring everything they own onto the plane in wheelie bags and ram these into my knee as they go down the aisle. This luggage is to be dropped on my head after it fails to fit into the overhead bins, then crammed into the under-seat space in front of *my* feet. Everyone, please be sure to insist on having a conversation if I'm trying to read and also sneeze and cough frequently, get up to go to the toilet every five minutes if you're in the window seat in my row, or kick the seat back rhythmically for hours if you're in the row behind. And no matter what your age or the climate at your destination you must dress as if you're a nine-year-old headed for summer camp. Apparently shorts and T-shirts are what one wears when one is having fun. I don't seem to own any fun outfits. I travel in a coat and tie. This is useful in negotiating customs and visa formalities, police barricades, army checkpoints, and rebel roadblocks.

"Halt!" say border patrols, policemen, soldiers, and guerrilla fighters in a variety of angry-sounding languages.

I say, "Observe that I am importantly wearing a jacket and tie."

"We are courteously allowing you to proceed now," they reply.

This doesn't work worth a damn with the TSA.

Then there's the problem of writing about travel fun, or fun of any kind. Nothing has greater potential to annoy a reader than a writer recounting what fun he's had. Personally—and I'm sure I'm not alone in this—I have little tolerance for fun when other people are having it. It's worse than pornography and almost as bad as watching the Food Channel. Yet in this manuscript I see that, as a writer, I'm annoying my reader self from the first chapter until the last sentence. I hope at least I'm being crabby about it. Writers of travelogues are most entertaining when—to the infinite amusement of readers—they have bad things happen to them. I'm afraid the best I can do here is have a bad attitude.

That's not hard for me. What is this thing called fun? It's harder to parse than that thing called happiness. To judge by traveling with my wife and daughters fun has something to do with shopping for clothes. But I already have clothes; otherwise I'd be standing there in Harrod's naked. Or maybe it has to do with eating in fancy restaurants. I like a good meal and often, in the midst of one, I'll begin to reminisce about dining on raw lamb brains in Peshawar, and suddenly nobody's eating. My son Buster's idea of fun is a frightening amusement park ride. I'm a professional coward. I make my living by being terrified. I shouldn't pay somebody when I get on Space Mountain; somebody should pay me when I get off.

The word "fun" is not found anywhere in the Bible. According to the *Oxford English Dictionary,* "fun" first occurs circa 1700 as slang for a trick, hoax, or practical joke. It may derive from the Middle English "fon," meaning to cheat. Dr. Johnson called it "a low cant word."

In his *Dictionary of Catch Phrases,* the eminent lexicographer Eric Partridge lists a number of expressions concerning fun. They don't indicate that much is being had. "Ain't we got fun!" comes from the lyrics of a 1920 song by Richard A. Whiting: "Not much money/But, oh, honey/Ain't we got fun!" Probably not for long. "Having fun?" is a question posed only to those who clearly aren't. A more kindly version is the existential query that the cartoonist Bill Griffith had Zippy the Pinhead make, "Are we having fun yet?," which Eric Partridge died too soon to note. "It's all good clean fun" means it isn't. And we mustn't forget "more fun than a barrel of monkeys." How long have the monkeys been in the barrel? Does the barrel have air holes?

Googling "fun" in March 2011 I got, first: "Due to a scheduling conflict, **fun** will not be performing at the June 25th Panic at the Disco show in Portland, OR." And, second: "FunBrain is the #1 site for online educational games for kids of all ages (math, grammar, science, spelling, history)."

And *Bartlett's* has only a dozen quotations concerning fun, none of which are fun to quote except a stanza from the poem "Hi!" by Walter de la Mare, which takes me back to my days as a shithole specialist.

Bang! Now the animal
Is dead and dumb and done.
Nevermore to peep again, creep
again, leap again,
Eat or sleep or drink again, oh,
what fun!

Republicans Evolving

The Galápagos Islands, April 2003

It is sometimes thought that Republicans are not environmentally conscious, that we are not concerned about the planet or, as we call it, the outdoors. This is not true. We love the outdoors and carefully instruct our children in its manifold splendors. For example, the son of a Republican friend of mine, when asked by his preschool teacher if he could name the four seasons, proudly said, "Dove, duck, deer, and quail!"

We Republicans respect and revere the natural world—and all its natural laws and truths we hold to be self-evident. We're particularly respectful of that aspect of the natural world known as Darwinian selection, whatever you may have heard to the contrary in our churches. Creationism is all well and good on Sunday, but it's "survival of the most market-oriented" the rest of the week and also in the voting booth. Thus it was that some Republican friends of mine and I made a pilgrimage to that ecological treasure and living monument to Charles Darwin, the Galápagos Islands.

Several million years ago the Galápagos Islands popped, volcanically, out of the Pacific Ocean. The South American mainland being six hundred miles away and nothing else nearby, each island was a tabula rasa. Various birds, lizards, sea mammals, and seeds blew in and washed up. Biological colonization occurred by dumb luck. Very dumb luck, to judge by how the local critters flap, crawl, and paddle up and present themselves to visiting omnivore bipeds for examination of gustatory potential. Pirates, whalers, and other nonmembers of the World Wildlife Federation had an estimated 100,000 friendly, curious Galápagos giant tortoises for lunch.

Isolation allowed unusual life-forms to flourish. It's an experiment we all made, when we were single, with Chinese takeout left in the refrigerator for six months. Interesting what happens when all the ecological niches except the shelf the beer is on are empty. General Tso's chicken can develop into something that fills the whole fridge. Darwin may have noticed this in the fridge of the HMS *Beagle*. Anyway, when the *Beagle* arrived in the Galápagos, Darwin—perhaps after a heavy lunch of giant tortoise and beer—formulated his theory of evolution, which may be restated for Republicans as: if you're slow and edible and I have a gun, the situation will evolve.

Unfortunately, now that the *Beagle* has been decommissioned, going to the Galápagos in style is something of a problem. For the most part the only way to see the islands is as a tourist on a cruise. There is a kind of tourist who takes this kind of cruise. This tourist loves nature in unnatural ways. An awful prospect presented itself of vegan fare at the captain's table and conversation about earth being in the balance, never mind that the earth has a mass of 5.97×10^{24} kilograms while Al Gore weighs little more than 250 pounds.

Fortunately, I know a Texan couple with the Texan energy and Republican ingenuity needed to tackle this downside of a Galápagos excursion. George and Laura (not their real names) spent a year juggling the busy schedules of fifty-some pals who adore nature's glories especially when a covey of them is pointed by our bird dogs. George and Laura then balanced the juggled schedules with the sailing dates of the MS *Polaris,* owned by that paragon organizer of exotic trips Lindblad Expeditions. We arrived in the Galápagos not as tourists but as a floating house party. We had booked the whole ship. A vessel that might have flown the Greenpeace un-jolly roger now, in effect, hoisted the happy burgee of a yacht. If our dinner seating included members of PETA, we could tell the cruise director, "Throw these vegetarians to the sharks!" Not that Lindblad Expeditions has cruise directors. Lindblad has naturalists with advanced degrees in wildlife biology. Each day these guides took us, by Zodiac boats, to a different Galápagos island. There they delivered talks on Galápagos flora and fauna, giving us important ecology lessons.

On Fernandina Island, our guide said, "The vestigial wings of the flightless cormorant evolved due to a lack of natural predators." Significant glances were exchanged among my shipmates. Being Republicans, we *are* natural predators. A nearby flightless cormorant spread stumpy and functionless appendages that looked to make him eligible for membership in the Feather Club for Birds.

"That's what happens to you without free-market competition," said Laura.

"The flightless cormorant is endemic to the Galápagos islands of Fernandina and Isabela," said our guide. ("Endemic" is wildlife biologist talk for "doesn't get out much" or "stuck there.")

"Notice how close we can get to the birds, even when they are nesting," our guide continued. "This is because they have no experience with humans; they are truly wild."

"Of course!" said a Dallas lawyer. "I should have realized that a long time ago—in my junior year of college—wild equals stupid."

It was an insight that dominated shipboard sundowner gin and tonic chatter.

"Into the stupid blue yonder."

"Call of the stupid."

"Stupid Kingdom."

"Stupid thing, you make my heart sing, you make everything . . . stupid."

The Galápagos are an Ecuadorian national park and a UNESCO World Heritage Site. Strict preservation of the pristine stupidity of the wilderness allowed us to experience a close communion with the animal world that you can't get even from Rover, no matter how stupid he is. The endemic waved albatross let us in on its every Dr. Phil moment. The birds mate for life, then immediately separate. They go off alone for months at sea and return to Española Island in the Galápagos to breed. But before the albatross husband gets back together with his albatross wife, he rapes the other wives. There is an elaborate reconciliation with squawking and slapping of beaks ending in mutual embrace—perfect for daytime bird television. They have an egg, probably to strengthen the relationship. Then they take turns sitting on it for up to a week at a time. When Al Junior is hatched he gets as much as four and a half pounds of food regurgitated down his throat in a single feeding. By five months the chick weighs more than its parents. Feminist issues, family leave, childhood obesity—on Española we had found a place where Hillary Clinton truly could make a difference.

Speaking of objects of ridicule, there is the foolishly waddling, risibly yclept blue-footed booby. The boobies' webbed toes are as funny-colored as a UN flag. Their mating dance is a disco polka. They give each other pebbles.

Boobies share their inshore feeding waters with the noble frigate bird. The frigate birds soar and loop on vast scimitar wings and grace the sky with acrobatics. It's impossible not to admire the one and disparage the other, until it's time for work. The boobies are skilled divers. Plunging from a hundred feet in the air into water sometimes only eighteen inches deep, they harvest whole schools of fish. Then the frigate birds grab the boobies by their tails in midair and bite them and shake them until the boobies cough up their food. "Back on the ground," said our guide, "the male frigate birds have a very large red throat pouch which they puff full of air to attract . . ."

"Voters, I'll bet," said a woman who'd survived a political appointment in the Bush père administration. "Observe the frigate birds," she said, "and you know everything you need to know about Democratic presidential candidates."

"The blue-footed boobies need rebranding," said a marketing consultant from New York. "Those feet—they're a skateboard sneaker franchise crying out for a licensing deal."

"Look," said our guide, "a lava gull." He pointed to a bird that was more like a dove than the airborne sanitation engineer that we call a gull. "They're very rare," said the guide, "maybe only four hundred in the world."

"They must be delicious," said one of our more avid bird hunters. Our shipboard party was of the opinion that extinction probably has as much to do with flavor as with pollution or climate change. Whenever a new creature was spotted, our first question was, "How do they taste?"

It took all week to get one of our guides to admit that he knew how giant tortoise tastes. Not personally, of course, but he was born in the Galápagos and "a long, long time ago my parents had some."

"Well?" we said.

"Good."

The food on the *Polaris* was good, too, albeit lacking in turtle chops and breast of lava gull. The crew was cheerful. The cabins were not too boat-size. And every night the Lindblad guides delivered further informative talks on Galápagos flora and fauna, giving us more important ecology lessons.

Some of us preferred to spend the evenings on the fantail in consultation with Professor Dewar's and Dr. Montecristo. Inside, a Lindblad guide was explaining how young the Galápagos Islands are, in geological time. Outside, George was suggesting that setting our watches to geological time could lessen stress and keep *us* young. "I'll get back to you on that right away—in geological time."

Mornings we snorkeled—an abrupt and effective hangover cure. Commercial fishing is banned in the Galápagos. The island waters are a fish Calcutta. So many giant angelfish appeared that I felt like the bubbling deep-sea diver in the aquarium of a pet store that just can't make a sale. Tiny, silver pizza toppers swam in schools the size of Little Italy. Parrot fish, damselfish, and wrasses exhibited the same obliviousness to our presence as the wave albatross and, mercifully, so did the white-tipped sharks (who'd already gorged themselves, perhaps, on vegetarians). Manta rays in watery flight winged by and had a look, as did gringo fish, so called by the locals because they're pale in the water and turn bright red in the sun.

Back in the Zodiac (and rather pink ourselves) we were told by our guide, "You'll notice the puffer fish is particularly friendly—because it is poisonous."

"Typical," said a Houston hostess who has to endure a lot of political fund-raisers.

Young sea lions came out and dived with us. They did barrel rolls around our torsos, nibbled our swim fins, and played tug-of-war with the Zodiac's lifesaver ring. They are aqua-puppies. On the lava shore of Santiago

Island we saw a little fellow who'd just been born. Like a well-bred American Kennel Club dam, his mother allowed us an up-close look. No one asked, "How do they taste?"

At that evening's fantail colloquium, fly casters asked bird hunters, "Is there a reason we couldn't train sea lions to flush bonefish in the Florida Keys?"

The adult male sea lions, the bulls, wouldn't be much use. They spend their lives guarding a particular stretch of beach from sea lion pool boys, sea lion UPS drivers, etc. Meanwhile their wives come and go as they please. "I tell my clients," said the Dallas lawyer, "just *give* her the house."

Not that our tour group meant to introduce collars and kennels or animal divorce courts into the Galápagos. There's been enough disturbance of nature's balance. Feral goats, let loose by settlers from the mainland, ate the giant tortoise habitat. On the smaller islands the goats have now cashed in their 401(k)s, but Santiago still has tens of thousands. The Charles Darwin Foundation, the World Wide Fund for Nature, and other organizations are spending millions on goat eradication. We volunteered to do it for free. Well, not exactly for free. But give us the goat-hunting rights and we'd sell trips to the Galápagos to wealthy American sportsmen offering unlimited trophy goat opportunities. The Lindblad people looked dubious.

The Galápagos Islands do need assistance, however. The government of Ecuador does its best but is hampered by being, frankly, the government of Ecuador. Send lawyers, guns, and money. Actually, our group had the lawyers and guns. Send just the money to donations@darwinfoundation.org. Think of those giant tortoises. They date back to the age of the dinosaurs. They have movie-star good looks. (*E.T.* was a huge hit.) And there's something about the giant tortoises that's just so . . . so . . . "Extinctable," said Laura. "When life-forms that had more on the ball than dinosaurs arrived, they thought, 'It comes in its own casserole dish!'"

On Santa Cruz Island we saw a few tortoises in the wild. They're easy enough to find, being in exactly the same place they were when the last Lindblad tour came through. Top speed is approximately zero. And we saw a turtle herd at the Charles Darwin Biological Research Station, where a tortoise dating service is attempting to reestablish various subspecies and repopulate the Galápagos. According to research station literature, "When hormonal levels are running high, male tortoises have even been known to try mounting rocks."

"Ugggh, *men*!" said the women in our group.

"Mating is very vigorous," the research station biologist said. He pointed to the last male of the *pinta* subspecies. "We knew that this one was sexually dysfunctional when he copulated for only twenty minutes."

"Ooooo, *turtles*!" said the women.

And then there is the pure beauty of nature in the Galápagos. One afternoon, steaming between islands, we encountered a pod of a thousand dolphins, jumping in undulations, Baryshnikoving above the waves. Even the Buchanan Republicans among us held their breath in awe and thereby briefly honored the Kyoto Protocol on climate change. Out beyond the dolphins was a basking sperm whale, such a magnificent creature that, we all concurred, harming it would be as bad as seeing a SAVE THE WHALES bumper sticker on your congressman's car.

"This trip really *is* educational," said the Dallas lawyer. "Suddenly I want to read *Moby-Dick,* and not the CliffNotes, either."

"And forty years after the fact, I finally understand my statistics class," said George. He was referring to the penguins and flamingos we'd seen the previous day. This is the only place on earth that has both. The Galápagos are on the equator, so they're tropical, but the icy Humboldt Current cools the air, forming a dense foggy mist called a *garúa* that gets everything cold and soaking wet even though the Galápagos are desert islands. The climate is perfect—if you average it. Confusing "average" with "median," as we all did in statistics class, penguins and flamingos both arrived.

I think we were also supposed to be learning something from the famous Darwin finches. But, to tell the truth, they're small, drab, and boring. It is a mark of Darwin's genius that he noticed them at all. Then, by observing the various evolutionary modifications in their little beaks, Darwin somehow discovered that men are descended from monkeys, although he would have known this already if he'd asked the men's wives.

Which goes to show that not all lessons in ecology are edifying. The marine iguana, for example. Washing ashore from the mainland, it learned to go with the flow. It became the only seagoing lizard. It eats nothing but algae. Here is the lizard version of moving to Humboldt County, California, growing your own vegetables, and weaving your clothes from hemp. Marine iguanas are as dull as folk songs and as ugly as unglazed pottery. They spend all day lying on top of each other in big iguana group gropes.

Looking at the marine iguanas, the Dallas lawyer said to his wife, "Honey, do you think we should have left the teenagers home by themselves?"

A Horse of a Different Color

Kyrgyzstan, July 2006

I was standing in the stirrups, stretched over the horse's neck. The reins were clenched in my teeth. I was gripping the mane with my left hand and swinging a quirt with my right, whipping the horse up a steep, grassy mountainside. There were hundreds of feet to climb to the top and a thousand feet to fall to the bottom. It had been raining all night. The grass was slick. Hooves churned. Forelegs milled in the air. Hind legs buckled. The horse was on the verge of flipping backward. And that was the least of my worries.

In the first place, I don't know how to ride. I can't ride a horse up a mountain. I can barely ride a horse at all. Until shortly before doing this impression of Sir Edmund Hillary as Roy Rogers my equestrian experience was limited to going around in circles to calliope music on a pony with a pole through its middle.

In the second place, I was somewhere in Kyrgyzstan. Not only didn't I know what I was doing, I didn't know where I was doing it. And I wasn't in the Westernized, cosmopolitan part of Kyrgyzstan—such as it is—with hospitals and ambulances. I was in the part with no roads, electricity, or cell towers. A satellite phone was in my saddlebag, but I couldn't get a satellite connection. Even by the standards of outer space Kyrgyzstan is remote. If something happened to my horse it would be shot. For me, the medical treatment wouldn't be that sophisticated.

Furthermore, there were blond hairs all over my clothes and luggage. How would I explain this to my redheaded wife? I had a love affair in Kyrgyzstan. Not only that, but with a male. His legs are so beautiful. And he has four of them.

All this began—as such things tend to—over a couple of drinks. I was having them in London with my friend Adrian Dangar, whose surname is only slightly misspelled. Adrian, besides writing about hunting for *The Field,* runs a small, bespoke travel agency called Wild and Exotic. I was telling him that I planned to go to Kyrgyzstan, one of the former Soviet Republics in Central Asia, to write about how, or if, democracy is developing in places with no democratic traditions. This seemed a safer way to investigate the question than going to Fallujah. I was wrong.

"Funny you should mention Kyrgyzstan," Adrian said. He told me that he was organizing a horse trek across the mountains there in the coming summer, with Alexandra Tolstoy and her husband, Shamil Galimzyanov. Alexandra is the great-great-great- (give or take a great-) niece of the author. Though English by birth, she speaks Russian and lives in Moscow. Shamil is a Tartar from Uzbekistan whose family has been training horses since horses were the diminutive things with toes that we see in the Natural History Museum evolution exhibit. Shamil knows the region. So does Alexandra. A few years earlier, she and three girlfriends from college had retraced the Silk Road on horses and camels for five thousand miles from Merve, near the Iranian border, to Xi'an, China.

"We'll have a great trip," said Adrian. "Come along. You'll see parts of Kyrgyzstan the Kyrgyz haven't seen."

"But I can't ride," I said.

Adrian has been riding since he was in utero. He's been Master of Hounds for several particularly neck-breaking foxhunts. He's ridden across the Serengeti and over the Andes. "Nonsense," said Adrian, "a horse trek is just backpacking on someone else's back."

At home in New Hampshire, I told Mrs. O., "I'm taking a horse trek across the mountains of Kyrgyzstan."

"No you're not," she said.

"Come on," I said, "it's not like the mountains of Kyrgyzstan are such a dangerous place."

"No," she said.

"I've been to lots more dangerous places than that."

"No."

"I was a war correspondent for twenty years, for gosh sake."

"You've *been* to a war," Mrs. O. said. "You've never *been* on a horse."

She relented, at last, on the condition that I take some months of riding lessons. This I dutifully did, from a dressage instructor in an indoor ring atop horses named Elmer's and Mucilage. And that is how I ended up in a tent camp in the heights of Central Asia. Kyrgyzstan is a nation the size of South Dakota that's all but lost among the Tian Shan Mountains, the "Heavenly Mountains," that divide China from the trans-Ural steppes. It is north of Kashmir and Afghanistan, beyond the Hindu Kush and the Pamirs, past what even Alexander the Great considered worth conquering. The country is, or might as well be, the "Kafiristan" of Kipling's *The Man Who Would Be*

King. (And, over the next two weeks, my horse would try to crown me with any number of tree branches overhanging our trail.)

A fellow named Djuman Kul, who looked like Genghis Khan and was wearing a felt hat as tall and amazing and elaborately embroidered as anything the pope dons for Easter, was choosing my mount from a herd of wild Kyrgyz horses. They were wild enough, at least, that nobody had bothered to name them. I had been picturing something on the order of a shaggy little Mongolian pony that would let my feet drag reassuringly on the ground. But these horses were fifteen hands high. That is, they were five feet tall at the shoulder, and thin and bony-headed as fashion models but sinewy like a California governor left outdoors to eat grass all winter. And the horses were stallions, with Floyd Landis levels of testosterone. Like Floyd and Tour de France officials, they were kicking and biting each other.

Djuman Kul led the lone palomino forward. He told me in Kyrgyz, Shamil translating, "This horse is strong, but kind." I wish I had not overheard Djuman telling each of the other trekkers, "This horse is strong, but kind."

I dubbed the horse "Trigger" and hopped aboard. There is a trick to this. You turn the left stirrup backward, place your left foot in it, and, springing with your right leg, swing yourself up so that you . . . slam your whole body smack into the side of the horse. Shamil helped me up. I had an excellent, if precarious, view of Kyrgyzstan. It looks like the American West. Not the dry-gulch western-movie American West (for which I had, without long underwear or adequate rain gear, packed), but the whole West—purple mountain majesties, fruited plain, noble forest spires, canyons as grand as grand can be, packed into one place with about as much sign of human habitation as Lewis and Clark saw. (Sacagawea, please go to the satellite phone.) It would have taken my breath away if I hadn't been too scared to breathe.

Not that Trigger was giving me much to be scared of. Per my riding lessons, I assumed a proper "seat," placing the balls of my feet on the stirrup treads with heels down and foot, hip, and shoulder aligned. I held the reins low, threaded over my pinkies and up into my hands, "carried like two flutes of champagne," as I'd been taught. I felt for the correct gentle contact with Trigger's bit. I applied a subtle pressure with my lower legs and gave the reins the requisite slight flick. Trigger stood there. I tried all of the above a little more forcefully. Trigger stood there. I tried more forcefully yet. Trigger stood even more there. Everyone else was riding away. Djuman Kul handed me the quirt. He pantomimed a ferocious Patrick O'Brian novel shipboard lashing. It is one thing to beat a miscreant of about one's own size who has been firmly tied to a mast. Beating a nine-hundred-pound critter that could buck you to China and run over there before you landed and then kick and bite you is another. Trigger received the sort of spanking that a six-year-old gets on a birthday. He ambled off, thankfully in the right direction.

That direction was onto the middle of a bridge over a small but Napoleonic mountain stream. I'd noticed the bridge earlier. What I'd noticed was that I wouldn't care to cross it on foot. It was made of several logs arranged like the losing turn in a game of pick-up-sticks. I cared a lot less to cross it on six feet, two of which had come out of their stirrups.

"Trust the horse!" Shamil yelled. "Let the horse do the thinking!" It is an experience, the first time you stake your life on a brain to which you wouldn't assign the simplest task such as keeping the lawn short without destroying the flower beds. I endured a mortal version of the fear my wife feels whenever she sees me on the rider mower.

On the other side of the bridge was a cliff, 500 or 600 feet high. The horses went right up it. Trigger found each tiny notch in the rocks by feeling around with his horseshoe as though he were typing a blog. Then, when his posting seemed to be put strongly enough—DEATH TO REPUBLICANS ON OUR BACKS!!!—he pressed "send." I didn't die, because there was always one part of Trigger that held still enough for desperate clinging to. His withers were firmly planted as his backside fluttered in the breeze. His loins stayed solid while everything up front gyrated in scree.

Trigger climbed hoof-over-hoof. And here was an excellent idea for yuppie sports marketing, if I survived, horseback climbing walls. Indoor facilities could be built in Southampton, Palm Beach, and Beverly Hills. A rider and steed, in one big harness, are top-roped and belayed by a dozen climbing coaches. "Left rear hoof on the red hoofhold," shouts the climbing coach. "Hook your right front pastern over the blue. Don't look down!"

Or up. Because at the top of the cliff there was no top. There was more and steeper cliff. Traversing this was a path the width of a dollar bill. The landscape had been turned 180 degrees. The horizon was viewed by ignoring the climbing coach's advice.

I don't own a hunting cap, and I wasn't about to show up in Kyrgyzstan wearing my daughter Poppet's pink Hello Kitty bicycle helmet. Now I saw that headgear was necessary only to preserve enough dental work to make the corpse identifiable. I rode with one stirrup banging against the cliff face like the knell of doom and the other a footrest on the bottomless pit.

Beyond the cliff were forest glades of the kind that, at an American ski resort, put an end to Michael Kennedy. He had it easy. The wet clay of Kyrgyzstan is deeper and faster than Rocky Mountain powder and Trigger is more self-willed than any pair of Rossignols. We went up, which was bad; then down, which was worse. Plummeting through a boulder-choked chute, there were times when Trigger was beyond vertical, when my boot heels were out past his ears, and, no, I didn't need a haircut, that was Trigger's tail flopping over my face.

After nine hours we reached camp on the Arkit Sai River. Shamil and Alexandra have two seven-ton, six-wheel-drive ex-military trucks, surplus from the Soviet Union's Afghan war. One is rigged as a kitchen and the other carries the gear. A camp staff of half a dozen rode in these down logging skids and sheep tracks and across country to meet us each evening. Tents were up. Latrines had been dug. A table was set with a line of vodka bottles down the middle. A local lamb was roasting. And I was splayed on the riverbank reveling in my good fortune. I wasn't dead. And I wasn't dead in a magnificent place. And I magnificently wasn't dead among splendid people, whom I've neglected to mention because I've been too busy being scared.

There were fourteen of us, including Adrian, Alexandra, and Shamil. It was such an intrepid cast of characters on such a thrilling journey during which I got beaten to such a pulp that introductions may be made according to pulp thriller conventions.

Andrew Stott—senior executive for Nestlé, UK, master of camp craft and avid foxhunter, who could lead a charge of the Light Brigade every bit as well as he charges (quite reasonably) for coffee and cocoa.

Ettie Boyd—superb athlete and corporate headhunter, the horsewoman who saved me from my own "Into the Valley of Death" experience by tactfully pointing out that whipping Trigger while yanking on his reins was making him as confused and stupid as . . .

"Me?" I suggested.

Claire Morrissey—North Dublin colleen possessed of the Irish way with dumb animals, sits on a horse with the same aplomb and authority as Tip O'Neill sat in the House of Representatives (but cuts a much finer figure).

Jennie Crohill—Norfolk countrywoman and seemingly an unassuming farm inspector for the British government but actually the hero who shot the last feral coypu in England. (It would sound more thrillerish if I left that unexplained, but a coypu is a nutria, a giant South American aquatic rat with a body two feet long. They were raised for fur, escaped, bred in the wild, and were playing merry hell with the Norfolk marshes.)

Bahar Ghaffari—exquisite Persian miniature, looks nineteen but is a Master of the Universe investment banker in Hong Kong, juggling equity derivatives so complex they make Alan Greenspan's head throb.

Camilla Coventry—raised on a ranch in Australia, but she and Crocodile Dundee are from the outback the way Lauren Bacall and Mel Brooks are from New York. Studied theater and can produce and direct *Annie Get Your Gun* and do all the stunt work, too.

Jean Baptiste Oldenhove de Guertechin and Gaetane Schaeken Willemaers, Belgians with educations as elaborate as their names. He a global management consultant with a degree in civil engineering and an MBA from the Wharton School of Business. She an international finance lawyer and the former counsel to Belgium's minister of foreign affairs. They are on their honeymoon.

Harold van Lier—another Belgian, a movie producer turned hotelier because guest towels have more wit than entertainment executives. He is on his honeymoon as well.

Emily—Harold's beautiful English bride, a relief worker specializing in third world sanitation problems (of which I was one at the moment). She has given up international aid work to come to the aid of, well, people such as ourselves, at the Grand Hotel des Bains in Brittany. As the name implies, it has plenty of sanitation.

"In your article about Kyrgyzstan," said Harold, "you must not use the term 'tour group.' It is as if we had silly Americans along in pink Hello Kitty bicycle helmets. None of us would ever join a 'tour group.' We are a 'tour horde.' We will sweep down upon Samarkand, Bukhara, and Tashkent and pillage . . . since some of us are Belgians . . . their chocolate and lace."

"You had better have another vodka," said Shamil, "because tomorrow the riding becomes difficult."

We rode through the village of Kizel Kel', where Djuman Kul and our horses were from. A lone electrical wire and a notional road connected it to the world. And even this much civilization the Kyrgyz leave, spring through fall, to graze their herds in the mountain pastures. Stay-behind women and kids and the eighty-year-old blacksmith (who had "about forty" grandchildren) came out to say hello and feed us apricot jam.

We went up into a cartoon-beautiful forest, climbing with animation—feature-length animation—through Shrek-colored fern glades with sunlight pixilating in the tree leaves. Irish Claire herself had never seen anything so green. We emerged to a view that looked even less real and left me faint with a wish that it weren't. We were on a scythe blade of a ridge, thousands of feet in the air. Snowcapped mountains loomed, but they loomed below us. We could see rivers, in extremely small scale—threads of blue monofilament. Milewide turquoise lakes glinted minutely, beads lost in a shag rug. We were at the top of the Chakal range of the Tian Shan, above everything.

Above almost everything. Obese thunderheads materialized on top of us. Jovian flatulence erupted. The sky would have been black if it hadn't been bright orange with lightning. Gaetane's curly hair stood on end, making a nimbus three times the size of her head.

"It is an interesting phenomenon, an effect of ionization," said Jean Baptiste.

"You look like Medusa," said Harold, "But much prettier, of course, and without the snakes."

"@#$%! GET DOWN!" screamed the nervous person from a country with frequently toasted golfers.

The best we could do was a thicket of stunted trees with a lush undergrowth of stinging nettles. It poured. It blew. The temperature dropped thirty degrees. The nettles were enjoyed by the horses. Ettie and Claire got under their mounts. This, if you've seen a horse relieve itself, was a calculated risk of a worse wetting. Camilla said, "I know what—*The Sound of Music.*"

The hills are alive with the sound of . . .

KA-BOOM

"@#$%! GET DOWN!"

Doe, a deer, a female deer,

Ray, a drop of golden . . .

KA-BOOM

"@#$%! GET DOWN!"

The path descending from the ridge was washed out. Shamil found a crevasse leading . . . somewhere. It was too muck-sunk and brush-filled to ride. We had to lead the horses. An enormous creature is behind you, threatening at every moment to add the mud luge to the list of Olympic equestrian events. Taking a fall on a horse is just a matter of one's own slobby body mass index hitting the ground. It is not to be compared to having a horse take a fall on you. There were places where leading was impossible. We had to jump and slide on our own, then call the horses like dogs, asking them to perform stunts that Lassie would have left Timmy down the well rather than attempt.

Trigger, who'd shown no previous inclination to obey, or even notice, me turned petlike and followed with puppyish devotion. The crevasse opened into a gorge, and the gorge opened into a canyon, and once, when he and I were stuck on a ledge, Trigger gave me a little nudge away from the abyss. (Though it's possible Trigger is dyslexic and was pushing in the wrong direction.)

The rain kept on and so did we, in a trail-breaking slog until our spirits had descended as far as we had. And there on the canyon floor were our trucks. Using a frayed old Soviet topo map, drivers Valeri and Andrei had guessed where we might emerge. The cook, Tyota Vera, and her helpers Nadia and Lyuda had a hot meal ready. A tarp was stretched over the table.

"You had better have another vodka," said Shamil, "because tomorrow the riding becomes *very* difficult."

It did. We climbed three thousand feet up a slope like a graph of crude oil prices to have lunch with the shepherds of Kizel Kel'. Their yurts are streamlined for the mountain winds—Airstream trailers made of felt but with more spacious and contemporary open-plan interiors. We ate yogurt and little balls of goat cheese fermented in burlap sacks hanging outside the yurts, and we drank the whey that dripped from the bags. The Kyrgyz bring little with them by way of provisions except their livestock. There was a lot of gawking, mostly from the Kyrgyz. Being nomads, they are sightseers themselves, and after a wet night in camp and a long ride we were a sight. Emily, with her background in relief work, was relieved to see no relief was needed. The camp's three families and their fourteen kids were smiling and fit. Either they lead much healthier lives than we do or they roll their sick down the hill. I imagined the size of the saddlebag needed to carry to the mountaintop my family's sunblock, bug spray, asthma inhalers, orthodontic retainers, vitamins, dietary supplements, and bottles of shampoo and conditioner formulated to correct high-altitude dryness and split ends.

We rode out through a canyon with walls that will dwarf the luxury resort that is going to be built there someday, through clouds of blue butterflies where the parking lot will be, and under a natural bridge, naming rights available. The striated sediment in the sandstone cliffs had been bent by mountain building into a gargantuan taffy pull. Owners of leisure homes will be sure to frame this view in the master suite's Palladian window. Hundreds of feet up, ibex skittered across the openings of unexplored caves. Unexplored cave tours at ten, noon, and two. Shamil, reconnoitering the canyon on foot a month before, had seen a Tian Shan brown bear and the spoor of a snow leopard. Call the concierge for safari bus reservations.

"This canyon is one vast herbaceous border," said Jennie, standing by a yard-wide clump of irises and naming a dozen other plants. "All these have to be so carefully tended in England, and here they just grow."

"Herbaceous Boarder" is a clever name for the upscale bed-and-breakfast that will cater to the more ecologically conscious visitors.

We vilified progress all the way to our cooked meal, distilled beverages, and double-walled synthetic fabric expedition tents. The river at the mouth of the canyon will survive—sweeping fly fishermen and kayakers straight to perdition. We tried to take a bath in it. Ettie had the guts to go first, lowering herself into water the temperature of decompressing Freon and being beaten by the roil of pebbles in the current. "Yow," she said, "this is worse than a spa. You know, there are people who pay thousands for things like this."

"Us among them," said Andrew.

We rode for two days through the Chakal Range's meadow fairways, not one of them less than a par ninety-nine. Golf would be a more exciting sport if it had been invented by the Kyrgyz instead of the Scots. You'd hit a horse instead of a ball, and it would be you that would wind up in a hole in the ground, six feet under if you weren't careful.

Being careful on Trigger wasn't hard. The other horses were galloping around. But for Trigger, as for many of the world's great beauties, being beautiful was a career. Doing anything else that he didn't have to was a waste of his valuable talents. Trigger would go where the other horses went with a Kate Moss vacuity. But out on his own, on open ground, he'd prance, flare his nostrils, arch his neck nobly, gaze at the fields of wildflowers, and eat them.

Trigger and I were married or—I'll have to check the laws of Kyrgyzstan on this point—joined in a civil union. Anyway, there I was on top going "Yes, Dear." Of course the other riders were skilled and accomplished. Although some of them said they weren't.

"I haven't ridden since I was a kid," said Bahar.

"Bahar," I said, "you *are* a kid."

"Jean Baptiste has spent only two hours before on a horse," said Gaetane. Jean Baptiste blushed with modest embarrassment at being a natural athlete and quick study.

I am neither. And I'm pushing sixty with a short stick. And I was chafed and sore in surprising places. In unsurprising places, too. Do not wear jeans on a hundred-some-mile ride through a graduate course in geography. You'll have permanent raised seams right where Levi's do. But I was also rubbed raw in my belly button from where the pommel of my saddle had dug into my gut going uphill and in the small of my back from where the saddle's cantle had caught me going downhill, and the bottoms of my feet ached because I'd been unconsciously pressing on the stirrups with an old automobile driver's instinctive hope that one of these things was the brake. Yet every night, after half a bottle of vodka or so, I became a brilliant rider. In fact we all became generally brilliant. Adrian and Andrew figured out exactly where Osama bin Laden was hiding—in the unexplored cave where we'd seen the ibex. They trapped him there, put an end to terrorism, and forged a lasting peace in the Middle East, although they were somewhat fuzzy on the details the next morning.

Jean Baptiste discovered that he could play the guitar. Camilla staged a production of *Grease*, complete with choreography.

Tell me more. Tell me more.
Did you get sore, of course?
Tell me more. Tell me more.
Like, does he have a horse?

A week into our trip we awoke below the mountain where Trigger would experience near-gymnastics. It stood at the end of a seemingly endless meadow. Blossoms of clouds drifted down from its peak on sunbeam stems arranged in an urn of celadon mist, or something like that. It was a scene to make me wax as florid as the nature poets of the Romantic era, although, compared with Kyrgyzstan, the Lake District of England looks like a rest stop on I-95.

"I think," said Shamil, "when we die this is what we see."

I'm glad to say that's not the means by which I saw it. Trigger didn't tumble. We made it to the top. And I could ride Trigger after all. He didn't change direction with leg pressure. It was reins on his neck that made him turn. The quirt was no punishment, just a memo from middle management. I couldn't post; that is, I couldn't rise rhythmically with Trigger's trot. His gait was too much like a hoppy toad's. But I could canter if I kept my mind—and my behind—on what I was doing.

And I had other epiphanies up there. I wasn't scared. I was still a coward, but I'd run out of fear. The grassy slope had depleted my proven reserves of trepidation, vast as they were. I'd also run out of adjectives. My ability to describe was as exhausted as my ability to worry. We went through a bunch-of-superlatives countryside down to a highly-evocative-metaphor valley and on to our campsite that was, oh, darn nice.

Except there was no camp. The trucks and the crew weren't there. The rain had been causing landslides on their routes. Alexandra's horse had gone lame and she'd ridden in one of the trucks that day. Shamil was grim with worry. It began to rain again. There was no food. Our canteens were empty. The sun set. It rained harder.

Miles down the valley was a government forestry station, intermittently occupied. The horses were worn out. We hobbled them and began to walk. The flashlights were with the camping gear.

Hours later, at that moment in a cold, wet, dark hike to an uncertain destination when the soul cries out for a cozy office cubicle and a job making unsolicited dinnertime phone calls asking people to switch their cable service, Alexandra appeared. Indeed there had been a landslide. She and the camp staff carried the supplies and equipment to the other side of the debris. They commandeered a logging truck. And they brought, thank God, the vodka.

The weather cleared the next day and so, eventually, did our heads. We rode on through mountains, fields, and forests. The Mongols and the Huns and Shamil's ancestors must have felt like this. They didn't really mean to overrun the known world and sack it; they just didn't want to stop riding.

And one afternoon on the banks of a lake called the Sary Chelek, the "Golden Bowl," I galloped Trigger. A real gallop with all hooves—and not me!—launched in the air. We ran for a mile and a half along the lakeside. We were a centaur. Trigger was Pegasus. I was Alexander on Bucephalus, conquering Kyrgyzstan after all.

Now I know what it is to be a *chevalier,* to be the Man on Horseback. I'm making the patio into a paddock. I'm building a stable in the garage. I'm getting Trigger a green card. I'm learning to jump so I can go foxhunting.

There are plenty of foxes just an hour and a half away from my house, in the suburbs of Boston. And a hell of a hunt it will be because every hedge has a swimming pool on the other side. I wear my new jodhpurs around the house, and all that I talk is horse sense.

"One small sore butt for man," says Mrs. O. "One giant pain in the ass for mankind."

A Journey to . . . Let's Not Go There

Summer 2008

Part 1

I looked death in the face. All right, I didn't. I glimpsed him in a crowd. I was diagnosed with cancer, of a very treatable kind. I'm told I have a 95 percent chance of survival. Come to think of it—as a drinking, smoking, saturated-fat-hound of a reporter—my chance of survival has been improved by cancer.

I still cursed God, as we all do when we get bad news and pain. Not even the most faith-impaired among us shouts, "Damn quantum mechanics!" "Damn organic chemistry!" "Damn chaos and coincidence!"

I believe in God. God created the world. Obviously pain had to be included in God's plan. Otherwise we'd never learn that our actions have consequences. Our cave-dwelling ancestors, finding fire warm, would conclude that curling up to sleep in the middle of the flames would be even warmer. Cave bears would dine on roast ancestor, and we'd never experience any pain because we wouldn't be here.

But God, Sir, in Your manner of teaching us about life's consequential nature, isn't death a bit . . . um . . . extreme, pedagogically speaking? I know the lesson that we're studying is difficult. But dying is a harder final exam than I was counting on. Also, it kind of messes up my vacation planning. Can we talk after class? Maybe if I did something for extra credit . . .

Seeing things from God's point of view is difficult for a mortal. The more so for a mortal who's just received an updated mortality scheduling memo from the pathology department.

Seeing things from God's point of view is the purpose of conventional religion, in my opinion. And I am a conventionally religious person. But I feel the need to think through a few things before I unload my gripes on Father Hoolihan. He's got a busy parish and he isn't as young as he used to be. In fact Father Hoolihan doesn't look well himself. Perhaps, if I can get my thoughts straight, he can unload his gripes on me. I can't give him last rites, but I can give him a whiskey.

Why can't death—if we must have it—be always glorious, as in *The Iliad*? Of course death continues to be so, sometimes, with our military heroes in Fallujah and Kandahar. But nowadays death more often comes drooling on the toilet seat in the nursing home or bleeding under the crushed roof of a teen-driven SUV or breathless in a deluxe hotel suite filled with empty drug bottles and a minor public figure whose celebrity expiration date has passed. I have, of all the inglorious things, a malignant hemorrhoid. What color bracelet does one wear for that? And where does one wear it? And what slogan is apropos? Perhaps that slogan can be sewn in needlepoint around the ruffle on a cover for my embarrassing little doughnut buttocks pillow.

Furthermore, I am a logical, sensible, pragmatic Republican, and my diagnosis came just weeks after Teddy Kennedy's. That *he* should have cancer of the brain, and *I* should have cancer of the ass . . . Well, I said a rosary for him and hoped he had a laugh at me. After all, what would I do, ask God for a more dignified cancer? Pancreas? Liver? Lung?

Which brings me to the nature of my prayers. They are, like most prayers from most people, abject self-pleadings. But praying for oneself has disturbing implications. There's Saint Teresa's warning about answered prayers or, for our atheistic friends, the tale of "The Monkey's Paw."

And I can't be the only person who feels like a jerk saying, "Please cure me, God. I'm underinsured. I have three little children. And I have three dogs, two of which will miss me. And my wife will cry and mourn and be inconsolable and have to get a job. P.S. Our mortgage is subprime."

God knows this stuff. He's God. He's all-knowing. What am I telling Him, really? "Gosh, You sure are a good God. Good—You own it. Plus, You're infinitely wise, infinitely merciful, but . . . Look, everybody makes mistakes. A little cancer of the behind, it's not a big mistake. Not something that's going on Your personal record. Let's not think of it as a mistake. Let's think of it as a teachable moment. Nobody's so good that He or She can't improve, so . . ."

It's one universe, entire, God's creation and all of a piece. There's a theory about how the fluttering of a butterfly's wing can somehow eventually cause a cyclone in the Bay of Bengal or something like that. What if the flatulence of me in a radiation therapy session eventually causes . . . I mean, suppose Saint Peter had my fax number and faxed me: "P.J., we did the math. We can get you a 100 percent survival rate instead of 95 percent, but twenty years from now a volcanic eruption in Honduras will kill 700,000 people." What do I fax back? "Dear Saint Peter, Thank God. That's a real shame about Honduras. I promise I'll donate $1,000 to the International Red Cross."

I think I'll pray for fortitude instead and, maybe, for relief from gas.

No doubt death is one of those mysterious ways in which God famously works. Except, upon consideration, death isn't mysterious. Do we really want *everyone* to be around *forever*? I'm thinking about my own family, specifically a certain stepfather I had as a kid. Sayonara, you SOB. On the other hand, Napoleon was doubtless a great man in his time; at least the French think so. But do we want even Napoleon extant in perpetuity? Do we want him always escaping from island exiles, raising fanatically loyal troops of soldiers, invading Russia, and burning Moscow? Well, at the moment, considering Putin et al., maybe. But, century after century, it would get old. And what with Genghis Khan coming from the other direction all the time and Alexander the Great clashing with a Persia that is developing nuclear weapons and Roman legions destabilizing already precarious Israeli-Palestinian relations—things would be a mess.

Then there's the matter of our debt to death for life as we know it. I believe in God. I also believe in evolution. If death weren't around to "finalize" the Darwinian process, we'd all still be amoebas. We'd eat by surrounding pizzas with our belly flab and have sex by lying on railroad tracks waiting for a train to split us into significant others. I consider evolution to be more than a scientific theory. I think it's a call to God. God created a free universe. He could have created any kind of universe He wanted. But a universe without freedom would have been static and meaningless—a taxpayer-funded-art-in-public-places universe.

Rather, God created a universe full of cosmic whatchamajiggers and subatomic whosits free to interact. And interact they did, becoming matter and organic matter and organic matter that replicated itself and life. And this life was completely free, as amoral as my cancer cells.

Life-forms could exercise freedom to an idiotic extent, growing uncontrolled, thoughtless, and greedy to the point that they killed the source of their own fool existence. But, with the help of death, matter began to learn right from wrong—how to save itself and its ilk, how to nurture, how to love (or, anyway, how to build a Facebook page), and how to know God and His rules.

Death is so important that God visited death upon His own Son, thereby helping us learn right from wrong well enough that we may escape death forever and live eternally in God's grace. (Although this option is not usually open to reporters.)

I'm not promising that the pope will back me up about all of the above. But it's the best I can do by my poor lights about the subject of mortality and free will. Thus, the next time I glimpse death . . . Well, I'm not going over and introduce myself. I'm not giving the grim reaper fist dibs. But I'll remind myself to try, at least, to thank God for death. And then I'll thank God, with all my heart, for whiskey.

Part 2

A diagnosis of cancer raises deep metaphysical questions such as, "Is God a nice guy?" and "Will my bird dog go to heaven or do I flush the quail of paradise with seraphim, cherubim, and putti?"

But after a while diagnosis wears off. It's time for an intermission in the self-dramatization of "I Have a Life-Threatening Disease." I wasn't able to play the role to its full tragical effect anyway. The kind of cancer I had was too treatable and too ridiculous.

It's not every time you get diagnosed with cancer and it makes you laugh. I'd had a hemorrhoid operation (possibly not unconnected to my horseback journey through Kyrgyzstan). Two days later the colorectal surgeon called. "I'm sorry to tell you," he said, "your hemorrhoid was malignant."

"Malignant hemorrhoid?" I said. "There's no such thing as a malignant hemorrhoid."

"In almost every case you'd be right," the surgeon said and paused in a moment of sympathetic hesitation and of unintentional comic timing. "But . . ."

I laughed but I wanted to argue. "Malignant hemorrhoid" is something somebody gets called on Rush Limbaugh talk radio. "Malignant Hemorrhoid" is a Dave Barry rock band. But I still had to get treated. Going from the metaphysical to the all-too-physical reminded me of my gratitude to God. You have immediate access to the top specialist in all fields when you pray. (Do polytheists have difficulties with this?) Plus I had the good fortune to be in Washington, D.C.—a city full of flaccid old guys like myself who spend their time blowing smoke out of you-know-where and being full of you-know-what and sitting on their duffs. Consequently the town is full of medical expertise about the body part in question.

It turns out what I had was a skin cancer, squamous cell carcinoma. Practically every melanin-deficient (let alone Irish) person who spends time in the sun gets this if he or she lives long enough. "I call it 'adult acne' when it turns up on the face or arms," the oncologist said. But why it occasionally turns up where it turned up on me is something of a medical mystery. I mean, I was naked a lot in the 1960s but not *that* naked.

There's a considerable loss of dignity involved in trading the awe-inspiring fear of death for the perspiration-inducing fear of treatment. There are hells on earth. Until a generation ago the cure for anal cancer was a colostomy. Doctors have gotten over that. Most of the time. Now, with God's grace, the cure is radiation and chemotherapy. Would I have to go to some purgatorial place for this? To Sloan-Kettering in New York, a city I detest? Or out to the Mayo Clinic, although I have a phobia about hospitals named after sandwich toppings? "No," the oncologist said. "The treatment protocol is standardized and is successfully used everywhere."

I named my local New Hampshire hospital (and large animal veterinary clinic).

"Almost everywhere," the oncologist said.

I asked about the Dartmouth-Hitchcock Medical Center, ninety miles from my home but still on the planet New Hampshire. Dr. Marc Pipas at Dartmouth-Hitchcock's Norris Cotton Cancer Center came strongly recommended. Dr. Pipas is an avid bird hunter and an advocate of reintroducing the prairie chicken to the Eastern Seaboard. So he and I had something to talk about in addition to my behind. I'd need radiation therapy every day for six weeks. (Every day, that is, Monday through Friday—the radiology department has to play golf, too.) And I would undergo two four-day stints of around-the-clock chemotherapy, carrying a fanny pack of poisonous chemicals to be pumped into my body through a surgically implanted mediport. (Dr. Pipas persuaded the infusions department to install this on the left side of my chest so that it wouldn't interfere with mounting a shotgun.)

In theory I could get my radiation treatments elsewhere, within easy commuting distance. But it's worthwhile to find out what a doctor himself would do if he had your medical problem. And he probably thinks he does. Several doctor friends have told me you can't get through medical school without being convinced that you have every disease in the textbooks, including elephantiasis, beriberi, and guinea worm infestation. Dr. Pipas immediately said that, for anal cancer, he'd go to the radiologist Dr. Bassem Zaki at Dartmouth-Hitchcock's Norris Cotton Cancer Center.

Dr. Zaki is a Coptic Christian who immigrated from Egypt in his late teens. He and I talked about Middle Eastern politics, which, as far as I'm concerned, is the second most interesting blood sport after upland-game shooting.

Dartmouth-Hitchcock Medical Center is a sparkling edifice, full of light and air and surprisingly good art for a nonprofit institution. The architectural style is higgledy-piggledy 1980s modern—2 million square feet, every one of which is between you and where you have an appointment. Finding your way around is a trial run for Alzheimer's but a small price to pay for the pleasant surroundings. Even the food in the cafeteria is good. Various scientific studies have shown that patients recover better and faster in cheerful environments. Duh.

The staff at DHMC is also cheerful, but not *too* cheerful. The staff members don't make you feel like a small child at the receiving end of an overambitious preschool curriculum. Perhaps they know better because DHMC is a teaching hospital. The Dartmouth Medical School is the fourth-oldest in the nation, founded in 1797. DHMC is venerable as well as modern. But not *too* venerable. It doesn't use leeches.

Being at a teaching hospital puts a patient in a comfortable equation with the institution. People are expecting to learn something from you, not just do something to you. But let's not push the idea of equality too far. There's a current notion that you should "take charge of your disease." No thanks. I'm busy. I've got cancer. I'm willing to face having cancer. I'm not willing to face having cancer with homework. I promised Dr. Pipas and Dr. Zaki that I wouldn't show up with sheaves of printouts from the Internet containing everything on Wikipedia about malignancies. They each laughed with detectable notes of relief. (Although I suspect my wife has made her way into the health blog ether. Fish oil pills, raw kelp, and other untoward substances started showing up on the dinner plates after I was diagnosed.)

Dr. Pipas and Dr. Zaki combined had something like half a century of medical experience. God wants us to have faith in what we can't see. Therefore He certainly wants us to have faith in what we can. I could see the diplomas on the doctors' office walls.

"I've got cancer" is more than an excuse for rational ignorance about medicine. It's an excuse for everything. From niece's wedding to daughter's piano recital to IRS audit, you're off the hook. I even tried my excuse on the pope. I couldn't go to Mass because of the effect that germ-swapping Vatican II "sign of peace" handshakes could have on my radiation-weakened immune system. And I continued to employ cancer as an excuse until an exasperated spouse finally shouted, "You're curable! You *can too* put your dirty dishes in the sink!"

The radiation treatments weren't bad—twenty minutes propped on a machine in a humiliating posture. Most of me was exposed and the nurses were embarrassingly pretty. But it's interesting, the connection that physical modesty has with physical vanity. Once past sixty you can reasonably abandon both. This was one of the life lessons with which having cancer abounds. I hate life lessons. Consider all the I-hope-you've-learned-your-lesson experiences: skinned knees, high school romances, wreckage of dad's car, flunked college courses, horrible hangovers, failed marriages. I tell my children, "Avoid life lessons. The more important the lesson, the more you should avoid it."

The chemotherapy was worse than the radiation. The pump in the fanny pack of poisonous chemicals made a whining whirr every minute or so—not frequently enough to get used to and too frequently to let me sleep. A long plastic tube that attached the fanny pack to my mediport allowed me to bury the pump and its noise in a mound of pillows. But then I'd forget that I was connected. As with all attempts to forget one's troubles, I was courting disaster. I'd get up in the middle of the night to go to the bathroom and be yanked back to the mattress by the tubing. The fanny pack came with a bag of protective clothing and instructions for dealing with chemical spills. According to these instructions I was supposed to do, by myself, what the entire U.S. government had done during the 2002 national anthrax panic.

The cumulative effects of the treatments were unpleasant. The loss of my previously full, thick head of ungrayed hair met with no sympathy from my age cohort of males. I developed fatigue, mouth sores, and a rash around my loins as if I'd been dressed in nothing but hip boots and an Eisenhower jacket and turned on a spit in a tanning salon. Suffering makes us question God. My question was: What evolutionary purpose does the itch serve? Indeed, an itch may be an argument for intelligent design. Maybe we itch not for biological purposes but to give us a moral lesson about surrendering to our strongest passions. I had the strongest passion to scratch certain parts of my body. If, however, I had scratched these parts of my body near a school or playground, I would be sent to jail.

Dr. Pipas, Dr. Zaki, and the Dartmouth-Hitchcock staff were attentive to my complaints and gave me generous doses of things to turn complaints into complaisance. But I was nagged by a concern about the quality of my medical care. Was it too good? I'm well insured and passably affluent. I asked Jason Aldous, Dartmouth-Hitchcock's media relations manager, "What if I weren't?"

"We're a charitable institution," Aldous said. "No one will ever be refused care here. On the other hand, we have to keep the lights on. We do try to find any possible means of payment—government programs, private insurance, et cetera."

The hospital has a whole department devoted to that. "In about sixty percent of cases," Aldous said, "people who think they aren't eligible for any assistance actually are." Then there are the people who have income but no savings, or assets but no income. Discounts are provided and payment plans worked out. Failing all else, treatment is simply given free—$63 million worth in 2007.

I asked Aldous about who gets what treatment from which doctor. Do your means affect the hospital's ways?

"The doctors," he said, "don't know how—or if—you're paying."

What Jason Aldous told me seemed true from what I could see of the hospital's patients, a cross section of Yankees, flinty and otherwise. The Norris Cotton Cancer Center alone treats more than five thousand people a year. And we were all amiable in the waiting rooms. Anytime someone new came in and sat down he or she was tacitly invited to spend about three minutes telling everyone what was wrong. Then the conversation was expected to return to general topics. The general topic of choice during the summer of 2008 was how the Democrats would destroy the private health care system that was saving our lives. When medicine was socialized we'd have to sit in waiting rooms forever, if we lived. (The exception to the three-minute rule was for a child patient. Then there was unlimited interest and upbeat chat.)

In my case at least, the amiability had something to do with painkilling drugs, of which I was on plenty. Opiates are a blessing—and a revelation. Now when I see people on skid row nodding in doorways I am forced to question myself. Have they, maybe, chosen a reasonable response to their condition in life? Being addicted to drugs is doubtless a bad plan for the future, but having cancer also lets you off the hook about taking long-term views.

I'm sure that various holy martyrs and pious ascetics will disagree, but I saw no point to adding suffering to my suffering. And I can't say I had a sign from God that I should, at least not if God was speaking through my old friend Greg Grip.

Greg was baching it in a cottage on Lake Mascoma, fifteen minutes from Dartmouth-Hitchcock. He's divorced and his college-age daughter was away at a summer job. "I'm not saying you can stay at the cottage while you get treated," Greg said. "I'm saying I will be deeply offended if you don't."

Dr. Zaki arranged my radiation treatments, late on Monday afternoons and early on Friday mornings. My wife and children were spared self-pitiful weekday grousings. And I missed them, so I was on good behavior over weekends.

Greg is a splendid Weber grill cook. Charcoal fires produce carcinogens, but the chemotherapy had that covered. Dr. Pipas said I could have one measured Scotch each evening. But he failed to specify the measure. I think the pint is a fine old measure, although the liter is more up-to-date.

I couldn't tolerate the sun, but Greg's cottage is on the southwest shore of Mascoma. The patio was in shade all afternoon. I read a lot, mostly histories of World War II concerning the Russian front. Everyone on the Russian front in World War II was having it worse than I was.

Tony Snow, the former Bush administration press secretary, wrote an essay about dying from colon cancer. Tony said that the sense of mortality promoted "the ability to sit back and appreciate the wonder of every created thing." Every created thing put on a wonderful show for me at Lake Mascoma. A family of mergansers with six ducklings was living under the dock. A pair of mallards had taken up residence in the shrubbery. Beavers swam up and down the lake; I don't know why—Mascoma has a concrete dam. There were bird sightings—hawks, turkey vultures, kingfishers, a bald eagle, even an extremely wayward pelican. A hummingbird visited the patio every evening. Skinny-dipping sightings were also made at a nature reserve across the lake. Water skiers and Jet Ski riders took amusing falls. Not to engage in the pathetic fallacy, but the weather itself was kind and cool. Greg's pointer Weezy slept on my bed each night, though this may have had less to do with doggy compassion than the fact that Greg won't let her sleep on his. Weezy's dulcet snoring drowned out the chemo fanny pack pump.

I'm doing fine now. Anal cancer can be invasive, but mine seems to have had a wimpy EU-style foreign policy. The cancer is gone, as far as can be told. I still have a colonoscopy to worry about and a CAT scan to dread and six-month checkups to fret over. I'll be okay. Or I won't. Or I'll go through it all again.

This summer was not the worst summer of my life—loving family, kind friends, skilled and considerate care, a big warm dog in the bed. The worst summer of my life was forty years ago when I was young and healthy and didn't have a care in the world. But there was this girl, and a novel that refused to write itself, and anomie, and angst, and weltschmerz . . . Nothing brings us closer to God than age and illness. I only hope the Almighty doesn't mind having nothing but sick old people around.

The Seventy-Two-Hour Afghan Expert

Kabul, July 2010

If you spend seventy-two hours in a place you've never been, talking to people whose language you don't speak about social, political, and economic complexities you don't understand, and you come back as the world's biggest know-it-all, you're a reporter. What do you want to know about Afghanistan, past, present, or future? Ask me anything.

As all good reporters do, I prepared for my assignment with extensive research. I went to an Afghan restaurant in Prague. Getting a foretaste—as it were—of my subject, I asked the restaurant's owner (an actual Afghan), "So what's up with Afghanistan?"

He said, "Americans must understand that Afghanistan is a country of honor. The honor of an Afghan is in his gun, his land, and his women. You take a man's honor if you take his gun, his land, or his women."

And the same goes for where I live in New Hampshire. I inquired whether exceptions could be made, on the third point of honor, for ex-wives.

"Oh yes," he said.

Afghanistan—so foreign and yet so familiar and, like home, with such wonderful lamb chops. I asked the restaurateur about other similarities between New Hampshire and Afghanistan.

"I don't know," he said. "Most of my family lives in LA."

In Kabul I was met at the airport by M. Amin Mudaqiq, bureau chief for Radio Free Europe/Radio Liberty's Afghan branch, Radio Azadi. "Our office is just down the main road," he said, "but since it's early in the morning we'll take the back way, because of the Suicides." That last word, I noticed, was pronounced as a proper noun, the way we would say "The Beatles" slightly differently than "the beetles." And, in a sense, suicide bombers do aspire to be the rock stars of the Afghan insurgency (average career span being about the same in both professions).

"The Suicides usually attack early in the morning," Amin said. "It's a hot country and the explosive vests are thick and heavy."

I'd never thought about suicide bombing in terms of comfort. Here's some guy who's decided to blow himself gloriously to bits and he's pounding the pavement all dressed up in the blazing sun, sweat running down his face, thinking, "Gosh, this thing itches, I'm pooped, let's call it off."

"It's the same with car bombs," Amin said. "You don't want to be driving around the whole day with police everywhere and maybe get a ticket."

Imagine the indignity of winding up in traffic court instead of the terrorist equivalent of the Rock and Roll Hall of Fame.

Kabul is a walled city, which sounds romantic except the walls are precast reinforced concrete blast barriers, ten feet tall and fifteen feet long and moved into place with cranes. The walls are topped with sandbags and the sandbags are topped with guard posts from which gun barrels protrude.

Amin pointed out the sights. "There's UN headquarters." All I could see was blast barriers, sandbags, and gun barrels. "There's the German embassy"—barriers, bags, and barrels. "There's the embassy of China"—barriers, bags, and barrels. I spotted a rough-hewn stone fort on a hilltop, looking more the ancient way Kabul should look. "Oh, nineteenth-century British," Amin said.

Security, in various senses of the term, was all over the place. I have never seen so many types and kinds of soldiers, policemen, and private security guards or such a welter of uniforms, each in a different pattern of camouflage every one of which stuck out like a toreador's suit of lights against the white blast walls. Some of this security was on alert, some was asleep, some was spit-and-polish, some had its shoes untied, and some, rather unaccountably, was walking around without weapons.

None of the security was American. Americans don't patrol Kabul. The American military is suffering its usual fate, the same as it does at an army base in Georgia—shunted off to places the locals don't care to go.

The Kabul cityscape looks like a cornfield maze version of the old Berlin Wall without the graffiti, or like an unshelled Verdun gone condo with high-rise trenches. Afghanistan's capital is located in a grand hollow, as if someone had closed the Rockies in tight around Denver. On the slopes of Kabul's mountains there is another cityscape of small stone houses. They could be from the time of the Prophet, although they all seem to have aluminum window frames. This is where the poor live, with panes of glass to keep out the winter winds but not much else. At night you can see how far the electric wires run uphill—not very far. The water pipes don't go up at all, and residents—women and children residents, I'm sure—must climb from the bottom with their water.

Then, around the corner from the blast walls, there's a third Kabul, an ordinary city with stores and restaurants open to the street and parking impossible to find. The architecture is overseas modern in concrete and chrome with some leftover Soviet modern in just concrete. It looks a bit worn and torn but less so than Detroit or trans-Anacostia Washington, D.C. People are going about their business in Kabul with no apparent air of knowing that "people are going about their business in Kabul" is considered a very special thing at the U.S. State Department.

Security here is merely ubiquitous as opposed to omnipresent. Men, women, and children mingle. Women cover themselves in public but not more than my Irish great-aunts did at Mass. An occasional down-to-the-ground burka is seen but not as often as in London. In the malls, clothing shops predominate. Men's and women's clothes are shinier and more vividly colored than those seen in a traditional society such as New Hampshire.

Traditionalism being one of the things that makes Afghanistan so hard for Americans to understand. We Americans have so many traditions. For instance, our political traditions date back to the twelfth-century English Parliament if not to the Roman Senate. Afghans, on the other hand, have had the representative-democracy kind of politics for only six years. Afghanistan's political traditions are just beginning to develop. A Pashtun tribal leader told me that a "problem among Afghan politicians is that they do not tell the truth." It's a political system so new that this needed to be said out loud.

In the matter of opinion polling, however, Afghanistan is fully up-to-date. Concerning the popularity of President Hamid Karzai, the tribal leader said, "He is welcomed by bullets in many provinces." Of course, in America, this would be a metaphorical statement—except in 1865, 1881, 1901, 1963, 1981, etc.

The Pashtun tribal leader was one of a number of people whom Amin Mudaqiq arranged for me to interview. Tribalism is another thing that makes Afghanistan hard to understand. We Americans are probably too tribal to grasp the subtlety of Afghan tribal concepts. The Pashtun tribal leader was joined by a Turkmen tribal leader who has a PhD in sociology. I asked the Turkmen tribal leader about the socioeconomic, class, and status aspects of Afghan tribalism.

"No tribe is resented for wealth," he said. So, right off the bat, Afghans show greater tribal sophistication than Americans. There is no Wall Street Tribe upon which the Afghan government can blame everything.

I asked the Turkmen, "Did either the Communists or the Taliban try to use one tribe against another?"

"No," he said, "I didn't notice such a policy with the Soviets. And the Taliban does not publicly use tribalism."

Even the worst of Afghan governments never acquired the special knack of pitting tribe against tribe that is vital to American politics—the Squishy Liberal Tribe versus the Kick-Butt Tribe, the Indignantly Entitled Tribe versus the Fed-Up Taxpayer Tribe, the Smug Tribe versus the Wipe-That-Smirk-Off-Your-Face Tribe.

"We are all one nation," said the Pashtun tribal leader. "In the name of Afghan is included all the tribes of Afghanistan. Outsiders create divisions to serve their own interests." Better than having insiders create divisions to serve their own interests. President Obama, take note.

"Are there land issues between the tribes?" I asked the Turkmen. He told me there are land issues between *everybody*. Land titles are a mess in Afghanistan, or, as the Turkmen put it with a nice PhD turn of phrase, "Definition of ownership is originally ambiguous." The situation is so confused that the Soviets, of all people, attempted to impose private property in Afghanistan. "They tried to change the law, but the period was too short. Afghanistan," the Turkmen said, and laughed, "did not use the benefits of colonialism."

The problem in Afghanistan is really not so much land as water. It's a dry country with ample amounts of water running through it but not to good enough effect. "We have a law to distribute water but not to *manage* water," the Turkmen said. This lack of management combines with the age-old managerial conflicts between nomads who need watered pastures and farmers who need irrigation. Partly this is a nontribal matter, since there are both nomads and farmers in various tribes. But partly it is a tribal matter because of the different ways that tribes decide to cease to be nomads and become farmers.

"The Turkmen," said the Turkmen, "settle close to the desert. The Pashtuns settle close to the source of the water." Downstream and upstream. It's the plot of *Chinatown*. If you don't understand Afghanistan, blame Robert Towne.

Both the Pashtun tribal leader and the Turkmen tribal leader were unenthusiastic about the use of the word "tribal" and felt that "ethnic groups" is a better way to describe the differences among Afghans.

I held forth on American patriotism, how it had to do with our own ethnic groups, and the attempt to give American immigrants of the late nineteenth and early twentieth centuries a sense of nationhood. The tribal leaders understood exactly what I meant, which is more than I can say for our NATO allies on the subject of American patriotism.

"Fifty years ago," the Turkmen said, "things in Afghanistan were going in the same direction as the U.S. growth of patriotism. These systems were disturbed by the events of the last thirty years. Also, the geographical location of Afghanistan is not helpful to building national ideals. The focal points of the tribes are outside the country."

But not far enough outside. The Turkmen have their heartland in Turkmenistan, the Uzbeks in Uzbekistan, the Tajiks in Tajikistan and Iran. Even the Pashtuns, who are the largest ethnic group in Afghanistan, making up about 40 percent of the population, count Peshawar in the Northwest Territories of Pakistan as their cultural capital. And the language spoken by most educated Afghans, Dari, is a dialect of Persian. It is as if, around the time Emma Lazarus was penning "Give me your tired, your poor, your huddled masses yearning to breathe free," Dublin and Naples and Warsaw and Minsk had been moved—complete with every palace, slum, monument, gutter, princeling, priest, bum, thug, and man-at-arms—to Ellis Island, and all of America's schools had started teaching their lessons in French.

Nonetheless Afghan patriotism obtains. Maybe because, as the Turkmen tribal leader pointed out, every "old country" to which an Afghan ethnic might turn manages—somewhat extraordinarily—to be a worse place than Afghanistan.

There's that and what the Pashtun tribal leader had to say: "If Afghanistan is divided, why do we keep defeating outsiders?" He went on in that vein, like Lincoln but with a thousand more years of history to go on, dating back to the twelfth-century outsider-defeating Afghan empire of Alauddin Husain, known as the "World-Burner." In the Pashtun's words, "A divided country cannot win."

Earlier in the day I'd heard a mullah become heated on the subject of ethnocentric politics. He accused a politician in the Karzai government of being a "national traitor" for doing what in the United States would be called playing the Charlie Rangel card. The politician is a member of the Hazara tribe (the Afghan politician, that is, though I'm sure Charlie Rangel would be glad to claim Hazara descent if it got him a tribal casino in New York's Fifteenth Congressional District). "Why I called him a national traitor," said the mullah, "is because he said he would shed his blood in favor of Hazaras. Instead of saying this was a judicial matter, he said it was a fighting matter. He broke his constitutional obligation."

The mullah represents another thing that makes Afghanistan hard to understand for Americans, although only for elite Americans who've had prestigious schooling and hold advanced opinions about everything. We ordinary Americans, far from such centers of heathen unbelief as the Brookings Institution, get the drift of a deeply religious polity.

I interviewed two mullahs at once. This might have been awkward, as they were opposite types, but they seemed fond of each other and the quieter mullah even took a few notes while the more voluble mullah was talking.

The quiet mullah was quietly dressed and modestly bearded, his close-cut hair topped with a simple turban. He was immediately recognizable as "mainstream." I don't mean he was hopelessly mainstream to the post-religious point, like some American clergy. I'd compare him to a solid Methodist or Presbyterian or picket-fence Baptist, not unwilling to make his sermons socially relevant but no electric guitars in the choir loft.

"Preaching isn't limited to the mosque," he said, and told me how he spends time sitting with shopkeepers, listening to complaints about price gouging, and talking about the Islamic view of these matters. It is, by the way, things like price gouging that the Taliban casts itself as a defender against—the free market being one more of modernity's villains.

"I make the subjects of my sermons both Islamic and scientific," said the quiet mullah. "People are the enemy of those things they do not know." He talked about peace, not harping on its somewhat obvious convenience for individuals, but speaking of "the importance of peace to *Islam*." There's something more than mortal men at stake in peace—God demands it.

Along with peace, the mullah said, one of the most frequent topics of his sermons is leadership. He tries to explain, as a prayer leader, how to select a political leader. This is an easy enough colloquy to have with fellow Muslims. There is no generally accepted earthly hierarchy in Islam, especially in Sunni Islam, and there's certainly no pope. A Muslim may pray on any piece of ground. A mosque is an institution that adheres to the definition of a church given by Jesus: "Where two or three are gathered together." Muslims choose their own mosque, and, ideally at least, those who pray at that mosque choose their own mullah. People who say the Muslim world isn't ready for democracy ignore, among other things, the fact that Muslims already have it.

Two of the criteria that the quiet mullah gave for political leadership would eliminate most U.S. politicians: "Be educated. Know the society." But the first criterion was to be Muslim.

The more voluble mullah explained, "Since the time of Adam until now there are four books from God." (Muslims, like Jews, separate the Pentateuch from the rest of the Old Testament.) "This is our constitution."

It's a little long, I suppose—even longer than the proposed EU Constitution. But there are worse documents by which to live and govern—the proposed EU Constitution, for example.

Being a person who believes in God-given rights, I don't find a God-given constitution very disturbing. But some Americans—Americans involved in Afghan policy — apparently do. The next night I had dinner with the governor of a province that has its share of Taliban troubles. Talking about the hindrances he faces in getting assistance from the United States, the governor protested against something that he must have been told by some American, that there is a "ban on religion" in the U.S. Constitution.

"Disarm the Taliban," the governor said. "Take the Islamic weapon away from them." He wasn't talking about secularization.

"The best reason for belief," said the voluble mullah, "is that every country has its own laws. The death of a person is the beginning of another, greater journey—more dangerous than the journey you're taking now. Like police at the airport when you leave here, Allah will be asking the same way, 'Have you obeyed the law?'"

This mullah was a splendid figure, a big man in a bright white *shalwar kameez* with a magnificence of beard in elaborate curls and a turban that looked as if it would take all night to unwind and all day to wind up again. He was an evangelical. I say that in the original complimentary Gospel way. (I'm Low Church Protestant on my mother's side.) I was swept up with his eloquence before its translation arrived, when I didn't even know what he was saying. What he was saying was, "There is God. There is no rival to God, or there would have been an election or a coup d'état."

He was concerned that I'd made it only three-quarters of the way through the four books from God since the time of Adam. I was concerned that if I spent another twenty minutes with him I'd be in trouble with my parish priest.

I asked both mullahs about the idea of a "clash of civilizations" between Islam and the West. The quiet mullah thought there might be some truth in the notion, arising from three things: inappropriate behavior of Muslims, materialism (in the metaphysical sense) of non-Muslims, and mutual ignorance.

"Maybe," I volunteered, "the real clash of civilizations is between people who believe in God and people who don't."

The voluble mullah said, "There are those who don't believe in God. Fortunately neither Muslims or Afghans or Americans are among them." I hope he's not being too optimistic about the last named. (Later I would get a more dismissive answer to the question about the clash of civilizations, from a member of the Afghan parliament. He said, "Chinese, Muslims, Jews, Europeans—they work together in international finance markets every day.")

As the mullahs were departing, an Afghan journalist gestured toward the more prepossessing of the two. "He's a drone problem," said the journalist. "They see the clothes and the turban from up in the air and they think, 'Taliban!' And he *is* like Taliban, but on the good side."

Yet someone in Afghanistan must think the Taliban on the other side are good for something, too. Otherwise there wouldn't be an "Afghan issue."

The Taliban offer bad law—chopping off hands, stoning desperate housewives, the usual things. Perhaps you have to live in a place that has had no law for a long time—since the Soviets invaded in 1979—before you welcome bad law as an improvement. An Afghan civil society activist, whose work has put him under threat from the Taliban, admitted, "People picked Taliban as the lesser of evils." He explained that lesser of evils with one word, "stability."

A woman member of the Afghan parliament said that it was simply a fact that the Taliban insurgency was strongest "where the government is not providing services." Rule of law being the first service a government must provide.

The member of parliament who laughed at the clash of civilizations laughed as well at what has passed for rule of law in Afghanistan. "Sure, Afghanistan is unruly," he said. "Afghans don't like rules. No one likes rules. And that is what we have been—*ruled*. We have been *ruled*, not *governed*."

"The insurgency is also strongest," the woman member of parliament said, "where private security is stirring up trouble."

United States and NATO forces are also seen to have a hand in the churning. A Shia candidate for parliament said, "The Afghan people hate your troops when they support a corrupt governor or a warlord."

A journalist for Radio Azadi said, "Afghans were happy *in principle* that Americans brought peace and democracy. But when rival tribes began to use the U.S. to crush each other, the attitude of the Afghan people changed."

Afghans think Americans have sided with the wrong people. It's not that Afghans think Americans have sided with the wrong people in a systematic, strategic, or calculated way. It's just that we came to a place that we didn't know much about, where there are a lot of sides to be on, and we started siding with this side and that side and the other side. We were bound to wind up on the wrong side sometimes. We're outsiders in Afghanistan, and this is Occam's razor for explaining the Taliban. Imagine if America were a country beset with all sorts of intractable difficulties. Or don't imagine it—America *is* a country beset with all sorts of intractable difficulties. Our government is out of control, wantonly interfering in every aspect of our private lives and heedlessly squandering our national treasure at a time when Americans are suffering grave economic woes. Meanwhile vicious tribal conflicts are being fought for control of America's culture and way of life. (I've been watching FoxNews.)

What if some friendly, well-meaning, but very foreign power, with incomprehensible lingo and outrageous clothes, were to arrive on our shores to set things right? What if it were Highland Scots? There they go marching around wearing skirts and purses and ugly plaids, playing their hideous bagpipe music, handing out haggis to our kiddies, and offending our sensibilities with a lack of BVDs under their kilts. Maybe they do cut taxes, lower the federal deficit, eliminate the Department of Health and Human Services and the EPA, give people jobs at their tartan factories, and launch a manhunt for Harry Reid and the UC-Berkeley faculty. We still wouldn't like them. In New Hampshire there'd be more than one neighbor of mine up in his tree stand taking potshots at the Scotties with his deer rifle, especially if Jock left a nickel tip at the local diner for the neighbor's waitress wife.

Maybe my neighbor doing the shooting at silly ribboned bonnets isn't my favorite neighbor. Maybe he's the neighborhood jerk. But you can suppose how I might feel about my fellow Granite State nutcases, and I can suppose how Afghans might feel about the Taliban. They're assholes, but they're *our* assholes.

The Pashtun tribal leader said, "I tell my own tribesmen to not support the Taliban, but they don't listen. They see the Taliban as fighting invaders."

It's not just an invasion by soldiers that the Taliban could be seen as fighting. It's an invasion by a whole outlandish other world, as alien to Afghans as a lot of cable TV is to me. Indeed, the provincial governor said that people in villages will ask him, "Why is a naked fellow on television?" I said I'd like to know myself.

The journalist with Radio Azadi said, "When people felt they were dishonored, they needed revenge. The Taliban gave them revenge."

To fully sympathize with the dishonor an Afghan might feel, foreign government, UN, and NGO aid agencies must be considered. A myriad of them operate in Afghanistan, staffed by people from around the globe. So it's not just that you've got Highland Scots marching in hairy-kneed formations up and down your subdevelopment's cul-de-sac. Many of the most ordinary functions of your society have been taken over by weird strangers. When you need a flu shot or a dog license or a permit to burn leaves, you have to go see Bulgarians and Bolivians and Nigerians and Fiji Islanders. Some Mumbai babu is sitting on your zoning board saying, "Oh my gosh golly no, it is most inefficient use of land to forbid parking of the camper vans on war memorials."

Afghanistan's minister of education, Farooq Wardak, is no friend of the Taliban, but he did sound like a potential recruit for the Tea Party. "I am absolutely unhappy with the U.S. role in Afghan education," he said. "Zero percent of U.S. aid to Afghan education is spent through the Afghan government."

"Why?" I asked.

"Because the Ministry of Education is not certified by USAID because no one from USAID has evaluated me or my ministry in the two years that I've held the job." Without the evaluation he can't get the certification.

He said that the U.S. government wanted to spend money on a program called "Community-Based Education." But that was a program the ministry had developed when the Taliban were attacking girls' schools across Afghanistan. It was a way to provide, he said, "covert education for girls. Now we need overt schools."

The U.S. also wants to spend money, he complained, on "accelerated teacher training" when what Afghanistan needs is just plain teacher training.

"Either give the money to us or align with the program," he said. "This accelerated training leaves no bricks and mortar behind. You are spending U.S. tax dollars building something taxpayers can't see." His pocket critique of U.S. aid: "Everything is air, nothing is on the ground." I didn't have the heart to tell him about No Child Left Behind back in America.

But the Taliban aren't winning much love, either—otherwise we and our NATO allies would have already gone the way of the Soviets. The civil society activist had a very Afghan insult for the Taliban: "The Taliban has the power to kill, and people still don't like them."

Radio Liberty's Pakistan bureau, which broadcasts in Pashto, had just run a story about the Taliban being as clumsy as the United States in dealing with tribalism—as clumsy but much more brutal. Unable to penetrate Pashtun tribal hierarchies, the Taliban had, according to the report, begun killing tribal elders, with more than one thousand murdered so far.

"The older tribal leaders are everyone's target," the woman member of parliament said. She also described how the Taliban, in areas under their control, go to villagers and demand, "Son or money." This insistence on either payoff or cannon fodder (drone fodder, I suppose) must undercut the Taliban's reputation for incorruptibility. But corruption in the Afghan government remains a raw material of insurgency.

As I mentioned, there's a lot of security in Kabul. The only place I saw that lacked any security—not a gun or a goon to be seen—was at the office of the Shia candidate for parliament, Ramazan Bashardost. He has a reputation for fanatical opposition to corruption. And, actually, he doesn't have an office; he refuses to have an office. Instead he has a tent pitched across the street from the parliament building, a large, simple nomad's tent staked in an empty lot and without so much as a carpet on the stony ground.

Bashardost has something of the look of a young Ralph Nader, with that Nader gleam of indignation in his eyes and that Nader tendency to pull out thick sheaves of documentation concerning each subject he's indignant about. He had been in the parliament before. He quit over what might seem a fine point. "I left Parliament because Karzai said salaries should run through September when Parliament had ended in May."

He had also been minister of planning. "I left the Ministry of Planning for my values," he said. He pointed to the pavement between his tent and the fortified parliament building. The four-lane avenue was completely torn up, littered in construction machinery, and nearly impassable. "We are three years into a six-month road project."

Asked to summarize corruption in Afghanistan, he said, "It is a Mafia economy disguised as a market economy."

Not that Bashardost is at all like Ralph Nader is his attitude toward a market economy. He has a PhD in economics and believes Afghanistan should be using private investment for development rather than international aid. But, he said, "Afghans hate a 'market economy' because it equals corruption." (Being fluent in English, he put "market economy" into phonetic quotation marks. He did the same with "democracy.") "Afghans hate 'democracy' because democracy equals power of the warlords, equals power of corruption, equals no rule of law."

If Americans claim not to understand Afghan corruption, we're lying. Bribery has been a dominant part of our foreign policy in Afghanistan, the way it's been a dominant part of everyone's foreign policy in Afghanistan, including al-Qaeda's. What we Americans don't understand about Afghan corruption is why it's so transparent, just a matter of taking money. Don't the Afghans know that you should take bribes indirectly—by collecting publicity, popularity, public recognition, prestige, influence, and, most of all, power? Then big corporations put you on their boards of directors and *that's* when you get the money. Meanwhile you've been riding in government cars, flying on government planes, eating out of the government pork barrel (lamb barrel in Afghanistan), so why worry about payoffs up front?

Afghans have failed to move their corruption from the Rod Blagojevich model, which we all deplore, to the Barack Obama model, which we all admire. Afghanistan should, as the minister of education says, "align with the program."

How can we know what America should do in Afghanistan? I've returned fully informed on this subject as well. We should stay. The member of parliament who dismissed the clash of civilizations said, "It's like buying a beautiful home somewhere and letting your neighborhood deteriorate."

Really, seriously, we should stay. Otherwise, Ramazan Bashardost said, "You'll see Chinese soldiers in the street. We have a border with China. They're a very rich country. We're very poor people—in a most strategic region."

We should leave. The Pashtun tribal leader said, "We don't have war. What we have is instability. Armies create instability. If you try this for twenty more years you'll never succeed."

We should do both. One of the journalists with Radio Azadi said, "There's the same feeling in Afghanistan as there is in the U.S. We worry about the U.S. staying, and we worry about the U.S. leaving."

The Afghan people are pro-American. The woman member of parliament said, "We say, 'Our enemy is their enemy.'"

The Afghan people are anti-American. Ramazan Bashardost said, "Frankly, people are generally against the U.S." But he tries to argue with them. "I say U.S. troops are in Afghanistan for values, not for oil—there is not enough of it."

Afghans know that we're still committed to our mission in Afghanistan. The minister of education said, "I have complete faith. But whether we are able and smart enough to express this mission to the people of Afghanistan . . ." He let his words trail off.

Afghans don't know that we're still committed to our mission in Afghanistan. The provincial governor said, "If perception is created by your actions that democracy is against Islam, that a controlled insurgency is all that's wanted, that Afghanistan is being used as a jump point for other geopolitical concerns—that justifies the insurgency."

Afghans hope like heck that we're still committed to our mission in Afghanistan. The woman member of parliament said, "From 2001 to 2004 people were very optimistic. With the switch to Iraq things began to change."

Afghans can't live on hope alone. The voluble mullah said, "There is a saying, 'A blind man will not lose his stick twice.' But the people of Afghanistan have lost their stick twenty times."

We should talk to the Taliban. The Pashtun tribal leader said, "Accept the fact that we cannot eliminate all Taliban from Afghanistan."

We shouldn't talk to the Taliban. The governor said, "Talks further strengthen the enemy's position."

We must fight the war the Afghan way. The governor said, "The Taliban are very quick. Our current units need too much preparation to move."

We must fight the war the American way. The governor also said, "There is an Arab proverb about fear as a tactic: 'I win the war a month away.'" And the U.S. military has been doing some fearsome things for month upon month in Afghanistan.

The Afghan government can be reformed from within. The governor said, "Blaming corruption is just a way to put blame on others for our own shortcomings. Internal strategies are needed to strengthen military and civil society."

The Afghan government can't be reformed from within. Bashardost proposed something like what General MacArthur did in Japan after World War II.

Poverty is the root of Afghanistan's problems. Bashardost said, "We are ready to support you for three hundred years. *If* we have electricity. *If* we have a life."

Poverty is not the root of Afghanistan's problems. "Or Haiti would be the most terroristic country in the world," the governor said.

There must be *something* in Afghanistan that we've got right. There is. Radio Azadi, the Afghan bureau of Radio Free Europe/Radio Liberty, is on the air twelve hours a day, seven days a week, half the time in Pashto, half the time in Dari. What Radio Azadi does is known as "surrogate broadcasting," meaning the content is Afghan-produced as a way for Afghans to get news and views in a place where, otherwise, these have to be delivered mostly face-to-face. And there is no agenda except to be factual (although facts are an agenda item if you care about freedom, which is what Azadi means in Dari).

Radio Azadi's bureau chief, and my host in Kabul, Amin Madaqiq, has 120 staff members and freelancers. They produce news bulletins, news in depth, and features on social, political, and economic topics, plus a couple of hours a day of Afghan music and even some comedy: "Police announced today that all the people who have passed their driver's license test must now learn to drive."

A missing persons program, *In Search of a Loved One,* tries to reunite families separated by decades of chaos. A medical program is hosted by doctors with eminent specialists, often from overseas, as guests. *Azadi and Listeners* is devoted to getting individuals individual responses from government ministries.

The call-in shows are popular. On a day when I was in the studio Afghanistan's minister of communications and minister of the interior were taking random phoners, trying to clear up confusion about a confusing-sounding system of national ID cards. I don't think it's likely that the head of the FCC and a member of President Obama's cabinet would spend two hours in a spartan, airless broadcast booth helping people who are unable to read through a form-filling process and suggesting work-arounds when local government corruption is encountered.

The quiet mullah told me that the day before an elderly religious scholar had asked for help buying a radio so that Azadi could be listened to in his mosque.

The Pashtun tribal leader said, "Azadi is doing very well because they are telling the facts." He griped that other media were insensitive to religion and culture.

The civil society activist thought that wisdom and social relationships were best established in person, but second best was radio. "Radio can pass wisdom," he said.

The woman member of parliament told me about how, after the fall of the Taliban, Radio Azadi had conducted four hours a week of open political debate. "The Afghans *got it,*" she said. She praised Azadi's "diversity of opinion" and the fact that it sometimes has "the government getting upset."

"Even the U.S. ambassador is afraid of our show," an Azadi journalist told me with a big smile.

"Any feeling of censorship from the U.S.?" I asked Amin.

"We haven't felt any," he said.

"A good channel," the minister of education called it. "An important institution. I've never had the feeling it was unnecessarily taking sides in the Afghan conflict. It maintains its impartiality."

"I wasn't sure what you'd hear from the minister," a journalist with Radio Azadi told me later. "We've been critical of him."

The member of parliament to whom I'd talked about clashing civilizations and deteriorating neighborhoods was a bit surprised at America sponsoring Azadi, the more so, I think, because he's an American. That is, he lived for a long time in America, where he spent ten years as a commercial airline pilot.

"America," he said, not without pride, "is spending money for you to express your opinions—not to twist your opinions but to *express* your opinions."

Ramazan Bashardost's only complaint about Radio Azadi was that he wasn't on it often enough. He was reminded that, only recently, he had been named by Radio Azadi as "Person of the Year."

"Yes," he said, and apologized for bringing too much documentation to radio interviews. "One positive point in Afghanistan is media," he said. "And the only positive point in Afghanistan is media."

Even the Taliban call in to Radio Azadi—to argue with the hosts and guests.

"We know you are funded by the U.S. Congress," a Taliban spokesman told Amin. "But we judge you by your deeds."

"The Taliban call to argue—this is *good*," said the woman member of parliament.

"The Taliban fights the U.S. militarily," said the former airline pilot, "but uses the U.S. media to express themselves." He chuckled. "I say to them, 'If this system is bad, you are using it! When you had your radio, would you let *us* call in?'" He saw the Taliban as caught in a trap by the logic of freedom. "This is a format that must be expanded."

The governor thought the Taliban itself might accidentally expand it. He recalled the days before Radio Azadi, during Taliban rule, when the only outside media was the BBC Afghan service. "The Taliban told people that they would go to hell if they listened to the BBC. Then *everyone* listened."

There was one other point that people in Kabul agreed on. Whatever it is that America does in Afghanistan, America should proceed with wisdom. The governor told a story about wisdom.

There was a student who had been studying for many years at a madrassa. He had memorized the Qu'ran and learned all the lessons his teacher taught. One day he went to his teacher and said, "I am ready to leave and go be a mullah."

His teacher said, "I think you should stay here for a few more years."

"Why?" asked the student. "Is there some additional degree or higher certificate that I will get?"

"No," said the teacher, "all you will get is wisdom."

"But I'm ready to be a mullah now," said the student. And he left the madrassa and wandered from village to village looking for a mosque where he could be the prayer leader.

Finally the student came to a village where a corrupt old mullah was using the mosque as a stall for his cow. The student was outraged. He gathered the villagers together and told them, "I have studied at a madrassa. I have memorized the Qu'ran. It is a great sacrilege for your mullah to use the mosque as a stall for his cow." The villagers beat him up.

The student limped back to the madrassa and told his teacher what had happened. The teacher said, "Follow me." They went back to the village where the mullah was using the mosque as a stall.

The teacher gathered the villagers together and told them, "I see you have a beautiful cow being kept in your mosque. It must be a very blessed animal. And I hear the cow belongs to your mullah. He must be a very holy man. In fact, I think that this cow is so blessed and your mullah is so holy that if you were to take one hair from the cow's hide and one hair from the mullah's beard and rub them together, you would be assured of paradise."

The villagers ran into the mosque and began plucking hairs from the cow's hide. The cow started to buck and kick and it bolted from the mosque and disappeared. Then the villagers ran to the corrupt old mullah's house and began plucking hairs from his beard. And they tugged and they yanked so hard at the mullah's beard that he had a heart attack and died.

"You see," said the teacher to the student. "No cow in the mosque and a need for a new mullah—*that* is wisdom."

THE BABY BOOM

How It Got That Way . . .
And It Wasn't My Fault . . .
And I'll Never Do It Again

(2014)

Thou shalt not answer questionnaires
Or quizzes upon World-Affairs,
Nor with compliance
Take any test. Thou shalt not sit
With statisticians nor commit
A social science.

—W. H. Auden,
"Under Which Lyre"

Prologue: We Are the World

We are the generation that changed everything. Of all the eras and epochs of Americans, ours is the one that made the biggest impression—on ourselves. But that's an important accomplishment because we're the generation that created the self, made the firmament of the self, divided the light of the self from the darkness of the self, and said let there be self. If you were born between 1946 and 1964, you may have noticed this *your*self.

That's not to say we're a selfish generation. Selfish means "too concerned with the self," and we're not. Self isn't something we're just, you know, concerned with. We *be* self.

Before us, self was without form and void, like our parents in their dumpy clothes and vague ideas. Then we came along. Now the personal is the political. The personal is the socioeconomic. The personal is the religious and the secular, science and the arts. The personal is every thing that creepeth upon the earth after his (and, let us hasten to add, her) kind. If the Baby Boom has done one thing it's to beget a personal universe.

And our apologies to anyone who personally happens to be a jerk. Self is like fish, proverbially speaking. Give a man a fish and you've fed him for a day. Teach a man to fish and, if he turns into a dry-fly catch-and-release angling fanatic up to his liver in icy water wearing ridiculous waders and an absurd hat, pestering trout with three-pound test line on a thousand-dollar graphite rod, and going on endlessly about Royal Coachman lures that he tied himself using muskrat fur and partridge feathers . . . well, at least his life partner is glad to have him out of the house.

We made the universe personal, and we made the universe new. New in the sense of juvenescent. We have an abiding admiration for our own larval state.

We saw that the grown-ups were like primitive insects. They never underwent metamorphosis. They didn't emerge from their home and office cocoons with brilliant, fluttering wings. They just continued to molt, getting more gross, lumpy, and bald and, as it were, bugging us. Better that we should stay nymphs and naiads. Plus we were having more fun than the adults of the species.

"Don't ever change!" we wrote in each other's high school yearbooks. "Stay just the way you are!" What strange valedictions to give ourselves on the threshold of life. Imagine if we had obeyed them, and now everyone possessed the resolute solipsism of adolescence with its wild enthusiasms, dark lethargies, strong lusts, keen aversions, inner turmoils, and uncontained impulses. Life would be exactly like it is today. You're welcome.

So here we are in the Baby Boom cosmos, formed in our image, personally tailored to our individual needs, and predetermined to be eternally fresh and novel. And we saw that it was good. Or pretty good.

We should have had a cooler name, the way the Lost Generation did. Except good luck to anybody who tries to tell us to get lost. Anyway it's too late now, we're stuck with being forever described as exploding infants. And maybe it's time, now that we've splattered ourselves all over the place, for the Baby Boom to look back and think. "What made us who we are?" "And what caused us to act the way we do?" "And WTF?" Because the truth is, if we hadn't decided to be young forever, we'd be old.

The youngest Baby Boomers, born in the last year when anybody thought it was hip to like Lyndon Johnson, are turning fifty. Those of us who were born when postwar birthrates were highest, even before Ike was liked, won't (statistics tell us) have to wait as long for death as we had to wait to get laid.

We'd be sad about this if we weren't too busy remarrying younger wives, reviving careers that hit glass ceilings when children arrived, and renewing prescriptions for drugs that keep us from being sad. And we'll never retire. We can't. The mortgage is underwater. We're in debt up to the Rogaine for the kids' college education. And it serves us right—we're the generation who insisted that a passion for living should replace working for one.

Nonetheless it's an appropriate moment for us to weigh what we've wrought and tally what we've added to and subtracted from existence. We've reached the age of accountability. The world is our fault. We are the generation that has an excuse for everything—one of our greatest contributions to modern life—but the world is still our fault. This is every generation's fate. It's a matter of power and privilege demography. Whenever anything happens anywhere, somebody over fifty signs the bill for it. And the Baby Boom, seated as we are at the head of life's table, is hearing Generation X, Generation Y, and the Millennials all saying, "Check, please!"

In the Doldrums of Fun

School, given the amount of childhood that's spent in it, should form a greater part of this story. But it doesn't. School was just there, inexorable, inevitable, and almost escape-proof. In our childhood, school life held the place that real life would occupy in our adulthood. You could avoid school but only by doing things that were worse or had worse consequences such as getting sick or telling wild lies, the juvenile equivalents of dying or going to Promises Malibu.

There were public schools and Catholic schools, mostly indistinguishable except that in the latter you learned about the infinite mercy of the Blessed Virgin Mary and got your knuckles whacked.

Schools were big buildings. They resembled fortifications or castles. But they had been carefully designed to avoid any suggestion of the romance associated with citadels, strongholds, and keeps. The windows were large, to give children plenty of the healthy sunlight that didn't use to cause skin cancer and lots of air during the climate change that happened only twice a year, spring and fall, instead of all the time. Through those large windows we learned what a wide and wonderful world it is and how much we'd love to be out in it.

Some of the massive public schools that were built in the first third of the twentieth century haven't yet been torn down or repurposed. But their windows have been replaced with insulated panels that leave just a slit of casements for students to peer through. And we wonder at the increase in childhood suicide rates.

School started at 8:30. Before the doors opened children were expected to form two lines, one for the boys and one for the girls. The boys pushed each other. The girls teased each other. We would have been better behaved if we'd been mixed together, but the people who insist on organizing life and the people who have no idea how life is organized were and always will be the same people.

Classrooms were well populated. I count forty-two children in my third-grade class picture. The teacher was, until junior high, invariably a woman, usually single, and alone at her station of command. Teachers' aides had not yet been sent to the aid of teachers. Busybody parents weren't sticking their noses in from the back row. Elected representatives of the school board weren't visiting to make sure that the curriculum was conformist, or that the curriculum was nonconformist, according to which kind of nut won the school board election. Not that our teachers needed such assistance. They wielded the kind of unalloyed power that God used to have in the Old Testament before 1950s Sunday school teachers got to Him.

Corporal punishment was not unknown in public schools. But its infrequency and the seemingly random nature of its application made it less a deterrent than a suburban legend. Someone being paddled gave us a sort of campfire story to tell on the way home from school. "And *then* he was sent to the principal."

The more effective disciplinary measure was to send us to sit in the hall. A break from the crowded, busy classroom would have been a relief to a sensible generation, but we are a sens*itive* generation and can't stand to be isolated. The worst penalty we could devise, when we got children of our own, was to give them a "time-out." Probably the tykes were thinking—like many people who have had experience with our generation—"Please, make it two."

Our teachers were not old bats by any means. Many were fresh from their El Ed major at state universities and full of innocent enthusiasm. Others were old bats. Pedagogical methods combined the hopelessly old-fashioned with the hopelessly newfangled. There was still copious rote learning and much copying of things from blackboards. We were made to memorize the alphabet both forward and backward, the latter being something I most certainly can't do to this day. I didn't have much success with the former either. When I use the dictionary I'm still singing the "ABC Song." My parents bought the 45 and I played it on a little red record player. I used to catch myself, among Y and Z words, mouthing the lyrics of the final verse—*Now I know my ABCs/Aren't you very proud of me?*—sometimes aloud, which occasioned looks in the college library.

We were taught to read with flash cards. "You can remember it's the word *look* because it has two eyes in the middle." This is not conducive to good spelling. It's no accident that SpellCheck is a product of the Baby Boom, and no accident that we misspelled "spell check." Anything to get out of liiking up words in the dictionary.

On the other hand, History and Geography had been replaced with Social Studies. By the end of grade school we were well prepared to go out and take Margaret Mead's place in Samoa, if we'd known where Samoa was. We studied the handicrafts, songs, and square dances of the American pioneers. We knew everything about frontier life except when it happened and why. There was a great fad for coonskin caps thanks to the Walt Disney show's Davy Crockett episodes, which were only slightly less historically inaccurate than Margaret Mead. We understood that pioneers wore coonskin caps. We didn't understand that they'd had to eat the raccoon first.

One lesson the Baby Boom did learn was that we were being bored on purpose. Until we understood school we regarded boredom as an accident—nobody to play with, nothing but *Name That Tune* on TV. At its worst, during Thanksgiving dinner with a relentlessly joshing Uncle Timmy, or on a visit to Grandma's ancient friend who was under the impression that children liked horehound candy, boredom was the result of mistakes in attempts to entertain us. Being boring was a fault, not a vice. It had never occurred to us that boredom could be premeditated.

Our generation does not believe in original sin. But we do believe that Adam and Eve were boring. We take it on faith that humankind has fallen from divine enjoyment of life. We carry the burden of blasé and are continually tempted to ennui in thought and deed. We can be restored to an Edenic state only by the grace of the Interesting.

We know this from school and from Sunday school, Scouting, summer camp, and organized sports. If you weren't bored by these institutions and activities, you weren't paying attention.

Let us not commit an intentional fallacy. The grown-ups bored us. They had a purpose for doing so. Therefore they bored us on purpose. That is not to say they *meant* to bore us. Quite the contrary with Sunday school teachers, who tried everything to make religion entertaining. God, how they failed.

The tedium of Sunday school, though less frequent and prolonged than the tedium of school, produced greater hopelessness and despair. It was a theft from the heavenly gift to us kids, the weekend. In church basements all over America the Gospel of Mark 10:14 was being invoked, "Suffer the little children to come unto me," leaving little children wondering what they'd done to deserve the suffering (". . . and the children shall rise up against their parents," Matthew 10:21, but that verse was never taught).

Jesus should have been frightfully interesting. He was undead. He wore his bathrobe outdoors. He had a beard. The halo thing meant he glowed in the dark. But by the time the Sunday school teachers were finished with Him all the gee whiz had been taken out of Jesus. He was always patient, kind, gentle, and understanding. The people we knew who were like that were really dull, except Mom. And Mom would give us hell sometimes while Jesus, we were told, was giving us the other place.

The glory of the other place was so vaguely described that it's easy to understand why our generation would mistake getting high on drugs for it.

Hell should have been fascinating. But the Sunday school teachers explained it as a sort of absence, without an excuse, from meeting God. Meeting

God, this sounded worrisome. But hell went on forever. This sounded like Sunday school.

Despite my name, both my parents were milquetoast Protestants. The O'Rourkes had been Catholic but in the 1920s my widower grandfather divorced his lunatic second wife. She'd put her stepchild—my dad's baby brother, later to become overjocular Uncle Timmy—out on the back steps in the snow as punishment for wetting his pants. His underwear froze.

The Catholic Church refused to grant an annulment. Granddad got so angry that he joined the Freemasons, the Republican Party, and the Lutheran Church, all in one day. It's a family story that is, as we journalists say, too good to check. Mom came by her Presbyterianism honestly.

During the 1950s denominations of the Lutheran, Presbyterian, Methodist, and Episcopalian kind had fitted the Light of the World with a lampshade so it wouldn't produce distracting salvational glare and dampened the fires of perdition to avoid spiritual smoke inhalation. A stillness of the soul and a quiet reverence during church services had been turned into sitting still and being quiet.

Catholic kids had the advantage of scary nuns, still in full habits. Did they have hair? Did they have *feet*? Priests, performing the mumbo jumbo of the Latin Mass, were almost as impressive as stage magicians. A Catholic priest could probably pull a quarter out of your ear. (That he could do something else in some other place of yours was not yet a popular article of faith.) And saints were all over the place with special powers like comic book superheroes but more numerous and more outlandishly costumed although beset with really a lot of Kryptonite causing them to be martyred all the time.

And there were kids, like Johnny MacKay, who went to the other kind of Protestant church, the kind in a cement block building with a clever sign out front.

CH RCH TODAY
WHAT'S MISSING?
U ARE

Never mind that much of the congregation and maybe the preacher hadn't finished high school, here was learning and culture. Worshippers were the heirs of Jonathan Edwards, one of colonial America's great religious thinkers, and conversant with the brilliant prose style of his "Sinners in the Hands of an Angry God."

"Consider the fearful danger you are in: 'tis a great furnace of wrath, a wide and bottomless pit, full of the fire of wrath . . . you hang by a slender thread, with the flames of divine wrath flashing about it . . ." Their religion had special effects.

My religion had specific evasions. The more specific the query I made, the more evasive was the response. How come Santa doesn't visit the crèche on Christmas? Baby Jesus is getting presents from the Three Wise Men but nothing from Santa? Does the Easter Bunny come before or after Jesus rises? When the rock was rolled back was the candy inside or outside the tomb? What does the Holy Ghost dress up as on Halloween?

Baby Boomers mock born-agains (or we do until we get cancer, go to jail, or reach the "Higher Power" part of the 12-step program). But Christian fundamentalists can answer these questions and we can't.

Scouting was Sunday school with mission creep. There was God *and* Country and for some reason both were in the Great Outdoors. The proper way to show respect for God and Country when They were outdoors was to adopt pseudomilitary dress and behavior.

We liked wearing the uniforms until we realized, immediately, that they looked stupid. We did not actually go outdoors much. Most Scouting was done in the church gymnasium, but at least it was on a weeknight. I remember maybe three camping trips in my five years of desultory participation in the Boy Scouts. It rained.

"Boy Scout" was not a term of endearment among the Greatest Generation. They'd had enough of military dress and behavior, pseudo- or otherwise. There was no superabundance of dads volunteering to be Scoutmasters. Organizational details were left to high school–aged Eagle Scouts who didn't—even we could tell—have much of a life at high school.

Cub Scouts got no male supervision at all. Den Mothers did their best. As a crafts project for our den, Johnny MacKay's mother chose painting china figurines of choirboys. She had the figurines glazed in the kiln belonging to Mrs. Furstein who lived one block over and was arty. I don't think this was what Baden-Powell had in mind.

When we graduated to the Boy Scouts proper there was the knot tying. What a tangled skein of cordage had to do with God and Country was not clear. What was to be done in the Great Outdoors with a big snarl of rope wasn't clear either. Study of the classics was not a strong point in 1950s education. If we'd known the legend of Alexander the Great and the Gordian knot we would have used our Scout knives on something besides our little brother's hair and sliced right through the hopeless clumps of failed half hitches, sheet bends, and bowlines. Or, anyway, we would have cut ourselves free from the Boy Scouts. As it was, the knottiness prefigured a generational tendency to find the most complex solutions to our problems. Health care reform, variable rate subprime mortgages, and Microsoft Word come to mind.

First aid was also taught. If you need it you'd better hope someone my age doesn't get to you first. And there were weak attempts to memorize semaphore flag signals and do other things that didn't engage our attention, followed by Battleball.

Steve Penske and I were charged with forming a new patrol. We chose the name Bat Patrol. We had the coolest patrol badge. Our patrol's call was an "EEEEEEE," inaudible to human ears.

We weren't any good at going to summer camp either, as Woodstock was to prove. Summer camp was basic—leaky forest, dense cabins, mucky mess hall, and a lake that smelled like greasy food. In time our generation would become fans of the primitive, the rustic, the crude, and the clumsily handmade. But not when our parents approved of it.

We played Capture the Flag at summer camp. The point of the game was to lose the unpopular kids in the woods. At my camp everyone was unpopular.

Summer camp was an exercise in doing things we didn't want to do with people we didn't know. A nature hike with a bunch of strangers was a lot like going to work. We in the Baby Boom put that off for as long as we could, but when we did go to work—on politics, finance, media, and the Internet—we did so with such a will that we almost wrecked the country, so summer camp must have been a suitable preparation.

Organized sports, as they were foisted upon us, had only a tenuous relationship to real sports, the kind we and our dads rooted for on radio and television. My friends and I didn't make a mental connection between Little League and the Cleveland Indians or even between Pop Warner football and the athletic glories on display from September through Thanksgiving in our local high school stadium.

Part of the problem was the fan base. Our parents didn't come down from the stands at our games and hit coaches, opposing players, and each other in swell melees that went viral and got, like, a million hits on YouTube. Such behavior was inconceivable. It would have meant that our parents had come to our games.

Our parents were home getting a little peace and quiet while sports "kept us out of trouble." Meanwhile, we could imagine ourselves as sports stars, but not while playing under adult supervision. There was too much supervising. We had just crossed the finish line and won the Indianapolis 500 in our Soap Box Derby racer when somebody yelled, "Fly ball, you dummy!"

Our parents imagined us as sports stars, too, when they bothered to take time off from imagining sports were keeping us out of trouble. (That playing sports is a way to meet kids who are real trouble is something we never told Mom and Dad.) Our parents imagined, "If the kid has talent maybe he'll get a scholarship to Youngstown State." But even if the dream came true, sports were regarded as a likely road to an income in the high four figures teaching gym someplace with the summer off for standing in the weeds at a public park yelling, "Fly ball, you dummy!"

We suffered from an emphasis on good sportsmanship. We weren't allowed to pump our fists in the air, exchange high fives, do sack dances, or prance around in the end zone as if we had Deep Heat in our jockstraps. We were reduced to bragging to smaller children out of adult earshot. (And the purchase of a first jockstrap was a painful humiliation. Our mothers hovered nearby. The size we required was invariably "small.")

We worshipped our sports heroes, collected their bubble gum pack baseball cards, followed their exploits in the sports pages as well as we could in the balderdash of sports writing, and argued about whether, if Rocky Marciano played baseball and Mickey Mantle was a boxer, who would win. We worshipped our sports heroes, but we didn't identify with them. Wearing an imitation item of Stan Musial's uniform to school would have been as odd as wearing Batman's cape. We'd be laughed at. And sent home. Maybe pro athletes are more approachable in the guilty minds of boys now that "felony indictment" has become a sports statistic.

We were never asked whether we liked sports. Some of us did. Billy and Bobby Stumf were good at sports. For the rest of us . . .

"Pat's batting. Everybody move in!"

"Jerry's on your team. He was on our team last time."

"Bobby, run the buttonhook. Billy, fall back and pass. And Steve and Johnny, you two, uh, go deep."

Liking sports wasn't the point. But, the adults informed us, being good at sports wasn't the point either. This left quite a few of us wondering, "What's the point?"

The point was to learn teamwork and leadership. The Greatest Generation was big on teamwork. I can't think why. They'd just lost China with their Chiang Kai-shek team, been stalemated in Korea on the UN team, and were in the middle of a Cold War that was the result of having been former teammates with the Soviet Union. When corporations teamed up it was called a monopoly and needed to be stopped with antitrust laws. When workers teamed up it was called Jimmy Hoffa and needed to be investigated by the FBI. But out on the sports field we were told, "There is no 'I' in team." And what with the way we were taught to spell in the 1950s, we had to think about that one.

Our parents were also big on leadership while, at the same time, being grossly cynical about leaders. They would say things like, "Ike wanted to be president because then he'd get *two* pensions when he retired." They'd impute base motives to those in positions of even the least authority. "The paperboy knows the Ryans are on vacation so he delivered their paper to us and saved himself three cents." And they knew what happened to youthful leaders. Our parents remembered D-day. They themselves were experts in "leading from behind," preferably from behind a beer at home while we played Little League. Maybe all generations want their children to have what they did not. Or maybe they didn't love us as much as we think.

The point of organized sports was teamwork and leadership. As far as I could tell from questioning adults, the point of everything they cajoled us into doing—sports, Scouting, religious instruction, summer camp—was teamwork and leadership.

I wonder what kind of leader I was supposed to become by getting beaned at home plate, making granny knots, being paired on the buddy system in the lake at camp with a kid who ran away and hid in the latrine, and thinking up three questions to ask Jesus if He came to our church bake sale. And I wonder what kind of team would want a semiconscious, tangled-up, soaking-wet, agnostic team member.

When you hear, these days, that there's no teamwork or leadership in Congress, the White House, business, industry, education, civil society, or at home when it's time to decide who's making dinner, it's because the Baby Boomers would rather have been watching TV. Even *Name That Tune*.

And, by the way, why is it that the TV of the 1950s, along with the suburbs and the tail fins, takes so much grief from deep thinkers? In a 1961 speech the chairman of the Federal Communications Commission, Newton N. Minow (now *there's* a name for a deep thinker), told the National Association of Broadcasters, right to its face, that television was "a vast wasteland." As if, before TV, my family spent the evening playing chess and Tchaikovsky.

Leave It to Beaver is still taking a beating as the exemplar of all that's tepid and bogus in our Baby Boom cultural heritage. This pleasantly written and acted diversion featured a masterful portrayal of Silent Generation Iago Lite in Eddie Haskell. Is the depiction of middle-class Baby Boom life in *Leave It to Beaver* less acute and penetrating than the depiction of middle-class Elizabethan life in Shakespeare's *Merry Wives of Windsor*? Which entertainment winks more often at moral turpitude? And, tell the truth, which would you rather sit through?

Not to go off on another digression (although the Baby Boom has always been inclined to wander from the main subject whenever we can get a hall pass), but unfounded objections to tract houses, DeSotos, and Beaver Cleaver make you fear for the mental well-being of intellectuals. We are not a highly intellectual generation and who can blame us.

Baby Boom girls didn't mind the boredom as much as Baby Boom boys. Girls could see into the future. This was evident in the way girls played with dolls that had dollhouses full of sinks, toilets, bassinets, and other items of real futurity plus doll clothes and somebody's older brother from down the block who'd rip Barbie's blouse off to look at her breasts. Meanwhile boys were playing "war," something that, a few years later, none of us would take a part in if we could help it.

Girls knew that the tedium of school was a necessary preparation for the tedium of home and family. And Baby Boom girls had an intuition that their tedium would extend beyond home and family to professions, corporate management, and the State Department. They'd better get ready to be bored.

Boys were driven crazy—literally crazy, as defined in the current edition of the American Psychiatric Association's *Diagnostic and Statistical Manual of Mental Disorders*. The "diagnostic criteria" for Attention Deficit/Hyperactivity Disorder include:

> makes careless mistakes in schoolwork
> does not seem to listen
> is often easily distracted
> fidgets with hands or feet or squirms in seat
> runs about or climbs excessively
> has difficulty playing or engaging in leisure activities quietly

These boys have been accurately diagnosed as boys. Now there are drugs to treat it. The medications are what Baby Boomers would call uppers. The recommended therapy for ADHD is, essentially, dating fat girls to get their diet pills to study for exams.

It's a shame, although not because Ritalin, Adderall, Vyvanse, Concerta lead to a lifetime of drug dependency and squalor. I came of age in the 1960s. A lifetime of drug dependency and squalor has its points. But kids are sitting still after the bell, engrossed in their schoolwork, and being denied the benefits of the fantasy life induced by utter boredom.

Our school's classrooms and halls had two-tone paint based on some theory that was current about what was good for eyesight: a pale bile green above a nose-high watermark with a darker cheese mold green below. The school is filling up with water, right to the watermark level. Miss Burbage's big wooden desk and chair are floating away and Miss Burbage with them. We have to tread water or we'll drown. "Get back in your seat," says Miss Burbage.

Our school is indeed a fortress. Other kids from other schools are attacking it. We rain Miss Burbage's potted African violets down upon their heads. They break through the girls' entrance with a teeter-totter battering ram. We fence with wooden rulers. They throw blackboard erasers. Our only hope is to retreat to the auditorium and barricade the stage with cardboard straw, cardboard twigs, and cardboard bricks from the first grade's performance of *Three Little Pigs*. "Get back in your seat," says Miss Burbage.

My desk is a helicopter. Mary Ritter sits in front of me. Her dual braids spin, *whup, whup, whup*. Jack Gertin sits behind me, a round boy, the tail rotor. I have twin .50-caliber Number 2 pencils. Oh no, ack-ack at twelve o'clock high. Good thing I've got a parachute in my book bag. "For the last time," says Miss Burbage, "get back in your seat."

And every couple of months we'd have a real air raid drill and get under our desks to protect ourselves from nuclear holocaust. Nowadays the kids, their minds made literal by drug-induced obsession with doing long division, would be scared they were going to die. But we, in the sure and certain hope of fantasy life, knew that atomic bombs only killed grown-ups and probably caused school to be let out early. Billy and I and Johnny and Steve and Bobby and Jerry would survive, like in *Lord of the Flies* but without the flies. Not that I'd read the book, or heard of it. But when I did read it I was impressed anew with the capacity of adults like William Golding to spoil things.

The Prelude

Bliss was it in that dawn to be alive, but to be young was very heaven, as William Wordsworth said when he got his driver's license.

The Baby Boom's first social movement was cruising. This is not to be confused with "Crusin'"— adolescence on wheels as it is poorly remembered in popular culture and badly reenacted in Plymouth Belvederes by old bald guys. I never saw a carhop wearing roller skates. The idea was as stupid then as it is now.

Nor did we cruise in the singles bar or Chistopher Street sense, loitering with sexual intent. We were full of sexual intentions. And we could loiter. But we had a broader agenda.

We drove around and around. Our parents didn't understand cruising. They thought we were driving around to find a place to drink and make out. Not that we weren't. But the Greatest Generation, with its dull powers of fancy, never suspected that our goal was to have no goal at all. Life is a journey, not a destination, as Ralph Waldo Emerson said when he got his driver's license.

We had the perfect pointless joy of freedom. It wasn't just our parents who didn't understand; neither do we anymore. We as grown-ups tell ourselves as kids (and tell our own kids), "Freedom is a serious responsibility" or, "Freedom means making important choices" or, if we've had a couple of drinks and are listening to an oldies station, "Freedom's just another word for nothing left to lose." We as kids tell ourselves as grown-ups, "No, it's not" and "No, it doesn't." And our kids tell us that Janis Joplin needed Auto-Tune. I leave it to others to decide whether, over the years, the Baby Boom has gained sophistication concerning the ontological question of free will.

We drove around and around. There were a few little red sports cars, hot rods, custom jobs, and bitching sets of wheels. Very few. Turning sixteen caused our parents to break out in a rash of vehicular insipidity. (Any good Baby Boom boy my age can testify that the oomph went out of American family car design in 1963.) Dad bought Mom a snappy convertible back about the time of the Nixon-Kennedy debates. When we got our driver's license, he traded it in on a station wagon.

Only rich kids with indulgent parents and poor kids with after-school jobs had their own cars. And thus began the political trend of Angry Middle-Class Resentment. The middle class is furious, or at least as furious as middle-class proprieties allow. You've seen it in the firebrand—well, Weber grill charcoal lighter—demagoguery and the crass rabble-rousing (though we're not rabble, so call it Babbitt-rousing) of recent elections and on *Morning Joe*.

Once the Baby Boom had gone through all its rudimentary phases of ideological development, from revolutionary pimples to Reaganite hip replacement, the true politics of our generation would be revealed. In America the reasonably well-off and moderately comfortable are the angry masses. It has to do with borrowing Mom's car.

Jim Fisk tried to make the best of things. He showed everybody how one pull on a lever caused the whole front seat of his mother's Nash Rambler to fold down into a bed.

Ana Klein said, "You're going to pull the lever and some girl's going to flip over backward and break her neck."

"No girl," said Al Bartz, "is willing to be seen dead in a Nash Rambler."

Turning sixteen caused us to break out in a rash of unwonted helpfulness. "I'll go to the supermarket, Mom. We're almost out of paprika."

We drove around and around. The cars got bad mileage. But gas was 31 cents a gallon. We could get to where all the other kids were by looking under the couch cushions. Unspoken consensus made driving up and down certain streets obligatory and parking in certain places required. Sometimes when we parked we were "parking," as the art of love was called, and sometimes when we parked we were parked. We got out of our cars to talk to each other. We're a talkative generation, and only so much can be shouted from a car window.

We got out of our cars but not away from them. That would have been like separating the body from the soul. Or, not to overstate the case, it would have been like getting too far from a bathroom for the males among us fifty years later. We lounged against the fenders. We perched on the trunk lids. We stood in the open doors with one foot resting on the sill and an elbow cocked on the roof, looking cool. It wasn't just our cool friend Leo Luhan who thought he was cool. Now we all did. And the cars of those days didn't ruin looking cool with nagging ding-dong noises if you left the car door open and the keys in the ignition.

It's heavy lifting conducting light flirtations. Much effort goes into crafting an effortless guise. We worked up an appetite. Drive-in burger restaurants played a crucial role in cruising. They were parking lots with food.

We had plenty to talk to each other about and plenty of each other to talk to. The Baby Boom was discovering itself—and not in the tiresome way that we would keep doing for the rest of our lives until, by now, every rock in our psyche has been overturned and each wiggling thing we've found underneath has been squashed or made into a pet. Youth was discovering youth. Not only were there lots of us, there were lots more of us. Other kids went to other high schools. The boys were almost as cool. The girls were even cuter.

Driving around was our Facebook. We never thought to monetize it. Generational vice? Or generational virtue?

We drove around and around and we talked and talked. We talked about what's cool and what's uncool. No one listens when teenagers talk, including the teenagers themselves most of the time. But teenagers were (and still are in present-day text messages) having an ancient colloquy of deep significance.

What we discussed appears in the Revised Standard Version of the Bible, Proverbs 17:27, "he who has a cool spirit is a man of understanding." Cool. The *Oxford English Dictionary* cites a line from a Chaucer poem, "thynkist in thyn wit that is ful cole." Spelling bees are uncool. In 1938 Eric Partridge, the twentieth century's preeminent lexicographer of slang, gave a cool definition of *cool* in *A Dictionary of Slang and Unconventional English*: "impertinent, impudent, audacious, especially if in a calm way." This was in common use by the mid-1820s, standard English by the mid-1880s, and exactly what we were talking about by the mid-1960s. In 2010 Partridge's lexicographic heir Jonathon Green, author of the 6,000-page *Green's Dictionary of Slang,* devoted eighteen column inches to *cool* and said, "As with a number of slang's (rare) abstract terms, it is less than simple to draw hard-and-fast lines between the senses."

We've been out of our senses a lot. The Baby Boom was always less than simple. Forget the hard-and-fast lines. We are a fiery generation, heated in our affection, feverish in our action, blistering in our scorn—and obsessed with being cool. Later we'd be a fat generation—obsessed with being fit. We still think we're cool. That isn't all. We still think we're hot.

Good thing we talked this out while we were driving around.

The music we listened to was cool. The power of our generation is our music. But, in the interest of speaking truth to power, I looked at the Billboard Top 100 for the year I went from junior to senior in high school. We liked "Everybody Loves Somebody" by Dean Martin (no. 6) better than we liked the Beatles' "Can't Buy Me Love" (no. 52). We liked "We'll Sing in the Sunshine" by Gale Garnett (no. 8) better than we liked the Kinks' "You Really Got Me" (no. 78). The Rolling Stones didn't make the chart. Leo Luhan had mentioned them. He said you could tell their music was influenced by the Kingsmen's "Louie Louie." Here are the actual lyrics to "Louie Louie" as posted on the Internet, a medium that does not spare our sensibilities.

Louie Louie, oh no
Me gotta go
Aye-yi-yi-yi, I said
Louie Louie, oh baby
Me gotta go

And more of the same. If it's any comfort the previous year's Billboard Top 100 was worse: "Hello Muddah, Hello Faddah, Here I am at Camp Granada . . ." and "Blame It on the Bossa Nova" by Eydie Gorme.

There were three AM stations playing the same songs. This was good because when one station finished playing a song we could push the buttons on the car radio and find the same song being played on another station. We enjoyed hearing songs over and over. As with wearing clothes like everyone else's and belonging to a clique and driving around to the same places at the same times, it forged individual identity.

A lot of identical individual identities were forged. We saw nothing ironic about this. So far the Baby Boom had only a mild, *Playboy* cartoon caption case of the ironic. Irony wouldn't become chronic and severe until the 1970s when we ran out of cool things that we all agreed on and disco happened.

AM radio was the sound track of our life. That was a cool thing that we all agreed on. Leo Luhan considered himself a talented composer of the sound track of his life. He made suggestions to the manager of the drive-in burger restaurant about what should be on the jukebox.

The restaurant had tables and booths inside, where we went when it was too cold to be cool outside. There was a sophomore we knew, driving around with us. He didn't have his driver's license. Leo convinced him to go into the burger restaurant and feed the jukebox so that the right sound track theme song would be playing when Leo walked through the door. Other kids had fed the jukebox. Twenty minutes passed before "Louie Louie" came on. We had to get up on our knees in the restaurant booth and frantically signal to Leo who was waiting in the car and had trouble seeing us through his sunglasses. By the time he got there the jukebox was playing "We'll Sing in the Sunshine."

Everything adults thought we were supposed to do was uncool. Especially if we were supposed to do it for fun. Adults had a peculiar sense of fun. My wife's book club meets at our house tonight. They're reading a self-help book called *My Life Sucks, I Hate You*. I intend to spend the evening in my basement workshop sorting a coffee can full of screws into small trays according to size and whether they are slotted or Phillips head. Adults retain a peculiar sense of fun.

Homecoming was all sorts of fun. The Homecoming Game was the West Side Cowboys versus their traditional rival the North Side Polar Bears.

"The West Side Cowboys," said Al Bartz, "and the North Side Polar Bears and the East Side Yankees. The school system was really thinking it through."

At the Homecoming Dance, balloons (sunset orange and buffalo brown, the school colors) were put in the basketball nets. Rented tuxedos made sure the fun was special. No shoes allowed made sure the gym floor wasn't damaged. The chaperones' efforts to curtail lewd personal contact were conducted on principles opposite of today's. Kids pressed together tightly with low lights in slow dances—this was considered sweet. Wild gyrations of the hully gully, the jerk, and the watusi performed four feet from a partner—these were glared at.

Joe Brody had the idea of using a hypodermic needle to inject vodka into a watermelon. Ideas, we were beginning to understand, were important for their own sake. That is, we didn't know where to get a hypodermic needle. Even Joe's parents would miss a whole bottle of vodka. It was November, there weren't any watermelons. And why would anyone bring a watermelon to a homecoming dance? We were almost ready for ideas of peace and love.

The homecoming parade had a float. A flatbed trailer was borrowed from the local plant nursery. Two-by-fours were nailed together to make a framework on the trailer. Chicken wire was bent around the two-by-fours more or less in the shape of a giant, almost-four-foot-tall cowboy boot. "Boot the Bears" was the homecoming theme.

To get a Rose Bowl parade float effect, wads of Kleenex were stuffed into the chicken wire. Kleenex did not make brown or orange Kleenex. The local stationery store donated a roll of brown tissue paper and a roll of orange. BOOT THE BEARS was spelled out in brown and orange on the boot top although with some spacing difficulties so that what paradegoers saw was BOOTT HEB EARS.

I don't remember why I was helping stuff Kleenex into chicken wire. I may have thought, wrongly, that Marsha Matthiessen would be helping stuff Kleenex into chicken wire. I do remember a sudden and strong feeling of being uncool. I am in my middle sixties. I have a teenage daughter. The feeling was stronger than that. The parade float looked like chicken wire with Kleenex stuffed into it.

Ana Klein, by dint of her many dance classes, had been chosen as one of the Tumbleweed Girls. They performed gymnastics on the sidelines at football games dressed alike in western outfits purchased at the local Western Wear store. Al Bartz asked Ana, "Is there a Midwestern Wear store?" She quit.

Tim Minsky ran for student council. His platform was based on a simple formula. Student council had no power. Therefore, if he was elected, he'd do nothing. He won. We'd soon loose our sense of humor about politics. It wouldn't come back until Watergate. When the Baby Boom's sense of humor about politics returned it acted like it had been sleeping in alleys and eating out of garbage cans.

We'd already lost our sense of humor about our parents. If we'd had one. Anything a parent said or did we took personally. (I don't think our children have made this mistake. The lesson in the Baby Boom's lifelong fascination with personhood, personality, and persons is that people shouldn't be taken personally.)

Our parents were generally pathetic. When they were specifically pathetic the pain was intense. Dr. Klein told Ana, Tim Minsky, and me, "I like that Beatles group. Some of the songs those young men sing show that they have genuine musical talent."

"I think they're cute!" said Mrs. Klein.

There was nothing of the remote about our parents. Meaning *remote* as a noun. They couldn't push our buttons from a distance. They had to come right up and try to switch to the channel we were on. They should have stuck with *remote* as an adjective.

We would have detested the twenty-first century's remote-control connectivity—cell phones, texting, Twitter. Parents everywhere, like God? (A god that couldn't tell George from Ringo.) The horror is unimaginable to the mid-1960s teenage mind. Parents with a Facebook page. Like a newspaper page but never thrown away. Parents "posting" things, as in a poster, as in a billboard, as in a billboard on a busy street where we were cruising. With things about us on it. With things about our parents. And last summer's snapshots. When I still had a crew cut and my sisters were teasing their hair.

Then we, the Baby Boom, invented electronic personal communication devices. We, of all people. TV that watches you. It's as if we read *Nineteen Eighty-Four,* and said, "Good idea!"

We didn't need connectivity. We were where all the other kids were, cruising West End Avenue, at the drive-in burger restaurant, watching submarine races by the pond in Pondside Park.

The Internet is a universally shared thought process. We had one already. When we were juniors the accepted, indeed required, dress for boys was penny loafers, white Levi's, a madras long-sleeved shirt, and white wool socks. On the first day of senior year Leo Luhan—with that deliberate flaunting of convention for which the Baby Boom is known—would come to school wearing penny loafers, white Levi's, a madras long-sleeved shirt. And black dress socks. The rest of us had come to school the same day wearing penny loafers, white Levi's, madras long-sleeved shirts. And black dress socks.

It wasn't like we hated the grown-ups. Yet. We were capable of real feelings for adults, as long as they had nothing to do with our lives.

In the fall of my junior year John F. Kennedy was shot in Dallas, and in American literature class. The school PA system—not an electronic personal, or any other kind of, communication device—made the details incomprehensible but the situation clear. There was no mistaking the sober tone and poignant halts in the loudspeaker static for an Al Bartz prank.

Our parents and teachers were shocked because John Kennedy was one of them the way John Lennon was (although, born in 1940, he really wasn't) one of us. That is, they were shocked because John Kennedy was one of them and then some, them more so, them to a greater—and not just presidential—power. Them richer than a king and admirably schooled in every grace.

We were shocked by all the emotion. Embarrassment, crushes, and embarrassment about crushes (and erections) were emotions as we knew them. Most of us had never lost a parent. Most of us had never even lost a parent to a woman younger than Mom. Not being allowed to borrow the car was our understanding of loss. Bereavement was annoying fellow grade school student Sonny Merton run over by a truck.

The emotions were so strong that we forgot to be cool. Not that there wasn't something cool about the strength of the emotions and their uninhibited display.

Mr. Entwhistle the American literature teacher knew a lot of poetry by heart. He began to recite "Richard Cory" by Edwin Arlington Robinson.

He was a gentleman from sole to crown,
Clean favored and imperially slim.
And he was rich—yes richer than a king—
And admirably schooled in every grace.

A wildly inappropriate poem, ending,

So on we worked, and waited for the light,
And went without the meat, and cursed the bread;
And Richard Cory, one calm summer night,
Went home and put a bullet through his head.

I think Mr. Entwhistle meant to recite "To an Athlete Dying Young" by A. E. Housman, because he did recite that the next time we were in American literature class (even though it wasn't American literature).

Now you will not swell the rout
Of lads that wore their honors out,
Runners whom renown outran
And the name died before the man.

Which we did not exactly understand because West Side High had a trophy case, and everybody who'd won something had his name engraved on a cup or a bowl or the base of a statuette.

But we understood the Kennedy assassination was a significant event for our generation. The significance being that the Kennedy assassination was Pearl Harbor scaled down to the level of the Baby Boom's understanding of actions having consequences.

The consequence of the assassination was only another president, more successful at pushing a legislative agenda—with which Kennedy is wrongly credited—and more effective at pressing a foreign policy—from which Kennedy is wrongly excused. Then myth took hold, in an early 1960s way. *Camelot,* starring Richard Burton and Julie Andrews, had recently closed on Broadway after 873 performances.

Don't let it be forgot
That once there was a spot
Where the president was fun
And he's remembered as having something to do with a drunk actor and a singing nun.

A generational truth was discovered. How people feel about things is as important as things. Feelings are real. And now so were girls. You could feel them. Eventually. But you had to talk to them about feelings first. (For girls, boys got real too—until talking to us about feelings got unreal at the end of the first marriage.)

I talked about feelings to my high school girlfriend Karen. Although she wasn't my girlfriend yet. She had to be talked into it. I don't mean by me, I mean by the power of talk in general. "They talked themselves into it" is the motto of the Baby Boom. Or maybe "They talked themselves out of it." But we're saving that for our epitaph.

Karen and I talked about feelings in a memorable way. I can't remember any of it. The fragments of our chat that have stuck in my mind for half a century—Karen explaining tampons—can't have been representative of our conversation. They sound more like intimate talk from toward the end of our being a couple, when we were promising to stay together while going to colleges far apart. We weren't talking about tampons in our kiss-on-the-lips-but-no-tongue stage. Nor were we talking about feeling cool and uncool. A boy doesn't speak to a girl about that. To mention being cool to the object of being cool is worse than uncool. It's the quarterback leaving the huddle to join the Tumbleweed Girls. Karen and I just talked. Words are Baby Boom pheromones.

One school night, when I'd borrowed the car and was supposed to be at the library and actually was at the library, Karen and I were sitting across from each other not studying. It was a week or ten days since we'd started talking between classes, in the cafeteria, at the drive-in burger restaurant, on the phone for an hour at a time. I was smiling at her. She was smiling at me. And then I felt an ankle-socked toe just above the vamp of my penny loafer and moving toward the hem of my white Levi's. The erotic shock was so intense that today I am at a loss to explain why I don't have a fetish for toes, ankle socks, or my old left penny loafer.

For a couple of years the Baby Boom was blessed with sure and certain hope. What we hoped for was sex and drugs. Hopes that would come too true but, in our blessed state, not for a little while.

We'd heard about drugs. The marijuana scare preceded the marijuana. We were never able to find any. Leo Luhan and I went to a jazz club downtown and sat through a set by somebody who somebody said sounded something like Charles Mingus. I had no idea a bass fiddle could be that noisy. The drug pusher seemed to have had the night off.

However, the fat girl Joe Brody was dating (fat by the ethereal standards of the era and, come to that, we were entering an era where all standards were ethereal) shared her diet pills. Joe stayed up all night writing a paper on *The Scarlet Letter* and the next day, still going, he insisted on reading it aloud in American literature class, taking up most of the period describing the ways Nathaniel Hawthorne's plot and character development would be transformed if Hester Prynne and Arthur Dimmesdale committed the six other deadly sins, starting with gluttony.

Sex, too, was had in occasional and limited doses. Fumbling anticipation generated a kind of prolonged bliss that fumbled completion has rarely matched. We were tantric when Buddha was still a porker on a shelf over the bar in Phillip Woo's parents' restaurant. No one's life was left in a mess by sex. Although some of our clothing was. What ever happened to the hand job?

It was an existence upon which no improvement could be made except, of course, for elimination of prejudice, poverty, war, and injustice and Dad buying us an Austin-Healey.

We were aware of, if not the nature, the prevalence of evil. "Black humor" was in vogue. There was Lenny Bruce, Paul Krassner's *The Realist,* ice-nine in Kurt Vonnegut's *Cat's Cradle,* and Al Bartz saying, "How do you unload a truck full of dead babies?"

We were sensitive to grim realities. "*With a pitchfork.*" In our college application essays we pointed out that prejudice, poverty, war, and injustice should be eliminated.

Meanwhile it would also be nice to have a place of our own, a "pad." But who'd iron our madras shirts? (And *not* our white Levi's. "Mom, they aren't *supposed* to have a crease!")

And it would be great if there was no school. But we skipped a lot. Grades don't count after the first semester of senior year. Ana Klein did a good mom voice. "Pat's not feeling too well." We were going to state colleges anyway. Except for Tim Minsky who would be studying math at Yale, to the mystification of most of our parents. "It's so far away," my mother said. "If he went to Ohio State he could come home on weekends."

Perhaps there were as many troubled adolescents then as there are now. But young people are sensitive to fashion trends, and being troubled wasn't in style. Girls weighed ninety pounds and barfed after eating a whole half gallon of butter pecan ice cream. Boys drove cars into phone poles at seventy miles an hour. But anorexia, bulimia, and teenage suicide were unheard of.

We were having fun. The stories we could tell—and do tell and will tell and have told and keep telling in movies, songs, TV shows, memoirs, blogs (though not much in poems and novels—literature is the enemy of fun), and to spouses, children, each other, and to ourself now that we've started talking to that person. There was the time Jim Fisk and I drove overnight to Hell, Michigan, a 422-mile round-trip, so we could say that we'd "been to hell and back." We left right after school on a Wednesday and . . . Oh shut up.

There's proof that it was a wonderful moment for our generation in the very fact of how boring our stories are. Every description of paradise is boring. According to the Bible, Adam and Eve didn't even notice they were naked and spent all day naming animals. It's a shame how the Baby Boom has never learned to appreciate boredom. It would make this current part of our lives more interesting.

Teenage 1960s middle-class America was a shining suburb on a hill. Almost twenty years would go by before we realized that. We've been trying to walk or fly or bum a ride back there since the first John Hughes movie came out.

It wasn't just fun. It was a state of grace. We wanted to bestow our state of grace upon the world. Youth was a virtue. We pitied the moral lapse of those who lacked it. Life was good. We were living. Therefore we were good. Since we were good, and we were mankind, then mankind was good. We'd make mankind as good as itself and living as fun as life. We'd change everything. And we'd write in each other's high school yearbooks, "Don't ever change!"

Ripeness Is All

Everything's all right. It turned out okay. Better than okay. Life has been much more fun since the Baby Boom took over. "Mommy, why are there scarves tied to the bedposts in Daddy's and your bedroom?" And there are plenty of fun tales to be told about the Baby Boom in the 1980s, the '90s, the '00s, and today. But we're saving them for psychotherapy sessions. If you go to a psychotherapy session and just sit there saying nothing it makes it seem like something's wrong with you, psychologically.

By the end of the 1970s the Baby Boom character had been formed. Our last youthful exuberance, "Punk," came just before Generation X's first youthful exuberance, "Goth"—a subtle shift from "fuck you" to "I'm fucked" that indicates the Baby Boom will remain in control for a long time to come.

We're still opposed to prejudice, poverty, war, and injustice—when they happen to us. But at least we're opposed to them. There have been times and places—the 1960s South, Benedictine monasteries, the 1860s South, and divorce court—where previous generations made strong arguments in favor of prejudice, poverty, war, and injustice, which you won't hear us doing. At least not very often except in divorce court or during hostile corporate takeovers or when Iran has nuclear weapons or looks like it maybe does or wants to.

If the Baby Boom went around being prejudiced against races, religions, ethnic groups, genders, and sexual orientations, date night would be pretty much down to a dose of Cialis and a box of tissues on the bedside table.

Who would invest in our BabyBoondoggle IPO if poverty meant nobody had enough money to buy the worthless stock?

War is wrong—itchy uniforms and ugly shoes.

We don't like injustice. We don't like justice either. Because we're the generation that's *not judgmental*. And who the hell put traffic surveillance cameras at every goddamned intersection? (Oops. That was us. We put surveillance cameras everywhere when we remembered how Joe Brody and Billy and Bobby Stumf and Johnny MacKay and Steve Penske and Jerry Harris and I were going to vandalize North Side High's football field with weed killer.)

The Baby Boom has had politics figured out since at least 1980. An American and a Russian are talking about Ronald Reagan and Leonid

Brezhnev. The American says, "I hate Reagan so much I pissed on his limousine." The Russian says, "I hate Brezhnev so much I *shit* on his limousine." The American says, "Well, to tell the truth, Reagan wasn't in the limousine when I pissed on it." The Russian says, "Well, to tell the truth, my pants weren't down."

The key is inept leadership. This makes things easy on followers. The Baby Boom has always gone in for following inept leaders. Follow Keith Richards and you can wind up in some sort of trouble. But follow Napoleon and you can wind up in Moscow.

Prior generations didn't have politics figured out. When my 100-year-old godmother was a freshman in high school she began to read the *Atlantic Monthly* in the school library. One night at dinner she announced, "I think Coolidge is a dope." Her father made her stand in the front hall closet for half an hour for showing disrespect to the president of the United States. Meanwhile I have it on good authority that President Reagan told the limousine joke himself.

Prior generations didn't have diversity figured out either. There was another joke, considered quite hip in 1962, yet the laugh line was almost the same as what the serious pundits were saying about who was most likely to be elected president in 2008. A man dies and goes to heaven but doctors resuscitate him and he comes back to life and everybody wants to know what's God like. "She's black."

Being different wasn't always considered normal, if not obligatory. Not even in the freewheeling sixties. When Tim Minsky was a senior at Yale he shared an off-campus apartment with a roommate who was diabetic. This was before the ready availability of disposable needles and the roommate was supposed to boil his syringe after every insulin injection. One of the kids with whom Tim and I had gone to high school, a serious type named Danny Phelps, was applying to grad school at Yale and stopped by to visit Tim. Danny glanced into the pot of water boiling on the stove and gave Tim a puzzled look.

Tim said, "Danny, there's a confession I've been wanting to make for a long time. I've never told this to anyone. I'm a heroin addict."

Danny sat down at the kitchen table, burst into tears, and said, "Tim, there's a confession I've been wanting to make for a long time. I've never told this to anyone. I'm a homosexual."

If Tim had been thinking quick he would have said, "So's Anderson Cooper and Barney Frank and Rufus Wainwright and Alexander the Great and Gomer Pyle and the mutant superhero Northstar in Marvel Comics' X-Men (a perfect Baby Boom touch—identity politics for secret identities). But Tim couldn't think that quick because none of those people were out of the closet in 1968. Tim didn't know what to say and felt like a jerk.

And feminism is so far along among Baby Boomers that women aren't even bothering to make men feel like jerks anymore, outside of marriage. As far as I can tell "third wave feminists" are mainly arguing about whether women can be simultaneously managing director of the International Monetary Fund, chancellor of Germany, Nobel laureate, Supreme Court justice, author of the best-selling book series in history, CEO of Xerox, and mother of three when there are only so many hours in the day. I understand that House Minority leader Nancy Pelosi is lobbying Congress to lengthen the day to seventy-two hours. Meanwhile Baby Boom men are left to wonder (but never aloud) whether—hand that rocks the cradle and all that—feminism hasn't always been a matter of women having a leg wrestling match with their own other leg.

There are some things the Baby Boom has done that we're not proud of. We used up all the weird. It has always been the special prerogative of youth to look and act strange, to alarm and surprise their elders with peculiar dress and manners. Cicero mentioned it. "O tempora! O mores!" So did my mom, although in English. But the Baby Boom exhausted the available supply of peculiar. Weird clothes, we wore them. Weird beards, we grew them. Weird words and phrases, we said them. Weird attitudes, we had them. Thus when it came time for the next generation to alarm and surprise us with their peculiarities they were compelled to pierce their extremities and permanently ink their exposed flesh. That must have hurt. We apologize.

The Baby Boom unleashed the safety hysteria on the world. I recently bought a stepladder so festooned with stickers warning of the types and kinds of peril entailed in operating this device that it lacked only bold capital letters stenciled in signal orange upon each stepladder step: DO NOT STEP ON LADDER.

I cannot get into my car without setting off a panic among admonitory bells and buzzers cautioning me to buckle this, close that, and lock the other thing.

Of course each child must be accompanied by a full-scale parental security detail on every visit to a sporting event, school activity, shopping mall, public restroom, Scout jamboree, and Catholic Mass, especially if the tyke is within inappropriate touching distance of a priest or Scoutmaster.

We bother and control our older children and interfere in every aspect of their lives because we don't want them horning in on the fun of being juvenile, which rightfully belongs in perpetuity to the Baby Boom. Although I also blame the kids. In "The Helicopter Parent/Air-Support Child" relationship, it takes two to "Tango Hotel Papa to Alpha Sierra Charlie: debit card deposit in-bound at zero-nine-hundred hours."

And despite the fact that we are now at the age when our generation has full control of the levers and pulleys of the American political mechanism, we ourselves haven't done much to legalize drugs except print up some "Medical Marijuana Makes Me Sick" bumper stickers.

"Safety" is so inconsistent with the spirit of the Baby Boom that it's like hearing the Clash performing Gilbert and Sullivan at the Nixon Library. Perhaps post-traumatic stress disorder explains the Baby Boom's safety hysteria. Doing the things our generation did and coming through them safely—that's hysterical.

Anyway, we grew up. We got married. We found true love. This wrecked the marriage. But we're a caring generation. We sometimes take care of the kids on weekends.

We got jobs. We made money. We spent it on cocaine. Then we made money with junk bonds for leveraged buyouts. Until the LBO market collapsed and the savings and loan crisis happened and some of us such as Michael Milken had to go to jail. Then we made money in the dot.com bubble. Hope you're not still waiting for the Webvan grocery delivery or the chew toy you ordered from Pets.com. Then we made money with subprime mortgage lending securitization and collateralized debt obligations. Sorry about the foreclosure. One thing about moving the family back to Mom's house, she may be getting a little dotty but she still makes a great meat loaf. Now we'll make money with category-killer SmartPhone apps.

But whatever it is that the Baby Boom has and hasn't done, it's worked.

First, look at the butcher's bill. When the Greatest Generation took charge of America in 1961, their esteemed John F. Kennedy and his pals began a war that, according to the Department of Defense, left some 58,200 Americans dead from battle and its attendant accidents, incidents, and disease. And this for a purpose that has yet to be explained.

That's not as completely horrible as what the Idiot Generation preceding the Greatest Generation did. They killed 405,399 Americans in World War II and another 36,576 in the Korean War. True, the idiots didn't start the wars, but they did fuck-all to prevent or preempt them, and may they rot in hell.

The Baby Boom took charge of America (and hence, for all intents and purposes, the world) in 1988. That's when we decided to skip a generation of political leadership. We bypassed the ever-risible Silent Generation represented by bobble-head Michael Dukakis trying to take a ride in a tank. (Younger readers should consult YouTube—a laugh is guaranteed.) We elected, as a sort of stand-in father figure, George H. W. Bush. And soon we'd have a Bill Clinton White House full of the Baby Boom and a Newt Gingrich Congress equally full of it.

Three hundred and eighty-two Americans died in the Persian Gulf War, 4,488 in the Iraq War, and 2,170 in Afghanistan as of this writing. That's an improvement. We do have blood on our hands. But there will be less

"Out, damned spot! out, I say!" when our conscience performs its Act V of *Macbeth*. Although let us not let ourselves off too easily. What with allowing villainous slaughter to run amok in the Balkans for most of a decade, staying seated in the bleachers during the Rwanda butchery, being perfectly oblivious to the oncoming catastrophic attack on New York and Washington by militant Islamic fundamentalists, giving no thought to what the Pandora's box of the Iraq War contained for Iraqi civilians, and so on, we'll probably rot in hell, too, but in an upscale neighborhood of it.

Now look at the balance sheet. The size of the world economy has more than tripled since Baby Boom students quit paying attention in economics class. World trade has grown enormously. I don't want to take all the credit myself, but I did buy a cheap Indian batik bedspread after I got my first job. The per capita gross domestic product of India, in 2013 dollars, was $691 in 1972 and is $1,734 now. Then I bought some cheap Japanese stereo equipment. Japan's per capita GDP went from $5,104 to $47,783 in the same period. Chinese electronics were even cheaper. China's per capita GDP has gone from $724 to $6,741. And we haven't done so badly ourselves with inflation-adjusted U.S. per capita GDP growing by $18,725 to reach a current figure of $51,248 on the Baby Boom's watch.

More to the point, morally speaking, there's the World Bank's index of global extreme poverty. By which they do mean extreme—people living on less than $1.25 a day. You can't even buy anything at the Dollar Store for $1.25 these days. In 1981, 52 percent of people in the developing world were that poor. By 1990 it was 43 percent. By 2008 (the last year for which the World Bank has complete data) it was 22 percent. This still leaves 1.29 billion people in starving and ragged misery. You might want to move the decimal point one place to the right on your check to Save the Children. But World Bank preliminary estimates indicate that, despite a worldwide economic slowdown, extreme poverty continues to abate.

The Baby Boom is more famous for repeatedly declaring that we're moral than for repeatedly acting that way, but the earth's increase in widespread well-being and decrease in widespread war couldn't have happened without a generation of self-indulgent Americans avid for all the good things in life and disinclined to put themselves—and hence, for all intents and purposes, the world—to too much trouble.

There have been some glitches in the Baby Boom's beneficent self-indulgence, especially when we were young and impetuous. The murder rate per 100,000 Americans went from 5.1 in 1960 to 10.2 in 1980 when the Baby Boom was between sixteen and thirty-four and buying blow and Quaaludes from shady characters in the disco parking lot. We've gotten a grip on ourselves since then (and put a trigger lock on the pistol in the desk drawer). The murder rate is back to where it was in the halcyon 1950s.

We've had a generational tendency to "liberate" things. Incidence of property crime—burglaries, larcenies, and petty thefts—was at a rate of 1,534.3 per 100,000 in 1960. The rate was 3,309.0 by 1971. The rate peaked in 1980 at 4,851.1 and is now down to 2,703.1 although I don't know if Bear Stearns, Lehman Brothers, and Fannie Mae are counted in that figure.

And we always stole a lot of cars. When we were in our early teens the rate per 100,000 was already 183.0 and by 1989 it had reached 630.4. But that was during the "Bush Recession" just after we'd all splurged on BMWs, and how many of us parked them in a bad part of town with the windows down, took the bus home, and called Allstate?

A more persistent problem with the Baby Boom's beneficence is that we aren't as good as we claim we mean to be at spreading the benefits around. Although America's per capita wealth is 37 percent greater than it was when the Baby Boom began its rise to national domination, 15.1 percent of American families are now living below the official federal poverty level. In 1972 the percentage was 11.9.

This is not the World Bank's "extreme poverty." The U.S. government 2013 poverty threshold for a family of four is $23,550—food stamps, Medicaid, and housing subsidies not included. In 1950 dollars $23,550 would have been $2,436.43 or a weekly wage of $46.85. According to *Historical Statistics of the United States,* the average weekly salary of people employed in "finance, insurance, and real estate" was $50.52 in 1950, and the average salary of people in "retail trade" was $39.71.

If you're poor in America today you're making a little less than Billy and Bobby Stumf's dad was making selling whole life and term before his reserve unit got called up and he went off to fight in Korea for peanuts. And you're making a little more than Jerry Harris's dad was making managing the produce department at a grocery store.

But wherever we draw the poverty line, having 15.1 percent of the country below it is nothing to be complimented upon. And before we Baby Boomers indulge ourselves in some canned indignation about the gross inequities of corporate capitalism and how Warren Buffett's income tax rate is lower that his secretary's, let us pause to consider what our generation has left in its tracks. The fragile naifs who stayed at the sixties ball too long. The muddled goofs still beguiled by Large Thoughts. The drug-sodden burnouts. The poor souls who flunked their sexual license exams and were left with the illegitimate children and debilitating diseases. The way we failed to keep our eye on our sense of shame, which jumped bail and has been on the lam ever since. The swarm of divorces and slews of late and paltry child support payments. And the struggling immigrants who help us around the house and in the yard and whom we pay under the table and not damn much. It's a wonder 151 percent of the country isn't below the poverty line.

And yet we are the best generation in history. Which goes to show history stinks. But at least we are fabulous by historical standards.

The Baby Boom was a carefully conducted scientific experiment. The empirical results are us. Take the biggest generation in the most important country, put them in excessively happy families, give them too much affection, extravagant freedom, scant responsibility, plenty of money, a modicum of peace (if they dodged the draft), a profusion of opportunity, and a collapse of traditional social standards.

You get better people. Well, not *better*. Taken one by one, we're as maddeningly smug as Abel and as vile as Cain, the way people always have been. But we're better behaved. Although better behaved isn't the right way to put it either.

We're willful, careless, rash, vain, indulged, and entitled. We're "mad, bad, and dangerous to know," as Lady Caroline Lamb said of the poet, but she was an ex-girlfriend and ex-girlfriends say those things especially if you marry their cousin Annabella who had a few choice words about the poet herself, but she was an ex-wife and ex-wives say those things. The point here is that "a bunch of rhyme-less Lord Byrons" is a good description of the Baby Boom and the romantic, disorderly, harum-scarum lives we've led.

Except, of course, modern medicine cured the clubfoot, and we never slept with our sister—come on, there were plenty of other people to sleep with and it wasn't like we didn't have cars and couldn't get out of the house. And we haven't embarked on a campaign to liberate Greece. The EU has a central bank for that. Not that we didn't give the Greeks a few bucks to see the Parthenon and knock back some ouzos when we embarked on our Carnival cruise through the Aegean to Athens. And we didn't die of diarrhea at Missolonghi. The cruise ship gift shop had Imodium. Also our poetry is awful. The name Baby Boom poetry will be given in future literary anthologies is probably *worse libre*.

Other than that we're a lot like Lord Byron—larger than life personalities, providing the world with amusement, hearts in the right place even when our private parts aren't, thinking noble thoughts somewhat thoughtlessly, and being high-minded in a mindless sort of way.

We leave a mess behind, like Lord Byron did, but compare it to the mess that a generation previous left behind, like the generation previous to Lord Byron, which was Napoleon Bonaparte. You won't catch us—or George Gordon, 6th Baron, either—taking credit for plunging all of Europe into bloodshed by putting our own name on a bunch of wars or posing for pictures while groping ourselves with our hand someplace where there's nothing to grope or not leaving Moscow until it's on fire and it's winter and nobody has plowed the roads or letting the Battle of Waterloo be won on the playing fields of Eaton, which is nowhere near Belgium, or being the person everybody in the lunatic asylum is being. I mean, if I'm in the lunatic asylum, I'm just being me.

It's not a bad idea to have spoiled brats rule the world. The rulers of the ancient world may have been brats, but they weren't spoiled, if the Spartan mother admonishment to sons on their way to an all-guy outing—"Come back with your shield or on it"—is any indication.

Ancient potentates seemed to have had a firm sense of purpose rare among us pampered Baby Boomers eager for instant gratification. Mrs. Pharaoh must have popped her ankh when she caught Mr. Pharaoh blowing the IRA on a 455-foot Pyramid of Cheops for "his next stage in life." But he kept at it for twenty years. We'd never pull something like that, especially if our Queen of the Nile happened to be the principal breadwinner in the family and was already on the phone to the partner in her law firm who handles community property settlements.

And the mighty of yore must not have been doted upon sufficiently to make them emotionally needy and desirous of being liked by absolutely everybody. If Pontius Pilate had been a Baby Boomer, when he ordered the Crucifixion he would have given Christ a "safe word."

Barbarian hordes used to run the ancient world too or, at any rate, run frequently into large parts of the ancient world to rape and pillage. The Baby Boom would make a lousy barbarian horde, no matter what Athenians had to say after we'd knocked back some ouzos. We'd be galloping across the Mongolian steppes sneezing because we're allergic to horse dander, going, "What, no sushi?" and living off the fat of the land when we're trying to cut down on the fat in our diet. Then it's time to rape and pillage. Rape is very wrong. Also it's damaging to self-esteem. When somebody cries "Rape!" it's a rejection, not just of your actions and attitudes at the moment but of you as a whole person. Baby Boom barbarian horde members would be smiling shyly at the cowering womenfolk, asking, "Get pillaged often?" Then we'd start fiddling with the firebrand instead of burning the houses down and explain that we were trying to stop smoking. Plus pillaging means lugging all that stuff back with you before there were wheelie bags. And wheelie bags are probably hard to roll along the Mongolian steppes while you're galloping on a horse.

I don't think we would have been much use in the Middle Ages either, going on the Crusades by hitchhiking with flowers in our hair. Then we'd gather in a circle holding hands and try to levitate Jerusalem. If we'd had a be-in while Saladin was around I doubt he would have just let it be. We probably would have fared worse with the sultan in the Levant than we did with the National Guard at Kent State.

In fact, the Baby Boom wouldn't have been much good at committing any of history's atrocities, history being mostly a record of atrocities, and this may be why we got a D in it. Our generation would have discovered the New World, got a whiff of tobacco, said, "We can start smoking again!," moved in with the Indians, and convinced them to take their wigwams condo.

A Baby Boom Cortés, eyeing Montezuma, would have been thinking, "Gold? Nah. Got that hedged with long calls in precious metal commodities. How about an emerging market fund invested in outsourcing high-priced domestic Spanish Inquisition torture to low-cost overseas Aztec human sacrifice?"

The notorious triangle trade—sugar/rum/slaves—likewise would have been in Chapter 11 if operated by the Baby Boom. We use NutraSweet and Splenda. Rum means a Jimmy Buffett concert. And then we're so hungover we sleep right through the slave auction. Not that we ever would have brought Africans to America as human chattel. We would have brought Africans to America to make sure we never had to listen to "Turkey in the Straw" again.

History would have been very different—a C+ at least—if the Baby Boom had ruled the world.

Big Damn Messy Bundle of Joy

And we will. Because the American Baby Boom is the future. We'll all turn into us eventually, as soon as families get excessively happy and start feeling too much affection for their kids. Unless, of course, extravagant freedom, scant responsibility, plenty of money, and a modicum of peace lead to such a high rate of carbon emissions that we all fry or drown. But you can't have everything. And you can have a profusion of opportunity and a collapse of traditional social standards.

Western Europe and the wealthiest parts of Asia and Latin America have had them already. And they're almost as useless as we are, meaning useless in the best abundant disposable income with ample leisure time to devote to pointless activities that don't harm anybody much except ourselves way.

Baby Boom–like places all seem to be engaged in bellicose national political deadlock the way we are in America. There's much tut-tutting about bellicose national political deadlock. But it's an improvement on bellicose national political purpose. World conquest, for example. "Mine eyes have seen the glory of the coming of the [insert name of deity or national leader whom you dislike most]/He is trampling out the vintage where the grapes of wrath are stored/He hath loosed the fateful lightning of his terrible swift sword . . ." That doesn't sound like any fun at all, except maybe the vintage trampling part.

We and our kindred generation of European Baby Boomers brought down the Berlin Wall. Reagan and Thatcher and Gorbachev get the kudos. But it was the Baby Boom that did the job.

In my foreign correspondent days I spent some time behind the Iron Curtain, in the USSR, Poland, and East Germany. Everything, including the toilets, was made of crumbling concrete. Buildings were constructed without benefit of plumb bob or spirit level. There were wire mesh nets around the tops of the taller structures because pieces of the crumbling concrete kept falling off. Furniture looked as if it had been made by the seventh grade shop class. Food was a lard sandwich except they were out of bread. Roads were paved with random bucketloads of asphalt dumped in the right-of-way.

Cars, trucks, and buses had been reverse engineered from Tootsie Toys and went bumping down moon-cratered streets sputtering, misfiring, and burping clouds of smoke. You could have made a fortune standing on a Moscow street corner with a screwdriver and a timing light, had fortunes been allowed to be made.

"Cosmos" brand filter cigarettes had to be held upright or the tobacco dribbled out the end of the paper tube. Matches didn't work. After you struck a match you put it back in the matchbox because it was just as likely to light as any other match in there. The dial telephones buzzed with static. Assuming they were all tapped there must be reams of telephone conversation transcriptions somewhere in the KGB files reading: "zzzzzzz Nyet zzzzzzz Da zzzzzzz."

There was nothing to do but drink bad vodka and a lot of it. The Poles had a joke about a man from Warsaw who visits his brother in America. The brother says, "Would you like a drink?"

"Of course."

So the American brother goes to the liquor cabinet, gets out a bottle of vodka, and pours them both a drink.

"And then," says the man from Warsaw, "do you know what my brother did? *He put the cap back on the bottle!*"

The Soviets may have been a nuclear power but all they ever blew up was Chernobyl. I was in Poland not long after it happened. I said to a Pole, "I understand that because of the fallout we're supposed to avoid fresh vegetables."

He said, "*Fresh vegetables?*"

As ugly as Chernobyl was, it was nothing compared to commie couture. Older men wore Harry Truman suits but looking as if they'd been fitted to Harry and worn by Hervé Villechaize on *Fantasy Island*. Older women wore housedresses so ugly and so flowered that our grandmothers, even in their most muttering-to-themselves-in-the-kitchen mode, would have recoiled in horror. Young people tried to be hep. But it didn't work. One youthful Soviet minder, who'd been assigned to me as my translator, wore a pair of blue jeans in the most wrong possible blue and as un-jean-like in cut and as denimless as a burka. On the back of these was a patch of fake leather, imitating the Levi's patch except three times too large, upon which was emblazoned "Dakota Jean" with *Dakota* misspelled in several places.

The Baby Boom was laughing at the communists. Finally, on November 9, 1989, the East German communists, being sensitive to ridicule the way Germans are, gave up on Marxist/Leninism, and the Berlin Wall came down.

For totalitarianism to work everybody has to keep a straight face. Dictators don't stand a chance with the Baby Boom—the Hitler snot comb mustache, the Mussolini beanie, Mao lacking only a gold chain to be dressed like a fat swinger in a Nehru jacket, plus all those silly dictator arm gestures.

Baby Boomers would be Photoshopping their cats. Notice how the leaders of today's China are careful to appear in public looking like they're headed to a funeral—probably their own. I'll bet "Chairman Meow" memes are all over Chinese microblogs. And not to bring Jimmy Buffett into this again, but did you ever notice how Stalin kind of looks like Jimmy when Buffett had hair and a mustache? If the Russians had posted videos of Stalin lip-syncing "Margaritaville," Uncle Joe would have had to go gulag his own bad self.

The Baby Boom is the generation of the mocking tongue. The pen may be mightier than the sword but not once you get people howling with laughter. A couple of spit takes and the ink runs, the sword rusts, and the Baby Boom triumphs.

It will take a while to turn the whole world into Baby Boomers. For one thing, due to declining birthrates, they won't be a boom like we were with the same weight of numbers on their side. On the other hand, aging populations in places such as Russia and China will let these babies speak in booming voices. And a lot of the world is still stuck in the Idiot Generation and hasn't progressed to Greatest let alone attained the glory of B.B. But Muammar Gaddafi's clothes, grooming, and arm gestures were so dictator-ridiculous that even the fool Libyans shot him.

Also, there's a little bit of the Baby Boom in everyone. I was in Lebanon in 1984 during the civil war, and I was stopped at a checkpoint manned—or I should say boyed—by fifteen- and sixteen-year-old members of the militant Islamic fundamentalist Hezbollah.

One of them demanded my passport. When he saw that I was an American he subjected me to a twenty-minute tirade, at gunpoint, about America Satan Devil and how the United States had caused the Lebanese civil war, colonialism, imperialism, Zionism, and every other problem he could think of. Then he handed my passport back and said, "As soon as I get my green card I am going to dentist school in Dearborn, Michigan."

Militant Islamic fundamentalism probably had a tough time surviving the karaoke nights and Craigslist personals of the Detroit metropolitan area. I bet the teenager who pointed the gun at me is now a wealthy orthodontist living in Bloomfield Hills.

Noxious politics will disappear as all the world's political science classes happily degenerate into hour-long shouting matches. It's hard to remain truly noxious when you like being obnoxious better.

Stupid notions of central planning, nationalization, and protectionist trade barriers will fall by the wayside when everyone is paying as little attention in econ. as I was.

And sooner or later the 1.29 billion people making $1.25 a day, the way I was selling pot (smoked the profits), are going to figure out there's a better way. In fact, I just received an e-mail from Nigeria about a rather large amount of money needing to be transferred to an American bank and requiring only modest assistance on my part.

There will be no religious fanaticism. We're not a generation who listens to anybody, God included. In our defense, I doubt God minds us not bothering about Him. Very few of the people we've bothered—parents, college deans, the police, LBJ, the psychiatrist at my draft physical, supervisors, bosses, attractive types in bars—have minded when we quit bothering them.

Religious fanatics must be pesky from a heavenly point of view. "Now what?" thundered the Lord. We're more sports fanatics. Yahweh hikes the ball to Jesus. Does Jesus hand off to Muhammad for short yardage? Buddha and Krishna are covered midfield. Secular Humanism is wide open for a long pass but he seems to be chatting with a cheerleader.

There will be no suicide bombings. Baby Boomers aren't going to strap explosive vests around our middles; it would make us look fat.

There will be no genocide or ethnic cleansing. One thing about the coddling and cosseting and doting upon that goes into creating a generation of spoiled brats is that it leaves us with a sentimental streak. Killing a whole race or ethnicity would involve doing away with quaint old people who possess time-honored wisdom (even if they are crabby with the kids in the neighborhood) and those kids in the neighborhood, too, not to mention major babes and ripped dudes. Plus a wholesale, warehouse store–type of hatred like that is too down-market for the Baby Boom. When it comes to hating people, we like brand names. Furthermore, consider the progress science has made. Nowadays genocide would require everyone to be subjected to DNA testing. All those cotton swabs, what a bother.

There may be some outbreaks of sixties behavior in unexpected places. Perhaps that's what the Arab Spring is. Doesn't look too groovy to me, but whatever turns you on. A Saudi Arabian sit-in would be interesting because I've never seen the Saudis do anything but sit around anyway.

World peace is probably too much to ask. But it will be hard to assemble those huge conscripted armies that used to fight wars. We'll all have a letter from our doctor about our deep-seated psychiatric problems and drug use.

The hippie doctor who wrote mine happened to be a good doctor despite a practice constrained by crab lice. I was having some kidney problem and he sent me to a hospital for tests. A decade later the problem recurred. I had more tests and an appointment with an elderly kidney specialist. Looking into my medical file he began to back his chair away from mine. "Your kidneys are all right," he said. "But . . . do you need help?"

I had no idea what he was talking about, for a moment. Then I said, "Did the doctor's letter I took to my draft physical wind up in my medical files?"

"Aha!" said the elderly kidney specialist. "I wrote a lot of draft physical letters. But I never wrote one *this* good!"

Besides, war is about power. Baby Boomers are not power hungry. Power comes with that kicker, responsibility. We're greedy for love, happiness, experience, sensation, thrills, praise, fame, adulation, inner peace, and, as it turns out, money. Health and fitness too. But we're not greedy for power. Observe the Baby Boomers who have climbed to its ascendency in Washington. The best and the brightest? They're over at Goldman Sachs.

When we really are the world the place will be chaos. A universal Baby Boom will be running around everywhere doing anything they want at all hours of the day and night with nobody left to clean up. It may be a bad world.

But it will be a worse world for the Leaders of Men, looking around for their followers and wondering why everyone is following Keith Richards. It will be a terrible world for Authority. The Baby Boom will not countenance it. We turn our face from Authority. Indeed we turn our ass toward it. We moon Dominion.

Woe to you who have oppressed mankind with your theologies and your ideologies, your bigotries, doctrines, dogmas, and no sex until after we're married. Desolation awaits you who have foisted war upon us, subjugated us, yoked us, fettered us, and told us we can't get down and boogie.

You shall be as the ants beneath our magnifying glasses, the sand wasps affronted with our tennis rackets, the frogs ingesting our fireworks, the cats between our garages, the birdbaths, garden gnomes, and glass gazing balls at the mercy of our Wham-O slingshots. Flaming bags of dog poop shall be set upon your front porches.

Think how we made a misery of the lives of our parents. If we can do that to our dearest beloved, think what we can do to you. For that matter think what we did to ourselves. You shall spend eternity at a "Model UN." You shall listen forever to lectures of Margaret Mead. You shall, under the influence of LSD, sit upon a staircase inside a giant evil eel for all time. And if you go upstairs you'll be chewed by giant eel teeth. And if you go downstairs you'll be eel shit.

We are an obdurate generation. Our whim is iron. What we will to do is done. You, eel shit members of the Chinese politburo, have had a taste of this in Tiananmen Square. You remember the fellow blocking the tank. But do you remember the crucial detail? He was carrying *shopping bags*. Not only were you violating his human liberties, you were interfering with his shopping, a Baby Boom birthright. One man is a majority with shopping on his side.

You loathsome communists got away with it in Tiananmen Square. But for how long? The vengeance of the Baby Boom can be delayed but not denied. There will come a day, Xi Jinping, when the power and the dignity of your office shall be rendered so low that you shall appear as guest host on *Saturday Night Live*.

And what about you, detestable Taliban and al-Qaeda and Osama wannabes cowering in your Waziristan, Kandahar, Yemen, and Mali hidey-holes? You who are pursued by those things perfectly christened with the name Baby Boomers have so often been called, drones. And when it comes to Baby Boom lethal technology, drones are nothing. How will things be with you when your bevy of wives discover vibrators?

And you, contemptible Putin? How long will your shirtless self escape the LGBT float in the Greenwich Village Halloween Parade?

And all the rest of you tyrannical, despotic, overbearing squares and wet smacks with your two-bit autocracies in the butt ends of the world? You shall gather in finished basements while your revered elders stand at the top of the basement stairs yelling, "I think something's on fire down there!" Your stereos shall play Blue Cheer. You shall spend your treasure on cocaine and rehab. Your junk bonds shall default. You shall form over-age garage bands and try to play "Margaritaville." Your third spouse shall acquire an American Express Black Card with a credit limit higher than the Greek national debt. Your daughters shall wear nose rings. Your sons shall have pagan symbols indelibly marked upon their necks. (Unless you belong to one of those cultures where daughters wear nose rings and sons have pagan symbols indelibly marked upon their necks, in which case they shall not.) You shall be perplexed by the Internet. You shall grow old and addled enough to vote for Ron Paul in a presidential primary.

There is no escape from happiness, attention, affection, freedom, irresponsibility, money, peace, opportunity, and finding out that everything you were ever told is bullshit. Behold the Baby Boom, ye mighty, and despair.

Acknowledgments

Come we now here to a part of a book that is never, ever read. Well, that's not completely true. If the author is an ignoramus politician (but I repeat myself) with a high public profile, we reporters will root around in the acknowledgments seeking the clue to who actually wrote the thing: "And this book would truly not have been made possible at all if it weren't for my dear, close friend and patient confidante who was always there for me, May Sue Sadhack."

But otherwise a writer can dump anything whatsoever in these paragraphs and it will never be noticed. Some reptiles have two dicks. This is the kind of thing you find out when you unleash your inner thirteen-year-old and Google "Lizard Penis." It's right there on Wikipedia.

> *A hemipenis (plural hemipenes) is one of a pair of intromittent organs of male squamates (snakes, lizards and worm lizards). Hemipenes are usually held inverted, within the body, and are everted for reproduction via erectile tissue, much like that in the human penis. Only one is used at a time, and evidence indicates males alternate use between copulations as a behavioral means of increasing sperm transfer when the interval between copulations is relatively brief.*

Now that I have your attention ("intromittent organs . . . alternate use between copulations . . . when the interval is brief"), there are some people whom I should acknowledge. Limited space and, more to the point, limited capacity for recall will make the list brief. Too brief for my conscience but, no doubt, too long for the reader.

The late Doug Kenny gave me my first assignment at *National Lampoon*. (It stunk.) Matty Simmons hired me at that magazine. (I sucked.) Jann Wenner spent fifteen years giving me the best job in the world, roaming ditto for *Rolling Stone*. (I wasn't as much trouble as Hunter S. Thompson, but who ever was?) The late and much-missed Michael Kelly gave me the next best job in the world at the *Atlantic Monthly*. And now it is John Avalon's turn at the *Daily Beast*. Gentlemen, you are and were delightful, fine, and patient people.

The late (I see a pattern and I swear it has to do with my age and not my driving people to their graves) David E. Davis Jr. taught me to be an automotive journalist at *Car and Driver* and *Automobile*. More important to us both, he taught me to be a reasonably decent shot in the hunting field.

To the editors and publishers of the *American Spectator, World Affairs,* and, most of all, the *Weekly Standard* I owe . . . I owe to you even more than I owe to you already in advances, kill fees, and fishy expense account submissions.

My debt is larger still to Don Epstein and everyone at my lecture agency, Greater Talent Network.

And my most profound thanks go to my friend Morgan Entrekin who has edited and published every one of my books—for better, for worse, for richer, for poorer, in sickness and in health.

To all of you and many, many others:

Beefsteak when you're hungry,
Whiskey when you're dry,
All the intromittent organs you ever need.
And heaven when you die.